JAZZ
RECORDS
1942-80

A discography

D1496749

Edited by Erik Raben

VOL.4: Cla-Da

Dedicated to the music of

Louis Armstrong, Albert Ayler,

Sidney Bechet, John Coltrane, Duke Ellington,

Gil Evans, Charlie Parker and Lester Young

Published by *Stainless/Wintermoon* ISBN: 87 - 88043 - 13 - 4
Copyright © 1993 *JazzMedia ApS*

Distributed by *JazzMedia ApS*
Dortheavej 39, DK-2400 Copenhagen NV, Denmark

CONTENTS

Preface

A discography is a compilation of information in standardized format about
recorded performances and their issue in the form of sound recordings. The
main sources of information on the performances are sleeve notes, record companies, collectors and musicians; the main sources of information on the
issued recordings are the recordings themselves (label and sleeve), record
company catalogues, magazines and collectors.

The information in JAZZ RECORDS 1942-80 has been derived from the sources
mentioned above, but, as with all other discographies, it is far from complete.

JAZZ RECORDS 1942-80 - the discographical background

The JAZZ RECORDS 1942-80 project started in 1972 and during the following
years an updated and corrected version of J.G. Jepsen's JAZZ RECORDS was
circulated to 20 - 25 collectors and/or discographies from several countries
all over the world. Additional countries were covered by means of national
jazz discographies and information from collectors and discographers in those
countries.

A small group of people has formed the "core" of the project:

    Chris Clark / Paul Wilson (UK)
    Michael Cuscuna (US)
    Mona Granager (Denmark)
    Mitsuo Johfu (Japan)
    Rainer E. Lotz (Germany)
    William R. Miner (US)
    Bob Porter (US)
    Michel Ruppli (France)

It is not possible to list all the persons who have contributed to the project; nevertheless we should like to mention the following (some of whom have
passed away in the meantime):

Lloyd Anderson (US)
Kazatumi Aoki (Japan)
Arne Astrup (Denmark)
Jerry L. Atkins (US)
Anthony Barnett (UK)
Louis Barnewitz (Denmark)
Jordi Beltrán (Spain)
Gabriel Benites (Peru)
Jan Beránek (Czechoslovakia)
Ed Berger (US)
Johs Bergh (Norway)
Gerard Bielderman (The Netherlands)
Per Borthen (Norway)
Walter Bruyninckx (Belgium)
Tom Buhmann (Denmark)
Henryk Z. Cholinski (Poland)
Julian Claes (Belgium)
L.C. Clavié (France)
Michael N. Clutten (UK)
Derek Coller (UK)

Gerhard Conrad (Germany)
Hugo de Craen (Belgium)
Ian Crosbie (UK)
Charlie Crump (UK)
Bill Daniels (US)
Martin Davidson (Canada)
Charles Delaunay (France)
Abel Deusebio (Argentine)
Steve Didymus (UK)
James M. Doran (US)
Kai Lykke Ewald (Denmark)
Rolph Fairchild (US)
Herbert Flügge (Germany)
Will Friedwald (US)
Peter Friedman (US)
Yasuhiro Fujioka (Japan)
Shinjiro Furusho (Japan)
Jack Goodwin (UK)
Robert Gordon (US)
David Griffiths (UK)

Gösta Hägglöf (Sweden)
Dieter Hartmann (Switzerland)
Dennis Hess (US)
J.-R. Hippenmeyer (Switzerland)
Ray Holland (UK)
George Hulme (UK)
Shinichi Iwamoto (Japan)
Bent Kauling (Denmark)
Erhard Kayser (Germany)
Larry Kiner (US)
Hans-Georg Klauer (Germany)
Keith Knox (Sweden)
Karl Emil Knudsen (Denmark)
Dietrich H. Kraner (Austria)
Werner Krozewski (Austria)
Peter Langhorn (Denmark)
Arnold Laubich (US)
Mike Leadbitter (UK)
Lars Linderoth (Sweden)
Jack Litchfield (Canada)
Jan Lohmann (Denmark)
Jacques Lubin (France)
Mario Luzzi (Italy)
Teo Macero (US)
Johnson McRee (US)
Jack Mitchell (Australia)
Dan Morgenstern (US)
Giorgio Mortarino (Italy)
Jan Mulder (The Netherlands)
Harry Nicolausson (Sweden)
John Norris (Canada)

Hugues Panassié (France)
Lothar Polomski (Germany)
Brian Priestley (UK)
Julian Purser (UK)
José Domingo Raffaelli (Brazil)
Henri Renaud (France)
Lars Rick (Denmark)
Howard Rye (UK)
James D. Shacter (US)
Bo Scherman (Sweden)
Todd Selbert (US)
Max Seligmann (Argentine)
Chris Sheridan (UK)
Roy Simonds (UK)
Ray Spencer (US)
Ruggero Stiassi (Italy)
Mike Sutcliffe (Australia)
Naoki Suzuki (Japan)
Jim Taylor (US)
Barry Tepperman (Canada)
Ib Skovsted Thomsen (Denmark)
Paul Vande Velde (Belgium)
Malcolm Walker (UK)
Roger Wernboe (Sweden)
Hans Westerberg (Finland)
Erik Wiedemann (Denmark)
David Wild (US)
Ove Wilson (Sweden)
Dick Wright (US)
Art Zimmerman (US)
George Ziskind (US)

References

Among the main sources for the preparation of JAZZ RECORDS 1942-80 are the jazz magazines; other important sources are the "Schwann" catalogue and the German "Bielefelder Katalog - Jazz". Since it is impossible to give a complete list of the magazines we have checked, this section only lists the discographies - or bio-discographies - used.

Allen,Walter C.: Hendersonia - The Music of Fletcher Henderson (1973)
Astrup,Arne: The Stan Getz Discography (1991)
Astrup,Arne: The John Haley (Zoot) Sims Discography (1980)
Astrup,Arne: The Gerry Mulligan Discography (1989)
Berger,M. & Berger,E. & Patrick,J.: Benny Carter - A Life In American Music (1982)
Bielderman,Gerard: Chris Barber Discography 1949-75 (1975)
Bowen,Michael: Michael Daniels and the Delta Jazzmen (1982)
Bruyninckx,Walter: Modern Jazz Discography (1984 etc.)
Bruyninckx,Walter: Modern Big Band Discography (1984 etc.)
Bruyninckx,Walter: Progressive Jazz Discography (1984 etc.)
Bruyninckx,Walter: Swing Discography (1985 etc.)
Bruyninckx,Walter: Traditional Discography (1987 etc.)
Bruyninckx,Walter: The Vocalists - Singers And Crooner (1988 etc.)
Cabanowski,Marek & Cholinski,Henryk: Polska dyskografia 1955-1972 (1974)
Clutten,Michael: A Bruce Turner Discography
Conrad,Gerhard: Discographie der Jazz- und Semijazzaufnahmen im Bereich der heutigen Volksdemokratien (1982 etc.)

Connor,Russell & Hicks,Warren: B.G. On The Record - A Bio-Discography Of
  Benny Goodman (1978 etc.)
Cuscuna,Michael & Ruppli,Michel: The Blue Note Label - A Discography (1988)
Daniels,Bill: The American 45 and 78 RPM Record Dating Guide 1940-1959 (1984)
De Craen,Hugo & Janssens,Eddy: Marion Brown Discography (1985)
Doran,James M.: Erroll Garner - The Most Happy Piano (1985)
Doruzka,Lubomir & Polednak,Ivan: Ceskoslovensky Jazz (1967)
Engelen,Piet van: Where's the Music - The Discography of Kai Winding (1985)
Evensmo,Jan & Borthen,Per & Thomsen,Ib Skovsted: Benny Carter 1927-46 (1982)
Fujioka,Yasuhiro: John Coltrane - A Discography and Musical Biography (1993)
Furusho,Shinjiro: Riverside Jazz Records (1984)
Garrod,Charles: Charlie Barnet and his Orchestra (1984)
Garrod,Charles: Les Brown and his Orchestra 1936-1960 (1986)
Garrod,Charles: Bob Crosby and his Orchestra (1987)
Hippenmeyer,Jean-Roland: Swiss Jazz Disco (1977)
Hofmann,Coen & Bakker,Erik M.: Shorty Rogers A Discography (1983)
Hofmann,Coen: Man of Many Parts - A Discography of Buddy Collette (1985)
Iwamoto,Shinichi: Hank Jones - A Discography (1988)
Janssens,Eddy & De Craen,Hugo: Art Ensemble Of Chicago - Discography (1983)
Jasen,David A.: Recorded Ragtime 1897-1958 (1973)
Jepsen,Jørgen Grunnet: Jazz Records 1942-68 (1963-69)
Kleinhout,Henk: The Wallace Bishop Story (1981)
Koster,Piet & Bakker,Dick M.: Charlie Parker 1940-1955 (1976)
Koster,Piet & Sellers,Chris: Dizzy Gillespie (1985)
Laing,Ralph & Sheridan,Chris: Jazz Records - The Specialist Labels (1981)
Lange,Horst H.: Die Geschichte des Jazz in Deutschland (1960)
Larsen,Peter H.: Turn On the Stars - Bill Evans (1984)
Leadbitter,Mike & Slaven,Neil: Blues Records - 1943 to 1970 (1987)
Lerfeldt,H.H. & Sjøgren,Th.: Chet - Discography of Chesney Henry Baker (1985)
Lindenmaier,H.L.: 25 Years Of Fish Horn Recordings - Steve Lacy (1982)
Litchfield,Jack: The Canadian Jazz Discography 1916-1980 (1982)
Lohmann,Jan: The Sound of Miles Davis - The Discography (1992)
Lombardi,Giorgio: Eddie Condon on Record - 1927-71 (1987)
Lotz,Rainer & Neuert,Ulrich: The AFRS "Jubilee" Transcriptions (1985)
Mackenzie,Harry & Polomski,Lothar: (AFRS) One Night Stand Series (1991)
McCarthy,Albert J. & Carey,Dave: Jazz Directory (1949-57)
Meeker,David: Jazz In The Movies (1981)
Middleton,Tony: Joe Daniels - a Discography (1982)
Millar,Jack: Born To Sing - A Discography of Billie Holiday (1979)
Mitchell,Jack: Australian Jazz On Record 1925-80 (1988)
Raftegard, Bo: The Kenny Dorham Discography (1982)
Ruppli,Michel: Atlantic Records - A Discography (1979)
Ruppli,Michel: The Prestige Label - A Discography (1980)
Ruppli,Michel: The Savoy Label - A Discography (1980)
Ruppli,Michel: Charles Mingus Discography (1981)
Ruppli,Michel: The Chess Labels - A Discography (1983)
Ruppli,Michel: The King Labels - A Discography (1985)
Ruppli,Michel: The Clef/Verve Labels - A Discography (1986)
Rust,Brian: Jazz Records 1897-1942 (1970 etc.)
Sears,Richard S.: V-Discs - A History and Discography (1980)
Selchow,Manfred & Lohmann,Karsten: Edmond Hall - a Discography (1981)
Shacter,James D.: Piano Man - The Story of Ralph Sutton (1975)
Sheridan, Chris: Count Basie - A Bio-Discography (1986)
Simon,Géza Gábor: Hungarian Jazz Records 1912-1984 (1985)
Simonds,Roy: King Curtis - A Discography (1984)
Simosko,V. & Tepperman,B.: Eric Dolphy - Biography and Discography (1974)
Sjøgren,Thorbjørn: The Duke Jordan Discography (1964)
Skovgaard,Ib & Traberg,Ebbe: Sonny Clark - A Discography (1984)
Stagg,Tom & Crump,Charlie: New Orleans - The Revival (1973)
Strateman,K.: Negro Bands On Film - Big Bands 1928-1950 (1981)

Sugita,Seiichi: Gil Evans Discography 1941-82 (1983)
Suzuki,Naoki: Herbie Hancock 1961-69 - A Discography (1988)
Teubig,Klaus: Staighten Up And Fly Right - A cronology/dicography of Nat "King" Cole jazzrecordings from 1936-1950 (1987)
Trolle,Frank H.: James P. Johnson - Father of the Stride Piano (1981)
Van Eyle,Wim (ed.): The Dutch Jazz & Blues Discography 1916-1980 (1981)
Villetard,Jean Francois: Coleman Hawkins 1922-1969 (1984)
Wachtmeister,Hans: A Discography & Bibliography of Anthony Braxton (1982)
Weir,Bob: Clifford Brown Discography (1985)
Weir,Bob: Buck Clayton Discography (1989)
Westerberg,Hans: Boy from New Orleans - Louis "Satchmo" Armstrong (1981)
Westerberg,Hans: A Finnish Jazz Discography 1932-1976 (1977)
White,Bozy: The Eddie Condon "Town Hall Broadcasts" 1944-45 (1980)
Wiedemann,Erik: Jazz i Danmark - i tyverne, trediverne og fyrrene (1982)
Wild,David & Cuscuna,Michael: Ornette Coleman 1958-1979 A Discography (1980)
Wild,David: The Recordings Of John Coltrane (1978)
Zoli,Arrigo: Storia del Jazz Moderno Italiano (1983)

The content of JAZZ RECORDS 1942-80

This discography lists jazz recordings from the period 1942 - 1980. Issues and reissues have been included whenever information has been available, but the listing of reissues on CD is far from complete. They have been included primarily for titles and takes which were previously unissued.

In many cases it has been difficult to decide where the boundaires to blues, R&B, dance-oriented big band music, pop-vocal music, jazz/rock fusion music and Latin music should be drawn. In some cases non-jazz recordings are included to "complete" the discography of a musician or a group/band.

As a general rule live recordings, broadcasts and transcriptions are only included when one or more titles have been - or are intended to be - issued on record. In some cases a complete series of broadcasts have been included even if a few of them are unissued. Broadcasts introduce a special problem since it is not always known whether the date listed is the date of the recording or the date of the broadcast (if it was broadcast at a later date).

Each volume includes an index with a reference to each page a musician's name is mentioned in the discography. An exception is the reference to a musician's own discography - in this case there is only a reference to the first page.

Order of headings for musicians/groups

Headings for each session leader or group/band are listed alphabetically. If there are two or more leaders, the session will be entered under the first-named musician with cross reference(s) from the other name(s). When a recording has been issued under the name of one of the musicians who was not the session leader, there will be a reference. References are generally given before the session entries, but there may be references in a note after a particular session. In has not always been possible to enter a session under the name of a musician or a group/band; in these cases, the session is entered under an appropriate heading - e.g. JAM SESSION (Norman Granz).

The note "List of equivalents" before the session entries indicates a list of equivalents after the last session.

The alphabetical ordering takes into account the various national languages and name spellings:

Definite articles as part of a name
When a name starts with the definite article (The, Der, Die, Das, Le, La, Les, El, Los, Las etc.) it will be disregarded and the name will be filed in the discography, and in the index, under the following word, e.g. Les Double Six and The **F**ive Bops. Exceptions are English/American names where the definite article is part of the family name, e.g. Scott LaFaro and Pete LaRoca.

Prepositions
When a name starts with a preposition (Von, Van, Ver, Van der, Van den, De etc.) it will be listed according to the last part of the name when it is a **German** or a **Dutch/Flemish** name, e.g. von **S**chlippenbach and Van **R**egteren Altena. Musicians of other nationalities will be listed according to the preposition-part of the name, e.g. **V**er Plack, **D**eFranco and **V**an Eps.

The alphabetical order of the discographies
The **Nordic countries** consider **Ä/Æ** and **Ö/Ø** as original letters - i.e. **not** as A-umlaut and O-umlaut - placed at the end of the alphabeth. This principle is followed for musicians from these countries.
Other countries consider **Ä** as **A-umlaut**, **Ö** as **O-umlaut** and **Ü** as **U-umlaut**, i.e. they are placed after the relevant letter (**without** umlaut). This principle is followed - e.g. Karl Haüss is listed after Karl Hauss but before Karl Hawss (if these names exist!).

The alphabetical order of the index.
Contrary to the listing of the discographies of musicians the order of listing in the index is - for technical reasons - the following:

A, B, C, D, E, ... S, T, U, Ü, V, W, X, Y, Z, Æ, Ø, Å, Ä, Ö.

Organization of information about the recordings

The recordings are listed chronologically under each name heading.

When information has been available, the recording venue and date have been entered for each session. The recording venue is given as the name of the city and state (US recordings) or the name of the city and country (non-US recordings). The name of the state is not included for larger US cities and the name of the country is not included for the capital of the country concerned. NYC and LA are used for the New York City and the Los Angeles area (including Hollywood). Concerts and other live recordings are listed as "Live recordings".

Information concerning a session is listed after the session (as a note or as information on issues of - some of - the titles).

Instrumental abbreviations

acc	accordion
alth	alto horn
arr	arranger
as	alto saxophone
b	bass
barh	baritone horn
bars	baritone saxophone
band-vcl	vocal by members of the band
bassax	bass saxophone
bcl	bass clarinet
bg	bongo drum(s)
bj	banjo
btb	bass trombone
btp	bass trumpet
cg	conga drum(s)
cl	clarinet
C-mels	C-melody saxophone
cnt	cornet
comp	composer
cond	conductor
dr	drum(s)
el	electical amplified instrument
enh	English horn
fl	flute(s)
flh	fluegelhorn
frh	French horn
g	guitar (acoustic and/or eletrical)
hca	harmonica
hsc	harpsichord
keyb	keyboards
ldr	leader
mand	mandolin
mar	marimba
mcs	maracas
mel	mellophone
org	organ
p	piano
perc	percussion
picc	piccolo flute
sax	(unspecified) saxophone(s)
ss	soprano saxophone
synth	synthesizer
tamb	tambourine
tb	trombone
timb	timbales
tp	trumpet
ts	tenor saxophone
tu	tuba
tymp	tympani
vbs	vibraphone (vibraharp/vibes)
vcl	vocal
vla	viola
vln	violin
vtb	valve trombone
wbd	washboard
xyl	xylophone

Nationality abbreviations

Nationality abbreviations are used to indicate non-US issues and to indicate US issues on labels owned by non-US record companies. In some cases it has not been possible to list the nationality of a non-US issue.

A	Austrian
Am	American (US)
Arg	Argentinean
Au	Australian
B	Belgian
Br	Brazilian
Bu	Bulgarian
Ca	Canadian
Cz	Czech
D	Danish
Du	Dutch
E	English/British
Eu	European Continent
F	French
Fi	Finnish
G	German (BRD and DDR)
Hu	Hungarian
I	Italian
Ind	Indian
J	Japanese
N	Norwegian
NZ	New Zealand
P	Polish
Ro	Roumanian
SA	South African
Sov	Soviet
Sd	Swedish
Sp	Spanish
Sw	Swiss
Y	Yugoslavian

Additional abbreviations

acc. by	accompanied by
alt. (take)	alternate take
CD	Compact Disc
coll. pers.	collective personnel
ed.	edited version
incompl.	incomplete version
LA	Los Angeles area
NYC	New York City area

THE CLAYTON BROTHERS

Jeff Clayton(ts),Patrice Rushen(p),Ron Eschete(g),John Clayton(b,vcl),Jeff Hamilton(dr).
                                        San Francisco.November 1978

Big Foot	Concord CJ89	
Blues For B.S.	-	
Walkin' Blues(jc)	-	
Cherokee	-	
Sometimes We Can't See Why	-	
Yo'mama	-	
Watergate Blues	-	

Jeff Clayton(ts,as,oboe),Roger Kellaway(p),Emily Remler(g),John Clayton(b),Jeff Hamilton
(dr).   Venice,Calif.June 1980

Broadway	Concord CJ138
Emily	-
Cannon	-
The Masquerade Is Over	-
Remembering You	-
Estate	-
Things Ain't What They Used To Be	-
If I Were A Rich Man	-

BUCK CLAYTON

See also LEONARD BERNSTEIN,JOE BUSHKIN,CAFE SOCIETY BAND/ALL STARS,DIXIELAND ALL STARS,
HARRY EDISON,ESQUIRE ALL AMERICAN AWARD WINNERS,ART FORD'S JAZZ PARTY,NANCY HARROW,COLEMAN
HAWKINS,HELEN HUMES,JAZZ AT THE PHILHARMONIC,JAZZ FROM A SWINGING ERA,MEZZ MEZZROW,NEWPORT
JAZZ FESTIVAL ALL STARS,PANASSIÉ STOMPERS,JIMMY RUSHING,WILLIE "THE LION" SMITH.

BUCK CLAYTON QUINTET:
Buck Clayton(tp),Flip Phillips(ts),Teddy Wilson(p),Slam Stewart(b),Danny Alvin(dr).
                                        NYC.June 7,1945

MR105	Diga Diga Doo	Melrose 1201,Vogue(F)LD063,Jazztone J1024,J1221, Guilde du Jazz(F)J1024
MR106	Love Me Or Leave Me	Melrose 1201,Vogue(F)LD063,Jazztone J1024,J1221, Guilde du Jazz(F)J1024
MR107	We're In The Money (The Golddigger's Song)	Melrose 1202,Jazztone J1024,J1221,Guilde du Jazz (F)J1024
MR108	B.C. Blues (Melrose Blues)	Melrose 1202,Vogue(F)LD063,Jazztone J-SPEC100, J-SPEC101,Concert Hall J-SPEC100,Guilde Int. du Disque(F)J100,Club Nat. du Disque(F)JSP100

All titles also on Dial LP213,Onyx OR1213,Polydor(E)2344.045,(Eu)2310.342.
Note:Reissues on Dial LP213 as by TEDDY WILSON AND HIS ALL STARS.

BUCK CLAYTON'S BIG FOUR:
Buck Clayton(tp),Scoville Brown(cl),Tiny Grimes(g),Sid Weiss(b).
                                        NYC.June 26,1946

1042-1	Dawn Dance	HRS 1024,Allegro LP4121,Riverside RLP142,Jazz Selection(F)JS537
1043-3	Wells-A-Poppin'	HRS 1025,Allegro LP4121,Riverside RLP142
1044-2	On The Sunny Side Of The Street	HRS 1026,1051,Vintage Jazz Classics VJC1009(CD)
1045-2	It's Dizzy	HRS 1024,Allegro LP4121,Riverside RLP142
1046-2	Basie's Morning Bluesicale	HRS 1025 - - ,Jazz Selection(F)JS537

All titles on RLP142 also on Original Jazz Classics OJC1709,OJCCD1709-2 (CD).

BUCK CLAYTON'S BIG EIGHT:
Buck Clayton(tp),Dicky Wells,Trummy Young(tb),George Johnson(as),Billy Taylor(p,celeste),
Brick Fleagle(g),Al McKibbon(b),Jimmy Crawford(dr).
NYC.July 24,1946

1047	Saratoga Special	HRS 1027,Jazz Selection(F)JS507	
1048	Sentimental Summer	- ,Riverside RLP142	
1049	Harlem Cradle Song	HRS 1028,	-
1050	My Good Man Sam	-	- ,Jazz Selection(F)JS507
1051	I Want A Little Girl	HRS 1029,	- ,Musica Jazz(I)2MJP1054

All titles - except "I Want A Little Girl" - also on Allegro LP4121,LP1643,Halo RPM50229,
Ultraphonic 8043.
All titles on RLP142 also on Original Jazz Classics OJC1709,OJCCD1709-2 (CD).

BUCK CLAYTON SEXTET:
Buck Clayton,Merrill Stepter(tp),Don Byas(ts),Charlie Lewis(p),Georges Hadjo(b),Wallace
Bishop(dr).   Paris.October 10,1949
RJS900-2 High Tide   Royal Jazz(F)719,Jazz Selection(F)719
RJS901   Swingin' At Sundown   Vogue(F)V5063,(E)V2361,LAE12032,Jazz Selection(F)
                                          LDM30021
RJS902-3 Who's Sorry Now   Royal Jazz(F)720
RJS903-2 Sugar Blues(1)   - ,Vogue(F)LD053,(E)LAE12032,Pop(F)
                                          SP017056,CBM60016,Mode(F)CMDINT9516,Jazz
                                          Selection(F)LDM30021,Dial LP306
RJS904-1 Blues In First(1,2)   Royal Jazz(F)721,Jazz Selection(F)721,Vogue(F)
                                          LD053,VG405.500115,(E)EPV1101,LAE12032,Dial
                                          LP306,Jazz Parade(E)B5,Pye(Au)ILP1032,Jazz
                                          Selection(F)LDM30021
RJS904-2 Blues In Second(1,2)   Royal Jazz(F)721,Jazz Selection(F)721,Vogue(E)
                                          EPV1101,Jazz Parade(E)B5
RJS905-2 Don's Blues   Royal Jazz(F)719,Jazz Selection(F)719,Vogue(F)
                                          VG405.500115,Jazz Selection(F)LDM30021

-1.Omit Stepter.
-2.Omit Byas.

All titles/takes also on Vogue(F)DP73,VG304.400073,Hispavox(Sp)26005,Bellaphon(G)BJS40181.

BUCK CLAYTON AND HIS ORCHESTRA:
Buck Clayton,Bill Coleman,Merrill Stepter(tp),Alix Combelle,Armand Conrad(ts),George
Kennedy(as,bars),André Persiany(p),Georges Hadjo(b),Wallace Bishop(dr).
Paris.November 21(?),1949
RJS919-2 Uncle Buck   Royal Jazz(F)734,Bellaphon(G)BJS40181
RJS920-2 Buck Special   Royal Jazz(F)731,Vogue(F)CLD737,VG403.500893,
                                          CLD893
RJS921-1 Night Life   Royal Jazz(F)731,Bellaphon(G)BJS40181
RJS922-2 Perdido   Royal Jazz(F)734,   -
RJS923-4 B.C. And B.C.(1,2)   Royal Jazz(F)738,Vogue(E)EPV1101, -
RJS924   Sweet Georgia Brown(2)   -   - ,Bellaphon(G)
                                          BJS40181

-1.Omit Stepter.
-2.Omit Combelle,Conrad,Kennedy.

All titles also on Vogue(F)DP73,VG304.400073,Hispavox(Sp)26005.
Note:Rec.date may be November 23 or 28,1949.
    "Sweet Georgia Brown" as by BUCK CLAYTON AND HIS TRIO OF TRUMPETS.

BUCK CLAYTON WITH MARLOWE MORRIS TRIO:
Buck Clayton(tp),Marlowe Morris(org),Jerome Darr(g),Les Erskine(dr).
NYC.February 18,1953
(session cont. next page).

```
(session cont. from previous page):
CO49002-1 I Want A Little Girl          Okeh 6968,4-6968
CO49003-1 Blue Moon                          -       -
CO49004   Basic Organ Blues,I          Epic EG7009
CO49005   Basic Organ Blues,II              -
CO49006   Hammond Stomp                  unissued
CO49007   'S Wonderful,I               Epic EG7009
CO49008   'S Wonderful,II                   -
CO49009   It's Only A Paper Moon         unissued
```

BUCK CLAYTON ORCHESTRA:
Buck Clayton(tp),"Big Chief" Russell Moore(tb),Red Richards(p),Pierre Michelot(b),Kansas
Fields(dr).   Paris.April 2,1953
```
53V4499 Sweethearts On Parade   Vogue(F)V5154,(E)V2285
53V4500 Patricia's Blues                  - ,(E)V2361,Concert Hall M2340,Explo-
                                       sive(F)528.006
53V4501 Special  B.C.           Vogue(F)V5178
53V4502 She's Funny That Way              -
53V4503 Lazy River              Vogue(F)V5182,LD156,(E)V2286,Mode(F)CMDINT9598,
                                       Jazz Selection(Sd)JS4042,Pax LP6009,Baronet
                                       B108,Explosive(F)528.006,Concert Hall M2340
53V4504 West End Blues(1)       Vogue(F)V5182,LD156,(E)V2286,Mode(F)CMDINT9598,Pax
                                       LP6009,Jazztone J1258,Jazz Greats JG603,Con-
                                       cert Hall M2340,(F)SMS7132,Polydor(J)LPPM1022
                                       Explosive(F)528.006
```

-1.MEZZ MEZZROW - BUCK CLAYTON ORCHESTRA;add Mezz Mezzrow(cl).

All titles also on Vogue(E)LAE12032,Jazz Selection(F)LDM30021,Jazztone J1225,Concert Hall
CHJ1225.
All titles - except "Lazy River" and "West End Blues" - also on Vogue(F)LD157,(E)EPV1043,
LDE102,Jazztone J1267,Pax LP6015.

Note:See MEZZ MEZZROW for additional titles from this session.
     The above titles also issued as by BUCKEROO'S ALL STARS:

BUCK CLAYTON WITH ALIX COMBELLE'S ORCHESTRA:
Buck Clayton(tp,arr),Alex Renard,Pierre Sellin,Aimé Hanuche,André Simon(tp),René Godard,
Jean-Jacques Léger(as),Alix Combelle(ts,arr),Henri Bernard(ts),Henri Jouot(bars),Jean-
Claude Pelletier(p),Roger Chaput(g),Yvon Le Guen(b),Christian Garros(dr),Chonanard(bg).
                                        Paris.October 20/21,1953
```
53V4758 Qui (Who)               Vogue(F)V3417,LD182,Storyville STLP906
53V4759 Relax Alix                        -       -                   -
        Bonds Et Rebonds
          (Jumping On The Rebound)        -                           -
        Blues En Cuivres
          (Blues In Brass)                - ,(E)V2230,               -
        Pulsation Du Rythme
          (Beatin' The Count)             -       -                   -
        Chocs Sonores (Basie Days)        -                           -
        Sahiva Boogie                     -
        Promenade Blues
          (Strolling Blues)               -
```

All titles also on Vogue(F)DP73,VG304.400073,(E)LDE140,Hispavox(Sp)26005.

BUCK CLAYTON WITH DAVE POCHONET AND HIS ALL STARS:
Buck Clayton(tp,arr),Guy Longnon -1(tp),Benny Vasseur(tb),André Ross -2(ts),Michel De
Villers(bars,cl),André Persiany(p),Jean-Pierre Sasson(g),Billy Banks(b),Gérard "Dave"
Pochonet(dr).   Paris.November 6,1953
(session cont. next page).

(session cont. from previous page):
```
OLA6710 Some Of These Days(2)          HMV(F)FFLP1022
OLA6726 Studio A(2)                     unissued
OLA6727 Blues For Hazel(1)(no tb)      HMV(F)7EMF57(ed.),FFLP1022,(E)7EG8279,Electrola
                                          (G)E41357,7EGW8650
OLA6728 Stompin' At The Savoy(1)       HMV(F)7EMF57,(E)7EG8279,Electrola(G)E41357,
                                          7EGW8650
```

Buck Clayton(tp,arr),Roger Guérin -1(tp),Charles Verstraete -2,Benny Vasseur(tb),José
Germain(as),André Ross(ts),Michel De Villers(bars,cl),André Persiany(p,arr),Charles
Blareau(b),Dave Pochonet(dr).   Paris.November 12,1953
```
        Swingin' The A.P. Blues         HMV(F)FFLP1022,FELP105
        Sur Les Quais Du
            Vieux Paris(1,2)(no as)     HMV(F)FELP125
        Fleur De Papillon(1),(no as)    unissued
        Confessin'(2)                   HMV(F)7EMF57,FFLP1022,(E)7EG8279,Electrola(G)
                                          E41357,7EGW8650,Club National du Disque(F)
                                          CND580
```

BUCK CLAYTON AND HIS FRENCH STARS:
Buck Clayton(tp),Michel De Villers(as,bars),André Persiany(p),Jean-Pierre Sasson(g),
Charles Blareau(b),Dave Pochonet(dr).   Paris.November 15,1953
```
        Sugar(no as/bars,p)             Club Francais du Disque(F)unissued
        Easy To Riff(no as/bars,p)      Club Francais du Disque(F)HF6
        Fast But Soft                                      -
        Buck's Bon Voyage Blues                            -
        Gift For The Club
            (I Found A New Baby)                           -
        Please Don't Talk
            About Me When I'm Gone(no g)                   -
```

All titles - except "Sugar" - also on Musidisc(F)JA5202,Omega OML1052,Deutscher Schall-
plattenclub(G)CO3,Opera(G)3120 (as BUCK CLAYTON'S JAZZ SIX).

BUCK CLAYTON JAM SESSION:
Buck Clayton,Joe Newman(tp),Urbie Green,Benny Powell(tb),Lem Davis(as),Julian Dash(ts),
Charlie Fowlkes(bars),Sir Charles Thompson(p),Freddie Green(g),Walter Page(b),Jo Jones
(dr).   NYC.December 14,1953
```
C050436 Moten Swing               Columbia 5-1956/57(ed.),CL6325,Philips(Eu)B07905R
C050437 Sentimental Journey              - (ed.),    -  ,(J)EM33
```

Both titles also on Columbia CL567,Fresh Sound(Sp)FS268,FSR1000,Philips(E)BBL7040,(Eu)
B07032L,CBS(J)SOPZ33.
Note:Columbia 5-1956/57 issued as a 2x45 rpm set (B439).

Henderson Chambers(tb) replaces Powell;Thompson plays (p,celeste).
                                         NYC.December 16,1953
```
C050531-6 Lean Baby               Columbia CL882,CJ44291,CBS(Eu)463336-1,463336-2
                                          (CD),(Sp)980081-1,Fresh Sound(Sp)FS272,FSR593
                                          Philips(E)BBL7129,(Eu)B07163L
C050532   The Hucklebuck          Columbia 5-1872/73,B1836(ed.),CL548,(J)EM5(ed.)
C050533   Robbins' Nest           Columbia B1836(ed.),           -
C050534   Christopher Columbus    Columbia 5-2073/74,CL614,CL919(see note),JC2L614,
                                          Philips(E)BBL7068,(Eu)B07059L,CBS(Du)88031,
                                          (J)20AP1827
```

Both titles on CL548 also on Fresh Sound(Sp)FS326,Philips(E)BBL7032,BBL7446,(Eu)B07022L,
Realm(E)RM52078,CBS(Eu)52078,21112,(J)20AP1435(?),XM24C,Coronet(Au)KLP654.
(session cont. next page).

(session cont. from previous page):
Note:Columbia 5-2073/74 issued as a 2x45 rpm set (B483).
    All issues of "Lean Baby" are prob. edited; CJ44291 and CBS(Eu)463336-1/2 use the
    same take as the original issue but insert different versions of some of the solos
    (after the second chorus).
    The issued version of "Robbins' Nest" was spliced from takes -1 and -2.
    All issues of "Christopher Columbus" are edited.
    9 seconds of "Christopher Columbus" is incl. on Leonard Bernstein's "What Is Jazz"
    (CL919 - and equivalents).

Buck Clayton,Joe Thomas(tp),Urbie Green,Trummy Young(tb),Woody Herman(cl),Lem Davis(as),Al
Cohn,Julian Dash(ts),Jimmy Jones(p,celeste),Steve Jordan(g),Walter Page(b),Jo Jones(dr).
                                      NYC.March 31,1954

CO51243	How Hi The Fi	Columbia 5-1958/59(ed.),5-2287(ed.),CL6326,CL567, CL777(ed.),CB4(ed.),CBS(J)SOPZ33,SONP50413, Fresh Sound(Sp)FS268,FSR1000,Phil.(E)BBL7040, (Eu)B07032L,(SA)ALD6033(ed.),Coron.(Au)KLP500
CO51244	Blue Moon	Columbia B1958(ed.),CL6326,CL567,CBS(J)SOPZ33, SONP50413,Fresh Sound(Sp)FS268,FSR1000, Philips(E)BBL7040,(Eu)B07032L
CO51245-1	Jumpin' At The Woodside	Columbia B2089,CL701,JC2L614,(J)PL5074,CBS(Du) 88031,Philips(E)BBL7087,(Eu)B07106L

Note:Columbia 5-1958/59 issued as a 2x45 rpm set (B440).
    All LP issues of "Jumpin' At The Woodside" - except B2089 - use a version spliced
    from part of the March 31,1954 recording and part of the August 13,1954 recording.

BUCK CLAYTON'S BAND FEATURING RUBY BRAFF:
Buck Clayton(tp),Ruby Braff(cnt),Benny Morton(tb),Buddy Tate(ts),Jimmy Jones(p),Steve Jor-
dan(g),Aaron Bell(b),Bobby Donaldson(dr).   NYC.July 1,1954
      Just A Groove(no tb,ts)   Vanguard VRS8008,(J)SR3048
      Kandee   - ,(J)SR3103
      I Can't Get Started   - ,(J)SR3048
      Love Is Just Around The Corner   -   -

All titles also on Vanguard VRS8517,(E)PPT12006,(F)519.057,VSD103/4,(J)LAX3074,Amadeo(Eu)
VRS7002,Family(I)SFR-VN729(10"),SFR-VN727(12").

BUCK CLAYTON JAM SESSION:
Buck Clayton,Joe Newman(tp),Urbie Green,Trummy Young(tb),Lem Davis(as),Coleman Hawkins
(ts),Charlie Fowlkes(bars),Billy Kyle(p,celeste),Freddie Green(g),Milt Hinton(b),Jo Jones
(dr).   NYC.August 13,1954

CO51245-2	Jumpin' At The Woodside	Columbia CL701,JC2L614,(J)PL5074,CBS(Du)88031, Philips(E)BBL7087,(Eu)B07106L
CO52505	Don't Be That Way	Columbia 5-2075/76,CL614,JC2L614,(J)PL5074,Philips (E)BBL7068,(Eu)B07059L,CBS(Du)88031,(J) 20AP1827
CO52506	Undecided	Columbia 5-2075/76,CL614,JC2L614,C3L236,(J)PL5074, Philips(E)BBL7068,(Eu)B07059L,CBS(Du)88031, (J)20AP1827
CO52507	Blue And Sentimental	Columbia CL701,JC2L614,CBS(Du)88031,Philips(E) BBL7087,(Eu)B07905R,B07106L

Note:All LP issues of "Jumpin' At The Woodside" use a version spliced from part of the
    March 31,1954 recording and part of the August 13,1954 recording.

Buck Clayton(tp),Ruby Braff(cnt),Bennie Green,Dick Harris(tb),Coleman Hawkins,Buddy Tate
(ts),Al Waslohn(p),Steve Jordan(g),Milt Hinton(b),Jo Jones(dr).
                                  NYC.March 15,1955

(session cont. next page).

(session cont. from previous page):
```
C052630   Rock-A-Bye Basie(1)         Columbia CL701,CBS(J)SONP50413
C052631-1 Out Of Nowhere              Columbia CJ44291,CBS(Eu)463336-1,463336-2(CD)
C052631-? Out Of Nowhere              Columbia CL882,(J)PL5074,CBS(J)SONP50413,Philips
                                               (Eu)B07905R
C052632   Blue Lou(alt.take)          Columbia CJ44291,CBS(Eu)463336-1,463336-2(CD)
C052632   Blue Lou                    Columbia CL882
C052633   Broadway                    Columbia B528,CL701,Philips(I)B07595/96L
```

-1.Add Jack Ackerman(tap-dance).

All titles on CL701 also on Columbia JC2L614,CBS(Du)88031,Philips(E)BBL7087,(Eu)B07106L.
All titles on CL882 also on CBS(Sp)980081-1,Fresh Sound(Sp)FS272,FSR593,Philips(E)BBL7129,
(Eu)B07163L.

JIMMY RUSHING - ADA MOORE WITH BUCK CLAYTON AND HIS ORCHESTRA:
Buck Clayton(tp,arr),Emmett Berry(tp),Dicky Wells(tb),Eddie Barefield(as),Budd Johnson(ts)
Willard Brown(as,bars),Sir Charles Thompson(p),Steve Jordan(g),Milt Hinton(b),Jo Jones(dr)
Jimmy Rushing,Ada Moore(vcl).   NYC.August 18,1955
```
        Any Place I Hang
          My Hat Is Home(am)        Columbia CL778
        You're My Thrill(am)                 -
        Between The Devil
          And The Deep Blue Sea(am)          - ,Philips(E)BBE12150,(Eu)429.263BE
        Gee,Baby,Ain't I Good To You(jr) Columbia 5-2299,CL778,       -        -
```

Aaron Bell(b) replaces Hinton.   NYC.August 19,1955
```
        Any Place I Hang
          My Hat Is Home(am)        Columbia CL778
        Pretty Little Baby(jr)      Columbia 5-2297,CL778
        I've Got A
          Feeling I'm Falling(am)   Columbia CL778,Philips(E)BBE12150,(Eu)429263BE
        If I Could Be With You(jr,am) Columbia 5-2298,CL778,        -        -
        Ain't She Sweet             Columbia CL778
```

Buck Clayton(tp,arr),Emmett Berry(tp),Dicky Wells(tb),Eddie Barefield(cl,as),Budd Johnson
(ts),Willard Brown(as,bars),Ken Kersey(p),Steve Jordan(g),Aaron Bell(b),Osie Johnson(dr),
Jimmy Rushing,Ada Moore(vcl).   NYC.August 23,1955
```
        Cool Breeze Woman(jr)       Columbia 5-2298,CL778
        I Can't Give You
          Anything But Love         Columbia CL778
        Any Place I Hang
          My Hat Is Home(am)                 -
        After You've Gone(jr)       Columbia 5-2297,CL778,CBS(J)SONP50413
        The Blues                   Columbia CL778
        Closing Theme(1)                     -
```

-1.Prob. from this session.

All titles on CL778 also on CBS(Sp)980081-1,Fresh Sound(Sp)FS269,FSR1001,Philips(E)BBL7105
(Eu)B07154L.
Note:CL778 issued as "Cat Meets Chick - A Story In Jazz" (incl. comments by Clayton, Moore
     and Rushing to introduce the tunes played).

FRANKIE LAINE(vcl) WITH BUCK CLAYTON AND HIS ORCHESTRA:
Buck Clayton(tp,arr),Ray Copeland(tp),Urbie Green(tb),Hilton Jefferson(as),Budd Johnson,
George Nicholas(ts),Dave McRae(bars),Sir Charles Thompson(p),Skeeter Best(g),Milt Hinton
(b),Jo Jones(dr).   NYC.October 24,1955
```
        Baby,Baby All The Time      Columbia B8081,CL808
        S'Posin'                    Columbia B8082,    -
        That Old Feeling                     - ,      -
```
(session cont. next page).

(session cont. from previous page):
        You Can Depend On Me   Columbia B8083,CL808
        Stars Fell On Alabama   -   -

FRANKIE LAINE(vcl) WITH BUCK CLAYTON AND HIS ORCHESTRA:
Buck Clayton(tp,arr),Ray Copeland(tp),Lawrence Brown,J.J. Johnson -1,Kai Winding -1(tb),
Hilton Jefferson(as),Budd Johnson,George Nicholas(ts),Dave McRae(bars),Al Lerner(p),Skee-
ter Best(g),Milt Hinton(b),Bobby Donaldson(dr).
                                         NYC.October 25,1955
        Roses Of Picardy(1)   Columbia B8081,CL808
        You'd Be So Nice
            To Come Home To(2)(no vcl)   unissued

-2.Sir Charles Thompson(p) replaces Lerner.

Dicky Wells(tb),Al Sears(ts) replace Brown,Nicholas.
                                         NYC.October 26,1955
        If You Were Mine   Columbia CL808
        Until The Real Thing Comes Along Columbia B8081,CL808
        Taking A Chance On Love(1)   Columbia B8081, -
        My Old Flame(2)(no vcl)   -

-2.Sir Charles Thompson(p) replaces Lerner.

All titles on CL808 also on Columbia JCL808,CBS(E)32413,(J)SOPZ22,Philips(E)BBL7080,(Eu)
B07129L,Coronet(Au)KLP512.

BUCK CLAYTON JAM SESSION:
Buck Clayton,Billy Butterfield(tp),Ruby Braff(cnt),J.C. Higginbotham(tb),Tyree Glenn -1
(tb,vbs),Coleman Hawkins,Julian Dash(ts),Ken Kersey(p),Steve Jordan(g),Walter Page(b),
Bobby Donaldson(dr),Jimmy Rushing(vcl).   NYC.March 5,1956
CO55544-1 All The Cats Join In(1)   Columbia CL882,CJ44291,CJ44380,(J)PL5074,CBS(Eu)
                                             463336-1,463336-2(CD),(J)SONP50413,Philips(G)
                                             B080405L(ed.),(Eu)429.411BE
CO55545-5 After Hours(1)   Meritt 10,Columbia CJ44291,CBS(Eu)463336-1,463336
                                             -2(CD)
CO55546-? Don't You Miss Your Baby(jr)   Columbia CL882,CBS(Eu)465192-2(CD),(J)SONP50413,
                                             Philips(Eu)429.411BE
CO55546-5 Don't You Miss Your Baby(jr)   Columbia CJ44291,CBS(Eu)463336-1,463336-2(CD)

All titles on CL882 also on CBS(Sp)980081-1,Fresh Sound(Sp)FS272,FSR593,Philips(E)BBL7129,
(Eu)B07163L.

Note:All issues of "All The Cats Join In" - except CJ44291, CJ44380, CBS(Eu)463336-1/2 -
     are edited and prob. some solos from another take have been used (via splicing).
     B080405L only contains an extract from Hawkins' solo on "All The Cats Join In".

BUCK CLAYTON'S ALL STARS:
Buck Clayton(tp),J.J. Johnson(tb),Coleman Hawkins(ts),Dick Katz(p),Benny Moten(b),Gus
Johnson(dr).   Live.Newport Jazz Festival,R.I.July 6,1956
CO56793 You Can Depend On Me   Columbia CL933,Philips(F)V2
Co56794 In A Mellotone   -
CO56795 Newport Jump   - ,Philips(Eu)429.315BE

All titles also on Columbia(J)PL5043,Philips(E)BBL7152,(Eu)B07208L,CBS(Eu)84420,M62614,(J)
20AP1452,Coronet(Au)KLP572.

JAZZ FESTIVAL ALL STARS:
Buck Clayton(tp),Jimmy Hamilton(cl),Paul Gonsalves(ts),Hank Jones(p),Sidney Gross(g),Jimmy
Woode(b),Sam Woodyard(dr).   Live.Connecticut Jazz Festival,Westport.July 28,1956
        Tea For Two   Queen(I)Q-044,I.A.J.R.C. LP45
        Jazz Festival Blues
        (Ad Lib Blues)   -   -

BUCK CLAYTON SEPTET:
Buck Clayton(tp),Vic Dickenson(tb),Earl Warren(as),Hank Jones(p),Kenny Burrell(g),Aaron
Bell(b),Jo Jones(dr).   NYC.March 14,1957
        Buck Huckles   Vanguard VRS8514
        Claytonia   -
        Cool Too   -
        Squeeze Me   -
        Good Morning Blues   -
        Ballin' The Jack   -
        Blues Blase   -
        The Queen's Express   -

All titles also on Vanguard(F)VSD103/04,(E)PPL11010,(J)SR3074,LAX3068,K20P6188,KIJJ2028,
Fontana(E)FJL407,(Eu)688.906JCL.

BUCK CLAYTON ALL STARS:
Buck Clayton(tp),Vic Dickenson(tb),Buddy Tate(ts),Dick Katz(p),Walter Page(b),Bobby
Donaldson(dr).   NYC.October 4,1957
C059022 Jive At Five   Philips(E)BBL7217
C059023 Cookin' Joe C   -
C059024 Love Drop   -
C059025 Wooster-shire   -

Same.   NYC.October 8,1957
C059021 (You Can't Fight)
        The Satellite Blues   Philips(E)BBL7217
C059030 Thou Swell   -
C059031 I Hadn't Anyone Till You   -
C059032 At Sundown   -
C059033 Makin' Whoopee   -

All titles on BBL7217 also on Jazz&Jazz(I)JJ608,CDJJ608 (CD).
Note:The issued version of "(You Can't Fight) The Satellite Blues" is prob. a re-make.

BUCK CLAYTON AND HIS ALL STARS:
Buck Clayton(tp,arr),Emmett Berry(tp),Dicky Wells(tb),Earl Warren(as,cl),Buddy Tate(ts),Al
Williams(p),Gene Ramey(b),Herbie Lovelle(dr).
                                     NYC.November 25,1958
C061795 Sunday   Columbia CL1320
C061796 Swingin' Along On Broadway   -
C061797 Night Train   -
C061798 Buckini   -
C061799 Moonglow   -
C061800 Swinging At The Copper Rail Columbia JJ1,JS1,CL1320,(J)SL3045,Philips(E)
                                       BBE12352,(Du)429.616BE
C061801 Mean To Me   Columbia CL1320,Philips(E)BBE12352,(Du)429.616BE
C061802 Outer Drive   -   -   -

All titles also on Columbia CS8123,Philips(E)BBL7317,SBBL533,(Eu)BO7150L,840.039BY.

BUCK CLAYTON ALL STARS - JIMMY RUSHING:
Add Jimmy Rushing(vcl).   Live.Copenhagen.September 17,1959
    Outer Drive   SteepleChase(D)SCC6006/7
    Swinging At The Copper Rail   -
    Moonglow   -
    Night Train   -
    Swingin' Along On Broadway   -
    Exactly Like You(jr)   -
    I Want A Little Girl(jr)   -
    Everyday I Have The Blues(jr)   -
    'Deed I Do(jr)   -
    Goin' to Chicago(jr)   -
    Sent For You Yesterday(jr)   -
    Sent For You Yesterday (enc.)(jr)   -

All titles also on SteepleChase(D)SCCD36006/7 (CD),Edigsa(Sp)09A0178.

Same.   Live.Olympia Théâtre,Paris.October 17,1959
    Swingin' The Blues   Palm Club(F)26
    Goin' To Chicago(1)(jr)   -
    Sent For You Yesterday(1)(jr)   -
    On The Sunny Side
      Of The Street(jr)   -
    Night Train   -
    Outer Drive   -
    Moonglow   unissued
    I Want A Little Girl(jr)   -

-1.George Wein(p) replaces Williams.

BUCK CLAYTON QUINTET:
Buck Clayton(tp),Jean-Claude Pelletier(p,org),Jean Bonal(g),Roland Lobligeois(b),Kansas
Fields(dr).   Paris.November 16/17,1959
    Lonesome (Si Tu Vois Ma Mère)   Pop(F)PIPO 01,MPO3013,POMS71.005,Vogue(F)EPL45-45,
                                        (J)LP63009,YX6002,Polydor(J)DP1192,LPP1078
    I've Got My Love To Keep Me Warm Pop(F)PO.134,STPCH501,MPO3013,POMS71.005,Vogue(F)
                                        STP045-07,EPL45-45,(J)VLP3009
    Premier Bal   Pop(F)PO.134,MPO3013,POMS71.005,Vogue(F)V45-1574,
                                        STP045-07,EPL45-45,CLVLX342,VG304.400342,(J)
                                        SJET1832,SJET8043,SWG7130,VLP3009,Polydor(J)
                                        DP1180,LPP1070,LPP1078LPPM1018,LPPM1052
    Louise   Pop(F)CBM6000730,MPO3013,POMS71.005,Vogue(F)
                                        EPL45-45,(J)VLP3009,Polydor(J)DP1188
    Tenderly   Pop(F)PO.202,STEP45-77004,MPO3039,POMS71.005,Vogue
                                        (F)V45-1575,EPL7778,(J)SWG7130,SJET8043,
                                        VLP3009,Polydor(J)DP1188,LPP1090
    Black and Blue   Pop(F)MPO3039,POMS71.005,Pye(Au)IPL1006,Vogue(F)
                                        V45-1574,SCK02,Polydor(J)DP1192
    These Foolish Things   Pop(F)STEP45-77501,MPO3039,CBM60035,POMS71.005,
                                        Vogue(F)EPL7780,(J)VLP3009,SJET8043
    I'm In The Mood For Love   Pop(F)MPO3039,POMS71.005,Vogue(F)V45-1575,(J)
                                        VLP3009,SWG7130,SJET8043,Polydor(J)LPP1090
    Rosetta   Pop(F)POMS71.005,CBM60035-30
    Sugar   Pop(F)POMS71.005,Polydor(J)DP1180
    Pennies From Heaven   Pop(F)POMS71.005
    Stompin' At The Savoy   Pop(F)PO.202,POMS71.005,Vogue(J)VLP3009,SJET8043

All titles also on Pop(F)POST19.001,Mode(F)MDINT9207,Vogue(J)UPS5090,Pye(Au)ILP1005,Mondio
Universalle(F)MM44,Inner City IC7019,IC7200,Polydor(J)LPPM1003,SLPM39.

BUCK CLAYTON - BUDDY TATE:
Buck Clayton(tp),Buddy Tate(ts),Sir Charles Thompson(p),Gene Ramey(b),Mousey Alexander
(dr).   NYC.December 20,1960
2766   High Life   Swingville SVLP2017,Prestige(J)SMJ7551
2767   Can't We Be Friends   -
2768   Birdland Betty   -
2769   Kansas City Nights   - ,Prestige P24111,2301(CD)
2770   When A Woman Loves A Man(no ts)   - ,Prestige(J)SMJ7551
2771   Thou Swell   -

All titles also on Prestige P24040,(E)PR24040,(J)MJ7033,Fontana(Eu)688.404ZL,Originial
Jazz Classics OJCCD757-2 (CD).

BUCK CLAYTON ALL STARS:
Buck Clayton(tp,arr),Emmett Berry(tp),Dicky Wells(tb),Earl Warren(cl,as),Buddy Tate(ts),
Sir Charles Thompson(p,celeste),Gene Ramey(b),Oliver Jackson(dr),Kenny Graham(arr).
                                            NYC.April 10,1961
        Night Ferry   Columbia(E)33SX1390
        I Can't Give You Anything But Love   -,Aves(G)INT156.511
        One For Buck   -   -
        Mr. Melody Maker   -
        Blue Mist   -
        Prince Eagle Head   -

All titles also on Metronome(Sd)MLP15075,World Record Club(E)(S)T601,Philips(Eu)6369.204.

Same.   Live.Olympia Théâtre,Paris.April 22,1961
        Outer Drive   Vogue(F)LD544,VG651.600160(CD)
        Robbins' Nest   Vogue(F)LD544(ed.),VG651.600160(CD)
        Swingin' At The Copper Rail   Vogue(F)VG651.600161(CD)
        Unknown title(s)(p,b,dr only)   -

All titles on LD544 also on Vogue(F)JL54,VG405.500054(E)VJD527,(J)YX4034.
Note:See JIMMY WITHERSPOON for additional titles from this concert.

Same.   Live.Olympia Théâtre,Paris.April 23,1961
        Night Train   Vogue(F)VG651.600160(CD)
        Moonglow   Vogue(F)LD544(ed.),VG651.600160(CD)
        Stompin' At The Savoy
          (tp,p,b,dr only)   Vogue(F)VG651.600160(CD)
        Swingin' The Blues   Vogue(F)LD544(ed.),VG651.600160(CD)
        Polka Dots And
          Moonbeams(ts,p,b,dr only)   Vogue(F)LD544,VG651.600160(CD),Mode(F)CMDINT9517
        Swingin' At The Copper Rail(1) Vogue(F)LD544,VG651.600160(CD)

-1.Mistitled as "Swingin' At The Camarillo" on LP issues.

All titles on LD544 also on Vogue(F)JL54,VG405.500054(E)VJD527,(J)YX4034.
Note:See JIMMY WITHERSPOON for additional titles from this concert.

BUCK CLAYTON QUINTET:
Buck Clayton(tp),Sir Charles Thompson(p,org),Jean Bonal(g),Gene Ramey(b),Oliver Jackson
(dr).   Paris.May 15/16,1961
        I Can't Believe
          That You're In Love With Me   Pop(F)POMS71009,Vogue(J)SJET8043,VLP3005
        I Surrender Dear   -   - ,YX6002
        Them There Eyes   - ,Vogue(J)YX6002
        When Your Lover Has Gone   -   -
        Georgia On My Mind   - ,Vogue(J)SJET8043,YX6002,SWG7130,
                                        Polydor(J)SLPM1123
        I've Got The World On A String Pop(F)POMS71009
(session cont. next page).

(session cont. from previous page):

I Cried For You	Pop(F)POMS71007,Vogue(J)YX6002
I Cover The Waterfront	Pop(F)MP03072,POMS71007, -
Night And Day	Pop(F)POMS71009,Vogue(J)SJET8043,VLP3005
Night And Day(alt.take)	- ,Vogue(J)SWG7130
Body And Soul	Pop(F)POMS71007,Vogue(J)SJET7999,SWG7130,VLP3005
I Want A Little Girl	Pop(F)POMS71009,Vogue(J)YX6002
I Want A Little Girl(alt.take)	-
Baby Won't You Please Come Home	Pop(F)POMS71007
Sleepytime Gal	- ,Vogue(J)SJET7999,SWG7130,YX6002
My Funny Valentine	- - - - , Polydor(J)SLPM1102
Rose Room	Pop(F)POMS71009,Vogue(J)YX6002
Rose Room(alt.take)	-
I Gotta Right To Sing The Blues	Pop(F)POMS71007,Vogue(J)SJET7999
Ma Gigolette	Pop(F)MP03072,POMS71007
Green Eyes	Pop(F)POMS71007,Vogue(J)SJET7999,SWG7130,YX6002, Polydor(J)SLPM1102
You Go To My Head	Pop(F)POMS71009,Vogue(F)VG304.416039,(J)SJET8043, VLP3005,Mode(F)MDINT9461
Passport To Paradise	Pop(F)MP03072,POMS71007,Vogue(J)SJET7999
Please Be Kind	Pop(F)POMS71007
Petite Fleur	Pop(F)POMS71009,Vogue(J)JET1832,SJET8043,SWG7130, VLP3005,Polydor(J)SLPM1123
Tangerine	Pop(F)MP03072,POMS71007
Nous Deux	unissued

All titles on POMS71007 also on Vogue(F)JL88,VG405.500088,(J)UPS5049,K23P6759,Mode(F)
CMDINT9410,Inner City IC7009,IC7100,Polydor(J)LPPM1084,SLPM1031.
All titles on POMS71009 also on Vogue(F)VG405.500106,Polydor(J)SLPM1043.
Note:Unissued alternate takes exist for several of the above titles.
    Inner City IC7100 is a 10xLP set.

BUCK CLAYTON - BUDDY TATE:
Buck Clayton(tp),Buddy Tate(ts,cl),Sir Charles Thompson(p),Gene Ramey(b),Gus Johnson(dr).
                                  NYC.September 15,1961

3209	Dallas Delight	Swingville SVLP2030
3210	Blue Ebony	-
3211	A Swinging Doll	-
3212	Don't Mind If I Do	-
3213	Rompin' At Red Bank	- ,Prestige(J)SMJ7581
3214	Blue Creek	- -
3215	Blue Breeze	-

All titles also on Prestige P24040,(E)PR24040,(F)FELP15.001,XTRA(E)XTRA5021.

BUCK CLAYTON QUARTET:
Buck Clayton(tp),Georges Arvanitas(org),Pierre Sim(b),Charles Bellonzi(dr).
                           Live.Salle Wagram,Paris.December 15,1962

Indiana	I Giganti del Jazz(I)GJ17,Europa Jazz(I)EJ1014
St. Louis Blues	- -
Stompin' At The Savoy	I Giganti del Jazz(I)GJ29,Europa Jazz(I)EJ1023

Note:"Stompin' At The Savoy" issued with erroneously personnel listed.

BUCK CLAYTON AND HIS BAND:
Buck Clayton(tp),Georges Arvanitas(org),Harry Kett,Pierre Urban(g),Georges Megalos(el-b),
Pierre Sim(b),Charles Bellonzi(dr).   Paris.December 17,1962

Barbara	Pop(F)MP03101,POMS71010,Mode(F)MDINT9117
September Blues	
Daniel(no el-b)	-

(session cont. next page).

(session cont. from previous page):

Cavalier	Pop(F)POMS71010
Grand'-Mere	Pop(F)MP03101,POMS71010
C'Est A L'Amour Auquel Je Pense	- -
Blueberry Hill	Mode(F)MDINT9409,Vogue(J)YX6004,SWG7130,SJET7999
La Colline Du Delta	- -
That's My Home	- -
Frankie And Johnny(no el-b)	- -

Note:Unissued alternate takes exist for several of the above titles.

Buck Clayton(tp),Georges Arvanitas(p,org),Harry Kett -1,Roger Terrien-2(g),Georges Megalos
-3(el-b),Pierre Sim(b),Philippe Combelle(dr).

Paris.December 18,1962

Nuages	Pop(F)POMS71010
Tous Les Garcons Et Les Filles	Pop(F)MP03101,POMS71010
Girl's Dance(1)	Pop(F)POMS71010
En Flanant Dans	
Les Rues De Paris(1)	- ,Mode(F)CMDINT9841
Laura(1,2)	Mode(F)MDINT9409
The Way You Look Tonight	- ,Vogue(J)SJET7999
Full Of Dreams(1,3)	-
It Ain't Necessarily So(1,3)	- ,Vogue(J)SJET7999
La Vie En Rose	unissued

Note:Unissued alternate takes exist for several of the above titles.

Buck Clayton(tp),Georges Arvanitas(p,org),Harry Kett -1,Roger Terrien(g),Georges Megalos
-2(el-b),Pierre Sim(b),Charles Bellonzi(dr). Paris.December 19,1962

La Vie En Rose	POP(F)POMS71010,Vogue(J)SWG7130,SJET8043
Promenade Aux Champs-Elysées	-
I'm Confessin'	Mode(F)MDINT9409,Vogue(J)SJET7999
Flamingo(2)	-
Stardust	- ,Vogue(J)SWG7130,SJET7999
Goodnight Sweetheart(1)	- - -

All titles on MDINT9409 also on Vogue(J)YX6004.
Note:Unissued alternate takes exist for several of the above titles.

BUCK CLAYTON WITH HUMPHREY LYTTELTON AND HIS BAND:
Buck Clayton(tp),Humprey Lyttelton(tp,tenor-h),Danny Moss(ts),Joe Temperley(bars),Ian
Armit(p),Pete Blannin(b),Eddie Taylor(dr).   London.July 5,1963

Tam	World Record Club(E)T/ST324,Philips(E)838.764-1,
	838.764-2(CD)
Stardust(1)	World Record Club(E)T/ST324
Humph And Me(2)	-
Fondu Head	-
Sentimental Journey	-
Me And Buck(2)	-
Autumn Leaves(1)	-
Cotton Tail	-

-1.Omit Lyttelton,Temperley.
-2.Omit Moss,Temperley.

Note:For contractual reasons the above session was issued as having been recorded in
    Interlaken, Switzerland.

BUCK CLAYTON AND THE COUNT BASIE ALL STARS:
Buck Clayton(tp),Earl Warren(as),Sir Charles Thompson(p),Tommy Potter(b),Jackie Williams
(dr).   Toronto.July 23,1963
      Smiley's Blues (theme)   Discus(Ca)DS-MM/VS63/2
      Canadian Capers   -
      Blue Goose Special   -
      Canadian Sunset   -
      North Atlantic Squadron   -
      Alouette(1)(ob)   -
      Thousand Islands Song   -
      Saskatchewan   -
      Squid Jiggin' Ground   -

-1.Add Olive Brown(vcl);Warren plays (fl).

BUCK CLAYTON WITH HUMPHREY LYTTELTON AND HIS BAND:
Buck Clayton,Humphrey Lyttelton(tp),Tony Coe(ts),Joe Temperley(bars),Eddie Harvey(p,tb),
Pete Blannin(b),Eddie Taylor(dr).   London.November 19,1964
      The Green Tiger   "77"(E)LEU12/11
      Red Barrel Blues   -
      Unbooted Character   -
      Talk Of The Town   -
      The Wrestler's Tricks(no ts,bars)   -
      Blues In The Afternoon   -
      The Huckle Buck   -
      One Hour   -
      Carole's Caper   -
      You Can Depend On Me   -

All titles also on Polydor(E)423.213,Harlequin(E)HQ3005.
Note:For contractual reasons the above session was issued as having been recorded in
     Interlaken, Switzerland.

BUCK CLAYTON SEPTET:
Buck Clayton(tp),Vic Dickenson(tb),Tommy Newsom(ts),Hank Jones(p),Kenny Burrell(g,vcl),
Milt Hinton(b),Osie Johnson(dr,vcl).   Live.Connecticut.Spring 1965
      Medley: Private issue(unnumb.)
          I Can't Get Started
          Stella By Starlight
          Imagination
          In A Sentimental Mood
          You Are Too Beautiful
          Li'l Darling
        Satin Doll   -
        Manhattan   -
        Everything Happens To Me(oj)   -
        Rose Room/In A Mellotone   -
        I Cover The Waterfront   -
        It's You Or No One(oj)   -
        How High The Moon   -
        Sunday   -
        The Girl From Ipanema   -
        Sweet Georgia Brown   -
        Just You,Just Me   -
        Where Or When(kb)   -
        Stompin' At The Savoy   -

Note:The above titles were recorded at a private party and issued on an unnumbered 3xLP
     set ("Jazz At J.J.'s").

BUCK CLAYTON QUINTET/ALL STARS:
Buck Clayton(tp),Vic Dickenson(tb),Benny Waters -1,Alix Combelle -1(ts),Joe Turner(p),
Jimmy Woode(b),Kenny Clarke(dr).   Broadcast.Paris.May 13,1965
         Keeping Out Of Mischief Now
         All Of Me
         Perdido(1)   I Giganti del Jazz(I)GJ29,Europa Jazz(I)EJ1023

Note:See Joe Turner(vcl) for additional titles from this broadcast.

BUCK CLAYTON - JOE TURNER WITH THE ZAGREB JAZZ QUARTET:
Buck Clayton(tp),Bosko Petrovic(vbs),Davor Kajfes(p),Kresimir Remeta(b),Silvije Glojnaric
(dr),Joe Turner(vcl).   Zagreb.June 2,1965
         Honeysuckle Rose   Black Lion(G)28455
         I'm In A World
           Of Trouble(no tp)(jt)   -
         I Can't Get Started   - ,157.000
         Feel So Fine(no tp)(jt)   -
         Perdido   -
         I Want A Little Girl(no tp)(jt)   -
         Too Late,Too Late(jt)   -

All titles also on Black Lion(E)BLP30145,2460.202,BLCD760170 (CD),(G)127.023,(F)BL278.089,
Freedom(F)BLP30145,Fontana(Eu)826.200QY,Audio Fidelity BL202,Intercord(G)28455.

Buck Clayton(tp),Michel Pilet(ts),Henri Chaix(p),Isla Eckinger(b),Wallace Bishop(dr).
                              Broadcast.Baden,Switzerland.February 6,1966
        Unknown titles   Sackville SKCD2028(CD)

BUCK CLAYTON AND HIS SWISS ALL STARS:
Buck Clayton(tp),Raymond Droz(tb),Werner Keller(cl),Michel Pilet(ts),Henri Chaix(p),Alain
Dubois(g),Isla Eckinger(b),Johnny Burrows(dr).
                            Zurich,Switzerland.March 14,1966
         Clayton Place   Decca(G)SLK16-431
         Casa Bar   -
         I Want A Little Girl   -
         Tune For Buck   -
         Swingin' The Blues(1)   -
         Candy's Tune   -
         Topsy   -

-1.Vince Benedetti(p) replaces Chaix.

BUCK CLAYTON AND FRIENDS:
Buck Clayton(tp),Hal Singer(ts),Joe Turner(p),Mickey Baker(g),Roland Lobligeois(b),Wallace
Bishop(dr).   Paris.March 16,1966
         Groovy Sunday   Polydor(Eu)423.221/623.221
         I Can't Think   -
         Juggi Buggi(1)   -
         Georgia On My Mind(no ts,g)   -
         Boo Boo   -
         Just You,Just Me   -
         One For Bonnie   -
         Blue Boy   -
         Pat's Party   -
         Come With Me   Polydor(F)LP74566
         These Foolish Things   unissued
         Spanish Fly   -
         Rosetta   -

-1.Bernard De Bosson(p) replaces Turner.
(session cont. next page).

(session cont. from previous page):
Note:"Juggi Buggi" poss. recorded May 2,1966 - this may also be the rec. date for "Come
     With Me" and the three unissued titles.

BUCK CLAYTON WITH HUMPHREY LYTTELTON AND HIS BAND:
Buck Clayton(tp,arr),Humphrey Lyttelton(tp),Chris Pyne(tb),Kathy Stobart(ts),Eddie Harvey
(p,arr),Dave Green(b),Tony Taylor(dr).   London.May 25,1966

Say Forward,I'll March	"77"(E)LEU12/18,Harlequin(E)HQ3002		
Russian Lullaby		-	-
Talkback		-	-
One For Buck		-	-
An Evening In Soho(1)		-	-
The Jumping Blues		-	-
Blue Mist		-	-
The Swingin' Birds		-	-
Poor Butterfly(2)		-	-
Bernie's Tune(3)	Harlequin(E)HQ3002		

-1.Harvey plays (tb).
-2.Omit Lyttelton,Pyne.
-3.Omit Lyttelton,Stobart.

Note:For contractual reasons the above session was issued as having been recorded in Paris
     (on the above date).

BUCK CLAYTON WITH HUMPHREY LYTTELTON AND HIS BAND:
Buck Clayton(tp,arr),Humphrey Lyttelton(tp),John Mumford(tb),Tony Coe(ts),Eddie Harvey
(p),Ron Rubin(b),Tony Taylor(dr).   Live.Musikhalle,Hamburg,Germany.May 4,1969
          Swinging At The Copper Rail   Wam(G)MLP15.402,JL8013

Note:See Humphrey Lyttelton for one additional title (without Clayton) from this concert.

BUCK CLAYTON JAM SESSION:
Joe Newman,Doc Cheatham(tp),Urbie Green(tb),Earl Warren(as),Budd Johnson(ts,ss),Zoot Sims
(ts),Joe Temperley(bars),Earl Hines(p),Milt Hinton(b),Gus Johnson(dr),Buck Clayton(arr).
                              NYC.March 25/26,1974

Boss Blues	Chiaroscuro CR132,CRD132(CD)		
Case Closed		-	-
Easy Blue(1)		-	-
Jayhawk	Chiaroscuro CR163,	-	,Vogue(E)VJD540

-1.As "Lazy Blues" on CRD132 (CD).

All titles on CR132 also on Vogue(E)VJD520,Overseas(J)ULS1848V.

Joe Newman,Harold "Money" Johnson(tp),Vic Dickenson,George Masso(tb),Lee Konitz,Earl War-
ren(as),Budd Johnson(ts,ss),Buddy Tate,Sal Nistico(ts),Tommy Flanagan(p),Milt Hinton(b),
Mel Lewis(dr),Buck Clayton(arr).   NYC.June 5/6,1975

Sidekick	Chiaroscuro CR143	
Change For a Buck	-	
The Duke We Knew(1)	-	
Glassboro Blues	Chiaroscuro CR163,Vogue(E)VJD540	

-1.Listed as "The Duke" on the label; "The Duke We Knew" is a Clayton original (i.e. not
   Dave Brubeck's "The Duke").

All titles on CR143 also on Vogue(E)VJD520,Overseas(J)UPX49.

Harry Edison,Marvin "Hannibal" Peterson(tp),Vic Dickenson,Jimmy Knepper(tb),Bob Wilber
(ss),Lee Konitz,Earl Warren(as),Budd Johnson,Buddy Tate(ts),Hank Jones(p),Richard Davis
(b),Bobby Rosengarden(dr),Buck Clayton(arr). NYC.September 13,1976
(session cont. next page).

(session cont. from previous page):
```
        Jazz Party Time              Chiaroscuro CR152
        Kansas City Style                    -
        Even Steven                          -
        Band Wagon                           -
```

All titles also on Vogue(E)VJD540.

JAMES "KID" CLAYTON

James "Kid" Clayton(tp,vcl),Joe Avery(tb),Albert Burbank(cl),"Sweet" Emma Barrett(p),
George Guesnon(b,vcl),Sylvester Handy(b),Alex Bigard(dr).
```
                                      New Orleans.August 20/21,1952
        The Sheik Of Araby(1)(alt.take)  Folkways FJ2859
        See See Rider(1)(alt.take)                -
        Gettysburg March              Folkways FA2463,FJ2859,Topic(E)12T55
        Coquette(gg)                  Folkways FJ2859
        The Sheik Of Araby            Folkways FA2465,FJ2859
        Bye Bye Blackbird             Folkways FJ2859
        See See Rider(kc)                     -
        Corrine Corrina(kc,gg)        Folkways FA2463,FJ2859,Topic(E)12T55
        In The Groove(kc)                     -       -        -
        Jimmy's Blues(kc)                     -       -        - ,Supraphon(Cz)
                                      DV15138
        Shake It And Break It         Folkways FA2465,FJ2859
```

-1.Omit Clayton.

KID CLAYTON'S HAPPY PALS:
Kid Clayton(tp,vcl),Bill Matthews(tb),Albert Burbank(cl),Charlie Hamilton(bj),August La-
noix(b),Abby "Chinee" Foster(dr,vcl).   New Orleans.Poss. September 1962
```
        Corrine Corrina(af)           Icon LP12
        Don'Cha Carry My
          Gal Out Fishin'(kc)                 -
        Jimmy's Blues (638 Blues)(kc)         -
        In The Groove(kc)                     -
        Azules De San Luis
          (St.Louis Blues)
        Song Of The Islands
```

Note: "Song Of The Islands" was prob. recorded at a public performance.

Alex Bigard(dr) replaces Foster.   New Orleans.September 19,1962
```
        You Tell Me Your Dreams       Icon LP12
        Who's Sorry Now(1)(kc)                -
        High Society                          -
        High Society (alt.take)       Archoolie F1013
        Chinee's Blues                Icon LP12
```

-1.The issued version is spliced from two takes.

All titles on Icon LP12 also on Jazzology JCE22.

JAY CLAYTON

(vcl) acc. by Jane Ira Bloom(ss,as),Larry Karusch(p),Harvie Schwartz(b),Frank Clayton(dr).
                                      NYC.October 1980
(session cont. next page).

(session cont. from previous page):
```
        Badadadat                     Anima 1J35
        Random Mondays                   -
        Lonely Woman(vcl,dr only)        -
        2-5-1                            -
        7/8 Thing(1)                     -
        Fragments                        -
        All Out                          -
```

-1.Add Bill Buschen(kalimba),Shelley Hirsch,Becca Armstrong,Sally Swisher(vcl).

JEFF CLAYTON

See CLAYTON BROTHERS.

JOHN CLAYTON

See CLAYTON BROTHERS.

KID CLAYTON

See JAMES "KID" CLAYTON.

(VAALBLEEK) CLEANSING DEPARTMENT ORCHESTRA / GEMEENTE REINIGINGSORKEST (Dutch)

Toon de Gouw(tp),Hans Sparla(tb),Paul van Kemenade(as),Henk Koekkoek(ts),Willem Kühne(p),
Peter Mingaars(g),Niko Langenhuijsen(b,ldr),Frans van Grinsven(dr).
```
                                      Hilvarenbeek,The Netherlands.July 7/8,1980
        Flattery In All Keys          BV Haast(Du)030
        Chessmash                        -
        Song For Carry Rabbit            -
        P.O. (Pech Onderweg)             -
        Diarréggae                       -
        Invensie                         -
        Vaalbleek Suite                  -
```


RUPERT CLEMENDORE (Trinidad)

RUPERT CLEMENDORE COMBO:
```
No details.                           Prob. Port Of Spain,Trinadad.  1950's
        Unknown titles                Cook LP(S)1082
```

Sunny Denner(ts),Bert Innis(p),Les Sargent(g),Gerald Charles(b),Randolph Lewis(dr),Rupert
Clemmendore(dr,vbs,vcl),Calvin Lorelike(cg),Clayton Peters(timba-dr).
```
                                      Prob. Port Of Spain,Trinidad.  1950's
        Mambo Chop Suey(no ts)(rc)    Cook LP(S)10850
        Mambo Metronome(no ts)           -
        Easter Congo                     -
        Off Beat                         -
        If Sorrow Fills My Heart         -
```
(session cont. next page).

(session cont. from previous page):
```
        Clem's Confession(rc)          Cook LP(S)10850
        Drummer's Mood                      -
        Doris,Oh!                           -
        Eight Hours A Day                   -
        Short Pants Saga                    -
        Mambo Ebonier                       -
        Eulogie                             -
        Progressive Calypso                 -
```

ROD CLESS

ROD CLESS QUARTET:
Sterling Bose(tp),Rod Cless(cl),James P. Johnson(p),Pops Foster(b).
                                       NYC.September 1,1944
```
BW33    Froggy Moore                   Black & White 29,Pickwick(J)PJFD15001(CD)
BW34-1  Make Me A
        Pallet On The Floor            Black & White 8,30,Crispus-Attucks PB 101,Pickwick
                                       (J)PJFD15001(CD)
BW35-1  I Know That You Know           Black & White 8,30,Pickwick(J)PJFD15001(CD)
BW36    Have You Ever Felt That Way    Black & White 29,               -
```

All titles - except "I Know That You Know" - also on Jazztone(Eu)J1039,Guilde du Jazz(F)
J1039 (issued as JAMES P. JOHNSON QUARTET).

JIMMY CLEVELAND

See also GIGI GRYCE.

JIMMY CLEVELAND AND HIS ALL STARS:
Ernie Royal(tp),Jimmy Cleveland(tb),Jerome Richardson(ts),Cecil Payne(bars),Wade Legge(p),
Barry Galbraith(g),Paul Chambers(b),Joe Harris(dr),Quincy Jones(arr).
                                       NYC.August 4,1955
```
11968   I Hadn't Anyone Till You       EmArcy MG36066
11969   See Minor                           -
11970-9 Our Love Is Here To Stay       Mercury(J)25PJ60(824116-1),EmArcy(J)195J55
```

Ernie Royal(tp),Jimmy Cleveland(tb),Lucky Thompson(ts),Cecil Payne(bars),John Williams(p),
Barry Galbraith(g),Paul Chambers(b),Max Roach(dr),Quincy Jones(arr).
                                       NYC.August 12,1955
```
11997   Hear Ye!Hear Ye!               EmArcy MG36066
11998   You Don't Know What Love Is    EmArcy EP1-6534,MG36066
11999   Little Beaver                  EmArcy MG36066,MG36085
```

Ernie Royal(tp),Jimmy Cleveland(tb),Lucky Thompson(ts),Cecil Payne(bars),Hank Jones(p),
Barry Galbraith(g),Oscar Pettiford(b),Osie Johnson(dr),Quincy Jones(arr).
                                       NYC.November 22,1955
```
12310   My One And Only Love           EmArcy MG36066
12311   Our Love Is Here To Stay            -
12312   Vixen                               -
12313   Count 'Em                      EmArcy EP1-6534,MG36066
12314   Bone Brother                   EmArcy MG36066
```

All titles on EmArcy MG36066 also on EmArcy(J)195J55,Mercury(E)MMB12012,Trip TLP5575.

JIMMY CLEVELAND QUARTET:
Jimmy Cleveland(tb),Billy Taylor(p),Oscar Pettiford(b),Kenny Clarke(dr).
                                          NYC.March 13,1956
5143   Embraceable You   ABC-Paramount ABC115,HMV(E)7EG8382

JIMMY CLEVELAND QUINTET:
Jimmy Cleveland(tb),Hank Jones(p),Barry Galbraith(g),Milt Hinton(b),Osie Johnson(dr).
                                          NYC.June 25,1956
CO56248 Wolf's Talk   Epic LN3297,Fresh Sound(Sp)LSP15597
CO56249 Sahara   -   -
CO56250 Blues   -   -
CO56251 Jimmy's Tune   Epic LN3339,Fontana(E)TFL5008

JIMMY CLEVELAND (SEPTET):
Art Farmer(tp),Jimmy Cleveland(tb),Don Butterfield(tu),Benny Golson(ts),Wynton Kelly(p),
Eddie Jones(b),Charlie Persip(dr).   NYC.December 12,1957
16460 Out Of This World   EmArcy MG36126
16461 All This And Heaven Too   EmArcy EP1-6557,MG36126
16462 Goodbye Ebbets Field   -   -

Jay McAllister(tu) replaces Butterfield.   NYC.December 13,1957
16463 Posterity   EmArcy EP1-6556,MG36126
16464 A Jazz Ballad   EmArcy MG36126
16465 Long Ago And Far Away   EmArcy EP1-6556,MG36126
16466 Jimmy's Tune   -   -

All titles on MG36126 also on Mercury MG20553,SR60121,(J)EXPR1019,15PJ17.

Ray Copeland(tp),Ernie Royal(flh),Jimmy Cleveland(tb),Don Butterfield(tu),Jerome Richard-
son(fl,ts),Junior Mance(p),Bill Crow(b),Art Taylor(dr),Ernie Wilkins(arr).
                                          NYC.December 16,1958
17432 Marie   Mercury MG20442
17433 Stardust   -

Same   NYC.December 17,1958
17434 The Best Things
       In Life Are Free   Mercury MG20442
17435 A Hundred Years From Today   -

Same   NYC.December 18,1958
17436 Jimmy's Old Funky Blues   Mercury MG20442
17437 Swing Low,Sweet Chariot   -
17438 Jay Bird   -

All titles on MG20442 also on Mercury SR60117,(E)MMC14023,(J)MC33.

Art Farmer(tp),Jimmy Cleveland(tb),Benny Golson(ts,arr),Jerome Richardson(fl,ts,bars),Hank
Jones(p),Milt Hinton(b),Osie Johnson(dr),Gigi Gryce(arr).
                                          NYC.c. February 1959
18130 Our Delight   Mercury MG20450,EmArcy MGE26003/SRE66003
18131 Crazy Rhythm   -   -
18132 Reminiscing   -   -
18133 We Never Kissed   -   -
18134 Old Reliable   -   -
18135 Tricrotism   -   -
18136 Tom-Kattin'   -   -

Jimmy Cleveland(tb),Benny Golson(ts),Eddie Costa(p),Ben Tucker(b),Eddie Campbell(dr).
                                    Westerley,R.I.September 1959
       Blues   Phoenix LP16

Note:See COLEMAN HAWKINS for additional titles from the above session.

JAY CLEVER

See JACK KLUGER.

DUD CLEWS (British)

DUD CLEWS JAZZ ORCHESTRA:
John Fallcon,Brian Bates(tp),Derek Habberjam(tb,tu,ldr),Bob Caldwell(as),Colin Wharton
(cl,ts),Mac Randle(cl,ss,ts),Tom Holt(as,bars),Ron Glen(p),Bernard Overton(g,bj),Ian
Hamilton(b),John Astle(dr).   London,November 14,1965

Stockholm Stomp	VJM(E)LC5	
Lament	-	
Cincinnati Daddy	-	
Baby Won't You Please Come Home	-	
Susie	-	
Radio Rhythm	-	
Panama	-	
New Call Of The Freaks	-	
Saratoga Shout	-	
Creole Love Call	-	
Deep Henderson	-	
Shout 'em,Aunt Tillie	-	

Note:Dud Clews died in 1964, but the name of the band was retained.

Brian Walther(p,vcl),Brian Bates(tp),Paul Munnery(tb),Mac Randle(ss,cl,as),Bob Caldwell
(as,cl),Colin Wharton(ts,cl),Terry Perry(bars,cl),Ron Glen(p),Bernard Overton(bj,g),John
Nuddings -1(bj),Derek Habberjam(tu,ldr),John Astle(dr).
                                          Coventry,England,October 18,1968

Wa, Wa Wa	Harlem(E)1101	
When You're Smiling	-	
Slue Foot	-	
Low Down On The Bayou	-	
Rhythm Club Stomp	-	
Song Of The Swanee	-	
Congo Love Song	-	
Take It Easy	-	
You Rascal You(bw)	-	
Rent Party Blues	-	
Jungle Blues(1)	-	
Black And Tan Fantasy(1)	-	
Mercer Stomp(1,2)	-	
Sugar(bw)(1,2)	-	

-2.Omit Overton.

CLIMAX JAZZ BAND (Canadian)

Bob Erwig(tp),Geoff Holmes(tb,vcl),Bruce Bakewell(cl,vcl),Juergen Hesse(bj),Chris Daniels
(b,vcl),Craig Barrett(dr).   Toronto.April 7,1973

Tight Like That(cd)	Tormax(Ca)33001	
La Harpe Street Blues	-	
Whistlin' Rufus	-	
St. James Infirmary(cd)	-	
Davenport Blues	-	
Climax Shake	-	
C Jam Blues	-	

(session cont. next page).

(session cont. from previous page):

Down Home Rag	Tormax(Ca)33001
Delia's Gone(bb)	-
As Long As I Live	-
Chimes Blues	-
Ice Cream(gh)	-
Introductory Blues(cd)	-

Note:Name of the record company and issueno. do not appear on the label.

Same.   Toronto.March 1974

The Entertainer	United Artists(Ca)UALA254
Everybody Loves My Baby	-
Let Me Be There	-
Dauphine Street Blues	-
Bloor Street Breakdown	-
1919 March	-
You're Sixteen	-
Swipsey Cakewalk	-
Inspiration	-
East Coast Trot(cl,bj,b only)	-
Perdido Street Blues	-
Chrysanthemum Rag	-

Ken Colyer(tp,vcl),Bob Erwig(cnt),Geoff Holmes(tb),Bruce Bakewell(cl,vcl),Jack Vincken
(bj),Chris Daniels(b),Al Mayers(dr).   Live."Malloney's Tavern",Toronto.April 19,1975

Too Busy(bb)	Tormax(Ca)33005
Baby Won't You	
Please Come Home(kc)	-
Oh!You Beautiful Doll	-
The Curse Of An Aching Heart(kc)	-
See See Rider(kc)	-
I Can't Escape From You	-

Bob Erwig(cnt),Geoff Holmes(tb),Bruce Bakewell(cl),Graeme Bell(p),Mike Warmsley(bj,g),Jack
Vincken(b),Al Mayers(dr,vcl).   Live."Malloney's Tavern",Toronto.June 28,1975

Swanee River	Tormax(Ca)33004,Festival(Au)L35927	
Memphis Blues	-	-
Malloney's Boogie(p,g,b,dr only)	-	-
Black And Blue	-	-
Tishomingo Blues	-	-
I Want A Little		
Girl(no tb,cl)(am)	-	-
Muskrat Ramble(p,bj,b,dr only)	-	-
Greenville Street Blues	-	-
China Boy(no cnt,tb)	-	-
Yellow Dog Blues	-	-

Bob Erwig(cnt),Geoff Holmes(tb,vcl),Jim Buchmann(cl,saxello,as),Jack Vincken(bj),Chris
Daniels (b,vcl),Steve Tattersall(dr).   Live."Harbourfront",Toronto.March 27,1977

Red Wing	Tormax(Ca)33006
Ostrich Walk	-
Stranger On The Shore	-
We Shall Walk	
Through The Valley(cd)	-
Dans Les Rues d'Antibes	-
Hiawatha Rag	-
I'm Crazy 'Bout My Baby(gh)	-
Les Oignons	-
Auf Wiedersehen	-

Note:Name of the record company and issueno. do not appear on the label.

Same.   Toronto.December 1977
    Sobbin' Blues   Labyrinth(Ca)LBR1000
    Sweet Like This   -
    Bobby Shafto   -
    Le Vendeur De Poissons   -
    Stevedore Stomp   -
    Chimes Blues   -
    Snake Rag   -
    Salutation March   -

Same.   Toronto.c. 1977
    The Chant   Baby Grand(Ca)SE1030
    Georgia Bobo   -
    Lord,Lord,Lord   -
    Big Noise From Winnetka   -
    Bienville Blues   -
    Didn't He Ramble   -
    Thriller Rag   -
    Baby Brown   -
    Washington And Lee Swing   -
    Majella Blues   -
    Snake Rag   -
    A Chicken Ain't
      Nothin' But A Bird   -

Max Littlejohns(dr) replaces Tattersall;add Tony Pringle(cnt).
                                               Live.Denver,Co.August 27,1978
    Algiers Strut   Denver Jazz Club DJC1

Omit Pringle.   Toronto.February 27/March 12,1979
    Revival   Tormax(Ca)33007
    Papa De Da Da   -
    Mad Dog   -
    Petite Fleur(no cnt,tb)   -
    Merrydown Rag   -
    Oh,Didn't He Ramble(cd)   -
    The Favorite   -
    Precious Lord(cd)   -
    Summerset(no cnt,tb)   -
    Sporting Life Blues(gh)   -
    Bluebells Goodbye   -

CLIMAX JAZZ BAND (German)

Peter Nusse(cnt,vcl),Peter Weiss(tb,vcl),Gunter Steidl(cl,as,vcl),Fatty Olberg(bj),Norbert
Kleinen(b),Christoph Hagmann(dr).   Live.Cologne,Germany.August 1,1974
    Down Home Rag   CJB(G)F65.311
    Saratoga Swing   -
    Over In Gloryland   -
    The New Orleans Wiggle   -
    High Society   -
    Bourbon Street Parade   -
    Sweet Emmalina   -
    On A Persian Market   -
    Riverside Blues   -
    We Sure Do Need Him Now   -
    Stevedore Stomp   -

CLIMAX JAZZ BAND (German)

Same.   Cologne,Germany.September 10,1975
        Entertainer Rag   (see note)

Note:The above title issued on a Rheinische Post LP.

Cliff Wren(tp),Peter Weiss(tb),Gunter Steidl(cl,as),Barry Dew(bj),Mike Dieck(b),Christoph
Hagmann(dr),Heinz Lauter(vcl).   Mönchengladbach,Germany.October 6,1976
        Mönchengladbach Ist "In"(hl)   MO Musikproduktion(unknown issueno.)
        Thekensomg(hl)   -

CLIMAX JAZZ BAND (New Zealand)

Bruce Haley(tp),Lindsay Brighouse(tb),Tony Ashby(cl),Denis Costello(p),Joe Rutledge(b),Max
Bayley(dr).   Tauranga,New Zealand.June 1968
        Green Green Grass Of Home   Tauranga(NZ)526

ALEX CLINE

See NELS CLINE,JAMIL SHABAKA.

NELS CLINE

THE QUARTET:
Jeff Gautier(vln),Nels Cline(g,mand),Eric von Essen(b),Alex Cline(perc).
                                LA.March 15/16,1980
        Morning Raga   Nine Winds 0106
        The Mad Goat   -
        Bill Evans   -
        2 Sevens   -
        The Tightrope Walkers (for N.V.E)   -

Note:The above LP is a recording by a collective group.

NELS CLINE - ERIC VON ESSEN:
Nels Cline(g,recorder,vcl),Eric von Essen(b).
                            LA.September 13/14,1980
        Talunis   Nine Winds 0105
        Two Improvisations: B&B,S&S   -
        Dedication: Charlie Haden   -
        Harlequin   -
        Love Song   -
        Darabsha Road   -

BOB CLITHEROW

BOB CLITHERO AND HIS CAVALIERS/ORCHESTRA:
Bob Clitherow,Paul Pickard(tp),Chick Bothelho(tb),Frank J. Casino(ts),Paul Harriman(p),
Thomas J. Davis(g),George J. Raso(b),Leon Graham(dr).
                              Prague.October 13,1945
44431 Rosetta   Ultraphon(Cz)B14312,Supraphon(Cz)C23184
44432 Sentimental Journey   Ultraphon(Cz)B14313,Supraphon(Cz)B22234
44433 I've Found A New Baby   -   -
44434 Boogie Woogie   Ultraphon(Cz)B14312,Supraphon(Cz)C23184

Note:The above musicians were U.S. servicemen stationed in Europe.

ROSEMARY CLOONEY

See also BILL BERRY,LES BROWN,DUKE ELLINGTON,BENNY GOODMAN,HARRY JAMES,NAT PIERCE.

Rosemary Clooney(vcl) acc. by JOHNNY GUARNIERI QUINTET:
Johnny Guarnieri(p),rest unknown.   Unknown location/date
      Thou Swell
      I Had A Talk With
        The Wind And The Rain
      Chicago
      Can't Help Loving That Man
      If I Were Your Girl
      Bye Bye Baby

Note:The above titles are from Voice Of America transcription (PV22).

(vcl) acc. by unknown orchestra,Frank Comstock(cond).
                                    LA. 1956
      Doncha' Go Way Mad(1)   Columbia CL1006
      Love Letters   -
      I'm In The Mood For Love   -
      Together(1)   -
      Everything Happens To Me   -
      What Is There To Say(1)   -
      I'm Glad There Is You   -
      How About You(1)   -

-1.Add The Hi-Lo's(vcl).

All titles also on Memoir MOIR114,CBS(J)32DP671 (CD).
Note:Additional titles on the above LP are without Clooney.

(vcl) acc. by THE BUDDY COLE TRIO:
Buddy Cole(p),rest unknown.   LA.December 26,1958
      'Deed I Do   Coral CRL(7)57266
      You Took Advantage Of Me   -
      Blue Moon   -
      Sing You Sinners   -
      A Touch Of The Blues   -
      Goody,Goody   -
      Too Close For Comfort   -
      Do Nothin' Till You Hear From Me   -
      Moonlight Mississippi   -
      I Wish I Were In Love Again   -
      Sunday In Savannah   -
      This Can't Be Love   -

All titles also on MCA(J)VIM4104,Jasmine(E)JASM1502.

(vcl) acc. by THE BUDDY COLE TRIO/QUARTET:
Buddy Cole(p),unknown g,b,dr.   Unknown location/date
      'Deed I Do   Star Line SLC61165
      A Touch Of The Blues   -
      I Feel A Song Coming On   -
      That's How It Is With Me   -
      Sunday In Savannah   -
      Goody,Goody   -

Note:The above titles are prob. from unknown transcription(s).
     SLC61165 is a cassette issue; additional tracks on SLC61165 are not included.

(vcl) acc. by Bill Berry(tp),Scott Hamilton(ts),Nat Pierce(p),Monty Budwig(b),Jake Hanna
(dr).   LA.June 7,1977

I Cried For You	Concord CJ47
More Than You Know	-
How Am I To Know(no vcl)	-
I Can't Get Started	-
A Foggy Day	-
I've Got A Crush On You	- ,CJ278
Hey There	-
As Time Goes By	-
All Of Me(no vcl)	-
Do You Know What It Means To Miss New Orleans	-

All titles also on Concord(J)LCJ2001.

(vcl) acc. by Scott Hamilton(ts),Nat Pierce(p),Cal Collins(g),Monty Budwig(b),Jake Hanna
(dr).   LA.January 6,1978

But Beautiful	Concord CJ60
Pennies From Heaven	-
Blue Skies	-
I Surrender,Dear	-
Where The Blue Of The Night	-
It's Easy To Remember	-
Swinging On A Star	-
Just One More Chance	-
I Wished On The Moon	-
Too-Ra-Loo-Ra-Loo-Ra	-

All titles also on Concord(J)LCJ2002.

(vcl) acc. by Warren Vaché(cnt),Scott Hamilton(ts),Nat Pierce(p),Cal Collins(g),Monty
Budwig(b),Jake Hanna(dr).   San Francisco.September 1978

I Cover The Waterfront	Concord CJ81
Good Morning,Heartache	-
Mean To Me	-
Lover Man	-
Don't Explain(no cnt)	-
Comes Love	-
He's Funny That Way	-
God Bless The Child(g,vcl only)	-
Them There Eyes	-
Everything Happens To Me	-

All titles also on Concord(J)ICJ70181,LCJ2041.

(vcl) acc. by Warren Vaché(cnt,flh),Roger Glenn(fl),Scott Hamilton(ts),Nat Pierce(p),Cal
Collins(g),Chris Amberger(b),Jeff Hamilton(dr).
                                          San Francisco.October 1979

But Not For Me	Concord CJ112
Nice Work If You Can Get It	-
How Long Has This Been Going On	-
Fascinating Rhythm	-
Love Is Here To Stay	-
Strike Up The Band	-
Long Ago And Far Away	-
They All Laughed	-
The Man That Got Away	-
They Can't Take That Away From Me	-

All titles also on Concord(J)LCJ2042.

(vcl) acc. by Warren Vaché(cnt,flh),Scott Hamilton(ts),Cal Tjader(vbs),Nat Pierce(p),Cal Collins(g),Bob Maize(b),Jake Hanna(dr).   San Francisco.November 1980

Just The Way You Are	Concord CJ144
The Way We Were	-
Alone At Last	-
Come In From The Rain	-
Meditation	-
Hello Young Lovers	-
Just In Time	-
Tenderly	-
Will You Still Be Mine	-

All titles also on Concord(J)CP35-3048,ICJ80198,LCJ2043.
Note:Additional recordings by this artist are not included.

POL CLOSSET (Belgian)

POL CLOSSET AND HIS DIXIELAND GAMBLERS:
Pol Closset(tp),Honoré d'Utrecht (Herman Veltman)(tb),André Ronsse(cl),Jean-Claude Pil (p),Etienne Boyens(b),Andrien Ransy(dr),Roger "Big Brown" Sauvenier(vcl).
                                        Brussels. 1959/60

My Testament	Palette(B)PB40088
Baby Blues(1)	-
Tityre,Tu Patulae(2)	Palette(B)PB40112
Menin,Aeide Thea(2)	- ,EPP7235
Hey Ba Ba Re Bop(bb)	Palette(B)PB40126
Hello,Mr. Brown(3)(bb)	-

-1.Pierre Lacroix(dr) replaces Ransy.
-2.Add unknown(ts).
-3.Add Willy Albimoor(org).

Pol Closset(tp),Honoré d'Utrecht(tb),Jean Daliers(cl),André Van Lint(p),Jean-Pierre Liénard(g,bj),Yves "Tif" Aerts(b),Gus Rogny(dr).
                                        Brussels.March 8,1968

Doctor Jazz	New Music Corporation(B)10.007
I'm Coming Virginia	-

Mike Pointon(tb) replaces d'Utrecht;add Pol Lenders(vcl).
                                        Buizingen,Belgium. 1971

Ice Cream(pl)	Smoke(B)S007
TVA Blues(pl)	-

Pol Closset(tp),André Knapen(tb),André Ronsse(cl),Marc Hérouet(p),Peter Welsh (Pierre Willems)(bj,vcl),Jean-Louis Rassinfosse(b),Bob Dartsch(dr).
                                        Brussels.March 23,1973

La Brabanconne(no p)	Vogue(B)VB257,CPRVB037
Florio	-

Same.   Brussels.July 24,1973

Down By The Riverside	Vogue(B)CPRVB037
Alexander's Ragtime Band	-
Saint James Infirmary	-
It's A Long Way To Tipperary	-
Happy Birthday	-
When The Saints Go Marching In	-
My Bonnie	-
A La Russe	-

(session cont. next page).

(session cont. from previous page):
```
        All The Time            Vogue(B)CPRVB037
        Walkin' With God                -
        Moi Y'en A Bien Aimer Ca        -
```

Pol Glosset(tp),Mike Pointon(tb),Michel Thiry(cl),Marc Hérouet(p),Terry Devos(b),Gus Rogny (dr).   Brussels.March 6,1978
```
        Canal Street Blues       Vogue(B)VBL9010
        That Da Da Strain               -
        South                           -
        Diga Diga Doo                   -
```

Pol Closset(tp),Honoré d'Utrecht(tb),Jean Daliers(cl),André Van Lint(p),Jean-Pierre Liénard(g)(g),Tif Aerts(b),Gus Rogny(dr).   Brussels.March 7,1978
```
        Doctor Jazz              Vogue(B)VBL9010
        I'm Coming Virginia             -
```

Pol Closset(tp),Michel Thiry(cl),Marc Hérouet(p),Jean-Pierre Liénard(g),Terry Devos(b),Bob Dartsch(dr).   Brussels.March 28/April 11,1978
```
        I Can't Give You
          Anything But Love      Vogue(B)VBL9010
        Ragtime Mama                    -
        I've Found A New Baby            -
        D.G. Blues                      -
        Just A Closer Walk With Thee    -
        There'll Be Some Changes Made   -
```

CLAUDE CLOUD

See also SAM TAYLOR.

CLAUDE CLOUD AND HIS THUNDERCLAPS:
Unknown -1(tp), Sam Taylor(ts),Haywood Henry(bars),Freddie Washington(p),Leroy Kirkland (g),Lloyd Trotman(b),Claude Cloud(dr).   NYC. 1954
```
54XY369  One Bone               MGM 55003
54XY468  Bang-Up(1)(band-vcl)   MGM 55008,E281,(E)EP517
54XY486  High Winds                -        -  ,XLP1127
54XY488  Cloudburst(1)          MGM EP281,(E)EP517
         Flip And Skip(1)       MGM 55003,EP281,(E)EP517
         The Big Horn(1)           -        -
         Close Out                 -  ,XLP1127
         The Beat(band-vcl)     MGM
         Should I               MGM
         Moanin'                MGM XLP1127
         Beginner's Mambo       MGM 11847,XLP1127
         If I Can Live To See      -
```

All titles - except "One Bone" and "If I Can Live To See" - also on MGM E3466.
All titles on E281 also on MGM(E)D142.
Note:Dick Harris(tb) on unknown titles (but definitely not on titles marked -1).

Unknown big band,Ernie Wilkins(arr).   NYC. 1954
```
         The Double Whammy      MGM E3466
         Around The Horn           -
```

RUSTY CLOUD

(section cont. next page).

Jim Clouse(ss,ts,cl),Rusty Cloud(p,el-p),Rick Kilburn(b,el-b),Tom Wailey(dr).

	NYC(?).c. 1980
Westering	Mu RC100
Karuna	-

Dave Scott(tp),Vince Prudente(tb),Jim Clouse(ss,ts,cl),Rusty Cloud(p,el-p),Rick Kilburn(b,el-b),Jeff Hirshfield(dr).

	Same date
Peace,Rahsaan	Mu RC100
Blessing	-

THE CLOUDS (Belgian)

See also JACK SELS.

Johnny Scott,Prosper Credo(fl),Frans L'Eglise(as),Jean Evans(p),Robert De Rijke(org),Freddy Sunder(g,ldr),Clement De Mayer(b),Armand Van De Walle(dr).

	Brussels.c. 1965
Cecilia	Nederlandse Pocketplaat(Du)NPP6006
Schoon Lief	
Twee Konigskinderen	-
Vier Weverkens	-
Sneeuwwitje Vogeltje	-
Island Bedroefde Kust	-
Heer Halewijn	-

Poss. omit Scott,Credo,L'Eglise.

	Prob. Brussels.c. 1965
Free Blowing	BRT EP19
Allegria	-
From Three To Four	-
Pinky	-
Springtime	BRT EP21

CLARENCE CLUMP

See BENNY CARTER.

THE CLYDE VALLEY STOMPERS (British)

Charlie Gall(tp),Ian Menzies(tb),Jim Doherty(cl),John Doherty(p),Norrie Brown(bj),Louis Reddie(b),Bobby Shannon(dr,wbd),Mary McGowan(vcl).

	Live.Glasgow.June 30,1956
Uist Tramping/Song (Come Along)	Beltona(E)BL2648,ABL524
Keep Right On To	
The End Of The Road	- -
I Love A Lassie	Beltona(E)BL2649,ABL519
Old Rustic Bridge By The Mill	- ,ABL524
Old Time Religion(1)(mmg)	Beltona(E)BL2650
Pearly Gates(1)(mmg)	-
Très Moutarde	Beltona(E)ABL519
When The Saints	
Go Marching In(mmg)	- ,Decca(I)MOR12

-1.Acc. by bj,b,wbd only.

All titles also on Eclipse(E)ECM2007,Ace Of Clubs(E)ACL1075.

Douggie Kerr(tp),Maurice Rose(cl,ss) replace Gall,Doherty.
London.February 15,1957

Teddy Bears' Picnic	Beltona(E)ABL524	
The Eyes Of Texas	-	
I Wish I Could Shimmy Like My Sister Kate(mmg)	-	
Struttin' With Some Barbecue	-	
Milenberg Joys(mmg)	- ,Decca F-J10897	
Bill Bailey,Won't You Please Come Home(mmg)	-	-

All titles also on Eclipse(E)ECM2007,Ace Of Clubs(E)ACL1075.

IAN MENZIES AND HIS CLYDE VALLEY STOMPERS:
Malcolm Higgins(tp),Ian Menzies(tb),Forries Cairns(cl),John Cairns(p),Norrie Brown(bj),
Andrew Bennie(b),Bobby Shannon(dr),Lonnie Donnegan(vcl).
London.April 1959

Polly Wolly Doodle	Pye(E)7NJ2027,Metronome(G/Sd)B1350,Vogue(F)45PV15062
In A Persian Market	Pye(E)7NJ2027,Metronome(G/Sd)B1350,Vogue(F)45PV15062
Roses Of Picardy	Pye(E)NJE1071
Beale Street Blues	- ,GH669
Gettysburg March	- -
Swingin' Seamus	-
Sailing Down Chesapeake Bay(ld)	Pye(E)7N15223,Metronome(G/Sd)B1365,Vogue(F)45PV15074,PNV24059
Ace In The Hole(ld)	unissued

All titles on NJE1071 also on Metronome(G/Sd)MEP1755,Vogue(F)PNV24064.

John Little(b) replaces Bennie;add Fiona Duncan(vcl).
London.September 10/11,1959

Bill Bailey(fd)	Pye(E)7NJ2028,NJL23 '
Savoy Blues	- ,GH644
The Soldier's Dream	- ,Vogue(F)45PV15103
Mack The Knife(fd)	-
Just A Closer Walk With Thee(fd,ld)	-
The World Is Waiting For The Sunrise	- ,GH644
Très Moutarde	- ,Vogue(F)PNV24060
There'll Be A Hot Time In The Old Town Tonight(fd)	Pye(E)7NJ2028,NJL23,Vogue(F)45PV15082,PNV24060
Yellow Dog Blues	- ,GGL0259,GH526
Irish Black Bottom	- ,Vogue(F)PNV24060
Ice Cream(ld,band-vcl)	- , - ,45PV15082
Royal Garden Blues	-

All titles also on Metronome(G/Sd)MLP15042.

Bill Bain(b) replaces Little;omit Donnegan. London.May 9-14,1960

Barnyard Blues	Pye(E)NJL26
Blues My Naughty Sweetie Gives To Me(fd)	-
The Fish Man	Pye(E)7NJ2031,NJL26,Vogue(F)45PV15103
I Can't Give You Anything But Love(fd)	Pye(E)NJL26
Il Trovatore	-
Battle Hymn Of The Republic	-
High Society	-

(session cont. next page).

```
(session cont. from previous page):
        Salty Dog(fd)                     Pye(E)7NJ2031,NJL26
        Prelude In C Sharp Minor          Pye(E)NJL26
        Five Foot Two,Eyes Of Blue(fd)        -
        Twelfth Street Rag                    -
        Scotland The Brave                    -

Similar.                                  London.c.January   1961
        Black Angus                       Pye(E)7NJ2041
        The Big Man                           -
        Play To Me Gypsy                  Pye(E)7NJ2044
        Trombones To The Fore                 -
        Taboo                             Pye(E)7NJ2046
        Auf Wiedersehen                       -
```

THE CLYDE VALLEY STOMPERS:
Malcolm Higgins(tp),Ian Menzies(tb),Pete Kerr(cl),Jim Douglas(bj),Bill Bain(b),Robin
Winter(dr).   Live.Worthing,England.May 17,1961

```
        Royal Garden Blues                Ember(E)CJS804
        Scotland The Brave                    -
        Silver Threads Among The Gold         -
        High Society                          -
        St. Louis Blues                       -
        Trombones To The Fore                 -
        Whistling Rufus                       -
        Lover Come Back To Me                 -
```

Prob. Joe McIntyre(tp),Peter Hodge(tb),Pete Kerr(cl),Ronnie Duff(p),Jim Douglas(bj),Ron
Mathewson(b),Sandy Malcolm(dr).   London.c.June 1962
```
7XCE16892 Peter And The Wolf             Parlophone(E)45R4928
7XCE16893 Loch Lomond                         -
```

Malcolm Higgins(tp) prob. replaces McIntyre. London.c. October 1962
```
        On The Beat                       Parlophone(E)45R4985
        Marching Dixielanders                 -
        Casbah                            Parlophone(E)45R5043,Columbia(E)33SX1537,SCX3486
```

Ian Hunter-Randall(tp),John Howlett(tb),Roy Pellett(cl),Les Muscutt(bj),Matt Paton(b),
Ernie O'Malley(dr).   London.May 14,1963
```
        Istanbul                          Parlophone(E)45R5043
```

Malcolm Higgins(tp),John McGuff(tb),Pete Kerr(cl),Edith Elliott(vcl),rest unknown.
                                        Edinburgh.c.August 1967
```
        Unknown titles                    Prob. unissued
```

Note:The jazz content of some of the above titles may be limited.

JEFF CLYNE (British)

See also GORDON BECK.

JEFF CLYNE - IAN CARR:
Ian Carr (tp,flh),Trevor Watts(as),Jeff Clyne(b),John Stevens(dr).
                                        London.June 4,1966
```
        Helen's Clown                     Polydor(E)545.007
        Ou Sont Les Neiges d'Antan            -
        Ballad                            rejected
```

Same.   London.August 27,1966
        Springboard   Polydor(E)545.007
        Love Was Born   -
        Crazy Jane   -
        Ballad   -
        C.4   -

CM4 (Swiss)

Jean-Luc Barbier(sax),Francois Lindemann(p),Olivier Magnenat(b),Olivier Clerc(dr).
                                    Live.Montreux,Switzerland.June 1975
        For John Tchicai   Evasion(Sw)EB100819
        4.3.74   -
        Tranquillity   -
        Queen   -
        Thursday Suite   -

Pierre-Francois Massy(b) replaces Magnenat;Barbier plays (as,ss,fl).
                                    Unknown location.c. 1976
        Isabel's Walk With Popof Evasion(Sw)EB100823
        Populet Free   -
        Up!   -
        It Seems Easy   -
        Monday   -
        Friday   -
        Tantot-Tango-Tantot-Go   -

JOHNNY COATES (Jr.)

Johnny Coates(p),Wendell Marshall(b),Kenny Clarke(dr).
                                    NYC.November 17,1955
69089   Between The Devil
        And The Deep Blue Sea   Savoy MG12082
69090   Skylark   -
69091   Stompin' At The Savoy   unissued
69092   Coated Oats   Savoy MG12082

Same.   NYC.April 23,1956
69186   Let's Get Lost   Savoy MG12082
69187   Love Is The Sweetest Thing   -
69188   Little Girl Blue   -
69189   Ding Dong The Witch Is Dead   -
69190   If I Love Again   -

Same.   NYC.May 21,1956
69207   Sha-Ga-Da-Ga   Savoy MG12082
69208   Unknown title   -
69209   Unknown title   -
69210   Unknown title   -

All titles on MG12082 also on Savoy(J)KIJJ2019.
Note:"This Is My Lucky Day" and "If There Is Someone Lovelier Than You" - issued on Savoy
     MG12082 - are two of the titles listed as unknown.

Johnny Coates(p),DeWitt Kay(b),Glen Davis(dr).
                                 Live.Northampton Community College,Penn.February 3,1974
(session cont. next page).

(session cont. from previous page):
```
        Love Is Enough                    Omnisound N1004
        Tune No. 4(p-solo)                     -
        A Minor Waltz                          -
        Deep Strings                           -
        Yesterday(p-solo)                      -
        Little Rock Getaway                    -
```

All titles also on Philips(J)RJ7480.

(p-solo).   Live."Deer Head Inn",Delaware Water Gap,Penn.June 24,1977
```
        Prologue (no.39)                  Omnisound N1015
        When It's Sleepy Time Down South       -
        Never Have Known An Esther             -
        Sketch                                 -
        Mixed Feelings                         -
```

(p-solo).   Live.East Stroudsburg,Penn.June 30,1977
```
        The Price                         Omnisound N1015
```

(p-solo).   Live."Deer Head Inn",Delaware Water Gap,Penn.July 1,1977
```
        Homage                            Omnisound N1015
        Something Kinda Silly                  -
        The End Of The Beginnings              -
```

All titles on N1015 also on Philips(J)RJ7444,18PJ2008,ULS6097,Baybridge(J)30CP22 (CD).

(p-solo).   Live.State College,East Stroudsburg,Penn.March 5,1978
```
        Black Is The Color
            Of My True Love's Hair        Omnisound N1021
```

(p-solo).   Live."Deer Head Inn",Delaware Water Gap,Penn.March 24,1978
```
        Game Dance                        Omnisound N1021
        My Song                                -
        Going To School On A Mule              -
        In Seach.../After The Before           -
        My Melancholy Baby                     -
        Goodbye                                -
```

All titles on N1021 also on Philips(J)RJ7460.

(p-solo).   Live."Deer Head Inn",Delaware Water Gap,Penn.December 16,1978
```
        Prance                            Omnisound N1022
        Love For Sale                          -
        Don't Know                             -
        Themette                               -
        Goodbye,Old Friend                     -
        In The Open Space                      -
        Friday Morning Desperation        Omnisound N1024
```

(p-solo).   Live."Deer Head Inn",Delaware Water Gap,Penn.December 23,1978
```
        Expression Of Hope                Omnisound N1022
        (Interlude)                            -
        Down Home Rag                          -
        Song Sung Blue                         -
        Right As The Rain                      -
        Send In The Clowns                Omnisound N1024
        Sandu                                  -
```

(p-solo).   Live."Deer Head Inn",Delaware Water Gap,Penn.December 30,1978
```
        Impressions                       Omnisound N1022
        Virus No.10 (Type AC)             Omnisound N1024
```

JOHNNY COATES

(p-solo).   Live."Deer Head Inn",Delaware Water Gap,Penn.March 3,1979
      The Church Of My Youth   Omnisound N1024
      "Take Off" Rag   -

(p-solo).   Live."Deer Head Inn",Delaware Water Gap,Penn.March 5,1979
      Sing A Rainbow   Omnisound N1024

All titles on N1022 also on Philips(J)BT8106-7.
All titles on N1024 also on Philips(J)RJ7497.

(p-solo).   Live.Seibu Theater,Tokyo.November 28,1979
      Willow Weep For Me   Omnisound N1032
      Supplication   -
      Encouragement   -
      Doxy   -
      Nameless   -
      Defune   -

All titles also on Philips(J)25PJ6.

Phil Woods -1(as,cl),Johnny Coates(p),Harry Leakey -2(g),Steve Gilmore -3(b).
               Live."Deer Head Inn",Delaware Water Gap,Penn.December 15,1980
    Two Degrees East,
      Three Degrees West(2)   Omnisound N1038
    Singing With You(1,3)   -
    More Than You Know(3)   -
    Some Changes(1)   -
    How Can We Be Wrong (1st v.)(2,3)   -
    How Can We Be Wrong (2nd v.)(1,3)   -
    Why Shouldn't I(1)   Omnisound N1045

Urbie Green(tb),Johnny Coates(p).
               Live."Deer Head Inn",Delaware Water Gap,Penn.December 16,1980
    The More I See You   Omnisound N1038
    Lady Be Good   -
    Pete Kelly's Blues   Omnisound N1045

(p-solo).   Live."Deer Head Inn",Delaware Water Gap,Penn.December 17,1980
    To Be Named Later   Omnisound N1038
    Requirement   -
    A Strain   -
    Now And Then   -
    Sing Song   -
    Resolution   -
    From Somewhere To Somewhere   -
    Prayer Of Thanks   -
    Tune No.10   Omnisound N1045
    Notion   -
    Why   -

Johnny Coates(p),Harry Leakey -1(g),Steve Gilmore -2(b).
               Live."Deer Head Inn",Delaware Water Gap,Penn.December 18,1980
    Brazilian Stew (No.13)(1,2) Omnisound N1045
    Like Someone In Love(1)   -
    Hymn To Her(2)   -

George Young(picc,sopranino-sax),Johnny Coates(p).
               Live."Deer Head Inn",Delaware Water Gap,Penn.December 19,1980
    The Very Thought Of You   Omnisound N1038

Add Steve Gilmore(b).   Live."Deer Head Inn",Delaware Water Gap,Penn.December 20,1980
    For A Friend   Omnisound N1038
    Our Love Is Here To Stay   Omnisound N1045

All titles on N1038 also on Philips(J)ULS1916/17.
All titles on N1045 also on Baybridge(J)UPS2167.

ARNETT COBB

See also MILT BUCKNER,EDDIE "LOCKJAW" DAVIS,AL GREY,ILLINOIS JACQUET.

ARNETT COBB WITH THE HAMP-TONE ALL STARS:
Wendell Culley,Joe Morris(tp),Herbie Fields,Arnett Cobb(ts),Charlie Fowlkes(bars),Milt
Buckner(p),Billy Mackel(g),Charlie Harris(b),George Jenkins(dr).
                                  LA. 1946
HJ001 Down Home   Hamp-Tone 102
HJ002 Jenny   Hamp-Tone 107
HJ003 Gate Serene Blues   -
HJ004 Shebna   Hamp-Tone 102

Note:Masters HJ001 and HJ003 were issued as by MILT BUCKNER and HERBIE FIELDS respec-
     tively.

ARNETT COBB AND HIS ORCHESTRA:
Dave Page(tp),Al King(tb),Arnett Cobb(ts),George Rhodes(p),Walter Buchanan(b),George Jones
(dr).   NYC.May 13,1947
R1231-4 Walkin' With Sid   Apollo 770,Jazz Selection(F)JS538,Vogue(F)CLDAP768
R1232   Still Flying   Apollo 772,EP603,Jazz Selection(F)JS519,Queen(I)
                              Q-058
R1233   Cobb's Idea   Apollo 772,LP105,Jazz Selection(F)JS519,Vogue(E)
                              EPV1054,(F)CLDAP768,Queen(I)Q-058
R1234-2 Top Flight   Apollo 770,LP105,Jazz Selection(F)JS538,Vogue(F)
                              CLDAP768

All titles also on Vogue(F)VG405.500116.
All titles on CLDAP768 also on Vogue(F)VG403.500768,(J)YX7023.

Booty Wood(tb) replaces King.   NYC.August 1947
R1253   When I Grow Too Old
        To Dream I(band-vcl)   Apollo 775,EP601,LP105,Jazz Selection(F)JS560
R1254   When I Grow Too Old
        To Dream II(band-vcl)   -   -   -   -
R1255   Cobb's Boogie   Apollo 781,LP105,Jazz Selection(F)JS766,Vogue(E)
                              EPV1054
R1256   Cobb's Corner   Apollo 792,Jazz Selection(F)JS769

All titles also on Vogue(F)LD088,CLDAP768,VG403.500768,VG405.500116,(J)YX7023.

Same.   NYC.Autumn. 1947
R1277-1 Dutch Kitchen Bounce   Apollo 778,EP601,LP105,Jazz Selection(F)JS528,
                            Vogue(E)EPV1054,Vogue(F)LD088,CLDAP768
R1278-3 Go,Red,Go   Apollo 778,EP601,LP105,Jazz Selection(F)JS528,
                            Vogue(F)V5528,LD088,CLDAP768,VG304.416039
R1279   Pay It No Mind   Apollo 792,EP603,Jazz Selection(F)JS769

All titles also on Vogue(F)VG405.500116.
All titles on CLDAP768 also on Vogue(F)VG403.500768,(J)YX7023.

Add Milt Larkins(vcl).　　　　　　　　　　NYC.Autumn. 1947
R1280　Chick She Ain't
　　　　　Nowhere(ml,band-vcl)　　　Apollo 784,EP603,Jazz Selection(F)JS771,Vogue(F)
　　　　　　　　　　　　　　　　　　　　　　CLDAP768,VG405.500116
R1281　Arnett Blows For 1300　　　Apollo 781,EP603,LP105,Jazz Selection(F)JS766,
　　　　　　　　　　　　　　　　　　　　　　Vogue(E)EPV1054
R1282　Running With Ray (Going Home)　　Apollo 784,LP447,Jazz Selection(F)JS771,Vogue(F)
　　　　　　　　　　　　　　　　　　　　　　VG405.500116
R1283　Flower Garden Blues(ml)　　Apollo 394,Vogue(F)CLDAP768,VG405.500116
R1284　Big League Blues(ml)　　　　　-　　　　　　-　　　　　-

All titles on CLDAP768 also on Vogue(F)VG403.500768,(J)YX7023.
Note:The track "Arnett Blows For 1300" issued on VG405.500116 in fact plays "Cobb's Cor-
　　　ner" (so the latter tune appears twice on the LP and "Arnette Blows For 1300" is not
　　　heard on VG405.500116).

Dave Page(tp),Booty Wood(tb),Arnett Cobb(ts),Charlie Fowlkes(bars),George Rhodes(p),Walter
Buchanan(b),George "Butch" Ballard(dr).　　NYC.September 12,1950
C044335 Smooth Sailing　　　　　　Columbia 39040,Okeh 8630,Epic EG37315
C044336 Your Wonderful Love　　　　　-　　　　　-
C044337 That's All,Brother　　　Columbia 39139
C044338 Bee-Bee　　　　　　　　　　　-

All titles also on Jazz Circle Basel(Sw)JC-01.

Lammar Wright,Sr.(tp),Booty Wood(tb),Arnett Cobb(ts),Charlie Fowlkes(bars),George Rhodes
(p),Carl Pruitt(b),Al Walker(dr).　　　NYC.January 19,1951
C045044 Holy Smoke　　　　　　　　Columbia 39369
C045045 Willow Weep For Me　　　Columbia 39247
C045046 Run For The Hills　　　　　-
C045047 Lunar Moon　　　　　　　　Columbia 39369

All titles also on Jazz Circle Basel(Sw)JC-01.

Willie Moore(tp),Dick Harris(tb),Arnett Cobb(ts),Johnny Griffin(bars),George Rhodes(p),
Walter Buchanan(b),Al Walker(dr).　　　NYC.August 7,1951
C046835 Cocktails For Two　　　　Okeh 6823
C046836 Walkin' Home　　　　　　　　-　,Epic EG37315
C046837 Jumpin' The Blues　　　　Okeh 6872,　　　-
C046838 I'm In the Mood For Love　Okeh 6851,　　-

All titles also on Jazz Circle Basel(Sw)JC-01.

Ed "Tiger" Lewis(tp),Dick Harris(tb),Arnett Cobb(ts),Willard Brown(ts,bars),George Rhodes
(p),Gene Wright(b),Al Walker(dr).　　　NYC.November 20,1951
C047171 Without A Word Of Warning　Okeh 6872
C047172 Whispering　　　　　　　　Okeh 6887,Epic EG37315
C047173 Charmaine　　　　　　　　Okeh 6851
C047174 Open House　　　　　　　　Okeh 6887,Epic EG37315

All titles also on Jazz Circle Basel(Sw)JC-01.

Prob. Ed Lewis(tp),Dick Harris(tb),Arnett Cobb(ts),George Rhodes(p),Walter Buchanan(b),Al
Walker(dr).　　　　　　　　　　　　　Live.NYC.June 27,1952
　　　Jumpin' The Blues　　　　　Phoenix LP18
　　　Cocktails For Two　　　　　　-
　　　Smooth Sailin'　　　　　　　-
　　　Someone To Watch Over Me　　-
(session cont. next page).

```
(session cont. from previous page):
      The Shy One                 Phoenix LP18
      Go,Red,Go                        -
      When I Grow Too Old
         To Dream(band-vcl)            -
      I Got It Bad(1)(dw)              -
```

-1.Add Cootie Williams(tp),Dinah Washington(vcl).

Note:See Dinah Washington for additional titles from this concert.

```
Prob. same;add Charlie Ferguson(bars,ts).   NYC.July  1952
C048014 Li'l Sonny                Okeh 69028,Epic EG37315
C048015 The Shy One               Okeh 6912,        -
C048016 Someone To Watch Over Me(1)   -
C048017 Linger A While            Okeh 6928
```

-1.Add Joe Van Loan,Warren Suttles' Dreamers(vcl).

```
Similar;add The Uninhibited Four(vcl).   NYC.June 14,1953
9468    Congratulations To Someone   Mercury 70101
9469    Poor Butterfly(uf)           Mercury(J)25PJ58
9470-3 Operation                     Mercury(J)25PJ58
9470-5 Operation                          -
9470-7 Operation                          -
```

```
Similar.                          NYC.September  1953
9684    Apple Wine(uf)            Mercury 70171
9685    The Traveler                  -
```

```
Ed Lewis(tp),Al Grey(tb),Arnett Cobb(ts),Charlie Ferguson(bars,ts),George Rhodes(p),Walter
Buchanan(b),Al Walker(dr).        NYC.April 19,1954
A1258   Night                     Atlantic 1031,5031
A1259   Horse Laff                Atlantic 1042
A1260   No Child,No More          Atlantic 1031,5031
A1261   Mr. Pogo                  Atlantic 1042,LP8013
```

```
Similar.                          NYC.January 19,1955
A1421   Perfidia                  Atlantic unissued
A1422   Flying Home Mambo         Atlantic 1056,5037,LP8013
A1423   Light Like That               -      -       -
```

```
Ed Lewis(tp),Al Grey(tb),Arnett Cobb(ts),Harold Cumberbatch(bars,as),Lloyd Mayers(p),Jimmy
Mobley(b),Al Jones(dr),Danny Cobb(vcl).   Chicago.February 17,1956
56-420 I Pray For Your Love(dc)   Vee-Jay unissued
56-421 Someday(dc)                     -
56-422 No Dues                    Vee-Jay 190,Top Rank(F)RLP100,Atlantis ATSD14(?)
56-423 Slats                           -       -
```

Note:Masters 56-420/21 recorded under Danny Cobb's name.

```
Arnett Cobb,Eddie Davis(ts),Wild Bill Davis(org),George Duvivier(b),Arthur Edgehill(dr).
                                  NYC.January 9,1959
1702    Dutch Kitchen Bounce      Prestige 45-133,PRLP7151,Metronome(Sd)MEP488
1793    Go,Red,Go                      -
1704    When I Grow Too Old To Dream   Prestige 45-133,  -
1705    The Eely One                   -
1706    Go Power                       -
1707    The Fluke                      -    ,Metronome(Sd)MEP488
```

All titles also on Prestige PR7835,Esquire(E)32-114.

Buster Cooper(tb),Arnett Cobb(ts),Austin Mitchell(org),George Duvivier(b),Osie Johnson
(dr).   NYC.February 27,1959
1730   Blues In My Heart   Prestige PRLP7184
1731   Ghost Of A Chance   -
1732   Let's Split   -
1733   Smooth Sailing   Prestige 45-185,PRLP7184,PR7711
1734   Charmaine   -
1735   Cobb's Mob   -
1736   Blues Around Dusk   -

All titles also on Original Jazz Classics OJC323.

Arnett Cobb(ts),Ray Bryant(p),Wendell Marshall(b),Art Taylor(dr),Ray Barretto(cg).
                                         NYC.May 14,1959
1780   Cocktails For Two   Prestige PRLP7165
1781   Flying Home   - ,PR7711
1782   When My Dreamboat Comes Home Prestige 45-133,PRLP7165,PR7711,Franklin Mint 71
1783   Lonesome Road   -   -
1784   Blues In The Closet   -
1785   Party Time   -
1786   Slow Poke(no cg)   -

All titles also on Original Jazz Classics OJC219,Esquire(E)32-154.

Arnett Cobb(ts),Tommy Flanagan(p),Sam Jones(b),Art Taylor(dr),Danny Barrajanos(cg).
                                         NYC.February 16,1960
2021   Swanee River   Prestige PRLP7165
2022   Blue Lou   -
2023   Blue Me   -
2024   Sometimes I'm Happy
2025   Fast Ride   Prestige PRLP7216,PR7711
2026   Lover Come Back To Me   Prestige 45-172,PRLP7175

All titles on PRLP7175 also on Esquire(E)32-184.

Bobby Timmons(p),Buck Clarke(cg) replace Flanagan,Barrajanos.
                                         NYC.February 17,1960
2027   Exactly Like You   Prestige PRLP7216
2028   Down By The Riverside   Prestige PRLP7175,PR7711,Esquire(E)32-184.
2029   Softly As In A Morning Sunrise Prestige PRLP7216
2030   The Nitty Gritty   - ,PR7711
2031   Walkin'   -
2032   All I Do Is Dream Of You   -
2033   Ghost Of A Chance   Prestige 45-185,PRLP7216
2034   The Shy One   -

Arnett Cobb(ts),Red Garland(p),George Tucker(b),J.C. Heard(dr).
                                         NYC.October 31,1960
2631   The Way You Look Tonight   Prestige PRLP7227
2632   Sizzlin'   -
2633   Black Velvet   - ,PR7711
2634   Sweet Georgia Brown   -
2635   Blue Sermon   -
2636   Georgia On My Mind   -

All titles also on Prestige(J)VIJ5063.

Same;Garland plays (p,celeste).   NYC.November 1,1960
2637   Hurry Home   Moodsville MVLP14
2638   Blue And Sentimental   -
2639   Willow Weep For Me   -
(session cont. next page).

(session cont. from previous page):
```
2640   Darn That Dream                Moodsville MVLP14
2641   Why Try To Change Me Now           -
2642   P.S. I Love You                    -
2643   Your Wonderful Love                -
```

Arnett Cobb(ts),Milt Buckner(org),Clarence "Gatemouth" Brown(g),Michael Silva(dr).
```
                                       Paris.July 23,1973
       Tight Like That            Black&Blue(F)33.052,59.052-2(CD)
       Cobb's Blues                       -      -
       Deep Purple(no g)                  -      -
       Willow Weep For Me                 -      -
       Swanee River                       -      -
       Cobb's Boogie                      -      -
       Claude Of Mine              Black&Blue(F)950.500,  -
```

ARNETT COBB - TINY GRIMES QUINTET:
Arnett Cobb(ts),Lloyd Glenn(p),Tiny Grimes(g),Roland Lobligeois(b),Panama Francis(dr).
```
                                       Live.Paris.April 28,1974
       Smooth Sailing             France's Concert FC133,FCD133(CD)
       El Fonko                          -      -
       Body And Soul                     -      -
       Jumpin' At The Woodside           -      -
       Just You,Just Me                  -      -
       Willow Weep For Me                -      -
       The Nearness Of You        France's Concert FCD133(CD)
       Flying Home                       -
```

Same.   Paris.May 21,1974
```
       Jumpin' At The Woodside    Black&Blue(F)33.175
       I Don't Stand A Ghost Of A Chance   -
       Blues For The Hot Club Of France    -
       I Want A Little Girl               -
       Jumpin' In France                 -
       Salty Mama Blues                  -
       On The Sunny Side Of The Street  Black&Blue(F)59.099-2(CD),233.099-2(CD)
       Take The A Train                  -              -
```

All titles on Black&Blue(F)33.175 also on Black&Blue(F)59.175.

Wallace Davenport(tp),Buster Cooper(tb),Earl Warren(as),Arnett Cobb,Eddie Chamblee(ts),
Milt Buckner(org,vbs,vcl),André Persiany(p,arr),Roland Lobligeois(b),Panama Francis(dr).
```
                                       Paris.April 30,1976
       Twenty Years After         Black&Blue(F)33.097
       Gone                              -
       Stompin' At The Savoy             -
       A Pretty Song                     -
```

Same.   Toulouse,France.May 6,1976
```
       Jacques,That's The Blues   Black&Blue(F)33.097
       Smooth Sailing             Black&Blue(F)33.099
       Flying Home No.2                  -
```

Same.   Paris.May 12,1976
```
       Tenor Duet                 Black&Blue(F)33.097
       Encore Flyin' Home                -
       New Green Onions(mb)              -
       Blowing In Paris                  -
       Where Or When              Black&Blue(F)33.099
       I Don't Stand A Ghost Of A Chance  -
       Blowing In Paris No.2      Black&Blue(F)59.099-2(CD),233.099-2(CD)
       Hey,Ba Ba Re Bop           Black&Blue(F)333.095
```

ARNETT COBB

Same.   Paris.May 20,1976
        The Nearness Of You   Black&Blue(F)33.099

Same.   Paris.May 30,1976
        Dutch Kitchen Bounce(1)   Black&Blue(F)33.099,950.506/7

-1.Prob. Cobb(ts),org,b,dr only.

All titles on Black&Blue(F)33.099 also on Black&Blue(F)59.099-2 (CD),233.099-2 (CD),
Classic Jazz CJ102.
Note:Black&Blue(F)33.097 was issued under Chamblee's name.

Arnett Cobb(ts),Derek Smith(p),George Mraz(b),Billy Hart(dr).
                                          NYC.June 27,1978
        Flying Home   Progressive(J)KUX113
        Big Red's Groove   -
        Big Red's Groove(alt.take)   Progressive PCD7037(CD),(J)30CP48(CD)
        Cherry   Progressive(J)KUX113
        Sweet Georgia Brown   -
        (I Don't Stand A)
          Ghost Of A Chance   -
        Blues For Shirley   -
        Blues For Shirley(alt/rehearsal) Progressive PCD7037(CD),(J)30CP48(CD)
        Take The "A" Train   Progressive(J)KUX113
        September Song   Progressive PRO7020

All titles on KUX113 also on Progressive PRO7037,(J)ULS1670,ULS6084,30CP48 (CD).

ARNETT COBB AND THE MUSE ALL STARS:
Arnett Cobb(ts),Buddy Tate -1(ts),Eddie "Cleanhead" Vinson -2(as),Ray Bryant(p),George
Duvivier(b),Alan Dawson(dr).   Live."Sandy's Jazz Revival",Beverly,Mass.August 25/26,1978
        Just A Closer Walk With Thee   Muse MR5191
        Blue And Sentimental   -
        On The Sunny Side Of The Street   -
        September Song   -
        Broadway(1,2)   -
        Blues For Lester(1)   Muse MR5236
        Go,Red,Go(1)   -
        Smooth Sailin'(2)   -
        Flying Home No.2(1)   -

All titles on MR5191 also on Muse(J)IXJ70187 (CD).

Arnett Cobb(ts),Derek Smith(p),Ray Drummond(b),Ronnie Bedford(dr).
                                          NYC.January 22,1980
        Jumpin' At The Woodside   Progressive(J)KUX142
        Satin Doll   -
        Georgia On My Mind   -
        Funky Butt   -
        I Got Rhythm   -
        September In The Rain   -
        Isfahan   -
        Radium Springs Swings   -

All titles also on Progressive PRO7054,(J)ULS6034.

ARNETT COBB - GUY LAFITTE:
Arnette Cobb,Guy Lafitte(ts),Roland Hanna(p),Jimmy Woode(b),Eddie Locke(dr).
                                          Live.Chateauneuf du Pape,France.March 16,1980
        I Got Rhythm   Black&Blue(F)33.306
        Go,Red,Go   -
        Jumpin' At The Woodside   -

Same.   Live.Deauville,France.March 29,1980
         On Green Dolphin Street   Black&Blue(F)33.306
         Climb Every Mountain   -
         Blues Abrupt   -

All titles on Black&Blue(F)33.306 also on Black&Blue(F)59.306.

DANNY COBB

See ARNETT COBB,LUCKY THOMPSON.

JUNIE COBB

JUNIE COBB'S NEW HOMETOWN BAND:
Fortunatus "Fip" Ricard(tp),Harlem Floyd(tb),Leon Washington(cl,ts),Junie Cobb(p,vcl),Ikey
Robinson(bj),Walter Cole(b),Red Sanders(dr),Annabel Calhoun(vcl).
                                          Chicago.September 8,1961
376   I'm Gonna Have You(ac)   Riverside RLP(9)389,RLP(9)415
377   Just Because Of You(jc,ac)   -
378   Be Mine   -
379   Once Or Twice   Riverside RLP(9)390,   -
380   Belligerent Blues(ac)   -
381   Mister Blues   -
382   Swing Your Hurdy Gardy   -
383   Just Squeeze Me(ac)   -

BILLY COBHAM

Jan Hammer(el-p,p,synth),Tommy Bolin(g),Lee Sklar(el-b),Billy Cobham(perc).
                                          NYC.May 14/15,1973
26750 Quadrant 4   Atlantic SD7268,19238-2(CD),7.81711-1,7.81711-2
                                          (CD),Amiga(G)8.55.834
26751 Searching For The Right Door   Atlantic SD7268
26753 Anxiety   -
26754 Taurian Matador   -
26755 Stratus   Atlantic 2998(ed.),SD7268,781.907-1,19238-2(CD),
                                          Amiga(G)8.55.834
26756 To The Women In My life   Atlantic SD7268
26758 Snoopy's Search   - ,19238-2(CD),Amiga(G)8.55.834(?)
26759 Red Baron   -   -
27104 Jam   unissued

Note:Atlantic 7.81711-1 and 7.81711-2 (CD) are part of 7.81712-1 (LPset) and 7.81712-2
     (CD set) respectively.

Jimmy Owens(tp,flh),Joe Farrell(fl,as,ss),Jan Hammer(el-p,p,synth),John Tropea(g),Ron
Carter(b),Billy Cobham(dr),Ray Barretto(cg). NYC.May 16,1973
26752 Spectrum   Atlantic SD7268
26757 Le Lis   Atlantic 3014(ed.),SD7268

All titles on SD7268 also on Atlantic(Eu)ATL40506,7.81434-1,(J)P6460,P8386.

Randy Brecker(tp,el-tp),Garnett Brown(tb),Michael Brecker(ss,ts,fl),George Duke(el-p),John
Abercrombie(g),John Williams(b,el-b),Billy Cobham(perc),Lee Pastora(perc).
                                          NYC.January 1974
(session cont. next page).

(session cont. from previous page):

28211	Spanish Moss	Atlantic SD7300,19238-2(CD),Amiga(G)8.55.834
28212	Flash Flood	-
28213	Heather	unissued
28214	Wah Wah Bass	-
28215	Savannah The Serene(1)	Atlantic SD7300
28216	Sugar Loaf Island	unissued
28217	The Pleasant Peasant	Atlantic SD7300,19238-2(CD),Amiga(G)8.55.834
28218	Heather	-
28219	Crosswinds	Atlantic 3014(ed.),SD7300
28220	Storm(2)	-

-1.Omit Randy Brecker,Michael Brecker,Lee Pastora.
-2.Cobham(perc-solo).

All titles also on Atlantic(Eu)ATL50037,(J)P6461,P8449.
Note:Masters 28211, 28212, 28215 and 28220 as "Spanish Moss: A Sound Portrait" on the LP.

Randy Brecker(tp,flh),Glenn Ferris(tb,btb),Michael Brecker(fl,ss,ts),Milcho Leviev(keyb),
Cornell Dupree -1,John Abercrombie(g),Alex Blake(el-b),Billy Cobham(dr,tymp,p),David Earle
Johnson -2(cg),Sue Evans -3(mar).   NYC. 1974
            Solarizations: Atlantic SD18121

29728	Solarization(2,3)	
29729	Second Phase	
29730	Crescent Sun	
29731	Voyage	
29732	Solarization-Recapitulation	
29733	Lunarputians	-
29734	Total Eclipse	-
29735	Bandits	Atlantic 3250(ed.),SD18121
29736	Moon Germs(1,2)	- - ,19238-2(CD),Amiga(G)
		8.55.834
29737	The Moon Ain't Made Of Green Cheese	Atlantic SD18121
29738	Sea Of Tranquility	-
29739	Last Frontier	-

All titles also on Atlantic(Eu)ATL50098,(J)P6462,P8539.

Omit Dupree,Johnson,Evans.   Live.Montreux,Switzerland.July 4,1974
30052 Taurian Matador   Atlantic SD18139

Same.   Live.Rainbow Theatre,London.July 13,1974
30049	Red Baron	Atlantic SD18139
30050	Tenth Pin	-
30051	Shabazz	-
30182	Heather(1)	unissued

-1.Prob. same concert.

All titles on SD18139 also on Atlantic(Eu)ATL50147,(J)P10022.

John Scofield(g) replaces Abercrombie;Cobham plays (perc,synth).
                              San Francisco.c.March 1975
31195	Panhandler(1)	Atlantic SD18149,19238-2(CD),Amiga(G)8.55.834
31196	Sorcery	-
31197	A Funky Thide Of Sings(1,2)	-
31198	Thinking Of You	-
31199	Some Skunk Funk	-
31200	Light At The End Of The Tunnel	-
31201	A Funky Kind Of Thing	-
31202	Moody Modes	-

(session cont. from previous page):
-1.Add Walt Fowler(tp),Tom Malone(tb,picc),Larry Schneider(sax),"Rebop" Kwaku Baah(cg).
-2.Omit Randy Brecker,Ferris,Michael Brecker.

All titles also on Atlantic(Eu)ATL50189,(J)P10079.
Note:Fowler,Malone,Schneider were rec. later in Philadelphia; Baah was recorded in London.

George Duke (as "Dawilli Gonga")(keyb),Alan Zavod -1(org),John Scofield(g),Doug Rauch(b),
Billy Cobham(perc,synth).   NYC.c. 1976

31644	Earthlings	Atlantic SD18166
31645	Song For A Friend,pt.1	-
31646	On A Natural High	-
31647	Song For A Friend,pt.2	-
31648	Life And Times(1)	-
31649	29	-
31650	Siesta(2,3)/Wake Up!	
	That's What You Said(3)	-
31651	East Bay	-

-2.Add Phil Bodner(fl,bcl),Richard Davis(b),Gene Orloff(vln),Al Brown(vla),Kermit Moore
   (cello),Arif Mardin(arr).
-3.Issued as part of "Life And Times".

All titles also on Atlantic(E/Eu)K/ATL50253,(J)P10183.

BILLY COBHAM - GEORGE DUKE BAND:
George Duke(keyb,vcl),John Scofield(g),Alphonso Johnson(el-b,vcl),Billy Cobham(dr,synth,
vcl),Jon Lucien(narration).   Live.Europe.July 1976

32619	Hip,Pockets	Atlantic 3370(ed.),SD18194			
32620	Ivory Tatoo	-			
32621	Space Lady(gd)	-			
32622	Almustfa The Beloved(jl,gd,aj)	-			
32623	Do What Cha Wanna(gd,aj,bc)	Atlantic 3370(ed.),	-	,19238-2(CD),Amiga(G)	
		8.55.834			
32624	Frankenstein Goes To The Disco	Atlantic SD18194			
32625	Sweet Wine	-			
32626	Juicy(gd)	-			

All titles also on Atlantic(Eu)ATL50316,(J)P10282.
All titles on Atlantic 19238-2(CD) also on Atlantic(Eu)ATL50620,7.81558-1,7.81558-2(CD).
Note:The above titles poss. rec. Montreux,Switzerland (July 6) and London (July 27/29).

Randy Brecker(tp),Jimmy Owens(tp,flh),Julian Priester(tb),Ernie Watts,Michael Brecker
(reeds),Ruth Underwood(xyl,mar),George Duke (as "Dawilli Gonga")(keyb),John Scofield(g),
John Williams(b),Billy Cobham(dr).   San Francisco. 1976

32495	Nickels And Dimes	Atlantic SD19174,Franklin Mint 99
32497	Arryo(keyb,g,b,dr only)	-
32498	Inner Conflicts(1)	-

-1.Cobham(dr,perc,synth) solo.

Julian Priester(tb),Don Grolnick(keyb),Steve Khan(g),Alphonso Johnson(b),Billy Cobham(dr),
Pete Escovedo,Sheila Escovedo,Jose Najeira(perc).
                                             San Francisco. 1976

32496	El Barrio	Atlantic SD19174
32499	The Muffin Talks Back(no tb)	-

All titles on SD19174 also on Atlantic(Eu)ATL50475,(J)P10530.

No details.   San Francisco. 1976

32958	Night Flight	Atlantic unissued
32959	New Rock & Roll	-

No details.   NYC(?). 1977
34674 Bright Eyed Lady   Atlantic unissued
34675 Skin Flick   -

Alvin Batiste -1(cl,vcl),Joachim Kühn -2(p,elp,synth),Mark Soskin -3(p,el-p,tack-p,synth),
Pete Maunu(g),Randy Jackson(b),Billy Cobham(dr,perc,vcl),Pete Escovedo -4(timb,vcl),Sheila
Escovedo -5(cg),Kathleen Kaan(vcl).   NYC.July 1977/Toronto. 1977
        On A Magic Carpet Ride(2,3)   Columbia JC34939,JC36400
        AC/DC(1,4,5)   -
        Leaward Winds(3)   -
        Puffnstuff(1,3)(bc)   - ,JC36400
        "Anteres" - The Star(1,3,4,5)   -   -
        Magic (Reflections In The
            Clouds)/(Recap.)(2,3)(pe,kk)   -

All titles also on CBS(Eu)82277,(J)25AP832.

Tom Scott(ts,ss,lyricon,perc),Mark Soskin(p,el-p,clavinet,synth),Steve Khan(g),Alphonso
Johnson(b),Billy Cobham(perc).   Live(?).NYC.November 12,1977
        "Antares" - The Star   Columbia JC35349
        Bahama Mama   -
        Shadows   -
        Some Punk Funk   -
        Spindrift   -
        On A Magic Carpet Ride   -

All titles also on CBS(Eu)82813,(J)25AP1111.
Note:The above recording is a CBS "All Star" issue - "ALIVEMUTHERFORYA".

Don Grolnick(keyb),Barry Finnerty(g),Tim Landers(n),Billy Cobham(dr).
                                        Live.Cologne/Stuttgart,Germany.June 1980
        Flight Time   Sandra(G)2112
        Antatres   -
        Six Persimmons   -
        Day Grace   -
        The Whisperer   -
        Princess   -
        Jackhammer   -

All titles also on In-Akustik(G)INAK8616 (CD).
Note:Additional recordings by this artist are not included.

COBLENTZ JAZZ ENSEMBLE

COBLENTZ JAZZ ENSEMBLE AND SYMPHONY ORCHESTRA:
Unknown jazz band,symphony orchestra,Charles Horton(cond).
                                        Unknown location.c. 1978
        Concerto For Big Band
            And Symphony Orchestra   Aries LP1616
        Contrasts For Piano And Orchestra   -
        Jazz Concerto   -

BILL COBURN

BILL COBURN'S COLONY CLUB COMBO:
Bob Wingett(tp,vcl),Bill Coburn(tb,vcl),Syl La Fata(cl),Vic Tooker(bj,vcl),"Wink" Black(b)
Jim Ross(dr).   Dayton,Ohio.Poss. 1970/71
(session cont. next page).

(session cont. from previous page):
    Clementine(bw)   Request 71056
    Memories Of You   -
    Caravan   -
    Way Down Yonder In New Orleans(bc)   -
    Dixie Banjo Medley   -
    Sweet Georgia Brown(vt)   -
    Jazz Me Blues   -
    Satin Doll(bw)   -
    Waitin' For Robert E. Lee   -
    Wolverine Blues   -

CHARLES COCHRAN

(vcl) with unknown acc.   Unknown location.c. 1963
    Unknown titles   Ava (S)25

(vcl) with unknown acc.   Unknown location.c. 1964
    'Round Midnight   Ava (S)44
    I've Got Your Number   -
    I Think I Fell   -
    Just Friends   -
    Spring Can Really
       Hang You Up The Most   -
    The Late,Late Show   -
    On Green Dolphin Street   -
    Sunday   -
    All The Things You Are   -
    I'm Afraid The Masquerade Is Over -

(vcl) acc. by Richard Rodney Bennett(p),Steve LaSpina(b),Tony Tedesco(dr).
                        Unknown location.Prob. 1970's
    Our Love Rolls On   Audiophile AP177
    I'm In Love Aagin   -
    Sure You're Born   -
    Haunted Heart   -
    If I Love You Again   -
    Peg O'My Heart   -
    Street Of Dreams   -
    I Never Went Away   -
    Make Me Rainbows   -
    In Love In Vain   -
    The Lady's In Love With You -
    Maybe September   -

TODD COCHRAN (BAYETÉ)

Fred "Mulobo" Berry,Oscar Brashear(tp,flh),Wayne Wallace(tb),Dave "Mganda" Johnson(ss,vcl)
Hadley Caliman(ts,fl),Bobby Hutcherson(vbs),Bayeté (Todd Cochran)(p,el-p,clavinet),James
Leary III(b,el-b),Thabo Vincar (Michael Carvin)(dr).
                        NYC.April 1972
    It Ain't   Prestige PR10045
    Free Angela (Thoughts And
      All I've Got To Say)(dj,tc) -
    Njeri
    I'm On It(dj,tc)
    Bayete   -
    Eurus   -

TODD COCHRAN (BAYETÉ)

Fred Berry(tp,flh,vcl),Dave Johnson(ss,fl,perc,vcl),Todd Cochran(p,el-p,clavinet,vcl),
Hoza Phillips(el-b,vcl),Augusta Lee Collins(dr,perc).
NYC(?).September 18/October 2,1972

Let It Take Your Mind	Prestige PR10062	
The Time Has Come	-	
Think On,The People		
Arise/Mulobo/People Arise!!!	-	
Don't Need Nobody	-	
Pruda's Shoes:	-	
Duet		
Trio		
Ensemble		
Finale		

COCORO STEEL BAND (French)

Didier Hussenot(tb),Alfredo Espinoza(cl,sax),Charly Congrega(bj,g),Gilles Chevaucherie(b).
Live.Montigny-sur-l'Hallue,France.June 23/24,1973

Them There Eyes	Promophone(F)PROM2
Hé(!) La-Bas	-

André Villeger(ss,as) replaces Espinoza;Congrega also (vcl).
Paris.November 10,1973

Shim Me Cha(!) Wabble	Pragmaphone(F)PRGLP12
Madame Bécassine	-
At The Jazz Band Ball	-
I Can't Give You Anything But Love	-
Wild Cat Blues	-
Suey	-

Same.
Paris.December 27,1973

Waitin' For Charly	Pragmaphone(F)PRGLP12
Mandy,Make Up Your Mind	-
Of All The Wrongs	-
Cake Walking Babies From Home	-
Doin' The New Lowdown	-
Maple Leaf Rag	-

CODONA

See DON CHERRY.

PETER COE (British)

THE PETER COE BIG BAND:
Charlie Evans,Ronnie Johnson,Frank Walsh,Bev Gordon,Bob Tomkins(tp),Dennis Bayton,Norman
Bull,Robin Sedgeley,Grahame Humphrey(tb),Mike Wilcox,Peter Aburrow,Morris Pritchard(as,
fl),Peter Coe(ts,fl),Brian Wales(ts,el-vln),Don Locke(bars),Alf Knight(p,el-p),Dick Ham-
mett(b),John Turner(dr).
London. 1976

Moon Stone	JAM(E)647
Don't Count	-
Pastel Theme	-
September Song	-
Switch In Time	-
Hay Burner	-

(session cont. next page):

(session cont. from previous page):
```
        Rain Stopped Play          JAM(E)647
        Quincy And The Count         -
        This Is Loneliness           -
        Hang In There                -
        You Gotta Try                -
        Summit Soul                  -
```

Barry Morris(tp),Alan Tidbury,Dennis Hymes(tb),Bob Cleall(dr) replace Johnson,Tomkins,
Sedgeley,Humphrey,Turner.   Live."The Leather Bottel",Merton Park,London. 1978
```
        Fourth Floor Walk Up       JAM(E)650
        Nobody's Perfect             -
        What Are You Doing
           The Rest Of Your Life     -
        Feelin' Free                 -
        Girl Talk                    -
        Hoops                        -
        Dark Orchid                  -
        Bundle Of Funk               -
        Doc's Holiday                -
        Blues In My Shoes            -
        April In Paris               -
```

TONY COE (British)

See also DEREK BAILEY,AL GREY.

TONY COE QUINTET:
John Picard(tb),Tony Coe(cl),Ian Armit(p),Brian Brocklehurst(b),Eddie Taylor(dr).
```
                                    London.March 14,1958
        Bali Ha'i                   Nixa(E)NJL20,Marble Arch(E)MALS1167
        Sans Humph                   -
        5/8ths                       -
```

TONY COE QUARTET:
Tony Coe(cl),Colin Purbrook(p),Lennie Bush(b),Lennie Hastings(dr).
```
                                    London.May  1961
        Love For Sale               Nixa(E)NJE1081
        Time's A Wastin'                     -   ,Pye(E)GH649
        Satin Doll                           -          -
        Sweet Georgia Brown                  -          -
```

TONY COE QUINTET:
John Picard(tb),Tony Coe(cl,as,ts),Colin Purbrook(p),Spike Heatley(b),Derek Hogg(dr).
```
                                    London.July 2,1962
DR29565 Gee,Baby,Ain't I Good To You  Decca(E)LK4512
DR29566 Hanid                        -
```

Same.
```
                                    London.July 10,1962
        Sunday Morning              Philips(E)B10784L
        Wrap Your Troubles In Dreams         -
        Not So Blue                          -
        I Can't Get Started                  -
        Sack O'Woe                           -
        Stomping At The Savoy                -
        Swingin' Till The Girls Gome Home    -
        Blue Lou                             -
        St. Thomas                           -
```

John Picard(tb),Tony Coe(ts,as,cl),Colin Purbrook(p),Peter Ind(b),Jackie Dougan(dr).
　　　　　　　　　Live."Student Onion Hall",Bristol University,England.November 18,1966

Jeep Is Jumpin'	"77"(E)LEU12/21	
Blues We Played Last Night	-	

Moe Miller -1(frh),Tony Coe(ts,as,cl,fl),Tommy Whittle -2(ts),Bill LeSage(p,vbs),Dennis
Bowden(b),Barry Morgan(dr),Monty Babson -3(bg),string quartet,David Mack(arr).
　　　　　　　　　London.June 1967

Baby Blue	Columbia(E)SX/SCX6170	
The Midnight Sun Will Never Set	-	
Murmurio(2,3)	-	
Ghost Of Yesterday(1)	-	
Baby Doll I Love You	-	
Lady Sings The Blues(2)	-	
Whisper It Slow	-	
Never Love A Stranger(1)	-	
Tony's Basement	-	

TONY COE - BRIAN LEMON TRIO:
Tony Coe(ts,cl),Brian Lemon(p),Dave Green(b),Phil Seaman(dr).
　　　　　　　　　Live."Ronnie Scott's",London.January 25,1971

Aristotle Blues	"77"(E)SEU12/41	
Regrets	-	
Reza	-	
Line Up Blues	-	
Together	-	
Some Other Autumn	-	

Incl. Henry Lowther,Kenny Wheeler(tp,flh),Chris Pyne(tb),Tony Coe(cl,bcl,ss,ts),Pat Smythe
(p,el-p,org),Bob Cornford(p,cond),Daryl Runswick(b,el-b),Trevor Tompkins,Frank Ricotti
(perc),Mary Thomas,Norma Winstone(voices).　London.July 29/30,1976

Zeitgeist(mt,nw)	EMI(E)EMC3207	

Tony Coe(ts,ss,cl),John Horler(p),Ron Rubin(b),Tervor Tompkins(dr),Frank Ricotti(perc).
　　　　　　　　　London.June 1978

Rio Vermelho	Lee Lambert(E)LAM100	
Loverman		
Killer Joe	-	
Don't Get Around Much Anymore	-	
Voce	-	
What Are You Doing		
The Rest Of Your Life	-	
Lee Thompson's Blues	-	
I'm Getting Sentimental Over You	-	

Note:Additional recordings by this artist are not included.

BASIL "MANNENBERG" COETZEE (South African)

Basil "Mannenberg" Coetzee(ts),Monty Weber(dr),Tete Mbambisa,Zulu Pindi(unknown instr.).
　　　　　　　　　South Africa. 1977

Unknown titles	Unknown label(SA)ML4258	

BILL COFFMAN

See KNOCKY PARKER.

COHELMEC ENSEMBLE (French)

Jean Cohen(ss,as,ts),Evan Chandlee(fl,bcl),Joseph Dejean(g),Francois Mechali(b,el-b),Jean-Louis Méchali(dr,perc,vbs).   Paris.c.   1971
    Teotihuacan   Saravah(F)SH10007
    Nadine O Sort - Colchique
        Dans Les Près - ...!   -
    Desert Angel   -
    Culculine d'Ancone   -
    Danse Finlandaise   -
    Le Passeur   -
    Boa Constrictor: -
       Le Boa Constrictor
       Le Héron Chagriné
       L'Ours Qui Frappe Du Pied
       Ligeïa's Alabaster Azalea
    Fouchtra   -
    Ant-Blues Coarazien   -

Dominique Elbaz(p) replaces Dejean.   Paris. 1970'es
    Adventures
      Terrestes Et Acquatiques   Saravah(F)SH10024
    Asia Minor   -
    Soupir   -
    Tarpotom   -
    Hippotigris Zebra
      Zebra (Terreste)   -
    Callompin' Bambin   -
    For Paule   -
    Silences - La Marche De Satan   -
    Lude - Panama Red   -
    Hippotigris Zebra
      Zebra (Acquatigue)   -

Jean-Francois Canape(tp,flh,fl),Jean Cohen(ss,as,ts,fl),Joseph Dejean(g),Francois Méchali (b,el-b),Jean-Louis Méchali(dr,perc,vbs).   Live.Paris.October 5,1974
    Cohelmec 20 H 45   Chevance(F)74606/07
    Les Cloches De Montoinuo   -
    La Croix Fry 1:   -
      Teotihuacan 1
      Teotihuacan 2
    Saturations   -
    The Alpaca Cassok   -
    Eparpiller Sa Mémoire
      Dans Une Fureur D'Aveux   -
    Colhelmec 21 H 50   -
    La Croix Fry 2: Fouchtra   -

ALAN COHEN (British)

ALAN COHEN BAND:
George Chisholm,Kenny Wheeler,Harry Beckett(tp),Henry Lowther(tp,vln),Malcolm Griffiths, Chris Pyne(tb),Geoff Perkins(btb),Olaf Vas(as,ss,cl),John Williams(as),Dave Gelly(ts,cl) Alan Skidmore(ts),John Warren(bars),Brian Priestley(p),Dave Markee(b),Alan Jackson(dr), Alan Cohen(arr,cond),Norma Winstone(vcl).   London.October 19,1972
    Work Song   Argo(E)ZDA159
    The Blues(nw)   -

ALAN COHEN

Greg Bowen(tp) replaces Chisholm.   Same date
      Come Sunday   Argo(E)ZDA159
      Light(no p)   -

George Chisholm,David Hancock,Les Condon(tp),Robin Gardner,Michael Gibbs(tb),Art Themen
(ts) replace Bowen,Wheeler,Lowther,Pyne,Perkins,Skidmore.
                                London.December 1,1972
      Beige   Argo(E)ZDA159
      West Indian Dance   -
      Emancipation Celebration -

All titles on ZDA159 also on Monmouth Evergreen(E)MES7077.
Note:Titles on ZDA159 are from Duke Ellington's "Black,Brown And Beige" suite.

JEAN COHEN (French)

See COLHELMEC ENSEMBLE.

MARC COHEN

FRIENDS:
Marc Cohen(el-as,ts),John Abercombie(g),Clint Houston(b,el-b),Jeff Williams(dr).
                                NYC.December 1972
      5/8 Tune   Oblivion OD3
      Black Vibrations   -
      Nursey Rhyme   -
      Loose Tune(no g)   -

All titles also on Virgin C1511.

Marc Cohen(p,sax).   NYC(?).July 16,1976
      Sparrow(1)   All Seasons 001
      Funk Pluck(1)   -
      Improvisation For
         Four Saxophones(1)   -
      6 unknown titles   -

-1.Overdubbing used on these titles.

MIKE COHEN

Warren Gale(tp),Marty Krystall(ts,fl),Mike Cohen(p),David Storrs(g),Kenneth Jenkins(b),
Dave Crigger(dr),Myron Ort(perc),Kathryn Thompson(vcl).
                              LA(?).August 8/9,1979
      3/4   Pacific Arts 7-137
      Red Star Mambo   -
      Funk(p,b,dr only)   -
      Hommage To Kenny   -
      The Search   -
      Rain Blues(kt)   -

AL COHN
(section cont. next page).

See also BIRDLAND STARS,BILLY BYERS,COLORADO JAZZ PARTY,FOUR BROTHERS,DEXTER GORDON,DON
HARPER,JAZZ COMMITTEE FOR LATIN AMERICAN AFFAIRS,JAMES MOODY,HENRI RENAUD,TENOR CONCLAVE,
KAI WINDING,WINNERS CIRCLE,XANADU ALL STARS.

Note:All recordings issued as by AL COHN - ZOOT SIMS or as by ZOOT SIMS - AL COHN are
     listed in this section.

AL COHN QUARTET:
Al Cohn(ts),George Wallington(p),Tommy Potter(b),Tiny Kahn(dr).
                                      NYC.July 29,1950
T103   Groovin' With Gus   Triumph 812,Progressive 106,PLP3002,Savoy XP8121,
                                            MG12048,Esquire(E)10-213,Metronome(Sd)B527
T103   Groovin' With Gus(alt.take)   Progressive PLP3002,Savoy SJL2210
T104   Infinity   Triumph 811,Progressive 105,PLP3002,Savoy XP8121,
                                            MG12048,Esquire(E)10-166,Metronome(Sd)B552
T104   Infinity(alt.take)   Progressive PLP3002,Savoy SJL2210
T105   How Long Has This Been Going On   Triumph 811,Progressive 105,PLP3002,Savoy XP8121,
                                            MG12048,Esquire(E)10-166,Metronome(Sd)B552
T106   Let's Get Away From It All   Triumph 812,Progressive 106,PLP3002,Savoy XP8121,
                                            MG12048,Esquire(E)10-213,Metronome(Sd)B527
T106   Let's Get Away From It All(alt.) Savoy SJL2210

All titles on MG12048 also on Savoy SJL1126,(Eu)WL70508,(J)SOPU16,Realm(E)RM155.
All titles - except the alternative takes - also on Esquire(E)ESQ320.

AL COHN QUINTET:
Nick Travis(tp),Al Cohn(ts),Horace Silver(p),Curley Russell(b),Max Roach(dr).
                                      NYC.June 23,1953
        I'm Tellin' Ya   Progressive PLP3004,Savoy XP8122
        Jane Street   -   -   ,Byg(F)529.607
        Ah-Moore   - ,Savoy XP8123,Franklin Mint 61
        That's What You Think   -   -
        That's What You Think(alt.take) Savoy SJL1126

All titles also on Savoy MG15036,MG12048,SJL1126,(Eu)WL70508,(J)SOPU16,Realm(E)RM155.

Hal Stein(as),Al Cohn(ts),Harvey Leonard(p),Red Mitchell(b),Christy Febbo(dr).
                                      NYC.July 29,1954
        Broadway(take 1)   Progressive PLP1003
        Broadway(take 2)   -
        Red Mitchell's Blues(1)   -
        Suddenly It's Spring(take 1)   -
        Suddenly It's Spring(take 2)   -
        Ballad Medley: -
            These Foolish Things(no ts)
            Everything Happens To Me(no as,ts)
            Sweet Lorraine(as,ts)
            When It's Sleepy Time Down South(no as)

-1.As "Help Keep Your City Clean Blues" on PR7819.

All titles also on Prestige PR7819.

AL COHN AND HIS "CHARLIE'S TAVERN" ENSEMBLE:
Joe Newman(tp),Billy Byers,Eddie Bert(tb),Hal McKusick,Gene Quill(as),Al Cohn(ts,arr),Sol
Schlinger(bars),Sanford Gold(p),Billy Bauer(g),Milt Hinton(b),Osie Johnson(dr).
                                      NYC.October 26,1954
E4VB5854 Inside Out   RCA-Victor LJM1020,(F)PM42043,HMV(E)7EG8130
E4VB5855 Serenade For Kathy   - ,HMV(E)7EG8113
E4VB5856 Autumn Leaves   - ,(F)PM42043,HMV(E)7EG8130

All titles also on Fresh Sound(Sp)NL45962.

Joe Newman(tp),Billy Byers(tb),Gene Quill(as),Al Cohn(ts,arr),Sol Schlinger(ts),Sanford
Gold(p),Buddy Jones(b),Osie Johnson(dr),Manny Albam,Ralph Burns,Johnny Carisi(arr).
                                        NYC.December 1954
E4VB6098 Cabin In The Sky   RCA-Victor LJM1024
E4VB6099 Breakfast With Joe   -   ,HMV(E)DLP1107
E4VB6100 This Reminds Me Of You   -   -
E4VB6101 Lullaby Of Birdland   RCA-Victor EPA672,LPM1146,(Eu)NL89278
E4VB6102 Cohn My Way   RCA-Victor LJM1024

Joe Newman(tp),Billy Byers,Frank Rehak(tb),Hal McKusick,Gene Quill(as),Al Cohn(ts,arr),Sol
Schlinger(bars),Sanford Gold(p),Billy Bauer(g),Milt Hinton(b),Osie Johnson(dr).
                                        NYC.December 22,1954
E4VB6178 Move   RCA-Victor LJM1024
E4VB6179 Never Never Land   -

Jimmy Raney (as "Sir Osbert Haberdasher") replaces Bauer.
                                        NYC.December 23,1954
E4VB6180 Count Every Star   RCA-Victor LJM1024
E4VB6181 Something For Lisa   -
E4VB6182 La Ronde   -

All ttles on LJM1024 also on RCA(F)PM42043,(J)RGP1051.

THE NATURAL SEVEN:
Joe Newman(tp),Frank Rehak(tb),Al Cohn(ts,arr),Nat Pierce(p),Freddie Green(g),Milt Hinton
(b),Osie Johnson(dr,vcl),Manny Albam,Ernie Wilkins(arr).
                                        NYC.February 3,1955
F2JB1238 Count Me In   RCA-Victor EPC1116-2,LPM1116
F2JB1239 Pick A Dilly   -   -
F2JB1240 Doggin' Around   RCA-Victor EPC1116-1, -
F2JB1241 A Kiss To Build A Dream On   -   -
F2JB1242 Jump The Blues Away   RCA-Victor EPC1116-2, -
F2JB1243 A.C. Meets Osie   RCA-Victor EPC1116-3, -
F2JB1244 9:20 Special   -   -
F2JB1245 The Natural Thing To Do   -   -
F2JB1246 Baby Please   -   -
F2JB1247 Osie's Blues(oj)   RCA-Victor EPC1116-1, -
F2JB1248 Jack's Kinda Swing   RCA-Victor EPC1116-2, -
F2JB1249 Freddie's Tune   RCA-Victor EPC1116-1, -

All titles - except "A.C. Meets Osie" - also on RCA(Eu)NL89278,(J)RGP1062.
All titles - except "A Kiss To Build A Dream On" and "Osie's Blues" - also on RCA 6465-2RB
CD).

AL COHN AND HIS ORCHESTRA:
omit Rehak;add strings,Ralph Burns(arr).   NYC.May 6,1955
F2JB3718 That Old Feeling   RCA-Victor LPM1207
F2JB3719 Trouble Is A Man   -
F2JB3720 Willow Weep For Me   -
F2JB3721 Gone With The Wind   -

  same.   NYC.May 11,1955
F2JB3722 Azure-Te (Paris Blues)   RCA-Victor LPM1207
F2JB3723 I'll Take Romance   -
2JB3724 I'll Be Around   -
2JB3725 Sweet And Lovely   -

  same.   NYC.May 13,1955
2JB3726 In A Mellow Tone   RCA-Victor LPM1207
2JB3727 Soft As Spring   -
2JB3728 Honey Blonde   -
2JB3729 Swingin' The Blues   -

THE JAZZ WORKSHOP (FOUR BRASS/ONE TENOR):
Thad Jones (as "Burt Valve"),Joe Newman,Joe Wilder(tp),Nick Travis(tp,vtb),Al Cohn(ts,arr)
Dick Katz(p),Freddie Green(g),Buddy Jones(b),Osie Johnson(dr),Manny Albam(arr).

		NYC.May 1955		
F2JB3730	Every Time	RCA-Victor EPB1161,LPM1161,LEJ-9,		
F2JB3731	Just Plain Sam		-	-
F2JB3732	Rosetta		-	-
F2JB3733	Alone Together	RCA-Victor EPA696,		-

Note:Rec. date for the above session may be May 9,1955.

Same.

		NYC.May 14,1955	
F2JB3734	A Little Song	RCA-Victor EPA696,LPM1161	
F2JB3735	The Song Is Ended	RCA-Victor EPB1161,	-
F2JB3736	Cohn Not Cohen		-	-
F2JB3737	Foggy Water	RCA-Victor EPA696,	-

Phil Sunkel(tp) replaces Glow.

		NYC.May 16,1955	
F2JB3738	Sugar Cohn	RCA-Victor EPA696,LPM1161	
F2JB3739	I'm Coming Virginia	RCA-Victor EPB1161,	-
F2JB3740	Haroosh		-	-
F2JB3741	Linger Awhile		-	-

All titles on LPM1161 also on RCA(F)PM45164.

COHN - KAMUCA - PERKINS (THE BROTHERS):
Al Cohn,Bill Perkins(ts,arr),Richie Kamuca(ts),Hank Jones(p),Barry Galbraith(g),John Beal
(b),Chuck Flores(dr),Bob Brookmeyer,Nat Pierce(arr).

		NYC.June 24,1955	
F2JB5011	Blue Skies	RCA-Victor EPB1162-1,LPM1162	
F2JB5012	Gay Blade	RCA-Victor EPB1162-2,	-
F2JB5013	Rolling Stone		-	-
F2JB5014	Memories Of You	unissued	
F2JB5015	Slightly Salty	-	
F2JB5016	Three Of A Kind	RCA-Victor LPM1162	
F2JB5017	Pro-Ex	-	
F2JB5018	Kim's Kaper	RCA-Victor EPB1162-1,LPM1162	

Jimmy Raney (as "Sam Beethoven")(g) replaces Galbraith;add Bill Potts(arr).

		NYC.June 25,1955	
F2JB5019	Chorus For Morris	RCA-Victor unissued	
F2JB5020	Hags!	RCA-Victor EPB1162-1,LPM1162	
F2JB5021	Blixed		-	-
F2JB5022	Strange Again	RCA-Victor LPM1162	
F2JB5023	Cap Snapper		
F2JB5024	Sioux Zan	RCA-Victor EPB1162-2,LPM1162	
F2JB5025	Saw Buck	unissued	
F2JB5026	The Walrus	RCA-Victor EPB1162-2,LPM1162	

All titles on LPM1162 also on RCA(Eu)PM43240.

AL COHN - ZOOT SIMS SEXTET:
Dick Sherman(tp),Al Cohn, Zoot Sims(ts),Dave McKenna(p),Milt Hinton(b),Osie Johnson(dr).

		NYC.January 23,1956
G2JB1114	Mediolistic	RCA-Victor unissued
G2JB1115	Sandy's Swing	-
G2JB1116	Crimea River	RCA-Victor LPM1282

Same.   NYC.January 24,1956
G2JB1114 Mediolistic   RCA-Victor LPM1282
G2JB1115 Sandy's Swing   -
G2JB1117 A New Moan   -
G2JB1118 A Moment's Notice   -
G2JB1119 My Blues   -
G2JB1119 My Blues(alt.take)   RCA Bluebird 6469-2RB(CD)
G2JB1120 Sherm's Terms   RCA-Victor LPM1282
G2JB1121 More Bread   -
G2JB1121 More Bread(alt.take)   RCA Bluebird 6469-2RB(CD)

AL COHN - ZOOT SIMS QUINTET:
Omit Sherman;Hank Jones(p) replaces McKenna. Same date.
G2JB1122 Tenor For Two Please,Jack   RCA-Victor LPM1282
G2JB1122 Tenor For Two
         Please,Jack(alt.take)   RCA Bluebird 6469-2RB(CD)
G2JB1123 Somebody Loves Me   RCA-Victor LPM1282
G2JB1123 Somebody Loves Me(alt.take)   RCA Bluebird 6469-2RB(CD),(Eu)ND86469(CD)
G2JB1124 East Of The Sun   RCA-Victor LPM1282,(G)LPM9861
G2JB1125 From A To Z   -

All titles on LPM1282 also on RCA Bluebird 6469-2RB (CD),RCA(Eu)PM42302,(F)NL89644,(J)
RGP1166,RA5404,(J)JCM1-8327.
All tiitles on RCA Bluebird 6469-2EB (CD) also on RCA(Eu)ND86469(CD),(J)R32J1079(CD).

AL COHN QUARTET:
Al Cohn(ts),Billy Taylor(p),George Duvivier(b),Percy Brice(dr).
                                  NYC.March 21,1956
5175   There Will Never Be Another You ABC-Paramount ABC-111,(J)PC7,HMV(E)7EG8367.

Note:See Billy Taylor for an additional title (without Cohn) from this session.

AL COHN AND THE SAX SECTION:
Sam Marowitz,Gene Quill(as),Al Cohn,Ed Wasserman(ts),Sol Schlinger(bars),John Williams(p),
Milt Hinton(b),Osie Johnson(dr).   NYC.May 24,1956
C056057 Shazam   Epic LN3278,Philips(E)BBL7208,(Eu)B07227L
C056058 Solsville   -
C056059 Double Fracture   -
C056060 Tears By Me Out The Heart   -

Romeo Penque,Phil Bodner(as),Al Cohn,Boomie Richman,Peanuts Hucko(ts),Charlie O'Kane
(bars),John Williams(p),Milt Hinton(b),Osie Johnson(dr).
                                            NYC.June 5,1956
C056093 Don't Worry 'Bout Me   Epic LN3278
C056094 Villa Rowboats   -
C056095 Shutout   - ,Fontana(E)TFE17006,(Eu)462.108TE
C056096 While My Lady Sleeps

Al Cohn,Ed Wasserman,Zoot Sims(ts),Sol Schlinger(bars),Hank Jones(p),Milt Hinton(b),Don
Lamond(dr).   NYC.June 28,1956
C056269 Shorty George   Epic LN3278
C056270 The Return Of The Redhead(1)   - ,LA16001,CBS(Eu)S66403,Fontana(E)
                                            TFE17006,(Eu)462.108TE,Supraphon(Cz)0152114
C056271 Blue For The High Brow   Epic LN3278,CBS(Eu)S66403,Fontana(E)TFE17006,
                                            (Eu)462.108TE
C056272 The Mellow Side   Epic LN3278,CBS(Eu)S66403,Fontana(E)TFE17006,
                                            (Eu)462.108TE

-1.Listed as "Red Boys" on the label of LSP15622.

All titles also on Fresh Sound(Sp)LSP15622.

```
AL COHN QUINTET:
Frank Rehak -1(tb),Al Cohn(ts),Hank Jones(p),Milt Hinton(b),Osie Johnson(dr).
                                      NYC.September 29,1956
         Abstract Of You               Dawn DLP1110,Biograph BCD120(CD)
         Be Loose(1)                     -
         Blue Lou                        -  ,Biograph BCD120(CD),unk.label SMS7145
         Good Old Blues(1)               -  ,unknown label SMS7145,SMS7152
         Idaho(1)                        -  ,DLP1123,        -
         Singing The Blues               -  ,Biograph BCD120(CD)
         Softly As In A Morning Sunrise  -  ,Biograph BCD120(CD),unk.lab. SMS7145,
                                       SMS7152
         The Things I Love              Dawn DLP1110
         When Day Is Done                -  ,unknown label SMS7145
         We Three                        -
         Them There Eyes(1)             Jazztone J1245
```

All titles on DLP1110 also on Dawn(J)SL5133,YW7603,Biograph BLP12063,Fun House(J)22WB7004,
32WD7004 (CD).

```
Bob Brookmeyer(vtb),Al Cohn(ts),Mose Allison(p),Teddy Kotick(b),Nick Stabulas(dr).
                                      NYC.December 4/5,1956
101060 S-h-i-n-e                       Coral CRL57118
101061 The Lady Is A Tramp              -
101062 Back To Back                     -
101063 Good Spirits                     -
101064 Chlo-e                           -
101065 Lazy Man Stomp                   -
101066 I Should Care                    -
101067 Ill Wind                         -
101068 So Far So Good                    -
101069 Bunny Hunch                      -
101070 Winter                           -
101071 A Blues Serenade                 -
```

All titles also on MCA/Coral(G)PCO7181,6.21813,MCA(F)510.173,(J)MCA3125.

```
Zoot Sims(ts) replaces Brookmeyer.      NYC.March 26/27,1957
102100 You're A Lucky Guy               Coral CRL57171
102101 Halley's Comet                    -
102102 Chasing The Blues                 -
102103 Two Funky People(1)               -  ,MCA MCA2-4069
102104 The Wailing Boat                  -
102105 Brandy And Beer                   -
102106 Gone With The Wind               Coral CRL57149,(E)LVA9089,MCA MCAD31372(CD),
                                          (J)3037
102107 Just You Just Me                 Coral CRL57171
102108 It's A Wonderful World            -
```

-1.Cohn,Sims play (cl).

All titles on CRL57171 also on Coral(E)LVA9074,MCA MCAD31372 (CD),(F)510.164,(J)MCA3037,
VIM5508.

```
(ZOOT SIMS - AL COHN SEPTET):
Nick Travis(tp),Jimmy Cleveland(tb),Zoot Sims(ts,cl),Al Cohn(bars,cl),Elliot Lawrence(p),
Milt Hinton(b),Osie Johnson(dr),Bill Elton(arr).
                                      NYC.c. 1957/58
         I Get Along
            Without You Very Well      Jass JASS TWELVE
         Old Rockin' Chair              -
         Skylark                        -
(session cont. next page).
```

(session cont. from previous page):
```
        The Nearness Of You              Jass JASS TWELVE
        Georgia On My Mind                        -
        Up A Lazy River                           -
        Two Sleepy People                         -
        Stardust                                  -
```

All titles also on Jass JCD5 (CD),DIW(J)DIW1235,Vogue(F)VG651.600262 (CD).
Note:The above titles issued as THE ZOOT SIMS - AL COHN SEPTET; nevertheless it was recor-
     ded as an Elliot Lawrence session.

Jack Kerouac(recitation) acc. by Al Cohn,Zoot Sims(ts).
```
                                         NYC.c. spring 1958
        American Haikus                  Hanover HM/S5006,Rhino "Wordbeat" R70939(CD)
        Hard-Hearted Old Farmer(1)                -                            -
        The Last Hotel(1)                         -                            -
        Some Of The Dharma                        -                            -
        Poems From The
            Unpublished "Book Of Blues"           -                            -
        Old Western Movies               Rhino "Wordbeat" R70939(CD)
        Conclusion Of The Railroad Earth          -
```

-1.Cohn(!) plays (p).

ZOOT SIMS - AL COHN QUINTET:
Zoot Sims,Al Cohn(ts),Mose Allison(p),Knobby Totah(b),Paul Motian(dr).
```
                                         NYC.February 6/7,1959
        Lover Come Back To Me            United Artists UAL4040/UAS5040
        It Had To be You                          -
        Wee Dot(1)                                -
        After You've Gone(1)                      -                 ,UAL4085,UAS5085
```

-1.Add Phil Woods(as).

All titles also on United Artists(J)GXC3139,SR3042,LAX3115,Blue Note(F)BNP25105,HMV(E)
CLP1471,CSD1381,(F)FELP227.

Al Cohn,Zoot Sims(ts,cl),Mose Allison(p),Bill Crow(b),Nick Stabulas(dr).
```
                                         Broadcast."Birdland",NYC.March 4,1960
        Halley's Comet                   Chazzer 2004
        Ah-Moore                                  -
        Gone With The Wind                        -
        Just You,Just Me                          -
        Jumpin' With
            Symphony Sid/Morning Fun              -
```

Al Cohn,Zoot Sims(ts),Mose Allison(p),Major Holley(b),Osie Johnson(dr).
```
                                         NYC.June 1/3,1960
20110  The Note                          Mercury MG20606
20111  You'd Be So Nice To Come Home To          -      ,Verve 845.708-2(CD)
20112  A Pair Of Deuces                 unissued
20113  You 'N Me                         Mercury MG20606
20114  On The Alamo                              -
20115  The Opener                                -
20116  Angel Eyes(1)                             -
20117  Awful Lonely                              -
20118  Love For Sale                             -
20119  Improvisation For Unaccompanied
           Saxophones(no p,b,dr)                 -
```

-1.Cohn,Sims play (cl).
(session cont. next page).

(session cont. from previous page):
All titles also on Mercury SR60606,(E)MMC14071,SMWL21030,SM134.590,(Eu)6336.523,(J)15PJ19,
EXPR1001,EJD3041 (CD),Trip TLP5548.

AL COHN AND HIS ORCHESTRA:
Nick Travis,Bernie Glow,Jimmy Maxwell,Clark Terry(tp),Frank Rehak,Bob Brookmeyer,Urbie
Green,Dick Hixon(tb),John Barrows,Jimmy Buffington(frh),Romeo Penque,Zoot Sims,Gene Quill,
Eddie Caine,Sol Schlinger(sax),Hank Jones(p),Mundell Lowe(g),Buddy Clark,George Duvivier
(b),Louis Hayes,Jimmy Cobb,Mel Lewis,Charlie Persip,Don Lamond(dr,perc),Al Cohn(arr,cond).

	NYC.August 24,1960	
L2PB3830 Son Of A Drum	RCA-Victor LPM/LSP2312	
L2PB3831 Brushmanship		-
L2PB3832 Dr. Skin And Mr. Hide		-

Gus Johnson(dr) replaces Hayes.

	NYC.August 26,1960	
L2PB3833 Five Drums In Four-Four	RCA-Victor LPM/LSP2312	
L2PB3834 Drums Loco		-
L2PB3835 Drum Smoke		-

Note:The titles from the August 24/26 sessions issued as "Son Of A Drum Suite".

AL COHN - ZOOT SIMS:
Al Cohn, Zoot Sims(ts),Mose Allison (as "Old Grand Happy")(p),Bill Crow(b),Gus Johnson
(dr),Cecil "Kid Haffey" Collier(vcl).

	NYC.February 1961	
P-Town	Fred Miles Presents FM-1	
I Like It Like That(kh)		-
Sweet Lorraine(kh)		-
Autumn Leaves		-
The Thing		-
I'm Tellin' Ya		-
Nagasaki(kh)		-
Morning Fun		-

All titles also on Fred Miles(J)KUX-IV,Zim ZMS2002,Baybridge(J)30CP74 (CD),Evidence
ECD22007-2 (CD).

Jimmy Maxwell,Marky Markowitz(tp),Willie Dennis(tb),Phil Woods(as,cl),Jerry Dodgion
(as,fl),Zoot Sims(ts),Gene Allen(bars),Eddie Costa(p),Bill Crow(b),Mel Lewis(dr),Al
Cohn(arr,cond).

	NYC.July 12,1962	
Mission To Moscow	Colpix (S)CP433	
The Sochi Boatmen		-
Midnight In Moscow		-
Let's Dance		-
Russian Lullaby		-
Red,White And Blue Eyes		-

All titles also on Ghent GS5003.

Al Cohn(ts),George Salisbury(p),Charles Matthews(b),Vince Bilardo(dr).

	Live.Kansas City.March 28,1965	
These Foolish Things	WDAF-KC610	

AL COHN - ZOOT SIMS - RICHIE KAMUCA SEXTET:
Al Cohn,Zoot Sims,Richie Kamuca(ts),Dave Frishberg(p),Tommy Potter(b),Mel Lewis(dr).

	Broadcast."Half Note",NYC.October 29,1965	
Tickle Toe	Pumpkin 108	
Broadway		-

Note:See Jimmy Rushing for additional titles from the above broadcast (and from other
October 1965 broadcasts with Cohn and Sims).

AL COHN - ZOOT SIMS:
Al Cohn,Zoot Sims(ts),Peter King(as,ts),Jack Sharpe(ts,bars),Stan Tracey(p),Rick Laird(b),
Jackie Dougan(dr).   London.November 1965
      Shoft   World Record Club(E)T/STP714
      Haunted Jazzclub   -
      Zoot's Tune   -
      Cockle Row   -
      Pete's Tune No.1   -
      Flaming June   -
      Mr. George   -
      Pete's Tune No.2   -

AL COHN - ZOOT SIMS:
Al Cohn,Zoot Sims(ts),Jaki Byard(p),George Duvivier(b),Mel Lewis(dr).
                                     NYC.March 23,1973
      Doodle-Oodle   Muse MR5016,Franklin Mint 71
      Emily   -
      Samba Medley: -
         Recado Bossa Nova
         The Girl From Ipanema
         One Note Samba
      Mama Flosie   -
      Body And Soul   -
      Jean(1)   -
      Blue Hodge   -

-1.Sims plays (ss).

All titles also on Muse MCD5356 (CD),(J)YP7044,IXJ80107,Vogue(F)VG651.600601 (CD),Seven
Seas(J)K22P6004.

Al Cohn,Zoot Sims(ts),Horace Parlan(p),Hugo Rasmussen(b),Svend-Erik Nørregaard(dr).
                                Stockholm.November 25,1974
        Stockholm - L.A.   Sonet(E)SNTF684
        My Funny Valentine   -
        Yardbird Suite(1)   -
        Motoring Along   -
        Fallin'   -
        What The World Needs Now   -

-1.Sims plays (ss).

All titles also on Sonet(E)SNTCD684 (CD),(J)UXP38,Vogue(F)VG408.SNTF684,Seven Seas(J)
K23P6078.

AL COHN QUARTET:
Al Cohn(ts),Barry Harris(p),Larry Ridley(b),Alan Dawson(dr).
                                NYC.June 19,1975
        You're My Everything   Xanadu 110
        Lover   -
        Play It Now   -
        Irresistible You   -
        Georgia On My Mind   -
        It's Sand,Man   -

All titles also on Xanadu(F)FDC5171 (CD),(J)JC7010,YS7105.

AL COHN QUARTET:
Al Cohn(ts),Barry Harris(p),Sam Jones(b),Leroy Williams(dr),
                                NYC.December 6,1976

(session cont. next page).

(session cont. from previous page):
```
        America The Beautiful        Xanadu 138,5001,(F)FDC5172(CD),(Eu)197150
        Night And Day                    -                -
        My Shining Hour                  -                -
        Bright                           - ,(F)FDC5171(CD)
        Skylark                          -                -
        Woody 'N' You                    -                -
        Comin' In Home                   -                -
```

All titles also on Xanadu(J)ULX487,ULX98.

AL COHN - JIMMY ROWLES:
Al Cohn(ts),Jimmy Rowles(p).   NYC.March 15,1977
```
        Them There Eyes              Xanadu 145
        Sweet And Lovely                 -
        I Hadn't Anyone Till You         -
        Taking A Chance On Love          -
        These Foolish things             -
        Bar Talk                         -
```

All titles also on Xanadu(J)ULX617,ULX81.

Al Cohn(ts),Barry Harris(p),Steve Gilmore(b),Walter Bolden(dr).
```
                                        NYC.December 18,1979
        Fred                         Xanadu 179
        Danielle                         -
        All The Things You Are           -
        Zoot Case                        -
        Sophisticated Lady(ts,p only)    -
        Mood Indigo                      -
        Three Little Words               -
```

All titles also on Xanadu(F)FDC5172 (CD),(J)BRJ4532 (CD).

DOLO COKER

See also XANADU ALL STARS.

Blue Mitchell(tp,flh),Harold Land(ts),Dolo Coker(p),Leroy Vinnegar(b),Frank Butler(dr).
```
                                        LA.December 26,1976
        Dolo                         Xanadu 139
        Affair In Havanna                -
        Lady Hawthorne,Please            -
        Field Day                        -
        Never Let Me Go(no tp/flh,ts)    -
        Smack Up                         -
```

Art Pepper(as,ts) replaces Land.   LA.December 27,1976
```
        Jumping Jacks                Xanadu 142,5001,(Eu)197.150
        Gone With The Wind               -
        Roots 4FB                        -
        Mr. Yohe                         -
        Gone Again(1)                    -
        Tale Of Two Cities               -
        'Round Midnight              Xanadu 171
```

-1.Omit Mitchell,Pepper.

All titles also on Xanadu(J)BRJ4560 (CD).
All titles on Xanadu 142 also on Xanadu(Eu)197.118,(J)KUX69,YS7094.

Dolo Coker(p),Leroy Vinnegar(b),Frank Butler(dr).
                                    LA.November 18,1977
    You Won't Let Me Go   Xanadu 153
    Third Down   -
    This Is All I Ask   -
    Groovin' High   -
    There Is No Other Way   -

Add Harry Edison(tp).   Same date
    Sweet Coke   Xanadu 153
    Out Of Nowhere   -

(p-solo).   NYC.November 28,1978
    Reflections   Xanadu 178
    Sine And Cosine   -
    Just You   -
    Cabin In The Sky   -
    All Alone   -
    The Things You Never Said   -
    Spectrum   -
    Try A Little Tenderness   -

JERRY COKER

Jerry Coker,Bob Cowart,Louis Ciotti(ts),Jack Coker(p),Monk Montgomery(b),Charles Mastro-
paolo(dr).   Bloomington(?),Indiana.July 1955
    Limehouse Blues   Fantasy EP4056,LP3-214
    This Is Always(1)   -   -
    Red Kelly's Blues   -
    You Gotta Show Me   -

-1.Omit Ciotti.

Add Freddy Fox,Roger Pemberton(bars). Bloomington(?),Indiana.July 1955
    Clare-ity   Fantasy EP4056,LP3-214
    Jack's Acts   -   -
    Old Crinkletoes   -
    Opus No.1   -

Add Alan Kiger -2(tp),Jim Hewitt -3(tb). Bloomington(?),Indiana.July 1955
    It's You Or No One(2)   Fantasy LP3-214
    Kigeria(2)   -
    Lost April(3)   -
    Nancy (With The Laughing Face)(3)   -

All titles on LP3-214 also on Metronome/Fantasy 0902116.

Alan Kiger(tp),Jerry Coker(ts),Eddie Duran(g),Dean Riley(b).
                                    San Francisco.November 1956
    Waters Edge   San Francisco JAZZ RECORDS-1
    You'll Stay   -
    Giggling Oysters   -

GEORGE "KID SHEIK" COLA

See also STEVE ANGRUM,BOVISA NEW ORLEANS JAZZ BAND,JOHN HANDY,BARRY MARTYN.
(section cont. next page).

GEORGE "KID SHEIK" COLA

KID SHEIK'S SWINGSTERS:
Kid Sheik Cola(tp),Eddie Sommers(tb),Harold "Duke" Dejan(as,vcl),John Smith(p,vcl),Fred
Minor(bj),Alcide "Slow Drag" Pavageau(b),Alex Bigard(dr).

New Orleans.February 11,1961

Gloryland	Music Of New Orleans rejected
The Sheik Of Araby(dd)	Music Of New Orleans MNLP1
The Sheik Of Araby(alt.take)(dd)	"77"(E)LA12/16,Jazz Crusade JC2001
Keeps Raining Blues(js)	Music Of New Orleans MNLP1
Down In Honky Tonk Town	-
Down In Honky Tonk Town(alt.take)	"77"(E)LA12/16,Jazz Crusade JC2001
Lord,Lord,Lord,	
You've Sure Been Good To Me	Music Of New Orleans MNLP1,Jazz Crusade JC2001
Duke's Blues(dd)	-
I'm Confessin'	-
Song Of The Island(incompl.)	-
How Long Blues(1)	-
Sheik's Blues(1)	unissued

-1.Cola(p),Bigard(dr) only.

All titles on MNLP1 also on Jazzology JCE31.

Kid Sheik Cola(tp,vcl),Albert Warner(tb),"Captain" John Handy(as,cl,vcl),Louis Gallaud(p),
"Papa" John Joseph(b),Josiah "Cie" Frazier(dr).

Cleveland,Ohio.September 28,1961

Some Of These Days(incompl.)(1)	Music Of New Orleans MNLP13
The Sheik Of Araby(ksc)	-
Shake It And Break It	-
When The Saints	
Go Marching In(ksc,jh)	-
I Want To Be Happy	-
Eh La Bas(jh)	-
Cap's Blues	-

-1.This title was not included on the first pressing of MNLP13.

KID SHEIK COLA WITH BARRY MARTYN:
Kid Sheik Cola(tp,vcl),Jack Wedell(tb),Sammy Rimington(cl),Paul Seely(bj),Barry Richardson
(b),Barry Martyn(dr).

Egham,England.June 12,1963

Careless Love	Jazz Crusade LP2003
Tulane Swing	-
When Your Hair	
Has Turned To Silver	-
Baby Face	-
Willie The Weeper	-
Take Your Burden To The Lord	-
The Waltz You Saved For Me	-
Sheik's Blues	-

All titles also on G.H.B. GHB187.

KID SHEIK AND HIS SHEIKS:
Same.

Prob.England. 1963

Put On Your Old Grey Bonnet	Jazzology JCE6
You Broke Your Promise	-
Take Your Burden To The Lord	-
The Sheik Of Araby	-

All titles also on G.H.B. GHB45.

GEORGE "KID SHEIK" COLA

Kid Sheik Cola(tp),Pete Dyer(tb),Jack McMahon(cl),John Coles(g,bj),Brian Turnock(b),Barry
Martyn(dr).   Willesden,London.March 5,1966
        The Bucket's Got A Hole In It   Rhythm(E)RY102
        Alexander's Ragtime Band   -
        Tin Roof Blues   -
        Swanee River   -
        Darktown Strutters' Ball   -
        Deslonde Street Blues   -
        When You And I Were Young Maggie   -
        See See Rider   -
        We Shall Walk Through
            The Streets Of The City   -

All titles also on G.H.B. GHB47.

Kid Sheik Cola(tp),"Cuff" Billett(tp,vcl),Pete Dyer(tb),John Handy(as,vcl),Richard Simmons
(p),Brian Turnock(b),Barry Martyn(dr).   Ghent,Belgium.March 11,1966
        Rebecca(cb)   "77"(E)LEU12/15
        Last Night On The Back Porch(ksc)   -
        Ice Cream   -
        Black And Blue   -
        Eh La Bas(jh)   -
        In The Groove(cb)   -
        Little Richard's Blues   -
        Grey Bonnet(ksc)   -
        Panama   -

Add Frank Booker(ts).   Willesden,London.March 1966
        Bogalusa Strut   G.H.B. GHB38
        Everybody's Talking 'Bout Sammy   -
        Down By The Riverside   -
        Mobile Stomp   -
        Over In Gloryland   -
        Short Dress Gal   -
        Steppin' On The Gas   -
        Sing On   -

Kid Sheik Cola(tp),John Handy(as,vcl),Richard Simmons(p),Brian Turnock(b),Barry Martyn
(dr).   London.March 31,1966
        I Want To Be Happy   NoLa(E)LP1
        Waltz Medley: -
            The Waltz You Saved For Me
            Sometime
            When Your Hair
                Has Turned To Silver
        Cap's Blues   -
        Bye Bye Blackbird(ksc)   -
        Boogie Woogie And Encore   -
        Last Night On The Backporch(ksc)   -
        Sheik's Blues   -
        Baby Face   -
        Song Of The Islands   -

KID SHEIK'S BAND/SAN JACINTO SIX:
Kid Sheik Cola(tp),Paul Barnes(cl,as),Earl Humphrey(tb),Lars Edegran(p),Chester Zardis(b),
Barry Martyn(dr).   New Orleans.November 2,1966
        Royal Telephone
            (Telephone To Glory)   Dixie(E)LP3
        Yes Sir,That's My Baby   -
        Yes Sir,That's My Baby(alt.take) Dixie(E)LP10
(session cont. next page).

(session cont. from previous page):
```
        Crying Time(ksc)                    Dixie(E)LP3
        Some Of These Days(pb)                   -
        St. Louis Blues                          -
        Darktown Strutters' Ball                 -
        Blues (Blues For Buster Holmes)          -
        Blues                                    -
        Indiana(pb)                              -
        Dipsey Doodle                       Dixie(E)LP10
        Angry                                 unissued
        Sister Kate                              -
```

Kid Sheik Cola(tp,vcl),Louis Nelson(tb),John Handy(as),James "Sing" Miller(p),Fred Minor
(bj),Chester Zardis(b),Alex Bigard(dr).   Broadcast.Boston,Mass.February 22,1967
```
        Yes Sir,That's My Baby             Golden Sunset GS102
        Last Night On The Back Porch(ksc)        -
        Muskrat Ramble                           -
        Boogie Woogie                            -
        The Sheik Of Araby(ksc)                  -
        Song Of The Islands                      -
```

KID SHEIK AND HIS CREOLE JAZZ BAND:
Kid Sheik Cola(tp),Louis Nelson(tb),John Handy(as),Dick Cook(cl),Dave Duquette(bj),Bill
Sinclair(p),Chester Zardis(b),Sammy Penn(dr).
```
                        Live."Wachusett Country Club",West Boylston,Mass.March 15,1968
        Blueberry Hill                 Music Of The Mass. Traditional Jazz Club (unnumb.)
        Just A Little While To Stay Here
        Girl Of My Dreams                                                        -
```

Kid Sheik Cola(tp,vcl),Pete Dyer(tb),Dick Douthwaite(cl,as),Jon Marks(p),Brian Turnock(b),
Barry Martyn(dr).   London.October 16,1968
```
        Some Of These Days                 Dixie(E)LP1
        Over The Waves                           -
        Yearning,Just For You                    -
        Honky Tonk Town No.1                     -
        Frankie And Johnny                       -
        Honky Tonk Town No.2                     -
        Carless Love                             -
        Blue Heaven                              -
        The Spinning Wheel                       -
        Jesus,Keep Me Near The Cross             -
```

Kid Sheik Cola(tp,vcl),Luciano Invernizzi(tb),Gigi Cavicchioli -1(cl),Beppe Aliprandi -2
(as),Jon Marks(p),Fabio Turazzi(bj),Eugenio Pateri(b),Barry Martyn(dr).
```
                        Live."La Speranza",Milan,Italy.October  1968
        Alexander's Ragtime Band           Rusty(I)RR402
        Sister Kate(1)                           -
        Ting A Ling(2)                           -
        Royal Telephone(1)                       -
        Birth Of The Blues(2)                    -
        Tulane Swing(1)(ksc)                     -
        Darktown Strutters' Ball(1)              -
```

Omit Cavicchioli;Aliprandi(as) on all titles.
```
                        Live.Milan,Italy.October  1968
        Yes Sir,That My Baby               Rusty(I)RR402
        St. Louis Blues(ksc)                     -
        Tin Roof Blues                           -
        Joe Avery's Piece                        -
```

SHEIK - ROBINSON NEW ORLEANS STOMPERS:
Kid Sheik Cola(tp),Jim Robinson(tb),Sammy Rimington(cl,as),Derek "Griff" Griffith(bj),Dick
McCarthy(b),Bill Bissonette(dr).   Unknown location.c. 1975
     Dipsey Doodle   G.H.B. GHB76
     My Darling Nellie Grey   -
     Whoopie Blues   -
     Birth Of The Blues   -
     Back Home Again In Indiana   -
     When You And I Were Young,Maggie   -
     Down By The Riverside   -
     Angry   -
     Hindustan   -

KID SHEIK AND JEGGPAP NEW ORLEANS JAZZBAND:
Kid Sheik Cola(tp),Joris De Cock(tp),Denis Vereecken(tb),Bert Heuvinck(cl),Norbert Detaye
(p),Flip Hermans(bj),Paul Van Den Durpel(b),Miel Leybaert(dr).
           Live.St. Vincentius Institute,Dendermonde,Belgium.September 8,1976
     Streets Of The City   HT1003
     I Can't Escape From You   -
     Old Rugged Cross   -
     Telephone To Glory   -
     Last Night On The Back Porch   -
     Just A Little
        While To Stay Here(1)   -
     Tipperary(1)   -
     If I Had To Live My Life Over(1)   -
     Beslonde Street Blues(1)   -
     Crying Time(1)   -

-1.Cola plays (p).

CRISTIAN COLAN (Roumanian)

CRISTIAN COLAN TRIO:
Cristian Colan(p),Johnny-Cretu Raducanu(b),Dumitru Manaila(dr).
               Bucharest.c. May/August 1967
     Papusa De Satin (Satin Doll)   Electrecord(Ro)EDD1164

RIC COLBECK (British)

Ric Colbeck(tp),Byard Lancaster(as,bcl),Bennie Maupin(ts),Joel Friedman(cello),Sonny
Sharrock(g),Sirone (Norris Jones)(b),Sunny Murray(dr).
               Live.NYC.October 4,1966
     Unknown titles   Pixie unissued

Ric Colbeck(tp),Mike Osborne(as),Jean-Francois Jenny-Clark(b),Selwyn Lissack(dr).
               London.January 19/20,1970
     Aphrodite   Fontana(E)6383.001
     Subdued   -
     The Sun Is Coming Up   -
     Lowlands   -

JOHN COLBOURNE-VEEL (Australian)
(section cont. next page).

JOHN COLBOURNE-VEEL'S BAND:
Geoff Bull(cnt),John Colbourne-Veel(tb),Barry Wratten(cl),Gary Walford(p),Geoff Holden(bj)
Don Heap(b),Viv Carter(dr).   Ballarat,Australia.December 30,1969
        Alone   East(Au)EASC40

Note:See GEOFF BULL for one additional title from this session.

Cliff Reese(tp),John Colbourne-Veel(tb),Paul Furniss(cl,ss,as),Hans Karssemeyer(p),Stan
Kenton(b),Mal McGillivray(dr).   Sydney.December 22,1980
        A Monday Date   unissued(?)
        Way Down Yonder In New Orleans
        Kenny's Cakewalk
        Stomping The Davil
        Shadows
        The Woogie Boogie
        Nevertheless
        Song Of The Night Before
        Alone
        Prelude To The Night
        The Jeep Is Jumping
        Don't Be That Way

MARK COLBY

Mark Colby(ts,ss),Bob James(keyb,arr,cond),Hiram Bullock -1(g,vcl),Steve Khan -2,Eric Gale
-3(g),Gary King(b),Steve Gadd(dr),Rubens Bassini(perc),Jay Chattaway,Bill Eaton(arr,cond).
                                        NYC.c. 1977
        Serpentine Fire(1,2,6)   Columbia/Tappan Zee JC35298
        Daydreamer(2,3,7)   -
        On And On(2,3,5,6,7,8)   -
        King Tut(2)   -
        Renegade(1,4,6,7)(hb)   -
        Rainbow Wings(2)   -

-4.Steve Jordan(dr) replaces Gadd.
-5.Add Bob Militello(fl,picc),Clifford Carter(keyb);omit Bassini.
-6.Add brass incl. Jon Faddis(tp).
-7.Add strings.
-8.Add unknown voices.

Mark Colby(ts,ss,vcl),Mike Mainieri(vbs),Barry Miles,Biff Hannon,Bob James(keyb),Eric Gale
Hiram Bullock,Steve Khan,Randy Bernsen(g),Gary King(b),Steve Jordan,Steve Gadd(dr),Jimmy
Maelen,Portinho(perc).   NYC. 1979
        Skat Talk   Columbia/Tappan Zee JC35725
        Macbeth (For Folon)(1)   -
        Peace Of Mind   -
        Song For My Daughter   -
        Village Zoo   -
        Capativa   -

-1.Gordon Johnson(b) replaces King.

MICHAEL COLDIN

MICHAEL COLDIN SEPTET:
No details.   NYC.February 18/19,1959
(session cont. next page).

(session cont. from previous page):

What Is this Thing Called Love	Everest LPBR5038/SDBR1038
Caravan	-
My Reverie	-
Lullaby Of Birdland	-
'S Wonderful	-
La Cinquantaine (Golden Wedding)	-
I've Got You Under My Skin	-
Lullaby Of The Leaves	-
Mack The Knife	-
Stella By Starlight	-
A Foggy Day	-

RICHARD COLDMAN (British)

(g-solo,vcl,etc.).   London.April 11,1979

Fret Buzz	Incus(E)31
Breaking Through	-
Nose Trouble	-
High Notes	-
One-Man-Band	-

COL D'ORCIA JAZZ (Italian)

Tony Scott(cl),Gianni Basso(ts),Renato Sellani(p),Julius Farmer(el-b),Giancarlo Pillot
(dr),Nicola Arigliano,Lilian Terry(vcl).   Live.Montalcino,Siena,Italy.October 1977

Dolphin Dance	C.D.(I)01
Sete Di Bene	-
Blue For Charlie Parker	-
I Love Montalcino	-
One For My Baby	-
Sixteen Tons	-
The Lady Is a Tramp	-
That Old Black Magic	-
Stardust	-
What A Difference A Day Made	-
Georgia On My Mind	-
St. Louis Blues	-
Brunello Scatt	-
Billie's Bounce	-

BILL COLE

Bill Cole(Ghanian-fl,Chinese usette,Indian shenai,voice),Sam Rivers(ts,p),Warren Smith
(dr,perc).   Live.Dartmouth.August 1,1975

The First Cycle	Music From Dartmouth D100

COZY COLE

See also JAZZ AT THE METROPOLE,GENE KRUPA,BOB MARSHALL,NICE ALL STARS,HERMAN SANDY,SAINTS
AND SINNERS.
(this section cont. next page).

COZY COLE ALL STARS:
Joe Thomas(tp),Trummy Young(tb),Coleman Hawkins(ts),Earl Hines(p),Teddy Walters(g),Billy
Taylor(b),Cozy Cole(dr).   NYC.February 22,1944
HLK17-1 Blue Moon   Keynote 1300,(J)18PJ1053,Mercury(F)ME4005,EmArcy
                                                    EP1-6036,Blue Star(F)205
HLK17-2 Blue Moon   Keynote(J)18PJ1053
HLK18-1 Father Co-operates   -
HLK18-2 Father Co-operates   -
HLK18-5 Father Co-operates   -
HLK18-6 Father Co-operates   Keynote 1301,(J)18PJ1053,Mercury 1089,71385,(E)
                                                    SMWL21034,AMT1015,EmArcy EP1-6037,MG36071,
                                                    (E)FJL1277,Blue Star(F)167,Metronome(Sd)
                                                    B45-764,Verve 845150-2(CD)
HLK19-1 Just One More Chance   Keynote(J)18PJ1053
HLK19-2 Just One More Chance   Keynote 1300,(J)18PJ1053,Mercury(E)SMWL21034,(F)
                                                    ME4005,EmArcy(E)EP1-6036,Blue Star(F)205,
                                                    Tulip TLP105
HLK20-1 Thru' For The Night   Keynote(J)18PJ1053,Mercury(Am)830.124
HLK20-2 Thru' For The Night   Keynote 1301,(J)18PJ1053,Mercury 1089,(E)SMWL21034
                                                    (Eu)6336.025,EmArcy EP1-6037,MGE26011,Blue
                                                    Star(F)167,Trip TLP5515,Amiga(G)8.55.487,Fon-
                                                    tana(I)6430.096,Franklin Mint 92,Album 23,
                                                    Time-Life STL-J12

All titles/takes also on Mercury(Am)830.124,830.960-2 (CD).
All takes originally issued on Keynote also on EmArcy MG26023,MG36047,(E)EJL751,Mercury
MG25018,(E)MLP7059,(Eu)134.599MFY,(J)BT2020,BT5262,Trip TLP5538,Fontana(E)FJL131,(Eu)
683.280.
Note:Some of the reissues are edited versions.
    Keynote(J)18PJ1053 and Mercury(Am)830.124 are part of the 21-LP albums 18PJ1051/71
    and 830.121-1 respectively.

Lammar Wright,Sr.(tp),Ray Conniff(tb),Ben Webster(ts),Johnny Guarnieri(p),Teddy Walters
(g),Billy Taylor(b),Cozy Cole(dr),Fred Norman(arr).
                                                NYC.March 13,1944
5410   Jericho   Savoy 502,575,Musidisc(F)CV969
5411   Talk To Me   Savoy 501
5412   Concerto For Cozy   Savoy 575,Musidisc(F)CV969
5413   Body And Soul(1)   Savoy 501,XP8088,MG9008,Royale 1854,Albyme AL1634,
                                                    Musidisc(F)CV969
5413   Body And Soul(alt.take)(1)   Savoy SJL2220,(Eu)WL70812,(F)1C.148-60966/67

-1.Omit Wright,Conniff.

All titles - except "Body And Soul" alt.take - also on Savoy MG12197,MG14010,SJL2218,(F)
1C.148-61047/48,(E)WL70533,Musidisc(F)JA5161.

Omit Webster.   Same date
5426   Nice And Cozy   Savoy 502,SJL2218,Musidisc(F)JA5161

COZY COLE ORCHESTRA:
Emmett Berry(tp),Walter Thomas(as,ts),Budd Johnson,Coleman Hawkins(ts),Johnny Guarnieri
(p),Max Shopnick(b),Cozy Cole(dr).   NYC.May 1,1944
5450   Old Man River   Savoy 512,MG9029,(F)MG90290,Musidisc(F)CV969,Byg
                                                    (F)529.168,Halo LP50242,Harlem Hitparade
                                                    HHP5011
5451   Wrap Your Troubles In Dreams   Savoy 512,MG15039,DGR(Du)2004
5452   Riding The Riff   Savoy 513,583,MG15039
5453   Flat Rock   Savoy 583,MG9029,(F)MG90290,Musidisc(F)CV969,Byg
                                                    (F)529.168

(sesion cont. next page).

(session cont. from previous page):
All titles also on Savoy MG12197,MG14010,SJL2218,(F)1C.148-61047/48,(E)WL70533,Musidisc
(F)JA5161.
Masters 5450/51 also on Rondolette A31,Allegro AL1631(?),Royale LP18154,Archives Of Folk&
Jazz FS331,Top Rank 25-008.

Eddie Barefield(as),Sid Weiss(b) replace Johnson,Shopnick.
                                      NYC.June 14,1944
5466   Jersey Jump Off   Savoy 519,XP8076,MG9029,(F)XP80760,MG90290
5467   Stomping At The Savoy   Savoy 518,550,MG9008,Byg(F)529.168,Musidisc(F)
                                        CV969
5468   On The Sunny Side Of The Street Savoy 519,550,XP8076,MG9008,(F)XP80760,Byg(F)
                                        529.168,Musidisc(F)CV969
5469   Jump Awhile (Jump Street/
        Jam Session At Savoy)   Savoy 518,MG9030

All titles also on Savoy MG12197,MG14010,SJL2218,(F)1C.148-61047/48,(E)WL70533,Musidisc
(F)JA5161.

COZY COLE AND HIS ORCHESTRA:
Charlie Shavers(tp),Hank D'Amico(cl),Walter Thomas(as,ts),Coleman Hawkins(ts),Clyde Hart
(p),Tiny Grimes(g),Slam Stewart(b),Cozy Cole(dr).
                                      NYC.November 14,1944
3275   Willow Weep For Me   Continental 6001,Royal Jazz(F)713
3276   Look Here (Cool Jive)   Continental 6000,CLP16007,Paris P122,Plymouth
                                        12-113,12-115,Remington RLP1032,Mastersound
                                        MSLP55,Stqryville(G)6.28474,Pontiac LP534
3277   I Don't Stand
        A Ghost Of A Chance   Continental 6000,Royal Jazz(F)736
3278   Take It On Back(1)   Continental 6001,CLP16007,Paris P122,Mastersound
                                        MSLP33,Royal Jazz(F)713,Storyville(G)6.28474

-1.Issued on Polydor(E)423.236 as "When Day Is Done" and on 423.237 as "Esquire Jump".

All titles also on Black&Blue(F)33.009,Xanadu 111.
All titles - except master 3277 - also on Continental CLP16006,Sonet(D)SLP1003,Storyville
(D)SLP818,(F)ST21028,(J)ULS1592,Polydor(E)423.236.

Don Byas(ts),Johnny Guarnieri(p) replace Thomas,Hart.
                                      NYC.November 21,1944
3283   Memories Of You(1)   Continental 6004
3284-1 Comes The Don   Continental 6004,Plymouth 12-113,12-115,Remington
                                        RLP1031
3284-2 Comes The Don(2,3)   Continental CLP16006,CLP16007,Plymouth 12-146,
                                        Masterseal MSLP5013,Palace PST793,Paris P122,
                                        Pontiac LP534
3285   When Day Is Done(4)   Continental 6014,CLP16006,Palace PST675,Ember(E)
                                        CJS826,Jazz Selection(F)JS777
3286   The Beat(The Drag)(5)   Continental 6014,CLP16007,Plymouth 12-113,12-115,
                                        Remington RLP1031,Palace PST675,Paris P122,
                                        Black&Blue(F)950.501,Ember(E)CJS826,Jazz
                                        Selection(F)JS777,Pontiac LP534,Gozo LP796

    1.Issued on Polydor(E)423.237 as "Thanks For The Memory".
    2.Issued on Palace 793 as "Booker T. Highway Blues".
    3.Issued on Polydor(E)423.237 as "Memories Of You".
    4.Issued on Polydor(E)423.236 as "Take It On Back".
    5.Issued on Pontiac LP534 as "The Rhythm".

    ll titles/takes also on Xanadu 111.
    ll titles - except master 3284-1 - also on Continental CLP16006,Sonet(D)SLP1004,Story-
    ille(D)SLP819,(F)ST21029,(J)ULS1593,Polydor(E)423.237,Black&Blue(F)33.009.

```
Shorty Rogers(tp),Vernon Brown(tb),Aaron Sachs(cl),Don Byas(ts),Bill Rowland(p),Billy
Taylor(b),Cozy Cole(dr).                      NYC.February 2,1945
HL78-2 Lover Come Back To Me    Keynote(J)18PJ1062,Mercury(Am)830.133
HL79-2 Smiles                        -              -
HL80-2 All Of Me                     -              -
HL81-3 They Didn't Believe Me   Keynote 656,(J)18PJ1062,Mercury 1099,MG25013,
                                      830.133,(E)SMWL21026,EmArcy EP1-6043,MG26026
```

Note:Keynote(J)18PJ1062 and Mercury(Am)830.133 are part of the 21-LP albums 18PJ1051/71
    and 830.121-1 respectively.

```
Don Byas(ts),prob. Billy Taylor(p),Tiny Grimes(g),Billy Taylor(b),Cozy Cole(dr),June Haw-
kins(vcl).                                    NYC.March 19,1945
601     Hallelujah                  Guild 119
602     Stompin' At The Savoy       Guild 118
603     Dat's Love(The Habanera)(jh)     -
604     Through For The Night(jh)    Guild 119
```

```
Same.                                         NYC.April  1945
615     Strictly Drums              Guild 129
616     Night Wind(jh)              Guild 130
617     Why regret(jh)              Guild 129
618     Now's The Time              Guild 130
```

COZY COLE'S CU-BOPPERS:
Joe Wilder(tp),Tony Acquaviva(cl),George "Big Nick" Nicholas(ts),Reuben Jay Cole(p),Billy
Taylor(b),Cozy Cole(dr),Diego Iborra(cg),Bill Alvarez(bg).
                                              NYC.February 1949
            Stardust   Candy 3002
            La Danse   -
            Mosquito Brain   unissued(?)
            Batao   -

Jonah Jones(tp,vcl),Aaron Sachs(cl,ts),Reuben Jay Cole(p),Ted Sturgis(b),Cozy Cole(dr).
                                              NYC.February 24,1954
            Hound Dog Special   MGM 11794,(E)EP622,(F)EPF16
            A Terrible Sight(jj)   -   -   -
            Someday You'll Be Sorry(jj)   -   -   -
            Drum Fantasy   -   -   -

COZY COLE'S BIG SEVEN:
Rex Stewart(tp),Tyree Glenn(tb),Coleman Hawkins(ts),Claude Hopkins(p,celeste),Billy Bauer
(g),Arvell Shaw(b),Cozy Cole(dr).   NYC. 1955/56
            Caravan   Grand Award 45-1023,LP33-334,Waldorf MH45-205,
                                        Supraphon(Cz)C33-4949
            Sweethearts On Parade   Grand Award LP33-334,Waldorf MH45-205,Supraphon
                                        (Cz)C33-4949
            My Blue Heaven   Grand Award LP33-334,Waldorf MH45-206
            Honeysuckle Rose   -   - ,Supraphon
                                        (Cz)C33-4949
            Organ Grinder's Swing   Grand Award LP33-334,Supraphon(Cz)C33-4949
            Perdido   -

All titles also on Waldorf MH33-162,Columbia(F)33FPX151.

COZY COLE AND HIS ORCHESTRA:
Bernie Privin(tp),Urbie Green(tb),Peanuts Hucko(cl,ts),Burton "Burt" Farber(p),Dick Hyman
(org),Al Caiola(g),Jack Lesberg(b),Cozy Cole(dr).
                                              NYC. 1958
(session cont. next page).
```
```

(session cont. from previous page):
```
SAL5003  Topsy I                          Love 5004,LP500,London(E)HL8750,Barclay(F)72.283,
SAL5004  Topsy II                          -      -            -                    -
         Deed I do                        Love 5007
         Turvy I                          Love 5013,LP500,Barclay(F)72.283
         Turvy II                          -      -            -
SAL5015  Bad                              Love 5016(?),-  ,Artistique 606,6124,Barclay(F)
                                          72.361
         Topsy-Turvy I                    Love 5016,LP500,LP505
         Topsy-Turvy II                    -(?)   -     -
SAL5023  Charleston                       Love 5023,   -  ,Artistique 606,6124,Barclay(F)
                                          72.361
SAL5024  Late And Lazy                    Love LP500,Barclay(F)72.361
         Crescendo                         -                   -
         Afro-Caravan                      -  ,LP505
```

COZY COLE SEPTET:
Lou Jones(tp),Walter "Phatz" Morris(tb,hca),Alva McCain(ts),Reuben Jay ("June") Cole(p),
Dickie Thompson(g,vcl),Pete Compo(b),Cozy Cole(dr).
```
                                          NYC.February 7,1958
         Caravan                          Felsted 8545,FAJ7002
         Phatz' Blues(dt)                  -
         Margie                            -
```

All titles also on Felsted SJA2002,Affinity(E)AFF167,Decca(E)820.605-2 (CD).

COZY COLE WITH ALAN HARTWELL ORCHESTRA:
No details.
```
                                          Unknown location.  1959
         A La Topsy,pt.3                  Random 602
         A la Topsy,pt.4                   -
```

COZY COLE AND HIS ORCHESTRA:
Edwin Kelly(ts),Harry Sheppard(vbs),Reuben Jay Cole(p),Fred Jordan,John Faire(g),Ivan
'Loco' Rolle(b),Cozy Cole(dr),Evalene Cole(vcl).
```
                                          Cincinnati.May 26,1959
K10371   Playtime Blues                   King 5265
K10372   Boy Meets Girl                    -
K10373   D-Mitri                          King 5287,LP673
K10374A  Blop-Up(no vbs)                  King 5222,   -  ,Odeon(F)SOE3557
K10374B  Blop-Down(no vbs)                 -       -            -
K10375   Stained Glass                    King 5287,   -
K10376   The Pogo Hop                     King 5390,   -
```

George Kelly(ts),Gene Redd(vbs,tp),John Thomas(p),Fred Jordan,John Faire(g),Edwyn Conley
(b),Cozy Cole(dr).
```
                                          Cincinnati.June 18,1959
K4280    Lover's Stroll                   King LP673
K4281    Ha-Ha Cha Cha (Big Boss)         King 5390,LP673,Bethlehem 3067
K4282    "D" Natural Rock(1)              King 5242,   -
K4283    Play Cozy Play                   King 5303
K4284    Cozy's Mambo (Cozy And Bossa)     -  ,Bethlehem 3067
K4285    Teen Age Ideas(1)                King 5316,LP673
```

1.Add unknown(ts).

same.
```
                                          Cincinnati.June 19,1959
K4286    Soft                             King 5254,LP673,Odeon(F)SOE3557
K4287    Strange                          King 5242,   -            -
K4288    Bag Of Tricks                    King 5337
K4289    Blockhead                        King 5316
K4290    Melody Of A Dreamer              King 5254,LP673
K4291    Drum Fever (Song)                King 5337,Guest Star GS1425
```

```
Similar.                              NYC.May 17,1960
K4614  Little Eva                     King unissued
K4615  Red Ball                       King 5363
K4616  Fantasy                             unissued
K4617  Cozy's Corner                  King 5363
```

George Holt(tp),Bernie Privin(tp,flh),Jerome Richardson(cl,bars,bcl),John Hafer(ts),Al
Klink(ts,bcl),Bob Hammer(p,org),Dick Hyman(org,arr),Milt Hinton/Jack Lesberg(b),Cozy Cole
(dr),Phil Kraus,Douglas Allen(perc).   NYC. 1961/62
```
       Prelude                        Charlie Parker PLP403(S)
       Chorus Of Street Boys                     -     ,CP823,Archives Of Jazz
                                      AJ508,Olympic(Am)OL7135,Pathé(F)2C.062-95823
       Habanera                       Charlie Parker PLP403(S),Jazzbox JLEP110
       Sequidilla                                 -
       Entr'Acte I/II                             -
       Gypsy Song                                 -
       Castanet Dance                             -
       Flower Song                                -
       Sextet                                     -
       Entr'Acte III/IV                           -
```

All titles also on Summit(E)AJS1,Musidisc(F)CV977,CV9770,Trip TLX5054.
All titles - except "Sequidilla" and "Entr'acte I/II" - also on Archives of Folk/Jazz
FS288.

```
No details.                           NYC(?).  1961/62
       Cozy Groove,I                  Charlie Parker 202
       Cozy Groove,II                            -
```

Incl. Cozy Cole,Gene Krupa -1,Ray McKinley -2(dr),Henry Jerome(cond).
```
                                      NYC.September 26,1962
       I Love Paris(1)                Coral CRL(7)57423
       You're The Top(2)                         -
       I Could Have Danced All Night(1)          -
       Night And Day(2)                          -
       I'll Get By(2)                            -
       Begin The Beguine(1)                      -
       Once In Love With Amy(2)                  -
       What Is This Thing Called Love(1)         -
```

Incl. Cozy Cole,Panama Francis(dr),Henry Jerome(cond).
```
                                      NYC.September 27,1962
       Dream                          Coral CRL(7)57423
       You Do Something To Me                    -
       Smoke Gets In Your Eyes                   -
       Dancing In The Dark                       -
```

All titles also on CRL(7)57423 also on Coral(E)LVA9213.

Incl. Cozy Cole,Gary Chester(dr),Henry Jerome(cond).
```
                                      NYC.  1964
       Big Noise From Winnetka,I      Coral 62339,CRL(7)57457,(E)45Q72457
       Big Noise From Winnetka,II                -           -        -
       Sing Sing Sing                 Coral 62379,          -
       Rockin' Drummer                           -          -
       Christopher Columbus           Coral 62395,          -
       Ol' Man Mose                              -          -
       North Beach                    Coral 62417,          -
       A Cozy Beat                               -          -
       Indian Love Call,I             Coral 65571,          -
       Indian Love Call,II                       -          -
(session cont. next page).
```

```
(session cont. from previous page):
114814 Topsy,I                    Coral 65584,CRL(7)57457
114815 Topsy,II                       -            -
       Let There Be Drums                          -

Bill Doggett(org),Tiny Grimes(g),Cozy Cole(dr),rest unknown.
                                  NYC.February 11,1966
C089253 Cozy Cosa                 Columbia CL2553/CS9353
C089254 Organ Grinders Swing          -            ,Epic 22.030
C089255 Huckle Buck                   -
C089256 Whole Lotta Shakin'       Columbia 4-44657,CL2553/CS9353

Same.                             NYC.March 2,1966
C089106 After Hours               Columbia CL2553/CS9353,Epic 22.030
C089109 I's A Rocking Thing           -

same.                             NYC.March 4,1966
C089119 Robbins Nest              Columbia CL2553/CS9353
C089120 Wailing Waltz                 -
C089122 Java Jive                     -
C089123 Luma                          -
C089124 Watch It                  Columbia 4-43657,CL2553/CS9353

(dr-solo).                        NYC.June 30,1970
       Cozy's Drum(ed.)           Jazz Odyssey(F)002,005,010
```

Note:The above title is from the "L'Aventure Du Jazz" film soundtrack.
     See BUDDY TATE for additional titles from this session.

COZY COLE - MARTY NAPOLEON:
Johnny Letman(tp),"Big Chief" Russell Moore(tb),Joe Muranyi(cl,ss),Lionel Hampton(vbs,vcl)
Marty Napoleon(p),Arvell Shaw(b),Cozy Cole(dr).

```
                                  NYC.October 5,1977
       Cabaret                     Who's Who Is Jazz WWLP21003
       Someday You'll Be Sorry                     -
       Louis' Dream                                -
       Short Ribs                                  -
       Mack The Knife                              -
       Do You Know What It Means
          To Miss New Orleans                      -
       Black And Blue                              -
       Back Home Again In Indiana                  -
       Jeepers Creepers          Who's Who Is Jazz WWLP21008,Toledo(G)147.408
       Hello Dolly(no tp,tb,cl)(lh)                -
       Sleepy Time Down South    Who's Who Is Jazz WWLP21012
```

All titles also on Philips(Eu)9123.604,Toledo(G)147.508,Fortune 3006.

EDDIE COLE

```
Eddie Cole(b,vcl),rest unknown.      Philadelphia.  1949/50
       I Want Somebody            Gotham 207
       Alabahip                        -
       Police                     Gotham 220
       Wiggle And Giggle               -
       News For You Baby          Gotham 238
       That's Right                    -
```

Eddie Cole,Billy Cole(vcl) acc. by JOE DARENSBOURG - RENE HALL'S ORCHESTRA:
Joe Darensbourg(cl),Rene Hall(g),rest unknown.

LA.   1959

Sweet Someone	Lark 4512
You Took Your Love From Me	-

FREDDY COLE

(vcl,p) acc. by Kenny Wheeler(tp,flh),Derek Watkins,Kenny Baker,Tony Fisher(tp),Nat Peck,
Ken Goldie,Don Lusher,Bobby Lamb(tb),Tony Coe(ss),Roy Willox,Bob Efford,Ronnie Ross,Vic
Ash(sax,fl),Gordon Beck(p),Daryl Runswick(b),Ronnie Stephenson(dr),Tony Carr(perc),Jerry
van Rooyen(arr,cond).   Fairfax,Va./London.c. 1976

Theme From Mahagony	Decca(E)SKL-R5279
Sing	-
For Once In My Life	-
Tristeza	-
You Are The Sunshin Of My Life	-
On A Clear Day	-
Michelle	-
Homefried Potatoes	-
You've Let Yourself Go	-
If I Had Your Love	-
Cabaret	-

(vcl,p(?)) acc. by Buddy Cooner(g),Ed Edwards(b),Paul Avery(dr).

Unknown location/date

Correct Me If I'm Wrong	Audiophile AP123
Moving On - Place In The Sun	-
Wild Is Love	-
A Man Shouldn't Be Lonely	-
Brother,Where Are You	-
Miss Otis Regrets	-
Live For Life	-
He'll Have To Go	-
Medley:	-
I Keep Going Back To Joe's	
Walter(?) Ask The	
Man To Play The Blues	

Note:Additional recordings by this artist are not included; the jazz content of the above
recordings may be limited.

JIMMY COLE (COE)

Note:Real name Jimmy Coe (but listed in the King files as Jimmy Cole).

JIMMY COLE AND HIS ORCHESTRA:
Joe Mitchell(tp),Jimmy Cole(as),Robert Darby(ts),Stanley "Stash" O'Laughlin(p),Jimmy Cox
(unknown instr.),William Boyd(b),Earl Walker(dr),Flo Garvin(vcl).

NYC.January 11,1952

K9100	I'm On The Outside Looking In(fg)	King 4518
K9101	Let Me Keep You Warm(fg)	-
K9102	I Got It Bad And That Ain't Good	King 4531,Vogue(F)V3125
K9103	Cole Tater	- -

Note:King 4518 was issued under Flo Garvin's name.

KING COLE BOOGIES (South African)

KING COLE BOOGIES WITH THE BB ALL STAR BAND:
Unknown cl,acc,p,b,dr,vcl-group.   Johannesburg. 1951/52
      Ndasuka Ekhayo (I Left Home)   BB(SA)BB633,Harlequin(E)HQ2020

NAT "KING" COLE

See also CAPITOL INTERNATIONAL JAZZMEN,DEXTER GORDON,WOODY HERMAN,THE KEYNOTERS,JAZZ AT
THE PHILHARMONIC,METRONOME ALL STARS,GENE NORMAN,ANITA O'DAY,JO STAFFORD,SUNSET ALL STARS,
SARAH VAUGHAN,LESTER YOUNG.

Note:List of equivalents (Capitol).

    The Nat Cole section was prepared by Michael Cuscuna, Will Friedwald, Gord Grievesen,
Roy Holmes, Bill Miner, Michel Ruppli and Klaus Teubig.

    This section only includes recordings of the King Cole Trio and of jazz-oriented ses-
sions led by Nat Cole. In addition to commercial recordings, Cole Trio performances
are found on many transcription recordings during the 1940's and on numerous broadcasts and film soundtracks. All known Cole Trio transcriptions, broadcasts and film
soundtracks are listed here, whether they have been issued to date or not.
Original recording dates for some of this non-commercial material are not known - or
are debatable. For most AFRS transcriptions, for example, only "date(s) of dubbing"
or "AFRS release date(s)" are generally documented; therefore AFRS original recording
dates given in this section are all estimated. Reliability of dating for other material varies; notes will indicate dating difficulties.

THE KING COLE TRIO:
Nat Cole(p,vcl),Oscar Moore(g),Red Callender(b).
                        LA.October 11,1942
RR8113-C Vom Vim Veedle(nc,trio-vcl)   Excelsior 102,Capitol(E)CL13096
RR8114-C All For You(nc)   Excelsior 103,V-Disc 286,Navy 66,Kat Wisker Prod.
                        NC1002

Both titles also on Capitol 139,Tampa TP134,Mosaic MR27-138,MD18-138 (CD).
Note:Excelsior 102/103 issued as one 78 rpm.
    On the V-Disc issues "All For You" is edited and used as part of a medley together
    with "I Can't See For Lookin'" (rec. December 15,1943).

Nat Cole(p,vcl),Oscar Moore(g),unknown(b).   LA.c. November/December 1942
      Unknown title(s)

Note:The unknown title(s) are from AFRS "Mail Call" transcription No.16.

Nat Cole(p,vcl),Oscar Moore(g),unknown(b).   LA.c. December 1942/January 1943
      Hip,Hip Hooray(nc)   Vintage Jazz Classics VJC1044(CD)
      I Know That You Know   -

Note:The above titles are from AFRS "Jubilee" transcription No.5.

Nat Cole(p,vcl),Oscar Moore(g),unknown(b).   LA.c. December 1942/January 1943
      Unknown title(s)

Note:The unknown title(s) are from AFRS "Jubilee" transcription No.10.

Nat Cole(p,vcl),Oscar Moore(g),unknown(b).   Broadcast."331 Club",LA.c. 1942/43
        I'm Gonna' Move To The
            Outskirts Of Town(nc)   Vintage Jazz Classics VJC1044(CD)

Nat Cole(p),Oscar Moore(g),unknown(b).   Unknown location/date
        Nice Work If You Can Get It   Vintage Jazz Classics VJC1044(CD)

THE KING COLE TRIO:
Nat Cole(p,vcl),Oscar Moore(g),Johnny Miller(b).
                                      LA.March 1,1943
AMO2961 Let's Spring One(trio-vcl)   Excelsior SC107,Design DLP3095,Parlophone(E)R3056,
                                          (Sw)PZ11179,Odeon(F)279745,S&H SH4547,Koala
                                          LP14143,Nap LP11004
        Beautiful Moons Ago(nc)   Excelsior MC106,Design DLP3095,Spinorama LP105,
                                          Parlophone(E)R3095,(Sw)PZ11185,Koala LP14143
AMO2963 Pitchin' Up
        A Boogie(trio-vcl)   Excelsior 104,BC104,Parlophone(E)R3095,(Sw)PZ11185
                                          S&H SH4547,Koala LP14143,Nap LP11004
AMO2966 I'm Lost(nc)   Excelsior 105,LC105,Design DLP3095,Spinorama LP105
                                          Parlophone(E)R3056,(Sw)PZ11179,Odeon(F)279745
                                          Columbia GS5334,S&H SH4546,SH4547,Kat Wisker
                                          Prod. NC1002,Nap LP11004

All titles also on Design DLP162,Vogue(F)VG655.650120 (CD),Mosaic MR27-138,MD18-138 (CD),
Laserlight 15 750 (CD),15 915 (5xCD),Savoy ZDS1205 (CD).
Note:Excelsior 104/105 issued as one 78 rpm; Excelsior 106/107 issued as one 78 rpm.
    The SH4547 reissue of master AMO2963 has Bill Oglesby(dr) and synthesized strings
    overdubbed.

Same.   LA.c. May/June 1943
        Honeysuckle Rose
        Slender,Tender And Tall(nc)

Note:The above titles are from AFRS "Jubilee" transcription No.29.

Same.   LA.c. July 1943
        Unknown title(s)

Note:The unknown title(s) are from AFRS "Jubilee" transcription No.36.

Same.   LA.August 1943
        Straighten Up And
            Fly Right(nc,trio-vcl)

Note:The above title is from the "Here Comes Elmer"/"Hitch-Hike To Happiness"(alt. title)
    feature film soundtrack.

Same.   LA.c. mid-late 1943
        I'm An Errand Boy For Rhythm(nc)

Note:The above title is from the "Pistol Packin' Mama" feature film soundtrack.

Same.   LA.c. September 1943
        Solid Potato Salad(nc,trio-vcl)

Note:The above title is from AFRS "Command Performance" transcription No.87.

Nat Cole(p,vcl),Oscar Moore(g),Johnny Miller(b).
                                        Prob. LA.c. September 1943
        Slender,Tender And Tall(nc)

Note:The above title is from AFRS "Jubilee" transcription No.45.

Same.   LA.c. October 1943
        Cool Down,Papa (Straighten Up
            And Fly Right)(nc,trio-vcl)   Biac(B)BRAD10528
        I'm An Errand Boy For Rhythm(nc)   -

Note:The above titles are from AFRS "Jubilee" transcription No.51.

Same.   LA.November 2,1943
IA2078 F.S.T.(1)   Premier 100,Atlas KC100
IA2079 My Lips Remember Your Kisses(nc)   -   - ,Kat Wisker Prod. NC1002
IA2080 Got A Penny,Benny(nc,trio-vcl) Premier 103,Atlas KC102,KC106,S&H SH4546
IA2081 Let's Pretend(2)(nc)   - ,Atlas KC106

-1.This title is an abbreviation of "Fine,Sweet And Tasty".
-2.Included twice on S&H SH4547.

All titles also on Koala LP14143,S&H SH4547,Wyncote LPW9107,Mosaic MR27-138,MD18-138 (CD).
Note:KC100 issued with wrong masternumber (IA2101) for IA2079.
     The S&H reissue of masters IA2079-81 has Bill Oglesby(dr) and synthesized strings
     overdubbed as well as narration between the tracks.

Same.   LA.November 30,1943
123-4   Straighten Up And
            Fly Right(nc,trio-vcl)   Capitol 154,1613,F1613,F6036,15284,F15509(CCF213),
                                      20009 (BD8),EBF/L/H213,N16261,CDP7.93590-2
                                      (CD),PRO2000,(F)406,C.152-81746/48,T20097,
                                      1551.863,(G)C80197,K83950,1C.056-85611,(Au)
                                      SCA076,Kat Wisker Prod. NC1002,Giants Of Jazz
                                      (I)LJT14,CD53005(CD),(E)CD0231(CD),New World
                                      NW261,Delta 11086(CD),Jazzline JL20815,DejaVu
                                      (I)DVLP2048,Rhino E2.71009(CD),Starlite(E)
                                      1003(CD)

124-4   Gee,Baby,Ain't
            I Good To You(nc)   Capitol 169,15284,F15511 (CCF213),EBF/L/H213,
                                      T2311,N16260,(F)T20097,1551.863,(G)LCA213,
                                      K83950,V-Disc 339,Navy 137,Oxford(I)OX3020,
                                      Krém(Hu)SLPXL17780,Music For Pleasure(E)
                                      MFP50177,Marifon(G)47956,Laserlight 15 718
                                      (CD),Delta 11044(CD),Jazzline JL20808,Rhino
                                      E2.71009(CD)

125-2   Jumpin' At Capitol   Capitol 10038 (CE19),F15643 (CDF242),EBF/H242,
                                      CDP7.98299-2(CD),(E)CL13204,LC6527,(F)449,
                                      (G)C80153,LCA242,Delta 11086(CD),Jazzline
                                      JL20815,Official(D)3026,83026(CD),Rhino
                                      E2.71009

126-1   If You Can't Smile
            And Say Yes (Please
            Don't Cry And Say No)(nc) Capitol 192,(E)ST23480,(F)1551.863,Rhino E2.71009
                                      (CD)

All titles also on Mosaic MR27-138,MD18-138 (CD).
Note:Master 126 issued with wrong speed on Capitol(F)1551.863 and Rhino E2.71009 (CD).

THE KING COLE TRIO WITH IDA JAMES:
Nat Cole(p,vcl),Oscar Moore(g),Johnny Miller(b),Ida James(vcl).
                                        LA.c. late 1943/early 1944

        I'm A Shy Guy(nc)
        Is You Is Or
           Is You Ain't My Baby(ij)
        Who's Been Eating My Porridge(ij)

Note:The above titles are from "Soundie" short film soundtracks. Exact original date(s) of
    filming are not known.

Note:The Cole trio recorded extensively for the C.P. MacGregor Radio Transcription Library
    throughout 1944 - or prob. over a slightly longer period incl. late 1943 (and maybe
    also early 1945). A total of 17 transcription programs (15 min.) featuring The King
    Cole Trio are known. Since no exact dates are available for the original MacGregor
    recording sessions this discography separates the MacGregor material into three esti-
    mated basic time periods: a) c. late 1943/early 1944, b) c. mid-1944 and c) c. late
    1944/early 1945. Additionally, the Cole Trio backed vocalist Anita Boyer on a number
    of McGregor transcriptions which are not included in this discography section.

THE KING COLE TRIO WITH IDA JAMES:
Nat Cole(p,vcl),Oscar Moore(g),Johnny Miller(b),Ida James(vcl).
                                        LA.c. late 1943/early 1944

        No Love,No Nothin'(ij)
        Knock Me A Kiss(ij)
        I Can't See For Lookin'(ij)
        People Will Say We're In Love(ij)
        Shoo Shoo Baby(ij,nc)

Note:The above titles are from MacGregor transcription LB4.

THE KING COLE TRIO:
Nat Cole(p,vcl),Oscar Moore(g),Johnny Miller(b).
                                        LA.c. late 1943/early 1944

      Is You Is Or Is
        You Ain't My Baby(nc)   Mark56 739,Jazz Anthology(F)JA5219,Sounds Rare
                                    SR5003,Kings Of Jazz(I)KLJ20029,Deja Vu(I)
                                    DVLP2048,Star Line SLC61014(?)

      I Can't Give You
        Anything But Love   Mark56 739,Jazz Anthology(F)JA5219,Kings Of Jazz
                                    (I)KLJ20029,Star Line SLC61014(?)

      Shoo Shoo Baby(nc)   Mark56 739
      Solid Potato Salad(nc,trio-vcl) -
      Miss Thing   - Sounds Rare SR5003

The above titles also on Laserlight 15 747 (CD),15 915 (5xCD),Fresh Sound(Sp)FSR-CD139
(CD).
Note:The above titles are from MacGregor transcription LB13.
    This version of "Solid Potato" was poss. used also for AFRS "King Cole Trio - Perso-
    nal Album" transcription No.227 (c. mid-1944).
    SLC61014 is a cassette-only issue.

Same.   LA.December 15,1943
139-1 Sweet Lorraine(nc)   Capitol 20009 (BD8),15564 (CCN220),1613,F15564
                                (CCF220),F1613,EBF/H220,T591,N16260,SKA02944,
                                CDP7.98931-2(CD),(E)LC6569,(F)T20097,20009356
                                1551.863,251.984-2(CD),(G)C20009,K60681,(J)
                                Z30,TOCJ5326(CD),(Au)SCA076,ENC9082,Blue Note
                                B2-96582(CD),V-Disc 359,Rhino E2.71009(CD),
(session cont. next page).   Giants Of Jazz(I)LPJT14

(session cont. from previous page):
140-1 Embraceable You(nc)   Capitol 20009 (BD8),15566 (CNN220),883,1650,F883,
     F1650,F15566 (COF220),EBF/H220,H9103,T591,
     T2311,T9103,N16260,(E)LC6587,(F)T20097,
     1551.863,251.684-1,251.984-2(CD),(G)C20009,
     K83950,(J)Z22,TOCJ3526(CD),TOCJ5027(CD),EMI
     (J)TOCP9101(CD),Krém(Hu)SLPXL17780,Music For
     Pleasure(E)MFP50177,Oxford(I)OX3020,Marifon
     (G)47957,Jazz Club(F)2M.056-64866,Delta(G)
     DK29004,11044(CD),Laserlight 15 718(CD),Rhino
     E2.71009(CD),Giants Of Jazz(I)LPJT14
140-2 Embraceable You(nc)   V-Disc 365,(I)VDL1012
141-4 It's Only A Paper Moon(nc)   Capitol 20012 (BD8),15564,883,1650,F883,F1650,
     F15564 (CFF220),EBF/H220,T591,N16261,(E)
     LC6569,(F)306,T20097,1551.863,251.984-2,(J)
     Z22,TOCJ5326(CD),(Aus)SCA076,ENC9082
     V-Disc 359,Deja Vu(I)DVLP2048,Kat Wisker Prod
     NC1002,Lotus(I)LOP14077,Delta 11086,(CD),
     Jazzline JL20815,Rhino E2.71009(CD),Giants Of
     Jazz(I)LPJT14
142-1 I Can't See For Lookin'(nc)   Capitol 154,15311,1033,F1033,(E)E-ST23480,(F)442,
     1551.863,251.683-1,Official(D)83026(CD),(Au)
     SCA076,V-Disc 286,Navy 66

All titles/takes also on Mosaic MR27-138,MD18-138 (CD).
Note:It has not been confirmed that master 140-2 was issued on Capitol(F)356.
     On the V-Disc issues "I Can't See For Lookin'" is used as part of a medley together
     with an edited version of "All For You" (rec. October 11,1942).

Same.   LA.January 17,1944
182-1 The Man I Love   Capitol 20010 (BD8),15565 (CCN220),F15565(CCF220),
     T2311,N16260,(F)354,T20097,251.984-2(CD),(G)
     C20010,K60681,K83950,Telefunken(D)A18021,
     Smithsonian PG21010,Deja Vu(I)DVLP2048,Giants
     Of Jazz(I)LPJT14,Delta 11044(CD),Laserlight
     15 718(CD)
183-1 Body And Soul   Capitol 20010 (BD8),15565 (CNN220),F15563(CCF220),
     T2311,N16261,(F)354,251.683-1,251.984-2(CD),
     T20193,(G)C20010,K60681,K83950,Telefunken(D)
     A18021,Jazz Club(F)2M.056-64866,Kat Wisker
     Prod. NC1002
184-1 Prelude In C Sharp Minor   Capitol 20011 (BD8),(E)CL13535,(F)251.682-1,
     251.984-2(CD),Laserlight 15 718(CD),Delta
     11044(CD)
185-1 What Is This Thing Called Love   Capitol 20011 (BD8),15566 (CCN220),F15566(CCF220),
     CDP7.98931-2(CD),(F)C.152-81746/8,(G)K60681,
     V-Disc 365,(I)VDL1012,Giants Of Jazz(I)LPJT14
     GOJCD53005(CD),(E)CD0231(CD),Kat Wisker Prod.
     NC1002,Deja Vu(I)DVLP2048,Delta 11044(CD),
     Laserlight 15 718(CD),Starlite(E)1003(CD)

All titles also on Capitol EBF/H220,T592,(F)C.054-81261,1551.863,CDP7.98299-2 (CD),(J)
TOCJ5326 (CD),Mosaic MR27-138,MD18-138 (CD).

IDA JAMES WITH THE KING COLE TRIO:
(vcl) acc. by Nat Cole(p),Oscar Moore(g),Johnny Miller(b).
     LA.c. late 1943/early 1944

     On The Sunny Side
       Of The Street
     Stormy Weather
     Close To You
(session cont. next page).

(session cont. from previous page):
       Who's Been Eating
         My Porridge(1)
       Honeysuckle Rose

-1.James(vcl) with (trio-vcl).

Note:The above titles are from MacGregor transcriptions LB28,409,611.

Same.
                                        LA.c. late 1943/early 1944
     My Heart Tells Me
     Harlem Sandman
     Speak Low
     Them There Eyes
     Hit That Jive,Jack

Note:The above titles are from MacGregor transcriptions LB14,114,410,602.

THE KING COLE TRIO:
Nat Cole(p,vcl),Oscar Moore(g),Johnny Miller(b).
                                        LA.c. late 1943/early 1944
     Mexico Joe(nc)   Mark56 739
     Lester Leaps In   -
     Just Another Blues(nc)   -
     Wild Goose Chase   -

All titles also on Laserlight 15 748 (CD),15 915 (5xCD),Fresh Sound(Sp)FSR-CD139 (CD).
Note:The above titles are from MacGregor transcriptions LB41,612.

Same.
                                        LA.c. late 1943/early 1944
     Little Joe From Chicago(nc)   Mark56 739,Giants Of Jazz GOJ1031,Sounds Rare
                                   SR5003(ed.),Remember(Eu)RMB75022(CD),Record.
                                   Arts LZCD343(CD),Laserlight 15 746(CD),
                                   15 915(CD)
     Rhythm Sam(nc)   Mark56 739,Laserlight 15 746(CD),15 915(CD)
     Have Fun
     On The Sunny Side
       Of The Street(nc,trio-vcl)   Mark56 739,Jazz Anthology(F)JA5219,Kings Of Jazz
                                     (I)KLJ20029,Giants Of Jazz GOJ1031,Star Line
                                   SLC61014(?),Recording Arts LZCD343(CD),
                                   Laserlight 15 747(CD),15 915(?)(CD),
     Indiana   Mark56 739,Giants Of Jazz GOJ1031,Remember(Eu)
                                   RMB75022(CD),Star Line SLC61014(?),Recording
                                   Arts LZCD343(CD),Laserlight 15 746(CD),
                                   15 915(CD)

All titles also on Fresh Sound(Sp)FSR-CD139 (CD).
Note:The above titles are from MacGregor transcriptions LB31,581.

Same.
                                        LA.c. January 1944
     I'm An Errand Boy For Rhythm(nc)

Note:The above title is from AFRS "Jubilee" transcription No.65.

THE KING COLE QUINTET:
Shad Collins(tp),Illinois Jacquet(ts),Nat Cole(p),Gene Englund(b),J.C. Heard(dr).
                                        LA.February 1944
D504-1010 Heads   Disc 2010,Melodisc(E)8011
D505-1011 Pro-sky   Disc 2011,Melodisc(E)8012
D506-1012 It Had To Be You   Disc 2010,Melodisc(E)8011
(session cont. next page).

(session cont. from previous page):
D507-1013 I Can't Give You
            Anything But Love   Disc 2011,Melodisc(E)8012

All titles also on Phoenix LP5,Spotlite(E)SPJ136.
Note:Disc 2010/11 was issued as a 78 rpm album (Disc 506); the Disc album title was "Nor-
     man Granz Presents King Cole Quintet". The secondary masternumbers (i.e. 101x) appear
     to be Granz's own series.

THE KING COLE TRIO:
Nat Cole(p,vcl),Oscar Moore(g),Johnny Miller(b).
                             LA.March 6,1944

211-2 After You Get What You
        Want,You Don't Want It(nc) Mosaic MR27-138,MD18-138(CD)
212-2 Look What You've Done To Me(nc) Capitol 20064 (BD29),Mosaic MR27-138,MD18-138(CD)
213-2 Easy Listening Blues   Capitol 20012 (BD8),EBF/H220,T592,CDP7.98299-2
                                      (CD),(F)306,T20193,1551.863,251.984-2(CD),
                                      (J)TOCJ5326(CD),Deja Vu(I)DVLP2048,Franklin
                                      Mint 49,Mosaic MR27-138,MD18-138(CD),Giants
                                      Of Jazz(I)LPJT14,Laserlight 15 718(CD),Delta
                                      11044(CD)
214-4 I Realize Now(nc)   Capitol 169,ST310,(E)E-ST23480,(F)1551.863,V-Disc
                                      339,Navy 137,Mosaic MR27-138,MD18-138(CD),
                                      Franklin Mint 49

Note:Issues on Capitol ST310 (and equiv.) were edited into stereo versions with new rhythm
     section and orchestra overdubbed (1969).

Same.   LA.Early 1944
        Jumpin' At The Jubilee

Note:The above title is from the "Stars On Parade" feature film soundtrack.

Same.   LA.c. May/June 1944
        The Man On The
            Little White Keys(nc)   Vintage Jazz Classics VJC1044(CD)
        Straighten Up And
            Fly Right(nc,trio-vcl)   -

Note:The above titles are from AFRS "Mail Call" transcription No.96.

Add Les Paul(g),Bing Crosby,The Andrews Sisters,Judy Garland(vcl).
                             LA.c. June/July 1944
        Unknown titles

Note:The unknown titles are from AFRS "Command Performance" transcription No.129.

THE KING COLE TRIO:
Nat Cole(p,vcl),Oscar Moore(g),Johnny Miller(b).
                             LA.c. June/July 1944
        I (Just) Can't See
            See For Lookin'(nc)   Joyce LP5006,Jazz Anthology(F)JA5219,Kings Of Jazz
                                     (I)KLJ20029,Deja Vu(I)DVLP2048
        Hit That Jive,Jack(nc,trio-vcl) Joyce LP5006,Jazz Anthology(F)JA5219,Kings Of Jazz
                                     (I)KLJ20029

Note:The above titles are from AFRS "Jubilee" transcription No.85.

```
Same.                                  LA.c. June/July  1944
        Fuzzy Wuzzy(nc,trio-vcl)
        Straighten Up And Fly Right(nc)
```

Note:The above titles are from AFRS "Jubilee" transcription No.89.

ANITA O'DAY WITH THE KING COLE TRIO:
(vcl) acc. by Nat Cole(p),Oscar Moore(g),Johnny Miller(b).

```
                                       LA.c.  mid-1944
        Ain't Misbehavin'              Laserlight 15 749(CD),15 915(CD)
        When We're Alone
          (Penthouse Serenade)              -           -
        The Lonesome Road                   -           -
        I Can't Give You
          Anything But Love                 -           -     ,Star Line SLC61014
        Rosetta                             -           -
```

Note:The above titles are from MacGregor transcription LB45 (issued under O'Day's name).
     Since all commercial issues are under Cole's name this session has nevertheless been
     included here.

THE KING COLE TRIO:
Nat Cole(p,vcl),Oscar Moore(g),Johnny Miller(b).

```
                                       LA.c.  mid-1944
        Besame Mucho(nc)               Giants Of Jazz GOJ1031,Remember(Eu)RMB75022(CD),
                                       Star Line SLC61118,Record. Arts LZCD343(CD),
                                       Laserlight 15 746(CD)
        Please Consider Me(nc)         Laserlight 15 746(CD)
        The Man I Love                 Giants Of Jazz GOJ1031,Recording Arts LZCD343(CD)
                                       Laserlight 15 747(CD)
        That'll Just
          'Bout Knock Me Out(nc)       Giants Of Jazz GOJ1031,Remember(Eu)RMB75022(CD),
                                       Star Line SLC61118,Record. Arts LZCD343(CD),
                                       Laserlight 15 747(CD)
```

All titles also on Laserlight 15 915 (5xCD).
Note:The above titles are from MacGregor transcription LB27.
     Star Line SLC61014 and SLC61118 are cassette-only issues.

```
Same.                                  LA.c.  mid-1944
        I Realize Now(nc)              Mark56 739,Star Line SLC61014
        Too Marvelous For Words(nc)         - ,Jazz Anthology(F)JA5219,Giants Of Jazz
                                       GOJ1031,Star Line SLC61014,SLC61118,Remember
                                       (Eu)RMB75022(CD),Recording Arts LZCD343(CD)
        I May Be Wrong                 Mark56 739
        You Must Be Blind(nc)               - ,Star Line SLC61014
```

All titles also on Laserlight 15 748 (CD),15 915 (5xCD),Fresh Sound(Sp)FSR-CD139 (CD).
Note:The above titles are from MacGregor transcriptions LB32,603.

```
Same.                                  LA.c.  mid-1944
        This Will Make You Laugh(nc)   Mark56 739,Star Line SLC61014
        Do Nothing 'Til
          You Hear From Me(nc)              -           -
        The Old Music Master(nc)            - ,Sounds Rare SR5003
        After You've Gone                   - ,Star Line SLC61014
```

All titles also on Laserlight 15 749 (CD),15 915 (5xCD),Fresh Sound(Sp)FSR-CD139 (CD).
Note:The above titles are from MacGregor transcription LB40.

Nat Cole(p,vcl),Oscar Moore(g),Johnny Miller(b).

LA.c. mid-1944

D-Day(nc)	Joyce JRC1209
Don't Blame Me(nc)	Sounds Rare SR5003(?),Joyce JRC1209
Smooth Sailing	Sounds Rare SR5003, -
You're So Different(nc)	Joyce JRC1209
Sweet Georgia Brown	Sounds Rare SR5003,Jazz Anthology(F)JA5219,Kings Of Jazz(I)KLJ20029

Note:The above titles are from MacGregor transcription LB67.

Same.

LA.c. mid-1944

Wouldn't You Like To Know(nc,trio-vcl)	Giants Of Jazz GOJ1031,Recording Arts LZCD343(CD), Laserlight 15 748(CD)
Barcarolle	Giants Of Jazz GOJ1031,Remember(Eu)RMB75022(CD), Recording Arts LZCD343(CD),Laserlight 15 748 (CD)
I Tho't You Ought To Know(nc)	Laserlight 15 748(CD)
Bring Another Drink(nc)	-

All titles also on Laserlight 15 915 (5xCD).
Note:The above titles are from MacGregor transcription LB68.

Same.

LA.c. mid-1944

Solid Potato Salad(nc,trio-vcl)	Laserlight 15 747(CD)
I Know That You Know	
Straighten Up And Fly Right(nc,trio-vcl)	
Honeysuckle Rose	

Note:The above titles are from AFRS "King Cole Trio - Personal Album" transcription No.227
This transcription also incl. "Slender,Tender And Tall" dubbed from AFRS "Jubilee" transcription No.29 (c. May/June 1943).
"Solid Potato Salad" may be dubbed from McGregor transcription LB13 (late 1943/early 1944).

Same.

LA.c. late 1944/early 1945

Poor Butterfly	Sounds Rare SR5003
These Foolish Things	-
Rosetta	- ,Laserlight 15 747(CD),15 915 (CD)
The Man I Love	Laserlight 15 747(CD),15 915(CD),Remember(Eu) RMB75022(?)
Liza	Laserlight 15 747(CD),15 915(CD)
I'm In The Mood For Love	Sounds Rare SR5003,Jazz Anthology(F)JA5219,Kings Of Jazz (I)KLJ20029,Laserlight 15 747(CD), 15 915(CD)

Note:The above titles are from MacGregor transcription LB71.
Sounds Rare SR5003 does not list "Rosetta" on the LP's cover or label.

Same.

LA.c. late 1944/early 1945

Don't Blame Me	Sounds Rare SR5003,Laserlight 15 746(CD)
Three Little Words	- -
Body And Soul	
How High The Moon	Sounds Rare SR5003,Laserlight 15 746(CD)
I Got Rhythm	Laserlight 15 746(CD)
Sweet Lorraine	-

All titles - except "Body And Soul" - also on Laserlight 15 915 (5xCD).
Note:The above titles are from MacGregor transcriptions LB47,72.

THE BARRIE SISTERS WITH THE KING COLE TRIO:
(vcl) acc. by Nat Cole(p),Oscar Moore(g),Johnny Miller(b).

                                        LA.c. late 1944/early 1945
            Someone's In
              The Kitchen With Dinah
            Basin Street Blues
            On The Sunny Side
              Of The Street
            I've Got Those
              Mad About Him Blues
            I've Heard That Song Before

Note:The above titles are from MacGregor transcriptions LB46,73.

THE KING COLE TRIO:
Nat Cole(p,vcl),Oscar Moore(g),Johnny Miller(b,vcl).

                                        LA.c. late 1944/early 1945
            It Only Happens Once(nc)   Sounds Rare SR5003,Joyce JRC1209
            Swingin' The Blues   - ,Jazz Anthology(F'
                                        JA5219,Kings Of Jazz(I)KLJ20029,Deja Vu(I)
                                        DVLP2048,Recording Arts LZCD343(CD),Giants
                                        Of Jazz GOJ1031
            Baby (Is What She Calls Me)(nc) Joyce JRC1209
            Baby,Won't You
              Please Come Home(nc)   Sounds Rare SR5003,Joyce JRC1209,Jazz Anthology(F'
                                        JA5219,Kings Of Jazz(I)KLJ20029,Deja Vu(I)
                                        DVLP2048
            Boogie A La King   Sounds Rare SR5003,Joyce JRC1209,Kings Of Jazz(I)
                                        KLJ20029,Deja Vu(I)DVLP2048(?)

All titles also on Laserlight 15 747(CD),15 915 (5xCD).
Note:The above titles are from MacGregor transcription LB74.
    Giants Of Jazz GOJ1031 does not list "Swingin' The Blues" on the LP's cover or label

Same.   LA.c. late 1944/early 1945
            'Tain't Me(nc,jm)   Sounds Rare SR5003,Laserlight 15 748(CD)
            Laura(nc)   - ,Kat Wisker Prod. NC1002(ed.),
                                        Laserlight 15 748(CD)
            Keep Knockin' On Wood(nc)   Laserlight 15 748(CD)
            If Yesterday
              Could Only Be Tomorrow(nc)   -
            Blues And Swing   -

All titles also on Laserlight 15 915 (5xCD).
Note:The above titles are from MacGregor transcription LB171.

Same.   LA.c. late 1944/early 1945
            It's Only A Paper Moon(nc) Sounds Rare SR5003,Laserlight 15 746(CD)
            What Can I Say
              After I Say I'm Sorry(nc) Laserlight 15 746(CD)
            I Wanna' Turn Out My Light(nc)   -
            You Call It Madness(nc)   -
            If I Had You   -

All titles also on Laserlight 15 915 (5xCD).
Note:The above titles are from MacGregor transcriptions LB175,394.

Same.   LA.November 28,1944
334   There,I've Said It Again(nc)   Capitol rejected
335-5 Please Consider Me(nc)   Mosaic MR27-138,MD18-138(CD)
336-6 Bring Another Drink(nc)   Capitol 192,(F)1551.863,Mosaic MR27-138,MD18-138
                                          (CD)

Nat Cole(p,vcl),Oscar Moore(g),Johnny Miller(b,vcl).

NYC.February 27,1945

If You Can't Smile And Say Yes(1)(nc)	V-Disc 437,(I)VDL1020,Navy 217,Elec(J)KV302,Dan(J) VC5011,Laserlight 15 915(CD)
A Pile Of Cole	V-Disc 437,Navy 217,Elec(J)KV302,Dan(J)VC5011, Laserlight 15 915(CD)
Any Old Time(nc)	V-Disc 455,Navy 235,Star Line SLC61118
Bring Another Drink(nc)	- -
Candy(nc)	V-Disc 499,Star Line SLC61118,CTPL(F)003,Laser- light 15 915(CD)
A Trio Grooves In Brooklyn	V-Disc 499,Laserlight 15 915(CD)

-1.Incl. spoken introduction by the members of the Trio (except on VDL1020).

All titles also on Giants Of Jazz GOJ1031.
All titles - except "Bring Another Drink" - also on Laserlight 15 749 (CD).
Note:"Any Old Time" is a mis-titling of "I'd Love To Make Love To You".
"A Trio Grooves In Brooklyn" recorded October 18,1945 as "This Way Out".
Star Line SLC61014 is a cassette only issue.

Same.   LA.March 1945
    The Man On The
        Little White Keys(nc)   Giants Of Jazz GOJ1013,Remember(Eu)RMB75022(CD)

Note:The above title is from AFRS "Mail Call" transcription No.132.

Same.   LA.c. March 1945
    It's Only A Paper Moon(1)(nc) Joyce LP5007,Black Jack(G)LP3003,Aura A1030
    Comedy routine(1)   -
    Sweet Lorraine(2)(nc)   - ,Black Jack(G)LP3003

1.Talking by Cole,Ernie "Bubbles" Whitman,Benny Carter,Arthur Treacher.
2.Add Benny Carter's orchestra for the last few bars.

Note:The above titles are from AFRS "Jubilee" transcriptions No.126,207,297.

Same.   LA.c. March/April 1945
    If You Can't
        Smile And Say Yes(nc)   Jazz Anthology(F)JA5219,Kings Of Jazz(I)KLJ20029
    Medley:
        Miss Thing   Giants Of Jazz GOJ1013,Classic Series PB55005,Jazz
                                Anthology(F)JA5219,Kings Of Jazz(I)KLJ20029
        On The Sunny Side
            Of The Street(nc,trio-vcl) Giants Of Jazz GOJ1013,Classic Series PB55005

All titles also on Biac(B)BRAD10528.
Note:The above titles are from AFRS "Jubilee" transcriptions No.129,220.

Same.   Broadcast.LA.April 5,1945
    It's Only A Paper Moon(nc) Giants Of Jazz GOJ1013,Bonsard 601

Note:The above title is from a Bing Crosby "Kraft Music Hall" radio program; both LP is-
    sues also include Cole and Crosby talking.

Same.   LA.April 13,1945
12-5 I'd Love To Make Love To You(nc) Mosaic MR27-138,MD18-138(CD)
13-1 I'm A Shy Guy(nc)   Capitol 208,(Au)SCA076,Mosaic MR27-138,MD18-138(CD
14-1 Katusha(nc)   Mosaic MR27-138,MD18-138(CD)
15-1 It Only Happens Once(nc)   - -
(session cont. next page).

(session cont. from previous page):
Note:Master 613 issued with wrong speed on Capitol(F)1551.863,Rhino E2.71009 (CD),Official
     (D)83026 (CD).

Nat Cole(p,vcl),Oscar Moore(g),Johnny Miller(b,vcl).
                                             Broadcast."Trocadero",LA.April 26,1945
         The Man On The Little
             White Keys(nc) (theme)   Giants Of Jazz GOJ1013
         If You Can't
             Smile And Say Yes(nc)   -
         The Trouble With Me Is You(1)(nc)   - ,Aura A1030,Classic Series
                                             PB55005
         Sweet Georgia Brown   Giants Of Jazz GOJ1013
         Satchel Mouth Baby(trio-vcl)   - ,Classic Series PB55005
         Closing Instrumental Riff   -

-1.This is not the same tune as "(It's Easy To See) The Trouble With Me Is You" recorded
   September 17,1946 and August 8,1947.

All titles - except "Closing Instrumental Riff" - also on Object(E)OR0075 (CD),Four Star
FS40047 (CD).
All titles - except "The Man On The Little White Keys" and "Closing Instrumental Riff" -
also on Remember(Eu)RMB75022 (CD),Topline(E)TOP112,CD508(CD).

Same.   Broadcast."Trocadero",LA.c. April 1945
         I'm Thru With Love(nc)   Swing House(E)SWH12,Recording Arts LZCD343(CD),
                                             Dance Band Days DBD15,DBCD15(CD)

Same.   LA.c. April/May 1945
         Candy(nc,trio-vcl)
         Sweet Lorraine(nc)(1)

-1.Add Andy Kirk's orchestra for the last few bars.

Note:The above titles are from AFRS "Jubilee" transcription No.133.

Same.   LA.c. early May 1945
         The Man On The
             Little White Keys(nc)
         Fuzzy Wuzzy(nc,trio-vcl)

Note:The above titles are from the "See My Lawyer" feature film soundtrack.

Same.   Live.LA.May 3,1945
         If You Can't
             Smile And Say Yes(nc)   Giants Of Jazz GOJ1013
         Sweet Georgia Brown   - ,Classic Series PB55005

Both titles also on Bonsard 601,Remember(Eu)RMB75022.
Note:The above titles are from a Bing Crosby "Kraft Music Hall" radio program dress
     rehearsal; both titles were transcribed for - but never issued on - V-Disc.
     Giants Of Jazz GOJ1013 and Bonsard 601 also include Cole and Crosby talking.

Same.   LA.May 19,1945
643-3 You're Nobody 'Til
           Somebody Loves You(nc)   Capitol T2529,N16260,(F)1551.863,251.684-1,
                                             251.984-2(CD),Mosaic MR27-138,MD18-138(CD)
644-1 Don't Blame Me(nc)   Capitol 15110,1032,F1032,(E)LC6594,(F)429,Music
                                             For Pleas.(E)MFP1129,MFP5004,Mosaic MR27-138,
                                             MD18-138(CD)
645-2 I'm In The Mood For Love(nc)   Mosaic MR27-138,MD18-138(CD)
(session cont. next page).

(session cont. from previous page):
646-1 What Can I Say
        After I Say I'm Sorry(nc)   Capitol T591,N16261,(F)251.683-1,251.984-2(CD),
                                      (Au)ENC9082,SCA076,Mosaic MR27-138,MD18-138
                                      (CD)
647-1 I'm Thru With Love(nc)   Capitol 20064 (BD29),T591,T2311,(F)1551.863,(G)
                                      (G)K83950,(J)TOCJ5326,(Au)ENC9082,Music For
                                      Pleasure(E)MFP50177,Mosaic MR27-138,MD18-138
                                      (CD),Jazz Club(F)2M.056-64866,Oxford(I)OX3020
                                      Krém(Hu)SLPXL17780,Laserlight 15 718(CD),
                                      Delta 11044(CD),Jazzline JL20808

Nat Cole(p,vcl),Oscar Moore(g),Johnny Miller(b,vcl).
                                      LA.May 23,1945
651-4 Barcarolle   Mosaic MR27-138,MD18-138(CD)
652-1 To A Wild Rose   -   -
653-1 Sweet Georgia Brown   Capitol 239,1037,F1037,T592,CDP7.98299(CD),(F)427,
                                      1551.863,251.683-1,251.984-2(CD),(G)C239,(J)
                                      TOCJ5326(CD),Mosaic MR27-138,MD18-138(CD),
                                      Giants Of Jazz(I)LPJT14,Telefunken(D)A18010,
                                      Deja Vu(I)DVLP2048,Delta 11044(CD),Jazz Club
                                      (F)2M.056-64866
654-5 I Tho't You Ought To Know(nc)   Capitol 208,(E)E-ST23480,(F)1551.863,Mosaic
                                      MR27-138,MD18-138(CD)
655-3 It Only Happens Once(nc)   Capitol 15358,(E)E-ST23480,(F)1551.863,Mosaic
                                      MR27-138,MD18-138(CD)

Same.   LA.c. May 1945
        It's Only A Paper Moon

Note:The above title is from AFRS "Command Performance" transcription No.177.

Same.   Live.LA.June 21,1945
        Satchel Mouth Baby(trio-vcl)   V-Disc 508,Navy 268,Vintage Jazz Classics VJC1044
                                        (CD)
        Solid Potato Salad(nc,trio-vcl) V-Disc 508,Navy 268,Vintage Jazz Classics VJC1044
                                        (CD),Elec(J)KV123,CTPL(F)003

Note:The above titles are from a Bing Crosby "Kraft Music Hall" radio program dress
    rehearsal.

Nat Cole(p,vcl),Johnny Miller(b).   LA.c. July 1945
        Sweet Lorraine(nc)   Giants Of Jazz GOJ1013,Sunbeam SB222,Classic Ser.
                                      PB55005,Remember(Eu)RMB75022(CD)(?),Topline
                                      (E)TOP112,CD508(CD)

Note:The above title is from AFRS "Jubilee" transcription No.144.

THE KING COLE TRIO:
Nat Cole(p,vcl),Oscar Moore(g,vcl),Johnny Miller(b).
                            Live."Casa Manana",LA.c. July/August 1945
        Hit That Jive,Jack(nc,trio-vcl) Vintage Jazz Classics VJC1044(CD)
        I Found A New Baby   -
        I Tho't You Ought To Know(nc)   -
        'Tain't Me(nc,om)   -
        After You've Gone   -
        Perdido (and theme)   -

Note:The above titles are from AFRS "Magic Carpet" transcription No.37.

Same.   LA.August 2,1945
750-5 (I Call My Papa)
        Fla-Ga-La-Pa(nc)   Mosaic MR27-138,MD18-138(CD)
751-3 It Is Better To
        Be By Yourself(nc,trio-vcl)   -   -

Note:The above titles were recorded for Capitol.

Same.   NYC.October 9,1945
        It's Only A Paper Moon(nc)   Vintage Jazz Classics VJC1044(CD)
        I Found A New Baby   -

Note:The above titles are from AFRS "Supper Club" transcription No.172; source: a Perry
     Como radio program.

Same.   NYC.October 11,1945
765-9 It Is Better To Be
        By Yourself(nc,trio-vcl)   Capitol 239,Telefunken(D)A18010,Official(D)3026,
                                       83026(CD)
766-7 Come To Baby,Do(nc)   Capitol 224,
767-3 The Frim Fram Sauce(nc)   - ,F15510 (CCF213),EBF/L/H213,T2529,ST31,
                                       N16261,(E)LC6587,(F)427,T20097,1551.863,Kat
                                       Wisker Prod. NC1002,Rhino E2.21009(CD)

All titles also on Mosaic MR27-138,MD18-138 CD).
Note:Issues on ST310 (and equiv.) were edited into stereo versions with new rhythm section
     and orchestra overdubbed (1969).

Same.   LA.October 18,1945
773-16 Homeward Bound(nc)   Mosaic MR27-138,MD18-138(CD)
774-9 I'm An Errand Boy For Rhythm(nc) Capitol EAP2/H1/W514,(E)EMS1142,(F)T20193,1566.251,
                                       Mosaic MR27-138,MD18-138(CD)
775-2 This Way Out   Capitol 20061 (BD29),1038,F1038,T592,CDP7.98299-2
                                       (CD),(F)C446,T20097,1566.251,C.152-81746/48,
                                       251.684-1,251.984-2(CD),(J)TOCJ5326(CD),
                                       Giants Of Jazz(I)LPJT14,GOJCD53005(CD),(E)
                                       CD0231(CD),Deja Vu(I)DVLP2048,Mosaic MR27-138,
                                       MD18-138(CD)
776-2 I Know That You Know   Capitol 20062 (BD29),1037,F1037,(F)441,Mosaic
                                       MR27-138,MD18-138(CD)

Same.   Broadcast.NYC.November 28,1945
        The Frim Fram Sauce(nc)   V-Disc 614,(I)VDL1004,SIAE(I)CT7196-7,Vintage Jazz
                                       Classics VJC1044(CD)
        I Found A New Baby(1)(fs)   Chairman 6011,Oscar(E)OSC102,Meteor(E)MTBS001,
                                       CDMTBS001/3(CD),JRC C1418,PJ004,Vintage Jazz
                                       Classics VJC1044(CD)

-1.Add Frank Sinatra(vcl).

Note:The above titles are from an AFRS transcription of a Frank Sinatra radio program
     ("Songs By Sinatra").

Same.   LA.December 4,1945
840-2 But She's My Buddy's Chick(nc) Mosaic MR27-138,MD18-138(CD)
840-3 But She's My Buddy's Chick(nc)   -   -
841-3 Oh,But I Do(trio-vcl)   Capitol(Au)SCA076,Mosaic MR27-138,MD18-138(CD)
842-3 How Does It Feel(nc)   Capitol ST310,   -   -
843-1 You Must Be Blind(nc)   Mosaic MR27-138,MD18-138(CD)
844-2 Loan Me Two Till Tuesday(nc)   -   -

Note:Issues on ST310 (and equiv.) were edited into stereo versions with new rhythm section
     and orchestra overdubbed (1969).

Nat Cole(p,vcl),Oscar Moore(g,vcl),Johnny Miller(b).

	LA.Poss. 1945/46
I'm An Errand Boy For Rhythm(nc)	Recording Arts JZCD343(CD),JCVC106,Storyville(D) SLP6003
Got A Penny,Benny(nc,trio-vcl)	Storyville(D)SLP6003
The Frim Fram Sauce(nc)	
Come To Baby,Do(nc)	Recording Arts JZCD343(CD),JCVC106,Storyville(D) SLP6003

Note:The above titles are from "Soundie" short film soundtracks. Exact original date(s) of
    filming are not known - some titles could have been produced as early as 1943.

Same.   LA.January 14,1946
    It Is Better To
        Be By Yourself(nc,trio-vcl)
    Satchel Mouth Baby(trio-vcl)

Note:The above titles are from the "Breakfast In Hollywood" feature film soundtrack.

Same.   Broadcast."Ritz Theater",NYC.January 16,1946
    After You've Gone   Session Disc 125
    Sweet Lorraine(nc)   -

Note:The above titles are from a broadcast of the third annual "Esquire All American Jazz
    Concert".

Same.   LA.c. January/February 1946
    Come To Baby,Do(nc)

Note:The above title is from AFRS "Jubilee" transcription No.171.

Same.   LA.March 13,1946
    Route 66(nc)   Vintage Jazz Classics VJC1044(CD)
    Exactly Like You(1)(nc,fs)   Chairman 6011,Deja Vu(I)DVLP2051,Meteor(E)MTBS001,
                                  JRC1418,PJ004,Vintage Jazz Classics VJC1044
                                  (CD)

-1.Add Frank Sinatra(vcl).

Note:The above titles are from an AFRS transcription of a Frank Sinatra radio program
    ("Songs By Sinatra").

Same.   LA.March 15,1946
1027-2 I'm In The Mood For Love(nc) Capitol 20063 (BD29),1032,F1032,(E)LC9594,(F)447,
                                  (G)C20063,Music For Pleasure(E)MFP1129,Mosaic
                                  MR27-138,MD18-138(CD),Deja Vu(I)DVLP2048(?)

1028-5 I Don't Know Why(nc)   Mosaic MR27-138,MD18-138(CD)
1028-6 I Don't Know Why(nc)   Capitol 20062 (BD29),1030,F1030,Mosaic MR27-138,
                                  MD18-138(CD)

1029-1 (Get Your Kicks On) Route 66(nc) Capitol 256,15511,F15511 (CCF213),EBF/H/L213,
                                  N16260,SKAO2944,DNFR7620,(E)CL13722,SM131,(F)
                                  406,1551.863,T20097,C.154-85330,C.166-50335,
                                  (G)C80107,LAC213,Mosaic MR27-138,MD18-138(CD)
                                  Jazzline JL20815,Rhino E2-71009(CD),Delta
                                  11086(CD)

1030-1 Everyone Is
        Sayin' Hello Again(nc)   Capitol 256,(E)LC6594,Mosaic MR27-138,MD18-138
                                  (CD),Official(D)3026,83026(CD)

Nat Cole(p,vcl),Oscar Moore(g,vcl),Johnny Miller(b).
                                        LA.March 1946
            The Frim Fram Sauce(nc)   Giants Of Jazz GOJ1013,Remember(Eu)RMB75022(CD)

Note:The above title is from AFRS "Jubilee" transcription No.172.
     Giants Of Jazz GOJ1013 also incl. a spoken introduction by Ernie "Bubbles" Whitman,
     Lena Horne and Cole.

Same.   LA.c. March 1946
            It Is Better To Be
                By Yourself(nc,trio-vcl)
            This Way Out
            Don't Blame Me(nc)
            After You've Gone

Note:The above titles are from AFRS "Magic Carpet" transcription No.287.

Same.   LA.c. March 1946
            It Is Better To Be
                By Yourself(nc,trio-vcl)
            This Way Out
            I'm Thru With Love(nc)
            Swingin' The Blues

Note:The above titles are from AFRS "Magic Carpet" transcription No.295.

Same.   LA.c. March 1946
            Route 66(nc)
            Take The "A" Train
            Baby,Baby All The Time(nc)
            After You've Gone

Note:The above titles are from AFRS "Magic Carpet" transcription No.306.

Same.   LA.c. March 1946
            I'm In The Mood For Love(nc)
            Somebody Loves Me
            How Deep Is The Ocean(nc)
            Honeysuckle Rose

Note:The above titles are from AFRS "Magic Carpet" transcription No.313.

Same.   LA.c. March 1946
            F.S.T. (opening theme)   Mosaic MR27-138,MD18-138(CD)
            F.S.T. (closing theme)   -   -   ,Echo Jazz EJLP08,
                                           EJCD08(CD)

Note:The above "F.S.T." recordings were used to open and close the Capitol transcriptions
     for radio broadcast.

Same.   LA.March 20,1946
ET795-2 Just You,Just Me(alt.take)(1)   Mosaic MR27-138,MD18-138(CD)
ET796-1 Just You,Just Me   -   -   ,Echo Jazz EJLP08
ET796-2 I've Got The
            World On A String(nc)   -   -   -
ET797-2 Rex Rhumba (Rhumba A La King)   -   -   -
ET798-1 But She's My Buddy's Chick(nc)   -   -   -
ET798-2 Chant Of The Blues(nc)   -   -
ET799-1 Rock-A-Bye Basie(1)   -   -
ET799-3 Lester Leaps In   -   -   -
ET800-1 I Don't Know Why
            (I Just Do)(1)(nc)   -   -
(session cont. next page).

(session cont. from previous page):
ET800-2 I Want To Be Happy(1)   Mosaic MR27-138,MD18-138(CD)
ET800-3 I Know That You Know   -   -   ,Echo Jazz EJLP08

Titles on EJLP08 also on Echo Jazz EJCD08 (CD).
Note:The above titles were recorded for Capitol transcriptions and used for transcriptions
     B157,B158,B160 - except titles/takes marked (1).

Nat Cole(p,vcl),Oscar Moore(g,vcl),Johnny Miller(b).
                                       LA.c. March/April 1946
        Sweet Georgia Brown

Note:The above title is from AFRS "Jubilee" transcription No.184 - see LESTER YOUNG for
     additional titles (incl. the Cole Trio) from this transcription.

Same.   LA.c. April 1946
       (Get Your Kicks On) Route 66(nc) V-Disc 705
       Sweet Georgia Brown

Note:The above titles are from AFRS "Jubilee" transcription No.186.
     See JAZZ AT THE PHILHARMONIC for additional titles from this session.

Same.   LA.April 5,1946
1069-4 What Can I Say After
       I Say I'm Sorry(nc)   Mosaic MR27-138,MD18-138(CD)
1069-5 What Can I Say After
       I Say I'm Sorry(nc)   Capitol 20061 (BD29),1034,F1034,DNFR7620,(F)441,
                                           1551.863,(G)C9018,(J)TOCJ5326(CD),Oxford(I)
                                           OX3020,Jazz Club(F)2M.056-64866,Delta 11044
                                           (CD),Mosaic MR27-138,MD18-138(CD),Laserlight
                                           15 718,Krém(Hu)SLPXL17780,Jazzline JL20808
                                           (CD)
1070-1 To A Wild Rose   Mosaic MR27-138,MD18-138(CD)
1070-2 To A Wild Rose   Capitol 20063 (BD29),(E)CL13535,E-ST23480,(G)
                                           C20063,Mosaic MR27-138,MD18-138(CD),Official
                                           (D)3026,83026(CD)
1071-2 Baby,Baby All The Time(nc)   Mosaic MR27-138,MD18-138(CD)

Same.   LA.April 11,1946
ET1015-1 I Don't Know Why
         (I Just Do)(nc)   Mosaic MR27-138,Echo Jazz EJLP08,EJCD08(CD)
ET1015-2 This Way Out   - ,Echo Jazz EJLP18,EJCD18(CD)
ET1016-1 Baby,Baby All The Time(nc)   - ,Echo Jazz EJLP08,EJCD08(CD)
ET1016-2 Somebody Loves Me   -   -   -   ,Kings
                                       Of Jazz(I)KLJ20029,Jazz Anthology(F)JA5219,
ET1017-1 Too Marvelous For Words(nc)   Mosaic MR27-138
ET1018-1 Honeysuckle Rose   - ,Echo Jazz EJLP18,EJCD18(CD)
ET1018-2 How Does It Feel(nc)   -   -   -
ET1019-2 Loan Me Two Till Tuesday(nc)   -   -   -
ET1020-1 What Can I Say
         After I Say I'm Sorry(nc)   -   -   -
ET1020-2 You Name It   -   -   -

All titles on MR27-138 also on Mosaic MD18-138 (CD).
Note:The above titles were recorded for Capitol transcriptions and used for transcriptions
     B157,B160,B161,B162(?),B226.

Same.   LA.April 17,1946
1080-2 Could 'Ja(nc)   Mosaic MR27-138,MD18-138(CD)
1080-4 Could 'Ja(nc)   Capitol 20128 (BD58),Mosaic MR27-138,MD18-138(CD)
(session cont. next page).

(session cont. from previous page):
1081-3 Baby,Baby All The Time(nc)   Mosaic MR27-138,MD18-138(CD)
1081-4 Baby,Baby All The Time(nc)   Capitol 15165,T2529,N16261,(F)1551.863,254.681-1,
                                         254.984-2(CD),(Au)SCA076,Mosaic MR27-138,
                                         MD18-138(CD)
1082-1 Oh,But I Do(trio-vcl)   Capitol 274,(E)E-ST23480,(G)C274,Mosaic MR27-138,
                                         MD18-138(CD),Official(D)3026,83026(CD)
1083-4 Rex Rhumba (Rhumba A La King)   Capitol 15240,1038,F1038,(E)CL13028,(F)441,
                                         1551.863,Mosaic MR27-138,MD18-138(CD),
                                         Official(D)83026(CD)

Nat Cole(p,vcl),Oscar Moore(g,vcl),Johnny Miller(b).
                                       LA.April 18,1946
ET1040-1 How High The Moon   Mosaic MR27-138,Echo Jazz EJLP18,EJCD18(CD)
ET1040-2 You Call It Madness(nc)   -   -   -
ET1041-1 Tiny's Exercise(1)   -
ET1042-2 After You Get What You
           Want,You Don't Want It(nc)   - ,Echo Jazz EJLP08,EJCD08(CD)
ET1043-1 Body And Soul   - ,Echo Jazz EJLP18,EJCD18(CD)
ET1043-2 On The Sunny Side
           Of The Street(nc)   - ,Echo Jazz EJLP08,EJCD08(CD)
ET1044-1 I'd Love To Make
           Love To You(nc)   -
ET1044-2 Homeward Bound   - ,Echo Jazz EJLP08,EJCD08(CD)

All titles on MR27-138 also on Mosaic MD18-138 (CD).
Note:The above titles were recorded for Capitol transcriptions and used for transcriptions
     B157,B160,B161,B225,B226 - except title marked (1).

Same.   LA.April 24,1946
ET1058-1 What Is This
           Thing Called Love   Mosaic MR27-138,Echo Jazz EJLP18,EJCD18(CD)
ET1059-1 Mabel,Mabel(nc)   - Echo Jazz EJLP08,EJCD08(CD)
ET1059-3 Swingin' The Blues   -

All titles on MR27-138 also on Mosaic MD18-138 (CD).
Note:The above titles were recorded for Capitol transcriptions and used for transcriptions
     B159,B160,B225.

Same.   LA.April 25,1946
ET1060-1 Beautiful Moons Ago(nc)   Mosaic MR27-138
ET1060-2 I Got Rhythm   - ,Echo Jazz EJLP08,EJCD08(CD)
ET1061-1 Could 'Ja(1)(nc)   -
ET1061-2 One O'Clock Jump   - ,Echo Jazz EJLP18,EJCD18(CD)
ET1062-2 How Deep Is The Ocean(nc)   - ,Echo Jazz EJLP08,EJCD08(CD)
ET1063-1 Route 66(nc)   - ,Echo Jazz EJLP18,EJCD18(CD)
ET1063-2 Cole Slaw   -

All titles on MR27-138 also on Mosaic MD18-138 (CD).
Note:The above titles were recorded for Capitol transcriptions and used for transcriptions
     B159,B161,B226 - except title marked (1).
     "Route 66" also issued on Capitol CDP7.93590-2 (CD) - erroneously listed as recorded
     March 15,1946.

Same.   LA.May 1,1946
1095-3 But She's My Buddy's Chick(nc) Capitol 328,T2529,(E)EMS1142,(F)1566.251,Mosaic
                                         MR27-138,MD18-138(CD)
1096-3 You Call It Madness(nc)   Capitol 274,F15510 (CCF213),EBF/H/L213,T2311,
                                         ST310,(F)429,(G)K83950,Oxford(I)OX3020,Music
                                         For Pleasure(E)MFP50177,Delta(G)20808,29037,
                                         Mosaic MR27-138,MD18-138(CD),Krém(Hu)
(session cont. next page).   SLPXL17780

- 91 -

NAT "KING" COLE

(session cont. from previous page):
1097-1 Homeward Bound   Mosaic MR27-138,MD18-138(CD)
1098-3 Chant Of The Blues
        (Dog-gone Unlucky Blues)(nc)   -   -

Note:Issues on ST310 (and equiv.) were edited into stereo versions with new rhythm section
    and orchestra overdubbed (1969).

Nat Cole(p,vcl),Oscar Moore(g,vcl),Johnny Miller(b).
                            Broadcast."Trocadero",LA.May 5,1946
        Could 'Ja(nc)   Vintage Jazz Classics VJC1044(CD)
        This Way Out   -
        How Deep Is The Ocean(nc)   -
        How High The Moon   -
        F.S.T. (closing theme)   -

Same.   NYC.May 9,1946
        Unknown titles

Note:The unknown title(s) are from AFRS "Supper Club" transcription No.312; source: a
    Perry Como radio program.

Same.   Broadcast.NYC.May 16,1946
        Linger In My Arms
          A Little Longer,Baby(nc)
        I'd Love To Make Love To You(nc)

Note:During the summmer of 1946, The King Cole Trio replaced Bing Crosby as the headliner
    act in the "Kraft Music Hall" radio program schedule for 13 weeks - beginning with
    the above program. The Cole Trio performed on every show, along with Edward Everett
    Horton and Eddie Duchin occasionally.

Same.   NYC.June 14,1946
956-5 The Christmas Song(nc)   Electrola/Capitol(G)1C.056-85613,Mosaic MR27-138,
                                        MD18-138(CD)
957-3 You Should Have Told Me(nc) Mosaic MR27-138,MD18-138(CD)

Same.   Broadcast.NYC.July 19,1946
        Mabel,Mabel(nc)
        Oh,But I Do(trio-vcl)

Note:The above titles are from a "Kraft Music Hall" radio program (also incl. comedy talk
    by Trio members and Edward Everett Horton).

Same.   Broadcast.NYC.Summer 1946
        I'm An Errand Boy For Rhythm(nc)

Note:The above title is from a "Kraft Music Hall" radio program (also incl. comedy talk
    by Trio members and Edward Everett Horton).

Same.   Broadcast.NYC.Summer 1946
        Comin' Through The Rye(nc,eeh)

Note:The above excerpt is from a "Kraft Music Hall" radio program - it is a vocal duet
    performance by Cole and Edward Everett Horton.

Same.   Broadcast.NYC.August 15,1946
        Mabel,Mabel(nc)
        I'm In The Mood For Love(nc)

Note:The above titles are from a "Kraft Music Hall" radio program (also incl. comedy talk
    by Trio members and Eddie Duchin).

Nat Cole(p,vcl),Oscar Moore(g),Johnny Miller(b),Jack "The Bear" Parker -1(dr).
                                        NYC.August 19,1946
980-4   The Best Man(1)(nc)   Capitol 304,T2529,(E)LC6594,EMS2142,(F)1566.251
981-2   The Christmas Song(2)(nc)   Capitol 311,15201,3561,57/54-90036,CDP7.93590-2
                                         (CD),(E)CL13010,EAP1-20151,LC6587,(F)355,(G)
                                         C80065,Kat Wisker Prod. NC1002
982-3   You Should Have Told Me(nc)   Capitol 356,Official(D)3026,83026(CD)

-2.Add strings,harp,Charlie Grean(arr).

All titles also on Mosaic MR27-138,MD18-138 (CD).
Note:The above original studio performance of "The Christmas Song" was used for the AFRS
     "Jubilee" Christmas Show 1947 transcription - applause was overdubbed. This edited
     version also on Vintage Jazz Classics VJC1016 (CD).

THE KING COLE TRIO:
Nat Cole(p,vcl),Oscar Moore(g),Johnny Miller(b).
                                        NYC.August 22,1946
983-5   (I Love You) For
           Sentimental Reasons(nc)   Capitol 304,1033,1674,15311,F1033,F1674,EAP1-357,
                                         EBF/H/T357,N16261,CDP7.46736-2,CDP7.93590-2
                                         (CD),(E)LC6587,EAP1-20151,(F)447,1551.863,(G)
                                         K83066,Kat Wisker Prod.NC1002,Giants Of Jazz
                                         (I),GOJCD53005(CD),(E)CD0231(CD),Starlite(E)
                                         1003,Mosaic MR27-138,MD18-138(CD),Rhino
                                         E2.71009(CD)

Same.   NYC.September 6,1946
987-9   In The Cool Of The Evening   Capitol 311,(G)C80065
988-3   That's The
           Beginning Of The End(nc)   Capitol 328,(E)E-ST23480

Both titles also on Mosaic MR27-138,MD18-138 (CD),Official(D)3026,83026(CD).

Same.   NYC.September 17,1946
995-4   If You Don't Like My Apples(nc) Mosaic MR27-138,MD18-138(CD)
996-4   (It's Easy To See) The
           Trouble With Me Is You(nc)   Capitol rejected

Same.   Broadcast."Hotel La Salle",Milwaukee,Wisconsin.September 21,1946
        Oh,But I Do(trio-vcl)
        I'm Thru With Love(nc)
        C Jam Blues
        My Sugar Is So Refined(nc)

Same.   Broadcast."Hotel La Salle",Milwaukee,Wisconsin.September 22,1946
        I'm In The Mood For Love(nc)
        I Found A New Baby
        I Don't Know Why(nc)
        If You Can't Smile And Say Yes(nc)

Same.   Broadcast."Hotel La Salle",Milwaukee,Wisconsin.September 23,1946
        Oh,But I Do(trio-vcl)
        Sweet Georgia Brown
        Sweet Lorraine(nc)
        My Sugar Is So Refined(nc)

Same.   Broadcast."Hotel La Salle",Milwaukee,Wisconsin.September 25,1946
        It's Only A Paper Moon(nc)
        One O'Clock Jump
        Everyone Is Sayin' Hello Again(nc)
        My Sugar Is So Refined(nc)

Note:From October 1946 until April 1948 Wildroot Cream Oil sponsored a weekly live NBC
     radio program titled: "King Cole Trio Time". A brief phrase from "Straighten Up And
     Fly Right" was used as theme at the beginning of each show. The "Wildroot Cream Oil
     Charlie" jingle was performed by the Trio in each show - a full version, and later
     a brief reprise.

     The following programs (with guest artists listed in parenthesis) were broadcast be-
     fore AFRS began transcribing - and re-broadcasting - these shows from January 1947
     onward:
     October 19. (Jo Stafford), 26. (June Christy)
     November 2. (Frances Wayne), 9. (Peggy Mann), 16. (The Dinning Sisters), 23. (Stan
     Kenton), 30. (Maxine Sullivan)
     December 7. (Johnny Mercer), 14. (The Pied Pipers), 21. (Mel Torme), 28. (Fontaine
     Sisters).

Nat Cole(p,vcl),Oscar Moore(g),Johnny Miller(b).
                                        Broadcast.NYC.October 19,1946

          Straighten Up And Fly Right(nc)
          Five Minutes More(nc)
          Sweet Lorraine(nc)
          The Best Man(nc)
          On The Sunny Side
             Of The Street(1)(js)

-1.Add Jo Stafford(vcl) - guest artist.

Note:The above titles are from the premiere Wildroot "King Cole Trio Time" radio program.
     It is not known if a recording of this program exists - the above information is from
     a review of the broadcast.

Same.   NYC.October 30,1946
1263-4 Smoke Gets In Your Eyes   Capitol 10074 (CD41),15502,F15502(CCF210),EBF/H210
                                        T592,T2311,CDP7.98299-2(CD),(E)LC6578,(F)
                                        1551.863,251.684-1,251.984-2(CD),(G)K83950,
                                        (J)TOCF5326(CD),Mosaic MR27-138,MD18-138(CD)

Same.   Broadcast.NYC.November 30,1946
          Straighten Up And Fly Right(nc)
          Need I Say(nc)
          I Found A New Baby
          Wildroot Cream Oil
             Charlie(trio-vcl)
          Unknown title(1)(ms)
          For Sentimental Reasons(nc)

-1.Add Maxine Sullivan(vcl) - guest artist.

Note:The above titles are from a Wildroot "King Cole Trio Time" radio program.

Same.   Broadcast.NYC.c. late 1946
          Straighten Up And Fly Right(nc)
          Medley:
             It's Only A Paper Moon(nc)
             Gee,Baby,Ain't
                I Good To You(nc)
          The Frim Fram Sauce(nc)

Note:The above titles are prob. from a Wildroot "King Cole Trio Time" radio program.

Nat Cole(p,vcl),Oscar Moore(g),Johnny Miller(b).

NYC.December 18,1946

1268-5 I Want To Thank Your Folks(nc)   Capitol 356,Mosaic MR27-138,MD18-138(CD),Official (D)3026,83026(CD)

1269-5 You're The
      Cream In My Coffee(nc)   Capitol 10086 (CD49),1030,F1030,T2529,(E)LC6587, EMS1142,(F)439,1566.251,Music For Pleasure(E) MFP50177,Mosaic MR27-138,MD18-138(CD),Oxford (I)OX3020,Krém(Hu)SLPXL17780,Bella Musica(G) LP3004,Jazz Club(F)2M.056-64966,VM(G)43004, Europa(G)11535.9,Delta(G)20808,29004,11044 (CD)

1270-2 Come In Out Of The Rain(nc)   Capitol 418,Mosaic MR27-138,MD18-138(CD),Kings Of Jazz(I)KLJ20029(?),Official(D)3026,83026(CD)

Note:Masters 1271 and 1272 are not Cole recordings.

Same.

NYC.December 19,1946

1273-2 You Don't Learn
      That In School(nc)   Capitol 393,(E)CL13767,Mosaic MR27-138,MD18-138 (CD),Official(D)3026,83026(CD)

1274-3 You Be You
      (But Let Me Be Me)(nc)   Mosaic MR27-138,MD18-138(CD)

1275-2 Can You Look Me In The Eyes
      (And Say We're Through)(nc)   Capitol 418,Mosaic MR27-138,MD18-138(CD),Official (D)3026,83026(CD)

Note:Master 1274 was originally recorded for Capitol transcriptions A71,B566.

Same.

Broadcast.Harrisburg,Penn.December 28,1946

      Straighten Up And Fly Right(nc)
      (Give Me) Five Minutes More(nc)
      Wildroot Cream Oil
        Charlie(trio-vcl)
      That's The
        Beginning Of The End(nc)
      Missouri Waltz(1)(fs)
      What Is This Thing Called Love

-1.Add The Fontaine Sisters(vcl-group) - guest artists.

Note:The above titles are from a Wildroot "King Cole Trio Time" radio program.

Same.

Broadcast.Baltimore.January 4,1947

      Straighten Up And Fly Right(nc)
      You're The Cream In My Coffee(nc)
      Come In Out Of The Rain(nc)   Biac(B)BRAD10528
      I'm Thru With Love(nc)
      Sleep,Kentucky Baby(1)(tv)
      Somebody Loves Me
      Crazy Rhythm

-1.Add The Vagabonds(vcl-group) - guest artists.

Note:The above titles are from a Wildroot "King Cole Trio Time" radio program (AFRS "King Cole Trio" transcription No.1).

Same.

Broadcast.Philadelphia.January 11,1947

      Straighten Up And Fly Right(nc)
      A Gal In Calico(nc)
(session cont. next page).

(session cont. from previous page):
        I'll Close My Eyes(nc)
        September Song(1)(tc)
        Cecilia(nc)
        Crazy Rhythm

-1.Add Thelma Carpenter(vcl) - guest artist.

Note:The above titles are from a Wildroot "King Cole Trio Time" radio program (AFRS "King
     Cole Trio" transcription No.4).

Nat Cole(p,vcl),Oscar Moore(g),Johnny Miller(b).
                                        Broadcast.NYC.January 18,1947
        Straighten Up And Fly Right(nc)
        Need I Say(nc)
        Hoodle Addle(1)(pk,tm)
        Talking by W.C. Handy and Cole
        St. Louis Blues(nc)
        I Found A New Baby

-1.Add Paula Kelly(vcl),The Modernaires(vcl-group) - guest artists.

Note:The above titles are from a Wildroot "King Cole Trio Time" radio program (AFRS "King
     Cole Trio" transcription No.2).

Same.   NYC.January 21,1947
1287-3 Give Me Twenty Nickels(nc)   Mosaic MR27-138,MD18-138(CD)
1288-3 Meet Me At No Special Place(nc) Capitol 393,(E)E-ST23480,(Au)SCA076,Mosaic
                                          MR27-138,MD18-138(CD),Official(D)3026,
                                          83026(CD)
1289-2 If You Don't Like My Apples(nc) Mosaic MR27-138,MD18-138(CD)

Same.   Broadcast.Washington,D.C.January 25,1947
        Unknown titles

Note:The unknown titles are from a Wildroot "King Cole Trio Time" radio program incl. Sam
     Donahue as guest artist. No information on poss. AFRS transcription.

Same.   Broadcast.Boston.February 1,1947
        Straighten Up And Fly Right(nc)
        You're The Cream In My Coffee(nc)
        Wildroot Cream Oil Charlie(nc)
        For Sentimental Reasons(nc)
        The Girl That I Marry(1)(rd)
        I'll Close My Eyes(nc)
        After You've Gone
        Straighten Up And
          Fly Right(nc)

-1.Add Ray Dorey(vcl) - guest artist.

Note:The above titles are from a Wildroot "King Cole Trio Time" radio program (AFRS "King
     Cole Trio" transcription No.10).

Same.   Broadcast.NYC.February 8,1947
        Straighten Up And Fly Right(nc)
        A Gal In Calico(nc)
        My Heart Is A Hobo(nc)
        I Want To Thank Your Folks(nc)
        Just A Gigolo(1)
        Honeysuckle Rose
(session cont. next page).

(session cont. from previous page):
     Prelude In C Sharp Minor

-1.Add the Joe Mooney Quartet - guest artists.

Note:The above titles are from a Wildroot "King Cole Trio Time" radio program (AFRS "King
    Cole Trio" transcription No.12).

Nat Cole(p,vcl),Oscar Moore(g),Johnny Miller(b).
                                      Broadcast.Hartford,Conn.February 15,1947
     Straighten Up And Fly Right(nc)
     I'd Love To Make Love To You(nc)
     Oh,Kickeroonie(nc)
     There Is No Greater Love(nc)
     Memories Of You(1)
     On The Sunny Side
       Of The Street(nc)
     I Know That You Know

-1.Add Sonny Dunham(tp,tb) - guest artist.

Note:The above titles are from a Wildroot "King Cole Trio Time" radio program (AFRS "King
    Cole Trio" transcription No.9).

Same.   Broadcast.Detroit.February 22,1947
     Unknown titles

Note:The unknown titles are from a Wildroot "King Cole Trio Time" radio program incl. June
    Richmond(vcl) as guest artist. No information on poss. AFRS transcription.

Same.   Broadcast.Chicago.March 1,1947
     Straighten Up And Fly Right(nc)
     Give Me Twenty
       Nickels For A Dollar(nc)   Vintage Jazz Classics VJC1011(CD)
     You're The Cream In My Coffee(nc)
     For Sentimental Reasons(nc)   Vintage Jazz Classics VJC1011(CD)
     Tired(1)(pb)   -
     I'm Thru With Love(nc)
     Crazy Rhythm   Vintage Jazz Classics VJC1011(CD)

-1.Add Pearl Bailey(vcl) - guest artist.

All titles on VJC1011 (CD) also on Milan(F)CH335 (CD).
Note:The above titles are from a Wildroot "King Cole Trio Time" radio program (AFRS "King
    Cole Trio" transcription No.13).

Same.   Broadcast.Cleveland.March 8,1947
     Straighten Up And Fly Right(nc)
     I'm In The Mood For Love(nc)
     Sweet Lorraine(nc)
     I Can't Believe
       It Was All Make-Believe(nc)
     Dorsey Brothers medley:
       Tangerine(nc)
       Yes,Indeed(nc)
     Love's Got Me In A Lazy Mood(nc)
     The Trouble With Me Is You(nc)

Note:The above titles are from a Wildroot "King Cole Trio Time" radio program (AFRS "King
    Cole Trio" transcription No.11). The medley is repeated on AFRS "King Cole Trio"
    transcription No.15. (Jimmy and Tommy Dorsey had been the scheduled guest artists
    but did not make the broadcast).

Nat Cole(p,vcl),Oscar Moore(g),Johnny Miller(b).

Broadcast.Cincinnati.March 15,1947

    Unknown titles

Note:The unknown titles are from a Wildroot "King Cole Trio Time" radio program incl.
    Sonny Dunham as guest artist. No information on poss. AFRS transcription.

Same.

Broadcast.Chicago.March 22,1947

    Unknown titles

Note:The unknown titles are from a Wildroot "King Cole Trio Time" radio program incl.
    Sarah Vaughan as guest artist. No information on poss. AFRS transcription.

Same.

Broadcast.Chicago.March 29,1947

    Straighten Up And Fly Right(nc)
    You're The Cream In My Coffee(nc)
    Prelude In C Sharp Minor
    I Want To Thank Your Folks(nc)
    My Adobe Hacienda(1)(ds)
    I Can't Believe
      It Was All Make-Believe(nc)
    I Know That You Know
    Crazy Rhythm

-1.Add The Dinning Sisters(vcl-group) - guest artists.

Note:The above titles are from a Wildroot "King Cole Trio Time" radio program (AFRS "King
    Cole Trio" transcription No.21).

Same.

Broadcast.Detroit.April 12,1947

    Unknown titles

Note:The unknown titles are from a Wildroot "King Cole Trio Time" radio program. No infor-
    mation on poss. AFRS transcription.

Same.

Broadcast.Chicago.April 19,1947

    Unknown titles

Note:The unknown titles are from a Wildroot "King Cole Trio Time" radio program. No infor-
    mation on poss. AFRS transcription.

Same.

Broadcast.St. Louis,Missouri.April 26,1947

    Straighten Up And Fly Right(nc)
    Across The Alley
      From The Alamo(nc)
    I'm In The Mood For Love(nc)
    Mamselle(nc)
    Hines medley(1):
      You Can Depend On Me
      Everything Depends On You
      Rosetta
    On The Sunny Side Of The Street(nc)
    Crazy Rhythm

-1.Earl Hines(p-solo) - guest artist.

Note:The above titles are from a Wildroot "King Cole Trio Time" radio program (AFRS "King
    Cole Trio" transcription No.15). Also on AFRS No.15 is an additional "Dorsey Brothers
    Medley" - not from this broadcast (see note after the March 8,1947 broadcast).

Nat Cole(p,vcl),Oscar Moore(g),Johnny Miller(b).

                                    Broadcast.Dallas,Texas.May 3,1947
      Unknown titles

Note:The unknown titles are from a Wildroot "King Cole Trio Time" radio program. No infor-
    mation on poss. AFRS transcription.

Same.   Broadcast.LA.May 10,1947
      Unknown titles

Note:The unknown titles are from a Wildroot "King Cole Trio Time" radio program incl. Mel
    Torme(vcl) as guest artist. No information on poss. AFRS transcription.

Same.   Broadcast.LA.May 17,1947
      Unknown titles

Note:The unknown titles are from a Wildroot "King Cole Trio Time" radio program incl. Tony
    Pastor as guest artist. No information on poss. AFRS transcription.

Same.   Broadcast.LA.May 24,1947
      Unknown titles

Note:The unknown titles are from a Wildroot "King Cole Trio Time" radio program incl. June
    Christy(vcl) as guest artist. No information on poss. AFRS transcription.

Same.   Broadcast.LA.May 28,1947
      You Don't Learn
         That In School(nc)   Sunbeam HB309
      You're The Cream In My Coffee(nc)   -
      I Ain't Mad At You(1)(nc,ds,pl,plh)   -

-1.Add Dinah Shore,Peggy Lee,Peter Lind Hayes(vcl).

Note:The above titles are from a "Dinah Shore Show" radio program.

Same.   Broadcast.LA.May 31,1947
      Straighten Up And Fly Right(nc)
      Movie Tonight(nc)
      After You've Gone
      I Wonder,I Wonder,I Wonder(nc)
      Cocktails For Two(1)
      The Trouble With Me Is You(nc)
      Give Me Twenty
         Nickels For A Dollar(nc)

-1.Add Benny Carter(as) - guest artist.

Note:The above titles are from a Wildroot "King Cole Trio Time" radio program (AFRS "King
    Cole Trio" transcription No.16).

Same.   Broadcast.LA.June 7,1947
      Straighten Up And Fly Right(nc)
      I'm In The Mood For Love(nc)
      Midnight Masquerade(nc)
      That's My Desire(1)(fl)
      A Gal In Calico(nc)
      I Found A New Baby

-1.Add Frankie Laine(vcl) - guest artist.

Note:The above titles are from a Wildroot "King Cole Trio Time" radio program (AFRS "King
    Cole Trio" transcription No.14).

Nat Cole(p,vcl),Oscar Moore(g),Johnny Miller(b).

LA.June 13,1947

2050-4 Naughty Angeline(nc)	Capitol 437,(E)LC6594
2051-2 I Miss You So(nc)	Capitol 444,1672,F1672,ST310
2052-3 That's What(nc)	Capitol 437,1036,F1036,(F)444

All titles also on Capitol T2529,(E)EMS1142,(F)1566.251,Mosaic MR27-138,MD18-138(CD).
Note:Issues on ST310 (and equiv.) were edited into stereo versions with new rhythm section
   and orchestra overdubbed (1969).

Same.   Broadcast.LA.June 14,1947
      Straighten Up And Fly Right(nc)
      It Takes Time(nc)
      Crazy Rhythm
      Dreams Are A Dime A Dozen(nc)
      I Got A Gal Named Nettie(1)(cc)
      Cecilia(nc)
      Somebody Loves Me

1.Add Cab Calloway(vcl) - guest artist.

Note:The above titles are from a Wildroot "King Cole Trio Time" radio program (AFRS "King
   Cole Trio" transcription No.17 with "I Found A New Baby" - not from this broadcast -
   added).

Same.   Broadcast.LA.June 21,1947
      Straighten Up And Fly Right(nc)
      Cecilia(nc)
      What Can I Say After
         I Say I'm Sorry(nc)
      You Should Have Told Me(nc)
      What More Can A Woman Do(1)(pl)
      On The Sunny Side
         Of The Street(1)(nc,pl)
      I Know That You Know

1.Add Peggy Lee(vcl) - guest artist.

Note:The above titles are from a Wildroot "King Cole Trio Time" radio program (AFRS "King
   Cole Trio" transcription No.3).

Same.   Live.Civic Auditorium,Pasadena,Calif.June 23,1947
      Sweet Lorraine(nc)
      I Know That You Know
      Don't Blame Me(nc)
      My Fair Lady(nc)
      Loan Me Two 'Til Tuesday(1)(nc)
      Patootie Pie(nc)
      Mabel!Mabel!(nc)

1.Listed as "I Will Dig You,Jack".

Note:The above titles are from a Gene Norman "Just Jazz" concert (AFRS "Just Jazz" transcriptions No.1,7,17). These transcriptions also incl. the studio recordings (November 24,1947) of "I've Got A Way With Women" and "Put 'Em In A Box".
   See GENE NORMAN for additional titles from this concert.

Nat Cole(p,vcl),Oscar Moore(g),Johnny Miller(b).
                                    LA.June 25,1947
2085-5 Honeysuckle Rose   Capitol 10102 (CC59),F15728 (CCF59),EBF/H59,T592,
                                        CDP7.98299-2(CD),(F)T20193,1551.863,251.984-2
                                        (CD),(J)TOCJ5326(CD),Mosaic MR27-138,MD18-138
                                        (CD),Giants Of Jazz(I)LPTJ14,CD53005(CD),(E)
                                        CD0231(CD),Laserlight 15 718(CD),Delta 11044
                                        (CD),Starlite(E)1003(CD),Deja Vu(I)DVLP2048
2086-4 Thanks For You(nc)   Mosaic MR27-138,MD18-138(CD)
2093-2 It's Kind Of
       Lonesome Out Tonight(nc)   Capitol(Au)SCA076,Mosaic MR27-138,MD18-138(CD)
2097-1 For Once In Your Life(nc)   Mosaic MR27-138,MD18-138(CD)

Note:Masters 2093 and 2097 were used for Capitol transcriptions A71,B566.

Same.   Broadcast.LA.June 28,1947
       Unknown titles

Note:The unknown titles are from a Wildroot "King Cole Trio Time" radio program incl. The
     Starlighters(vcl-group) as guest artists. No information on poss. AFRS transcription.

Same.   LA.July 3,1947
2101-2 I Think You Get What I Mean(nc) Capitol 444,T2529,(E)EMS1142,(F)1566.251,Pickwick
                                        SPC3071,PTP2002,Mosaic MR27-138,MD18-138(CD)
2102-1 (Everyone Has Someone)
       But All I've Got Is Me(nc)   Capitol EAP3-514,H2/W514,(E)EMS1142,(F)T20193,
                                        1566.251,Giants Of Jazz(I)LPJT62,GOJCD53005
                                        (CD),(E)CD0231(CD),World Record Club(E)TP315
                                        Mosaic MR27-138,MD18-138(CD),Starlite(E)1003
                                        (CD)
2103-1 Now He Tells Me(nc)   Mosaic MR27-138,MD18-138(CD)

2104-2 I Can't Be Bothered(nc)   Capitol EAP4-514,H2/W514,Music For Pleasure(E)
                                        MFP5201,Mosaic MR27-138,MD18-138(CD),Official
                                        (D)3026,83026(CD)

Same.   Broadcast.LA.July 5,1947
       Straighten Up And Fly Right(nc)
       Naughty Angeline(nc)   Vintage Jazz Classics VJC1011(CD)
       Ask Anyone Who Knows(nc)   -
       Bloop Bleep(1)(wh)   -
       You're The Cream In My Coffee(nc)
       Aunt Hetty(1)(nc,wh)   Vintage Jazz Classics VJC1011(CD)
       I Know That You Know

-1.Add Woody Herman(cl,vcl) - guest artist.

All titles on VJC1011 (CD) also on Milan(F)CH335 (CD).
Note:The above titles are from a Wildroot "King Cole Trio Time" radio program (AFRS "King
     Cole Trio" transcription No.8 - this transcription also incl. the studio recording of
     "I Want To Thank Your Folks" rec. December 18,1946). AFRS No.8 was reissued on an
     AFRS "Here's To Veterans" transcription.

Same.   Broadcast.San Francisco.July 12,1947
       Straighten Up And Fly Right(nc)
       I Believe(nc)
       On The Sunny Side
           Of The Street(nc)
       There's That Lonely
           Feeling Again(nc)
(session cont. next page).

(session cont. from previous page):
    When I Write My Song(1)(hj)
    Count Me Out(nc)
    Give Me Twenty
       Nickels For A Dollar(nc)
    Crazy Rhythm

-1.Add Herb Jeffries(vcl) - guest artist.

Note:The above titles are from a Wildroot "King Cole Trio Time" radio program (AFRS "King
    Cole Trio" transcription No.18).

Nat Cole(p,vcl),Oscar Moore(g),Johnny Miller(b).
                            Broadcast.Seattle.July 19,1947
    Straighten Up And Fly Right(nc)
    Oh,Kickeroonie(nc)
    Somebody Loves Me
    Just An Old Love Of Mine(nc)
    Honeysuckle Rose
    Sweet Lorraine(nc)

Note:The above titles are from a Wildroot "King Cole Trio Time" radio program (AFRS "King
    Cole Trio" transcription No.5); there were no guest artists for this show.

Same.   Broadcast.LA.July 26,1947
    Straighten Up And Fly Right(nc)
    My Heart Is A Hobo(nc)
    You're The Cream In My Coffee(nc)
    Love's Got Me In a Lazy Mood(nc)
    You're Not The Kind(1)(sv)
    Cecilia(nc)
    The Trouble With Me Is You(nc)

1.Add Sarah Vaughan(vcl) - guest artist.

Note:The above titles are from a Wildroot "King Cole Trio Time" radio program (AFRS "King
    Cole Trio" transcription No.6).

Same.   LA.August 6,1947
134-3 When I Take My Sugar To Tea(nc) Capitol 813,F813,T2529,DNFR7620,(E)LC6587,EMS1142,
                                    SM131,(F)439,1566.251,Oxford(I)OX3020(?),
                                    Joker(I)SM4050,Music For Pleasure(E)MFP50177,
                                    Jazz Club(F)2M.056-64866,Delta(G)20808,11044
                                    (CD),Kat W. Prod. NC1002,Mosaic MR27-138,
                                    MD18-138(CD),Krém(Hu)SLPXL17780,Laserlight
                                    15 718(CD),Rhino E2.71009(CD)
135-1 Rhumba Azul   Capitol 10103 (CC59),F15730 (CCF59),EBF/H59,T592,
                                    M11803,CDP7.98299-2(CD),(F)307,1551.863,
                                    251.683-1,251.984-2(CD),(J)TOJC5326,DejaVu(I)
                                    DVLP2048,Giants Of Jazz(I)LPJT14,GOJCD53005
                                    (CD),(E)CD0231(CD),Delta 11044(CD),Mosaic
                                    MR27-138,MD18-138(CD),Laserlight 15 718(CD),
                                    Starlite(E)1003(CD)
136-2 What'll I Do(nc)   Capitol 15019,EAP1-357,EBF/H/T357,SN16162,
                                    CDP7.46736-2(CD),(E)E-ST23480,(G)K40581,
                                    Mosaic MR27-138,MD18-138(CD)
137-3 I Never Had A Chance(nc)   Mosaic MR27-138,MD18-138(CD)

Note:Master 2137 was used for Capitol transcription B392.

Nat Cole(p,vcl),Oscar Moore(g),Johnny Miller(b).

LA.August 7,1947

2138-4 This Is My Night To Dream(nc)   Capitol 10103 (CC59),1669,F1669,F15730 (CCF59),
EBF/H/T59,T591,(E)LC6594,(F)307,1551.863,
251.684-1,251.984-2(CD),(G)LCA59,(Au)ENC9082,
(J)TOCJ5326(CD),Mosaic MR27-138,MD18-138(CD),
Joker(I)SM4054

2139-3 Makin' Whoopee(nc)   Capitol 10101 (CC59),1669,F1669,F15728 (CCF59),
EBF/H59,T591,N16261,CDP7.93252-2(CD),(E)
LC6569,(F)1551.863,T20193,(G)LCA59,(Au)SCA076
ENC9082,Encore(E)ENC102,Joker(I)SM4051,Star-
line(E)SRS5039,Mosaic MR27-138,MD18-138(CD)

2140   Laguna Mood   rejected

2141-1 There,I've Said It Again(nc)   Capitol EAP1-514,H1/W514,ST310,(F)F3,(Arg)353091,
World Record Club(E)TP315,Mosaic MR27-138,
MD18-138(CD),Kat Wisker Prod. NC1002,Official
(D)3026,83026(CD),Music For Pleasure(E)5201

Note:Issues on ST310 (and equiv.) were edited into stereo versions with new rhythm section
and orchestra overdubbed (1969).

Same.   LA.August 8,1947

2142-3 I'll String Along With You(nc)   Capitol 10102 (CC59),F15729 (CCF59),EBF/H59,T591,
ST310,(E)LC6594,SRS5039,(F)1551.863,251.984-2
(CD),(G)LCA59,(J)TOCJ5326,(Au)ENC9082,SCA076,
Mosaic MR27-138,MD18-138(CD),Encore(E)ENC102
Starline(E)SRS5039

2143-5 Oh,Kickeroonie(nc)   Mosaic MR27-138,MD18-138(CD)

2144-3 (It's Easy To See) The
    Trouble With Me Is You(nc)   Capitol 57-680,F680,(E)CL13415,(F)333,World Rec.
Club(E)TP202,Mosaic MR27-138,MD18-138(CD),
Official(D)3026,83026(CD)

2145-1 Too Marvelous For Words(nc)   Capitol 10101 (CC59),F15729 (CCF59),EBF/H59,T591,
N16260,(E)LC6587,(F)T20097,1551.863,251.684-
(G)LCA59,(J)TOCJ5326(CD),(Au)ENC9082,SCA076,
Jazz Club(F)2M.056-64866,Music For Pleasure
(E)MFP50177,Bella Musica(G)LP3004,Delta(G)
20808,Joker(I)SM4053,Mosaic MR27-138,MD18-13
(CD),Krém(Hu)SLPXL17780,Delta 11044(CD),Lase
light 15 718(CD)

Note:Issues on ST310 (and equiv.) were edited into stereo versions with new rhythm sectio
and orchestra overdubbed (1969).

Same.   Broadcast.LA.August 9,1947

    Straighten Up And Fly Right(nc)
    Cecilia(nc)
    Crazy Rhythm
    Count Me Out(nc)
    I Surrender Dear(1)
    Unknown instrumental
    That's What(nc)

-1.Add Red Norvo(vbs) - guest artist.

Note:The above titles are from a Wildroot "King Cole Trio Time" radio program (AFRS "King
Cole Trio" transcription No.7).

Nat Cole(p,vcl),Oscar Moore(g),Johnny Miller(b).
                                    LA.August 13,1947
2147-1 Three Little Words   Capitol 10190 (CC135),54-530 (CCF156),EBF/L/H156,
                                       54-530,(E)CL13391,(G)LCA156,Regal(E)REG1019
2153-3 Moonlight In Vermont   Capitol EBF/L/H156,T2311,N16261,CDP7.98299-2(CD),
                                       (E)LC6593,(F)1551.863,(G)K83950,LCA156
2154-1 Poor Butterfly   Capitol EBF/L/H156,(E)LC6593,(G)LCA156
2155-2 How High The Moon   Capitol 10191 (CC135),54-531 (CCF156),EBF/L/H156,
                                       CDP7.98299-2(CD),(E)CL13204,(F)449,(G)80153,
                                       LCA156
2156-1 I'll Never Be The Same   Capitol 10190 (CC135),54-530 (CCF156),EBF/L/H156,
                                       T2311,N16260,CDP7.98299-2(CD),(E)LC6593,(F)
                                       1551.863,251.984-2(CD),(G)LCA156,K83950
2157-1 These Foolish Things   Capitol 10189 (CC135),54-529 (CCF156),EBF/L/H156,
                                       T2311,CDP7.98299-2(CD),(E)LC6593,EMS1142,(F)
                                       T20193,1566.251,(G)LCA156,K83950
2158-3 Cole Capers   Capitol 10189 (CC135),54-529 (CCF156),EBF/L/H156,
                                       (F)T20193,(G)LCA156,(J)CR8810,Echo EJCD08(CD)
2159-1 Blues In My Shower   Capitol 10191 (CC135),54-531 (CCF156),EBF/L/H156,
                                       (G)LCA156,Smithsonian P621010

All titles also on Mosaic MR27-138,MD18-138 (CD).
Note:All titles - except master 2155 - were used for Capitol transcriptions B393,B394.
     Masterno. 2148-2152 are not Cole items.

Nat Cole(p,celeste,vcl),Oscar Moore(g),Johnny Miller(b).
                                    LA.August 15,1947
2163-3 I Wanna' Be A
          Friend Of Yours(nc)   Capitol H3070
2164-3 Ke Mo Ky Mo(nc)   Capitol 7-25009 (DC89),F32009 (CCF3070),H3070,(E)
                                       EMS1142,(F)T20193(G)LCA213
2165-3 Three Blind Mice(nc)   Capitol H3070

All titles also on Mosaic MR27-138,MD18-138 (CD).
Note:Master 2163 was used for Capitol transcriptions A71,B566.
     Master 2164 was retitled "Kee-Mo Ky-Mo" and the introduction removed - this version
     was assigned masterno. 3493 and issued on Capitol 15240,1613,F1613,EBF/L/H213,(E)
     CL13181,(F)1566.251,(Eu)T20193,(J)Z30.

Same; Cole plays (p,vcl).   Broadcast."The Bocage",LA.August 16,1947
     Straighten Up And Fly Right(nc)
     Midnight Masquerade(nc)
     I Miss You So(nc)
     He's A Real Gone Guy(1)(nl)
     I'm In The Mood For Love(nc)
     Naughty Angeline(nc)

-1.Add Nellie Lutcher(p,vcl) - guest artist.

Note:The above titles are from a Wildroot "King Cole Trio Time" radio program (AFRS "King
     Cole Trio" transcription No.22).

JOHNNY MERCER AND THE KING COLE TRIO:
Nat Cole(p,vcl),Oscar Moore(g),Johnny Miller(b),Johnny Mercer(vcl).
                                    LA.August 20,1947
2184-3 Save The Bones
          For Henry Jones(nc,jm)   Capitol 15000,(E)CL13051,Music For Pleasure(E)
                                       MFP1432,MFP5198,Kat Wisker Prod. NC1002,
                                       Official(D)12003,812003(CD)
2185-3 My Baby Likes To Be-Bop(nc,jm) Capitol 15026
2186-2 Harmony(nc,jm)   Capitol 15000,Official(D)12003,812003(CD)
(session cont. next page).

(session cont. from previous page):
2187-5 You Can't Make
        Money Dreamin'(nc,jm)   Capitol 15026,(E)CL13051

All titles also on Capitol CDP7.96693-2 (CD),Mosaic MR27-138,MD18-138 (CD).

THE KING COLE TRIO WITH FRANK DEVOL'S ORCHESTRA:
Nat Cole(p,vcl),Oscar Moore(g),Johny Miller(b),unknown orchestra,Frank De Vol(arr,cond).
                                     LA.August 22,1947
2172-3 There's A Train
        Out For Dreamland(1)(nc)   Capitol 7-25011 (DC89),F32008 (CCF3070),H3070,(E)
                                   CL13180,Mosaic MR27-138,MD18-138(CD)

2191-2 (Go To Sleep) My
        Sleepy Head(1)(nc)   Capitol 7-25010 (DC89),F32007 (CCF3070),H3070,
                                   Mosaic MR27-138,MD18-138(CD)

2192   Wiegenlied
        (Brahms' Lullaby)(4)(nc)   Capitol CDP7.94685-2(CD),Official(D)12003,812003
                                   (CD)

2193-1 Nature Boy(2)(nc)   Capitol 15054,1663,F1663,F15509 (CCF213),EBF/H213,
                                 H6068(?),DF505,SN16033,S/W1926,CDP7.93590-2
                               (CD),(E)CL13010,CL13028,T20100,(F)395,(G)
                               LCA213,1C.056-85615,Pickwick(E)PTP2058,Mosaic
                               MR27-138,MD18-138(CD),Kat Wisker Prod. NC1002

2197-2 Wildroot Charlie(3)(nc)   Mosaic MR27-138,MD18-138(CD)

-1.Add Buddy Cole(celeste).
-2.Buddy Cole(p) replaces Nat Cole.
-3.Omit orchestra.
-4.Omit trio.

THE KING COLE TRIO:
Nat Cole(p,vcl,Oscar Moore(g),Johnny Miller(b).
                          Broadcast."The Bocage",LA.August 23,1947
        Straighten Up And Fly Right(nc) Joyce LP1076
        Kate(nc)
        You're The Cream
           In My Coffee(nc)   Joyce LP1076
        Ain't Cha Ever Coming Back(nc) -
        Variations On
           "Artistry In Rhythm"(1)   -
        This Is My Night To Dream(nc) -
        An Apple Blossom Wedding(nc)   -
        I Know That You Know   -

-1.Stan Kenton(p) - guest artist - replaces Cole.

Note:The above titles are from a Wildroot "King Cole Trio Time" radio program (AFRS "King
    Cole Trio" transcription No.23).

Same.   LA.August 27,1947
2210-2 Nursery Rhymes(nc)   Capitol 7-25010 (DC89),F32007 (CCF3070),H3070,(E)
                                   CL13181
2211-3 Old MacDonald Had A Farm(nc) Capitol 7-25009 (DC89),F32009 (CCF3070),H3070,(E)
                                   CL13180
2212-2 The Three Trees(nc)   Capitol 7-25011 (DC89),F32008 (CCF3070),H3070,(E)
                                   CL13180
2213-2 Laguna Mood   Capitol 15201,(F)355

All titles also on Mosaic MR27-138,MD18-138 (CD).
Note:Sound effects added on first 3 titles.
    Master 2213 was used for Capitol transcription B394.

Nat Cole(p,vcl,Oscar Moore(g),Johnny Miller(b).
                                    LA.August 28,1947
2220-3 I'm A Little Ashamed(nc)   Mosaic MR27-138,MD18-138(CD)
2221-3 Now He Tells Me(nc)   Capitol 15011,Mosaic MR27-138,MD18-138(CD)
2222-2 That's A Natural Fact(nc)   Capitol 15320,(E)CL13077,Pickwick SPC3046,Mosaic
                                        MR27-138,MD18-138(CD)

Same.   LA.August 29,1947
2226-4 Lament In Chords   Mosaic MR27-138,MD18-138(CD),Echo Jazz EJLP18,
                                        EJCD18(CD)

2227-3 You've Got Another
          Heart On Your Hands(nc)   Mosaic MR27-138,MD18-138(CD)
2228-2 Baby,I Need You(nc)   -   -
2229-3 Those Things Money Can't Buy(nc) Capitol 15011,Mosaic MR27-138,MD18-138(CD)

Note:Master 2226 was used for Capitol transcription B392.
     The version of "Route 66" on Capitol(Au)SCA076 was erroneously credited to this
     session - the correct rec.date is March 23,1961.

Same.   Broadcast.LA.August 30,1947
      Straighten Up And Fly Right(nc)
      Naughty Angeline(nc)
      For Sentimental Reasons(nc)
      I Miss You So(nc)
      Save The Bones For
         Henry Jones(1)(nc,jm)
      I Know That You Know

-1.Add Johnny Mercer(vcl) - guest artist.

Note:The above titles are from a Wildroot "King Cole Trio Time" radio program (AFRS "King
     Cole Trio" transcription No.19 - this transcription also incl. "Aunt Hetty" from the
     July 5,1947 show plus a closing "After You've Gone" from an unknown source).

Same.   Broadcast.McCormack General Hospital,Pasadena,California.c. August/September 1947
         I Apologize(nc)   Biac(B)BRAD10528
         I'm In The Mood For Love(nc)   -
         Somebody Loves Me   -
         I Found A New Baby   -

Note:The above titles are from AFRS "Jubilee" transcription No.256.

Same.   Broadcast.Salt Lake City,Utah.September 6,1947
         Unknown titles

Note:The unknown titles are from a Wildroot "King Cole Trio Time" radio program; there
     were no guest artists for this show. No information on poss. AFRS transcription.

Same.   Broadcast.Louisville,Kentucky.September 13,1947
         Unknown titles

Note:The unknown titles are from a Wildroot "King Cole Trio Time" radio program; there
     were no guest artists for this show. No information on poss. AFRS transcription.

Same.   Broadcast.Davenport,Iowa.September 20,1947
      Kate(nc)
      Wildroot Cream Oil Charlie(nc)
      Sweet Lorraine(nc)
      Sweet Georgia Brown
      Wildroot Cream
         Oil Charlie (encore)(nc)
(session cont. next page).

(session cont. from previous page):
    Tangerine(nc)
    Naughty Angeline(nc)
    Straighten Up And
      Fly Right(nc,trio-vcl)

Note:The above titles are from a Wildroot "King Cole Trio Time" radio program; there were
    no guest artists for this show. No information on poss. AFRS transcription.

Nat Cole(p,vcl,Oscar Moore(g),Johnny Miller(b).
                                    Broadcast.Cincinnati,Ohio.October 4,1947
    Straighten Up And Fly Right(nc)
    Give Me Twenty
      Nickels For A Dollar(nc)
    I Can't Believe It
      Was All Make-Believe(nc)
    I Miss You So(nc)
    I Found A New Baby
    Count Me Out(nc)
    For Once In Your Life(nc)
    The Trouble With Me Is You(nc)

Note:The above titles are from a Wildroot "King Cole Trio Time" radio program (AFRS "King
    Cole Trio" transcription No.24); there were no guest artists for this show.

Same.   Broadcast.Detroit.October 11,1947
    Unknown titles

Note:The unknown titles are from a Wildroot "King Cole Trio Time" radio program (unknown
    guest artists). No information on poss. AFRS transcription.

THE KING COLE TRIO:
Nat Cole(p,vcl),Irving Ashby(g),Johnny Miller(b).
                                     Broadcast.NYC.October 18,1947
    Unknown titles

Note:The unknown titles are from a Wildroot "King Cole Trio Time" radio program (unknown
    guest artists). No information on poss. AFRS transcription.

Same.   Broadcast.NYC.October 25,1947
    Unknown titles

Note:The unknown titles are from a Wildroot "King Cole Trio Time" radio program incl. Nel-
    lie Lutcher(vcl) as guest artist. No information on poss. AFRS transcription.

Same.	NYC.October 28,1947
1749-5 The Love Nest(nc)	Capitol EAP3-514,H2/W514,(E)EMS1142,T20193,(F)
	1566.251,Music For Pleasure(E)MFP5201,World
	Record Club(E)TP315
1950-3 Dream A Little Dream Of Me(nc)	Capitol EAP1-514,H1/W514,(E)EMS1142,(F)1566.251,
	T20193,Music For Pleasure(E)MFP5201,World
	Record Club(E)TP315,Joker(I)SM4054
1951-3 Then I'll Be Tired Of You(nc)	Capitol ST310

All titles also on Mosaic MR27-138,MD18-138 (CD).
Note:Masters 1950 and 1951 were used for Capitol transcriptions B391,B392.
    Issues on ST310 (and equiv.) were edited into stereo versions with new rhythm section
    and orchestra overdubbed (1969).

Nat Cole(p,vcl),Irving Ashby(g),Johnny Miller(b).
                                    Broadcast.NYC.November 1,1947

      Straighten Up And Fly Right(nc)
      Kate(nc)
      Ballerina(nc)
      And Mimi(1)(mt)
      This Is My Night To Dream(nc)
      Save The Bones For
         Henry Jones(1)(nc,mt)

-1.Add Mel Torme(vcl) - guest artist.

Note:The above titles are from a Wildroot "King Cole Trio Time" radio program (AFRS "King
    Cole Trio" transcription No.27).

	NYC.November 3,1947
Same.	
1952-6 Money Is Honey(nc)	Mosaic MR27-138,MD18-138(CD)
1953-1 Little Girl(nc)	Capitol 15165,1034,F1034,EBF/H177,T591,N16260,
	CDP7.93252-2(CD),(E)CL13008,(F)441,T20097,
	1551.863,251.683-2(CD),251.984-2(CD),(J)
	TOCJ5326(CD),(Au)ENC9082,Mosaic MR27-138,
	MD18-138(CD),Joker(I)SM4052,Echo Jazz EJLP18,
	EJCD18(CD)
1954-2 Who's Telling You Lies(nc)	Mosaic MR27-138,MD18-138(CD)
1955-3 No Moon At All(nc)	Capitol 15358,5-1673,F1673,(E)E-ST23480,(Au)
	SCA076,Mosaic MR27-138,MD18-138(CD)

Note:Master 1953 was used for Capitol transcription B391.

	NYC.November 4,1947
Same.	
1956-5 I Feel So Smoochie(nc)	Capitol 15019,(E)CL13008,E-ST23480,Mosaic
	MR27-138,MD18-138(CD)
1957-1 A Boy From Texas - A	
Girl From Tennessee(nc)	Capitol 15085,(E)CL13025,(Au)SCA076,Mosaic
	MR27-138,MD18-138(CD)
1958-2 When You Walked Out	
With Shoes On(nc)	Mosaic MR27-138,MD18-138(CD)
1959-2 That's The Kind Of	
Girl I Dream Of(nc)	- -

Same.	NYC.November 5,1947
1960-3 It's The	
Sentimental Thing To Do(nc)	Capitol 15080,Telefunken(D)A18004,Mosaic MR27-138,
	MD18-138(CD)
1961-2 I've Only Myself To Blame(nc)	Capitol 15036,Mosaic MR27-138,MD18-138(CD)
1962-2 It's Like Taking	
Candy From A Baby(nc)	Mosaic MR27-138,MD18-138(CD)
1963-2 You've Changed(nc)	- -

Same.	NYC.November 6,1947
1964-4 The Geek	Capitol 15036,Franklin Mint 49,Mosaic MR27-138,
	MD18-138(CD)
1965-3 Confess(nc)	Mosaic MR27-138,MD18-138(CD),Echo Jazz EJLP18,
	EJCD18(CD)
1966-1 If I Had You(nc)	Capitol 813,F813,EBF/H59,EBF/H177,T591,N16261,
	ST310,(E)CL13279,E-ST23480,(F)1551.863,
	251.684-1,251.984-2(CD),(G)LCA59,(J)TOCJ5326
	(CD),Music For Pleasure(E)MFP50177,Jazz Club
	(F)2M.056-64866,Mosaic MR27-138,MD18-138(CD),
	Oxford(I)OX3020,Krém(Hu)SLPXL17780,Jazzline
	JL20808

(session cont. next page).

(session cont. from previous page).
Note:Master 1965 was used for Capitol transcription B391.
    Issues on ST310 (and equiv.) were edited into stereo versions with new rhythm section and orchestra overdubbed (1969).

Nat Cole(p,vcl),Irving Ashby(g),Johnny Miller(b).

NYC.November 7,1947

1967-7	Flo And Joe(nc)	Capitol 15320,Mosaic MR27-138,MD18-138(CD),Echo Jazz EJLP18,EJCD18(CD)
1968-2	If You Stub Your Toe On The Moon(nc)	Capitol 15418,54-584 (F584),(E)CL13077,(F)309, Mosaic MR27-138,MD18-138(CD)
1969-2	I'm Gonna Spank My Heart(nc)	Mosaic MR27-138,MD18-138(CD)
1970-2	I See By The Papers(nc)	- -
1971-1	Return Trip	Capitol F15843 (CCF323),H323,(E)LC6559,(G)LCA323, Mosaic MR27-138,MD18-138(CD)
1995-3	A Woman Always Understands(nc)	Capitol 15224,ST310,(E)CL13044,(F)308,Mosaic MR27-138,MD18-138(CD)

Note:Master 1967 was used for Capitol transcription B392.
    Issues on ST310 (and equiv.) were edited into stereo versions with new rhythm section and orchestra overdubbed (1969).

Same.   Broadcast.NYC.November 8,1947
    Straighten Up And Fly Right(nc)
    Gonna' Get A Girl(nc)
    There's That
        Lonely Feeling Again(nc)
    Those Things Money Can't Buy(nc)
    I Still Get Jealous(1)(gm)
    Kate(nc)
    Naughty Angeline(nc)

-1.Add Gordon MacRae(vcl) - guest artist.

Note:The above titles are from a Wildroot "King Cole Trio Time" radio program (AFRS "King Cole Trio" transcription No.28).

Same.   Broadcast.NYC.November 15,1947
    Straighten Up And Fly Right(nc)
    Ballerina(nc)
    For Once In Your Life(nc)
    How Soon(nc)
    I Wish I Didn't
        Love You So(1)(pm)
    I Know That You Know
    Oh,Kickeroonie(nc)
    After You've Gone(nc(?))

-1.Add Peggy Mann(vcl) - guest artist.

Note:The above titles are from a Wildroot "King Cole Trio Time" radio program (AFRS "King Cole Trio" transcription No.26).

Same.   NYC.November 24,1947

2529-6	Put 'Em In A Box, Tie 'Em With A Ribbon(nc)	Capitol 15080,(E)CL13044,(E)E-ST23480,Telefunken (D)A18004,Mosaic MR27-138,MD18-138(CD)
2530-2	Blue And Sentimental(nc)	Mosaic MR27-138,MD18-138(CD)
2531-4	I've Got A Way With Women(nc)	Capitol 15110,EBF/H59,(E)CL13422,EMS1142,(F) T20193,1566.251,Mosaic MR27-138,MD18-138(CD)
2532-2	My Fair Lady(nc)	Capitol 15085,Mosaic MR27-138,MD18-138(CD)

Nat Cole(p,vcl),Irving Ashby(g),Johnny Miller(b).
NYC.November 29,1947
2544-3 I Wish I Had The Blues Again(nc) Mosaic MR27-138,MD18-138(CD)
2545-4 Didn't I Tell You So(nc)   -   -
2546-5 Lost April(nc)   -   -

Note:Master 2546 was used for Capitol transcriptions B391,B392.

Same.   Broadcast.NYC.November 29,1947
        Straighten Up And Fly Right(nc)
        Naughty Angeline(nc)
        I'm In The Mood For Love(nc)
        Let's Be Sweethearts Again(nc)
        You Made Me Love You(1)(ch)
        That's What(nc)
        The Trouble With Me Is You(nc)

-1.Add Connie Haines(vcl) - guest artist.

Note:The above titles are from a Wildroot "King Cole Trio Time" radio program (AFRS "King
     Cole Trio" transcription No.25).

Same.   Broadcast.Cincinnati.December 6,1947
        Straighten Up And Fly Right(nc) Vintage Jazz Classics VJC1011(CD)
        When I Take My Sugar To Tea(nc)   -
        Let's Be Sweethearts Again(nc)   -
        Those Things Money Can't Buy(nc)   -
        Variations On "Mood Indigo"(1)   -
        For Once In Your Life(nc)   -
        You're The Cream In My Coffee(nc)   -
        I Know That You Know(incompl.)   -

-1.Duke Ellington(p-solo) - guest artist.

All titles also on Milan(F)CH335 (CD).
Note:The above titles are from a Wildroot "King Cole Trio Time" radio program (AFRS "King
     Cole Trio" transcription No.29).

Same.   Broadcast.Cincinnati.December 13,1947
        Straighten Up And Fly Right(nc)
        Ballerina(nc)
        Ask Anyone Who Knows(nc)
        And Mimi(nc)
        Rhumba Azul
        Naughty Angeline(nc)
        Save The Bones
           For Henry Jones(nc)

Note:The above titles are from a Wildroot "King Cole Trio Time" radio program (AFRS "King
     Cole Trio" transcription No.30); there were no guest artists for this show.

Same.   NYC.December 20,1947
2928-3 Lost April(1)(nc)   Capitol 15054,1035,1627,F1035,F1627,EAP2-357,
                                           EBF/H/T/SM357,DT357,SN16162,CDP7.46736-2(CD),
                                           (E)CL13025,(F)395,(Du)1A.146-1822693,(Sw)
                                           CL200,(G)C15054,K40581,Mosaic MR27-138,
                                           MD18-138(CD),Kat Wisker Prod. NC1002
2929-5 Lillette(nc)   Capitol 15224,(E)CL13044,(F)308,1551863,(G)C80134
                                           (Sd)C9011,Pickwick(E)SPC3046,Mosaic MR27-138,
                                           MD18-138(CD),Official(D)83026(CD)

(session cont. next page).

```
(session cont. from previous page):
2930-2 Monday Again(nc)               Mosaic MR27-138,MD18-138(CD)
2931-3 Lulubelle(nc)                  Capitol EAP2-514,H1/W514,(E)LCT6003,(F)CAP3,F3,
                                        T20097,Mosaic MR27-138,MD18-138(CD),World Rec
                                        Club(E)TP315
2932-1 It's So Hard To Laugh
       (It's So Easy To Cry)(nc)      Mosaic MR27-138,MD18-138(CD)
```

-1.Add strings,Carlyle Hall(arr,cond).

Nat Cole(p,vcl),Irving Ashby(g),Johnny Miller(b).
                                      Broadcast.NYC.December 20,1947
       Unknown titles

Note:The unknown titles are from a Wildroot "King Cole Trio Time" radio program incl. the
    Stan Kenton Orchestra and June Christy(vcl) as guest artists. No information on poss.
    AFRS transcription.

Same.   Broadcast.Buffalo,N.Y.December 27,1947
       Unknown titles

Note:The unknown titles are from a Wildroot "King Cole Trio Time" radio program; there
    were no guest artists for this show. No information on poss. AFRS transcription.

Same.   LA.Prob. late 1947
       Oh,Kickeroonie(nc)   JCVC106
       Now He Tells Me(nc)
       Breezy And The Bass

Note:The above titles are from the "Killer Diller" feature film soundtrack. The dating is
    estimated: date is assumed to be post-October since Irving Ashby is seen playing (g).

Same.   Broadcast.Hartford,Conn.January 3,1948
       Straighten Up And Fly Right(nc)
       Almost Like Being In Love(nc)
       At The Candlelight Cafe(nc)
       What'll I Do(nc)
       You've Changed(1)(re)
       Rhumba Azul
       The Best Things
          In Life Are Free(nc)

-1.Add Ray Eberle(vcl) - guest artist.

Note:The above titles are from a Wildroot "King Cole Trio Time" radio program (AFRS "King
    Cole Trio" transcription No.34).

Same.   Broadcast.Washington,D.C.January 10,1948
       Straighten Up And Fly Right(nc)
       Ballerina(nc)
       The Trouble With Me Is You(nc)
       At The Candlelight Cafe(nc)
       Golden Earrings(1)(jd)
       Rhumba Azul
       Return Trip

-1.Add Johnny Desmond(vcl) - guest artist.

Note:The above titles are from a Wildroot "King Cole Trio Time" radio program (AFRS "King
    Cole Trio" transcription No.32).

Nat Cole(p,vcl),Irving Ashby(g),Johnny Miller(b).
                                    Broadcast.NYC.January 17,1948
        Straighten Up And Fly Right(nc)
        I'll Dance At Your Wedding(nc)
        You're The Cream In My Coffee(nc)
        What'll I Do(nc)
        When I Write My Song(1)(hj)
        I Found A New Baby
        I Feel So Smoochie(nc)

1.Add Herb Jeffries(vcl) - guest artist.

Note:The above titles are from a Wildroot "King Cole Trio Time" radio program (AFRS "King
    Cole Trio" transcription No.31).

Same.   Broadcast.Cleveland.January 24,1948
        Straighten Up And Fly Right(nc)
        I Feel So Smoochie(nc)
        But Beautiful(nc)
        Pianissimo(nc)
        Your Red Wagon(nc)
        This Is My Night To Dream(nc)
        A-N-G-E-L Spells Mary(nc)
        Too Marvelous For Words(nc)
        The Geek

Note:The above titles are from a Wildroot "King Cole Trio Time" radio program (AFRS "King
    Cole Trio" transcription No.39); there were no guest artists for this show.

Same.   Broadcast.Unknown location/date
        Straighten Up And Fly Right(nc)
        This Is My Night To Dream(nc)
        I'm In The Mood For Love(nc)
        Near You(nc)
        Rhumba Azul
        You're Driving Me Crazy(1)(mt)
        I'm Thru With Love(nc)
        Crazy Rhythm

1.Add Mel Torme(vcl) - guest artist.

Note:The above titles are from a Wildroot "King Cole Trio Time" radio program (AFRS "King
    Cole Trio" transcription No.40).

Same.   Broadcast.Cleveland,Ohio.January 28,1948
        Almost Like Being In Love(nc)   Vintage Jazz Classics VJC1044(CD)
        Those Things Money Can't Buy(nc)   -

Note:Both titles are from Treasury Department "Guest Star" transcription No.52.

Same.   Broadcast.Philadelphia.January 31,1948
        Straighten Up And Fly Right(nc)
        Almost Like Being In Love(nc)
        I Feel So Smoochie(nc)
        But Beautiful(nc)
        Gonna Get A Girl(nc)
        Rhumba Azul
        Beg Your Pardon(nc)
        Wildroot Bebop(1)
        Rhumba Azul (encore)
(Session cont. next page).

(session cont. from previous page):
-1."Wildroot Bop" is a re-titling of "The Geek".

Note:The above titles are from a Wildroot "King Cole Trio Time" radio program (AFRS "King
    Cole Trio" transcription No.38); there were no guest artists for this show.

Nat Cole(p,vcl),Irving Ashby(g),Johnny Miller(b).
                                        Broadcast.Baltimore.February 7,1948
        Straighten Up And Fly Right(nc)
        I'll Dance At Your Wedding(nc)
        When I Take My Sugar To Tea(nc)
        What'll I Do(nc)
        My Blue Heaven(1)(drb)
        You're The Cream In My Coffee(nc)
        Let's Be Sweethearts Again(nc)
        Too Marvelous For Words(nc)

-1.Add The Delta Rhythm Boys(vcl-group) - guest artists.

Note:The above titles are from a Wildroot "King Cole Trio Time" radio program (AFRS "King
    Cole Trio" transcription No.35).

Same.   Broadcast.Fort Wayne,Indiana.February 14,194▌
        Straighten Up And Fly Right(nc)
        Beg Your Pardon(nc)
        But Beatiful(nc)
        Wildroot Boogie

Note:The above titles are from a Wildroot "King Cole Trio Time" radio program; there were
    no guest artists for this show. No information on poss. AFRS transcription.

Same.   Broadcast.Louisville,Kentucky.February 21,194▌
        Unknown titles

Note:The unknown titles are from a Wildroot "King Cole Trio Time" radio program; there
    were no guest artists for this show). No information on poss. AFRS transcription.

Same.   Broadcast.Chicago.February 28,1948
        Straighten Up And Fly Right(nc)
        My Baby Likes To Bebop(nc)
        Tea For Two
        Fool That I Am(nc)
        My Cousin Louella(nc)
        I'll Dance At Your Wedding(nc)
        What Is This Thing Called Love(1)
        Ballerina(nc)

-1.Add Alice Hall(acc) - guest artist.

Note:The above titles are from a Wildroot "King Cole Trio Time" radio program (AFRS "King
    Cole Trio" transcription No.36).

Same.   Broadcast.Chicago.March 6,1948
        Straighten Up And Fly Right(nc)   Vintage Jazz Classics VJC1011(CD)
        Sunday(nc)   -
        Laroo,Laroo,Lily Bolero(nc)
        I May Be Wrong(nc)
        Wildroot Cream Oil Charlie(nc)   Vintage Jazz Classics VJC1011(CD)
        What'll I Do(nc)   -
        I've Got A
            Feeling I'm Falling(nc)   -
(session cont. next page).

(session cont. from previous page):
<pre>
     Peg O' My Heart(1)(cd)   Vintage Jazz Classics VJC1011(CD)
     You're The Cream In My Coffee(nc)   -
     Straighten Up And Fly Right(nc)   -
</pre>

-1.Add Clark Dennis(vcl) - guest artist.

ll titles on VJC1011 (CD) also on Milan(F)CH335 (CD).
ote:The above titles are from a Wildroot "King Cole Trio Time" radio program (AFRS "King
     Cole Trio" transcription No.41 - this transcription also incl. "Body And Soul" (with
     an unknown (ts) added) dubbed in from another source.

Nat Cole(p,vcl),Irving Ashby(g),Johnny Miller(b).
<pre>
                                     Broadcast.Chicago.March 13,1948
     Straighten Up And Fly Right(nc) Vintage Jazz Classics VJC1011(CD)
     Your Red Wagon(nc)   -
     Ballerina(nc)
     I've Only Myself To Blame(nc)   Vintage Jazz Classics VJC1011(CD)
     The Dickey Bird Song(nc)   -
     Almost Like Being In Love(nc)
     Beg Your Pardon(1)(ds)   Vintage Jazz Classics VJC1011(CD)
     The Geek   -
     Straighten Up And Fly Right(nc)   -
</pre>

1.Add The Dinning Sisters(vcl-group) - guest artists.

ll titles on VJC1011 (CD) also on Milan(F)CH335 (CD).
ote:The above titles are from a Wildroot "King Cole Trio Time" radio program (AFRS "King
     Cole Trio" transcription No.37).

same.
<pre>
                                     Broadcast.Chicago or NYC.March 20,1948
     Straighten Up And Fly Right(nc)
     It's The Sentimental
          Thing To Do(nc)
     Laroo,Laroo,Lily Bolero(nc)
</pre>

ote:The above titles are from a Wildroot "King Cole Trio Time" radio program; there were
     no guest artists for this show). No information on poss. AFRS transcription.

same.
<pre>
                                     Broadcast.NYC.March 27,1948
     Unknown titles
</pre>

ote:The unknown titles are from a Wildroot "King Cole Trio Time" radio program incl. Tony
     Pastor as guest artist. No information on poss. AFRS transcription.
     The April 3,1948 Wildroot broadcast did not include the King Cole Trio.

same.
<pre>
                                     Broadcast.Chicago.April 10,1948
     Straighten Up And Fly Right(nc)
     Too Marvelous For Words(nc)
     Wildroot Cream Oil Charlie(nc)
     I've Only Myself To Blame(nc)
     My Fair Lady(nc)
     The Dickey Bird Song(nc)
     Nature Boy(1)(nc)
</pre>

1.Cole(vcl,p) acc. by frh,harp,strings,Frank De Vol(arr).

ote:The above titles are from the final Wildroot "King Cole Trio Time" radio program
     incl. an instrumental group of Chicago musicians. No information on poss. AFRS
     transcription.

THE KING COLE TRIO:
Nat Cole(p,vcl),Irving Ashby(g),prob. Joe Comfort(b).
                                        Broadcast.LA.September 30,1948
        Little Girl(nc)

Note:The above title is from an AFRS "Supper Club" transcription.

Same.   LA.c. October 1948
        The Trouble With Me Is You(nc)

Note:The above title is from the "Make Believe Ballroom" feature film soundtrack.

Nat Cole(p,vcl),Irving Ashby(g),Joe Comfort(b).
                                        NYC.December 21,1948
3808-2 Portrait Of Jenny(1)(nc)   Mosaic MR27-138,MD18-138(CD)
3809-4 It Only Happens Once(nc)   -   -
3810-1 My Mother Told Me(nc)   -   -
3811-4 Bang Bang Boogie(nc)   -   -

-1.Add woodwinds,strings,prob. Carlyle Hall(arr,cond).

Same.   NYC.January 14,1949
3381-3 Portrait Of Jenny(1)(nc)   Capitol 15387,1035,F1035,6179,EAP1-357,T948,
                                        EBF/H/T/SM357,DT357,SN16162,CDP7.46736-2(CD)
                                        (E)CL13096,E-ST21139,EMTV9,(F)350,(G)C80103,
                                        (Du)1A.146-1822693,(J)TOCP9069(CD),Starline
                                        (E)SRS5039,Mosaic MR27-138,MD18-138(CD),Kat
                                        Wisker Prod. NC1002
3382-1 Don't Cry,Cry Baby(nc)   Capitol 15418,54-584,F584,(F)309,(G)C80103,Mosaic
                                        MR27-138,MD18-138(CD),Pickwick(E)SPC3046
3383-3 An Old Piano Plays The Blues(nc) Capitol 15387,(F)350,(G)C80063,Mosaic MR27-138,
                                        MD18-138(CD)
3384-2 How Lonely Can You Get(nc)   Mosaic MR27-138,MD18-138(CD)

-1.Add strings,Carlyle Hall(arr,cond).

NAT KING COLE AND HIS TRIO:
Nat Cole(p,vcl),Irving Ashby(g),Joe Comfort(b),Jack Costanzo(bg).
                                        NYC.March 22,1949
3741-2 Laugh,Cool Clown   Capitol 57-643,F643 (CC139),F15554 (CCF177),
                                        EBF/H177,T592,CDP7.98299-2(CD),(F)251.683-1
3742-2D Bop-Kick   Capitol 57-641,F641 (CC139),F15555 (CCF177),T592
                                        EBF/H177,CDP7.98299-2(CD),(F)T20193,251.684
                                        Giants Of Jazz(I)LPJT14,GOJCD53005(CD),(E)
                                        CD0231(CD),Delta 11044(CD),Starlite(E)1003
                                        (CD),Laserlight 15 718(CD)
3743-1D For All We Know(no bg)(nc)   Capitol 57-643,1663,F643 (CC139),F15553 (CCF177)
                                        F1663,EBF/H177,T591,T2311,N16260,(E)LC6594,
                                        (G)K83950,(Au)ENC9082,Music For Pleasure(E)
                                        MFP1129,Oxford(I)OX3020,Krém(Hu)SLPXL17780,
                                        Delta(G)20808,Joker(I)SM4053,Delta 11044(CD
                                        Laserlight 15 718(CD)

All titles also on Capitol(F)1551.863,251.982-2,(J)TOCJ5326(CD),Mosaic MR27-138,MD18-138
(CD),Jazz Club(F)2M.056-64866.

Same.   NYC.March 29,1949
3750-3 Land Of Love(1)(nc)   Capitol 57-716,F716,(E)CL13187,Regal(E)REG1019
3751-3 Lush Life(1)(nc)   Capitol 57-606,1672,F606,F1672,EBF/L/H213,(E)
                                        CL13149,(F)677,(G)LCA213,Regal(E)REG1019,
                                        Music For Pleasure(E)MFP1049

(session cont. next page).

NAT "KING" COLE

session cont. from previous page):
```
752-3 Lillian(no bg)(2)(nc,akv)        Capitol 57-606,F606,(F)677
753-2 'Tis Autumn(no bg)(nc)           Capitol 57-642,F642 (CC139),F15553 (CFF177),
                                            EBF/H177,ST310,(E)LC6587,(F)T20097,Oxford(I)
                                            OX3020,Music For Pleas.(E)MFP50177,Jazz Club
                                            (F)2M.056-64866,Delta(G)20808,DK29037,11044
                                            (CD),Krém(Hu)SLPXL17780,Laserlight 15 718
                                            (CD)
754-3 Yes Sir,That's My Baby(nc)       Capitol 57-642,57-716,F642 (CC139),F716,F15552
                                            (CCF177),EBF/H177,(E)CL13384,(F)426,T20097,
                                            Kat Wisker Prod. NC1002
755-1 I Used To Love You (But
         It's All Over Now)(nc)        Capitol 57-641,F641 (CC139),F15552 (CCF177),
                                            EBF/H177,(E)EMS1142,(F)1566.251,T20193,
                                            1566.251,Delta(G)11086(CD),Jazzline JL20815,
                                            Laserlight 15 718(CD),15 915(CD)
```

1.Add Al Richman(frh),Sid Cooper(cl,fl),Mel Zelnick(dr),strings,Pete Rugolo(arr,cond).
2.Add Alyce King's Vokettes(vcl).

11 titles also on Mosaic MR27-138,MD18-138 (CD).
ote:Issues on ST310 (and equiv.) were edited into stereo versions with new rhythm section
    and orchestra overdubbed (1969).

t Cole(p,vcl),Irving Ashby(g),Joe Comfort(b),Jack Costanzo(bg).
```
                                       NYC.March 30,1949
56-5 Etymology(nc)                     Mosaic MR27-138,MD18-138(CD)
57-2 Peaches                           Capitol EAP4-514,H2/W514,CDP7.98299-2(CD),Giants
                                            Of Jazz(I)LPTJ62,GOJCD53005(CD),(E)CD0231(CD)
                                            Mosaic MR27-138,MD18-138(CD),Starlite(E)1003
                                            (CD),World Record Club(E)TP315
58-3 Last,But Not Least                Mosaic MR27-138,MD18-138(CD)
59-3 I Wake Up Screaming,
         Dreaming Of You(nc)                    -          -
```

me.   Broadcast."Bop City",NYC.May 7,1949
```
   (An) Old Piano
      Plays The Blues(nc)              Alto AL709
   Yes Sir, That's My Baby(nc)         Alto AL709,Kat Wisker Pr. NC1002,Remember(Eu)
                                            RMB75022(?)(CD),Classic Series PB55005(CD)
   Last,But Not Least                  Alto AL709,Remember(Eu)RMB75022(?)(CD)
   Don't Cry,Cry Baby(nc)                   -                -(?)         ,Classic
                                            Series PB55005(CD)
   (It's Only A) Paper Moon(nc)        Alto AL709,Classic Series PB55005(CD)
   Body And Soul                            - ,Remember(Eu)RMB75022(?)CD),Classic
                                            Series PB55005(CD)
   Cole's Bop Blues                    Alto AL709
   Nat Meets June(1)(jc,nc)                 -
```

.Add June Christy(vcl),Milt Jackson(vbs) - plus the Machito orchestra (heard on the
    out-chorus only).

titles also on Jazz Anthology(F)JA5175.
titles - except "An Old Piano Plays The Blues" and "Nat Meets June" - also on Topline
)TOP112,CD508 (CD).

ne.   NYC.May 20,1949
```
38-5 It Was So Good While
         It Lasted(no bg)(1)(nc)       Capitol 818,F818,(E)E-ST23480,Mosaic MR27-138,
                                            MD18-138(CD)
```

ssion cont. next page)

(session cont. next page):
3790-5 I Get Sentimental Over
        Nothing(no bg)(1)(nc,akv)   Capitol 57-705,F705,(E)CL13149,Music For Pleasure
                                       (E)MFP5201,Mosaic MR27-138,MD18-138(CD)
3791-3 Who Do You
        Know In Heaven(no bg)(nc)   Capitol 57-680,F680,(E)CL13187,(F)333,Mosaic
                                       MR27-138,MD18-138(CD),Regal(E)REG1019
3792-1 Your Voice(2)(nc,mc)   Capitol 57-705,F705,(E)CL13200,(F)426,Mosaic
                                       MR27-138,MD18-138(CD)
3793-2 A Little Yellow Ribbon(nc)   Mosaic MR27-138,MD18-138(CD)

-1.Add Alyce King's Vokettes(vcl).
-2.Add Maria Cole(vcl).

Note:One additional (non-jazz) title from this session is not included.

Nat Cole(p,vcl),Irving Ashby(g),Joe Comfort(b),Jack Costanzo(bg).
                                       LA.July 26,1949
4980   My Mother Told Me(no bg)(nc)   Capitol 57-70050,(E)E-ST23480,Mosaic MR27-138,
                                       MD18-138(CD)
4981   Exactly Like You(nc)   Capitol 57-70050,1036,F1036,DNFR7620,(E)LC6594,
                                       SM136,Music For Pleasure(E)MFP1129,Giants Of
                                       Jazz(I)LPTJ62,GOJCD53005(CD),CDO231(CD),
                                       Mosaic MR27-138,MD18-138(CD),Kat Wisker
                                       Prod.NC1002,Lotus(I)LOP14077
       Part Of Me(no bg)(nc)   Mosaic MR27-138,MD18-138(CD)
       What You Got In
         Those Eyes(no bg)(nc)   -   -
       Top Hat Bop   -   -
       Go Bongo   -   -
       Rhumba Blues   -   -
       Boulevard Of Broken Dreams(nc)   -   -

Note:The above titles were originally recorded for Capitol transcriptions No.B447,B448.

Johnny Miller(b) replaces Comfort.   Live.Shrine Auditorium,LA.July 29,1949
       Top Hat Bop
       Yes Sir,That's My Baby(nc)   Swing House(E)SWH12
       Tiny's Exercise   -
       Gee,Baby,Ain't
         I Good To You(nc)   -
       Body And Soul
       Flo And Joe(nc)   Swing House(E)SWH12
       Go Bongo   -
       That's What(nc)
       Blabber(nc)
       Lush Life
       Baby,I Need You(nc)   Swing House(E)SWH12
       Bop Kick   -
       How High The Moon(1)

-1.Only the introduction is played by the Cole group - the rest is played by the Woody
   Herman Orchestra.

All titles on SWH12 also on Dance Band Days DBD15,DBCD15 (CD).
Note:The above titles are from a Gene Norman "Just Jazz" concert (AFRS "Just Jazz" tran-
     scriptions No.75,76,79).
     Johnny Miller replaced Comfort for this concert only.

'AT KING COLE AND HIS TRIO WITH THE STARLIGHTERS:
at Cole(p,vcl),Irving Ashby(g),Joe Comfort(b),Jack Costanzo(bg),The Starlighters(vcl).
LA.August 2,1949

754-4 All I Want For Christmas
Is My Two Front Teeth(nc,ts)   Capitol 57/54-90036,2955,F2955,EAP1-9026,T9030,
CDP7.94685-2(CD),(E)CL13200

755-2 You Can't Lose A
Broken Heart(no bg)(nc,ts)   Capitol 57-749,F749,(E)CL13880
756-1 Bang Bang Boogie(nc)   Capitol 818,F818,(E)CL13370,(F)439

ll titles also on Mosaic MR27-138,MD18-138 (CD).

.nit The Starlighters.   LA.September 9,1949
976-1 (Here Is My Heart) Nalani(1)(nc) Capitol 57-749,F749
977-1 The Horse Told Me(2)(nc) Capitol 852,57-90063,F852,(E)CL13279
978-1 Don't Shove,I'm Leaving(nc) Capitol 852,F852,(E)CL13369
976-1 Calypso Blues(3)(nc)   Capitol 915,1627,F915,F1627,EAP1-852,(E)CL13384,
CL14709,(F)239,(Sw)200,Pickwick SPC3071,
PTP2002,Starline(E)SRS5010

1.Add unknown vcl-group.
2.Cole plays prepared-p;Ashby and Costanzo play rhythm effects.
3.Cole(vcl),Costanzo(bg) only.

ll titles also on Mosaic MR27-138,MD18-138 (CD).

)ODY HERMAN WITH NAT KING COLE AND HIS TRIO:
at Cole(p,vcl),Irving Ashby(g),Joe Comfort(b),Jack Costanzo(bg),Woody Herman(vcl).
NYC.November 7,1949
314-4 Mule Train(1)(nc,wh)   Capitol 57-787,F787,Kat Wisker Prod. NC1002
315-4 My Baby Just Cares For Me(nc,wh)   -   - ,Official(D)12003,812003(CD)

..Add Gene Orloff(vln).

•th titles also on Capitol CDP7.96693-2 (CD),(E)CL13229,Mosaic MR27-138,MD18-138 (CD),
usic For Pleasure(E)MFP1432,MFP5198.
•te:"Mule Train" issued on Capitol 57-787,F787,(E)CL13229 as by KING COLE AND HIS MULE-
SKINNERS.

•te:Post-1949 recordings are included here only when they are Trio performances, or feature jazz artists or Cole playing piano. Only a small number of post-1949 Cole recordings can be classified as jazz music - therefore the last part of this Cole section
does not always list all titles recorded at a session, and only selected sessions are
included.
Nat Cole disbanded the Trio (as a basic working unit) late in 1951.

.T KING COLE - NELLIE LUTCHER:
nie Royal(tp),Charlie Barnet(ts),Nat Cole(p,vcl),Irving Ashby(g),Joe Comfort(b),Earl
.de(dr),Nellie Lutcher(vcl).   LA.January 5,1950
66-3 For You,My Love(nc,nl)   Capitol 847,F847,(E)CL351,12CL351,Kat Wisker Prod.
NC1002,Music For Pleasure(E)MFP5198

71-4 Can I Come In
For A Second(nc,nl)   Capitol 847,F847

th titles also on Capitol CDP7.96693-2 (CD),(E)CL13275,Mosaic MR27-138,MD18-138 (CD),
ficial(D)12003,812003(CD).
te:Masters 5367-70 are not Cole recordings.

T KING COLE AND HIS TRIO:
t Cole(p,vcl),Irving Ashby(g),Joe Comfort(b).
LA.January 1950
ession cont. next page).

(session cont. from previous page):
     Almost Like Being In Love(nc)   Swing House(E)SWH12,Recordings Arts JZCD343(CD),
                                         Dance Band Days DBD15,DBCD15(CD)

     Baby,Won't You
        Say You Love Me(nc)
     It's Only A Paper Moon(nc)   Swing House(E)SWH12,Recordings Arts JZCD343(CD),
                                         Dance Band Days DBD15,DBCD15(CD)

Note:The above titles are from Treasury Department "Guest Star" transcription No.170.

Add Jack Costanzo(bg).   LA.January 1950
     Oh,Kickeroonie(nc)   VJC LEV-KC6
     Route 66(nc)   -
     Congaroo   -

Note:The above titles are from the "King Cole And His Trio" short film soundtrack; on eac▮
    title the Benny Carter Orchestra is heard in the final bars.
    LEV-KC6 is a limited-edition video cassette of the entire short film.

NAT KING COLE WITH THE STARLIGHTERS:
Nat Cole(p,vcl),Irving Ashby(g),Joe Comfort(b),poss. Lee Young -1(dr),Jack Costanzo -1(bg
The Starlighters(vcl).   LA.February 9,1950
5159-2 Baby,Won't You
        Say You Love Me(nc,ts)   Capitol 889,F889,(E)CL13308,Music For Pleasure(E)
                                    MFP5201,World Rec. Club(E)T202
5160-2 I Almost Lost My Mind(2)(nc) Capitol 889,F889,(E)CL13370,LC6587
5161-2 A Little Bit Independent(2)(nc) Capitol 1068,F1068,(E)CL13415,(F)398,Music For Pl▮
                                    (E)MFP1049,MFP5201
5162-2 I'll Never Say "Never
        Again" Again(1)(nc,ts)   Capitol 1068,F1068,(E)CL13501,E-ST23480,Regal(E)
                                    REG1019
5526-1 Twisted Stockings(1)(nc,ts) Capitol 915,F915,(E)CL13369,(F)239

-2.Add unknown female vcl-trio.

All titles also on Mosaic MR27-138,MD18-138 (CD).

NAT KING COLE AND HIS TRIO:
Nat Cole(p,vcl),Irving Ashby(g),Joe Comfort(b),Jack Costanzo(bg).
                                NYC.March 9,1950
     If I Were You,
        Baby,I'd Love Me(no bg)(nc) Mosaic MR27-138,MD18-138(CD)
     Third Finger Left Hand(no bg)(nc)   -   -
     After My Laughter
        Came Tears(no bg)(nc)   -   -
     Calico Sal(nc)   -   -
     Peaches   -   -
     Don't Let Your Eyes Go
        Shopping (For Your Heart)(nc)   -   -
     All Aboard   -   -
     Oh,Kickeroonie(nc)   -   -
     'Deed I Do(nc)   -   -

Note:The above titles were used for Capitol transcriptions B467,B468.

Add Lee Young(dr).   LA.March 11,1950
5665-4 The Greatest
        Inventor Of Them All(1)(nc) Capitol 1010,F1010,(F)352
5666-1 Who's Who(nc)   Capitol(E)EMS1279

-1.Add Lex Baxter Chorus(vcl).
(session cont. next page).

(session cont. from previous page):
Both titles also on Mosaic MR27-138,MD18-138 (CD).
Note:Additional (non-jazz) titles from this session are not included.

Add unknown orchestra,vcl-group.   TV-cast.LA.May 7,1950
        The Greatest
            Inventor Of Them All(nc)   Alto AL709,Jazz Anthology(F)JA5175

Note:The above title is from an "Ed Sullivan Show" TV program.

Al Richman(frh),Sid Cooper(fl,cl),Irving Ashby(g),Joe Comfort(b),Mel Zelnick(dr),strings,
Pete Rugolo(arr,cond),Nat Cole,Alyce King' Vokettes(vcl).
                                           NYC.May 19,1950
5755-5 Time Out For Tears(nc,akv)   Capitol 1270,F1270,(F)532,Pickwick SPC3352,Mosaic
                                               MR27-138,MD18-138(CD)

Note:Additional (non-jazz) titles from this session are not included.

NAT KING COLE - STAN KENTON AND HIS ORCHESTRA:
Maynard Ferguson,Jim Salko,Buddy Childers,Chico Alvarez(tp),Shorty Rogers(tp,arr -2),Milt
Bernhart,Harry Betts,Bob Fitzpatrick,Johnny Halliburton,Herbie Harper(tb),Bud Shank,Art
Pepper(as),Bob Cooper,Bart Caldarell(ts),Bob Gioga(bars),Nat Cole(p,vcl),Irving Ashby -1,
Laurindo Almeida -2(g),Joe Comfort -1,Don Bagley -2(b),Shelly Manne(dr),Jack Costanzo(bg),
Pete Rugolo -1(arr),Stan Kenton(cond).   LA.August 16,1950
6513-6 Orange Colored Sky(1)(nc)   Capitol 1184,F1184,CDP7.98931-2(CD),Franklin Mint
                                              BBE 57,Amiga(G)8.55.077,Kat Wisker Prod.
                                          NC1002
6514-6 Jam-Bo(2)   Capitol 1184,F1184

Both titles also on Capitol CDP7.96259-2 (CD),(E)CL13392,(F)409,(G)C80111,Mosaic MR27-138,
MD18-138 (CD).

Nat Cole(p,vcl),Irving Ashby(g),Joe Comfort(b),Shelly Manne(dr),Jack Costanzo(bg),unknown
orchestra,Pete Rugolo(arr,cond).   LA.August 25,1950
6543-2 Get To Gettin'(1)(nc)   Capitol 1270,F1270,(E)CL13744,(F)532,Mosaic
                                              MR27-138,MD18-138(CD)

-1.Add unknown vcl-group.

Note:Additional (non-jazz) titles from this session are not included.

NAT KING COLE AND HIS TRIO:
Nat Cole(p,vcl),Irving Ashby(g),Joe Comfort(b),Jack Costanzo(bg).
                                          LA.August/September 1950
        Calypso Blues(no p,g,b)(nc)   Camay CA3004(A)
        The Trouble With Me Is You(nc)   Camay CA3004(A/B),JCVC106(?)
        Route 66(nc)   -
        Little Girl(nc)   -
        You Call It Madness(no bg)(nc)   Camay CA3004(B),Recordings Arts JZCD343(CD)(?)
        That's My Girl(nc)
        This Is My Night
            To Dream(no bg)(nc)   -   ,Recordings Arts JZCD343(CD)(?)
        For Sentimental   unissued
            Reasons(no bg)(nc)   -
        Mona Lisa(no bg)(nc)   -
        Sweet Lorraine(no bg)(nc)   -

Note:The above titles are from Snader Telescription short film soundtracks.
    Two versions of CA3004 (both 12" LP) have been issued - with different covers. The
    listing above therefore adds "A" and "B" to the issue number given.

Nat Cole(p,vcl),Irving Ashby(g),Joe Comfort(b),Jack Costanzo(bg).

Live.Konserthuset,Stockholm.October 16,1950

    Nothin' To Fret About
    Too Marvelous For Words(nc)
    Poor Butterfly
    My Foolish Heart(no bg)(nc)
    Tiny's Exercise
    Lilette(nc)
    Home(no bg)

Note:The above titles were transcribed from the concert and broadcast by the Swedish
    Radio.

Same.   Live.Kongresshaus,Zürich,Switzerland.October 19,1950
    Nothin' To Fret About   Duke(I)D1014
    Tea For Two(no bg)
    Body And Soul(no bg)   Duke(I)D1014
    Too Marvelous For Words(nc)   -
    Bop Kick   -
    St. Louis Blues   -
    St. Louis Blues (encore)   -
    In The Cool Of The Evening(no bg) -
    Go Bongo(trio-vcl)   -
    How High The Moon
    Medley(no bg):   Duke(I)D1014
        Summertime
        Embraceable You(nc)
    Poor Butterfly   -
    Little Girl(nc)   -
    Sweet Lorraine(no bg)(nc)   -
    Route 66(nc)   -

Note:The above titles were transcribed from the concert and broadcast by the Swiss Radio.

Add unknown orchestra,Neal Hefti(arr,cond). LA.December 11,1950
6240-4 Paint Yourself
       A Rainbow(no p)(nc)   Capitol(E)CL13744,Mosaic MR27-138,MD18-138(CD)
6241-3 Destination Moon(nc)   Capitol 1401,F1401,(F)615,   -   -

Note:One additional (non-jazz) title from this session is not included.

NAT KING COLE AND HIS TRIO / PLUS (GERALD WILSON) STUDIO ORCHESTRA:
Nat Cole(p,vcl),Irving Ashby(g),Joe Comfort(b),Jack Costanzo(bg).
                                    LA.c. 1950/51
    Destination Moon(1)(nc)   JCVC106,VJC LEV-KC6
    Too Young(nc)   -
    That's My Girl(1)(nc)   JCVC106,   -

-1.Add unknown orch.,Gerald Wilson(tp,cond),Neal Hefti,Pete Rugolo(arr); Cole(vcl) only.

Note:The above titles are from the "Nat King Cole and Joe Adams' Orchestra" short film
    soundtrack.
    LEV-KC6 is a limited-edition video cassette of the entire short film.

THE KING COLE TRIO PLUS STRINGS:
Nat Cole(p,vcl),Irving Ashby(g),Joe Comfort(b),strings,Nelson Riddle(cond).
                                    LA.c. January 1951
    Nature Boy(nc)   Camay CA3004(A/B)
    Too Young(nc)   -
    Because Of Rain(nc)   -
    Always You(nc)   -
(session cont. next page).

(session cont. from previous page):
     Mona Lisa(nc)   Camay CA3004(B)
     Home(nc)   -

Note:The above titles are from Snader Telescription short film soundtracks. It has been
    reported that a second version was filmed.
    Two versions of CA3004 (both 12" LP) have been issued - with different covers. The
    listing above therefore adds "A" and "B" to the issue number given.

Nat Cole(p,vcl),Irving Ashby(g),Joe Comfort(b),unknown orchestra,Pete Rugolo(arr,cond).
                               LA.February 1,1951
7050-9 That's My Girl(nc)   Capitol 1449,F1449,(E)CL13564,EAP20151,(F)418,(G)
                            C80158,Mosaic MR27-138,MD18-138(CD)

NAT KING COLE AND HIS TRIO:
Same (as session February 1,1951);add Jack Costanzo -1(bg).
                                LA.February 12,1951

7110-8 Wish I Were
      Somebody Else(2)(nc)   Capitol EAP4-514,EBF2-514,H2/W514,Mosaic MR27-138,
                          MD18-138(CD)
7119-10 You Can't Make
      Me Love You(2)(nc)   Mosaic MR27-138,MD18-138(CD)
7136-9 Poor Jenny Is A Weepin'(1)(nc) Mosaic MR27-138,MD18-138(CD)

-2.Add vcl-group.

Note:The jazz content of the above Trio titles is limited; additional (non-jazz) titles
    from this session are not included.

Nat Cole(p,vcl),Irving Ashby(g),Joe Comfort(b),Jack Costanzo -1(bg),unknown(dr).
                                LA.March 9,1951
6275-3 A Robin And A Rainbow
      And A Red,Red Rose(1,2)(nc) Mosaic MR27-138,MD18-138(CD)
6276-3 The Lighthouse
      In The Sky(1,3)(nc,rcs)   -   -
6277-4 Pigtails And Freckles(nc)   -   -

-2.Add strings,Joe Lippman(arr).
-3.Add The Ray Charles Singers(vcl).

Note:The jazz content of the above Trio titles is limited; additional (non-jazz) titles
    from this session are not included.

Nat Cole(p,vcl),John Collins(g),Charlie Harris(b),Jack Costanzo -1(bg),unknown orchestra,
Pete Rugolo(arr,cond).   LA.January 11,1952
9224-7 It's Crazy(1)(nc)   Capitol 5-2897,W9122,(F)1374
9249-6 You Stepped
      Out Of A Dream(1)(nc)   Capitol T/DT420,Pickwick SPC3105,PTP2002,Starline
                        (E)SRS5039,Starlite(E)1003(CD)
9572-2 Where Were You(1)(nc)   Capitol EAP3-514,EBF2-514,H2/W514
9579-5 Summer Is Comin' In(nc)   Capitol 5-1994,(E)CL13729,E-ST23480
9580-3 Funny(nc)   Capitol 2130,EAP1-9110,H/T9110,DWBB252,W1574,
                        T1891,(E)CL13878,(F)988,(G)C80268

All titles also on Mosaic MR27-138,MD18-138 (CD).

Nat Cole(p),John Collins(g),Charlie Harris(b),Bunny Shawker(dr),Jack Costanzo -1(bg).
                                LA.July 18,1952
(session cont. next page).

(session cont. from previous page):
```
9472-23 Penthouse Serenade            Capitol 15868 (CCN332),F15868 (CCF332),EAP1-332
9473-22 Rose Room(1)                  Capitol EAP1-332,(E)LC6593
9474-21 Polka Dots And Moonbeams      Capitol 15870 (CCN332),F15870 (CCF332),EAP2-332
9475-23 Somebody Loves Me(1)          Capitol 15869 (CCN332),F15869 (CCF332),EAP1-332,
                                            (E)LC6593
9476-25 Once In A Blue Moon(1,2)      Capitol EAP2-332,(E)LC6593
9477-21 If I Should Lose You          Capitol 15868 (CCN332),F15868 (CCF332),EAP1-332
9478-23 Down By The Old Mill Stream(1) Capitol 15869 (CCN332),F15869 (CCF332),EAP2-332
9479-35 Laura                         Capitol 15870 (CCN332),F15870 (CCF332),    -  ,
                                            (E)LC6593
```

-2.Subtitled "Based on Rubinstein's Melody In F".

All titles also on Capitol EBF/H/T332,(J)TOCJ5363 (CD),Mosaic MR27-138,MD18-138 (CD).
Note:The above titles were originally recorded - with same pers. - March 31 or April 3,
     1952 but the original versions were rejected.

Add orchestra,Nelson Riddle(arr,cond);omit Shawker,Costanzo.
                                      LA.July 24,1952
10436-3 Don't Let Your Eyes Go
          Shopping(For Your Heart)(nc) Capitol 5-2346,F2346,(E)CL13880,(F)1082,(G)C80352,
                                            Mosaic MR27-138,MD18-138(CD)

Note:The acc. orchestra is the RAY ANTHONY ORCHESTRA - additional titles from this session
     are by Ray Anthony.

Nat Cole(p,vcl),John Collins(g),Charlie Harris(b),Jack Costanzo(bg),unknown orchestra,
Nelson Riddle(arr,cond).   LA.January 28,1953
10850-6 Almost Like Being In Love(nc) Capitol EAP1-420,EBF/H/DT420,CDP7.46650-2(CD),(E)
                                            LC6627,Mosaic MR27-138,MD18-138(CD),Pickwick
                                            SPC3046
11082-2 This Can't Be Love(nc)   Capitol EAP1-420,EBF/H/DT420,CDP7.46650-2(CD),(E)
                                            LC6627,Mosaic MR27-138,MD18-138(CD)
11083-7 Don't Hurt The Girl(no bg)(nc) Mosaic MR27-138,MD18-138(CD)

Nat Cole(p,vcl) acc. by unknown orchestra,Pete Rugolo(arr).
                                      LA.c. mid-1953
          It's Crazy   VJC LEV-KC6

Note:The above title is from the "Nat King Cole and Russ Morgan's Orchestra" short film
     soundtrack.
     LEV-KC6 is a limited-edition video cassette of the entire short film.

Nat Cole(p,vcl),John Collins(g),Charlie Harris(b),unknown orchestra,Nelson Riddle(arr,
cond).   LA.August 24,1953
11726-11 The Christmas Song(nc)   Capitol 5-2953,5-3561,93741,EAP1-9026,EAP1-1346,
                                            H/T9026,(S)W1927,T9030,(E)EAP1036,(F),
                                            STTX340.492,C.062-80482,Music For Pleasure
                                            (E)MFP5224,Mosaic MR27-138,MD18-138(CD)

Note:Additional (non-jazz) titles from this session are not included.

Nat Cole(p,vcl),John Collins(g),Charlie Harris(b),Lee Young(dr),unknown orchestra,Nelson
Riddle(arr,cond).   LA.c. 1955
          Straighten Up And Fly Right
          Sweet Lorraine
          Route 66

Note:The above titles are from the "Nat King Cole Musical Story" soundtrack; additional
     (non-jazz) titles from the soundtrack are not included.

Nat Cole(p) acc. by TOMMY DORSEY AND HIS ORCHESTRA:
Incl. Tommy Dorsey(tb),Jimmy Dorsey(cl).   TV-cast.LA.March 19,1955
     Stomping Down Broadway   Magic(E)AWE30,DATOM5(CD),Festival(F)ALB223,Accord
                             (F)302232,Laserlight 15 750(CD),15 915(CD),
                             Delta 11086(CD),Delta/Jazzline 20815

Note:The above titles are from a Tommy Dorsey TV-cast; additional (non-jazz) titles are
    not included.

Nat Cole(p),unknown orchestra,Nelson Riddle(cond).
                             LA.June 7,1955
13980 I Hear Music   Capitol EAP1-689,(S)W689,(E)LC6830,Pickwick
                           (S)PC3187
13981 My Heart Stood Still(1)   Capitol EAP1-689,(S)W689,(E)LC6830,Pickwick
                           (S)PC3187
13982 I Never Knew   Capitol EAP2-689,(S)W689
13983 Tea For Two   Capitol EAP1-689,(S)W689,(E)LC6830,Pickwick
                           (S)PC3187,(Sp)1.76-82048/49

-1.All commercial issues - except Capitol CDP7.81203-2 (CD) - are edited; the unedited
    master was originally issued only on the US Government "Guard Session" transcription
    No.187; the Capitol CD issue also includes the edited version.

All titles also on Capitol CDP7.81203-2 (CD).
Note:Two additional (non-jazz) titles from this session are not included.
    The personnel for the June and August 1955 "The Piano Style of Nat King Cole" ses-
    sions includes: Juan Tizol(vtb),George Roberts(btb),Willie Smith(as),John Collins
    (g),Charlie Harris(b),Lee Young(dr).

Same.   LA.June 11,1955
13995 What Can I Say
       After I Say I'm Sorry   Capitol EAP3-689,(S)W689,(E)LC6830
13995 Taking A Chance On Love   Capitol EAP4-689,   -   -

Both titles also on Capitol CDP7.81203-2 (CD).
Note:One additional (non-jazz) title from this session is not included.

NAT KING COLE AND HIS TRIO:
Nat Cole(p),John Collins(g),Charlie Harris(b),Lee Young(dr).
                             LA.July 14,1955
14180-3 Don't Blame Me   Capitol T332,Mosaic MR27-138,MD18-138(CD),Music
                           For PLeasure(E)MFP1129
14192-9 It Could Happen To You   Capitol T332,Mosaic MR27-138,MD18-138(CD)
14206-1 I Surrender Dear(no g)   Mosaic MR27-138,MD18-138(CD)
14206-2 I Surrender Dear(no g)   Capitol T332,Mosaic MR27-138,MD18-138(CD)
14207-3 Little Girl   -   -   -

All titles - except master 14206-1 - also on Capitol(J)TOCJ5363.

Nat Cole(p),unknown orchestra,Nelson Riddle(cond).
                           LA.August 18,1955
14317 Imagination   Capitol EAP2-689,(S)W689
14318 April In Paris   Capitol EAP4-689,   - ,(E)LC6830,Pickwick
                           (S)PC3187
14319 Love Walked In   Capitol EAP1-689,(S)W689,(E)LC6830,Pickwick
                           (S)PC3187
14320 I See Your Face Before Me   Capitol EAP3-689,(S)W689
14325 Stella By Starlight(1)   -   - ,(E)LC6830,(F)2C.152-81746
                      Pickwick (S)PC3187

-1.Add strings.

All titles also on Capitol CDP7.81203-2 (CD).

```
Add strings.                           LA.August 23,1955
14342  I Didn't Know What Time It Was  Capitol EAP4-689,(S)W689,(E)LC6830,Pickwick
                                         (S)PC3187
14343  If I Could Be With You          Capitol EAO2-689,(S)W689
14345  I Get A Kick Out Of You                   -       -
```

All titles also on Capitol CDP7.81203-2 (CD).
Note:One additional (non-jazz) title from this session is not included.

```
Omit strings.                          LA.August 27,1955
14382  Just One Of Those Things        Capitol EAP3-689,(S)W689,(F)2C.152-81746,Pickwick
                                         (S)PC3187
14383  I Want To Be Happy              Capitol EAP4-689,(S)W689,(E)LC6830,Pickwick
                                         (S)PC3187
```

All titles also on Capitol CDP7.81203-2 (CD).
Note:Two additional (non-jazz) titles from this session are not included.

NAT KING COLE AND HIS TRIO:
Nat Cole(p,vcl),John Collins(g),Charlie Harris(b),Lee Young(dr).
                                       LA.c. Summer/autumn 1956
        I Was A Little Too Lonely (And
          You Were A Little Too Late)(nc)

Note:The above title is from the "Istanbul" feature film soundtrack; one additional (non-jazz) title from this soundtrack is not included.

NAT KING COLE AND HIS TRIO PLUS GUESTS:
Harry Edison(tp),Nat Cole(p,vcl),John Collins(g),Charlie Harris(b),Lee Young(dr).
                                       LA.August 15,1956
```
15788-10 You Can Depend On Me(nc)      Capitol(E)EMS1103,(Au)CEP004(?)
15789-8  Candy(nc)                               -          -
15790-4  Sweet Lorraine(nc)           Capitol EAP2-782,EBF1-782,W782,(E)CL15323,EMS1103,
                                         (G)K60681,(J)TOCJ5027(CD),TOCP9069(CD),Giants
                                         Of Jazz(I)GOJCD53005(CD),(E)CD0231(CD)
15791-5  It's Only A Paper Moon(nc)    Capitol EAP4-782,EBF2-782,W782,CDP7.98931-2(CD),
                                         (E)EMS1103,(G)EPK40627,(J)TOCJ5027(CD),Giants
                                         Of Jazz(I)GOJCD53005(CD),(E)CD0231(CD),Delta
                                         11086(CD),Emidisc(F)C.048-40707
15792-3  Route 66(nc)                  Capitol EAP3-782,EBF2-782,W782,(E)EMS1103,(G)
                                         EPK40627,(J)TOCJ5027(CD),Giants Of Jazz(I)
                                         LPJT62,GOJCD53003(CD),(E)CD0231(CD)
```

All titles also on Capitol CDP7.48328-2 (CD),Mosaic MR27-138,MD18-138 (CD).

NAT KING COLE AND HIS TRIO PLUS GUESTS:
Willie Smith(as),Nat Cole(p,vcl),John Collins(g),Charlie Harris(b),Lee Young(dr).
                                       LA.September 14,1956
```
15895-10 Don't Let It
           Go To Your Head(nc)         Capitol EAP4-782,EBF2-782,W782,(G)EPK40627,Music
                                         For Pleasure(E)MFP1129,Giants Of Jazz(I)
                                         JLPT62,GOJCD53005(CD),(E)CD0231(CD),Mosaic
                                         MR27-138,MD18-138(CD)
15896-?  You're Looking At Me(nc)      Capitol EAP3-782,EBF2-782,W782,(G)K60681,Music
                                         For Pleasure(E)MFP1129,Giants Of Jazz(I)
                                         LPJT62,GOJCD53005(CD),(E)CD0231(CD)
15896-11 You're Looking At Me(nc)      Mosaic MR27-138,MD18-138(CD)
15897-7  Just You,Just Me(nc)          Capitol EAP1-782,EBF1-782,W782,T1034,(S)T2943,
                                         (G)EPK40602,Music For Pleasure(E)MFP1129,
                                         Giants Of Jazz(I)LJPT62,GOJCD53005(CD),(E)
                                         CD0231(CD),Mosaic MR27-138,MD18-138(CD)
```

(session cont. next page).

session cont. from previous page):
5898-8 I Was A Little Too
        Lonely (And You Were
        A Little Too Late)(nc)   Capitol(E)EMS1103,Mosaic MR27-138,MD18-138(CD)

ll titles - except master 15896-11 (alt. take) - also on Capitol CDP7.48328-2 (CD),(E)
MS1103.

NAT KING COLE AND HIS TRIO PLUS GUESTS:
Juan Tizol(vtb),Nat Cole(p,vcl),John Collins(g),Charlie Harris(b),Lee Young(dr),Jack
Costanzo -1(bg,cg).   LA.September 21,1956
15920-5 Caravan(1)   Capitol EAP3-782,EBF2-782,W782,(G)EPK40602,(J)
                                   TOCJ5027(CD),Giants Of Jazz(I)LPJT62,
                                   GOJCD53005(CD),(E)CD0231(CD)
15921-11 Lonely One(1)(nc)   Capitol EAP2-782,EBF2-782,W782,Music For Pleasure
                                   (E)MFP1129,Giants Of Jazz(I)GOJCD53005(CD),
                                   (E)CD0231(CD)
15922-1 Blame It On My Youth(nc) Capitol EAP4-782,EBF2-782,W782,Music For Pleasure
                                   (E)MFP1129
15923-11 What Is There To Say(nc) Capitol(E)EMS1103,Pickwick SPC3105

All titles also on Capitol CDP7.48328-2 (CD),(E)EMS1103,Mosaic MR27-138,MD18-138 (CD).

NAT KING COLE AND HIS TRIO PLUS GUESTS:
Stuff Smith(vln),Nat Cole(p,vcl),John Collins(g),Charlie Harris(b),Lee Young(dr).
                                   LA.September 24,1956
15936-5 Sometimes I'm Happy(nc)   Capitol EAP1-782,EBF1-782,W782,Music For Pleasure
                                   (E)MFP1129
15937-3 I Know That You Know(nc) Capitol EAP2-782,EBF1-782,W782,Music For Pleasure
                                   (E)MFP1129,Giants Of Jazz(I)LPJT62,GOJCD53005
                                   (CD),(E)CD0231,Franklin Mint
15938-11 When I Grow
         Too Old To Dream(nc)   Capitol EAP1-782,EBF1-782,W782,Music For Pleasure
                                   (E)MFP1129,Giants Of Jazz(I)LPJT62,GOJCD53005
                                   (CD),(E)CD0231
15939-14 Two Loves Have I(nc)   Capitol(E)EMS1103

All titles also on Capitol CDP7.48328-2 (CD),(E)EMS1103,Mosaic MR27-138,MD18-138 (CD).

Juan Tizol(vtb),Nat Cole(p,vcl),John Collins(g),Charlie Harris(b),Lee Young(dr),Jack
Costanzo(bg).   TV-cast.Chicago.Autumn 1956
        Caravan(nc)

Note:The above title is from an "Nat King Cole Show" TV program.

Nat Cole(p),prob. John Collins(g),Charlie Harris(b),Mel Torme(dr),June Christy(vcl).
                                   TV-cast.LA.c. 1956
        How High The Moon(jc)

Note:The above title is from a "Nat King Cole Show" TV program.

Nat Cole(p,vcl) acc. by orchestra,Gordon Jenkins(cond).
                                   TV-cast.LA.November 5,1956
        Tea For Two(1)(nc)   Sandy Hook SH2054,Delta 11086(CD),Laserlight
                                   15 750(CD),15 915(CD),Festival(F)ALBUM223,
                                   Accord(F)302.232(CD)

-1.Add unknown(vcl-group).

Note:Additional (non-jazz) titles from this NBC TV-cast are not included.

Same.   TV-cast.November 12,1956
         This Is The End Of A
             Beautiful Friendship(1)(nc)   Magic(E)DATOM5(CD),Warwick(E)U2026,Sandy Hook
                                               SH2054
         (I'll See You In) C-U-B-A(nc)   Magic(E)DATOM5(CD)

-1.Add unknown(vcl-group).

Both titles also on Sunbeam SB222,Festival(F)ALBUM223,Accord(F)302.232 (CD).
Note:The above titles are from a "Nat King Cole Show" TV program; additional (non-jazz)
     titles from this TV-cast are not included.

Nat Cole(p,vcl),prob. John Collins(g),Charlie Harris(b).
                                          TV-cast.LA.November 19,1956
       It Is Only A Paper Moon(nc)   Festival(F)ALBUM223,Magic(E)DATOM5(CD),Warwick(E)
                                              U2026,Accord(F)302.232(CD)

Note:The above title is from a "Nat King Cole Show" TV program; additional (non-jazz)
     titles from this TV-cast are not included.

Nat Cole(p,vcl) acc. by orchestra,Gordon Jenkins(cond).
                                          TV-cast.LA.November 26,1956
         Stella By Starlight

Note:The above title is from a "Nat King Cole Show" TV program; additional (non-jazz)
     titles from this TV-cast are not included.

Nat Cole(p) acc. by orchestra,Gordon Jenkins(cond),Nelson Riddle(arr).
                                          TV-cast.LA.December 3,1956
       Just One Of Those Things   Festival(F)ALBUM223,Accord(F)302.232(CD),Interdis〈
                                              (Du)76.006,Magic(E)DATOM5(CD),Warwick(E)U202〈
                                              (CD),Spectrum(F)U3013-2(CD)

Note:The above title is from a "Nat King Cole Show" TV program; additional (non-jazz)
     titles from this TV-cast are not included.

Nat Cole(p),prob. John Collins(g),Charlie Harris(b).
                                          TV-cast.LA.December 10,1956
         Too Marvellous For Words

Note:The above title is from a "Nat King Cole Show" TV program; additional (non-jazz)
     titles from this TV-cast are not included.
     Cole did not play piano on "Nat King Cole Show" TV programs cast during the period
     December 17,1956 - February 4,1957.

Nat Cole(p) acc. by orchestra,Nelson Riddle(cond).
                                          TV-cast.LA.February 11,1957
         Tea For Two

Note:The above title is from a "Nat King Cole Show" TV program; additional (non-jazz)
     titles are not included.

NAT KING COLE WITH "JAZZ AT THE PHILHARMONIC" GUESTS:
(vcl) acc.by Roy Eldridge -1(tp),Flip Phillips -2,Illinois Jacquet -3,Stan Getz -4,Coleman
Hawkins -5(ts),Oscar Peterson -6(p),Herb Ellis(g),Ray Brown(b),Jo Jones(dr),unknown studio
orchestra.   TV-cast.LA.October 15,1957
         (Norman Granz announcements)   Sunbeam SB222
         It's Only A Paper Moon(2)(nc)   - ,Sandy Hook SH2054
         Sweet Lorraine(5,6)(nc)   -
(session cont. next page).

(session cont. from previous page):
     C Jam Blues(1,2,3,6)   Sunbeam SB222,Koala LP14143
     I Want To Be Happy(1,4,7)   -
     With You On My Mind(2,3)(nc)   -
     Stompin' At The
         Savoy(1,4,5,6)(nc)   -
     Tenderly(6)(nc)   -
     Shadow Waltz (theme)(7)   -

-7.Cole also plays (p).

Note:The above titles are from a "Nat King Cole Show" TV program.

Nat Cole(p,vcl),prob. John Collins(g),Charlie Harris(b),Lee Young(dr),Billy Eckstine(vcl).
                                  TV-cast.NYC.December 24,1957

     Life Is Just A
         Bowl Of Cherries(be)
     Rosetta(1)(nc,be)

1.Eckstine also plays (tp,vtb,valve-sax).

Note:The above titles are from a "Nat King Cole Show" TV program.

NAT KING COLE WITH THE COUNT BASIE ORCHESTRA:
vcl) acc. by John Anderson,Wendell Culley,Thad Jones,Joe Newman,Snooky Young(tp),Henry
oker,Al Grey,Benny Powell(tb),Marshall Royal(as,cl),Frank Wess(as,fl),Frank Foster,Billy
itchell(ts),Charlie Fowlkes(bars),Gerald Wiggins(p),Freddie Green(g),Eddie Jones(b),Sonny
ayne(dr),Dave Cavanaugh(cond,arr).   LA.June 30,1958
9550 She's Funny That Way   Capitol (S)W1120,SWAK11355,(Eu)C.064-81120
9551 Any Time,Any Day,Anywhere   - ,EAP1-1120
9552 I Want A Little Girl   -
9553 Mood Indigo   - ,(J)TOCJ5027(CD)

ll titles also on Capitol CDP7.96259-2 (CD).
ote:Count Basie is not present on these sessions.

ame.   LA.July 1,1958
9569 The Blues Don't Care   Capitol (S)W1120
9570 Avalon   - ,EAP1-1120,(J)TOCJ5027(CD)
9571 Baby,Won't You Please Come Home   - ,(J)TOCJ5027(CD)
9572 The Late Late Show   - ,EAP1-1120
9573 Welcome To The Club   -   -

ll titles also on Capitol CDP7.96259-2 (CD).

ame.   LA.July 2,1958
9589 Look Out For Love   Capitol (S)W1120
9590 Wee Baby Blues   -
9591 Madrid   Capitol F4125

ll titles also on Capitol CDP7.96259-2 (CD).

at Cole(p),John Collins(g),Charlie Harris(b),Lee Young(dr),unknown(tamb),vocal chorus,
ve Cavanaugh(arr,cond).   LA.September 2,1959
2320-5 Whatcha' Gonna' Do   Capitol 4325,(E)45CL15111,Mosaic MR27-138,
                                        MD18-138(CD)
2321-4 In A Mellow Tone   Mosaic MR27-138,MD18-138(CD)

ote:"In A Mellow Tone" prob. issued on a Capitol promotional album (PRO6303).
     Additional (non-jazz) titles from this session are not included.

NAT KING COLE WITH THE STAN KENTON ORCHESTRA:
(vcl) acc. by Bud Brisbois,Frank Huggins,Pete Candoli,Jack Sheldon,Conte Candoli(tp),Bob
Fitzpatrick,Kent Larsen,Tom Shepard,Jim Amlotte,Bob Knight(tb),Lennie Niehaus(as),Ronnie
Rubin,Jay Migliori(ts),Jack Nimitz,Marvin Holladay(bars),Stan Kenton(p),Don Bagley(b),Mel
Lewis(dr).   LA.March 9,1960
33412 Steady(nc)   Capitol 4393,(E)45CL15144
33413 My Love(1)(nc)   -   -

-1.Add Plas Johnson(ts),Jack Marshall,Bill Pittman,John Collins(g),Charlie Harris(b),Lee
   Young(dr),vocal chorus.

Both titles also on Capitol CDP7.96259-2 (CD),(E)CL15144.

Nat Cole(p),John Collins(g),Charlie Harris(b),Lee Young(dr),orchestra,Dave Cavanaugh(arr)
Antonio Morelli(cond).   Live."The Sands",Las Vegas.June 14,1960
55355 Where Or When   Capitol SMAS2434,CDP7.93786-2(CD),(E)EMS1110,
                                            Mosaic MR27-138,MD18-138(CD)

Note:Additional (non-jazz) titles from this session are not included.

THE KING COLE TRIO:
Nat Cole(p,vcl),John Collins(g),Charlie Harris(b).
                                            NYC.March 22,1961
23549-21 It's Only A Paper Moon(nc)   Capitol 93741,Amiga(G)8.55.077
23550-14 Sweet Lorraine(nc)   - ,SLB6803,SLB6808,(E)W20664,Lotus(I)
                                            LOP14077

Both titles also on Capitol SWCL1-1613 (SW1926),SN16033,CDP7.95129-2 (CD),Mosaic MR27-138
MD18-138 (CD).

Same.   NYC.March 23,1961
23551-21 Route 66(nc)   Capitol SWCL1-1613 (SW1926),(E)W20664,(Au)SCA076,
                                            Deja Vu(I)DVLP2048,Mosaic MR27-138,MD18-138
                                            (CD)
23564-9 Straighten Up
         And Fly Right(nc)   Capitol 6036,93741,SWCL1-1613 (SW1926),(J)TOCP90■
                                            (CD),Mosaic MR27-138,MD18-138(CD)
23565-12 For Sentimental Reasons(nc)   Capitol 93741,SWCL1-1613 (SW1926),SLB6803,DT357,
                                            SM357,Mosaic MR27-138,MD18-138(CD),Scana(G)
                                            GH83021,Picturedisc(G)PD30033,Giants Of Jazz
                                            (I)LJPT14,Lotus(I)LOP14077
23566-10 Embraceable You(nc)   Mosaic MR27-138,MD18-138(CD)

All titles - except "Embraceable You" - also on Capitol SN16033,CDP7.95129-2 (CD).
Note:Additional (non-jazz) titles from these March 1961 sessions are not included.
    The version of "Route 66" issued on SCA076 was erroneously credited to the August 2
    1947 session.

NAT KING COLE WITH THE STAN KENTON ORCHESTRA:
(vcl) acc. by Dalton Smith,Bud Brisbois,Marvin Stamm,Bob Rolfe,Bob Behrendt(tp),Bob Fitz
patrick,John Spurlock,Bud Parker,Jim Amlotte,Dave Wheeler(tb),Gabe Baltazar(as),Sam Dona
hue,Paul Renzi(ts),Marvin Holladay,Wayne Dunsten(bars),Paul Smith(p),Al Hendrickson(g),R
Mitchell or Joe Comfort(b),Jerry McKenzie(dr),Larry Bunker,George Acevedo(perc),Pete Rug
lo(arr).   LA.July 6,1961
36115 Orange Colored Sky   Capitol SWCL1-1613 (SW1926),SN16033,CDP7.96259-2
                                            (CD),(E)SI/SWI1613,SW20664

(vcl) acc. by Mike Pacheco(bg).   LA.July 19,1961
36204 Calypso Blues(nc)   Capitol SWCL1-1613 (SW1926),SN16033,CDP7.95129-2
                                            (CD),(E)SI/SWI1613,Pickwick(E)SPC3071

Note:Additional (non-jazz) titles from these two sessions are not included.

ING COLE WITH THE GEORGE SHEARING QUINTET:
vcl) acc. by Warren Chiasson(vbs),George Shearing(p,arr),Israel Crosby(b),Vernell Four-
ier(dr),Armando Peraza(cg),strings,Ralph Carmichael(arr,cond).
                                        LA.December 19,1961
6894 Azure-Te   Capitol (S)W1675,(E)EMS1113
6895 A Beautiful Friendship   -   - ,(E)45CL15588
6896 Everything Happens To Me   Capitol(E)EMS1113

ll titles also on Capitol CDP7.48332-2 (CD).

ame.   LA.December 20,1961
6942 Pick Yourself Up   Capitol (S)W1675,Smithsonian Institute RD048-4(CD)
6943 September Song   - ,(E)ST21874,(F)C.152-81746/8
6944 Let There Be Love   - ,(E)CL15257,ST21139
6945 I Got It Bad And That Ain't Good   -

ll titles also on Capitol CDP7.48332-2 (CD),(E)EMS1113.

ame.   LA.December 21,1961
6951 Serenata   Capitol (S)W1675,CDP7.48332-2(CD),(E)EMS1113
6952 The Game Of Love   Capitol CDP7.48332-2(CD)
6953 (In Other Words)
        Fly Me To The Moon   Capitol (S)W1675,CDP7.48332-2(CD),(E)EMS1113
6954 Guess I'll Go Back Home   Capitol CDP7.48332-2(CD),(E)EMS1113

ame.   LA.December 22,1961
6957 I'm Lost   Capitol (S)W1675,(E)CL15257
6958 Don't Go   -
6959 There's A Lull In My Life   -
6960 Lost April   -

ll titles also on Capitol CDP7.48332-2 (CD),(E)EMS1113.

T COLE - List of Capitol equivalents:

pitol(U.S.):		Capitol(E):	Capitol(Eu):	Capitol(J):	Other labels:
iginal:	Reissue:				
'310			1C.048-80213		
32				ECJ50099,	
				TOCJ5363(CD)	
357	SM357		2S.066-85531		
57	CDP7.46736	EMS1100			
	(CD)				
20		LC6627			
20		EMS1101	260.771-1		
14		LCT6003		ECJ50080	
91				ECJ50062,	
				ECP88163	
92	M11033		5C.052-80804	ECJ50057	OneUp(E)0U2007
)W689		T689,			
		EMS1271			

ont. next page).

NAT COLE - List of Capitol equivalents (cont.):

Capitol(U.S.): Original:	Reissue:	Capitol(E):	Capitol(Eu):	Capitol(J):	Other labels:
W782	SM11796	LCT6133	260.896-1	CR8061, ECJ50019	
(S)W993	(S)W1713, (S)W1929	(S)LCT6156			Music For Pl.(E)MFP1277, Music For Pl.(F)MFP5102, Regal(E)REG111, World Rec.Club(E) (S)T4(
(S)W1120	(S)SW1724	LCT6176, EMS1107		2LP3026, ECJ6013, TOCJ5392(CD)	
(S)W1675				ECJ50020	Music For Pl.(E)MFP5612
(S)W1926			STTX340.491, C.062-81134		
CDP7.48328-2 (CD)		CDEMS1103(CD)		CP32-5308(CD)	
CDP7.48332-2 (CD)				CP32-5557(CD)	
CDP7.93252-2 (CD)		CDEMS1370(CD)			

All titles on Music For Pleasure(E)MFP1129 also on Music For Pleasure(F)5004.

RICHIE COLE

See also REUBEN BROWN,MARK MURPHY.

Richie Cole(as),Gerald Price(p),Steve Gilmore(b),Al Jackson(dr).
Live."Lanzi's Lounge,Trenton,N.J.May 5,1975

Waltz For A Rainy Bebop Evening	Progressive P.R.1001
Last Tango In Paris	-
Naima(1)	-

-1.The title is misspelled "Niema" on the LP.

Richie Cole(as),Gerald Price(p),Benny Nelson(b),Al Jackson(dr),Doni Johnson(cg).
Trenton,N.J.November 16,1975

Harold's House Of Jazz	Progressive P.R.1001
Trenton Makes,The World Takes	-
Tokyo Rose Sings The Blues	-
It's The Same Thing Everywhere	-

RICHIE COLE - ERIC KLOSS:
Richie Cole,Eric Kloss(as),Mickey Tucker(el-p),Rick Laird(b),Eddie Gladden(dr).
Live."The Tin Palace",NYC.March 26,1976

Ebony Godfather	Muse MR5082
Robin	-
Libra	unissued
Last Tango In Paris	Seven Seas(J)K26P6250
Waltz For A Rainy Bebop Evening	-

aird plays (el-b).   Live."The Tin Palace",NYC.March 27,1976
     D.C. Farewell   Muse MR5082
     Harold's House Of Jazz   -
     It's The Same Thing Everywhere   Seven Seas(J)K26P6250
     'Round Midnight(1)   -
     Libra   unissued

1.Omit Cole.

11 titles on MR5082 also on Seven Seas(J)K22P6031.
ote:See EDDIE JEFFERSON for additional titles from the above sessions.

ichie Cole(as),Mickey Tucker(p,el-p),Vic Juris(g),Rick Laird(b,el-b),Eddie Gladden(dr),
ay Mantilla(perc),Eddie Jefferson(vcl).   NYC.October 13,1976
     Dorothy's Den   Muse MR5119
     Waltz For A Rainy
       Bebop Evening(ej)   -
     Alto Madness   -
     New York Afternoon   -
     It's The Same
       Thing Everywhere(ej)   -
     Stormy Weather (Trenton Style)   -
     You'll Always Be My Friend   -

11 titles also on Seven Seas(J)K22P6023.

arold Mabern(p) replaces Tucker;add Steve Gilmore(b).
                                            NYC.December 1977
     Cole's Nocturne   Muse MR5155
     The Price Is Right   -
     The Common Touch(ej)   -
     Last Tango In Paris   -
     Island Breeze   -
     Big Bo's Paradise   -
     Remember Your Day Off   -
     Moody's Mood '78(ej)   -

.1 titles also on Muse MCD5155 (CD),(J)BRJ4505 (CD),Seven Seas(J)K18P9423,K22P6024.

.chie Cole(as),Harold Mabern(p),Vic Juris(g),Rick Laird(b,el-b),Eddie Gladden(dr),Eddie
•fferson(vcl).   NYC.September 6,1978
     As Time Goes By   Muse MR5192
     I Can't Get Started   -
     Keeper Of The Flame   -
     Harold's House Of Jazz(ej)   -
     Holiday For Strings   -
     New York Afternoon(ej)   -
     Strange Groove(1)   -

..Add The Alt-Tettes (Cole,Mabern,Juris,Laird,Gladden,Joe Fields,David Lahm,Terry
  Silverlight)(vcl).

1 titles also on Seven Seas(J)K18P9421,K22P6001.

chie Cole(as),Dick Hindman(p),Bob Magnusson(b),Les DeMerle(dr),Michael Spiro(perc).
                                            LA.April 25,1979
     Hooray For Hollywood   Muse MR5207

chie Cole(as),Dick Hindman(p),Bruce Forman(g),Marshall Hawkins(b),Les DeMerle(dr),
chael Spiro(perc),Eddie Jefferson,Manhattan Transfer(vcl).
                                            Same date
ession cont. next page).

(session cont. from previous page):
```
        Hi Fly(ej,mt)                    Muse MR5207
        Tokyo Rose Sings
            The Hollywood Blues                   -
        Relaxin' At The Camarillo(ej)            -
        Malibu Breeze                            -
        I Love Lucy(1)(mt)
        Waiting For Waits(ej,mt)         Muse 45005,MR5207
        Hooray For Hollywood(ej,mt)     Muse MR5207
```

-1.Add Jeep Duquesne(perc).

All titles on MR5207 also on Muse MCD5207 (CD),(J)BRJ4501 (CD),Seven Seas(J)K18P9422,
K22P6014.

RICHIE COLE - PHIL WOODS:
Richie Cole,Phil Woods(as),John Hicks(p),Walter Booker(b),Jimmy Cobb(dr).
```
                        Live.The Historic Paramount Theatre,Denver,Colorado.July 25/26,198
        Save Your Love For Me(1)         Muse MR5237
        Naugahyde Reality(2)                     -
        Scrapple From The Apple
        Rain Go Away                     Muse CD6016(CD),(J)BRJ4514(CD)(?)
        Donna Lee                        Muse MR5237
        Polka Dots And Moonbeams(3)              -
        Eddie's Mood/Side By Side                -
```

-1.Add Eddie "Lockjaw" Davis(ts).
-2.Woods(as),Cole(as,vcl) only.
-3.Omit Woods.

All titles on MR5237 also on Muse CD6016 (CD),BRJ4514 (CD),Seven Seas(J)K26P6055.

ROCKY COLE

See MICHAEL "ROCKY" COLUCCIO.

BILL COLEMAN

See also RICHARD BENNETT,CAPITOL INTERNATIONAL JAZZMEN,BUCK CLAYTON,JACK DIEVAL,DIXIELAND
PIPERS,STEPHANE GRAPPELLI,NICE ALL STARS,MARY LOU WILLIAMS.

BILL COLEMAN'S QUARTET:
Bill Coleman(tp),Billy Taylor(p),Matty Chapin(b),Specs Powell(dr).
```
                                        Live.Town Hall.NYC.June 9,1945
        Stardust                        Commodore FL20027,(E)8.26169(CD),(G)6.26169,
                                        Mainstream M56010,M56027,"77"(E)LA12/10,
                                        Columbia(F)FP1101,Atlantic SD2-310,London
                                        (E)HMC5002,Mosaic MR20-134
```

BILL COLEMAN - DON BYAS QUINTET:
Bill Coleman(tp),Don Byas(as),Bernard Peiffer(p),Jean Bouchety(b),Roger Paraboschi(dr).
```
                                        Paris.January 4,1949
8001    Just You Just Me               Jazz Selection(F)10.001,506
8002    Bill Brother's Blues                    -        -
8003    Idaho                          Jazz Selection(F)10.002
8004-2  All The Things You Are(no tp)           -
8005    Bill Coleman Blues             Jazz Selection(F)513
```
(session cont. next page).

session cont. from previous page):
Note:Master 8004 issued as by DON BYAS BIG FOUR.

ame.   Paris.January 5,1949

SW562-1	What Is This Thing Called Love	Swing(F)295,Prestige PR7598
SW563-1	Yesterdays(no tp)	Pathé(F)45EA28
SW563-2	Yesterdays(no tp)	Swing(F)300,Pathé(F)2C.054-16027,Prestige PR7598
SW564-1	St. Louis Blues	Swing(F)302,Prestige PR7598
SW565-1	Lover Man	-
SW566-1	Liza	Swing(F)300, -
SW567-1	Blues At Noon	Swing(F)295, -

ote:Master OSW563 issued as by DON BYAS BIG FOUR.

ILL COLEMAN AND HIS ORCHESTRA:
ill Coleman(tp,vcl),Bill Tamper(tb,arr),Jay Cameron(as),William Boucaya(bars),Art
immons(p),Jean-Pierre Sasson(g),Guy DeFatto(b),Gérard "Dave" Pochonet(dr).
                        Paris.November 9,1951

676	Jumpin' At Pleyel(1)	Philips(F)72043H,P76100R
677-2	Si Jolie	Philips(F)72044H,P76101R
678-3	The Blues Jumped Up And Got Me(bc)	-
679-1	I'm Comin' Virginia	Philips(F)72045H,P76100R
680	Come On A My House(bc)	Philips(F)72043H,P76101R
681-1	Tenderly	Philips(F)72045H,P76100R

1.tp,g,b,dr only.

ILL COLEMAN AND HIS SWING STARS:
ill Coleman(tp,vcl),Dicky Wells(tb),Guy Lafitte(cl,ts),Randy Downes(p),Buddy Banks(b),
atty Singleton(dr).   Live."Salle Pleyel",Paris.October 18,1952

340	St. Louis Blues,I	Philips(F)72131H
341	St. Louis Blues,II	-
343	Tea For Two	Philips(F)72130H
344	Drum Face	- ,P70900H,P76008R(?),Rarities(E)10
346	Muskrat Ramble	Philips(F)72128H, -
347	Black And Blue	- ,P76006R,Rarities(E)10
20	Perdido	Philips(F)72143H,P76008R,Rarities(E)10
21	The Sheik Of Araby	- ,P76006R, -
	St. James Infirmary(bc)	- -
	Out Of Nowhere(p,b,dr only)	-
	Royal Garden Blues	- ,Rarities(E)10
	One O'Clock Jump	- -
	Ghost Of A Chance	-
	Knuckle Head	Philips(F)72129H,P76008R,Rarities(E)10
	When The Saints Go Marching In(band-vcl)	- -
	Baby Won't You Please Come Home	- ,Rarities(E)10
	Solitude	- -
	Red Top	- -

11 Coleman(tp,vcl),Bill Tamper(tb),Benny Waters(cl,as,ss),Jack Starling(p),Eddie de Haas
),Wallace Bishop(dr).   Live."Cluny Palace",Paris.October 23,1953

	Summertime	Pathé(F)unissued
	Boogie Blues	-
	Lover	Pathé(F)ST1047,TRS1003
	Alexander's Ragtime Band	unissued
	Honeysuckle Rose	-
	I Surrender Dear(bc)	Pathé(F)ST1047,TRS1003
	Bugle Call Rag	unissued

ession cont. next page).

(session cont. from previous page):

Royal Garden Blues	Pathé(F)ST1047,TRS1003
Some Of These Days	unissued
Mood Indigo	Pathé(F)ST1047,TRS1003
Old Maid Blues(bc)	-
When The Saints	
Go Marching In(bc)	unissued
St. Louis Blues(bc)	Pathé(F)ST1047

All titles on ST1047 also on Trianon(F)5-302.
Note:Tommy Brookins is listed on the sleeve as vocalist - but not heard on the LP.

BILL COLEMAN AND HIS BAND/ORCHESTRA:
Bill Coleman(tp,vcl),Michel De Villers(as),Guy Lafitte(ts),André Persiany(p),Paul Rovère
(b),Teddy Martin(dr).   Paris.December 15,1955

Them There Eyes	Columbia(F)ESDF1078,(E)SEG7684
I've Got My Love To Keep Me Warm	- -
Wrap Your Troubles In Dreams	- -
Metro Jazz	- -

Same.   Paris.December 21,1955

If I Had You	Columbia(F)ESDF1079,(E(SEG7645
Yes Sir That's My Baby	- -
Confessin' I/II(bc)	- -

Roger Paraboschi(dr) replaces Martin;add Cecily Ford(vcl).
                                 Paris.March 13,1956

St. Louis Baby	Columbia(F)ESDF1100,(E)SEG7722
Basin Street Blues(bc)	- -
Lullaby Of Birdland(cf)	- -
Ding Dong Boogie(cf)	- -

BILL COLEMAN AND HIS FOUR:
Bill Coleman(tp,vcl),Jean-Claude Pelletier(p),George Duvivier(b),Roger Paraboschi(dr).
                                 Paris.May 24,1956

Tin Roof Blues	Columbia(F)ESDF1119
I Got A Right	
To Sing The Blues(bc)	-
Blues In My Heart	-
Draggie Mama Blues(bc)	-

All titles also on Swing(Am)SW8410.

BILL COLEMAN AND HIS SEVEN:
Bill Coleman(tp,vcl),Fernand Verstraete(tb),Jacques Hendrix,Guy Lafitte(ts),Armand Migian
(bars),Jean-Claude Pelletier(p),George Duvivier(b,arr),Roger Paraboschi(dr).
                               Paris.September 12,1956

5534	All Too Soon	Columbia(F)FP1093
5535	My Ideal	-
5536	B And G Bounce	-
5537	Reunion In Paris	-
5538	Just A Gigolo(bc)	-
5539	Dinah(bc)	-
5540	Walking My Baby Back Home(bc)	-
5541	Jump For Joy(bc)	-

All titles also on Swing(Am)SW8410.

Bill Coleman(tp),Jean-Claude Pelletier(p),George Duvivier(b,arr),Christian Garros(dr),
strings.   Paris.September 17,1956
(session cont. next page).

(session cont. from previous page:
```
5542   Basel In Spring                     Columbia(F)FP1096
5543   April In Paris                          -
5544   A Foggy Day In London Town(bc)          -
5545   Chicago(bc)                             -
5546   The Golden Gate (San Francisco)         -
5547   Overhead On Stockholm                   -
5548   A Night In Rio                          -
5549   Autumn In New York
```

BILL COLEMAN AND THE NEW ORLEANS WILDCATS:
Bill Coleman(tp,vcl),Francis Bonjour(tp),Fred De Coulon(tb),Jean-Paul Augsburger(cl,as),
Claude Joly(p),Alain Dubois(g),Arnold Hoffmänner(b),Pierre Bouru(dr).
                          Live."Cinéma Bel-Air",Yverdon,Switzerland.November 6,1957
```
       Back Home Again In Indiana(bc)    Black&Blue(F)33.182
       Blues In My Heart(1)(bc)                -
       Basin Street Blues(bc)                  -
       Limehouse Blues                         -
       I'm Confessin'(bc)                      -
       N'embrassez Pas Ma Femme(bc)            -
       Saint Louis Blues(bc)                   -
```

-1.Coleman(tp,vcl) acc. by p,g,b,dr only.

BILL COLEMAN WITH THE TREMBLE KIDS:
Bill Coleman(tp,vcl),Edward Jegge(tp),Walter Leibundgut(tb),Werner Keller(cl),Jean Bionda
(p),Rolf Cizmek(b),Charly Antolini(dr).   Zürich,Switzerland.November 13,1957
```
       Sugar(bc)                         Columbia(Sw)SCMZ3003,SEGZ2017,33ZS102
       Sweet Lorraine(bc)(1)                   -            -            -
       Sweet Georgia Brown               Columbia(Sw)SEGZ2017,33ZS102
       Some Of These Days                      -            -
       Blues For Lilly(1)                Columbia(Sw)33ZS102
       Pennies From Heaven(bc)           Columbia(Sw)33ZS102
       Somebody Loves Me                       -
       If I Had You                            -
```

-1.Omit Jegge,Leibundgut,Keller.

All titles also on Trianon(F)CTRY7165.

Bill Coleman(tp,vcl),Claude Bolling(p),Roland Lobligeois(b),Kansas Fields(dr).
                                         Prob. Paris.c. 1958
```
       Indiana                           Giganti del Jazz(I)GJ22,Europa Jazz(I)EJ1019
       I Got Rhythm(1)                         -                        -
```

-1.Add unknown tb,ts.

Bill Coleman(tp),Quentin Jackson(tb),Budd Johnson(ts),Patti Bown(p),Les Spann -1(g),George
"Buddy" Catlett(b),Joe Harris(dr).   Paris.January 21,1960
```
       Have Blues,Will Play 'Em(1)       Brunswick(F)87.905
       From Boogie To Funk,
          pt.2 (The Boogie)(1)                 -
```

Same.   Paris.January 22,1960
```
       Bill,Budd And Butter              Brunswick(F)87.905
       Afromotif In Blue                       -
       Colemanology                            -
       From Boogie To Funk,
          pt.1 (The Blues)(1)                  -
```

All titles on Brunswick(F)87.905 also on Polydor(Eu)2445.035,837.235-2 (CD).

BILL COLEMAN AND HIS ORCHESTRA:
Incl. Bill Coleman(tp),Maurice Vander(p),Jean Bouchety(b,arr),Roger Paraboschi(dr).
Paris.October 14,1960
```
Hé,Vous,Avec Ces Beaux Yeux    Polydor(F)21.753
Connais-Tu                                -
Ma Petite Symphonie                       -
Pardonne-Moi                              -
```

BILL COLEMAN AND HIS ORCHESTRA:
Bill Coleman(tp,vcl),Henri Carels(tp),Léo Delsemme(tb,arr),Roger Demael(as,cl),Fernand
Durey(ts),Johnny Dover(bars),Jean-Pol Manderborght(p),Jean Warland(b),Léon Demeuldre(dr).
Brussels. 1960
```
Petite Fleur                   RCA(F)unissued
Alright,Okay,You Win                       -
Indiana                                    -
```

Bill Coleman(tp,vcl),Georges Bence,Louis Laboucarie,Jean Baissat,Tony Russo,Jean Liesse
(tp),André Feraud,Francois Guin,André Siot,Charles Orieux(tb),Claude Lénissois(cl),Hubert
Fol(as),Jef Gilson(org,arr),Gilbert Rovère,Jack Sewing(b),Gaëtan Dupenher,Alain Dahan(dr)
Tshura,Jacques Degor,unknown choir(vcl).   Paris. 1966
```
Jericho(bc)                    Unidisc(F)30.145
Pax                                       -
Sometimes I Feel
   Like A Motherless Child     Unidisc(F)30.146
Agnus Dei                                 -
```

Bill Coleman(tp,flh,vcl),Georges Bence,Louis Laboucarie(tp),Christian Guizien,Francois
Guin,Claude Gousset,Charles Orieux(tb),Eddie Louiss(org),Guy Pedersen(b),Lionel Magal(dr)
Jef Gilson(arr,cond).   Paris.May 8/9/10,1968
```
Let My People Go               Jazztone/Concert Hall(F)SJS1269
Blow Ye,The Trumpet Blow                   -
Dark Was The Night                         -
Nobody Knows The Trouble I've Seen         -
```

Bill Coleman(tp,vcl),Eddie Louiss(org),Jean-Charles Capon(cello),Gilbert Rovère(b),Lionel
Magal(dr),poss. others strings,Jeff Gilson(arr,cond).
Same dates
```
Swing Low Sweet Chariot        Jazztone/Concert Hall(F)SJS1269,SJS1303
Jericho                                    -
Old Time Religion                          -
Sometimes I Feel
   Like A Motherless Child                 -
```

Add Annie Vassiliu,Helène Devos,France Laurie(vcl).
Same dates
```
Salvation                      Jazztone/Concert Hall(F)SJS1269
Down By The Riverside                       - ,SJS1303
We Praise Thee,O God                       -
When The Saints
   Go Marching In(bc)                      -
```

All titles on SJS1269 also on Palm(F)PALM15.

BILL COLEMAN - BEN WEBSTER:
Bill Coleman(tp,flh,vcl),Ben Webster -1(ts),Fred Hunt(p),Jim Douglas(g),Ronnie Rae(b),
Lennie Hastings(dr).   London.April 27,1967
```
Bill Coleman(1)                Black Lion(E)2460.128
But Not For Me                             - ,2661.006,(G)157.001,(Am)
                               BLP20101
```
(session cont. next page).

(session cont. from previous page):
```
        Pound Horn(1)              Black Lion(E)2460.128,(G)157.000
        Sunday(bc)                           -
        For All We Know(2)                   -
        Satin Doll(bc)                       -
        For Max(1)                           -
```

-2.Omit Coleman.

All titles also on Black Lion(F)BLP30127,(Am)BL128,(G)28441,127.019,(Sp) (S)4.285.

BILL COLEMAN - BUDDY TATE:
Bill Coleman(tp,flh,vcl),Buddy Tate(ts),Georges Arvanitas(p,org),Pierre Sim(b),Charles
Bellonzi(dr).   Paris.December 5,1968
```
        L 'n' L Blues              Pathé(F)CPTX240863
        Impulsive                            -
        Isn't It Romantic                    -
        Cute                                 -
        Together At Last                     -
        Métro Jazz                           -
        Memories Of You(bc)                  -
        Stompin' At The Savoy                -
```

BILL COLEMAN PLUS FOUR:
Bill Coleman(tp,flh),Francois Guin(tb),Michael Garrett(p),Jean-Francois Catoire(b),Art
Taylor(dr).   Paris.January 30/31,1969
```
        For Me And My Gal          "77"(E)SEU12/34
        Satin Doll                           -
        Don't Blame Me                       -
        How High The Moon(1)                 -
        If I Had You                         -
        I'm In The Mood For Love             -
        Rosetta                              -
        Stairway To The Stars(1)             -
        I Believe In Miracles                -
        I Ain't Got Nobody                   -
```

-1.Omit Coleman,Guin.

BILL COLEMAN WITH RAYMOND FONSEQUE ORIGINAL BAND:
Bill Coleman(tp,flh,vcl),Marcel Bornstein(tp),Raymond Fonsèque(tb,cond),Jacques Caroff(cl)
Patrick Deroide(bassax),Philippe Baudoin(p),Jean-Paul Murile(bj),Claude Pou(wbd).
                                       Paris.April 5/29,1971
```
        Tenderly                   Jazztone/Concert Hall(F)SJS1335
        Let Me Dream                         -
        I'm Tipsy                            -
        Travelin' On A Cloud                 -
        Tomorrow Is Sunday                   -
        Bill And The Boys                    -
        Memories Of Old Days                 -
        Summernight's Dream                  -
        Looking Back                         -
        Feeling Fine                         -
```

Add Bernard Gremier(bj).   Montmagny,France.June 4,1971
```
        When The Saints
           Go Marching In(bc)      National(F)16169
        Hot Club Blues                       -
        Royal Garden Blues                   -
        Saint James Infirmary(bc)            -
```

Marc Richard(cl,ts) replaces Caroff;omit Gremier.

Taverny,France.September 26,1971
```
        After You've Gone(bc)        National(F)16169
        Sweet Georgia Brown                     -
```

BILL COLEMAN WITH LINO PATRUNO AND HIS FRIENDS:
Bill Coleman(tp,flh,vcl),Paolo Tomelleri -1(ts),Sergio Rigon -2(ts,fl),Mario Rusca(p),
Lino Patruno(b),Giorgio Vanni(dr).   Milan,Italy.December 1,1972
```
        Perdido(1)(bc)               Durium(I)A77313
        I Want A Little Girl(2)(bc)             -
```

Omit Rusca;add Giancarlo Cinti(b);Patruno plays(g).

Same date
```
        Out Of Nowhere(2)            Durium(I)A77313
        Pennies From Heaven(2)(bc)              -
```

Bill Coleman(tp,flh,vcl),Gianni Acocella(tb),Bruno Longhi(cl),Paolo Tomelleri -1,Sergio
Rigon -2(ts),Mario Rusca(p),Lino Patruno(g),Giancarlo Cinti(b),Giorgio Vanni(dr).

Milan,Italy.December 2,1972
```
        I've Found A New Baby(1)     Durium(I)A77313
        Honeysuckle Rose(2)(bc)                 -
```

Omit Cinti;Patruno plays(b).   Same date
```
        Basin Street Blues(bc)       Durium(I)A77313
        Perdido(1)(no tb,cl)(bc)        unissued
```

All titles on Durium(I)77313 also on Durium(F)C.062-94651.

BILL COLEMAN - GUY LAFITTE QUINTETTE:
Bill Coleman(tp,flh,vcl),Guy Lafitte(ts),Marc Hemmeler(p),Jack Sewing(b),Daniel Humair
(dr).   Live.Montreux Jazz Festival,Switzerland.July 4,197
```
        Blue Lou                     Black Lion(E)2460.212,
        Idaho                                   -
        Sur Les Quais Du Vieux Paris(1)         -
        L & L Blues(no ts)                      -
        Tour De Force                           -
        Montreux Jump                           -
        I Want A Little Girl(bc)     Black Lion(E)2460.213,(E)BLP30148
        I Know That You Know                    -                    -
```

-1.Omit Coleman.

All titles on Black Lion(E)2460.212 also on Black Lion(E)BLP30150,(G)28469,127.025,(Am)
BL212,(Sp) (S)4.287.
All titles on Black Lion(E)2460.213 also on Black Lion(G)28464,(Am)BL213,(Sp)4.286.

Bill Coleman(tp,flh),Vincent Casino,Louis Vézant,Georges Gay,Pierre Sellin(tp),Francis
Lussier,Emile Vilain,Benny Vasseur,Charles Verstraete(tb),Pierre Gossez,Georges Grenu,Jea
Aldegon,Jo Hrasko,Georges Bessières(sax),Guy Boyer,Jacques Larue,Alain Fougeret(p,vbs),
Francis Le Maguer,Pierre Cullaz(g),Alphonse Masselier,Pierre Sim(b),Jean-Marie Hauser,
André Arpino(dr),Jerry Mengo(cond)(coll.pers.).
                                Paris.November 15/16,1973
```
        Blowing For The Cats         Music For Pleasure(F)2M.056-64822
        One Room Flat                           -
        Twenty Turtles On A Tree                -
        Eve's Apple                             -
        Serenade For Two                        -
        Saucy Suzy                              -
        Gentle Storm                            -
        Blues Is How You Feel                   -
```
(session cont. next page).

(session cont. from previous page):
Take A Trip To The Stars	Music For Pleasure(F)2M.056-64822
Blow Them Sound	-
Sweet Lily Of Mine	-
Jumping On The Moon	-

All titles also on DRG SL5200.

Bill Coleman(flh),Gilbert Rost(tp),Raymond Fonsèque(tb),Olivier Frank(ss),Jean Poinsot(cl)
Philippe Baudoin(p),Ricardo Galeazzi(b),Claude-Alain Du Parquet(dr).
Paris.January 26,1975

Please Don't Talk About Me	Flame 1003/4
Sugar	-

Note:The above titles are from a Hugues Pannassié memorial concert; the rec. date may be
January 26,1976.

BILL COLEMAN WITH THE NEW RAGTIME BAND:
Bill Coleman(tp,vcl),Robert Antenen(tp),Pierre Descoeudres(tb),Jacques "Jacky" Milliet
(cl),Erwin "Vino" Montavon(p),Bernard Moritz(bj,g),Hans Schlaepfer(b),Rolf Siedler(dr).
Geneva,Switzerland.June 13,1976

Down By The Riverside(bc,band-vcl)	Vogue(F)406-LSDE5505
Blue Turning Grey Over You(bc)	-
Sweet Georgia Brown(bc)	-
That's A Plenty	-

All titles also on Vogue(F)VG407.505505.
Note:Additional titles on this LP are not by Bill Coleman.

BILL COLEMAN - DANY DORIZ:
Bill Coleman(tp,flh,vcl),Rolf Bührer(vtb),Dany Doriz(vbs),Patrice Authier(p),Henry
Tischitz(b),Michel Denis(dr).   "Caveau de la Huchette",Paris.March 21,1979

Goody,Goody(bc)	Jazzmosphere(F)JZ79.03
Cheek To Cheek(bc)	-
Lover Man(bc)	-

same.   "Caveau de la Huchette",Paris.March 22,1979

Cave's Blues(bc)	Jazzmosphere(F)JZ79.03
Bye Bye Blackbird(bc)	-
In A Mellotone	-

11 titles on JZ79.03 also on Adda 590.026 (CD).

BILL COLEMAN - RAYMOND FONSÈQUE:
Bill Coleman(tp),Raymond Fonsèque(tb),Daniel Huck(as),Dan Girard(bj),Alain Huguet(b,tu),
Claude Pou(dr).   Paris.May 7,1979

Whoopee,You're Mine	Milan Jazz(Sw)873.121(CD)
Don't Worry,Lily(?)	-
That's Where I Left My Heart	-
Sunny Side Up	-
Mr.Bill And Doctor Ray	-
Bla-Bla	-
Dancing Close Together	-
That's All	

Olivier Frank(ss) replaces Huck.   Paris.September 23,1979

Caravan	Milan Jazz(Sw)873.121(CD)
Petite Fleur	-

Bill Coleman(tp,flh,vcl),Guy Lafitte(ts),Red Richards(p),Bill Pemberton(b),Panama Francis (dr).

Toulouse,France.May 15,1980

Crazy Rhythm	Black&Blue(F)33.162
You've Changed(bc)	-
Tinto Time	-
On The Trail	-
Hello Babe	-
Really I Do	-
She's Funny That Way(bc)	-
I've Got My Love To Keep Me Warm	-
Montreux Jump	-

All titles also on Black&Blue(F)59.162-2 (CD).

DAVE COLEMAN

Tommy Ball(tp),Bud Pearson(as),Pepper Adams(bars),Dick Wetmore(vln),Pat Petracco(g),Everett Evans(b),Paul Drummond(cl),Dave Coleman(composer,arr,cond).

Boston.November 7,1956

Backstreet	Transition TRLP30,(J)GXF3126
Unknown titles	unissued

Note:The unknown titles were scheduled for Transition TRLP12 but this LP was never issued.

EARL COLEMAN

See also GENE AMMONS,CHARLIE PARKER.

(vcl) acc. by Miles Davis(tp),Gene Ammons(ts),Linton Garner(p),Connnie Wainwright(g),Tommy Potter(b),Art Blakey(dr).

LA.October 18,1946

168-1	Don't Sing Me The Blues	Black Lion(E)BLP60102
168-2	Don't Sing Me The Blues	-
169-1	Don't Explain To Me,Baby	-
169-2	Don't Explain To Me,Baby	-
169-3	Don't Explain To Me,Baby	-
169-4	Don't Explain To Me,Baby	-

All titles also on Black Lion(E)BLCD760102 (CD).
Note:See ANN HATHAWAY for additional titles from this session.

(vcl) acc. by unknown(p),Al Casey(g),Gene Ramey(b).

NYC.June 23,1948

S35128	It's A Crying Shame	Savoy unissued
S35129	Polka Dots and Moonbeams	-
S35130	Please	Savoy 672
S35131	Pennies From Heaven	-
S35132	My Old Flame	unissued

(vcl) acc. by LINTON GARNER'S ALL STARS:
Incl. Allen Eager(ts),Linton Garner(p),Kenny Clarke(dr).

NYC.October 25,1948

155	You're The One For Me	Atlantic unissued
156	I Won't Tell A Soul I Love You	-
157	Don't Bring Your Troubles To Me	Atlantic 872
158	I Hadn't Anyone 'Till You	-

Similar.   NYC.October/November 1948
161   I Don't Need You Now   Atlantic unissued
162   I Give You My Word   -

(vcl) acc. by Fats Navarro(tp),Don Lanphere(ts),Linton Garner(p,celeste),Al Casey(g),Jimmy
Johnson(b),Max Roach(dr).   NYC.November 29,1948
D1161 I Wished On The Moon   Dial 756
D1162A Guilty   - ,1049,Prestige 905
D1163C Yardbird Suite   Dial 753
D1164A A Stranger In Town   -
D1165A As Time Goes By   Dial 1049,LP212,Prestige 905

All titles - except "I Wished On The Moon" also on Xanadu 120,(J)JC7008,Spotlite(E)SPJ133.
Note:See FATS NAVARRO for an additonal title from this session.

(vcl) acc. by Billy Taylor(p),John Collins(g),Gene Ramey(b),Kelly Martin(dr).
                                             NYC. 1948
M-4001-5 Searching Blues   Jade 704
M-4002-2 Nightingale   -
         You're All That Matters Now   unissued
         When You Smile   -

(vcl) acc. by Art Farmer(tp),Gigi Gryce(as),Hank Jones(p),Oscar Pettiford(b),Shadow Wilson
dr).   NYC.March 2,1956
456   No Love,No Nothin'   Prestige PRLP7045
457   It's You Or No One   -
458   Come Rain Or Come Shine   -

vcl) acc. by Art Farmer(tp),Hank Jones(p),Wendell Marshall(b),Wilbert Hogan(dr).
                                             NYC.June 8,1956
11   Social Call   Prestige PRLP7045
12   Reminiscing   -
13   Say It Isn't So   -

ll titles on PRLP7045 also on Prestige(J)VIJ5023,Original Jazz Classics OJC187.

vcl) acc. by Harry Edison(tp),Tommy Flanagan(p),Reggie Workman(b),Gus Johnson(dr).
                                             NYC.1960
       Unknown titles   Gigi unissued

vcl) acc. by big band incl. Jerome Richardson(fl),Billy Taylor(p),Frank Foster,Tom
cIntosh(arr).   NYC.August 16,1966
0663   People   Atlantic LP/SD8172
0664   The Song Is You   unissued
0665   Work Song   Atlantic LP/SD8172
0666   I've Got You Under My Skin   -

vcl) acc. by Eddie Williams(tp),Billy Taylor(p),Gene Bertoncini(g),Reggie Workman(b),
obby Thomas(dr).   NYC.February 26,1967
1778   Manhattan Serenade   Atlantic LP/SD8172
1779   When Did You Leave Heaven   -
1780   A Day In The Life Of A Fool   -
1781   Charade   -
1782   There's No You   - ,7.81706-1,7.81706-2(CD)
1783   I Won't Tell A Soul (I Love You)   -
1784   I Wish I Knew   -

Note:Atlantic 7.81706-1 and 7.81706-2 (CD) are part of 7.81712-1 (LPset) and 7.81712-2
     (CD set) respectively.

(vcl) acc. by Al Cohn -1(ts),Hank Jones(p),George Duvivier(b),Leroy Williams(dr).
                                         NYC.September 9,1977
     A Song For You(1)   Xanadu 147
     What Are You Doing
        The Rest Of Your Life   -
     Two Different Worlds(1)   -
     My Funny Valentine   -
     All In Love Is Fair   - ,5001,(Eu)197.150
     The Very Thought Of You(1)   -
     Wave   -
     Dark Shadows(1)   -

All titles also on Xanadu(Eu)197.119,(J)KUX71.

EARL COLEMAN - TED DUNBAR:
(vcl) acc. by Harris Simon(p),Ted Dunbar(g),George Duvivier(b),Leroy Williams(dr).
                                         NYC.January 12,1979
     It's A Cryin' Shame   Xanadu 175
     I Love You   -
     I Need A Shoulder To Cry On   -
     Lover   -
     Embraceable You   -
     You Don't Know What Love Is   -
     I Got It Bad
        (And That Ain't Good)   -
     I Guess It's The Mood I'm In   -
     Moonlight In Vermont   -
     There's Something
        About An Old Love   -

All titles also on Xanadu(J)BRJ4544 (CD).

GEORGE COLEMAN

See also WYNTON KELLY.

GEORGE COLEMAN - TETE MONTOLIU DUO:
George Coleman(ts),Tete Montoliu(p).
                                         Weesp,The Netherland.February 20,1977
     Lisa   Timeless(Du)SJP110
     Dynamic Duo   -
     First Time Down   -
     Waltzing At Rosa's Place   -
     Meditation   -
     Sophisticated Lady   -

All titles also on Timeless(Am)TI312.

THE GEORGE COLEMAN OCTET:
Danny Moore(tp,flh),Frank Strozier(as),George Coleman,Junior Cook(ts),Mario Rivera(bars),
Harold Mabern(p),Lisle Atkinson(b),Idris Muhammad(dr).
                                         NYC.November 2/3,1977
     On Green Dolphin Street   Catalyst(J)KUX73
     Frank's Tune   -
     Big George   - ,Atlantis(E)ATSD14
     Joggin(1)   -
     Body And Soul   -
     Revival   -

-1.Add Azzedin Weston(perc).
(session cont. next page).

(session cont. from previous page):
ll titles also on Affinity(E)AFF52,AFF178,CD766 (CD),Charly(E)83 (CD),Collection Thésis
Jazz(F)THJ82032,VeeJay(J)30YD7015 (CD).

George Coleman(ts),Hilton Ruiz(p),Sam Jones(b),Billy Higgins(dr).
NYC.December 29,1978

Amsterdam After Dark	Timeless(Du)SJP129	
New Arrival	-	
Lo-Joe	-	
Autumn In New York	-	
Apache Dance	-	
Blondie's Waltz	-	

ll titles also on Timeless(J)30R2-10 (CD).

eorge Coleman(ts),Hilton Ruiz(p),Ray Drummond(b),Billy Higgins(dr).
Live."Ronnie Scott's",London.April 19/20,1979

Blues Inside Out	Pye(E)N121
Walking	-
Stella By Starlight	-

ll titles also on Vogue(F)VG408-N121.

ame.
Live."Ronnie Scott's",London.April 1979

Laura	Jazz House(E)JH002,JHCD002(CD)		
Siorra	-	-	,NARCD1(CD)
Moment's Notice	-	-	
Oleo	Debut(E)1/2		

LORIA COLEMAN

eo Wright(as),Gloria Coleman(org),Grant Green(g),Pola Roberts(dr).
NYC.May 21,1963

1498	Hey Sonny Red	Impulse A(S)47
1499	My Lady's Waltz	-
1500	Melba's Minor	-
1501	Funky Bob	-
1502	Que Baby	-
1503	Sadie Green	-

y Copeland -1(flh),Dick Griffin -1(tb),James Anderson(ts),Gloria Coleman(org,vcl),Earl
nbar(g),Charlie Davis(dr).
NYC.c. 1965

Bugaloo For Ernie	Mainstream MRL322
Sunday,Monday Or Always(1)	-
Fungi Mama	-
You Better Go Now(1)	-
Blues For Youse	-
Blue Bossa(1)	-
Love Nest(1)	-
Fly Me To The Moon	-

NETTE COLEMAN

e also PAUL BLEY,CHARLIE HADEN,LENOX STUDENT SMALL GROUP/LARGE ENSEMBLE,JAMES "BLOOD"
MER.
ection cont. next page).

- 144 -

ORNETTE COLEMAN

Note:List of equivalents (Atlantic Records).
  When Don Cherry started recording he was playing a pocket-cornet - which he calls a
  pocket-trumpet - but later he changed (at least for some years) to a full-sized cornet. On most recordings his instrument is listed as pocket-trumpet; this discography
  lists the instrument as cornet (cnt).

Don Cherry(cnt),Ornette Coleman(as),Walter Norris(p),Don Payne(b),Billy Higgins(dr).
                                        LA.February 10,1958
        Alpha   Contemporary M3551/C3551
        Jayne   -
        Chippie   -
        The Time Is Now   unissued
        McB   -

Same.   LA.February 22,1958
        The Blessing   Contemporary M3551/C3551
        The Sphinx   -
        Embraceable You   unissued
        Invisible   Contemporary M3551/C3551
        When Will The Blues Leave   rejected
        Angel Voice   Contemporary M3551/C3551
        The Disguise   -

Same.   LA.March 24,1958
        McB   Contemporary rejected
        The Disguise   -
        When Will The Blues Leave   Contemporary M3551/C3551

All titles on M3551/C3551 also on Contemporary S7551,(F)CHTX240489,(J)LAX3024,GXC3181,
SR3143,VDJ1664 (CD),Vogue(E)LAC12170,Original Jazz Classics OJC163,OJCCD163-2 (CD),Bopli-
city(E)COP024.

ORNETTE COLEMAN QUARTET:
Don Cherry(cnt),Ornette Coleman(as),Red Mitchell(b),Shelly Manne(dr).
                                        LA.January 16,1959
        Lorraine   Contemporary M3569

Same.   LA.February 23,1959
        Turnaround   Contemporary M3569
        Endless   -

Percy Heath(b) replaces Mitchell.   LA.March 9/10,1959
        Tears Inside   Contemporary M3569
        Tomorrow Is The Question   -
        Compassion   -
        Giggin'   -
        Rejoicing   -
        Mind And Time   -

All titles on M3569 also on Contemporary S7569,(F)HTX40389,99.972 (CD),(J)LAX3025,GXC3182,
VDJ1634 (CD),Vogue(E)LAC12228,Original Jazz Classics OJC342,OJCCD342-2 (CD),Boplicity(E)
COP002.

Don Cherry(cnt),Ornette Coleman(as),Charlie Haden(b),Billy Higgins(dr).
                                        LA.May 22,1959
3507   Focus On Sanity   Atlantic LP/SD1317
3508   Chronology(1)   - ,(Sd)EP80.016,(I)2K60010
3509   Peace   - ,(I)2K60010
3510   Congeniality(2)   - ,(Sd)EP80.016,(I)2K60010,Smith-
                                        sonian Inst. P6.11891,RD033-5(CD)
(session cont. next page).

ORNETTE COLEMAN

(session cont. from previous page):

511	Lonely Woman	Atlantic LP/SD1317,SD1558,781709-1,781709-2(CD), (F)30.013,(I)2K60010,Smithsonian Institute P6.11891,RD033-5(CD)
512	Monk And The Nun(3)	Atlantic SD1588
513	Just For You	Atlantic SD1572,790978-2(CD)
514	Eventually	Atlantic LP/SD1317,781709-1,781709-2(CD)

1.Originally listed as "Step In".
2.Originally listed as "Nomad".
3.Originally listed as "C.C.".

11 titles also on Atlantic(J)30XD1032 (CD).

same.   LA.October 8,1959

865	Una Muy Bonita	Atlantic 5008(ed),LP/SD1327,SD1558,SD2-316,(Sd) EP80.035,(F)30.013,940.031
866	Bird Food	Atlantic LP/SD1327,(Sd)EP80.035,(I)2K60010
867	Change Of The Century	-
868	Music Always	Atlantic(J)P10085,790978-2(CD)
869	The Face Of The Bass	Atlantic LP/SD1327,(I)2K60010

Note:The seven compositions issued on P10085 were assigned new titles by Coleman at the
      time of release. In the playing sequence these seven titles form a poem ("Music Al-
      ways/Brings Goodness/To Us/All/P.S. Unless One Has/Some Other/Motive For Its Use").
      Unfortunately this title assignment has created some confusion, since at least two
      of the compositions already had other titles.

same.   LA.October 9,1959

870	Forerunner	Atlantic LP/SD1327
871	Untitled original	unissued
872	Free	Atlantic LP/SD1327
869	The Face Of The Bass	rejected
873	The Circle With A Hole In The Middle(1)	Atlantic SD1572,790978-2(CD)
865	Una Muy Bonita	rejected
874	Ramblin'	Atlantic LP/SD1327,SD1558,781709-1,781709-2(CD), (F)30.013,Franklin Mint 97

1.Originally listed as "Crossroads" (and appeared under that title on recordings by
  PAUL BLEY).

Note:Atlantic 7.81709-1 and 7.81709-2 (CD) are part of 7.81712-1 (LPset) and 7.81712-2
     (CD set) respectively.

Don Cherry(cnt),Ornette Coleman(as),Charlie Haden(b),Ed Blackwell(dr).
                                           NYC.July 19,1960

23	Little Symphony(2)	Atlantic SD1588
24	Kaleidoscope	Atlantic LP/SD1353
25	Untitled original	unissued
26	Untitled original	-
27	Blues Connotation	Atlantic LP/SD1353,SD1558,(F)30.013
27	P.S. Unless One Has(1)	Atlantic(J)P10085
28	Untitled original	unissued
29	Untitled original	-

1.This title is in fact an alternate version of "Blue Connotation" (see note after ses
  sion October 8,1959).
2.Originally listed as "Skyline".

Note:Some - or all - of the above tunes listed "Untitled original" were poss. recorded
     July 26,1960.

Same.   NYC.July 26,1960
4734   Joy Of A Toy(1)   Atlantic SD1588
4735   To Us   Atlantic(J)P10085
4736   Humpty Dumpty(2)   Atlantic LP/SD1353
4736   The Fifth Of Beethoven(2)   Atlantic SD1572,790978-2(CD)
4737   Motive For Its Use   Atlantic(J)P10085
4738   Moon Inhabitants   Atlantic SD1572,790978-2(CD)
4739   The Legend Of Be-Bop   -   -
4740   Some Other   Atlantic(J)P10085
4741   Embraceable You   Atlantic LP/SD1353,SD1558,(F)30.013
4742   Dawn   Atlantic unissued
       All(3)   Atlantic(J)P10085
       Brings Goodness(4)   -   ,790978-2(CD)

-1.Originally listed as "Royalty".
-2."Humpty Dumpty" is a diff. take of "The Fifth Of Beethoven" - with part of the composi-
   tional material omitted. "The Fifth Of Beethoven" was also recorded in 1966 - entitled
   "Atavism".
-3.This title was recorded June 28,1960 by John Coltrane and Don Cherry as "Cherryco".
-4.Poss. rec. July 19,1960.

Same.   NYC.August 2,1960
4764   Untitled original   Atlantic unissued
4765   Folk Tale   Atlantic LP/SD1353
4766   Untitled original   unissued
4767   Poise   Atlantic LP/SD1353
4768   Untitled original   unissued
4769   Untitled original   -
4770   Untitled original   -
4771   Untitled original   -
4772   Untitled original   -
4773   Beauty Is A Rare Thing   Atlantic LP/SD1353,(I)2K60010
4774   Untitled original   unissued
4775   Untitled original   -
4776   Untitled original   -
4777   Untitled original   -
4778   Untitled original   -
4779   Untitled original   -

Note:Some of the above unissued titles are re-recordings of titles recorded July 19 and
     July 26,1960.

ORNETTE COLEMAN DOUBLE QUARTET:
Don Cherry(cnt),Freddie Hubbard(tp),Ornette Coleman(as),Eric Dolphy(bcl),Charlie Haden,
Scott LaFaro(b),Ed Blackwell,Billy Higgins(dr).
                                               NYC.December 21,1960
5247-1 Free Jazz(1)   Atlantic SD1588
5247-2 Free Jazz   Atlantic LP/SD1364

-1.Issued as "First Take".

Both takes also on Atlantic 7.81347-2 (CD),(J)30XD1031 (CD).
Note:An excerpt from master 5247-2 also on Smithsonian Inst. P6.11891(ed.),RD033-5 (CD).

ORNETTE COLEMAN QUARTET:
Don Cherry(cnt),Ornette Coleman(as),Scott LaFaro(b),Ed Blackwell(dr).
                                               NYC.January 31,1961
5316   Untitled original   Atlantic unissued
5317   W.R.U.   Atlantic LP/SD1378
5318   Check-Up   Atlantic SD1588
(session cont. next page).

(session cont. from previous page):

5319	T. & T.	Atlantic LP/SD1378
5320	C. & D.	- ,SD1558
5321	R.P.D.D.	-
5322	The Alchemy Of Scott LaFaro	Atlantic SD1572,790978-2(CD)

Don Cherry(cnt),Ornette Coleman(<u>ts</u>),Jimmy Garrison(b),Ed Blackwell(dr).
                                        NYC.March 22,1961

5417	Untitled original	Atlantic unissued
5418	Eos	rejected
5419	Ecars	-
5420	Untitled original	unissued
5421	Cross Breeding	rejected

Same.   NYC.March 27,1961

5427-1	Enfant	Atlantic LP/SD1394
5428-2	Ecars	-
5429-4	Eos	-
5430-4	Cross Breeding	-
5431-3	Untitled original(1)	unissued
5432-1	Harlem's Manhattan	Atlantic SD1572,790978-2(CD)
5433	Mapa	rejected
5434	Harlem's Manhattan	-
5435	Ecars	-
5436-1	Mapa	Atlantic LP/SD1394

-1.The above tune is the same as played on master 5417 from session March 22,1961.

ORNETTE COLEMAN DOUBLE QUARTET:
Don Cherry(cnt),Bobby Bradford(tp),Steve Lacy(ss),Ornette Coleman(as),Jimmy Garrison,Art
Davis(b),Charles Moffett,Ed Blackwell(dr).   NYC.c. June 1961
        Unknown titles   unissued

Note:Atlantic masterbooks and session files do not list this session; the information is
     based on a note - and a photo - in Down Beat, but it has not been possible to verify
     that a recording actually took place.

STRING QUARTET:
Selwart Clarke,Nathan Goldstein(vln),Julian Barber(vla),Kermit Moore(cello).
                                        Live.Town Hall,NYC.December 21,1962
        Dedication To Poets And Writers ESP 1006,1006-2(CD)

ORNETTE COLEMAN TRIO:
Ornette Coleman(as),David Izenzon(b),Charles Moffett(dr).
                                        Same concert

Story Teller	(Blue Note BST84210 - see note)
Sadness	ESP 1006,1033(ed),1006-2(CD),Musica Jazz(I)MJP1018
The Ark	- ,1006-2(CD)
Opus D (Taurus)(b-solo)	ESP 1006-2(CD)
I Don't Love You	- ,(Blue Note BST84210 - see note)
Children's Book	- -

Add Chris Towns(p),Nappy Allen(g),Barney Richardson(el-b).
                                        Same concert

Blues Misused	unissued

Omit Towns,Allen,Richardson.   Same concert

Architect	unissued
Play It Straight	(Blue Note BST84210 - see note)
Doughnut	ESP 1006,1006-2(CD)

(session cont. next page).

(session cont. from previous page):
All titles on ESP 1006 also on ESP(J)7420,SFX10727,BT5001,15PJ2019,Fontana(E)SFJL923,Magic
Music 30010 (CD),Base(I)1006.
Note:Blue Note originally scheduled to issue 2 LPs (BST84210, BST84211) from this concert
   because of legal problems these LPs were never released. The content of BST84210 is
   listed above while BST84211 duplicates ESP 1006 - with the addition of "Opus D" (Tau-
   rus)".

ORNETTE COLEMAN - ALBERT AYLER:
Ornette Coleman(tp),Charles Tyler(C-mels),Albert Ayler(ts),Fred Lyman(g),Norman Butler
(cello,as),Earle Henderson(b).   NYC.c. December 1963
      Unknown titles   unissued

Note:The above was a private recording.

Ornette Coleman(as),rest unknown.   Unknown location.c. 1963
      Unknown titles

Note:The unknown titles are from the "Soundtrack for Improvisation" short film soundtrack

Ornette Coleman(as),Pharoah Sanders(ts),David Izenzon(b),Charles Moffett(dr),unknown
brass,strings,Joseph Tekula(cond).   NYC.June 15/16/17,1965
      Chappaqua Suite,Parts I-IV   CBS(F)62896/62897,(Eu)BPG66203,S66403(ed.),(J)
                                       SONP50249/50,SOPW13/14,Supraphon(Cz)0152114,
                                       SUA15998,SUA ST55998

Note:"Chappaqua Suite" was written and recorded as the soundtrack for the Conrad Rooks
   film "Chappaqua" but was later rejected and not used; the issued version is edited.

THE VIRTUOSO ENSEMBLE:
John Burden(frh),Edward Walker(fl),Derek Wickens(oboe),Sidney Fell(cl),Cecil James(bassoon),Ornette Coleman(comp).   Live.Fairfield Hall,Croydon,England.August 29,196
      Sounds And Forms For
         Wind Quartet,movements 1-10   Polydor(E)623.246

ORNETTE COLEMAN TRIO:
Ornette Coleman(as-1,tp-2,vln-3),David Izenzon(b),Charles Moffett(dr).
                                         Same concert
      Sadness(1)   Polydor(E)623.246,I Grandi del Jazz(I)GdJ11
      The Clergyman's Dream(1)   -   -
      Falling Stars(2,3)   Polydor(E)623.247,   -
      Silence(1)   -
      Happy Fool(1)   -
      Ballad(1)   -   ,I Grandi del Jazz(I)GdJ11
      Dough Nuts(!)(2)   -   ,Arista LP1,   -

All titles also on Vogue(F)VG405.511017.
All titles on Polydor(E)623.246/47 also on Polydor(E)2383.090/91,(J)SMP9022/23,Freedom(G)
BL28427/1-2,157.300,(F)FLP40102/03,FLP4100/01,(J)32JDF170 (CD),Arista(Am)1900,(J)PA9741/4
Black Lion(E)BLM51503/04,Discophon(Sp)4265,Trio(J)PAP9207/08.
Note:Arista LP1 is a sampler which was not issued commercially.

ORNETTE COLEMAN TRIO:
Ornette Coleman(as-1,tp-2,vln-3),David Izenzon(b),Charles Moffett(dr).
                                         Live.Sportpalast,Berlin.October 30,1965
      Sadness(1)
      Falling Stars(1,2,3)
      The Clergyman's Dream(1)
      Ballad(1)

ORNETTE COLEMAN

Same.   Live.Tivoli's Koncertsal,Copenhagen.October 31,1965
      Lonely Woman(1)   Magnetic(G)MRCD131(CD)
      The Clergyman's Dream(1)   -
      Falling Stars(2,3)   -
      Sadness(1)   -

Note:MRCD131 also incl. an interview with Coleman.

Same.   Live.Stockholm.November 2,1965
      The Clergyman's Dream(1)
      Sadness(1)
      The Happy Fool(1)
      Falling Stars(2,3)

Same.   Live.Paris.November 4,1965
      Sadness(1)   Magnetic(G)MRCD122(CD)
      Lonely Woman(1)   -
      Falling Stars(2,3)   -
      The Clergyman's Dream(1)   -

Same.   Paris.November 1965
      January(1,2,3)   Atmosphere(F)IRI5006
      Sortie Le Coquard(1)   -
      Dans Le Neige(1,2,3)   -
      The Changes(1,2,3)   -
      Better Get Yourself
         Another Self(1,2,3)   -
      The Duel,Two Psychic
         Lovers And Eating Time(1,2,3)   -
      The Mis-used Blues (The
         Lovers And The Alchemist)(1)   Atmosphere(F)IRI5007
      The Poet(2,3)   -
      Wedding Day And Fuzz(1)   -
      Fuzz,Feast,Breakout,
         European Echoes,
         Alone And The Arrest(1,3)   -

All titles also on Affinity(E)AFFD102,Trio(J)PAP9254/55.
Note:The above titles are from the "Who's Crazy" film soundtrack.

Same.   Broadcast."Gyllene Cirkeln",Stockholm.November 22,1965
      Sadness(1)
      The Clergyman's Dream(1)
      Lonely Woman(1)

Note:Rec.date poss. December 3,1965.

Same.   TV-cast.Stockholm.November/December 1965
      Sadness(1)
      The Clergyman's Dream(1)
      Falling Stars(2,3)

Note:The above titles were broadcast December 9,1965.

Same.   Live."Gyllene Cirkeln",Stockholm.December 3,1965
      The Blessing(1)   Blue Note unissued
      Dee Dee(1)   -
      Faces And Places(1)   -
      Antiques(1)   Blue Note BLP4225/BST84225
      Dawn(1)   unissued
(session cont. next page).

(session cont. from previous page):
```
      European Echoes(1)                     unissued
      The Riddle(1)                          -
      Morning Song(1)             Blue Note BLP4225/BST84225,Franklin Mint 36
      Snowflakes And Sunshine(2,3)           unissued
      Dee Dee(1)                             -
      Dawn(1)                     Blue Note BLP4224/BST84224
```

```
Same.                           Live."Gyllene Cirkeln",Stockholm.December 4,196
      Dee Dee(1)                Blue Note unissued
      Faces And Places(1)                    -
      European Echoes(1)        Blue Note BLP4224/BST84224,BST89904,LA160,Liberty
                                             (Eu)LBS83443
      Dawn(1)                                unissued
      The Riddle(1)                          -
      Snowflakes And Sunshine(2,3)           -
```

Note:The above titles are from the afternoon performance.

```
Same.                           Live."Gyllene Cirkeln",Stockholm.December 4,196
      Morning Song(1)           Blue Note unissued
      Antiques(1)                            -
      The Clergyman's Dream(1)               -
      Dawn(1)                                -
      Dee Dee(1)                             -
      Faces And Places(1)                    -
      European Echoes(1)                     -
      The Riddle(1)             Blue Note BLP4225/BST84225
      Antiques(1)                            unissued
      Dee Dee(1)                Blue Note BLP4224
      Snowflakes And Sunshine(2,3)  Blue Note BLP4225/BST84225
      Faces And Places(1)       Blue Note BLP4224/BST84224
      Dawn(1)                                unissued
      European Echoes(1)                     -
      Dee Dee(1)                             -
```

All titles on BLP4224 also on Blue Note BCT84224 (CD),CDP7.84224-2 (CD),(E)BNS40021,(J)
GXK8107,GXF3018,BNJ71045,CP32-9539 (CD).
All titles on BLP4225 also on Blue Note BCT84225 (CD),CDP7.84225-2 (CD),(E)BNS40022,(J)
GXK8108,BNJ71046,CP32-9540 (CD).
Note:The above titles are from the evening performance.

```
Same.                           Broadcast.Paris.February 18,1966
      The Happy Fool(?)
      Dee Dee(1)
      Sadness(1)
      Doughnut(1,4)             Trio(J)PA7169/70
      Unknown ballad(?)
      The Clergyman's Dream(1)
      Unknown title(2,5)        Trio(J)PA7169/70
      Unknown title(3,6)                     -
```

-4.As "All Day Affair" on Trio(J)PA7169/70.
-5.As "14 Juillet" on Trio(J)PA7169/70.
-6.As "Reminiscense" on Trio(J)PA7169/70.

Note:The last two titles are prob. from this concert.

```
Same.                           Live.Maison de l'ORTF,Paris.February 26,196
      The Clergyman's Dream(1)
      European Echoes(1)
      Doughnut(1)
```

Same.   Live.San Remo Jazz Festival,Italy.March 27,1966
          Atavism(1,4)
          Snowflakes And Sunshine(2,3)
          Sadness(1)
          European Echoes(1)
          Dee(1)

-4.A.k.a. "The Fifth Of Beethoven".

Same.   NYC(?).c. August 1966
          Unknown titles

Note:The unknown titles are from the Canadian "Population Explosion / Explosion Demogra-
     phique" film (animated cartoon) soundtrack.

ORNETTE COLEMAN TRIO:
Ornette Coleman(as-1,tp-2,vln-3),Charlie Haden(b),Ornette Denardo Coleman(dr).
                                   NYC.September 9,1966
1780   The Empty Foxhole(2)   Blue Note BLP4246/BST84246
1781   Freeway Express(2)   -
1782   Zig Zag(1,4)   -
1783   Faithful(1)   -
1784   Sound Gravitation(3)   -
1785   Good Old Days(1)   -

-4.Originally listed as "Play Ground".

All titles also on Blue Note(J)GXK8149.

ORNETTE COLEMAN QUARTET:
Ornette Coleman(as-1,tp-2,vln-3,musette -4),Charlie Haden,David Izenzon(b),Charles Moffett
(dr).   Live."Village Theatre",NYC.March 17,1967
          The Little Symphony(1)   unissued
          Just For You(2)   -
          A Capella For Three
             Wise Men And A Saint(2,3)   -
          Bhudda's Blues(4)   -
          Love And Sex(1)   -
          Atavism(1)   -
          European Echoes(1)   -

Note:The above titles were prob. recorded by RCA-Victor.

ORNETTE COLEMAN AND THE PHILADELPHIA WIND QUINTET:
Ornette Coleman(tp,comp),Mason Jones(frh),Murray Panitz(fl,picc),John DeLancie(oboe,enh),
Anthony Gigliotti(cl,bcl),Bernard Garfield(bassoon).
                                   Same concert
URAI-1475 Forms And Sounds   RCA LM/LSC2982

Note:During the above concert the Philadelphia Wind Quintet also performed - without Cole-
     man - "En Forme De Choros" (comp. by Villalobos) and "Titles" (comp. by Coleman and
     F.A. Chambers).

THE CHAMBER SYMPHONY OF PHILHARMONIC QUARTET:
Stuart Canin,William Steck(vln),Carlton Cooley(vla),Willem Stokking(cello),Ornette Coleman
(composer).   NYC.March 31,1967
URAI-1494 Space Flight   RCA LM/LSC2982,Franklin Mint 64
URAI-1495 Saints And Soldiers   -

All titles on LM/LSC2982 also on RCA 6561-2 (CD),(E)RD/SF7944,(Eu)ND86561 (CD),(J)RCA6023.

Ornette Coleman(as),David Izenzon,Charlie Haden(b),Charles Moffett(dr).
NYC.July 21,1967
   Holiday For A Graveyard   Flying Dutchman FDS-104

Note:The above title was recorded at John Coltrane's funeral and issued under Bob Thiele's
  name.

Same.   Live.Monterey Jazz Festival.September 17,1967
    Haight Ashbury
    Unknown title
    Unknown title

Note:The above titles were poss. recorded.

Ornette Coleman(as-1,tp-2,musette-3),David Izenzon,Charlie Haden(b),Ed Blackwell(dr).
Live.Teatro Lirico,Milan,Italy.February 5,1968
    Holiday For A Graveyard
    Forgotten Children
    Haight Ashbury
    New York   Jazz Up(I)JU310(CD)
    Buddah's Blues(3)
    Three Wise Men And A Sage Jazz Up(I)JU310(CD)
    Tutti   -
    Sunrise

Same.   Live.Rome.February 8,1968
    Lonely Woman(1)   Joker(J)UPS2061
    Unknown title(1,4)   -
    Let's Play(2,5)   -
    Buddah's Blues(3)   -

-4.As "Monsieur Prince" on LP.
-5.As "Forgotten Children" on LP.

All titles also on Lotus(I)LOP14.074,Passport Lotus(I)LPPS11.116.

Same.   Paris.February 12,1968
    4 unknown titles

ORNETTE COLEMAN QUARTET:
Ornette Coleman(as-1,tp-2,vln-3,musette-4),David Izenzon,Charlie Haden(b),Ed Blackwell
(dr),Yoko Ono(vcl).   Rehearsal.London.February 29,1968
    Aos (Emotion Modulation)(2)(yo) Apple SW3373,SAPCOR17

Note:The above title was issued as by YOKO ONO.

Same.   Live.Royal Albert Hall,London.February 29,1968
    Emotion Modulation(2,3)(yo) Apple(?)unissued
    Sunrise(2)   -
    Forgotten Children(1)   -
    Long Time No See(1)   -
    Lonely Woman(1)   -
    Haight Ashbury(1)   -
    Budda's Blues(4)   -
    Three Wise Men And The Sage(3) -

Note:It is not known if some - or all - of the above titles were recorded.

ORNETTE COLEMAN QUARTET:
Ornette Coleman(as-1,tp-2,vln-3),Dewey Redman(ts),Jimmy Garrison(b),Elvin Jones(dr).
NYC.April 29,1968

We Now Interrupt		
For A Commercial(3,4)	Blue Note Blue Note BST84287,B2-84287(CD)	
Love Call(2)	Blue Note B2-84356(CD)	
The Garden Of Souls(1,5)	Blue Note BST84287,B2-84287(CD)	
Open To The Public(1)	Blue Note BST84356,B2-84356(CD)	
Toy Dance(1)	Blue Note BST84287,B2-84287(CD)	
Check Out Time(1)	Blue Note B2-84356(CD)	
Airborne(1)	Blue Note BST84356,B2-84356(CD)	
Broad Way Blues(1)	Blue Note B2-84287(CD)	

-4.On the LP version the voice of Mel Fuhrman was overdubbed for the announcements - on
   the CD version the original announcements by the band are restored.
-5.The opening theme from the rejected May-version was used.

Same.   NYC.May 7,1968

Love Call(2)	Blue Note BST84356(ed.),B2-84356(CD)	
Just For You(2)	Blue Note B2-84356(CD),(Eu)BOX5	
Broad Way Blues(1)	Blue Note BST84287,B2-84287(CD),(Du)1A.158-83401/4	
Check Out Time(1)	Blue Note BST84356,B2-84356(CD)	
The Garden Of Souls(1)	rejected(see above note 5)	
Round Trip(1)	Blue Note BST84287,B2-84287(CD)	

All titles on B2-84287 (CD) also on Blue Note(Eu)CDP7.84287-2 (CD).
All titles on B2-84356 (CD) also on Blue Note(Eu)CDP7.84356-2 (CD).
Note:Several of the titles on the LP issues were edited - the CD issues restore the ori-
   ginal versions.

ORNETTE COLEMAN QUARTET:
Ornette Coleman(as-1,tp-2,vln-3),Dewey Redman(ts),Charlie Haden(b),Ornette Denardo Coleman
(dr).   Live.Hearst Greek Amphitheatre,University of Cal.,Berkeley,Cal.August 11,1968

C.O.D.(1)	Impulse AS9178	
Rainbows(2)	-	
New York(1)	-	
Bells And Chimes(3)	-	
Sun Suite Of San Francisco(1)	unissued	

-1.Add Bobby Bradford,Allan Smith(tp),John Mosher(b),Jerry Granelli(perc),members of the
   San Francisco Symphony Orchestra.

All titles also on AS9178 also on Impulse(E)MIPL/SIPL518,(I)IMP442,(J)YP8601.

ORNETTE COLEMAN QUINTET:
Add Don Cherry(cnt).   Live.Loeb Student Center,New York University,NYC.March 22,1969

91059	Broken Shadows(1)	Impulse AS9187
	Who Do You Work For	unissued
	The Anthem	-
91060	Comme It Faut(1)	Impulse AS9187
91061	Space Jungle(1,4)	-
91062	Song For Che(1)	- ,AS9253(ed.)
	Unknown title	unissued
91063	Trouble In The East(1)	Impulse AS9187

-4.Cherry plays (Indian-fl),Redman plays (cl).

All titles on AS9187 also on Impulse(E)IMPL8002,(I)3C.064-95722,(J)YP8602.
Note:Mastersnumbers were added later by Impulse.

Ornette Coleman(as-1,tp-2,vln-3),Dewey Redman(ts),Charlie Haden(b),Ed Blackwell(dr).
                              NYC.June 7,1969
91045 Man On The Moon(1,4)   Impulse 45-275,Pathé(F)2C.006-90643
91046 Growing Up(1,2)   -   -

-4.Add Emmanuel Ghent(electronics).

Note:(tp) on "Growing Up" was overdubbed.

Ornette Denardo Coleman(dr) replaces Blackwell.
                     Live.Loeb Student Center,New York University,NYC.June 20,1969
          Unknown titles

Ornette Coleman(as-1,tp-2,vln-3),Dewey Redman(ts),Charlie Haden(b),Ed Blackwell(dr).
                              Live.Bilzen,Belgium.August 24,1969
          Space Jungle(2,3,4)   Moon(I)MLP022-1
          Comme Il Faut(1,5)   -
          Song For Che(1)   -
          Broken Shadows(1)   -
          Tomorrow(1,6)   -

-4.This is not the same composition as "Space Jungle" from the March 22,1969 concert.
-5.As "As It Should Be" on Moon issues.
-6.As "Count Down" on Moon issues.

All titles also on Moon(I)MCD022-2 (CD).

Ornette Coleman(as-1,tp-2,vln-3,musette-4),David Izenzon,Charlie Haden(b),Charles Moffett
(dr).   Live.Boston University,Mass.November 30,1969
          Sadness(1)
          Buddah's Blues(4)
          The Good Life(1)
          Unknown titles

Ornette Coleman(as-1,tp-2,vln-3),Dewey Redman(ts),Charlie Haden(b),Ed Blackwell(dr).
                              Live.NYC.February 14,1970
          Friends And Neighbors(3,4)   Flying Dutchman FDS123
          Friends And Neighbors(3)   -
          Long Time No See(1)   -
          Let's Play(2)   -
          Forgotten Songs(1)   -
          Tomorrow(1)   -

-4.Add vocal-chorus by the session audience.

All titles also on FD10123,(Eu)PL43548,(J)SR3080,PG77.
Note:The above titles were recorded at Coleman's loft-studio on Prince Street,N.Y.C.

Same.   Live."Village Gate";NYC.July 4,1970
          5 unknown titles

Don Cherry(cnt),Bobby Bradford(tp),Ornette Coleman(as),Dewey Redman(ts,musette),Charlie
Haden(b),Ed Blackwell(dr).   Live."Slug's",NYC.September 3,1971
          Civilization Day
          Broken Shadows
          Happy House
          Street Woman
          The Good Life
          Elizabeth
          Unknown title

ORNETTE COLEMAN

Same.   Live."Slug's",NYC.September 5,1971
        Unknown title
        Law Years
        The Good Life
        Unknown title(1)
        Unknown title
        Happy House

-1.Coleman plays (tp,vln).

Don Cherry(cnt),Bobby Bradford(tp),Ornette Coleman(as),Dewey Redman(ts,musette),Charlie
Haden(b),Ed Blackwell,Billy Higgins(dr).   NYC.September 9,1971
CO 112012 Happy House   Columbia FC38029
CO 112013 Broken Shadows   -
CO 112014 Written Word   unissued
CO 112015 Elizabeth   Columbia FC38029

Omit Bradford,Redman,Blackwell.   Same date
CO 112016 Civilization Day   Columbia KC31061
CO 112017 Country Town Blues   Columbia FC38029
CO 112018 Street Woman   Columbia KC31061

Bobby Bradford(tp),Ornette Coleman(as),Dewey Redman(ts),Charlie Haden(b),Ed Blackwell
(dr).   Same date
CO 112019 School Work   Columbia FC38029
CO 112020 The Jungle Is A Skyscraper   Columbia KC31061
CO 112021 Law Years   -

All titles on FC38029 also on CBS(Eu)S85934,(J)25AP2779.
Note:The Columbia files erroneously date the above session November 9,1971.
      "School Work" is also known as "Tutti", "The Good Life" and "Theme From A Symphony".

Don Cherry(cnt),Bobby Bradford(tp),Ornette Coleman(as),Dewey Redman(ts),Charlie Haden(b),
Billy Higgins,Ed Blackwell(dr),David Henderson(recitation).
                                         NYC.September 10,1971
CO 112022 What Reason Could I Give   Columbia rejected
CO 112023 All My Life   -
CO 112024 Science Fiction(dh)   Columbia KC31061
CO 112025 Light House   Columbia unissued

Gerard Schwarz,Carmine Fornarotto(tp),Ornette Coleman(as),Dewey Redman(ts),Charlie Haden
(b),Billy Higgins,Ed Blackwell(dr),Asha Puthli(vcl).
                                         NYC.September 13,1971
CO111482 What Reasons Could I Give(ap)   Columbia KC31061
CO111483 All My life   -

Ornette Coleman(tp,vln),Dewey Redman(ts,musette),Charlie Haden(b),Ed Blackwell(dr).
                                         Same date
CO111482 Rock The Clock   Columbia KC31061

All titles on KC31061 also on Columbia CG33669,CBS(Eu)S64774,(J)SOPL18.

ORNETTE COLEMAN QUARTET:
Ornette Coleman(as-1,tp-2,vln-3),Dewey Redman(ts,musette),Barre Phillips(b),Ed Blackwell
(dr).   Live.Bologna,Italy.October 16,1971
        Unknown titles

Charlie Haden(b) replaces Phillips.   Live.Teatro Lirico,Milan,Italy.October 20,1971
        Unknown title(1)
        Broken Shadows(1)
        Rock The Clock(2,3)
        Street Woman(1)

Same.   Live.Rotterdam,The Netherlands.October 30,1971
      Who Do You Work For(1)
      Broken Shadows(1)
      Rock The Clock(2,3)

Same.   Live.Berlin.November 5,1971
      Whom Do You Work For(1)   Unique Jazz(I)UJ13
      Broken Shadows(1)
      Street Woman(1)   Unique Jazz(I)UJ13
      Song For Che(1)   -
      Rock The Clock(2,3)   -
      Happy House(1,4)   -

-4.As "Written Word" on UJ13.

Same.   Live.Cologne,Germany.November 1971
      Broken Shadows(1)
      Street Woman(1)
      Song For Che(1)
      Rock The Clock(2,3)
      Happy House(1)

Same.   Live.Tivoli's Koncertsal,Copenhagen.November 9,1971
      Broken Shadows(1)
      Street Woman(1)
      Song For Che(1)

Same.   Live.Uppsala,Sweden.November 10,1971
      Broken Shadows(1)
      Street Woman(1)
      Song For Che(1)
      Rock The Clock(2,3)
      Happy House(1)

Same.   Live.Prob. Paris.November 1971
      Street Woman(1,4)   Trio(J)PA7169/70
      Unknown title(1,5)   -
      Unknown title(1,6)   -
      Rock The Clock(2,3,7)   -

-4.As "Second Fiction" on PA7169/70.
-5.As "Summer Thang" on PA7169/70.
-6.As "Silhouette" on PA7169/70.
-7.As "Fantasy 77" on PA7169/70.

Ornette Coleman(as-1,composer),unknown(dr),The London Philharmonic Orchestra,David Measham
(cond).   London.April 17/18/19,1972
CO112442 Skies Of America   Columbia KC31562
CO112443 Native Americans   -
CO112444 The Good Life   -
CO112445 Birthdays And Funerals   -
CO112446 Dreams   -
CO112447 Sounds Of Sculpture   -
CO112448 Holiday For Heroes(2)   -
CO112449 All Of My Life   -
CO112450 Dancers   -
CO112451 The Soul Within Woman   -
CO112452 The Artist In America(1) -
CO112453 The New Anthem   -
CO112454 Place In Space   -
CO112455 Foreigner In A Free Land(1) -
(session cont. next page).

```
(session cont. from previous page):
CO112456 Silver Screen(1)              Columbia KC31562
CO112457 Poetry(1)                           -
CO112458 The Men Who Live
            In The White House(1)            -   ,KG31574
CO112459 Love Life(1)                        -      -
CO112460 The Military                        -
CO112461 Jam Session                         -
Co112462 Sunday In America                   -
```

-2.A.k.a. "Forgotten Songs".

All titles on KC31562 also on Columbia CG33669,CBS(Eu)S65147,(J)SOPL111.
Note:The above titles are the "Skies Of America" suite; the suite was performed live at
     Philharmonic Hall (NYC) on July 4,1972 with Coleman's regular quartet and the Ameri-
     can Symphony Orchestra cond. by Leon Thompson.

Ornette Coleman(as),Dewey Redman(ts),Cedar Walton(p),Jim Hall(g),Charlie Haden(b),Ed
Blackwell(dr),woodwind quintet,Webster Armstrong(vcl).
                                          NYC.September 1972
```
CO112661 Good Girl Blues(wa)           Columbia FC38029
CO112662 Is It Forever(wa)                   -
CO112663 Rubber Gloves(1)                    -
```

-1.Coleman,Redman,Haden,Blackwell only.

All titles on FC38029 also on CBS(Eu)S85934,(J)25AP2779.

Don Cherry(cnt),Ornette Coleman(as),Dewey Redman(ts,musette),Charlie Haden(b),Ed Blackwell
(dr).   Live.Prob. "Artist's House",NYC.September 22,1972
```
         The Word Became Music       J For Jazz JF803
         Unknown Races                       -
         Love Eyes                           -
         The Good Life                       -
         Skies Of America                    -
         Unknown title                       -
```

All titles also on Jazz Anthology(F)JA5248.
Note:The titles listed above are played on the A-side of JF803 and JA5248; the B-sides
     have the same titles (and same versions) - except for the "Unknown title" (which
     is not played on the B-side). Each LP has 6 tracks on the A-side, but JF803 splits
     "Love Eyes" between tracks 3 and 4 while track 6 has "Skies Of America" plus the
     "Unknown title".

Same.   Live."Artist's House",NYC.September 23,1972
```
         The Word Became Music
         Unknown Races
         Love Eyes
         The Good Life
         Skies Of America
         Stand By For The News
```

Ornette Coleman(as,p-1) solo.   Live.Philharmonic,Berlin.November 4,1972
```
         Unknown title/Love Eyes(1)
         Who Do You Work For
```

ORNETTE COLEMAN QUARTET:
Ornette Coleman(as-1,tp-2,vln-3),Dewey Redman(ts,musette),Charlie Haden(b),Ed Blackwell
(dr).   Live.Smithsonian Institute,Washington,D.C.November 12,1972
```
         Who Do You Work For
         Unknown Races
(session cont. next page).
```

(session cont. from previous page):
        Love Eyes
        Street Woman
        Skies Of America
        The Good Life
        Song For Che

Robert Palmer(cl,wood-fl),Ornette Coleman(as-1,tp-2,vln-3),Master Musicians Of Joujouka
(reeds,strings,dr).   Joujouka,Morocco.January 1973
        Midnight Sunrise(1)   Horizon SP722,(E)AMLJ722,(J)GP3518,HOJ2008,A&M(E)
                                              CDA0807(CD),(F)396.999-2(CD),(J)D32Y3020,
                                              C28Y3025(CD),D22Y3908(CD)
        Music From The Cave(2)   unissued
        Unknown titles   -

ORNETTE COLEMAN QUARTET:
Ornette Coleman(as-1,tp-2,vln-3),Dewey Redman(ts,musette),Charlie Haden(b),Ed Blackwell
(dr).   Queensborough Community College,NYC.February 18,1973
        Unknown title(1)
        Broken Shadows(1)
        Unknown title(1)
        Song For Che(1)
        Unknown title(2)
        The Word Became Music(1)
        Lonely Woman(1,4)
        Unknown titke/The Good Life(1)
        Skies Of America(1)
        Unknown title(2,3)

-4.Omit Redman.

Same.   Live.New York University,NYC.April 23,1973
        Essu
        Unknown title
        To See And To Hear My Love
        Unknown title
        Little Orphan Annie
        Skies Of America
        Unknown title
        Unknown title
        Song For Che

ORNETTE COLEMAN SEXTET:
Ornette Coleman(as-1,tp-2,vln-3),Dewey Redman(ts),James "Blood" Ulmer(g),Charlie Haden(b),
Billy Higgins(dr),Soloman Olonari(perc),Webster Armstrong(vcl).
                              Live.Ann Arbor Blues and Jazz Festival,Michigan.September 9,1973
        Unknown title(1)
        Unknown title(1)
        To See And Hear My Love(1)
        Unknown blues(1)
        Unknown title(1)
        Unknown title(2,3)

ORNETTE COLEMAN TRIO:
Ornette Coleman(as-1,tp-2,vln-3),Dewey Redman(ts,musette),Charlie Haden(b).
                                           Live.Europe.c. 1973
        Unknown title(1)
        Something To Listen To(1)
        Song For Che(1)
        Unknown title(2)
        Law Years(1)
        Unknown title(1)

ORNETTE COLEMAN QUARTET:
Ornette Coleman(as-1,tp-2,vln-3),James "Blood" Ulmer(g),Sirone (Norris Jones)(b),Billy
Higgins(dr).   Live.Theatro dell' Arte,Milan,Italy.April 15,1974 (1st concert)
      Unknown titles

Same.   Live.Theatro dell' Arte,Milan,Italy.April 15,1974 (2nd concert)
      Long Time No See(1)
      What Reason Could I Give(1)
      The Good Life(1)
      Unknown title(1)
      Something To Listen To(1)
      Unknown title(2)
      Comme Il Faut(1)
      Skies Of America(1)

Same.   Live.Milan,Italy.April 22,1974
      Unknown titles

Same.   Live.Willisau,Switzerland.April 27,1974
      Unknown titles

Same.   Live."Hotel National",Bern,Switzerland.April 28,1974
      Who Do You Work For(?)
      The Good Life(?)
      Unknown title
      Something To Listen To
      4 unknown titles

Same.   Live.Theatro S. Pio X,Padova,Italy.May 4,1974
      Tutti(1)   Osaka Jazz League(I)P10085
      Love Call(2)   -
      What Reason Could I Give(1)   -
      The Story Of The King And Queen(1)   -
      Harloff(1)   -
      Comme Il Faut(1)   -
      Bells And Chimes(3)   -
      Something To Listen To(1)   -

Same.   TV-cast.Rome.May 7,1974
      New York(incompl.)(1)
      Comme Il Faut(1)
      The Good Life(1)

Same.   Live.Unknown loaction/date
      Unknown titles   Craws unnumbered(?)

Ornette Coleman(as-1,tp-2,vln-3),James "Blood" Ulmer(g),Charlie Haden(b),Billy Higgins -4,
   Blackwell -5(dr).   Live(?).Artist's House,NYC.June 27,1974
      Unknown title I(4)
      Unknown title II(4)
      Unknown title III(4)
      Unknown title IV(4)
      Unknown title V(5)
      Unknown title VI(5)

Cut Blackwell.   Live(?).Artist's House,NYC.June 28,1974
      Unknown title I(4)
      Unknown title II(4)
      Unknown title III(4)
      Unknown title IV(4)
      Unknown title V(4)
      Unknown title VI(4)

ORNETTE COLEMAN QUARTET:
Ornette Coleman(as-1,tp-2.vln-3),James "Blood" Ulmer(g),David Willliams(b),Ornette Denard
Coleman(dr).   Live.Laren,The Netherlands.August 10,1974
        Harlowe(1)
        The Garden Of Soul(1)
        Something To Listen To(1)
        The Good Life(1)
        Sound Into That(2,3)

Same.   Live.Antwerpen,Belgium.Augsut 17,1974
        Harlowe(1)
        The Garden Of Soul(1)
        Something To Listen To(1)
        The Good Life(1)
        Sound Into That(incompl.)(1)

ORNETTE COLEMAN QUINTET:
Add Barbara Huey(perc);Coleman plays (as,tp,vln,p,synth).
                                          NYC.October 23,1974
        Unknown titles

Note:13 titles/takes were recorded.

Same.   NYC.October 25,1974
        Unknown titles

Charlie Haden(b) replaces Williams.   Live."Five Spot",NYC.May 13,1975
        Hamdulillah
        Voice Poetry
        Uncle Sam
        Skies Of America
        Long Time No See

CLAUDE NOUGARO:
Claude Nougaro(vcl) acc. by Ornette Coleman(as),Maurice Vander(p),Luigi Trussardi(b),
Charles Bellonzi(dr).   Paris.November 20,1975
33723 Gloria   Barclay(F)90025

Note:Additional titles (without Coleman) from this LP are not included.

ORNETTE COLEMAN GROUP:
Ornette Coleman(as),Bern Nix,Charles Ellerbee(g),Rudy McDaniel (Jamaaladeen Tacuma)(b),
Ronald "Shannon" Jackson(dr).   Paris.December 28,1975
        Fou Amour   Artists House AH1
        Voice Poetry   -
        Home Grown   -
        Macho Woman   -
        European Echoes   -
        Theme From A Symphony,var.1   Horizon SP722
        Theme From A Symphony,var.2   -
        Ghetto Kid   unissued

All titles on SP722 also on Horizon(E)AMLJ722,(J)GP3518,HOJ2008,A&M(E)CDA0807 (CD),
(F)396.999-2 (CD),(J)D32Y3020,C28Y3025 (CD),D22Y3908 (CD).
All titles on AH1 also on AH(Ca)AH7401,(J)GP3167,Sonopresse(F)2S.068-62555.

ORNETTE COLEMAN QUARTET:
Don Cherry(cnt),Ornette Coleman(as),Charlie Haden(b),Billy Higgins(dr).
                                          NYC.December 21,1976
        Without Name Or Number   Artists House unissued/rejected
        Don't Know
(session cont. next page).

(session cont. from previous page):
        Night Worker
        The Adjuster
        Energy,Mind And Matter

Same.   NYC.December 22,1976
        The Adjuster   Artists House unissued
        Energy,Mind And Matter
        Without Name Or Number
        Don't Know
        Night Worker
        The Adjuster

ORNETTE COLEMAN SEXTET:
Ornette Coleman(as,tp,vln),rest unknown.   Live.South Hill Park,Brackwell,England.c. 1976
        Unknown titles

ORNETTE COLEMAN - CHARLIE HADEN:
Ornette Coleman(ts-1,tp-2),Charlie Haden(b). NYC.January 30,1977
        Mary Hartman,Mary Hartman(1)   Artists House AH-6
        Human Being(1)   -
        Soaps Suds(1)   -
        Sex Spy(1)   -
        Some Day(2)   -

All titles also on Artists House(J)GP3174.

Don Cherry(cnt),Ornette Coleman(as),Dewey Redman(ts),James "Blood" Ulmer(g),Buster Williams,David Izenzon(b),Ed Blackwell,Billy Higgins(dr).
                                         Live.Avery Fisher Hall,NYC,June 30,1977
        Name Brain   Artist House unissued
        The Black House
        Mr. And Mrs. Dream
        Race Face
        Sound Amoeba

ORNETTE COLEMAN AND THE PRIME TIME BAND:
Ornette Coleman(as,tp,vln,bassoon),Bern Nix,Charles Ellerbee(g),Albert McDowell(el-b),
Shannon Jackson,Ornette Denardo Coleman(dr). Same concert
        Writing In The Streets   Artist House unissued
        Mukami
        Sleep Talking
        What Reason Could I Give
        Song X

Note:The JAMES "BLOOD" ULMER QUARTET also appeared at the above concert.

ORNETTE COLEMAN DUO:
Ornette Coleman(as),Ornette Denardo Coleman(dr).
                                 Live.The White House,Washington,D.C.June 18,1978
        Earth Souls/Meta

ORNETTE COLEMAN SEXTET:
Ornette Coleman(as-1,tp-2,vln-3),Bern Nix,Charles Ellerbee(g),Charlie Haden(b),Jamaaladeen
Tacuma(el-b),Shannon Jackson,Ornette Denardo Coleman(dr).
                                 Live.Carnegie Hall,NYC.June 24,1978
        The Night Stick People(1,2)
        Earth Souls(1,2,3)
        Macho Woman(1,2)
        Asa(1)
        Meta(1,3)

ORNETTE COLEMAN SEXTET:
Ornette Coleman(as-1,tp-2,vln-3),Bern Nix,James "Blood" Ulmer(g),Fred Williams(el-b),Shan-
non Jackson,Ornette Denardo Coleman(dr).   Live.Kongsberg,Norway.June 30,1978
          Mukami(1,2,3)
          Song X(1,2,3)
          Macho Woman(1,2)
          Dream Talking(1,3)

Same.   Live."Quartier Latin",Berlin.July 4,1978
          Dream Talking(1,2,3)
          Mukami(1,2,3)
          Macho Woman(1)
          Song X(1,2,3)

Same.   Live.Innsbruck,Austria.July 5,1978
          Writing In The Streets
          Dream Talking
          Mukami
          Macho Woman
          Asa
          The Night Stick People
          Song X(incompl.)

Same.   Live.Kristianstad,Sweden.July 6,1978
          Writing In The Streets(1,2,3)
          Dream Talking(1,2)
          Mukami(1,2,3)
          Macho Woman(1)
          Asa(1)

Same.   Live.Hamburg,Germany.July 7,1978
          Unknown titles

Same.   Live.Bracknell,England.July 8,1978
          Macho Woman(1,2,3)
          Asa(1,3)

Same.   Live.Pori,Finland.July 13-15,1978
          Writing In The Streets(1)
          Dream Talking(1,2,3)
          Macho Woman(1)

Same.   Live.Congresgebrouw,Den Haag,The Netherlands.July 16,197
          Song X(1,2,3)
          Mukami(1,2,3)
          Writing In The Streets(1,3)
          Macho Woman(1,2)
          Asa(1)

Same.   Live.Munich,Germany.July 17,1978
          Song X
          Mukami
          Asa(1)

Same.   Live.Ansbach,Germany.July 18,1978
          Dream Talking(1,2,3)
          Writing In The Streets(1,2,3)
          Mukami(1,2,3)
          Macho Woman(1,2)

Same.   Live.Antibes Jazz Festival,Juan Les Pins,France.July 22,1978
     Song X(1,2,3)
     Macho Woman(1)

Note:Additional titles were recoded - but not broadcast - by the French National Radio.

Same.   Live.Nevi,Italy.July 23,1978
     Dream Talking(1,2,3)
     Song X(1,2,3)
     Mukami(1,2,3)
     Macho Woman(1,2)
     Asa(1)

Same.   Live.Wiesen,Germany.July 28,1978
     Dream Talking(1,2,3)
     Song X(1,2,3)
     Mukami(1,2)
     Macho Woman(1)
     Asa(1)

Same.   Live.Bregenz,Germany.July 29,1978
     Writing In The Streets
     Mukami
     Macho Woman
     Dream Talking
     Asa
     The Night Stick People

ORNETTE COLEMAN AND THE PRIME TIME BAND:
Ornette Coleman(as),Bern Nix,Charles Ellerbee(g),Jamaaladeen Tacuma(el-b),Shannon Jackson,
Ornette Denardo Coleman(dr).   NYC.March 1979
     Unknown titles   Artists House unissued

Same.   TV-cast.NYC.April 14,1979
     Unknown title(1)
     Writing In The Streets(1)

Calvin Weston(dr) replaces Jackson.   NYC.April 25,1979
     Sleep Talk (Dream Talking)   Antilles AN2001
     Jump Street   -
     Him And Her   -
     Air Ship (Meta)   -
     What Is The Name Of That Song   -
     Job Mob   -
     Love Words   -
     Times Square   -
       (Writing In The Streets)   -

All titles also on Antilles(G)802.385-425,(J)25S300,J33D20002 (CD)..
Note:"What Is The Name Of That Song" is based on "Love Eyes" and "Forgotten Songs" (a.k.a.
    "Holiday For Heroes").

ORNETTE COLEMAN AND THE PRIME TIME BAND:
Ornette Coleman(as,tp,vln),Bern Nix,Charles Ellerbee(g),Jamaaladeen Tacuma,Albert McDowell
(el-b),Calvin Weston,Ornette Denardo Coleman(dr).
                                    Live.Rome.March 6,1980
     Unknown titles

poss. Shannon Jackson(dr) replaces Weston;poss. omit McDowell.
                              NYC.c. April 1980
     Unknown titles   Artists House(?) unissued

ORNETTE COLEMAN DUO:
Ornette Coleman(as-1,tp-2,vln-3),Ornette Denardo Coleman(dr).
Live.Verona,Italy.June 5,1980

      Emolodic Playing(1,2)
      Dance Work(1,3)
      Thinking(1,4)

-4.Ornette Denardo Coleman plays (el-b).

ORNETTE COLEMAN - list of equivalents (Atlantic Records):

Atlantic: Orig.:	Reissue:	Atlantic(E):	Atlantic(F):	Atlantic(G):	Atlantic(J):	London(E):
LP/SD1317		587.022, S588.022	332.010, 40.441, 781.339-2(CD)		P6004, P7510	
LP/SD1327			332.062		P6076	LTZ-K15199 SAH-K6099
LP/SD1353					P6095	LTZ-K15228 SAH-K6181
LP/SD1364		K50240	412.008, 781.347-2(CD)	ATL50240	P6059, P7511	
LP/SD1378	Jazzlore 29		850.007			LTZ-K15241 SAH-K6235
LP/SD1394		588.121	432.069		P6105	
SD1558			940.031			
SD1572		2400.109, K40112	60.043		P8006	
SD1588	SD8810	K40278	40.278 60.043		P8165	

JOHNNY COLES

See also COMPOSERS WORKSHOP ENSEMBLE.

JOHNNY COLES QUARTET:
Johnny Coles(tp),Kenny Drew -1,Randy Weston -2(p),Peck Morrison -1,George Tucker -2(b),
Charlie Persip(dr).   NYC.April 10,1961
CO66515 Hi-Fly(2)   Epic LA16015
CO66516 Come Rain Or Come Shine(1)   -
CO66517 Pretty Strange(2)   -
CO66518 If I Should Lose You(1)   -

Same.   NYC.April 13,1961
CO66581 Room 3(1)   Epic LA16015
CO66582 Where(2)   -
CO66583 Babe's Blues(2)   Columbia FC38509

All titles on LA16015 also on Epic(F)EPC80072,(J)ECPZ10,CBS(J)SONP50412.
Note:The above information is listed acc. to the Columbia files.

ohnny Coles(tp),Leo Wright(as),Joe Henderson(ts),Duke Pearson(p),Bob Cranshaw(b),Walter
erkins(dr).   NYC.July 18,1963
    Little Johnny C   Blue Note BLP4144
    Hobo Joe   -
    Jano   -
    So Sweet My Little Girl   rejected

ete LaRoca(dr) replaces Perkins;Wright plays (as,fl).
                              NYC.August 9,1963
    Heavy Legs   Blue Note BLP4144
    My Secret Passion   -
    So Sweet My Little Girl   -

ll titles on BLP4144 also on Blue Note BST84144,(J)GXK8204,BN4144.

ohnny Coles(tp,flh),Ashley Fennel(tb),Howard Johnson(tu),Gregory Herbert(ts),Cedar Walton
o,el-p),Reggie Workman(b,el-b),Bruce Ditmas(dr).
                              NYC. 1971
    Never Can Say Goodye   Mainstream MRL346
    September Of My Years   -
    728(no tb,tu)   -
    Petits Machins   -
    Betty's Bossa   -
    Funk Dumplin'(no tb,tu)   -

AURY COLES (Canadian)

as-solo).   Live.The Music Gallery,Toronto.November 5,1977
    Yonge Street Traveller   Onari(Ca)003
    Hats Off   -
    Goasts Hill Road   -
    Tip Top Pop   -
    Prepared Plastic Number One   -

LGATE HI-FIVE

xter Morill(tp),Dan Hammalian(tb),Vic Strite(cl),Arnold Eriksen(p),Stieg Reichert(b),
m Wade(dr).   NYC.March 12,1959
    Muskrat Ramble   Golden Crest CR3099
    Tin Roof Blues   -
    Is It True What
        They Say About Dixie   -
    Monday Date   -
    Royal Garden Blues   -
    Jazz Me Blues   -
    Black And Blue   -
    Battle Hymn Of The Republic   -
    Copenhagen   -
    That's A Plenty   -
    Blues For Five   -

YMOND COLIGNON (Belgian)

ymond Colignon(p),unknown b,dr.   Brussels. 1950's
ession cont. next page).

(session cont. from previous page):
          Bandstand Boogie   Philips(B)P19171H
          The Varsity Drag   -

Note:Additional recordings by this artist are not included.

ALBERTO COLLATINA (Italian)

See also MODERN JAZZ GANG.

(p-solo).   Milan,Italy.May 8,1953
CMT315 Way Down Yonder In New Orleans Pathé(I)MG166

Alberto Collatina(p),Boris Morelli(b),Roberto Trillo(dr).
                                       Milan,Italy.May 3,1954
CMT417 Honeysuckle Rose   Pathé(I)MG226

Note:See JUNIOR DIXIELAND GANG for additional titles from the above 1953/54 sessions.

LE COLLECTIF LE TEMPS DES CERISES (French)

Manu Ferrier,Pierre Ferrier,Jean Mereu(tp),Poc(tb),Michel Marre(bars,ts,cnt),Claude Marre
(prob. bassax),Gérard Tamestit(vln),Guy Oulchen,Alain Hako,Alain Bruhl,Joël Grasset,Deni
Levaillant,Francois Tusques(perc),Carlos Andreu,Boussaba,choir(vcl).
                              Prades Le Lez,France.July/August 1974/Paris.November 19
          Les Faux Touristes,
          Les Partisans ...   Unknown label/issueno.
          Versailles   -
          Le Front Uni De Travailleurs   -
          Nous Allons Vous Conter
             (Intercommunal Blues)   -
          L'Internationale   -

THE COLLECTIVE STAR

Similar to next session.   NYC. 1970's
     Unknown titles   Unanimous Anonymous UNAN999

Charles McGhee(tp),John Gerber(sax,fl),David Klein(hca),Ron Burton(p,el-p),Paul Silbey
(g,org,vcl),Jim Crozier(el-b),Tulsi(tamboura,perc,vcl),Howard Hirsch,Roger Dawson(perc).
                                  NYC.December 28,1973
          Circle Around   Unanimous Anonymous UNAN1000(?)
          Listen   -
          God Of Beauty   -
          Bliss (Ananda)   -

Similar.   NYC. 1975
          Less Resistance   Unanimous Anonymous UNAN1001
          We're Alive   -
          Reborn To Return   -
          Cosmic Boogie   -
          Listen   -

Similar.

	Live.Boston. 1975
	Unanimous Anonymous UNAN1001
Introductory Om	
Letter From Kierwaan	-
Toward The One	-

COLLECTION DE HOT CLUB DE FRANCE (French)

Raymond Cicurel(tp),Maurice Meunier(cl),Eddie Bernard(p),Jean-Pierre Sasson(g),Georges
Hadjo(b),Gaston Leonard(dr).   Paris.October 10,1947
4779	Nobody Likes Me	Blue Star(F)57
4780	Somebody Loves Me	-
4781	Good Time Blues	Blue Star(F)58
4782	Old Time Blues	-

COLLEGE ALL-STARS

See STAN RUBIN.

COLLEGE OF THE REDWOODS STAGE BAND

Randy Carrico,Bill Allen,Randy Ames,Dick Titterington,Jim Sernesky(tp,flh),Dana Wheaton,
Lawrence Mooney,Charles Richards,Gary Stipek,Jan Stout(tb),Michael Moore,Candace Tinkler,
Barry Block,Joe DeAndries,Darcy Christenson(reeds,fl),Jim Royer(p(?)),Ian Cone(b),Charles
Bulla,David Burn,Alvirino Camillo(perc),Jerrold Moore(cond).
                                      California(?). 1974
Bossa Nuts	Custom Fidelity CFS3511
April	-
St. Thomas	-
These Are Eyes Of Rain	-
Meridian West	-

Randy Carrico,Bill Allen,Jim Sernesky,Steve Horton,Steve Parmenter(tp,flh),Dana Wheaton,
Lawrence Mooney,Charles Richards,Pat Spurling(tb),Michael Moore,Candace Tinkler,Barry
Block,Joe DeAndries,Ken McCall(reeds,fl),Jim Royer(p(?)),Nick Kirgo(g),Alvirino Camillo,
Michael Vatcher,John May,Bill Roth(perc),Jerold Moore(cond).
                                      San Francisco.April 3,1975
Romo	Custom Fidelity GSR-CR1975
Arby's Tinge	-
A Handful Of Futures	-
Flintstones	-
The Family Of Man	-

COLLEGIATE NEOPHONIC ORCHESTRA OF SOUTHERN CALIFORNIA

Tony Farrell,Jack Caudill,Greg Wallen,Gary Pack,Lee Coffey(tp),Steve Spiegl(tp,arr),Jeff
Apmadoc,Tom Baker,Bob Grove,Nat Patterson(tb,btb),Ron Applegate,Jerry Mansanger,Jacob van
Velzen,Starn Steele,Marni Johnson,Kathy Tapla(frh),Davis Coy(tu),Adrian Tapia,Mark Shrode,
Ron Foster,Jim Snodgrass,Philip Ayling,Mike Francis(reeds,fl),Greg Mathiesen(p),Tom Morell
(g),Clana Stein(b),Bill van Ravensberg(el-b),Wynn Smith(dr),Ruth Ritchie,Gene Strimmling
(perc),Jack Wheaton(cond),James Hill,Alf Clausen,Willie Maiden,John Prince,Al Davis,Bill
Fritz(arr).   California. 1970s
(session cont. next page).

COLLEGIATE NEOPHONIC ORCHESTRA OF SOUTHERN CALIFORNIA

(session cont. from previous page):
```
        Tribute To A Poltergeist      Custom SZB3308/09
        Phrygia                            -
        Marche                             -
        Three Sounds For
            Neophonic Orchestra            -
        Bygones                            -
        Neophonic Portrait                 -
        Toccata                            -
        Neophonic Funk                     -
        Orange Grease(1)                   -
        Lamentations(1)                    -
```

-1.Add Mike Vaccaro(as,ts).

Note:This band also issued another LP (Neo 6701) - no details are available.

BUDDY COLLETTE

See also MAX ALBRIGHT,CHARLES KYNARD,LATIN ALL STARS,HERBIE MANN,DICK MARX,DON RALKE.

BUDDY COLLETTE QUARTET:
Buddy Collette(as),Jimmie O'Brien(p),Harper Cosby or David Bryant(b),Chuck Thompson(dr).
```
                                      LA.  1948/49
        It's April                    Dolphins Of Hollywood (unknown issueno.)
```

Unknown horns,Buddy Collette(sax),Jimmie O'Brien(p),Chuck Norris(g),unknown(b),Chuck
Thompson(dr).   LA. 1951/52
```
        Blue Strings                  Crest 111
        Jimmy's Boogie                     -
```

Gerald Wilson(tp),Dave Wells(tb,btp),Buddy Collette(fl,as,ts),Bill Green(as),Jewell Grant
(bars),Ernie Freeman(p),Red Callender(b),Max Albright(dr).
```
                                      LA.February 13,1956
        Cycle                         Contemporary C3522
        Ruby                          Contemporary 45-362,C3522
        Slappy's Tune                      -
        Santa Monica                       -
```

Buddy Collette(fl,as,ts),Gerald Wiggins(p),Gene Wright(b),Bill Richmond(dr).
```
                                      LA.February 24,1956
        Makin' Whoopee                Contemporary 45-362,C3522
        Sunset Drive                       -
        Jazz City Blues                    -
        Frenesi                            -
```

Buddy Collette(fl,as,ts,cl),Ernie Freeman(p),Barney Kessel(g),Joe Comfort(b),Larry Bunker
(dr).   LA.April 17,1956
```
        St. Andrew's Place Blues      Contemporary C3522
        Cheryl Ann                         -
        Jungle Pipe                        -
        Zan                                -
```

All titles on C3522 also on Vogue(E)LAC12090,Original Jazz Classics OJC239.

Buddy Collette(fl,bcl),rhythm,strings.   LA.August 1956
```
704     Someone To Watch Over Me      Vogue 100
705     Moonrail                           -
```

Note:The above - LA-based - label is not connected to the French or British Vogue labels.

John Anderson(tp),Buddy Collette(fl,cl,as,ts),Gerald Wiggins(p),Jim Hall(g),Curtis Counce
(b),Chico Hamilton(dr).   LA.September/October 1956
     Green Dream   Dig J101
     It's You   -
     A Walk In The Veldt   -
     How Long Has This Been Goin' On   - ,Vintage Jazz JVR31736
     The Blindfold Test   -
     Jungle Pogo Stick   -
     Tanganyika   -
     Wagnervous   -
     And So Is Love   -
     Coming Back For More   -

All titles also on Tampa TP34,VSOP 20.
Note:The above group poss. recorded another 1956 session for the Dig label.

BUDDY COLLETTE QUARTET:
Buddy Collette(fl,cl),Don Friedman(p),John Goodman(b),Joe Peters(dr).
                                      LA.November 6,1956
     A Nice Day   Contemporary C3531
     Over The Rainbow   -

Same.   TV-cast.LA.Poss. November 19,1956
     Makin' Whoopee   Calliope CAL3014
     Fall Wind   -
     I'll Remember April   -

Note:The above titles are from a Bobby Troup "Stars of Jazz" TV-show.

Buddy Collette(fl,cl,as),Dick Shreve(p),John Goodman(b),Bill Dolney(dr).
                                      LA.November 29,1956
     Minor Deviation   Contemporary C3531
     Change It   -
     I'll Remember April   -
     Blues For Howard   -
     Fall Winds   -

All titles on C3531 also on Contemporary(J)VDJ1632 (CD),Vogue(F)LDM30098,(E)LAC12092,King
(J)GXC3174,Original Jazz Classics OJCCD747-2 (CD).

Same;Collette plays (fl,cl,as,ts).   LA.January 16,1957
9428 Three And One   ABC-Paramount ABC179
9429 Night In Tunisia   - ,HMV(E)7EG8356
9430 Johnny Walks   -   -
9431 Perfidia   -
9432 Morning Jazz   -

Same.   LA.January 24,1957
9436 Winston Walks   ABC-Paramount ABC179
9437 If She Had Stayed   -
9438 They Can't Take That Away From Me   -
9439 Undecided   - ,HMV(E)7EG8356
9440 Flute In "D"   -   -
9441 The Continental   -

All titles on ABC179 also on W&G(Au)BJN548.

Buddy Collette(as,ts,cl),Calvin Jackson(p),Leroy Vinnegar(b),Shelly Manne(dr).
                                      LA.February 18,1957
(session cont. next page).

(session cont. from previous page):
    There Will Never Be Another You Contemporary C3531
    Moten Swing -
    Buddy Boo -

All titles on C3531 also on Contemporary(J)VDJ1632 (CD),Vogue(F)LDM30098,(E)LAC12092,King
(J)GXC3174,Original Jazz Classics OJCCD747-2 (CD).

Buddy Collette(fl,cl,as),Dick Shreve(p),Gene Wright(b),Bill Richmond(dr).
                                  LA.May 1957
    Orlando   Challenge CHL603
    Soft Touch -
    Old School -
    Debbie -

Buddy Collette(fl,cl,as),Gerald Wiggins(p),Howard Roberts(g),Gene Wright(b),Bill Richmond
(dr).   LA.May 1957
    Tasty Dish   Challenge CHL603
    I Still Love You -
    Mrs. Potts -
    You Better Go Now -

All titles on CHL603 also on Fresh Sound(Sp)FSR506.

Gerald Wilson(tp),Buddy Collette(fl,as,ts),Al Viola(g),Wilfred Middlebrooks(b),Earl Palmer
(dr).   TV-cast.LA.Poss. December 16,1957
    Tasty Dish   Calliope CAL3009
    Soft Touch -
    Under Paris Skies -

Note:The above titles are from a Bobby Troup "Stars of Jazz" TV-show.

Same;Collette plays (fl,cl,as,ts).   LA. 1957
    Soft Touch   Dooto DTL245,Bel Canto SR1004
    Walkin' Willie - ,   -
    Changes - ,DTL856
    My Funny Valentine -
    The Cute Monster - ,Bel Canto SR1004
    Orlando Blues -
    Blue Sands - ,Bel Canto SR1002
    It's You - ,DTL856,Bel Canto SR1002

Note:"Walkin' Willie" as "Bass Rock" on Bel Canto SR1004.

BUDDY COLLETTE AND THE POLLWINNERS:
Buddy Collette(fl,bcl,arr),Gerald Wiggins(org),Pete Jolly(acc),Jim Hall(g),Red Callender
(tu),Louis Belson(dr).   LA. 1957
    (Bess,Oh) Where Is My Bess Interlude MO505
    My Man's Gone Now -
    Summertime -
    It Ain't Necessarily So - ,S&H SH4546
    I Got Plenty Of Nuttin' -
    There's A Boat
       Leavin' For New York -
    Bess You Is My Woman Now -
    A Woman Is A Sometime Thing -

All titles also on Interlude ST1005,Top Rank(E)25/003,Charlie Parker CP825 (under Pete
Jolly's name).
Note:"It Ain't Necessarily So" issued on SH4546 under Bellson's name.

BUDDY COLLETTE AND THE JAZZ GREATS:
ank Rosolino(tb),Buddy Collette(fl,cl,as,ts,arr),Howard Roberts(g),Red Mitchell(b),Bill
.chmond(dr).   LA.January 24,1958
    Pigalle   Speciality SP5002
    La Vie En Rose   -
    La Vie En Rose(alt.take)   Original Jazz Classics OJCCD1764-2(CD)
    C'est Si Bon   Speciality SP5002
    Domino   -
    Under Paris Skies   -

ank Rosolino(tb),Buddy Collette(fl,as,ts,arr),Red Callender(tu),Howard Roberts(g),Red
.tchell(b),Bill Douglas(dr).   Same date
    I Love Paris   Speciality SP5002
    Darling,Je Vous Aime Beaucoup   -
    Darling,Je Vous
       Aime Beaucoup(alt.take) Original Jazz Classics OJCCD1764-2(CD)
    Mam'selle   Speciality SP5002
    Mam'selle(alt.take)   Original Jazz Classics OJCCD1764-2(CD)
    The Song From "Moulin Rouge" Speciality SP5002
    The Last Time I Saw Paris   -
    The Last Time
       I Saw Paris(alt.take)   Original Jazz Classics OJCCD1764-2(CD)

.l titles on SP5002 also on Original Jazz Classics OJCCD1764-2 (CD).

JDDY COLLETTE'S SWINGING SHEPHERDS:
iddy Collette,Paul Horn,Bud Shank(picc,fl,arr),Harry Klee(picc,fl),Bill Miller(p),Joe
)mfort(b),Bill Richmond(dr),Pete Rugolo(arr).
                                      LA.March 5/7,1958
5881 Pony Tale   EmArcy MG36133
5882 Flute Diet   - ,Mercury EP1-6559,(Du)957.127
5883 Short Story   -   -
5884 Machito   -
5885 The Funky Shepherds   - ,Mercury(Du)957.127
5886 The Four Winds Blow   - ,Mercury EP1-6559
5887 Tasty Dish   -
5888 Improvisation,II(1)   -
5889 Improvisation,I(2)   -

1.Collette,Horn,Shank,Klee unaccompanied.
2.Collette,Horn,Shank,Klee acc. by Richmond(cg) only.

11 titles also on EmArcy SR80005,Mercury MG20519,SR60196,(E)MMB12001.

JDDY COLLETTE QUINTET:
erald Wilson(tp),Buddy Collette(fl,as,ts),Al Viola(g),Wilfred Middlebrooks(b),Earl Palmer
ir).   TV-cast.LA.Poss. September 29,1958
    Soft Touch   Calliope CAL3009
    Moonlight In Vermont   -
    It's You   -

ll titles also on Calliope CAL3034.
)te:The above titles are from a Bobby Troup "Stars of Jazz" TV-show.
    CAL3009 lists date as September 29,1858 - CAL3034 lists date as July 7,1958.
    "It's You" is an original composition - i.e. not "It's You Or No One".

erald Wilson(tp),Buddy Collette(fl,cl),Gene Cipriano(oboe,enh,bcl),Al Viola(g,bj),Justin
iTullio(cello),Red Callender(b,tu),Earl Palmer(dr),Robert Sorrels(narration).
                                      LA. 1959
session cont. next page).

(session cont. from previous page):
```
        Taboo                     Music&Sound (S)1001
        Polynesian Suite(rs):                       -
            Tennin
            Barbarian
            Mistress
            Anchorage
            Corpse
            Sleeping Gipsy
            Room With Skies
        Japanese Suite(rs)                          -
```

Billy Bean(g),Ed Lustgarten(cello),Marni Nixon(vcl) replace Viola,DiTullio,Sorrels.
```
                                  LA.  1959
        Flight(mn)                Music&Sound (S)1001
        Gauguin(mn)                                 -
        Singapore Sling                             -
```

BUDDY COLLETTE AND HIS SWINGING SHEPHERDS:
Buddy Collette,Paul Horn,Bud Shank(picc,fl,arr),Harry Klee(picc,fl),Bill Miller -1,John
Williams -2(p),Jim Hall(g),Red Mitchell(b),Shelly Manne -3,Earl Palmer -4(dr),Pete Rugolo
(arr).
```
                                  LA.  1959
18153  Intermezzo                Mercury MG20447/SR60132
18154  I Can't Believe That
       You're In Love With Me                       -
18155  The Bad And The Beautiful
       (Love Is For The Very Young)                 -
18156  The Trolley Song          unissued
18157  Laura                     Mercury MG20447/SR60132
18158  Smile(1,3)                                   -
18159  Invitation(2,4)                              -
18160  The Shrike(2,3)                              -
18364  Ruby(1,4)                                    -
18365  Colonel Bogey/
       River Kwai March(1,4)                        -
18366  Swingin' On A Star                           -
18367  The Trolley Song(1,4)                        -
```

Note:Information on pianist and drummer is not available for all titles.

Buddy Collette(ts),Gerald Wiggins(p),Joe Comfort(b),Bill Douglas(dr).
```
                                  LA.  1959/60
        What's Up                 Crown CLP5278/CST278,CLP5424/CST424
        Hideaway                         -                    -
        Reunion                          -                    -
        Evergreen                 Crown CLP5284/CST284,CLP5415
        Bye-Bye                          -
        The Groove                       -
        Lucky Me                         -
        Joggin'                   Crown CLP5289/CST289,CLP5411,Ember(E)CJS811
```

Note:CLP5278 and CLP5424 issued as by WARDELL GRAY; CLP5284 issued as by STAN GETZ.

Gerald Wilson(tp),Buddy Collette(picc,fl,cl,bars),Red Callender(b,tu),Earl Palmer(dr).
```
                                  LA.  1960
        Briefcase Intrigue        (see note)
        Tidal Riff
        The Bahamian Bit
        Opus In G-3
        Mysticfied
```
(session cont. next page).

(session cont. from previous page):
```
    Speedy
    Seafair Chanty
    Wisconsin Wonderland
    Jazzpar
    Swingin' On The Skis
    Playback Catalog
```

Note: The above titles are from the "Glasspar Makes Your 1960 Sales Picture" film soundtrack; they were issued on an unnumbered 10" Glasspar promotional LP ("Selling Boats
And All That Jazz").

Dusko Goykovich(tp),Buddy Collette(fl,cl,as,ts),Renato Sellani(p),Franco Cerri(b),Jimmy
Pratt(dr).   Milan,Italy.March 10,1961

Slavic Mood	Music(I)LPM2095
San Carlo	-
Pickford Street	Music(I)LPM2091
Paddi	-

Add George Joyner (Jamil Nasser)(b);Cerri plays (g).
                                              Same date

Blues For Nicola	Music(I)LPM2091
A Taste Of Fresh Air	-
Everything Happens To Me	Music(I)LPM2095

Buddy Collette(fl,cl,as,ts),Gianni Basso(cl,ts),Renato Sellani(p),Franco Cerri(b),Jimmy
Pratt(dr).   Milan,Italy.March 14,1961

I Forgot	Music(I)LPM2095
I Wished On The Moon	unissued
Miss Helen	-

Dino Piana(tb),Buddy Collette(fl),Renato Sellani(p),Franco Cerri(b),Jimmy Pratt(dr),Norman
Shobey,poss. Armshed(?) Shobey(perc).   Milan,Italy.March 15,1961

Orfeo Negro	Music(I)LPM2091
Mounya Labeli Matatoo	-

All titles on LPM2091 also on Stella(I)LPS6108,Joker(I)SM3215.

BUDDY COLLETTE WITH QUINTETTO BASSO - VALDAMBRINI:
Oscar Valdambrini(tp),Buddy Collette(as,cl,fl),Gianni Basso(ts,cl),Renato Sellani(p),
Giorgio Azzolini(b),Gianni Cazzola(dr).   Milan,Italy.March 16,1961

Hunt And Peck	Ricordi(I)MRJ8001
Room With Skies	-
Inverness	-

Same.   Milan,Italy.March 17,1961

Santa Tecla	Ricordi(I)MRJ8001
Buddy Boo	-

Same.   Milan,Italy.March 18,1961

One For The Air	Ricordi(I)MRJ8001
Nice Day	-
My Funny Valentine	- ,MRJ8005

All titles on MRJ8001 also on Family(I)SFR-RI625.

Buddy Collette(fl,as,cl),Gianni Basso(ts,cl),Renato Sellani(p),George Joyner(b),Jimmy
Pratt(dr).   Milan,Italy.March 20,1961

Skater For Mater	Music(I)LPM2091
The Blues	-

(session cont. next page).

(session cont. from previous page):
        Softly As In A Morning Sunrise   unissued
        That's All   -
        Eh Oh   -
        The Power Of The Winds   -

All titles on LPM2091 also on Stella(I)LPS6108,Joker(I)SM3215.

Buddy Collette,Jacques Pelzer(fl),Renato Sellani -1,Amadeo Tommasi -2(p),George Joyner -3,
Giovanni Tommaso -4(b),Buster Smith(dr).   Milan,Italy.March 23,1961
        Jake(1,3,5)   Music(I)unissued
        Hannie's Dream(2,3)
        Kelly(2,4)

-5.Add Sergio Fanni(tp).

Note:"Jake" and "Kelly" were issued on stereo cartridges (Ampex E8180 and E8179 respecti-
    vely).

BUDDY COLLETTE WITH LA SCALA STRING QUARTET:
Buddy Collette(fl),Franco Cerri(g),George Joyner(b),Jimmy Pratt(dr),string quartet.
                                    Milan,Italy.March 24,1961
        Soft Touch   Music(I)LPM2095
        Skylark   -
        Santa Monica   -
        Stella By Starlight   -

Sergio Fanni(tp),Buddy Collette,Jacques Pelzer(fl,as),Renato Sellani(p),George Joyner(b),
Buster Smith(dr).   Milan,Italy.March 25,1961
        Just Friends   Music(I)unissued
        Spectacular
        It Could Happen To You
        Speak Low
        Lonely Flute
        I'll Remember April
        You Are Too Beautiful

Buddy Collette(fl,ts),Howard Roberts(g),Jim Helms(g,arr,cond),Mel Pollan(b),Leo Acosta,
poss. Emil Richards(perc).   LA. 1961
        It Never Can Be   Crown CST460,CLP5302
        Noise Of The Night
          (Background For Buddy)   -   -
        Turtle Samba   -   -
        Mischievous Lady   -   -
        At Midnight   -   -
        Blue Samba   -   -
        Skin Of Ivory   -   -
        Why Do You Linger   Crown CLP5302

Note:Additional titles on CST460 ("The Girl From Ipanema","I Left My Heart In San Fran-
    cisco" and "Fly Me To The Moon") - listed on the cover as Collette items - are with
    an unknown tenorsax acc. by p,g,b,dr (i.e. without Collette).
    CLP5302 (which also lists titles in Portuguese) may be the original issue - under the
    name of Jim Helms.

Buddy Collette(fl,cl,sax),Frank Marocco(acc),Al Viola(g),Jimmy Bond(b),Milt Holland,Emil
Richards(dr,perc).   LA. 1961/62
        Unknown titles   unissued

Note:The above titles - which are scheduled for release on the R.G.B. label - are from the
    "Trauma" film soundtrack.

uddy Collette(fl,cl,as,ts),Jack Wilson(p),Al Viola(g),Jimmy Bond(b),Bill Goodwin(dr),
rene Kral(vcl).   LA. 1962

A Taste Of Fresh Air	Studio West No.104CD
Hunt And Peck	-
Emaline's Theme	-
The Meaning Of The Blues(ik)	-
Laura	-
Just Friends(ik)	-
There Will Never Be Another You	-
Spring Can Really	
Hang You Up The Most(ik)	-
Tenderly	-
Nobody Else But Me(ik)	-
Road Trip	-
Detour Ahead(ik)	-
Soft Touch	-
It's A Wonderful World(ik)	-

ote:The above titles are from "The Navy Swings" transcription(s).

JDDY COLLETTE - CHARLES KYNARD:
iddy Collette(fl,arr),Johnny Rae(vbs,timb),Charles Kynard(org),Al McKibbon(b),Doug Sides
ir),Nick Martinis,Armando Peraza,Bill Fitch(perc).
                                         LA. 1964

Strong Breeze	World Pacific WP/ST1823
Mamblues	-
Blue Sands	-
Warm Winds	-
Cubano Chant	-
Watermelon Man	-
Satin Doll	-
Gauchi Gauro	-

te:1965/66 recordings with - pre-recorded - p,g,b,dr,strings are not included.

DDY COLLETTE AND THE WEST COAST JAZZ QUINTET:
 Aarons(tp),Buddy Collette(fl,as,ts),John Collins(g),Al McKibbon(b),Earl Palmer(dr).
                                    Live.LA.November 17,1973

Billie's Bounce	R.G.B. 2001
Autumn Leaves	-
Like Someone In Love(g,b,dr only)	-
On The Trail	-

 Aarons(tp),Grover Mitchell(tb),Buddy Collette(fl,arr),Al Viola(g),Red Callender(tu),
roy Vinnegar(b),Frank Severino(dr).   LA. 1973

Fun City	Legend LGS1004
Safari West	-
Shatara	-

 Aarons(tp),Grover Mitchell(tb),Buddy Collette(fl,as,ts,arr),Al Viola(g),Red Callender
),Frank Chavez(dr),Patrick Boyle(arr). LA. 1973

Veda	Legend LGS1004
J. Power Buzzard	-
Now And Then	-
Andre	-

idy Collette(fl,ts,cl),Kohnosuke Saijoh,Budd Johnson(ts),Nat Pierce(p),Mundell Lowe(g),
orge Duvivier(b),Gus Johnson(dr).   Tokyo.April 1978
ession cont. next page).

```
(session cont. from previous page):
        Blues For Terry              King(J)SKA3017
        E.K.E.'s Blues                       -
        Ballad Medley:                       -
            Polka Dots And Moonbeams
            Sophisticated Lady
            Yesterdays
        Blues For Buddy                      -
        Fancy Kind Of Blues                  -
        Ballad Medley:                       -
            Body And Soul
            Sweet Lorraine
            Tenderly
```

Note:The above musicians - except for Saijoh - toured with Benny Carter in Japan; the LP
     ("Blues For Friends") were poss. not issued under Collette's name.

BUDDY COLLETTE - VERLYE MILLS:
Buddy Collette(fl),Verlye Mills(harp),Llewellyn Matthews(p),Buell Neidlinger(b),Roy
McCurdy(dr).   LA.July/August 1980
```
        Danse Lente                  R.G.B. 2003
        Conversation                         -
        A Matter Of Time                     -
        Marcell                              -
        Brazilian Baby                       -
        Seaside Stroll                       -
```

Note:It is not known if R.G.B. 2003 was released.

MAX COLLIE (Australian/British)

MAX COLLIE'S RHYTHM ACES:
Phil Mason(cnt),Max Collie(tb,vcl),Cy Laurie(cl),Jim McIntosh(bj),John Healy(b,vcl),Ron
McKay(dr,vcl).   Live."Winterhuder Führhaus",Hamburg,Germany.May 7,19
```
        Too Busy                     WAM(G)MLP15418
        Fidgety Feet                         -
        Perdido Street Blues                 -
        Shine                                -
        The Chant                            -
        Papa Dip                             -
        Creole Love Call                     -
        Ice Cream(band-vcl)                  -
```

Same.   Live."Die Glocke",Bremen,Germany.September 28,19
```
        Flat Foot                    Reality(G)R105.1W
        Grandpa's Spell                      -
        Bourbon Street Parade(mc)            -
        Perdido Street Blues                 -
        Shine(rmk)                           -
        Stevedore Stomp                      -
        Trouble In Mind(mc)                  -
        Ice Cream(mc)                        -
```

All titles also on Creative World AL7082.

Jack Gilbert(cl) replaces Laurie.   Schellerten,Germany,May 8,1972
```
        Petulia(mc,jh)          WAM(G)MLP15455,2002 Metronome(G)DALP2/1960
        Willie The Weeper(rmk)               -
(session cont. next page).
```

(session cont. from previous page):

Aunt Hagar's Blues	WAM(G)MLP15455	
Walking With The King(rmk)	-	
Black Bottom Stomp	-	,2002 Metronome(G)DALP2/1960
Let The Light From		
The Lighthouse Shine(rmk)	-	-
Steamboat Stomp	-	
I Wonder Who's Kissing Her Now	-	
Bourbon Street Parade(mc)	-	
Snake Rag	-	

All titles also on WAM WAM/O No.2,2001 Metronome(G)201.603.

Phil Mason(cnt),Max Collie(tb,vcl),Jack Gilbert(cl),Jim McIntosh(bj),Trevor Williams(b),
Ron McKay(dr,vcl).   Live."Deutsches Schauspielhaus".Hamburg,Germany.February 14,1973

Runnin' Wild	Happy Bird(G)HB5012	
At A Georgia Camp Meeting	-	
Shim-Me-Sha-Wabble	-	
Bluebells Goodbye	-	
Tiger Rag	-	,F/90062,Time Wind DB50120,
	Tobacco Road(G)B/2581	
Yellow Dog Blues	Happy Bird(G)HB5012	
Ice Cream(mc)	-	,Time Wind DB50120

All titles also on Happy Bird(G)B/90029,Tobacco Road(G)B/2561.

Same.   Hamburg,Germany.February 20,1973

Stomp Off Let's Go	Happy Bird(G)HB5002,HB5013,Marifon 296.095-241	
Chimes Blues	-	
Doctor Jazz(rmk)	-	,HB5013
Brown Skin Mama	-	
High Society	-	,F/90062,Time Wind DB50120
Snag It(mc)	-	
Moarie	-	,HB5028,Time Wind DB50120
Baby Brown(rmk)	-	,HB5013
Cake Walking Babies Back Home(rmk)	-	

All titles also on Happy Bird(G)B/90001,Tobacco Road(G)B/2579,White Elephant(E)PE877067.

Same.   Live."Trafalgar",London.April 8,1973

Shim-Me-Sha-Wabble	Reality(G)R106
All The Girls Go Crazy(mc)	-
Beale Street Blues(rmk)	-
Red Wing	-
The Entertainer	-
Panama	-
Ballin' The Jack	-
St. Philip Street	
Breakdown(cl,bj,b only)	-
Alexander's Ragtime Band(rmk)	-
Weather Bird Rag	-
Some Of These Days	-
Yellow Dog Blues	-
Gettysburg March	-
Tiger Rag	-
There'll be Some	
Changes Made(rmk)	-

All titles also on Espérance(F)ESP155.109.

Same.   Live."Big Horn Underground",Atlanta,Georgia.March 15,1974
     Original Tuxedo Rag   G.H.B. GHB63
     Savoy Blues   -
     All The Girls Go Crazy
       'Bout The Way I Ride(mc)   -
     Too Busy   -
     I Found A New Baby   -
     Stockyard Strut   -
     Baby Brown(rmk)   -
     Over In The Gloryland   -
     Mabel's Dream   -
     Cake Walkin' Babies(rmk)   -

Same.   Live.Wethersfield,Conn.May 4,1974
     The Ragtime Dance   Connecticut Traditional Jazz Club SLP10
     Snake Rag   -

Same;Gilbert plays (cl,as).
                Live.Bix Beiderbecke Memorial Jazz Festival.Davenport,Iowa.July 25,1975
     Steamboat Stomp   Bix Lives Vol.5
     Salutation March   -
     Panama Rag   -
     I Can't Escape From You   -
     Streets Of Antibes   -
     Dinah(rmk)   -
     Snake Rag   -

Same.   Live.Kortrijk,Belgium.September 7,1975
     Harlem Rag   Unknown label KRM617

Same.   Live."Bird's Nest",London.March 29,1976
     Too Bad   Black Lion(E)BLPX12137
     Sweet Like This   -
     Salutation March   -
     'S Wonderful(cl,bj,b,dr only)   -   ,(G)155.032
     I'm Crazy 'Bout My Baby   -   ,BLPX12170,BLP30403/04,
                               (G)155.024
     Didn't He Ramble(mc,rmk)   Black Lion(E)BLPX12137
     The Ragtime Dance   -   ,BLP30401/02
     Dans Les Rues D'Antibes   -
     Fidgety Fingers   -   ,BLPX12170
     Winin' Boy Blues   Black Lion(E)BLPX12138
     Ostrich Walk   -
     When My Dreamboat Comes Home   -
     The Martinique   -
     Algiers Strut   -
     Mandy,Make Up Your Mind   -
     Cheek To Cheek   -   ,(G)155.024
     Avalon   -   -

All titles also on Black Lion(G)172.000.

Same.   Live.Ystad,Sweden.August 10,1976
     Travelling Blues   Sweet Folk&Country(E)SFAX108
     When My Dreamboat Comes Home(rmk)   -
     East Coast Trot   -
     Pretty Baby(mc)   -
     Original Dixieland One Step   -
     Summertime   -
     Black Cat On A Fence   -
     Mad Dog   -
(session cont. next page).

(session cont. from previous page):

The World Is Waiting For The Sunrise	Sweet Folk&Country(E)SFAX108
Wabash Blues	-
Cheek To Cheek(rmk)	-
Snag It(mc)	-
The Martinique	-
The Ostrich Walk	-
Short Dress Gal	-
The Entertainer	-
Light From The Lighthouse(rmk)	-

same;Gilbert plays (cl,as,ss). London.April 3,1977

Gospel Train(mc,rmk)	Black Lion(E)BLP12147	
Over The Rainbow	-	
Nobody Knows You When You're Down And Out(mc)	-	
Woodworm Stomp	-	
My Blue Heaven(rmk)	-	,(G)155.032
Lullaby	-	
After You've Gone(rmk)	-	
Clarinet Marmalade	-	,(G)155.032
The Jazz Band Ball	Black Lion(E)BLP12168	
That's My Desire(rmk)	-	
Milenberg Joys	-	
East Coast Trot	-	
Dinah(rmk)	-	
New Orleans	-	
You Took Advantage Of Me(rmk)	-	
Martha	-	

11 titles on BLP12147 also on Black Lion(G)147.007.

same. Live.Longjumeau,Paris.November 24,1977

Original Dixieland One Step	Espérance(F)ESP165.511
Gospel Train(rmk)	-
Stardust	-
Saratoga Shout	-
Les Oignons	-
When I Leave The World Behind(rmk)	-
Somebody Stole My Gal	-
Passport To Paradise	-
You Don't Understand	-

11 titles also on Sonodisc(F)577.30.34.

same. London.November 28,1978

When You're Smiling(mc)	Black Lion(E)BLP12181
Passport To Paradise	-
Doctor Jazz(rmk)	-
Summertime	-
Begin The Beguine	-
Just A Gigolo(rmk)	-
Les Onions(band-vcl)	-
Willie The Weeper(rmk)	-
As Time Goes By	-
Maryland,My Maryland	-
Margie(rmk)	-
Once In A While	-
Pretty Baby(mc)	-
Tres Moutarde	-

Add Jan Sutherland(vcl).   Live.Dongen,The Netherlands.January 5,1980
    I Ain't Gonna Tell Nobody   Beerendonk(Du)9996/97
    The Sheik Of Araby(rmk)   -
    Buddy Bolden Blues(mc)   -
    Frog-I-More Rag   -
    That's A Plenty   -
    Careless Love(js)   -
    There's A Rainbow
      'Round My Shoulder(rmk)   -
    Lou-isi-a-ni-a(rmk)   -
    Blame It On The Blues   -
    Nobody Knows
      The Trouble I've Seen(rmk)   -
    Blues My Naughty
      Sweetie Gives To Me(js)   -
    Down Home Rag   -
    Shine(rmk)   -
    The Thriller Rag   -
    St. James Infirmary(rmk)   -
    I Am Sailing(rmk)   -
    Algiers Strut   rejected

Omit Sutherland.   Llanfair Caereinion,Powys,Wales,U.K.February 12/13,1980
    Georgia Grind(rmk)   Sweet Folk&Country(E)SFAX118
    Give Me Your Telephone Number   -
    I Guess I'll Have
      To Change My Plans   -
    Dippermouth Blues   -
    Everybody Loves My Baby(rmk)   -
    I'm Gonna Sit Right Down And
      Write Myself A Letter(rmk)   -
    Girl In Clover   -
    Beautiful Dreamer   -
    Hindustan   -
    Ace In The Hole(rmk)   -
    Dallas Blues   -
    Buddy's Habits/Kneedrops   -
    Jumping Jack Sax   -
    (There's A) Rainbow
      'Round My Shoulder(rmk)   -
    Cieolito Lindo   -
    Wolverine Blues   -
    Hi Lili,Hi Lo(rmk)   -
    Everybody Loves My Baby(1)   -

-1.The tune played is "Don't Forget Our Monday Date".

GRAHAM COLLIER (British)

Kenny Wheeler(tp,flh),Mike Gibbs(tb),Dave Aaron(as,fl),Karl Jenkins(bars,fl),Phil Lee(g),
Graham Collier(b),John Marshall(dr).   London.January 15/18,1967
    El Miklos   Deram(E)DML/SML1005
    Conversations   -
    Deep Dark Blue Centre   -

Harry Beckett(tp,flh) replaces Wheeler.   London.January 24,1967
    Blue Walls   Deram(E)DML/SML1005
    Hirayoshi Suite   -
    Crumblin' Cookie   -

arry Beckett(tp,flh),Nick Evans(tb),Stan Sulzmann(as,ts),Karl Jenkins(oboe,p),Graham
ollier(b,arr),John Marshall(dr,chimes).   London.March 21,1969
    Down Another Road   Fontana(E)SFJL922
    Aberdeen Angus   -
    The Barley Mow   -

ame.   London.March 22,1969
    Danish Blue   Fontana(E)SFJL922
    Lullaby For A Lonely Child   -
    Molenwrench   -

arry Beckett(tp,flh),Derek Wadsworth -1(tb),Alan Wakeman(ts,ss),Tony Roberts,Alan Skid-
ore -2(ts),Bob Sydor(ts,as),John Taylor(p),Phil Lee -3(g),Graham Collier(b),John Webb
(r).   London.January/February 1970
    Songs For My Father: Fontana(Eu)6309.006
        Song One (Seven-Four)(1,2,3)
        Song Two (Ballad)(1)
        Song Three
          (Nine-Eight Blues)(1)
        Song Four (Waltz In Four-Four)
        Song Five (Rubato)(2)
        Song Six (Dirge)
        Song Seven (Four-Four
          Figured)(1,2,3)

rry Beckett(tp,flh),Alan Wakeman(ss,ts),Bob Sydor(as,ts),Geoff Castle(b),Graham Collier
),John Webb(dr).   London.December 8,1970
    Mosaics: Philips(Eu)6308.051
        Piano Cadenza - Theme 1
        Theme 1
        Duet - Theme 4
        Theme 2
        Drum Cadenza - Theme 3
        Fluegel Cadenza - Theme 4
        Theme 6
        Tenor Cadenza
        Piano Cadenza - Theme 2
        Theme 8

ck Pearce(flh),Peter Hurt(as),Geoff Castle(p),Ed Speight(g),Graham Collier(b),John Webb
r).   London.November 16/17,1972
    And Now For Something
        Completely Different   Saydisc(E)SDL244
    Portraits   -

rry Beckett(tp,flh),Derek Wadsworth(tb),Geoff Castle(el-p),Ed Speight(g),Graham Collier
),John Webb(dr).   Live.Cranfield,Bedfordshire,England.March 13,1974
    Darius,pt.I-V   Mosaic(E)GCM741
    A New Dawn   -

ger Dean(p) replaces Castle.   London.February 17,1975
    Midnight Blue   Mosaic(E)GCM751
    Adam   -
    Cathedra   -

rry Beckett(tp,flh),Derek Wadsworth(tb),Geoff Castle(p,el-p),Ed Speight(g),Graham Col-
er(b),John Webb(dr).   Unknown location,England.c. 1975
    (The Rhythm Section)
        (el-p,b,dr only)   Cambridge University Press 0521.20560-3(cass.tape)
    (Jazz Lecture Concert)   Cambridge University Press 0521.20563-8
    (Jazz Illustrations)   Cambridge University Press 0521.20564-6
ession cont. next page).

(session cont. from previous page):
Note:The above recordings were released as educational material.
      The "Jazz Lecture Concert" (0521.20563-8) has four parts (incl. part one of Collier'
      composition "Darius").

Harry Beckett(tp,flh),Henry Lowther,Pete Duncan(tp),Malcolm Griffiths(tb),Mike Page(as),
Art Themen,Alan Wakeman(ts,ss),Roger Dean(p),Ed Speight(g),Graham Collier(b),John Webb(d
John Mitchell(perc).   Nettlebed,Oxfordshire,England.June 2/3,1976
            New Conditions: Mosaic(E)GCM761
               Introduction
               Parts 1 - 8
               Finale

Tony Roberts(ts) replaces Wakeman.   London.November 7,1976
         Symphony Of Scorpions,pt.1-4   Mosaic GCM773

Same.   London.March 10,1977
         Forest Path To The Spring   Mosaic GCM773

Harry Beckett,Henry Lowther,Peter Duncan(tp,flh),Malcolm Griffiths(tb),Mike Page(ss,as),
Art Themen(ss,ts),Alan Wakeman(ss,bcl,ts),Roger Dean(p,el-p),Graham Collier(keyb,cond),E
Speight(g),Roy Babbington(b,el-b),Ashley Brown(dr,perc),John Carbery(narration).
                                         Nettlebed,Oxfordshire,England.March/April 19
         The Day Of The Dead,pt.1-8(1)   Mosaic GCMD783/4
         October Ferry   -

-1.Add Alan Jackson(dr) on pt. 6.

RON COLLIER (Canadian)

RON COLLIER QUINTET:
Ron Collier(tb),Bernie Piltch(as),Ed Bickert(g),Carne Bray(b),Ron Rully(dr),CBC Symphony
Orchestra,Victor Feldbrill(cond).   Toronto.May 25,1959
         Concerto Grosso For
            Jazz Quintet And Orchestra   CBC(Ca)RCI181,RM222

Note:CBC is Canadian Broadcasting Corporation.

Omit CBC Symphony Orchestra.   Toronto.December 9,1959
         Quintet   CBC(Ca)RCI181
         Weary   CBC(Ca)JFC7
         Blue Boy   -
         Blues On One Theme   -

RON COLLIER JAZZ QUINTET(!):
Guido Basso,Jack Long(tp),Ron Collier(tb),Bernie Piltch(as),Bill Goddard(ts),Jack Taylor
(bars),Maury Kaye(p,frh),Bill Britto(b),Bud Hill(tu),Archie Alleyne(dr).
                                         Toronto.July 13,1961
         Strate(!) Ahead   CBC(Ca)RM33
         Blues On One Theme   -
         The Myth Of Marsays   -
         Home   -
         Lee's Lament   -

THE RON COLLIER SEPTET:
Guido Basso(tp),Ron Collier(tb),Bernie Piltch(as),Jack Taylor(bars),Ed Bickert(g),Bill
Britto(b),Archie Alleyne(dr).   Toronto. 1962
         Theme   CBC(Ca)RM82
         Barbados   -
(session cont. next page).

(session cont. from previous page):
```
        Two Shades Of Blues          CBC(Ca)RM82
        Come Sunday                     -
        Autumn Haze                     -
        Walking Out                     -
```

THE RON COLLIER TENTET:
Guido Basso,Fred Stone(tp,flh),Ron Collier,Butch Watanabe,Ron Hughes(tb),Bernie Piltch,
Mort Ross(sax,cl,fl),Ed Bickert(g),Bill Britto(b),Archie Alleyne(dr).
```
                                     Toronto.March 12,1965
        I Feel Pretty                CTL(Ca)M1059/S5059
        Hockey Theme                    -      ,DM/DS103
        Come Sunday                     -
        Walking Out                     -
        Days Of Wine And Roses          -
        Lee's Lament                    -
        I Believe In You                -
        Relaxin'                        -
        The Thrill Is Gone              -
        Fair Wind                       -
        Charade                         -
```

Note:CTL is Canadian Talent Library.

THE RON COLLIER JAZZ ORCHESTRA:
Erich Traugott(tp),Guido Basso,Fred Stone(tp,flh),Butch Watanabe,Ron Hughes,Ray Sikora(tb)
Bernie Piltch(sax,cl,fl),Gary Morgan(bars,bcl),Ed Bickert(g),Lenny Boyd(b),Jerry Fuller
(dr),Ron Collier(cond).
```
                                     Live.Montreal.July 21,1967
        Centim                       CBC(Ca)EXPO-25
        Requiem For J.F.K.              -
        Waterfront                      -
        Stone Poem                      -
        Just About Now                  -
        Silent Night,Lonely Night       -
        Collage                         -
        Psycolliergy                    -
```

THE RON COLLIER JAZZ ORCHESTRA WITH DUKE ELLINGTON:
Duke Ellington(p),Lenny Boyd,Sam Levine(b),strings,Ron Collier(cond).
```
                                     Toronto.July 24,1967
        Nameless Hour                Decca DL75069,CBC(Ca)RM222
```

Erich Traugott,Dick Van Evera(tp),Guido Basso(tp,flh),Fred Stone(flh),Butch Watanabe,Ray
Sikora(tb),Ron Hughes(btb),Mary Barrow(frh),Bernie Piltch(sax,cl,fl),Moe Koffman(as,fl),
Rick Wilkins,Eugene Amaro(ts),Gary Morgan(bars,bcl),Peter Appleyard(vbs,perc),Duke Elling-
ton(p),Ed Bickert(g),Lenny Boyd(b),Jerry Fuller(dr),strings,Ron Collier(cond).
```
                                     Same date
        Aurora Borealis              Decca DL75069
```

Erich Traugott(tp),Guido Basso(tp,flh),Fred Stone(flh),Butch Watanabe,Ray Sikora(tb),Ron
Hughes(btb),Bernie Piltch(sax,cl,fl),Gary Morgan(bars,bcl),Duke Ellington(p),Ed Bickert
(g),Lenny Boyd(b),Jerry Fuller(dr),Ron Collier(cond).
```
                                     Toronto.July 25,1967
        Song And Dance               Decca DL75069
        Fair Wind                       -
        Collage No.3                    -
        Silent Night,Lonely Night       -    ,CBC(Ca)RM222
```

All titles on DL75069 also on MCA(E)MUPS372,MPS/BASF(G)21.21704,(E)MDLP12361,(Am)
BASF21704,(J)UXP53.

Note:Additional recordings by this artist are not included.

SHEILA COLLIER (British)

SHEILA COLLIER'S SMOKY CITY JAZZ BAND:
(vcl) acc. by Dave Barrett(tp),Dai Davies(tp,tb),Eric Briley(tb),John Hunt(cl,as,ts,fl),
Jon Gillespie(keyb),John Slaughter,Colin Goldring,Stewart Goldring(g),Rick Kemp(el-b),Ni-
gel Pegrum(dr).   Unknown location. 1973
          A Change Is Gonna Come   Plant Life(E)PLJ005
          On My Way   -
          I've Had It   -
          Why Don't You Do Right   -
          What A Day For A Daydream   -
          Blues Get Off My Shoulder   -
          Do Your Duty   -
          Harmony Alone   -
          Sweet Man   -
          On Revival Day   -
          Am I Blue   -

(vcl) acc. by Bill Smith(tp,flh),Terry Brunt(tb,euphonium),John Hallam(cl,as,ss,fl),Roger
Godfrey(p),Roy Tweedie(g,bj),Brian Morrison(b),Bob Jones(dr).
                                               Unknown location. 1970's
          Georgia Swing   Small(E)PET2609
          Ce M'sieu Qui Parle   -
          You Took Advantage Of Me   -
          T'Aint What You Do   -
          Mood Indigo   -
          Jackass Blues   -
          Comin' Home Baby   -
          Jelly Bean Blues   -
          Was I Drunk,Was He Handsome
             And Did Mama Give Me Hell   -
          Black And Tan Fantasy   -
          Ostrich Walk   -
          Wrought Iron Rag   -
          A Hundred Years From Today   -
          Can't Trust Nobody   -

Charlie Bentley(g,bj) replaces Tweedie.   Live.Rotterdam,The Netherlands.October 20,1979
          Perdido Street Blues(no vcl)   Harbour Jazz Club(Du)HJL001
          Going To Town(no vcl)   -
          Just A Closer Walk With Thee   -
          Blues On Parade(no vcl)   -
          Cake Walking Babies From Home   -
          Bourbon Street Parade(no vcl)   -
          The Mooche(no vcl)   -
          Mean Mistreater   -
          Dardanella(no vcl)   -
          Hiawatha Rag(no vcl)   -

TOM COLLIER

TOM COLLIER - DAN DEAN (WHISTLING MIDGETS):
Ernie Watts(ts) or Gary Berbig(ss,ts,as,bars),Tom Collier(mar,vbs),Don Grusin(el-p),Norman
Durkee(synth,org),John Morton(g),Dan Dean(b),Moyes Lucas(dr),Alex Acuna(dr,perc).
                                               LA. 1980/81
          San Juan   Inner City IC1126
          Sunrise   -
          Old Friends And Relatives   -
(session cont. next page).

(session cont. from previous page):
Fog Tight	Inner City IC1126
Whistling Midgets	-
Cora,Like A Rose	-
A Song For M	-
Hagen's Hoedown	-
Cowboys And Christians	-

AL "JAZZBO" COLLINS

(vcl) acc. by Lou Stein(p).   NYC.c. 1953
84492 Little Red Riding Hood	Brunswick 80226
84493 Three Little Pigs	-

(narration) acc. by Clark Terry(tp),Phil Bodner,George Berg(sax),Eddie Costa(vbs),Lou Stein(p),Barry Galbraith(g),Wendell Marshall(b),Don Lamond(dr).
                                               NYC. 1960/61
Purple Grotto Blues	Old Town LP2001
It Don't Mean A Thing	-
It's A Wonderful World	-
Wang Tut	-
My One And Only Love	-
When Your Lover Has Gone	-
Harrison The Owl	-
Christopher Columbus	-
Purple Mood	-

(narration) acc. by Terry Gibbs(vbs),Steve Allen(p),Mel Brown,Al Casey(g),Ron Brown(el-b), Hal Blaine,Paul Humphrey(dr).   LA.May 31,1967
90792 Little Red Riding Hood	Impulse AS9150
90793 Goldilox And Three Bears	-
90794 Jazz Mass	-
90795 The Power Of The Flower	-
90796 Sonny Cool	-
90797 Three Little Pigs	-
90798 Jack The Beanstalk	-
90810 The Swearing In Of The Bandidos	-

Note:Additional recordings by this artist are not included.

BURT COLLINS

See also MUSIC MINUS ONE.

COLLINS/SHEPLEY GALAXY:
Burt Collins,Joe Shepley(tp,flh),Bernie Glow(tp,picc-tp),Garnett Brown(tb),Paul Faulise (btb),Joe De Angelis(frh),Tony Price(tu),Jerry Dodgion(fl,ss),Mike Abene(p,arr,cond),Bob Cranshaw(b),Mickey Roker(dr).   NYC.c. 1968
Time,Space And The Blues	MTA NWS2
Apogee	-
Blue Interlude	-
Docking Maneuver	-
Module 3	-
Soft Landing	-
Susan Moon	-
Fourth Dimension	-

Add Herbie Hancock(el-p);Abene (arr,cond) only;Collins,Shepley,Glow play (tp,flh,picc-tp).

	NYC.c. 1969		
She's A Woman	MTA NWS4		
Lady Madonna	-		
Hey Jude	-		
Penny Lane	-		

Myron Youles(btb) replaces Faulise.

	NYC.c. 1969
Eleanor Rigby	MTA NWS4
Eight Days A Week	-

Lloyd Michels(tp) replaces Glow.

	NYC.c. 1969
Norwegian Wood	MTA NWS4
Magical Mystery Tour	-

CAL COLLINS

See also CONCORD ALL STARS,CONCORD SUPER BAND.

CAL COLLINS QUINTET:
Carmen Leggio(ts),John Bunch(p),Cal Collins(g),Michael Moore(b),Connie Kay(dr).

	NYC. 1977
Limehouse Blues	Famous Door HL123
For All We Know	-
'Tis Atumn	-
Young And Foolish	-
A Pretty Girl	-
You're My Everything	-
Cincinnati Capers	-
Bernie's Tune	-

Cal Collins(g),Monty Budwig(b),Jake Hanna(dr).

	LA.January 5,1978
Soon	Concord CJ59
Easy Living	-
If I Had You	-
I Hear A Rhapsody	-
Willow Weep For Me	-
Close Your Eyes	-
I Fall In Love Too Easily	-
The Touch Of Your Lips	-
A Child Is Born	-
My Old Flame	-

All titles also on Concord(J)ICJ70167.

Jeff Hamilton(dr) replaces Hanna.

	San Francisco.July 25,1978
Blue Haze	Concord CJ71
How Long Has This Been Going On	-
Laura	-
Sometimes I'm Happy	-
Miles' Theme	-
Blue Prelude	-
Exactly Like You	-
Deep In A Dream	-
So What	-

All titles also on Concord Jazz(J)ICJ70178,LCJ2019.

CAL COLLINS

Larry Vuckovich(p),Cal Collins(g),Bob Maize(b),Jeff Hamilton(dr).
                                    San Francisco.April 1979
    Blues On My Mind   Concord CJ95,CJ160
    Imagination   -
    Softly As In A Morning Sunrise   -
    I Love You,Samantha   -
    Marie   -
    Dream A Little Dream Of Me   -
    My Melancholy Baby   -
    Ruby   -

All titles also on Concord(J)ICJ70192.

(g-solo).   San Francisco.December 1979
    By Myself   Concord CJ119
    Where Are You   -
    What Is This Thing Called Love   -
    Stairway To The Stars   -
    No Moon At All   -
    P.S. I Love You   -
    Sunrise,Sunset   -
    The Gypsy   -
    All The Things You Are   -
    The Nearness Of You   -
    Route 66   -
    Jackson County Blues

CAL COLLINS - HERB ELLIS:
Cal Collins,Herb Ellis(g),Ray Brown(b),Jake Hanna(dr).
                                    San Francisco(?).August 1980
    Besame Mucho   Concord CJ137
    I'll Be Seeing You   -
    People Will Say We're In Love   -
    That's Your Head   -
    Trica's Fantasy   -
    I Got It Bad And That Ain't Good   -
    Limehouse Blues   -

DICK COLLINS

See also NAT PIERCE.

THE RUNAWAY HERD:
Dick Collins(tp),Med Flory(as),Al Cohn,Dick Hafer(ts),Bill Perkins(ts,fl),Jack Nimitz
(bars),Nat Pierce(p),Red Kelly(b),Chuck Flores(dr).
                                    NYC.May 22/23,1954
    I'd Know You Anywhere   RCA-Victor LJM1019
    Angel Eyes   -
    Tricky Dick   -
    Stairway To The Stars   -
    Very Shifty   -
    Just As You Are   -
    The Long Night   -
    What A Little Moonlight Can Do   -
    My One And Only Love   -
    No Soap   -
    Why Was I Born   -
    Please Don't Talk About Me When   -

All titles also on RCA/Fresh Sound(Sp)NL45632.

Dick Collins,Al Porcino,Charlie Walp or John Howell(tp),Billy Byers,Sonny Russo(tb),Dick
Meldonian(as),Al Cohn(ts,arr),Richie Kamuca,Bill Perkins(ts),Jack Nimitz(bars),Nat Pierce
(p,arr),Herb Ellis(g),Red Kelly(b),Chuck Flores(dr).

		NYC.November 27/28,1954
Strike Up The Band	RCA-Victor LJM1027
The Winter Of My Discontent	-
Hold Me,Hold Me,Hold Me	-
As Long As I Live	-
It's Love	-
They Can't Take That Away From Me	-
Donna Mia	-
Northern Comfort	-
Lullaby Of Birdland	RCA-Victor EPA672,LPM1146

All titles on LJM1027 also on RCA(Au)L10058,RCA/Fresh Sound(Sp)NL45745.
Note:Herb Ellis listed as "Bunny Harris" on LJM1027 and as "Irving von Edith" on LPM1146.
     Charlie Walp plays on the November 27,1954 session and John Howell plays on the No-
     vember 28,1954 session.

JOHN COLLINS

See IRVING ASHBY.

JOYCE COLLINS

Joyce Collins(p),Ray Brown (as "Roy Green")(b),Frank Butler(dr).

		LA.June 1/2,1960
Walkin'	Jazzland JLP(9)24
I Let A Song Go Out Of My Heart	-
Just In Time	-
I Get Along Without You Very Well	-
The End Of A Love Affair	-
Day In,Day Out	-
Somethings Gotta Give	-
Ah,Moore	-
Blue Jay	-

LEE COLLINS

See also MEZZ MEZZROW.

Lee Collins(tp),rest unknown.   Chicago.March 1948
     Nobody Knows You
          When You're Down And Out   "Soundsheet" MAL741

Note:"Soundsheet" MAL741 is a 7" LP incl. in Collins' biography ("Oh,Didn't He Ramble").

Lee Collins(tp),George Winn(tb),Scotty McGlory(cl),Don Ewell(p),Booker Washington(dr).
                                    Live."Gaffers Lounge",Chiago.July 7,1951
     Panama   New Orleans NOR7203
     (On The) Sunny Side Of The Street   -
     Struttin' With Some Barbecue   -
     Sleepy Time Down South   -
     Ain't Gonna Give Nobody
          None Of My Jelly Roll   "Soundsheet" MAL741

Lee Collins(tp),Jeep Robinson(ts),Bill "Nose" Thompson(p),Anderson Saucier(dr),Charlie
McBride(vcl).   Live."Victory Club",Chicago.Summer 1951
       Storyville Blues   New Orleans NOR7203
       If You Were Mine   -
       A-Flat Blues   -
       Sister Kate   -
       Blue Turning Grey Over You(cmb)   -

Note:"Royal Garden Blues" is listed in some catalogues from New Orleans Records but does
     prob. not appear on the LP (though it may be listed on the sleeve).

LEE COLLINS - RALPH SUTTON'S JAZZOLA SIX:
Lee Collins(tp),Burt Johnson(tb),Pud Brown(cl,ss,ts),Ralph Sutton(p),Deacon Jones(b),Smo-
key Stover(dr).   Live."Hangover Club",San Francisco.August 1,1953
       Do You Know What It
          Means To Miss New Orleans   Rarities(E)LP31
       Panama   - ,"Soundsheet" MAL741
       After You've Gone   -
       Little Rock Getaway(1)   -
       West End Blues   -
       Indiana   -

-1.Joe Sullivan(p-solo).

Same.   Live."Hangover Club",San Francisco.August 8,1953
       Do You Know What It
          Means To Miss New Orleans   Rarities(E)LP31
       Down In Jungle Town   -
       St. James Infirmary   -
       Honeysuckle Rose(1)   -
       Johnson Rag   -
       (On The) Sunny Side Of The Street   -
       Hindustan   -

-1.Joe Sullivan(p-solo).

Same.   Live."Hangover Club",San Francisco.August 15,1953
       Do You Know What It
          Means To Miss New Orleans   Rarities(E)LP32
       I Found A New Baby   -
       Buddy Bolden's Blues   -
       Muskrat Ramble   -
       Monday Date   -
       Clarinet Marmalade   -

Bob McCracken(cl),Don Ewell(p) replace Brown,Sutton.
                          Live."Hangover Club",San Francisco.August 22,1953
       Do You Know What It
          Means To Miss New Orleans   Rarities(E)LP32
       Fidgety Feet   -
       Chinatown,Chinatown   -
       Viper's Drag(1)   -
       Basin Street Blues   -
       Big Butter And Egg Man   -

-1.Ralph Sutton(p-solo).

Lee Collins(tp),Jack Delaney(tb),Harry Shields(cl),Jeff Reddick(p),Richard Alexis(b),
Albert "Abbie" Brunies(dr).   Live(?).New Orleans.October 31,1953
       Fidgety Feet   Storyville(D)SLP6017,STLD6017(CD)
       Royal Garden Blues   -   -

TOM COLLINS (British)

THE TOM COLLINS JAZZ BAND:
Tom Collins(cnt),Dick Mayhew(tb),Phil Butler(cl),Mel Cox(bj,g),Alan Arnold(b,el-b),Jon Heard(dr).   Ipswich,England.c. 1977

Fidgety Feet	Sweet Folk&Country(E)SFA067
Saratoga Swing	-
Charleston	-
Bugle Boy March	-
King Of The Road	-
Bei Mir Bist Du Schoen	-
Savoy Blue	-
Big Butter And Egg Man	-
Summertime	-
Gonna Travel On	-

Same;Collin plays (cnt,flh).   Ipswich,England.May 1979

Give Me Sunshine	Sweet Folk&Country(E)SFA107
Saturday Night Function	-
Milo's Other Samba	-
Cotton Fields	-
Tuxedo Junction	-
Lou-isi-a-ni-a	-
Midnight Special	-
Wabash Blues	-
Fish Seller	-
Struttin' With Some Barbecue	-
Wolverine Blues	-
If I Had You	-
Hindustan	

JERRY COLONNA

(p,vcl) prob. acc. by The International Sweethearts Of Rhythm.
                                               LA.c. May 1944

You Are My Everything	Sunbeam SB212

Note:The above title is from AFRS "Jubilee" transcription No.84.
    Jerry Colonna playing piano on this session is believed to be the same person as the trombone player listed for the next sessions.

JERRY COLONNA WITH HIS DIXIE HIGHWAYMEN:
Dick Cathcart,Clyde Hurley(tp),Jerry Colonna,Moe Schneider,Billy Schaeffer(tb),Matty Matlock(cl),Eddie Miller(ts),Stan Wrightsman(p),George Van Eps(g),Morty Corb(b),Nick Fatool(dr).   LA.July 19/20/21,1956

Dixieland Highway	Liberty SL9004
Soft Shoulders	-
Tallahassee Detour	-
Post No Bills	-
Caution-Go Slow	-
Dangerous Curves	-
Coffee Stop	-
Wait Outside	-
Slippery When Wet	-
Watch Out For Wild Life	-
Keep Off The Grass	-
Tourists Welcome	-
22 Miles To Conchita's	-

(session cont. next page).

session cont. from previous page):
Big Fat Minnie	Liberty SL9004
Dim Your Lights	-
Hurry Back	-

ERRY COLONNA AND HIS DIXIELAND BAND:
anny Klein(tp),Jerry Colonna(tb),Matty Matlock(cl),Eddie Miller(ts),Paul Sells(p),Morty
orb(b),Johnny Williams(dr).   LA. 1958

Ballin' The Jack	Design DLP78
Waltz Me Around	-
August And Azusa	-
U.S. Moon	-
Three Trees	-
Big Fat Minnie	-
Bowser	-
I Like!You Like!	-
Coffeebreak	-
I Came To Say Goodbye	-

ıknown(tp),Jerry Colonna(tb),Phil Gomez(cl),Bill Campbell(p),unknown b,dr,perc.
                                            LA. 1958

7837	New Orleans Cha Cha	Wing MGW12153
7838	Ebb Tide	-
7839	Carolina In The Morning	-
7840	Singin' In The Rain	-
7841	Black And White Rag	-
7842	Long Long Intro	-
7843	Chicago Style	-
7844	When The War Breaks Out In Mexico	-
7845	Waterfront Blues	-
7846	Mardi Gras Parade	-

1 titles also on Wing SRW12500,SRW16300.

te:The jazz content of some of the above titles may be limited.

CHEL COLOMBIER

chael Brecker(ts),Tom Scott(lyricon),Michel Colombier(p,el-p,clavinet),Herbie Hancock
l-p,synth,clavinet),Michael Boddicker(synth),Larry Carlton,Ray Parker Jr.,Lee Ritenour
),Jaco Pastorius,Jerry Knight(el-b),Steve Gadd,Peter Erskine(dr),Airto Moreira(perc).
                                            NYC.c. 1979

Sunday	Chrysalis CHR1212
Take Me Down	-
Dreamland	-
Queens Road	-
Overture	-
Bird Song	-
Layas	-
Do It	-
Spring	-
The Dancing Bull	-
Autumn Land(1)	-

.Colombier(p-solo).

1 titles also om Chrysalis(J)WWS81222.

EUGENIO COLOMBO (Italian)

See MARTIN JOSEPH,GIANCARLO SCIAFFINI,STRUTTURE DI SUPPORTO QUARTETTO,VIRTUOSI DI CAVE.

COLORADO JAZZ PARTY

Clark Terry(tp,flh),Flip Phillips(ts),Victor Feldman(p),Lyn Christie(b),Cliff Leeman(dr).
                          Live."Broadmoor Hotel",Colorado Springs,Colorado.September 5,197
    Just Squeeze Me   MPS(G)49.21699-1
    Medley: -
      I'm Getting
        Sentimental Over You
      Georgia On My Mind
    Billie's Bounce   -

All titles also on MPS/BASF(E)BAP5068,(Am)MD25099,(J)ULX70,Pausa PR7024,(J)SLS5093/95.

Kai Winding,Urbie Green,Carl Fontana,Trummy Young(tb),Dick Hyman(p),Lyn Christie(b),Bobby
Rosengarden(dr).   Same date
    Undecided   MPS(G)49.21699-2
    Lover Come Back To Me   -

Both titles also on MPS/BASF(E)BAP5068,(Am)MD25099,(J)ULX71,Pausa PR7025,(J)SLS5093/95.

Carl Fontana(tb),James Moody(ts),Ross Tompkins(p),Larry Ridley(b),Mousey Alexander(dr).
                                          Same date
    Emily(no ts)   MPS(G)49.21699-2
    Oleo   -

Both titles also on MPS/BASF(Am)MD25099,(J)ULX71,Pausa PR7025,(J)SLS5093/95.

Harry Edison,Joe Newman(tp),Teddy Wilson(p),Larry Ridley(b),Gus Johnson(dr).
                                          Same date
    Moten Swing   MPS(G)49.21699-3
    Yesterday(1)   -
    Caravan   -

-1.Omit Newman.

All titles also on MPS/BASF(J)ULX72.

Al Cohn(ts),Ross Tompkins(p),Lyn Christie(b),Alan Dawson(dr).
                          Live."Broadmoor Hotel",Colorado Springs,Colorado.September 6,19
    Samba De Orfeo   MPS(G)49.21699-3
    These Foolish Things   -
    Lester Leaps In   -

All titles also on MPS/BASF(Am)MD25099,(J)ULX72,Pausa(J)5093/95.

Flip Phillips(ts),Ross Tompkins(p),Lyn Christie(b),Duffy Jackson(dr).
                                          Same date
    Sweet And Lovely   MPS(G)49.21699-3
    Jumpin' At The Woodside   -

All titles also on MPS/BASF(J)ULX72,Pausa(J)5093/95.

Clark Terry,Harry Edison(tp),Kai Winding,Urbie Green(tb),Zoot Sims(ts),Budd Johnson(bars, ss),Victor Feldman(p),Lyn Christie(b),Alan Dawson(dr).
                                        Same date
    On The Trail   MPS(G)49.21699-1
    The Hymn   -

Both titles also on MPS/BASF(Am)MD25099,(J)ULX70,Pausa PR7024,(J)SLS5093/95.

Clark Terry(tp),Carl Fontana(tb),Benny Carter(as),Victor Feldman(p),Lyn Christie(b),Alan Dawson(dr).   Live."Broadmoor Hotel",Colorado Springs,Colorado.September 1971
    Terry Cloth   unissued
    When I Fall In Love
    The Shadow Of Your Smile
    My Foolish Heart
    A Time For Love
    Rifftide

Benny Carter(as),Dick Hyman(p),Larry Ridley(b),Duffy Jackson(dr).
                                        Same date
    All The Things You Are   unissued
    What's New
    Stompin' At The Savoy

Joe Newman(tp),Vic Dickenson(tb),Benny Carter(as),James Moody,Bob Wilber(reeds),Dick Hyman p),Larry Ridley(b),Alan Dawson(dr).   Same date
    In A Little Spanish Town   unissued
    Body And Soul
    It's The Talk Of The Town
    Laura
    You've Changed
    Tangerine
    Lester Leaps In

Benny Carter(as),Teddy Wilson(p),Milt Hinton(b),Cliff Leeman(dr).
                                        Same date
    Rosetta   unissued
    I Can't Get Started
    'S Wonderful
    Makin' Whoopee

Note:Carter refused to allow any of his performances from the 1971 Colorado Jazz Party to be issued.

DEGOKE STEVE COLSON

DEGOKE STEVE COLSON AND THE UNITY TROUPE:
Douglas Evert(sopranino-sax,bcl),Wallace McMillan(fl,ts,bars),Joseph Jarman(bcl,bassax), Adegoke Steve Colson(p,as,musette),Reggie Willis(b),Dushun Mosley(perc),Iqua Colson(vcl).
                                   Evanston,Ill.April 1978
    Cidigie-Dicesui   Silver Sphinx SS01
    For Paul   -
    Unknown   -

Wallace McMillan(fl,ts),Adegoke Steve Colson(p,vcl),Reggie Willis(b),Dushun Mosley(perc), Iqua Colson(vcl).   Evanston,Ill.August 1979
    Lateen   Silver Sphinx SS01
    Triumph Of The Outcasts,Coming   -
    Temple At Dendera(p-solo)   -

Wallace McMillan(ss,as,ts,picc,perc),Adegoke Steve Colson(p,ts),Reggie Willis(b),Dushun
Mosley(perc),Iqua Colson(vcl).   Milan,Italy.July 22/23,1980
      Family Members   Black Saint(I)BSR0043
      Teachers/World Heroes   -
      Clockwork   -
      Thought From Duke   -
      Patch No. 2   -

ALICE (McLEOD) COLTRANE

Pharoah Sanders(ts,fl,bcl,bells),Alice Coltrane(p),Jimmy Garrison(b),Ben Riley(dr).
                             NYC.January 29,1968
      The Sun(1)   Coltrane AU4950,Impulse AS9232-2
      Lord Help Me To Be   -
      Ohnedaruth   Impulse A(S)9156

-1.John Coltrane,Pharoah Sanders (spoken introduction).

Both titles on AU4950 also on Coltrane CRC5000,Impulse A(S)9148,(E)MIPL/SIPL515,(J)
IMP88158,YP8568,MCA29025,WEA(J)WMC5-115 (CD).

Alice Coltrane(p,harp),Jimmy Garrison(b),Rashied Ali(dr),Pharoah Sanders(bells).
                             NYC.June 6,1968
      Gospel Trane   Impulse A(S)9156,ASH9272-3
      I Want To See You   - ,AS9232-2
      Lovely Sky Boat   - , -
      Oceanic Beloved(1)   -
      Atomic Peace   -

-1.John Coltrane(spoken introduction).

All titles on A(S)9156 also on Impulse(J)YP8579.

Alice Coltrane(p,harp),Ron Carter(b),Rashied Ali(dr).
                             NYC.May 14,1969
91018 Jaya Jaya Rama   Impulse AS9185
91019 IHS   -
91020 Via Sivanandagar   -
91021 Paramhansa Lake   -
91022 Turiya   -
91041 Huntington Ashram Monastery   -

Pharoah Sanders(ts,fl,bells),Joe Henderson(ts,fl),Alice Coltrane(p,harp),Ron Carter(b),Ben
Riley(dr),Chuck Stewart(bells).   NYC.January 26,1970
91141 Blue Nile   Impulse AS9196,AS9232-2(ed.),IMP1972
91142 Mantra   - ,ASH9253-3
91143 Turiya/Ramakrishna(p,b,dr only)   -
91144 Ptah,El Daoud   -

Pharoah Sanders(ss),Alice Coltrane(harp),Vishnu Wood(oud),Charlie Haden(b),Rashied Ali
(dr).   Live."Village Gate",NYC.July 4,1970
      Isis And Osiris   Impulse AS9203,MCA 33119(CD)

No details.   NYC.October 27,1970
91182 Unknown title   Impulse unissued
91183 Sivanandagar
91184 Unknown title
91185 Leo
91186 Unknown title

Pharoah Sanders(ss,perc),Alice Coltrane(p,harp),Tulsi(tamboura),Cecil McBee(b),Rashied Ali
(dr),Majid Shabazz(perc).   NYC.November 8,1970
91170 Journey In Satchidananda   Impulse AS9203,AS9232-2(ed.)
91201 Shiva-Loka   -
91202 Stopover Bombay   -
91203 Something About John Coltrane   -

All titles also on MCA 33119 (CD).

John Blair,Leroy Jenkins,Julius Brand,Joan Kalisch(vln),Alice Coltrane(org,harp),Jimmy
Garrison(b),Jack DeJohnette(dr).   NYC.April 6,1971
       Universal Consciousness   Impulse AS9210
       Oh,Allah   - ,AS9232-2(ed.)

add Tulsi(tamboura),Clifford Jarvis(dr) replaces DeJohnnette.
                                       NYC.April 6 or May 14,1971
       Hare Krishna   Impulse AS9210

Note:String sections were orchestrated by Ornette Coleman.

Alice Coltrane(org,harp),Tulsi(tamboura),Jimmy Garrison(b),Clifford Jarvis(dr).
                                       NYC.May 14,1971
       Sita Ram   Impulse AS9210,AS9232-2(ed.)

Alice Coltrane(org,harp),Rashied Ali(dr).   NYC.June 19,1971
       Battle At Armagedon   Impulse AS9210,AS9232-2
       The Ankh Of Amen-Ra   -

Frank Lowe(ts,ss,perc),Leroy Jenkins(vln),Alice Coltane(p,org,harp,tamboura,perc),Reggie
Workman(b),Ben Riley(dr),Elayne Jones(tympani),strings,Swami Satchidananda(vcl),David
Jackson(cond).   NYC.November 15/16,1971
1262 Galaxy Around Olodumare   Impulse AS9218,AS9232-2(ed.)
1263 Leo   unissued
1264 My Favorite Things   Impulse AS9218
1265 A Love Supreme(ss)   - ,AS9232-2(ed.)
1266 Galaxy In Satchidananda   -   -
1267 Galaxy In Turiya   -   -   ,IMP1972

All titles on AS9218 also on Impulse(J)YP8580.

Alice Coltrane(p,org,harp,tympani,perc),Charlie Haden(b),Ben Riley(dr,perc),strings,Murray
Adler(cond).   LA.July 5-13,1972
       Andromeda's Suffering   Impulse AS9224,AS9232-2(ed.)
       Sri Rama Ohnedaruth   -   -
       Excerpts From The Firebird   -   -
       Lord Of Lords   -
       Going Home   -

All titles also on Impulse(E)IMPL8009.

ALICE COLTRANE - CARLOS SANTANA:
Jules Broussard(ss,fl),Alice Coltrane(org,harp),Tom Coster(org,p),Carlos Santana(g),Phil
Browne(tamboura),Dave Holland(b),Jack DeJohnette(dr,perc),Phil Ford(tabla),Armando Peraza
(g),strings.   Unknown location. 1974
       Guru Shi   Columbia PC32900
       Chinmoy Aphorism   -
       Angel Of Air   -
       Angel Of Water   -
       Bliss:The Eternal Now   -
       Angel Of Sunlight   -
       Illuminations   -
All titles also on CBS(Eu)S69063.

Alice Coltrane(org),Charlie Haden(b),Ben Riley(dr),Armando Peraza(cg),Ed Michel -1,unknown
(perc).
　　　　　　　　　　　　　　　　　　　　　LA.August 13,1975
　　　　Los Caballos　　　　　　　　Warner Bros. BS2916
　　　　Morning Worship(1)　　　　　　　　　-

Paul Hubinon,Oscar Brashear(tp),Charles Loper,George Bohanon(tb),Marilyn Robinson,Alan
Robinson(frh),Tommy Johnson(tu),Hubert Laws,Fred Jackson(fl),Jerome Richardson(ss,fl),
Jackie Kelso,Terry Harrington(ts,cl),Don Christlieb,Jack Marsh(bassoon),Alice Coltrane
(org),Charlie Haden(b),Ben Riley(dr,perc),strings.
　　　　　　　　　　　　　　　　　　　　　LA.August 15,1975
　　　　Spiritual Eternal　　　　　　Warner Bros. BS2916
　　　　Spring Rounds From
　　　　　"Rite Of Spring"(1)　　　　　　　-

-1.Add Vince DeRosa,Arte Maebe(frh),Louise Di Tullio(picc),Gene Cipriano,John Ellis(oboe),
Ernie Watts(enh),Julian Spear(bcl),Jo Ann Caldwell(contra-bassoon).

(harp-solo).　　　　　　　　　　　　　LA.September 5,1975
　　　　Wisdom Eye　　　　　　　　　　Warner Bros. BS2916

Alice Coltrane(el-p),vocal-group(vcl).　　　LA.October 15,1975
　　　　Om Supreme　　　　　　　　　　Warner Bros. BS2916

All titles also on Warner Bros.(E)K56198,(J)P10156.

Alice Coltrane(org,el-p,perc),Sita Coltrane -1(tamboura),Arjuna John Coltrane,Jr. -2 (dr)
Indian musicians(vcl,perc).　　　　　Sausalito,Calif.August 5/6,LA.August 23/28,197
　　　　Govinda Jai Jai　　　　　　　Warner Bros. BS2986
　　　　Ganesha(1)　　　　　　　　　　　　　-
　　　　Prema Muditha　　　　　　　　　　　-
　　　　Hare Krishna　　　　　　　　　　　　-
　　　　Om Namah Sivaya(2)　　　　　　　　-

All titles also on Warner Bros. WB56333.

Alice Coltrane(el-p,org),Sita Coltrane(vcl,perc),Indian musicians(vcl,tamboura,perc).
　　　　　　　　　　　　　　　　　　　　　LA.May 5,1977
　　　　Ghana Nile　　　　　　　　　　Warner Bros. BS3077
　　　　Bhaja Govindam　　　　　　　　　　-
　　　　Sri Nrsimha　　　　　　　　　　　　-

Alice Coltrane(org),Indian musicians(vcl,tamboura,perc).
　　　　　　　　　　　　　　　　　　　　　LA.May 6,1977
　　　　Trancendence　　　　　　　　Warner Bros. BS3077

Alice Coltrane(harp) acc. by the Satori Quartet(strings).
　　　　　　　　　　　　　　　　　　　　　LA.May 18,1977
　　　　Radha-Shyam　　　　　　　　　Warner Bros. BS3077

Alice Coltrane(harp,tamboura,tambourine,perc).
　　　　　　　　　　　　　　　　　　　　　LA.May 20,1977
　　　　Vrindavana Sanchara　　　　Warner Bros. BS3077

Alice Coltrane(org,p,arr),Reggie Workman(b),Roy Haynes(dr),strings.
　　　　　　　　　　　　　　　　　　　Live.UCLA,LA.April 16,1978
　　　　Transfiguration　　　　　　Warner Bros. 2WB3218
　　　　One For The Father　　　　　　　　-
　　　　Krishnaya　　　　　　　　　　　　　-
　　　　Prema(p-solo)　　　　　　　　　　　-
　　　　Affinity　　　　　　　　　　　　　-
　　　　Leo　　　　　　　　　　　　　　　　-

JHN COLTRANE

ee also ART BLAKEY,KENNY BURRELL,PAUL CHAMBERS,DEXTER CULBERTSON (U.S. NAVY BAND),RAY
RAPER,TOMMY FLANAGAN,RED GARLAND,WILBUR HARDEN,MILT JACKSON,PRESTIGE ALL STARS,PAUL
JINICHETTE,CECIL TAYLOR,TENOR CONCLAVE,MAL WALDRON.

te:List of equivalents.

JHN COLTRANE SEXTET:
ohnny Splawn(tp),John Coltrane(ts),Sahib Shihab(bars),Mal Waldron(p),Paul Chambers(b),Al
eath(dr).   NYC.May 31,1957

92	Straight Street	Prestige PRLP7105,PRP-2,Original Jazz Classics OJCCD1203-2(CD),Metronome(Sd)MEP403
93	While My Lady Sleeps(no bars)	Prestige PRLP7105,Moodsville MVLP2,Fontana(Eu) 469.203TE,688.200ZL,Musica Jazz(I)2MJP1051
94	Chronic Blues	Prestige PRLP7105,Top Rank(J)RANK1093

l titles also on Giants Of Jazz(I)LPJT72,CD53058 (CD),Jazz Roots 56018.

d Garland(p) replaces Waldron.   Same date

95	Bakai	Prestige PRLP7105,New Jazz NJLP8292,Giants Of Jazz (I)LPJT72,CD53058(CD),Jazz Roots 56018
96	Violets For Your Furs(no tp,bars)	Prestige PRLP7105,PR7426,(J)SMJ9013/15,VDJ1587, VDP5204,VDP9015/16,SMJX10030,VICJ23049(CD), VDJ28047(CD),Top Rank(J)RANK5047/49,Excelent (J)EX012,Metronome(Sd)MEP403
97	Time Was(no tp,bars)	Prestige 45-107,PRLP7105,(J)MJ1021/25,Top Rank(J) MJ1023
98	I Hear A Rhapsody	Prestige PRLP7188,PRP-2

HN COLTRANE TRIO:
hn Coltrane(ts),Earl May(b),Art Taylor(dr).
                                              NYC.August 16,1957

34-1	Trane's Slow Blues	Prestige PRLP7188,PR24094
34-2	Slowtrane (Trane's Slo Blues)	Prestige PRLP7378, -
35	Like Someone In love	Prestige PRLP7188,PR7426
36	I Love You	Prestige 45-249,45-415,PRLP7188,PR7426,FCD60-014 (CD)

HN COLTRANE WITH RED GARLAND TRIO:
hn Coltrane(p),Red Garland(p),Paul Chambers(b),Art Taylor(dr).
                                              NYC.August 23,1957

37	You Leave Me Breathless	Prestige 45-415,PRLP7123,PR7426,(J)VICJ23049(CD), VDJ28047(CD),Metronome(Sd)MEP417,Esquire(E) EP239
38	Bass Blues	Prestige PRLP7123,Metronome(Sd)MEP417,Esquire(E) EP239
39	Soft Lights And Sweet Music	Prestige PRLP7123,FCD60-014(CD),(J)SMJ9013/15, SMJ9028/29,Transition(E)SAM3,Metronome(G) JEB1001,Musica Jazz(I)2MJP1043,Fantasy FCD60-041(CD)
0	Traneing In	Prestige 45-119,PRLP7123,PRP-1
1	Slow Dance	Prestige PRLP7123

N COLTRANE SEXTET:
 Morgan(tp),Curtis Fuller(tb),John Coltrane(ts),Kenny Drew(p),Paul Chambers(b),Philly
 Jones(dr).   NYC.September 15,1957

ssion cont. next page).

(session cont. from previous page):
```
        Lazy Bird                       Blue Note BLP1577
        Moments Notice                  Blue Note 45-1718,BLP1577
        Blue Train                      Blue Note 45-1691,BLP1577,BST89903,BN-LA159,(J)
                                        NP9020,Liberty(Eu)LBS83442,Sunset(G)SLS50229
                                        United Artists(G)UAS29816
        Locomotion                      Blue Note BLP1577,(J)K18P9125,Sunset(G)SLS50229,
                                        SLD55031/32,United Artists(G)UAS29816
        I'm Old Fashioned               Blue Note BLP1577,Sunset(G)SLD55031/32
```

All titles also on Blue Note BST81577,CDP7.46095-2 (CD),(I)BNST36506,(Eu)5C.038-60094,(J)
LNJ80067,GXF3010,GXK8055,CP32-5231 (CD),CP35-3088 (CD),(Br)31C.152-53712,Mobile Fidelity
547 (CD).

JOHN COLTRANE QUARTET:
Donald Byrd(tp),John Coltrane(ts),Red Garland(p),Paul Chambers(b),Louis Hayes(dr).
```
                                              NYC.January 10,1958
1434    Lush Life                       Prestige 45-249,PRLP7188
1435    The Believer                    Prestige 45-315,PRLP7292
1436    Nakatini Serenade                        -           -
1437    Come Rain Or Come Shine         Prestige PRLP7378,PR24094
1438    Lover                                    -           -
```

All titles also on Prestige FCD60-014 (CD).

JOHN COLTRANE WITH RED GARLAND TRIO:
John Coltrane(ts),Red Garland(p),Paul Chambers(b),Art Taylor(dr).
```
                                              NYC.February 7,1958
1460    Russian Lullaby                 Prestige PRLP7142,PRP-1,FCD60-014(CD),(J)MBK4021
                                        MJ7047,SMJ7361/62,SMJ7363/64,SMJ9013/15,
                                        SMJX10030,Esquire(E)EP229,Top Rank(J)MJ2006
                                        Musica Jazz(I)2MJP1051,Barclay(F)74.054
1461    Theme For Ernie                 Prestige PRLP7142,(J)VICJ23049(CD),Metronome(Sd)
                                        MEP464,Boplicity BOPM10
1462    You Say You Care                Prestige PRLP7142,Esquire(E)EP229,Metronome(Sd)
                                        MEP464,Barclay(F)74.054
1463    Good Bait                       Prestige 45-139,PRLP7142,(J)MJ7035,SMJ7361/62,
                                        SMJ9013/15,Top Rank(J)MJ2006
1464    I Want To Talk About You        Prestige 45-177,PRLP7142,(J)VDJ1587(CD),VDJ28047
                                        (CD),VICJ8005(CD),VICJ23049(CD)
```

```
Same.                                         NYC.March 26,1958
1488    Rise And Shine                  Prestige PRLP7213
1489    I See Your Face Before Me                -  ,(J)VICJ23049(CD)
1490    If There Is
        Someone Lovelier Than You                -
1491    Little Melonae                           -
1492    By The Numbers                  Prestige 45-394,PRLP7378
```

All titles also on Prestige PR24094.

JOHN COLTRANE QUINTET:
Donald Byrd(tp),John Coltrane(ts),Red Garland(p),Paul Chambers(b),Art Taylor(dr).
```
                                              NYC.May 23,1958
1513    Black Pearls                    Prestige 45-373,PRLP7316
1514    Lover Come Back To Me           Prestige PRLP7316
1515    Sweet Sapphire Blues                     -
```

Wilbur Harden(tp,flh),John Coltrane(ts),Red Garland(p),Paul Chambers(b),Jimmy Cobb(dr).

NYC.July 11,1958

1541	Spring Is Here	Prestige PRLP7243,PRLP7322,Moodsville MVLP32, Fontana(Eu)469.203TE,688.204ZL,Stateside(E) SL10111
1542	Invitation	Prestige PRLP7243,FCD60-014(CD)
1543	I'm A Dreamer (Aren't We All)(1)	Prestige PRLP7353
1544	Love Thy Neighbour	Prestige 45-267,PRLP7268
1545	Don't Take Your Love From Me(1)	Prestige PRLP7243
1546	Stardust	Prestige 45-267,PRLP7268,PRLP7298
1547	My Ideal	Prestige PRLP7353
1548	I'll Get By	Prestige PRLP7243

-1.The mastertake prob. edited from two or more takes.

All titles also on Prestige P24056,PCD24056-2 (CD).

JOHN COLTRANE QUARTET:
John Coltrane(ts),Red Garland(p),Paul Chambers(b),Art Taylor(dr).

NYC.December 26,1958

1696	Do I Love You Beacause You're Beautiful(1)	Prestige PRLP7292
1697	Then I'll Be Tired of You(1)	Prestige PRLP7268
1698	Something I Dreamed Last Night(2,3)	Prestige PRLP7353,
1699	Bahia	-
1700	Goldsboro Express(no p)	-
1701	Time After Time(3)	Prestige PRLP7268,PR7426

-1.Add Freddie Hubbard(tp).
-2.Add Wilbur Harden(flh).
-3.Jimmy Cobb(dr) replaces Taylor.

All titles - except master 1696 - also on Prestige PR24110.

JOHN COLTRANE QUARTET:
John Coltrane(ts),Cedar Walton(p),Paul Chambers(b),Lex Humphries(dr).

NYC.April 1,1959

4420	Giant Steps	Atlantic SD1668,1311-2(CD)
4421	Naima	- -
4422	Like Sonny	- ,1354-2(CD)

JOHN COLTRANE QUARTET:
John Coltrane(ts),Tommy Flanagan(p),Paul Chambers(b),Art Taylor(dr).

NYC.May 4,1959

4469	Cousin Mary	Atlantic 45-5003,LP/SD1311,SD1541,1311-2(CD), (F)232.016,Supraphon(Cz)11153286ZD
4469	Cousin Mary(alt.take)	Atlantic SD1668,1311-2(CD)
462	Spiral	Atlantic LP1311,1311-2(CD)
463	Sweet Sioux	unissued

Note:"Cousin Mary" was the first tune recorded at this session.
"Sweet Sioux" may be the same tune as "Count Down".

same.

NYC.May 5,1959

464	Count Down	Atlantic LP/SD1311,SD2-313,1311-2(CD),(E)EP80020, (F)232.016
464	Count Down(alt.take)	Atlantic SD1668,1311-2(CD)
465	Naima	unissued

session cont. next page).

(session cont. from previous page):
```
3466   Syeeda's Song Flute            Atlantic LP/SD1311,SD2-313,1311-2(CD)
3466   Syeeda's Song Flute(alt.take)  Atlantic SD1668,1311-2(CD)
3467   Mr. P.C.                       Atlantic LP/SD1311,1311-2(CD)
3468   Giant Steps                    Atlantic LP/SD1311,SD1541,SD2-313,SD2-316,1311-2
                                         (CD),(E)EP80020,(F)232.016,(E)ATL20082,(I)
                                         RMM26012,Franklin Mint 70,Grandi del Jazz(I)
                                         GdJ10,Supraphon(Cz)11153286ZD
```

JOHN COLTRANE QUARTET:
John Coltrane(ts),Wynton Kelly(p),Paul Chambers(b),Jimmy Cobb(dr).
```
                                      NYC.November 24,1959
3883   Fifth House                    Atlantic rejected
3884   Some Other Blues                  -
3885   I'll Wait And Pray             Atlantic LP/SD1354,1354-2(CD),Supraphon(Cz)
                                         11153286ZD
3885   I'll Wait And Pray(alt.take)   Atlantic SD1668,1354-2(CD)
3886   Little Old Lady                Atlantic LP/SD1354,1354-2(CD)
```

Same.
```
                                      NYC.December 2,1959
3891   Like Sonny                     Atlantic LP/SD1354,SD2-313,1354-2(CD),Supraphon
                                         (Cz)11153286ZD
3892   Harmonique                     Atlantic LP/SD1354,1354-2(CD),Supraphon(Cz)
                                         11153286ZD
3893   The Night Has Thousand Eyes    unissued
3894   Equinox                           -
3895   My Shining Hour                Atlantic LP/SD1354,SD2-313,1354-2(CD)
3896   Naima                          Atlantic 45-5003,LP/SD1311,SD1541,1311-2(CD),(I)
                                         RMM26012,Franklin Mint 70,Grandi del Jazz(I)
                                         GdJ10,Supraphon(Cz)11153286ZD
3897   Some Other Blues               Atlantic LP/SD1354,1354-2(CD)
3898   Fifth House                                 -  ,1354-2(CD),Supraphon(Cz)
                                         11153286ZD
```

JOHN COLTRANE QUARTET:
John Coltrane(ts),Wynton Kelly(p),Paul Chambers(b),Jimmy Cobb(dr).
```
                              Live."Rheinhalle",Düsseldorf,Germany.April 4,1960
       On Green Dolphin Street
       Walkin'
       The Theme
```

Note:It has not been possible to verify that the above titles were recorded in Düsseldorf
     Germany.

JOHN COLTRANE - DON CHERRY:
Don Cherry(cnt),John Coltrane (ts-1,ss-2),Charlie Haden(b),Ed Blackwell(dr).
```
                                      NYC.June 28,1960
4662   Cherryco(1)                    Atlantic LP/SD1451
4663   The Blessing(2)                   -
4664   The Invisible(1,2)             unissued
```

Percy Heath(b) replaces Haden.   NYC.July 8,1960
```
4688   Focus On Sanity
          (Near And Far)(1)           Atlantic LP/SD1451
4689   The Blessing(1)                unissued
4690   The Invisible(1,2)             Atlantic LP/SD1451,SD2-313
4691   Bemsha Swing(1)                   -
```

JOHN COLTRANE QUARTET:
John Coltrane(ts),McCoy Tyner(p),Steve Davis(b),Billy Higgins(dr).
                                      LA.September 8,1960

15343	One And Four (Mr. Day)	Roulette (S)R52094,(Sd)REP1037,Vogue(F)CLVLXR401
15344	Exotica	Roulette (S)R52094,(Sd)REP1037,Vogue(F)CLVLXR600, VG304.400600,Mode(F)MDINT9200
15344	Exotica(alt.take)	Roulette B2-93901(CD),CDP793901-2(CD),Vogue(E) VJD560-2(?)(CD)
15411	Simple Like (Like Sonny)	Roulette (S)R52094,Vogue(F)CLVLXR399,VG603.000103, Joy(E)JOYS203,VeeJay VJS2501

All titles - ecxept "Exotica" (alt.take) - also on Roulette (S)RB2,RE120,B2-93901 (CD),
CDP793901-2 (CD),(E)ROU1012,CDROU1012 (CD),(I)RAD15009/10,(J)YS7089,YW7511,YW7811,YS2697,
Vogue(E)VJD560-2 (CD),(F)LD662,CLDR889,VG409.500889,Dunhill(F)DZ.SO12 (CD),Columbia(E)
33SX1399,Trip TLX5001,TLX5038,Bellaphon(G)BLST6537,Accord SN7227.

JOHN COLTRANE QUARTET:
John Coltrane(ts-1,ss-2),McCoy Tyner(p),Steve Davis(b),Elvin Jones(dr).
                                      NYC.October 21,1960

5118	Village Blues(1)	Atlantic LP/SD1354,1354-2(CD),(I)2K60009,Supra- phon(Cz)11153286ZD
5119	Equinox(1(?))	unissued
5120	My Favorite Things(2)	Atlantic 45-5012(ed.),LP/SD1361,SD1541,SD2-313, (Eu)781.907-1,Grandi del Jazz(I)GdJ10
5121	The Night Has A Thousand Eyes(1(?))	unissued

Same.   NYC.October 24,1960 (afternoon session)

5126	Central Park West(2)	Atlantic LP/SD1419,SD1541,SD2-313,1419-2(CD),(I) ST05517
5127	Mr. Syms(2)	Atlantic LP/SD1382,1382-2(CD),(I)2K60009
5128	Exotica(2)	Atlantic SD1553,1382-2(CD)
5129	Summertime(1)	Atlantic LP/SD1361,(I)2K60009,RMM26012
5130	Body And Soul(1)	Atlantic LP/SD1419,SD2-313,1419-2(CD)
5130	Body And Soul(alt.take)(1)	Atlantic SD1668,1419-2(CD)

Note:"Exotica" issued as "Untitled original".
     See McCoy Tyner for two additional titles - without Coltrane - from this session.

Same.   NYC.October 24,1960 (evening session)

5133	Mr. Knight(1)	Atlantic LP/SD1382,SD2-313
5134	Blues To Elvin(1)	- ,(I)2K60009
5135	Mr. Day(1)	-
5136	Blues To You(no p)(1)	-
5137	Blues To Bechet(no p)(2)	- ,SD2-313,Supraphon(Cz)11153286ZD
5138	Satellite(no p)(1)	Atlantic LP/SD1419,1419-2(CD)

All titles - except "Satellite" - also on Atlantic 1382-2 (CD).

Same.   NYC.October 26,1960

5139	Ev'rytime We Say Goodbye(2)	Atlantic LP/SD1361
5140	26-2(1,2)	Atlantic SD1553,1419-2(CD)
5141	But Not For Me(1)	Atlantic LP/SD1361
5142	Liberia(1)	Atlantic LP/SD1419,1419-2(CD)
5143	The Night Has Thousand Eyes(1)	- -
5144	Equinox(1)	- ,SD1541,SD1559,1419-2(CD),(I) ST05517

JOHN COLTRANE ORCHESTRA:
Booker Little,Freddie Hubbard(tp),Charles Majid Greenlee,Julian Priester(euphonium),Jimmy
Buffington,Julius Watkins,Donald Corrado,Bob Northern,Robert Swisshelm(frh),Eric Dolphy
(as,fl,bcl,arr),John Coltrane(ts-1,ss-2),Garvin Bushell(reeds,woodwinds),Pat Patrick(bars)
McCoy Tyner(p),Reggie Workman -3,Paul Chambers -4(b),Elvin Jones(dr).
```
                                    NYC.May 23,1961
        Greensleeves(2,3)            Impulse A(S)6,AS9223-2,GRD3-119-2(CD),(E)IMPL8015,
                                       MCA MCAD42001(CD)

        Song Of The
            Underground Railroad(1,4)  Impulse AS9273,MCA MCAD5541(CD),MCAD42001(CD)
        Greensleeves(alt.take)(2,3)         -  ,(F)68060/066,MCAD42001(CD)
        The Damned Don't Cry(1,2,3,5)  Impulse IZ9361/2
        Africa(1,3,4)                       -
```
-5.Add Cal Massey(arr),Romulus Franceschini(cond).

All titles also on Impulse(J)MVCI-23010/11 (CD).
Note:The above titles are listed in the order of recording.
    "Song Of The Underground Railroad" as "The Drinking Gourd" on session tapes.

JOHN COLTRANE GROUP:
Freddie Hubbard(tp),John Coltrane(ts-1,ss-2),Eric Dolphy (as "George Lane")(as,fl),McCoy
Tyner(p),Reggie Workman -3,Art Davis -4(b),Elvin Jones(dr).
```
                                    NYC.May 25,1961
5556   Olé(2,3,4)                    Atlantic LP/SD1373,Grandi del Jazz(I)GdJ10
5557   Dahomey Dance(1,3,4)                 - ,(I)2K60009,RMM26012
5558   Aisha(1,3)                           - ,SD2-313,        -
5559.  To Her Ladyship(1,4)         Atlantic SD1553
```
All titles also on Atlantic 1373-2 (CD).
Note:"To Her Ladyship" issued as "Original untitled ballad" on SD1553.

JOHN COLTRANE ORCHESTRA:
Booker Little(tp),Britt Woodman(tb),Carl Bowman(euphonium),Julius Watkins,Donald Corrado,
Bob Northern,Robert Swisshelm(frh),Bill Barber(tu),Eric Dolphy(fl,as,bcl,arr),John Col-
trane(ts),Pat Patrick(bars),McCoy Tyner(p),Reggie Workman,Art Davis(b),Elvin Jones(dr).
```
                                    NYC.June 7,1961
        Africa(alt.take)            Impulse AS9273
        Africa                      Impulse A(S)6,AS9200-2(ed.),(E)IMPL8015,(F)
                                       68060/66,(J)SR3026-28
        Blues Minor(1)              Impulse A(S)6
```
-1.Omit Art Davis.

All titles also on Impulse(J)MVCI-23010/11 (CD),MCA MCAD42001 (CD).

JOHN COLTRANE QUARTET:
John Coltrane(ts-1,ss-2),McCoy Tyner(p),Reggie Workman(b),Elvin Jones(dr).
```
                               Live.Newport Jazz Festival,R.I.July 1,1961
        Impressions(1)              Musica Jazz(I)2MJP1051
        Naima(1)
        My Favorite Things(2)       Musica Jazz(I)2MJP1051
```
JOHN COLTRANE GROUP:
John Coltrane(ts-1,ss-2),Eric Dolphy(as,bcl),McCoy Tyner(p),Jimmy Garrison -3,Reggie Work-
man -4(b),Elvin Jones(dr).
```
                               Live."Village Vanguard",NYC.November 1,1961
        India(2,3,4,5)              Impulse rejected
        Chasin' The Trane(1,4)(no p) Impulse AS9325
        Impressions(2,3)            Impulse IZ9361/2,(F)68060/66
        Spiritual(2,4)              Impulse AS9325,(F)68060/66,Rare LP11/15(?),CD012
                                       (CD)(?)
```
(session cont. next page).

(session cont. from previous page):
10570 Miles' Mode
            (The Red Planet)(1,4)   Impulse IZ9361/2
         Naima(1,4)   -   ,GRD3-119-2(CD)
         Brasilia(1,4)   Impulse AS9325

-5.Add Ahmed Abdul-Malik(oud).

All titles - except "India" - also on Impulse(J)MVCI-23001 (CD).
Note:"Brasilia" was issued as "Untitled original" with Garrison incorrectly listed as the
     bassist.
     Masternumbers for the November 1961 sessions were added later.

Same.   Live."Village Vanguard",NYC.November 2,1961
         Chasin' Another Trane(1,4,5)   Impulse IZ9361/2
10572 Softly As In A
            Morning Sunrise(2,4)   Impulse A(S)10,AS9200-2,(J)YS8526,Probe(E)SBP1025,

10576 Chasin' The Trane(1,3)
            (no as/bcl)   Impulse A(S)10,ASH9278-2,GRD3-119-2(CD),(J)
                                            SR3926-28,Crusader Jazz Masterworks(I)CJZLP2
         India(2,3,4,6)   MCA MCAD5541(CD),Impulse(J)45XD2009(CD)
         Spiritual(2,4,7)   -
10573 Greensleeves(2,4)(no as/bcl)   Impulse AS9325
         Impressions(1,3)   Impulse IZ9361/2

-5.Roy Haynes(dr) replaces Jones.
-6.Add Garvin Bushell(oboe),Ahmed Abdul-Malik(oud).
-7.Add Garvin Bushell(contrabassoon).

All titles also on Impulse(J)MVCI-23002/3 (CD).
Note:Impulse A(S)10 incorrectly lists Workman as the bassists on "Chasin' The Trane".

Same.   Live."Village Vanguard",NYC.November 3,1961
         Spiritual(1,2,4)   Impulse A(S)10,ASD9228-3(ed.),ASH9306-2,GRD3-119
                                            (CD)
10574 Naima(1,4)   rejected
10575 Impressions(1,3)(no as/bcl)   Impulse A(S)42,ASH9283-2,GRD3-119-2(CD),(F)
                                            68060/66,Franklin Mint 70,Crusader Jazz
                                            Masterworks(I)CJZLP2(?)
         India(2,3,4)   Impulse A(S)42,AS9223,AS9306,Crusader Jazz Master-
                                            works(I)CJZLP3(?)
         Greensleeves(2,4)(no as/bcl)   Impulse IZ9361/2
         Miles' Mode
            (The Red Planet)(1,3,4)   rejected

All titles - except "Naima" and "Miles' Mode" - also on Impulse(J)MVCI-23004/5 (CD).
Note:A(S)42 (and equivalents) incorrectly gives November 5,1961 as the rec.date for the
     above versions of "Impressions" and "India".

Same.   Live."Village Vanguard",NYC.November 5,1961
10556 India(2,3,4,5)   Impulse AS9325
10557 Spiritual(1,2,4,6)   -

-5.Add Garvin Bushell(oboe),Ahmed Abdul-Malik(oud).
-6.Add Garvin Bushell(contrabassoon).

Both titles also on Impulse(J)MVCI-23004/5 (CD).

JOHN COLTRANE QUINTET:
John Coltrane(ts-1,ss-2),Eric Dolphy(as,bcl,fl),McCoy Tyner(p),Reggie Workman(b),Elvin
Jones(dr).   Live."L'Olympia",Paris.November 18,1961 (1st concert)

Impressions(1)	Jazzway(I)LTM1503
I Want To Talk About You(1,3)	-
Blue Trane(1)	-
My Favorite Things(2)	-

-3.Omit Dolphy.

All titles also on Magnetic(Eu)MRCD114 (CD).

Same.   Live."L'Olympia",Paris.November 18,1961 (2nd concert)

Blue Trane(1)	Magnetic(Eu)MRCD115(CD)
I Want To Talk About You(1,3)	-
My Favorite Things(2)	-

-3.Omit Dolphy.

Same.   Live."Falkonercentret",Copenhagen.November 20,1961

Delilah(2)	Magnetic(Eu)MRCD116(CD)
Everytime We Say Goodbye(2)	-
Impressions(1)	-
Naima(1)	-
My Favorite Things(2)	-

Same.   Live."Konserthuset",Stockholm.November 23,1961

My Favorite Things(2)	Historic Perform.(Sd)HPLP1,Oppex 10,Jazzbird
	JAZ2006,Jazz Club CDDRIVE(G)3513(CD)
Impressions(1)	Historic Perform.(Sd)HPLP1, -
Naima(incompl.)(1)	-
My Favorite Things(2)	Historic Perform.(Sd)HPLP5
Blue Trane(1)	-,Bandstand(I)BDLP1514,
	Affinity(E)AFF764(CD)
Impressions(1)	Historic Perform.(Sd)HPLP5,Bandstand(I)BDLP1514
Naima(incompl.)(1)	- -

All titles on HPLP1 also on Beppo(E)BEP504.
All titles on HPLP5 also on Byg(J)YX8006,YX4006,YX2063/65,Affinity(E)AFF14,(J)RJL3001,
Charly(E)CDCH117 (CD),Ariston(I)PROM20,King(J)K18P6233/34.
All titles on BDLP1514 also on Bandstand(I)BDCD1514 (CD),(J)32JDB199 (CD).
Note:The above titles are from two performances.
    "Naima" - which incl. only the theme and bcl solo - is prob. from the above concert.
    Historic Performances LPs were released without any identifying information on the
    covers or the labels (which were blank). Information on each LP was given only in the
    advertising sheets which identified Coltrane as "Blue Train" (HPLP1 and HPLP5 were
    issued as "The Eric Dolphy Quintet featuring Blue Train").

Same.   TV-cast.Baden-Baden.November 26,1961

My Favorite Things(2)	Jazz Connoisseur(I)JC112,Bandstand(I)BDLP1514	
Everytime We Say Goodbye(2,3)	-	-
Impressions(1)	-	-
Unknown blues(4)		

-3.Omit Dolphy.
-4.Omit Coltrane,Dolphy.

All titles on BDLP1514 also on Bandstand(I)BDCD1514 (CD),(J)32JDB199 (CD).

Same.   Live."Kongreshalle",Frankfurt am Main,Germany.November 27,1961
        My Favorite Things(2)
        Impressions(1)
        Everytime We Say Goodbye(2,3)

-3.Omit Dolphy.

Same.   Live."Liederhalle",Stuttgart,Germany.November 29,1961
        Impressions(1)
        Everytime We Say Goodbye(2,3)
        My Favorite Things(2)

-3.Omit Dolphy.

Same.   Live.Freie Universität,Berlin.December 2,1961
        Impressions(1)

JOHN COLTRANE QUARTET:
John Coltrane(ts-1,ss-2),McCoy Tyner(p),Reggie Workman(b),Elvin Jones(dr).
                                   NYC.December 21,1961
10669 Greensleeves(2)   Impulse 45-203
10670 It's Easy To Remember(1)   - ,A(S)32,(J)MVCI-23006(CD)

Both titles also on Impulse(J)Q-1 (an EP incl. in the set SR3026-28),Karussel(Sd)KFF388,
Artone(Du)AP122.129.

JOHN COLTRANE QUINTET:
John Coltrane(ts-1,ss-2),Eric Dolphy(as,fl),McCoy Tyner(p),Jimmy Garrison(b),Elvin Jones
(dr).   Live."Birdland",NYC.February 10,1962
        Mr. P.C.(1,3)   Session 114,Crusader Jazz Masterw.(I)CJZLP3(ed),
                                     Rare LP11/15,CD14(CD),Unique Jazz(I)UJ26,
                                     Giganti del Jazz(I)GJ16,Europa Jazz(I)EJ1013,
                                     Il Jazz(I)SdMJ090(?),Accord(F)556.632,139.230
                                     (CD),Telstar(I)TDS3600(CD)

        Miles' Mode
          (The Red Planet)(1,4)   Session 114,Rare LP11/15,CD15(CD),Unique Jazz(I)
                                     UJ26,Crusader Jazz Masterworks(I)CJZLP3,Tel-
                                     star(I)TDS3600(CD)
        My Favorite Things(2,5)   Session 114,Unique Jazz(I)UJ26

-3.Issued as "Mr. R.C.M. Jr." or "Improvisations" on some issues.
-4.Issued as "Man Made Miles" on some issues.
-5.Issued as ""Stuff" I'm Partial Too" on some issues.

All titles also on Ozone 10,Musidisc(F)JA5184,Vee Jay(J)UXP88,RJL6011,Affinity(E)AFF79,
Charly(E)CDCH68 (CD),Festival(F)378,Collection Thesis Jazz THJ82031.

JOHN COLTRANE QUINTET:
Same;Dolphy plays(as,bcl,fl).   Live."Birdland",NYC.February 16 or 17,1962
        The Inchworm
        Mr. P.C.
        My Favorite Things

JOHN COLTRANE QUARTET:
John Coltrane(ts-1,ss-2),McCoy Tyner(p),Jimmy Garrison(b),Elvin Jones(dr).
                                   NYC.April 11,1962
10873 Soul Eyes(1)   Impulse unissued
10874 The Inchworm(2)   Impulse A(S)21,(J)MVCI-23012(CD)
10875 Big Nick(2)   Impulse A(S)99,(G)1C.052-90806,(J)SH3037,YC8501,
                                     45XD2009(CD),(J)MVCI-23012(CD),HMV(E)CLP1798,
                                     Philips(Eu)632.092BL,843.503BY,MCA MCAD5541
                                     (CD),(J)VIM4633

```
Same.                                    NYC.April 12,1962
10876  Soul Eyes(1)                      Impulse unissued
10877  Excerpt (Impressions)(1)                   -
10878  Body And Soul(1)                           -
10879  Neptune(1)                                 -
```

Note:"Neptune" also known as "Brasilia".

```
Same.                                    Live."Birdland",NYC.June 2,1962
       My Favorite Things(2)             Alto AL724,Cool&Blue CD101(CD)
       Body And Soul(1)                  Alto AL724,Affinity(E)AFF79,Vee Jay(J)UXP88,
                                              RJL6011,Rare LP11/15,CD15(CD),Crusader Jazz
                                              Masterworks(I)CJZLP2(?),Collection Thesis
                                              Jazz THJ82031,Telstar(I)TDS3600(CD),Cool&Blue
                                              CD101(CD)
       Cousin Mary(incompl.)(1)
```

All titles also on Affinity(E)AFF16.
Note:"My Favorite Things" was issued as "Cousin Mary" on AL724; however the "Cousin Mary"
     played during the above performance remains unissued.

```
Same.                                    NYC.June 19,1962
10979  Untitled                          Impulse unissued
10980  Out Of This World(1)              Impulse A(S)21,ASH9253-3,(J)SR3026-28,MVCI-23012
                                              (CD)
10981  Soul Eyes(1)                      Impulse A(S)21,AS9200-2,ASH9306-2,GRD107-2(CD),
                                              GRD3-119-2(CD),(J)YS8526,MVCI-23012(CD),MCA
                                              MCAD5541(CD)
10982  Excerpt (Impressions)(1)          unissued
```

Note:For some of the unissued recordings it has not been possible to list which instrument
     Coltrane plays.

```
Same.                                    NYC.June 20,1962
10983  Untitled                          Impulse unissued
10984  Miles' Mode(1)                    Impulse A(S)21,AS9223-2,MVCI-23012(CD),GRD3-119-2
                                              (CD),Jazzbox 119
10985  Two,Three,Four                    unissued
10986  Excerpt (Impressions)(1)                   -
```

```
Same.                                    NYC.June 29,1962
10992  Tunji(1)                          Impulse A(S)21,(J)MVCI-23012(CD)
10993  Out Of This World(1)              unissued
```

```
Same.                                    NYC.September 18,1962
11092  Nancy With The Laughing
          Face(1)                        Impulse 45-212,A(S)32,ASH9306-2,GRD107-2(CD)
11093  What's New(1)                              -       -    ,     -       -
                                              GRD3-119-2(CD),(J)YS8526,SR3026-28
11094  Up 'Gainst The Wall(1)(no p)      Impulse A(S)42,ASH9278-2
```

All titles also on Impulse(J)MVCI-23006(CD).

DUKE ELLINGTON - JOHN COLTRANE:
John Coltrane(ts-1,ss-2),Duke Ellington(p),Aaron Bell -3,Jimmy Garrison -4(b),Sam Woodyard
-5,Elvin Jones -6(dr).   NYC.September 26,1962
```
11114  Stevie(2,3,5)                     Impulse A(S)30
11115  In A Sentimental Mood(2,3,6)              - ,ASH9306-2,GRD2-101-2(CD),GRD107-2
                                              (CD),GRD3-119-2(CD),(E)IMPD901,(F)68.060/066,
                                              (J)Y117,YX8801,YS8526,Franklin Mint 70
11116  Angelica(2,4,6)                   Impulse A(S)30
```
(session cont. next page).

(session cont. from previous page):
```
11117  Big Nick(1,4,6)                 Impulse A(S)30,AS9223-2,MCA MCAD5541(CD),Victor
                                          Family Club(J)229
11118  My Little Brown Book(2,3,5)     Impulse A(S)30,ASH9306-2,GRD107-2(CD),(E)IMPD901
11119  The Feeling Of Jazz(2,3,5)         -  ,ASH9285-2,MCA MCA2-8028
11120  Take The Coltrane(2,4,6)          -  ,AS256-2,GRD3-119-2(CD)
```

All titles on A(S)30 also on Impulse IA9350.

JOHN COLTRANE QUARTET:
John Coltrane(ts-1,ss-2),McCoy Tyner(p),Jimmy Garrison(b),Elvin Jones(dr).
                              NYC.November 13,1962
```
11161  Too Young To Go Steady(1)       Impulse A(S)32
11162  All Or Nothing At All(1)          -  ,ASH9283-2
11163  I Wish I Knew(1)                  -
11164  They Say It's Wonderful(1)      unissued
11165  You Don't Know What Love Is(1)  Impulse A(S)32,(J)SR3026-28
11166  Say It Over And Over Again(1)     -
```

All titles - except "They Say It's Wonderful" - also on Impulse(J)MVCI-23006(CD).

same.   Live."L'Olympia",Paris.November 17,1962
```
       Bye Bye Blackbird(1)
       Mr. P.C.(1)
       Inchworm(2)
       Naima(1)
       Traneing In(1)
       My Favorite Things(2)
```

same.   Live."Konserthuset",Stockholm.November 19,1962 (1st concert)
```
       Bye Bye Blackbird(1)     Magnetic(Eu)MRCD108(CD)
       The Inchworm(2)          Duke(I)D1016,    -
       Mr. P.C.(1)              Historic Perform.(Sd)HPLP2,Magnetic(Eu)MRCD108(CD)
       Naima(1)                 Historic Perform.(Sd)HPLP3,          -
       Traneing In(1)           Historic Perform.(Sd)HPLP3,Magn.(Eu)MRCD109(CD),
                                  Pablo 2308.227,2308.227-2(CD),(J)28MJ3064,
                                  VICJ23052(CD),Orig. Jazz Classics OJCCD681-2
                                  (CD),Crusader Jazz Masterworks(I)CJZLP5
       Impressions(1)           Duke(I)D1016,Magnetic(Eu)MRCD109(CD)
       My Favorite Things(2)       -                -
```

11 titles also on Jazz Door 1210 (CD).

same.   Live."Konserthuset",Stockholm.November 19,1962 (2nd concert)
```
       Bye Bye Blackbird(1)     Historic Perform.(Sd)HPLP2,Pablo 2308.227,2310.886
                                  2404.417,2308.227-2(CD),2405.417-2(CD),(J)
                                  28MJ3064,VICJ23052(CD),Oppex 10,Rare LP11/15,
                                  CD13(CD),Orig. Jazz Classics OJCCD681-2(CD),
                                  Jazzbird JAZ2006,Crusader Jazz Masterworks(I)
                                  CJZLP4,Magnetic(Eu)MRCD127(CD)
       The Inchworm(2)          Historic Perform.(Sd)HPLP2,Oppex 10,Magnetic(Eu)
                                  MRCD127(CD)
       Naima(1)                 Magnetic(Eu)MRCD127(CD)
       I Want To Talk About You(1)   -
       Impressions(1)           Historic Perform.(Sd)HPLP3,Magnetic(Eu)MRCD127(CD)
       Mr. P.C.(1)              Magnetic(Eu)MRCD128(CD)
       My Favorite Things(2)       -
       Everytime We Say Goodbye(2)  Magnetic(Eu)MRCD127(CD)
       Traneing In(1)           Magnetic(Eu)MRCD128(CD)
```

All titles on HPLP2 also on Beppo(E)BEP500,WIF(E)101.
All titles on HPLP3 also on Beppo(E)BEP507.

Same.   Live."Falkonercentret",Copenhagen.November 22,1962
   Bye Bye Blackbird(1)
   Chasin' The Trane(no p)(1)   Ingo(I)Four,Jazzup(I)JU316(CD)
   The Inchworm(2)   Ingo(I)Seven,   -
   Everytime We Say Goodbye(2)   Ingo(I)Four,   -   ,Jazz Door 1210(CD)
   Mr. P.C.(1)   -   -
   I Want To Talk About You(1)   -   -   ,Jazz Door 1210(CD)
   Traneing In(1)
   Impressions(1)
   My Favorite Things(2)

Same.   Live."Stefaniensaal",Graz,Austria.November 28,1962
   Bye Bye Blackbird(1)   Magnetic(Eu)MRCD104(CD)
   The Inchworm(2)   Unique Jazz(I)UJ32,Magnetic(Eu)MRCD104(CD),Accord
                                      (F)556.632,139.230(CD),Festival(F)378
   Autumn Leaves(2)   Magnetic(Eu)MRCD104(CD)
   Everytime We Say Goodbye(2)   Unique Jazz(I)UJ32,Magnetic(Eu)MRCD104(CD),Accord
                                      (F)556.632,139.230(CD),Festival(F)378
   Mr. P.C.(1)   Magnetic(Eu)MRCD104(CD)
   I Want To Talk About You(1)   Ingo(I)Seven,Magnetic(Eu)MRCD105(CD)
   Impressions(1)   Unique Jazz(I)UJ32,Ingo(I)Seven(ed.),Magnetic(Eu)
                                      MRCD105(CD),Accord(F)556.632,139.230(CD),
                                      Festival(F)378
   My Favorite Things(2)   Magnetic(Eu)MRCD105(CD)

All titles on UJ32 also on Musidisc(F)JA5242,Natasha Imports 4003 (CD).

Same.   Live."Teatro dell'Arte",Milan,Italy.December 2,196
   Everytime We Say Goodbye(2)
   The Inchworm(2)   Ingo(I)Seven
   Mr. P.C.(1)
   Chasin' The Trane(incompl.)(1)

Same.   Live."Birdland",NYC.February 23,1963
   I Wanna' (Want To)
     Talk About You(1)   Session 115,Chiaroscuro CR2035,Cool&Blue CD101(CD
   One Up And One Down(1,3)   -   -   -
   The Inchworm(incompl.)(2,4)   -

-3.As "The Colt Gallops" on Session 115.
-4.As "Tran Stops In The Night" on Session 115.

All titles also on Ozone 21,Yadeon 501 (CD).
Note:The above "One Up And One Down" is not the same tune as "One Down,One Up" recorded
    1965.
    "One Up And One Down" appears twice on CR2035; both versions are identical - except
    that the first one is edited.
    Yadeon 501 (CD) lists only "I Wanna' Talk About You" and "The Inchworm" but "One Up
    And One Down" is also included.

Same.   Live."Birdland",NYC.March 2,1963
   Mr. P.C.(1,3)   Alto AL724
   My Favorite Things(incompl.)(2,4)   -

-3.As "Interpretations" on Alto AL724.
-4.As "March 2nd On The Books" on Alto AL724.

Same.   NYC.March 6,1963
11382 Vilia(2)   Impulse AS9101,(J)YC8503,YW8541,SR3011,32XD576(C
                                  MVCI-23008(CD),MCA MCAD5541(CD),(J)VIM4633,
                                  HMV(E)CLP1931

(session cont. next page).

(session cont. from previous page):
```
1383  Untitled original                    unissued
1384  Nature Boy(1)                         -
1385  Untitled original                     -
1386  Untitled original                     -
1387  Untitled original                     -
1388  Untitled original (slow blues)        -
```

JOHN COLTRANE - JOHNNY HARTMAN:
John Coltrane(ts-1,ss-2),McCoy Tyner(p),Jimmy Garrison(b),Elvin Jones(dr),Johnny Hartman vcl).
                                          NYC.March 7,1963
```
1400  They Say It's Wonderful(1)(jh)    Impulse A(S)40,(J)SR3026-28,MCA(J)ICD7(CD)
1401  Lush Life(1)(jh)                  Impulse 45-218(ed.),A(S)40,ASH9306-2,GRD107-2(CD),
                                          (E)IMPD901,MCA MCA2-8026
1402  My One And Only Love(1)(jh)       Impulse 45-218(ed.),A(S)40,ASH9306-2,GRD2-101-2
                                          (CD),GRD107-2(CD),GRD3-119-2(CD),(E)IMPD901,
                                          (J)SR3026-28,Y117,Excellent(J)EX012
1403  Autumn Serenade(1)(jh)            Impulse A(S)40,Excellent(J)EX012
1404  Dedicated To You(1)(jh)                 - ,ASH9278-2
1405  Afro-Blue(3)                      unissued
1406  You Are Too Beautiful(1)(jh)      Impulse A(S)40
```

3.It is not known if there is vocal (by Hartman) on this title.

11 titles - except "Afro Blue" also on Impulse(J)32XD576 (CD),MVCI-23008 (CD).

JOHN COLTRANE QUARTET:
John Coltrane(ts-1,ss-2),McCoy Tyner(p),Jimmy Garrison(b),Roy Haynes(dr).
                                          NYC.April 29,1963
```
1466  After The Rain(1)                 Impulse A(S)42,IZ9346/2,GRD107-2(CD),GRD3-119-2
                                          (CD),GRD120-2(CD)
1467  All The Things You Are            unissued
1468  Dear Old Stockholm(1)             Impulse A(S)100,IZ9346/2,GRD120-2(CD),(J)YC8502,
                                          YS8526,MCA(J)VIM4633,HMV(E)CLP1889
```

Note:A(S)100 incorrectly lists Elvin Jones(dr).

same.   Live.Newport Jazz Festival,R.I.July 7,1963
```
0965  My Favorite Things(1,2)           Impulse AS9161,ASH9200-2(ed.),IZ9346/2,Crusader
                                          Jazz Masterworks(I)CJZLP5,Rare LP11/15,CD15
                                          (CD),At Ease MD6707,Hör Zu(G)SHZE906BL,
0966  I Want To Talk About You(1)       Impulse AS9161,IZ9346/2,Crusader Jazz Masterworks
                                          (I)CJZLP4(?),MCA(J)VIM4632
      Impressions(1)                    Impulse IZ9346/2
```

1 titles also on MCA(J)VIM4632.

JOHN COLTRANE QUARTET:
John Coltrane(ts-1,ss-2),McCoy Tyner(p),Jimmy Garrison(b),Elvin Jones(dr).
                                          Live."Birdland",NYC.October 8,1963
```
0001  The Promise(2)                    Impulse A(S)50,AS9223-2,(J)SR3026-28
0002  Afro-Blue(2)                          - ,ASH9306-2,GRD3-119-2(CD),(E)IMPD901
                                          Crusader Jazz Masterworks(I)CJZLP3
0003  I Want To Talk About You(1)       Impulse A(S)50,AS9200-2,GRD107-2(CD),GRD3-119-2
                                          (CD),Probe SBP1025
0004  Mr. P.C.(1)                       unissued
0005  Rockin'                           -
```

Same.   Live."Konserthuset",Stockholm.October 22,196
    Traneing In(1)   Historic Perf.(Sd)HPLP6,Jazz Club CDDRIVE(G)3513
                                         (CD),Coll. Thesis Jazz THJ82033,Telstar(I)
                                         TDS3600(CD)
    Mr. P.C.(1)   Historic Perf.(Sd)HPLP6,(ed.),Pablo 2308.222,Col-
                                         lection Thesis Jazz THJ82033
    Naima(1)   Pablo 2308.222
    The Promise(2)   Pablo 2308.222,2310.886,2405.417,2310.886-2(CD),
                                         2405.417-2(CD)
    Spiritual(1,2)   Historic Perf.(Sd)HPLP6,Pablo 2620.101,2620.101-2
                                         (CD),(J)MTZ8501/02,VICJ40039/40(CD),Jazz Clu
                                         CDDRIVE(G)3513(CD),Coll. Thesis Jazz THJ8203
    Impressions(1)   Historic Perf.(Sd)HPLP1,Pablo 2620.101,2620.101-2
                                         (CD),(J)MTZ8501/02,VICJ40039/40(CD)
    I Want To Talk About You(1)   Historic Perf.(Sd)HPLP6,Pablo 2308.222,Atlantis(F
                                         ATSD14,Telstar(I)TDS3600(CD),Affinity(E)
                                         CDPRO1(CD),Coll. Thesis Jazz THJ82033

All titles on HPLP1 also on Beppo(E)BEP504.
All titles on HPLP6 also on Affinity(E)AFF16,(J)RJL3006,Charly(E)CDCH33 (CD),Byg(J)YX8007
YX2063/65,Seven Seas(J)K18P6233/34.
All titles on Pablo 2308.222 also on Pablo 2308.222-2 (CD),(F)98.844 (CD),(J)MTF1821,
VICJ23051 (CD).

Same.   Live."Tivolis Koncertsal",Copenhagen.October 25,196
    Mr. P.C.(1)
    Impressions(1)   Tempo di Jazz(I)CDTJ701(CD)
    The Promise(2)   -
    Afro-Blue(2)   -
    Naima(1)   -
    My Favorite Things(2)   -

Same.   Live."Salle PLeyel",Paris.November 1,1963
    Chasin' The Trane(1)
    My Favorite Things(2)
    Afro Blue(2)

Same.   Live.Freie Universität,Berlin.November 2,19
    Lonnie's Lament(1)   Pablo 2620.101,Rare LP11/15,RARECD11/15(CD)
    Naima(1)   -   -   -
    Chasin' The Trane(1)   - ,2310.886,-   -
    My Favorite Things(2)   -
    Afro-Blue(2)   - ,2310.886,Rare LP11/15,RARECD11/15
                                   (CD)
    Cousin Mary(1)   - ,Rare LP11/15,RARECD11/15(CD)
    I Want To Talk About You(1)   -   -   -
    Mr. P.C.(1)   Pablo 2308.217
    The Inchworm(2)   -
    Ev'rytime We Say Goodbye(2)   - ,2310.886

All titles on Pablo 2308.217 also on Pablo 2308.217-2 (CD),(J)MTF1816,VICJ23050 (CD).
All titles on Pablo 2310.886 also on Pablo 2405.417,2310.886-2 (CD),2405.417-2 (CD).
All titles on Pablo 2620.101 also on Pablo 2620.101-2 (CD),2405.417-2 (CD),(J)MTZ8501/02
VICJ40039/40 (CD).
Note:Pablo 2620.101 erroneously lists rec. date as October 26,1963.
    The last three titles listed are prob. from the above concert.

Same.   Live."Liederhalle",Stuttgart,Germany.November 4,19
(session cont. next page).

session cont. from previous page):

Afro-Blue(2)	Jazz Galore(I)1001	
The Promise(2)	-	
Impressions(1)		
I Want To Talk About You(1)	Jazz Galore(I)1001	
My Favorite Things(2)	-	
Mr. P.C.(1)		
Everytime We Say Goodbye(2)		

11 titles on Jazz Galore(I)1001 also on Jazz&Jazz(I)CDJJ613 (CD).

ame.   NYC.November 18,1963

0017	Your Lady(2)	Impulse A(S)50,ASH9283-2
0018	Alabama(1)	- ,ASH9200-2,ASH9306-2,GRD107-2(CD),
		GRD3-119-2(CD),(E)IMPD901,Probe(E)SBP1025,
		Smithsonian Inst. P6.11891,RD033-5(CD)

ote:The first release of A(S)50 included two takes of "Alabama" - take 4 (2:40) and take
5 (2:23); ASH9200-2 and CD reissues of A(S)50 also include both takes. Later editions
of A(S)50 - as well as ASH9306-2,GRD107-2(CD) and GRD3-119-2(CD) - only incl. take 5.

ame.   TV-cast.San Francisco.c. December 1963

Afro-Blue(2,3)	Session 126		
Alabama(1,4)	-,Blue Parrot(E)AR700,Moon(I)MCD035-2(CD)		
Impressions(1)	-	-	-

3.Issued as "African Blues".
.Issued as "Alabama Stomp".

te:The above titles are from a "Jazz Casual" TV-show (prob. broadcast February 23,1964).

ame.   NYC.April 27,1964

081	Crescent(1)	Impulse unissued
082	Lonnnie's Lament(1)	Impulse A(S)66
083	The Drum Thing(1)	- ,ASH9272-3
084	Wise One(1)	- ,ASH9306-2,GRD107-2(CD),(E)IMPD901
085	Bessie's Blues	unissued
086	Song Of Praise(1)	-

me.   NYC.June 1,1964

127	Crescent(1)	Impulse A(S)66,AS9278-2,GRD3-119-2(CD)
128	Bessie's Blues(1)	- ,AS9200-2,GRD3-119-2(CD),At Ease
		MD6707

me.   NYC.December 9,1964

	A Love Supreme:	
243	Pt.1:Acknowledgement(1)	Impulse A(S)77,ASD9228-3,GRD3-119-2(CD)
244	Pt.2:Resolution(1)	-
245	Pt.3:Pursuance(1)	- ,ASH9283-2(ed.)
245	Pt.4:Psalm(1)	- ,AS9200-2

1 titles also on Impulse(J)SR3027 (part of the set SR3026-28).
te:90245 is the masternumber for both "Pursuance" and "Psalm".

HN COLTRANE SEXTET:
hn Coltrane,Archie Shepp(ts),McCoy Tyner(p),Jimmy Garrison,Art Davis(b),Elvin Jones(dr).
                                        NYC.December 10,1964

	A Love Supreme:	Impulse unissued
246	Pt.1:Acknowledgement	
	Pt.2:Resolution	
	Pt.3:Pursuance	
	Pt.4:Psalm	

JOHN COLTRANE QUINTET:
John Coltrane(ts-1,ss-2),McCoy Tyner(p),Jimmy Garrison,Art Davis(b),Elvin Jones(dr).
                                        NYC.February 17,1965
90253 Nature Boy(1)   Impulse IZ9345/2
90254 Feelin' Good(1)   rejected
90255 Chim Chim Cheree(2,3)   -

-3.Omit Davis.

Same.   NYC.February 18,1965
90256 Nature Boy(1)   Impulse A(S)85,GRD3-119-2(CD)
90257 Feelin' Good(1)   Impulse IZ9345-2,MCA(J)VIM4633

Both titles also on Impulse(J)MCVI-23015 (CD).

JOHN COLTRANE QUARTET:
John Coltrane(ts-1,ss-2),McCoy Tyner(p),Jimmy Garrison(b),Elvin Jones(dr).
                                        Live."Half Note",NYC.March 19(?),1965
       Chim Chim Cheree(2)   J For Jazz JFJ800,Rare LP11/15,CD13(CD)
       Impressions(1)   -   - ,CD14(CD)

Both titles also on Chiaroscuro CR2023.

Same.   Live."Village Gate",NYC.March 28,1965
90374 Nature Boy(1)   Impulse A(S)90,ASH9278-2,(J)YW8541,HMV(E)CLP193
                                        MCA(J)VIM4633

Same.   Live."Half Note",NYC.April 2,1965
       Untitled original(1,3)   Blue Parrot(E)AR700,Chiaroscuro CR2033,Moon(I)
                                        MCD035-2(CD)
       I Want To Talk About You(1)   Chiaroscuro CR2035
       Afro-Blue(2)

-3.As "Creation" on AR700 and MCD035-2(CD).

Same.   Live."Half Note",NYC.May 7,1965
       Song Of Praise(1,3)   Ozone 21,Blue Parrot(E)AR700,Blue Labor LP705,
                                        Cool&Blue CD101(CD)
       My Favorite Things(2)   Blue Parrot(E)AR700,Blue Labor LP705

-3.As "Brasilia" on AR700 and Blue Labor LP705.

Same.   NYC.May 17,1965
90305 Chim Chim Cheree(2)   Impulse A(S)85,AS9223-2,GRD3-119-2(CD),(J)YS852
                                        SR3926-28
90306 Brasilia(1)   Impulse A(S)85
90307 Song Of Praise(1)   - ,ASH9284-3

All titles also on Impulse(J)MCVI-23015 (CD).

JOHN COLTRANE QUARTET:
John Coltrane(ts-1,ss-2),McCoy Tyner(p),Jimmy Garrison(b),Roy Haynes(dr).
                                        NYC.May 26,1965
90308 After The Crescent(1)   Impulse IZ9346/2,GRD120-2(CD)
90309 Dear Lord(1)   - ,AS9195,AS9278-2,ASH9306-2,IMP19
                                        GRD107-2(CD),GRD3-119-2(CD),GRD120-2(CD),(
                                        45XD2009(CD),MCA MCAD5541(CD)
90310 One Down,One Up(1)   Impulse IZ9346/2,GRD120-2(CD)
90311 Welcome(1)   rejected

JOHN COLTRANE QUARTET:
John Coltrane(ts-1,ss-2),McCoy Tyner(p),Jimmy Garrison(b),Elvin Jones(dr).
                                            NYC.June 10,1965
90312 Welcome(1)   Impulse AS9106,AS9235-2,AS9278-2,ASH9306-2,
                                        GRD107-2(CD),GRD3-119-2(CD)
90313 The Last Blues   unissued
90314 Untitled original(1)   Impulse IZ9345/2
90315 Transition(1)   Impulse AS9195
90316 Suite(1):   -
           Pt.1:Prayer And
                 Meditation:Day
           Pt.2:Peace And After
           Pt.3:Prayer And
                 Meditation:Evening
           Pt.4:Affirmation
           Pt.5:Prayer And
                 Meditation:4 A.M.

ame.   NYC.June 16,1965
0317   Living Space(1)   Impulse AS9225,ASH9278-2,IZ9345/2,GRD3-119-2(CD)
0318   Dusk Dawn(1,2,3)   Impulse IZ9345/2
0319   Vigil(no p,b)(1)   Impulse AS9106,AS9283-2
0320   Untitled original(1)   Impulse IZ9345/2

ote:"Living Space" has percussion and strings overdubbed (April 16/17,1972 - arranged and
     conducted by Alice Coltrane) on AS9225,ASH9278-2.

OHN COLTRANE ORCHESTRA:
reddie Hubbard,Dewey Johnson(tp),John Tchicai,Marion Brown(as),John Coltrane,Archie Shepp
haroah Sanders(ts),McCoy Tyner(p),Jimmy Garrison,Art Davis(b),Elvin Jones(dr).
                                            NYC.June 28,1965
0321-1 Ascension,pt.1   Impulse A(S)95,ASD9228(ed.),(J)SR3026/28
0322-1 Ascension,pt.2   - ,(J)SR3026/28
0321-2 Ascension,pt.1   - ,ASD9223-2(ed.)
0322-2 Ascension,pt.2   -

oth takes also on Impulse GRD2-113-2 (CD),(J)MVCI-23016 (CD).
ote:Each take was recorded as one continuous piece. The first edition (thousand copies or
     so) of A(S)95 used take 1 - later releases used take 2.

OHN COLTRANE QUARTET:
ohn Coltrane(ts-1,ss-2),McCoy Tyner(p),Jimmy Garrison(b),Elvin Jones(dr).
                                      Live.Newport Jazz Festival,R.I.July 2,1965
0350   One Down,One Up(1)   Impulse A(S)94,AS9235-2,(J)IMP88071,YP8524,YW8541,
                                        SH3075,WMC5-114(CD),MCA MCA29019,(J)VIM4633,
                                        Jasmine(E)JAS22,HMV(E)CLP/CSD3551,EMI(I)
                                        064-92920
       My Favorite Things(2)   Impulse IZ9345/2,MCA MCA2-4138,(J)VIM4632

oth titles also on Impulse GRD1-105-2(CD),(J)MVCI-23017.

ame.   Live.Antibes,France.July 26,1965
       A Love Supreme: France's Concert(F)FC106
           Pt.1: Acknowledgement(1)
           Pt.2: Resolution(1)
           Pt.3: Pursuance(1)
           Pt.4: Psalm(1)

A Love Supreme" pt. 1-4 also on France's Concert(F)FCD106 (CD),Ingo(I)Eleven(incompl.),
rusader Jazz Masterworks(I)CJZLP1,Rare LP11/15,CD012(CD),DejaVu(I)DVCD2037(CD)(incompl),
)MCD2011 (CD),Giants Of Jazz(I)CD53068 (CD).
t.3: Pursuance" also on Jazz Connoisseur(I)JC112.

Same.   Live.Juan Les Pins,France.July 27,1965
    Naima(1)   Byg(J)YX4001/02,France's Concert(F)FC119,FCD119
                           (CD),Giants Of Jazz(I)CD53068(CD),Jazz Club
                           CDDRIVE(G)3513(CD),Telstar(I)TDS3600(CD),
                           Toshiba(J)TOLW3113,Jazz Hour(I)JHR73538(CD)
    Blue Valse(1)   France's Concert(F)FC119(incompl.),FCD119(CD),
                           Toshiba(J)TOLW3113
    Drum solo   France's Concert(F)FCD119(CD)
    My Favorite Things(2)   France's Concert(F)FC119,FCD119(CD)(incompl.),
                           Jazz Hour(I)JHR73538(CD)
    Impressions(1)   Byg(J)YX4001/02,France's Concert(F)FC119,
                           FCD106(CD),Giants Of Jazz(I)CD53068(CD),
                           Jazz Hour(I)JHR73538(CD)

All titles also on Telstar(I)TDS3600 (CD).
Note:FCD119 and TDS3600 also incl. the presentation of the musicians at the beginning of
    the concert.
    Byg(J)YX4001/02 (and equiv.) does not incl. the bass-introduction (10:05) to "Impres-
    sions".

Same.   Live."Salle Pleyel",Paris.July 28,1965
    Afro-Blue   Byg(J)YX4001/02,France's Concert(F)FCD119(CD)
                           (incompl.)
    Impressions   Byg(J)YX4001/02,France's Concert(F)FCD119(CD)
    Blue Valse   -

All titles on YX4001/02 also on Byg(J)YX2026/27,YX2063/65,PCD2001 (CD),Affinity(E)AFFD24,
(J)RJL3011/12,Charly(E)CDCH87 (CD),Thesis Jazz THJ82035 (CD),Seven Seas(J)K18P6253.

Same.   Live.Comblain-la-Tour,Belgium.August 1,1965
    Untitled original
    Naima
    My Favorite Things

Note:"Naima" and "My Favorite Things" issued on video cassette only.

JOHN COLTRANE QUINTET:
John Coltrane(ts-1,ss-2),Archie Shepp(ts),McCoy Tyner(p),Jimmy Garrison(b),Elvin Jones
(dr).   Live.Down Beat Jazz Festival,Chicago.August 15,196
    Unknown original
    Nature Boy

JOHN COLTRANE QUARTET:
Omit Shepp.
90363 Dearly Beloved(1)   NYC.August 26,1965
90364 Attaining(1)   Impulse AS9211
90365 Sunship(1)   - ,ASH9283-2
90366 Ascent(1)   - ,ASH9235-2
90367 Amen(1)   -

Note:One of the releases of AS9211 erroneously included unknown non-Coltrane material on
    the B-side of the LP.

Same.   NYC.September 2,1965
90379 Meditations,pt.1:   Impulse AS9332
       Love(1)
       Compassion(1)
       Joy(1)
90380 Meditations,pt.2:   -
       Consequences(1)
       Serenity(1)
(session cont. next page).

(session cont. from previous page):
All titles also on Impulse GRD118-2 (CD).
Note:The above version of "Meditations" was issued as "First Meditations (For Quartet)".
      This version differs compositionally from the original issued one (rec. November 23,
      1965).

Same.   San Francisco.September 22,1965
        Joy(1)   Impulse AS9225,IZ9345/2,GRD118-2(CD)

Note:"Joy" has Alice Coltrane(keyb),Charlie Haden(b),strings overdubbed (April 16/17,
      1972 - arranged and conducted by Alice Coltrane) on AS9225.

JOHN COLTRANE SEXTET:
John Coltrane(ts-1,ss-2),Pharoah Sanders(ts),Donald Garrett(bcl,b),McCoy Tyner(p),Jimmy
Garrison(b),Elvin Jones(dr).   Live."The Penthouse",Seattle,Washington.September 30,1965
91198 Cosmos(1)   Impulse AS9202-2,AS9267-2,ASH9278-2
91199 Out Of This World(1,2)   -
91120 Evolution(1)   -
       Tapestry In Sound(b-solo)   -
       Body And Soul(1)   unissued
       Afro Blue(incompl.)   -
       Kalimba-solo(3)   -
       Unknown title (incompl.)(4)   -

-3.Kalimba ("thumb piano") played by unknown musician.
-4.This title (30:00) was broadcast only and not recorded by Impulse.

All titles on AS9202-2 also on WEA(J)WMC5-116 (CD).

JOHN COLTRANE GROUP:
Add Joe Brazil(fl).   Lynwood,Washington.October 1,1965
90435 Om,pt.1(1)   Impulse AS9140
90436 Om,pt.2(1)   - ,AS9200-2(ed.)

Both parts also on Impulse GRD2-113-2 (CD) (played as one continuous piece).
Note:The HMV(E) CLP/CSD3617 reissues of AS9140 was erroneously numbered and covers printed
      for "Kulu Se Mama"; these were withdrawn and replaced with corrected titles.

JOHN COLTRANE GROUP:
John Coltrane,Pharoah Sanders(ts),Donald Garrett(bcl),McCoy Tyner(p),Jimmy Garrison(b),
Elvin Jones(dr),Frank Butler(dr,perc),Juno Lewis(perc,vcl).
                                         LA.October 14,1965
90676 Kula Se Mama   Impulse AS9106,AS9200-2(ed.),Probe(E)SBP1025
90677 Selflessness   Impulse AS9161

Both titles also on Impulse GRD2-113-2 (CD).
Note:See note after session October 1,1965.

No details.   Unknown location/date
        Om   WEA(J)WMC5-116(CD)

JOHN COLTRANE SEXTET:
John Coltrane,Pharoah Sanders(ts),McCoy Tyner(p),Jimmy Garrison(b),Elvin Jones,Rashied Ali
(dr).   NYC.November 23,1965
90413 Meditations,pt.1:
       The Father,The Son
          And The Holy Ghost   Impulse AS9110,AS9223-2(ed.)
       Compassion   -
(session cont. next page):

(session cont. from previous page):
90414 Meditations,pt.2:
            Consequences   Impulse AS9110,AS9283-2(ed.)
            Serenity   - ,AS9235-2(ed.)
            Love   -

Note:See note after session September 2,1965.

JOHN COLTRANE SEXTET:
John Coltrane(ts-1,bcl-2),Pharoah Sanders(ts,picc,wooden-fl,perc),Alice Coltrane(p),Jimmy
Garrison(b),Rashied Ali(dr),Ray Appleton(perc).
                                        San Francisco.February 2,1966
90986 Manifestation(1)   Coltrane AU4950,Impulse AS9223-2
90987 Reverend King(1,2)   - ,Hör Zu(G)SHZE906BL
            Peace On Earth(1)   Impulse AS9225,IA9360
            Leo(1)   - ,ASD9228(ed.),AS9266-2

All titles on AU4950 also on Coltrane CRC5000,Impulse A(S)9148.

Note:On "Leo" and "Peace On Earth" Alice Coltrane(keyb),Charlie Haden(b) overdubbed - and
     replaced - the original keyboard and bass parts (LA.April 16/17,1972). On AS9225 and
     ASD9228 strings and percussion was also overdubbed (LA.April 16/17,1972 - arranged
     and conducted by Alice Coltrane).

JOHN COLTRANE GROUP:
Donald Ayler(tp),Carlos Ward(as),John Coltrane(ts-1,ss-2),Pharoah Sanders,Albert Ayler
(ts),Alice Coltrane(p),Jimmy Garrison(b),Rashied Ali,J.C. Moses(dr).
                                        Live."Philharmonic Hall",NYC.February 19,1966
            My Favorite Things(2)
            Om(1)

JOHN COLTRANE QUINTET:
John Coltrane(ts,ss,bcl),Pharoah Sanders(ts,fl),Alice Coltrane(p),Jimmy Garrison(b),
Rashied Ali(dr).   NYC.April 21,1966
90536 Darkness   Impulse unissued
90537 Lead Us On
90538 Leo
90539 Peace On Earth

Same.   NYC.April 28,1966
90540 Call   Impulse unissued
90541 Leo

JOHN COLTRANE SEXTET:
John Coltrane(ts-1,ss-2,bcl-3),Pharoah Sanders(ts,picc),Alice Coltrane(p),Jimmy Garrison
(b),Rashied Ali(dr),Emaniel Rahim(perc).   Live."Village Vanguard",NYC.May 28,1966
90644 My Favorite Things(2,3,4)   Impulse AS9124,(J)SR3026-28
90645 Naima(1)   - ,AS9200-2

-4.The first part (a bass-solo) issued as "Introduction To My Favorite Things".

JOHN COLTRANE QUINTET:
Omit Rahim.   Live.Newport Jazz Festival,R.I.July 2,1966
            My Favorite Things(2)
            Peace On Earth(1)
            Leo(1)

Same.   Live."Sankei Hall",Tokyo.July 11,1966
            Afro-Blue(2)   Impulse(J)YB8508-10,MCA(J)VIM4630/31
            Peace On Earth(1)   -
(session cont. next page).

Crescent(1)	Impulse(J)YB8508-10,MCA(J)VIM4630/31	
Leo (theme)(1)	-	-

All titles also on Impulse GRD4-102-2 (CD),(J)55XD579/80 (CD),MVCI-23019/22 (CD),MCA
MCA254620,MAPS9765,(Eu)254620-2 (CD).
Note:Impulse(J)Q-1 (an EP incl. in the set SR3026-28) has an interview with John Coltrane
    (rec. Tokyo.July 18,1966).

Same.   Live."Koseinenkin Hall",Tokyo.July 22,1966
        Peace On Earth(1)   Impulse(J)IMR9036-38,(Am)AS9246/2
        My Favorite Things(2,4)   -   ,VIM4628/29,SR3060
        Meditations(1)/Leo(1,4)   -   - ,(Am)AS9246/2,
                                   AS9266(ed.),IMP1973(ed.),(F)68.060/066

-4.Coltrane and Sanders also play (as).

All titles also on Impulse GRD4-102-2 (CD),(J)YB8501/03,55XD573/74 (CD),MVCI-23019-22 (CD)
(Eu)254610-2 (CD).

JOHN COLTRANE GROUP:
John Coltrane(ts,ss),Pharoah Sanders(ts),Alice Coltrane(p),Jimmy Garrison,Lionel "Sonny"
Johnson(b),Rashied Ali(dr),Omar Ali,Algie DeWitt(perc).
                                    Live."Village Theatre",NYC.December 26,1966
        Unknown original
        Hymn
        Unknown original
        My Favorite Things

JOHN COLTRANE QUINTET:
John Coltrane(ts,fl),Pharoah Sanders(fl,picc),Alice Coltrane(p),Jimmy Garrison(b),Rashied
Ali(dr).   Prob.NYC.February 15,1967
90769 To Be   Impulse AS9120,(J)SR3026-28
90770 Offering   - ,ASH9253-3,GRD3-119-2(CD)

Both titles also on Impulse(J)MVCI-23023 (CD).

JOHN COLTRANE - RASHIED ALI:
John Coltrane(ts,bells),Rashied Ali(perc,dr).
                                      NYC.February 22,1967
90771 Mars   Impulse ASD9277
90772 Leo   Impulse IA9360
90773 Venus   Impulse ASD9277
       Jupiter Variation   Impulse IA9360
       Jupiter   Impulse ASD9277,Franklin Mint 70
       Saturn   -

All titles also on Impulse GRD110-2 (CD).

JOHN COLTRANE QUINTET:
Marion Brown(as),John Coltrane(ts),Alice Coltrane(p),Jimmy Garrison(b),Rashied Ali(dr).
                                      NYC.February 27,1967
90774 E Minor   Impulse unissued
90775 Half Steps

JOHN COLTRANE QUARTET:
Omit Brown.   NYC.March 7,1967
90776 Number One   Impulse IS9360
90777 Ogunde   Impulse AS9120,AS9223-2

Both titles also on Impulse(J)MVCI-23023 (CD).
Note:The rec.date for "Ogunde" is incorrectly listed as March 17,1967 in the cover notes.

```
Same.                               NYC.March 29,1967
90784  Number Eight                 Impulse unissued
90785  Number Seven
90786  Number Six
90787  Number Five
90788  Number Four
90789  Number Two
```

JOHN COLTRANE SEXTET:
Pharoah Sanders(as),John Coltrane(ts),Alice Coltrane(p),Jimmy Garrison(b),Rashied Ali(dr),
Algie DeWitt(bata-dr).   Live.Olatunji Center Of Afican Culture,NYC.April 23,1967
        Ogunde(incompl.)
        My Favorite Things(incompl.)

Note:Additional titles from the group's - two - performances that day were taped.

```
Same.                               NYC.May 17,1967
90790  None Other                   Impulse unissued
90791  Kaliedoscope
```

JOHN COLTRANE QUARTET:
Omit Sanders,DeWitt.   NYC.Spring 1967
        Expression   Impulse AS9120,AS9278-2,(J)MVCI-23023(CD)

Note:The rec.date for "Expression" is incorrecly listed as March 17,1967 in the cover
     notes - the correct rec.date is prob. February 27, March 29 or - most likely - May
     17,1967.

Pharoah Sanders(fl),Alice Coltrane(p),Jimmy Garrison(b),Ben Riley(dr).
                                     NYC.January 29,1968
        The Sun(1)   Coltrane AU4950,CRC5000,Impulse A(S)9148,AS9232-2,
                              Hör Zu(G)SHZE906

-1.John Coltrane,Pharoah Sanders (spoken introduction).

Note:The above title (recorded after the death of Coltrane) was included in the John Col-
     trane album "Cosmic Music" - see Alice Coltrane for additional titles from the above
     session.

JOHN COLTRANE - list of equivalents:

Prestige: Orig.:	Reissue:	Stateside/ Esquire(E):	HMV/Carère/ Barclay(F):	Bella- phon(G):	Prestige(J):	Other labels:
PRLP7105	PR7609, PR24014	32-079		BJS40126, BLST6527	PJ12-7105, SMJ6547, LPJ70027, VIJ217, VDJ1511(CD), VICJ23508(CD)	Orig.Jazz Cl.OJC020 OJCCD020-2(CD)
PRLP7123	PR7651, PR24003	32-091		BJS40148, BLST6513	MJ7135, SMJ6548, LPR88023, VIJ245, VDJ1636(CD), VICJ23621(CD)	Prestige(Eu)81107, Orig.Jazz Cl.OJC189 OJCCD189-2(CD)

JOHN COLTRANE - list of equivalents (cont.):

Prestige: Orig.:	Reissue:	Stateside/ Esquire(E):	HMV/Carère/ Barclay(F):	Bella- phon(G):	Prestige(J):	Other labels:
PRLP7142	PR7531, PR24003	32-089	84.078	BJS4063 BLST6513	MJ7094, SMJ6559, LPR88002, VIJ201, VDJ1502(CD), VICJ23507(CD)	Prestige(Du)PPR070, Prest.(E)CDRIVM003, Prestige(Eu)81107, Prest.(F)98373(CD), Orig.Jazz Cl.OJC021 OJCCD021-2(CD), Top Rank(J)RANK5013
PRLP7188	PR7581, PR24014	32-129	84.086, 68.343	BJS40121, BLST6527	MJ7113, SMJ6505, LPR8896, VIJ225, VDJ1544(CD), VICJ23573(CD)	Prestige(Du)PPR071, Prest.(E)CDJZD001, Prest.(F)98442(CD), Orig.Jazz Cl.OJC131 OJCCD131-2(CD), Top Rank(J)RANK5083
PRLP7213	PR7746			BJS40155	SMJ6560, SMJ7551, LPJ80016, VIJC23623(CD)	Orig.Jazz Cl.OJC078 OJCCD078-2(CD), Top Rank(J)RANK7025
PRLP7243	PR7825	32-179		BJS40163	SMJ6562, LPP88109, VDJ1667(CD), VICJ23625(CD)	Orig.Jazz Cl.OJC246 OJCCD246-2(CD)
PRLP7268			FELP10.004		SMJ6564, LPR88056, VIJ226, VDJ1608(CD), VICJ23548(CD)	
PRLP7292	PR24037		FELP10.016		SMJ6558, SMJ7246, LPJ70004, VICJ23627	Prest.(Du)PR/M5007, Prest.(Du)MPRS3026
PRLP7316	PR24037	SL10124			SMJ6561, SMJ7252, LPP88122, VICJ23628(CD)	Prest.(Du)PR/M5001, Prest.(Du)MPRS3027, Orig.Jazz Cl.OJC352 OJCCD352-2(CD)
PR7353		SL10162	99.996		SMJ6563, SMJ7353, LPP88051, VICJ23629(CD)	Prest.(Du)PR/M5008, Prest.(Du)PPR072, Orig.Jazz Cl.OJC415 OJCCD415-2(CD)
PR7378					SMJ6557, VICJ23630	Prest.(Du)PR/M5009, Prest.(Du)MPRS3028, Orig.Jazz Cl.OJC394 OJCCD394-2(CD)

Note:All Coltrane's recordings for Prestige - except for the Miles Davis recordings - also on Prestige PCD4405-2 (16xCD set),(J)VICJ40017-34 (18xCD).

JOHN COLTRANE - list of equivalents (cont.):

Atlantic: Orig.:	Reissue:	Atlantic(E):	Atlantic(F):	Atlantic(G):	Atlantic(J):	London(E):
LP/SD1311		588.168, K50239	332.017, WEA50.239, 40.376	ATL50239, ATL40376	P6003, P7502	LTZ-K15197
1311-2(CD)			7.81337-2(CD)		AMCY1001(CD)	
LP/SD1354			332.032, 40.391		P6044, P7503, SMJX2, MJ7005/6, SMJ7008/9	LTZ-K15219, SAH-K6162
1354-2(CD)			7.81344-2(CD)		AMCY1002(CD)	
LP/SD1361	1361-2 (CD)	588.146, ATL/SAL5022	332.037, 40.287, 7.81346-2(CD)		P6030, P7505, SMJX2, MJ7005/6, SMJ7008/9, AMCY1004(CD)	
LP/SD1373			332.048, 40.286	ATL40286	P6052, P7507, MJ7040	LTZ-K15239, SAH-K6223
1373-2(CD)					AMCY1007(CD)	
LP/SD1382			332.056, S372.010, 40.288		P6068, P7504	HA/SH-K8017
1382-2(CD)					AMCY1005(CD)	
LP/SD1419		587.039, S588.039,	40.388		P6083, P7506, SMJ7219	
1419-2(CD)			7.81358-2(CD)		AMCY1006(CD)	
LP/SD1451	Jazzlore No.7, 90041-1, 90041-2 (CD)	587.004, S588.004,		ATL50523, 30017,	P6013, P4545, SMJ7378, AMCY1003(CD)	
SD1553			940.032	ATL40120	P6108, MT2034	
SD1668	Jazzlore No.24, 90462-1, 90462-2 (CD)			ATL50115	P6128, P7502	
SD2-313		K60052		ATL60052	P5096/97, P4501/02	

JOHN COLTRANE - list of equivalents (cont.):

Impulse/MCA: Orig.:	Reissue:	HMV(E):	Impulse/MCA/ Jasmine(E):	Impulse/ MCA(Eu)	Impulse/ MCA(J):	Other labels:
A(S)6	MCA29007, MCA42231, MCA254638	CLP1548, CSD1431	JAS8	1C.052-90805, 3C.064-90805, (I)IMP423	IMP88090, YS8501, YP8571, MH3012, SH3018, SNY3, SR3071, VIM4609 32XD589(CD)	World Rec.Club(E)ST996, Philips(Eu)P632.060L, HMV(I)QELP8049, HMV(I)CSDQ6264,
A(S)10	MCA29009, MCA254627 MCAD39136 (CD)	CLP1590, CSD1456	IMPL8041, JAS9	(F)IMP10, 254627-2(CD)	IMP88073, YP8521, MH3014, SH3021, SNY10, SR3096, VIM4611, 32XD582(CD)	
A(S)21	MCA29011, MCA254609 MCAD5883 (CD),	CLP1629, CSD1483	IMPL8028, JAS10	3C.064-95770, 254609-2(CD)	IMP88095, YS8502, YP8572, MH3001, SH3001, VIM4644 32XD572(CD)	Philips(Eu)P632.070L
A(S)30	MCA29032, MCA254636 MCAD39103 (CD)	CLP1657, CSD1502	IMPL8045, JAS4	3C.064-95767, (I)IMPL4087, (I)IMPL5019, 254636-2(CD)	IMP88091, YS8503, YP8573, MH3003, SH3003, SR3111, VIM4608, 32XD587(CD), MVCI-23009 (CD)	
A(S)32	MCA29012, MCA5885, MCA254607, MCAD5885 (CD)	CLP1647, CSD1496	JAS37	(F)IMP32, C.062-96321, 254607-2(CD)	IMP88096, YS8504, YP8574, SH3008, VIM4606, 32XD570(CD)	World Rec.Club(E)ST670
A(S)40	MCA29013, MCA5661, MCA254617, MCAD5661 (CD)	CLP1700		(I)IMPL5028	IMP88079, YS8505, YP8575, SH3019, SR3112, VIM4607	
A(S)42	MCA29014, MCA254628 MCAD5887 (CD)	CLP1695, CSD1509	JAS39	3C.064-95769, (F)IMP42, (I)IMP432, 254628-2(CD)	IMP88067, YP8522, SH3020, VIM4612, 32XD583(CD)	

JOHN COLTRANE - list of equivalents (cont.):

Impulse/MCA: Orig.:	Impulse/MCA: Reissue:	HMV(E):	Impulse/MCA/ Jasmine(E):	Impulse/ MCA(Eu)	Impulse/ MCA(J):	Other labels:
A(S)50	MCA29015, MCA254637 MCAD33109 (CD)	CLP1741, CSD1544	JAS11	(F)IMP50, 254637-2(CD)	IMP88078, YP8523, SH3036, VIM4622, 32XD588(CD), MVCI-23013 (CD)	
A(S)66	MCA29016, MCA254608 MCA5889, MCAD5889 (CD)	CLP1799, CSD1567	JAS41	(F)IMP66 254608-2(CD)	IMP88097, YS8506, YP8576, SH3041, VIM4623, 32XD571(CD), MVCI-23014 (CD)	
A(S)77	MCA29017, MCA254557 MCA5660, MCAD5660 (CD)	CLP1869, CSD1605	IMPL8001, (E)MCL1648	(I)IT2001, (I)IMP414, 254557-2(CD)	IMP88060, YP8527, SH3063, SR3006, VIM4610, 32XD595(CD), MVCI-23007 (CD)	
A(S)85	MCA29018, MCA254619 MCAD33110 (CD)	CLP1897, CSD1619		254619-2(CD)	IMP88103, YP8528, VIM4652, 32XD578(CD)	
A(S)95 (take 1)	MCA254745	CLP3543, CSD3543	JAS45	(F)9563, 254745-2(CD)	VIM4666, SH3076, 32XD584(CD)	
A(S)95 (take 2)	MCA29020, MCA254618		JAS44	(I)IMPL5002, (I)IMP424, IMP424(CD), 264618-2(CD)	IMP88119, YP8529, VIM4624, 32XD577(CD)	
AS9106	MCA29021, MCA254645	CLP3617, CSD3617	JAS51	254645-2(CD)	IMP88125, YP8564, SR3005, VIM4625, 32XD596(CD)	
AS9110	MCA29022, MCA254621 MCAD39139 (CD)	CLP3575, CSD3575	M/SIPL515, JAS80	254621-2(CD)	IMP88149, YP8567, SH3084, VIM4667, 32XD581(CD)	
AS9120	MCA29023, MCA254646		M/SIPL502, JAS73	254646-2(CD)	IMP88157, YP8570, SR6071, VIM4626, 32XD597(CD)	
AS9124	MCA29010, MCA254647	CLP3599, CSD3599	JAS16	254647-2(CD)	IMP88110, YP8569, SH3085, VIM4627 32XD598(CD), MVCI-23018 (CD)	

JOHN COLTRANE - list of equivalents (cont.):

Impulse/MCA: Orig.:	Reissue:	HMV(E):	Impulse/MCA/ Jasmine(E):	Impulse/ MCA(Eu)	Impulse/ MCA(J):	Other labels:
AS9140	MCA29024, MCA254640 MCAD39118 (CD)	CLP3617, CSD3617		(I)IMP434, (I)IMPL5006, 254640-2(CD)	IMP88142, YP8566, VIM4668, 32XD592(CD), MCVI-23061 (CD)	Probe(E)SPB1025
AS9148	MCA29025	MIPL/SIPL515			IMP88158, YP8568	WEA(J)WMC5-115(CD)
S9161	MCA29026, MCA254629	SIPL522	254629-2(CD)		IMP88104, YP8561, SR3121, 32DX585	
AS9195	MCA29027, MCA254611			(I)IMP425(CD) 254611-2(CD)	IMP88115, YP8562, SR3118, VIM4661, 32XD575(CD)	
S9200-2	MCA2-4131					
S9202	MCA2-4134			(I)AIMP25042	IMP88069/70, YP8504/05, MCVI-23060(CD)	
S9211	MCA29028 MCA254630			254630-2(CD)	IMP88129, YP8565, VIM4669, 32XD586(CD)	
S9223-2	MCA2-4132					
S9225					YIMP88175, YP8563	WEA(J)WMC5-117(CD)
S9246/2	MCA2-4135, NCA254610			1C.064-96422	VIM4628/29	
S9273	MCA29008, MCA42232, MCA254648		JAS59	3C.064-95813	IMP88195, YP8577, YS8507, 32XD599(CD)	Melodij(Sov)S60-19423
D9277	MCA29029			064-96079	IMJ80013, YP7585, YP8578	WEA(J)WMC5-118(CD)
S9278-2	MCA2-4133					
H9306	MCA2-4136					
9325	MCA2-4137			254639-2(CD)	YB8506/07, VIM4613/14, 55XD590/1(CD)	
9332	MCA29030				YX8506	
9345/2	MCA2-4138 MCA254641			254641-2(CD)	YB8511/12, 55XD593/94(CD)	
9346/2	MCA2-4139					
9360	MCA29031, MCA254649			254649-2(CD)	YX8511, 32XD600(CD)	
9361/2	MCA2-4140, MCA254650			0082.711	VIM4615/16, 55XD601/2(CD)	

MICHAEL "ROCKY COLE" COLUCCIO

"Rocky Cole"(p,vcl) acc. by AL COHN'S ORCHESTRA:
Incl. Al Cohn(ts,arr,cond),Zoot Sims,Frank Socolow(ts),Steve Perlow(bars).

	NYC.May 1960
Will You Still Be Mine	Roulette (S)R25113
The Glory Of Love	-
I Wish I Were In Love Again	-
I Can't Get Started	-
Squeeze Me	-
Little Girl	-
C'est La Vie	-
Let's Do It	-
P.S. I Love You	-
I Remember You	-
The Late Late Show	-
Caravan	-

COLUMBIA ALL STARS (French)

Guy Lafitte(ts),Géo Daly(vbs),Jean-Claude Pelletier(p),Jean-Pierre Sasson(g),Paul Rovère
(b),Christian Garros(dr).

	Paris.June 18,1956
Dans Un Vieux Livre	Columbia(F)ESDF1125
Flying Back	-
What A Funny Moon	-
Partnership Boys	-

CHRIS COLUMBUS

KRAZY KRIS AND THE SWINGIN GENTLEMEN:
Johnny Grimes(tp),Jimmy Tyler(ts),John Wiegand(p),Floyd Smith(g),Chris Columbus(dr).

		NYC.October 13,1956
K8814	Floyd's Guitar Blues	King 4991
K8815	I Let A Song Go Out Of My Heart	unissued
K8816	Wishy Washy	King 4991
K8817	Jack's Idea	unissued

Gil Askey(tp),Jimmy Tyler(ts),Johnny "Hammond" Smith(g),Floyd Smith(g),Chris Columbus(dr

		Cincinnatti.January 4,1957
K9918	Oh Yeah,I(band-vcl)	King 5012
K9919	Oh Yeah,II(band-vcl)	-

CHRIS COLOMBO QUINTET:
Incl. Johnny "Hammond" Smith(org),Chris Columbus(dr).

	NYC. 1963
Summertime	Strand 15056,SL(S)1044
Minerology	-
Happy House	-
Teach Me Tonight	-
Things Ain't What They Used To Be	-
All The Way	-
What A Difference A Day Makes	-
I Let A Song Go Out Of My Heart	-
Mr. Wonderful	-
Sha-Gong	-
My Melencholy Baby	-
Bernie's Tune	-

KEN COLYER (British)

See also GRAEME BELL,KEITH CHRISTIE,CRANE RIVER JAZZ BAND,GOLDEN RIVER CITY JAZZ BAND,
GEORGE LEWIS,MARYLAND JAZZBAND.

COLYER - DAVIES TRIO:
Ken Colyer(cnt,g),John R.T. Davies(g,org),Bill Colyer(wirebrushes).
                                        Poss. Burnham,England. 1950
        Muddy Old River   "77"(E)LEU12/7

Note:The above title issued as by CRANE RIVER JAZZ BAND.

Same.   Burnham,England.November 1951
        Sister Kate   Ristic(E)unissued
        Mama Don't Allow   -
        Midnight Special   -
        Tell Me Your Dreams   -
        How Long Blues   -
        Bucket's Got A Hole   -
        Faraway Blues   -
        Tishomingo Blues   -
        Our Lil(1)   -
        Ja Da   "77"(E)LEU12/7

1.Ken Colyer(vcl,g) only.

Note:"Ja Da" issued as by CRANE RIVER JAZZ BAND.

Ken Colyer(cnt),Jack Delaney(tb),Raymond Burke(cl),Stanley Mendelsohn(p),Lawrence Marrero
(bj),Alcide "Slow Drag" Pavageau(b),Abbie Brunies(dr).
                                        New Orleans.December 8,1952
        Panama   Nola LP15
        Blues   -
        High Society   -
        Indiana   -
        The World Is
            Waiting For The Sunrise   -

Ken Colyer(cnt),Raymond Burke(cl),Billy Huntington(bj),Chas. Merriweather(dr).
                                        New Orleans.February 13,1953
        Make Me A Pallet On The Floor   unissued
        Willie The Weeper
        Blues
        Tishomingo Blues

KEN COLYER AND HIS NEW ORLEANS BAND:
Ken Colyer(cnt,vcl),Harrison Brazlee(tb),Emile Barnes(cl),Billy Huntington(bj),Albert
Glenny(b),Albert Jiles(dr).   New Orleans.February 23,1953
        New Orleans Hop Scop Blues   Vogue(E)unissued
        Climax Rag   -
        Gravier Steet Blues   Vogue(E)V2344,EPV1202,LDE161,Dawn Club DC12025
        Black Cat On The Fence   Vogue(E)LDE161,Dawn Club DC12025
        That's A Plenty   Vogue(E)EPV1202,LDE161,Dawn Club DC12025
        How Long Blues(kc)   Vogue(E)LDE161,Dawn Club DC12025

George Fortier(b) replaces Glenny.   New Orleans.February 24,1953
        Winter Wonderland   Vogue(E)EPV1202,LDE161
        New Orleans Hop Scop Blues   -
        Frankie And Johnny   Vogue(E)EPV1202,   -
        Ciriribin   Vogue(E)V2345,   -
        How Long Blues No. 2(kc)   - ,EPV1102
(session cont. next page).

(session cont. from previous page):
      Buddy Bolden's Blues(kc)   Vogue(E)V2344,EPV1102
      Mile's Blues   -
      Panama Rag   -

All titles also on Dawn Club DC12025.
Note:LDE161 was originally issued as unnumbered "Special Edition" LP.

KEN COLYER'S JAZZMEN:
Ken Colyer(cnt,vcl),Chris Barber(tb),Monty Sunshine(cl),Lonnie Donegan(bj),Jim Bray(b),Ro
Bowden(dr).   Copenhagen.April 11,1953
KC24   Tiger Rag   Storyville(D)SEP301,SLP144,(G)DALP2/1941,108.602,
                                   Tempo(E)EXA53,LAP11

Same.   Copenhagen.April 12,1953
KC6   I Can't Escape From You   Storyville(D)SEP392,SLP144,(G)DALP2/1941,108.602
KC7   The Sheik Of Araby   rejected
KC8   Breeze(no tb,cl)   Storyville SLP144,(G)DALP2/1947,108.602

Note:See MONTY SUNSHINE for additional titles (without Colyer) from this session.

Same;Bray plays (b,sousaphone).   Copenhagen.April 19,1953
KC13 Just A Closer Walk With Thee Storyville(D)A45054,SEP301,(G)DALP2/1947,Tempo(E)
                                 A117,EXA53,LAP11
KC14 Bucket's Got A Hole In It(1)(kc) Storyville(D)KB209,SEP309,SEP392,(G)DALP2/1947,
                                 Tempo(E)A126,EXA31,LAP11
KC15 We Sure Do Need Him Now   Storyville(D)SEP392
KC16 Shine   Storyville(D)KB201,SEP305,(G)DALP2/1947,Tempo(E)
                                 (E)EXA26,LAP11
KC17 If I Ever Cease To Love   Storyville(D)KB206,A45001,SEP309,SEP412,Tempo(E)
                                 (E)A120,EXA26,LAP11
KC18 Isle Of Capri   Storyville(D)KB200,A45001,SEP305,Tempo(E)A120,
                                 EXA26,LAP11
KC19 Wabash Blues   Storyville(D)KB209,SEP309,Tempo(E)A126,LAP11
KC20 Saturday Night Function   Storyville(G)DALP2/1947
KC21 The Sheik Of Araby   Storyville(D)SEP301,Tempo(E)A117,EXA53,LAP11
KC22 Blue Bells Goodbye   Storyville(D)A45054,SEP412,(G)DALP2/1947

-1.Vocal edited out on some issues.

All titles - except master KC13 - also on Storyville(G)DALP2/1941.
All titles - except master KC21 - also on Storyville SLP144,(G)108.602.
Note:See CHRIS BARBER for one additional title from this session.
    "The Sheik Of Araby" (master KC21) is not on SLP144 and DALP2/1947 although
    the covernotes and the labels list this title.

Same.   London.September 2,1953
DR18118 Isle Of Capri   Decca(E)F10241,LF1152,(G)DX2140,DS3202/1-2,(Au)
                                Y6607
DR18119 Harlem Rag   Decca(E)LF1152,(G)DS3202/1-2
DR18120 Too Busy   Decca(E)F10332,LF1152,(G)DX2140,DS3271/1-2,(Au)
                                Y6621
DR18121 Goin' Home(kc)   Decca(E)F10241,LF1152,(G)DX2140,DS3202/1-2,(Au)
                                Y6607,Ace Of Clubs(E)ACL1154
DR10822 La Harpe Street Blues   Decca(E)F10332,LF1152,(G)DS3202(1-2,(Au)Y6621
DR10823 Cataract Rag   Decca(E)F10504,   - ,(G)D18133,F46133,DS3271/1-
DR10824 Stockyard Strut   Decca(E)LF1152,(G)DX2140,DS3202/1-2
DR10825 Early Hours   Decca(E)F10504,LF1152,LK4139,(G)D18133,F46133,
                                DS3202/1-2

(session cont. next page).

session cont. from previous page):
11 titles also on London(Am)LB904,LL1340,Lake(E)LA5014,Decca(G)6.25013,Limelight(G)
20.879-1,820.879-2 (CD).
11 titles - except "Too Busy" - also on Decca(G)BLK16438.
11 titles on DS3202/1-2 also on Decca(G)6.28130 .
11 titels on DS3271/1-2 also on Decca(G)6.28146.

EN COLYER'S JAZZMEN:
en Colyer(tp,vcl),Ed O'Donnell(tb),Bernard "Acker" Bilk(cl),Johnny Bastable(bj),Mickey
shman(b),Eric Skinner(dr).   London.June 25,1954
R19275 Sing On   London(Am)LB1089
R19276 Lord,Lord,Lord,You
        Sure Been Good To Me(kc)   -
R19277 Faraway Blues   -
R19278 Shim-Me-Sha-Wabble   -
R19279 Saturday Night Function   -
R19280 Moose March   -

EN COLYER'S JAZZMEN:
en Colyer(tp,vcl),Ed O'Donnell(tb),Bernard "Acker" Bilk(cl),William "Diz" Disley(bj),Dick
mith(b),Stan Greig(dr).   London.September 10,1954
19539 Sing On   Decca(E)LF1196,(G)DS3202/1-2,6.28130
19540 Lord,Lord,Lord,You
        Sure Been Good To Me(kc)   -   -   - ,BLK16438
19541 Faraway Blues   - ,(G)BLK16438,London(Am)LL1340
19542 Moose March   - ,London(Am)LL1340
19543 Saturday Night Function   -
19544 Shim-Me-Sha-Wabble   -

    1 titles also on Decca(G)6.25013,Lake(E)LA5014,Limelight(G)820.879-1,820.879-2 (CD).

me.   Live.Royal Festival Hall,London.October 30,1954
20027 Postman's Lament(kc)   Decca(E)LK4088
20028 Tuxedo Rag   - ,(G)DS3271/1-2,6.28146

th titles also on Decca(G)BLK4088,London(Am)LL1184,(J)LLB20008,Lake(E)LA5004.

n Colyer(tp,vcl),Mac Duncan(tb,vcl),Ian Wheeler(cl),Johnny Bastable(bj),Dick Smith(b),
an Greig(dr).   London.April 19,1955
20558 The Sheik Of Araby(md)   Decca(E)DFE6268,(G)DS3202/1-2,BLK16438,London(Am)
                                       BEP6277,Lake(E)LACD21(CD)
20559 Cradle Song   Decca(E)DFE6299,(G)DS3271/1-2,London(Am)BEP6278,
                                       Lake(E)LACD21(CD)
20560 The Entertainer   Decca(E)F10519,(Du)M33894,Lake(E)LA5001
20561 Hiawatha   Decca(E)DFE6268,(G)DS3202/1-2,London(Am)BEP6277,
                                       Lake(E)LACD21(CD)
20562 If I Ever Cease To Love You   Decca(E(F10519,(Du)M33894,(G)DS3271/1-2,Lake(E)
                                       LA5001
20563 It Looks Like A Big Time
        Tonight   Decca(E)F10565,DFE6299,(G)DS3271/1-2,Telefunken(G)
                                       S14.784,6.21367,Lake(E)LACD21(CD)
20564 Corrine,Corinna(kc)   Decca(E)DFE6299,(G)DS3202/1-2,London(Am)BEP6278,
                                       Telefunken(G)S14.784,6.21367,Lake(E)LACD21
                                       (CD)
20565 Red Wing   Decca(E)F10565,DFE6299,(G)DS3271/1-2,Lake(E)LACD21
                                       (CD)
20566 Dallas Blues(kc)   Decca(E)DFE6268,(G)DS3202/1-2,BLK16438,London(Am)
                                       BEP6277,Lake(E)LACD21(CD)

    titles on DS3202/1-2 also on Decca(G)6.28130.
    titles on DS3271/1-2 also on Decca(G)6.28146.

KEN COLYER'S JAZZMEN:
Ken Colyer(tp),Mac Duncan(tb),Ian Wheeler(cl),Johnny Bastable(bj),Dick Smith(b),Colin Bow
den(dr).   London.March 8,1956
DR21769 Dippermouth Blues   Decca(E)F10755,LK4205,Ace Of Clubs(E)ACL1105
DR21770 The Girls Go Crazy   -
VOG688 Maryland My Maryland   Tempo(E)A136
VOG689 The World Is
          Waiting For The Sunrise   -

All titles also on Lake(E)LA5001.
Masters DR21769-70 also on Decca(G)D18403,F46403,DS3271/1-2,6.28146.
Masters VOG688-89 also on Decca(G)DS3202/1-2,6.28130,Telefunken(G)A11883.

Ron Ward(b) replaces Smith.
                 Live."Railway Hotel",Hampstead,Endland.October 4/November 16,195
DR22671 Uptown Bumps
          (Bucket's Got A Hole In It) Decca(E)LK4178
DR22672 Blame It On The Blues   - ,(G)DS3202/1-2,6.28130
DR22674 Chrysanthemum Rag   -   -   -   -
DR22675 Snag It(kc)   -   -   -
DR22676 Thriller Rag   - ,(G)DS3271/1-2,6.28146
DR22677 Black Cat On The Fence   -
DR22678 The Rugged Old Cross   -
DR22679 Walking With The King(kc)   - ,(G)DS3202/1-2,6.28130
DR22680 Home Sweet Home/Auf
          Wiederseh'n Sweetheart   -

All titles also on London(Am)LL1618,Lake(E)LA5006.
Note:The above session was recorded "live" before a selected audience.

KEN COLYER'S JAZZMEN WITH GEORGE LEWIS:
Ken Colyer(tp),Mac Duncan(tb),George Lewis -1,Ian Wheeler -2(cl),Johnny Bastable(bj),Ron
Ward(b),Colin Bowden(dr).   Live."Clarendon Hotel",Manchester,England.April 8,19
          Over The Waves(1)   K.C.(E)KC1
          Walking With The King(1)(kc)   -
          Corrine,Corrina(1,2)   -
          Ice Cream(1,2)(kc)   -

Same.   Live.Free Trade Hall,Manchester,England.April 17,19.
          Bucket's Got A Hole In It(2)   Blank label LP1
          It Looks Like A
            Big Time Tonight(2)   -
          Creole Song(2)   -
          Gotta See Mama Every Night(2)   -
          Thriller Rag(2)   -
          Just A Little
            While To Stay Here(2)   -
          Basin Street Blues(1,2)
          Weary Blues(1)   Blank label LP2
          Shine(1)(kc)   -
          Tin Roof Blues(1)   -,NoLa(E)LP15
          Bugle Boy March(1)   -   -
          Burgundy Street Blues(4)   -
          St. Philip Street Breakdown(4)   -,NoLa(E)LP15
          Nobody Knows The Way I Feel This
            Morning/Old Rugged Cross(4)   -   -
          Over The Waves(1)(kc)   -   -
(session cont. next page).

session cont. from previous page):
      Ice Cream(1)(kc)   Blank label LP3
      Corrine,Corrina(1,2)(kc)   -,NoLa(E)LP15
      Mama Don't Allow/When The
        Saints Go Marching In(1,2)(kc)   -
      Home Sweet Home/Auf Wiedersehn   -

4.Lewis(cl),bj,b,dr only.

EN COLYER'S JAZZMEN:
nit Lewis;Wheeler(cl) is playing on all titles.

                             Live."Eel Pie Island Hotel",Twickenham,England.May 30,1957
      Running Wild   K.C.(E)KC1
      The Happy Wanderer   -
      Gatemouth   -
      Working Man Blues   -
      One Sweet Letter From You   -
      Dusty Rag   -
      Sensation   -
      Heebie Jeebies   K.C.(E)KC2
      Tin Roof Blues   -
      Red Wing   -
      Aunt Hagar's Blues   -
      Maryland,My Maryland   -
      Old Miss Rag   unissued
      Bluebells Goodbye   -
      Bugle Boy March   -
      Yellow Dog Blues   -
      Don't Go Away Nobody   -
      Over The Rainbow   -
      Eh La Bas(incompl.)   -
      Walking With The King   -
      Dippermouth Blues   -
      Auf Wiedersehn   -

N COLYER'S OMEGA BRASS BAND:
n Colyer,Bob Wallis(tp),Sonny Morris(cnt),Mac Duncan,Mick Clift(tb),Ian Wheeler(cl),Dave
ir(as),Derek Easton(ts),Maurice Benn (as "Mo")(tu),Colin Bowden(snare-dr),Neal Millett
ass-dr).   London.September 8,1957
23778 Over In Gloryland   Decca(E)DFE6435,LF1301,(G)DS3202/1-2,6.28130
23779 Bugle Boy March   -   -
23780 Jambalaya   -   - ,(G)DS3202/1-2,6.28130
23781 Just A Closer Walk With Thee -   -   -   -
23782 Isle Of Capri   Decca(E)LF1301
23783 Panama Rag   -
23784 Tiger Rag   -
23785 Gettysburg March   - ,(G)DS3202/1-2,6.28130

l titles also on Lake(E)LACD21 (CD).

N COLYER'S JAZZMEN:
n Colyer(tp,vcl),Mac Duncan(tb,vcl),Ian Wheeler(cl),Ray Foxley(p),Johnny Bastable(bj),
n Ward(b),Colin Bowden(dr).   London.January 16,1958
24112 Kinklets   Decca(E)DFE6466
24113 Fig Leaf Rag
24114 Heliotrope Bouquet   -
24115 Sensation   -

l titles also on Decca(G)DS3271/1-2,6.28146,Lake(E)LA5001.

Same.   Live."Curio-Haus",Hamburg,Germany.March 3,195▩
```
        Gatemouth                     Decca(G)BLK16092
CP2057 Bourbon Street Parade               -    ,(E)LF1319
CP2058 Dauphin Steet Blues                 -       -
CP2059 Bill Bailey(md)                     -       -
CP2063 Bye And Bye                         -       -
        When The Saints Go Marching In(kc) -       -    ,Ace Of Clubs(E)ACL1154
```

All titles also on Lake(E)LA5004.
Note:Masters CP2060-62 (with KEN COLYER'S SKIFFLE GROUP) are not included.

Same.   Live."Railway Hotel",Hampstead,England.June 19,185▩
```
 DR24948 Pretty Baby                 Lake(E)LA5010
ZDR24950 Bluebells Goodbye                -
 DR24951 Over The Rainbow                 -
ZDR24952 Under The Bamboo Tree
 DR24954 Oh,You Beautiful Doll       Decca(I)MOR12,Lake(E)LA5010
ZDR24956 Swanee River                Lake(E)LA5010
 DR24957 Lonesome Road                    -
 DR24958 All Of Me(md)                    -
ZDR24963 Dinah(kc)                        -
```

Same.   London.August 5,1958
```
DR24963 Oh,You Beautiful Doll       Decca(E)LK4294
DR24968 Over The Rainbow                 -
DR24969 When You Wore A Tulip            unissued
DR24970 Under The Bamboo Tree       Decca(E)LK4294,(G)DS3274/1-2,6.28148
DR24971 Winter Wonderland                unissued
DR24972 Red Sails In The Sunset          -
DR24973 Bluebells Goodbye           Decca(E)LK4294,(G)DS3274/1-2,6.28148
DR24974 Swanee River                     -       -    ,(I)MOR12
DR24975 All Of Me(md)                    -    ,(G)DS3271/1-2,6.28146,    -
DR24976 The Curse Of An Aching Heart(kc) -    ,(G)DS3274/1-2,6.28148,Lake(E)LA50▩
DR24977 Dinah(kc)                        -    ,(G)DS3271/1-2,6.28146,(I)MOR12
DR24978 Pretty Baby                      -
```

All titles on LK4294 also on Decca(G)BLK1657.
Note:LK4294 - and BLK1657 - issued as a live recording (applause was dubbed on later).

KEN COLYER'S JAZZMEN WITH GEORGE LEWIS:
Same.   Live.Düsseldorf,Germany.March 15,1959
```
        Swanee River                K.C.(E)KC3
        In The Evening
            When The Sun Goes Down   -
        Willie The Weeper(1)         -
        Red Wing(1)                  -
        St. Philip Street Breakdown(1,2) -
        Bourbon Street Parade(1)     -
        Cheek To Cheek               -
        If I Ever Cease To Love      -
```

-1.George Lewis(cl) replaces Wheeler.
-2.George Lewis(cl),p,bj,b,dr only,

KEN COLYER'S JAZZMEN:
Same.   London.May 8,1959
```
DR25940 Gravier Street Blues        Decca(E)DFE6645
DR25941 Canal Street Blues               -
DR25942 Beale Street Blues               -
DR25943 Perdido Street Blues             -
```

All titles also on Decca(E)STO143,Lake(E)LA5001.

KEN COLYER AND HIS JAZZMEN:
Same.   London.September 22,1959
    Papa Dip   Columbia(E)SEG8104,33SX1220,Metronome(G)HLP10012,
                                 200127,Bertelsmann(G)36860,Philips(Eu)
                                 830.788-2(CD)
    Papa Dip(alt.take)   Philips(Eu)830.782-2(CD)
    Dusty Rag   Columbia(E)SEG8038,33SX1220,Encore(E)ENC158,
                                 Philips(Eu)830.782-2(CD)

    Heebie Jeebies   Columbia(E)SEG8104,33SX1220,Philips(Eu)830.782-2
                                 (CD)
    Somebody Stole My Gal   Columbia(E)33SX1220,Encore(E)ENC158,Philips(Eu)
                                 830.788-2(CD)
    Somebody Stole My Gal(alt.take) Philips(Eu)830.782-2(CD)

Same.   London.September 23,1959
    Hilarity Rag   Columbia(E)SEG8104,33SX1220
    Salutation March   Columbia(E)SEG8038,33SX1220,Encore(E)ENC158,Aves
                                 (G)89002-2,156511
    Nobody Knows The
       Trouble I've Seen(kc) Columbia(E)33SX1220,Encore(E)ENC158
    Working Man's Blues   -   -

All titles also on Philips(Eu)830.782-2 (CD).

Same.   London.September 29,1959
    Sweet Fields   Columbia(E)SEG8038,33SX1220,Encore(E)ENC158,
                                 Bertelsmann(G)36860,Philips(Eu)830.782-2(CD)
    Riverside Blues   Columbia(E)SEG8038,33SX1220,Encore(E)ENC158,
                                 Metronome(G)HLP10012,Philips(Eu)830.782-2(CD)
    Cheek To Cheek   Columbia(E)33SX1220,Encore(E)ENC158,Philips(Eu)
                                 830.787-2(CD)
    Cheek To Cheek(alt.take) Philips(Eu)830.782-2(CD)
    At A Georgia Camp Meeting Columbia(E)SEG8104,33SX1220,Philips(Eu)830.782-2
                                 (CD)

All titles on 33SX1220 also on Metronome(Sd/G)MLP15037.

KEN COLYER'S JAZZMEN:
Ken Colyer(tp,vcl),Graham Stewart(tb),Sammy Rimington(cl),Ray Foxley(p),Johnny Bastable
(bj),Ron Ward(b),Colin Bowden(dr).   London.August 22,1960
    South   Columbia(E)SEG8145,33SX1297,Philips(Eu)818.651-2
                                 (CD)
    Ballin' The Jack   Columbia(E)SEG8145,33SX1297,Metronome(G)HLP10012,
                                 200127,Verve(Eu)831.375-2(CD)
    When I Grow To Old To Dream(kc) Columbia(E)33SX1297,Polydor(G)834.745-1,834.745-2
                                 (CD)
    When I Leave The World Behind Columbia(E)33SX1297

Same.   London August 23,1960
    Get Out Of Here And Go On Home Columbia(E)SEG8145,33SX1297,Aves(G)89002-2,
                                 Philips(Eu)818.651-2(CD),Polydor(G)834.745-1,
                                 834.745-2(CD)
    Mabel's Dream   Columbia(E)SEG8145,33SX1297,Philips(Eu)818.651-2
                                 (CD)
    Blanche Touquatoux   Columbia(E)33SX1297,Polydor(G)834.745-1
    Savoy Blues   -
    Gonna Get Along Without Ya Now   - ,Polydor(G)834.745-1

```
Same.                                 London.August 25,1960
        Sweet Sue Just You            Columbia(E)33SX1297,HLP10012,200127,Philips(Eu)
                                      818.651-2(CD),Polydor(G)834.745-1,834.745-2
                                      (CD)
        Sweet Lorraine(kc)            Columbia(E)33SX1297
        There'll Come Another Day              - ,Polydor(G)834.745-1
```

All titles on 33SX1297 also on Columbia(E)SCX3360,Metronome(Sd/G)MLP15067,Philips(Eu)
6459.223.

```
Omit Foxley.                          London.November 22,1960
        The Happy Wanderer            Columbia(E)DB4676
        Maryland My Maryland                   -
```

Both titles also on Encore(E)ENC158,Metronome(G)B1449,Philips(Eu)830.782-2.

```
Same.                                 London.December 7/8,1960,January 4,1961
        St. Louis Blues               Columbia(E)33SX1363
        Aunt Hagar's Blues                     - ,(J)SL3091
        The Breeze(kc)                         -
        Tishomingo Blues                       -
        Sobbin' Blues                          - ,Aves(G)89002-2,156511
        See See Rider(kc)                      -
        Chimes Blues                           - ,Philips(Eu)830.787-2(CD)
        Sentimental Journey(kc)                -
        When The Sun Goes Down(kc)             -
        Take It Easy(kc)                       -
```

All titles also on Columbia(E)SCX3406,Metronome(G)MLP15077.

```
Ken Colyer(tp,vcl),Geoff Cole(tb),Sammy Rimington(cl),Johnny Bastable(bj),Ron Ward(b),
Pete Ridge(dr).                       London.November 21,1961
        Too Busy                      Columbia(E)DB4783,SEG8180,Aves(G)89002-2,OneUp(E)
                                      OU2074,Metronome(G)B1532
        Maple Leaf Rag                Columbia(E)SEG8180
        Cielito Lindo(kc)                      -
        Postman's Lament(kc)          Columbia(E)DB4783,SEG8180,Metronome(G)B1532
        Darkness On The Delta         Philips(Eu)830.782-2(CD)
```

All titles also on Philips(Eu)830.782-2 (CD).

```
KEN COLYER'S JAZZ BAND:
Same.                                 London. 1962
        Teasing Rag                   Society(E)SOC914
        After You've Gone                      -
        Highway Blues(kc)                      -
        Dardanella                             -
        I Can't Escape From You                -
        You Always Hurt The One You Love       -
        Creole Bo-Bo                           -
        Honeysuckle Rose                       - ,Presto(E)PRE657,ARC51,Boulevard
                                      (E)4131
        Barefoot Boy(kc)              Society(E)SOC914
```

```
Same.                                 Nottingham,England.November 24,1962
        Mahogany Hall Stomp           Society(E)SOC914
        The Old Spinning Wheel(no tp) Lake(E)LACD19(CD)
```

Same.   Live.Nottingham,England.March 2,1963
       When I Leave The World Behind   Lake(E)LACD19(CD)
       Mabel's Dream   -
       Dr. Jazz(kc)   -
       Wabash Blues   -
       Down Home Rag   -
       Darkness Of The Delta   -
       Old Black Joe   -
       Careless Love(kc)   -
       After You've Gone   -
       Give Me Your Telephone Number   -
       Who's Sorry Now(incompl.)   -
       Working Man Blues   unissued
       Too Busy   -
       I Can't Escape From You   -
       Till We Meet Again/Auf Wiedersehn   -

KEN COLYER'S JAZZMEN:
Ken Colyer(tp,vcl),Geoff Cole(tb),Sammy Rimington(cl),Pat Hawes(p),Johnny Bastable(bj),
Ron Ward(b),Pete Ridge(dr).   Live.Willesden,London.February 27,1964
       Down Home Rag   "77"(E)LEU12/10
       Someday Sweetheart   -
       As Long As I Live   -
       Chilly Winds(kc)   -
       King Porter Stomp   -
       Wolverine Blues   -
       The Entertainer   -
       Swipsey Cakewalk   -
       Michigan Water Blues(kc)   -
       Give Me Your Telephone Number   -

Ken Colyer(tp,vcl),Geoff Cole(tb),Sammy Rimington(cl),Richard Simmons(p),Johnny Bastable
(bj),Bill Cole(b),Bryan Hetherington(dr).   London.c. April 1965
       Out Of Nowhere   K.C.(E)GN0101
       The Lady Is A Tramp   -
       Lily Of The Valley   -
       Melancholy Blues(kc)   -
       Darktown Strutters' Ball   -
       Indiana   -
       Eccentric Rag   -
       There's Yes Yes In Your Eyes   -
       Ole Miss Rag   -
       You're Driving Me Crazy   unissued
       You've Got To
          See Mama Every Night   -
       We Shall Walk Through
          The Streets Of The City   -
       Yearning   -
       I Said I Wasn't
          Going To Tell Nobody   -
       Darkness On The Delta   -

Ken Colyer(tp,vcl),Geoff Cole(tb),Tony Pyke(cl),Johnny Bastable(bj),Bill Cole(b),Bryan
Hetherington(dr).   Live.Hamburg University,Germany.October 13,1966
       Over In Gloryland(kc)   Polydor(G)623.231
       You've Got To See
          Mama Every Night   -
       Lady Be Good   -
       I Said I Wasn't Goin'
          To Tell Nobody(kc)   -
(session cont. next page).

(session cont. from previous page):
```
        Down Home Rag                 Polydor(G)623.231
        Hindustan                          -
        Struttin' With Some Barbecue       -
```

All titles also on 2001Metronome(G)200.194,Storyville(G)DALP2/1941.
Note:Additional titles from this concert (with KEN COLYER'S SKIFFLE GROUP) are not inclu-
     ded.

Malcolm Murphy(dr) replaces Hetherington.   Live.Hamburg University,Germany.October 13,1967
```
        Creole Bobo                   WAM(G)JEP0468
        My Life Will Be Sweeter Someday    -
        In A Sweet Bye And Bye             -
```

All titles also on CSA(D)CEP201.

Add Ray Smith(p).   Live.Hamburg University,Germany.November 5,1968
```
        We Shall Walk Through
            The Streets Of The City   WAM(G)JL8014
        Salutation March                   -
        Magnetic Rag(p-solo)               -
        Winin' Boy Blues(kc)               -
        Swanee River                       -
        Martha                             -
        Georgia Bobo                       -
        Ory's Creole Trombone              -
```

All titles also on WAM(G)MLP15399,WAM No.3,2001Metronome(G)201.064.
Note:Additional titles from this concert (with KEN COLYER'S SKIFFLE GROUP) are not inclu-
     ded.

Omit Smith.   Live."Dancing Slipper Ballroom",Nottingham,England.February 1,1969
```
        Yellow Dog Blues(kc)          VJM(E)unissued
        Sweet Fields                  VJM(E)LC35
        That Teasin' Rag                   -
        The Entertainer                    unissued
        Harlem Rag                    VJM(E)LC35
        Hiawatha Rag                       unissued
        Birth Of The Blues            VJM(E)LC35
        Drop Me Off At Harlem              -
        Running Wild                       unissued
        The Barefoot Boy(kc)          VJM(E)LC35
        Salutation March                   -
        Shoe Shine Boy                     -
        The Peanut Vendor                  -
        Isle Of Capri                      unissued
        Chimes Blues                       -
        High Society                  VJM(E)LC35
        Hindustan                          unissued
        Home Sweet Home/Auf Wiedersehen VJM(E)LC35
        Get Out Of Here And Go Home        -
```

Same.   Hampton Court,England.February 5,1969
```
        Royal Garden Blues            Joy(E)JOYS140
        High Society                       -
        Drop Me Off In Harlem              -
        Bougalousa Strut                   -
        One For My Baby
            (And One For The Road)(kc)     -
```
(session cont. next page).

session cont. from previous page):
```
    Stardust                          Joy(E)JOYS140
    Tiger Rag                              -
    Black And Blue                     unissued
    Carolina Moon                          -
    Poor Butterfly                         -
    Make Me A Pallet On The Floor          -
```

11 titles on JOYS140 also on Joy(E)JOYCD1 (CD),(G)800.976.

en Colyer(tp,vcl),Geoff Cole(tb),Tony Pyke(cl),Johnny Bastable(bj),Ken Ames(b),Malcolm
urphy(dr).   Hampton Court,England.February 5,1970
```
    Till Then                         Joy(E)JOYS164
    One Sweet Letter From You(kc)          -
    Arkansas Blues(kc)                     -
    Poor Butterfly                         -
    Bugle Boy March                        -
    If You're A Viper(kc)                  -
    Runnin' Wild                           -
    My Gal Sal(kc)                         -
    Black And Blue(kc)                     -
    Swipesy Cake Walk                      -
```

11 titles also on Joy JOYCD3 (CD),(G)800.974.

ame.   Hampton Court,England.May 29,1970
```
    Milneburg Joys                    Joy(E)JOYS170
    Lowland Blues(kc)                      -
    Trombonium                             -
    Short Dress Gal                        -
    Blue Skies                             -
    Glory Of Love                          -
    Hindustan                              -
    Hiawatha Rag                           -
```

11 titles also on Joy(E)JOYCD4 (CD).

ame.   Hampton Court,England.August 20/27,1970
```
    Cataract Rag                      Joy(E)JOYS194
    Grace And Beauty                       -
    Minstrel Man                           -
    Chrysanthemum Rag                      -
    Tuxedo Rag                             -
    Joplin' Sensation                      -
    Harlem Rag                             -
    Heliotrope Bouquet                     -
    Fig Leaf Rag                           -
    Kinklets                               -
    Thriller Rag                           -
    We Shall Walk Through
        The Streets Of The City       Joy(E)JOYS235
    Darkness On The Delta                  -
    It's Nobody's Fault But Mine(kc)       -
    My Life Will Be Sweeter Someday        -
    Were You There When
        They Satisfied My Soul(kc)         -
    Sometimes My Burden
        Is So Hard To Bear(kc)             -
    Old Rugged Cross                       -
    Ghost Soldier(kc)                 Joy(E)JOYS236
```
session cont. next page).

(session cont. from previous page):
```
        Precious Lord(kc)              Joy(E)JOYS236
        In The Sweet Bye And Bye          -
        Ain't You Glad(kc)                -
        Sing On                           -
        Just A Closer Walk With Thee(kc)  -
        Lead Me Saviour                   -
```

All titles on JOYS194 also on Joy(E))JOYCD2 (CD).
All titles on JOYS235 also on Joy(E))JOYCD5 (CD).
All titles on JOYS236 also on Joy(E))JOYCD6 (CD).
Note:JOYS194 and JOYCD2 (CD) also incl. two piano solos ("Pineapple Rag" and "Ragtime
     Oriole") rec. by Ray Smith c. December 1970.

KEN COLYER AND HIS HANDPICKED JAZZMEN:
Ken Colyer(cnt,vcl),Mike Sherbourne(tb),Jack Gilbert(cl,as),Jim McIntosh(bj),Ray Holland
(b),Tony Scriven(dr).   Morden,Surrey,England.January 25,1972
```
        Some Of These Days            Ken Colyer Trust(E)KCT2R
        Gatemouth                         -
        Over In Gloryland(kc)             -
        Blame It On The Blues             -
        Lord,Lord,Lord,You've
           Sure Been Good To Me(kc)       -
        Michigan Water Blues(kc)          -
        Bugle Boy March                   -
        Panama Rag                        -
        Pretty Baby                   Ken Colyer Trust(E)KCTCD3(CD)
        Sing On                           -
        Snag It(kc)                       -
        Wabash Blues                      -
        Louisian-I-Ya(kc)                 -
        Tishomingio Blues(kc)             -
        Black Cat On The Fence            -
        High Society                      -
        Winter Wonderland             unissued
        Tiger Rag(incompl.)               -
```

KEN COLYER AND WHITE EAGLE NEW ORLEANS BAND:
Ken Colyer(tp,vcl),Harald Blöcher(tb),Peter Müller(cl),Klaus P. Czikowski(p),Klaus D.
Sonntag(bj),Bert Greve(b),Gerhard Tenzer(dr).
                                       Schellerten,Germany.May 5/6 or 6/7,1972
```
        Isle Of Capri                 WAM(G)MLP15434
        Dippermouth Blues                 -
        Winter Wonderland(kc)             - ,2001Metronome(G)DALP2/1960
        Midnight Hour Blues(kc)           -                              -
        Mahogany Hall Stomp               -
        Sportin' Life Blues(kc)           -
        Walking With The King(vcl)        - ,2001Metronome(G)DALP2/1960
```

All titles also on WAM(G)WAM/O No.9.

KEN COLYER AND THE PHOENIX JAZZ BAND:
Ken Colyer(tp),Barry Weston(tb),Peter Curtis(cl),Colin Martin(p),Bill Stotesbury(bj),Dave
Grey(b),Pete Lay(dr).   Live."The Mitre",Greenwich,England.July 26,1973
```
        Beale Street Blues            Medway(E)MR/MD001
        Margie                            -
```

KEN COLYER WITH CHRIS BLOUNT'S NEW ORLEANS JAZZ BAND:
Ken Colyer(tp,vcl),Dave Vickers(tb),Chris Blount(cl),Pete Trevor(p),John Bly(bj),Harry
Slater(b),Mike Ellis(dr).   Live."Grandstand Hotel",Derby,England.October 21,1973
```
        Basin Street Blues(kc)        Ken Colyer Trust(E)KCT5CD(CD)
        Till We Meet Again                -
```

KEN COLYER AND THE PHOENIX JAZZ BAND:
Ken Colyer(tp),Barry Weston(tb),Ivan Gandon(cl),Alan Bradley(p),Dave Straker(bj),John
Tubby Spicer(b),Pete Lay(dr).   Live."The Men Of Kent",Rainham,England.March 12,1974
        Willie The Weeper   Medway(E)MR/MD001

Ken Colyer(tp,vcl),Barry Weston(tb),Ivan Gandon(cl),Alan Bradley(p),Bill Stotesbury(bj),
John Tubby Spicer(b),Pete Lay(dr).
                                Live."Good Companions Club",Rochester,England.May 14,1974
        I Can't Escape From You   Medway(E)MR/MD001
        Weary Blues   -
        Buddy Bolden's Blues(kc)   -
        Bugle Boy March   -

Note:MR/MD001 also incl. one title without Colyer ("I Got Rhythm").

KEN COLYER AND THE STORYVILLE JAZZ BAND:
Ken Colyer(tp,vcl),Cor Fabrie(tb),Pierre Claessens(cl,fl),Eddy Lokersen(p),Jos Koster(bj),
Ad van Beerendonk(b),Hein Trimbosch(dr).
                     Live.Technische Hogeschool,Eindhoven,The Netherlands.November 7,1974
        Storyville Blues   (see note)
        Bugle Boy March
        Highway Blues
        Weary Blues
        Climax Rag
        Darkness On The Delta
        High Society
        Winter Wonderland(kc)
        Jambalaya

Note:The above titles were issued on cassette (no label or number).

KEN COLYER'S ALL STAR JAZZMEN:
Ken Colyer(tp,vcl),Lennie Baldwin(tb),John Wurr(cl),Ray Smith(p),Bill Stotesbury(bj),Annie
Hawkins(b),Colin Bowden(dr).   Hamburg,Germany.May 12/13,1975
        I Want To Be Happy   Happy Bird(G)5016
        Go Down Sunshine(kc)   -
        Sister Kate   -
        Basin Street Blues(kc)   - ,Marifon(G)296095-241
        Hot Time In The Old Town Tonight   -
        Cheek To Cheek   -
        It's Only A Paper Moon   -
        One Sweet Letter From You(kc)   -

All titles also on Tobacco Road(G)B/2571.

Gerry Turnham(cl),Paul Rosenberg(dr) replace Wurr,Bowden.
                                      Hamburg,Germany.November 16,1975
        Darktown Strutters' Ball(kc) Happy Bird(G)5021
        Tishomingo Blues(kc)   -
        Shine(kc)   -
        Going Home To New Orleans(kc)   -
        Celito Lindo(kc)   -
        Louisiany L.A.
          (Lou-easy-an-i-ay)(kc)   -
        K.C. Moan(kc)   -
        Doctor Jazz(kc)   - ,Time Wind(G)DB50.120
        St. James Infirmary(kc)   - ,F90062,   -

All titles also on Happy Bird B90016,Tobacco Road(G)B/2569.
Note:The cover notes incorrectly list John Wurr(cl).

KEN COLYER WITH CHRIS BLOUNT'S NEW ORLEANS JAZZ BAND:
Ken Colyer(tp,vcl),Dave Vickers(tb),Chris Blount(cl),Pete Trevor(p),Dave Brennan(bj),Harry
Slater(b),Mike Ellis(dr).   Live."Rutland Hotel",Ilkeston,England.July 13,1976
  Indiana   Ken Colyer Trust(E)KCT5CD(CD)
  Ice Cream(kc)   -
  Sporting Life Blues(kc)   -
  Red Wing,My Red Wing   -

Ken Colyer(tp,vcl),Cor Fabrie(tb),Butch Thompson(cl),Jos Koster(bj),Ad van Beerendonk(b),
Miel Leybaert(dr).   Live."Koetshuis",Eindhoven,The Netherlands.November 16,1976
  Cielito Lindo(kc)   Beerendonk(Du)9999
  Bogalusa Strut   -
  Tishomingo Blues(kc)   -
  There's Yes,Yes,In Your Eyes   -
  Postman's Lament(kc)   -
  Panama Rag   -
  Winin' Boy Blues(kc)   -
  Goin' Home(kc)   -

KEN COLYER WITH CHRIS BLOUNT'S NEW ORLEANS JAZZ BAND:
Ken Colyer(tp,vcl),Dave Vickers(tb),Chris Blount(cl),Pete Trevor(p),Dave Brennan(bj),Harry
Slater(b),Mike Ellis(dr).   Live."Bell Hotel",Derby,England.January 2,1977
  Too Busy   Ken Colyer Trust(E)KCT5CD(CD)
  Rum And Coco Cola(kc)   -
  Nobody's Fault But Mine   -

Same.   Live."Bell Hotel",Derby,England.December 18,1977
  Black And Blue   Ken Colyer Trust(E)KCT5CD(CD)
  Lord,Lord,Lord(kc)   -
  Cielito Lindo   -

KEN COLYER'S JAZZMEN:
Ken Colyer(cnt,vcl),Lennie Baldwin(tb),Gerry Turnham(cl),Ray Smith(p),Bill Stotesbury(bj),
Arthur Bird(b),Paul Rosenberg(dr).
                               Live."Strathallan Hotel",Birmingham,England.January 22,1978
1366 Some Of These Days   Neovox(E)No.521
1367 Yearning   -
1368 I Wish I Could Shimmy
   Like My Sister Kate   -
1369 The Birth Of The Blues   -
1370 Ace In The Hole(kc)   -
1371 Down In Honky Tonk Town   -
1372 Black And Blue(kc)   Neovox(E)No.522
1373 Black Cat On The Fence   Neovox(E)No.521
1374 At The Jazz Band Ball   Neovox(E)No.522
1375 Lead Me Saviour   unissued
1376 Short Dress Gal   -
1377 Cataract Rag   Neovox(E)No.522
1378 Kinklets   Neovox(E)No.521
1379 Thriller Rag   Neovox(E)No.522
1380 Aunt Hagar's Blues   -
1381 Jungle Blues(p-solo)   unissued
1382 Pep(p-solo)   -
1383 When I Leave The World Behind   Neovox(E)No.522
1384 Just A Closer Walk With The(kc)   -
1385 Too Busy   -
  Auf Wiedersehn   unissued

Note:Neovox(E)No.521 and 522 are cassette issues.

Dave Brennan(bj) replaces Stotesbury;Colyer plays (tp).

Live.Kulturpalast,Dresden,Germany.May 6,1978

   Give Me Your Telephone Number Amiga(G)8.55.637

KEN COLYER ALL STARS:
Ken Colyer(cnt,vcl),Barry Palser(tb),Dave Bailey(cl),Ray Smith(p),Louis Lince(bj),Annie
Hawkins(b),Colin Bowden(dr). Live(?).Saffron Walden Parish Church,England.November 4,1978

Just A Little	
While To Stay Here(kc)	CMJ CD12(CD)
Saturday Night Function	-
Lead Me On(kc)	-
Lily Of The Valley	-
Sometimes My Burden	
Is So Hard To Bear(kc)	-
Lord,Lord,Lord(kc)	-
Just A Closer Walk With Thee(kc)	-
Nobody's Fault But Mine(kc)	-

Ken Colyer(tp,vcl),Mike Sherbourne(tb),Tony Pyke(cl),Ray Smith(p),Bill Stotesbury(bj),Bill
Cole(b),Paul Rosenberg(dr).

Live.North Sea Jazz Festival,The Hague,The Netherlands.July 14,1979

Lord,Lord,Lord,You've	
Sure Been Good To Me(kc)	Black Lion(E)BLP12136
Darkness On The Delta	-
Yaaka Hula Hickey Dula	-
Gettusburg March	-
Deep Bayou Blues	-
Shine(kc)	-
Auf Wiedersehen	-

Ken Colyer(cnt,vcl),Mike Sherbourne(tb),Bruce Bakewell(cl),Ray Smith(p),Bill Stotesbury
(bj),Alyn Shipton(b),Colin Bowden(dr). London.October 6,1979

Should I Reveal	Black Lion(E)BLCD760501(CD)
Painting The Clouds With Sunshine	-
When I Grow To Old To Dream	-
Jungle Town	-
Uptown Bumps	-
Snag It(kc)	-
The Entertainer Rag	unissued
Everywhere I Go	-
Twilight Time	-
When You Leave The World Behind	-
It's A Long Way To Tipperary	-
Over The Waves	-
Burgundy Street Blues	-
Liza	-
Sweet Lorraine	-
Tiger Rag	-
Goin' Home	-
Running Wild	-

Note:Additional recordings by this artist are not included.

STUFF COMBE (Swiss)

STUFF COMBE BIG BAND AND RHYTHM:
Poul Schmassmann,Eric Brooke,R. Parisod(tp),Jacques Barraud,J.Stupin(tb,vbs,perc),Luc
Hoffmann(reeds,perc),Tony D'Adario,Jean-Pierre Dupuis,Robert Croisier(reeds),Achille Scot-
(org),Pierre Cavalli(g),Bob Jacquillard(b,perc),Stuff Combe(dr).
(session cont. next page).

(session cont. from previous page):

	Geneva(?). 1960's	
Caravan	Avedis Zildjian SZ1001,Jazztone(F)SJS1303	
Watermelon Man	-	
Love For Sale	-	
River Kwai March	-	
Carioca	-	
Yesterday	-	
Ride The Rhythm	-	
Summertime	-	
Crotale's Riff	-	
New St. Louis Blues	-	
Moon River	-	
Istanbul	-	

Benny Bailey(tp),Tony D'Adario(ts),Francy Boland(p),Bob Jacquillard(b),Stuff Combe(dr).
                                        Geneva.September 28,1973
Space Trip	"M"(Sw)MLP10205
Bossa Turquoise	-
Eastern Blues	-
St. Thomas	-

ALIX COMBELLE (French)

See also BUCK CLAYTON,JAM SESSION(French),JAZZ DE PARIS,JONAH JONES.

ALIX COMBELLE ET LE "JAZZ DE PARIS"
Christian Bellest,Jean Lemay,Charles Suire(tp),Jean-Louis Jeanson(tb),Pierre Delhoumeau
Charles Lisée(as),Alix Combelle,Gaston Etienne,Roby Davis (Robert David)(ts),Henri Gau-
thier(p),Tony Rovira(b),Jerry Mengo(dr).   Brussels.June 1942
16238	Alma Marceau	Rythme(B)RB5027
16239	Automne	-
16240	La Ta Ta Da	Rythme(B)RB5028
16241	Fariboles	-

ALIX COMBELLE ET SON ORCHESTRE:
Christian Bellest(tp),Alix Combelle(cl,ts),John Ouwerx(p),Tony Rovira(b),Jerry Mengo(dr)
                                        Brussels.June 1942
16242	Chuchotements (Whispering)	Rythme(B)RB5029
16243	Gare Du Nord	-
16244	Improvistaion En Moderato	Rythme(B)RB5031
16245	Bizare	-

ALIX COMBELLE ET SON ORCHESTRE:
Christian Bellest,Jean Lemay,Charles Suire(tp),Jean-Louis Jeanson(tb),Hubert Rostaing(as
cl),Pierre Delhoumeau(as),Roby Davis,Alix Combelle(ts,arr,vcl),Roger Chaput(g),Emmanuel
Soudieux(b),Pierre Fouad(dr).   Paris.July 3,1942
OSW292-1 La Da Da La La(ac)	Swing(F)144
OSW293-1 Ma Chanson Triste	Swing(F)189
OSW294-1 Fariboles	Swing(F)144

Alix Combelle(ts,arr,vcl),Roby Davis(ts),Léo Chauliac(p),Lucien Gallopain(g),Lucien Si-
moens(b),Armand Molinetti(dr).   Paris.September 8,1942
OSW299-1 Ecoutez Ca(ac,band-vcl)	Swing(F)148
OSW300-1 Oui(ac,band-vcl)	-
OSW301-1 Rue Duperré	EMI/Jazz Time(F)251.282-2(CD)
OSW302-1 Encore	Swing(F)189, -

Note:The first issue of Swing(F)148 used masters OSW299/300; later issue(s) used masters
     OSW320/21 (session February 16,1943).

ALIX COMBELLE

Raoul Coucoule(tp),Georges Galavielle,Michel Donnay(as),Alix Combelle(ts,arr,vcl),Jacques
Diéval(p),Roger Chaput(g),Lucien Simoens(b),Armand Molinetti(dr).
                                        Paris.February 5,1943
OSW316-1 Elle Et Lui(ac)   Swing(F)163
OSW317-1 Echo(ac)   -

same.   Paris.February 16,1943
OSW318-1 Riff En Crescendo(1)   Swing(F)171
OSW319-1 Riff En Diminuendo(1)   -
OSW320-1 Ecoutez-Ca(ac,band-vcl)   Swing(F)148,EMI/Jazz Time(F)780.380-2(CD)
OSW321-1 Oui(ac,band-vcl)   - ,Pathe(F)C.054-16024,2C.154-15919,
                                        EMI/Jazz Time(F)794.247-2(CD)

1.Add Maurice Moufflard,Alex Caturegli,Christian Bellest(tp),Maurice Gladieu,Pierre Rémy,
  Julien Layat,André Lafosse(tb),Pierre Delhoumeau,Charles Lisée(as).

Note:Masters OSW320/21 - see note after session September 8,1942.
     It is not known if "Oui" on EMI/Jazz Time(F)794.100-2(CD) is the above version or the
     version recorded September 8,1942.

Christian Bellest(tp),Christian Wagner(as,cl),Alix Combelle(ts,arr,vcl),Georges Galavielle
(ts),Jacques Diéval(p),Roger Chaput(g),Ernest Fuggi(b),Jean-Pierre Dariel(dr).
                                        Paris.September 9,1943
SW373-1 Ca S'fait Pas(ac,band-vcl)   Swing(F)181,Pathé(F)C154-15919
SW374-1 Ce Qu'Il Faut
          Démontrer(ac,band-vcl)   - ,Pathé(F)C154-15918

ALIX COMBELLE AND HIS ORCHESTRA/ET SA MUSIQUE:
Christian Bellest(tp),Maurice Gladieu(tb),Robert Luinet,Georges Galavielle(as),Roby Davis
(ts),Alix Combelle(ts,arr,vcl),Cléo Plateaux(bars,as),Pierre Guillot(p),Pierre Gérardot
(g),Jean Bouchety(b),André Jourdan(dr).   Paris.July 5,1945
OSW402-1 One O'Clock Jump   Swing(F)193
OSW403-1 Flying Home   -
CL8032-1 Daisy(ac)   Columbia(F)DF3036
CL8033-1 Patte De Lapin(ac)   -

Note:Swing(F)193 was never issued.
     Masters CL8032-33 were prob. rec. same date as masters OSW402-03.

ALIX COMBELLE ET LA JAM SESSION No.1:
Christian Bellest(tp),Michel De Villers(as),Alix Combelle(ts,arr),Jacques Diéval(p),Roger
Chaput(g),Jean Bouchety(b),Jerry Mengo(dr),Django Reinhardt(arr).
                                        Paris.October 21,1946
CK1-1 Daphné   Swing(F)unissued
CK2-1 Blues,Look Out There   Swing(F)227
CK3-1 Bring That Bottle,Pops!   Swing(F)250
CK4-1 Take That Last Note   Swing(F)227

ALIX COMBELLE ET SON ORCHESTRE:
Jean Lemay,Alex Caturegli,prob. Christian Bellest,unknown(tp),Pierre Rémy,Julien Layat,
unknown(tb),Robert Luinet(as),Roby Davis,Georges Galavielle(ts),Alix Combelle(ts,arr),
Jes Raynal(bars),Jean Gruyer(p,arr),Pierre Gérardot(g),Jean Bouchety(b),unknown(dr),(vcl-
group).   Paris.December 13,1950
CB8899-2 Rag Mop(vcl-group)   Columbia(F)BF364,FB687,FS1002
CB8900-2 Ca,C'est Mieux   Columbia(F)BF343,FS1001
CB8901-2 Sam's Song   -   -
CB8902-2 Pour Chanter
          Le Jazz(ac,vcl-group)   Columbia(F)BF364,FB687,FS1002

```
Similar.                              Paris.June 7,1951
CL8985-2 Rose,Rose,I Love You         Columbia(F)BF399,FS1001
CL8986-2 Orange Colored Sky                    -
CL8987-2 Pour Danser                  Columbia(F)BF392,FS1001
CL8988-2 Rose Pompon Et Papillon               -
```

ALIX COMBELLE,SON TENOR-SAX ET SON ORCHESTRE:
Jean Mauclaire,Alex Renard,Pierre Sellin,Fernand Verstraete,Roland Vincent(tp),Gaby Vilai
André Paquinet,Charles Verstraete(tb),René Godard,Jean-Jacques Léger(as),Alix Combelle,
Henri Bernard,Michel Donnay(ts),Henri Jouot(bars),Jean-Claude Pelletier(p),Jean-Pierre
Sasson(g),Yvon Le Guen(b),Gérard "Dave" Pochonet(dr).

```
                                      Paris.May 13,1954
54V4841 Moonlight Serenade            Vogue(F)V3464,V45-66,EPL7056,LD223
54V4842 Music Box Tango               Vogue(F)V3465,V45-117,EPL7080
54V4843 In The Mood                   Vogue(F)V3464,V45-66,EPL7056
54V4844 Confidentially (Alix Talks)   Vogue(F)V3465
```

ALIX COMBELLE QUINTET:
Alix Combelle(ts),Jean-Claude Pelletier(p),Jean Bonal(g),Alix Bret(b),Gérard "Dave"
Pochonet(dr).   Paris.June 18,1954

```
        Don't Be That Way             Vogue(F)EPL7144
        Blues Des Deux Alix                    -
        My Melancholy Baby                     -
        Blue Moon                              -
```

Note:The bassplayer may be Roland Lobligeois.

ALIX COMBELLE ET SON ORCHESTRE:
Incl. Alex Renard(tp),Alix Combelle(ts),Jacky Cnudde(p),Jean Bonal(g),Roland Lobligeois
(b),Philippe Combelle(dr).   Paris. 1957/58

```
        Hot Toddy                     Philips(F)B76046R,P10175L
        Make Yourself Comfortable             -        -    ,N72254H
        Skokiaan                              - ,432.021BE,P72252R
        Malaguena                     Philips(F)P72252R
        Rock At The Apollo            Philips(F)B372.389F,432.129BE,B79089R,P77110L
        Rock A Go Go                          -        -       -      -   ,
                                      P76152R
        Sleeping Car Blues            Philips(F)B372.505F,432.188BE,P76152R
        Marche A La Rock                      - ,P76152R
        Only You                      Philips(F)B372.493F,432.188BE,P76152R
        Joseph                                -        -        -
        Pour Garder Le Tempo          Philips(F)432.232BE,P76152R
        Charleston 58                         -        -
        Le Jour Our La Pluie Viendra          -        -
        On Dit                                -        -
        Shah Shah Persan              Philips(F)432.153BE,P10191L,P76152R
```

Claude Gousset(tb),Alix Combelle(ts,arr),Georges Arvanitas(p),Jean Bonal(g),Roland Lobli
geois(b),Philippe Combelle(dr).   Paris. 1960

```
        On The Alamo(no tb)           Club Francais du Disque(F)HF242
        All Of Me(no tb)                       -
        Sent For You Yesterday                 -
        Christopher Columbus                   -
        Bruno Blues                   Club Francais du Disque(F)HF243
        Don't Be That Way                      -
        L'Autre Boogie                         -
```

Note:Additonal recordings by this artist are not included.

OMBO FH (Czech)

ilan Sladek(bassoon),Oldrich Svoboda(fl),Borek Suchy(ss),Daniel Fikejz(p,el-p,perc,ldr),
aroslav Hönig(g),Petr Hajek(el-b,b),Vit Ondracek(dr,perc),Petr Krecan(perc),Martha Elef-
eriadu(vcl).   Czechoslovakia.October 4/20,1976
    Kopytem Ruzne   Panton(Cz)330415
    Horizontálni Louceni(me)   -
    Jogurt Az Jindy(no bassoon)   -

ote:Additional recordings by this group are not included.

OMBO 50 (Finnish)

atti Pirtinheimo(ts),Jukka Haavisto(vbs),Lasse Mårtenson(p),Sami Ahokas(g),Tauno Suojärvi
b),Eric Forsman(dr).   Helsinki.June 12/13,1978
    All Of Me   SMMY(Fi)unnumbered
    E 4(no vbs)   -

MBO 4 BRATISLAVA (Czech)

ktor Hidvegy(p),Karel Ondreicka(g,ldr),Gustav Riska(b),Peter Mraz(dr).
                              Bratislava,Czechoslovakia.January 8 or April 27,1963
    Vituv Tanec (St. Vitus Dance)   Supraphon(Cz)DV10142,SUA15584

MBO JAZZ (Italian)

avio Boldro(tp),Giorgio Andrizzi(tb),Claudio Montafia(fl),Maurizio Gianotti(as,bars),
audio Bonadé(ts,cl),Aldo Ridone(p,el-p),Gigi Venegoni(b),Giorgio Marotti,Pippo Calvagna
l-b),Giorgio Diaferia(dr).   Torino,Italy. 1979
    Verona   MU(I)UM105
    Blue Bossa   -
    No Speed   -
    Pag.1   -
    Teachers   -
    Walking   -

MMAND ALL STARS

cl. Pee Wee Erwin(tp),Terry Snyder(vbs).   NYC.c. 1959
    You're The Top   Grand Award 33-806/806SD
    Somebody Loves Me   -
    Blues In The Night   -
    Perhaps,Perhaps,Perhaps   -
    Love For Sale   -
    Fascinatin' Rhythm   -
    'S Wonderful   -
    Mood Indigo   -
    Ain't Misbehavin'   -
    The Man I Love   -
    Song Of India   -
    Mad About The Boy   -

. titles also on Command(F)RSSD806.

No details.   NYC.c. 1960/61
        Unknown titles   Grand Award 33-820/820SD

THE COMMANDERS/THE COMMANDERS WITH EDDIE GRADY

See also LOUIS ARMSTRONG.

Billy Butterfield,Andy Ferretti,Carl Poole(tp),Cutty Cutshall,Phil Giardina,Lou McGarity,
Jack Satterfield(tb),Hymie Schertzer(as,cl,bars),Al Klink/Russell Banzer(ts,bars),Bernie
Leighton(p),Carmen Mastren(g),Bob Haggart/Sandy Block(b),Eddie Grady(dr),Toots Camarata
(arr).   NYC.February 27,1953
84025 Swanee Boogie   Decca 28659
84026 Honey On The Horn   -

Both titles also on Decca ED2099,DL5525,Brunswick(E)05128,(G)82765.

Same.   NYC.June 29,1953
84784 "O"   Decca 28779
84785 Meet The Brass   -

Both titles also on Decca ED2099,DL5525,Brunswick(E)05164,(G)82788.

Same.   NYC.July 13,1953
84858 When I'm With You   Decca 28848,ED2217,DL8117,Brunswick(E)05216
84859 Hors D'Oeuvre   - ,ED2219,ED2393,DL8117,DL8313,(J)JDL60●
                                         Brunswick(E)05216
84860 Jim'ny Crickets   Decca 29093,ED2219,DL8117

Same.   NYC.October 18,1953
85347 It's A Wonderful World   Decca 29093,ED2218,ED2393,DL8117,DL8313,(J)JDL60●
85348 Davy Jones   Decca 28966,ED2140,DL5525

Add Neal Hefti(arr).   NYC.November 5,1953
85486 March Of The Commanders   Decca 29209,ED2217,DL8117
85487 I Want A Little Girl   Decca 28966,ED2140,DL5525,Brunswick(E)05491

Same.   NYC.February 2,1954
85822 Make Love To Me   Decca 29048,ED2140,DL5525,Brunswick(E)05279
85823 Dixie Flyer   Decca 29652
85824 Kentucky Boogie   Decca 29048,ED2140,DL5525,Brunswick(E)05279

All titles on DL5525 also on Brunswick(E)LA8683.
Note:Additional titles with this band are not included.

COMMITMENT

Will Connell,Jr.(as,bcl,fl),Jason Hwang(vln),William Parker(b),Takeshi Zen Matsuura(dr).
                                         Unknown location.October 13/14,1980
        Montain Song   Flying Panda C1001
        The Web Of Forces   -
        Famine   -
        Grassy Hills   -
        The Sun   -
        No Name   -

COMMODORE JAZZ BAND (Dutch)

Jan van de Berg(cnt,tp,flh),Paul Woesthuis(tb),Hans Schraders(cl,as),Jack Koppels(p,ldr),
Wim Boelhouwer(b),Ton Lucassen(dr).   Live.Heerde,The Netherlands.August 23,1980
     Beale Street Blues   Eurosound(Du)ES46.488

Henk Gunneman(p) replaces Koppels.   Live.Ermelo,The Netherlands.September 26,1980
     Indiana   Killroy(Du)16995
     I Can't Believe That
       You're In Love With Me   -
     Commodore Blues   -
     That Da Da Strain   -
     New Orleans   -
     Undecided   -

THE COMMODORES (Canadian)

Frank Howard,Sr.,Jim Elliott(tp),Stan Wiggins(tp,vcl),Jim Large,Jim Belair(as),Larry Brown
(ts,ldr),Bud Haines(ts),Phil Huddleston(p),Max Caldwell(b),Reg Scriven(dr).
                    Peterborough,Ontario,Canada.July   1945
     I Can't Get Started(sw)   Nomadic(Ca)NR7001

COMPANY

Note:Derek Bailey organises and directs the group COMPANY.

Evan Parker(ss,ts),Derek Bailey(g),Tristan Honsinger(cello),Maarten van Regteren Altena
(b).   London.May 9,1976
     No South(no ss/ts)   Incus(E)21
     No North(no g)   -
     No East(no b)   -
     No West(no cello)   -

Anthony Braxton(ss,as,cl),Evan Parker(ss,ts),Derek Bailey(g).
                    London.August 22,1976
     Za'Id   Incus(E)23
     Akhrajat   -
     Al   -
     Mutala   -
     Hiq   -

Derek Bailey(g),Han Bennink(dr,vln,bj,cl,vcl).
                    London.September   1976
     In The Dead Of The Night
       I Gotta Go Where You Are   Incus(E)25
     The Song Is Ended (Medley)   -
     Umberto Who   -
     Tether End 1   -
     A Fine Mesh   -
     Stanley   -
     Tether End 2   -

Steve Lacy(ss),Derek Bailey(g).   London.November 11,1976
     Once Upon A Time   Incus(E)26
     Abandoned 1   -
     Abandoned 2   -
     Step 1   -
     Step 2   -
     Happily Ever After   -

Leo Smith(tp,fl),Steve Lacy,Lol Coxhill(ss),Anthony Braxton(sopranino-sax,as,cl,fl),Evan
Parker(ss,ts),Steve Beresford(p),Derek Bailey(g),Tristan Honsinger(cello),Maarten van Reg
teren Altena(b),Han Bennink(dr,perc,vla).   London.May 25/26/27,1977

LS/MR/DB/TH/AB/SL/EP	Incus(E)28
SL/AB 1	-
SL/AB 2	-
EP/TH/AB 1	-
EP/TH/AB 2	-
LS/TH/AB/SL/MR	Incus(E)29
EP/HB/DB(1)	-
SB,MR,HB,LC	-
MR/SL	-
HB/AB/DB	-
LC/TH/LS	-
AB/EP	Incus(E)30
TH/MR/SB/HB/DB	-
SL/EP/AB/LC	-
LC/AB/MR	-
TH/LS	-
HB/LC/MR/TH	-
EP/LS/DB	-

-1.An edited part of a longer piece.
Note:The titles on Incus 28/29/20 are derived from the initials of the musicians playing.

Lol Coxhill(ss,vcl),Misha Mengelberg(p,celeste),Steve Beresford(p,vcl),Derek Bailey(g),Ia
Croall(vcl).   London.August 1977

The 1st Hackney Scroll:	Incus(E)38
a.Theology	
b.Otology	
c.Speak Up,Lad	
The 2nd Hackney Scroll:	-
a.So Few	
b.So Many	
c.So So	
d.So What	
e.So Long	

George Lewis(tb),Evan Parker(ss,ts),Derek Bailey(g),Dave Holland(b).
                                            London.May 17/18,1980

ATG 4	Incus(E)36
ATG 6	-
ATG 3	-
ATG 13	-
ATG 2	-
ATG 9	-

COMPARED TO WHAT (Australian)

KERRIE BIDDELL AND COMPARED TO WHAT:
(vcl) acc. by Graham Jesse(fl,ss,as,ts),Michael Bartolomei(p,el-p,synth),Alan Freeman
(el-b),Nick Lister(dr).   Sydney.September 7,1979

33/48 You're Joking(no vcl)	Studios 301(Au)SS301
How Do You Say Auf Wiedersehn	-
Superwoman	-
The Masquerade Is Over	-
Three To Feel(no vcl)	-
Steamroller	-

COMPLOT OF SIX (Polish)

Zbigniew Czwojda(tp),Leszek Paszko(tb),Wlodzimierz Winski(ts,bars),Boguslaw Razik(p),
Andrzej Pluszcz(g),Adam Bielawski(dr).   Wroclaw,Poland.March 1975
         Wizje   Musa(P)SXL1221
         Amorphous   -
         Pieprzem I Sola   -
         Epitaphium   -

COMPOSERS WORKSHOP ENSEMBLE

Johnny Coles(tp),Jack Jeffers(btb),Julius Watkins(frh),Howard Johnson(tu,bars),Al Gibbons
(ts),Bross Townsend(p),Herb Bushler(b),Warren Smith(dr,ldr).
                                   NYC. 1972
         Lament (What Does It Mean)   Strata-East SES1972/3
         Sub Structure   -
         Blues By Monk   -
         Introduction To The Blues   -
         Blues For E.L.C.(1)   -
         Hello Julius   -

-1.Jimmy Owens(tp) replaces Coles.

Jack Jeffers(btb,tu),Sharon Freeman(frh),Howard Johnson(tu),George Barrow(ts),Courtney
Wynter(reeds),Bross Townsend(p),Herb Bushler(b),Warren Smith(dr,perc,ldr),Omar Clay(dr,
perc),Greg Maker,Norman Spiller(perc).   NYC. 1974
         (We've Been) Around   Strata-East SES7422
         Screamer   -
         I Know The Scenery By Heart   -
         Love In The Open   -

COMPOST

Harold Vick(ts,fl),Jack DeJohnette(org,vbs,el-clavinet,dr),Jack Gregg(b),Bob Moses(dr),
Jumma Santos(cg,perc).   NYC. 1971/72
         Take Off Your Body   Columbia C31176
         Thinkin'   -
         Bwaata   -
         Happy Peace   -
         Country Song   -
         Sweet Berry Wine   -
         Funky Feet(bm)   -
         Inflation Blues   -

All titles also on CBS(Eu)S64935.

Harold Vick(ts,fl.el-ts,perc),Jack DeJohnette(p,org,chimes,el-clavinet,dr,perc,vcl),Roland
Prince(g),Ed Finney(g,perc),Jack Gregg(b),Bob Moses(dr,el-clavinet,org,vbs),Jumma Santos
(cg,perc),Jeanne Lee,Lou Courtney(vcl).   NYC. 1971/72
         Seventh Period   Columbia KC32031,CBS(Eu)S65326
         Moonsong   -   -
         Compost Festival   -   ,KG31574, -
         The Ripper   -   -
         Buzzard Feathers   -   -
         Changing Streams   -   -
         Mon Cherry Popsocool   -   -
         Restless Wave   -   -
         Life Is Round   -   -

FRANK COMSTOCK

See TONY RIZZI.

PETER COMTON (British)

PETER COMTON BIG BAND:
John Burnett,Dave Mowatt,Ian Fenby(tp),Mike Carroll(tb),Ray Warleigh -1(as),Peter Ward
(as,ts),Keith Thomas,Art Themen(ts),Peter Comton(bars),Colin Parnell(p),Peter Hughes(b),
Chuck Smith(dr).   London.September 30,1965

C Jam Blues	"77"LEU12/14	
Da Capo	-	
By Request(1)	-	
Clea	-	
Djinn(1)	-	
Sound Of Eleven	-	
Over The Rainbow(1)	-	
Mountolive And Balthazar(1)	-	
Nessim	unissued	
Tonk	-	
The Hard School	-	

CONCERT JAZZ FIVE (Hungarian)

See GABOR RADICS.

CONCORD ALL STARS / FESTIVAL ALL STARS / SUPER BAND

CONCORD FESTIVAL ALL STARS:
Harry Edison(tp),Plas Johnson(ts,as),George Duke(p),Herb Ellis(g),Ray Brown(b),Jake Hanna
(dr).   Live.Concord Festival,Concord,Calif.August 2,1974

After You've Gone	Concord CJ6	
Mitch's Lament	-	
Home Grown	-	
Mood Indigo	-	
Detour Ahead(g,b only)	-	
Fatty McSlatty	-	
Flintstones II	-	

CONCORD SUPER BAND:
Warren Vaché(cnt,flh),Scott Hamilton(ts),Ross Tompkins(p),Cal Collins(g),Monty Budwig(b),
Jake Hanna(dr).   Live.Yubin Chokin Hall,Tokyo.September 15,1978

I Would Do Anything For You	Concord CJ80	
Blue Lester	-	
Nuages	-	
Don't Blame Me	-	
Blue Lou	-	
You're Drivin' Me Crazy	-	
Blue And Sentimental	-	
I'm Gonna Go Fishin'	-	
When It's Sleepy Time Down South	-	
Take The "A" Train	-	
Undecided	-	

CONCORD ALL STARS / FESTIVAL ALL STARS / SUPER BAND

CONCORD ALL STARS:
Snooky Young(tp),Marshall Royal(as),Ross Tompkins(p),Cal Collins(g),Ray Brown(b),Jake
Hanna(dr).   Live.Concord Festival,Calif.August 1979

Moten Swing	Concord CJ117
Don't Get Around Much Anymore	-
Willow Weep For Me(no tp)	-
I Want A Little Girl(no as,g)	-
Sleeping Bee(no tp,as,p)	-
Summer Wind(no tp,as,g)	-
Exactly Like You	-
Pavilion Blues	-

CONCORD SUPER BAND:
Warren Vaché(cnt,flh),Scott Hamilton(ts),Dave McKenna(p),Cal Collins(g),Phil Flanigan(b),
(b),Jake Hanna(dr),Anli Sugano(vcl).   Live.Koseinenkin Kaikan Hall.Tokyo.December 5,1979

Crazy Rhythm	Concord CJ120
Gone With The Wind	-
Nancy(no cnt/flh)	-
Limehouse Blues(p-solo)	-
Out Of Nowhere(ts,p,dr only)	-
Oh Baby	-
Just Friends	-
Summertime(g,b,dr only)	-
In A Mellow Tone	-
My Romance(no ts)	-
On The Sunny Side	-
Of The Street(as)	
Drum Boogie	-
The King	-

EDDIE CONDON

See also BOYCE BROWN,"CHICAGO AND ALL THAT JAZZ",BING CROSBY,DIXIELAND ALL STARS,BOBBY
HACKETT,MANASSAS JAZZ FESTIVAL,JOE MARSALA,STARS OF JAZZ.
Note:Condon does not always play guitar on the sessions recorded - or broadcast - under
his name, but acts as conductor/coordinator.

EDDIE CONDON AND HIS BAND:
Max Kaminsky(cnt),Brad Gowans(vtb),Pee Wee Russell(cl),Joe Sullivan(p),Eddie Condon(g),Al
Morgan(b),George Wettling(dr).   NYC.January 28,1942

R4305-3 Don't Leave Me Daddy	Commodore C542,FL20019,FL30013,XFL16568,Melodisc (E)MLP12-126,Mosaic MR23-123
R4306-3 Fidgety Feet	Commodore XFL16568,Mosaic MR23-123
R4306-4 Fidgety Feet	Commodore C542,FL20019,FL30013,XFL15658,Melodisc (E)MLP12-126,Mosaic MR23-123,Mainstream M56024
R4306-5 Fidgety Feet	Mosaic MR23-123
R4307-1 Mammy O'Mine	Commodore 1509,XFL16568,London(J)SLC446,Mosaic MR23-123,Time-Life STL-J27
R4307-2 Mammy O'Mine	Commodore XFL16568,Mosaic MR23-123
R4308-1 Lonesome Tag Blues	Commodore 1510,XFL16568,London(J)SLC446,Mosaic MR23-123
R4308-3 Tortilla B Flat	Commodore 1509,XFL16568,London(J)SLC446,Mosaic MR23-123
R4308-4 More Tortilla B Flat	Commodore 1510,Mosaic MR23-123

All titles on XFL16568 also on London/Commodore(G)6.25526.

Henry "Red" Allen(tp,vcl),Max Kaminsky(tp),Muggsy Spanier(cnt),J.C. Higginbotham,George
Brunies,Brad Gowans(tb),Irving Fazola,Edmond Hall,Pee Wee Russell(cl),Billy Kyle,Mel
Powell,Joe Sullivan(p),Eddie Condon(g),John Kirby(b),Zutty Singleton,Cozy Cole(dr)(coll.
pers.).   Live.Town Hall,NYC.March 7,1942

> She Hollored Brother,If
> You Want(ha)
> I Smell Something Cooking(ha)
> I Found A New Baby
> Squeeze Me
> Strut Miss Lizzie
> China Boy
> Love Is Just Around The Corner
> Davenport Blues
> Gin Mill Blues(1)
> Honeysuckle Rose(1)
> Impromptu Ensemble

-1.Sullivan(p-solo).

EDDIE CONDON'S SEXTET AND QUINTET:
Billy Butterfield(tp),Ernie Caceres(bars),Dave Bowman(p),Eddie Condon(g),Bob Haggart(b),
George Wettling(dr),Lee Wiley(vcl).   NYC.April 1943
2111-A Down With Love   Monmouth Evergreen MES6807
2111-B Stormy Weather   -
2212   Between The Devil
       And The Deep Sea   -
2113   I've Got The World On A String   -

All titles also on Ember(E)CJS829,Audiophile AP10,Schirmer 2008,MIST 104/3

EDDIE CONDON AND HIS ORCHESTRA:
Bobby Hackett(cnt),Lou McGarity,Vernon Brown,Buddy Morrow(tb),Ernie Caceres(bars),Dave
Bowman(p),Eddie Condon(g),Bob Haggart(b),George Wettling(dr),Lee Wiley(vcl).
                                             NYC.April 1943
2115   Fun To Be Fooled   Monmouth Evergreen MES6807
2216   You Said It   -
2117   Let's Fall In Love   -
2118   Moanin' In The Morning   -

All titles also on Ember(E)CJS829,Audiophile AP10,Schirmer 2008,MIST 104/3

EDDIE CONDON'S BARRELHOUSE GANG:
Yank Lawson(tp),Brad Gowans(tb),Pee Wee Russell(cl),James P. Johnson(p),Eddie Condon(g),
Bob Haggart(b),Tony Sbarbaro (Spargo)(dr). NYC.November 20,1943
T1901 Squeeze Me   Signature 28130
T1902 That's A Plenty   -

Both titles also on Riverside RLP2509,Bob Thiele Music BTM1-0941,Joker(I)SM3244.
Note:See Yank Lawson for additional titles from this session.

EDDIE CONDON AND HIS BAND:
Max Kaminsky(tp),Benny Morton(tb),Pee Wee Russell(cl),Joe Bushkin(p),Eddie Condon(g),Bob
Casey(b),Sidney Catlett(dr).   NYC.December 2,1943
A4687-1 Nobody Knows You
        When You Are Down And Out Mosaic MR23-123
A4687-2 Nobody Knows You
        When You Are Down And Out Commodore C603,FL20017,FL30010,Ace Of Hearts(E)
                                   AH178,Stateside(E)SL10010,London(J)SLC442,
                                   Top Rank(Sd)HJA16507,Mosaic MR23-123
A4688-1 Rose Room   Commodore C603,FL20017,FL30010,London(J)SLC442,
                                   Melodisc(E)MLP12-126,Mosaic MR23-123

(session cont. next page).

```
(session cont. from previous page):
A4688-2  Rose Room                    Mosaic MR23-123
A4689-1  Basin Street Blues           Commodore C1513,FL30006,Ace Of Hearts(E)AH179,
                                        Stateside(E)SL10005,London(J)SLC446,Top Rank
                                        (Sd)HJA16504,Mainstream M56024,S6024,Mosaic
                                        MR23-123

A4689-BD Basin Street Blues           Mosaic MR23-123
A4690-1  Oh,Katharina                 Commodore C1513,FL30006,Ace Of Hearts(E)AH179,
                                        Stateside(E)SL10005,London(J)SLC446,Top Rank
                                        (Sd)HJA16504,Mainstream M56024,S6024,Mosaic
                                        MR23-123

A4690-2  Oh,Katharina                 Mosaic MR23-123
```

Note:Commodore 603-605 also issued as an album (CR12).

```
Max Kaminsky(tp),Brad Gowans(tb),Pee Wee Russell(cl),Joe Bushkin(p),Eddie Condon(g),Bob
Casey(b),Tony Sbarbaro (Spargo)(dr).          NYC.December 8,1943
A4695-1  Pray For The Light           Mosaic MR23-123
A4695-2  Pray For The Light           Commodore C568,FL20017,FL30010,Ace Of Hearts(E)
                                        AH178,Stateside(E)SL10010,Top Rank(Sd)
                                        HJA16507,Mosaic MR23-123

A4695-?  Pray For The Light           Mosaic MR23-123
A4696-1  Tell 'Em About Me            Mosaic MR23-123
A4696-2  Tell 'Em About Me            Commodore C604,FL20017,FL30010,Ace Of Hearts(E)
                                        AH178,Stateside(E)SL10010,Top Rank(Sd)
                                        HJA16507,Mosaic MR23-123

A4697-1  Mandy,Make Up Your Mind      Mosaic MR23-123
A4697-2  Mandy,Make Up Your Mind      Commodore C604,FL20017,FL30013,Melodisc(E)
                                        MLP12-126,Mosaic MR23-123

A4698-1  Singin' The Blues            Commodore C568,Mosaic MR23-123

A4698-2  Singin' The Blues            Mosaic MR23-123
A4698-?  Singin' The Blues            Mosaic MR23-123
```

Note:"Singin' The Blues" issued on FL20017,FL30013,Melodisc(E)MLP12-126,Mainstream M56003,
     S6003 is either from master A4698-2 or A4698-? (i.e. not from master A4698-1).
     Commodore 603-605 also issued as an album (CR12).

```
Max Kaminsky(tp),Lou McGarity(tb),Pee Wee Russell(cl),Gene Schroeder(p),Eddie Condon(g),
Bob Casey(b),George Wettling(dr).             NYC.December 11,1943
A4699-1  Back In Your Backyard        Mosaic MR23-123
A4699-2  Back In Your Backyard        Commodore C551,FL20019,FL30013,Mainstream M56026,
                                        S6026,Melodisc(E)MLP12-126,Fontana(E)TFL5271,
                                        London(J)SLC456,Mosaic MR23-123

A4699-?  Back In Your Backyard        Mosaic MR23-123
A4700-1  Of All The Wrongs
            You've Done To Me         Mosaic MR23-123
A4700-?  Of All The Wrongs
            You've Done To Me         Commodore C551,FL20019,FL30013,Melodisc(E)
                                        MLP12-126,London(J)SLC456,Mosaic MR23-123

A4701-1  You Can't Cheat A Cheater    Mosaic MR23-123
A4701-?  You Can't Cheat A Cheater    Commodore C605,FL20017,FL30013,Melodisc(E)
                                        MLP12-126,London(J)SLC456,Mosaic MR23-123
A4702-1  Save Your Sorrow             Commodore C605,FL20017,FL30010,Ace Of Hearts(E)
                                        AH178,Mainstream M56024,S6024,Stateside(E)
                                        SL10010,Top Rank(Sd)HJA16507,Mosaic MR23-123
A4702-?  Save Your Sorrow             Mosaic MR23-123
```

Note:Commodore 603-605 also issued as an album (CR12).

EDDIE CONDON ALL STARS - GEORGE GERSHWIN:
George Gershwin(p),rest unknown.   NYC(?). 1944
        I Got Rhythm

Note:The above title is from the soundtrack of the "Music In America" film series (March
    Of Time Vol.10 issue 12).

EDDIE CONDON AND HIS ORCHESTRA:
Incl. James P. Johnson(p),Eddie Condon(g),Bob Casey -1(b),George Wettling(dr).
                                            Live.Town Hall,NYC.February 19,1944
        Inprovisation On
          A 32 Bar Standard
        The Boogie Woogie Stride
        The Gut Stomp
        Flamingo(1)

EDDIE CONDON AND HIS JAZZ BAND:
Sterling Bose(tp),Miff Mole(tb),Pee Wee Russell(cl),Gene Schroeder(p),Eddie Condon(g),Bob
Casey(b),Joe Grauso)dr).   NYC.March 8,1944
        Uncle Sam's Blues(1)(hlp)   V-Disc 191,Palm Club(F)09,Foxy(F)9005/06,Fonit
                                        Cetra(I)1018
        Tin Roof Blues   V-Disc 211,Palm Club(F)09,FDC(I)1019,Ariston(I)
                                        AR/LP12030,Fonit Cetra (I)1018
        Ballin' The Jack   V-Disc 211,FDC(I)1019,Ariston(I)AR/LP12030,Fonit
                                        Cetra (I)1018
        Peg O' My Heart   unissued
        Fidgety Feet   -
        Royal Garden Blues   -
        I Ain't Gonna Give
          Nobody None Of My Jelly Roll -

-1.Add Hot Lips Page(tp,vcl).

EDDIE CONDON JAM SESSION:
Max Kaminsky(tp),Bobby Hackett -1(cnt),Miff Mole(tb),Pee Wee Russell(cl),Cliff Jackson(p),
Eddie Condon -2(g),Pops Foster(b),George Wettling(dr).
                                        Live.NYC.Town Hall,March 11,1944
        Darktown Strutters' Ball   Jass J-CD634(CD)
        Dear Old Southland   -
        Jada(1)   -
        Muskrat Ramble(1,2)   -
        St. Louis Blues(3)(p,dr only)   -
        Honeysuckle Rose(3)(p,dr only) -

-3.Kansas Fields(dr) replaces Wettling.

Joe Bushkin(p),Bob Casey(b) replace Jackson,Foster.
                                        Same concert
        She's Funny That Way(4)   Jass J-CD634(CD)
        It's Been So Long(5)   -
        Nobody Knows And Nobody Seems
          To Care(1)(cnt,p,b,dr only)   -
        Serenade In Thirds(1)(p,dr only) -
        Unknown title(1)(p,dr only)   -
        China Boy(5)   -

-3.Kansas Fields(dr) replaces Wettling.
-4.Billy Butterfield(tp),p,b,dr only.
-5.Edmond Hall(cl),p,b,dr only.

Max Kaminsky(tp),Hot Lips Page(tp,vcl),Bobby Hackett(cnt),Miff Mole(tb),Pee Wee Russell
(cl),Cliff Jackson(p),Bob Casey,Pops Foster(b),George Wettling(dr).
                                        Same concert
        Uncle Sam Blues(hlp)   Jass J-CD634(CD)
        Impromptu Ensemble(1)   -

-1.Add Billy Butterfield(tp),Joe Bushkin(p),Eddie Condon(g),Kansas Fields(dr).

Note:Some of the above titles are from Columbia transcriptions (Programme 8,9,10,14); some
     of the titles were later reissued on Voice Of America transcription No.31.

EDDIE CONDON AND HIS TOWN HALL JAZZ BAND:
Wild Bill Davison(cnt),George Lugg(tb),Pee Wee Russell(cl),Joe Bushkin(p),Eddie Condon(g),
Pops Foster(b),Kansas Fields(dr),Jimmy Rushing(vcl).
                                        NYC.March 12,1944

        Honeysuckle Rose(incompl.)
        Honeysuckle Rose   Aircheck 31,I.A.J.R.C. 28
        (Warm Up)
        On The Sunny Side Of The Street
        I Ain't Gonna Give Nobody
           None Of My Jelly Roll(1)   Aircheck 31
        I Ain't Gonna Give Nobody
           None Of My Jelly Roll(alt.)(1)   -
        Tin Roof Blues(1,2)
        (Ad Lib) Blues(1,2)(jr)   Aircheck 31
        Baby,Won't You
           Please Come Home(1,2,3)
        Someday Sweetheart(1,2,3)
        Old Fashioned Love(2)
           (p-duet,b,dr only)

-1.Add Edmond Hall(cl).
-2.Add James P. Johnson(p).
-3.Omit Russell,Bushkin.

Note:The above titles were recorded for O.W.I. (Office of War Information) and later
     mastered for V-Disc - but not issued.

EDDIE CONDON AND HIS JAZZ BAND:
Max Kaminsky(tp),Wilbur De Paris(tb),Pee Wee Russell(cl),Joe Bushkin(p),Eddie Condon(g),
Bob Casey(b),George Wettling(cl),Red McKenzie(vcl).
                                        NYC.March 30,1944
N2023-1 Save Your Sorrow(incompl.)   Jazzology J101/102
N2023-2 Save Your Sorrow(incompl.)   -
N2023-3 Save Your Sorrow   Jazum 77,Jazzology J101/102
N2024-1 Rose Room   Jazzology J101/102
N2024-2 Rose Room   -
N2024-3 Rose Room(incompl.)   -
N2024-4 Rose Room   Jazum 77,Jazzology J101/102
N2025-1 Back In Your Backyard(rmk) Jazzology J101/102
N2025-2 Back In Your Backyard(rmk)   -
N2025-3 Back In Your Backyard(incompl.) -
N2025-4 Back In Your Backyard(rmk) Jazum 77,Jazzology J101/102
N2026-1 Darktown Strutters'
           Ball(incompl.)(rmk)   Jazzology J101/102
N2026-2 Darktown Strutters' Ball(rmk) -
N2026-3 Darktown Strutters'
           Ball(incompl.)(rmk)   -
N2026-4 Darktown Strutters' Ball(rmk) Jazum 78,Jazzology J101/102
(session cont. next page).

(session cont. from previous page):
N2027-1 Everybody Loves My Baby(incom.) Jazzology J101/102
N2027-2 Everybody Loves My Baby   -
N2027-3 Everybody Loves My Baby(incom.)   -
N2027-4 Everybody Loves My Baby(incom.)
N2027-5 Everybody Loves My Baby(incom.)   -
N2027-6 Everybody Loves My Baby   Jazum 78,Jazzology J101/102
N2028-1 Of All The Wrongs
        You've Done To Me   Jazzology J101/102
N2028-2 Of All The Wrongs
        You've Done To Me(incompl.)   -
N2028-3 Of All The Wrongs
        You've Done To Me   Jazum 78,Jazzology J101/102
N2029-1 Mandy,Make Up Your Mind   -   -
N2030-1 Blues For Pee Wee   Jazum 77,   -

Note:The above titles were recorded for World transcriptions No.12,13.

Note:The "Eddie Condon Blue Network" Town Hall broadcasts started on May 21,1944 and
      continued almost weekly till April 7,1945. The final tune on each show - "Impromptu
      Ensemble" also as "Carnegie Leap", "Carnegie Blues" or "Ensemble Blues".
      Condon's guitar is heard only on some of the titles from the shows.

EDDIE CONDON JAM SESSION:
Max Kaminsky(tp),Miff Mole(tb),Pee Wee Russell(cl),Gene Schroeder(p),Eddie Condon(g),Bob
Casey(b),Joe Grauso(dr),Liza Morrow(vcl).   Live.Town Hall,NYC.May 20,1944
        Sweet Georgia Brown   Jazzology JCE1001/02
        Peg O' My Heart   -
        Carolina Shout(1)   -
        (Interview)   -
        Wherever There's Love(2,5)   -
        Uncle Sam Blues(3)(hlp)   -
        Someone To Watch Over Me(4,5)(lm)   -
        Impromptu Ensemble(2,3,4)   -

-1.James P. Johnson(p-solo).
-2.Add Billy Butterfield(tp).
-3.Add Hot Lips Page(tp,vcl).
-4.Add Bobby Hackett(cnt).
-5.Omit Kaminsky.

All titles also on Jazzology JCECD1001/02 (CD).
Note:The above titles are from the "Blue Network Show 1".

EDDIE CONDON JAM SESSION:
Max Kaminsky -1(tp),Hot Lips Page -2(tp,vcl),Bobby Hackett -3,Rex Stewart -4(cnt),Miff
Mole(tb),Pee Wee Russell(cl),Ernie Caceres(bars),Gene Schroeder(p),John Kirby(b),Sonny
Greer(dr),Liza Morrow(vcl).   Live.Town Hall,NYC.May 27,1944
        At The Jazz Band Ball(1)   Jazum 4,10,Kings Of Jazz(I)KLJ20028,Baybridge(J)
                                         UXP126
        I Must Have That Man(1,3)   Jazum 4,Good Music JRR3
        (Interview)   Jazzology JCE1001/02
        The Sheik Of Araby(1,2)(hlp)   Jazum 4,Foxy(F)9007/08,Baybridge(J)UXP126,Good
                                         Music JRR3
        Za-za(4)(cnt,p,b,dr only)   Jazum 4
        Time On My Hands(3)   -   -
        I'll Get By(3,5)(lm)   Jazum 24,Foxy(F)9007/08,Good Music JRR3
        Impromptu Ensemble(1,2,3,4)   Jazum 4,   -   -

-5.Omit Russell;Caceres plays (bars,cl).
-6.Add James P. Johnson(p).
(session cont. next page).

(session cont. from previous page):
All titles also on Jazzology JCE1001/02,JCECD1001/02 (CD).
All titles - except the interview - also on Kings Of Jazz(I)KLJ20018,Baybridge(J)UPS2255.
Note:The above titles are from the "Blue Network Show 2" (AFRS "Eddie Condon" transcrip-
    tion no. 1).
    "Ballin' The Jack" (on the same AFRS transcription) is from the June 3,1944 show.

EDDIE CONDON JAM SESSION:
Hot Lips Page -1(tp,vcl),Billy Butterfield -2(tp),Bobby Hackett(cnt),Benny Morton(tb),Pee
Wee Russell(cl),Ernie Caceres(bars,cl),Gene Schroeder(p),Bob Casey(b),Joe Grauso(dr),Liza
Morrow(vcl).   Live.Town Hall,NYC.June 3,1944
        Ballin' The Jack   Jazum 4(ed.),Jazzology JCE1001/02,JCECD1001/02
                                            (CD),Kings Of Jazz(I)KLJ20018

        Whatcha Doin'
            After The War(no tb)(1)(hlp) Jazum 10,Jazzology JCE1001/02,JCECD1001/02(CD)
        I'm Coming Virginia   Jazzology JCE1001/02,JCECD1001/02(CD)
        It's Been So Long(3)   Jazum 72,Jazzology JCE1001/02,JCECD1001/02(CD)
        What's New(2)   Jazum 10,   -   -
        (Interview)   Jazzology JCE1001/02,JCECD1001/02(CD)
        The One I Love Belongs
            To Somebody Else(2(?))(lm)   -   -
        Impromptu Ensemble
            (Ol' Miss)(1,2)   -   -

3.Edmond Hall(cl),p,b,dr only.

ote:The above titles are from the "Blue Network Show 3".
    The above show was not issued on AFRS "Eddie Condon" transcriptions - but some of the
    titles was used as "fill" in the transcriptions from other shows.

DDIE CONDON AND HIS ORCHESTRA:
Bobby Hackett(cnt),Pee Wee Russell(cl),Ernie Caceres(bars),Gene Schroeder(p),Eddie Condon
(g),Bob Haggart(b),Joe Grauso(dr).   NYC.June 8,1944
        Ballin' The Jack   Design DLP47,DLP148,Pickwick Int.PR111,Gala GLP342
                                            Trip TLP5800,Jazz Club(F)1652.371,Olympic(E)
                                            OL7122,DJM(E)DJML065,Vogue(F)DP35,Allegro(E)
                                            ALL791,Everest 924730,Archive Of Folk&Jazz
                                            FS274,Jazz Bird(E)JAZ2012,Music For Pleasure
                                            165.237,Murray Hill S53958/5,Stash ST-CD530
                                            (CD)
        That's A Plenty   Design DLP47,DLP148,Pickwick Int.PR111,Gala GLP342
                                            Trip TLP5800,Jazz Club(F)1652.371,Olympic(E)
                                            OL7122,DJM(E)DJML065,Vogue(F)DP35,Allegro(E)
                                            ALL791,Everest 924730,Archive Of Folk&Jazz
                                            FS274,Jazz Bird(E)JAZ2012,Music For Pleasure
                                            165.237,Murray Hill S53958/5,Stash ST-CD530
                                            (CD)
        Cherry(take 1)   Stash ST-CD530(CD)
        Cherry(take 2)(incompl.)   -
        Cherry(take 3)   Design DLP47,Gala GLP342,Trip TLP5800,Jazz Club(F)
                                            1652.371,Olympic(E)OL7122,DJM(E)DJML065,Vogue
                                            (F)DP35,Allegro(E)ALL791,Everest 924730,Arch.
                                            Of Folk&Jazz FS274,Jazz Bird(E)JAZ2012,Music
                                            For Pleasure 165.237,Murray Hill S53958/5,
                                            Stash ST-CD530(CD)
        Sweet Georgia Brown   Gala GLP342,Trip TLP5800,Olympic(E)OL7122,DJM(E)
                                            DJML065,Vogue(F)DP35,Jazz Bird(E)JAZ2012,
                                            Stash ST-CD530(CD)
        At The Jazz Band Ball   Stash ST-CD530(CD)

Add Billy Butterfield(tp),Hot Lips Page -1(tp,vcl).
                                          Same date
      When The Sugar Walks Down
        The Street(take 1)(1)(hlp)   Stash ST-CD530(CD)
      When The Sugar Walks Down
        The Street(take 2)(1)(hlp)   Trip TLP5800,Olympic(E)OL7122,DJM(E)DJML065,Jazz
                                          Bird(E)JAZ2012,Murray Hill S53968/5,Stash
                                          ST-CD530(CD)
      Uncle Sam Blues(take 1)(1)(hlp) Stash ST-CD530(CD)
      Uncle Sam Blues(take 2)(1)(hlp) Trip TLP5800,Olympic(E)OL7122,DJM(E)DJML065,Jazz
                                          Bird(E)JAZ2012,Foxy(I)9007/08,Stash ST-CD530
                                          (CD)
      Someone To Watch Over Me(lm)   Trip TLP5800,Olympic(E)OL7122,DJM(E)DJML065,Jazz
                                          Bird(E)JAZ2012,Stash ST-CD530(CD)
      The One I Love
        Belongs To Somebody Else(lm) Trip TLP5800,Olympic(E)OL7122,Jazz Bird(E)JAZ2012
                                          Vogue(F)DP35,Stash ST-CD530(CD)
      Wherever There's Love(2)   Design DLP47,DLP148,Pickwick Int.PR111,Gala GLP34
                                          Trip TLP5800,Jazz Club(F)1652.371,Olympic(E)
                                          OL7122,DJM(E)DJML065,Vogue(F)DP35,Allegro(E)
                                          ALL791,Everest 924730,Archive Of Folk&Jazz
                                          FS274,Music For Pleasure 165.237,Murray Hill
                                          S53958/5,Stash ST-CD530(CD)

-2.Poss. omit Hackett.

Note:Butterfield and Russell are not audible on all titles.

Add Benny Morton(tb).   Same date
      What's New(take 1)(incompl.)   Stash ST-CD530(CD)
      What's New(take 2)   Palm(E)P30-08,Stash ST-CD530(CD)
      Jada(take 1)   Stash ST-CD530(CD)
      Jada(take 2)   Design DLP47,Pickwick Int.PR111,Gala GLP342,Jazz
                                          Club(F)1652.371,Allegro(E)ALL791,Everest
                                          924730,Archive Of Folk&Jazz FS274,Murray Hil
                                          S53958/5,Stash ST-CD530(CD)
      Time On My Hands
        (take 1)(incompl.)   Stash ST-CD530(CD)(?)
      Time On My Hands
        (take 2)(incompl.)   Stash ST-CD530(CD)(?)
      Time On My Hands(take 3)   Palm(E)30-08,Stash ST-CD530(CD)
      Royal Garden Blues   Wax 105(E),Design DLP47,DLP148,DLP213,Pickwick
                                          Int. PR111,Gala GLP342,Jazz Club(F)1652.371
                                          Allegro(E)ALL791,Everest 924730,Archive Of
                                          Folk&Jazz FS274,Music For Pleasure 165.237,
                                          Murray Hill S53958/5,Stash ST-CD530(CD)
      Muskrat Ramble(1)   Stash ST-CD530(CD)

Note:Morton is not audible on all titles.
     The above titles are from Associated Program Service transcriptions No.A60598,
     A60634,A60635,A60645,A60802.

EDDIE CONDON JAM SESSION:
Max Kaminsky -1(tp),Hot Lips Page -2(tp,vcl),Bobby Hackett -3(cnt),Bill Harris(tb),Pee W
Russell(cl),Ernie Caceres(bars),Clyde Hart(p),Bob Haggart(b),Joe Grauso(dr),Liza Morrow
(vcl).   Live.Town Hall,NYC.June 10,1944
      Muskrat Ramble(1)   Jazum 25(ed.),72
      Mean To Me(3)   Jazum 72
      When My Sugar Walks Down
        The Street(2,3)(hlp)   Chiaroscuro CR113,(J)ULX54,Foxy(I)9007/08
(session cont. next page).

session cont. from previous page):
```
     Body And Soul(3)                   Jazum 72
     Jada(1,3)                              -
     Back In Your Own Back Yard(1)          -
     You Don't Know
        What Love Is(3)(lm)                 -
     Impromptu Ensemble
        (Ol' Miss)(1,2,3)                   -
```

ll titles also on Baybridge(J)UPS2255,Jazzology JCE1001/02,JCECD1001/02 (CD).
ote:The above titles are from the "Blue Network Show 4" (AFRS "Eddie Condon" transcrip-
     tion no. 2).
     "It's Been So Long" (on the same AFRS transcription) is from the June 3,1944 show.

DDIE CONDON JAM SESSION:
ot Lips Page -1(tp,vcl),Bobby Hackett -2(cnt),Bill Harris(tb),Pee Wee Russell(cl),Ernie
aceres(bars),Gene Schroeder(p),Bob Haggart(b),Joe Grauso(dr).
```
                                       Live.Town Hall,NYC.June 17,1944
     The Joint Is Jumpin'(1,2,3)(hlp) Pumpkin 117,Jazzology JCE1003/04,JCECD1003/04(CD)
     Squeeze Me(2)                     Jazzology JCE1003/04,JCECD1003/04(CD)
     Willow Tree(4)                           -            -      ,Storyville
                                       (D)SEP307,Tempo(E)EXA65
     Chocolate Bar(4,5)               Jazzology JCE1003/04,JCECD1003/04(CD),Storyville
                                       (D)SEP307,Tempo(E)EXA65
     I'm Crazy 'Bout My Baby(4)       Jazzology JCE1003/04,JCECD1003/04(CD),Storyville
                                       (D)SEP307,Tempo(E)EXA65
     Ain't Misbehavin'(2)             Jazzology JCE1003/04,JCECD1003/04(CD)
     Honeysuckle Rose(1,2)                    -            -
     If It Ain't Love(2)                      -            -
     Impromptu Ensemble (Ol' Miss/
        Buy Bonds Blues)(1,2,3)(hlp)          -            -
```

.Add James P. Johnson(p).
.James P. Johnson(p-solo).
.Erroneous announced as "Candied Sweets".

te:The above titles are from the "Blue Network Show 5" - they were prob. not recorded by
    AFRS.

DIE CONDON JAM SESSION:
x Kaminsky -1(tp),Hot Lips Page -2(tp,vcl),Bobby Hackett -3(cnt),Pee Wee Russell(cl),
nie Caceres(bars),Gene Schroeder(p),Eddie Condon -4(g),Bob Haggart(b),Joe Grauso(dr).
```
                                       Live.Town Hall,NYC.June 24,1944
     I Found A New Baby(1,4)          Jazum 4,Kings Of Jazz(I)KLJ20018,Good Music JJR1
     What Is There To Say(5)(p-solo)         -                      -
     St. Louis Blues(5)(p,dr only)           -                      -
     Chinatown My Chinatown(1,2)(hlp) Jazum 10
     Cherry(3)                               -,Rhapsody(E)RAL6028
     Jazz Me Blues(1)                 Jazum 4,Kings Of Jazz(I)KLJ20018
     Keepin' Out Of
        Mischief Now(1,2,3,6)(hlp)    Jazum 10
     Impromptu Ensemble
        (Ol' Miss)(1,2,3,7)                  -(ed.)
```

.Willie "The Lion" Smith(p) replaces Schroeder.
.Page (vcl) only.
.Add Willie "The Lion" Smith(p).

l titles also on Jazzology JCE1003/04,JCECD1003/04 (CD).
l titles - except "Impromptu Ensemble" - also on Baybridge(J)UPS2256.
:e:The above titles are from the "Blue Network Show 6" (AFRS "Eddie Condon" transcrip-
    tion no. 4).

EDDIE CONDON JAM SESSION:
Max Kaminsky -1(tp),Jonah Jones -2(tp,vcl),Bobby Hackett -3(cnt),Benny Morton -4(tb),Pee
Wee Russell,Joe Marsala -5(cl),Ernie Caceres(bars),Gene Schroeder(p),Sid Weiss(b),Gene
Krupa(dr).   Live.Town Hall,NYC.July 1,1944
    The Lady's In Love With You(3,6) Jazzology JCE1003/04,JCECD1003/04(CD)
    China Boy(1,3,4)   -   -
    Baby Won't You Please
      Come Home(1(?),2,3(?),4)(jj)   -   -
    Clarinet Chase(1,3,5,7)   -   -   ,Swaggie(Au)
                        JCS33776
    Pennies From Heaven(1,3,4)   Jazzology JCE1003/04,JCECD1003/04(CD)
    Impromptu Ensemble(1,2,3,4,5,8)   -   -   ,Baybridge
                      (J)Bonus E-1

-6.Add Eddie Condon(g).
-7.Caceres plays (cl).
-8.Add Willie "The Lion" Smith(p).

All titles - except "Baby Won't You Please Come Home" - also on Chiaroscuro CR108,(J)
ULX53,Storyville(D)SLP509.
Note:The above titles are from the "Blue Network Show 7" (AFRS "Eddie Condon" transcrip-
    tion no. 5).
    The title "Clarinet Chase" for the improvisation by the three clarinets was assigned
    later (for the Swaggie release).

EDDIE CONDON JAM SESSION:
Billy Butterfield -1(tp),Jonah Jones -2(tp,vcl),Bobby Hackett -3(cnt),Benny Morton(tnb),
Pee Wee Russell,Edmond Hall -4(cl),Ernie Caceres(bars),Gene Schroeder(p),Johnny Williams
(b),Joe Grauso(dr).   Live.Town Hall,NYC.July 8,1944
    Struttin' With Some Barbecue(3) Jazum 72,Swaggie(Au)JCS33776,Good Music JJ3,Bay-
                           bridge(J)Bonus E-1
    You Can Depend On Me(2,3)(jj)   Jazum 72
    High Society(4,5)   -,Baybridge(J)Bonus E-1
    Royal Garden Blues(1,4,5)   -,Swaggie(Au)JCS33776,Storyville(D)SEP506
    Singing' The Blues(1(?),3)   Jazum 26,Good Music JRR2
    Impromptu Ensemble(1,2,3,4)   Jazum 73

-5.Omit Russell,Caceres.

All titles also on Jazzology JCE1003/04,JCECD1003/04 (CD).
Note:The above titles are from the "Blue Network Show 8" (AFRS "Eddie Condon" transcrip-
    tion no. 6).
    "Royal Garden Blues" issued on SEP506 as by BILLY BUTTERFIELD'S DIXIELAND BAND.

EDDIE CONDON JAM SESSION:
Max Kaminsky -1(tp),Jonah Jones -2(tp,vcl),Bobby Hackett -3(cnt),Benny Morton(tb),Pee Wee
Russell(cl),Ernie Caceres(bars),Gene Schroeder(p),Bob Haggart(b),George Wettling(dr).
                                Live.Town Hall,NYC.July 15,1944
    That's A Plenty(1)   Jazum 52(ed.),Baybridge(J)UXP126
    I'm A Ding Dong
      Daddy From Dumas(1,2)(jj)   Jazum 73
    Echoes Of Spring(4)   -
    Polonaise(4)   -
    Caravan(5)   Jazum 11,Chiaroscuro CR113,(J)ULX54,Good Music
                         JRR1
    New Orleans(1,3)   Jazum 24
    Wolverine Blues(3)   Jazum 11(ed.),26,Swaggie(Au)JCS33776,Spook Jazz
                        SPJ6607(ed.),Gazell GJ1045
    Impromptu Ensemble(1,2,3)   Jazum 73
(session cont. next page).

session cont. from previous page):
4.Willie "The Lion" Smith(p-solo).
5.Edmond Hall(cl),p,b,dr only.
6.Add Edmond Hall(cl).

ll titles also on Jazzology JCE1005/06,JCECD1005/06 (CD),Baybridge(J)UPS2256.
ote:The above titles are from the "Blue Network Show 9" (AFRS "Eddie Condon" transcrip-
    tion no. 7).

DDIE CONDON JAM SESSION:
ax Kaminsky -1(tp),Sterling Bose -2(cnt),Benny Morton(tb),Pee Wee Russell(cl),Ernie Cace-
es(bars),Gene Schroeder(p),Bob Haggart(b),Gene Krupa -3,Joe Grauso -4(dr).
                                    Live.Town Hall,NYC.July 22,1944
        Fidgety Feet(2,3)   Jazum 10,Swaggie(Au)JCS33776,Storyville(D)SLP133,
                                        (J)ULS1564
        Oh Katharina(1,3)   Jazum 10,Rhapsody(E)RAL6028
        Davenport Blues(5)   -,Baybridge(J)Bonus E-1
        I'd Climb The Highest
           Mountain(4)(no tb,bars)   Jazum 24,Chiaroscuro CR108,(J)ULX53,Storyville(D)
                                        SLP509
        In A Mist(6)   Jazum 10
        Candelight(6)   Jazum 24
        Jazz Me Blues(1,2,4)   Jazum 10,Rhapsody(E)RAL6028

5.Carl Kress,Tony Mottola(g-duet).
5.Harry Gibson(p-solo).

.1 titles also on Jazzology JCE1005/06,JCECD1005/06 (CD),Rare Broadcast 479.
ote:The above titles are from the "Blue Network Show 10" (AFRS "Eddie Condon" transcrip-
    tion no. 8).

DIE CONDON JAM SESSION:
x Kaminsky(tp),Bobby Hackett -1(cnt),Benny Morton(tb),Pee Wee Russell,Edmond Hall -2
1),Ernie Caceres(bars),Gene Schroeder(p),Bob Haggart(b),Gene Krupa -3,Joe Grauso -4
r).   Live.Town Hall,NYC.July 29,1944
        Swing That Music(3)   Jazum 11,Radiola MR1042,Good Music JRR1
        Avalon(2,3,5)   -,Chiaroscuro CR113,(J)ULX54,Good Music
                                        JRR1
        Between The Devil And
           The Deep Blue Sea(6)   Jazum 11,Chiaroscuro CR113,(J)ULX54
        The Sneakaway(6)   -
        Big Boy(4)   -,Radiola MR1042,Good Music JRR2
        I Ain't Gonna Give Nobody
           None Of My Jelly Roll(4)   -,Spook Jazz(E)SPJ6607
        I'm Coming Virginia(1,2,4)   -,Good Music JJR1
        Impromptu Ensemble(1,2,4,7)   -

.Hall(cl),p,b,dr only.
.Willie "The Lion" Smith(p-solo).
.Add Willie "The Lion" Smith(p).

1 titles also on Jazzology JCE1005/06,JCECD1005/06 (CD).
te:The above titles are from the "Blue Network Show 11" (AFRS "Eddie Condon" transcrip-
    tion no. 10 - out of sequence!).

DIE CONDON JAM SESSION:
x Kaminsky(tp),Bobby Hackett -1(cnt),Benny Morton(tb),Pee Wee Russell,Edmond Hall -2,
1),Ernie Caceres(bars),Jess Stacy(p),unknown(b),Gene Krupa -3,Joe Grauso -4(dr),Lee
ley(vcl).   Live.Town Hall,NYC.August 5,1944
ession cont. next page).

(session cont. from previous page):

I Got Rhythm(3)	Jazum 26
Someone To Watch Over Me(3)(p,dr only)	Aircheck 26,Jazum 52
Lady Be Good(2,3,5)	- -
Summertime(1,2,4,6)	Jazum 52
I've Got A Crush On You(1,2,4,6)(lw)	Totem 1033,Jazum 52,Baybridge(J)UPS2280
Soon(1,4)	Jazum 52
Sweet And Lowdown (1,2(?),4,6)(lw)	Totem 1033,Jazum 52,Baybridge(J)UPS2280

-5.Hall(cl),p,b,dr only.
-6.Poss. omit Kaminsky.

All titles also on Jazzology JCE1005/06,JCECD1005/06 (CD).
Note:The above titles are from the "Blue Network Show 12" (AFRS "Eddie Condon" transcrip-
    tion no. 9 - with the number out of sequence!).

EDDIE CONDON JAM SESSION:
Muggsy Spanier -1,Bobby Hackett -2(cnt),Benny Morton(tb),Pee Wee Russell(cl),Ernie Caceres
(bars,cl),Gene Schroeder(p),Bob Haggart(b),Gene Krupa -3,Joe Grauso -4(dr),Lee Wiley(vcl).
                                         Live.Town Hall,NYC.August 12,1944

Everybody Loves My Baby(1,3)	Jazum 11,Spook Jazz(E)SPJ6607,Good Music JRR1, Gazell(Sd)GEP8
You're Lucky To Me(1,2,3)(lw)	Totem 1033,Jazum 11,Kings Of Jazz(I)KLJ20036,Dan (J)VC5020,Tono TJ6004,Baybridge(J)UPS2280
Limehouse Blues(3,5)	Jazum 11,Good Music JRR1,Baybridge(J)Bonus E-1
Just Before Daybreak(6)	Chiaruscuro CR113,(J)ULX54,Kings Of Jazz(I) KLJ20028,Storyville(D)SEP307,Tempo(E)EXA65
Caprice Rag(6)	Chiaruscuro CR113,(J)ULX54,Kings Of Jazz(I) KLJ20028,Storyville(D)SEP307,Tempo(E)EXA65
Black And Blue(1,4)	Jazum 24,Chiaroscuro CR108,(J)ULX53,Storyville(D) SLP133,SLP509,(J)ULS1564,Gazell(Sd)GEP8
Wherever There's Love(1,2,4)(lw)	Jazum 24,26,Baybridge(J)UPS2280
Impromptu Ensemble(1,2,4,7)	-

-5.Carceres(cl),p,b,dr only.
-6.James P. Johnson(p-solo).
-7.Add James P. Johnson(p).

All titles also on Jazzology JCE1007/08,JCECD1007/08 (CD).
Note:The above titles are from the "Blue Network Show 13" (AFRS "Eddie Condon" transcrip
    tion no. 11).

EDDIE CONDON JAM SESSION:
Billy Butterfield -1(tp),Bobby Hackett -2(cnt),Benny Morton(tb),Pee Wee Russell,Edmond
Hall -3(cl),Ernie Caceres(bars),Gene Schroeder(p),Bob Casey(b),Gene Krupa -4,Joe Grauso
(dr),Lee Wiley(vcl).   Live.Town Hall,NYC.August 19,1944

Clarinet Marmalade(2,4)	Jazum 24,Swaggie(Au)JCS33776,Storyville(D)SLP133 (J)ULS1564
On The Sunny Side Of The Street(1(?),2,4)(lw)	Totem 1033,Jazum 24,Kings Of Jazz(I)KJL20036,Dan (J)VC5020,Napoleon NLP11091,Baybridge(J) UPS2280,Tono TJ6004
Rose Room(3,4,6)	Chiaroscuro CR113,Kings Of Jazz(I)KJL20028,Story ville(D)SLP133,(J)ULS1564
I'll Follow You(7)	Chiaroscuro CR113,Kings Of Jazz(I)KJL20028
Here Comes The Band(7)	- -
Muskrat Ramble(1,5)	Jazum 24,Kings Of Jazz(I)KJL20028

(session cont. next page).

session cont. from previous page):

Sugar(1,2,5,8)(lw)	Totem 1033,Jazum 24,Kings Of Jazz(I)KJL20036,Dan (J)VC5020,Napoleon NLP11091,Baybridge(J)Bonus E-1,UPS2280,Tono TJ6004
Impromptu Ensemble(1,2,3,5,9)	Ciaroscuro CR113

6.Hall(cl),p,b,dr only.
7.Willie "The Lion" Smith(p-solo)
8.Omit Russell;Caceres plays (cl).
9.Add Willie "The Lion" Smith(p).

11 titles also on Jazzology JCE1007/08,JCECD1007/08 (CD).
11 titles on CR113 also on Chiaroscuro(J)ULX54.
ote:The above titles are from the "Blue Network Show 14" (AFRS "Eddie Condon" transcrip-
     tion no. 12).

ODIE CONDON JAM SESSION:
ax Kaminsky -1(tp),Bobby Hackett -2,Muggsy Spanier -3(cnt),Bill Harris(tb),Pee Wee Rus-
ell,Joe Marsala -4(cl),Ernie Caceres(bars,cl),Gene Schroeder(p),Bob Haggart(b),Gene Krupa
dr).   Live.Town Hall,NYC.August 26,1944

California,Here I Come(1)	Jazum 24
I Know That You Know(4,6)	-
Beale Street Blues(5)	Jazum 25
Dinah(3)	-,Baybridge(J)UXP126,Rhapsody(E)RAL6029
Clarinet Jam(1,4)	-
Soon(1,2)	-
Impromptu Ensemble(1,2,3,4,7)	-,Rhapsody(E)RAL6028

5.Art Hodes(p-solo).
5.Marsala(cl),p,b,dr only.
7.Poss. add Art Hodes(p).

11 titles also on Jazzology JCE1007/08,JCECD1007/08 (CD),Baybridge(J)UPS2257.
te:The above titles are from the "Blue Network Show 15" (AFRS "Eddie Condon" transcrip-
     tion no. 13).
     The title "Clarinet Jam" for the improvisation by the three clarinets was assigned
     later (for the Jazum release) - as "Clarinet Chase" on Jazzology issues.

ODIE CONDON JAM SESSION:
onah Jones -1(tp,vcl),Bobby Hackett -2(cnt),Miff Mole(tb),Pee Wee Russell,Edmond Hall -3
l),Ernie Caceres(bars),Gene Schroeder(p),Eddie Condon -4(g),Sid Weiss(b),Gene Krupa -5,
e Grauso -6(dr).   Live.Town Hall,NYC.September 2,1944

Walkin' The Dog(2,4,5)	Jazum 73,Jazzology JCE1007/08,JCECD1007/08(CD)
I Can't Give You Anything But Love(1,2,5)(jj)	- - -
	Good Music JRR1
The Sheik Of Araby(3,5,7)	Chiaroscuro CR113,Jazzology JCE1007/08, JCECD1007/08(CD)
Peg Of My Heart(2,6)	Jazum 73,Jazzology JCE1007/08,JCECD1007/08(CD)
There'll Be Some Changes Made(8)	Chiaroscuro CR113,Jazzology JCE1007/08, JCECD1007/08(CD)
Jada(2,6)	Jazum 73,Jazzology JCE1007/08,JCECD1007/08(CD)
Impromptu Ensemble(incompl.)(9)	Jazzology JCE1007/08,JCECD1007/08(CD)

.Hall(cl),p,b,dr only.
.Cliff Jackson(p-solo).
.Prob. played by the full band.

1 titles on CR113 also on Chiaroscuro(J)ULX54.
te:The above titles are from the "Blue Network Show 16" (AFRS "Eddie Condon" transcrip-
     tion no. 14).

EDDIE CONDON JAM SESSION:
Max Kaminsky -1,Billy Butterfield -2(tp),Muggsy Spanier -3(cnt),Miff Mole(tb),Pee Wee Rus-
sell(cl),Ernie Caceres(bars),Gene Schroeder(p),Bob Haggart(b),Gene Krupa -4,Joe Grauso -5
(dr).   Live.Town Hall,NYC.September 9,1944
        Love Nest(1,4)   Jazum 25,Spook Jazz(E)SPJ6607,Good Music JJR2,
                                         Rhapsody(E)RAL6028,Gazell GJ1015
        Big Noise From Winnetka(6)   Jazum 25,Good Music JJR2
        Big Butter And Egg Man(3,5)   -   -,Rhapsody(E)RAL6028,
                                         Baybridge(J)Bonus E-1
        The Blues By Pee Wee Russell(7) Chiaroscuro CR108,(J)ULX53,Storyville(D)SLP509
        Hebbie Jeebies(1,2,5)   Jazum 25,Gazell(Sd)GEP6
        Impromptu Ensemble(1,2,3,5,8)   -,Storyville(D)SLP133,(J)ULS1564

-6.Haggart(b,whistling),Krupa(dr) only.
-7.Russell(cl),p,b,Grauso(dr).
-8.Add Cliff Jackson(p).

All titles also on Jazzology JCE1009/10,JCECD1009/10 (CD),Radiola MR1042.
Note:The above titles are from the "Blue Network Show 17" (AFRS "Eddie Condon" transcrip-
    tion no. 15).
    "The Blues By Pee Wee Russell" issued as "Pee Wee Blues" on CR108.
    "Impromptu Ensemble" issued as "Presenting The Blues" on SLP133,ULS1564.

EDDIE CONDON AND HIS ORCHSTRA:
Muggsy Spanier(cnt),Miff Mole(tb),Pee Wee Russell(cl),Ernie Caceres(bars),Gene Schroeder
(p),Eddie Condon -1(g),Jack Lesberg(b),Gene Krupa(dr),Red McKenzie(vcl).
                                         Live.Town Hall,NYC.September 16,1944
        Rosetta(1)   Chiaroscuro CR108,(J)ULX53,Storyville(D)SLP509,
                                         Jazzology JCE1009/10,JCECD1009/10(CD)
        Memphis Blues   Chiaroscuro CR108,(J)ULX53,Storyville(D)SLP509,
                                         Jazzology JCE1009/10,JCECD1009/10(CD)
        There'll Be
            Some Changes Made(rmk)   Jazzology JCE1009/10,JCECD1009/10(CD)
        I Would Most Anything For You   Jazum 26,   -   -

Note:The above titles are from the "Blue Network Show 18" (AFRS "Eddie Condon" transcrip
    tion no. 16 - except "There'll Be Some Changes Made").

EDDIE CONDON JAM SESSION:
Max Kaminsky -1(tp),Bobby Hackett -2,Muggsy Spanier -3(cnt),Miff Mole(tb),Pee Wee Russel
Edmond Hall -4(cl),Ernie Caceres(bars,cl),Jess Stacy(p),Sid Weiss(b),Gene Krupa(dr),Red
McKenzie,Lee Wiley(vcl).   Live.Town Hall,NYC.September 23,1944
        That's A Plenty(1)   Jazum 78,Jazzology JCE1009/10,JCECD1009/10(CD)
        Sentimental Baby(1,2,5)(rmk)   -   -   -   -
        Euphonic Sounds(6)   -   -   -
        If Dreams Come True(6)   Pumpkin 117,Jazzology JCE1009/10,JCECD1009/10(CD
        Easter Parade(2)   Jazzology JCE1009/10,JCECD1009/10(CD)
        Untitled improvisation
            (bars,p,b,dr only)   Jazum 78,Jazzology JCE1009/10,JCECD1009/10(CD)
        Relaxin' At The Touro(3)   Jazum 52,78,   -   -
        Untitled improvisation(4)
            (cl,p,b,dr only)   Jazzology JCE1009/10,JCECD1009/10(CD)
        Poor As A Churchmouse(3)   Jazum 78,Jazzology JCE1009/10,JCECD1009/10(CD)
        Wherever There's Love(1,2)(lw)   -   -   -   -   ,
                                         Tono TJ6004
        Impromptu Ensemble(1,2,4(?),7)   Jazum 78,Jazzology JCE1009/10,JCECD1009/10(CD)

-5.Omit Russell.
-6.James P. Johnson(p-solo).
-7.Add James P. Johnson(p).
(session cont. next page).

(session cont. from previous page):
Note:The above titles are from the "Blue Network Show 19" (AFRS "Eddie Condon" transcrip-
     tion no. 17).
     "That's A Plenty" erroneously as "Muskrat Ramble" on Jazum 78.

EDDIE CONDON JAM SESSION:
Max Kaminsky -1(tp),Muggsy Spanier -2(cnt),Miff Mole(tb),Edmond Hall(cl),Ernie Caceres
(bars),Gene Schroeder(p),Sid Weiss(b),Cozy Cole(dr),Red McKenzie(vcl).
                                         Live.Town Hall,NYC.September 30,1944

At The Jazz Band Ball(2)	Jazum 52,Jazzology JCE1009/10,JCECD1009/10(CD)			
I Would Do Anything For You(2)(rmk)	Jazum 73,	-		-
Rosetta(2,3)	Aircheck 26,	-		-
I Want To Be Happy(1,4) (cl,p,b,dr only)	Chiaroscuro CR113,ULX54,	-		-
Keep Smiling At Trouble(1,4)	Jazzology JCE1009/10,JCECD1009/10(CD)			
Waiting For The Evening Mail(1,2,4)	Jazum 74,	-		-
Impromptu Ensemble (Bugle Call Rag)(1,2,5)	-	-		-

-3.Jess Stacy(p),Cole(dr) - except for the coda.
-4.Jess Stacy(p) replaces Schroeder.
-5.Add Jess Stacy(p).

Note:The above titles are from the "Blue Network Show 20" (AFRS "Eddie Condon" transcrip-
     tion no. 18).

EDDIE CONDON JAM SESSION:
Max Kaminsky -1(tp),Muggsy Spanier -2(cnt),Miff Mole(tb),Edmond Hall(cl),Ernie Caceres
(bars),Gene Schroeder(p),Jack Lesberg(b),Cozy Cole(dr),Lee Wiley(vcl).
                                         Live.Ritz Theatre,NYC.October 7,1944

At Sundown(1,3)	Jazum 37
Squeeze Me(1)	-,Baybridge(J)Bonus E-1
Concentratin'(4)(p-solo)	-
It's Been So Long(cl,p,b,dr only)	-,Good Music JJR2
Mandy Make Up Your Mind(2)	-
Someone To Watch Over Me(1,5(?))(lw)	-,Baybridge(J)UPS2280,Dan(J)VC5020
Impromptu Ensemble(1,2,3,6)	-

-3.Add Eddie Condon(g).
-4.Willie "The Lion" Smith(p) replaces Schroeder.
-5.Add Dick Cary(tp).
-6.Add Willie "The Lion" Smith(p).

All titles also on Jazzology JCE1011/12,JCECD1011/12 (CD).
Note:The above titles are from the "Blue Network Show 21" (AFRS "Eddie Condon" transcrip-
     tion no. 19).

EDDIE CONDON JAM SESSION:
Billy Butterfield -1,Max Kaminsky -2(tp),Benny Morton(tb),Pee Wee Russell(cl),Ernie
Caceres(bars),Gene Schroeder(p),Bob Casey(b),George Wettling(dr),Lee Wiley,Red McKenzie
-vcl).   Live.Ritz Theatre,NYC.October 14,1944

Muskrat Ramble(1)	Jazum 26,Good Music JJR2,Baybridge(J)UXP126
Sweet Lorraine(1,2)(rmk)	-
Sweet Georgia Brown(3) (p,b,dr only)	
Honeysuckle Rose(3,4) (cl,p,b,dr only)	-
Sugar(2)	-

(session cont. next page).

(session cont. from previous page):
```
        Don't Blame Me(2,3)(lw)          Jazum 26,Baybridge(J)UPS2280,Totem 1033
        Impromptu Ensemble(1,2,5,6)      -
```

-3.Jess Stacy(p) replaces Schroeder.
-4.Edmond Hall(cl) replaces Russell.
-5.Add Jess Stacy(p).
-6.Add Edmond Hall(cl).

All titles also on Jazzology JCE1011/12,JCECD1011/12 (CD).
All titles - except "Honeysuckle Rose" - also on Baybridge(J)UPS2257.
Note:The above titles are from the "Blue Network Show 22" (AFRS "Eddie Condon" transcrip-
     tion no. 20).
     "Honeysuckle Rose" is incomplete on AFRS transcription and Jazum 26.

EDDIE CONDON JAM SESSION:
Max Kaminsky -1,Billy Butterfield -2,Dick Cary -3(tp),Miff Mole(tb),Pee Wee Russell(cl),
Ernie Caceres(bars),Gene Schroeder(p),Bob Casey(b),Joe Grauso(dr),Red McKenzie,Lee Wiley
(vcl).   Live.Ritz Theatre,NYC.October 21,1944
```
        Royal Garden Blues(1)           Jazum 37,Baybridge(J)UXP126
        Little High Chairman(2,3)(rmk)  -
        Three Little Words(4,5)         Aircheck 26,Jazum 37
        Yesterdays(2)(tp,p,b,dr only)   Jazum 38
        Struttin' With Some Barbecue(2) Jazum 37,Storyville(D)SLP133,(J)ULS1564,Gazell(Sd)
                                        GEP7,Good Music JRR3,Baybridge(J)UXP126
        Old Folks(2,3,4)                Jazum 38,Baybridge(J)UPS2280,Dan(J)VC5020
        Impromptu Ensemble(1,2,6)       -
```

-4.Jess Stacy(p) replaces Schroeder.
-5.Caceres(cl),p,b,dr only.
-6.Add Jess Stacy(p).

All titles also on Jazzology JCE1011/12,JCECD1011/12 (CD),Baybridge(J)UPS2258.
Note:The above titles are from the "Blue Network Show 23" (AFRS "Eddie Condon" transcrip-
     tion no. 21).

EDDIE CONDON'S JAZZ CONCERT ORCHESTRA:
Billy Butterfield(tp),Edmond Hall(cl),Ernie Caceres(bars),Jess Stacy(p),Eddie Condon(g),
Bob Haggart(b),George Wettling(dr).   NYC.October 24,1944
```
        It's Been So Long
          (take 1)(incompl)(1)          Stash ST-CD530(CD)
        It's Been So Long(take 2)(1)    Stash ST-CD530(CD),Design DLP47,Gala GLP342,Palm
                                           (E)P30-08,Palm Club(F)1652.371,Archives Of
                                           Folk&Jazz FS274
        The Man I Love
          (take 1)(incompl.)(1)         Stash ST-CD530(CD)
        The Man I Love(take 2)(1)       -          ,Palm(E)P30-08
        S'Wonderful(take 1)(incompl.)   -
        S'Wonderful(take 2)(incompl.)   -
        S'Wonderful(take 3)             -
```

-1.Hall(cl),p,b,dr only.

Add Lou McGarity(tb).   Same date
```
        Just You,Just Me                Stash ST-CD530(CD)
```

Add Max Kaminsky(tp),Pee Wee Russell -2(cl),Lee Wiley(vcl);omit Hall.
                                        Same date
```
        Old Folks(take 1)(incompl.)(lw) Stash ST-CD530(CD)
        Old Folks(take 2)(lw)           -          ,Palm(E)P30-08,Tono TJ6004
        You're Lucky To Me(2)(lw)       -          -              -
```

Max Kaminsky -1(tp),Muggsy Spanier -2(cnt),Lou McGarity(tb),Pee Wee Russell(cl),Ernie
Caceres -3(bars),Jess Stacy(p),Eddie Condon(g),Bob Haggart(b),George Wettling(dr).
                                              Same date
      I Want A Big Butter And
         Egg Man(take 1)(incompl.)(2)
      I Want A Big Butter And
         Egg Man(take 2)(incompl.)(2)
      I Want A Big Butter And
         Egg Man(take 3)(incompl.)(2)
      I Want A Big Butter And
         Egg Man(take 4)(2)
      Carnegie Leap(take 1)
         (incompl.)(1,2,4)
      Carnegie Leap(take 2)(1,2,4)   Wax 105,Palm(E)P30-08
      At Sundown(1,3)
      Sugar(take 1)(incompl.)(1)
      Sugar(take 2)(1)   Design DLP47,Gala GLP342,Palm(E)P30-08
      Muggsy's Serenade
         (take 1)(incompl.)(1,2,3,5)
      Muggsy's Serenade
         (take 2)(1,2,3,5)   Palm(E)P30-08

-4.Add Edmond Hall(cl)
-5.Add Billy Butterfield(tp).

Omit Spanier,Russell;Caceres plays (cl).   Same date
      Back In Your Backyard
         (take 1)(prob. incompl.)(1)
      Back In Your Backyard(take 2)(1) Design DLP47,DLP213,Gala GLP342,Palm(E)30-08
      If I Had You(1)   Palm(E)P30-08
      Indiana(1)   Design DLP47,DLP148,DLP213,Gala GLP342,Palm(E)
                                         P30-08,Palm Club(F)1652.371,Pickwick Int.
                                         PR111

Note:The above titles are from Associated Program Service transcriptions No.A60634,
      A60635,A60636,A60645,A60802.

EDDIE CONDON JAM SESSION:
Max Kaminsky,Dick Cary -1(tp),Lou McGarity(tb),Pee Wee Russell(cl),Ernie Caceres(bars),
Jess Stacy(p),Sid Weiss(b),George Wettling(dr),Red McKenzie(vcl).
                                       Live.Ritz Theatre,NYC.October 28,1944
      Sweet Georgia Brown   Jazum 52,Jazzology JCE1011/12,JCECD1011/12(CD)
      I Ain't Gonna Give
         Nobody None Of My Jelly Roll Chiaroscuro CR108,(J)ULX53,Storyville(D)SLP509,
                                         Spook Jazz(E)SPJ6607,Jazzology JCE1011/12,
                                         JCECD1011/12(CD)

      Keepin' Out Of
         Mischief Now(p,b,dr only)   Jazum 52,Jazzology JCE1011/12,JCECD1011/12(CD)
      Wolverine Blues(2)   Jazzology JCE1011/12,JCECD1011/12(CD)
      'S Wonderful(3)   I.A.J.R.C. 36,Jazzology JCE1011/12,JCECD1011/12
                                         (CD)
      It's The Talk
         Of The Town(1,4)(rmk)   Jazzology JCE1011/12,JCECD1011/12(CD)
      Impromptu Ensemble(1,5)   I.A.J.R.C. 38,Jazzology JCE1011/12,JCECD1011/12
                                         (CD)

-2.Joe Marsala(cl),b,dr only.
-3.Omit Russell;Caceres plays (cl).
-4.Poss. omit Russell.
-5.Add Joe Marsala(cl).

Note:The above titles are from the "Blue Network Show 24" (prob. no AFRS "Eddie Condon"
      transcription exists from this show).

EDDIE CONDON JAM SESSION:
Billy Butterfield -1,Dick Cary -2(tp),Muggsy Spanier -3(cnt),Lou McGarity(tb),Pee Wee
Russell(cl),Ernie Caceres(bars,cl),Gene Schroeder -4,Jess Stacy -5(p),Bob Casey(b),George
Wettling(dr),Lee Wiley,Red McKenzie(vcl).   Live.Ritz Theatre,NYC.November 4,1944
```
        My Blue Heaven(1,4)              Rarities(E)44,Jazum 53
        Through A Veil Of
           Indifference(1,2,4,6)(rmk)         -
        After You've Gone(5)(p,b,dr only)      -
        Untitled improvisation(5)
           (cl,p,b,dr only)             Chiaroscuro CR108,(J)ULX53,Storyville(D)SLP509,
                                          Rarities(E)44
        Riverside Blues(1,3,4)           Rarities(E)44
        Wherever There's
           Love(1,2,5)(lw)               Jazum 63,Rarities(E)44,Tono TJ6004
        Impromptu Ensemble(1,2,3,4,5)    Rarities(E)44
```
-6.Poss. omit Russell.

All titles also on Jazzology JCE1013/14,JCECD1013/14 (CD).
Note:The above titles are from the "Blue Network Show 25" (AFRS "Eddie Condon" transcrip-
     tion no. 23).
     "Untitled Improvisation" issued as "Pee Wee's Town Hall Stomp" and "Pee Wee Origi-
     nal".

EDDIE CONDON JAM SESSION:
Max Kaminsky(tp),Pee Wee Russell(cl),Ernie Caceres(bars),Jess Stacy(p),Bob Casey(b),Joe
Grauso(dr).   Live.Ritz Theatre,NYC.November 11,1944
```
        Easter Parade               Jazzology JCE1013/14,JCECD1013/14(CD)
        Cherry(1)                   Aircheck 26,      -            -
        Someday Sweetheart          Jazzology JCE1013/14,JCECD1013/14(CD)
        Impromptu Ensemble              -            -
```
-1.Caceres(cl),p,b,dr only.

Note:The above titles are from the "Blue Network Show 26" (prob. no AFRS "Eddie Condon"
     transcription exists).

EDDIE CONDON JAM SESSION:
Billy Butterfield(tp),Lou McGarity(tb),Pee Wee Russell(cl),Ernie Caceres(bars),Jess Stacy
(p),Bob Casey(b),George Wettling(dr).   Live.Ritz Theatre,NYC.November 18,1944
```
        'Way Down Yonder In New Orleans  Jazum 74
        Three Little Words(p,b,dr only)      -
        Song Of The Wanderer                 -
        Impromptu Ensemble                   -
```
All titles also on Jazzology JCE1013/14,JCECD1013/14 (CD).
Note:The above titles are from the "Blue Network Show 27" (prob. no AFRS "Eddie Condon"
     transcription exists).

EDDIE CONDON JAM SESSION:
Billy Butterfield -1,Dick Cary -2(tp),Muggsy Spanier -3(cnt),Lou McGarity(tb),Pee Wee
Russell(cl),Ernie Caceres(bars),Jess Stacy(p),Bob Casey(b),Johnny Blowers(dr),Lee Wiley
(vcl).   Live.Ritz Theatre,NYC.November 25,1944
```
        September In The Rain(1)    Jazum 38,Rhapsody(E)RAL6028
        I Got Rhythm(4)                 -
        I've (Never) Been
           Around(bars,p,b,dr only)     -
        The Lady's In Love With You(3)  -
        Old Folks(1,2)(lw)              -
```
(session cont. next page).

(session cont. from previous page):
    Medley(1,2,3,5):   Chiaroscuro CR113,(J)ULX54,Foxy 9007/08
        Impromtu Ensemble
        Uncle Sam Blues(hlp)
        Ol' Miss

-4.Jimmy Dorsey(cl),p,b,dr only.
-5.Add Hot Lips Page(tp,vcl).

All titles also on Jazzology JCE1013/14,JCECD1013/14 (CD).
Note:The above titles are from the "Blue Network Show 28" (AFRS "Eddie Condon" transcrip-
    tion no. 26).

EDDIE CONDON JAM SESSION:
Max Kaminsky -1(tp),Wingy Manone -2(tp,vcl),Bobby Hackett -3(cnt),Jack Teagarden(tb,vcl),
Pee Wee Russell(cl),Ernie Caceres(bars),Cliff Jackson(p),Jack Lesberg(b),George Wettling
(dr).   Live.Ritz Theatre,NYC.December 2,1944
        Teaser (Makin' Friends)
          (tb,p,b,dr only)   Pumpkin 106
        I Found A New Baby(1)   - ,Baybridge(J)UPS2258,UXP126,Good Music
                                        JJR3
        Little Rock Get-A-Way(1,4)   Pumpkin 106,   -
        Memories Of You(1,4)   Jazum 74,Stash ST109
        The Sheik Of Araby(2)   Pumpkin 106,Baybridge(J)UPS2258
        Baby,Won't You
          Please Come Home(1)(jt)   -   - ,UXP126
        Impromptu Ensemble
          (1,2,3,5)(wm,jt)   -   -

-4.Norma Teagarden(p) replaces Jackson.
-5.Add Norma Teagarden(p).

All titles also on Jazzology JCE1013/14,JCECD1013/14 (CD).
Note:The above titles are from the "Blue Network Show 29" (AFRS "Eddie Condon" transcrip-
    tion no. 26).
    "Impromptu Ensemble" as "Big T And Wingy Blues" on Pumpkin 106.

McKENZIE - CONDON CHICAGOANS:
Red McKenzie(vcl) acc. by Max Kaminsky(tp),Jack Teagarden(tb),Pee Wee Russell(cl),Gene
Schroeder(p),Eddie Condon(g),Bob Casey(b),Joe Grauso(dr).
                             NYC.December 8,1944
N2914-1 Ida,Sweet As
        Apple Cider(incompl.)   Jazzology J110
N2914-2 Ida,Sweet As Apple Cider   -
N2914-3 Ida,Sweet As Apple Cider   -
N2914-4 Ida,Sweet As Apple Cider   -
N2915-1 I Would Do Anything
        For You(incompl.)   -
N2915-2 I Would Do Anything
        For You(incompl.)   -
N2915-3 I Would Do Anything
        For You(incompl.)   -
N2915-4 I Would Do Anything
        For You(incompl.)   -
N2915-5 I Would Do Anything For You -
N2916-1 I've Got The World On A String -
N2916-2 I've Got The World On A String -
N2917-1 Exactly Like You   -
(session cont. next page).

(session cont. from previous page):
```
N2918-1 Basin Street Blues               Jazzology J110
N2918-2 Basin Street Blues(incompl.)            -
N2918-3 Basin Street Blues                      -
N2919-1 Baby Won't You Please Come Home         -
N2919-2 Baby Won't You Please Come Home         -
N2920-1 Sweet Lorraine(incompl.)                -
N2920-2 Sweet Lorraine(incompl.)                -
N2920-3 Sweet Lorraine                          -
N2920-4 Sweet Lorraine                          -
N2921-1 Dinah(incompl.)(no vcl)                 -
N2921-2 Dinah                                   -
N2922-1 After You've Gone(incompl.)             -
N2922-2 After You've Gone(incompl.)             -
N2922-3 After You've Gone                       -
N2923-1 'Way Down Yonder In New Orleans         -
N2923-2 'Way Down Yonder In New Orleans         -
N2923-3 'Way Down Yonder In
        New Orleans(incompl.)                   -
N2923-4 'Way Down Yonder In
        New Orleans(incompl.)                   -
N2923-5 'Way Down Yonder In New Orleans         -
```

Note:There was no Eddie Condon "Blue Network Show" on December 9,1944.

EDDIE CONDON AND HIS ORCHESTRA:
Billy Butterfield,Max Kaminsky(tp),Bobby Hackett(cnt),Jack Teagarden(tb,vcl),Pee Wee
Russell(cl),Ernie Caceres(bars),Gene Schroeder(p),Eddie Condon(g,vcl),Bob Haggart(b),
George Wettling(dr),Lee Wiley(vcl).   NYC.December 12,1944

```
W72619-A When Your Lover Has Gone(1)    Decca 23393,27471 (A836),91776 (ED413),9-27471
                                          (9-216),DL5195,DL8282,(J)JDL6013,AL12044,
                                          (Sd)BML8549,Brunswick(E)O4303,LA8549,MCA
                                          MCA2-4071,Franklin Mint 48
W72620-A Wherever There's Love(1)(lw)   Decca 23393,27471 (A836),91776 (ED413),9-27471
                                          (9-216),DL5195,DL8282,(J)AL12044,(Sd)BML8549,
                                          Brunswick(E)O4303,O4988,LA8549,MCA(J)MCA3160,
                                          Tono TJ6004
W72621-A Impromptu Ensemble(jt)         Decca 23718 (A490),91527 (ED722),91712 (ED843),
                                          DL5203(?),DL5218,DL8244,DL8281,(J)JDL2060,
                                          JDL6037,(Sw)M30464,(Sd)BKL8124,BML8577,
                                          Brunswick(E)LA8577,LAT8124,(F/G)LPBM87003/08,
                                          MCA BA212,MCA2-4071,(F)510.206,(J)MCA3019,
                                          MCA3061,Ace Of Hearts(E)AH100,Affinity(E)
                                          AFS1021,Tono TJ6004,Festival(Au)CFR10-521
W72622-A The Man I Love(2)(lw)          Decca 23432 (A398),91051 (ED539),DL5137,DL8304,
                                          DL(7)9234,DXF140,DXSF7140,(Sd)BML8518,(J)
                                          JDL7,Brunswick(E)LA8518,MCA(J)MCA3019,
                                          MCA3160,CID(F)233043,Tono TJ6004
W72623-A 'S Wonderful(3)                Decca 23430 (A398),91050 (ED539),DL5137,DL(7)9234,
                                          (Sd)BML8518,(J)JDL7,Brunswick(E)O4304,LA8518,
                                          MCA(J)MCA3019,CID(F)233043
```

-1.Omit Russell.
-2.Hackett poss. plays (tp).
-3.Omit Kaminsky,Hackett.

All titles also on MCA(J)MCA3100 (part of 3xLP set).

Same.		NYC.December 14,1944
N2944-1	Jam Session Jump(incompl.)	Jazzology J101/2
N2944-2	Jam Session Jump	-
N2944-3	Jam Session Jump	Jazum 78, -
N2945-1	Jam Session Blues(incompl.)	-
N2945-2	Jam Session Blues	-
N2945-3	Jam Session Blues	-
N2945-4	Jam Session Blues	-
N2946	Someone To Watch	
	Over Me (W72630)(lw)	Decca 23422 (A398),91051 (ED539),DL5137,DL(7)9234,
		(J)JDL7,(Sd)BML8518,Brunswick(E)LA8518,MCA(J)
		MCA3005,MCA3019,MCA3160,CID(F) 233043,Tono
		TJ6004,Jazzology J101/2
N2947	The Sheik Of Araby	
	(W72631)(jt,ec)	Decca 23718 (A490),91527 (ED722),DL450,DL5203,
		DL5218,DL8281,DL8304,(Sw)M30464,(J)JDL2060,
		JDL2066,JDL5082,JDL6037,JDL6077,(Sd)BKL8229,
		BML8577,Brunswick(E)LA8577,LAT8229,MCA BA227,
		(F)510.206,(J)3019,MCA-Coral(G)COPS3442,
		6.21851,Ace Of Hearts(E)AH28,Affinity(E)
		AFS1021,Festival(Au)CFR10-521,Jazzology
		J101/2
N2948	The Man I Love (W72632)(lw)	Jazzology J101/2
N2949	Somebody Loves Me (W72633)(jt)	Decca 23430 (A398),91050 (ED539),DL4540,DL5137,
		DL4540,DL8304,DL8400 (DXSF7140),DL(7)9234,
		DL78383/6,(J)JDL7,JDL5082,JDL6025,JDL6077,
		(Sd)BKL8168,BKL8229,BML8518,(Arg)XLTM9260/63,
		Brunswick(E)04305,LA8518,LAT8168,LAT8229,
		(F/G)87016,(Du)349500DXY,MCA BA227,MCA2-4062,
		(F)510.206,MCA-Coral(G)COPS3274,COPS3442,
		6.21851,(I)ORL8166,Ace Of Hearts(E)AH28,Fonit
		(I)DL8400,Festival(Au)FAL3,CID(F)233.043,
		Jazzology J101/2

Masters N2946-49 also on MCA(J)MCA3100 (part of 3xLP set).

Note:The above titles were rec. and issued by World Transcriptions No.JS42B,JS43A,JS358.
    Decca masternumbers for masters N2946-49 are listed in parenthesis.
    It has not been confirmed that master N2948 ("The Man I Love") was ever issued by
    Decca (etc.).

EDDIE CONDON JAM SESSION:
Billy Butterfield -1,Max Kaminsky -2(tp),Bobby Hackett -3(cnt),Jack Teagarden(tb,vcl),Pee
Wee Russell(cl),Ernie Caceres(bars),Gene Schroeder(p),Sid Weiss(b),Johnny Blowers(dr),Lee
Wiley,Eddie Condon(vcl).   Live.Ritz Theatre,NYC.December 16,1944

Ballin' The Jack(2)	Pumpkin 106,Baybridge(J)UPS2259
The Sheik Of Araby(2)(jt,ec)	- -
China Boy(4)(ss,p,b,dr only)	Baybridge(J)UPS2259
There's A Small Hotel(2,3,5)	-
Royal Garden Blues(1)	Pumpkin 106, -
Wherever There's	
Love(1(?),3,5)(lw)	- - ,Dan(J)VC5020
Impromptu Ensemble(1,2,3,4,5)	- -

-4.Add Sidney Bechet(ss).
-5.Poss. add Dick Cary(tp).

All titles also planned for issue on Jazzology JCE1015/16,JCECD1015/16 (CD).
Note:The above titles are from the "Blue Network Show 30" (AFRS "Eddie Condon" transcrip-
    tion no. 28).

EDDIE CONDON JAM SESSION:
Max Kaminsky -1(tp),Wingy Manone -2(tp,vcl),Bobby Hackett -3(cnt),Pee Wee Russell(cl),
Ernie Caceres(bars),Jess Stacy(p),Bob Casey(b),George Wettling(dr),Lee Wiley(vcl).
Live.Ritz Theatre,NYC.December 23,1944

Jingle Bells(1,2(?))(no bars)	Jazzology JCE1015/16,JCECD1015/16(CD)
On The Sunny Side Of The	
Street(1,2)(no bars)(wm)	Jazum 74,Jazzology JCE1015/16,JCECD1015/16(CD)
D.A. Blues(cl,p,b,dr only)	Aircheck 26,Chiaroscuro CR108,(J)ULX53,Storyville
	(D)SLP509,Jazzology JCE1015/16,JCECD1015/16
	(CD)
Blue Skies(1,2)(no bars)	Jazum 74,Jazzology JCE1015/16,JCECD1015/16(CD)
Rosetta(p,b,dr only)	- - -
Exactly Like You(1(?),2,3,4)	-,Baybridge(J)Bonus E-1,Jazzol. JCE1015/16,
	JCECD1015/16(CD)
Jada(1,3)	Jazum 74,Jazzology JCE1015/16,JCECD1015/16(CD)
You're Lucky To Me(1(?),3)(lw)	- - -
Impromptu Ensemble	
(1,2,3(?),5)(incompl.)	Jazzology JCE1015/16,JCECD1015/16(CD)

-4.Gene Schroeder(p) replaces Stacy.
-5.Add Gene Schroeder(p).

Note:The above titles are from the "Blue Network Show 31" (AFRS "Eddie Condon" transcrip-
    tion no. 29).
    Jazzology JCE1015/16,JCECD1015/16(CD) are planned for issue.

EDDIE CONDON JAM SESSION:
Max Kaminsky(tp),Benny Morton(tb),Pee Wee Russell(cl),Ernie Caceres(bars),Jess Stacy(p),
Jack Lesberg(b),George Wettling(dr),Lee Wiley(vcl).
Live.Ritz Theatre,NYC.December 30,1944

Walkin' The Dog	Jazum 53,Good Music JJR3,Rhapsody(E)RAL6028
I Ain't Got Nobody(p,b,dr only)	- -
Strut Miss Lizzie	-,Rhapsody(E)RAL6029
I Know That You Know(1)	
(ss,p,b,dr only)	-,Good Music JJR3
Sweet Georgia Brown	-,65,Good Music JJR3,FDC(I)1012,Musidisc(F)
	CCV2522(?)
When Your Lover Has Gone(lw)	Jazum 53,Good Music JJR2,Totem 1033,Baybridge(J)
	UPS2280
Impromptu Ensemble(1)	Jazum 53,64(?)

-1.Add Sidney Bechet(ss).

All titles also on Baybridge(J)UPS2259.
All titles planned for issue on Jazzology JCE1015/16,JCECD1015/16 (CD).
Note:The above titles are from the "Blue Network Show 32" (AFRS "Eddie Condon" transcrip-
    tion no. 30).

EDDIE CONDON AND HIS ORCHESTRA:
Max Kaminsky(tp),Miff Mole(tb),Pee Wee Russell(cl),Ernie Caceres(bars),Jess Stacy(p),Eddie
Condon(g),unknown b,dr,Lee Wiley(vcl).   NYC.Late 1944

Easter Parade	Jazum 66
Old Folks(lw)	
Rosetta(p,g,b,dr only)	Jazum 66
On The Sunny Side	
Of The Street(lw)	
On The Sunny Side	
Of The Street (reprise)	
'S Wonderful	Jazum 66
Someone To Watch Over Me	
Lady Be Good(1)	

(session cont. next page).

(session cont. from previous page):
      Somebody Loves Me(lw)   Jazum 66
      Somebody Loves Me (reprise)   -

-1.Edmond Hall(cl),p,g,b,dr only.

Note:The above titles are from the auditions for two Chesterfield Cigarettes radio pro-
     grams; later (1945) these programs were edited and combined to one program.

EDDIE CONDON AND HIS ORCHESTRA:
Max Kaminsky(tp),Miff Mole(tb),Pee Wee Russell(cl),Cliff Jackson,unknown(p),Eddie Condon
(g),Pops Foster,unknown(b),George Wettling,unknown(dr),Lee Wiley(vcl).
                                    Live(?).Town Hall,NYC.Late 1944
        Dear Old Southland
        Peg O' My Heart

Note:The above titles are from Columbia transcription No.13.

Max Kaminsky(tp),Miff Mole(tb),Pee Wee Russell(cl),James P. Johnson(p),Eddie Condon(g),
Pops Foster(b),George Wetling,poss. Sidney Catlett -1(dr).
                                  Live(?).Town Hall,NYC.Late 1944
        Indiana
        Finger That Bass

Note:The above titles are from Voice Of America transcription.

Max Kaminsky(tp),Rex Stewart(cnt),Miff Mole(tb),Pee Wee Russell(cl),prob. Joe Bushkin(p),
prob. Eddie Condon(g),unknown b,dr.   Live.NYC.Late 1944
        The World Is
          'Waiting For The Sunrise
        I'm Confessin'
        Cherry

Note:The above titles are from Voice Of America "Notes On Jazz" transcriptions No.13,16.
     "Cherry" as "September In The Rain" on No.13 and "Improvisation - Cherie" on No.16.

Max Kaminsky(tp),poss. Rex Stewart(cnt),prob. Benny Morton(tb),Pee Wee Russell(cl),Ernie
Caceres -1(bars),Jess Stacy -1,poss. Joe Bushin -2(p),Eddie Condon(g),unknown(b),George
Wettling -1,Zutty Singleton -2(dr).   Live.NYC.c. 1944/45
        Squeeze Me(1)
        I Found A New Baby(2)

Note:The above titles are from Voice Of America "Notes On Jazz" transcription No.16.

Max Kaminsky(tp),Benny Morton(tb),Pee Wee Russell(cl),poss. Gene Schroeder(p),Eddie
Condon(g),unknown(b),poss. Dave Tough(dr).   NYC.c. 1944/45
        I Got Rhythm
        It's Been So Long(1)
        Stardust

1.Edmond Hall(cl),poss. Jess Stacy(p),b,dr.

Note:The above titles are from Voice Of America "Notes On Jazz" transcription No.18.

EDDIE CONDON JAM SESSION:
Billy Butterfield -1,Max Kaminsky -2,Dick Cary -3(tp),Tommy Dorsey(tb),Pee Wee Russell
(cl),Ernie Caceres(bars),Jess Stacy(p),Sid Weiss(b),George Wettling(dr),Lee Wiley,Jack
Eberle(vcl).   Live.Ritz Theatre,NYC.January 6,1945
(session cont. next page).

(session cont. from previous page):
```
      Sunday(1,4)                      Rarities(E)37,Gazell(Sd)GEP5
      How Come You Do Me
         Like You Do-Do-Do(1)             -              -,Good Music JJR3
      Every Night(1,3,5)(je)              -
      Keep Smiling At Trouble(2)          - ,Spook Jazz(E)SPJ6607
      That's A Plenty(1,2)                - ,Good Music JJR3
      Sugar(1,3)(lw)                   Memories Lightest LWIL403,Rarities(E)37,Good Music
                                          JJR3
      Impromptu Ensemble(1,2,3(?),6)   Chiaroscuro CR108,(J)ULX53,Rarities(E)37,Story-
                                          ville(D)SLP509,Good Music JJR3
```

-4.Add Eddie Condon(g).
-5.Omit Russell;Caceres plays (bars,cl).
-6.As "Why Is Leonard So Modest".

All titles also on Baybridge(J)UPS2260.
All titles planned for issue on Jazzology JCE1015/16,JCECD1015/16 (CD).
Note:The above titles are from the "Blue Network Show 33" (AFRS "Eddie Condon" transcrip-
     tion no. 31).
     Memories Lightest LWIL403 is record no. 178 in the Nostalgia Greats series.

EDDIE CONDON JAM SESSION:
Billy Butterfield -1,Dick Cary -2(tp),Muggsy Spanier -3(cnt),Tommy Dorsey(tb),Pee Wee
Russell(cl),Ernie Caceres(bars),Jess Stacy(p),Sid Weiss(b),George Wettling(dr),Lee Wiley
(vcl).   Live.Ritz Theatre,NYC.January 13,1945
```
      September In The Rain(1)         Rarities(E)37,Good Music JJR3
      Body And Soul(tb,p,b,dr only)       -,44,          -
      Rose Room(1,3)                      -,Baybridge(J)UXP126,Gazell GJ1044(ed
      A Monday Date(4)                 Chiaroscuro CR113,(J)ULX54,Rarities(E)37,Good
                                          Music JJR3
      At The Jazz Band Ball(1,3)       Rarities(E)37,Spook Jazz(E)SPJ6603,Storyville(D)
                                          SEP506,Good Music JJR3,Saga(E)PAN6917,Joker
                                          (I)SM3575,Gazell GJ1048
      How Long Has This
         Been Going On(1,2,6)(lw)      Totem 1033,Rarities(E)37,Dan(J)VC5020
      Impromptu Ensemble(1,2(?),3,5,7) Rarities(E)37
```

-4.Earl Hines(p),Wettling(dr) only.
-5.Add Earl Hines(p).
-6.Poss. omit Dorsey,Russell.
-7.As "What Makes Leonard So Modest" or "Muggsy's Serenade".

All titles also on Baybridge(J)UPS2260.
All titles - except "A Monday Date" - also on Sunbeam SB231.
All titles planned for issue on Jazzology JCE1017/18,JCECD1017/18 (CD).
Note:The above titles are from the "Blue Network Show 34" (AFRS "Eddie Condon" transcrip-
     tion no. 32).
     "At The Jazz Band Ball" issued on SEP506 as by MUGGSY SPANIER'S DIXIELAND BAND.

EDDIE CONDON JAM SESSION:
Max Kaminsky -1(tp),Wild Bill Davison -2(cnt),Tommy Dorsey(tb),Pee Wee Russell(cl),Ernie
Caceres(bars),Jess Stacy(p),Sid Weiss(b),George Wettling(dr),Lee Wiley(vcl).
                                         NYC.January 20,1945
```
      Jazz Me Blues(2)
      Smoke Gets In Your
         Eyes(tb,p,b,dr only)
      At Sundown(1)
      Rosetta(3)(p,b,dr only)
```
(session cont. next page).

session cont. from previous page):
      Dear Old
         Southland(4)(ss,p,b,dr only) Chiaroscuro CR113,(J)ULX54
      The Sheik Of Araby(2,3,4(?))
      Don't Blame Me(1)(lw)
      Impromptu Ensemble(1,2,4,5)

3.Earl Hines(p) replaces Stacy; full band at coda.
4.Add Sidney Bechet(ss).
5.Add Earl Hines(p).

11 titles planned for issue on Jazzology JCE1017/18,JCECD1017/18 (CD).
ote:The above titles are from the "Blue Network Show 35" (no AFRS "Eddie Condon" trans-
    cription exists).

DDIE CONDON JAM SESSION:
ax Kaminsky -1,Billy Butterfield -2,Dick Cary -3(tp),Lou McGarity(tb),Joe Marsala(cl),
rnie Caceres(bars,cl),Gene Schroeder(p),Sid Weiss(b),George Wettling(dr),Red McKenzie,
ee Wiley(vcl).   Live.Ritz Theatre,NYC.January 27,1945
      St. Louis Blues(1)   Joyce LP1035,Baybridge(J)Bonus E-1
      (Al Jarvis guest spot)
      Blues improvisation(2,4,5)(wh)   Joyce LP1035,Baybridge(J)Bonus E-1,Good Music
                                         JJR2
      Indiana(2)   Joyce LP1035,Storyville(D)SLP133,(J)ULS1564
      It's The Talk Of
         The Town(2,3)(rmk)   -
      Back In Your Backyard(1)   Jazum 75
      Ghost Of A Chance(2,3)(lw)   Totem 1033,Jazum 75,Memories Lightest LWIL403,Dan
                                     (J)VC5020
      Impromptu Ensemble(1,2,3(?),4) Jazum 75

4.Add Woody Herman(cl,vcl).
5.Untitled but issued as "Blues 'Round My Head" on Joyce LP1035.

11 titles planned for issue on Jazzology JCE1017/18,JCECD1017/18 (CD).
ote:The above titles are from the "Blue Network Show 36" (AFRS "Eddie Condon" transcrip-
    tion no. 34 - except the Al Jarvis guest spot).
    Lou McGarity was presented as "Johnny Pesci" on the above and the following shows.
    Memories Lightest LWIL403 is record no. 178 in the Nostalgia Greats series.

DIE CONDON JAM SESSION:
lly Buttterfield -1,Max Kaminsky -2(tp),Lou McGarity(tb),Edmond Hall(cl),Ernie Caceres
ars),Jess Stacy(p),Sid Weiss(b),George Wettling(dr),Lee Wiley(vcl).
                               Live.Ritz Theatre,NYC.February 3,1945
      It's Been So Long(1)   Jazum 75
      Sweet Lorraine(p,b,dr only)   Aircheck 26
      Sunday(1 or 2)   Jazum 75
      Don't Get Around Much
         Anymore(3)(ss,p,b,dr only)   -
      Alice Blue Gown(1)   -
      My Blue Heaven(2,3)   -
      How Long Has This
         Been Going On(1,4)(lw)   -
      Impromptu Ensemble(1,2,3,4)   -

.Add Sidney Bechet(ss).
.Add Dick Cary(tp).

1 titles - except "Sweet Lorraine" - also on Baybridge(J)UPS2261.
1 titles planned for issue on Jazzology JCE1017/18,JCECD1017/18 (CD).
te:The above titles are from the "Blue Network Show 37" (AFRS "Eddie Condon" transcrip-
    tion no. 35).

EDDIE CONDON JAM SESSION:
Yank Lawson -1(tp),Muggsy Spanier -2(cnt),Lou McGarity(tb),Hank D'Amico(cl),Jess Stacy(p)
Bob Casey(b),George Wettling(dr),Lee Wiley(vcl).

Live.Ritz Theatre,NYC.February 10,1945

Should It(2)	Jazum 38,64(ed.),Good Music JRR2
Song Of The Wanderer(2)	-
Sister Kate(3)(ss,p,b,dr only)	-
Indiana(1)	Jazum 63,Storyville(D)SEP506,Baybridge(J)Bonus E-
Relaxin' At The Touro(2)	Jazum 63,Spook Jazz(E)SPJ6603
I Can't Get Started	
(vcl,p,b,dr only)(lw)	Totem 1033
Impromptu Ensemble(1,2,3)	Jazum 63(ed.)

-3.Add Sidney Bechet(ss).

All titles planned for issue on Jazzology JCE1019/20,JCECD1019/20 (CD).
Note:The above titles are from the "Blue Network Show 38" (AFRS "Eddie Condon" transcrip-
    tion no. 36).
    "Indiana" issued on SEP506 as by YANK LAWSON'S DIXIELAND BAND.

EDDIE CONDON JAM SESSION:
Max Kaminsky -1,Billy Butterfield -2,Dick Cary -3(tp),Lou McGarity(tb),Pee Wee Russell
(cl),Ernie Caceres(bars),Jess Stacy(p),Jack Lesberg(b),George Wettling(dr),Red McKenzie,
Lee Wiley(vcl).

Live.Ritz Theatre,NYC.February 17,1945

Strut Miss Lizzie(1)	Jazum 75,Baybridge(J)UPS2261
Time On My Hands(1 or 2,3)(rmk)	- - ,Palm(E)P30-08(?)
Ain't Misbehavin'(2)	Jazum 76, - ,Spook Jazz(E)SPJ6607
	Baybridge(J)UXP126,Gazell GJ1050
There'll Be Some Changes	
Made(4)(ss,p,b,dr only)	Jazum 76,Baybridge(J)UPS2261
At The Jazz Band Ball(1,2,4)	Baybridge(J)UPS2261
Someone To Watch	
Over Me(2,5)(lw)	Totem 1033,Jazum 63,Baybridge(J)UPS2261
Impromptu Ensemble(1,2,4)	Jazum 76,Spook Jazz(E)SPJ6607,Baybridge(J)UPS226:

-4.Add Sidney Bechet(ss).
-5.Omit Russell.

All titles planned for issue on Jazzology JCE1019/20,JCECD1019/20 (CD).
Note:The above titles are from the "Blue Network Show 39" (AFRS "Eddie Condon" transcrip-
    tion no. 37).

EDDIE CONDON JAM SESSION:
Billy Butterfield -1,Max Kaminsky -2(tp),Tommy Dorsey(tb),Jimmy Dorsey(cl),Ernie Caceres
(bars),Jess Stacy(p),Sid Weiss(b),George Wettling(dr),Lee Wiley(vcl).

Live.Ritz Theatre,NYC.February 24,1945

Honeysuckle Rose(1)	Jazum 53
Baby Won't You	
Please Come Home(1)	- ,Storyville(D)SLP133,(J)ULS1564,Good
	Music JRR2
China Boy(3)(ss,p,b,dr only)	Aircheck 26,Chiaroscuro CR113,(J)ULX54
I Can't Believe That	
You're In Love With Me(2)	Jazum 63,
Royal Garden Blues(1)	-
Any Old Time	
(vcl,tb,p,b,dr only)(lw)	Totem 1033,Jazum 63,Memories Lightest LWIL403,Day
	(J)VC5020,Baybridge(J)UPS2280
Impromptu Ensemble(1,2,3)	Jazum 63

-3.Add Sidney Bechet(ss).
(session cont. next page).

,ll titles also on Baybridge(J)UPS2262,Rarities(E)44 ("Impromptu Ensemble" is edited).
ll titles planned for issue on Jazzology JCE1019/20,JCECD1019/20 (CD).
ote:The above titles are from the "Blue Network Show 40" (AFRS "Eddie Condon" transcription no. 39).
   Memories Lightest LWIL403 is record no. 178 in the Nostalgia Greats series.

DDIE CONDON JAM SESSION:
ax Kaminsky -1,Dick Cary -2(tp),Muggsy Spanier -3(cnt),Lou McGarity(tb),Sidney Bechet
ss),Ernie Caceres(bars,cl),Jess Stacy(p),Sid Weiss(b),Johnny Blowers(dr),Lee Wiley,Red
cKenzie(vcl).   Live.Ritz Theatre,NYC.March 3,1945
    I Found A New Baby(3)   Jazum 63
    Just Friends(1(?),2)(no ss)(rmk)   -
    (Guest spot with Tommy Dorsey)
    That's A Plenty(1)   Jazum 63
    High Society(ss,p,b,dr only)   Jazum 64
    Someday Sweetheart(3)   -
    The Man I Love
       (1(?),2)(no ss)(lw)   Totem 1033,Jazum 64,Dan(J)VC5020,Baybridge(J)
                                   UPS2280
    Impromptu Ensemble(1,2(?),3)   Jazum 64(ed.)

.l titles - except the guest spot - also on Baybridge(J)UPS2262.
.l titles planned for issue on Jazzology JCE1019/20,JCECD1019/20 (CD).
)te:The above titles are from the "Blue Network Show 41" (AFRS "Eddie Condon" transcription no. 40).

DIE CONDON JAM SESSION:
lly Butterfield -1,Max Kaminsky -2,Dick Cary -3(tp),Lou McGarity(tb),Pee Wee Russell
1),Ernie Caceres(bars),Joe Bushkin(p),Jack Lesberg(b),Rollo Laylan(dr),Red McKenzie
cl).   Live.Ritz Theatre,NYC.March 10,1945
    Sweet Georgia Brown(1)   Jazum 64,Storyville(D)SLP133,(J)ULS1564
    Serenade In Thirds(p,dr only)   -
    Sugar(2)   - ,Baybridge(J)UXP126
    Cherry(4)   -
    Love Is Just Around The Corner(1)   - ,Storyville(D)SLP133,(J)ULS1564
    Can't We Be Friends(1,3)(rmk)   -
    (Guest spot with Bunk Johnson) Fat Cat's Jazz FCJ001
    Impromptu Ensemble(1,2,3(?))   Jazum 64

.Caceres(cl),p,b,dr only.

l titles also on Baybridge(J)UPS2263.
l titles planned for issue on Jazzology JCE1021/22,JCECD1021/22 (CD).
te:The above titles are from the "Blue Network Show 42" (AFRS "Eddie Condon" transcription no. 41).
   The guest spot with Condon and Bunk Johnson talking was included on a Sidney Bechet
   LP (FJC001).

DIE CONDON JAM SESSION:
lly Butterfield -1(tp),Muggsy Spanier -2(cnt),Lou McGarity(tb),Pee Wee Russell(cl),Ernie
:eres(bars),Joe Bushkin(p),Sid Weiss(b),Johnny Blowers(dr),Lee Wiley(vcl).
                                              Live.Ritz Theatre,NYC.March 17,1945
    When Irish Eyes Are Smiling(1,3) Jazum 66
    As Long As I Live(1)   -
    Tin Roof Blues(2)   - ,Baybridge(J)UXP126
    Culver City Suite (1st mvt.)(1) Jazum 76
    Three Little Words(1)   Jazum 65(ed.)
    Why Shouldn't I
       (vcl,p,b,dr only)(lw)   Jazum 66,Dan(J)VC5020,Baybridge(J)UPS2280
ssion cont. next page).

(session cont. from previous page):
     My Honey's Lovin' Arms(2)   Jazum 76
     The Lady's In Love With You(1)   -
     Impromptu Ensemble(1,2)   -

-3.Only a few bars are played.

All titles also on Baybridge(J)UPS2263.
All titles planned for issue on Jazzology JCE1021/22,JCECD1021/22 (CD).
Note:The above titles are from the "Blue Network Show 43" (AFRS "Eddie Condon" transcrip-
    tion no. 42).

EDDIE CONDON JAM SESSION:
Billy Butterfield -1,Max Kaminsky -2(tp),Lou McGarity(tb),Pee Wee Russell(cl),Ernie Cace-
res(bars,cl),Joe Bushkin(p),Jack Lesberg(p),Danny Alvin(dr),Lee Wiley(vcl).
                             Live.Ritz Theatre,NYC.March 24,1945
     Struttin' With Some Barbecue(1) Jazum 65,Baybridge(J)UPS2264
     When Your Lover Has Gone(1,3,4)   -   -
     Jazz Me Blues(1,2,4)   -   -
     You're Driving Me
       Crazy(p,dr only)(4)   Aircheck 26,Jazum 65,   -
     Clarinet Marmalade(2)   Jazum 65,   - ,Rhapsody(E)RAL6029
     Wherever There's Love(1,2,4)(lw) Baybridge(J)UPS2264
     Impromptu Ensemble(1,2,5)

-3.Bushkin plays (tp).
-4.Jess Stacy(p) replaces Bushkin.
-5.Bushkin plays(tp,p);add Jess Stacy(p).

All titles planned for issue on Jazzology JCE1021/22,JCECD1021/22 (CD).
Note:The above titles are from the "Blue Network Show 44" (AFRS "Eddie Condon" transcrip-
    tion no. 43 - except "Impromptu Ensemble").

EDDIE CONDON JAM SESSION:
Billy Buttterfield -1(tp),Muggsy Spanier -2(cnt),Lou McGarity(tb),Pee Wee Russell(cl),
Ernie Caceres(bars),Gene Schroeder(p),Sid Weiss(b),Sidney Catlett(dr),Lee Wiley(vcl).
                             Live.Ritz Theatre,NYC.March 31,1945
     Easter Parade(1)
     I Ain't Gonna Give Nobody
       None Of My Jelly Roll(2)   Jazum 65,Baybridge(J)UPS2264,Rhapsody(E)RAL6029
     You're Lucky To Me(2)   -   - ,Spook Jazz(E)SPJ660
                             Gazell GJ1045
     Down With Love(1)
       (tp,p,b,dr only)(lw)   Totem 1033,Jazum 65,Baybridge(J)UPS2264,UPS2280,
                             Dan(J)VC5020
     California Here I Come(1)   Jazum 66,Baybridge(J)UPS2264
     I've Got The
       World On A String(3)   Jazum 65,   -
     Impromptu Ensemble(1,2)   Jazum 66,   -

-3.Caceres(cl),p,b,dr only.

All titles planned for issue on Jazzology JCE1021/22,JCECD1021/22 (CD).
Note:The above titles are from the "Blue Network Show 45" (AFRS "Eddie Condon" transcrip-
    tion no. 44).

EDDIE CONDON JAM SESSION:
Billy Butterfield -1,Max Kaminsky -2(tp),Muggsy Spanier -3(cnt),Vernon Brown(tb),Joe Dix
(cl),Ernie Caceres(bars),Dave Bowman(p),Jack Lesberg(b),Sidney Catlett -4,George Wettlin
-5(dr).   Live.Ritz Theatre,NYC.April 7,1945
(session cont. next page).

(session cont. from previous page):
    Ballin' The Jack(2,4)   Jazum 66
    Jada(1,4)   -
    Limehouse Blues(5)
      (bars,p,b,dr only)   -
    Bugle Call Rag(3,4)   -,Storyville(D)SLP133,(J)ULS1564
    Peg Of My Heart(5)
      (cl,p,b,dr only)   -
    I Found A New Baby(2,5)   -
    Impromptu Ensemble(1,2,3,4,5)

.ll titles planned for issue on Jazzology JCE1023,JCECD1023 (CD).
Note:The above titles are from the "Blue Network Show 46" (AFRS "Eddie Condon" transcrip-
    tion no. 45) - which was the final show in this series.

DDIE CONDON AND HIS ORCHESTRA:
illy Butterfield,Yank Lawson(tp),Bobby Hackett(cnt),Lou McGarity(tb),Edmond Hall(cl),Joe
ixon(bars or bassax),Joe Bushkin(p),Eddie Condon(g),Sid Weiss(b),George Wettling(dr).
                             NYC.May 17,1945

72865-A I'll Build A
      Stairway To Paradise(1)   Decca 23433 (A398),91051 (ED539),DL5137,DL9234,
                            (Sd)BML8518,(J)JDL7,Brunswick(E)LA8518,MCA(J)
                            MCA3019,MCA3100,MCA-Coral(G)6.22424
72866-A Lady Be Good,I   unissued(?)
72867-A Lady Be Good,II   unissued(?)
72868-A My One And Only   Decca 23431 (A398),91050 (ED539),DL5137,DL9234,
                            (Sd)BML8518,(J)JDL7,Brunswick(E)LA8518,MCA(J)
                            MCA3019,MCA3100,MCA-Coral(G)6.22424

.Omit Butterfield,Hackett.

ote:Acc. to a note in Downbeat (1946) Hackett plays (tp) on "My One And Only".

DIE CONDON AND HIS ORCHESTRA:
x Kaminsky(tp),Lou McGarity(tb),Joe Dixon(cl),Jess Stacy(p),Eddie Condon(g),Jack
esberg(b),Johnny Blowers(dr).   NYC.June 14,1945
72933-A Lady Be Good   Decca 23431 (A398),91050 (ED539),Brunswick(E)04304
72934-B Swanee(1)   Decca 23433 (A398),91051 (ED539),Brunswick(E)04305
                            Coral(G)COPS7807/1-2

.Billy Butterfield(tp) replaces Kaminsky.

th titles also on Decca ED539,DL5137,DL9234,(Sd)BML8518,Brunswick(E)LA8518,MCA(J)
A3100.

DIE CONDON'S JAZZ BAND:
cl. Wild Bill Davison(cnt),Brad Gowans(tb),Dave Tough(dr).
                           NYC(?). 1946
    Unknown titles

te:The unknown titles are from the soundtrack of the "Music In America" film series
    (March Of Time Vol.12 issue 8).

DIE CONDON AND HIS ORCHESTRA:
ld Bill Davison(cnt),Brad Gowans(tb),Tony Parenti(cl),Gene Schroeder(p),Eddie Condon(g),
ck Lesberg(b),Dave Tough(dr).   NYC.March 27,1946
3480-A Farewell Blues   Decca 23719 (A490),91527 (ED722),DL5218,DL8281,
                            (Sd)BLM8577,(J)JDL2060,Brunswick(E)LA8577,
                            Festival(Au)CFR10-521,MCA BA212,MCA2-4112

ession cont. next page).

(session cont. from previous page):
W73481-A Improvisation
      For March Of Time   Decca 23600,27470 (A836),9-27470 (9-216),DL5195,
                                    DL8282,(J)JDL6013,MCA MCA2-4071

Both titles also on Brunswick(E)O4306,Ace Of Hearts(E)AH100,MCA(F)510.206,(J)MCA3100,
Affinity(E)AFS1021.

EDDIE CONDON AND HIS ORCHESTRA:
Billy Butterfield,Max Kaminsky(tp),Wild Bill Davison(cnt),Brad Gowans,Lou McGarity(tb),Joe
Dixon(cl),Bud Freeman(ts),Joe Bushkin(p),Eddie Condon(g),Jack Lesberg(b),Dave Tough(dr).
                                      Same date
W73482-A She's Funny That Way   Decca 23600,27470 (A836),9-27470 (9-216),DL5195,
                                    DL8282,(J)JDL6013,Brunswick(E)O4302
W73483-A Stars Fell On Alabama(1)   Decca 23719 (A490),91527 (ED722),DL5203,DL5218,
                                    DL8281,(Sd)BLM8577,(J)JDL2060,(Au)Y6041,
                                    Brunswick(E)LA8577,Festival(Au)CFR10-521

-1.Omit Kaminsky,Davison,Gowans,McGarity.

Both titles also on Ace Of Hearts(E)AH100,MCA MCA20013,(J)MCA3101,Affinity(E)AFS1021.

EDDIE CONDON AND HIS ORCHESTRA:
Max Kaminsky(tp),Fred Ohms(tb),Joe Dixon(cl),Gene Schroeder(p),Eddie Condon(g),Jack
Lesberg(b),Dave Tough(dr),John "Bubbles" Sublett(vcl).
                                      NYC.July 17,1946
W73646-A Some Sunny Day   Decca 23721,MCA MCA20013
W73647-A Just You,Just Me(1)   Decca 23720,(F)MU60027,(Au)Y6041,Brunswick(E)
                                    03793,(G)87008LPBM,MCA BA212,MCA2-4071,
                                    MCA2-4112,(F)510.206,Affinity AFS1035
W73648-A Atlanta Blues(1)(bs)   Decca 23720,(F)MU60027,(Au)Y6041,Brunswick(E)
                                    03793,(G)87008LPBM,MCA BA212,MCA2-4071
W73649-A The Way You Look Tonight   Decca 23721,MCA MCA20013

-1.James P. Johnson(p) replaces Schroeder.

All titles also on Decca A490 (23720/21),DL5203,DL5218,DL8281,(J)JDL2060,Brunswick(E)
LA8577,(F)87008,MCA(F)(J)MCA3101,Festival(Au)CFR10-521.

EDDIE CONDON AND HIS ORCHESTRA:
Bobby Hackett,Max Kaminsky(tp),Jack Teagarden(tb,vcl),Peanuts Hucko(cl),Ernie Caceres
(bars),Joe Bushkin(p),Eddie Condon(g),Jack Lesberg(b),George Wettling(dr).
                                      NYC.August 5,1947
W74023-A My Melancholy Baby(jt)   Decca 24218,DL8282,Brunswick(E)O4302,MCA BA212,
                                    MCA2-4071
W74024-A Tulip Time In Holland(jt) Decca 24218,DL8282,Brunswick(E)O4302,MCA MCA2-407
W74025-A Nobody Knows(jt)   Decca 24217,DL8281,Brunswick(F)87008,Ace Of Hear
                                    (E)AH100,MCA 20013,Affinity(E)AFS1021
W74026-A We Called It Music(jt)   Decca 24217,DL8281,(E)LAB542,Brunswick(F)510.206
                                    Ace Of Hearts(E)AH100,MCA BA212,MCA2-4071,
                                    Affinity(E)AFS1021

All titles also on Decca DL5246,Brunswick(E)LA8542,MCA(J)MCA3101.

EDDIE CONDON AND HIS ORCHESTRA:
Wild Bill Davison(cnt),Jack Teagarden(tb,vcl),Pee Wee Russell(cl),Gene Schroeder(p),Eddi
Condon(g),Morris Rayman(b),Johnny Blowers(dr).
(session cont. next page).

(session cont. from previous page):
                                        NYC.August 6,1947
W74030-A Aun't Hagar's Blues(jt)   Decca 24220,DL8281,DL8304,(Sd)BKL8229,Brunswick(E)
                                        04303,LAT8229,Ace Of Hearts(E)AH28,MCA BA212,
                                        MCA2-4064,MCA2-4071,20013,(F)510.206,(J)
                                        MCA3101,Affinity(E)AFS1021

W74031-A Down Among The
            Sheltering Palms(jt)   Decca 24219,DL8282,Brunswick(E)03964,Ace Of Hearts
                                        (E)AH100,MCA BA212,MCA2-4064,MCA2-4071,20013,
                                        (F)510.206,(J)MCA3101,Affinity(E)AFS1021

W74032-A Rose Of Rio Grande   Decca 24220,DL4540,DL8281,DL8304,(Sd)BKL8229,
                                        Brunswick(E)04303,Ace Of Hearts(E)
                                        AH28,MCA BA212,(F)510.206,(J)MCA3102

W74033-A Ida,Sweet As Apple Cider   Decca 24219,DL8282,(J)JDL6013,Brunswick(E)03964,
                                        MCA(J)MCA3102

All titles also on Decca DL5246,Brunswick(E)LA8542.

Note:The first Eddie Condon "Floor Show" TV series started on September 7, 1948 and conti-
    nued weekly till (prob.) November 23, 1948.

EDDIE CONDON JAM SESSION:
Incl. Sidney Bechet(ss),Joe Bushkin(p).   TV-cast.NYC.October 26,1948
        Tin Roof Blues
        Summertime   FDC(I)1012(?),Musidisc(F)CCV2522(?)
        Unknown titles

Note:The above titles are from a "Condon's Floor Show" TV-show.

EDDIE CONDON JAM SESSION:
Louis Armstrong(tp,vcl),Jack Teagarden(tb,vcl),Peanuts Hucko(cl),Dick Cary(p),Arvell Shaw
(b),Sidney Catlett(dr).   TV-cast.NYC.November 23,1948
        Lover
        Tap Dance(1)
        Mop Mop
        Rockin' Chair(la,jt)
        King Porter Stomp   Jazz Society(Sd)AA530,Palm Club(F)PALM23,Windmill
                                        (E)WMD215,Saga(E)PAN6931,Jazz Anthology(F)
                                        JA5155,Parade(F)LDP501245,Intercord(G)125.400
                                        Boulevard(E)BD3001,Amiga(G)8.50.807,Laser-
                                        light(G)15700(CD)

        A Song Is Born
        Muskrat Ramble
        Don't Worry About Me
        Where The Blues
            Were Born In New Orleans   Palm Club(F)PALM23,Windmill(E),WMD215,Saga(E)
                                        PAN6931

-1.Add Teddy Hale(tap-dance).

Note:The above titles are from a "Condon's Floor Show" TV-show.
    Some of the above titles were issued under Armstrong's name.

EDDIE CONDON JAM SESSION:
Charlie Shavers(tp),Benny Morton(tb),Peanuts Hucko(cl),Joe Bushkin(p),Bob Haggart(b),Buddy
Rich(dr,vcl).   TV-cast.NYC.Late 1948/early 1949
        Three Little Words(br)   Joyce LP1035
        These Foolish Things   -
        Stompin' At The Savoy(1)   -
        I Cover The Waterfront(2)(sv)   -
        Love Or Leave Me(2)(sv)   -
        (Royal Garden) Blues(3)   -

-1.Add Teddy Hale,Rich(tap-dance).
-2.Sarah Vaughan(vcl) acc. by Jimmy Jones(p),Haggart(b),Rich(dr).
-2.Add Charlie Barnet(as).

Note:The above titles are prob. from a "Condon's Floor Show" TV-show.

EDDIE CONDON JAM SESSION:
Roy Eldridge(tp,vcl),Joe Bushkin(p),Bob Haggart(b),Buddy Rich(dr).
                              TV-cast.NYC.Late 1948/early 1949
            Boot Whip(re)
            Unknown titles

Note:The above titles are prob. from a "Condon's Floor Show" TV-show.

EDDIE CONDON JAM SESSION:
Incl. Roy Eldridge(tp),Mary Lou Williams(p),Eddie Condon(g),Buddy Rich(dr).
                              TV-cast.NYC.Late 1948/early 1949
            Unknown titles

Note:The unknown titles are prob. from a "Condon's Floor Show" TV-show.

EDDIE CONDON'S ALL STARS:
Incl. Wild Bill Davison(cnt),Brad Gowans(tb),Dave Tough(dr).
                              NYC(?). 1949
            Unknown titles

Note:The unknown titles are from the soundtrack of the "Music In America" film series
     (March Of Time Vol.15 issue 6).

Note:The second Eddie Condon "Floor Show" TV series started on (prob.) January 1, 1949 and
     continued weekly till September 24, 1949.

EDDIE CONDON JAM SESSION:
Roy Eldridge,Billy Butterfield(tp),Cutty Cutshall(tb),Peanuts Hucko,Pee Wee Russell(cl),
Freddie Slack(p),Jack Lesberg(b),Gene Krupa(dr),Liza Miles(vcl).
                              TV-cast.NYC.January 15(?),1949
            After You've Gone   Broadcast Tribute 0001
            Brown Danube   -
            Boogie Woogie   -
            I Can't Get Started   -
            The Boot Whip   -
            I've Got The World On A String   -
            Slow Blues   -

Note:The above titles are from a "Condon's Floor Show" TV-show.

EDDIE CONDON JAM SESSION:
Hot Lips Page(tp,vcl),Max Kaminsky(tp),Peanuts Hucko(cl),Sidney Bechet(ss),Bud Freeman(ts
Gene Schroeder(p),Jack Lesberg(b),Jimmy Crawford(dr).
                              TV-cast.NYC.Poss. January 1949
            The Blues
            Unknown titles

Note:The above titles are from a "Condon's Floor Show" TV-show.

EDDIE CONDON JAM SESSION:
Jonah Jones(tp,vcl),Bobby Hackett(cnt),Cutty Cutshall(tb),Peanuts Hucko(cl),Sidney Bechet
(ss),Joe Bushkin(p),Jack Lesberg(b),Tiny Kahn(dr),Rosemary Clooney,Kingdom Choir(vcl),
Charlie King(cond),Peter Nugent(tap-dance). TV-cast.NYC.March 5,1949
(session cont. next page).

(session cont. from previous page):
      Way Down Yonder In New Orleans
      When The Saints Go Marching In/
         Medley of religious songs(kc)
      But Not For Me
      Baby Won't You Please Come Home
      Medley(1):   Queen(I)Q-031
         Muskrat Ramble
         Birth Of The Blues
         Louisiana
         New Orleans
         High Society(ss,p,b,dr only)
      Do You Know What It Means
         To Miss New Orleans(rc)
      Ad-lib Blues
      I Found A New Baby

-1.Buddy Rich(dr) replaces Kahn;omit Hacket.

Note:The above titles are from a "Condon's Floor Show" TV-show.
     Bechet may be playing on the medley only.

EDDIE CONDON JAM SESSION:
Wild Bill Davison(cnt),Cutty Cutshall(tb),Peanuts Hucko(cl),Sidney Bechet(ss),Dick Cary,
Ralph Sutton(p),Jack Lesberg(b),Buddy Rich(dr),Rosemary Clooney,Kingdom Choir(vcl),Charlie
King(cond),Peter Nugent(tap-dance).   TV-cast.NYC.March 12,1949
      Just One Of Those Things(no cl) Queen(I)Q-029
      I Know That You
         Know(ss,p,b,dr only)
      Call Of The Wild(ss,p,b,dr only)
      As Time Goes By(1)(p-solo)   Queen(I)Q-030
      Running Wild(1)(cl,p,b,dr only)   -
      Old Man River(kc)
      There'll Be Some Changes Made(rc)
      Jam Session

-1.Teddy Wilson(p).

Note:The above titles are from a "Condon's Floor Show" TV-show.

EDDIE CONDON JAM SESSION:
Hot Lips Page(tp,vcl),Bobby Hackett(cnt),Cutty Cutshall(tb),Peanuts Hucko(cl),Sidney
Bechet(ss),Gene Schroeder,Ralph Sutton(p),Eddie Condon(g),Jack Lesberg(b),Buddy Rich(dr),
poss. Helen Ward(vcl).   TV-cast.NYC.March 19,1949
      Swing That Music(hlp)
      Lover Come Back To Me(1)
      Why Was I Born
      I Know That You
         Know(ss,p,g,b,dr only)   Queen(I)Q-029
      Jada(2)   Queen(I)Q-030
      Old Man River
      The Gentleman Is A Dope
      Blues (Ol' Miss)(3)(hlp)   Queen(I)Q-029

-1.Sutton(p-solo).
-2.Omit Page,Bechet,Condon;Schroeder plays (p).
-3.Omit Hackett,Condon.

Note:The above titles are from a "Condon's Floor Show" TV-show.
     This TV-show poss. also incl. "Why Do I Love You" played by Sutton,b,dr.

EDDIE CONDON JAM SESSION:
Jimmy McPartland(tp),Muggsy Spanier -1(cnt),Cutty Cutshall(tb),Peanuts Hucko(cl),Sidney
Bechet -2(ss),Dick Cary(p),Eddie Condon(g),Jack Lesberg(b),Buddy Rich(dr),Helen Ward(vcl),
Baby Lawrence(tap-dance).   TV-cast.NYC.March 26,1949
        Thou Swell
        Squeeze Me(3)
        September Song(2)
          (ss,p,b,dr only)   Queen(I)Q-029
        Just You,Just Me
        Relaxing At The Touro(1)(no tp) Queen(I)Q-031
        Argonne Stomp(2)
        Dixieland Band(hw)   Queen(I)Q-031
        My Funny Valentine
          (cl,p,b,dr only)(hw)   Queen(I)Q-030
        Jam session(1(?),2(?))

-3.Cliff Jackson(p) replaces Cary.

Note:The above titles are from a "Condon's Floor Show" TV-show.

EDDIE CONDON JAM SESSION:
Billy Butterfield(tp),Cutty Cutshall(tb),Ernie Caceres(cl),Dick Cary(p),Eddie Condon(g),
Jack Lesberg(b),Buddy Rich(dr,vcl).   TV-cast.NYC.April 2,1949
        St. Louis Blues
        Unknown title(1)
        Yesterday
        Heat Wave(br)
        Bechet's Bounce(2)

-1.Joe Bushkin(p),Rich(dr) only.
-2.Add Sidney Bechet(ss) - poss. acc. by p,b,dr only.

Note:The above titles are from a "Condon's Floor Show" TV-show.

EDDIE CONDON JAM SESSION:
Bobby Hackett(cnt),Cutty Cutshall(tb),Ernie Caceres(cl),Sidney Bechet -1(ss),Dick Cary
(p,org),Eddie Condon(g),Jack Lesberg(b),J.C. Heard(dr),Helen Ward(vcl).
                                        TV-cast.NYC.April 16,1949
        Gershwin Medley(hw):   Queen(I)Q-030
          Fascinatin' Rhythm
          I Got A Crush On You
          'S Wonderful
          They Can't Take
            That Away From Me
          The Man I Love
          Embraceable You
          I Got Rhythm
        Summertime(1)(ss,p,b,dr only)   Queen(I)Q-029
        Sweet And Lowdown
        But Not For Me(2)(hw)   Queen(I)Q-031
        Lady Be Good
        Jam Session(1(?))

-2.Ward(vcl) acc. by Hackett(cnt),p,b,Buddy Rich(dr).

Note:The above titles are from a "Condon's Floor Show" TV-show.

EDDIE CONDON JAM SESSION:
Billy Butterfield(tp),Jonah Jones -1(tp,vcl),Will Bradley(tb),Peanuts Hucko(cl),Sidney
Bechet -2(ss),Ernie Caceres(bars),Joe Bushkin(p),Eddie Condon(g),Ray Brown(b),Buddy Rich
(dr).   TV-cast.April 23,1949
(session cont. next page).

(session cont. from previous page):
        Our Monday Date
        At The Front Page Ball(2)
        I'm A Ding Dong Daddy(1)(jj)
        Easter Parade(3)
        My Romance(tb,p,b,dr only)
        The Blues (Ole Miss)(1,2)

-3.Ella Fitzgerald(vcl) acc. by p,b,dr only.

Note:The above titles are from a "Condon's Floor Show" TV-show.

EDDIE CONDON JAM SESSION:
Bobby Hackett(cnt),Ray Deal(tb),Peanuts Hucko(cl),Ernie Caceres(cl),Dick Cary(p),Eddie
Condon(g),Jack Lesberg(b),Buddy Rich(dr),Helen Ward,Buck & Bubbles (Buck Washington,John
Bubbles)(vcl).   TV-cast.NYC.May 7,1949
        California,Here I Come
        Unknown titles

Note:The above titles are from a "Condon's Floor Show" TV-show.

EDDIE CONDON JAM SESSION:
Billy Butterfield(tp),Cutty Cutshall(tb),Ernie Caceres(cl,bars(?)),Joe Bushkin(p),Eddie
Condon(g),Irving Manning(b),Buddy Rich(dr,vcl),Thelma Carpenter(vcl),Baby Lawrence(tap-
dance).   TV-cast.NYC.May 14,1949
        Oh!Baby
        Buckner's Boogie(1)
        The Hucklebuck(br)
        Flying Home(2)

-1.Milt Buckner(p) replaces Bushkin.
-2.Add Milt Buckner(vbs).

Note:The above titles are from a "Condon's Floor Show" TV-show.

EDDIE CONDON JAM SESSION:
Bobby Hackett(cnt),Cutty Cutshall(tb),Dick Cary(alth),Peanuts Hucko(cl),Ernie Caceres
(bars),Sidney Bechet -1(ss),Joe Bushkin(p),Eddie Condon(g),Jack Lesberg(b),Buddy Rich
(dr,vcl),Thelma Carpenter(vcl).   TV-cast.NYC.May 21,1949
        Fats Waller Medley(tc):   Queen(I)Q-031
            I've Got The
               Feeling I'm Falling
            Keepin' Out Of Mischief Now
            Handful Of Keys
            Squeeze Me
            The Joint Is Jumpin'
        I'm Crazy About My Baby
        Black And Blue(1)   Queen(I)Q-029
        Ain't Misbehavin'(tc)   Queen(I)Q-031
        Honeysuckle Rose(1,2)   Queen(I)Q-029
        Fats Waller Medley,II(3)

-2.Willie "The Lion" Smith(p) replaces Bushkin.
-3.Willie "The Lion" Smith,Henry Duncan(p-duet).

Note:The above titles are from a "Condon's Floor Show" TV-show.

EDDIE CONDON AND HIS TV DIXIELAND BAND:
Bobby Hackett(cnt),Will Bradley(tb),Dick Cary(alth),Peanuts Hucko(cl,ts),Ernie Caceres
(bars),Joe Bushkin(p),Eddie Condon(g),Jack Lesberg(b),Sidney Catlett(dr),Ruth Brown(vcl).
                                    NYC.May 25,1949

(session cont. next page).

(session cont. from previous page):
A236   Seems Like Old Times   Atlantic 661
A237   Time Carries On   -
A238   It's Raining(rb)   Atlantic 879,Route 66(Sd)KIX16
A239   So Long(rb)   - ,EP505,LP8004,Atco SD7009

Note:Masters A238-39 were issued under Ruth Brown's name.

EDDIE CONDON JAM SESSION:
Billy Butterfield(tp),Cutty Cutshall(tb),Dick Cary(alth),Peanuts Hucko(cl),Ernie Caceres
(bars),Joe Bushkin(p),Eddie Condon(g),Jack Lesberg(b),Sidney Catlett(dr),June Christy,
Johnny Desmond(vcl),unknown(tap-dance).   TV-cast.NYC.May 28,1949
        Ballin' The Jack(no alth)   Queen(I)Q-031
        In A Little Spanish
          Town(cl,p,g,b,dr only)   Queen(I)Q-030
        Everything
          Happens To Me(jc)   -
        My Old Flame   Queen(I)Q-031
        Look At Me Now(jc,jd)   Queen(I)Q-030
        Ol' Miss

Note:The above titles are from a "Condon's Floor Show" TV-show.

EDDIE CONDON JAM SESSION:
Hot Lips Page(tp),Cutty Cutshall(tb),Dick Cary(alth),Peanuts Hucko(cl),Ernie Caceres(bars)
Sidney Bechet(ss),Joe Bushkin -1,Bobby Tucker,Ralph Sutton(p),Eddie Condon(g),Jack Lesberg
(b),Sidney Catlett(dr).   TV-cast.NYC.June 4,1949
        Happy Feet
        Gone With The Wind
        High Society(1)   Queen(I)Q-029
        Mop Mop
        The Joint
        Alligator Crawl
        Hobson Street Blues
        The Blues

Note:The above titles are from a "Condon's Floor Show" TV-show.

EDDIE CONDON JAM SESSION:
Louis Armstrong(tp,vcl),Jack Teagarden(tb,vcl),Peanuts Hucko(cl),Ernie Caceres(bars,cl),
Joe Bushkin(p),Jack Lesberg(b),Sidney Catlett(dr).
                                     TV-cast.NYC.June 11,1949
        When It's Sleepy Time Down South Queen(I)Q-010
        Them There Eyes(la)   -
        St. James Infirmary(jt)   -
        Sweethearts On Parade(la)   -
        Do You Know What It Means
          To Miss New Orleans(la,jt) -
        Struttin' With Some Barbecue -
        When It's Sleepy Time Down South -

All titles also on Jazz Anthology(F)JA5222,Jazzline(G)JL20803.
Note:The above titles are from a "Condon's Floor Show" TV-show.
     Some of the above titles were issued under Armstrong's name.

EDDIE CONDON JAM SESSION:
Incl. Count Basie -1(org).   TV-cast.NYC.June 18,1949
        Unknown titles
        Unknown title(1)(org,g,b,dr only)
        Blues In E-flat(1)

Note:The above titles are from a "Condon's Floor Show" TV-show.

EDDIE CONDON JAM SESSION:
Bobby Hackett(cnt),Cutty Cutshall(tb),Dick Cary(alth),Peanuts Hucko(cl),Sidney Bechet -1
(ss),Ernie Caceres(bars),Joe Bushkin(p,tp,vcl),Jack Lesberg(b),Sidney Catlett(dr).
                                            TV-cast.NYC.June 25,1949

    In The Groove
    Sweet Georgia Brown(1)   Queen(I)Q-029
    I'm Gonna Sit Right Down And
      Write Myself A Letter(2,3)(jb)Queen(I)Q-030
    Seems Like A Old Times(2)   Queen(I)Q-031
    Ol' Miss(1(?))

-2.Buddy Rich(dr) replaces Catlett.
-3.Omit Hackett.

Note:The above titles are from a "Condon's Floor Show" TV-show.

EDDIE CONDON JAM SESSION:
Wild Bill Davison(cnt),Cutty Cutshall(tb),Peanuts Hucko(cl),Sidney Bechet -1(ss),Ernie
Caceres(bars),Gene Schroeder(p),Eddie Condon(g),Jack Lesberg(b),Sidney Catlett(dr),Lee
Wiley(vcl).   TV-cast.NYC.July 9,1949
    Blues   Queen(I)Q-030,Jazzline(G)JL20803
    Riverboat Shuffle   -   -
    Blues In My Heart
      (1)(ss,p,b,dr only)   Queen(I)Q-029,   -
    Hotter Than That   Queen(I)Q-030,   -
    All Of Me(2)   Jazzline(G)JL20803
    Blues(2)   -
    Alone With The Blues(1(?))(lw)   -
    Why Can't You Behave(1(?))(lw)   -
    Ol' Miss(1,3)   -

-1.Count Basie(p) replaces Schroeder.
-2.Poss. add Count Basie(p).

Note:The above titles are from a "Condon's Floor Show" TV-show.

EDDIE CONDON JAM SESSION:
Wild Bill Davison(cnt),Cutty Cutshall(tb),Peanuts Hucko(cl),Ernie Caceres(bars),Joe Bush-
kin(p),Jack Lesberg(b),George Wettling(dr). TV-cast.NYC.July 23,1949
    At The Jazz Band Ball   Queen(I)Q-030
    Stars Fell On
      Alabama(p,b,dr only)   Queen(I)Q-031
    Limehouse Blues   -
    Ma,He's Makin' Eyes At Me
    Ain't She Sweet
    The Hucklebuck
    The World Is
      Waiting For The Sunrise

Note:The above titles are from a "Condon's Floor Show" TV-show.
    Add Sidney Bechet(ss),Pearl Bailey(vcl) on some of the unissued titles.

EDDIE CONDON JAM SESSION:
Hot Lips Page(tp,vcl),Cutty Cutshall(tb),Ernie Caceres(cl),Joe Bushkin(p),Jack Lesberg(b),
Buddy Rich,George Wettling(dr).   TV-cast.NYC.August 6,1949
    The Sheik Of Araby(hlp)   Queen(I)Q-031
    Homeward Bound
    Buddy Bolden Stomp(1)   Queen(I)Q-029
    Blues
    Sister Kate
(session cont. next page).

(session cont. from previous page):
    Ol' Miss(2)
    Stompin' At The Savoy(3)
    Body And Soul(3)

-1."Big Chief" Russell Moore(tb),Sidney Bechet(ss),Sammy Price(p),Kansas Fields(dr).
-2.Poss. add Moore,Bechet,Price,Fields.
-3.CHARLIE VENTURA TRIO:Charlie Ventura(ts),rest unknown.

Note:The above titles are from a "Condon's Floor Show" TV-show.
    Moore and Bechet may be playing on some of the unissued titles; Rich plays on "The
    Sheik Of Araby" - the drummer for the additional unissued titles is not known.

EDDIE CONDON JAM SESSION:
Louis Armstrong(tp,vcl),poss. Bobby Hackett(cnt),Jack Teagarden(tb,vcl),rest unknown.
                                    TV-cast.NYC.Prob. August 20,1949
    I Can't Give You
       Anything But Love(la)   Saga(E)PAN6904,Archive Of Folk&Jazz FS312,Everest
                                    (E)3312,Vogue(F)SLDEV816,VG403.500816,COF15,
                                    VG603.000015,Ariston(I)ARI12010

Note:The above title is prob. from a "Condon's Floor Show" TV-show; it was issued under
    Armstrong's name.

EDDIE CONDON JAM SESSION:
Bobby Hackett(cnt),Cutty Cutshall(tb),Pee Wee Russell(cl),Joe Bushkin(p),Eddie Condon
(g,vcl),Jack Lesberg(b),George Wettling(dr),Billie Holiday(vcl).
                                      TV-cast.NYC.August 27,1949
    If I Could Be With You
       One Hour Tonight(ec)   FDC(I)1014
    Medley: - ,Saga(E)PAN6916
       Mandy Make Up Your Mind
       I Love A Piano
       Soft Lights And Sweet Music
       I Know That You Know(1)
       I Want A Little Girl
       The Man I Love
    I Got Rhythm   -   -
    Billie's Blues(2)(bh)   -   -
    Keeps On A-Rainin'(2)(bh)   FDC(I)1014,Saga(E)PAN6916,Avenue(E)AVINT1020,Black
                                      Elephant(Du)PE811006,Palm(E)30-17,ESP LP3002,
                                      (F)538101,Decca(G)PD12006,PAR(E)2001,Joker(I)
                                      SM3131,Amalgated 130,Rare LP01/3
    Lover Man(2)(bh)   FDC(I)1014,Saga(E)PAN6916,Avenue(E)AVINT1020,Black
                                      Elephant(Du)PE811006,Palm(E)30-17,ESP LP3002,
                                      (F)538101,Amalgated 130
    We Called It Music(3)(jt)   FDC(I)1014,Saga(E)PAN6916,Palm(E)30-17
    Chinatown,My Chinatown(3)   FDC(I)1014,Saga(E)PAN6916,Palm Club(F)PALM23,Jazz
                                      Society(Sd)AA551,(F)67401,67414,Jazz Antholog
                                      (F)JA5155,Saga(E)PAN6904,Archive Of Folk&Jazz
                                      FS312,Everest EK3,(E)3312,DJM(E)DJLMD8001,
                                      Trip X2,TLX5814,Jazz Trip JT10,Metronome(G)
                                      DALP2/1969,Vogue(F)SLDEV816,VG403.500816,
                                      COF15,VG603.000015,Ember(E)CJS838,Alamac
                                      QSR2436,(F)180053,Bulldog(E)BDL2007,Ariston
                                      (I)ARI12010,Quadrifoglio(I)VDS282,Discophon
                                      (Sp)S4271,Music For Pleasure(SA)MFP3518,
                                      Windmill(E)WMD266,Brad 10516/17

(session cont. next page).

(session cont. from previous page):
```
     Someday You'll Be
        Sorry(no cnt,cl)(3)(la,hc,st)  FDC(I)1014,Saga(E)PAN6916,Palm(E)30-17,Decca(G)
                                        PD12008,Jazz Society(F)67401,67414,Saga(E)
                                        PAN6916,Archive Of Folk&Jazz FS312,Everest
                                        EK3,(E)3312,DJM(E)DJLMD8001,Trip X2,TLX5814,
                                        Jazz Trip JT10,Metronome(G)DALP2/1969,Vogue
                                        (F)SLDEV816,VG403.500816,COF15,VG603.000015,
                                        Ember(E)CJS838,Bulldog(E)BDL2007,Ariston(I)
                                        ARI12010,Quadrifoglio(I)VDS282,Discophon(Sp)
                                        S4271,Music For Pleasure(SA)MFP3518,Joker(I)
                                        SM3133,Vintage(I)7841001,Brad 10516/17
     Three Little Bears(3,4)(la,hc,st)  FDC(I)1014,Saga(E)PAN6916,Palm(E)30-17
     Jam Session(5)                     FDC(I)1014,Saga(E)PAN6916
```

1.Add Sidney Bechet(ss).
2.Acc. by Hot Lips Page(tp),Horace Henderson(p),Jack Lesberg(b),George Wettling(dr).
3.Add Louis Armstrong(tp,vcl),Jack Teagarden(tb,vcl),Helen Cherell,The Swan-Tones(vcl).
4.Armstrong(narration);omit Hackett,Russell;Bushkin plays (org).
5.Add Hot Lips Page(tp,vcl).

ote:The above titles are from a "Condon's Floor Show" TV-show.
     Some of the above titles were issued under Armstrong's name.

DDIE CONDON JAM SESSION:
ild Bill Davison(cnt),Cutty Cutshall(tb),Peanuts Hucko(cl),Ernie Caceres(bars)Joe Bushkin
p),Eddie Condon(g),Jack Lesberg(b),George Wettling(dr),Billie Holiday(vcl).
```
                                        TV-cast.NYC.September 3,1949
     Walking My Baby Back Home          Queen(I)Q-011
     Fine And Mellow(bh)                       -
     I Loves You Porgy(bh)                     -
     Them There Eyes(bh)                       -
     Runnin' Wild                              -
     These Foolish Things(1)                   -
     Swing That Music(1,2,3)(la)        Queen(I)Q-011,Palm Club(F)PALM21,Jazz Society(F)
                                        67401,Saga(E)PAN6904,DJM(E)DJLMD8001,Trip X2,
                                        TLX5814,Jazz Trip JT10,Olympic 7124,Metronome
                                        (G)DALP2/1969,Ember(E)CJS850,Alamac QSR2436,
                                        (F)180053,Bulldog(E)BDL2007,Brad 10516/17,
                                        Ariston(I)ARI12010
     Aunt Hagar's Blues(1,3)(jt)        Queen(I)Q-011,Family(I)SFR-DP640
     Heebie Jeebies(2,3)(la)            Queen(I)Q-011,Palm Club(F)PALM21,Jazz Society(Sd)
                                        AA592,(F)67401,Saga(E)PAN6904,Ar.Of Folk&Jazz
                                        FS312,Everest EK3,(E)3312,DJM(E)DJLMD8001,
                                        Trip X2,TLX5814,Jazz Trip JT10,Metronome(G)
                                        DALP2/1969,Vogue(F)SLDEV816,VG403.500816,
                                        COF15,VG603.000015,Ember(E)CJS838,Alamac
                                        QSR2436,(F)180053,Bulldog(E)BDL2007,Ariston
                                        (I)ARI12010,AR038,Quadrifoglio(I)VDS282,
                                        Discophon(Sp)S4271,Music For Pleasure(SA)
                                        MFP3518,Windmill(E)WMD266,Brad 10516/17,
                                        Amiga(G)8.50.807
     Farewell To Storyville(2,3)(la)    Queen(I)Q-011,Palm Club(F)PALM21,Jazz Society(F)
                                        67401,Saga(E)PAN6904,DJM(E)DJLMD8001,Trip X2,
                                        TLX5814,Jazz Trip JT10,Olympic 7124,Metronome
                                        (G)DALP2/1969,Ember(E)CJS850,Alamac QSR2436,
                                        (F)180053,Bulldog(E)BDL2007,Brad 10516/17,
                                        Ariston(I)ARI12010
```

ession cont. next page).

(session cont. from previous page):
```
        Rockin' Chair(2,3)(1a,jt)          Queen(I)Q-011,Jazz Society(F)67401,Saga(E)PAN6904,
                                           DJM(E)DJLMD8001,Trip X2,TLX5814,Jazz Trip
                                           JT10,Olympic 7124,Metronome(G)DALP2/1969,
                                           Ember(E)CJS850,Alamac QSR2436,(F)180053,
                                           Bulldog(E)BDL2007,Brad 10516/17,Ariston(I)
                                           ARI12010
        I Love My Man(bh)                  Queen(I)Q-011
        Ol' Miss                           -
```

-1.Earl Hines(p) replaces Bushkin.
-2.Add Louis Armstrong(tp,vcl).
-3.Add Jack Teagarden(tb,vcl).

All titles also on Jazz Anthology(F)JA5223.
Note:The above titles are from a "Condon's Floor Show" TV-show.
     Some issues of "Farewell To Storyville" as "Storyville Blues".
     Some of the above titles were issued under Armstrong's name.

EDDIE CONDON JAM SESSION:
Louis Armstrong(tp,vcl),Bobby Hackett(cnt),Jack Teagarden(tb,vcl),Cutty Cutshall(tb),
Peanuts Hucko(cl,ts),Ernie Caceres(bars,cl),Joe Bushkin(p),Eddie Condon(g),Jack Lesberg
(b),George Wettling(dr).   TV-cast.NYC.September 10,1949
```
        Sweet Georgia Brown(1)             Queen(I)Q-010
        After You've Gone(1)               -
        Royal Garden Blues                 -
        Back O'Town Blues(1a)              Queen(I)Q-010,Jazz Society(F)67401,Saga(E)PAN6904
                                           DJM(E)DJLMD8001,Trip X2,TLX5814,Jazz Trip
                                           JT10,Metronome(G)DALP2/1969,Alamac QSR2436,
                                           (F)180053,Ariston(I)ARI12010
        Me And Brother Bill(1a)            Queen(I)Q-010,Jazz Society(F)67401,Olympic 7124,
                                           DJM(E)DJLMD8001,Trip X2,TLX5814,Jazz Trip
                                           JT10,Metronome(G)DALP2/1969,Ember(E)CJS850,
                                           Bulldog(E)BDL2007,Ariston(I)ARI12010
        Blues In B Flat(incompl.)          Queen(I)Q-010,Jazz Society(F)67401,Ariston(I)
                                           ARI12010
```

-1.Omit Armstrong,Teagarden.

All titles also on on Jazz Anthology(F)JA5222.
Note:The above titles are from a "Condon's Floor Show" TV-show.
     Some of the above titles were issued under Armstrong's name.

EDDIE CONDON'S JAZZ CONCERT ALL STARS:
Wild Bill Davison(cnt),Cutty Cutshall(tb),Peanuts Hucko(cl),Gene Schroeder(p),Eddie Condon
(g),Bob Casey(b),Buddy Rich(dr).   Broadcast.NYC.January 1950
```
        Riverboat Shuffle                  Jazum 76
        Charleston                         -
        Sweet Georgia Brown                -
        Blues                              -
        Shine                              -
```

Note:The above titles are from Voice Of America transcription No.76.

Buzzy Drootin(dr) replaces Rich.   Broadcast.NYC. 1950
```
        Everybody Loves My Baby
        Up The Lazy River
        Cheese Cake                        Jazum 77
        The Lady's In Love                 -
        Struttin' With Some Barbecue       -
```

Note:The above titles are from Voice Of America transcription No.78.

.alph Sutton(p) replaces Schroeder.   Broadcast.NYC. 1950
```
    When The Saints Go Marching In   Jazum 77
    She's Funny That Way             -
    After You've Gone                -
    When Your Lover Has Gone         -
    When You're Smiling              -
```
ote:The above titles are from Voice Of Ameria transcription No.84.

obby Hackett(cnt),Cutty Cutshall(tb),Peanuts Hucko(cl),Sidney Bechet(ss),Ralph Sutton(p),
ddie Condon(g),Jack Lesberg(b),Buddy Rich(dr).
```
                              Broadcast.NYC.  1950
    Thou Swell                Jazum 77
    September Song            -
    I Know That You Know      -
    This Is Romance           -
    Cottontail                -
```
ote:The above titles are from Voice Of Ameria transcription No.85.

ODIE CONDON AND HIS ORCHESTRA:
ild Bill Davison(cnt),Cutty Cutshall(tb),Peanuts Hucko(cl),Gene Schroeder(p),Eddie Condon
g),Jack Lesberg(b),Buzzy Drootin(dr),Jimmy Atkins(vcl).
```
                              NYC.March 20,1950
5988  Maple Leaf Rag(1)       Decca 27035,DL5195,DL8282,(Sd)BML8549,(J)JDL6013,
                              Brunswick(E)LA8549,Ace Of Hearts(E)AH100,MCA
                              BA212,(F)510.206,MCA(J)MCA3102,Affinity(E)
                              AFS1028,Herwin LP401
5989  Dill Pickles(1)         Decca 24987,DL5195,DL8282,(Sd)BML8549,(J)JDL6013,
                              Brunswick(E)04506,LA8549,Ace Of Hearts(E)
                              AH100,MCA BA212,(F)510.206,MCA(J)MCA3102,
                              Affinity(E)AFS1028
5990  Sweet Cider (Time)(ja)  Decca 27106,DL5196,MCA(J)MCA3102
```
.Ralph Sutton(p-solo).

me.
```
                              NYC.March 22,1950
000  At The Jazz Band Ball(ja)  Decca 24987,Brunswick(E)04506,Ace Of Hearts(E)
                              AH100,Affiniy(E)AFS1021
001  Jazz Me Blues(ja)        Decca 27035,MCA BA212,MCA2-4071(F)510.206
```
th titles also on Decca DL5195,DL8282,(Sd)BML8549,(J)JDL6013,Brunswick(E)LA8549,MCA(J)
A3102.

ggy Ann Ellis(vcl) replaces Atkins.   NYC.June 9,1950
```
473-5 Black Bottom(pae)        Decca 27095,Brunswick(E)04571
474-4 (Original) Charleston(pae)   - ,DL8655,        -
475   Yellow Dog Blues         Decca 27106,MCA BA212,(F)510.206
```
l titles also on Decca DL5196,(Sd)BML8549,Brunswick(E)LA8549,MCA MCA2-4071,(J)MCA3102.

DIE CONDON JAM SESSION:
ld Bill Davison(cnt),Cutty Cutshall(tb),Peanuts Hucko(cl),Gene Schroeder(p),Eddie Condon
),Sid Weiss(b),Buddy Rich(dr),Rosemary Clooney(vcl).
```
                              TV-cast.Poss. June 19,1950
    Blues
    I Found A New Baby
    Up A Lazy River
    Do You Know What It Means
        To Miss New Orleans(rc)
    Sweet Georgia Brown
```
ession cont. next page).

(session cont. from previous page).
Note:The above titles may be from a "Condon's Floor Show" TV-show.

Wild Bill Davison(cnt),Cutty Cutshall(tb),Bill Bognar(cl),Ralph Sutton(p),Eddie Condon(g)
prob. unknown(b),Buzzy Drootin(dr).   Broadcast.NYC.August 1,1950
        Fidgety Feet
        Squeeze Me
        Maple Leaf Rag
        I Want A little Girl
        The World Is
            Waiting For The Sunrise
        She's Funny That Way
        Black Bottom

Yank Lawson(tp),Cutty Cutshall(tb,vcl),Edmond Hall(cl),Gene Schroeder -1,Ralph Sutton -2
(p),Eddie Condon(g),Bill Goodall(b),Buzzy Drootin(dr).
                                            NYC.October 2,1950
76895 Raggin' The Scale(1,2)   Decca 27408
76896 Grace And Beauty(1,2)   - ,Ace Of Hearts(E)AH100,MCA BA212,(F)
                                            510.206
76897 Everybody Loves My Baby(1)(cc) Decca 27409
76898 A Hundred Years From Today(2,3)   -

-3.Johnny Windhurst(tp) replaces Lawson;Schroeder plays (celeste).

All titles also on Decca DL5196,MCA MCA2-4071,(J)MCA3102,MCA-Coral(G)6.22424.

Wild Bill Davison(cnt),Cutty Cutshall(tb),Edmond Hall(cl),Gene Schroeder(p),Bob Casey(b),
Buzzy Drootin(dr).   Live."At Condon's",NYC.April 17,1951
        The Lady's Is
            In Love With You(1)
        Crazy Rhythm
        On The Sunny Side Of The Street
        I Can't Believe That
            You're In Love With Me

-1.Add Bud Freeman(ts),Ernie Caceres(cl,bars).

Zutty Singleton(dr) replaces Drootin;add Eddie Condon(g).
                                            Live."At Condon's",NYC.May 21,1951
        Memphis Blues
        Blues My Naughty
            Sweetie Gives To Me
        I'm Forever Blowing Bubbles
        Jazz Me Blues

Wild Bill Davison(cnt),Cutty Cutshall(tb),Edmond Hall(cl),Gene Schroeder(p),prob. Eddie
Condon(g),unknown b,dr,Dolores Hawkins,Johnny Ray(vcl).
                                            Live."At Condon's",NYC.October 16,1951
        Improvisation
            For The March Of Time
        Eccentric Rag
        For You,My Love(dh)
        Improvisation
            For The March Of Time
        Tell The Lady I Say
            Goodbye(p,b,dr only)(jr)

Note:The above titles are from the "Eddie Condon's" soundtrack (from Columbia's "Cavalca
    of Broadway" series).

Wild Bill Davison(cnt),Cutty Cutshall(tb),Edmond Hall(cl),Gene Schroeder(p),Eddie Condon
(g),Bob Casey(b),Buzzy Drootin(dr).   Broadcast."At Condon's",NYC.December 10,1951
        Improvisation For The
            March Of Time (theme)
        Dippermouth Blues   Savoy XP8129,MG15029
        Keepin' Out Of Mischief Now   Savoy XP8128,MG15029
        Morning Air(1)
        Squeeze Me   Savoy MG15029
        Memphis Blues   Savoy XP8128,MG15029
        A-Flat Dream(1)
        I'm Forever Blowing
            Bubbles(incompl.)

1.Ralph Sutton(p-solo).

above titles on MG15029 also on Savoy MG12055,SJL2229,403,(E)WL70837,London(E)LZ-C14004,
Quality(Ca)V39,Trova(Arg)MG22055.
Note:From December 10,1951 to June 2,1952 the Condon band had weekly broadcasts in WMGM's
     "Dr. Jazz" series.
     SJL2229 was issued under Davison's name.

same.   Broadcast."At Condon's",NYC.December 17,1951
        Improvisation For The
            March Of Time (theme)
        That Dada Strain
        Black And Blue
        Somebody Stole My Gal(1)
        Beale Street Blues
        Basin Street Blues(incompl.)

1.Ralph Sutton(p-solo).

Bill Goodall(b),George Wettling(dr) replace Casey,Drootin.
                                            Broadcast."At Condon's",NYC.December 24,1951
        Improvisation For The
            March Of Time (theme)
        Royal Garden Blues
        Blue And Broken-Hearted
        Maple Leaf Rag(1)
        Do You Know What It
            Means To Miss New Orleans
        St. Louis Blues(1)
        Wolverine Blues
        Improvisation For The
            March Of Time (theme)

1.Ralph Sutton(p-solo).

Wild Bill Davison(cnt),Cutty Cutshall(tb),Edmond Hall(cl),Gene Schroeder(p),Eddie Condon
(g),Bob Casey(b),Buzzy Drootin(dr).   Broadcast."At Condon's",NYC.December 31,1951
        Improvisation For The
            March Of Time (theme)
        Beale Street Blues   Savoy MG15030,MG12055,403,London(E)LZ-C14024
        Mandy Make Up Your Mind   -   -   -   -   ,
                                            Byg(F)529.604
        Ain't Misbehavin(1)
        Blues For 1951 (Just The Blues)   Savoy MG15029,MG12055,London(E)LZ-C14004,Quality
                                            (Ca)V39
        Riverboat Shuffle(incompl.)   Savoy MG15030,London(E)LZ-C14024

1.Ralph Sutton(p-solo).
(session cont. next page).

(session cont. from previous page):
Above titles on MG15029 and MG15030 also on Savoy SJL2229,(E)WL70837,Trova(Arg)MG22055.
Note:SJL2229 was issued under Davison's name.

Omit Condon.   Broadcast."At Condon's",NYC.January 7,1952
        Improvisation For The
            March Of Time (theme)
        I Want To Be Happy
        If I Had You
        Snowy Morning Blues(1)
        Baby Won't You Please Come Home
        The Sheik Of Araby
        Oh,By Jingo

-1.Ralph Sutton(p-solo).

Same.   Broadcast."At Condon's",NYC.January 14,1952
        Improvisation For The
            March Of Time (theme)
        Original Dixieland One Step
        When My Sugar
            Walks Down The Street
        Keep Your Temper(1)
        Birth Of The Blues
        Medley: Savoy MG15030,MG12055,SJL2229,(E)WL70837,London(█
                                            LZ-C14024,Trova(Arg)MG22055

        Makin' Whoopee
        You Made Me Love You
        I Can't Give You
            Anything But Love
        Clothesline Ballet(1)
        That's A Plenty(incompl.)

-1.Ralph Sutton(p-solo).

Note:Savoy issues list the above medley as rec. December 31,1951.

Johnny Windhurst(tp),Cutty Cutshall(tb),Edmond Hall(cl),Gene Schroeder(p),Bob Casey(b),
Buzzy Drootin(dr).   Broadcast."At Condon's",NYC.January 21,1952
        Improvisation For The
            March Of Time (theme)
        At The Jazz Band Ball
        I Never Knew
        Dancing On The Ceiling(1)
        South
        If I Could Be With You
        If I Had You(1)
        Panama

-1.Don Abney(p-solo).

Wild Bill Davison(cnt) replaces Windhurst.   Broadcast."At Condon's",NYC.January 28,195█
        Improvisation For The
            March Of Time (theme)
        Sweet Georgia Brown   Savoy XP8129,MG15029,MG12055,SJL2229,403,(E)
                                            WL70837,London(E)LZ-C14004,Quality(Ca)V39,
                                            Trova(Arg)MG22055
(session cont. next page).

session cont. from previous page):
    The One I Love
        Belongs To Somebody Else   Savoy XP8129,MG15029,MG12055,SJL2229,(E)WL70837,
                            London(E)LZ-C14004,Quality(Ca)V39,Trova(Arg)
                            MG22055

    Makin' Whoopee(1)
    Blues My Naughty
        Sweetie Gave (Gives) To Me   Savoy MG15030,MG12055,SJL2229,403,(E)WL70837,
                            London(E)LZ-C14004,Trova(Arg)MG22055

    I Didn't Know What Time It Was(1)
    September In The Rain(incompl.)

1.Don Abney(p-solo).

ote:SJL2229 was issued under Davison's name.

ohnny Windhurst(tp),Cutty Cutshall(tb),Edmond Hall(cl),Gene Schroeder(p),Bob Casey(b),
uzzy Drootin(dr).   Broadcast."At Condon's",NYC.February 4,1952
    Improvisation For The
        March Of Time (theme)
    Easter Parade
    The Sheik Of Araby
    Yes Sir,That's My Baby
    Muskrat Ramble

ild Bill Davison(cnt),Don Lamond(dr) replaces Windhurst,Drootin.
                          Broadcast."At Condon's",NYC.February 11,1952

    Improvisation For The
        March Of Time (theme)
    Wolverine Blues
    Squeeze Me
    Sometimes I'm Happy(1)
    Medley:
        Stars Fell On Alabama
        Summertime
        Don't Blame Me
    That Da Da Strain(incompl.)

1.Don Abney(p),b,dr only.

ild Bill Davison(cnt),Cutty Cutshall(tb),Edmond Hall(cl),Gene Schroeder(p),Eddie Condon
g),Bob Casey(b),Cliff Leeman(dr).   Broadcast."At Condon's",NYC.February 18,1952
    Improvisation For The
        March Of Time (theme)
    Linger Awhile
    Blue And Broken
    Hearted
    Snowy Morning Blues(1)
    Medley:
        I Got It Bad
        September Song
        When Your Lover Has Gone
    Honeysuckle Rose(1)
    Singin' The Blues
    High Society(incompl.)

1.Ralph Sutton(p-solo).

```
Same.                                Broadcast."At Condon's",NYC.February 25,1952
        Improvisation For The
           March Of Time (theme)
        Original Dixieland One Step    Savoy XP8128,MG15029,MG12055,SJL2229,403,(E)
                                          WL70837,London(E)LZ-C14004,Quality(Ca)V39,
                                          Trova(Arg)MG22055
        Wrap Your Troubles In Dreams   Savoy MG15030,MG12055,SJL2229,403,(E)WL70837,
                                          London(E)LZ-C14024,Trova(Arg)MG22055
        Oh Baby(1)
        Eccentric Rag(incompl.)


-1.Hall(cl),Ralph Sutton(p),b,dr only.

Note:SJL2229 was issued under Davison's name.

Wild Bill Davison(cnt),Cutty Cutshall(tb),Edmond Hall(cl),Ralph Sutton(p),Eddie Condon(g)
Bob Casey(b),Cliff Leeman(dr).            Broadcast."At Condon's",NYC.March 3,1952
        Improvisation For The
           March Of Time (theme)
        Avalon
        If I Had You
        Dardanella(1)
        I Would Do Anything For You
        Alice Blue Gown
        Hindustan(incompl.)


-1.Hall(cl),Sutton(p),b,dr only.

Gene Schroeder(p),Buzzy Drootin(dr) replace Sutton,Leeman.
                                     Broadcast."At Condon's",NYC.March 10,1952
        Improvisation For The
           March Of Time (theme)
        Someday Sweetheart
        In The Dark(1)
        The Blues And Ol' Miss
        Sweet And Lovely(2)
        Baby Won't You Please Come Home
        Riverboat Shuffle(incompl.)


-1.Ralph Sutton(p-solo).
-2.Hall(cl),Ralph Sutton(p),b,dr only.

Dick Cary(tp),Cutty Cutshall(tb),Edmond Hall(cl),Gene Schroeder(p),Eddie Condon(g),Bob
Casey(b),Cliff Leeman(dr).            Broadcast."At Condon's",NYC.March 17,1952
        Improvisation For The
           March Of Time (theme)
        The Lady Is A Tramp
        It's Been So Long
        Love Me Or Leave Me(1)
        Danny Boy
        Ballin' The Jack(2)
        It All Depends On You
        Bill Bailey Won't You
           Please Come Home(incompl.)


-1.Ralph Sutton(p-solo).
-2.Hall(cl),Ralph Sutton(p),b,dr only.

Wild Bill Davison(cnt) replaces Cary.  Broadcast."At Condon's",NYC.March 31,1952
(session cont. next page).
```

(session cont. from previous page):
    Improvisation For The
        March Of Time (theme)
    Fidgety Feet
    Memphis Blues
    Fascination(1)
    Medley: Aircheck 31
        Don't Take Your Love From Me
        Willow Weep For Me
        I'm Comin' Virginia
    Somebody Stole My Gal(2)
    Oh,By Jingo(incompl.)   Aircheck 31

-1.Ralph Sutton(p-solo).
-2.Hall(cl),Ralph Sutton(p),b,dr only.

Buzzy Drootin(dr) replaces Leeman.   Broadcast."At Condon's",NYC.April 7,1952
    Improvisation For The
        March Of Time (theme)
    At The Jazz Band Ball   Aircheck 31
    Mandy,Make Up Your Mind   -
    Jitterbug Waltz(1)
    Easter Parade   Aircheck 31
    Avalon(2)
    Wolverine Blues

-1.Ralph Sutton(p-solo).
-2.Hall(cl),Ralph Sutton(p),b,dr only.

EDDIE CONDON AND HIS ALL STARS:
Wild Bill Davison(cnt),Jimmy Archey(tb),Edmond Hall(cl),Frank Signorelli(p),Pops Foster
(b),George Wettling(dr).   Live.Town Hall,NYC.April 12,1952
    Blue Skies
    I Can't Believe That
        You're In Love With Me
    Hindustan
    I Can't Give You
        Anything But Love
    When The Saints Go Marching In

EDDIE CONDON AND HIS ORCHESTRA:
Johnny Windhurst(tp),Cutty Cutshall(tb),Edmond Hall(cl),Gene Schroeder(p),Eddie Condon(g),
Bob Casey(b),Cliff Leeman(dr).   Broadcast."At Condon's",NYC.April 14,1952
    Improvisation For The
        March Of Time (theme)
    Bill Bailey
    It All Depends On You
    You Met The Nicest
        People In Your Dreams(1)
    Medley:
        More Than You Know
        Sleepy Time Gal
        Deep Purple
    Everybody Loves My Baby(2)
    That Da Da Strain(incompl.)

-1.Ralph Sutton(p-solo).
-2.Hall(cl),Ralph Sutton(p),b,dr only.

Same.   Broadcast."At Condon's",NYC.April 21,1952
        Improvisation For The
           March Of Time (theme)
        Struttin' With Some Barbecue
        Jada
        Honeysuckle Rose(1)
        Way Down Yonder In New Orleans
        Do You Know What It
           Means To Miss New Orleans
        I'm Forever Blowing Bubbles

-1.Hall(cl),Ralph Sutton(p),b,dr only.

Buzzy Drootin(dr) replaces Leeman.   Broadcast."At Condon's",NYC.April 28,1952
        Improvisation For The
           March Of Time (theme)
        Big Butter And Egg Man
        Keepin' Out Of Mischief Now
        Exactly Like You(1)
        Medley:
           Sweet Lorraine
           Red Sails In The Sunset
           Why Shouldn't I
        Riverboat Shuffle

-1.Hall(cl),Ralph Sutton(p),b,dr only.

Omit Condon.   Broadcast."At Condon's",NYC.May 5,1952
        Improvisation For The
           March Of Time (theme)
        Swing That Music
        Sentimental Journey
        Lulu's Back In Town(1)
        What's The Use
        Original Dixieland One Step

-1.Hall(cl),Ralph Sutton(p),b,dr only.

Same.   Broadcast."At Condon's",NYC.May 13,1952
        Improvisation For The
           March Of Time (theme)
        Struttin' With Some Barbecue
        I Ain't Got Nobody
        St. Louis Blues(1)
        The Sheik Of Araby
        Save It Pretty Mama
        I Never Knew

-1.Hall(cl),Ralph Sutton(p),b,dr only.

Same.   Broadcast."At Condon's",NYC.May 20,1952
        Improvisation For The
           March Of Time (theme)
        Bill Bailey
        Beale Street Blues
        I Would Do Anything For You(1)
        Basin Street Blues
        How Come You Do Me Like You Do
        St. Louis Blues(incompl.)

-1.Hall(cl),Ralph Sutton(p),b,dr only.

Johnny Windhurst(tp),Eddie Hubble(tb),Edmond Hall(cl),Gene Schroeder(p),Bob Casey(b),Cliff
Leeman(dr).   Broadcast."At Condon's",NYC.May 28,1952
   Improvisation For The
    March Of Time (theme)
   Clarinet Marmalade
   Memphis Blues
   Ain't Misbehavin'(1)
   Louisiana
   As Long As I Live

-1.Hall(cl),Ralph Sutton(p),b,dr only.

Johnny Windhurst(tp),Cutty Cutshall(tb),Edmond Hall(cl),Gene Schroeder(p),Bill Goodall(b),
Mort Herbert(dr).   Broadcast."At Condon's",NYC.June 2,1952
   Improvisation For The
    March Of Time (theme)
   My Monday Date
   I'm Gonna Sit Right Down
   Love Me Or Leave Me(1)
   Hindustan
   Ballin' The Jack
   The Blues/Ol' Miss

-1.Ralph Sutton(p-solo).

Note:The above was the last Condon broadcast in WMGM's "Dr. Jazz" series.

EDDIE CONDON AND HIS ALL STARS:
Wild Bill Davison(cnt),Cutty Cutshall(tb),Edmond Hall(cl),Gene Schroeder(p),Eddie Condon
(g),Walter Page(b),Cliff Leeman(dr).   NYC.November 24,1953
CO50396 Beale Street Blues   Columbia 5-1870,B396,B1835,CL547,(J)EM6,Philips(E)
              BBR8085,Eu)B07706R,B07148L

CO50397 Riverboat Shuffle   Columbia CL547
CO50398 Medley(1)   -
   Emaline
   Don't Worry 'Bout Me
   I Can't Give You
    Anything But Love
CO50399 Jam Session Blues/Ol' Miss(2) Columbia JPA52114/15,5-1871,B396,CL547,Philips(Eu)
              429.190BE

-1.Add Dick Cary(tp,p),Peanuts Hucko(cl).
-2.Add Dick Cary(tp,p),Lou McGarity(tb),George Wettling(dr).

All titles also on Columbia(J)PL5006,(Arg)8013,Philips(E)BBL7013,(Eu)B07023L,CBS(Eu)53348,
(J)20AP1485,Coronet(Au)KLP554.
Note:Columbia 5-1871 only contains "Jam Session Blues" - Philips(Eu)429.190BE only con-
  tains "Ol' Miss".

Wild Bill Davison(cnt),Billy Butterfield(tp),Cutty Cutshall,Lou McGarity(tb),Dick Cary
(alth),Edmond Hall,Peanuts Hucko(cl),Bud Freeman(ts),Gene Schroeder(p),Eddie Condon(g),Al
Hall(b),Cliff Leeman(dr).   NYC.June 24,1954
CO51636 Blues (My Naughty
    Sweetie Gives To Me)   Columbia B1967,CB8,CL616,KG31564 (C31565),Philips
              (E)BBE12049,(Eu)429.105BE,CBS(Eu)67273
CO51637 How Come You Do Me Like You Do Columbia 5-2058,B474,B1968,CL616,Philips(Eu)
              B07901R
CO51638 Medley: Columbia 5-2057,B474,B1969,CL616
   When My Sugar
    Walks Down The Street
   I Can't Believe That
    You're In Love With Me

Omit Cary.   NYC.July 1,1954
CO51141 There'll Be Some Changes Made   Columbia 5-2057,B474,B1967,CL616,Philips(E)
                                         BBE12049,(Eu)429.105BE
CO51142 Tin Roof Blues   Columbia 5-2058,B474,B1969,CL616

All titles on CL616 also on Columbia JCL616,(Arg)8029,Philips(E)BBL7031,(Eu)07044L,CBS(Eu)
88032,(J)SOPZ34.

Wild Bill Davison(cnt),Cutty Cutshall(tb),Edmond Hall(cl),Gene Schroeder(p),Eddie Condon
(g),Walter Page(b),George Wettling(dr).   TV-cast.December 22,1954
        Beale Street Blues
        Medley:
            Emaline
            Don't Worry 'Bout Me
            I Can't Give You Anything But Love
        Riverboat Shuffle

Note:The above titles are from Steve Allen's "Tonight Show" TV-show.

Bobby Hackett (as "Pete Pesci")(cnt),Cutty Cutshall(tb),Dick Cary(alth),Edmond Hall(cl),
Gene Schroeder(p),Eddie Condon(g),Walter Page(b),George Wettling(dr).
                                               NYC.April 20,1955
CO53225 Singin' The Blues   Columbia CL719,Philips(E)BBE12098,(Eu)429.203BE
CO53226 From Monday On   -   -   - ,
                                         BO7183L
CO53227 I'm Comin' Virginia   Columbia CL719,CL777,Philips(E)BBE12098,(Eu)
                                         429.203BE,Coronet(Au)KLP500
CO53228 I'll Be Friend With Pleasure   Columbia CL719,Philips(E)BBE12280,(Eu)BO7901R
CO53229 Royal Garden Blues   Columbia B2093,CL719,Philips(E)BBE12098,(Eu)
                                         429.203BE

Wild Bill Davison(cnt) replaces Hackett;omit Cary.
                                               NYC.April 22,1955
CO53234 At The Jazz Band Ball   Columbia B2083,CL719,Philips(E)BBE12365,(Eu)
                                         429.728BE,429.866BE
CO53235 Louisiana   Columbia 5-2185,B539,CL719,Philips(E)BBE12280,(Eu)
                                         BO7901R,Franklin Mint 66
CO53236 Ol' Man River   Columbia B2083,CL719,Philips(E)BBE12365,(Eu)
                                         429.728BE,429.866BE
CO63237 Fidgety Feet   Columbia 5-2186,B539,CL719,Philips(E)(E)BBE12280,
                                         (Eu)429.083BE,429.589BE,BO7901R
CO53238 Jazz Me Blues   Columbia 5-2185,CB8,CL719

All titles also on Columbia(Arg)1020,(Uruguay)107,Harmony(Arg)17194.
All titles on CL719 also on Columbia(J)PL5023,20AP1832,Philips(E)BBL7109,(Eu)BO7088L,CBS
(Eu)88032,21129,Coronet(Au)KLP525.

Wild Bill Davison(cnt),Lou McGarity(tb),Pee Wee Russell(cl),Gene Schroeder(p),poss. Eddie
Condon(g),Walter Page(b),George Wettling(dr).
                                         Live.Miami Beach,Florida.November 27-29,1955
        Beale Street Blues   Pumpkin 111
        Medley: -
            Judy
            I'm In The Market For You
            Rockin' Chair
        I Ain't Gonna Give
            Nobody None Of My Jelly Roll   -
        Struttin' With Some Barbecue   -
        Singin' The Blues   -
        Dippermouth Blues   -
        Squeeze Me   -
        I Want To Be Happy   -

Unknown(tp),Wild Bill Davison(cnt),Cutty Cutshall(tb),Edmond Hall -1,Peanuts Hucko -2(cl),
Ralph Sutton(p),Eddie Condon(g),Walter Page(b),Buzzy Drootin(dr).
Live."At Condon's",NYC.c. 1955/56

        When You're Smiling(1)
        Blues In Limbo(2)
        When My Dreamboat Comes Home(2)
        Medley(2)
        Just You,Just Me(1)

Note:An incorrect rec.date (January 22,1956) has been given for the above session.

Wild Bill Davison(cnt),Cutty Cutshall(tb),Pee Wee Russell(cl),Gene Schroeder(p),Eddie
Condon(g),Walter Page(b),George Wettling(dr).
                                 NYC.February 16,1956

CO54487 I'm Gonna Sit Right Down
        And Write Myself A Letter   Columbia CL881,Philips(Eu)429.233BE
CO54488 Don't Get Around Much Anymore   -
CO54489 Three-Two-One Blues   - ,Philips(Eu)429.233BE,Time-Life
                            STL-J717
CO54490 I'm Confessin'   Columbia CL881,Philips(E)BBE12365
CO54491 Sometimes I'm Happy   -

Add Billy Butterfield(tp),Peanuts Hucko(cl,ts).
                                 NYC.February 20,1956

CO54494 Since My Best
        Girl Turned Me Down   Columbia CL881,Philips(Eu)B07901R
Co54495 Just Friends   - ,Philips(E)BBE12280,(Eu)B07901R
CO54496 Someday You'll Be Sorry   -

Billy Butterfield(tp),Cutty Cutshall(tb),Peanuts Hucko(cl),Ralph Sutton(p),Eddie Condon
(g),Walter Page(b),George Wettling(dr). NYC.February 23,1956
CO55587 Duff Campbell's Revenge   Columbia CL881,Philips(E)BBL7207,(Eu)BF322.214,
                            B07226L
CO55588 I've Got A Crush On You   Columbia CL881,Philips(Eu)429.233BE
CO55589 I've Found A New Baby   - ,Philips(E)BBE12365,(Eu)BF322.214,
                            429.233BE
CO55590 Original Dixieland One-Step   Columbia CL1020,Philips(E)BBL7184,(Eu)B07260L,
                            Coronet(Au)KLP687

All titles on CL881 also on Columbia(J)TD1006,Phillips(E)BBL7131,(Eu)B07193L,Coronet(Au)
KLP673.

Wild Bill Davison(cnt),Lou McGarity(tb),Peanuts Hucko(cl),Bud Freeman(ts),Gene Schroeder
(p),Eddie Condon(g),Jack Lesberg(b),Cliff Leeman(dr).
                           Live.Newport Jazz Festival,R.I.July 5,1956
CB56799 Dippermouth Blues   Columbia CL931
        At The Jazz Band Ball   unissued
CO56800 Bye And Bye   Columbia CL931,Philips(Eu)429.314BE
CO56801 Squeeze Me   -
CO56802 Struttin' With Some Barbecue   - ,Philips(Eu)429.314BE
CO56803 Big Butter And Egg Man   -

All titles - except "At The Jazz Band Ball" - also on Philips(E)BBL7151,(Eu)B07206L,
Coronet(Au)KLP571.
Note:The above concert also on Voice Of America transcriptions No.73,74.

Wild Bill Davison(cnt),Cutty Cutshall(tb),Bob Wilber(cl),Gene Schroeder(p),Eddie Condon
(g),Leonard Gaskin(b),George Wettling(dr). Live.Unknown location.c. 1956/57
(session cont. next page).

(session cont. from previous page):
    At The Jazz Band Ball   Jazzology J10
    Squeeze Me   -
    Sentimental Journey   -
    High Society   -
    Limehouse Blues   -
    Snowy Morning Blues   -
    Love Me Or Leave Me   -
    Mean To Me   -
    I Can't Give You
       Anything But Love   -
    I Ain't Gonna Give
       Nobody None Of My Jelly Roll -
    When The Saints Go Marching In -

Billy Butterfield(tp) replaces Davison.   NYC.June 28,1957
CO58207 What-Cha-Call-Em Blues   Columbia CL1089,Philips(E)JAZ115
CO58208 Heebie Jeebies   - ,(J)ZL1010,   -
CO58209 Chimes Blues   -   -
CO58210 My Monday Date   -   - ,Philips(Eu)BF322.275

Wild Bill Davison(cnt),Vic Dickenson(tb) replace Butterfield,Cutshall.
                            NYC.August 19,1957
CO59524-4 Wolverine Blues   Columbia CL1089,CK45145(CD),(J)ZL1010
CO59525-2 China Boy   Columbia CK45145(CD)
CO59525-3 China Boy   Columbia CL1089,CK45145(CD),(J)ZL1010,Philips(E)
                          BBL7356,(Eu)B13602L,RTB(Y)LPV4300
CO59526-2 St. James Infirmary Columbia CL1089,CK45145(CD),(J)ZL1010
CO59527-1 That's A Plenty   -   -   -
CO59528-4 The Song Is Ended   Columbia AM/BM14396, -
CO59529-2 Hindustan   -   -

Billy Butterfield(tp),Cutty Cutshall(tb) replace Davison,Dickenson.
                            NYC.September 25,1957
CO59867-4 Put 'Em Down Blues   Columbia CL1089,CK45145(CD),Philips(Eu)BF322.275
CO59868-5 Davenport Blues   -   -
CO59869-3 Apex Blues   Columbia AM/BM14396,CK45145(CD)
CO59869-? Apex Blues   Columbia CL1089
CO59870-1 What's The Use   Columbia AM/BM14396,CK45145(CD)
CO59883-3 Wrap Your Troubles In Dreams -   -
CO59884-3 When A Woman Loves A Man   -   -
CO59885-2 Minor Drag   -
CO59885-3 Minor Drag   Columbia CL1089,CK45145(CD),(J)ZL1010
CO59886-2 Why Was I Born   Columbia AM/BM14396,CK45145(CD)

All titles on CL1089 also on Philips(E)BBL7227,(Eu)B07301L.
All titles on CK45145 (CD) also on CBS(Eu)465680-2 (CD).

Billy Butterfield(tp),Rex Stewart(cnt),Dick Cary(tp,alth),Cutty Cutshall(tb),Herb Hall,
Peanuts Hucko(cl),Bud Freeman(ts),Gene Schroeder(p),Eddie Condon(g),Leonard Gaskin(b),
George Wettling(dr).   NYC.June 10/11,1958
    Medley: Dot DLP3141
       Copenhagen
       Riverboat Shuffle
       Sugar Foot Stomp
       Fidgety Feet
    Medley:
       Little White Lies   -
       Louisiana
       Dinah
       Indiana
(session cont. next page).

(session cont. from previous page):
 Medley: Dot DLP3141,(J)DOT5050
  Original Dixieland One Step
  I've Found A New Baby
  China Boy
  South Rampart Street Parade
 Medley: - ,DLP25878,(J)DOT5050,Rediff.(F)0100174
  At The Jazz Band Ball
  That's A Plenty
 Medley: -
  Now That You're Gone
  Willow Weep For Me
  Blue Again
 Medley: -
  Sugar
  Liza
  There'll Be Some Changes Made
  Nobody's Sweetheart
 Medley: - ,DLP25878,(J)DOT5050,Rediff.(F)0100174
  Clarinet Marmalade
  High Society

All titles also on Dot DLP25141,London(E)LTZ-D15158,Rediffusion(F)ZS162.

EDDIE CONDON AND HIS BOYS:
Omit Hucko.   NYC. 1958
 Blue Lou   MGM E3651
 Wherever There's Love   -
 Newport News   -
 The Lady's In Love With You -
 The Albatross   -
 Ya Got Trouble   -
 Ain't Misbehavin'   -
 Third Street Blues   -
 Ginger Brown   - ,Verve 845146-2(CD)
 Everybody's Movin'(rs)   -
 Eddie And The Milkman   -
 St. Louis Blues   - ,Verve(Eu)2615.044,831375-2(CD)

All titles also on MGM(E)C768,Verve(E)2683.051,Metro(G)2356.133.

Omit Butterfield,Cary.   NYC or LA. 1958
 Reisenweber Rag   World Pacific WP(S)1292
 Ostrich Walk   -
 Livery Stable Blues   -
 Lazy Daddy   -
 Sensation Rag   -
 Bluin' The Blues   -
 Lazy River   -
 Tiger Rag   -

All titles also on World Pacific WP9268,(J)K18P9268,Vogue(E)LAE12249,Sunset SUS5542.
Note:"Reisenweber Rag" as "Original One Step" on LAE12249.

EDDIE CONDON AND HIS CHICAGOANS:
Max Kaminsky(tp),Cutty Cutshall(tb),Pee Wee Russell(cl),Bud Freeman(ts),Dick Cary(p),Eddie
Condon(g),Leonard Gaskin(b),George Wettling(dr).
         NYC.February 26,1959
B50230 There'll Be Some Changes Made Warner Bros. W(S)1315
B50231 I've Found A New Baby   Warner Bros. ED1315-1,W(S)1315
B50232 Oh Baby   Warner Bros. W(S)1315
B50233 Love Is Just Around The Corner -

```
Al Hall(b) replaces Gaskin.                    NYC.February 27,1959
B50234 Nobody's Sweetheart          Warner Bros. ED1315-1,W(S)1315
B50235 Chicago                                  -          -
B50236 Shim-Me-Sha-Wabble           Warner Bros. W(S)1315
B50237 Someday Sweetheart                       -
B50238 Friar's Point Shuffle                    -
B50239 Liza                         Warner Bros. ED1315-1,W(S)1315
```

All titles from W(S)1315 also on Warner Bros. 7.90461-2 (CD),(E)WM4009,WS8009,(Eu)90461-1
WEA68011,(J)SB1037.

EDDIE CONDON AND HIS ORCHESTRA:
Pee Wee Russell(cl),Johnny Varro(p),Eddie Condon(g),rest unknown.
```
                                    Live."London House",Chicago.September  1960
        September In The Rain        I.A.J.R.C. IAJRC28
```

EDDIE CONDON'S CHICAGOANS:
Jimmy McPartland(tp),Jack Teagarden(tb,vcl),Pee Wee Russell(cl),Bud Freeman(ts),Joe Sulli-
van(p),Eddie Condon(g),Bob Haggart(b),Gene Krupa(dr).
```
                                    NYC.October 30,1961
        China Boy                   Pumpkin 115
        After You've Gone                   -
        Indiana                             -
        Blues For Today                     -
        Royal Garden Blues                  -
```

Note:The above titles are prob. from the rehearsals for the NBC TV-show "Chicago And All
     That Jazz" (November 26,1961 - see vol. 3 for details).

```
Same.                               NYC.October 30,1961
61VK514 Logan Square(jt)            Verve MGV8441,Metro(F)2355.015,(Eu)2356.017
61VK515 Chicago                              -           -             -
61VK516 After You've Gone(jt)                - ,845144-2(CD),-          -
61VK517 China Boy                            - ,
```

All titles also on Verve(E)2683.051.

Add Blossom Sealey,Lil Armstrong(vcl);McPartland also (vcl).
```
                                    NYC.October 31,1961
61VK518 Take Me To The
        Land Of Jazz(jt,bs,la)      Verve MGV8441
61VK519 Sugar(jmp)                           - ,Metro(Eu)2356.017
61VK521 Nobody's Sweetheart                  -            -
61VK523 Wolverine Blues                      - ,(G)2615.044,  -
61VK524 Chicago(jt,bs,la)                    -            -
```

All titles also on Verve(E)2683.051,Metro(F)2355.015.
All titles on MGV8441 also on Verve V6-8441,(E) (S)VLP9003,(J)VL1049,MV2019,MV2535,
20MJ0092 (CD).
Note:See LIL ARMSTRONG for additional titles from this session.

EDDIE CONDON AND HIS ALL STARS:
Wild Bill Davison(cnt),Cutty Cutshall(tb),Peanuts Hucko(cl),Johnny Varro(p),Eddie Condon
(g),Joe Williams(b),Buzzy Drootin(dr).   NYC. 1961
```
        Royal Garden Blues          Storyville(D)SLP242
        Blue And Brokenhearted               - ,Extreme Rarities LP1008
        Big Ben Blues                        -
        Stealin' Apples                      -
        Little Ben Blues                     -
        Muskrat Ramble                       -
(session cont. next page).
```

(session cont. from previous page):
All titles also on Storyville(Am)SLP4005.
Note:The above titles are from the Goodyear Tyre Company's "Eddie Condon" film soundtrack.
        Issued as EDDIE CONDON ALL STARS WITH WILD BILL DAVISON.

EDDIE CONDON AND THE ALL STARS:
Bobby Hackett(cnt),Lou McGarity(tb),Peanuts Hucko(cl,tamb),Dick Cary(p,alth),Eddie Condon
(g),Jack Lesberg(b),Buzzy Drootin(dr).   NYC.January 27,1962
C069040 Midnight In Moscow   Epic LA16024
C069041 Meadowlands   -
C069042 Dark Eyes   -
C069043 Theme From Swan Lake   -
C069044 Londonderry Air   -
C069045 La Vie En Rose   -
C069046 Hindustan(1)   -
        Loch Lomond   -
C069048 The Sheik Of Araby(1)   -
C069049 Japanese Sandman(1)(no dr)   -

1.Knobby Totah(b) replaces Lesberg.

11 titles also on Epic BA17024.

Bobby Hackett(cnt),Lou McGarity(tb),Peanuts Hucko(cl),John Mortilaro(p),Eddie Condon(g),
Jack Lesberg(b),George Wettling(dr).   NYC.September 4,1962
075740-2 Baby Elephant Walk   Columbia AM/BM14396
075741-8 Over And Over Again   -
075742-4 Circus On Parade   -
075743-2 Tiger Rag   Columbia CL1970,CS8770,CBS(Eu) (S)BPG62141,Amiga
                                        (G)8.50.083

EODIE CONDON AND HIS ALL STARS:
Buck Clayton(tp),Vic Dickenson(tb),Pee Wee Russell(cl),Bud Freeman(ts),Dick Cary(p,alth),
Eddie Condon(g),Jack Lesberg(b),Cliff Leeman(dr),Jimmy Rushing(vcl).
                                     Live.Sydney Stadium,Sydney.March 13/14,1964
        Caravan
        Dinah(no tp,tb,cl)
        St. Louis Blues
        Sugar(no tb,ts)   I.A.J.R.C. IAJRC28
        Stompin' At The Savoy(no tb,c,ts)
        I Can't Get Started(no tb,cl,ts)
        Am I Blues(jr)
        When You're Smiling(jr)
        Medley(jr):
           Goin' To Chicago
           I'm Gonna Move To
              The Outskirts Of Town
           See See Rider
           St. Louis Blues
        Medley(jr):
           Sent For You Yesterday
           Rock And Roll
           Sent For You Yesterday(encore)
        That's A Plenty(incompl.)

same.   Live.Hibiya Kohkaidoh,Tokyo.March 24,1964
        Muskrat Ramble   Chiaroscuro(J)UPS2069/70
        Do You Know What It
           Means To Miss New Orleans   -
        Rose Room   Chiaroscuro CR154,   -
        Manhattan(no tp,cl,ts)   -   -
(session cont. next page).

```
Please Don't Talk About
    Me When I'm Gone(no tp,cl,ts) Chiaroscuro(J)UPS2069/70
Three Little Words(no tp,tb,cl)  Chiaroscuro CR154,      -
Caravan                          Chiaroscuro CRD154(CD),-
I Would Do
    'Most Anything For You       Chiaroscuro CR154,      -
St. Louis Blues                                          -
Basin Street Blues               Chiaroscuro CRD154(CD),-
I Can't Believe That
    You're In Love With Me       Chiaroscuro CR154,      -
Pee Wee Blues(no tp,tb,ts)           -               -
Stompin' At The
    Savoy(no tb,cl,ts)               -               -
I Can't Get Started(no tb,cl,ts)     -
All Of Me(jr)                    Chiaroscuro CR154,      -
Am I Blue(jr)                        -               -
When You're Smiling(jr)              -               -
Medley(jr):                      Chiaroscuro CRD154(CD),-
    Goin' To Chicago
    Every Day I Have The Blues
    See See Rider
    St. Louis Blues(1)
Royal Garden Blues               Chiaroscuro CR154,      -
```

-1.Prob. not on CRD154 (CD).

All titles also on Chiaroscuro(J)ULS1684/85.
All titles on CR154 also on Chiaroscuro CRD154 (CD).

Same.   Live.Festival Hall,Osaka,Japan.March 27,1964
```
    Muskrat Ramble
    St. Louis Blues
    Basin Street Blues
    Caravan
    Pee Wee Blues(no tp,tb,ts)
    Stompin' At The
        Savoy(no tb,cl,ts)
    All Of Me(jr)
    Am I Blue(jr)
    When You're Smiling(jr)
    Medley(jr):
        Goin' To Chicago
        I'm Gonna Move To
            The Outskirts Of Town
        See See Rider
        St. Louis Blues
    Medley(jr):
        Sent For You Yesterday
        Rock And Roll
        Sent For You Yesterday(encore)
```

Note:The above titles were issued in England (in a limited edition) on a "blank" label.

EDDIE CONDON AND HIS ALL STARS:
Wild Bill Davison(cnt),Cutty Cutshall(tb),Edmond Hall(cl),Dick Wellstood(p),Eddie Condon
(g),Willie Wayman(b),Hap Gormley(dr).   NYC. 1964
```
    The Sheik Of Araby             Storyville(D)SLP242
    Bugle Call Rag                       -
    Wild Bill Blues                      -
    Farewell Blues                       -
```

All titles also on Storyville(Am)SLP4005.

EDDIE CONDON AND HIS ALL STARS:
Wild Bill Davison(cnt),George Brunies(tb),Tom Gwaltney(cl),Don Ewell(p),Eddie Condon(g),
Bill Goodall(b),Frank Marshall(dr).   Live.Manassas Jazz Festival,Virginia.December 1,1968
        At The Jazz Band Ball   Jazzology J50
        Sister Kate   -
        Royal Garden Blues   -
        That's A Plenty   -
        Muskrat Ramble   -
        Medley:
            Ja Da   -
            When A Woman Loves A Man
            You Took Advantage Of Me
        Squeeze Me   -
        I've Found A New Baby   -

CONDON - McPARTLAND CHICAGOANS:
Jimmy McPartland(tp),Ed Hubble(tb),Johnny Mince(cl),Dill Jones(p),Eddie Condon(g),Bill
Pemberton(b),Gene Krupa(dr).   Live.Meriden,Conn.December 5,1969
        I've Found A New Baby   Connecticut Traditional Jazz Club SLP6

EDDIE CONDON AND HIS STROLLING REUNION COMMODORES:
Wild Bill Davison(cnt),George Brunies(tb,vcl),Tom Gwaltney(cl),John Eaton(p),Eddie Condon
(g),Bill Goodall(b),Cliff Leeman(dr),Johnson "Fat Cat" McRee(vcl).
                                    Live.Manassas Jazz Festival,Virginia.December 7,1969
        Blues My Naughty Sweetie Gives   Fat Cat's Jazz FCJ114
        Medley: -
            It Had To Be You
            When A Woman Loves A Man
            Ja Da
            You Took Advantange Of Me
        'S Wonderful   -
        Struttin' With Some Barbecue   -
        Angry(gb)   -
        Sunday   -
        Georgia On My Mind(fmr)   -
        Ghost Of A Chance   -

EDDIE CONDON ALL STARS:
Wild Bill Davison(cnt),Ed Hubble(tb),Johnny Mince(cl),Dill Jones(p),Eddie Condon(g),Jack
Lesberg(b),Cliff Leeman(dr).   NYC.c. 1970
        How Come You Do Me Like You Do   Jazzology J100
        Time After Time   -
        Crazy Rhythm   -
        Them There Eyes   -
        Eddie's Blues   -

EDDIE CONDON AND HIS ALL STARS:
Wild Bill Davison(cnt),Lou McGarity(tb),Tom Gwaltney(cl),John Eaton(p),Eddie Condon(g),
Bill Goodall(b),Cliff Leeman(dr).   Live.Manassas Jazz Festival,Virginia.December 6,1970
        Lazy River   Fat Cat's Jazz FCJ124,Storyville(D)SLP513
        Avalon   -   -
        I Want To Be Happy   -   -
        Sweet Georgia Brown   Fat Cat's Jazz FCJ126
        I Can't Get Started   -

EDDIE CONDON AND HIS ALL STARS:
Wild Bill Davison(cnt),Herb Gardner(tb,alth),Joe Muranyi(cl),Deane Kincaide(ts,bars),Art
Hodes(p),Eddie Condon(g),Van Perry(b),Skip Tomlinson(dr).
                                    Live.Manassas Jazz Festival,Virginia.December 5,1971
        Someday You'll Be Sorry   Fat Cat's Jazz FCJ141
        Avalon   -
        Love Is Just Around The Corner   -

Wallace Davenport(tp),Freddie Moore(dr) replace Davison,Tomlinson;omit Kincaide.
```
                                    Same date
        Darkness On The Delta       Fat Cat's Jazz FCJ141
        Washboard Blues(p-solo)                    -
        St. Louis Blues            Fat Cat's Jazz FCJ130
```

All titles on FCJ141 also on Jazzology J73.
Note:FCJ141 (and equivalents) also includes the title "Condon" performed by George Brunie
    (p,vcl) - this title was recorded in Manassas May 6,1973.

EDDIE CONDON AND HIS JAZZ BAND:
Wild Bill Davison(cnt),Kenny Davern(cl),Dick Wellstood(p),Eddie Condon(g),Gene Krupa(dr).
```
                              Live.New School For Social Research,NYC.April  197
        I Want To Be Happy         Chiaroscuro CR110
        Sugar                                  -
        Shim-Me-Sha-Wabble(no cnt)             -
        Avalon                                 -
        That Da Da Strain                      -
        Blues In C                             - ,CR204
        The Mooche(no cnt)                     -
        I Can't Believe That
            You're In Love With Me             -
        Struttin' With Some Barbecue Chiaroscuro CRD110(CD)
        China Boy                              -
```

All titles on CR110 also on Chiaroscuro CRD110 (CD),Storyville(D)SLP515.

LES CONDON (British)

See TUBBY HAYES.

ANDRE CONDOUANT (French)

Eddy Louiss(p),André Condouant(g),Percy Heath(b),Connie Kay(dr).
```
                                    Paris.November 4,1970
        Brother Meeting            Debs(F)HDD523
        Blues For Wes                          -
        Short B.N.                             -
        Poema                                  -
        Ballad For Annie                       -
        Astrakan                               -
```

Richard Raux(ts),Michel Graillier(p),André Coundouant(g),Sylvain Marc(el-b),Tony
Rabeson(dr),Jean-Pierre Coco(perc).   Paris.November 1979
```
        Happy Funk                 Debs(F)HDD662
        Super Chic                             -
        I Want Another Life                    -
        As You Like It                         -
        Flying Saucer                          -
```


CONFEDERATE COLONELS OF JAZZ

(section cont. next page).

Armin Kay(cnt),Bill Crais(tb,vcl),Jimmy Pugh(cl),Ralph "Buddy" Jackson(p),Edmond Souchon
(g),Howard "Bunny" Franks(b),Dick Johnson(dr).
New Orleans.August 10,1959

Beale Street Blues	Golden Crest(S)CR3063
I'm Coming Virginia	-
Mississippi Mud	-
Little Rock Getaway	-
Carolina In The Morning	-
Save Your Confederate Money(bc)	-
Missouri Waltz	-
Georgia On My Mind	-
On Miami Shores	-
Stars Fell On Alabama	-
Why Don't You Come	
Back To Louisiana(bc)	-
My Old Kentucky Home	-

ONFLUENCE (French)

ean Querlier(oboe,enh,fl,as,ss),Christian Escoudé(g),Jean-Charles Capon(cello),Didier
evallet(b),Merzak Mouthna,Armand Lemal(dr,perc).
Paris.December 20,1975/Villejuif,France.January 25,1976

Dakka	RCA(F)FPL1.0132
Convergences	-
Quatre Voyages	-

hristian Lété(dr) replaces Mouthana. Paris.May 1977

Après Le Désert	RCA(F)PL37109
A Propos De La Sorite	-
Les Quais En Automne	-
Eté D'sver(?)	-
Takssim	-
Arkham	-

ean Querlier(oboe,enh,fl,as),Philippe Petit(g),Denis Van Hecke(cello),Didier Levallet
),Christian Lété(dr),Yves Herwan-Chotard(perc).
Paris.October 23-26,1978

Chroniques Terrestres(1,2)	RCA(F)PL37239
Bolero Loco	-
Dans Mon Grenier(2)	-
Rumeurs	-

..Add Roger Guérin(flh).
..Add André Jaume(bcl).

RRY CONGER

RRY CONGER'S TWO RIVERS JAZZ BAND:
rry Conger(cnt,vcl),Charlie Bornemann(tb),Tommy Wicks(cl),Ralph Goodwin(p),Jim Spruill
j),John Haynes(b),Tony Torre(dr). Camden,South Carolina.December 12,1965

Atlanta Blues	Solo S101
Wise Guys(lc)	-
Chimes Blues	-
When I See All The Lovin'	
They Waste On Babies(lc)	-
Wolverine Blues	-

ession cont. next page).

(session cont. from previous page):
```
      Sailin' Down Chesapeake Bay(lc)   Solo S101
      Smokey Mokes                           -
      Auntie Skinner's
         Chicken Dinner(lc)                  -
      Hard Hearted Hannah(lc)                -
      Ory's Creole Trombone                  -
      New Orleans Shuffle                    -
```

Same.   Charlotte,North Carolina.April 7,1966
```
      Snake Rag                        Solo S102
      Something For Annie                   -
      Come Back For Papa                    -
      I Had Someone Else(lc)                -
      Yellow Dog Blues                      -
      Dallas Blues                          -
      Storyville Blues                      -
      Floatin' Down To Cotton Town          -
      Red Hot Mama(lc)                      -
      Swanee Sue                            -
```

Same.   Charlotte,North Carolina.October 19,1966
```
      Lowcountry Blues                 Solo S104
      Sobbin' Blues                         -
      Nobody Knows You When
         You're Down And Out(lc)            -
      Oriental Strut                        -
      My Heart (Will Always
         Lead Me Back To You)               -
      Milenburg Joys                        -
      Honky Tonk                            -
      Angry                                 -
      Two Rivers Rag                        -
      Lowcountry Blues(alt.take)            -
```

Same.   Unknown location.Poss. 1973
```
      Willie The Weeper                Audex AX101
      All The Wrongs You've Done To Me      -
      Irish Black Bottom                    -
      Kansas City Man Blues                 -
      Coney Island Washboard                -
      Fidgety Feet                          -
      See See Rider                         -
      Get It Right                          -
      Just A Closer Walk With Thee          -
      Canal Street Blues                    -
```

All titles also on Solo S106.

CHECCO CONIGLIO (Italian)

See DR. DIXIE JAZZBAND.

CONJUNTO "A" DEL HOT CLUB DE BUENOS AIRES (Argentinean)

Juan Martinez(tp),Carlos Blasi(tb),Antonio Sofia(cl),Rene Gilbert(p),Eduardo Rey(b),
Rodolfo Alchurron(g),Carlos Speroni(dr).
(session cont. next page).

CONJUNTO "A" DEL HOT CLUB DE BUENOS AIRES

(session cont. from previous page):
```
                                  Live(?).Teatro La Mascara.Buenos Aires.July 6,1954
     Lazy Daddy                   Odeon(Arg)LDS170
     Improvisation On Blues              -
     I've Found a New Baby               -
     At Sundowm                          -
     Someday Sweetheart                  -
```


CONJUNTO SANTA ANITA EN EL ALMA (Argentinean)

see SANTA ANITA.

UD CONLON

(vcl) acc. by RED NICHOLS AND HIS FIVE PENNIES:
Red Nichols(cnt),Ted Vesely(tb),Matty Matlock(cl),Joe Rushton(bassax),Stan Wrightsman(p),
ick Fatool(dr).   LA.February 1954
```
     Wrist Pin Charlie            DR 1001
     Readers Frank                      -
     Speed Shift Hal              DR 1002
     Draggin' Every Sunday              -
```
ote:Additional recordings by this artist are not included.

CONNECTICUT JAZZ FESTIVAL

see also DUKE ELLINGTON,WILLIE "THE LION" SMITH.

FESTIVAL ALL STARS:
ick Clayton(tp),Jimmy Hamilton(cl),Paul,Gonsalves(ts),Hank Jones(p),Sam Woodyard(dr).
```
                                  Live.Westport,Conn.July 28,1956
     Tea For Two(1)               I.A.J.R.C.  IAJRC45,Queen(I)Q-044
     Ad Lib Blues                       -                 -
```
..Add Sidney Gross(g),poss. Jimmy Woode(b).

GGY CONNELLY

(cl) acc. by RUSS GARCIA'S WIGVILLE BAND:
te Candoli,Stu Williamson(tp),Russ Cheever(ss),Charlie Mariano(as),Bill Holman(ts),Jimmy
uffre(bars),Al Hendrickson(g),Max Bennett(b),Stan Levey(dr),Russ Garcia(arr,cond).
```
                                  LA.January 16/17/18,1956
     That Old Black Magic         Bethlehem BEP128,BCP53,Parlophone(E)GEP8762
     Ev'ry Time We Say Goodbye           -        -
     Trav'lin Light                      -
     Ev'ry Time                          -
     It Never Entered My Mind            -
     Why Shouldn't I                     -
     Gentleman Friend             Bethlehem BEP128,   - ,Parlophone(E)GEP8762
     What Is There To Say                -        -
     He Was Too Good To Me               -
     I Got Plenty O'Nuttin'              - ,Parlophone(E)GEP8762
```
ession cont. next page).

(session cont. from previous page):
        Fools Rush In   Bethlehem BCP53
        Alone Together   - ,Parlophone(E)GEP8762

All titles also on Fresh Sound(Sp)FSR2018.

JACK CONNER

JACK CONNER AND HIS ORCHESTRA:
Hubert Rostaing(cl),André Ekyan(as),Jack Conner(vbs),Léo Chauliac(p),Paul Mattei(g),Emma-
nuel Soudieux(b),Pierre Fouad(dr).   Paris.July 10,1945
OSW406-1 After You've Gone   Swing(F)195,Pathe(F)C.054-16028
OSW407-1 Stompin' At The Savoy   - ,   -

RAY CONNIFF

Incl. Johnny Best(tp),Ray Conniff(tb),Skeets Herfurt(cl),Bill Moody(dr).
                                           Live.Germany.c. 1969
        Muskrat Ramble   CBS(Eu)S66219
        Tin Roof Blues   -

Johnny Best(tp),Ray Conniff(tb),Skeets Herfurt(cl),Johnny Guarnieri(p),unknown bj,b,Panar
Francis(dr).   Live."Sahara Hotel",Lake Tahoe,Calif.c. 19
        Muskrat Ramble   Columbia G30122
        South Rampart Street Parade   -

Note:Additional titles from the above LPs are not included - neither are other recording=
     by this artist.

CHRIS CONNOR

See also ART FORD'S JAZZ PARTY,CLAUDE THORNHILL.

(vcl) acc. by SY OLIVER ORCHESTRA:
Jim Bright,Red Solomon,Jimmy Nottingham(tp),Kai Winding,Vernon Friley,Frank Saracco,Ward
Silloway(tb),Sid Cooper,Milt Yaner(as),Boomie Richman,Sam Taylor(ts),Dave McRae(bars),Da
Martin(p),Sid Block(b),Jimmy Crawford(dr),Sy Oliver(arr,cond).
                                           NYC.December 17/18,1953
        Blue Silhouette   Bethlehem 1291,BEP114,BCP6004,EXLP-6
        Miser's Serenade   -   - ,BCP56,(J)33CY1641(CD),Lond
                                           (E)HBN1074
        Ask Me   Bethlehem 1293,BEP114,BCP6004,Ember(E)EMB3347
        Chiquita From Chi-Wah-Wah   -   -   -
        Indian Summer   Bethlehem BEP130,BCP56,(J)33CY1641(CD),London(E)
                                           HBN1074
        Everything I Love   Bethlehem BEP127,BCP56,(J)33CY1641(CD),London(E)
                                           HBN1074

All titles also on Bethlehem(J)MP2378.
All titles on BCP56 also on Bethlehem(J)22AP234,YP7102,PAP23024,COCY6491 (CD),Ember(E)
EMB3341,Angel(J)HV3011.
All titles on BCP6004 also on Bethlehem BR5021,BCP6004 (CD),(G)BTM6823,(J)SOPL283,YP710:
PAP23003,CY4592 (CD),30CY1432 (CD),Parlophone(E)PMC1082,Angel(J)HV3001.

(vcl) acc. by ELLIS LARKINS TRIO:
Ellis Larkins(p),Everett Barksdale(g),Beverley Peer(b).
NYC.August 9/11,1954

I Hear Music	Bethlehem BEP101A,BCP56,(J)33CY1641(CD),London(E) HBN1074,Affinity(E)AFF122,Charly(E)CD97(CD)
What Is There To Say	Bethlehem 11001,BEP101A,BCP6004,BCP6041,Affinity (E)AFF97
Come Back To Sorrento	Bethlehem 11005,BEP101A,BCP56,EXLP-6,(J)33CY1641 (CD),Stateside(J)SR7055,Affinity(E)AFF122
Why Shouldn't I	Bethlehem BEP101A,BCP6004,Affinity(E)AFF122
Lullaby Of Birdland	Bethlehem 3081,BEP101B,BCP6004,BCP6068,(J) 35C38-7345(CD),London(E)EZ-N19010,Stateside (J)SR7055,Affinity(E)AFF97,Charly(E)CD97(CD)
Try A Little Tenderness	Bethlehem 11001,BEP101B,BCP6004,BCP6041,(J) 35C38-7345(CD),London(E)EZ-N1901,Stateside (J)SR7055,Affinity(E)AFF97
All About Ronnie	Bethlehem 3081,BEP101B,BCP56,(J)35C38-7345(CD), 33CY1641(CD),London(E)HBN1074,EZ-N19010,Sta- teside(J)SR7055,Affinity(E)AFF122
Spring Is Here	Bethlehem BEP101B,BCP6004,London(E)EZ-N19010,Sta- teside(J)SR7055,Affinity(E)AFF97

All titles also on Bethlehem BCP1001,(J)MP2340,Charly(E)CD115 (CD).
All titles - except "Why Shouldn't I" - also on Bethlehem 2BP1001.
All titles on BCP56 also on Bethlehem(J)22AP234,YP7102,PAP23024,COCY6491 (CD),Ember(E)
EMB3341,Angel(J)HV3011.
All titles on BCP6004 also on Bethlehem BR5021,BCP6004 (CD),(G)BTM6823,(J)SOPL283,YP7103,
PAP23003,CY4592 (CD),30CY1432 (CD),Parlophone(E)PMC1082,Angel(J)HV3001.

(vcl) acc. by VINNIE BURKE QUARTET:
Ronnie Odrich(fl,cl),Don Burns(acc),Joe Cinderella(g),Vinnie Burke(b),Art Mardigan(dr).
NYC.August 21,1954

Lush Life	Bethlehem BEP102A,BCP56,BCP6006,2BP1001,(J) 33CY1641(CD),35C38-7345(CD),London(E)REN1093, Affinity(E)AFF122
Out Of This World	Bethlehem BEP102A,BCP56,2BP1001,(J),(J)33CY1641 (CD),Affinity(E)AFF122,Charly(E)CD97(CD)
A Cottage For Sale	Bethlehem BEP102A,BCP6004,BCP6041,Stateside(J) SR7055,Affinity(E)AFF122
How Long Has This Been Going On	Bethlehem BEP102A,BCP6004,Stateside(J)SR7055
Goodbye	Bethlehem BEP102B,BCP6004,BCP6041,(J)35C38-7345 (CD),Stateside(J)SR7055,Affinity(E)AFF122
Stella By Starlight	Bethlehem BEP102B,BCP6004,2BP1001,(J)35C38-7345 (CD),Stateside(J)SR7055,Affinity(E)AFF97
Gone With The Wind	Bethlehem BEP102B,BCP6004,2BP1001,(J)35C38-7345 (CD),Stateside(J)SR7055,Affinity(E)AFF97
He's Coming Home	Bethlehem BEP102B,BCP6004,Affinity(E)AFF122

All titles also on Bethlehem BCP1002,(J)MP2340,London(E)LZ-N14007,Charly(E)CD115 (CD).
All titles on BCP56 also on Bethlehem(J)22AP234,YP7102,PAP23024,COCY6491 (CD),Ember(E)
EMB3341,Angel(J)HV3011.
All titles on BCP6004 also on Bethlehem BR5021,BCP6004 (CD),(G)BTM6823,(J)SOPL283,YP7103,
PAP23003,CY4592 (CD),30CY1432 (CD),Parlophone(E)PMC1082,Angel(J)HV3001.
Note:Some discographies list an alternate take of "Lush Life" issued on AFF122; this is
not correct: AFF122 only has one track of "Lush Life" (with the same take as on other
issues).

(vcl) acc. by Herbie Mann(fl),Ralph Sharon(p),Joe Puma(g),Milt Hinton(b),Osie Johnson(dr).
NYC.April 1955

(session cont. next page).

(session cont. from previous page):

Blame It On My Youth	Bethlehem 11005,BEP129,BCP20,2BP1001,EXLP-6,(J) 35C38-7345(CD),Stateside(J)SR7055,Affinity (E)AFF97
Ridin' High	Bethlehem BEP129,BCP20,2BP1001,Parlophone(E) GEP8778,Affinity(E)AFF122
It's Alright With Me	Bethlehem 11012,BEP126,BCP20,BCP6006,2BP1001,(J) 35C38-7345(CD),London(E)REN1093,Stateside(J) SR7055,Parlophone(E)GEP8767,Affinity(E)AFF97
All Dressed Up With A Broken Heart	Bethlehem BEP126,BCP20,2BP1001,2BP1001,(J) 35C38-7345(CD),Parlophone(E)GEP8778,Affinity (E)AFF122
Trouble Is A Man	Bethlehem BEP130,BCP20,2BP1001,Stateside(J)SR7055, Affinity(E)AFF122
All This (Is Mine) And Heaven Too	Bethlehem 11012,BEP130,BCP20,BCP6006,Parlophone(E) GEP8778,Affinity(E)AFF122

All titles also on Bethlehem BCP6010(new series),(J)33CY1641 (CD).

Add Kai Winding,J.J. Johnson(tb).	NYC.April 1955
From This Moment On	Bethlehem BEP126,BEP130,BCP20,BCP56,BCP6010(new series),2BP1001,(J)35C38-7345(CD),Parlophone (E)GEP8767,Stateside(J)SR7055,Affinity(E) AFF122,Charly(E)AFF97
The Thrill Is Gone	Bethlehem BEP126,BCP20,BCP6006,BCP6010(new ser.), 2BP1001,(J)35C38-7345(CD),Stateside(J)SR7055, London(E)REN1093,Parlophone(E)GEP8778,Affini- ty(E)AFF97
Someone To Watch Over me	Bethlehem BEP129,BCP20,BCP6010(new series),(J) 35C38-7345(CD),Parlophone(E)GEP8767,Affinity (E)AFF122
I Concentrate On You	Bethlehem BEP129,BCP20,BCP6010(new ser.),2BT1001, (J)35C38-7345(CD),Stateside(J)SR7055,Affinity (E)AFF97
Don't Wait Up For Me	Bethlehem BEP127,BCP56,(J)MP2334,London(E)HBN1074
A Good Man Is A Seldom Thing	Bethlehem BEP127,BCP56,(J)MP2334,London(E)HBN1074
In Other Words (Fly Me To The Moon)	Bethlehem BEP127,BCP56,(J)MP2334,35C38-7345(CD), London(E)HBN1074,Affinity(E)AFF122

All titles also on Bethlehem(J)33CY1641 (CD).
All titles on BCP20 also on Bethlehem BR5017,BCP20 (CD),(J)MP2334,22AP233,YP7101,PAP23029,
CY3779 (CD),London(E)LZ-N14036.
All titles on BCP56 also on Bethlehem(J)22AP234,YP7102,PAP23024,COCY6491 (CD),Ember(E)
EMB3341,Angel(J)HV3011.

(vcl) acc. by unknown orchestra,Ralph Burns(arr,cond).
NYC.January 19,1956

1835	My April Heart	Atlantic EP577,LP/SD1228
1836	When The Wind Was Green	Atlantic LP/SD1228
1837	He Was Too Good For Me	Atlantic EP577,LP/SD1228,LP8082,(J)AMCY1078(CD)
1838	Something To Live For	Atlantic LP/SD1228,81817-1,81817-2(CD)

(vcl) acc. by John Lewis(p),Barry Galbraith(g),Oscar Pettiford(b),Connie Kay(dr).
NYC.January 23,1956

1853	Where Are You	Atlantic LP/SD1228
1854	I Get A Kick Out Of You	- ,81817-1,81817-2(CD),LP8082,(J) AMCY1078(CD)
1855	Ev'rytime	Atlantic LP/SD1228
1856	Almost Like Being In Love	-

(vcl) acc. by Nick Travis(tp),Sam Marowitz,Ray Beckenstein(as),Zoot Sims,Al Young(ts),
Danny Bank(bs),Moe Wechsler(p),Barry Galbraith(g),Milt Hinton(b),Osie Johnson(dr).
NYC.February 8,1956

1874	You Make Me Feel So Young	Atlantic EP577,LP/SD1228
1875	Anything Goes	Atlantic LP/SD1228,(J)MJ7020
1876	'Way Out There	Atlantic EP577,LP/SD1228
1877	Get Out Of Town	Atlantic LP/SD1228

All titles on LP/SD1228 also on Atlantic(J)ATL5002,P6012,AMCY1050(CD),London(E)HAK2020,
SAK-K6032.

(vcl) acc. by unknown orchestra,poss. Ray Ellis(arr).
NYC.February 15,1956

1878	Go 'Way From My Window	Atlantic 1097,LP8014,LP8082,(J)AMCY1078(CD)
1879	Past The Age Of Innocence	- -
1880	Speak Low	Atlantic LP8014
1881	My Ideal	-

All titles on LP8014 also on Atlantic(J)AMCY1059 (CD).

(vcl) acc. by unknown orchestra,Ralph Burns(arr,cond).
NYC.June 5,1956

2006	Round About	Atlantic LP/SD1240
2007	But Not For Me	- ,601-2(CD),(Eu)7.81980-2(CD),(J) AMCY1051/52(CD)
2008	Oh! You Crazy Moon	Atlantic LP/SD1240,LP8082,(J)AMCY1078(CD)
2009	High On A Windy Hill	-

(vcl) acc. by unknown orchestra,prob. Ralph Burns(arr).
NYC.June 6,1956

2010	Why Can't I	Atlantic LP/SD1240
2011	Suddenly It's Spring	-
2012	Angel Eyes	-
2013	You Stepped Out Of A Dream	-

All titles on LP/SD1240 also on Atlantic(J)AMCY1058(CD),London(E)HAK2060.

(vcl) acc. by unknown orchestra,prob. Ray Ellis(arr).
NYC.July 28,1956

2063	My Heart Is So Full Of You	Atlantic 1105,EP580,LP8014
2064	I Miss You So	- - - ,81817-1,81817-2(CD),(J) ACMY1078(CD)
2065	Radar Blues	Atlantic LP8014

All titles on LP8014 also on Atlantic(J)AMCY1059 (CD).

(vcl) acc. by unknown orchestra,prob. Ralph Burns(arr).
NYC.August 7,1956

2073	I Guess I'll Hang My Tears Out To Dry	Atlantic LP/SD1240
2074	Thursday's Child	-
2075	I Wonder What Became Of Me	-
2076	About The Blues	-

All titles on LP/SD1240 also on Atlantic(J)AMCY1058(CD),London(E)HAK2060.

(vcl) acc. by unknown orchestra.   NYC.October 16,1956

2158	Time Out For Tears	Atlantic 1121,EP580,LP8014
2159	Trust In Me	Atlantic 1138,LP8014
2160	Mixed Emotions	- -
2161	I Love You,Yes I Do	Atlantic 1121,EP580

(session cont. next page).

(session cont. from previous page):
All titles on LP8014 also on Atlantic(J)AMCY1059 (CD).

(vcl) acc. by Joe Wilder(tp),Al Cohn(ts),Eddie Costa(vbs),Ralph Sharon(p,arr),Oscar Petti-
ford(b),Osie Johnson(dr).   NYC.November 16,1956
2204   Poor Little Rich Girl   Atlantic LP/SD1286
2205   Everything I've Got   Atlantic EP615,LP/SD1286
2206   All I Need Is You   Atlantic LP/SD1286
2207   It Only Happens
       When I Dance With You   Atlantic EP615,LP/SD1286

(vcl) acc. by Sam Most(fl),Eddie Costa(vbs),Ralph Sharon(p,arr),Joe Puma(g),Oscar Petti-
ford(b),Osie Johnson(dr).   NYC.December 17,1956
2243   Lonely Town   Atlantic LP/SD1286
2244   Fancy Free   -
2245   Moon Ray   Atlantic EP615,LP/SD1286
2246   Driftwood   Atlantic LP/SD1286

(vcl) acc. by Al Cohn,Lucky Thompson(ts),Eddie Costa(vbs),Ralph Sharon(p,arr),Oscar Petti-
ford(b),Osie Johnson(dr),Chino Pozo(bg),Mongo Santamaria(cg).
                                              NYC.December 19,1956
2278   My Shining Hour   Atlantic LP/SD1286
2279   Just Squeeze Me   -
2280   I'm Shooting High   Atlantic EP615,LP/SD1286
2281   It's A Most Unusual Day   Atlantic LP/SD1286

All titles on LP/SD1286 also on Atlantic(J)ATL5017,P6130,P4576,AMCY1072 (CD),London(E)
LTZ-K15142.

(vcl) acc. by unknown orchestra.   NYC.January 31,1957
2320   Who Cares   Atlantic unissued
2321   Looking For A Boy
2322   Liza

(vcl) acc. by Joe Newman(tp),Al Cohn(ts),Eddie Costa(vbs),Ralph Sharon(p,arr),Milt Hinton
(b),Osie Johnson(dr),John Rodriguez(bg).   NYC.February 1,1957
2323   Of Thee I Sing   Atlantic LP/SD2-601
2324   Strike Up The Band   -
2325   I've Got A Crush On You   Atlantic EP593,   -
2326   Soon   Atlantic EP595,   -
2327   Liza   -
2328   Looking For A Boy   Atlantic EP594,   -
2329   I Got Rhythm   - ,(J)MJ4010

(vcl) acc. by Herbie Mann(fl),Ralph Sharon(p,arr),Barry Galbraith(g),Oscar Pettiford(b),
Ronnie Free(dr).   NYC.February 7,1957
2334   I've Got Beginner's Luck   Atlantic LP/SD2-601
2335   Slap That Bass   - ,Clarion LP/SD611
2336   For You,For Me,For Evermore   -   -
2337   Love Is Sweeping The Country   Atlantic EP596,   -

(vcl) acc. by Ralph Sharon(p,arr),Oscar Pettiford(b),Osie Johnson(dr).
                                              NYC.February 26,1957
2384   The Man I Love   Atlantic EP595,LP/SD2-601,(J)MJ4010,MJ7020
2385   'S Wonderful   Atlantic EP596,   -   -
2386   A Foggy Day   -   - ,Clarion
                                       LP/SD611
2387   Summertime   Atlantic EP594,LP/SD2-601,LP8082,(J)MJ4010,
                                       AMCY1078(CD),Clarion LP/SD611
2388   There's A Boat That's
       Leavin' Soon For New York   Atlantic EP595,LP/SD2-601
2389   I Love You,Porgy   Atlantic LP2-601,Clarion LP/SD611

(vcl) acc. Peanuts Hucko(cl),Herbie Mann,Sam Most(fl),Ralph Sharon(p,arr),Joe Puma(g),
Vinnie Burke(b),Osie Johnson(dr).   NYC.March 12,1957

2418	Our Love Is Here To Stay	Atlantic unissued
2419	Nice Work If You Can Get It	Atlantic EP595,LP/SD2-601,Clarion LP/SD611
2420	Blah,Blah,Blah	Atlantic EP593, -
2421	They Can't Take That Away From Me	Atlantic LP/SD2-601,(J)MJ7020,Clarion LP/SD611

(vcl) acc. by Jimmy Cleveland,Warren Covington,Jim Thompson(tb),Ed Wassermann(ts,bcl),Hank
Jones(p),Barry Galbraith(g),Wendell Marshall(b),Ed Shaughnessy(dr),Ray Ellis(arr).
     NYC.March 26,1957

2422	Clap Yo' Hands	Atlantic EP594,LP/SD2-601
2423	Little Jazz Bird	Atlantic LP/SD2-601
2424	I Was Doing All Right	Atlantic EP593,LP/SD2-601,Clarion LP/SD611
2425	My One And Only Love	Atlantic EP596, -

(vcl) acc. by Doc Severinsen(tp),Eddie Bert(tb),Al Cohn(ts),Danny Bank(bars),Stan Free(p),
Mundell Lowe(g),Wendell Marshall(b),Ed Shaughnessy(dr),Ray Ellis(arr).
     NYC.April 24,1957

2482	That Certain Feeling	Atlantic EP596,LP/SD2-601
2483	Fascinatin' Rhythm	Atlantic LP/SD2-601
2484	Our Love Is Here To Stay	- ,(J)MJ4010,Clarion LP/SD611
2485	They All Laughed	Atlantic LP8014,81817-1,81817-2(CD),601-2(CD), (Eu)7.81980-2(CD),(J)AMCY1051/52(CD)

(vcl) acc. by Milt Jackson(vbs),Stan Free(p,arr),Mundell Lowe(g),Milt Hinton(b),Ed Shaugh-
nessy(dr).   NYC.May 1,1957

2516	How Long Has This Been Going On	Atlantic EP595,LP/SD2-601
2517	I Can't Be Bothered Now	Atlantic EP594, -
2518	Love Walked In	Atlantic LP/SD2-601,Clarion LP/SD611
2519	Somebody Loves Me	Atlantic EP593,LP/SD2-601,(J)MP4010,Clarion LP/SD611
2520	Embraceable You	Atlantic LP2-601

All titles on LP/SD2-601 also on Atlantic 601-2(CD),(Eu)7.81980-2(CD),(J)P6080/81,P4552/53
AMCY1051/52 (CD).

(vcl) acc. by unknown p,b,dr.   Live.TV-cast.LA.Poss. May 27,1957

'S Wonderful	Calliope CAL3002
Love Walked In	-

Both titles also on Calliope CAL3030.
Note:The above titles are from a Bobby Troup "Stars of Jazz" TV-show.
    CAL3002 lists date as May 27,1957 - CAL3030 lists date as November 5,1956.

(vcl) acc. by Bobby Jaspar -1(fl),Stan Free(p),Mundell Lowe(g),Percy Heath(b),Ed Shaugh-
nessy(dr).   NYC.March 13,1958

2998	Here Lies Love(1)	Atlantic LP/SD1290
2999	The Night We Called It A Day(1)	- ,81817-1,81817-2(CD)
3000	Blow Gabriel,Blow	-
3001	Chinatown,My Chinatown	- ,(J)MJ7020

(vcl) acc. by Al Epstein(reeds),Stan Free(p),Mundell Lowe(g),George Duvivier(b),Ed Shaugh-
nessy(dr).   NYC.April 8,1958

3032	Be My All	Atlantic LP/SD1290
3033	One Love Affair	-
3034	Good For Nothin'	-
3035	On The First Warm Day	-

```
(vcl) acc. by unknown orchestra.              NYC.April 29,1958
3054   Under Paris Skies          Atlantic 1188,(J)P6135,AMCY1059(CD)
3055   Moon Ride                      -          -          -
3056   Long Hot Summer            Atlantic(J)P6135
3057   Circus                     Atlantic 2017,(J)P6135,AMCY1050(CD)


(vcl) acc. by Stan Free(p),Mundell Lowe(g),George Duvivier(b),Ed Shaughnessy(dr).
                                              NYC.May 23,1958
3067   Be A Clown                 Atlantic LP/SD1290
3068   Moonlight In Vermont          - ,81817-1,81817-2(CD),(J)MJ7020
3070   Johnny One Note               -
3069   Lover Man                     -


All titles on LP/SD1290 also on Atlantic(J)ATL5026,P4516,P6155,AMCY1062 (CD),London(E)
LTZ-K15151.


(vcl) acc. by unknown orchestra.              NYC.July 31,1958
3107   Flying Home                Atlantic 2017,(J)MJ7020,P6135,AMCY1050(CD)
3108   Hallelujah,I Love Him So   Atlantic 1198,LP8082,(J)AMCY1078(CD)
3109   I Won't Cry Anymore           - ,(J)P6135,      -
3110   Open Fire                  unissued


(vcl) acc. by Ernie Royal,Snooky Young,Harry Edison,Joe Newman(tp),Al Grey,Frank Rehak,
Eddie Bert(tb),Marshall Royal,Phil Woods(as),Frank Foster(ts),Seldon Powell(ts,fl),Charlie
Fowlkes(bars),Stan Free(p),Freddie Green(g),Eddie Jones(b),Sonny Payne(dr),Ralph Sharon
(arr,cond).                                   NYC.January 29,1959
3338   Bargain Day                Atlantic LP/SD1307,LP8082,(J)AMCY1078(CD)
3339   One For My Baby               -
3340   Good Morning Heartache       -
3341   Glad To Be Unhappy           -


(vcl) acc. by Wayne Andre,Willis Dennis,Frank Rehak,Dick Hixon(tb),Bobby Jaspar(fl),Stan
Free(p),Barry Galbraith(g),Don Payne(b),Ed Shaughnessy(dr),strings,Ralph Sharon(arr,cond).
                                              NYC.March 10,1959
3405   These Foolish Things       Atlantic LP/SD1307,LP8082,(J)MJ7020,AMCY1078(CD)
3406   I'm Afraid The
          Masquerade Is Over      Atlantic(J)P6135
3407   The End Of A Love Affair   Atlantic LP/SD1307
3408   Something I Dreamed Last Night      -


(vcl) acc. by Donald Byrd(tp),Bobby Jaspar,Steve Perlow,Stan Webb,Jerry Sanfino,Morton
Lewis(sax,woodwinds),Stan Free(p),Kenny Burrell(g),Don Payne(b),Billy Exiner(dr),strings,
Ralph Sharon(arr,cond).                       NYC.March 19,1959
3411   Ballad Of The Sad Cafe     Atlantic LP/SD1307
3412   I'm A Fool To Want You     unissued
3413   Lilac Wine                 Atlantic LP/SD1307


All titles on LP/SD1307 also on Atlantic(J)ATL5032,AMCY1067 (CD),London(E)LTZ-K15183.


(vcl) acc. by unknown orchestra.              NYC.September 6,1959
3655   Senor Blues                Atlantic 2037,(J)MJ7020,P6135,AMCY1072(CD)
3656   Misty                         - ,AMCY1072(CD)
3657   Fine And Dandy             unissued
3658   All About Ronnie              -


Note:"All About Ronnie" issued on Atlantic(J)AMCY1078 (CD) may be the above version or the
     September 13,1959 version.


(vcl) acc. by Bill Rubenstein(p),Kenny Burrell(g),Eddie de Haas(b),Lex Humphries(dr).
                                   Live."Village Vanguard",NYC.September 13,1959
(session cont. next page).
```

(session cont. from previous page):
	Introduction	Atlantic LP/SD8040
3747	Strike Up The Band	-
3748	Misty	- ,New World NW295
3749	Senor Blues	-
3750	Lover Come Back to Me	-
3751	All About Ronnie	-
3752	Hallelujah,I Love Him So	-
3753	Poor Little Rich Girl	-
3754	'Round Midnight	-
3755	Blow,Gabriel,Blow	unissued
3756	I Miss You So	-
3757	Got Out Of Town	-
3758	Fine And Dandy	Atlantic LP/SD8040
3759	Don't Worry 'Bout Me	-
3760	It Don't Mean A Thing	-
3761	Chinatown My Chinatown	-
3762	Angel Eyes	-

All titles on LP/SD8040 also on Atlantic(J)ATL5047,P4515,AMCY1063 (CD),London(E)
LTZ-K15195,SAH-K6088.

(vcl) acc. by Jimmy Nottingham,Bernie Privin,Bernie Glow,Ernie Royal(tp),Chauncey Welsch,
Frank Rehak,Morton Bullman,Bob Alexander(tb),George Berg,Phil Bodner,Jerry Sanfino,Romeo
Penque,Al Klink(sax,woodwinds),Hank Jones(p),Mundell Lowe(g),Milt Hinton(b),Don Lamond,Sol
Gubin(dr),Bobby Rosengarden(bg),Phil Kraus(perc),Richard Wess(arr,cond).
NYC.September 14,1959
3763	Witchcraft	Atlantic EP622,LP/SD8032,LP8082,(Sd)EP80018,(J) AMCY1078(CD)
3764	I Hear The Music Now	Atlantic EP622,LP/SD8032,LP8082,(Sd)EP80018,(J) AMCY1078(CD)
3765	Like A Woman	unissued
3766	You Don't Know What Love Is	Atlantic LP/SD8032,(Sd)EP80018

(vcl) acc. by Joe Cabot,Bernie Privin,Bernie Glow,Doc Severinsen(tp),Chauncey Welsch,Bob
Ascher,Morton Bullman,Bob Alexander(tb),George Berg,Phil Bodner,Jerry Sanfino,Romeo
Penque,Hymie Schertzer(sax,woodwinds),Hank Jones(p),Mundell Lowe(g),Milt Hinton(b),Don
Lamond(dr),Richard Wess(arr,cond).   NYC.September 21,1959
3773	Just In Time	Atlantic EP622,LP/SD8032,(Sd)EP80018
3774	Come Rain Or Come Shine	- ,(J)MJ7020
3775	I'll Never Be Free	Atlantic EP622, -
3776	How Little We Know	- ,(Sd)EP80018

(vcl) acc. by Fred Klein,Jimmy Buffington(frh),George Berg(as,fl),Phil Bodner(enh,ts,fl),
Hank Jones(p),Mundell Lowe(g),Milt Hinton(b),Osie Johnson(dr),Sol Gubin(vbs,perc),strings,
Richard Wess(arr,cond).   NYC.October 5,1959
3817	The Lady Sings The Blues	Atlantic LP/SD8032,(J)MJ7020
3818	Skyscraper Blues	-
3819	Baltimore Oriole	-
3820	When Sunny Gets Blue	-

All titles on LP/SD8032 also on Atlantic(J)ATL5037,P6155,AMCY1068 (CD),London(E)
LTZ-K15185.

(vcl) acc. by unknown orchestra.   NYC.December 22,1959
3984	Invitation	Atlantic 2073,(J)P6135,AMCY1059(CD)
3985	To Each His Own	Atlantic(J)P6135
3986	I Sold My Heart To The Junkman	Atlantic 2073,(J)P6135

```
(vcl) acc. by unknown orchestra.          NYC.January 28,1960
4238   I Heard A Bluebird               Atlantic(J)P6135
4239   Fortune Cookies                          -
4240   That's My Desire                 Atlantic 2053,(G)70014
4241   I Only Want Some                         -      -  ,(J)AMCY1059(CD)

(vcl) acc. by RONNIE BALL ORCHESTRA:
Danny Stiles,Burt Collins(tp),Willie Dennis(tb),Phil Woods(as),Ronnie Ball(p,arr,cond),
George Duvivier(b),Ed Shaughnessy(dr).    NYC.September 19,1960
4932   Day In,Day Out                   Atlantic LP/SD8046
4933   Soliloquy For Sidney                   unissued
4934   Alone Together                   Atlantic LP/SD8046
4935   Love                                     -

(vcl) acc. by JIMMY JONES ORCHESTRA:
Clark Terry(tp),Phil Bodner(reeds),Hank Jones(p),Barry Galbraith(g),Milt Hinton(b),Osie
Johnson(dr),strings,Jimmy Jones(arr,cond).  NYC.October 27,1960
5145   All Too Soon                     Atlantic LP/SD8046
5146   Harlequin                                -
5147   If I Should Lose You                     -
5148   Here's That Rainy Day                    -

Clark Terry(tp,flh),Jimmy Jones(p,arr),Barry Galbraith(g),George Duvivier(b),Ted Sommer
(dr).                                      NYC.November 16,1960
5177   Follow Me(1)                     Atlantic LP/SD8046
5179   Where Flamingo Fly                       - ,(J)MP7020,Franklin Mint 8
5178   I Gotta Right To Sing The Blues          -
5180   I'm Glad There Is You                    -
5181   You Go To My Head                      unissued
5182   Sweet William                    Atlantic LP/SD8046

-1.Harry Lookofsky(vln) replaces Terry.

All titles on LP/SD8046 also on Atlantic(J)SMJ7010,P7709,AMCY1073 (CD).

(vcl) acc. by MAYNARD FERGUSON AND HIS ORCHESTRA:
Maynard Ferguson(tp,flh,tb),Rolf Ericson,Chet Ferretti,Rick Kiefer(tp),Ray Winslow,Kenny
Rupp(tb),Lanny Morgan(as,fl),Joe Farrell(ts,ss,fl),Willie Maiden(ts,cl,arr),Frank Hittner
(bars,bcl),Jaki Byard(p),Charlie Saunders(b),Rufus Jones(dr),Don Sebesky(arr).
                                           NYC.December 5,1960
5215   The Lonesome Road                Atlantic 45-5014,LP/SD8049
5216   Two Ladies In De
       Shade Of De Banana Tree          Atlantic LP/SD8049
5217   Happy New Year                           -

All titles also on Atlantic(J)MJ4011.

Same.                                      NYC.December 14,1960
5224   Spring Can Really
       Hang You Up The Most             Atlantic LP/SD8049
5225   All The Things You Are                   - ,Atlantic(J)MJ4011
5226   It Never Entered My Mind         Atlantic 45-5018,LP/SD8049,    -
5227   Black Coffee                     Atlantic LP/SD8049,            -

All titles on LP/SD8049 also on Atlantic SD90143,(J)AMCY1074 (CD),London(E)LTZ-K15229,
SAH-K6190.

Same.                                      NYC.December 15,1960
15645  New York's My Home               Roulette (S)R52068
15646  The Wind                                 -
15647  When The Sun Comes Out                   -
```

CHRIS CONNOR

Same.		NYC.December 22,1960
15648	Guess Who I Saw Today	Roulette (S)R52068
15649	Where Do You Go	-

All titles on (S)52068 also on Columbia(E)33SX1377,SCX3415,Fresh Sound(Sp)FS93.
Note:S(R)52068 issued as MAYNARD FERGUSON - CHRIS CONNOR.

Bill Berry(tp) replace Kiefer.		NYC.January 23,1961
5292	I Only Have Eyes For You	Atlantic LP/SD8049,(J)MJ4011
5294	Summertime	Atlantic 45-5014,LP/SD8049,601-2(CD),(Eu)7.81980-2
		(CD),(J)MJ4011,AMCY1051/52(CD)
5295	That's How It Went All Right	Atlantic LP/SD8049

All titles on LP/SD8049 also on Atlantic SD90143,(J)AMCY1074 (CD),London(E)LTZ-K15229,
SAH-K6190.
Note:Master 5293 was not used for the above session.

Same.		NYC.January 30,1961
15650	Something's Coming	Roulette (S)R52068
15651	Send For Me	-
15652	I Feel A Song Coming On	-
15653	Deep Song	-
15654	Can't Get Out Of This Mood	- ,Blue Note B2.96583(CD)

All titles on (S)52068 also on Columbia(E)33SX1377,SCX3415,Fresh Sound(Sp)FS93.
Note:S(R)52068 issued as MAYNARD FERGUSON - CHRIS CONNOR.

vcl) acc. by Ronnie Ball(p),Ben Tucker(b),Dave Bailey(dr).
Live.Teatro Municipal,Rio de Janeiro,Brazil.July 16,1961

	Day In,Day Out	Imagem(Br)5041
	Hallelujah,I Love Him So	
	Spring Can Really	
	Hang You Up The Most	-
	Medley:	-
	I Got A Kick Out Of You	
	From This Moment On	
	Blow,Gabriel,Blow	-

All titles also on West Wind WW0025,WW2025 (CD).
Note:See JAZZ COMMITTEE FOR LATIN AFFAIRS for additional titles (without Connor) from this
concert.

Same.		Live."Village Gate",NYC.November 14/15,1961
	Unknown titles	Atlantic(?) unissued

vcl) acc. by Joe Newman(tp),Clark Terry(tp,flh),Phil Woods(as,cl),Oliver Nelson(ts,cl),
Sol Schlinger(bars),Ronnie Ball(p),Ben Tucker(b),Dave Bailey(dr),Al Cohn(arr,cond).
NYC.December 11,1961

357	Free Spirits	Atlantic LP/SD8061
358	I'm Gonna' Go Fishin'	- ,LP8082,(J)AMCY1078(CD)
359	Opportunity,Please Knock	Atlantic 45-5016,LP/SD8061
360	Nobody's Business	Atlantic(J)AMCY1077(CD)

vcl) acc. by Ernie Royal,Nick Travis(tp),Jimmy Cleveland(tb),Gene Quill(cl,as),Phil Woods
(as),Oliver Nelson(ts),Sol Schlinger(bars),Ronnie Ball(p),Milt Hinton(b),Gus Johnson(dr),
Al Cohn(arr,cond). NYC.March 19,1962

043	The Sweetest Sounds	Atlantic 45-5016,LP/SD1383,81817-1,81817-2(CD)
044	Look No Further	Atlantic LP/SD1383
045	No Strings	-
046	Nobody Told Me	-

(vcl) acc. by Joe Newman,Clark Terry(tp),Phil Woods(as,cl),Oliver Nelson(ts,cl),Sol
Schlinger(bars,bcl),Ronnie Ball(p),George Duvivier(b),Ed Shaughnessy(dr),Al Cohn(arr,
cond).   NYC.April 9,1962

6094	Milano	Atlantic LP/SD8061	
6095	Jump For Joy		- ,LP8082,(J)AMCY1078(CD)
6096	God Bless The Child	-	
6097	Lonely Woman	-	

Irving Markowitz(tp) replaces Terry.   NYC.April 30,1962

6186	Kansas City	Atlantic LP/SD8061
6187	Things Are Swingin'	-
6188	Night Bird	-
6189	Day Dream	-

All titles on LP/SD8061 also on Atlantic(J)AMCY1077 (CD).

(vcl) acc. by Ronnie Ball(p),Mundell Lowe(g),Richard Davis(b),Ed Shaughnessy(dr).
                                 Live."Village Gate",NYC. 1963

Lot Of Livin' To Do	FM 3002,LP(S)300
Anyplace I Hang My Hat Is Home	FM LP(S)300
All Or Nothing At All	-
Something's Coming	-
You Came A Long Way From St. Louis	-
Old Devil Moon	-
I Concentrate On You	FM 3002,LP(S)300
Black Coffee	FM LP(S)300
Goodbye	-
Only The Lonely	-
Ten Cents A Dance	-

All titles also on Roulette(J)SL5111,YW7515,YW7817,YS7080,RF7016,30CY1433 (CD),35C38-7220
(CD),TOCJ5332 (CD),Fresh Sound(Sp)FSR705.
Note:The liner notes use the term "the early show" for the first 6 titles and "the late
    show" for the last 5 titles.

(vcl) acc. by MICHEL COLOMBIER ORCHESTRA:
No details.   Paris.March 1963

It's Not For Me To Say	FM LP(S)312
Cry Me A River	-
I Could Go On Singing	-
I Love My Man	-
Hum Dum Blues	-
The Second Time Around	-
I Wish You Love	- ,Blue Note CDP7.99100-2(CD)
Chances Are	-
Meantime	-
Johnny	-

All titles also on Roulette(J)SL5059,YW7818,TOCJ5359 (CD).

(vcl) acc. by unknown orchestra,Pat Williams(cond).
                                 NYC. 1965

A Hard Day's Night	ABC-Paramount ABC(S)529
A Taste Of Honey	-
Downtown	-
Feeling Good	-
Shadow Of Your Smile	-
Who Can I Turn To	-

(session cont. next page).

(session cont. from previous page):

Can't Get Over The Bossa Nova	ABC-Paramount ABC(S)529	
Hush,Hush,Sweet Charlotte	-	
Dear Heart	-	
Baby,The Rain Must Fall	-	
Stranger On The Shore	-	
A Quiet Thing	-	

All titles also on HMV(E)CLP/CSD3515.

Note:The jazz content of the above record - and other recordings from the late 1960's and the early 1970's - is limited.

vcl) acc. by unknown orchestra,Don Sebesky(arr,cond).

NYC. 1967

Goin' Out Of My Head	ABC-Paramount ABC(S)585	
Carnival	-	
The Boys From Madrid	-	
Love Life	-	
Never On Sunday	-	
Autumn	-	
You're Gonna' Hear From Me	-	
The Shining Sea	-	
I'm Telling You Now	-	
Nowhere Man	-	
Strangers In The Night	-	
Who's Afraid	-	

11 titles also on ABC-Paramount(J)YW8508,YS8534.

vcl) acc. by Hideo Ichikawa(p),Shungo Sawada(g),Takashi Mizuhashi(b),George Ohtsuka(dr).

Tokyo.January 28/29,1969

Softly As In A Morning Sunrise	Victor(J)SMJ7511	
'Round About Midnight	-	
Cry Me a River	-	
Misty	-	
Someone To Watch Over Me	-	
Fool On The Hill	-	
I've Gotta' Be Me	-	
What The World Needs Now	-	
It's All Right With Me	-	
Good-bye	-	

vcl) acc. by unknown orchestra,Pat Rebillot,Alyn Ainesworth,George Barnes(arr).

NYC.c. March 1971

Hit 'Em In The Head With Love	Stanyan SR10029	
Make It With You	-	
More Today Than Yesterday	-	
We've Only Just Begun	-	
Time And Love	-	
Buy And Sell	-	
Fire And Rain	-	
As I Love My Own	-	
The Long And Winding Road	-	
Hi De Ho	-	
What Are You Doing The Rest Of Your Life	-	
Snowbird	-	
Hurry,Tuesday Child	-	
Ten Cents A Dance	-	

1 titles also on Bainbridge BT6230.

(vcl) acc. by Lee Konitz(as),Robert Kaye(p),Richard Davis(b),Grady Tate(dr).

	NYC.October 7,1976
This One's For You	CBS(J)25AP538
Riding On The Moon	-
Lush Life	-

(vcl) acc. by George Opalinsky -1(ts,fl),Robert Kaye(p),Richard Davis(b),Ed Soph(dr).

	NYC.October 12,1976
The Jazz Man(1)	CBS(J)25AP538
The Wind(1)	-
Good Morning,Heartache	-

(vcl) acc. by Mike Abene(p),Michael Moore(b),Jimmy Madison(dr).

	NYC.Octber 18,1976
The Way We Were	CBS(J)25AP538
The Gypsy In My Soul	-

(vcl) acc. by Mike Abene(p).

	NYC.Octber 19,1976
Feelings	CBS(J)25AP538
All Too Soon	-

(vcl) acc. by Jerry Dodgion(as,fl),Mike Abene(p),Michael Moore(b),Ronnie Bedford(dr).

	NYC.January 27,1978
Things Are Swinging	Progressive PR7028
Any Place I Hang My Hat Is Home	-
Just In Time	-
Here's That Rainy Day	-
The Sweetest Sounds	-
Where Flamingos Fly	-

Same.

	NYC.February 3,1978
Out Of This World(1)	Progressive PR7028
I've Got You Under My Skin(1)	-
I Wish You Love(1)	-
I Feel A Song Coming On	-
When Sunny Gets Blue	-

-1.Some kind of dubbing added February 28,1978.

All titles also on Progressive(J)KUX82,ULS6080,Century(J)CECC00353 (CD),Audiophile AP208

(vcl) acc. by Harold Danko(p),Ron McClure(b),Ed Soph(dr).

	NYC(?).December 22,1978
Come In From The Rain	Lobster(J)LDC1015
A Baby's Born	-
I'll Catch The Sun	-
Blue,Green,Grey And Gone	-
Fly Me To The Moon	-
More Today Than Yesterday	-
Alone Together	-
Baltimore Oriole	-
All Or Nothing At All	-

BILL CONNORS

(g-solo).   Oslo.November 1974
(session cont. **next page**).

session cont. from previous page):

Theme To The Guardian	ECM(G)1057
Childs Eyes	-
Song For A Crow	-
Sad Hero	-
Sea Song	-
Frantic Desire	-
Folk Song	-
My Favorite Fantasy	-
The Highest Mountain	-

11 titles also on ECM(J)PAP9032.

an Garbarek(ts,ss),Bill Connors(g),Gary Peacock(b),Jack DeJohnette(dr).

Oslo.December 1977

Meltin	ECM(G)1120
Not Forgetting	-
Face In the Water	-
Aubade	-
Cafe Vue	-
Unending	-

11 titles also on ECM(J)PAP9119.

g-solo).

Oslo.August 27/28,1979

Feet First	ECM(G)1158
Wade	-
Sing And Swim	-
Frog Stroke	-
Surrender To The Water	-
Survive	-
With Strings Attached	-
Breath	-

1 titles also on ECM(J)PAP9205.

NE "MIGHTY FLEA" CONNORS

te:On some LPs the surname is - erroneously - given as Conners.

ne "Mighty Flea" Connors(tb),rest unknown.

Unknown location. 1960's

Ode To Billy Joe	Eldo(?) 155
Unknown title(s)	-

ne Connors(tb,vcl),Mike Burney(ts),Bob Hall(p),Mickey Baker(g),Roger Hill(el-b),Pete
rk(dr).

London.August 24/25,1972

Let The Good Times Roll	Polydor(E)2460.185
Honky Tonk	-
T'Ain't Nobody's Business If I Do	-
Charley Stone	-
Bloodshot Eyes	-
Hi-Heel Sneakers	-
Goin' To L.A.	-
Let's Get Stoned	-
The Chocolate Cowboy Rides Again	-
GM Blues	-

Gene Connors(tb,vcl),Eddie Davis(ts),Wild Bill Davis(org),Billy Butler(g),Oliver Jackson
(dr).   Paris.February 1,1976
        Coming Home   Black&Blue(F)33.091
        See See Rider   -
        Georgia On My Mind(no ts)   -
        T'Ain't Nobody's Business If I Do   -
        Good Cooking Woman   -
        Let The Good Times Roll   -
        Ode To Billy Joe   unissued
        Concerto For Cootie   -

Bob Wulffers(tp),Gene Connors(tb,vcl),Henk van Muyen(tb),Sidney Pfeffer(ts,ss),Fred Hunt
(p),Pim Hogervorst(bj,tb),Jacques Kingma(b),Ted Easton(dr).
                                          Leiden,The Netherlands.April 24,1976
        China Boy   Riff(Du)659.032
        Creole Love Call   -
        Blues Mix(gc)   -
        The Preacher   -
        Wolverine Blues   -
        The Cripple Crab Crutch(gc)   -
        Satin Doll   -   ,659.026
        Basin Street Blues(gc)   -
        Mood Indigo   Riff(Du)659.026

Gene Connors(tb,vcl),Arnett Cobb(ts),Milt Buckner(org),Panama Francis(dr).
                                          Paris.May 30,1976
        I Wouldn't Give A
          Cribble Crab A Crutch(gc)   Black&Blue(F)33.091
        Tuxedo Junction   unissued
        The Masquerade Is Over   -

NORMAN CONNORS

Eddie Henderson(tp),Arthur Webb(fl),Gary Bartz(as,ss),Carlos Garnett(ts,ss),Herbie Hanco
(p,el-p),Stanley Clarke,Cecil McBee -1(b),Norman Connors(dr),Nat Bettis(African-perc,cg)
Tony Wiles,Babafemi -2(African-perc),Alphonse Mouzon -3,Billy Hart -4,Airto Moreira -4
(perc),The Universal Black Force Singers(vcl).
                                          NYC.June 26/27,1972
        Dance Of Magic(1,2,3)   Cobblestone CST9024
        Moonlight Change(1,4)   -
        Blue(3,4)   -
        Give The Drummer Some(4,5)   -

-5.Omit horns,p/el-p,b.

All titles also on Cobblestone(J)YZ24,Buddah BDS5674.

Eddie Henderson(tp),Arthur Webb(fl),Gary Bartz(as),Carlos Garnett(ts,ss),Herbie Hancock
(p),Cecil McBee(b),Norman Connors(dr),Warren Smith(perc),Lawrence Killian(cg),Dee Dee
Bridgewater,Ellen DeLeston,Michael Brown(vcl).
                                          NYC.December 13/14,1972
        Butterfly Dreams   Cobblestone CST9035
        Twilight Zone   -
        Song For Rosa   -
        Black Lightnin'(1)   -

-1.Onaje Allen Gumbs(p) replaces Hancock.

dd Ted Dunbar(g),strings;Buster Williams(b) replaces McBee.
                                    Same date

        Dark Of Light   Cobblestone CST9035

dd Alfred Williams(fl,bassoon);Elmer Gibson(el-p),Stanley Clarke(b),Henry Palmer,Gerald
oberts(perc) replace Hancock,Williams,Smith,Killian.
                                    Philadelpia.February 25,1973
        Laughter   Cobblestone CST9035

ll titles also on Cobblestone(J)YZ37,Buddah BDS5675.

ddie Henderson(tp,cnt,flh),Hubert Laws(fl),Gary Bartz(as,ss),Carlos Garnett(ts,ss),Herbie
ancock(p,el-p),Buster Williams(b),Norman Connors(dr),Kenneth Nash(perc),Dee Dee Bridgewa-
er(vcl).   San Francisco.October 1973
        Revelation(ddb)   Buddah BDS5142
        Carlos II   -
        Drums Around The World(1)   -
        Love From The Sun(2,3)(ddb)   - ,BDS5716
        Kuma Kusccha   -
        Holy Waters(3)(ddb)   -

1.Connors(dr),Nash,Bill Summers(perc) only.
2.Add Nathan Rubin(vln),Terry Adams(cello).
3.Add Onaje Allen Gumbs(el-p).

ll titles also on Cobblestone(J)YP7042.

ddie Henderson(tp,flh),Hubert Laws(fl),Gary Bartz(as,ss),Carlos Garnett(ts),Hubert Eaves
clavinet),Elmer Gibson(el-p,clavinet),Reggie Lucas(g),Ron Carter(b),Norman Connors(dr),
awrence Killian,Dom Um Romao,Skip Drinkwater(perc),Jean Carn(vcl).
                                    NYC.July 1974
        Mother Of The Future(jc)   Buddah BDS5611
        Welcome(1)(jc)   -
        Dreams   -

..Add Lonnie Liston Smith(p).

nthony Jackson(b) replaces Carter;omit Carn.
                                    NYC.July 1974
        Back On The Street   Buddah BDS5611
        Slew Foot   -
        Chuka   -
        Jump Street   -

l titles on BDS5611 also on Cobblestone(J)YX7016.

die Henderson(tp,flh),David Subke,William O. Murphy(fl),Gary Bartz(as,ss),Carlos Garnett
s),Nathan Rubin,Myra Bucky(vln),Nancy Ellis(vla),Terry Adams(cello),Onaje Allem Gumbs
,el-p,org,synth),Hubert Eaves(p,el-p,org,clavinet),Bernard Krause(synth),Reggie Lucas,
bert King(g),Michael Henderson(el-b,vcl),Norman Connors(dr),Kenneth Nash(perc),Jean Carn
cl).   San Francisco.May 1975
        Saturday Night Special   Buddah BDS5643
        Dindi   - ,BDS5716
        Maiden Voyage   -
        Valentine Love   -
        Akia   - ,BDS5716
        Skin Diver   -

rbie Hancock(p),Onaje Allen Gumbs(el-p),Buster Williams(b),Norman Connors(dr),Kenneth
sh,Bill Summers(perc).   San Francisco.May 1975
        Kwasi   Buddah BDS5643

(session cont. from previous page):
All titles on BDS5643 also on Buddah(J)YQ7520.

Shunzo Ohno(tp),Earl McIntyre(tb),Arthur Webb(fl),Gary Bartz(as,ss),Carter Jefferson
(ts,ss),Onaje Allen Gumbs(el-p,synth),Hubert Eaves(el-p,hsc),Ian Underwood(synth),Keith
Loving,Lee Ritenour -1(g),Michael Henderson(b,vcl),Anthony Jackson -2,Larry McRae-3(b),
Norman Connors(dr,vcl),Don Alias,Neil Clarke(perc),Phyllis Hyman,Tasha Thomas,Magretha
Styewart,Sharon Reed(vcl).   NYC.February/March 1976

We Both Need Each Other(1)	Buddah BDS5655,BDS5716	
Betcha By Golly Wow(2)	-	-
Bubbles(2)	-	
You Are My Starship	- ,BDS5716	
Just Imagine(2)	-	
So Much Love	-	
The Creator Has A Masterplan(3)(nc)	-	

All titles on BDS5655 also on Buddah(J)YQ7525.

Gary Bartz(as,ss),Pharoah Sanders(ts),Hubert Eaves,Ian Underwood(keyb),Lee Ritenour,Reggi
Lucas(g),Alphonso Johnson(b),Norman Connors(dr),Kenneth Nash,Bobby Hall,Victor Feldman
(perc),Phillip Mitchell,Ray Gomez,Jerry Peters,Eleanor Mills(unkn. instr.),horns,strings.
                                          LA. 1976

Once I've Been There	Buddah BDS5682,BDS5716	
Destination Moon	-	
Romantic Journey	- ,BDS5716	
Last Tango In Paris	-	
For You Everything	-	
Thembi	-	

No details.   Unknown location. 1977

This Is Your Life	Buddah BDS5716
Wouldn't You Like To See	-

Duke Jones(tp),Ralph "Buzzy" Jones(ts,ss,fl),Billy McCoy(p,keyb),Jacques Burvick(keyb),
Greg Hill(g),Alex Blake(el-b),Norman Connors(dr,perc),Lawrence Killian,Petro Bass(perc).
                         Live.Montreux Jazz Festival,Switzerland.July 22,19

Babylon	Arista Novus AN3021
Beyond A Dream	-

Add Pharoah Sanders(ts),Bobby Lyle(p).   Same date

Montreux Overture	Arista Novus AN3021
The End Of The Beginning	-
Casino Latino	-

Shunzo Ohno(tp),Gary Bartz(as,ss),Ralph "Buzzy" Jones(ts,ss,fl),Pharoah Sanders(ts),Bill
McCoy,Jacques Burvick(keyb),Lee Ritenour,Melvin "Wah Wah" Watson (Ragin),David T. Walker
(g),Norman Connors(dr),Kenneth Nash,Petro Bass(perc),Jean Carn(vcl),Richard Cummings,Jam
Robinson,Eleanor Mills(unkn. instr.),horns,strings.
                             Burbank,Calif.Late 1970's

Stella	Arista AL4177
Listen	-
This Is Your Life	-
Wouldn't You Like To See	-
Say You Love Me	-
Captain Connors	-
Butterfly	-
The Creator Has A Master Plan	-
You Make Me Feel Brand New	-

Note:Additional recordings by this artist are not included.

WILLIS CONOVER

See THE ORCHESTRA.

BARRY CONRAN (Australian)

John Kathner(tp,flh),John Costelloe(tb,vcl),Ken Roberts(cl,sax,fl),Barry Conran(p,vcl),
Don Rouse(g),John O'Hagan(el-b),Graeme Gilmour(dr,vcl),Tommy Clarke(vcl).
Sydney.c. 1974

	Wheel(Au)unnumbered
Tailgate Ramble	
Memories Of You	
After The Loving	
The Hustle	
Hasta Manana	
Eleanor Rigby	
American Patrol	
So Do I	
Mas Que Nada	
I'm Tired Lord	
Soulful Strut	
Sleepy Time Gal	

HANS CONRIED

(vcl) acc. by THE DIXIELAND ALL STARS:
Pee Wee Erwin(tp),Lou McGarity(tb),Kenny Davern(cl),Boomie Richman(ts),Billy Maxted(p),
George Barnes/Tony Gattusso(g),Harvey Phillips(b),Cliff Leeman(dr).
NYC. 1959

	Strand SL1001
Grumpy Grandpa	
Peter Meets The Wolf In Dixieland	-
Wild Wolf Wailing	-
Requiem For A Blue Duck	-
The Cat-Like Cat	-
In Defence Of The Wolf	-
Pete's Theme	-

BEN CONROY

BEN CONROY - CHARLIE BOOTY:
Ben Conroy -1,Charlie Booty -2(p).
Unknown location.c. 1979/80

	Dirty Shame DSR1239
Goldenrod(1,2)	
Pass The Jug(2)	-
Albert's Thing(1)	-
Melancholy(2)	-
Psalm 32-11(1)	-
Reminishing With Jimmy And Montana(1,2)	-
Hold 'Em Jay(1)	-
Down The Road A Piece(2)	-
Phantom Rag(?)	-
Holler Stomp(1)	-
Stompin' In Texas(2)	-
Montana's Lament(1,2)	-

MARIUS CONSTANT (French)

Marius Constant,Martial Solal(p),Cesarius Alvim(b),Daniel Humair(dr),Sylvio Gualda(perc),
Le Quintette de Cuivres Ars Nova.   Paris.December 1979
        Stress   Erato(F)STU71238

Katia Labèque,Marielle Labèque -1(p),Jean-Francois Jenny-Clark -2(b),Jean-Pierre Drouet-1,
Sylvio Gualda -1(perc).   Prob. same date
        Psyché(1)   Erato(F)STU71238
        Trois Complexes (Extraits)(2)   -

JEAN CONSTANTIN (French)

JEAN "FATS" CONSTANTIN ET SON ORCHESTRE:
Roger Guérin(tp),Benny Vasseur(tb),Charles Grenu(cl,ts),Jean Constantin,Eddie Bernard(p),
Pascal Gros(b),Teddy Martin(dr).   Paris.c. 1965
        Bye Bye Bye (Bye Bye Baby)   Vogue(F)EPL8344
        Le Tigre (Tiger Rag)   -
        Too Big Or Not Too Big
           (Your Feet's Too Big)   -
        Flic Flac Floc
           (Flat Foot Floogie)   -
        Cette Fleur (Sweetie Pie)   Vogue(F)EPL8366
        Cavian (K Cha Cha) For One
        Quelqu'un Ma Pris Ma Femme
           (Somebody Stole My Gal)   -
        Wodka For Two
           (The Spider And The Fly)   -

CONTACT TRIO (German)

Evert Brettschneider(g),Alys Kott(b,el-b),Michael Jullich(dr,mar,vbs,perc,fl).
                         Live.Jazz Festival Balver Höhle,Germany.July 27/28,1974
        Dig   JGO(G)39

Same.   Kirchhellen,Germany.July 1974/February 1975
        Rumpelstielzschen   Calig(G)30614
        Double Face   -
        Engelstanz   -
        Sonate   -

Same.   Ludwigsburg,Germany.January 1978
        Happy   Japo(G)60024
        Circle   -
        The Quick Brown Fox
           Jumps Over The Lazy Dog   -
        Stoned Tunes   -
        New Marks   -

Evert Brettschneider(g),Alys Kott(b,el-b),Peter Fischold(dr).
                         Ludwigsburg,Germany.October 1980
        Air Lines   Japo(G)60036
        String Games   -
        Daddy Longleg   -
        Simple Symphony   -
        Silence   -
        Elbow Dance   -

JOHN CONTE

(vcl) acc. by JOHN KIRBY'S ORCHESTRA:
Incl. CLarence Brereton(tp),Buster Bailey(cl),Russell Procope(as),John Kirby(b).
                                          NYC. 1946
T05   Down The Old Ox Road   Apollo 1028
T06   Merry Ha Ha   -

(vcl) acc. by JERRY JEROME'S ORCHESTRA:
John Giampietro(tb),Toots Mondello(as),Jerry Jerome(ts),Bernie Kaufman,Joe Dixon,Andy
Querze(sax),Bill Clifton(p),Morris Rayman(b),John Williams(dr),strings.
                                          NYC.February 17,1947
3065   Beware My Heart   Apollo 1044
3066   Midnight Masquerade   -

PAOLO (PAUL) CONTE (Italian)

Paolo Conte(vbs),Fred Mancini(p),Cosimo Occhiena(b),Giorgio Conte(dr).
                                          Italy. 1962
         Christopher Columbus   RCA(I)PME30485
         I Cover The Waterfront   -
         More Than You Know   -
         Out Of Nowhere   -

THE CONTEMPORARIES

See KENO DUKE.

THE CONTEMPORARY BRASS QUINTET

Bob Millikan,David Gale(tp),Gerald Chamberlain,Jim Morris(tb),Bill Hamilton(frh).
                                          Unknown location/date
         A Picture Of Dorian Blue   Classic Jazz CJ11
         Serial Stomp   -
         Suite For Brass   -
         1 x 1 x 5/Riff Rock   -
         Classical Jazz Suite   -
         Metropolitan Quintet   -
         Suite For Brass Quintet   Classsic Jazz CJ12
         Pointel/Mood   -
         Jaroque Waltz   -
         Simplis Sonor   -
         Theme And Waltz   -
         Better Days/Golden Gait   -
         Blues,Prelude And Fugue   -
         Morrisania Motion   -

Note:The jazz content of the above recordings may be limited.

THE CONTEMPORARY JAZZ ENSEMBLE

Bob Norden(tp),Bob Silberstein(as),Ed Summerlin(ts),Jim Straney(p),Neil Courtney(b),Bill
Porter(dr).   Rochester,N.Y.June 1953
(session cont. next page).

(session cont. from previous page):
```
494   Variation                    Prestige LP163
495   Prelude And Jazz                  -
496   Prelude:Go Forth                  -
497   Fantasia And Fugue:Poinciana      -
498   All The Things You Are            -
```

THE CONTEMPORARY JAZZ ENSEMBLE (diff. group)

See ERROLL PARKER.

CONTEMPORARY JAZZ OCTET

```
Lennie Niehaus(arr),rest unknown.        Unknown location/date
      Annie's Dance                Highland Music Co. 101
      Categene                               -
      Unknown titles                         -
```

THE CONTEMPORARY (JAZZ) QUARTET (American)

See CHARLES BELL.

THE CONTEMPORARY JAZZ QUARTET/QUINTET (Danish)

Hugh Steinmetz(tp),Franz Beckerlee(as),Steffen Andersen(b),Sonny Murray(dr).
```
                                    Copenhagen.October 1,1964
      Refraction                Debut(D)DEB143
      Action                              -
      Catalysm                            -
      In The Name Of Beauty               -
      Predetermination                    -
```

NIELS VIGGO BENTZON FEATURING THE CONTEMPORARY JAZZ QUARTET:
Add Niels Viggo Bentzon(p).   Copenhagen.September 4,1965
```
      Nylon(no tp,dr)           Fona(D)LPJ542
      Rush On(no tp,dr)                   -
      No Style(tp,b only)                 -
      It's Blowing Half
        A Gale(as,p only)                 -
      Music For Concrete Poetry           -
      Marcel Proust Vignet(no p,dr)       -
      There Are No Flowers In My Room     -
      Tuff Guy                            -
      Walking Monkey(p-solo)              -
      In The Old Candy Store(tp,p only)   -
      Bread And Butter                    -
      Rigomarole(no p)                    -
      Reel(no p)                          -
      Cakewalk                            -
      Charleston                          -
```

THE CONTEMPORARY JAZZ QUINTET:
Add Niels Harrit(el-ts,org);Beckerlee plays (el-as);omit Bentzon.
                                   Copenhagen.December 28,1968

Action 5:40	Debut(D)SDEB151
Action 18:06	-
Action 10:25	-
Action 11:25	-

CONTEMPORARY JAZZ QUINTET

See KENNY COX.

ROBERT CONTI

(g-solo).   LA(?).May 17,1979

A Time For Love	Trend TR519
My Funny Valentine	-
I've Grown	
Accustomed To Your Face	-
Theme From "Airport"	-
Feelings	-
Yesterday	-
All The Things You Are	-
A Man And A Woman	-
Live For Life	-
The Last Time	

THE CONTINENTAL JAZZ OCTETTE

Unknown tp,tb,as,ts/fl,bars,p,b,dr.   Prob. California. 1950s

Jumpin' With Symphony Sid	Crown CLP5212/CST227
Soft Shoe	-
Freeway	-
Confirmation	-
Popo	-
The Funky Shepherds	-
Robbins' Nest	-
Stuffy	-
Ornithology	-
Bounce With Me	Crown CLP5220/CST234
Big Girl	-
Walking Shoes(ts,bars,b,dr only)	-
Moose The Mooche	-
Jazz Clarinet Concerto	-
Bernie's Tune(ts,bars,b,dr only)	-
Dewey Square	-
Intermission Riff	-

CONTRABAND

Charles Orena(ts,ss,fl),Pete Robinson(p,el-p,org,melodica),Dave Pritchard(g),Bruce Cale
(b,el-b,vln),Brian Moffatt(dr,perc).   LA(?). 1971/72
(session cont. next page).

(session cont. from previous page):

Shadow On The Mountain	Epic E30814
Intune	-
Interlock	-
Reverie	-
To Miles	-
The One Who Knows	-
Crimson Sunsets	-
An Aborted Eddie Harris Tune	-

All titles also on Epic/CBS(Eu)EPC64736.

TINO CONTRERAS (Mexican)

Mario Contreras(tp),Cuco Valtierra(sax),Mario Patron(p),Victor Ruiz(b),Tino Contreras(dr),
Magda Leon,Alicia Gonzales(vcl). Prob. Paris. 1962

Good Beat	Festival(F)FLD291S
Mack The Knife	-
'Round Midnight	-
Tadd Lights	-
Tenderly	-
Imagination(ml)	-
Jazz En Riguz (Media Noche)	-
Beauty Lady	-
My Skin	-
Peter Gunn	-
Mon Homme(ag)	-
When The Saints Go Marching In	-

CONVECTION SECTION

Butch Hudson,Eddie Engels(tp),Richard Pullin,Frans van Luin(tb),Dick Vennik,Ferdinand
Povel(ts,as,fl),Jasper van 't Hof(p,el-p),Hans Hollestelle,Toto Blanke(g),Henk Haverhoek
(el-b),Eric Ineke(dr),Steve Boston(cg),Bruce Parsons(bg).
 Blaricum,The Netherlands. 1972

Psychadellic Sally	Munich(Du)6802814
Proud Mary	-
Autumn	-
Yasha's Mo-Sike-L	-
Evil Mike	-
Four Beat	-
A Letter	-
Summer	-
Bottle Neck	-

THE CONVENTION ALL STARS (Australian)

Tony Newstead(tp),Frank Traynor(tb),Johnny McCarthy,Peter Pretty(cl),Neville Sherburn(p),
Don Hardie(bj),Ray Price(g),Lou Silbereisen(b),Bob Leggett(dr).
 Sydney.December 30,1954

Canal Street Blues	Parlophone(Au)PMD07503
Convention Stomp	-

Ian Cuthbertson(cnt),John Costelloe(tb),Nick Polites(cl),Neville Stribling(as),Graham
Coyle(p),Willie Watt(bj),Mookie Herman(b),Gordon Hastie(dr),Paul Marks(vcl).
                                        Sydney.December 30,1958
          See See Rider(pm)   Columbia(Au)330SX7618
          Bill Bailey Won't
            You Please Come Home   -

CONVENTION STREET PARADE (Australian)

No details.   Sydney.December 1958
          Oh,Didn't He Ramble   Columbia(Au)330SX7618
          Just A Closer Walk With Thee   -

ROBERT CONVERS (Swiss)

ROBERT CONVERS ET SA GRANDE FORMATION:
Yves Herzinger,Jean-Claude Grillon,Paul Sautebin,Gérard Riat(tp),René Comment,Francois
Zemp(tb),Noël Broggia,Jean-Pierre Osiowski(as),Bernard Montandon,Christian Fischer(ts),
Gilbert Ricard(bars),Gérard Wyss(p),Roger Zemp(g),Pierre Baudin(b),René Bandel(dr),Robert
Convers(ldr).   Switzerland.Febaury 18,1966
          Salt Peanuts   Tempo/New Jazz Club(Sw)1
          Basie Boogie   -
          Dizzy Atmosphere   -
          Basie Blues   -

RY COODER

Earl Hines(p),Ry Cooder(g,vcl).   LA.c. 1974
          Diddy Wah Diddy   Warner Bros. MS2129

Earl Hines -1(p),Ry Cooder(g,mandolin,tiple,harp),Chuck Domanico -1(b),Mark Stevens -1
(dr),Tom Collier -1(mar).   LA.c. 1977
          The Pearls/Tia Juana   Warner Bros. BSK3197
          Flashes
          The Dream(1)   -

Harvey Pittel(as),David Sherr(bcl),Tom Collier(vbs),Ry Cooder(g),Tom Pedrini(b),Joseph
Byrd(arr).   LA.c. 1977
          In A Mist   Warner Bros. BSK3197
          Davenport Blues   -

Wilbur Schwarts(cl),Harvey Pittel(as),David Sherr(bcl),Tom Collier(vbs),John Rodby(p),Ry
Cooder(g),Chuck Berghofer(b),Mark Stevens(dr),Jimmy Adams,Bill Johnson,Simon Pico Payne,
Cliff Givens(vcl),Joseph Byrd(arr).   LA.c. 1977
          Shine   Warner Bros. BSK3197
          Nobody(g,vcl only)   -

Mario Guarnieri(cnt),Randy Aldcroft(tb),Harvey Pittel,Pat Rizzo(as),John Rodby(p),Ry
Cooder(g),Bill Hood(bassax),Mark Stevens(dr),Joseph Byrd(arr).
                                       LA.c. 1977

          Big Bad Bill Is
            Sweet William Now   Warner Bros. BSK3197

Oscar Brashear(tp),George Bohanon(tb),Barbara Starkey(pump-organ),Ry Cooder(g),David Lind-
ley(mandolin),Red Callender(tu),Mark Stevens(dr),Stuart Brotman(cymbal),Joseph Byrd(arr).
LA.c. 1977

      Face To Face
         That I Shall Meet Him   Warner Bros. BSK3197
      Happy Meeting In Glory
      We Shall Be Happy

All titles on BSK3197 also on Warner Bros.(E)K56488,(J)P10519.
Note:Additional recordings by this artist are not included.

ANN COOK

See "WOODEN" JOE NICHOLAS.

JIMMY COOK

JIMMY COOK AND HIS ORCHESTRA:
Al Porcino(tp,vcl),Billy Hodges,Bobby Steed,Charlie Walp,Eddie Butterfield(tp),Carl Fon-
tana(tb),Autie Goodman(as,vcl),Charlie McLean(as),Jimmy Cook(ts),Bob Enevoldsen(ts,arr),
Bob Lawson(bars),Eddie Weid(p),Carson Smith(b),Tom Montgomery(dr),Bill Holman,Bill Hood
(arr).   Las Vegas.November 25,1960
M3PB1956 Melancholy Serenade   Camden CAL(CAS)670
M3PB1957 Do Nothin' Till
         You Hear From Me   -
M3PB1958 St. Louis Blues   -
M3PB1959 Time After Time(ag)   -
M3PB1960 Posin'(ap)   -
M3PB1961 Alexander's Ragtime Band   -
M3PB1962 Polka Dots And Moonbeams   -
M3PB1963 Whisper Not   -
M3PB1964 It Could Happen To You(ag)   -
M3PB1965 Easy Living   -
M3PB1966 Jubilee(ap)   -
M3PB1967 Soon   -

JUNIOR COOK

See also LOUIS HAYES.

JUNIOR COOK QUINTET:
Blue Mitchell(tp),Junior Cook(ts),Dolo Coker(p),Gene Taylor(b),Roy Brooks(dr).
LA.April 10,1961

      Blue Farouq   Jazzland JLP(9)58
      Sweet Cakes   -
      Field Day   -

Ronnie Mathews(p) replaces Coker.   NYC.December 4,1961
      Mzar   Jazzland JLP(9)58
      Turbo   -
      Easy Living   -
      Pleasure Bent   -

Junior Cook(ts),Mickey Tucker(p),Cecil McBee(b),Leroy Williams(dr).
                                    NYC.November 1,1977
         Sweet Lotus Lips   Affinity(E)AFF53,AFF764(CD)
         Not Quite That   -
         Yardbird Suite   -
         Moment To Moment,pt.1   -
         Moment To Moment,pt.2   -

Juney Booth(b) replaces McBee.   NYC.November 2,1977
         The Crucifier   Affinity(E)AFF53
         The 8th Cat   -

All titles on AFF53 also on VeeJay(J)20YB6014,30YD7014 (CD).
All titles on AFF53 - except "The 8th Cat" - also on Affinity(E)AFF766 (CD).

Bill Hardman(tp,flh),Slide Hampton(tb,arr),Junior Cook(ts),Mario Rivera(bars),Albert
Dailey(p),Walter Booker(b),Leroy Williams(dr).
                                    NYC.June 7,1979
         J.C.   Muse MR5159
         I'm Getting Sentimental Over You -
         Play Together Again   -
         Waltz For Junior   -
         I Waited For You   -
         Mood   -

ARTY COOK

ARTY COOK AND THE NEW YORK SOUND EXPLOSION:
Arty Cook(tb,arr),Monty Waters(as),Seth Brothy(ts),Curtis Clark(p),Ratso Harris(b),John
Bethch(dr).   NYC.December 3,1979
         Flesh & Blood(no as,p)   Circle(G)RK21379/20
         For Those Who Loved Him(no as,ts) -
         O.C. & Montville(no p)   -
         Trance Suite: -
             Signs Of Times
             Trance
             Merry Death Dance

WILLIE COOK

See ENRIQUE VILLEGAS.

OB COOKE

PLATTE RIVER JAZZ BAND:
Ob Cooke(tp),Vern Beebe(tb),Bill Pontarelli(cl),Bill Murray(p),Dennis Condreay(bj),Al
Nisson(tu),Jack Cook(dr).   Prob. Denver. 1978/79
         River Boat Shuffle   Platte River Jazz Band 33014
         Perdido Street Blues   -
         Sidewalk Blues   -
         San Francisco Bay Blues   -
         Georgia Swing   -
         Frog-I-More Rag   -
         Nagasaki   -
         Savoy Blues   -
         New Orleans Stomps   -

SAM COOKE

(vcl) acc. by RENE HALL ORCHESTRA:
Gerald Wilson,Conte Candoli,Pete Candoli,Conrad Gozzo(tp),Milt Bernhart(tb),Benny Carter
(as),Plas Johnson(ts),Jackie Kelso,Buddy Collette,Jewell Grant(reeds),Ernie Freeman(p),
Rene Hall(g,arr,cond),Red Callender(b),Earl Palmer(dr).

LA.c. November/December 1959

God Bless The Child(1)	Keen A/S2004,Trip TLP8030,Trip Top 16-2,Up Front UPF160
She's Funny That Way(1)	Keen A/S2004,Trip TLP8030
I've Got A Right To Sing The Blues	Keen A/S2004,RCA APL1-0899,(E)HY1030,Trip TLP8030 Trip Top 16-2
Good Morning,Heartache(1)	Keen A/S2004,RCA APL1-0899,(E)HY1030,Trip TLX9517 Trip Top 16-2,Up Front UPF160
T'Ain't Nobody's Bizness (If I Do)	Keen A/S2004,RCA APL1-0899,(E)HY1030,Trip TLX9517 Trip Top 16-2,Up Front UPF160
Comes Love	Keen A/S2004,Trip TLP8030
Lover Girl (Man)	Keen A/S2004,RCA APL1-0899,(E)HY1030,Trip TLX9517 Up Front UPF160
Let's Call The Whole Things Off	Keen A/S2004,RCA APL1-0899,(E)HY1030,Trip TLX9517 Up Front UPF160,Springboard SPX6003
Lover Come Back To Me	Keen A/S2004,RCA APL1-0899,(E)HY1030,Trip TLP8030 Trip Top 16-2,Up Front UPF160
Solitude	Keen A/S2004,RCA APL1-0899,(E)HY1030,Trip TLP8030 Up Front UPF160
They Can't Take That Away From Me	Keen A/S2004,RCA APL1-0899,(E)HY1030,Trip TLP8030
Crazy In Love With You (Crazy She Calls Me)(1)	Keen A/S2004,RCA APL1-0899,(E)HY1030,Trip TLP8030 Up Front UPF160

-1.Add strings,vcl-group.

Note:Additional recordings by this artist are not included.

COOL AND THE CLONES

Incl. unknown as,p,dr.	Prob. Bethesda,Maryland. 1976-1982
For Stu Martin	Ejaz (cass. unnumbered)
Clone Medley	-
Clonal Unity Trio	-
Systems Of Thought	-
Eric's Birthday Party	-
Exon Blues	-
A Couple Of Jokes And Foxy Kremlins	-
For Philip Steinbeck RIP	-
People In Need Of Supervision	-
Phil's Ghost (Interlude)	-
Bassisms	-
Instant Insanity Pool	-
Piano Solo	-
Haig's Blues	-

Incl. Perry Robinson(cl),Mark Whitecage(as),Eric Ziarko(as,ts,cl,etc.),Scott Macauley
(synth),Charles Hooper(el-b),Janice Ziarko(dr,etc.).
(session cont. next page).

session cont. from previous page):

		Prob. Bethesda,Maryland. 1979-1983
Cloned Perry	Ejaz 03(cass.)	
Skins Win Bowl	-	
The Creek	-	
Destruction Of Jeff's Mandolin	-	
Interlewed(?)	-	
Disco Stone	-	
Hot Dogs Of The Fifth Dimension	-	
For Milton Suggs	-	
To Peter Sellers	-	
Jan's House	-	
Beet Red	-	
Hunger	-	

OOL GABRIELS

ick Travis,Bernie Glow,Conte Candoli,Don Stratton(tp),Elliot Lawrence(p,arr,ldr),Buddy
ones(b),Sol Gubin(dr).   NYC.June 1956
Elevation	Groove LG1003
Five O'Clock Shadow	-
Happy Hooligan	-
Spooky	-

id Phil Sunkel(cnt).   NYC.June 1956
Each Other's Arms	Groove LG1003
Swingin' Scots(take 1)	-
Swingin' Scots(take 2)	-
Nick	-

ick Travis,Al Derisi,Conte Candoli,Don Stratton,Dick Sherman(tp),Elliott Lawrence(p,arr,
ir),Buddy Jones(b),Sol Gubin(dr).   NYC.June 1956
Cupcake	Groove LG1003
Mostly Latin	-
Love Is Just Around The Corner	-
Something Blue	-

OL HAMBONE

e ROLF WIKSTRÖM.

E COOL SCANDINAVIANS

rgen Ryg(tp),Max Brüel(ss),Rolf Billberg(ts),Atli Bjørn(p),Erik Mølbak(b),William
hiöpffe(dr).   Copenhagen.February 13/14,1956
F1	El Domingo	Sonet(D)SXP2000
F5	The Lady Is A Tramp(1)	Sonet(D)SXP2001

.Omit Brüel.

th titles also on Storyville(D)SLP419.

it Billberg.   Copenhagen.February 19,1956
ession cont. next page).

(session cont. from previous page):
DGF13 Don't Blame Me(2)   Sonet(D)SXP2000
DGF15 Out Of Nowhere   Sonet(D)SXP2001
DGF17 Royal Garden Blues(1)   Sonet(D)SXP2000
DGF18 Fine And Dandy   Sonet(D)SXP2001

-1.Omit Brüel.
-2.Omit Ryg.

LESLIE COOL (Dutch)

Leslie Cool (Juriaan Andriessen)(p),Cor Baan(g),Henk Orthman(b),Gerard van Bezeij(dr).
                                    Amsterdam.September 21,1956
        Detour   Telefunken(Du)HX1016
        Takin' A Chance On love   -
        Steppin' Out With My Baby   -
        Embraceable You   -
        Jazz Tonic   -

COOLING'S TRADITIONAL JAZZMEN (Swedish)

Hans "Cooling" Carling(tp),Ulf Almarker(tb),Peter Svenfors(cl,ss),Dennis Johnson(bj),Joha
Munck(b),Nils-Ove Månsson(dr).   Copenhagen.December 4,1960
        Double Check Stomp   Heat Wave MMEP412
        Mood Indigo   -
        Riverboat Shuffle   -
        Ham And Eggs   -

Hans Carling(tp),Povel Randén(tb),Björn Franzen(tb),Frans Sjöström,Mikael Wiehe(sax),Bob
Stalin(p),Dennis Johnson(bj),Carl Otto Strand(dr).
                                    Copenhagen.November 5,1963
        In The Dark   Discus Celeste DCEF105
        Sentimental Baby   -
        Saratoga Shout   -
        The Pearls   -

LEO COOMANS

COOMANS - VINCK - DENHAENE:
Kris Vinck(tb),Leo Coomans(reeds),Marc Denhaene(g).
                        Live."King Kong",Antwerpen,Belgium.December 11/12,19
        Eight Intimate Poses   Stichting Vrijere Muziek SVM3

NIGEL COOMBES (British)

Nigel Coombes(vln),Steve Beresford(p).   London.March 24,1979
        White String's Attached 2   Bead(E)16

Same.   London.May 20,1979
        White String's Attached 1   Bead(E)16
        White String's Attached 3   -

BOB COOPER

See also JUNE CHRISTY,BUD SHANK.

BOB COOPER QUINTET:
Bob Cooper(ts),Bud Shank(bars),Howard Roberts(g),Joe Mondragon(b),Shelly Manne(dr).
LA.May 14,1954

2627	The Way You Look Tonight	Capitol H/L6501,(J)CR8806
2645	Polka Dots And Moonbeams	-
2726	Solo Plight	-
2727	Lisbon Lady	-

11 titles also on Capitol EBF6501 (2xEP set),Affinity(E)AFF65.

BOB COOPER SEXTET:
Bob Cooper(ts),Bud Shank(bars),Claude Williamson(p),Howard Roberts(b),Curtis Counce(b),
Stan Levey(dr).
LA.July 30,1954

2887	Group Activity	Capitol H/L6501,(J)CR8806
2888	She Didn't Say Yes	- -
2889	When The Sun Comes Out	-
2890	Excursion	- ,(J)CR8806

11 titles also on Capitol EBF6501 (2xEP set),Affinity(E)AFF65.

BOB COOPER SEPTET:
Stu Williamson(tp,vtb),Bob Enevoldsen(vtb,ts,bcl),Bob Cooper(ts,enh,oboe),Bud Shank(fl,
ts,as),Jimmy Giuffre(ts,cl,bars),Claude Williamson(p),Max Bennett(b),Stan Levey(dr).
LA.April 26,1955

3745	Hot Boy	Capitol EAP1-6513,T6513,(E)EAP1005
3746	It Don't Mean A Thing	- - -
3747	Strike Up The Band	Capitol EAP2-6513, - ,(E)EAP1021
3748	Sunset	Capitol EAP3-6513, - ,(E)EAP1039

John Graas(frh),Joe Mondragon(b),Shelly Manne(dr) replace Stu Williamson,Bennett,Levey.
LA.June 13,1955

3935	Hallelujah	Capitol EAP3-6513,T6513,(E)EAP1039
3958	Deep In A Dream	Capitol EAP2-6513, - ,(E)EAP1021
3966	It's De Lovely	Capitol EAP1-6513, - ,(E)EAP1005
3967	Drawing Lines	Capitol EAP3-6513, - ,(E)EAP1039

Ralph Pena(b) replaces Mondragon.
LA.June 14,1955

4644	All Or Nothing At All	Capitol EAP3-6513,T6513,(E)EAP1039
4645	'Round Midnight	Capitol EAP1-6513, - ,(E)EAP1005
4646	Tongue Twister	Capitol EAP2-6513, - ,(E)EAP1021

7 titles on T6513 also on Affinity(E)AFF59.

BOB COOPER WITH THE WESSEL ILCKEN TRIO:
Bob Cooper(ts,oboe),Pim Jacobs(p),Ruud Jacobs(b),Wessel Ilcken(dr).
Live."De Waakzaamheid",Koog aan de Zaan,The Netherlands.March 13,1957

Indiana	HMV(Du)7EGH125
That's All	-
All The Things You Are	-
It Could Happen To You	HMV(Du)7EGH146
Yesterdays	-

1 titles on 7EGH125 also on HMV(E)7EG8376,(?)7EG11-8434,Fresh Sound(Sp)FSR-CD179 (CD).

BOB COOPER AND RHYTHM:
Bob Cooper(ts,oboe),Hans Hammerschmid(p),Rudolf Hansen(b),Victor Plasil(dr).
Milan,Italy.April 30,1957

(session cont. next page).

(session cont. from previous page):
```
        Milano Blues                    Music(I)EPM20037,LPM2009
        I'm Through With Love                      -           -
        Tickle Toe                      Music(I)EPM20036,        -
        People Will Say We're In Love             -           -
        Angel Eyes                      Music(I)EPM20038        -
        Cappuccino Time                           -           -
        Fiera Di Milano                 Music(I)LPM2009
```

All titles also on Stella(I)LPS6104,Fresh Sound(Sp)FSR-CD179 (CD).

BOB COOPER SEXTET:
Frank Rosolino(tb),Victor Feldman(vbs),Bob Cooper(ts),Lou Levy(p),Max Bennett(b),Mel Lewi⌐
(dr).   LA.August 26/27,1957
```
        Confirmation                    Contemporary C3544
        Day Dream                                 -
        Easy Living                               -
        Frankie And Johnny                        -
        Somebody Loves Me                         -
        Jazz Theme And Four Variations:           -
            Main Theme: Sunday Mood
            1st variation: A Blue Period
```

Add Conte Candoli,Pete Candoli,Don Fagerquist(tp),John Halliburton(tb).
                                          Same date
```
        Jazz Theme And Four Variations:  Contemporary C3544
            2nd variation: Happy Changes
            3rd variation: Night Stroll
            4th variation: Saturday Dance
```

All titles on C3544 also on Contemporary S7012,S7544,Vogue(E)LAC12157,Original Jazz Clas
sics OJC161,OJCCD161-2 (CD).

BOB COOPER ORCHESTRA:
Conte Candoli(tp),Frank Rosolino(tb),Vincent DeRosa(frh),Bud Shank(fl,as),Buddy Collette
(fl,bars),Bob Cooper(ts,oboe),Pete Jolly(p),Al Viola(g),Joe Mondragon(b),Mel Lewis(dr).
                                        LA.c. February 1961
```
35325  All Of My Life                   Capitol (S)T1586
35326  It's Legitimate                            -
35327  Adventure                                  -
```

Bill Hinshaw(frh),Jack Nimitz(bars) replace DeRosa,Collette.
                                        LA.c. February 1961
```
35395  Ambition                         Capitol (S)T1586
35396  Fireworks                                  -
```

All titles on (S)T1586 also on Fresh Sound(Sp)054.2607961.
Note:See June Christy for additional titles on (S)T1586.

Bob Cooper(ts),Carl Schroeder(p),Bob Magnusson(b),Jimmie Smith(dr).
                                        Burbank,Calif.May 6,1979
```
        "Yo Yo"                         Trend TR518
        Punkin' Head                              -
        We'll Be Together Again                   -
        Juarez Saturday Night                     -
        Indy 500                                  -
        True Grits                                -
        Fat Tuesday (Mardi Gras)                  -
        I've Got The World On A String            -
```

All titles also on Trend TRCD543 (CD).

BOB COOPER WITH THE MIKE WOFFORD TRIO:
Bob Cooper(ts),Mike Wofford(p),Tom Azarello(b),Jim Plank(dr,perc).
LA.July 31,1980
Where's The Love	Discovery DS822
Watch What Happens	-
His Eyes,Her Eyes	-
Siren Song	-
To Love	-
What Are You Doing The Rest Of Your Life	-
Her Hair	-
Love Discover Me	-

All titles also on Discovery DSCD935 (CD).

HARRY COOPER

HARRY COOPER ET SON ORCHESTRE:
Harry Cooper(tp),Robert Mavounzy(cl,as),Sylvio Siobud,Félix Valvert(ts),Jacques Diéval
p),Pierre Gérardot(g),Lucien Simoens(b),Armand Molinetti(dr).
Paris.January 14,1943
SW310-1 Inspiration	Swing(F)178
SW311-1 Blues 43	Swing(F)155
SW312-1 Nuages	- ,Harlequin(E)HQ2018
SW313-1 La Cigale (Undecided)	Swing(F)178

Harry Cooper(tp),Chico Cristobal(as),Robert Mavounzy(ts),Robert Castella(p),Pierre Gérar-
ot(g),Lucien Simoens(b),Charles Delaunay (as "H.P. Chadel")(dr).
Paris.May 11,1943
SW344-1 Allegro	Swing(F)191
SW345-1 Nos (Mes) Impressions (Body and Soul)	Swing(F)173
SW346-1 Caprice En Ut	Swing(F)191
SW347-1 Lune Rousse	Swing(F)173

Harry Cooper(tp),Eddie Barclay(p),Jean-Pierre Sasson(g),Emmanuel Soudieux(b),Yvan Levine
dr),Louie Williams(vcl).
Paris.May 10,1947
078-1 Mop Mop	Blue Star(F)36,Barclay(F)81004
079-1 Sweet Lorraine(lw)	unissued
080-1 Hit That Jive,Jack(1)(lw)	Blue Star(F)35,Barclay(F)81004
081-1 Open The Door,Richard(lw)	unissued
082-1 Hya Ha 69(lw)	-
083-1 Blue Drag	-
Blues Boogie	-
Grooving High	-
Boogie Woogie No.2	-

1.Issued as LOUIE WILLIAMS AND HIS CRAZY RHYTHM.

JACKIE COOPER

JACKIE COOPER AND HIS COMBO:
nk Lawson(tp),Lou McGarity(tb),Bill Stegmeyer(cl),Boomie Richman(ts),Dick Hyman(p),
orge Barnes(g),Bob Haggart(b),Jackie Cooper(dr).
NYC.July 7/9,1958
ession cont. next page).

(session cont. from previous page):
```
        Gone With The Wind             Dot DLP3146
        River Kwai March                    -
        Who's Afraid Of The Big Bad Wolf    -
        Picnic                              -
        Let's Fall In Love                  -
        The Man With The Golden Arm         -
        Meet Me In St. Louis                -
        Gigi                                -
        St. Louis Blues                     -
        Top Hat,White Tie And Tails         -
        Fifty Second Street                 -
        Pennies From Heaven                 -
```

All titles also on Dot(J)DOT5032.

```
Similar.                               NYC.   1958
        Midnight Train                 Dot 15793
        When My Sugar Walks
            Down The Street                 -
```


JEROME COOPER

See also THE REVOLUTIONARY ENSEMBLE.

Frank Lowe(ts,whistle,bells),Kalaparusha Maurice McIntyre(ts,cl,wooden-fl),Jerome Cooper
(dr,gong,saw,wooden-fl,etc.).   Live.NYC(?).April 25,1977
```
        Movement (AA)                  Kharma PK3/4
        Movement (A)                        -
        Movement (B)                        -
        Movement (C)                        -
        Movement (C2)                       -
        Movement (D)                        -
        Movement (E)                        -
        Movement (F)                        -
        Movement (G)                        -
```

Jerome Cooper(balaphone,b-dr,cymbal).   NYC(?).April 14,1978
```
        Root Assumptions,pt.1,2        Anima 2J11C
```

Oliver Lake(as,fl,bells,voice),Jerome Cooper(dr,perc,whistle).
                                            Live."The Kitchen",NYC.May 12,1979
```
        Moments 1-6                    Hat Hut(Sw)1R07
```

Jerome Cooper(dr,perc,fl,whistle).   Live."The Soundscape",NYC.July 6,1979
        The Unpredictability
```
            Of Predictability:         About Time AT1002
                Movements A,B
                Movement C
                Movement C1
        Bert That Cat                       -
```


LINDSAY COOPER (British)

See also HENRY COW.

Phil Minton(tp,voice),Lindsay Cooper(bassoon,ss,sopranino-sax,oboe,fl,keyb,acc,dr),Fred
Frith(g),Georgie Born(b,cello),Chris Cutler(dr),Sally Potter(voice).
London. 1979/80

The Exhibition Of Fashions	RER LCD(E)unnumbered
Lots Of Larks	-
General Strike	-
Women's Wrongs 1	-
Women's Wrongs 2	-
The Charter	-
Parliment Catch	-
Women's Wrongs 3	-
Film Music	-
The Prostitution Song	-
1848	-
The Chartist Anthem	-
Cholera	-
Stitch Goes The Needle	-
A Young Lady's Vision	-
Pin Money	-
Women's Wrongs 4	-
The Song Of The Shirt	-

Note:The above titles are from "The Song Of The Shirt" film soundtrack.
Additional recordings by this artist are not included.

MIKE COOPER (British)

See also JOHNNY RONDO.

MIKE COOPER - JOANNA PYNE:
Mike Cooper(g,vcl),Joanna Pyne(vcl,dance).
Ghent,Belgium.February 1980

Hammers	Matchless(E)MR4

Same.
Live.Bremen,Germany.February 1980

Beginners	Matchless(E)MR4
Beginning	-
1,2,3,4	-
Breath/Toes	-
'Ave They Started Yet	-

ROY COOPER (British)

ROY COOPER'S STOMPERS:
Roy Cooper(tb),Eddie Hancock(cl),Fred Pay(p),Tony Bracegirdle(g),George Hopkinson(dr).
London.March 13,1949

p16-MG4 Ice Cream	Delta(E)8

ROY COOPER AND HIS JAZZ BAND:
Eddie Blackwell(tp),Roy Cooper(tb),Eddie Hancock(cl),Erick Lovell(p),Gordon Branderth(bj),
Neville Baxter(b),Tony Mather(dr).
Sheffield,England.Fenbruary 3,1950

WHC151 Jenny's Ball	Classic Jazz(E)0002
WHC152 Ory's Creole Trombone	-
Original Riverboat Rag	unissued
Savoy Blues	-

Same.   Sheffield,England.March 10,1950
        Down In Honky Tonk Town   Classic Jazz(E)unissued
        Camp Meeting Blues
        Savoy Blues

Note:Additional recordings by this artist are not included.

COOTAMUNDRA JAZZ BAND (Australian)

Lloyd Janssen(tp),John Costelloe(tb),Greg Gibson(cl),John Ansell(p,vcl),Bob Cowle(b),Kevin
McArthur(dr).   Sydney.December 1,1956
        Tin Roof Blues   Parlophone(Au)PMD07513
        In An Eighteenth Century
            Drawing Room(cl,p,dr only)   -
        Softly As In A
            Morning Sunrise(no tp,cl)   -
        Just A Little Street
            Where Old Friends Meet   -
        Swanee River   -
        I Found A New Baby   -
        The Song Is Ended   -
        Hello Lola   -
        Little Brown Jug   - ,Columbia(Au)330SX7630
        Ole Miss   -

Laurie Gooding(cl,ts,tu,whistle) replaces Gibson;Ansell plays (p,celeste,vcl).
                                         Sydney.August 8,1959
        Anchors Aweigh   Columbia(Au)330SX7620
        Fanfare:Shuffle Off To Buffalo   -
        How Ya Gonna Keep
            'Em Down On The Farm   -
        The Pub With No Beer   -
        McNamara's Band   -
        Red Wing   -
        O Gee,Say Gee   -
        Yes Sir That's My Baby   -
        Wabash Blues   -
        You Can't Stop Me From Dreaming   -
        When The Red Red Robin
            Comes Bob Bob Bobbin' Along   -
        Give My Regards To Broadway   -
        Hello,Hello Who's
            Your Lady Friend   -
        Diggers Song Medley   -
        King Chanticleer   -
        Fanfare   -

OS COPACABANAS (Brazilian)

Felix Wagner(tp),Gilberto Gagliardi(tb),Kuntz(cl),Quinas(ts),José Mariho(p),Juvenat(b),
Hugo ???(dr),Popeye(perc),Elda Magda(vcl).   Rio de Janeiro. 1962
S113   Wabash Blues   Sinter 00056
S114   Three Little Words   -

LINDSAY COPELAND (Australian)
(section cont. next page).

LINDSAY COPELAND QUINTETTE:
Bruce Groves(tp),Ken Pimblett(ts),Les Patching(p,vcl),Bob Ramage(b),Lindsay Copeland(dr,
vcl).   Melbourne. 1955
        Deep Purple   Paramount(Au)LPP02
        A Precious Thing Called Love   -
        Ain't She Sweet(lc)   -
        It's Only A Paper Moon   -
        Louise   -
        Embraceable You   -
        Hit That Jive Jack(no tp,ts)(lp)   -
        Isn't It Romantic   -

Same.   Melbourne. 1955
        Muskrat Ramble(lc)   Swaggie(Au)S4518
        Taking A Chance On love   -
        Putting On The Ritz(no tp,ts)(lp)   -

Same.   Melbourne.June 22,1956
        Blue Star   Swaggie(Au)S4506
        Get A Load Of That Crazy Walk(lc)   -
        Get Out Of The Car(lp)   -
        Flamingo   -
        Saturday Night Jump   Swaggie(Au)S4518

FRANCIS COPPIETERS (Belgian)

FRANCIS COPPIETERS QUARTET:
Claudio Szenkar(vbs),Francis Coppieters(p),Jean Warland(b),Charly Antolini(dr).
                                        Cologne,Germany.February 1969
        The Open Skyway   KPM(G)1166
        Funky Chimes   -
        Bright Blue Note   -
        To Shearing With Love   -
        Cross Talk   -
        Waltz On The Off Beat   -
        Blues In The Basement   -
        Sales Talk   -
        Kings Road Chelsea   -
        Samba De Negra   -

Note:Additional recordings by this artist are not included.

MORTY CORB

MORTY CORB AND HIS DIXIE ALL STARS:
Johnny Best(tp),Moe Schneider(tb),Heinie Beau(cl),Dave Harris(ts),Bob Hammack(p),George
Van Eps(g),Morty Corb(b),Jack Sperling(dr). LA.April 1957
        Bayou Blues   Tops L1581,Venise 7014,S10014
        Alexander's Ragtime band   -   -   -
        Pennies From Heaven   -   -   -
        South   - ,Golden Tone C4021,Venise 7014,S10014
        Ramble In   -
        Honeysuckle Rose   -
        Sugarcane Strut   -
        Baby,Won't You Please Come Home   - ,Venise 7014,S10014
        Indiana   - ,Golden Tone C4021
(session cont. next page).

(session cont. from previous page):
       Savannah Shakedown   Tops L1581
       Farewell Blues   - ,Venise 7014,S10014

All titles also on Mayfair 1581S.

HAROLD CORBIN

Harold Corbin(p),Spanky DeBrest(b),Eddie Campbell(dr).
                                      NYC.c. June 1961
16137 JAMF's   Roulette(S)R52079
16138 René   -
16139 Soul Sister   -
16140 Cheek To Cheek   unissued
16141 Soul Brother   Roulette(S)R52079
16142 The Gypsy   -
16143 Satin Doll   unissued
16144 Tunga   Roulette(S)R52079
16145 I've Never Been In Love Before   -
16146 The Girl In The Window   -
16147 Don't Blame Me   -
16148 Caroline   -

CORKY CORCORAN

See also JUBILEE ALL STARS:

CORKY CORCORAN'S COLLEGIATES:
Emmett Berry(tp),Willie Smith(as),Corky Corcoran(ts),Dodo Marmarosa(p),Allan Reuss(g),Ed
Mihelich(b),Nick Fatool(dr).   LA.May 15,1945
HL94-3 What Is This Thing Called Love   Keynote 621,Mercury 1108,MG25075
HL95-3 Minor Blues   -   - ,EmArcy MG36018,MG25075
HL96-2 You Know It   Keynote(J)18PJ1063,Mercury 830.134-1
HL96-5 You Know It   Keynote 654,Mercury 1097,MG25616,EmArcy MG26026
HL97-3 Lullaby Of The Leaves   EmArcy MG36023,Trip TLP5527

All titles/takes also on Keynote(J)18PJ1063,Mercury 830.134-1 (part of set 830.121),
830.923-2 (CD).
All titles - except master HL96-2 - also on Mercury(J)BT2022.

Corcy Corcoran(ts),Gary Jones(p),Al Turay(g),Milt Garred(b),Dave Coleman(dr).
                                  Seattle. 1958
       The Fid   Celestial 1
       Low Life   -
       The Last Day   -
       Happy Feet   -
       The Thrill Is Gone   -
       Rhumba A La Prez   -
       What 'Cha Doin' Now   -
       When I Am Alone With You   -
       By The River   -
       I Guess I'll Have
          To Go To Sleep Again   -
       Since Those Days   -
       You Know It   -

Corky Corcoran(ts),Jack Perciful(p),John Smith(b).
                                        Tokoma,Washington. 1972
       Something   RCS 2555
       My Funny Valentine   -
       Ah Moore   -
       How High The Moon   -
       Danny Boy   -
       Happy Reunion   -

Incl. Stu Burnett,Bobby Herriot,Don Clark,Bobby Hales(tp),Bob Hamper(tb),Corky Corcoran
(ts),Wally Snider,Fraser MacPherson(sax,fl),Oliver Gannon(g),Ray Sims(vcl),David Robbins,
Sam Donahue(arr).   Vancouver,B.C.,Canada.September 1973
       Everywhere   C.C. Productions 4012
       Dream Of You   -
       A Sinner Kissed An Angel   -
       Sophisticated Lady   -
       Some Saturday   -
       Days Of Wine And Roses   -
       It Never Entered My Mind   -
       Mobile Bay   -
       Glocca-Morra   -
       Topsy   -

Note:Additional recordings by this artist are not included.

CHICK COREA

See also GARY BURTON,JAM SESSION ("VILLAGE VANGUARD"),PETE LA ROCA,HUBERT LAWS.

Woody Shaw(tp),Joe Farrell(ts),Chick Corea(p),Steve Swallow(b),Joe Chambers(dr).
                                        NYC.November 30,1966
11242 Inner Space   Atlantic rejected
11243 Litha   Vortex 2004,Atlantic SD2-305,2-305-2(CD)
11244 Guijira   Atlantic SD2-305,2-305-2(CD)

Same.   NYC.December 1,1966
11254 Straight Up And Down   Vortex 2004,Atlantic SD2-305,2-305-2(CD)
11255 This Is New   - ,Atlantic SD1696,SD2-305,1696-2(CD),(G)
                                    ATL50326,781402-2(CD),(I)W50326
11256 Inner Space   Atlantic SD2-305,2-305-2(CD),(G)ATL20082
11257 Tones For Joan's Bones(no tp,ts) Vortex 2004,Atlantic SD1696,SD2-305,1696-2(CD),(G)
                                    ATL50326,781402-2(CD),(I)W50326

All titles on Vortex 2004 also on Atlantic(G)ATL50302,(J)P4558,Vortex(J)P6010.
All titles on SD2-305 also on Atlantic(E)K60081,(J)P5083/84.

Chick Corea(p),Miroslav Vitous(b),Roy Haynes(dr).
                                        NYC.March 14,1968
       The Law Of
         Falling And Catching Up   Solid State SS18039,Blue Note BN-LA395
       Bossa   Blue Note BN-LA472,(G)BST84555
       Matrix   Solid State SS18039,Blue Note BN-LA395,(J)W5510,
                                    K23P-6725,TOCJ5633(CD),(Indian)JAZ1
       My One And Only Love   Blue Note BN-LA472,(G)BST84555,TOCJ5633(CD)

All titles also on Blue Note CDP7.90055-2 (CD),(J)CJ32-5009 (CD),Solid State(J)TOCJ5355
(CD).

Same.   NYC.March 19,1968
    Gemini   Blue Note BN-LA472,(G)BST84555
    Now He Sings,Now He Sobs   Solid State SS18039,Blue Note BN-LA395,(J)TOCJ5633
                                     (CD)
    Fragments   Blue Note BN-LA472,(G)BST84555

All titles also on Blue Note CDP7.90055-2 (CD),(J)CJ32-5009 (CD),Solid State(J)TOCJ5355
(CD).

Same.   NYC.March 27,1968
    Windows   Blue Note BN-LA472,(J),TOCJ5633(CD)
    Samba Yantra   -
    I Don't Know   -
    Pannonica   - ,(Du)1A.158-83401/04,(J)TOCJ5633
                                     (CD)

All titles also on Blue Note CDP7.90055-2 (CD),(J)CJ32-5009 (CD),Solid State(J)TOCJ5355
(CD).
All titles on BN-LA472 also on Blue Note(G)BST84555,(J)CGSW3019/20.

Same.   NYC.March 1968
    Steps - What Was   Solid State SS18039
    Now He Beats The
      Drum - Now He Stops   -

All titles also on Blue Note CDP7.90055-2 (CD),(J)CJ32-5009 (CD).
All titles on SS18039 also on Solid State(E)USS7011,(J)SR3029,LAX3151,SR3157,GXC3165,
Pacific Jazz LN10057.

Woody Shaw(tp),Hubert Laws(fl,picc),Bennie Maupin(ts),Chick Corea(p,el-p),Dave Holland(b),
Jack DeJohnette(dr),Horacee Arnold(dr,perc). NYC.May 11/12/13,1969
    Is   Solid State SS18055,Blue Note BN-LA395
    This(1)   -   -
    This(alt.take)(1,2)   Chiaroscuro CR2021,America(F)AM6144,Denon(J)
                                        33C38-7969(CD),33C38-8519,LRC CD7969(CD),
                                        (J)YX7387
    It(picc,p only)   Solid State SS18055
    Jamala   - ,Blue Note BN-LA395,Denon(J)
                                        33C38-7969(CD),LRC CD7969(CD)
    Jamala(alt.take)(3)   Denon(J)33C38-7969(CD),LRC CD7969,(J)YX7387
    The Brain   Groove Merchant GM2022,Giganti del Jazz(I)GJ3,
                                        Europa Jazz(I)EJ1003,Quintessential Jazz
                                        QJ25011,Laserlight 15 751(CD)
    The Brain(alt.take)   Denon(J)33C38-7969(CD),LRC CD7969(CD),(J)YX7387
    Song Of The Wind(4)   Groove Merchant GM2022,Giganti del Jazz(I)GJ3,
                                        Europa Jazz(I)EJ1003,Quintessential Jazz
                                        QJ25011,Laserlight 15 751(CD)
    Song Of The Wind(alt.take)(4)   Chiaroscuro CR2021,America(F)AM6144,Denon(J)
                                        33C38-7969(CD),LRC CD7969(CD),(J)YX7387
    Converge   Groove Merchant GM2022,Giganti del Jazz(I)GJ3,
                                        Europa Jazz(I)EJ1003,Quintessential Jazz
                                        QJ25011
    Converge(alt.take)   Chiaroscuro CR2021,America(F)AM6144,Denon(J)
                                        33C38-7969(CD),LRC CD7969(CD),(J)YX7387
    Sundance(5)   Groove Merchant GM2022,Denon(J)33C38-7969(CD),
                                        DC8519,LRC CD7969,(J)YX7387,Quintessential
                                        Jazz QJ25011,Laserlight 15 751(CD)
    Sundance(alt.take)(5)   America(F)AM6144,Giganti del Jazz(I)GJ3,Europa
                                        Jazz(I)EJ1003
(session cont. next page).

(session cont. from previous page):
-1.Omit Shaw,Laws,Arnold.
-2.Erroneously listed as "Sundance" on Denon/LRC issues.
-3.Erroneously listed as "Dave" on Denon/LRC issues.
-4.Listed as "Waltz For Bill Evans" on America,Giganti del Jazz,Europa Jazz and Denon/LRC
   issues.
-5.Erroneously listed as "Vamp" on America,Giganti del Jazz,Europa Jazz and Denon/LRC
   issues.

All titles on SS18055 also on Solid State(J)SR3052,LAX3153,GXC3166.
All titles on Blue Note BN-LA395 also on Blue Note(G)BST84504.
All titles on GM2202 also on Groove Merchant 4406,(J)RCA6037,People(E)PLEO9.

CHICK COREA TRIO:
Chick Corea(p,perc),Dave Holland(b,perc),Barry Altschul(dr).
                                      NYC.April 7,1970
       Flesh   Blue Note BST84353
       Toy Room   - ,BN-LA395,(G)BST84504
       Nefertiti   -   -   - ,(J)
                             TOCJ5633(CD)
       Blues Connotation   Blue Note BN-LA472,(G)BST84555

All titles also on Blue Note CDP7.46401-2,CDP7.84353-2 (CD),(E)BNZ22 (CD),(J)CP32-9549
(CD).

Same.   NYC.April 8,1970
       Rhymes   Blue Note BST84353,CDP7.84353-2(CD)
       Ballad I   - ,BN-LA395,CDP7.84353-2(CD),(G)
                             BST84504
       Ballad II   Blue Note CDP7.84353-2(CD)
       Ballad III   Blue Note BST84353,BN-LA395,CDP7.84353-2(CD),(G)
                             BST84504
       Drone   Blue Note BN-LA882,CDP7.84353-2(CD),(J)GXF3026/27,
                             (F)2S.062-61900/01,

All titles also on Blue Note CDP7.46401-2,(E)BNZ22 (CD),(J)CP32-9549 (CD).
All titles on BST84353 also on Blue Note(E)BNS40030,(Portuguese)11C.076-83122,183122-1,
(J)BNJ71062,Solid State(J)SR3115,GXC3167.

CHICK COREA TRIO/QUARTET (CIRCLE):
Anthony Braxton(as,cl,contrabass-cl,fl),Chick Corea(p,perc),Dave Holland(b,g,cello,perc).
                                      NYC.August 13,1970
       Duet For Bass And Piano No.1(1) Blue Note BN-LA472
       Duet For Bass And Piano No.2(1)   -
       Dance For Clarinet
          And Piano No.1(2)   -
       Dance For Clarinet
          And Piano No.2(2)   -
       Chimes,pt.1   -
       Chimes,pt.2   -

-1.Omit Braxton.
-2.Omit Holland.

Add Barry Altschul(dr,perc).   NYC.August 19,1970
       Starp   Blue Note BN-LA472
       73 Degr. Kelvin   -
       Ballad   -
       Percussion Piece   Blue Note BN-LA882,CDP7.84465-2(CD),(J)GXF3026/27,
                             (F)2S.062-61900/01

All titles on BN-LA472 also on Blue Note CDP7.84465-2 (CD),(G)BST84555,(J)CGSW3019/20.

Same.   NYC.August 21,1970
    Quartet Piece No.1   Blue Note BN-LA882
    Quartet Piece No.2   -
    Quartet Piece No.3   -

All titles also on Blue Note(F)2S.062-61900/01,(J)GXF3026/27.

Steve Grossman(ts,musette),Chick Corea(p),Dave Holland(b),Jack DeJohnette(dr),Steve
Jackson,Teruo Nakamura -1(perc).   Live(?).Unknown location.September 14,1970
    Moon Dance   Express(J)ETP9016
    Slumber   -
    The Sun,pt.1,2   -
    The Moon   -

All titles also on Express(J)ETJ66004.
Note:It is not known if the above LP was recorded under Corea's name.

CIRCLE:
Anthony Braxton(reeds,perc),Chick Corea(p),Dave Holland(b,cello),Barry Altschul(dr,perc).
                                 Live.Iserlohn,Germany.November 28,1970
    Medley: CBS(J)SOPL19
        Toy Room
        Q And A
    There Is No Greater Love   -

Same.   Live.NYC(?). 1970/71
    Nefertiti   Oxford(I)OX/3005,Giganti del Jazz(I)GJ86

Chick Corea(p),Dave Holland(b),Barry Altschul(dr).
                                 Ludwigsburg,Germnay.January 11-13,1971
    Nefertiti   ECM(G)1009
    Ballad For Tillie   -
    A.R.C.   -
    Vadana   -
    Vadana(alt.take)   Trio(J)PA9701
    Thanatos   ECM(G)1009
    Games   -
    Country Song   Trio(J)PA9701

All titles on ECM(G)1009 also on ECM833.678-2 (CD),(J)MP2192,MPF1133,J28J20218 (CD),
J25J20327 (CD),POJC2018 (CD).

CIRCLE:
Anthony Braxton(reeds,perc),Chick Corea(p),Dave Holland(b,cello),Barry Altschul(dr,perc).
                                 Live."Maison de l'ORTF",Paris.February 21,1971
    Nefertiti   ECM 1018/19
    Song For The Newborn(b-solo)   -
    Duet(as,p only)   -
    Lookout Farm(dr,perc-solo)   -
    73 Degr. Kelvin (Var. 3)   -
    Toy Room - Q And A   -
    There Is No Greater Love   -

All titles also on ECM(J)SORJ19/20,POCJ2055/56 (CD).

(p-solo).   Oslo.April 21/22,1971
    Noon Song   ECM(G)1014
    Noon Song(alt.take)   Trio(J)PA9601
    Song For Sally   ECM(G)1014
    Ballad For Anna   -
    Song Of The Wind   -
(session cont. next page).

ession cont. from previous page):
```
    Sometime Ago                    ECM(G)1014
    Where Are You Now -
       A Suite In 8 Pictures            -
    After Noon Song                 ECM(G)1020
    Song For Lee Lee                    -
    Song For Thad                       -
    Trinkle Tinkle                      -
    Masquellero                         -
    Preparation 1                       -
    Preparation 2                       -
    Departure From Planet Earth         -
    A New Place:                        -
       Arrival
       Scenery
       Imps Walk
       Rest
    Strings                         Trio(J)PA9601
```

l titles on ECM(G)1014 also on ECM(J)MP2223,MPF1134,J33J20111 (CD),J25J20325 (CD),
CJ2016 (CD).
l titles on ECM(G)1020 also on ECM(J)MP2292,MPF1135,J28J20219 (CD),J25J20326 (CD),
CJ2001 (CD).
te:One of the above takes of "Noon Song" also on on ECM(G)825426-1.

RCLE:
thony Braxton(reeds,perc),Chick Corea(p),Dave Holland(b,cello),Barry Altschul(dr,perc).
```
                                    Live.NYC.May 17,1971
    Gathering,pt. 1,2               CBS(J)SOPL20
```

TURN TO FOREVER:
e Farrell(ts,fl,ss),Chick Corea(p,el-p),Stanley Clarke(el-b,b),Airto Moreira(dr,perc),
ora Purim(vcl,perc).   NYC.February 2/3,1972
```
    Return To Forever               ECM(G)1022
    Crystal Silence                    - ,Franklin Mint 99
    What Game Shall We Play Today      -
    Sometime Ago/La Fiesta             -
    Captain Marvel                  ECM(J)PA9601
```

l titles on ECM(G)1022 also on ECM(G)811978-2 (CD),(J)MP2273,MPF1136,25MJ3220,J33J20110
D),J28J20217 (CD),J25J29024 (CD).

```
me.                                 Live.NYC.  1972
    Sometime Ago/La Fiesta          Oxford(I)OX/3005,Giganti del Jazz(I)GJ86
```

```
me.                                 Live.Prob. "Carnegie Hall",NYC.May 13,1972
    Unidentified title(p,b,dr only) Session LP122
    Return To Forever                  -
    Sometime Ago/La Fiesta             -
```

te:The unidentified title issued as "Country Ripples/Summer Storm" and "Return To Forever" as "Future Return Trip".

```
me.                                 London.October  1972
    You're Everything               Polydor(Am)PD5525
    Light As A Feather                 - ,Verve(Eu)2367.074
    Captain Marvel                     - ,(Eu)831.365-2(CD),Verve
                                    831.376-2(CD)
    500 Miles High                  Polydor(Am)PD5525(Eu)831.365-2(CD)
    Children's Song                    -
    Spain                              - ,(Eu)831.365-2(CD),Verve
ession cont. next page).            (Eu)2367.074
```

(session cont. from previous page):
All titles also on Polydor(E)2310.247,(Eu)2482.497,827.148-2 (CD),(J)MP2304,MPF1171,
18MJ9003,25MJ3219.
Note:Verve(Eu)2367.074 is part of the 10 LP-set (2615.011).

RETURN TO FOREVER:
Chick Corea(p,el-p,org,hsc,gongs),Bill Connors(g),Stanley Clarke(b,el-b,perc),Lenny White
(dr,perc).   NYC.August 1973
        Hymn Of The Seventh Galaxy   Polydor(Am)PD5536
        After The Cosmic Rain   -
        Captain Senor Mouse   - ,Polydor(Eu)831.365-2(CD)
        Theme To The Mothership   -
        Space Circus,pt.1,2   -
        The Game Maker   -

All titles also on Polydor(E)2310.283,(F)2302.028,(J)MF1172,18MJ9007.

Al Di Meola(g,el-g) replaces Connors;Corea plays (p,el-p,org,synth,clavinet,perc);Clarke
also plays (org).   NYC.July/August 1974
        Vulcan Worlds   Polydor(Am)PD6509,(Eu)831.365-2(CD)
        Where Have I Loved You Before   -
        The Shadow Of Lo   -
        Where Have I
            Danced With You Before   -
        Beyond The Seventh Galaxy   -
        Earth Juice   -
        Where Have I Known You Before   -
        Song To The Pharoah Kings   -

All titles also on Polydor(E)2310.354,(F)2302.030,(J)MP2417,MF1173,18MJ9008,25MJ3223,
Supraphon(Cz)1151903.
All titles - except "Where Have I Danced With You Before" - also on Polydor(Eu)825.206-2
(CD),(J)J33P50001 (CD).

Chick Corea(p,el-p,org,synth,clavinet,perc,mar,vcl),Al Di Meola(g),Stanley Clarke(b,el-b
org,synth,vcl),Lenny White(dr,perc,cg,mar). NYC.January 1975
        Dayride   Polydor(Am)PD6512
        Jungle Waterfall   -
        Sofistifunk   -
        Flight Of The Newborn   - ,Balkanton(Bu)BTA1952
        Excerpt From The First
            Movement Of Heavy Metal   -
        No Mystery   - ,(Eu)831.365-2(CD),Balkanton(Bu
                                            BTA1952
        Interplay   Polydor(Am)PD6512
        Celebration Suite,pt.1,2   -

All titles also on Polydor(E)2310.378,(Eu)827.149-2 (CD),(J)MP2470,MPF1174,18MJ9006,
25MJ3224.

Danny Cahn,Bob Millikan,John Gatchell(tp),Bill Watrous,Wayne Andre(tb),Joe Farrell -1
(ss,fl,enh),Chick Corea(p,org,synth,perc),Eddie Gomez -2(b),Anthony Jackson -3(el-b),Ste
Gadd(dr),Gayle Moran(vcl),strings.   NYC. 1975
        Imp's Welcome   Polydor(Am)PD6062
        Lenore   -
        Reverie(4)(gm)   -
        Looking At The World(3)   -
        Nite Sprite(1,3)   -
        Soft And Gentle(2)   -
        Pixiland Rag   -
        Leprechaun's Dream(1,2,3)   -
(session cont. next page).

session cont. from previous page):

4.Corea,Moran only.

ll titles also on Polydor(F)2391.217,(J)MP2548,MPF1175,18MJ9004.

hick Corea(p,el-p,clavinet,synth,mar,perc),Al Di Meola(g,perc,whistle),Stanley Clarke
el-b,piccolo-b,b,perc),Lenny White(dr,perc).

	Caribou Ranch,Colorado.February 1976
Medieval Overture	Columbia PC34076
Sorceress	-
The Romantic Warrior	-
Majestic Dance	-
The Magician	-
Duel Of The Jester	
And The Tyrant,pt.1,2	-

ll titles also on Columbia CK46109 (CD),CBS(Eu)81221,(J)25AP55.

ohn Thomas,John Rosenberg,Stuart Blumberg(tp),Ron Moss(tb),Chick Corea(p,synth,org,el-p,
cl),Stanley Clarke -1(b),Steve Gadd(dr),Don Alias(perc),strings,Gayle Moran(vcl).

	Burbank,Calif.October 1976	
Love Castle	Polydor PD2-9003,(Eu)831.365-2(CD)	
The Gardens(1)	-	
Day Danse	-	
My Spanish Heart	-	
Night Streets	-	
The Hilltop(1)	-	
The Sky:		
Children's Song No.8		
Portrait Of		
Children's Song No.8		
Wind Danse(!)	-	
Armando's Rhumba(2)	-	,(Eu)831.365-2(CD)
Prelude To El Bozo	-	
El Bozo,pt.I-III	-	
Spanish Fantasy,pt.I-IV(1,3)	-	

2.Jean Luc Ponty(vln),Chick Corea(p,handclapping),Stanley Clarke(el-b),Narada Michael
Walden(handclapping).
3.Clarke plays on part I only.

l titles also on Polydor(Eu)2669.034,2672.031,(j)MPZ8103/04,30MJ9010/11.
l titles - except "The Sky" - also on Polydor(Eu)825.657-2 (CD),(J)J33P50002 (CD),
CJ1980 (CD).

hn Thomas(tp,flh),James Tinsley(tp,piccolo-tp),Jim Pugh(tb),Harold Garrett(tb,btb,barh),
e Farrell(ts,ss,fl,picc),Chick Corea(p,el-p,synth,vcl),Stanley Clarke(b,el-b,piccolo-b),
rry Brown(dr),Gayle Moran(vcl,keyb).

	Colorado.January/February 1977
The Musician	Columbia PC34682
Hello Again	-
Musicmagic	-
So Long Mickey Mouse	-
Do You Ever	-
The Endless Night	-

l titles also on Columbia CK34682 (CD),CBS(Eu)S81050,(J)25AP445.
te:The CBS(Eu) issue number may be S81959.

Add Ron Moss(tb);Garrett plays (btb,barh,tu).
```
                                    Live."Palladium Theatre",NYC.May 20/21,1977
        Opening '77               Columbia C4X35350
        The Endless Night         -
        The Musician              Columbia JC35281,C4X35350
        Hello Again               Columbia C4X35350
        So Long Mickey Mouse      Columbia JC35281,C4X35350
        Musicmagic                -           -
        Come Rain Or Come Shine   -           -
        Serenade                  Columbia C4X35350
        The Moorish Warrior
            And Spanish Princess  Columbia JC35281,C4X35350
        Chick's Piano Solo        -           -
        Spanish Fantasy           Columbia C4X35350
        On Green Dolphin Street   -
```

All titles on JC35281 also on CBS(Eu)82808.

Chick Corea(p,synth,mar),strings -1.   Burbank,Calif. 1977/78
```
        The Woods                 Polydor(Am)PD1-6130
        Tweedle Dee(1)            -
```

Joe Farrell(ts),Chick Corea(p),Eddie Gomez(b),Steve Gadd(dr).
```
                                          Burbank,Calif.  1977/78
        Humpty Dumpty             Polydor(Am)PD1-6130
```

John Thomas,Stuart Blumberg,John Rosenberg(tp),Ron Moss(tb),Joe Farrell(ts,fl,picc),Chick
Corea(p,mar,perc),Eddie Gomez(b),Steve Gadd(dr),strings,Gayle Moran(vcl).
```
                                          Burbank,Calif.  1977/78
        Falling Alice(gm)         Polydor(Am)PD1-6130
        Dear Alice(1)(gm)         -
        Mad Hatter Rhapsody(1,2)(gm)  -
```

-1.Omit Moss.
-2.Add Herbie Hancock(p).

Jamie Faunt(b),Harvey Mason(dr) replace Gomez,Gadd.
```
                                          Burbank,Calif.  1977/78
        The Trial(gm)             Polydor(Am)PD1-6130
        Prelude To Falling Alice  -
        Tweedle Dum
            (p,b,strings only)(gm)  -
```

All titles on PD1-6130 also on Polydor(Eu)2490.144(J)MPF1150,18MJ9002.

Joe Farrell(ts,fl),Chick Corea(p,el-p),Eddie Gomez(b),Steve Gadd(dr).
```
                                          Burbank,Calif.January  1978
        The One Step              Polydor PD1-6160
        Waltse(!) For Dave
            (Dedicated to Brubeck)  -
        Children's Song No.5      -
        Samba Song                -
        Friends                   -
        Sicily                    -
        Children's Song No.15     -
        Cappucino                 -
```

All titles also on Polydor(Eu)2391.366,(J)MPF1191,18MJ9001,POCJ1981 (CD).

CHICK COREA - LIONEL HAMPTON:
1 Vizzutti(tp),Ron Moss(tb),Lionel Hampton(vbs),Chick Corea(p),unknown b,dr,Gayle
oran(vcl).   Live.Cannes,France.Prob. January 22,1978
    Sea Breeze(1)   Who's Who In Jazz 21016
    Moments Notice   -
    Come Rain Or Come Shine
      (p,vcl only)(gm)   -
    Fiesta Piano Solo(p-solo)   -
    I Ain't Mad At You(2)(lh)   -

1.As "Sea Journey" on B690061,TJ039.
2.Hampton (p,vcl).

11 titles also on Kingdom Jazz Gate(E)7005,Fortune 3002,Philips(F)6313.265,Toledo(G)
47428,Happy Bird(G)B90061,Master(Du)CLCD5007 (CD),That's Jazz TJ039 (CD),Platinum(G)
LP31,Legends Of Music(J)RJL8004,Baystate(J)RJL2677.
ote:Vizzutti and Moss were overdubbed later.

CHICK COREA - HERBIE HANCOCK:
hick Corea,Herbie Hancock(p).   Live.San Francisco/LA/San Diego/Ann Arbor.February 1978
    Homecoming   Polydor PD2-6238
    Ostinato (Mikrokosmos)   -
    The Hook   -
    Bouquet(1)   -
    Maiden Voyage   -
    La Fiesta   -
    Someday My Prince Will Come   Columbia PC2.35663
    Liza   -
    Button Up(2)   -
    February Moment   -
    Maiden Voyage   -
    La Fiesta   -

..Omit Hancock.
..Omit Corea.

1 titles on PD2-6238 also on Polydor(Eu)2669.049,2672.049,835.680-2 (CD),(J)MPZ8125/26,
0J20243 (CD)POCJ1982 (CD).
1 titles on PC2.35663 (JG35664/5) also on CBS(Eu)88329,(J)40AP1182/83,40DP5533/34 (CD).
te:PD2-6238 was issued under Corea's name while JG35664 was issued under Hancock's name.
  Two versions of "Maiden Voyage" and of "Fiesta" were recorded.

 Vizzutti(tp,flh),Bob Zottola(tp),Jim Pugh,Ron Moss(tb),Joe Farrell(ts,ss,fl),Chick
rea(keyb),Bunny Brunel(b),Tom Brechtlein(dr),Airto Moreira(perc),strings,Al Jarreau,
yle Moran(vcl).   LA.June 1978
    The Golden Dawn   Polydor PD1-6176
    Slinky   -
    Mirage   -
    Drifting(gm)   -
    Glebe St. Blues(gm)   -
    Fickle Funk   -
    Bagatelle No.4(?)   -
    Hot News Blues(aj)   -
    Central Park   -

1 titles also on Polydor(Eu)2391.381,(J)MPF1220,18MJ9005.

-solo).   Delphian Foundation,Sheridan,Oregon.October 26/27,1978
ession cont. next page).

```
(session cont. from previous page):
        Delphi I-VIII                    Polydor PD1-6208
        Children's Song No.20                   -
        Stride Time I                           -
        Stride Time II (Soft Stride)            -
        Stride Time III (Soft Stride)           -
        Stride Time IV (Stride Bop)             -
        Stride Time V (Mr. T.)                  -
        Stride Time VI (Stride Out)             -
        Stride Time VII
            (Rhapsody For Mr. T.)               -
        New World I (Sad Song)           Polydor(J)28MJ3011
        New World II (Samba)                    -
        New World III (North Brasil)            -
        New World IV (Mountain Top)             -
        New World V (Voices)                    -
        New World VI (Spirits)                  -
        New World VII
            (Waltz For My Folks)                -
        Unicorns I-II                           -
        Maim I-II                        Polydor(J)28MJ3012
        Valley I-XII                            -
        Poem I (Concerto Flamenco)              -
        Poem II                                 -
        Poem III                                -
        Poem IV                                 -
        Poem V                                  -
```

All titles on PD1-6208 also on Polydor(E)2490.150,(Eu)2391.402,(J)MPF1255.

CHICK COREA - GARY BURTON:
Chick Corea(p),Gary Burton(vib).   Live.Zürich,Switzerland.October 28,1979
        Senor Mouse   ECM(G)1182/83
        Bud Powell   -
        Crystal Silence   -
        Tweak   -
        Medley: -
            I'm Your Pal
            Hullo,Bolinas
            Love Castle
        Falling Grace   -
        Mirror,Mirror   -
        Song To Gayle   -
        Endless Trouble,Endless Pleasure   -

All titles also on ECM(G)821.415/16-2 (CD),(J)PA6125/26,38MJ3320/21.
All titles - except "Medley" - also on ECM(J)J28J20246 (CD),J33J50004 (CD),POCJ2021 (CD)

Chick Corea(el-p,synth,clavinet),Bunny Brunel(b,el-b),Airto Moreira,Laudir Oliveira(perc
Flora Purim,Gayle Moran,Shelby Flint,Nani Villa Brunel(vcl).
                                              LA.December 1979/January 1980
        Samba L.A.(fp,gm,sf,nvb)   Warner Bros. BSK4325
        The Slide(1)   -

-1.Add Jamie Faunt(piccolo-b),Tom Brechtlein(dr),Don Alias(perc).

Al Vizzutti(tp,flh),Hubert Laws -1(fl),Joe Farrell(ts,ss),Chick Corea(p,el-p,synth,perc
Bunny Brunel(el-b),Tom Brechtlein(dr,perc),Don Alias -2(cg),Gayle Moran(vcl).
                                              Same dates

(session cont. next page).

(session cont. from previous page):
    The Embrace(1,2)(no ts/fl)(gm)   Warner Bros. BSK4325
        Tap Step   -
        Magic Carpet(2)   -
        Flamenco(1,3)   -

3.Add Joe Henderson(ts).

Chick Corea(el-p,synth),Bunny Brunel(el-b),Stanley Clarke(picc-b,talk-box),Tom Brechtlein
(dr).   Same dates
    Grandpa Blues   Warner Bros. BSK4325

11 titles on BSK3425 also on Warner Bros.(Eu)WB56801,(J)P10815.

CORNY STOMPERS (Swedish)

Magnus Granhed(tp),Sten Forsler(tb),Mats Granström(cl),Stefan Poluha(p),Staffan Åberg(bj,
cl),Sten Eriksson(b),Thomas Ohlsson(dr).   Stockholm.February 12,1966
        Darktown Strutters' Ball   Cornyphone(Sd)CO1
        Gärdeby Gånglåt   -
        Imse Vimse Spindel   -
        Just A Closer Walk With Thee   -

CORONA'S (Dutch)

Peter Bennink(sopranino-sax,as,ts),Ralph de Jongh(perc).
                                        Amsterdam.May 1980
        Corona 1   VR(Du)10597
        Corona 2   -
        Velocity Duet   -
        Corona 5 (Ain't Misbehavin')   -

CORONA SENIOR HIGH JAZZ ENSEMBLE

Mike Harlin,Jeff Ward,Steve Renfeldt,John Hardison,Sam Spiegel(tp),Bob Temple,Mike Zegler,
Kent Dastrup(tb),Louis West(btb),Ed Hull(btb,tu),Dan Kreuter(as),Rob Trantow(as,bars),Mike
Kelsey,Greg Huckins,Kent Ward(ts),Steve King(bars),Doug Phillips(p),Kurt Seidler(g),Kent
Hatch(b),Wes Bridgewater,Glenn Johnson,Richard West(dr,perc),Roger E. Rickson(cond).
                                        LA(?).c. 1971
        Chiapas   Custom Fidelity CFS2477
        Quickstep   -
        Malaga   -
        My Tosis   -
        Porgy And Bess   -

Mike Ernst,Jeff Ward(tp,flh),Eric Norland,Mark Hornberger,Mike Wuflestad(tp),Mike Danner,
Steve Holtman,Vernon Holmwood(tb),Vernon Whitt(btb),Steve Paulson(btb,tu),Dave Hlebo(as,
s,fl),Paul Pettit(as,bars,cl),Greg Huckins(ts,ss,fl,picc),Doug Flynn(ts,cl),Rob Trantow
(bars,cl),Steve Dahl(p,el-p),Jim Dell(g),Wade Lachman(b),Pat Wilson,Blake Gardner(dr,perc)
Roger E. Rickson(cond).   LA(?).June 9,1973
        Double Exposure   Custom Fidelity USR5751
        La Voz Del Viento   -
        Carte Blanche   -
        Illicit Debauchery
            And How To Cultivate It   -
(session cont. next page).

(session cont. from previous page):
    Blues Between And Betwixt   Custom Fidelity USR5751
    Dark Orchid   -
    Afterthoughts   -
    Porgy And Bess   -

CORONARIAS DANS (Danish)

Kenneth Knudsen(p),Peter Friis Nielsen(b),Claus Bøje(dr).
        Copenhagen.October 22/23,1970
    Start Off   Parlophone(D)E.062-38052
    Stay   -
    Smoke   -
    The 21 Cms Song   -
    Speaker   -
    Breathe,Your Queen Has Gone   -

Kenneth Knudsen(p,el-p),Peter Friis Nielsen(b),Ole Streenberg(dr).
        Copenhagen.January 15,1973
    Tired Waves   SteepleChase(D)SCS1032
    Morning(1)   -

-1.Add Morten Grunnet(tamboura).

Same.   Copenhagen.May 15,1973
    Sagittarius   SteepleChase(D)SCS1032
    Se Det   -
    Esrom(b-solo)   -

Add Claus Bøhling(g);Knudsen plays (p,el-p,bg).
        Copenhagen.November 11,1973
    Don't Know   SteepleChase(D)SCS1032
    Which Witch   -
    Visitor   -

All titles on SCS1032 also on SteepleChase(J)RJ7131,Inner City IC2032.

THE CORONETS

Note:Some issues as THE DUKE ELLINGTON AND BILLY STRAYHORN ALL-STARS and as DUKE ELLINGTON
AND THE ELLINGTONIANS.

Cat Anderson(tp),Juan Tizol(tb),Willie Smith(as),Paul Gonsalves(ts),Billy Strayhorn(p),
Wendell Marshall(b),Louis Bellson(dr).   NYC.April 17,1951
M4029   Night Walk (Cat Walk)   Mercer 1969,LP1005,Vogue(E)V2088,EPV1060,(F)LD49
        Jazz Selection(F)JS780
M4030-1 Moonlight Fiesta   Mercer 1967,Vogue(E)V2088,Jazz Selection(F)JS780
        (Sd)4004
M4030-2 Moonlight Fiesta   Mercer LP1005,Vogue(E)EPV1060
M4031-1 She (Sensuous)   Mercer 1967,LP1007,Vogue(E)V2087,(F)LD050,Jazz
        Selection(F)JS781
M4032   The Happening   Mercer 1969,LP1005,Vogue(E)V2087,EPV1060,(F)LD49
        Jazz Selection(F)JS781,I.A.J.R.C. IAJRC15

All titles/takes also on Vogue(E)VJD525,(F)DP19.
All titles - except master M4030-1 - also on Prestige P24103,PCD24103-2 (CD).
All titles on LP1005 also on Vogue(E)LDE035,(F)LD028.

Quentin Jackson,Britt Woodman,Juan Tizol(tb),Willie Smith(as),Billy Strayhorn(p),Wendell
Marshall(b),Louis Bellson(dr).   Boston.May 18,1951
M4033 Swamp Drums   Mercer LP1005
M4034 Sultry Serenade(1)   -
M4035 Indian Summer   Mercer 1968,LP1007,Vogue(E)V2080,(F)LD050,(D)782,
                                            Jazz Selection(F)JS782

M4036 Britt And Butter Blues   Mercer LP1005

-1.Duke Ellington(p) replaces Strayhorn.

All titles also on Vogue(E)VJD525,(F)DP19,Prestige P24103,PCD24103-2 (CD).
All titles on LP1005 also on Vogue(E)LDE035,(F)LD028.

Juan Tizol(tb),Willie Smith(as),Duke Ellington(p),Billy Strayhorn(org),Wendell Marshall
(b),Louis Bellson(dr),Norma Oldham(vcl).   NYC.June 1,1951
M4037 The Nearness Of You(no)   Mercer unissued
M4038 More Than You Know(no)   -
M4039 Caravan   Mercer 1968,LP1007,Vogue(E)V2080,EPV1060,VJD525,
                                            (F)LD050,LD497,DP19,(D)782,Jazz Selection(F)
                                            JS782,(Sd)4004,Prestige P24103,PCD24103-2(CD)

Add Jimmy Hamilton(cl,ts);omit Strayhorn.   NYC.June 19,1951
M4040 Alternate   Mercer LP1005,Vogue(F)LD497
M4041 Noppin (Hoppin') John   Mercer 1973(?),LP1007,Vogue(E)V2130,(F)LD050,Jazz
                                            Selection(F)JS808
M4042 Jumpin' With Symphony Sid(1)   Mercer 1973,LP1005,Vogue(E)V2130,Vogue(F)
                                            LD497,Jazz Selection(F)JS808

-1.Billy Strayhorn(p) replaces Ellington.

All titles also on Vogue(E)VJD525,(F)DP19,Prestige P24103,PCD24103-2 (CD).
All titles on LP1005 also on Vogue(E)LDE035,(F)LD028.

RICH CORPOLONGO

Rich Corpolongo(as,ss,cl,bcl,fl,picc,electronics),Doug Lofstrom(b,bamboo-fl,perc,vcl),Paul
Wertico(dr,perc,electronics).   Unknown location.July 11/14/22,1980
       Prelude   Spoco 12101
       Bird Dirge   -
       1 & 2   -
       Flutter-Wings   -
       Chinese New Year: -
          Spirit Play
          Dance
       No Survivors: -
          Fog-Bound
          Lost-At-Sea
       March Of The Scnatskis   -
       Stay Out - Or - I Thought
          I Told You To Take Those
          Roller Skates Off The Stairs

JUAN CARLOS CORREA (Argentinean)

(p-solo).   Unknown location/date
       St Louis Blues   Columbia(Arg)301046
       Lago De Ensueno (Lake Of Dreams)   -

CORTEX (French)

Alain Labib(as),Alain Mion(keybd,vcl,arr,ldr),Jean Claude "Le Boeuf" d'Agostini(g),Jean Grevet(b),Alain Gandolfi(dr,perc,vcl),Jo Pucheu(perc),Mireille Dalbray(vcl).

	Paris.July 15-16,1975
La Rue	Esperance(F)ESP155.524
Automne (Colchiques)	-
L'Enfant Samba	-
Troupeau Bleu	-
Prélude A "Go Round"	-
Go Round	-
Chanson D'Un Jour d'Hiver	-
Mary Et Jeff	-
Huit Octobre 1971	-
Sabbat 1ere, 2e Et 3e Parties	-
Mad Bass	-

JAYNE CORTEZ

(recitation) acc. by Richard Davis(b).	NYC.July 18,1974
Lead	Strata East SES7421
How Long Has Trane Been Gone	-
Essence Of Rose Solitude	-
Song For Kwane	-
Forreal	-
Festivals And Funerals	-
Solo	-
I Am New York City	-
Under The Edge Of February	-
Lynch Fragment 2	-
Ife Night	-
Homicide	-
3 Day New York City Blues	-
Remembrance	-
Do You Think	-
Making It	-
So Long	-
Lexington/96th Street Stop	-
I Won't Forget It	-

(recitation) acc. by Bill Cole(musette,nagaswarm),Bern Nix(g),Joe Daley(tu),Ornette Denardo Coleman(dr).

	NYC.October 1,1979
You Know	Bola Press BP8001
For The Brave Young Students In Soweto	-
Ogun's Friend	-
Brooding	-
In The Morning	-
The Red Pepper Poet	-

BOB CORWIN

BOB CORWIN QUARTET:
Don Elliott(tp),Bob Corwin(p),Ernie Furtado(b),Jimmy Campbell(dr).

NYC.June 1956

(session cont. next page).

(session cont. from previous page):
```
        My Shining Hour              Riverside RLP12-220,RLP12-267
        Isn't Is Romantic                       -
        I'll Remember April(no tp)              -
        I Remember You                          -
        Rico-Jico Joe                           -
        It Might As Well Be Spring              -
        I'll Take Romance(no tp)                -
        Gone With The Wind                      -
        It Could Happen To You                  -
        Pony Tail                               -
```

All titles also on Riverside(J)WWLJ7017.

LARRY CORYELL

See also JAZZ COMPOSERS ORCHESTRA,ARNIE LAWRENCE,STEVE MARCUS.

Larry Coryell(g,b,vcl),Bob Moses(dr).   NYC. 1968
```
        Herman Wright(lc)            Vanguard VSD6509
        Sunday Telephone(lc)                    -
        Two Minute Classical                    -
        Love Child Is Coming Home(lc)           -
        Lady Coryell                            - ,VSD75/76
        The Dream Thing                         -
        Treats Style(1,2)                       - ,(J)SR3168,K22P6134/35
        You Don't Know What Love Is             -
        Stiff Neck(2)                           - ,VSD75/76
        Cleo's Mood                             -
```

-1.Add Jimmy Garrison(b).
-2.Elvin Jones(dr) replaces Moses.

All titles also on Vanguard(E)SVRL19051,(F)VSD23017,(J)GXC3168,K20P6196.

Mike Mandel(org),Larry Coryell(g,vcl),Ron Carter(el-b),Steve Haas(dr),Ray Mantilla(perc).
```
                                          NYC.  1968
        Call To The Higher
          Consciousness(1)          Vanguard VSD79375
        Slow Blues                              - ,(J)K22P6134/35
        Friday Night                            -
        Half A Heart                            - ,(J)K22P6134/35
        Tyrone                                  -
        Organ Blues                             -
```

-1.Add unknown(ts) - prob. Jim Pepper or Steve Marcus.

All titles also on Vanguard(F)VSD23028.

Larry Coryell(g,p,vcl),Chuck Rainey(el-b),Bernard Purdie(dr).
```
                                      NYC.April 25,1969
        Sex                          Vanguard VSD6547
        Sex(alt.take)               Vanguard VSD79375,(F)VSD23028,(J)GP3114
        Elementary Guitar Solo 5(1) Vanguard VSD6547,VSD75/76,(J)K22P6134/35
        No One Really Knows,pt.1                -
        Morning Sickness                        -
```

-1.Add Mike Mandel(org,p).

Larry Coryell(p,el-p,g,vcl),Albert Stinson(el-b),Bernard Purdie(dr).

	Same date
Beautiful Woman(1)	Vanguard VSD6547,(J)SR3168
The Jam With Albert	- ,VSD75/76
The Jam With Albert(alt.take)	Vanguard VSD79375,(F)VSD23028,(J)GP3114
No One Really Knows,pt.2	Vanguard VSD6547
Ah Wuv Ooh(1,2)	-

-1.Ron Carter(el-b) replaces Stinson.
-2.Add Jim Pepper(fl).

All titles on VSD6547 also on Vanguard(E)SVRL19059,(F)VSD23030,519.026,(J)SR379.

Larry Coryell,John McLaughlin(g),Miroslav Vitous(cello,b),Billy Cobham(dr).

	NYC.Summer 1970	
Spaces (Infinite)	Vanguard VSD6558,VSD75/76,(J)SR3168	
Rene's Theme(g-duet)	-	- ,(J)K22P6134/35
Gloria's Step(1)	-	
Wrong Is Right	-	
Chris(1,2)	-	
New Year's Day In Los Angeles - 1968(3)		- ,(J)K22P6134/35
Tyrone(2)	Vanguard VSD79367	
Planet End	-	

-1.Omit McLaughlin.
-2.Add Chick Corea(el-p).
-3.Coryell(g-solo).

All titles also on Vanguard(J)240E6842 (CD).
All titles on VSD6558 also on Vanguard VSD79345,(E)VMLP5305,VMCD7305 (CD),(F)VSD23002,
519.031,(J)SR3109,LAX135,K20P6194.
All titles on VSD79367 also on Vanguard(F)VSD23022,(J)GP3047,K20P6198.

Larry Coryell(g,vcl),Mervin Bronson(el-b),Harry Wilkinson(dr),Julie Coryell(vcl).

	Live."Village Gate",NYC.January 20/21,1971
The Opening	Vanguard VSD6573,(J)SR3168,K22P6134/35
After Later	- ,VSD75/76,(J)SR3168
Entardecendo En Saudade	-
Can You Follow (Dance On The Green Hill)	-
Beyond These Chilling Winds(jc)	- ,(J)SR3168

All titles also on Vanguard(F)VSD23024,519.041.

Steve Marcus(ts,ss),Larry Coryell(g),Roy Haynes(dr),Lawrence Killian(cg),Harry Wilkinson (perc).

	NYC. 1971
Gypsy Queen	Flying Dutchman FD26012(ed.),FD10139
The Great Escape(1)	Flying Dutchman FD10139
Call To The Higher Conciousness(2)	-

-1.Add Mervin Bronson(el-b).
-2.Add Mike Mandel(p).

All titles also on Flying Dutchman(J)PG73,RJL2566,RCA AYL1-3961,(Eu)CL13961,Philips(Eu)
6369.407.
Note:FD26012 is a disc jockey 45 r.p.m.

Larry Coryell(g,vcl),Chuck Rainey(el-b),Bernard Purdie(dr),Julie Coryell(vcl).
                          Live.Montreux Jazz Festival,Switzerland.June 18,1971
    Soul's Dirge(1)(lc)   Mega M51-5000
    Eskdalemuir(2)   -
    All My Love's Laughter(lc,jc)   unissued
    Stones   Mega M51-5000
    Further Explorations
      For Albert Stinson   -

-1.Introduced by Coryell as "Struggles Gloom".
-2.Introduced by Coryell as "Destruction's Run".

All titles also on Mega MLPS607,Philips(Eu)6369.411,Flying Dutchman(J)LAX3054,PG72,
RJL2565,Zodiac 5003.

Steve Marcus(ts,ss),Mike Mandel(p,synth),Larry Coryell(g,synth,vcl),Mervin Bronson(b),
Harry Wilkinson(dr),Earl Derouen(cg),unknown horns -1,Julie Coryell(vcl),Bryan Wells(arr).
                                       NYC.c. 1972
    The Real Great Escape(1)(lc) Vanguard VSD79329
    Are You Too Clever(lc)   - ,VSD75/76
    Love Life's Offering(lc)   -
    Makes Me Wanna Shout(1)(lc)   -
    All My Love's Laughter(lc)   - ,(J)K22P6134/35
    Scotland II(lc)   -
    P.F. Sloan(1)(lc)   -

All titles also on Vanguard(F)VSD23019.

Steve Marcus(ss),Mike Mandel(el-p),Larry Coryell(g,vcl),Mervin Bronson(b),Harry Wilkinson
(dr).   NYC.January 17/18/20,1972
    Foreplay   Vanguard VSD79319,VSD75/76
    Ruminations
    Scotland I   - ,VSD75/76
    Offering   - ,(J)K22P6134/35
    The Meditation Of November 8th -
    Beggar's Chant(lc)   -

All titles also on Vanguard(F)VSD23001,(I)33045,(J)SR3156,GXC3169,K20P6195.

(LARRY CORYELL AND) THE ELEVENTH HOUSE:
Randy Brecker(tp),Mike Mandel(p,synth),Larry Coryell(g),Danny Trifan(b),Alphonse Mouzon
(dr).   NYC.March 1973
    Birdfingers   Vanguard VSD79342
    The Funky Waltz   -
    Low-Lee-Tah   -
    Adam Smasher   -
    Joy Ride   -
    Yin   - ,VSD75/76
    Theme For A Dream   -
    Gratitude "A So Low"   -
    Ism - Ejercicio   -
    Right On Y'All   -

All titles also on Vanguard 79342 (CD),(F)VSD23012,SVAL33033,(J)SR3175,K20P6199.

Michael Lawrence(tp) replaces Brecker. Live.Montreux Jazz Festival,Switzerland.July 4,1974
    Improvisations On Villa-Lobos: Vanguard VSD79410
      Prelude No 4 In E Minor
    Tamari
    Joyride   -
(session cont. next page).

(session cont. from previous page):
       Rasputin   Vanguard VSD79410
       Song For A New York Rainmaker   -
       The Eleventh House Blues
         (Struttin'With Sunshine)   -

All titles also on Vanguard(J)GP3171.

Same.   NYC. 1974
       Cover Girl   Vanguard VSD79367
       Rocks   -
       The Eyes Of Love(g-solo)   -

All titles also on Vanguard(F)VSD23022,(J)GP3047,K20P6198,240E6842 (CD).

Michael Lawrence(tp,flh),Mike Mandel(keybd),Larry Coryell(g),John Lee(el-b),Alphonse Mou-
zon(dr).   NYC. 1974
       Level One(1)   Arista AL4052
       The Other Side   -
       Diedra   -
       Some Greasy Stuff   -
       Nyctaphobia   -
       Suite: -
        a. Entrance
        b. Repose
        c. Exit
       Eyes Of Love   -
       Struttin' With Sunshine   -
       That's The Joint   -

-1.Add Steve Khan(g).

All titles also on Arista(E)ARTY113,(F)2C.066-96774.

Same.   Live.Europe 1974/75
       Birdfingers   LC-1
       Diedra   -
       The Funky Waltz   -
       Suite: -
        a. Entrance
        b. Repose
        c. Exit
       The Other Side   -
       Tamari   -
       Julie Lobelle/Scotland(g-solo) -

Note:The LP does not list the titles played.

Larry Coryell,Ralph Towner(g),Glen Moore(b),Collin Walcott(tabla,cg).
                   NYC. 1974/75
       Improvisations On Robert
        De Visee's Menuet II   Vanguard VSD79353
       Ann Arbor   -
       Pavane For A Dead Princess -
       Improvisation On
        Robert De Visee's Sarabande - ,VSD75/76
       Song For Jim Webb   -
       Julie La Belle   -
       The Restful Mind   -

All titles also on Vanguard(F)VSD23013,(J)GP3011,GXC3170,K25P4005.

Larry Coryell,Steve Khan(g).   Prob. Live.Montreux Jazz Festival,Switzerland.July 1975
    Serabond(1)   EGG(G)900558

(g-solo).   NYC. 1975/78
    Acoustic Solo   EGG(G)900558
    Improvisation   -

Michael Brecker(ts),Larry Coryell,Arthur Rhames(g),Glen Moore(b),Tony Williams(dr).
                                       NYC. 1975/78
    Octaves   EGG(G)900558
    Piscean Moon   -
    Aquarian Mode   -

David Sanborn(as),Michael Brecker(ts),Don Grolnick(keyb),Larry Coryell,Steve Khan(g),Will
Lee(b),Steve Gadd(dr).   NYC. 1975/78
    Memphis Underground   EGG(G)900558

All titles on EGG900.558 also on EGG 66048,(J)GP3222.

LARRY CORYELL AND THE ELEVENTH HOUSE:
Randy Brecker(tp),Terumasa Hino(tp,flh),David Sanborn(as),Michael Brecker(ts),Mike Mandel
(keyb,synth),Larry Coryell,Steve Khan(g),Danny Toan(rhythm-g),John Lee(b),Gerry Brown(dr),
Mtume(perc).   NYC. 1976
    Kowloon Jag   Arista AL4077
    Titus   -
    Pyramids   -
    Rodrigo Reflections   -
    Yin-Yang   -
    Woman Of Truth And Future   -
    Ain't It Is   -
    Aspects   -

All titles also on Arista(E)ARTY133,(F)2C.066-97823,(J)IES80578.

Mike Mandel(p,synth),Larry Coryell(g),Joe Beck(el-b,synth,g).
                                       North Brookfield,Mass. 1976
    Larry's Boogie   Arista AL4108
    Stravinsky   -
    Toy Soldiers(1)   -
    Short Time Around   -
    Improvisation On Bach Lute Prelude   -
    Song For My Friend's Children   -
    Bicentennial Head Fest   -
    The Fifties   -
    Domesticity   -
    The Lion And The Ram(2)   -

-1.Add Danny Toan(g).
-2.Add Michael Urbaniak(vln).

All titles also on Arista(E)ARTY154,(J)IES80786,15RS14.

LARRY CORYELL - STEVE KHAN:
Larry Coryell,Steve Khan(g).   NYC. 1976/77
    Spain   Arista AL4156
    Bouquet   -
    Son Of Stiff Neck   -
    Juju   -
    St. Gallen   -
    Footprints   -
    General Mojo's Well-Laid Plan   -
(session cont. next page).

(session cont. from previous page):
All titles also on Arista(J)IES81067,15RS9,25RS109.

LARRY CORYELL - PHILIP CATHERINE:
Larry Coryell,Philip Catherine(g).   London. 1976
    Ms. Julie   Atlantic(G)ATL50342
    Home Comings   -
    Airpower   -
    Twin House   -
    Mortgage On Your Soul   -
    Gloryell   -
    Nuages   -
    Twice A Week   -

Note:All titles also on Elektra 6E123.

(g-solo).   LA or San Francisco.October 11,1976
    Spain   MCA MCA2-6002
    Autumn In New York   -
    Toronto And The
       Sign Of The Capricorn   -

All titles also on MCA(F)410.068/69.

LARRY CORYELL - ALPHONSE MOUZON:
Larry Coryell(g,vcl),Philip Catherine(g),John Lee(b,vcl),Alphonse Mouzon(dr,vcl).
                         NYC. 1977
33525 Back Togther Again(jl,am)   Atlantic SD18220
33526 Reconciliation(1)(cp,ta)   -
33527 Transvested Express   -
33528 Crystallization   -
33529 Rock 'N Roll Lovers   Atlantic 3430,-
33530 Get On Up (We Gonna Boogie)(am) -
33531 Beneath The Earth   -
33532 The Phonse(lc)   -
33533 Mr. C   -
33534 High Love   -
33535 Get Up We're Gonna Boogie   unissued
33536 John's Tune   -

-1.Add Cheryl P. Alexander,Tawatha Agee(background-vcl).

All titles on SD18220 also on Atlantic(E)K50382,(G)ATL50382,(J)P10408.

LARRY CORYELL - PHILIP CATHERINE:
Larry Coryell,Philip Catherine(g),rest unknown.
                 Live.Montreux Jazz Festival,Switzerland.July 1977
    One Plus Blues   Atlantic unissued
    Rene's Theme
    A Quiet Day In Spring
    Transvested Express
    Nuages
    Miss Julie

(g-solo).   Unknown location.c. 1977
    Moon   Guitar Player 3003
    Octave   -

Note:Guitar Player 3003 is an instruction record.

LARRY CORYELL - PHILIP CATHERINE:
Larry Coryell,Philip Catherine(g).   Hamburg,Germany.February 1978
     One Plus Two Blues   Elektra 6E153
     Snowshadows   -
     Transvested Express   -
     Deus Xango(1)   -
     My Serenade   -
     No More Booze   -
     Father Christmas   -
     A Quiet Day In Spring   -
     The Train And The River   -

-1.Add Joachim Kühn(p).

All titles also on Electra(Eu)ELK52086.

CORYELL - CATHERINE - KÜHN:
Joachim Kühn(p),Larry Coryell,Philip Catherine(g).
                   Live.Paris,Berlin,Brussels,Vienna,Montreux (Switzerland). 1978
     O.D.(p-solo)   Elektra ELK52232
     My Serenade(no p)   -
     Gemstone File(no p)   -
     That's Rock 'N Roll(no p)   -
     Santa Cruz   -
     Deus Xango   -
     The Acoustic Tour Blues   -

g-solo).   Stuttgart,Germany.March 8-11,1978
     Discotexas   Mood(G)22888
     Excerpt From "A Lark
       Descending" (Vaughan Williams)   -
     Ravel   -
     Wonderful Wolfgang   -
     Piano Improvisation(1)   -
     Sweet Shuffle   -
     Moon   -
     Park It Where You Want   -
     Spritual Dance(2)   -

1.Coryell plays (p).
2.Add L. Subramaniam(vln,tambura).

11 titles also on Arista Novus AN3024,(J)25RS112.

g-solo).   Live.Montreux Jazz Festival,Switzerland.July 23,1978
     Overture/Greensleeves   Arista Novus rejected
     April Seventh   -
     Toronto Under
       The Sign Of Capricorn   Arista Novus AN3005
     For Philip And Django   -
     Rodrigo Reflections   -

g-solo).   NYC.August 17,1978
     April Seventh   Arista/Novus AN3005,BMG Novus 83072(CD)
     Copenhagen Impressions   -   -
     Silver Medley: -   -
       Song For My Father
       Sister Sadie
     Variations On A Theme   -   -

1 titles on AN3005 also on Arista/Novus(J)25RJ5,Novus Blue(J)BVCJ5012 (CD).

LARRY CORYELL AND THE BRUBECK BROTHERS:
Darius Brubeck(keyb,clavinet),Larry Coryell(g),Chris Brubeck(b),Danny Brubeck(dr,perc).
                                    Nashville,Tenn.August 29-31,1978
            Fire Serpent   Direct Disc DD109
            In A Spanish Mode   -
            The Midnight Sailor   -
            Mirth   -
            The Secret Me   -
            Just Like Being Born   -

Add Ray Mantilla(perc).   NYC.June 4/6,1979
            Cisco At the Disco   Vanguard VSD79426
            Rue Gregoire Du Tour   -
            Three Mile Island   -
            Return   -
            Sweet Shuffle   -
            Mediterranean Sundance/   -
                Entre Dos Aguas   -

All titles also on Vanguard(J)GP3212,K20P6197.

Larry Coryell,Joe Beck,John Scofield(g).   NYC.August 17/23,September 17/19,1979
            The File   Arista/Novus AN3017
            Mother's Day(1)   -
            Little B's Poem(2)   -
            Zimbabwe   -
            Solo On Wednesday(1,2)   -
            Thurman Munson   -
            Equinox   -
            Alster Fields   -

-1.Omit Scofield.
-2.Omit Beck.

All titles also on BMG Novus NL83072,ND83072 (CD),Novus Blue(J)BVCJ5012 (CD).

BILL COSBY

BUNIONS BRADFORD'S FUNERAL PARLOR MARCHING BAND:
Rudy Johnson(ts),Donald Bailey(hca),Gildo Mahones,Walter Bishop(el-p),Stu Gardner(org),
Jeff Kaplan,Otis Keys,Fred Robinson(g),Ron Johnson,Monk Montgomery(el-b),Jimmie Smith,
Teddy Edwards,Robert De Simone(perc),Big Black(cg),Bill Cosby(cond).
                                    LA.c. 1970
            Martin's Funeral   Uni 73080
            Hybish,Shybish   -

Note:Additional recordings by this artist are not included.

GIANNI COSCIA (Italian)

See also FLAVIO CRIVELLI.

QUINTTTO DE GIANNI COSCIA.
Larry Nocella(ts),Gianni Coscia(el-acc),Mario Rusca(p),Tony Parisi(b),Giancarlo Pillot
(dr).   Live."Club Capolinea",Milan,Italy.December 21/22,19
            Capolinea   Jazz Capolinea(I)JII1/2

GIANNI COSCIA

Annibale Modini(vbs),Gianni Coscia(el-acc),Mario Rusca(p),Paolo Tomelleri(b),Giancarlo
Pillot(dr).   Live."Club Capolinea",Milan,Italy.September 1975
      Shine   Jazz Capolinea(I)JII3

QUARTETTO COSCIA - CRIVELLI:
Gianni Coscia(el-acc),Flavio Crivelli(p),Sergio Pavone(b),Matteo Ottonello(dr).
                    Live."Louisiana Jazz Club",Genova,Italy.February 16 or June 21/22,1980
      El L'uomo Vive   Louisiana Jazz Club(I)LJR80

MARITO COSENTINO (Argentinean)

MARITO COSENTINY Y SU ORQUESTA:
Marito Cosentino(cl),rest unknown.   Buenos Aires. 1975
771   Summer Set   Vik(Arg)1Z2009
772   A Summer Place   -

MARITO COSENTINY Y SUS JAZZ CATS:
Adolfo Rossini(tp),Miguel Piccolo(tb),Marito Cosentino(cl,as),Enrique Varela(ts),Jorge
Navarro(p),Enrique Costa(g,bj),Ricardo Salas(b),Osvaldo "Pichi" Mazzei(dr).
                                      Buenos Aires. 1977
      Limehouse Blues   Columbia(Arg)19638
      And The Angels Sing   -
      12th Street Rag   -
      Mack The Knife   -
      Diga Diga Doo   -
      Hello Dolly   -
      Indiana   -
      Makin' Whoopee   -
      Charleston   -
      St. Louis Blues
      Bugle Call Rag   -
      At Sundown   -

VLADIMIR COSMA

Acl. Al Newman,Alain Hato(as),Tony Coe,Jean-Louis Chautemps(ts),Pepper Adams(bars),Mau-
rice Vander(p),Sam Woodyard(dr),Vladimir Cosma(cond).
                                      Paris.c. 1977
      Les Saxs Brothers   Deesse(F)DDLX157
      Jalousie Blues   -
      Nous Irons Tous Au Paradis   -
      Parker Par Coeur   -

Note:The above are from the "Nous Irons Tous Au Paradis" film soundtrack.
    Additional recordings by this artist are not included.

COSMIC EYE (British)

y Swinfield,Dave Grossmith,Chris Taylor(fl),Alan Branscombe(ss,perc),John Mayer(vln),
ancio D'Silva(g),Viran Jasani(sitar),Tony Campo(el-b),D. Wright(dr),Keshav Sathe(tabla).
                                      London(?). 1972
      Dream Sequence,pt.1,2   Regal Zonophone(E)SLRZ1030

THE COSMOPOLITAN REEDS AND RHYTHM

Eddie Barefield(cl,as,arr),Pete Clark(as,bars,fl,arr),Russ Andrews(ts,fl),Arthur "Babe" Clarke(ts,bars),George Kelly(ts,arr),Sonny White(p),Eddie Durham,Lucius Fowler(g),Lawrenc Lucie(el-b),Slick Jones(dr),Edgar Battle(arr).

	NYC. 1964	
Deep South	Cosmopolitan SLP535/36	
Dillinger(1)		-
K.C. Rhythm		-
Jump And Swing		-
Artichoke		-
Jumpin' Jack		-
South Of South		-
Tropical Mood		-
Endless Blues		-

-1.Add Eddie Swanston(org).

Add Floyd "Horse Collar" Williams(ts,arr).   Same date

Mr. K's Tune	Cosmopolitan SLP535/36	
Horse Collar		-

Harold Ashby(ts) replaces Kelly.   Same date

Huckleberry Finn(take 1)	Cosmopolitan SLP535/36	
Huckleberry Finn(take 2)		-
Huckleberry Finn(take 3)		-

Note:Side 1 and side 2 of the above LP as SLP535 and SLP536 respectively.
     The label erroneusly lists "Artichoke" as the first track on side 2 - in fact it is
     the seventh track on side 1.

RENE COSPITO (Argentinean)

RENE COSPITO Y SU ORQUESTRA ARGENTINA DE JAZZ:
Francisco Mazzeo,Juan Salazar,Loiacono(tp),Weselvicz(tb),Duke Daveda(cl,as),Raul Bozzo,
Castro(ts),Néstor Cospito(p),Ahmed Ratip(g),Carlos di Tata(b),Gustavo Tola(dr).

	Buenos Aires. 1945	
Red Bank Boogie	RCA(Arg)60-0647	
Basie Boogie		-

SCOTT COSSU

Christopher Kern(vbs),Scott Cossu(p),Philip Boulding(harp),Paul Scott-Sevilla(cello),Ala
Swenson(tamboura),Steve Clover(dr,perc),Michael Spiro(cg,perc).

	Unknown location.c. 1980	
The Raven's Dance	Music Is Medicine MIM9025	
Indian Prayer		-
Ode To Shiva		-
Daybreak Angelina		-
Song For A Blind Man		-
Still Moments		-

THE COSTA DEL ORO JAZZ BAND
(section cont. next page).

section cont. from previous page):
ruce Dexter(tp),Bill Carter(cl,vcl),Bill Mitchell(p),Ed Durant(bj,vcl),Bill Hawley(bj),
alt Sereth(wbd).   Live."Aldo's",LA.July 30,1954
     Cakewalking Babies(bc)   Epitaph No.1

DDIE COSTA

ee also MIKE CUOZZO,THE FIRST MODERN PIANO QUARTET,JOHN MEHEGAN.

DDIE COSTA - VINNIE BURKE TRIO:
die Costa(p),Vinnie Burke(b),Nick Stabulas(dr).
                                            NYC.February 1956
     Fascinating Rhythm   Jubilee LP1025
     Unison Blues   -
     Sweet And Lovely(1)   -
     Let's Do It   -
     Yesterdays   -
     Pile Driver   -
     It Could Happen To You   -
     Get Happy   -
     Jeepers Creepers   -

.Costa plays (vbs).

1 titles also on Jubilee(J)UPS525,YW7567,Josie JJM3509,President(F)KVP1025,Fresh Sound
p)LP1025,FSR-CD76 (CD),Roulette(J)TOCJ5397 (CD).

DIE COSTA TRIO WITH ROLF KUHN AND DICK JOHNSON:
die Costa(p),Ernie Furtado(b),Al Beldini(dr).
                                   Live.Newport Jazz Festival,R.I.July 6,1957
     Taking A Chance On Love   Verve MGV8237
     There Will Never Be Another You(1)   -
     I'll Remember April(1)   -

.Add Rolf Kühn(cl),Dick Johnson(as).

1 titles also on Verve(J)MV2023,MV2539,Columbia(E)33CX10108.

DIE COSTA QUINTET:
t Farmer(tp),Phil Woods (as),Eddie Costa(p),Teddy Kotick(b),Paul Motian(dr).
                                   NYC.July 13,1957
     Get Out Of The Road   Mode MOD-LP118,Sonet(D)SXP2852
     In Your Own Sweet Way(1)   - ,Sonet(D)SXP2844
     Big Ben   -
     Nature Boy   - ,Sonet(D)SXP2844
     Blues Plus Eight   -
     I Didn't Know What Time It Was   - ,Sonet(D)SXP2852
     Stretch In F   - ,Sonet(D)SXP2844

.Woods plays (p),Costa plays (vbs).

. titles also on Interlude MO508,ST1008,(J)35220-28,85040-30 (CD),Premier PM/PS2002,
onet B2002,Top Rank(E)25/017,Overseas(J)ULS1862,V.S.O.P. 7,Jazz Anthology(F)JA5239.
e:Some issues as ART FARMER QUINTET.

IE COSTA QUARTET:
lie Costa(vbs),Bill Evans(p),Wendell Marshall(b),Paul Motian(dr).
                                   NYC.January 15,1958
069 Guys And Dolls   Coral CRL57230,(E)FEP2018
070 I'll Know   -   -

Same.	NYC.January 16,1958	
104085 I've Never Been In Love Before	Coral CRL57230,(E)FEP2019	
104086 Luck Be A Lady	-	-

Same.	NYC.January 17,1958	
104087 Adelaide	Coral CRL57230,(E)FEP2020	
104088 If I Were A Bell	-	- ,MCA MCA2-4063,Affinity
	(E)AFS1035	

All titles on CRL57230 also on MCA(J)MCA2038.

EDDIE COSTA TRIO:
Eddie Costa(p),Wendell Marshall(b),Paul Motian(dr).
                                    NYC.January 29/February 2,1959

The House Of Blue Lights	Dot DLP3206	
My Funny Valentine	-	
Diane	-	
Annabelle	- ,DLP25879	
When I Fall In Love	-	
What's To Ya	-	

All titles also on Dot DLP25206,(J)5055,SMJ6092,YW8551,MCA(J)VIM4657.
Note:See Coleman Hawkins and Clark Terry for titles rec. at an Eddie Costa memorial con-
     cert (1962).

JOHNNY COSTA

See also THE FIRST MODERN PIANO QUARTET.

Johnny Costa(p),Gene Ramey(b),Kenny Clarke(dr).
                                    NYC.February 26,1955

SJC4674 Tea For Two	Savoy MG15056,MG12052	
SJC4675 Begin The Beguine	-	
SJC4676 Caravan	Savoy MG15056,MG12052	
SJC4677 Flamingo	-	-

(p-solo).	Same date	
SJC4678 Dancing In The Dark	Savoy MG12052	
SJC4679 La Mer	-	
SJC4680 Stella By Starlight	-	
SJC4681 Manhattan	Savoy MG15056,MG12052	
SJC4682 Just One Of Those Things	-	
SJC4683 There's A Small Hotel	Savoy MG12052	
SJC4684 Honeysuckle Rose	-	

Johnny Costa(p),Sandy Block(b),Jimmy Crawford(dr).
                                    NYC.July 18,1955

88399 Hallelujah	Coral CRL57020
88400 Autumn In New York	-
88401 Lover	-
88402 Stella By Starlight	-
88403 A Foggy Day	-
88404 Misty	-
88405 After You've Gone	-
88406 Love For Sale	-
88407 Holiday In Strings	-
88408 Tenderly	-

All titles also on Vogue(E)LVA9027.
Note:Additional recordings by this artist are not included.

JACK COSTANZO

(bg-solo).   LA.December 17,1954
2142   Mambo Costanzo   Norgran 132,MGN32,MGN1067,Verve MGV8157
2143   Mister Bongo   -

Rolf Ericson(tp),Herbie Steward(as),Bill Holman(ts),Gerald Wiggins(p),Joe Comfort(b),
Lawrence Marable(dr),Jack Costanzo(bg,cg).   Same date
2144   Bottlabud   Norgran EPN99
2145   Satin Doll   Norgran EPN100

Both titles also on Norgran MGN32,MGN1067,Verve MGV8157,Columbia(E)SEB10103.

John Anderson(tp),Herbie Steward(as),Tom Brown(ts),Gerald Wiggins(p),Jack Coughlan(b),
Albert Bartee(dr),Jack Costanzo(bg,cg).   Prob. same date
146   Yukon Mambo   Norgran EPN100
2147   Maggie   -
148   G And J Blues(1)   Norgran EP99,Columbia(E)SEB10103

1.Jackie Mills(dr) replaces Bartee.

All titles also on Norgran MGN32,MGN1067,Verve MGV8157.

JACK COSTANZO AND HIS AFRO-CUBAN BAND:
John Anderson(tp),Eddie Cano(p),Erneste Montez(b),Jack Costanzo(cg,bg),William Gillardo
(timb),Ramon Rivera(cg),Eddie Gomez(claves),Kaskara,Marda Saxon(vcl).
                                       LA.Late 1950's
         Caravan   Gene Norman Presents GNP19
         Melado De Cana   -
         La La La   -
         El Rebaloso   -
         Coco May May   -
         Chopsticks Mambo   Gene Norman Presents 124X,GNP19
         Abaniquito   -
         Just One Of Those Things Gene Norman Presents 124X,   -
         Goza Negra   -
         Dongo Festeris   - ,GNP25

All titles aso on Vocalion(E)VA-N160150.

Jack Costanzo(cg,bg,vcl),Manny Meyer(cg,vcl),"Speedy" Odaye(cg).
                                       London.August 24/25,1961
         Semliki Torrent   Fontana(E)TFL5190
         Afro-Cuban Concord(bg-solo)   -
         Bongo Montuno(bg-solo)   -
         African Congo Y Boleo(mm)   -
         Tribal Subpoena(1)   -

1.Add Harold McNair(?)(fl).

Shake Keane -1(flh),Harold McNair -2(fl),Malcolm Cecil -3(cello),Jack Costanzo(bg),Mirza
. Shariff -4(perc),Keefe West(vcl).   Same date
         Lament For Cello(3,4) Fontana(E)TFL5190
         Marital Sacrifice(1,2)   -
         Baccanale(1,2,4)(kw)   -
         Adjaye Adjaye(2)   -
         Question And Answer(5)   -

5.Phil Seamen(dr-solo).

1 titles also on Fontana(E)STFL598,(Eu)680.981TL,886.150TY.
te:Additional recordings by this artist are not included.

SVEND COSTER (Danish)

COSTER-KVARTETTEN:
Alex Hartmann(cl,ts,bars,bassoon),Svend Coster(p,vbs,vcl),Kurt Jensen(g),Arly Jensen(b).
Copenhagen.October 19,1942
CC1190 P.O. 13   Columbia(D)DD484
CC1191 Impromptu Monderne(1)   -

-1.Omit Hartmann.

Same.   Copenhagen.May 3,1943
CC1213 Yupy Ya(sc,band-vcl)   Columbia(D)DD488
CC1214 The Country Jail(sc,band-vcl)   -
CC1215 Andy Kirk   Columbia(D)DD489
CC1216 Studio I   -

Same.   Copenhagen.August 24,1943
CC1227 A Minor Tune   Columbia(D)DD496
CC1228 Swinging At Elsinore   -
CC1229 Idaho(sc)   Columbia(D)DD497
CC1230 Soft Shoe Shuffle(sc)   -

Valdemar Nielsen(cl,ts),Svend Coster(p,vbs,vcl),Kurt Jensen(g),Edvin Christiansen(b).
Copenhagen.November 30,1943
CC1235 Tuesday Morning At Ten   Columbia(D)DD498
CC1236 Two Ideas   -
CC1237 Shoo Fly(sc)   Columbia(D)DD499
CC1238 Long About Midnight(sc,band-vcl) -

Alex Hartmann(cl,ts,bars,bassoon),Svend Coster(p,vbs,vcl),Kurt Jensen(g),Arly Jensen(b).
Same as session October 19,1942.   Copenhagen.December 12,1944
CC1243 Undecided   Columbia(D)DD503
CC1244 Rose Room   -
CC1245 Will A Bassoon Do   Columbia(D)DD504
CC1246 Simpleton   -

Note:DD503 and DD504 were not issued.

RENE COSTY (Belgian)

René Heylbroeck(cl),René Costy(vln),Charles Belvaux(p),Marcel Mortier(g),Mischa Schwartz
man(b).   Brussels. 1955
18726 Texas Mary Lou   Elspor(B)5003
18727 Salt Peanuts Boogie   -

THE COSY CORNER STREET PARADERS (Dutch)

Peter Huysman(tp),George Kaatee(tb),Gerard Wehrmeyer,Frits Kaatee(cl),Hans Heinhuis(p),
Rudi Smit(bj,g),Ido Roeleven(b),Jaap Verhagen(dr).
Hilversum,The Netherlands.October 20 or November 4,1
De Zak Van Sinterklaas   Polydor(Du)S1195
Sinterklaas Is Jarig   -

Omit Wehrmeyer,Heinhuis;Rob Hageman(b) replaces Roeleven.
The Hague,The Netherlands.Autumn 1966
(session cont. next page).

(session cont. from previous page):
    (When) The Saints
        Go Marchin' In(1)(wc)   I.C.I.B.(Du)110876F
    Go Tell It On
        The Mountains(1)(wc)   -

-1.Add De Watnouweer-Club (choir)(vcl).

Add Margie Ball(vcl).   Soest,The Netherlands.June 14,1967
    Sweet Georgia Brown   CNR(Du)SKLP4246,385252,Quintessence QS900.013-2
                                  (CD)
    Blue Is Turning Grey Over You   CNR(Du)SKLP4246
    Willie The Weeper   -
    Hiawatha Rag(1)   -
    Oh,Miss Hannah   -
    I'm Coming Virginia   -

-1.Frits Kaatee(cl) was dubbed in June 15,1967.

Same.   Soest,The Netherlands.June 15,1967
    Bourbon Street Parade   CNR(Du)SKLP4246
    Stormy Weather(mb)   -
    Baby Doll   -
    Ain't Misbehavin'(mb)   -
    Blueberry Hill(cl,g,b,dr only)   -
    Maryland,My Maryland   - ,385252

COTTON CITY JAZZ BAND (Belgian)

See also MEZZ MEZZROW.

Jacques Cruyt(tp),Romain Vandriessche(tb),Rudi Balliu(cl,vcl,ldr),Walter de Troch(bj),Paul
Gevaert(b),Jean-Pierre Roelant(dr).   Ghent,Belgium.June 27/July 2,1969
    Ole Miss   Alpha(B)AL7001
    Tin Roof Blues   -
    Gettysburg March   -
    See See Rider   -
    Mahogany Hall Stomp   -
    In The Upper Garden(no tp,tb)   -
    I Wonder What Became Of Sally   -
    Shake It Or Break It   -
    Somebody Else Has Taken My Place -
    Loveless Love   -
    Ciribiribin   -
    When I Come To The
        End Of My Journey(rb)   -
    Dippermouth Blues   -
    Till We Meet Again   -

Emanuel Sayles(bj,vcl) replaces de Troch.   Ghent,Belgium.October 11,1969
    Just A Closer Walk With Thee(es) Alpha(B)AL7002
    Over The Waves   -
    Sister Kate   -
    I Ain't Gonna' Give Nobody
       None Of My Jelly Roll(es)   -
    Lou-easy-an-i-ya   -
    Corrine,Corrina   -
    Who's Sorry Now   -
    Should I Reveal(no tp,tb,cl)   -
    Doctor Jazz(es)   -

Walter de Troch(bj) replaces Sayles;add Alton Purnell(p,vcl).
                              Ghent,Belgium.February 23,1970
    Four Or Five Times(ap)   Alpha(B)AL7004
    Just A Closer Walk With Thee   -
    You Only Hurt
      The One You Love(ap)   -
    Heebie Jeebies   -
    The Old Rugged Cross   -
    Canal Street Blues   -
    Dallas Blues   -
    Bye And Bye(ap)   -
    Ain't Misbehavin'   -
    Chinatown,My Chinatown   -

Percy Humphrey(tp,talking) replaces Cruyt;omit Purnell.
                              Ghent,Belgium.November 2,1970
    Milenberg Joys   Alpha(B)AL7005
    Careless Love Blues   -
    Funeral Sequence(ph):   -
      Just A Little
        While To Stay Here
      Just A Closer Walk With Thee
      Oh,Didn't He Ramble
    Over In Gloryland
    Bucket's Got A Hole In It   -
    Old Grey Bonnet   -
    What A Friend We Have In Jesus   -
    Deep In The Heart Of Texas   -
    Somebody's Taking My Place(ph)   -

Jacques Cruyt(tp),Romain Vandriessche(tb),Rudi Balliu(cl,ts,ldr),Don Ewell(p),Walter de
Troch(bj),Paul Gevaert(b),Jean-Pierre Roelant(dr).
                              Ghent,Belgium.February 22,1971
    Runnin' Wild   Alpha(B)AL7006
    Don't Go 'Way Nobody   -
    Lady Be Good   -
    Savoy Blues   -
    Clarinet Marmalade   -
    Albert's Blues(cl,p,b,dr only)   -
    Blues For Brussels(p-solo)   -
    A Porter's Love
      Song(cl,p,b,dr only)   -
    Love Is Just Around
      The Corner(p-solo)   -
    Buddy Bolden's
      Blues(cl,p,b,dr only)   -
    Squeeze Me(p-solo)   -

Jacques Cruyt(tp),Louis Nelson(tb),Rudi Balliu(cl,as,ldr),Loek (Luc) van Hoeteghem(bj),
Paul Gevaert(b),Trevor Richards(dr).   Ghent,Belgium.March 28,1972
    Move The Body Over   Alpha(B)AL7007
    Lonesome Road   -
    When My Dreamboat Comes Home   -
    Just A Closer Walk With
      Thee/The Old Rugged Cross   -
    Four Leaf Clover   -
    One Night Of Love   -
    Marie   -
    Make Me A Pallet On The Floor   -
    Over The Waves   -
    Careless Love/Corrine,Corrina   -
    Say Si Si   -

Kid Thomas Valentine(tp),Louis Nelson(tb),Rudi Balliu(cl,as,ldr),Jon Marks(p),Loek van
Hoeteghem(bj),Paul Gevaert(b),Jean-Pierre Roelant(dr).
Ghent,Belgium.January 8,1973

Panama	Alpha(B)LP7010
Is It True What They Say About Dixie	-
Release Me	-
Jambalaya	-
The Bells Of St. Mary	-
Linger Awhile	-
Big Milkcow Blues	-
Cielito Lindo	-
Washington And Lee Swing	-
In The Shade Of The Old Apple Tree	-

Jacques Cruyt(tp),Romain Vandriessche(tb) replace Valentine,Nelson;omit Marks.
Gorcum,The Netherlands.October 11,1975

I'm Putting All My Eggs In One Basket	Beerendonk(Du)99914
Rhum And Coca Cola	-

Same.
Ghent,Belgium,October 25,1975

Rainbow Boogie	Cotton City Band I.V.P.3000
Colorful World	-

Freddie Kohlman(dr,vcl) replaces Roelant.   Ghent,Belgium.June 5,1976

Love	Alpha(B)LP7011
Do You Know What It Means To Miss New Orleans	-
Exactly Like You	-
The Second Line	-
Big Butter And Egg Man	-
Blueberry Hill	-
June Night	-
Rhum And Coca Cola	-
Freddie Kohlman's Blues	-

Jacques Cruyt(tp),Romain Vandriessche(tb),Rudi Balliu(cl,ldr),Walter de Troch(p),Loek van
Hoeteghem(bj),Paul Gevaert(b),Jean-Pierre Roelant(dr).
Live.Ghent,Belgium.June 12,1977

Buddy Bolden's Blues (introd.)	Flamingo(B)2004
Margie,I'm Always Thinking Of You	-
Alabama Jubilee	-
Sugar Blues	-
Original Dixieland One Step	-
The Entertainer	-
Blues For De De Pierce	-
Martha	-
Yes,Sir,That's My Baby	-

Rudi Balliu(cl,tp,ldr),Jean-Pierre Henkart(tb),Guido De Groen (Bill Greenow)(cl),Simon
Renard (Richard Simmons)(p),Walter de Troch(bj),Paul Gevaert(b),Maurice Van Eyck(dr).
Live."Lazy River Club",unknown location.c. 1977

Sensation Rag	Rhythm(B)LP3
I'm Alone Because I Love You	-
Smile,Darn You,Smile	-
Boogie Woogie	-
Salutation March	-
Panama	-

(session cont. next page).

(session cont. from previous page):
```
        Old Time Religion            Rhythm(B)LP3
        Put On Your Old Grey Bonnet    -
        Walter's Laughing Blues        -
        Say Si Si                      -
```

COTTON TOWN JAZZ BAND (Dutch)

Herman Loman(tp),Jochem Falk(tb),Gerard Koopman(cl),Ben Volkers(p,arr),Leon Kamerbeek
(bj,g),Jaap Flentrie(b),Ton Lucassen(dr).   Enschede,The Netherlands.December 17,1978
```
        From Monday On               CTE(Du)SLP7905
        Big Butter And Egg Man         -
        Someday Sweetheart             -
        Once In a While                -
        Olga                           -
        Shake It And Break It          -
        Mama's Gone Goodbye            -
        Blue Turning Grey Over You     -
```

Henk Wittenberg(tu) replaces Flentrie;add Jan Goossen -1(tp),Ruud Schuller(as,bcl).
```
                                     Same date
        Zonky Blues                  CTE(Du)SLP7905
        Eccentric(1)                   -
        Clarinet Marmelade             -
        What'cha Call 'Em Blues        -
```

MIKE COTTON (British)

THE MIKE COTTON JAZZMEN:
Mike Cotton(tp,vcl),John Beecham(tb),Jerry Williams(cl),Stu Morrison(g,bj),Geoff King(b),
Jimmy Garforth(dr).   London.April 27,1961
```
        Out Of Gallion               Columbia(E)SEG8144,Philips(Eu)830.788-2(CD)
        Sensation Rag                  -
        Savoy Blues                    -
        Sittin' In The Sun(mc)         -
```

Same.   London.June 7,1961
```
        Senora(band-vcl)             Columbia(E)45DB4697(ed(?))
        Senora(band-vcl)(1)          Philips(Eu)830.788-2(CD)
        The Colonel's Tune           Columbia(E)45DB4697
```

-1.Either an alternate take or an unedited version.

Same.   London.December 23,1961
```
        Ain't Misbehavin'(mc)        Columbia(E)45DB4779
        Sidewalk Blues                 -
```

Derek Tearle(b) replaces King.   London.March 22,1962
```
        Cobbler's Song               Columbia(E)45DB4821
        African Twist                  -
```

Same.   London.April 18,1962
```
        Zulu Warrior                 Columbia(E)45DB4910,SEG8190
        The Tinker                     -                    -
        Theme For Harry              Columbia(E)SEG8190
        Theme For Josie                -
```

John Crocker(cl,as,ts) replaces Williams;add Dave Rowberry(p,org).
                                 London.March 15,1963
          Heartaches   Columbia(E)DB7029
          Swing That Hammer   - ,Aves(G)89.002-2
          Sweet Briar Walk   Aves(G)89.002-2

Same.   London.September 18,1963
          Midnigth Flyer   Columbia(E)DB7134
          One Mint Julep   -

Mike Cotton(tp,hca,vcl),John Beecham(tb),John Crocker(cl,as,ts,vcl),Dave Rowberry(p,org),
Tony Pitt(g),Stu Morrison(el-b,vcl),Jimmy Garforth(dr).
                                 London.February 18,1964
          This Little Pig   Columbia(E)DB7267,33SX1647
          I Don't Wanna Know(mc)   -   -

Same.   London.April/June 1964
          Watermelon Man   Columbia(E)33SX1647
          Chinese Checkers   -
          Love Potion No.9(mc,jc)   -
          So What   -
          How Long Can This Go On(mc)   -
          Moanin'   -
          Night Train   -
          Pills(mc,jc)   -
          Pretty Thing(mc)   -
          Walk On The Wild Side   -

Similar.   London.September 1964
          'Round And 'Round   Columbia(E)DB7382
          Beau Dudley   -

LOUIS COTTRELL

See also ONWARD BRASS BAND.

LOUIS COTTRELL TRIO:
Louis Cottrell(cl),Emanuel Sayles(bj,g),Alcide "Slow Dreag" Pavageau(b).
                                 New Orleans.January 26,1961
196   Running Wild   Riverside unissued
197   Sheik Of Araby   -
198   Perdido   -
199   Three Little Words   -
200   Drag's Turnaround Blues   Riverside RLP(S9)385
201   Blues For Dixie(1)   -
202   What A Friend We Have In Jesus(1)   -
203   Rose Room(1)   -

-1.McNeal Breaux(b) replaces Pavageau.

Louis Cottrell(cl),Emanuel Sayles(bj,g,vcl),McNeal Breaux(b).
                                 New Orleans.January 27,1961
229   Perdido   Riverside RLP(S9)385
230   Bourbon Street Parade   -
231   Three Little Words   -
232   Sayles' Broken String Blues   -
233   The Sheik Of Araby   -
234   Yellow Dog Blues   -
235   Runnin' Wild   -
(session cont. next page).

(session cont. from previous page):
```
236    Down By The Riverside          Riverside RLP(S9)356
237    Down By The Riverside(es)          rejected
238    You Don't Love Me              Riverside RLP(S9)357
```

All titles on RLP(S9)385 also on Riverside(J)VIJ6350.

LOUIS COTTRELL AND HIS NEW ORLEANS JAZZ BAND:
Kid Howard(tp,vcl),Waldron "Frog" Joseph(tb,vcl),Louis Cottrell(cl,vcl),Lester Santiago
(p),Placide Adams(b),Paul Barbarin(dr).   New Orleans.November 15,1964

```
        When The Saints Go Marching In    Nobility LP703
        You Don't Love Me(lc)                     -
        Let's Take A
          Ferryboat To New Orleans                -
        Just A Closer Walk With Thee(wfj)         -
        Who's Sorry Now(wfj)                      -
        Back Home Again In Indiana                -
        Down By The Riverside(kh)                 -
        Clarinet Marmalade                        -
        Bogalusa Strut                            -
```

LOUIS COTTRELL'S HERITAGE HALL JAZZ BAND:
Alvin Alcorn(tp,vcl),Waldron "Frog" Joseph(tb),Louis Cottrell(cl),Walter Lewis(p),Placide
Adams(b),Louis Barbarin(dr),Blanche Thomas(vcl).
                                           New Orleans.c. 1973
```
        Bourbon Street Parade           GNP Dixieland Jubilee DJS512
        Slide Frog,Slide                          -
        Bill Bailey(bt)                           -
        Second Line                               -
        Petite Fleur                              -
        Bogalusa Strut                            -
        Muskrat Ramble(aa)                        -
        Tin Roof Blues                            -
        Basin Street Blues(bt)                    -
        Fidgety Feet                              -
        Tiger Rag                                 -
```

Same.   Live.Carnegie Hall,NYC.February 12,1974
```
        Wolverine Blues                 Viko(?)20011
        Tin Roof Blues                            -
        Darktown Strutters' Ball(bt)              -
        I Ain't Gonna Give Nobody
          None Of My Jelly Roll(bt)               -
        Bill Bailey(bt)                           -
        There'll Be Some Changes Made(bt)         -
        Tiger Rag                                 -
```

LOUIS COTTRELL - BARNEY BIGARD:
Teddy Riley(tp),Waldron "Frog" Joseph(tb),Louis Cottrell,Barney Bigard -1(cl),Walter Lewis
(p),Placide Adams(b),Freddie Kohlman(dr),Blanche Thomas(vcl).
                                           Live.Europe. 1975
```
        Second Line                     Rarities(E)No.71
        Fidgety Feet(1)                           -
        Jazz Me Blues(1)                          -
        Just A Little
          While To Stay Here(1)                   -
        A Good Man Is Hard To Find(bt)            -
        Slide,Frog,Slide                          -
        Royal Garden Blues                        -
```

Note:Freddie Kohlman erroneously listed as Freddy Coleman on the LP.

LOUIS COTTRELL QUINTET:
Louis Cottrell(cl),Bob Barton(p),Les Muscutt(g),Placide Adams(b),Andrew Hall(dr).
New Orleans.November 11,1976

```
I Can't Believe That
    You're In Love With Me      G.H.B. GBH156
Solitude                              -
Girl Of My Dreams                     -
In The Sweet Bye And Bye             -
Cottrell's Boogie Woogie             -
```

FRANK COUGHLAN (Australian)

FRANK COUGHLAN'S BAND:
Frank Coughlan(tp,tb),Ivan Halsall,Eric Warburton(cl,ts),Don Thompson(ts),Nancy Warren(p),
Frank Walsh(b),Charlie Blott(dr).   Melbourne.c. 1942
```
    Muskrat Ramble              Private recording unissued
    Blue Prelude
    Darktown Strutters' Ball
    Sister,You Can Spare A Dime
```

Incl. Frank Coughlan(tp,tb,vcl),Benny Featherstone(cl),Bob Tough(ts).
Melbourne. 1942/43
```
    Jazz Me Blues               Private recording unissued
    Basin Street Blues(fc)
```

Frank Coughlan(tp,tb,vcl),rest unknown.   Sidney. 1947
```
    When The Saints
        Go Marching In(fc)      MBS Jazz 8
    9:20 Special                unissued
```

FRANK COUGHLAN AND HIS LUCKY SEVEN:
Frank Coughlan(tp,tb,vcl),Les Dixon(tb),Andy McIntosh(cl),Ron Murray(ts),Jim Riley(p),
Dennis King(g),Tommy Wallis(b),Bobby Bell(dr).
Sydney.March 8,1950
```
MX33163 That Da Da Strain       Wilco(Au)0-112
MX33164 Slippin' Around(fc)     Wilco(Au)0-109
MX33165 Randwick Saturday Blues(fc)     -
MX33166 Where Ya Gonna' Get
            Another Sweetheart(fc)  Wilco(Au)0-112
MX33167 Just Because(fc)        Wilco(Au)0-111
MX33168 Carry Me Back To Old Virginia   -
```

Alan Lynch(p) replaces Riley.   Sydney.August 30,1950
```
MX36184 Alexander's Ragtime Band    Wilco(Au)0-119
MX36185 When You're Smiling(fc)     Wilco(Au)0-120
MX36186 Yes,We have No Bananas(fc)  Wilco(Au)0-121
MX36187 Milenburg Joys              Wilco(Au)0-120
MX36188 I've Been Floating
            Down That Old Green River   Wilco(Au)0-119
MX36189 Whistling Rufus(fc)         Wilco(Au)0-121
```

FRANK COUGHLAN'S COTTON PICKERS:
Max Hardy(tp),Frank Coughlan(tb),Don Smith(cl),Ron Rosenberg(p),Billy May(g),Don McFarlane
(b),Keith Cerche(dr).   Melbourne.September 14,1953
```
    The Sheik Of Araby          Spotlight Varieties(Au)SV16
    Jealous                             -
    My Sweetie Went Away
    Chinatown My Chinatown              -
    The Original Blues                  - ,SV233
```
(session cont. next page).

(session cont. from previous page):
    'Deed I Do   Spotlight Varieties(Au)SV16
    Sweet Little You   -
    Sloss Street Shuffle   -

FRANK COUGHLAN'S FAMOUS DANCE BAND:
Prob. Frank Coughlan(tp,tb,vcl),Bruce Kerr(tp,vcl),Jack Crotty,"Woody" Herman(tp),Les
Dixon(tb),Frank Smith,Norm Lloyd,Ron Murray,Gordon Scott(reeds),Emile Kew(p),John Weine
(g),Bruce Higginbotham(tb),Bobby Bell(dr).   Melbourne.February 6,1956
MX80366 Brave Don Pedro(fc)   Prestophone(Au)A56-9/10
MX80367 How Deep Is The Ocean(bk)   -
MX80368 I Got Rhythm   Prestophone(Au)A56-7/8
MX80369 I Haven't Heard A Word   -

FRANK COUGHLAN AND HIS DIXIELANDERS:
Ken Brentnall(tp),Frank Coughlan(tb,euphonium),Jim Ryan(cl),Ron Murray(ts),Col Nolan(p),Ed
Gaston(b),Johnny Sangster(dr).   Sydney.March 9,1965
S3RS0261 I'm Gonna' Sit Right Down
         And Write Myself A Letter   Readers Digest/RCA(Au)SP(S)8
S3RS0262 Pennies From Heaven   -
S3RS0263 Jeepers Creepers   -

Same.   Sydney.March 11,1965
S3RS0264 When My Dreamboat Comes Home   Readers Digest/RCA(Au)SP(S)8
S3RS0265 Jersey Bounce   -
S3RS0266 You Are My Lucky Star   -

Tom Bone(dr) replaces Sangster.   Sydney.March 12,1965
S3RS0267 March Of The Bobcats   Readers Digest/RCA(Au)SP(S)8
S3RS0268 Top Hat,White Tie And Tails   -
S3RS0269 A-Tisket,A-Tasket   -
S3RS0270 When The Saints Go Marching In   -

CLIFFORD COULTER

John Turk(tp),Gino Landry(as),Cornelius Bumpus(ts),Clifford Coulter(p,el-p,org,g,vcl),Mel
Brown,Jerry Perez(g),Jimmy Calhoun(el-b),Joe Provost(dr).
                                        San Francisco.April 8,1970
91152 East Side San Jose   Impulse AS9197
91153 Sal Si Puedes
       (Get Out If You Can)(cc)   -
91154 Do It Again(cc)   -
91155 Alum Rock Park   -
91156 Swingtime Blues   unissued

Billy Ingram(dr) replaces Provost.   San Francisco.April 9,1970
91157 Prayer Garden(1)   Impulse AS9197
91158 Cliff's Place   -

-1.Acc. to the LP notes Joe Provost plays (dr) on this title.

Same.   San Francisco.April 30,1970
91179 Big Fat Funky Shirley   Impulse AS9197

Harry Edison(tp),John Turk(tp,el-tp),Jimmy Cleveland(tb),Willie Ruff(frh),Bill Perkins
(as),Marshall Royal,Plas Johnson(reeds),Clifford Coulter(keyb,g,melodica,vcl),Sonny Glaze
(g),Jimmy Calhoun(el-b),Ron Beck(dr).   LA.May 24,1971
91214 Before The
       Morning Comes(no el-b)   Impulse AS9216
91215 Do It Now,Worry ('Bout It) Later   -,IMP1972

Clifford Coulter(g,tamb,melodica,vcl),Mel Brown,Sonny Glaze(g),Jimmy Calhoun(el-b),Ron
Beck(dr).   LA.May 25,1971
91250 Yodelin' In The Whatchamaname(1) Impulse AS9216
91251 Mr. Peabody   -

-1.Coulter(org,melodica,vcl),Ray Carthy(g),Beck(dr,cg).

Add John Turk(tp,el-tp,perc),chorus(vcl).   Same date
91252 Ridin' On Empty(1)   Impulse AS9216
91253 VJC(no el-b)   -

-1.Omit Glaze.

CURTIS COUNCE

CURTIS COUNCE GROUP:
Jack Sheldon(tp),Harold Land(ts),Carl Perkins(p),Curtis Counce(b),Frank Butler(dr).
                                      LA.October 8,1956
       Landslide   Contemporary C3526
       Landslide(alt.take)   Contemporary S7655,CCD7655-2(CD)
       Time After Time   Contemporary C3526,Vogue(E)EPC1242
       Time After Time(alt.take)   unissued
       Mia   -
       Sarah   -
       A Fifth For Frank   -
       Big Foot   Contemporary C3539

ame.   LA.October 15,1956
       Sonar   Contemporary C3526,Vogue(E)EPC1242
       Sonar(alt.take)   Contemporary S7655,CCD7655-2(CD)
       Stranger In Paradise   Contemporary C3539
       Woody'n You   Contemporary S7655
       Woody'n You(alt.take)   Contemporary CCD7655-2(CD)

ll titles on C3526 also on Contemporary S7526,(J)LAX3009,GXC3184,Vogue(E)LAC12073,Swing
(F)LDM30097,Original Jazz Classics OJCCD606-2 (CD).
Note:It is not known which take of "Woody'n You" was used for the issue on Original Jazz
     Classics OJCCD159-2 (CD).

ame.   LA.April 22,1957
       Pink Lady   Contemporary M3574
       Love Walked In   -
       Counceltation   Contemporary C3539
       Too Close For Comfort   -
       A Drum Conversation(dr-solo)   Contemporary CCD7655-2(CD)

ame.   LA.May 13,1957
       How Deep Is The Ocean   Contemporary C3539
       Complete   -

ame.   LA.August 29,1957
       Nica's Dream   Contemporary M3574
       How Long Has This Been Going On Contemporary S7655,CCD7655-2(CD)

ll titles on M3574 also on Contemporary S7574,(E)COP040,Vogue(E)LAC12263,Original Jazz
Classics OJC423,OJCCD423-2 (CD).

Same.   LA.September 3,1957
         Mean To Me   Contemporary C3539

All titles on C3539 also on Contemporary S7539,Vogue(E)LAG12263,Original Jazz Classics
OJC159,OJCCD159-2 (CD).

Jack Sheldon(tp),Harold Land(ts),Carl Perkins(p),Curtis Counce(b),Frank Butler(dr).
                                          La.January 6,1958
         I Can't Get Started   Contemporary M3574
         The Butler Did It(dr-solo)   -

Gerald Wilson(tp) replaces Sheldon.   Same date
         Larue   Contemporary M3574
         Carl's Blues   -
         A Night In Tunisia   Contemporary C7655,CCD7655-2(CD)

All titles on M3574 also on Contemporary S7574,(E)COP040,Vogue(E)LAC12263,Original Jazz
Classics OJC423,OJCCD423-2 (CD).

Elmo Hope(p) replaces Perkins.   Same date
         So Nice   Contemporary C7655,CCD7655-2(CD)
         Origin   -   -
         Bella Rosa   Contemporary CCD7655-2(CD)

CURTIS COUNCE QUINTET:
Rolf Ericson(tp),Harold Land(ts),Elmo Hope(p),Curtis Counce(b),Frank Butler(dr).
                                          LA.c. April 1958
         So Nice   Dooto DTL247
         Angel Eyes   -
         Into The Orbit   -
         Move   -
         Move(alt.take)   Belcanto LP26,SR1004
         Race For Space   Dooto DTL247
         Someone To Watch Over Me   -
         Exploring The Future   -
         The Countdown   -
         Chasin' The Bird   Belcanto LP26,SR1004,SR2000
         Head Gear   -   -

All titles on DTL247 also on Dooto(J)J33J20141 (CD),Boplicity BOP7.

COUNTRYSIDE JAZZ BAND (Dutch)

Henk Leeftink(tp,cnt,as,vcl),Robert Fisscher(tb),Job Zomer(cl,ss,as),Jan Kies(bj),Joop t
Hoedt(g),Hans Rombouts(b),Peter Verschoor(dr),Irene Allard(vcl).
                                          Heelsum,The Netherlands.June 2,1979
         Baby Won't You
            Please Come Home(ia)   Munich(Du)BM150229
         Ain't Misbehavin'(ia)   -
         Nobody Knows You When
            You're Down And Out(ia)   -
         Blues My Naughty
            Sweetie Gives To Me(ia)   -

Omit Allard.   Heelsum,The Netherlands.June 23,1979
         Gettysburgh March   Munich(Du)BM150229
         I'm Crazy 'Bout My Baby   -
         Gully Low Blues   -
(session cont. next page).

COUNTRYSIDE JAZZ BAND

session cont. from previous page):
```
      Alcoholic Blues                   Munich(Du)BM150229
      Lou-easy-i-an-i-a                        -
      When You And I Were Young Maggie         -
      Basin Street Blues                       -
```

same.   Heelsum,The Netherlands.June 28,1979
```
      Jackass Blues                    Munich(Du)BM150229
```


THE COUNT'S MEN

see EARL WARREN.

PIERRE COURBOIS (Dutch)

see also ASSOCIATION PC,EUROPEAN JAZZ QUINTET.

FREE MUSIC QUARTET:
Roy Raaymakers(tp,flh),Peter van de Locht(as,ss,picc,oboe),Erwin Somer(vbs,mar,vln),Ferdi
Rikkers(b),Pierre Courbois(dr).   Welsum,The Netherlands.June 24/25,1968
```
      Free Music I,II                  ESP 1083
```

Roy Raaymakers(tp,flh),Peter van de Locht(as,ss,fl),Erwin Somer(vbs),Oscar Gottlieb Blarr
(org),Ferdi Rikkers(b),Pierre Courbois(dr,bells),Egar M. Böhlke(speaker).
                         Arnhem,The Netherlands/Düsseldorf,Germany.October 13/14,1968
```
      Psalmus                          Schwann Verlag AMS Studio 505
      Kyrie                                    -
      Gloria For Percussions                   -
      Da Pacem                                 -
      Benedicamus Domino I,II                  -
```

Roy Raaymakers(tp,flh),Peter van de Locht(as,ss,hca),Henk Haverhoek(b),Pierre Courbois
(dr,vbs).   Arnhem(?),The Netherlands.April 21,1969
```
      Zand I,II                        Ketchup EP 3
```

Pierre Courbois(dr,gongs,synth,etc.).   Arnhem,The Netherlands.February 3/4/5,1975
```
      Beat And Bow                     Universe(Du)Hot109
      Myria' Poda                              -
      Mr. P. Aista And Mr. I. Banez            -
      Handycraft Center                        -
      Silence                                  -
      Crying With The
          Wolves In The Wood                   -
      Naar En Dorp                             -
      There Is A Hole In The Bassdrum          -
      Straight Shooter                         -
      Rock Will Never Die                      -
      Drums In The Lobau                       -
      Cymbal Symon                             -
```

Pierre Courbois(dr,cymbals,gongs,etc.).   Arnhem.December 15,1977
```
      Er Zijn Nog Acht
          Wachtenden Voor U            Varajazz 201
```

note:Additional titles on this LP are by Jasper van 't Hof (recorded April 6,1981).

JACQUES COURSIL (French)

Jacques Coursil(tp),Marion Brown(as),Scotty Holt(b),Eddie Marshall(dr).
                                    NYC.May 1967
        Unknown titles   ESP (S)1062

Note:ESP (S)1062 was never issued.

Jacques Coursil(tp),Arthur Jones(as),Anthony Braxton(contrabass-cl,ss),Burton Greene(p),
Beb Guérin(b),Claude Delcloo(dr).   Paris. 1969
        Black Suite,pt.1,2   America(F)AM6111,Byg(F)529.349

Note:Byg(F)529.349 lists rec.date as June 10,1969 - the actual date is prob. July 10,1969

Jacques Coursil(tp),Arthur Jones(as),Beb Guérin(b),Claude Delcloo(dr).
                                    Paris.July 7/8,1969
        Duke   Byg 529.319
        Fidel   -
        Paper   -

BERT COURTLEY (British)

See also THE JAZZ COMMITTEE.

COURTLEY - SEYMOUR ORCHESTRA:
Bert Courtley,George Boocock,Al Spoone,Doug Taylor(tp),Tony Russell,Eddie Harvey(tb),Jim
Walker(as),Norman Hunt,Jack Massey(ts),Gerry Gerke(bars),Don Innes(p),Jack Seymour(b),
Dougie Cooper(dr).   Live.Royal Festival Hall,London.November 10,19
DR22793 Struttin' With Some Barbecue   Decca(E)LK4180,London(Am)LL1639
DR22799 Stompin' At The Savoy   Decca(E)DFE6380

BERT COURTLEY JAZZ QUARTET:
Bert Courtley(tp),Eddie Harvey(p),Pete Blannin(b),Eddie Taylor(dr).
                                    London.August 21,1958
DR25022 Bertrand's Bugle   Decca(E)DFE6602
DR25023 New Blues For Old   Decca(E)DFE6537
DR25024 Sweet And Lovely   -
DR25025 Chocolate Shake   -

Bert Courtley(tp),Don Rendell(ts),Eddie Harvey(p),Pete Blannin(b),Jack Dougan(dr).
                                    London.March 24,1959
DR25727 Jones   Decca(E)DFE6602
DR25728 Tenderly   -

COUSIN JOE

See EARL BOSTIC,PETE BROWN,AL CASEY,LEONARD FEATHER,SAMMY PRICE,DICKY WELLS.

FRANCOIS COUTURIER (French)

Jean-Jacques Ruhlmann(ss,bcl,fl),Roland Merle(ts,cl),Francois Couturier(p,el-p,clavinet)
Christian Gentet(b),Bertrand Maillot(perc). Tours,France.October 27/28/29,1978
        Manèges   J.A.M.(F)CG1278
        Si Le Coeur Éclate   -
        Béla   -
(session cont. next page).

FRANCOIS COUTURIER

session cont. from previous page):
```
    Mont Dore(?)              J.A.M.(F)CG1278
    Musique Agacante                   -
    Le Vice Et La Paresse             -
```

COUTURIER - CELEA:
Francois Couturier(p,el-p),Jean-Paul Celea(b).
```
                             Paris.March  1980
    Pipo                     JMS(F)010
    Moderato Cantabile             -
    Mont D'Or                      -
    Ad Pandémonium                 -
    Sing Me Softly Of The Blues    -
    Jungle De Pierre               -
    Le Clé Des Chants              -
    Souffrir A Tout Prix           -
    Tempo Di Cane                  -
```

F COWARD (Canadian)

f Coward(p),Don Thompson(b),Terry Clarke(dr).
```
                             Toronto.September  1971
    Shem's Lullabye          Canadian Broadcasting Corp.(CA)LM137
    Just Found Out                 -
    Softly                         -
    Baby It's All Right            -
```

ANLEY COWELL

e also DAVE BURRELL,THE PIANO CHOIR.

anley Cowell(p,hsc,org),Reggie Johnson(b),Joe Chambers(dr).
```
                             London.January  1969
    Dave's Chant             Byg(F)unissued
    Ruth-Less
    Ungano
    The Killers
```

anley Cowell(p,el-p),Steve Novosel(b),Jimmy Hopps(dr).
```
                             London.June 2,1969
    Departure                Polydor(E)583.740
    Photon In A Paper World        -
```

te:See CHARLES TOLLIVER for additional titles from this session.

ne.
```
                             London.June 5,1969
    Sweet Song               Polydor(E)583.740
    The Shuffle                    -
    You Took Advantage Of Me(p-solo)  -
    Blues For Viet Cong            -
    Wedding March                  -
    Travellin' Man                 -
```

titles on Polydor(E)583.740 also on Arista/Freedom AL1032,Freedom(E)FLP41032,(J)
7093,32JDF174 (CD).

Woody Shaw(tp,maracas),Tyrone Washington(ts,fl,cl,tamb,maracas),Bobby Hutcherson(vbs),
Stanley Cowell(p),Reggie Workman(b,el-b),Joe Chambers(dr).
NYC.September 25,1969

Brilliant Circles	Polydor(Eu)2383.092
Earthly Heavens	-
Boo Ann's Grand	-
Bobby's Tune	-

All titles also on Arista/Freedom AL1009,Freedom(E)FLP40104,(G)28425,(J)PA7031.

Stanley Cowell(p,el-p,African thumb-p),Stanley Clarke(b,el-b),Jimmy Hopps(dr).
NYC.November 29,1972

Maimoun	ECM(G)1026
Ibn Mukhtarr Mustapha	-
Cal Massey	-
Miss Viki	-
Emil Danenberg	-
Astral Spiritual	-

All titles also on ECM(J)PA7082,ECM4005.
Note:The above titles are from "The Illusion Suite".

Stanley Cowell(p,el-p,African thumb-p.   NYC.October/December 10/11,1973

Abscretions	Strata-East SES1974/3
Equipoise	-
Prtayer For Peace	-
Emil Danenberg (from	
"The Illusion Suite")	-
Maimoun (from	
"The Illusion Suite")	-
Travellin' Man	-
Departure No.1	-
Departure No.2	-

All titles also on Strata-East(J)JC7501,Black&Blue(F)33.784.

Marion Brown -1(wooden-fl),Stanley Cowell -2(p,synth),Jerry Venable -2(g),Billy Higgins,
Blackwell,Aleke Kanonu(dr,African-perc),Glenda Barnes,Charles Fowlkes,Jr.(vcl).
White Plains,N.Y.April 27,1975

Trying To Find A Way(2)(gb,cf)	Strata-East SES1976/5
Shimmy Shewobble(1)	-

Marion Brown -1(wooden-fife,wooden-fl),Jimmy Heath -2(fl),Stanley Cowell(thumb-p,kora),
Bill Lee(b,el-b),Billy Higgins(African-perc),Nadi Quamar(African-perc,Madagascan-harp),
Charles Fowlkes,Jr.,Kareema(vcl).   Same date

The Gembhre	Strata-East SES1976/5
Travellin' Man(1,2)(cf,k)	-
Lullabye(2)(cf,k)	-

Psyche Wanzandae(fl),Jimmy Heath(ss),John Stubblefield(zuna),Stanley Cowell(kora),Bill
(b),Charles Fowlkes,Jr.(el-b),Billy Higgins,Ed Blackwell(perc),Aleke Kanonu,Kareema(vcl
Same date

Parlour Blues(1)	Strata-East SES1976/5
Thank You,My People	-

-1.Wanzandae(hca),Cowell(p) only.

All titles on SES1976/5 also on Strata-East(J)JC7515.

```
tanley Cowell(p,el-p,synth,clavinet,African thumb-p).
                                  Berkeley,Calif.July 6/7/8,1977
        Ragtime                   Galaxy GXY5104
        Boogie Woogie                    -
        Parisian Thoroughfare            -
        'Round Midnight                  -
        Spanish Dancers                  -
        Sienna:Welcome,My Darling        -
        Sienna: Waiting For The Moment   -
        Coup De Grass                    -
        Today,What A Beautiful Day       -
```

11 titles also on Galaxy(J)SMJ6216.

```
ddie Henderson(tp),Julian Priester(tb),Stanley Cowell(p,el-p,synth,thumb-p),Clifford
oulter(g),Keith Hatchel(el-b),Albert Heath(dr),Kenneth Nash(perc),Loretta Devine,Charles
owlkes,Jr.(vcl).                  Berkeley,Calif. 1977/78
        The Stoker                Galaxy GXY5111
        I Am Waiting                     -
        If You Let Me                    -
        What Do I Do                     -
        The Stoker(lc,cf)                -
        Talkin' 'Bout Love               -
        (Let Me Love You) Let Me Be Me   -
        Here I Am                        -
```

11 titles also on Galaxy(J)SMJ6258.

```
tanley Cowell(p),Cecil McBee(b),Roy Haynes(dr).
                                  Berkeley,Calif.November 28/29/30,1978
        Equipoise                 Galaxy GXY5125
        Lady Blue                        -
        Musa And Maimoun                 -
        Dr. Jackle(!)                    -
        November Mood                    -
        Dave's Chant                     -
```

11 titles also on Galaxy(J)VIJ6325.

```
ddie Henderson(tp,el-tp,flh),Julian Priester(tb,btb),Pat Patrick(picc,fl,cl,ts),Stanley
owell(p,el-p,prepared-p,thumb-p,org,chimes,vcl),Clifford Coulter(g),Nathan Rubin(vln),
erry Adams(cello),Cecil McBee(b),Roy Haynes(dr),Kenneth Nash(perc),Robert Mandolph,Linda
ndolph,Judy Lacey(vcl).      .    Berkeley,Calif.November  1978
        Come Sunday(1)            Galaxy GXY5131
        Ask Him(1)                       -
        Island Of Haitoo                 -
        I'm Trying To Find A Way(1)      -
        El Space-O                       -
        Sienna: Welcome
           To This World(p-solo)        -
```

.Vocal - by one of the above-mentioned vocalists.

A COX

```
cl) acc. by Roy Eldridge(tp),Coleman Hawkins(ts),Sammy Price(p),Milt Hinton(b),Jo Jones
r).                               NYC.April 11,1961
ession cont. next page).
```

(session cont. from previous page):
```
260    Hard Time Blues               Riverside RLP(S9)374
261    Wild Women Don't Have The Blues        -
262    Death Letter Blues                     -
263    Blues For Rampart Street               -
264    Cherry Pickin' Blues                   -
```

```
Same.                             NYC.April 12,1961
265    Fogyism                      Riverside RLP(S9)374
266    Mama Goes Where Papa Goes              -
267    Lawdy,Lawdy Blues                      -
268    St. Louis Blues                        -
269    Hard,Oh Lord                           -
```

All titles on RLP(S9)374 also on Rosetta RR1304,Original Jazz Classics OJC1758,OJCCD1758-(CD).
Note:Rec.dates are incorrectly given as April 12/13 on RLP(S9)374 (and at least some of the reissues).

JOHN COX (British)

FAT JOHN'S JAZZ BAND:
John Pritchard(tp),John Mumford(tb),Dave Castle(cl,as,ts),Ronnie Duff(p),Vernon Brown(b)
John Cox(dr).   London.July 2,1962
DR29559 Ghana   Decca(E)SKL4512
DR29560 Chicken 'N' Dumplings   -
DR29561 Theme   -

KENNY COX

KENNY COX AND THE CONTEMPORARY JAZZ QUINTET:
Charles Moore(tp),Leon Henderson(ts),Kenny Cox(p),Ron Brooks(b),Danny Spencer(dr).
                                  Detroit.December 9,1968
```
3050   Eclipse                      Blue Note BST84302
3048   Diahnn                                -
3047   Trance Dance                          -   ,(Du)1A.158-83401/4 (BOX5)
3049   Number Four                           -
3046   Mystique                              -
3051   You                                   -
```

Note:The above titles are listed in the order of recording; masternumbers were added lat
    by Blue Note.

```
Same.                             Detroit.November 26,1969
5587-4 Gravity Point               Blue Note BST84339
5588-3 What Other One                      -
5589-1 Smick In                            -
5590-2 Sojourn                             -
5591-1 Spellbound                          -
5592-1 Multidirection                      -
```

THE CONTEMPORARY JAZZ QUINTET:
Charles Moore(tp,flh,perc),Leon Henderson(ss,ts),Kenny Cox(p,el-p),Ron Brooks(el-b,b),
Danny Spencer(dr,perc).   Detroit.June 7,1970
       Noh Word   Strata SRI-1001-73

```
Same.                             NYC.August 23,1971
       Nguzo Saba (Struggle)       Strata SRI-1001-73
```

Charles Moore(tp,flh,perc),Leon Henderson(ss,ts),Kenny Cox(p,el-p),Charles Eubanks(el-p),
Ron Brooks(el-b,b),Bud Spangler.   NYC.March 17,1972
    Bang   Strata SRI-1001-73

Charles Moore(tp,flh,perc),Kenny Cox(p,el-p),Ron English(g),Ron Brooks(el-b,b),Bud Spangler,Danny Spencer(dr,perc).   NYC.August 26,1972
    Tao   Strata SRI-1001-73

Add Phil Mendelson(synth).   NYC.November 5,1972
    Inner Beckonning   Strata SRI-1001-73

Charles Moore(tp),Kenny Cox(p),Ron English(g),Ron Brooks(b),Bud Spangler,Danny Spencer
(dr).   Live.Ann Arbor Blues Festival,Michigan.September 8,1972
    Form Kinetic   Atlantic SD2-502

SONNY COX

THE THREE SOULS:
Sonny Cox(as),Ken Price(org),Gerald Sims -1(g),Louis Satterfield -1(el-b),Robert Shy(dr).
                                      Chicago.February 12,1965
13744 I Don't Want To Hear Any More(1) Cadet LP4044
13745 Walk On By(1)   -
13746 A House Is Not A Home(1)   -
13747 You're No Good(1)   Cadet 5514,LP4044
13748 Stack Mile   -
13749 Dear Old Stockholm   -
13750 Chitlins Con Carne   Cadet 5514, -
13751 Armageddon   -
13752 The Astronaut   -
13753 Big Jim   -

John Howell,Arthur Hoyle,Paul Serrano(tp),John Avant(tb),Sonny Cox(as),Rubin Cooper Jr./
Leonard Druss(bars),Ken Price(org),Bobby Robinson/Roland Faulkner(g),Cleveland Easton(b),
Maurice White(dr).   Chicago.December 10,1965
14393 Soulero   Cadet LP(S)765
14394 The Wailer   Cadet 5536, -
14395 The Retreat Song   -
14396 Come Rain Or Come Shine   -

Same.   Chicago.January 7,1966
14456 I'm Just A Lucky So And So   Cadet LP(S)765
14457 Berimbau   -
14458 For Sentimental Reasons   -
14459 Hoggin'   Cadet 5536, -

LOL COXHILL (British)

See also ANDREA CENTAZZO.

(ss-solo).   Charing Cross Railway Bridge,London.July 17,1970
    Hungerford   Dandelion(E)DSD8008

(ss-solo).   Live.Piccadilly,London.July 17,1970
    Open Piccadilly   Dandelion(E)DSD8008
    Piccadilly With Boots   -
    Mango Walk   -
    The Rhythmic Hooter   -
    Zoological Fun   -

Lol Coxhill(ss),David Bedford(org),Mike Oldfield,Kirwin Dear(g,perc).
                              London.July 17/18,1970
        A Collective Improvisation   Dandelion(E)DSD8008

Lol Coxhill(ss,ring modulator,fl).   Live.Hyde Park,London.July 18,1970
        Deviation Dance   Dandelion(E)DSD8008

Lol Coxhill(ss,ring modulator,fl).   Prob. Rotterdam,The Netherlands. 1970
        Feedback   Dandelion(E)DSD8008

Lol Coxhill(ss),David Bedford(org),Mike Oldfield,Dave Dufort,Kirwin Dear(g,perc).
                              Prob. Rotterdam,The Netherlands.July 1970
        Vorblifa Exit   Dandelion(E)DSD8008

Lol Coxhill(ss),David Bedford -1(p),Ted Speight -2(g).
                              Wimbledon (studio),London.January 1971
        Two Little Pigeons(1)   Dandelion(E)DSD8008
        Don Alfonso(1)   -
        Dat's Why Darkies Were Born(1)   -
        Insensatez(2)   -

Lol Coxhill(ts,mellotron).   Same date
        Lover Man   Dandelion(E)DSD8008
        Little Triple One Shot   -
        A Series Of Superbly
          Played Mellotron Codas   -
        I Am A Walrus(1)   -

-1.Coxhill(maracas,fl),children's chorus(vcl).

Lol Coxhill(ss,ring modulator,lotus-fl,vcl),Burton Greene,Jasper van 't Hof(keyb),Pierre
Courbois(dr,perc).   Live."Rasa",Utrecht,The Netherlands.January 13,1971
        Rasa Moods   Dandelion(E)DSD8008

All titles on DSD8008 also on Ampex C10132.

Lol Coxhill(ss),Jasper van 't Hof(p,el.p),Pierre Courbois(dr).
                              Live."De Toverbal",Maassluis,The Netherlands.May 4,1971
        Five To Four   Mushroom(E)150MR23
        Clompen Stomp   -
        Spirit Of Maasluis(!)   -
        Association   -
        Or Alternatively Nine   -
        One To Three   -
        P.C. One   -
        Toverbal   -
        Toverbal Sweet   -
        Jasper And Out   -
        The Un-Tempered
          Klavier And Heavy Friends   -

No details.   Live.Rotterdam,The Netherlands. 1973
        Gumbley's Creole Trombone   Caroline(E)C1514
        Blossom Time   -
        Expedition To The Lair Of The
          Terrifying Spider Boy ... Who
          Fortunately Was Not At Home   -
        An Awfully Romantic Duet For
          Possibly Blackbird And
          Definitely Saxophone   -

No details.   Live."Shaffy Theatre",Amsterdam. 1973
    Arena   Caroline(E)C1514

COXHILL - MILLER/MILLER - COXHILL:
Lol Coxhill(ss,as,org),Steve Miller(p,el-p,perc),Phil Miller(g),Richard Sinclair(b),Pip
Pyle(dr,perc),Archie Leggat(bg),Laurie Allen(perc).
                                     London. 1973
    Chocolate Field   Caroline(E)C1503
    One For You   -
    Portland Bill   -
    Will My Thirst Play Me Tricks/
        The Ant About To Be Crushed
        Ponders Not The Wherewithall
        Of Bootleather   -
    Maggots   -
    Bath '72   -
    Wimbledon Baths   -
    Gog Ma Gog   -

LOL COXHILL - STEVE MILLER:
Lol Coxhill(ss,org),Steve Miller(p,el-p),Kevin Ayers(g),Archie Leggat(el-b),Laurie Allen
(perc,dr),Robert Wyatt(perc,vcl).   Unknown location(s). 1973/74
    G Song   Caroline(E)C1507
    F Bit   -
    Songs Of March   -
    More G Songs   -
    Does This   -
    Or This   -
    Greatest Off-Shore
        Race In The World   -
    Reprise For Those
        Who Prefer It Slower   -
    Tubercular Bells   -
    Soprano Derivativo/Apicot Jam   -
    Oh Do I Like To Be
        Beside The Seaside   -
    In Memoriam - Meister Eckehart   -
    Fabulous Comedian   -

Phil Minton(tp,vcl),Lou Glandfield,Steve Gumbley(tb,perc),Liz Lockhart(fl,org),Cathy Kidd-
le(cl,org),Lol Coxhill(ss,ts,org,perc),Jane Durrant(ss,org),John Fox(as),Diana Davies(org,
perc),Penny Glandfield(perc),Boris Howarth(perc,org,vln,g,concertina),Peter Kiddle,John
Chapman(whistling),Sue Fox,Warner Var Wely(vcl)(see note).
                      Live.Welwyn Garden City,England.May 1975
    Mole Song   Caroline(E)C1514
    Little German Band   -
    Brig Out Your Skeletons   -
    Lady Howard Calypso   -
    Parade   -
    Tribal Drumming From
        The Nim Ram River Region   -
    Big German Band   -

Note:The personnel listed is prob. a collective one - for the above and the next session.

Similar.   Sheffield,England.August 1975
    The First Bit   Caroline(E)C1514
    Egal O.K.   -
    Le Tombeau De Ravel   -
    Rag   -
    Ghosts   -

```
No details.                              Unknown location(s)/date(s)
        Tuba Gallicalis              Caroline(E)C1514
        Egg Dance
        Mad Tom
        Luke Jamboree
        Skipton March
        Children Of The Evening
        Anne Marie
        W,S. Samba
        Yet Another Egal O.K.


Lol Coxhill(ss,as,synth,vcl),C.F. Fitzgerald -1(g),Ken Ellis(vcl).
                                 Newcastle,England/London.  1975
        Duet For Soprano And Guitar(1)  Caroline(E)C1515
        Hitherho Unrevealed Facts                 -
        Hints For Beginners                       -
        Three AM Modulations                      -
        Synalto                                   -
        Hurry Along Please(2)                     -
        Hurry Along
            Please/Don't Call Us(ke)              -


-2.Coxhill,local voices(vcl) only.


Lol Coxhil(ss),prob. Fred Frith(g).      Live.France/England.  1975/76
        Unknown title(s)             Random Radar(E)RRR666


Lol Coxhill(ss),Colin Wood -1(cello),Dave Green -1(b),John Mitchell -1(perc).
                                 London.January  1976
        Diver - Duet For Soprano
        Saxophone And Loose
            Floorboard (Unrelated)   Ogun(E)OG510
        Divers(1)                                 -


No details.                              London.January/May/August  1976
        "Toni Verde"                 Harvest 3C.064-18239


Lol Coxhill(ss,speaking).                    London.  1977
        Murder In The Air,Act 1,2    Chiltern Sound(E)CS100


THE COXHILL - BEDFORD DUO:
Lol Coxhill(ss,p),David Bedford(p).      Unknown location/date
        Pretty Little Annie          Polydor(E)unknown issueno.


THE JOHNNY RONDO TRIO:
Lol Coxhill(ss),David Holland(p),Colin Wood(cello).
                                 Unknown location/date
        La Bicicletas                Chiltern Sound(E)Rondo 1
        Frog Dance                                -


Lol Coxhill(ss),Veryan Weston(p),Michael Garrick(el-p),Richard Wright,Ken Shaw(g),Paul
Mitchell-Davidson(el-b).             Bretton Hall,Wakefield,England.  1978
        The Wakefield Capers         Ogun(E)OG525


Lol Coxhill(ss),Veryan Weston(p).        Hatfield Music Centre,Hatfield,England.  1978
        The Clück Variations:        Ogun(E)OG525
            1st mvt:Prelude To Familiarity
            2nd mvt:In Pursuit Of Rumble
            3rd mvt:Explanatory Passage
            4th mvt:Prelude To Paranoia
```

(ss-solo).   London. 1978
     Joy Of Paranoia Waltz   Ogun(E)OG525

Lol Coxhill(ss),Michael Garrick(el-p).   "Fairway Tavern",Panshanger,England. 1978
     Lover Man   Ogun(E)OG525
     Perdido   -

Lol Coxhill(ss),Simon Emmerson(electronics). Welwyn Garden City,England.May 11,1978
     11.5.78   Random Radar(E)RRR005

Lol Coxhill(ss),Veryan Weston(p).   Oxford,England.May 26,1978
     26.5.78   Random Radar(E)RRR005

Lol Coxhill(ss,mar).   Pistoia,Italy.July 1978
     Uno   Ictus(I)0011
     Due   -
     Tre   -
     Cinque   -
     Quatro   -
     The Frogs Of Gabbiano   -

LOL COXHILL - FRED FRITH:
Lol Coxhill(ss),Fred Frith(g).   Live.Limoges,France. 1978
     Limoges   A.A.A.(F)A02

Same.   Live.Poitiers,France.October 25,1978
     Poitiers   A.A.A.(F)A02

Note:The last title on A02 was recorded 1981 in Reims,France.

LOL COXHILL - MORGAN-FISHER:
Lol Coxhill(ss,vcl),Morgan-Fisher(g,b,p,vcl).
                         London.April/May 1980
        Que En Paz Descanse   Pipe(E)1
        Flotsam   -
        Vase   -
        Jetsam   -
        Matt Finish   -
        Slow Music   -
        Pretty Little Girl   -

(ss-solo).   Live.Reims,France.April/May 1980
     An End Of The Matter   Pipe(E)2

Note:The above title is edited from various performances at a festival in Reims.

THE JOHNNY RONDO DUO PLUS MIKE COOPER:
Lol Coxhill(ss),David Holland(p),Mike Cooper(g).
                        Live."Flöz",Berlin.May 3,1980
        Russian Dance   Free Music Production(G)SAJ29
        Flöz Variations IV   -
        Frog Dance   -
        Caucasian Splinter Mystery   -
        Flöz Variations V   -
        Scales   -
        Flöz Variations VI   -
        Flöz Variations VII   -
        Flöz Variations VIII   -
        Russian Dance (reprise)   -

LOL COXHILL - RAYMOND BONI - MAURICE HORSTHUIS:
Lol Coxhill(ss),Maurice Horsthuis(vln),Raymond Boni(g).
                                    Live.Chantenay-Villedieu,France.September 1980
         Chantenay 80   Nato(F)10

No details.   Live."Bimhuis",Amsterdam. 1980
         Unknown title   Recloose Organisation(E)LOOSE-001

GRAHAM COYLE (Australian)

See also MOOD INDIGO.

Graham Coyle(p),Peter Cleaver(bj),Ron Williamson(tu,b),Tony Johnson(dr).
                                    Melbourne.December 7,1955
         Kansas City Stomps   Swaggie(Au)S4507,S1221
         Froggie Moore Rag   -   -
         Perfect Rag   -   -
         Grandpa's Spells   - ,S1222
         Dill Pickles Rag   Swaggie(Au)S4514,S1325
         The Tickle Rag   - S1007,S1325

All titles also on Bill Haesler Collection(Au)H001.

Omit Johnson.   Melbourne.April 7,1956
         My Monday Date   Swaggie(Au)S4514

Note:See ADE MONSBOURGH for additional titles from this session.

(p-solo).   Melbourne.March 9,1974
         You've Got A Friend   Jazznote(Au)JNLP011/S
         If I Could Be With
            You One Hour Tonight   -
         Everything Happens To Me   -
         I Can't Get Started   -

THE CRANE RIVER JAZZ BAND (British)

See also KEN COLYER.

Ken Colyer(tp),Sonny Morris(cnt),John R.T.Davies(tb,vtb),Monty Sunshine(cl),Ben Marshall
(bj),Julian Davies(b,tu),Ron Bowden(dr),Bill Colyer(vcl).
                                    London.November 1949
         After Dark   Ristic(E)unissued
         Roll 'Em Thin
         Lowdown Blues
         Sister Kate(bc)

Same.   Longford,England.March 11,1950
CRJB-T Down By The Riverside   Ristic(E)unissued
CRJB-1 Just A Closer Walk With Thee   -
CRJB-2 Savoy Blues   "77"(E)LP17
CRJB-3 Savoy Blues   unissued
CRJB-4 The Whores All
            Love The Way I Ride   -
CRJB-5 Creole Love Call   "77"(E)LP17
CRJB-6 South   -
CRJB-7 Lowdown Blues(no cnt)   - ,LEU12/7
CRJB-8 Ostrich Walk   -

```
Same.                                    London.March 24,1950
MM336   Crane River Woman(bc)            Modern(E)MM335/6,Dormouse(E)DM18
        Bucket Got A Hole In It          "77"(E)LP18
        Down By The Riverside                 - ,Dormouse(E)DM18
```

Add John Shipcott(p);George Hopkinson(dr) replaces Bowden.
```
                                         Live.Park Theatre,Ealing,London.April 17,1950
MM335   Lowdown Blues                     Modern(E)MM335/6
        After Dark                        Ristic(E)16,"77"(E)LP18,LEU12/7
        One Sweet Letter From You         "77"(E)LP18
        You Always Hurt The One You Love     unissued
```

```
Pat Hawes(p) replaces Shipcott.          London.April  1950
        Bill Bailey(no cnt)              Modern(E)unissued
        Ice Cream(no tp,cnt)                  -
```

Ken Colyer(tp),Sonny Morris(cnt),John R.T.Davies(tb,vtb),Monty Sunshine(cl),Pat Hawes(p),
Ben Marshall(bj),Julian Davies(b,tu),Ron Hardy(dr).
```
                                         London.May 1,1950
        Blues                            unissued
        You Always Hurt The One You Love     -
```

```
John Westwood(dr) replaces Hardy.        London.June 10,1950
        (My) Old Kentucky Home(no cnt)   "77"(E)LP18,LEU12/7
        Just A Little While To Stay Here      -        -
        Moose March                      unissued
```

```
Omit Hardy.                              London.August 2,1950
PRS9    (My Old) Kentucky Home           Delta(E)D5,"77"(E)LP5,Dormouse(E)DM18
PRS10   Moose March                           -          -,LEU12/7,      -
PRS11   If I Ever Cease To Love          Delta(E)D6,     -              -
PRS12   Gypsy Lament
          (Play To Me Gypsy)(no cnt)          -          -,LEU12/7,      -
        Milneburg Joys                   Ristic(E)16,    -              -
        Bobby Shafto                     "77"(E)LP5
```

```
Same.                                    Cranford,Middlesex,England.November  1950
RCJB11  High Society                     Ristic(E)unissued
RCJB12  Over In Gloryland                     -
RCJB13  Dusty Rag(1)                          -
RCJB14  Get It Right                     Dormouse(E)DM18
RCJB15  Down By The River                unissued
RCJB16  Over In Gloryland                     -
RCJB17  Just A Closer Walk With Thee          -
RCJB18  When You Wore A Tulip                 -
```

Ken Colyer(tp,vcl),Sonny Morris(cnt),Ray Orpwood(tb),Monty Sunshine(cl),Pat Hawes(p,vcl),
Ben Marshall(bj),Julian Davies(b).   Cranford,Middlesex,England.March 1951
```
        A Miner's Dream Of Home          Dormouse(E)DM18
        Doctor Jazz                      "77"(E)LP4
RCRJB-21 In The Gloryland                     -
RCRJB-22 All The Whores Go Crazy              -
        Winin' Boy Blues(no cnt)(ph)     "77"(E)LEU12/7
        Yama Yama Blues(1)               unissued
        Ice Cream(1)                          -
```

-1.John R.T. Davies(tb) replaces Orpwood.

```
Add Cyril Louth(dr).                     London.March 19,1951
P-3-149 Eh La Bas(kc,band-vcl)           Esquire(E)12-013
```

Same.   London.March 22,1951
MEL125 Down By The River(band-vcl)   Melodisc(E)1165,EPM7-105
MEL126 Eh La Bas(sm(?),band-vcl)   Melodisc(E)1027,EPM7-59
MEL127 Dauphin Street Blues   Melodisc(E)1030,   -
MEL128 Just A Closer Walk With Thee   Melodisc(E)1027,   -
MEL129 Blanche Toucatoux(no cnt)   Melodisc(E)1165,EPM7-105
ME1130 Just A Little While To Stay Here Melodisc(E)1030,EPM7-59

Note:EPM7-59 issued as KEN COLYER WITH THE CRANE RIVER JAZZ BAND.

Omit Louth.   Cranford,Middlesex,England.April 15,1951
RCRJB31-1 A Miner's Dream Of Home   "77"(E)LP4,LEU12/7
RCRJB31-2 A Miner's Dream Of Home   Ristic(E)16
RCRJB32   Do What Ory Say(kc)   Crane River Jazz unnumbered,"77"(E)LP4,LEU12/7,
                                            Dormouse(E)DM18
RCRJB33   Dusty Rag(no tp)   Crane River Jazz unnumbered,"77"(E)LP4,LEU12/7,
                                            Dormouse(E)DM18
RCRJB34   Joshua Fit The Battle   Ristic(E)3,"77"(E)LP4
RCRJB35   Put On Your Old Grey Bonnet   "77"(E)LP4
RCRJB36   Dauphine Street Blues(2)   -,Dormouse(E)DM18
RCRJB37   Uptown Bump   -,LEU12/7,   -
          High Society(2)   unissued
          Maryland,My Maryland(3)   "77"(E)LEU12/7

-1.Omit Morris;issued as "Deep Bayou Blues" on DM18.
-2.John R.T. Davies(tb) replaces Orpwood.
-3.Add unknown(wbd);poss. not recorded at the above session.

Note:Several takes of "A Miner's Dream Of Home" were recorded; it is not known which take
     was used for the issue on Dormouse(E)DM18.

Ken Colyer,Sonny Morris(cnt),Ray Orpwood(tb),Monty Sunshine(cl),Pat Hawes(p),Ben Marshall
(bj),Denny Coffee(b),Bill Colyer(wbd).   Live.Royal Festival Hall,London.July 14,1951
CE13507 I'm Travelling   Parlophone(E)R3427,Decca(Am)DL5422,Dormouse(E)DM10
                                          Odeon(G)OBL37-29045,45-0-29045,0-20521
        Down By The River   unissued
        Sometimes My Burden's So Hard   -

Sonny Morris(cnt),Ray Orpwood(tb),Monty Sunshine(cl),Phil Dearle(p),Les Page(bj),Julian
Davies(b),Pete Appleby(dr).   London.November 7,1951
MEL234 Sheik Of Araby   Melodisc(E)1202
MEL235 Careless Love   Melodisc(E)1228
MEL236 Sobbin' Blues   Melodisc(E)1202
MEL237 Spicy Advice   Melodisc(E)1228

Stan Pearcy(b) replaces Davies.   London.April 22,1952
CE13948-1 Slow Drag Blues   Parlophone(E)R3567,GEP8652
CE13953-1 T'ain't Nobody's Business   -   -
CE13954-3 Lily Of The Valley   Parlophone(E)R3634,   - ,MSP6008
CE13955-1 Till We Meet Again   -   -   -

Ken Colyer(tp),Sonny Morris(cnt),John R.T. Davies(tb),Monty Sunshine(cl),Pat Hawes(p),Ben
Marshall(bj),Julian Davies(b).   Cranford,Middlesex,England.May 15,1953
RCRJB41 Creole Song   "77"(E)LP5,LEU12/7,Dormouse(E)DM18
RCRJB42 Get Out Of Here   -   -
RCRJB43 Tell Me Your Dreams   Ristic(E)16,   -
        Blues At Cranford   unissued
        Snag It   -

Add Colin Bowden(dr); Davies plays (tb,bass-cornet); Colyer (tp,vcl).

	Burnham,England.April 17,1972
Ballin' The Jack	Dawn Club(E)DC12026
Down By The Riverside(kc)	-
South	unissued
Just A Closer Walk With Thee	-
When You And I Were Young Maggie	-
Just A Little While To Stay Here	-
Hiawatha	-
I'm Travelling	-

same.

	Burnham,England.May 4,1972
Maryland,My Maryland	Dawn Club(E)DC12026
After Dark	-
Moose March	-
Canal Street Blues	-
Washington And Lee Swing	unissued

same.

	Burnham,England.June 1,1972
Winin' Boy Blues(kc)	Dawn Club(E)DC12026
Tell Me Your Dreams	-
Tishomingo Blues(kc)	-

same.

	Burnham,England.June 26,1972
When I Leave This World Behind	Dawn Club(E)DC12026
Saturday Night Function	-
Buddy Bolden's Blues	unissued
Tell Me Your Dreams	-
I Ain't Gonna Give Nobody None Of My Jelly Roll	-

same;John R.T. Davies plays (tb,as).

	Hamburg,Germany.May 12,1973
Moose March	Happy Bird(G)5003
Sometimes My Burden Is So Heard To Bear(kc)	- ,F90062,Time Wind(G)DB50120
Buddy Bolden's Blues(kc)	-
When You And I Were Young,Maggie	- ,Marifon(G)296095-241

Note:The above titles are studio recordings.

same.

	Live.Congress Centrum,Hamburg,Germany.May 12,1973
(Introduction)	Happy Bird(G)5003
Snag It(kc)	- ,Marifon(G)296095-241
I Can't Escape From You	-
Panama	-

All titles on Happy Bird(G)5003 also on Tobacco Road(G)B/2574.

similar.

	Live."100 Club",London. 1974/75
Unknown titles	Black Lion(E)unissued

Ken Colyer(cnt,vcl),Sonny Morris(cnt,vcl),Lennie Baldwin(tb),John R.T. Davies(tb,as),Monty Sunshine(cl),Pat Hawes(p),Ben Marshall(bj),Julian Davies(b),Colin Bowden(dr).

	Burnham,England.January 3,1977
Trombonium	Unknown label unissued
When Will I Leave The World Behind(sm)	
Sad Night In Harlem(kc)	
Working Man Blues	
Thriller Rag	

(session cont. next page).

(session cont. from previous page):
        Gettysburg March
        Winin' Boy Blues(kc)
        Hiawatha Rag
        Wa-Wa-Wa
        Jambalaya

BIXIE CRAWFORD

See LOUIS JORDAN.

HANK CRAWFORD

See also CTI ALL STARS.

HANK CRAWFORD SEPTET:
Phil Guilbeau(tp),John Hunt(tp,flh),Hank Crawford(as,p,arr),David Newman(ts),Leroy Cooper
(bars),Edgar Willis(b),Milton Tuner(dr).   NYC.October 7,1960
5084   Boo's Tune   Atlantic LP/SD1356,SD1557
5085   Angel Eyes   -   - ,SD2-315
5086   The Story(1)   -
5087   Misty   Atlantic 5013(ed.),LP/SD1356
5088   Four,Five,Six   Atlantic LP/SD1356
5089   What A Difference A Day Makes   -
5090   Sister Sadie   -
5091   Dat Dere   - ,SD2-315
5092   Bye Bye Blackbird   unissued

-1.Add Ray Charles(arr).

All titles also on Atlantic(F)332.058,(J)SMJ7018.

Bruno Carr(dr) replaces Turner.   NYC.February 24,1961
5360   Me And My Baby   Atlantic LP/SD1372
5361   Easy Living   Atlantic 5016(ed.),LP/SD1372,SD2-315
5362   Please Send Me Someone To Love Atlantic LP/SD1372,SD2-315

Same.   NYC.May 2,1961
5520   Playmates   Atlantic 5016(ed.),LP/SD1372
5521   Lorelei's Lament   Atlantic LP/SD1372,SD1557
5522   Blue Stone   -

All titles on LP/SD1372 also on Atlantic(F)332.049.

Same.   NYC.November 8,1961
5777   Sweet Cakes   Atlantic LP/SD1387
5778   What Will I Tell My Heart   -
5779   Baby,Let Me Hold Your Hand   -

Add Sonny Forriest(g).   NYC.April 13,1962
6150   The Peeper   Atlantic 5022,LP/SD1387,SD1557,SD2-315
6151   Don't Cry Baby   -   - ,SD2-315
6152   You've Changed   Atlantic LP/SD1387
6153   Sherry   -

Omit Forriest.   NYC.May 16,1962
6203   But On The Other Hand   Atlantic LP/SD1387
6204   Stoney Lonesome   - ,SD1557

Hank Crawford(as,ts),rhythm,strings,Marty Paich(arr,cond).

LA.February 16,1963

5836	I'm Getting Sentimental Over You	Atlantic LP/SD1405
5837	If I Didn't Care	-
838	Whispering Grass	Atlantic 5033, - ,SD1557,SD1559,SD2-315,(E) 781.907-1
839	Blueberry Hill	Atlantic 5030(ed.),LP/SD1405,SD2-315
840	Stormy Weather	Atlantic LP/SD1405
841	Star Dust	-

ame.

LA.February 20,1963

842	I Left My Heart In San Francisco	Atlantic LP/SD1405
843	Any Time	Atlantic 5030(ed.),LP/SD1405
844	There Goes My Heart	Atlantic LP/SD1405
845	Sweet Slumber	-
846	Time Out For Tears	-
847	Have A Good Time	-

11 titles on LP/SD1405 also on London(E)HA-K/S8103.

HANK CRAWFORD SEPTET:

Phil Guilbeau(tp),John Hunt(tp,flh),Hank Crawford(as),James Clay(ts),Leroy Cooper(bars), Sonny Forriest(g),Edgar Willis(b),Bruno Carr(dr).

NYC.June 7,1963

050	Read 'Em And Weep	Atlantic 5042,LP/SD1423
051	Two Years Of Torture	- ,SD2-315
052	Skunky Green	Atlantic 5042(ed.), -(ed.), -
053	Don't Go To Strangers	unissued
054	Save Your Love For Me	Atlantic LP/SD1423

Charlie Patterson,John Hunt(tp),Hank Crawford(as),Wilbur Brown(ts),Alexander Nelson(bars), Lewis Worrell(b),Carl Lott(dr).

NYC.October 9,1963

268	Shooby	Atlantic LP/SD1423
269	Got You On My Mind	-
270	Shake A Plenty	Atlantic 5039, - ,SD2-315

Julius Brooks,John Hunt(tp),Hank Crawford(as),Wilbur Brown(ts),Leroy Cooper(bars),Charlie Green(b),Milton Turner(dr).

NYC.March 19,1964

705	Mellow Down	Atlantic 5039,LP/SD1423
706	Merry Christmas,Baby	Atlantic 5042, -
707	Blues In Bloom	-

11 titles on LP/SD1423 also on Atlantic(E)ATL/SAL5017.

Edgar Willis(b),Bruno Carr(dr) replace Green,Turner.

NYC.April 13,1964

734	Hollywood Blues	Atlantic LP/SD1436
735	H.C. Blues	-
736	News Blues	-

Phil Guilbeau,Oliver Beener(tp),Hank Crawford(as,arr),Wendell Harrison(ts),Leroy Cooper (bars),Ali Mohammed(b),Bruno Carr(dr).

NYC.December 10,1964

92	These Tears	Atlantic LP/SD1436
93	Dig These Blues	- ,SD1557
94	The Crazy Saloon(1)	-
95	Untitled blues	unissued

.Crawford plays (p).

Marcus Belgrave,Jimmy Owens(tp),Hank Crawford(as,arr),Abdul Baari(ts),Howard Johnson(bars
Charlie Green(b),Milton Turner(dr).   NYC.February 11,1965
8615   Baby,Won't You
            Please Come Home   Atlantic LP/SD1436
8616   Bluff City Blues(1)   Atlantic 5049(ed.),LP/SD1436
8617   Don't Get Around Much Anymore   -   -

-1.Crawford plays (p).

All titles on LP/SD1436 also on Atlantic(E)ATL/SAL5033.

John Hunt,Fielder Floyd(tp),Hank Crawford(as),Wendell Harrison(ts),Lonnie Shaw(bars),
Charlie Green(b),Milton Turner(dr).   NYC.October 19,1965
9432   Special 2426   Atlantic unissued
9433   Smoky City   Atlantic 5079(ed.),LP/SD1470
9434   When Did You Leave Heaven   Atlantic LP/SD1455
9435   Fly Me To The Moon   unissued

Wilbert Hogan(dr) replaces Turner.   NYC.October 29,1965
9451   Someday You'll Want Me   Atlantic SD1503
9452   Hush Puppies   Atlantic 5079(ed.),LP/SD1470,SD2-315
9453   Mud Island Blues   Atlantic SD1503

Same.   NYC.November 17,1965
9599   Route 66   Atlantic LP/SD1470
9600   Teardrops   -
9601   Makin' Whoopee(1)   Atlantic LP/SD1455,SD2-315

-1.Crawford(p),b,dr only.

John Hunt,Fielder Floyd(tp),Hank Crawford(as,p),Wendell Harrison(ts),Howard Johnson(bars
Willie Jones(g),Ali Mohammed(b),Joe Dukes(dr).
                                        NYC.January 7,1966
9809   After Hours   Atlantic LP/SD1455,SD2-315
9810   The Black Slider   -   -
9811   Next Time You See Me
            Things Won't Be The Same   -

John Hunt,Fielder Floyd(tp),Hank Crawford(as),Wendell Harrison(ts),Howard Johnson(bars),
Sonny Forriest(g),Charles Lindsay(b),Wilbert Hogan(dr).
                                        NYC.January 14,1966
9840   Lonely Avenue   Atlantic LP/SD1470,SD2-315
9841   Junction   Atlantic LP/SD1455
9842   The Turfer   Atlantic LP/SD1470

Charles Dungey(b),Joe Dukes(dr) replace Lindsay,Hogan;unknown(vbs) replaces Forriest.
                                        NYC.January 19,1966
9856   Soul Shoutin'   Atlantic 5066,LP/SD1455,SD2-315
9857   Who Can I Turn To   Atlantic 5066(ed.),   -
9858   Danger Zone   Atlantic LP/SD1470

All titles on LP/SD1455 also on Atlantic(E)587026,S588026.

John Hunt,Fielder Floyd(tp),Hank Crawford(as),Wendell Harrison(ts),Lonnie Shaw(bars),
Sonny Forriest(g),Charlie Green(b),Isaac Walton(dr).
                                        NYC.March 21,1966
10046   Mr. Blues   Atlantic LP/SD1470,SD2-315
10047   On A Clear Day   -
10048   I Wish You Love   unisssued

oe Newman,Melvin Lastie(tp),Tony Studd(tb),Hank Crawford(as),David Newman(ts),Pepper
dams(bars),Carl Lynch(g),Jimmy Tyrell(el-b),Bruno Carr(dr).

NYC.November 20,1967

3508	I Can't Stand It	Atlantic SD1503
3509	Glue Fingers	Atlantic 2510,SD1503
3510	In The Heat Of The Night	Atlantic 2510(ed.),SD1503,SD2-315
3511	Double Cross	Atlantic SD1503,SD2-315
3512	Jimmy Mack	-
3513	The Second Time Around	-
3514	Untitled (uptempo) blues	

ank Crawford(as),David Newman(ts,fl),Paul Griffin(p,el-p),Eric Gale(g),Ron Carter(el-b),
ernard Purdie(dr),Arif Mardin(arr,cond).   NYC.February 12,1969

6300	Groovin'	Atlantic 2688,SD1523
6301	Never Let Me Go(1)	Atlantic SD1523
6302	Ain't No Way	Atlantic 2688,SD1523

1.Add Ernie Royal,Joe Newman,Snooky Young,Bernie Glow(tp),Jimmy Cleveland,Benny Powell
tb),Frank Wess(as),Seldon Powell(ts),Pepper Adams(bars) - overdubbed later.

erry Jemmott(el-b) replaces Carter.   NYC.February 12,1969

6303	I Can't See Myself Leaving You	Atlantic SD1523
6304	Since You've Been Gone	
	(Sweet,Sweet Baby)	-
6305	Goin' Down Slow	-

uck Rainey(el-b) replaces Jemmott.   NYC.February 13,1969

6306	Lady Soul	Atlantic SD1523
6307	Take A Look(1)	-
6308	Baby,I Love You	-
6309	Soul Serenade	-
6310	Goin' Down Slow	-

..Add strings,Gene Orloff(cond) - overdubbed later.

nk Crawford(as),Eric Gale/Cornell Dupree(g),Richard Tee(p),Chuck Rainey/Ron Carter(b),
ernard Purdie(dr).   NYC.December 10,1970

807	Sophisticated Soul	Cotillion SD18003
808	If Ever I Should Leave You	-
809	King Size Man	-
810	You're The One	-
811	Parker's Mood	-
812	Soulful Susie	unissued
813	The Hills Of Love	Cotillion SD 18003
814	It's A Funky Thing To Do(1)	- ,Atlantic SD2-315

.Pee Wee Ellis(p) replaces Tee.

DeRisi,Snooky Young(tp),Wayne Andre(tb),Hank Crawford(as),Grover Washington(ts),Pepper
ams(bars),Phil Kraus(vbs),Richard Tee(org,p),Eric Gale(g),Ron Carter(b),Idris
hammad(dr),Airto Moreira(perc),strings,Pee Wee Ellis(arr,cond).

NYC.August 1971

Ham	Kudu KU06

nk Crawford(as),Phil Kraus(vbs),Richard Tee(org,p),Margaret Ross(harp),Cornell Dupree
),Ron Carter(b),Bernard Purdie(dr),strings,Don Sebesky(arr,cond).

NYC.January 1972

Help Me Make It	
Through The Night	Kudu KU908,KU06
Brian's Song	- ,CTI CTS2
Uncle Funky	Kudu KU908, -

ession cont. next page).

(session cont. from previous page):
```
      In The Wee Small
          Hours Of The Morning     Kudu KU06,CTI(E)CTB200
      Go Away,Little Girl          -
      Imagine                      -
      The Sun Died                 -
```

All titles on KU06 also on Kudu(E)KUL4,(J)GP3062,LAX3257,CTI(J)SR3329.

Hank Crawford(as),unknown harp,rhythm,strings,Don Sebesky,Bob James(arr,cond).
                                     NYC.September/October 1972
```
      We Got A Good Thing Going    Kudu KU08
      Imagination                  -
      Down To Earth                -
      The Christmas Song           -
      Alone Again,Naturally        -
      I Don't Know                 -
      I'm Just A Lucky So And So    -
      Winter Wonderland            -
      A Little Tear                -
```

All titles also on Kudu(E)KUL7,(J)GP3060,SR3338,CBS ZK40820 (CD).

Bernie Glow,Alan Rubin,Marvin Stamm(tp),Wayne Andre,Paul Faulise,Tony Studd(tb),Jimmy Buf
fington,Brooks Tillotson(frh),Hank Crawford(as),Richard Tee(p,org),Joe Beck(g),Bob Cran-
shaw(b),Idris Muhammad(dr),Rubens Bassini,George Devens,David Friedman,Arthur Jenkins,Ph:
Kraus,Ralph MacDonald(perc),Bill Eaton,Hilda Harris,Randy Peyton,Maeretha Stewart(vcl),Bo
James(arr).   NYC.June 1973
```
      Corazon                      Kudu KU15
      Wildflower                   -
      Mr. Blues                    -
      You've Got It Bad Girl       -
      Good Morning Heartache       -
```

All titles also on Kudu KSQX15,(J)GP3064,SR3353,CBS ZK40709 (CD),(Eu)450566-2 (CD).

Hank Crawford(as),rest unknown.   NYC.June 1974
```
      Don't Worry 'Bout A Thing    Kudu KU19
      Jana                         -
      All Love Is Fair             -
      Sho Is Funky                 -
      Groove Junction              -
```

All titles also on Kudu(J)GP3065,SR3371,LAX3214.

Hank Crawford(as),Leon Pendarvis(keyb),Eric Gale(g),Gary King(el-b),Steve Gadd(dr),unkn
horns,strings,David Matthews(arr,cond). NYC.June/July 1975
```
      The Stripper                 Kudu KU26
      I Hear A Symphony            -
      I'll Move You No Mountain    -
      Madison ((Spirit/The Power)  -
      Hang It On The Ceiling       -
```

Richard Tee(keyb),Bernard Purdie(dr) replace Pendarvis,Gadd.
                                     Same date
```
      Sugar Free                   Kudu KU26
      Baby!This Is Love I Have     -
      Love Won't Let Me Wait       -
```

All titles on KU26 also on Kudu(J)GP3050,LAX3215.

Incl. Fred Wesley(tb),Jeremy Steig(fl),Hank Crawford(as),Richard Tee(el-p),Eric Gale(g),
Gary King(el-b),Andy Newmark(dr),Nicky Marrero(perc),Frank Floyd,Zachary Sanders,Ray Simp-
son(vcl).   NYC. 1976
    Funky Pigeon   Kudu KU33
    I Can't Stop Lovin' You   -
    You'll Never Find
      Another Love Like Mine   -

Anthony Jackson(el-b),Steve Gadd(dr) replace King,Newmark.
                                              NYC. 1976
    Canadian Sunset   Kudu KU33
    Midnight Over Memphis   -

ll titles on KU33 also on Kudu(J)GP3089.

Randy Brecker,Jon Faddis(tp),Jeremy Steig(fl),Hank Crawford(as),Michael Brecker(ts),Cliff
Carter(keyb),Eric Gale(g),Gary King(el-b),Steve Gadd(dr),Nicky Marrero,Sue Evans(perc),
strings,Frank Floyd,unknown backgrund-vcl(vcl),David Matthews(arr,cond).
                                              NYC.November 1976
    Tico Rico   Kudu KU35
    Lady Soul   -
    Lament   -
    Funky Rooster   -
    Lullaby Of Love   -
    Teach Me Tonight   -
    I've Just Seen A Face   -

All titles also on Kudu(J)GP3118,LAX3258.

Randy Brecker(tp),Fred Wesley(tb),Hank Crawford(as),Ronnie Cuber(bars),Cliff Carter,Steve
Robbins(keyb),Joe Caro,Hiram Bullock(g),Cliff Morris(bj),Will Lee(el-b),Steve Gadd(dr),Sue
Evans(perc),Vivian Cherry,Lani Groves,Yolanda McCullough(vcl).
                                              NYC.February/March 1978
    What A Difference
      You've Made In My Life   Kudu KU39
    I Don't Want No Happy Songs   -
    New York's One Soulful City   -
    Take This Job And Shove It   -
    Just The Way You Are   -
    Daytime Friends   -
    Evergreen   -
    Cajun Sunrise   -

l titles also on Kudu(G)63048,(J)GP3190.

HANK CRAWFORD - CALVIN NEWBORN:
Incl. Joe Shepley,Michael Lawrence(tp),Janice Robinson(tb),Hank Crawford(as,el-p),Alex
Foster(ts),Howard Johnson(bars),Warren Chiasson(vbs),Mario Sprouse(synth),Calvin Newborn
(g),Flip Greene(b),Billy Kaye(dr),Erroll Bennett(perc).
                                              NYC.October/November 1978
    Centerpiece   Buddah BDS5730
    Gee Baby,Ain't I Good To You   -
    Breezin'   -
    I Had A Dream   -
    I Can't Stand It   -
    Frame For The Blues   -

HANK CRAWFORD - JIMMY McGRIFF:
Incl. Hank Crawford(as),Eddie Daniels(ts),Jimmy McGriff(org),Jimmy Ponder(g).
                                              Unknown location.c. 1980
    Outside Looking In   Denon DC8520(CD)

PAUL CRAWFORD

CRAWFORD - FERGUSON NIGHT OWLS:
Jack Bachman(tp),Paul Crawford(tb),Hank Kmen(cl),Edmond Souchon(g,bj,vcl),Bill Humphries
(bj),Chink Martin,Sr. -1(tu),Sherwood Mangiapane(b,vcl),Len Ferguson(dr).

	New Orleans.June 7,1965	
Moose March	New Orleans Originals JM65-2	
Ida!Sweet As Apple Cider		-
Bedelia(1)		-
Bogalusa Street(1)		-
Bill Bailey(es)		-
Dr. Jazz(1)		-
Just A Little While To Stay Here		-
Working Man Blues		-
And They Called		
It Dixieland(1)(sm)		-
Melancholy		-
Once In A While		-

The above titles also on New Orleans Originals R2092.

Jack Bachman(tp),Paul Crawford(tb),Raymond Burke(cl),Henry Kmen(cl,ts),Nat Krasnoff(acc)
Bob Lee(bj),Chink Martin,Sr.(b),Len Ferguson(dr).

	New Orleans. 1970's	
Little Orphan Annie	Audiophile AP109	
Emaline		-
Taps Miller		-
Roamin'		-
San Antonio Shout		-
Chinatown,My Chinatown		-
Corrine Corrina		-
Tuck Me To Sleep In My Old 'Tucky Home		-
Underneath Hawaiian Skies		-
My Baby's Arms		-

RAY CRAWFORD

Johnny Coles(tp),Cecil Payne(bars),Junior Mance(p),Ray Crawford(g),Ben Tucker(b),Frank
Dunlop(dr).

	NYC.February 1961	
I Knew Pres	Candid(J)SONF01121	
Smooth Groove		-
Miss April		-
Impossible		-
The Compendium Suite		-

All titles also on Candid CS9028,CCD79028,(J)SMJ6196,32JDC144 (CD).

Ronnell Bright(keyb),Ray Crawford(g),Herbie Lewis(b),Donald Dean(dr).

	NYC. 1977	
It's About Time	Dobre DR1010	
Motherless Child		-
Pick Me Up		-
I'll Close My Eyes		-

Henry Franklin(b) replaces Lewis.

	NYC. 1978	
It Ain't Necessarily So	Dobre DR1021	
Almost Blue		-
Song For Cookie		-

(session cont. next page).

(session cont. from previous page):
    One Step At A Time   Dobre DR1021
    But Beautiful   -
    One For The Money   -

All titles also on United National UND1035.

CRAZY CLOWNS JAZZ BAND (Uruguayan)

Luis Trobo(tp),José Crespo(tb),Wilson De Oliveira(cl),Juan Laglere(p),Heber Carambula
(bj),Enrique Trobo(tu),Roberto Galletti(dr),Marcos Larghero(vcl).
                                       Montevideo. 1960
10041 St. Louis Blues   Orfeo(Uruguayan)40015
10042 Walking With The King(ml)   -

CREATIVE ART JAZZ ENSEMBLE

Peter Montalbano(tp),Pat O'Hara(tb),Bert Wilson(ss,ts),Rahim Roach(as),Dave Wilson(vbs),
Robin Young(p),Chris Amberger(b),Smiley Winters(dr).
                                Berkeley,Calif.October 31,1968
    Madness   Arhoolie ST8002
    Pretty Good   -
    Doris   -
    Nirvana   -
    Daniel   -
    Now   -

CREATIVE ARTS ENSEMBLE

Al White(tp),George Bohanon(tb),Dadesi Komolafe(fl),Gary Bias(as,ss),Wilbert Hemsley(ts),
Jeff Clayton(bars),Kaeef Ruzadu(p,ldr),Henry Franklin(b),Sonship Phaeus(dr),B.J. Crowley
(vcl,ldr).   LA.c. 1980
    One Step Out   Nimbus NS913
    Flashback Of Time   -
    All Praises Due   -
    Stars In Lightyear Time   -

CREATIVE CONSTRUCTION COMPANY

Leo Smith(tp,flh,frh,etc.),Anthony Braxton(as,ss,cl,fl,contrabass-cl,chimes),Leroy Jenkins
(vln,vla,recorder,hca,etc.),Muhal Richard Abrams(p,cello,cl),Richard Davis(b),Steve McCall
(dr).   Live.Washington Square Methodist Church,NYC.May 19,1970
    Muhal,pt.1,2:   Muse MR5071,Vedette(I)VPA8360,Seven Seas(J)
      Live Spiral   K18P9170
      Total Time
    No More White Gloves,pt.1,2
    (With Sand Under Your
    Shoes Doing A Dance)   Muse MR5097,Seven Seas(J)K18P9180

CREATIVE ORCHESTRA

See ANTHONY BRAXTON,ROSCOE MITCHELL,LEO SMITH.

TOM CREEKMORE

Tom Creekmore(ts,as),Joe Felix(p),Joe Diorio(g),Don Felix(b),Nick Martinis(dr).
                                        LA.August 18,1978
    Semi-Gymnopedia   Discovery DS791
    Strawberry Wine   -
    Stylin'   -
    She Is It   -
    Candy Lil   -
    40 Love   -
    No More   -
    Three For All   -

CREME FRAICHE (Danish)

Erik Tschentscher,Tim Hagans,Poul Nielsem,Egon Pedersen,Flemming Hansen(tp),Vincent Nilsson,Erling Kroner,Niels Neergaard(tb),Flemming Andreasen(btb),Jan zum Vohrde,Michael Hove
(ss,as,fl),Torben Enghoff,Ole Olsen(ts,fl),Niels Husum(bars,ss,fl,cl),Thomas Clausen(keyb)
John Sund(g),Mads Vinding(b),Bjarne Rostvold(dr),Peter Olesen(perc),Lars Togeby(arr,cond).
                                        Copenhagen.May 20-22,1978
    Creme Fraiche   Storyville(D)SLP1022
    That's It   -
    Maj Vals   -
    Himbeergeist   -
    Interlude   -
    Snow Drop   -
    Triade

CREOLE JAZZ BAND (Argentinean)

Roberto Canci(cnt),Jorge Mario Palmieri(tb),José Vanella(cl,as),Arturo Fernández(cl,ts),
Aldo Montilla(ss),Alfredo Desiata(as),Roberto Oscar Bottyan(p),José Luis Ruiz(bj),Horacio
Caccianini(tu),Carlos Fossaceca(dr).   Buenos Aires.November 3,1972
    Dr. Jazz   Eleité(Arg)77001
    Meanest Kind Of Blues   -
    Shooting The Pistol   -
    She's Crying For Me   -
    Dippermouth Blues   -
    Deep Henderson   -

Same.   Buenos Aires.November 7,1972
    Hop Off   Eleité(Arg)77001
    Black Bottom Stomp   -
    London Cafe Blues   -
    Wild Man Blues   -
    Sweet Lovin' Man   -

NEAL CREQUE

Neal Creque(p,keyb,arr),Billy Butler(g),Gene Taylor(b),Steve Berrios(dr,tymp),Richard
Landrum(perc),strings,The Ikinen Singers(vcl).
                                        NYC. 1972
    Rafiki   Cobblestone CST9005
    Years Of Regret(is)   -
(session cont. next page).

(session cont. from previous page):
         Sis Daisi   Cobblestone CST9005
         Nina   -
         What'cha Call It   -
         Black Velvet Rose   -
         Cease The Bombing   -
         Before The Rain Come   -

All titles also on Muse MR5226.

Neal Creque(p,el-p),Wally Richardson(g),Bill Salter(el-b),Freddie Waits(dr),Sonny Morgan,
Babba Famy(perc).   NYC.August 6,1973
         What Am I Gonna Do   Muse MR5029
         The Happiness I Found   -
         What'cha Wanna Do-Do It   -
         Yes I'm Your Friend   -
         In The Middle Of It All   -
         What Good Is Love
             That Cannot Start   -
         This Too Shall Pass   -
         Holding The Hand Of Time   -

CRESCENDO (KRESTSCHENDO) (Soviet)

QUINTET CRESCENDO:
Konstantin Bacholdin(tb),Alexej Zubov(ts),Boris Frumkin(p),Alexej Isplatovski(b),Valeri
Bulanov(dr).   Live.Moscow.May 30-June 4,1967
         Variations On The
             Azerbaijan Mugam "Chargyakh" Melodija(Sov)D020983/4,ST011885/6

KWARTET KRESTSCHENDO:
Omit Bacholdin.   Live.Moscow.June 1-4,1968
         Sjuta Na Russkie Temu   Melodija(Sov)D024283/4

KWARTET KRESTSCHENDO I LEONID GARIN:
Add Leonid Garin(vbs).   Moscow(?).February 5,1969
         Russkij Naigrisch   Melodija(Sov)D024296

ANSAMBL KRESTSCHENDO:
Incl. Alexej Zubov(ts),Leonid Garin(vbs). Moscow(?).May 13,1975
         Ballada   Melodija(Sov)S60-05897/8
         Russkij Naigrisch   -
         Bljus (Blues)   -

CRESCENT BAY JASS BAND

Al Colter(tp),Norm Shacker(tb),John Jewett(cl),Ron Ortmann(p),Pete O'Leary(bj),Buddy Burns
(b),Lee Wedberg(dr).   Live."Guys 'n Dolls",LA.May 27,1956
         Down By The Riverside   Epitaph No.1

CRESCENT CITY CRYSTALS

John Henry McNeil(tp,ldr),Buster Moore(tb),Albert Delone(ts),Harold Christopher(g),
Sylvester Handy(b),Dave Bailey(dr).   Harmony Inn,New Orleans.November 13,1963
         The Sheik Of Araby   "77"LA12/29,Jazz Crusade JC2001
         Tulane Swing   -

CRESCENT CITY JAZZ BAND (Dutch)

Henk Duymelink(cnt),Leo van Bokhoven(tb),Henk Schriks(cl),Hen van Bokhoven(bj),Wout Bombeeck(tu),Jan van Kemenade(dr).   Gorcum,The Netherlands.November 8,1975
     Everybody Loves My Baby   Beerendonk(Du)99914

Add Peter van Bokhoven(p).   The Netherlands.October/November 1979
    Wise Guy   Crescent City Jazz Band(Du)100180
    I Found A New Baby   -
    See See Rider   -
    King Porter Stomp   -
    Old Fashioned Love   -
    Careless Love Stomp   -
    Irish Black Bottom   -
    Peoria   -
    Bimbo   -
    The Chrysanthemum   -
    Ace In the Hole   -
    Blues My Naughty
      Sweetie Gives To Me   -

CURT CRESS

Ack van Rooyen(flh),Kristian Schultze(keyb),Volker Kriegel(g),Dave King(b),Curt Cress(dr).
                             Munich,Germany.c. 1975
    Cyclone   Atlantic(G)50079
    From The Back   -
    Fields   -
    Shuffle On Out   -
    Delphine   -
    451271   -
    No Answer   -
    Funk Off   -

CAROLE CREVELING

(vcl) acc. by Lou Levy(p),Max Bennett(b),Chuck Flores(dr).
                                 LA. 1950's
    Willow Weep For Me   Euterpean 45-5001
    Between The Devil
      And The Deep Blue Sea   -

(vcl) acc. by BILL BAKER QUARTET:
Bill Baker(p),Jimmy Wyble(g),Jack Coughlan(b),Bob Norris(dr).
                                 LA.c. 1957
    My Old Flame   Euterpean ETP101
    My Ship   -
    You Have Cast The
      Shadow On The Sea   -
    Better Luck Next Time   -
    Long Ago   -
    Star Eyes   -
    This Heart Of Mine   -
    One Morning In May   -
    Now We Know   -
    Nobody Else But Me   -
    Anything Can Happen With You   -
    There's No You   -

JOHNNY CRINER

(vcl) acc. by WILBERT BARANCO QUINTET:
Karl George(tp),Lucky Thompson(ts),Wilbert Baranco(p),Dave Barbour(g),Phil Stephens(b).
LA. 1945/46

GEM16	Sugar Mama Blues	Gem 16
GEM16	I've Been Drinking	-
GEM24	Railroad Man	G & G 1024
GEM24	I Got Money Blues	-
GEM25	Down Home Blues	G & G 1025
GEM25	Bring What Daddy Needs	-

ETTORE CRISOSTOMI (Italian)

See SISTINA STREET SWINGERS.

SONNY CRISS

See also WARDELL GRAY,HOLLYWOOD JAZZ CONCERT,JAM SESSION (SUPERSTARS OF JAZZ),JAZZ AT THE
PHILHARMONIC,AL KILLIAN,GENE NORMAN (JUST JAZZ).

Sonny Criss(as),Hampton Hawes(p),Iggy Shevack(b),Chuck Thompson(dr).
LA.September 22,1949

272-6	Calidad	Clef 8910,Mercury 8910,Karusell(Sd)K1041
273-4	Tornado (Allen's Alley/Wee)	Clef 8915
274-1	The First One	Clef 8910,Mercury 8910,Karusell(Sd)K1041
275-3	Blues For Boppers	Clef 8915

All titles also on Clef EPC115,Clef MGC122,Norgran MGN1065,Verve MGV8155,(J)70M3234/37,
Columbia(E)SEB10059,Fresh Sound(Sp)FSR403,FSR-CD64 (CD).

Sonny Criss(as),Gil Barrios(p),David Bryant(b),Billy Snyder(dr).
Live."Trade Winds",LA.Poss. September 4,1952

Strike Up The Band	Xanadu 200,DIW(J)32DIW302(CD)

Note:Xanadu 200 cover notes list the rec.date September 4,1952 as well as August 4,1952.

Sonny Criss(as),Kenny Drew(p),Barney Kessel(g),Bill (Buddy(?)) Woodson(b),Chuck Thompson
(dr).
LA.January 26,1956

IM981	Easy Living	Imperial LP9006,LP9205,LP12205
IM982	Criss Cross	-
IM983	Willow Weep For Me	Imperial 5694,LP9006,LP9205,LP9233,LP12205
IM984	Alabamy Bound	- - ,LP12205

Omit Kessel.
LA.February 24,1956

IM1012	Something's Gotta Give	Imperial LP9006,LP9205,LP12205
IM1013	These Foolish Things	Imperial LP9006,Polydor(F)27.004,27.706,657.026
IM1014	West Coast Blues(1)	Imperial 5694,LP9006,LP9233,Polydor(F)27.706
IM1015	Blue Friday	Imperial LP9006

-1.As "Blues Pour Flirter" on Polydor(F)27.706.

Same.
LA.March 23,1956

IM1034	More Than You Know	Imperial LP9006,LP9205,LP12205
IM1035	Sunday	- - -
IM1036	Sweet Georgia Brown	- - -
IM1037	Hamp's Blues	-

(session cont. next page).

(session cont. from previous page):
All titles on LP9006 also on Liberty(J)K18P9253,TOCJ5329 (CD).

Sonny Criss(as),Sonny Clark(p),Leroy Vinnegar(b),Lawrence Marable(dr).
                                        LA.July 10,1956
IM1084 Summertime   Imperial LP9020
IM1085 Memories Of You   -
IM1086 Wailin' With Joe   -
IM1087 How Deep is The Ocean   -
IM1088 The Blues For Rose   -
IM1089 The Man I Love   - ,LP9205,LP12205

Same.   LA.July 31,1956
IM1090 Until The Real
        Thing Comes Along   Imperial LP9020
IM1091 Blue Prelude   - ,LP9205,LP12205,Polydor(F)27.004,
                                        27.717
IM1092 After You've Gone   Imperial LP9020
IM1093 Come Rain Or Come Shine   - ,LP9205,LP12205,Polydor(F)27.704,
                                        27.717
IM1094 Ornithology(1)   Imperial LP9020
IM1095 If I Had You   - ,Polydor(F)27.004,27.717

-1.Listed as "How High The Moon" in Imperial files but the theme played is "Ornithology".

All titles on LP9020 also on Liberty(J)LLJ70018,(J)K18P9254,TOCJ5310 (CD).

Sonny Criss(as),Larry Bunker(vbs),Sonny Clark(p),prob. Buddy Woodson(b),Lawrence Marable
(dr).   LA.August 21,1956
IM1101 What Is This Thing Called Love   Imperial LP9024
IM1102 Night And Day   - ,LP9205,LP12205
IM1103 Love For Sale   - ,LP9205,LP12205
IM1104 Just One Of Those Things   -
IM1105 Anything Goes   -
IM1106 I Get A Kick Out Of You   - ,LP9205,LP12205

Sonny Criss(as),Larry Bunker(vbs),prob. Jimmy Bunn(p),prob. Teddy Smith(b),Lawrence Ma-
rable(dr).   LA.October 3,1956
IM1155 Easy To Love   Imperial LP9024
IM1156 It's Alright With me   -
IM1157 I Love You   -
IM1158 In The Still Of The Night   -

All titles on LP9024 also on London(E)LTZ-P15094,Liberty(J)K18P9255,TOCJ5330 (CD).

Sonny Criss(as),Hampton Hawes(p),Buddy Woodson(b),Chuck Thompson(dr).
                                        TV-cast.LA.November 25,1957
        Easy Living   Calliope CAL3024
        Willow Weep For Me   -
        Wailin' With Joe(1)   -

-1.Issued as "Wailin' For Joe".

All titles also on Fresh Sound(Sp)FSR403,FSR-CD64 (CD).

Note:The above titles are from a "Stars Of Jazz" TV-show.

Ole Hansen(tb),Sonny Criss(as),Wynton Kelly (as "Joe Scott")(p),Bob Cranshaw(b),Walter
Perkins(dr).   Chicago.Poss. March 1959
(session cont. next page).

(session cont. from previous page):
```
        Softly As In A Morning Sunrise   Peacock PLP91
        Sweet Lorraine(no tb)            Peacock 802P,PLP91
        Sylvia                                             -
        I Got It Bad(no tb)              Peacock 802P,     -
        Butts Delight                                      -
        Indiana                                            -
        You Don't Know
           What Love Is(no as)                             -
```

All titles also on Fresh Sound(Sp)252962,Impulse IA9337/2,(J)YW8560,MCA MCA2-4141.

SONNY CRISS QUARTET:
Sonny Criss(as),Henri Renaud(p),Michel Gaudry(b),Philippe Combelle(dr).
```
                                        Paris.October 10,1962
PEP3617 Mighty Low                      Brunswick/Polydor(F)27.004,657.026
PEP3618 Black Coffee                                      -
        Don't Blame Me                                   -
        We'll Be Together Again                          - ,657.026
```

All titles also on Onyx ORI22 (scheduled for release but never issued),Polydor(Eu)2445.034
Fresh Sound(Sp)FSR547.

SONNY CRISS QUINTET:
Sonny Criss(as),Georges Arvanitas(p,org),René Thomas(g),Pierre Michelot(b),Philippe Com-
belle(dr).   Paris.April 22,1963
```
        Blues Pour Flirter(1)           Polydor(F)27.049,(Eu)2445.034
        Once In A While                 Brunswick(F)87.519,Polydor(F)657.026,(Eu)2445.034
        Day Dream                                  - ,           -              - ,
                                        Verve 845702-2(CD)
```

-1.Originally issued as Blues Pour Flirter,No.2".

All titles also on Fresh Sound(Sp)FSR548.

```
Same.                                   Paris.April 23,1963
        Don't Get Around Much Anymore   Brunswick(F)87.519,Fresh Sound(Sp)FSR547
        St. Louis Blues                            - ,Fresh Sound(Sp)FSR548
        Early And Later,pt.1                       - ,Polydor(F)27.049,657.026,
                                        (Eu)2445.034,Fresh Sound(Sp)FSR548
        Early And Later,pt.2            Brunswick(F)87.519,Polydor(F)27.049,(Eu)2445.034,
                                        Fresh Sound(Sp)FSR548
```

SONNY CRISS QUARTET:
Omit Thomas;Arvanitas plays (p).
```
                                        Paris.April 25,1963
        God Bless The Child             Brunswick(F)87.519,Polydor(F)657.026,(Eu)2445.034,
                                        Fresh Sound(Sp)FSR547
        This Can't Be Love              Brunswick(F)87.519,Fresh Sound(Sp)FSR548
        On Green Dolphin Street                    -                        -
```

All titles on FSR547 and FSR548 also on Fresh Sound(Sp)BOX-2 (2xLP set).
Note:All titles recorded at the above April 1963 sessions - except "Blues Pour Flirter",
    "Early And Later,pt.1" - were scheduled for release on Onyx ORI22 but never issued.

Sonny Criss(as),Hampton Hawes(p),Clarence Johnson(b),Frank Butler(dr).
```
                                        LA.June 15,1965
        Saturday Morning                Xanadu 200
        When Sunny Gets Blue                       -
        The Masquerade Is Over                     -
        What's New                                 -
        Ursula(1)                                  -
```
(session cont. next page).

(session cont. from previous page):
-1.Criss plays (ss).

All titles also on DIW(J)32DIW302 (CD),EPM(F)FDC5163 (CD).

Sonny Criss(as),Walter Davis(p),Paul Chambers(b),Alan Dawson(dr).
                                    NYC.October 21,1966
    When Sunny Gets Blue   Prestige PR7511
    Days Of Wine And Roses   -
    Black Coffee   -
    Greasy   Prestige 45-435,PR7511
    Sunrise,Sunset   -   -
    Love For Sale   Prestige(J)VICJ23670(CD),Original Jazz Classics
                                    OJCCD430-2(CD)
    Skylark   Prestige PR7511
    Steve's Blues   -

All titles on PR7511 also on Prestige(J)SMJ6269,VICJ23670 (CD),Original Jazz Classics
OJC430,OJCCD430-2 (CD).

Same.   NYC.March 23,1967
    Blues In the Closet   Prestige PR7526
    On A Clear Day   - ,PR7742
    Smile   -
    A Million Or More Times   -
    Wee (Allen's Alley)   -
    God Bless The Child   -
    All The Things You Are   unissued

All titles on PR7526 also on Prestige(J)SMJ7480,VICJ23671 (CD),Original Jazz Classics
OJC655,OJCCD655-2 (CD).

Sonny Criss(as),Cedar Walton(p),Tal Farlow(g),Bob Cranshaw(b),Lennie McBrowne(dr).
                                    NYC.August 18,1967
    Up,Up And Away   Prestige PR7530,PR7742
    This Is For Benny   -
    Sunny   - ,PR7742
    Paris Blues   -
    Willow Weep For Me   -
    Scrapple From The Apple   - ,Franklin Mint 72

All titles also on Prestige(J)SMJ6268,SMJ7491,VIJ4057,VDJ1654 (CD),VICJ23577 (CD).

Sonny Criss(as),Cedar Walton(p),Bob Cranshaw(b),Alan Dawson(dr).
                                    NYC.January 12,1968
    Somewhere My Love (Lara's
      Theme From "Dr. Zhivago") Prestige PR7558
    The Beat Goes On   - ,PR7742
    Georgia Rose   -
    Ode To Billy Joe   - ,PR7742
    Calidad   -
    Yesterdays   -

All titles also on Prestige(J)SMJ7507,VICJ23672 (CD).

Conte Candoli(tp),Dick Nash(tb),Ray Draper(tu),David Sheer(as),Sonny Criss(as,ss),Teddy
Edwards(ts),Pete Cristlieb(bars),Tommy Flanagan(p),Al McKibbon(b),Everett Brown(dr),Horace
Tapscott(arr,cond).   LA.May 8,1968
    Sonny's Dream   Prestige PR7576
    Sonny's Dream(alt.take)   Original Jazz Classics OJCCD707-2(CD)
(session cont. next page).

(session cont. from previous page):

The Golden Pearl	Prestige PR7576
The Golden Pearl(alt.take)	Original Jazz Classics OJCCD707-2(CD)
The Black Apostles	Prestige PR7576
Ballad For Samuel	-
Daughter Of Cochise	-
Sandy And Niles	-

All titles on PR7576 also on Prestige(J)SMJ7516,VICJ23673 (CD),Original Jazz Classics OJCCD707-2 (CD).

Sonny Criss(as),Eddie Green(p),Bob Cranshaw(b),Alan Dawson(dr).
NYC.July 2,1968

Misty Roses	Prestige PR7610
Eleanor Rigby	Prestige 45-703,PR7610,PR7742
Rockin' In Rhythm	- - -
The Masquerade Is Over	Prestige PR7610
When The Sun Comes Out	-
Sonnymoon For Two	-

All titles also on Prestige(J)SMJ7521,VICJ23674 (CD).

Sonny Criss(as),Hampton Hawes(p),Monty Budwig(b),Shelly Manne(dr).
LA.January 20,1969

I'll Catch The Sun	Prestige PR7628
I Thought About You	- ,Ace(E)RIVM002,RIVM002CD(CD)
California Screamin'	-
Cry Me A River	-
Don't Rain On My Parade	-
Blue Sunset	-

All titles also on Prestige(J)SMJ7526,SMJ6200,VIJC23675 (CD),Bellaphon(G)40130.

SONNY CRISS WITH THE GEORGES ARVANITAS TRIO:
Sonny Criss(as),Georges Arvanitas(p),Jacky Samson(b),Charles Saudrais(dr).
Live.Bologna,Italy.January 28,1974

Tin Tin Deo	Fresh Sound(Sp)FSR401
Lover Man	-
Sonny's Blues	-
Summertime	-
Sunny	-
Willow Weep For Me	-

All titles also on Fresh Sound(Sp)FSR-CD67 (CD),DIW(J)DIW333 (CD).
Note:Poss. two additional titles on the CD issue.

Sonny Criss(as),Dolo Coker(p),Ray Crawford(g),Larry Gales(b),Jimmie Smith(dr).
LA.February 24,1975

The Isle Of Celia	Muse MR5068
Blues In My Heart	-
Blues In My Heart(alt. take)	Muse MCD6015(CD),(J)CRCJ7015(CD)
This Is For Benny	Muse MR5068
All Night Long	-
Crisscraft	-

All titles also on MR5068 also on Muse MCD6015 (CD),(J)YQ7505,CRCJ7015 (CD),Stateside(J)J80174,Seven Seas(J)K22P6061.

Sonny Criss(as),Barry Harris(p),Leroy Vinnegar(b),Lennie McBrowne(dr).
LA.March 1,1975

(session cont. next page).

```
(session cont. from previous page):
        Angel Eyes                      Xanadu 105
        Tin Tin Deo                         -
        Jeannie's Knees                     -
        Saturday Morning                    - ,5001,(Eu)197.150
        My Heart Stood Still(no as)         -
        Until The Real
            Thing Comes Along              -
```

All titles also on Xanadu(J)JC7004,ULX83,YS7092,DIW(J)32DIW301 (CD),EPM(F)FDC5163 (CD).

Sonny Criss(as),Dolo Coker(p),Larry Gales(b),Jimmie Smith(dr).
                                        LA.October 20,1975
```
        All The Things You Are     Muse MR5089,MCD6015(CD),(J)CRCJ7015(CD)
        The Dreamer                         -
        El Tiante                           -
        My Ideal                            -
        Out Of Nowhere                      -
        Brother Can You Spare A Dime        -
        The First One                       -
```

All titles on Muse MR5089 also on Muse MCD5089 (CD),(F)900.326,(J)BRJ4522 (CD),Stateside
(J)IXJ80127,Seven Seas(J)K18P9171.

Paul Hubinon,Chuck Findley,Bud Brisbois(tp,flh),George Bohanon,Lew McCreary(btb),Vincent
DeRosa(frh),Sonny Criss(as),Buddy Collette(ts,fl),Bill Green(bassax,fl),Dorothy Ashby
(harp),Clarence McDonald(keyb),Lee Ritenour(g),Scott Edwards(b),James Gadson(dr),Eddie
Brown(perc),strings.   LA.c. 1976
```
        Cool Struttin'             Impulse ASD9312
        Memories(1)                Impulse 31004,ASD9312
        Sweet Summer Breeze        Impulse 31007,    -
```

-1.Add Melvin "Wah Wah" Watson (Ragin)(g).

Sonny Burke(keyb),Dennis Budimir(g),Chuck Domanico(b) replace McDonald,Ritenour,Edwards.
                                        LA.c. 1976
```
        The Way We Were            Impulse ASD9312
        Bumpin                     Impulse 31004,ASD9312
        That's The Way Of The World(1) Impulse ASD9312
        Blues For Willie           Impulse 31007,ASD9312
```

-1.Add Melvin "Wah Wah" Watson (Ragin)(g).

All titles on ASD9312 also on Impulse(J)YQ8511.

Oscar Brashear(tp),George Bohanon,Garnett Brown,Ray Jackson(tb),George Byron Thatcher(bt
Robert L. Watt,Alan Robinson,Barbara E. Korn(frh),Sonny Criss(as),Ernie Watts(ts),Patric
Rushen,Bill King,Sonny Burke(p),McKinley Jackson(clavinet),Lee Ritenour,Mitch Holder(g),
Chuck Domanico,Scott Edwards,Henry E. Davis(b),James Godson(dr),Eddie Brown,Esmond Edwar
(perc),strings,Viola Jackson(vcl).   LA/Burbank,Calif.c. 1977
```
        You've Lost That Lovin' Feelin'  Impulse AS9326
        Don't You Worry 'Bout A Thing       -
        You Are So Beautiful                -
        Turn Me Loose                       -
        Stolen Moments(1)                   -
        Have A Talk With God(vj)            -
        Midnight Mellow                     -
```

-1.Add Blue Mitchell(tp).

All titles also on Impulse(J)YX8502.

CHICO CRISTOBAL (French)

CHICO CRISTOBAL AND HIS BOOGIE WOOGIE BOYS:
Alex Caturegli(tp),Hubert Rostaing(cl),Chico Cristobal(as),Jean Tesse(ts),Paul Goudeau
(bars),Bernard Peiffer(p),Jean-Pierre Sasson(g),Lucien Simoens(b),Jerry Mengo(dr,arr).

		Paris.November 15,1946
ST1719	Frog-Frog Boogie	Blue Star(F)21
ST1720	Bobby Soxer's Boogie	Blue Star(F)20
ST1721	Cow Cow Boogie	Blue Star(F)6
ST1722	Boogie Woogie On The St.Louis Blues(1)(jv)	Blue Star(F)12

1.Add Jackie Vermont(vcl).

Note:Acc. to the personnel listed on Blue Star(F)12 - and Vermont's vocal - the issued
     version of master ST1722 may have been recorded at the December 1,1946 session.

Jackie Vermont(tp,vcl),Alex Caturegli(tp),Hubert Rostaing(cl),Chico Cristobal(as),Cléo
Plateaux(ts),Paul Goudeau(bars),Bernard Peiffer(p),Jean-Pierre Sasson(g),Lucien Simoens(b)
Armand Molinetti(arr),André Lafosse,Jerry Mengo(arr).

		Paris.December 1,1946
ST1781	Drum Boogie	Blue Star(F)20,127
ST1782	Gee!You Got Eyes Babe	Blue Star(F)12
ST1783	Blues In The Night(1)(jv)	Blue Star(F)21
ST1784	Vieux jazz	unissued

1.Vermont only (vcl).

CRISTO CRISOBAL HOT BAND:
omit Caturegli,Plateaux,Goudeau.

		Same date
ST1785	Tea For Two	Blue Star(F)6,Barclay(F)81004/05

FLAVIO CRIVELLI (Italian)
(section cont. next page).

See also GIANNI COSCIA.

Cesare Marchini -1(as,ts),Gianni Coscia -2(el-acc),Flavio Crivelli(p),Luciano Ciucci(b),
Giovanni Cellerino(dr).   Live."Louisiana Jazz Club",Genova,Italy.November 29/30,197
     Dindi(2)   Louisiana Jazz Club(I)LJR75
     Lover Man(1)   -
     Opus De Funk(1,2)   -

Dany Lamberti,Franco Astuti,Ugo Priarone(ts),Flavio Crivelli(p),Allessandro Armanino(g),
Luciano Ciucci(b),Gino Bocchino(dr).
                            Live."Louisiana Jazz Club",Genova,Italy.November 29/30,197
     Chase   Louisiana Jazz Club(I)LJR75
     Moanin'   -
     Richie's Dilemma   -

Note:The above LP issued as "Jazz From Louisiana Jazz Club Of Genoa".

HENRI CROLLA (French)

TRIO HENRI CROLLA:
Henri Crolla(g),rest unknown.   Paris. 1953
     Mon Homme   Odeon(F)282.753
     C'est Mon Gigolo   -

HENRI CROLLA - STEPHANE GRAPPELLI QUARTETTE:
Stéphane Grappelli(vln),Henri Crolla(g),Emmanuel Soudieux(b),Baptiste Mac Kac Reilles(dr
                            Paris.December 30,1954
     Have You Met Miss Jones?   Ducretet-Thomson(F)460V068
     Just Can't Be Love   -
     Alembert's   Ducretet-Thomson(F)255V005,460V068,Vega(F)30S805
                            Pathe(F)153-15917/19
     Mano(1)   Ducretet-Thomson(F)260V044,Pathé(F)153-15917/19

-1.Grappelli plays (p).

All titles also on Jazztime(F)251286-2 (CD).

Same.   Paris.March 3,1955
     Swing 39   Ducretet-Thomson(F)250V004,Vega(F)30S805,Jazztim
                            (F)794100-2(CD)
     Belleville   Ducretet-Thomson(F)250V004,Pathé(F)153-15917/19
     Manoir De Mes Rêves   - ,Vega(F)30S805
     Djangology   - ,460V068,Vega(F)30S805

All titles also on Telefunken(G)UX4641,Jazztime(F)251286-2 (CD).

HENRI CROLLA ET SON ENSEMBLE:
Maurice Meunier(cl,ts),Michel Hausser(vbs),George Arvanitas(p),Henri Crolla(g),Emmanuel
Soudieux(b),Jacques David(dr).   Paris.June 1955
     The Continental   Vega(F)V45P1519,V35M703
     If I Had You   -   -
     Alembert's   Vega(F)V45P1520,   -
     All The Things You Are   -   -
     These Foolish Things   -   -
     There's A Small Hotel   Vega(F)V35M703   -
     Lullaby Of Birdland   - ,860.102
     Body and Soul   -   -

- 419 -

HENRI CROLLA

Maurice Vanderschueren(p) replaces Arvanitas;omit Hausser.
                                    Paris.June 1955
        Tenderly   Vega(F)V45P1519,V35M711,860.102
        Yardbird Suite   Vega(F)V45P1520,   -
        Love For Sale   Vega(F)V35M711
        September Song   - ,860.102
        Out Of Nowhere   -
        Sweet Georgia Brown   - ,860.102
        Solitude   -   -

oss. Lalo Schifrin(p),Henri Crolla(g),Emmanuel Soudieux(b),Jacques David(dr).
                                    Paris. 1955
        Mon Homme   Vega(F)V45P1503
        C'est Mon Gigolo   -
        Stardust   - ,860.102
        Sonny Boy   -   -
        The Man I Love   -   -

imilar.   Paris.November 1955
        If I Loved You   Vega(F)V45P1564
        Begin The Beguine   - ,Vega(F)860.102
        Little White Lies   -
        I'm In The Mood For Love   -

imilar.   Paris.December 1955
        Have You Met Miss Jones Vega(F)V45P1575
        Quand Refleuriront Les Lilacs   -
        Je Charcher Aprés Titine   -
        Maitre Pathelin   -
        Ay Ay Ay   -
        I Only Have Eyes For You   -

ENRI CROLLA ET SON QUINTETTE:
ger Guérin(tp),Hubert Rostaing(cl),Martial Solal(p,arr),Henri Crolla(g),Emmanuel Sou-
eux(b),Christian Garros(dr).   Paris.October 1956
        Jeepers Creepers   Vega(F)V45P1730,Vega(F)860.102
        What's New   -
        Hallelujah   -
        Night And Day   - ,Vega(F)860.102

ENRI CROLLA ALL STARS:
bert Rostaing(cl),André Ekyan(as),Stéphane Grappelly(vln),Géo Daly(vbs),René Urtréger/
urice Vanderschueren(p),Henri Crolla(g),Emmanuel Soudieux(b),Pierre Lamarchand/Al Levitt
r).   Paris. 1958
        Minor Swing   Vega(F)V30S805
        Swing 39   -
        Manoir De Mes Rêves   -
        Swing From Paris   -
        Artillerie Lourde   -
        Nuages   -
        Djangology   -
        Anouman   -
        Swing 42   -
        Place De Brouckère   -

te:Additional recordings by this artist are not included.

NY CROMBIE (British)
ection cont. next page).

See also FLAMINGO ALL STARS.

TONY CROMBIE AND HIS ORCHESTRA:
Dizzy Reece,Les Condon(tp),Joe Temperley,Sammy Walker(ts),Lennie Dawes(bars),Harry South
(p),Ashley Kozak(b),Tony Crombie(dr).   Live.Royal Festival Hall,London.October 30,195
DR20021 Good Bait   Decca(E)LK4087
DR20022 Ahmed   -
DR20023 Compos Mentis   -
DR20024 Down Under   -

All titles also on London(Am)LL1185.

Add Annie Ross,Bobby Breen(vcl).   London.November 18,1954
DR19821 Perdido   Decca(E)F10454,DFE6247
DR19822 Stop It   Decca(E)F10424, -
DR19823 Love You Madly(ar)   Decca(E)F10454, -
DR19824 All Of Mee(bb)   Decca(E)F10424, -

Jimmy Deuchar,Les Condon(tp),Ken Wray(tb),Derek Humble(as),Don Rendell,Al Cornish(ts),
Ronnie Ross(bars),Damian Robinson(p),Lennie Bush(b),Tony Crombie(dr),Art Baxter(vcl).
                                   London.March 31,1955
DR20513 Baby Mine(ab)   Decca(E)DFE6281

Omit Baxter.   London.May 17,1955
DR20746 Flying Home   Decca(E)F10547,DFE6281
DR20747 Early One Morning   -   -
DR20748 Tiptoe Through The Tulips Decca(E)DFE6281

Same.   London.July 7,1955
DR20890 Flying Hickory   Decca(E)F10592
DR20891 String Of Pearls   -

Add Annie Ross(vcl).   London.September 28,1955
DR21141 I Want You To Be My Baby Decca(E)F10637
DR21142 Hawk Eye   unissued
DR21143 Three Little Words   Decca(E)F10637

Jimmy Deuchar(tp),Derek Humble(cl,as),Tubby Hayes,Ronnie Scott(ts),Ronnie Ross(bars),Sta
Tracey(p),Lennie Bush(b),Tony Crombie(dr).   London.April 26,1956
        Wrong   unissued
        Danny's Hideaway   -
        Just As You Are   -
        My One Sin   -
        Some Folks Do   -
        I'd Love To Take
           You Home With Me Baby   -

Note:Since Crombie does not recall this - or the April 30,1956 - session (though he play
    with these musicians in the mid-1950's), he was prob. not leader on these dates.

Derek Humble(ts),Tubby Hayes,Ronnie Scott,Bob Efford(ts),Stan Tracey(p),Dave Goldberg(g)
Lennie Bush(b),Tony Crombie(dr).   London.April 30,1956
        Sometimes I Wonder   unissued
        Raindrops   -
        My Heart Jumps   -
        I Think Of You   -
        Something Tells Me   -
        My One And Only Love   -

TONY CROMBIE

Ronnie Scott(ts),Harry Klein(bars),Terry Shannon(p),Johnny Hawksworth(b),Tony Crombie(dr).
London.July 31,1956

Unknown titles	Tempo(E)unissued

Les Condon,Stan Roderick(tp),Bob Burns(as),Ronnie Scott(ts),Tubby Hayes(bars),Norman Sten-
falt(p),Lennie Bush(b),Tony Crombie(dr,arr). London.June 18,1958

Ninth Man	Columbia(E)SEG7918,33SX1119
Beryl's Bounce	Columbia(E)33SX1119
Panic Stations	-
Shapes	-
Copy-Cats	-

Jimmy Watson(tp),Tommy Whittle(ts) replace Roderick,Scott.
London.July 23,1958

St. James Infirmary	Columbia(E)SEG7918,33SX1119	
I'll Close My Eyes	-	-
Small Talk	Columbia(E)33SX1119	
Duke's Joke	-	
Invitation(1)	-	

1.Tubby Hayes(vbs),p,b,dr only.

Tubby Hayes(vbs),Tony Crombie(p),Jack Fallon(b).
London.July 30,1958

Stompin' At The Savoy	Columbia(E)SEG7918,33SX1119
Perpetual Lover	Columbia(E)33SX1119

ll titles on SEG7918 also on Columbia(E)ESG7753.
ll titles on 33SX1119 also on Columbia(E)33SCX3262,Renaissance(E)REN002.

TONY CROMBIE ORCHESTRA/JAZZ INC.:
Leon Calvert,Les Condon(tp),Al Newman(cl,as),Bobby Wellins(ts),Harry Klein(bars),Stan
Tracey(p,arr),Kenny Napper(b,arr),Tony Crombie(dr,arr).
London.January 6,1960

OG4795	Caravan	Tempo(E)TAP30
OG4796	Boo-Bah	-
OG4797	Lullaby	-
OG4798	Reelin'	-
OG4799	Li'l Ol' Pottsville	-
OG4800	Jamba	-
OG4801	I Let A Song Go Out Of My Heart	-
OG4802	Summertime	-

Bert Ezzard,Les Condon,Duncan Campbell,Bobby Pratt(tp),Don Lusher,George Chisholm,Harry
Roche,Ken Goldie(tb),Jimmy Buck Jr.(frh),Johnny Scott(fl),Ronnie Chamberlain,Les Gilbert
(as),Keith Bird(ts,cl),Victor Feldman(vbs,mar),Stan Tracey(p),Dave Goldberg/Jack Llewelyn
(g),Kenny Napper(b),Tony Crombie(dr),Jock Cummings(tymp,chimes).
London.July 5-8,1960

27260	So Rare	Decca(E)SKL4114
27261	Cocktails For Two	-
27262	Embraceable You	-
27263	I've Got The World On A String	-
27264	Summertime	-
27265	I Should Care	-
27266	Tulip Or Turnip	-
27267	Wrap Your Troubles In Dreams	-
27268	Percussion Staccato	-
27269	You Are My Lucky Star	-
27270	So Near So Far	-
27271	For You Alone	-

Harold McNair(as,fl),Tommy Whittle(ts),Gordon Beck(p,hsc),Malcolm Cecil(b),Tony Crombie
(dr).   London.August 1961
      Gut Bucket   Ember(E)JBS706,EMB3336
      Just Like Old Times   -   -
      Keep It Light   Ember(E)EMB3336
      Look For The Real Thing   -
      Flute Salad(1)   -
      Brazilia   -
      Penthouse Party   -
      Journey's End   -

-1.Whittle plays (bcl).

Harold McNair(as,fl),Bobby Wellins(ts),Gordon Beck(p),Malcolm Cecil(b),Tony Crombie(dr).
                                   London.August 1961
      Yodelin'   Ember(E)JBS706,EMB3336
      Stop That Man   Ember(E)EMB3336
      Round The 'Ouses   -
      The Gang-Busters   -

Note:Additional recordings by this artist are not included.

AUSTIN CROMER

(vcl) acc. by Hubert Laws(fl,g),Chick Corea(p),Richard Davis(b),Bruno Carr(dr).
                                   NYC.August 12,1964
8069 As Long As He Needs Me   Atlantic LP8107
8070 These Foolish Things   unissued
8071 The More I See You   Atlantic LP8107
8072 A Tree In The Meadow   -
8073 Laura   -
8074 This Love Of Mine   -
8076 I Wish I Knew   -
8077 There Is No Greater Love   -
8078 As Time Goes By   unissued

DICK CROOK

SHEDONI:
Chip Dabney(ss,ts,b,ldr),James Balley -1(ss,ts),Dick Crook(p,ldr),Andrew Stern -1(g),Dic
Dworkin -1(dr).
                                   San Francisco.November 1979
      Sun: Polar Bear PB1
         See Space Suite
         Gails Dance
         Nimbus
         Marigold
      Moon(1):   -
         Blew Meanie
         Nightown Rhythm
         Offering

BING CROSBY

See also LOUIS ARMSTRONG,COUNT BASIE,LES BROWN,NAT COLE,DUKE ELLINGTON.
(section cont. next page).

(vcl) acc. by WOODY HERMAN'S WOODCHOPPERS:
Cappy Lewis(tp),Neal Reid(tb),Woody Herman(cl,vcl),Tommy Linehan(p),Hy White(g),Walter
Yoder(b),Frank Carlson(dr).   LA.January 18,1942
DLA2827-A I Want My Mama(bc,wh)   Decca 18316,DL8143,DL8493,Brunswick(E)03971,
                                         LAT8228,LAT8579,Ace Of Hearts(E)AH24,AH31,
                                         Coral(E)CPS105
DLA2828-A Deep In The Heart Of Texas Decca 4162,29319,ED1700,DL9067,Brunswick(E)03971,
                                         LAT8055,MCA GRP16032(CD),Phontastic(Sd)
                                         PHONTCD7670(CD)
DLA2829-A I'm Thinking
          Tonight Of Blues Eyes   Decca 18316,18769,Brunswick(E)03456

(vcl) acc. by BOB CROSBY'S ORCHESTRA:
Yank Lawson,Lyman Vunk,Max Herman(tp),Elmer Smithers,Floyd O'Brien,Buddy Morrow(tb),Matty
Matlock(cl),Art Mendelsohn,Arthur Rando(as),Gil Rodin,Eddie Miller(ts),Jess Stacy(p),Nappy
Lamare(g),Bob Haggart(b),Ray Bauduc(dr).   LA.May 25,1942
DLA2989-B Lazy   Decca 18427,91620,DL8144,DL34002,Brunswick
                                         (E)03385,Ace Of Hearts(E)AH17
DLA2990-A Let's Start
          The New Year Right   Decca 18429,DL5092,Brunswick(E)03384,LA8592
DLA2990-B Let's Start
          The New Year Right   Decca 23823
DLA2991-A I've Got Plenty
          To Be Thankful For   Decca 18426,23823,DL5092,Brunswick(E)03383,LA8592

All titles - except master DLA2990-B - also on Decca DL4256,Brunswick(E)BING-7.

Same.   LA.May 27,1942
DLA2996-A I'll Capture Your
          Heart(1)(bc,fa,ml)   Decca 18427,23823,DL4256,DL5092,Brunswick(E)03383,
                                         LA8592,BING-7

DLA2998-A When My Dream
          Boat Comes Home(2)   Decca 18371,27505,DL5323,DL8493,(Au)Y5812,Brunsw.
                                         (E)04113,LA8579,LAT8228,Ace Of Heart(E)AH31,
                                         Coral(E)CPS105,Axis(Au)CDAX701594(CD),MCA
                                         GRP16032(CD)
DLA2999-A Walkin' The Floor Over You(2) Decca 18371,18770,23970,27505,DL5063,DL5323,DL8076
                                         DL8493,DL9067,(Au)Y5812,Brunswick(E)04360,
                                         LA8579,LAT8055,LAT8228,Ace Of Heart(E)AH31,
                                         Axis(Au)CDAX701594(CD),Coral(E)CPS105

-1.Add Fred Astaire,Margaret Lenhart(vcl).
-2.Acc. by BOB CROSBY'S BOB CATS:Lawson(tp),O'Brien(tb),Matlock(cl),Miller(ts),p,g,b,dr.

Note:Masters DLA2997 and DLA3000 are Fred Astaire items.

(vcl) acc. by LOUIS JORDAN AND HIS BAND/TYMPANI FIVE:
Eddie Roane(tp,),Louis Jordan(as,vcl),Arnold Thomas(p),Al Morgan(b),Slick Jones(dr).
                                      LA.July 26,1944
L3477-A My Baby Said Yes(1)   Decca 23417,(Au)Y5948,MCA(E)MCL1807,Brunswick(E)
                                         03744,Queen(I)Q-058
L3478-A My Baby Said Yes   MCA GRP16032(CD)
L3479-A Your Socks Don't Match   Decca 23417,(Au)Y6085,MCA GRP16032(CD),(E)MCL1807,
                                         Brunswick(E)03744,Queen(I)Q-058

-1.Vocal by Crosby,Jordan.

All itles also on Bear Family(G)BCD15557-3 (CD).

(vcl) acc. by EDDIE HEYWOOD'S ORCHESTRA:
Harry "Parr" Jones(tp),Vic Dickenson,Henry Coker(tb),Lem Davis(as),Eddie Heywood(p),Ernie
Shepard(b),William Purnell(dr).   LA.Augest 9,1945
L3910-A Save Your Sorrows For Tomorrow Decca 24595,Brunswick(E)04748,(G)82621
L3911-A Baby Won't You Please Come Home Decca 23636,DL8142,(Au)Y6145,Brunswick(E)04113,Ace
                                            Of Hearts(E)AH24

Same.   LA.August 17,1945
L3918-A That Little Dream Got Nowhere   Decca 23636,Brunswick(E)04746
L3919   Who's Sorry Now   unissued

Same.   LA.September 5,1945
L3949-A I've Found A New Baby   Decca 23530,Brunswick(E)04117
L3950-A Who's Sorry Now   - ,DL8142,Brunswick(E)03875,04117,Ace Of
                                            Hearts(E)AH24

(vcl) acc. by EDDIE CONDON AND HIS ORCHESTRA:
Wild Bill Davison(cnt),Brad Gowans(vtb),Joe Dixon(cl),Bud Freeman(cl),Gene Schroeder -1,
Joe Sullivan -2,Joe Bushkin -3(p),Eddie Condon(g),Bob Haggart(b),George Wettling(dr).
                                        NYC.January 16,1946
W73278 Blue And Brokenhearted(1)   Decca 24114,DL8493,(Au)Y6085,Brunswick(E)04119,
                                            LAT8228,Ace Of Heart(E)AH31,Coral(E)CPS105,
                                            Axis(Au)CDAX701594(CD),MCA GRP16032(CD)
W73279 After You've Gone(2)   Decca 24114,DL8493,(Au)Y6085(?),Y73269,Brunswick
                                            (E)04119,LAT8228,Ace Of Heart(E)AH31,Coral(E)
                                            CPS105,Axis(Au)CDAX701594(CD),MCA GRP16032
                                            (CD)
W73279 After You've Gone(2)(alt.take)   MCA GRP16032(CD)
W73280 Personality(3)   Decca 18790,(Au)Y5956,Brunswick(E)05016,Odeon(Arg)
                                            28631,GRP16032(CD)

(vcl) acc. by LIONEL HAMPTON ORCHESTRA:
Wendell Culley,Joe Morris,Dave Page,Lammar Wright,Jr.,Jimmy Nottingham(tp),Andrew Penn,
Booty Wood,James Wormick,Al Hayes(tb),Ben Kynard,Bobby Plater(as),Johnny Griffin,Arnett
Cobb(ts),Charlie Fowlkes(bars),Lionel Hampton(p,vbs,vcl),Milt Buckner(p),Billy Mackel(g),
Charlie Harris,Ted Sinclair(b),George Jenkins(dr).
                                        NYC.January 21,1946
73287   Pinetops Boogie Woogie   Decca 23843
73288   On The Sunny Side
            Of The Street(1)   -

-1.Vocal by Crosby,Hampton.

Both titles also on Brunswick(E)04120,(G)82539,Coral(G)COPS7186(?),MCA GRP16032 (CD).

BING CROSBY AND THE CHICKADEES(vcl) acc. by BOB CROSBY'S BOB CATS:
No details.   LA.December 17,1946
L4337-A That's How Much I Love You   Decca 23840,(Au)Y6011,Brunswick(E)04131
L4338-A Rose Of Santa Rosa   - ,Brunswick(E)04131

(vcl) acc. by BOB HAGGART BAND:
Yank Lawson(tp),Vernon Brown(tb),Hank D'Amico(cl),Art Drelinger(ts),Bubby Weed(p),Perry
Botkin(g),Bob Haggart(b),George Wettling(dr),The Jesters(vcl).
                                        NYC.May 8,1947
73909   A Feudin' And A Fightin'   Decca 23975,Brunswick(E)04364
73910   Goodbye My Love,Goodbye   - ,DL8493,Brunswick(E)03813,LAT8228,Cora
                                            (E)CPS105

Both titles also on Brunswick(E)LA8578.

(vcl) acc. by BOB HAGGART ORCHESTRA:
No details.   NYC.April 8,1950
76113 The Dixieland Band   Decca 27013,Coral(E)CPS105
76114 Jamboree Jones   -   -

(vcl) acc. by THE FIREHOUSE FIVE PLUS TWO:
No details.   Prob. Broadcast.LA. 1950's
       Yes Sir,That's My Baby"   Magic(E)AWE3

(vcl) acc. by JOHN SCOTT TROTTER'S DIXIELAND BAND:
Incl. Red Nichols -1(cnt).   NYC.February 14,1952
L6648 Ida Sweet As Apple Cider(1)   Decca DL8493,Coral(E)CPS105
L6649 Nobody's Sweetheart

(vcl) acc. by BUDDY BREGMAN ORCHESTRA:
Conrad Gozzo,Pete Candoli,Harry Edison,Maynard Ferguson(tp),Francis Howard,Milt Bernhart,
Lloyd Ulyate,George Roberts(tb),Bud Shank,Maurice Stein(as),Ted Nash,Bob Cooper(ts),Chuck
Gentry(bars),Paul Smith(p),Barney Kessel(g),Alvin Stoller(dr),woodwinds,strings,Buddy
Bregman(arr,cond).   LA.June 11,1956
20155-11 The Blue Room   Verve EPV5021,MGV2020
20156-8 Jeepers Creepers   Verve EPV5022,   - ,(Sd)VEP5010,HMV(E)7EG8405
20157-4 I've Got Five Dollars   Verve 10025,EPV5022,MGV2020,Sd)VEP5009,HMV(E)
                                        7EG8475
20158-1 'Deed I Do   Verve EPV5020,MGV2020,(Sd)VEP5010,HMV(E)7EG8475
20159-3 The Song Is You   -   -
20160-4 Nice Work If You Can Get It Verve EPV5022,   - ,(Sd)VEP5009,HMV(E)7EG8405

Same.   LA.June 12,1956
20161-3 They All Laughed   Verve EPV5021,MGV2020,(Sd)VEP5009,HMV(E)7EG8475
20162-4 Heat Wave   Verve 10089,EPV5020,MGV2020,HMV(E)7EG8405
20163-3 September In the Rain   - ,EPV5022,   - ,(Sd)VEP5010
20164-5 Cheek To Cheek   Verve EPV5021,MGV2020,(F)1625.061,   - ,HMV(E)
                                        7EG8405
20165-2 Have You Met Miss Jones   Verve EPV5021,MGV2020,(Sd)VEP5009
20166-5 Mountain Greenery   Verve 10025,EPV5020,MGV2020,HMV(E)7EG8475

All titles on MGV2020 also on Verve(J)MV2663,HMV(E)CLP1088.

(vcl) acc. by BOB SCOBEY AND HIS BAND:
Bob Scobey,Frank Beach(tp),Abe Lincoln(tb),Matty Matlock(cl),Dave Harris(ts),Ralph Sutton
(p),Clancy Hayes(g),Red Callender(b),Nick Fatool(dr).
                                     LA.February 19,1957
H2JB0321 Dream A Little Dream Of Me RCA-Victor EPC1473-2,LPM1473
H2JB0322 Some Sunny Day   -   -
H2JB0323 I'm Gonna Sit Right Down
           And Write Myself A Letter RCA-Victor EPC1473-1,   -
H2JB0324 Tell Me   RCA-Victor EPC1473-3,   -
H2JB0325 Exactly Like You   RCA-Victor EPC1473-1,   -
H2JB0326 Let a Smile Be Your Umbrella -   -

Same.   LA.February 29,1957
H2JB0327 Mama Loves Papa   RCA-Victor EPC1473-3,LPM1473
H2JB0328 Down Among The Sheltering Palms -   -
H2JB0329 Last Night On The Back Porch RCA-Victor EPC1473-2,   -
H2JB0330 Along The Way To Waikiki   RCA-Victor EPC1473-1,   -
H2JB0331 Whispering   RCA-Victor EPC1473-2,   -
H2JB0332 Mack The Knife   RCA-Victor EPC1473-3,   -

All titles on LPM1473 also on RCA(E)RD27032,(SA)33.121,JVC(J)PG62.

(vcl) acc. by BUDDY COLE AND HIS TRIO:
Buddy Cole(p),unknown b,dr.   LA.March 14,1957
L9926 When I Take My Sugar To Tea   Decca DL8575
L9927 Between The Devil
          And The Deep Blue Sea   -
L9936 Alabamy Bound   -
L9937 Georgia On My Mind   -
L9938 I'm Confessin'   -
L9939 If I Could Be With You   -
L9940 Avalon   -
L9941 Chinatown,My Chinatown   -
L9942 You're Drivin Me Crazy   -
L9943 On The Alamo   -
L9944 Chicago   -
L9945 Softly As In A Morning Sunrise   -

All titles also on Decca DL4415,MCA(J)MCA3120,Memoir(E)MOIR202.

Note:Additional recordings by this artist are not included.

BOB CROSBY

See also FRED ASTAIRE,BING CROSBY,DIXIELAND BIG BAND.

BOB CROSBY AND HIS ORCHESTRA:
Max Herman,Yank Lawson,Lyman Vunk(tp),Buddy Morrow,Floyd O'Brien,Elmer Smithers(tb),Matty
Matlock(cl,arr),Arthur Rando,Art Mendelsohn(as),Eddie Miller(ts,cl,vcl),Gil Rodin(ts),Jess
Stacy(p),Nappy Lamare(g,vcl),Bob Haggart(b,arr),Ray Bauduc(dr),Bob Crosby,Bob-O-Links(vcl)
Phil Moore(arr).   LA.January 20,1942
DLA2834-A Vultee Special   Decca 4397,Decca(E)F8302,Ace Of Heart(E)AH29,Joker
                                         (I)SM3243,Franklin Mint 95
DLA2835-B Russian Sailors Dance(bol) Decca 4397,(E)F8302,Bandstand BS7121,Swingfan
                                         LP1016,Joker(I)SM3243,Boogie Woogie LP1016(?)
DLA2836-A A Zoot Suit(nl)   Decca 4169,Decca(E)F8158
DLA2837-A Barrelhouse Bessie
          From Basin Street(em)   - ,Brunswick(E)04079
DLA2838-A Brass Boogie,I   Decca 18359,(E)F8444,MCA-Coral(G)COPS6845,6.28197
DLA2839-A Brass Boogie,II   -   -   -   -

All titles also on Ajaz LP402.

Same.   LA.January 27,1942
DLA2851-A Sugar Foot Stomp   Decca 4390,Coral CRL57089,(E)LVA9045,(G)EPC94099,
                                         Brunswick(E)03940,Festival(Au)C12-1302
DLA2852-A King Porter Stomp   Decca 4390,Brunswick(E)03940,Swingfan LP1016,
                                         Sounds Of Swing LP109,Boogie Woogie LP1016(?)
DLA2853-A Jimtown Blues   Decca 25475,GRD615-2(CD),Brunswick(E)04079,Coral
                                         EC81003,(G)EPC94039,Bandstand BS7121,Joker(I)
                                         SM4243
DLA2854-A The Eccentric Rag   Coral CRL57089,(E)LVA9045,(G)EPC94099
DLA2855-A Milenberg Joys   Decca 25293,GRD615-2(CD),Brunswick(E)03975,Joker
                                         (I)SM4243
DLA2856-A Original Dixieland One Step Decca 25475,Brunswick(E)04398,Coral EC81003,
                                         CRL57089,(E)LVA9045,(G)EPC94039,Bandstand
                                         BS7121

All titles - except "Eccentric Rag" - also on Ajaz LP402.

BOB CROSBY'S BOB CATS:
Yank Lawson(tp),Floyd O'Brien(tb),Matty Matlock(cl),Eddie Miller(ts,vcl),Jess Stacy(p),
Nappy Lamare(g,vcl),Bob Haggart(b),Ray Bauduc(dr).
LA.January 29,1942
DLA2867-A That Da Da Strain   Decca 25293,Brunswick(E)03975,Swaggie(Au)S1288,
                                        MCA(E)MCFM2695,Joker(I)SM3243,Ajaz LP402
DLA2868-A Sweethearts On Parade   Decca 18355,10017,Brunswick(E)04291,Ajaz LP402
DLA2869-A It's A Long Way to Tipperary   -   -   - ,MCA-Coral(G)
                                        COPS6845,6.28197,Ajaz LP402
DLA2870-A Tin Roof Blues   Coral CRL57089,(E)LVA9045,(G)EPC94099,Brunswick
                                        (E)04003,Swaggie(Au)S1288,Affinity(E)AFS1014,
                                        Ajaz LP423

Same.   LA.February 5,1942
DLA2885-A Way Down Yonder
          In New Orleans(nl,em)   Decca 4403,(Au)Y6037,Brunswick(E)04003,Swaggie(Au)
                                        S1245
DLA2886-A You'll Be Sorry(bc)   Decca 18373,10038,Brunswick(E)03723
DLA2887-A Tears On My Pillow(bc)   -   -
DLA2888-A I'll Be True
          To The One I Love(bc)   Decca 4357

All titles also on Ajaz LP423.

BOB CROSBY AND HIS ORCHESTRA:
Max Herman,Yank Lawson,Lyman Vunk(tp),Buddy Morrow,Floyd O'Brien,Elmer Smithers(tb),Matty
Matlock(cl,arr),Arthur Rando,Art Mendelsohn(as),Eddie Miller(ts,cl,vcl),Gil Rodin(ts),Jess
Stacy(p),Nappy Lamare(g,vcl),Bob Haggart(b,arr),Ray Bauduc(dr),Bob Crosby(vcl),Phil Moore
(arr).   LA.February 17,1942
DLA2907-A Black Zephyr   Decca 4415,Brunswick(E)03664,Sounds Of Swing LP109
                                        Franklin Mint BBE86
DLA2908-A Blue Surreal   Decca 4415,Brunswick(E)03664,Sounds Of Swing LP109
DLA2909-A Chain Gang   Decca 15064,29236,GRD615-2(CD),MCA MCA2-4083,Sound
                                        Of Swing LP109,Time-Life STBB14
DLA2910-A Ec-Stacy   Decca 15064,29236,Ace Of Heart(E)AH29

All titles also on Ajaz LP423,MCA(E)MCFM2578.

Add Muriel Lane(vcl).   LA.March 3,1942
DLA2928-A Poor You(1)(bc)   Decca 4316,(E)F8177
DLA2929-A I'll Keep The
          Lovelight Burning(1)(bc)   Decca 4290,25254
DLA2930-A Don't Sit Under
          The Apple Tree(1)(bc)   - ,(E)F8158
DLA2931-A Last Call For Love(1)(bc) Decca 4316,(E)F8177
DLA2932-A Dear Old Donegal(ml)   Decca 4305

-1.Crosby(vcl) acc. by unknown vcl-quartet.

All titles also on Ajaz LP423.

Lyn Wilde,Lee Wilde (The Wilde Twins)(vcl) replace Lane.
                                     Broadcast."Casa Manana",Culver City,Calif.May 23,1942
          Smokey Mary   Sunbeam SB229,Fanfare 6-106,Jasmine(E)JASM2512,
                                        Jazz Connoisseur(E)JC74
          Jersey Bounce   Sumbeam SB229
          Brass Boogie   - ,Jazz Connoisseur(E)JC74,Alamac
                                        QSR2403
          Blue Surreal   Alamac QSR2403

Note:Jazz Connoisseur(E)JC74 is a cassete tape issue.

Similar.   California.Spring/summer 1942
    Skylark
    Poor You(1)(bc)
    Last Call For Love(1)(bc)
    Don't Sit Under
      The Apple Tree(1)(bc)
    Barrelhouse Bessie
      From Basin Street(em)   Hindsight HSR192
    I'll Keep The Lovelight Burning
    Arthur Murray Taught
      Me Dancing In A Hurry
    I Fell In Love With
      The Leader Of The Band
    Somebody Nobody Loves
    I Remember You
    I've Got A Gal In Kalamazoo
    Jingle,Jingle,Jingle
    South Wind
    Lazy
    Easy To Dance With
    Knock Me A Kiss
    Hello Mom
    Don't Get Around Much Anymore   Hindsight HSR192
    Dearly Beloved
    Where Do We Go From Here   Hindsight HSR192
    I'm Gonna Move
      To The Outskirts Of Town(nl)   -
    Twilight Till Dawn
    The Song Is You
    Sugar Foot Stomp

-1.Crosby(vcl) acc. by unknown vcl-quartet.

Note:The above titles are from Standard Transcriptions (X-116,X-120,X-121,X-122).

Similar.   California.Spring/summer 1942
    Dear Old Donegal
    Mexicali Rose   Hindsight HSR192
    This Love Of Mine(bc)   -
    Just A Dream(em)   -
    Take It Easy
    Believe Me If All Those
      Endearing Young Charms
    Boogie Woogie Maxixe
    Two In Love
    Catalina Jump   Hindsight HSR192,Jazum 5
    Until I Live Again
    The Shrine Of St. Cecelia
    Black Zephyr
    Two Timin' Gal
    Blue Surreal
    Fighting Sons Of The Navy Blue
    I'm Just A Mile
      From Treasury Isle
    Marcheta   Hindsight HSR192,Jazum 5
    The Night Of My Life
    Hey Mabel!
    Dreamsville Ohio
    Swingin' On Nothin'   Hindsight HSR192
    Tell On A Star
(session cont. next page).

(session cont. from previous page):
        Angel Beware
        Vultee Special
        Russian Sailor Dance
        Love Turns Winter Into Spring
        A Zoot Suit(nl)   Hindsight HSR192
        Kiss Me Godnight For Tomorrow
        Livin',Lovin',Laughin'
        Mary
        Somewhere,Sometime
        The Memory Of This Dance
        AsWe Walk In The Sunset
        String Of Pearls   Jazum 5
        We're Riding For Uncle Sammy Now
        Soft Jive   Hindsight HSR192
        Yank's Lament
        Mirage   Hindsight HSR192
        Russian Winter
        I Left Me Heart At
            The Stagedoor Canteen
        When You Think Of Lovin' Baby,
            Think Of Me(bc,wt)
        Love Is A Song

Note:The above titles are from Standard Transcriptions (P-173,P-186,P-187,P-191,P-193,
    P-197 and - reissues on - Z-236).

Similar.   California.Spring/summer 1942
        Boogie Woogie Maxixe   Jazum 5
        Vultee Special   -
        Yank's Lament   -,Hindsight HSR192

Note:The above titles are from Standard Transcriptions (Z-236) - but may be the same ver-
    sions as listed earlier.

Max Herman,Yank Lawson,Lyman Vunk(tp),Pete Carpenter,Floyd O'Brien,Bruce Squires(tb),Matty
Matlock(cl,vcl),Arthur Rando(as),Ted Klein(bars,as),Eddie Miller(ts,cl,vcl),Gil Rodin(ts),
Jess Stacy(p),Nappy Lamare(g),Bob Haggart(b,arr),Ray Bauduc(dr),Bob Crosby,Lyn Wilde,Lee
Wilde (The Wilde Twins)(vcl),Billy May,Axel Stordahl(arr).
                                           LA.July 13,1942
L3090-A The Marine's Hymn   Decca 4385,25254,Franklin Mint BBE85
L3091-A Anchor's Aweigh   Decca 4395,MCA-Coral(G)6.22245
L3092-A Over There   Decca 4368,Phontastic(Sd)PHONTCD7670(CD)
L3093-A When You Think Of Lovin',Baby,
            Think Of Me(bc,wt,band-vcl)   Decca 4357

Same.   LA.July 19,1942
L3109-A When Do We Go From Here   Decca 4385
L3110-A The Caissons Go Rolling Along   Decca 4395
L3111-A Semper Paratus   Decca 4374

Same.   LA.July 20,1942
L3112-A Smile,Smile,Smile
            (Pack Up Your Troubles)(bc)   Decca 4368
L3113-A Army Air Corps Song(bc)   Decca 4374,25254

Similar.   LA.August 1942
        Big Noise From Winnetka(bc,wt)

Note:The above titles is from the "Reveille With Beverly" film soundtrack.

Add Judy Garland(vcl).   LA. 1942
        When You Think Of Lovin',
            Baby,Think Of Me(jg)   Caliban 6038
        Unknown title(jg)
        Paradise

Note:The above titles are from the "Presenting Lily Mars" film soundtrack.

Yank Lawson,Lyman Vunk,Johnny Best(tp),Floyd O'Brien,Bob Logan,Blaise Touri(tb),Matty Mat-
lock(cl,vcl,arr),Arthur Rando,Ted Klein(as),Eddie Miller(ts,cl,vcl),Bob Mario(bars),Jess
Stacy(p),Nappy Lamare(g,vcl),Bob Haggart(b,arr),Cody Sandifer(dr),Bob Crosby(vcl),Billy
May(arr).   Broadcast.Williamsport,Pennsylvania.December 3,1942
        King Porter Stomp   Sunbeam SB229
        It's A Long Way To Tipperary(1)   - ,Fanfare 6-106,Jasmine(E)JASM2512
        Paradise   -
        One O'Clock Jump   -
        Diga Diga Do   Fanfare 6-106,Jasmine(E)JASM2512,Alamac QSR2403

-1.Played by BOB CROSBY'S BOB CATS.

Note:The above titles are from AFRS "Spotlight Bands" transcription (No.64).
     "Diga Diga Doo" may be from another broadcast; Fanfare 6-106 and JASM2512 also incl.
     a closing theme ("Summertime") which prob. is from another date.

Same.   Broadcast(?).Unknown location.January 1943
        Unknown titles

Note:The above titles are from AFRS "Spotlight Bands" transcription (no.107).

Harry Uhlman(tb) prob. replaces Touri;add Virginia O'Brien,Gloria DeHaven,June Allyson
(vcl).   LA.April 1943
        In A Little
            Spanish Town(vob,gdh,ja)   Joyce LP3008,Hollywood Soundstage LP409

Note:The above title is from the "Thousands Cheer" film soundtrack.

Omit O'Brien,DeHaven,Allyson.   Broadcast.LA.July 18,1943
        What's The Good
            Word,Mr. Bluebird(bc)   V-Disc 36

Note:The above title is from NBC's "Old Gold" program.

Add Joy Hodges,The Pied Pipers(vcl).   Broadcast.San Francisco.August 28,1943
        Theme
        They're Either Too
            Young Or Too Old(bc,pp)
        Sugar
        Sunday,Monday Or Always(bc,pp)
        Somebody Loves Me(bc)
        I Heard You Cried
            Last Night(bc,pp)
        Get On Board Little Children(pp)
        Two O'Clock Jump   Golden Era LP15009

Note:The above titles are from AFRS "Spotlight Bands" transcription (No.294).

Similar.   LA.February 1944
        I'll Be Around(bc,pp)
        Cherry
        Red Grow The Roses(bc,pp)
(session cont. next page).

session cont. from previous page):
```
     Poinciana
     G.I. Jive(bc,pp)
     You Forgot About Me(bc,pp)
     As Long As I Live
     Goody Goody(bc,pp)
     Star Eyes(bc,pp)
     Rose Of Rio Grande            Golden Era LP15009
```

ote:The above titles are from AFRS "Downbeat" transcription (No.71).

imilar.   LA.February 1944
```
     Jazz Me Blues
     One O'Clock Jump
     Who's Sorry Now
```

ote:The above titles are from AFRS "Jubilee" transcription (No.70).

imilar.   Prob. LA. 1944
```
     Summertime (Theme)
     Do Nothin' Till You Hear From Me
     Rose Of Rio Grande
     Besame Mucho(pp)
     Take It Easy
     Lady Be Good(pp)
     Pavanne
     It's Love,Love,Love(pp)
     Snoqualomie Joe(?)(pp)
     Sweet Lorraine(pp)
     Goodnight Wherever You Are(pp)
```

te:The above titles are from AFRS "Basic Music Library" transcript. (P-95,P-102,P-117).

cl. Billy May(tp,arr),Steady Nelson,Phil Stephens,John Martel(tp),Matty Matlock(cl,arr),
b Poland(ts),Stan Wrightsman(p),Nappy Lamare(g,vcl),Elmer Snyder(b),Nick Fatool(dr),Bob
osby,Patty Long,The Pied Pipers(vcl).
                          Broadcast."Casa Manana",Culver City,Calif.April 7,1944
```
     No Love,No Nothing(pl,bc)
     I've Heard That Song Before
     It's Love,Love,Love(pp)
     You're Mine You(pl)
     Take It Easy(bc)
     I'll Get By
     A Lovely Way To Spend An Evening
     Darktown Strutters' Ball
     The Hour Of Parting
```

me.   Broadcast."Casa Manana",Culver City,Calif.April 8,1944
```
     San Fernando Valley(bc,band-vcl)
     No Love,No Nothing(pl,bc)
     I've Heard That Song Before(nl)
     It's Love,Love,Love(pp(?))
     You're Mine You(pl)
     Take It Easy(bc)
     I'll Get By
     Darktown Strutters' Ball
     Alexander's Ragtime Band
     It's Only A Paper Moon
```

te:The above titles are from AFRS "One Night Stand" trancription (No.203).

Similar.   NYC.April-June 1944
        Unknown titles

Note:The above titles are from AFRS "Downbeat" transcriptions (No.80,88,92)

Similar.   Broadcast."Casa Manana",Culver City,Calif.May 14,1944
        King Porter Stom
        Echoes Of Harlem
        Pavanne
        Long Ago And Far Away(1)(gn,bc)
        Alexander's Ragtime Band
        You're The Rainbow(bc)
        Cherry(nl)
        I Got Rhythm
        Jazz Me Blues(2)
        Ring Dem Bells(incompl.)

-1.Add Gloria Nelson(vcl).
-2.Played by BOB CROSBY'S BOB CATS.

Note:The above titles are from AFRS "One Night Stand" trancription (No.249).

Peggy Lee,The Town Criers(vcl) replace Long,The Pied Pipers.
                                NYC.June 30,1944
R9754 Java Junction   ARA RM103
R9755 Come With Me My Honey
          (Calypso Joe)(bc,tc)   -
R9756 It's Anybody's Spring(pl)   unissued
R9757 On The Atchison,
          Topeka And Santa Fe(bc,pl)   -

BOB CROSBY AND HIS V-DISC BOB CATS:
Yank Lawson(tp),Ward Silloway(tb),Hank D'Amico(cl),Boomie Richman(ts),Dave Bowman(p),Herb
Ellis(g),Bob Haggart(b),George Wettling(dr),Bob Crosby,Martha Tilton(vcl).
                                NYC.April 3,1945
        Pack Up Your Troubles(bc,mt) V-Disc 480,Navy 260,(I)VDL1005,Dan(J)VC5017,
                                      Vintage Jazz Classics VJC1036(CD)
        When I Grow Too Old To Dream(bc) V-Disc 508,Navy 268,Elec(J)KV115,Swinghouse(E)
                                      SWH34,Coll. de Hugues Panassié(F)CTPL003
        It's A Long Way
          To Tipperary(bc)   V-Disc 554,Elec(J)KV115,Swinghouse(E)SWH34,Dan(J)
                                      VC5017
        A Ghost Of A Chance   unissued
        Big Noise From
          Winnetka(b,dr only)   -

BOB CROSBY AND THE AFRS ORCHESTRA:
No details.   Unknown location. 1945
        In The Middle Of May
        Aren't You Glad You're You
        Love Letters
        It's Been A Long,Long Time

Note:The above titles are from AFRS "Basic Music Library" transcription (P-478).

BOB CROSBY AND HIS ORCHESTRA:
Similar to next session;incl. Bob Crosby,Jeri Sullivan,The Town Criers(vcl).
                                Prob. LA.late 1945
        You Forgot About Me(bc)
        Oh What It Seemed To Be(bc)
        Wait And See(js)
(session cont. next page).

(session cont. from previous page):
      Easy Street(tc)
      Gravy Train(bc)
      Sweet Molly Malone(bc,tc)
      Everybody Know But Me(bc)
      Alice From Nogales(bc)
      Don't Be A Baby,Baby(tc)
      The Gypsy(tc)
      Seems Like Old Times(tc)
      I Don't Know Enough Of You(js)
      I Found A Million Dollar Baby(tc)

Note:The above titles are from AFRD "Basic Music Library" transcriptions (No. P-535,P-581,
      P-624).

Claude Bowen,Jack Mootz,Jack Holmes(tp),Quig Quigley(tp,vcl),Warren Smith,Bud Jenkins,
Walter Benson,Bill Hearn(tb),Sid Bender(cl,as),Clint Neagley(as),Frank Myers,Don Brass-
field(ts),Bob Lawson(bars),Ernie Hughes(p),Bob Bain(g),Eddie Gilbert(b),Jimmy Felton(dr),
Bob Crosby,Bonnie Lou Williams(vcl),Van Alexander,George Siravo(arr).
                                        LA.December 1945

110	Let It Snow,Let It	
	Snow,Let It Snow(bc)	ARA RM129
111	I Wish I Could Shimmy	
	Like My Sister Kate(qq)	ARA RM131
112	The Same Old Story(bc)	-
113	In The Valley(blw)	ARA RM129

Murray McEachern(tb),Gus Bivona(cl,as) replace Smith,Bender.
                        Broadcast.Air Force Base,Walla Walla,Washington.December 21,1945
      Theme (Summertime)   Giants Of Jazz LP1021
      Alexander's Ragtime Band   -
      In The Valley(blw)   -
      I Can't Begin To Tell You(bc)   -
      One O'Clock Jump   -

Note:The above titles are from AFRS "Spotlight Bands" transcription (No.937).

Same.   Broadcast.Treasure Island,Calif.January 4,1946
      Theme (Summertime)
      Linger Awhile
      Oh What It Seemed To Be(bc)
      Come To Baby,Do(blw)
      Rip Van Winkle
      Perdido

Note:The above titles are from AFRS "Spotlight Bands" transcription (No.943).

Similar.   Unknown location(s).c. January 1946
      Gravy Train
      I'll Get By   Golden Era LP15009
      Lady Be Good
      Another Time   Golden Era LP15009
      G.I. Jive
      Poinciana(1)   Golden Era LP15009

.Add strings.

Note:The above titles are from AFRS "Downbeat" transcriptions (No.204,205)

Similar.   Unknown location/date
      Java Junction   Golden Era LP15009
      Bull Frog's Jump   -

Wilbur Schwartz(as),Tommy Todd(p,arr),Jimmy Stutz(b),Frank Carlson(dr),Jewell Hopkins(vcl
replace Neagley,Hughes,Gilbert,Felton,Williams.

	Broadcast."Hollywood Palladium",LA.February 10,1946
Theme (Summertime)	Giants Of Jazz LP1021
9:20 Special	- ,Jazz Anthology(F)JA5142,
	First Time FTR1517,Onward To Yesterd. OTY151
Gee,It's Good To Hold You(jh)	Giants Of Jazz LP1021
Always	-
I Wish I Could Shimmy	
Like My Sister Kate(qq)	-
He's Funny That Way(jh)	-
My Type(1)	-
Symphony	-(?)
Alexander's Ragtime Band	-

-1.Announced as "She's My Type".

Note:The above titles are from AFRS "One Night Stand" transcription (No.874).

Add Gordon Polk(vcl).   Broadcast."Hollywood Palladium",LA.February 14,1946
      Theme (Summertime)
      A Strings Of Pearls
      Hit That Jive,Jack(gp)
      I'll Buy That Dream(qq)
      I See Your Face Before Me
      Cement Mixer(gp)
      He's Funny That Way(jh)
      Begin The Beguine   Golden Era LP15009
      Personality(bc)
      The Whistler

Note:The above titles are from AFRS "One Night Stand" transcription (No.881).
    This transcription also incl. "9:20 Special" from February 10,1946.

Same.   Broadcast."Hollywood Palladium",LA.February 21,1946
      Theme (Summertime)
      The Whistler
      As Long As I Live(bc)
      Cement Mixer(gp)
      Embraceable You(jh)
      My Type(1)   Jazz Anthology(F)JA5142(ed.),First Time FTR1517
                               (ed.),Onward To Yesterday OTY1517(ed.)
      I'll Buy That Dream(qq)
      I Can't Begin To tell You(bc)
      Strictly Dynamics   Joyce LP1072,Golden Era LP15009

-1.Announced as "That's My Type".

Note:The above titles are from AFRS "One Night Stand" transcription (No.888).

Same.   Broadcast."Hollywood Palladium",LA.February 1946
      Perdido
      He's Funny That Way
      Let It Snow
      'S Wonderful

Note:The above titles are from AFRS "Magic Carpet" transcription (No.242).

same.   Broadcast."Hollywood Palladium",LA.February 1946
    The Whistler
    I'll Buy That Dream(qq)
    I Can't Begin To Tell You(bc)
    Fifty-Fifty   Joyce LP1072,Jazz Anthology(F)JA5142,First Time
                                        FTR1517,Onward To Yesterday OTY1517

Note:The above titles are from AFRS "Magic Carpet" transcription (No.254).

same.   Broadcast."Hollywood Palladium",LA.February 1946
    Blue Skies
    Don't Forget Tomorrow Night(bc)
    Always   Golden Era LP15009
    Hit That Jive,Jack(gp)

Note:The above titles are from AFRS "Magic Carpet" transcription (No.273).

same.   Broadcast."Hollywood Palladium",LA.February 1946
    Strictly Dynamics
    You Won't Be Satisfied
    Rip Van Winkle
    You Go To My Head(jh)

Note:The above titles are from AFRS "Magic Carpet" transcription (No.277).

same.   Broadcast."Hollywood Palladium",LA.February 1946
    Another Time
    As Long As I Live
    Always
    It's Anybody's Spring

Note:The above titles are from AFRS "Magic Carpet" transcription (No.285).

same.   Broadcast."Hollywood Palladium",LA.February 1946
    9:20 Special
    Don't Forget Tomorrow Night(bc)
    Cement Mixer(gp)
    Welcome To My Dreams

Note:The above titles are from AFRS "Magic Carpet" transcription (No.291).

same.   Broadcast."Hollywood Palladium",LA.February 1946
    Shoo Fly Pie
    It's Better To Be Yourslef(gp)
    Unknown title
    And Then I Looked At You

Note:The above titles are from AFRS "Magic Carpet" transcription (No.317).

same.   Broadcast."Hollywood Palladium",LA.February 1946
    Hollywood Rumpus   Jazz Anthology(F)JA5142,First Time FTR1517,Onward
                                        To Yesterday OTY1517
    I Don't Believe A Word You Said
    You Won't Be Satisfied
    Cement Mixer(gp)

Note:The above titles are from AFRS "Magic Carpet" transcription (No.324).

same.   Broadcast."Hollywood Palladium",LA.February 1946
(session cont. next page).

(session cont. from previous page):
       Hollywood Rumpus
       Shoo Fly Pie
       Prisoner Of Love(bc)
       My Type

Note:The above titles are from AFRS "Magic Carpet" transcription (No.330).

Same.   Broadcast."Hollywood Palladium",LA.February 23,194
       Theme (Summertime)
       Blue Skies   Golden Era LP15009
       Oh,What It Seemed To Be(bc)
       I Wish I Could Shimmy
           Like My Sister Kate(qq)
       You Go To My Head(jh)
       The Frim Fram Sauce(gp)
       It's Anybody's Spring
       You Won't Be Satisfied(bc)
       Drums Out Front

Note:The above titles are from AFRS "One Night Stand" transcription (No.909).

Poss. Claude Bowen,Jack Mootz,Jack Holmes(tp),Quig Quigley(tp,vcl),Bud Jenkins,Walter Ben
son,Bill Hearn,Warren Smith(tb),Clint Neagley,Sid Bender(as),Frank Myers,Don Brassfield
(ts),Bob Lawson(bars),Ernie Hughes(p),Bob Bain(g),Eddie Gilbert(b),Jimmy Felton(dr),Bob
Crosby,Gordon Polk,Jewell Hopkins(vcl),Tommy Todd,Van Alexander,George Siravo(arr).
                                         LA.March 4,1946
1136   Cement Mixer(gp)   ARA RM137
1137   On The Atchison,
           Topeka And Santa Fe(bc)   ARA RM114
1138   Where Did You Lear To Love(bc) ARA RM137
1139   Big Fat Ma   ARA RM143

Incl. Quig Quigley(tp,vcl),Walter Benson(tb),Gus Bivona(cl,as),Dave Pell(ts),Ernie Hughe
(p),Frank Carlson(dr),Bob Crosby,Gordon Polk,Jewell Hopkins(vcl).
                                  Broadcast."Hollywood Palladium",LA.March 5,19
       Theme (Summertime)
       Alexander's Ragtime Band
       Where Did You Learn To Love(bc)
       You've Got Me Crying Again
       It's The Talk Of The Town(jh)
       I Wish I Could Shimmy
           Like My Sister Kate(qq)
       (Just) My Type
       Oh,What It Seemed To Be(bc)
       One O'Clock Jump   Golden Era LP15009

Note:The above titles are from AFRS "One Night Stand" transcription (No.895).

Same.   Broadcast."Hollywood Palladium",LA.March 12,1
       Theme (Summertime)
       The Whistler
       Don't Forget Tonight Tomorrow(bc)
       The Honeydripper(qq)
       The Man I Love(jh)
       Nobody Wants To Sing(gp)
       A String Of Pearls
       A Gal In Nogales(bc)
       Blue Moon

Note:The above titles are from AFRS "One Night Stand" transcription (No.902).

Add Murray McEachern(tb),Wilbur Schwartz(as),Phyllis Lynne(vcl);Tommy Todd(p),Ralph Col-
lier(dr) replace Hughes,Carlson.
                    Broadcast."Meadowbrook Gardens",Culver City,Calif.April 20,1946
    Theme (Summertime)
    A String Of Pearls
    You Won't Be Satisfied(bc)
    I Didn't Mean A Word I Said(pl)
    Prelude To A Kiss(1)
    A Gal In Nogales(bc)
    The Frim Fram Sauce(gp)
    Oh,What It Seemed To Be(bc)
    Embraceable You(pl)

1.McEachern plays (ss).

Note:The above titles are from AFRS "One Night Stand" transcription (No.956).
    This transcription also incl. "Drums Out Front" from February 23,1946.

same.   Broadcast."Meadowbrook Gardens",Culver City,Calif.April 28,1946
    Theme (Summertime)   Joyce LP1072
    A String Of Pearls   -
    I'm Always Chasing Rainbowns(bc)   -
    Blue Room   - ,Jazz Anthology(F)JA5142,First Time
                                  FTR1517,Onward To Yesterday OTY1517
    In A Moon Mist(pl)   Joyce LP1072
    A Gal In Nogales(bc)   -
    Surprise Party(gp)   -
    Seems Like Old Times(bc)   -
    Drums Out Front(1)   -
    The Whistler(incompl.)   -

1.As "Drums Up Front" on LPs.

Note:The above titles are from AFRS "One Night Stand" transcription (No.998).

same.   Broadcast."Meadowbrook Gardens",Culver City,Calif.April 1946
    Unknown titles

Note:The above titles are from AFRS "Magic Carpet" transcription (No.337).

same.   Broadcast."Meadowbrook Gardens",Culver City,Calif.April 1946
    Pet My Pup(gp)
    Seems Like Old Times(bc)
    Tom Foolery   Jazz Anthology(F)JA5142,First Time FTR1517,Onward
                                  To Yesterday OTY1517
    Prisoners Of Love(bc)

Note:The above titles are from AFRS "Magic Carpet" transcription (No.345).

same.   Broadcast."Meadowbrook Gardens",Culver City,Calif.April 1946
    I Didn't Mean A Word I said(bc)
    It's Better To Be Yourself(gp)
    Atlanta,GA.(bc)
    Blue Skies
    Prisoner Of Love(bc)
    Unknown titles
    There's Good Blues Tonight(pl)
    It's Better To Be Yourself(gp)
    Give A Broken Heart A Break(bc)
    Tom Foolery

Note:The above titles are from AFRS "Magic Carpet" transcriptions (No.352,359,365,372).

Same.   Broadcast."Meadowbrook Gardens",Culver City,Calif.May 12 or 21,194
        Theme (Summertime)
        A String Of Pearls
        Don't You Remember Me(bc)
        I Don't Know Enough About You(pl)
        The Whistler
        In The Moon Mist(pl)
        The Frim Fram Sauce(gp)
        The Gypsy(bc)
        Drums Out Front   Jazz Anthology(F)JA5142(ed.),First Time FTR1517
                                           (ed.),Onward To Yesterday OTY1517(ed.)

-1.As "Drums Up Front" on LPs.

Note:The above titles are from AFRS "One Night Stand" transcription (No.977).
     This transcription also incl. "You Won't Be Satisfied" from April 20,1946.

Similar.   LA.May 21,1946
L4189 It's Better To Be Yourself(gp) Decca 18915,10380
L4190 Give A Broken Heart A Break(bc)   -   -
L4191 I've Never Forgotten   Decca 18909,10363,Brunswick(E)03682
L4192 Five Minutes More   -   -   -

Dale Pierce,Nick Buono,Dick Cathcart(tp),Quig Quigley(tp,vcl),Murray McEachern,Bill Hear
(tb),Phil Washburne(tb,vcl),Gus Bivona,Wilbur Schwartz(as),Frank Myers,Dave Pell(ts),Bob
Lawson(bars),Dodo Marmarosa(p),Bob Bain(g),Jimmy Stutz(b),Ralph Collier(dr),Bob Crosby,
Phyllis Lynne(vcl),Nelson Riddle(arr).
                            Broadcast."Meadowbrook Gardens",Culver City,Calif.June 1,19
        Theme (Summertime)
        Blue Moon
        Baby,Baby All The Time(pl)
        I've Never Forgotten(bc)
        As Long As It Gets A Laugh(gp)   Joyce LP1072
        I Don't Know Enough About You(pl)   -
        The Gypsy   -(?)
        A String Of Pearls

Note:The above titles are from AFRS "One Night Stand" transcription (No.1025).
     This transcription also incl. "Drums Out Front" from May 12 or 21,1946.

Similar;Dottie O'Brien(vcl) replaces Lynne. LA(?). 1946
        Give A Broken Heart A Break(bc)
        Ugly Chile(dob)
        For Sentimental Reasons(dob)
        Zip-A-Dee-Doo-Dah(bc)
        Ready To Go Steady(dob)
        So Would I(bc)
        Things We Did Last Summer(bc)
        It's All Over Now(dob)
        What Am I Gonna
           Do About You(bc)
        A Gal In Nogales(bc)

Note:The above titles are from Standard Transcriptions (X-228).

CONNIE BOSWELL(vcl) with BOB CROSBY ORCHESTRA:
No details.   LA.October 17,1946
73727 Zip-A-Dee-Doo-Dah   Decca 23748
73733 Too Many Times   -

No details.   LA(?). 1946
       Summertime
       Cloud Nine   Jazz Anthology(F)JA5142,First Time FTR1517,Onward
                                     To Yesterday OTY1517

       String Of Pearls   Jazz Anthology(F)JA5142,First Time FTR1517,Onward
                                     To Yesterday OTY1517

       Blue Moon   Jazz Anthology(F)JA5142,First Time FTR1517,Onward
                                     To Yesterday OTY1513,OTY1517

       I'll Never Be The Same   Jazz Anthology(F)JA5142,First Time FTR1517,Onward
                                     To Yesterday OTY1517

       Me And The Blues(dob)
       You Brought A New
          Kind Of Love To Me(dob)
       Romance
       Twilight Time

Note:The above titles are from Standard Transcriptions (X-228).

Similar.   LA(?). 1946
       What More Can I Ask For
       Gotta Get Me Somebody To Love
       There Is No Breeze
       Vem Vem
       A Gal In Galico(bc)
       Isn't This Better Than
          Walking In The Rain(dob)
       Didn't I Tell You So(bc)
       You Forgot About Me(bc)
       Winter Wonderland(bc)

Note:The above titles are from Standard Transcriptions (X-231).

No details.   Unknown loaction/date
       Summertime   Onward To Yesterday OTY2-2501
       Summertime   Swing Era LP1011

No details.   Broadcast(?)."Avalon Ballroom",LA.November 1946
       Romance
       Either It's Love Or It Isn't(dob)
       Winter Wonderland(bc)
       It's Only A Paper Moon
       Ugly Chile(dob)
       You're Mine You
       For Sentimental Reasons(dob)
       September Song
       Me And The Blues(dob)
       You Forgot About Me(bc)
       Oh,Kickeroonie(pw)
       Nigt And Day
       Me And The Blues(dob)
       Didn't I Tell You So(bc)
       Cotton Seed
       It's Only A Paper Moon
       September Song
       Ready To Go Steady(dob)
       You Forgot About Me(bc)
       Oh,Kickeroonie(pw)

Note:The above titles are from AFRS "Magic Carpet" transcriptions(No.532,539,543,547,559).

No details.   Broadcast(?)."Hollywood Palladium",LA.   1946
        Perdido
        You Win't Be Satisfied
        Rip Van Winkle
        Prelude To A Kiss

Note:The above titles are from AFRS "Magic Carpet" transcription (No.725).

No details.   Unknown locations. 1946
        You're Mine You   Jazz Anthology(F)JA5142,First Time FTR1517,Onward
                                         To Yesterday OTY1517
        Prelude To A Kiss   Jazz Anthology(F)JA5142,First Time FTR1517,Onward
                                         To Yesterday OTY1517
        It's Only A Paper Moon   Golden Era LP15009
        September Song   -
        Night And Day   -
        Perdido   -

Note:The titles are prob. from the above AFRS "Magic Carpet" transcriptions.

BOB CROSBY AND HIS ORCHESTRA:
No details;Bob Crosby,Marion Morgan(vcl).   LA.c. March 1949

HC03609 Don't Call Me
        Sweetheart Anymore(bc)   Columbia 38458
HC03610 An Old Fashioned Song(bc)   -
        Be My Little Bumble Bee(bc,mm) Columbia 38504
        Maybe It's Because(bc,mm)   -

BOB CROSBY AND HIS ORCHESTRA:
Yank Lawson,Billy Butterfield,Andy Ferretti(tp),Will Bradley(tb),Hank D'Amico(cl,as),Hymie
Schertzer(as),Hank Ross,Jimmy Lytell(ts),Paul Ricci(ts,bars),Dave Bowman(p),Carl Kress(g),
Bob Haggart(b),Norris "Bunny" Shawker(dr).   NYC.February 17,1950
75868   That's A Plenty(1)   Coral unissued(?)
75869   If You Can't Get A
        Drum With A Boom(2)   Coral 60171
75870   Rose Room   Coral CRL57089
75871   When My Sugar
        Walks Down The Street   Coral 60171

-1.Omit Ferretti,Schertzer,Ross.
-2.Add Fred Pfaff(tu).

BOB CROSBY'S BOB CATS:
Yank Lawson(tp),Cutty Cutshall(tb),Stan Webb(as),Ernie Caceres(bars),Joe Lipman(p),Carl
Kress(g),Bunny Shawker(dr).   NYC(?). 1950
        'Way Back Home
        Dear Hearts And Gentle People
        Politics
        Let's Go 'Round Together
        Sing To Me
        Fool's Paradise
        Bye Bye Baby
        Happy Times
        Charlie My Boy
        The Old Master Painter

Note:The above titles are from Standard Transcriptions (No.X-286).

BOB CROSBY AND HIS ORCHESTRA:
Incl. Yank Lawson(tp),Will Bradley(tb),Paul Ricci(as),Dave Bowman(p),Trigger Alpert(b).
NYC(?).c. March 1950

        Rag Mop
        The Wedding Samba
        Did Anyone Ever Tell You,Mrs. Murphy
        There's An "X" In The Middle Of Texas
        Half A Heart
        Zing-A-Zing-A Zing Boom
        Broken Down Merry-Go-Round
        Out Of A Clear Blue Sky
        But Me,I Love You
        Peter Cottontail
        I Don't Know Whether
            To Laugh Or Cry Over You
        Don't Say Goodbye

Note:The above titles are from Standard Transcriptions (No.X-290).

BOB CROSBY'S BOB CATS:
Billy Butterfield,Yank Lawson(tp),Cutty Cutshall(tb),Matty Matlock(cl),Eddie Miller(ts),
Dave Bowman(p),Carl Kress(g),Bob Haggart(b),Fred Pfaff(tu),George Wettling(dr),Bob Crosby
(vcl).   NYC.April 10,1950
76117 Washington Post March   Coral 60217,CRL56018,CRL57061,(G)EPC94008,Festival
                                          (Au)CFR10-728
76118 My Scandinavian Baby   Coral 60211
76119 Stars And Stripes Forever   Coral 60217,CRL56018,CRL57061,(G)EPC94008,Festival
                                          (Au)CFR10-728
76120 Your Heart Of Stone   Coral 60211
76121 Black Bottom(bc)   Coral 60254,EC81003,CRL57005,(G)EPC94039
76122 Charleston(bc)   -   -   -   -

BOB CROSBY AND HIS ORCHESTRA:
Billy Butterfield,Yank Lawson,Chris Griffin(tp),Cutty Cutshall(tb),Ernie Caceres(cl),Pea-
nuts Hucko(ts),Lou Stein(p),Carl Kress(g),Bob Haggart(b),Phil Kadaway(tu),Bunny Shawker
(dr).   NYC.May 22,1950
86401 Semper Fidelis   Coral 60280,CRL56018,CRL57061,(G)EPC94014
86402 El Capitan   -   -   -   ,(G)EPC94008
86403 The Thunderer   Coral CRL56018,CRL57061,(G)EPC94014

All titles also on Festival(Au)CFR10-728.

Jay Linn,Charlie Teagarden,Zeke Zarchy(tp),Lou McGarity(tb),Matty Matlock(cl),Eddie Miller
(ts),Stan Wrightsman(p),Nappy Lamare(g),Country Washburne(tu,b),Nick Fatool(dr),Bob Crosby
(vcl).   LA.October 9,1950
85868 King Cotton   Coral 60340,CRL56018,CRL57061,(G)EPC94014,Festival
                                          (Au)CFR10-728
85869 Hands Across The Sea   Coral 60340,CRL56018,CRL57061,(G)EPC94014,Festival
                                          (Au)CFR10-728
85870 Echo In The Cavern   Coral CRL57089,(G)EPC94100
85871 High School Cadets   Coral 60341,CRL56018,CRL57061,(G)EPC94008,Festival
                                          (Au)CFR10-728

All titles on CRL57089 also on Coral(E)LVA9045.

Same;add Connie Haines(vcl).   LA.December 18,1950
85962 Destination Moon(ch)   Coral 60370
85963 What Have You Done For Me(ch)   -
85964 Drop Another Bean In The Basket Coral 60368
85965 Sidewalk Shufflers   -

Note:Coral 60370 issued as by CONNIE HAINES.

Charlie Teagarden,Zeke Zarchy,Ray Linn(tp),Ted Vesely,Elmer "Moe" Schneider(tb),Matty
Matlock(cl),Wilbur Schwartz(as),Eddie Miller(ts),Bob Lawson(bars),Stan Wrightsman(p),Nappy
Lamare(g),Phil Stephens(b),Nick Fatool(dr),Bob Crsby(vcl).

		LA.March 19,1951
L6167	9:20 Special	Coral 60440
L6168	'Cause Of You	-
L6170	The Memphis Blues	Coral 60536,CRL56039,CRL57060,(G)EPC94061

Chuck Gentry(bars),Ray Bauduc(dr) replace Lawson,Fatool.

		LA.April 2,1951
L6189	St. Louis Blues	Coral 60535,CRL56039,(G)EPC94084,Sounds Of Swing LP109
L6190	Beale Street Blues	Coral 60537,CRL56039,(G)EPC94061
L6191	Loveless (Careless) Love	Coral 60535,CRL56039,(G)EPC94084,Sounds Of Swing LP109

All titles also on Coral CRL57060.

Same.   LA.April 16,1951

L6237	Joe Turner's Blues	Coral 60537,CRL56039,(G)EPC94061
L6238	Way Down South	Coral 60538, - , (G)EPC94084
L6239	Yellow Dog Blues	Coral 60536,61929,CRL56039,(G)EPC94061
L6240	Aunt Hagar's Blues	Coral 60538,CRL56039,(G)EPC94084

All titles also on Coral CRL57060.
All titles on CRL56039 also on Festival(Au)CFR10-342.

Same;add The Crew Chiefs(vcl).   LA.May 15,1951

7533	Shanghai(bc)	Capitol 1525,H9101,(E)CL13585
7534	That Naughty Waltz	- ,(S)T1556,(E)CL13598,Telefunken(G) C80161
7535	How About You	unissued
7536	L'Amour Toujours(bc,cc)	Capitol 1576,(E)CL13585,(Au)CP021,Telefunken(G) C80161
7559	I Don't Mind	Capitol 1576,(Au)CP021

Conrad Gozzo(tp),Jeanne Gayle(vcl) replace Linn,The Crew Chiefs;add Bob Haggart(arr).

		LA.June 13,1951
7651	Lone And Sorry	Capitol 1595,(S)T1556
7652	I'm Waiting Just For You	-
7653	Tales Of Hoffman	Capitol 1751,(S)T1556,(E)CL13598,Sounds Of Swing LP109,Telefunken(G)C80208
7654	Hobo Boogie(jg)	Capitol 1751,Telefunken(G)C80188

Charlie Teagarden,Zeke Zarchy,Ray Linn(tp),Ted Veseley,Moe Schneider(tb),Matty Matlock
(cl),Wilbur Schwartz(as),Eddie Miller(ts,cl),Chuck Gentry(bars),Stan Wrightsman(p),Nappy
Lamare(g),Phil Stephens(b),Nick Fatool(dr),Bob Crosby,The Dinning Sisters(vcl).

		LA.August 6,1951
7894	Ask Me(ds)	Capitol 1766,(E)CL13883
7895	Oklahoma Hills(ds)	-
7896	Bluin' The Blues	Capitol H/T293
7897	Once In A While	- ,(S)T1556
7898	Fidgety Feet	- ,TB01970-2,(E)EAP1-20112
7899	Ostrich Walk	- ,Il Jazz(I)SdMJ091
7903	Hors D'Oeuvre	Capitol 1778,(S)T1556,Capitol(E)CL13663
7904	99 Out Of A Hundred	- -

All titles on H293 also on Capitol EBF293 (2xEP),(E)LC6553.
Note:Masters 7894 and 7895 issued as by THE DINNING SISTERS.

Add Warren Smith(tb).   LA.September 18,1951
9027   Magnolia Street Parade   Capitol H/T293,T795,(E)EAP1-20112,(G)1J.060-80155,
                                              Il Jazz(I)SdMJ091
9028   Maryland,My Maryland   Capitol H/T293,(S)T1556,W2140,K83924,(E)EAP1-20112
                                              (Eu)C.048-50746,Il Jazz(I)SdMJ091
9029   Pennies From Heaven   Capitol F15654,H/T293,(E)EAP1-20112,Il Jazz(I)
                                              SdMJ091
9030   Cattin' On The Keys   Capitol H/T293,(E)EAP20112

All titles on H293 also on Capitol EBF293 (2xEP),(E)LC6553.

Add Gisele MacKenzie(vcl).   LA.September 21,1951
9059   I Was Never Loved
           By Anyone(bc,gmk)   Capitol 1826,(E)CL13663
9060   Sans Souci(bc,gmk)   -
9061   (It's A) Crying Shame(bc,gmk) Capitol 1894,(S)T1556

Billy Butterfield(tp),Murray McEachern,Moe Schneider,Ted Vesely(tb),Matty Matlock(cl),
Eddie Miller(ts),Jess Stacy(p),Nappy Lamare(g),Bob Haggart(b,arr),Ray Bauduc(dr),poss. The
Crew Chiefs(vcl).   LA.October 3,1951
9112   Bouquet Of Roses   Capitol 1850
9114   Just A Little Lovin'   -

BOB CROSBY'S BOB CATS:
Warren Smith(tb) replaces McEachern,Schneider,Vesely.
                                             Same date
9115   Savoy Blues   Capitol 1894,T293,(S)T1556
9116   Avalon   Capitol T293,(S)T1556,K83924,(Eu)C.048-50746

same.   LA.October 1951
        Who's Sorry Now   Camay CA3035
        Muskrat Ramble   -
        March Of The Bob Cats   -
        Panama Blues   -
        Savoy Blues   -
        Love's Got Me In A Lazy Mood
        Complainin'
        Big Noise From Winnetka

Note:The above titles are from Snader Telescriptions and were recorded as by BOBCATS(!).

JEANNE GAYLE(vcl) acc. by BOB CROSBY AND HIS ORCHESTRA:
Charlie Teagarden,Zeke Zarchy,Ray Linn(tp),Ted Veseley,Moe Schneider,Warren Smith(tb),
Matty Matlock(cl),Wilbur Schwartz(as),Eddie Miller(ts,cl),Chuck Gentry(bars),Stan Wrights-
man(p),Nappy Lamare(g),Phil Stephens(b),Nick Fatool(dr).
                                             LA.March 17,1952
871   Goody Goody(jg)   Capitol 2037,(E)CL13757,Telefunken(G)C80237
872   It's Been So Long(jg)   - ,(E)CL13764,   -

BOB CROSBY AND HIS BOB CATS:
omit Gayle.   Same date
873   Song Of The Islands   Capitol 2119,T293,(S)T1556,Telefunken(G)C80277(?)
874   Paducah Parade   -   -   -   -

BOB CROSBY AND HIS ORCHESTRA
Charlie Teagarden,Zeke Zarchy,Ray Linn(tp),Jack Teagarden,Ted Veseley,Moe Schneider(tb),
Matty Matlock(cl),Wilbur Schwartz(as),Eddie Miller(ts,cl),Chuck Gentry(bars),Stan Wrights-
man(p),unknown(g),Morty Corb(b),Nick Fatool(dr),Bob Crosby(vcl).
                                             LA.c. July 1952
(session cont. next page).

(session cont. from previous page):
```
     Forgive Me(bc)
     Watching The World Go By(bc)
     Here In My Heart(bc)
     Walking My Baby Back Home(bc)    Jazum 5
     My Inspiration                   Hindsight HSR209,Fanfare LP2-102
     The Naughty Waltz                      -                     -
     Cattin' On The Keys                    -
     I'm Yours(bc)
     Paducah Parade                   Hindsight HSR209,Fanfare LP2-102
     Barcarolle                             -                     - ,Concertone 2059,
                                      Ultraphone 5059,50268
```

All titles on Fanfare LP2-102 also on Jasmine(E)JASM2510.
All titles on HSR209 also on Hindsight(E)HUK209,(J)RJL3122,R28J3122 (CD).
Note:The above titles are from Standard Transcriptions (X-335).

Al Hendrickson(g) replaces unknown(g);add June Christy,Polly Bergen(vcl).
```
                                      LA. 1952
     It Had To Be You(bc)             Hindsight HCD245(CD)
     Lover                                  -
     Ostrich Walk                           -
     My Baby Just Cares For Me(bc)          -
     Over The Waves                         -
     Love Is Just
        Around The Corner(jc)               -
     Song Of The Islands
     Exactly Like You(bc)                   -
     Skater's Waltz
     Willow Weep For Me(jc)                 -
     Aunt Hagar's Blues                     -
     Let's Fall In Love(pb)                 -
     She's Funny That Way(bc)               -
     Tales From Hoffman
     Wolverine Blues                        -
     Fidgety Feet                           -
```

Note:The above titles are - prob. all - from U.S. Marine transcriptions (by BOB CROSBY AN▮
     ALL STARS.

Similar;omit Jack Teagarden.   Unknown location(s). 1952/53
```
     Ostrich Walk                     Hindsight HSR209
     The Grabber                            -
     Once In A While                        -
     Muskrat Ramble                         -
     Panama                                 -
     Beale Street Blues                     -
     9:20 Special                           -
     King Cotton March                      -
     Honeysuckle Rose                       -
```

All titles on HSR209 also on Hindsight(E)HUK209,(J)RJL3122,R28J3122 (CD).
Note:The above titles are from unknown transcription(s).

Similar.   Broadcasts.Unknown locations. 1952/53
```
     That's A Plenty                  Hindsight HSR241,HCD409(CD)
     Lazy Mood                              -      -
     March Of The Mustangs                  -      -
     March Of The Bob Cats                  -      -
     Ghost Of A Chance                      -      -
```
(session cont. next page).

(session cont. from previous page):

Washington And Lee Swing	Hindsight HSR241,HCD409(CD)		
Jazz Me Blues		-	-
High Society		-	-
Dixieland Shuffle		-	-
Sugar Foot Stomp		-	-
Mississippi Mud		-	-
Alabamy Bound		-	-
On The Alamo		-	-
My Monday Date		-	-
San Antonio Shout	Hindsight HCD409(CD)		
What's New		-	
Big Noise From Winnetka		-	
Stomp Mr. Henry Lee		-	
Medley:		-	
In A Sentimental Mood			
Solitude			
Rose Of Rio Grande		-	
Grandpa Spells		-	

Note:The above titles are from unknown transcriptions.

BOB CROSBY AND THE BOB CATS:
Unknown big(!) band;Bob Crosby(vcl).   NYC. 1953

The Happy Wanderer(1,2)(bc)	Bell 1045,Gala(E)45XP1017		
Steam Heat(1)		-	-

-1.Add unknown female(vcl).
-2.Add unknown male (vcl-group).

THE MODERNAIRES(vcl) with BOB CROSBY AND HIS ORCHESTRA:
No details.   LA.April 15,1955
L8332 Sloo Foot   Coral 61412
L8333 La Fiesta   Coral 61449
L8335 Wine,Women And Gold   Coral 61412

THE BOB CROSBY ORCHESTRA/BOB CATS:
Charlie Teagarden(tp,vcl),Moe Schneider(tb),Matty Matlock(cl,arr),Eddie Miller(ts),Al
Pellegrini(p),Al Hendrickson/Barney Kessel(g),Morty Corb/Ray Leatherwood(b),Larry Bunker/
Jack Sperling(dr),Bob Crosby,Paula Kelly,The Modernaires,Alan Copeland Singers(vcl).
                                         LA.November 8,1955
RHCO33609 I Can't Carry A Tune(tm)   Columbia CL766
RHCO33610 My Baby Just Cares For Me(acs)   -
RHCO33611 The Dum Dat Song(bc,pk)   -
RHCO33612 Lazy Bones(bc,jt)   -

Add Carol Richards(vcl).   LA.November 17,1955
RHCO33613 You Forgot About Me(bc,tm) Columbia CL766
RHCO33614 Whispering Hope(bc,cr)   -
RHCO33615 Look For The
             Silver Lining(bc,tm)   -
RHCO33616 My Mother's Pearls(cr)   -

Add Joanie O'Brien(vcl).   LA.January 3,1956
RHCO33663 He's The Last
             Word(job,cr,pk)(1)   Columbia CL766
RHCO33664 I Gotta Have My Baby Back(job)   -
RHCO33665 San Antonio Rose(2)   -
RHCO33666 Small Fry(bc,acs)   -

-1.O'Brien,Richards,Kelly as THE THREE KITTENS.
-2.Prob. incl. all the vocalists listed for the last three sessions.

BOB CROSBY'S BOB CATS:
Poss. Manny Klein,Clyde Hurley,Johnny Best(tp),Abe Lincoln,Moe Schneider,Warren Smith(tb),
Matty Matlock(cl),Eddie Miller,Babe Russin(ts),Joe Rushton(bars),Stan Wrightsman(p),George
Van Eps,Al Hendrickson(g),Nappy Lamare(bj),Morty Corb(b),Country Washburne(tu),Jack Sper-
ling,Nick Fatool(dr),Paula Kelly,The Modernaires(vcl).

		LA.c. 1956
	Paducah Parade	Black Jack LP3009
	Ain't She Sweet(pk,tm)	-
	Milenburg Joys	-

Note:The above titles are from Treasury Dept. "Guest Star" transcription (No.478).

BOB CROSBY AND HIS ORCHESTRA:
Conrad Gozzo,Frank Beach,Charlie Teagarden,Johnny Best(tp),Moe Schneider,Abe Lincoln,Joe
Howard(tb),Matty Matlock(cl),Jack Dumont(as),Eddie Miller,Jack Chaney(ts),Dent Eckels
(bars),Al Pellegrini(p),Al Hendrickson(g),Morty Corb(b),Jack Sperling(dr).

		LA.June 7,1956
L9273	Skater's Waltz	Coral EC81141,CRL57062
L9274	At The Jazz Band Ball	Coral CRL57089,(E)LVA9045,(G)EPC94100

Charles Gifford(tp) replaces Gozzo.

		LA.June 14,1956
L9308	Dogtown Blues	Coral CRL57062
L9309	Louise Louise	-
L9310	Smokey Mary	-
L9311	Milk Cow Blues	Coral 61714,CRL57062,MCA-Coral(G)COPS6845/1-2, 6.28197
L9312	South Rampart Street Parade	Coral EC81141,CRL57062,CRL57222,EPC94100(?),MCA-Coral(G)COPS6597/1-2,COPS6845/1-2,6.28195
L9313	Honky Tonk Train(1)	Coral 61714,CRL57062

-1.Marvin Ash(p-solo).

Conrad Gozzo(tp) replaces Gifford.

		LA.June 15,1956
L9314	Gin Mill Blues	Coral CRL57062,EC81141
L9315	What's New	Coral 61929,CRL57062
L9316	Vieni Vieni	Coral CRL57062,(G)EPC94100
L9317	Big Noise From Winnetka(1)	- ,EC81141,MCA-Coral(G)COPS6845/1-2, 6.28197
L9330	The Old Spinning Wheel(2)	Coral CRL57062,(G)EPC94098

-1.Charlie Teagarden(whistling).
-2.Marvin Ash(p) replaces Pelegrini.

All titles on CRL57062 also on Festival(Au)C12-1308.

Conrad Gozzo,Frank Beach,Charlie Teagarden,Johnny Best(tp),Ed Kusby,Moe Schneider,Si Zent-
ner(tb),Matty Matlock(cl),Jack Dumont(as),Eddie Miller,Babe Russin(ts),Clarence Karella
(basssax),Al Pellegrini(p),Nappy Lamare(g),Morty Corb(b),Jack Sperling(dr).

		LA.January 24,1957
L9815	Happy Valley Trek(!)	Coral CRL57061
L9816	Memphis March	-
L9817	Bobcats On Parade	-
L9818	Skippin' John	-

Dick Cathcart(tp),Hoyt Bohannon,Abe Lincoln(tb),Dent Eckels(as) replace Teagarden,Kusby,
Zentner,Karella;Jack Dumont plays(bars);add Billy May(arr).

		LA.March 15,1957
L9952	Ash Trays For Two	Coral CRL57060
L9953	Exodus Blues	-
L9954	Blues For Lou	-
L9955	Lost All My Blues (For You)	-

BOB CROSBY'S BOB CATS:
Johnny Best,Dick Cathcart(tp),Moe Schneider(tb),Matty Matlock(cl),Eddie Miller(ts),Al Pel-
legrini(p),Al Hendrickson(g),Morty Corb(b),Jack Sperling(dr),Nappy Lamare(vcl).

LA.May 1,1957

10080	Who's Sorry Now	Coral CRL57170,MCA-Coral(G)COPS6845/1-2,6.28197
10081	Do You Ever Think Of Me(nl)	-
10082	Don't Call Me Boy(nl)	-
10083	Coquette	-

Nappy Lamare(g) replaces Hendrickson.　　　LA.May 3,1957

10084	Fidgety Feet	Coral CRL57170
10085	Stumbling	-
10086	The Big Crash From China	-
10087	March Of The Bob Cats	- ,MCA-Coral(G)COPS6845/1-2,6.28197

Charlie Gifford(tp) replaces Cathcart.　　LA.May 5,1957

10088	Sweethearts On Parade	Coral CRL57170,MCA-Coral(G)COPS6845/1-2,6.28197
10089	Hindustan	-
10090	Five Point Blues	-
10091	Washington And Lee Swing	- ,MCA-Coral(G)COPS6845/1-2,6.28197

11 titles on CRL57170 also on Coral(E)LVA9083.

BOB CROSBY AND HIS ORCHESTRA:
Billy Butterfield,Yank Lawson(tp),Cutty Cutshall,Lou McGarity(tb),Peanuts Hucko(cl),Al
Klink(as),Bud Freeman(ts),Dean Kincaide(ts,bars),poss. Jerome Richardson(bars),Louis Stein
(p),Carl Kress(g),Bob Haggart(b),Cliff Leeman(dr).

NYC.June 1958

This Nearly Was Mine	Dot DLP3136,DLP25878,Rediffusion(F)0100174
There Is Nothing Like A Dame	-
Some Enchanted Evening	-
Happy Talk	-
Honey Bur	-
I'm Gonna Wash That 　　Man Right Out Of My Hair	-
Bali Hai	-
Younger Than Springtime	-
A Wonderful Guy	-

11 titles also on Dot DLP25136.

Bill Stegmeyer(cl) replaces Hucko;omit Klink,Kincaide,Richardson,Kress.

NYC.September 2/3/4,1958

Oh,I Can't Sit Down	Dot DLP3193,DLP25878,Rediffusion(F)0100174
Bess,You Is My Woman Now	-
It Ain't Necessarily So	-
It Takes A Long Pull To Get There	-
I Loves You Porgy	-
I Got Plenty Of Nothin'	-
There's A Boat Dat's 　　Leavin' Soon For New York	-
Oh Bess,Where's My Bess?	-
My Man's Gone Now	-
Summertime	-

11 titles also on Dot DLP25193.

BOB CROSBY'S BOB CATS:
Yank Lawson,Pee Wee Ervin,Chris Griffin(tp),Cutty Cutshall,Lou McGarity(tb),Bill Stegmeyer
(cl),Bud Freeman(ts),Ralph Sutton(p),Bob Haggart(b),Cliff Leeman(dr),Bob Crosby(vcl).

TV-cast."Americana Hotel",Bal Harbour,Florida.November 10,1958

(session cont. next page).

(session cont. from previous page):
```
        Royal Garden Blues(bc(?))            Sounds Great SG8011
        South Rampart Street Parade(1)                  - ,Kings Of Jazz(I)KLJ20026,Music
                                             For Pleasure(F)2M.056-78139,2M.146-13270,
                                             Windmill(E)WMD266,Phonic(Sp)PHL5505
```

-1.Add Louis Armstrong(tp).

Note:The above titles are from a Timex TV-show.

BOB CROSBY AND THE BOBCATS:
2 unknown(sax),rhythm group,vocal-group.   NYC. 1958
MW11541 Such A Long Night   Dot 15890,London(E)HL1498,MSD3297

Poss. same.   NYC. 1958
```
        El Bingo Rock                    Dot 15828
        Boogie Woogie Rock                     -
```

BOB CROSBY AND HIS ORCHESTRA:
Similar to session September 2/3/4,1958;Justin Gordon(cl) replaces Stegmeyer.
                                         NYC.Late 1958/January 1959
```
MW12363 Petite Fleur                     Dot 15890,DLP3170,London(E)HL1498
MW12435 South                            Dot 15907,    -
MW12438 Sweet Lorraine                        -       -
        Creole Love Call                 Dot DLP3170
        Smoke Rings                           -
        Stardust                              -
        Pretend                               -
        Peg O'My Heart                        -
        Out Of Nowhere                        -
        Poinciana                             -
        Moonglow                              -
        My Foolish Heart                      -
```

All titles on DLP3170 also on Dot DLP25170.

Similar;add Joanie O'Brien (vcl).   Unknown location. 1959
```
BAT15282 Steam Heat(job)                 Dot (unknown issueno.),Music Hall 15110
MB15303  Night Theme                     Dot 16141
MB15305  Theme From "The Dark
         At The Top Of The Stars"             -
```

Conrad Gozzo,Frank Beach,Johnny Best,Mickey Mangano(tp),Moe Schneider,Joe Howard,Si Zent-
ner(tb),Matty Matlock(cl,as),Eddie Miller(ts,cl),Babe Russin(ts),Chuck Gentry(bars),Bill
Maxted(p),Nappy Lamare(g,vcl),Bob Haggart(b),Ray Bauduc(dr).
                                         LA.February 1960
```
        Yancey Special                   Dot DLP3278,Hamilton HLP12142(?)
        South Rampart Street Parade           -
        Honky Tonk Train Blues                - ,Hamilton HLP12142
        Little Rock Getaway                   -           -
        Big Noise From Winnetka(1)            -           -
        Gin Mill Blues                        -           -
```

-1.Haggart(b,whistling),Bauduc(dr) only.

All titles on DLP3278 also on Dot DLP25278,London(E)HAD2293,SAHD6105,Rediffusion(F)01-17-

Conrad Gozzo,Frank Beach,Johnny Best,Mickey Mangano(tp),Moe Schneider,Warren Smith,Joe H-
ward(tb),Matty Matlock(cl),Philip Sobel(as),Eddie Miller,Babe Russin(ts),Butch Stone(bar-
Stan Wrightsman(p),George Van Eps(g),Morty Corb(b),Jack Sperling(dr).
                                         LA. 1960
(session cont. next page).

(session cont. from previous page):
      What's New   Dot DLP3288
      Boogie Woogie Maxie   -
      Sugar Foot Stomp   -

BOB CROSBY'S BOB CATS:
Johnny Best(tp),Moe Schneider(tb),Matty Matlock(cl),Eddie Miller(ts),Stan Wrightsman(p),
George Van Eps(g),Morty Corb(b),Jack Sperling(dr).
                                      LA. 1960
      March Of The Bob Cats   Dot DLP3288
      Washington And Lee Swing   -
      Muskrat Ramble   -

All titles also on Dot DLP25278,London(E)HAD2293,SAHD6105,Rediffusion(F)01-179.

Eddie Miller -1(ts,cl),Horace Henderson(org),William Swanston,Nappy Lamare(g),John Mackel
(b),Alvin Stoller(dr).   LA.January 26/30,1961
      Just A Closer Walk With Thee(1) Dot DLP3382
      Cherry Pink And
         Apple Blossom White   -
      Diane   -
      To Each His Own   -
      C'est Si Bon(1)   -
      Don't You Know   -
      Street Scene   -
      I Let A Song Go Out Of My Heart   -

Add Matty Matlock(cl);omit Miller.   Same dates
      Calcutta   Dot DLP3382
      Someday Sweetheart(2)   -
      Sentimental Journey   -
      Blue Moon   -

 -2.Henderson plays (p).

All titles on DLP3382 also on Dot DLP25382.

BOB CROSBY AND THE BOB CATS:
Yank Lawson(tp),Lou McGarity(tb),Matty Matlock(cl),Eddie Miller(ts),Ralph Sutton(p),Bob
Haggart(b),Don Lamond(dr),Bob Crosby(vcl).   Live."Rainbow Grill",NYC.November 18,1966
      Some Day You'll Be Sorry   Monmouth-Evergreen MES6815
      Basin Street Blues   -
      Battle Hymn Of The Republic   -
      Lazy Mood   -
      Keepin' Out Of Mischief Now   -
      St. James Infirmary   -
      Puzzy Cat   -
      I Loves You,Porgy   -
      Oh,Baby   -
      Summertime   -
      Mardi Gras Parade   Monmouth-Evergreen MES7026
      Ballin' The Jack   -
      Lazy River(bc)   -
      South   -
      C-Jam Blues   -
      I Ain't Gonna Give
         Nobody None Of My Jelly Roll   -
      Smile   -
      Tin Roof Blues   -
      Mardi Gras Parade   -

All titles on MES6815 also on Ember(E)CJS827.

Ray Linn(tp),Bob Manary(?)(tb),Peanuts Hucko(cl),Babe Russin(ts),Art Waggoner(?)(p),Harry
Babasin(b),Bill Smith(dr),Bob Crosby(vcl).   Evansville,Indiana.November 17,1972

> At The Jazz Band Ball
> Muskrat Ramble
> Big Noise From Winnetka
> Lazy River(bc)
> When The Saints Go Marching In(bc)

Note:The above titles may be from a - prob. unissued - private recording.

BOB CROSBY'S BOB CATS:
No details.   Unknown location(s)/date(s)

Little Rock Getaway	Bulldog(E)BDL2026
Big Noise From Winnetka	-
Gin Mill Blues	-
Lazy Mood	-
Summertime	-
Tin Roof Blues	-
Washington And Lee Swing	-
When The Saints Go Marching In	-
Jada	-
Tiger Rag	-
High Society	-
Pennies From Heaven	-
Georgy Girl	-
Thoroughly Modern Millie	-
Winchester Cathedral	-
Ballin' The Jack(1)	-
Java	-
March Of The Bob Cats	-
Mame	-
Patricia	-

-1.Played by a big band.

Note:It has not been possible to verify that the above titles were recorded by Bob Crosby
     and his orchestra or his Bob Cats; some of the titles may be reissues from the Novem-
     ber 18, 1966 and February 1960 Dot recordings.
     Additional recordings by this artist are not included; the jazz content of some of
     the recordings listed may be limited.

GARY CROSBY

See also LOUIS ARMSTRONG.

(vcl) acc. by BUD SHANK'S ORCHESTRA:
Jerry van Rooyen,Rob Pronk,Hans Schachtner(tp),Franz Simons,Erich Well(tb),Bud Shank(as,
fl,cond),Hans Koller,Rudy Brink(ts),Willy Sanner(bars),Roland Kovac(p),Attila Zoller(g),
Gary Peacock(b),Rudy Pronk(dr),Bill Holman,Johnny Mandel(arr).
                                     Remagen,Germany.May 20,1957

Please Send Me Someone To Love	World Pacific X640,WP2006	
There's No You		-
One For My Baby		-
The Nearness Of You		-
I Gotta Right To Sing The Blues		-
Exactly Like You		-
Skylark		-
If I Could Be With You		-
Blue Prelude		-
Love Is Just Around The Corner		-

(vcl) acc. by orchestra,Bunny Botkin(arr).   LA.September 5,1958
22493-10 The Things We Did Last Summer Verve unissued
22494-12 Cheatin' On Me   Verve 10153,(Sd)VEP5051
22495   Funny Feeling   unissued
22496-6 Judy,Judy   Verve 10153,(Sd)VEP5051

(vcl) acc. by orchestra,Marty Paich(cond).   LA(?).October 15/17/18,1958
22599-17 Blues In The Night   Verve MGV2112,HMV(E)7EG8530
22600-5 Mood Indigo   -
22601-10 Night Train   -
22602-11 Sentimental Journey   Verve 10163,MGV2112,(Sd)VEP5051,HMV(E)7EG8530
22603-3 After The Lights Go Down Low   -   -   -
22604-4 Breeze (Blow My
          Baby Back To Me)   Verve MGV2112
22605   What's Your Story,Morning Glory   - ,HMV(E)7EG8530
22606-13 I Miss You So   -
22607-3 In The Wee Small
          Hours Of The Morning   -
22608-7 I'm Gonna Move To
          The Outskirts Of Town   -
22609-5 St. Louis Blues   -
22610-8 Baltimore Oriole   - ,HMV(E)7EG8530

All titles also on Verve MGVS6018.

GARY CROSBY AND HIS ALL STARS:
(vcl) acc. by orch. incl. Pete Candoli(tp),Gene Estes(vbs),Paul Smith(p),Howard Roberts
(g),Joe Mondragon(b),Larry Bunker/Bill Richmond(dr),Bunny Botkin(arr)(coll. pers.).
                                    LA.April 8,1959
26313-9 I've Got My Love
          To Keep Me Warm   Verve MGV2121
26314-10 Manana   -
26315-9 I'll Never Be Free   -
26316-6 Old Buttermilk Sky   - ,HMV(E)7EG8573

Same.   LA.April 9,1959
26317-5 You Won't Be Satisfied
          Until You Break My Heart   Verve MGV2121,HMV(E)7EG8573
26318-4 Side By Side   -
26319-6 Undecided   - ,HMV(E)7EG8573
26320-7 I'm Beginning To See The Light   -

Same.   LA.April 10,1959
26321-10 The Happy Bachelor   Verve 10175,MGV2121
26322-4 Glow Worm   Verve MGV2121,HMV(E)7EG8573
26323-7 Into Each Life
          Some Rain Must Fall   - ,HMV(E)7EG8573(?)
26324-6 This Little Girl Of Mine   Verve 10175,MGV2121

All titles on MGV2121 lso on Verve MGVS6067,(J)MV2664.

Note:The jazz content of some of the above recordings may be limited.

ISRAEL CROSBY

ISRAEL CROSBY QUARTETTE:
Unknown ts,p,Israel Crosby(b),Jack Cooley(dr,vcl).
                                    Unknown location. 1947
(session cont. next page).

(session cont. from previous page):
R1240 I Feel The Blues(jc)   Apollo 405
R1241 The Death Of Piney Brown(jc)   Apollo 390
R1243 I Know The Blues(jc)   -
R1244 I Deal In Cats   Apollo 405

LEIGH AND VIRGINIA CROSBY DIXIEBOPPERS

Nick Cochrane(tp),Paul Wiegand(tb),Rosy McHargue(cl),Joe Rushton(bassax),Milt Golden(p),
Gus Von Camp(b),Nick Fatool(dr).   LA.December 1946
RR15251 Jazz Me Blues   C&F 1
RR15252 Sheik   C&F 2
RR15253 How Come You Do Me Like You Do C&F 3
RR15254 Dixieland One Step   C&F 4
RR15255 After You've Gone   C&F 5

Note:C&F 1 and 5 are backed; the other titles have non-jazz backings. The name of this
     group was added after the recording.

OCTAVE CROSBY

OCTAVE CROSBY'S RAGTIME BAND:
Alvin Alcorn(tp),Irvin Verret(tb),Albert Burbank(cl,vcl),Octave Crosby(p,vcl),Jim Davis
(b),Chester Jones(dr).   New Orleans.January 25,1954
DB110 Gettysburg March   Jazz Man 102
DB111 Ain't Gonna Give Nobody
       None Of My Jelly Roll(oc)   -
       Ting-A-Ling(ab)   Jazz Man 103
       Bourbon Street Blues   -

All titles on Southland SLP210,Tempo(E)EXA92,Storyville(D)SEP341.
Note:Rec.date may be January 1,1954.

OCTAVE CROSBY BAND:
Incl. Clement Tervalon(tb),Albert Burbank(cl),Octave Crosby(p).
                                      New Orleans.February 1960
       Alabama Jubilee   unissued
       Memphis Blues(incompl.)   -

PIERRE-JEAN CROSSET (French)

Pierre-Jean Crosset(el-lyre).
                        Live."Original Center",St. Michel-de-Provence,France.May 11,197
       Danse Dans Le Néant
          Des Grands Dieux Agiles: Atelier Musical(F)AM001
             First Hour
             Second Hour

EARL CROSS

EARL CROSS SEXTET:
Earl Cross(flh),Daoud Haroon(tb),Jimmy Vass(ss),Ronnie Boykins,Juma Sultan(b),Roger Blank
(dr).   NYC.July 3,1973
(session cont. next page).

session cont. from previous page):
        J.L. March   Circle RK7376/6
        Una Muy Bonita   -

AY CROSSE

AY CROSSE AND HIS ORCHESTRA:
ddie Harris(tp),Gay Crosse(ts,vcl),Charlie Ross(p),Edward Lee(g),John Latham(b),Walter
arson(dr).   Cincinnati.June 28,1946
5082 Gay's Blues(gc)   Queen/King 4132
5083 I'm In The Groove Tonight(gc)   unissued
5084 I'm A Fool(gc)   -
5085 My Heart(gc)   Queen/King 4132

imilar.   Chicago. 1947
36   The Door Is Wide Open(gc)   Mercury 8034
37   Bop-De-Bip(gc)   Mercury 8036
38   It's A Low Down Dirty Shame(gc)   -
39   Ain't Nobody Here
          But Us Chickens(gc)   Mercury 8034

AY CROSSE AND HIS GOOD HUMOR SIX:
o details.   LA.January 1949
884   Give It Up(gc)   Capitol 57-70008
886   Be-Bop Blues(gc)   -

ddie Harris(tp),Jewel Grant(as),Gay Crosse(ts,vcl),Charlie Ross(p),William Lewis(g),John
atham(b),Walter Carson(dr).   Chicago.August 16,1949
)VB1181 Saturday Night Fish Fry(gc)   Victor 22-0049,50-0033
)VB1182 It Ain't Gonna Be That Way(gc) Victor 22-0065,50-0050
)VB1183 Swallow Dollow(gc)   -   -
)VB1184 Pelican's Stomp   Victor 22-0049,50-0033

known(tp),John Coltrane(as,ts),Gay Crosse(ts,vcl),unknown p,b,Specs Wright(dr).
                                        Unknown location.c. 1951
:1   Fat Sam From Birmingham(gc)   Gotham 279
:2   Bittersweet(gc)   -

mmy Turrentine(tp),John Coltrane(as,ts),Gay Crosse(ts,vcl),Stash O'Laughlin(p),Alvin
ckson(b),Oliver Jackson(dr),Christine Kittrell(vcl).
                                        Nasville,Tenn. 1952
KW6072 Easy Rockin'   Republic 7027
KW6074 No Better For You(gc)   Republic 7008
KW6075 Tired Of Being
           Shoved Around(gc)   -
KB6076 Gotta Stop Loving You(gc,ck)   Republic 7026
KW6082 G.C. Rock   Republic 7027

OSSFIRE (Australian)

ck Kenny(tp,keyb),Don Reid(reeds),Jim Kelly(g),Greg Lyon(b,vcl),John Proud(dr),Ian Blox-
m(perc).   Sydney.July 1975
        Remember The Trees   Harvest(Au)SHVL616
        Nobody Nose   -
        Freddy Funkbump   -
        Perverted Pavanne   - ,EMI(Au)EME1028
ession cont. next page).

(session cont. from previous page):
```
        Inside Out              Harvest(Au)SHVL616
        Nada                             -
        Stygian Night                   -
        You Gotta Make It               -
```

Mick Kenny(flh,el-p),Don Reid(fl,reeds),Jim Kelly(g),Greg Lyon(b),Doug Gallagher(dr),Ian
Bloxsom(perc).   Sydney.July 1978
```
        It Coitainly Was        Trafalgar(Au)D2D001
        On The Wings Of An Albatrocity  -
        Fahannakookin'                  -
        Odd Ball                        -
        Satie                           -
```

Tony Buchanan(ts,ss,fl),Mick Kenny(keyb),Jim Kelly(g),Phil Scorgie(b),Steve Hope(dr),Ian
Bloxsom(perc).   Sydney.June 1980
```
        East Of Where           WEA(Au)600072
        Parade                          -
        Away In D Major                 -
        Malice In Wonderland            -
        Let Sco'                        -
        Bob's Ya Uncle                  -
        Roll The Ivory Dice             -
        Where's The Man In The Fat Suit -
```

All titles also on Headfirst HF9704.

MICHAEL FRANKS WITH CROSSFIRE:
Add Michael Franks(vcl).   Sydney/Auckland,New Zeeland.September 1980
```
        B'Wana - He Not Home    WEA(Au)600084
        Chain Reaction                  -
        The Lady Wants To Know          -
        Antonio's Song                  -
        Moneky See - Monkey Do          -
        Don't Be Blue                   -
        Pocsicle Toes                   -
        When The Cookie Jar Is Empty    -
```


CONNIE CROTHERS

CONNIE CROTHERS TRIO:
Connie Crothers(p),Joe Solomon(b),Roger Mancuso(dr).
```
                                Jamaica,N.Y.June 21,1974
        Incandecense            SteepleChase(D)SCS1022
```

Same.   Jamaica,N.Y.September 7,1974
```
        Three-Way               SteepleChase(D)SCS1022
```

Same.   Jamaica,N.Y.September 17,1974
```
        Hillside Avenue         SteepleChase(D)SCS1022
```

Same.   Jamaica,N.Y.September 24,1974
```
        Convergence             SteepleChase(D)SCS1022
        Images                          -
        Lennie's Scene                  -
```

(p-solo).   Jamaica,N.Y.October 25,1974
(session cont. next page).

(session cont. from previous page):
    Perceptism   SteepleChase(D)SCS1022
    Vibration   -
    Labyrinth   -
    Free-Way   -

All titles on SCS1022 also on SteepleChase(J)RJ7103,Inner City IC2022.

Nomi Rosen(fl),Connie Crothers(p).   Live.Town Hall,NYC.January 28,1979
    Confluence   Jazz JR3

Note:The above title was recorded at a Lennie Tristano memorial concert.

(p-solo).   Live.Unknown location.c. 1980
    All About Love   Jazz JR4
    A New Jazz Scene   -
    My One And Only Love(cc)   -
    The Straight Ahead Thing   -
    A Single Note(cc)   -
    Drums-Piano   -
    All About You   -
    Love Suite: -
       Roy Eldridge
       Sheila Jordan
       Max Roach
    I'm Getting Sentimental Over You -
    You Don't Know What Love Is(cc)   -
    How Deep Is The Ocean   -
    Breaking Through The Boundairies -

"SCAT MAN" (BENJAMIN SHERMAN) CROTHERS

(vcl) acc. by RIFF CHARLES AND HIS FRIENDS:
Incl. Vic Dickenson(tb).   LA. 1948
3234 Riff's Blues   Capitol 15220
3235 The Thing   Capitol 15076
3236 Mabel The Lush   Capitol 15220
3237 Dead Man's Blues   Capitol 15076

(vcl) acc. by unknown group.   LA(?). 1948
3502 Have You Got The Gumption Capitol 15431

(vcl) acc. by Gerald Wiggins(p),Danny Barker(g),John Simmons(b),Jesse Price(dr).
                              LA.January 10,1949
3839 Pretty Little Blue-Eyed Susie Capitol 15383
3844 Do Something   Capitol 15431
3845 I'd Rather Be A Humming Bird Capitol 15383

vcl) acc. by unknown group.   LA(?).c. 1950
    Shuffleboard Blues   Orchid 1

vcl) acc. by unknown group.   LA(?).c. 1950
    Television Blues   London(Am)30081
    I'd Rather Be A Rooster   -

vcl) acc. by RED CALLENDER SEXTET:
rob. incl. Maxwell Davis(ts),Red Callender(b).
                              LA.April 16,1951
session cont. next page).

(session cont. from previous page):
RR1667 King Berman's Stomp   Intro 6017
RR1668 A Gruntin' And A
          Groanin' (Wrestler's Song)   Intro 6016
RR1669 Free Samples   -
RR1670 Just Like Two Drops Of Water   Intro 6017

(vcl) acc. by unknown group.   LA(?). 1952/53
      Easy Money   Recorded In Hollywood 401
      Waiting For My Baby   -

(vcl) acc. by MATTY MATLOCK'S ALL STARS:
No details.   LA.September 8,1953
L7348 Walkin' My Baby Back Home   Decca 28895
L7349 Honeysuckle Rose   -
L7350 On The Sunny Side Of The Street Decca 29097
L7351 A Smile Will Go A Long Way   -

(vcl) acc. by unknown group.   LA(?). 1955
      Dearest One   Century 710
      Keep That Coffee Hot   -
      Pork 'N' Beans   Century 712
      When,Oh When   -

(vcl) acc. by unknown group.   LA(?). 1955/56
      Sweet Lips   MGM 12199
      Waitin' For My Baby   -

(vcl) acc. by Babe Russin(ts),Paul Smith(p),Al Hendrickson(g),Larry Breen(b),Milt Holland/
Jack Sperling(dr).   LA. 1956
      Exactly Like You   Tops L1511
      September Song   -
      St. James Infirmary   -
      Ghost Riders In The Sky   -
      My Blue Heaven   -
      I'm Gonna Sit Right Down
         And Write Myself A Letter   -
      I Got Rhythm   -
      Nobody Knows Why   -
      The Best Things In Blue Are Free -
      The Gal Looks Good   -
      Please Don't Talk
         About Me When I'm Gone   -
      Baby Won't You Please Come Home -
      Round And Round   Tops EP R304

(vcl) acc. by unknown group.   LA(?). 1958
      Take Your Time   Challenge 59028
      Rock,Roma,Rock It   -
      Planet Fazoo   Challenge 59065
      Good Times Will Come   -

(vcl) acc. by unknown p,g,b,dr,background vocals.
                                    Unknown location.c. 1973
      I'm A Melody Man   Motown M777L
      Elaine,Elaine(1)   -
      I Found Someone   -
      God Bless The Child(1,2)   -
      Nobody Knows Why   -
      Dead Man's Blues   -
(session cont. next page).

(session cont. from previous page):

Waiting For My Baby	Motown M777L
How Long,How Long Blues	-
Kansas City	-
Tell Me How Long That Train's Been Gone	-
Wondering(1)	-
Until The Real Thing Comes Along(1,2)	-
Hey Lawdy Mama(1)	-

-1.Add unknown(ts).
-2.No background vocal.

MIKE CROTTY

MIKE CROTTY AND THE SUNDAY MORNING JAZZ BAND:
Tom Bowen,Dave Russell,Tony Ebersole,Wayne Toyne,Steve Robinson(tp,flh),Ken Hedberg,Larry
Farris,Jim Templin(tb),Dallas Parker(btb),Mike Crotty(ss,as,fl,cl,arr),Mike Redford(as,fl)
Jack Wolfe(ts,ss,fl,picc),C.J. Landry(ts,cl,fl),Bill Schremp(bars,bcl),Paul Morawski(p,
el-p),Wiley Porter(g),Paul Langosch(b),Dave Palamar(dr).

	Springfield,Virginia.October 1980
Jeanine	Jazz Heritage Inc. JHI81001
Tone Poem For A Rainy Day	-
Sunlit Dreams	-
In Search Of The Phoenix	-
Soul Eyes	-
Well,You Needn't	-

RON CROTTY

RON CROTTY TRIO:
Vince Guaraldi(p,celeste),Eddie Duran(g),Ron Crotty(b).

	San Fransicso.August 4,1955
Ginza	Fantasy LP3213
The Night We Called It A Day	-
The Masquerade Is Over	-

11 titles also on Original Jazz Classics OJC272.

ICK CROUCH

ee PAZ.

OEL CROW (Australian)

OEL CROW'S JAZZMEN:
evin Keogh(tp),Jeff Hawes(tb,vcl),Noel Crow(cl),Dennis Tong(bj,g,vcl),Col Best(b),Geoff
llen(dr).

	Sydney.August 29,1978
Wolverine Blues	EMI(Au)EMC2681
You're Driving Me Crazy(jh)	-
Who Stole The Lock(jh)	-

session cont. next page).

(session cont. from previous page):
```
        Gee Baby,Ain't I Good To You(jh) EMI(Au)EMC2681
        South Rampart Street Parade           -
        Ballin' The Jack(jh)                  -
        Oh Gee,Say Gee(jh)                    -
        Original Dixieland One Step           -
        Skylark(df,jh)                        -
        Sailing Down Chesapeake Bay(dt)       -
        Panama Rag(1)                         -
        All The Girls Go Crazy(1)(df)         -
```

-1.Add Dave Ferrier(cnt,vcl).

Kevin Keogh(tp),Jeff Hawes(tb,vcl),Noel Crow(cl,ts),Verdon Morcum(p),Col Best(b),Geoff
Allen(dr).   Live.Forbes,Australia.December 27 or 29,1980
        Diga Diga Doo   Strad(Au)SSR047

R.J. CROWLEY

See CREATIVE ART ENSEMBLE.

HUGH CROZIER

```
(p-solo).                             London.c.  1970
        Late Night Stomp              Stomp(E)ROBB002
        Queen Of The South                    -
        Blues For You                         -
        Kaleidoscrope Rag                     -
        You've Got No Time For Me             -
        Classical Rag                         -
        Georgie                               -
        Jelly Roll Stomp                      -
        Olde London Ragge(!)                  -
        Lovely                                -
        Dunkirk Festival Stomp                -(?)
```


BOB CRUICKSHANKS (Australian)

BOB CRUICKSHANKS' QUARTET:
Johnny McCarthy(cl),Bob Cruickshanks(as),Jimmy Somerville(p),Neil Macbeth(dr).
                                      Live.Sydney.December 30,1958
        I Know The Feeling Well   Columbia(Au)330SX7618

ROBERT CRUM

```
Robert Crum(p),Barrett Deems(dr).       Chicago.  1946
1133    If I Had You                  Gold Star 103
1135    Who                                   -
        Crum-Boogie                   Gold Star 101
        The Very Thought Of You               -
        One O'Clock Boogie            Gold Star 102
        Alexanders's Ragtime Band             -
```

PAT CRUMLEY

See EDGE.

PHIL CRUMLEY

See NATURAL GAS JAZZ BAND.

TINY CRUMP

See also JEAN LA RUE.

TINY CRUMP TRIO:
Tiny Crump(p),Edward Young(g),Chalres Oden(b).

		LA. 1946
UR706	Crumpus Rumpus	Universal 704
	Boogie Joys	Universal 703

THE CRUSADERS

See THE JAZZ CRUSADERS.

JUANITA CRUSE

(vcl) acc. by Bill Green(fl,sax),Emil Richards(vbs),Gerald Wiggins(p),Dennis Budimir(g), Al McKibbon(b),Jackie Mills(dr),Jack Costanzo(bg).

	LA. 1960
Alone Together	Gene Norman Presents GNP51(ST)
Teach Me Tonight	-
I Love Paris	-
The Midnight Sun Will Never Set	-
Fine And Mellow	-
You'd Be So Nice To Come Home To	-
God Bless The Child	-
Sunset Eyes	-
Don't Explain	-
Stop Teasin' Me	-

CRYPTO (Dutch)

incl. Peter Schön(p,el-p),Bert Devies(g).   Unknown location.c. 1973

Labyrinth	The Natural Label NALS001
Jazztime	-

Peter Schön(el-p,p,synth),Bert Devies(g),Wim Dijkgraaf(el-b),Jan Nanning van der Hoop(dr, perc).   Nederhorst den Berg,The Netherlands.December 2/3/4/5/9,1974

Ribatejo	Pandora(Du)NR503
Masogistic Bonus Point	-
Funk For Farmers	-
My Bonnie	-

(session cont. next page).

(session cont. from previous page):
```
        Gallfly                  Pandora(Du)NR503
        Melon Cactus                    -
        Awakening                       -
        Tatus                           -
        Nova Zembla                     -
```

Note:Additional recordings by this group are not included.

THE CRYSTALETTE/LAMPLIGHTER ALL STARS

See also WINI BEATTY,KAY STAR.

Ray Linn(tp),Vic Dickenson(tb),Barney Bigard(cl),Willie Smith(as),Calvin Jackson(p),Allan
Reuss(g),Red Callender(b),Zutty Singleton(dr).
```
                                     LA.December 12,1945
A2989  My Melancholy Baby           Lamplighter 104

Same.                                LA.December 18,1945
S1280  Sweet Georgia Brown(no tb)    Crystalette 640,Lamplighter 104,Solid Sender
                                       SOL512
S1824  Night And Day                 Crystalette 608
S1920  Uncle Willie(no tp,tb,cl)     Crystalette 640,Solid Sender SOL512
```

Eddie Beal or Calvin Jackson(p),Allan Reuss(g),Red Callender(b),Zutty Singleton(dr).
```
                                     LA.  1945/46
S1282  Lantern Boogie                Crystalette 641,Solid Sender SOL512
```

CRYSTALETTE DIXIELAND ALL STARS:
```
Same.                                LA.  1945/46
        Panama                       Crystalette 646
        Who's Sorry Now                     -
```

CRYSTALLETTE ALL STARS ORCHESTRA:
Ray Linn(tp),rest unknown.
```
                                     LA.  1945/46
S1923  Roses Of Picardy              Crystalette 641,Solid Sender SOL512
```

CLAUDE TRENIER WITH THE LAMPLIGHTER ALL STARS:
Barney Bigard(cl),Eddie Beal(p),Allan Reuss(g),Red Callender(b),Zutty Singleton(dr),Claude
Trenier(vcl).
```
                                     LA.January 29,1946
A2994  Young Man's Blues,pt.1(ct)    Lamplighter 102
A2995  Young Man's Blues,pt.2(ct)           -
```

Both parts also on Crystalette 619,Solid Sender SOL512,Two Flats Disc TFD5002.

MONETTE MOORE WITH THE LAMPLIGHTER ALL STARS(?):
Monette Moore(vcl) replaces Trenier;poss. Eddie Beal(p).
```
                                     LA.  1946
        Rockin' Chair(mm)            Solid Sender SOL512
        I Want A Little Boy(mm)             -
```


GUSZTAV CSIK (Hungarian)

CSIKY - KOVACS - PEGE TRIO:
Gusztav Csik(p),Aladar Pege(b,arr),Gyula Kovacs(dr).
```
                                     Budapest.January 7,1964
6242   Blues                         Qualiton(Hu)LPX7279/80
6243   Dalia                                -
```

CSIK TRIO:
Gusztav Csik(org),Jenö Buri(b),Imre Közegi(dr).
                                        Budapest.March 13,1970
        Emlekeim (My Memories)   Hungaroton(Hu)SLPX17421

Laszlo Juhasz(tp,el-b),Kurt Weil(tb,vbs),Jean-Pierre Wuttke(ts,as),Gusztav Csik(org,ts),
Bernd Heil(g,el-b,vcl),Ralph Bloch(dr).   Cologne,Germany.December 1971
        Motives   EMI-Harvest(G)1C.062-29438
        Born To Wander   -
        I Hear You Call   -
        Send Me A Letter   -
        Share My World   -
        'Scuse Me   -
        Sunshine In My Eyes   -
        Thinking Of You   -
        Don't Get Me Wrong   -
        Circle Of Dreams

Same.   Prob. Cologne,Germany.July 1972
        Listen People   EMI-Harvest(G)1C.086-30272
        I Like How You Say It   -

Add Jerry Howell(el-b,vcl);Csik plays (org,el-p);Wuttke also (vcl).
                                        Cologne,Germany.January 1973
        Suite Hope: EMI-Harvest(G)1C.062-29483
           Hope For Mankind
           Hope For Children(jpw)
           Hope For Music
           Interlude
           Hope For The Universe
        Alchemy Is Good For You
           (Don't You Know It)   -
        Gone To The Dogs(jh)   -
        If You Know   -
        Gimme Some Lovin'   -
        So Sad   -

CSIK GUSZTAV ES EGYÜTTESE:
Gusztav Csik(el-p,synth),Janos Fogarasi(org),Balazs Berkes(b,el-b),Vilmos Javori(dr).
                                        Budapest. 1975
        Papirsarkany (Sky Papers)   Pepita(Hu)SLPX17506
        Ritsmusvaltasok (Rhytmic Changes)   -
        Almodozas (Reverie)   -
        Cameleon   -
        Babaszerenad (Doll
           Serenade)(no org)   -

CSULA

See CALIFORNIA STATE UNIVERSITY (LOS ANGELES).

CTI ALL STARS

Freddie Hubbard(tp),Hubert Laws(fl),Hank Crawford(as),Stanley Turrentine(ts),Johnny "Hammond" Smith(el-p,org),George Benson(g),Ron Carter(b),Billy Cobham(dr),Airto Moreira(perc).
                                        Live."Hollywood Bowl",LA.July 18,1971

(session cont. next page).

(session cont. from previous page):

Fire And Rain	CTI CTX2	
Red Clay,pt.1,2	-	
Sugar	-	
Blues West	-	
Leaving West	-	

All titles also on CTI(J)GW187/88.

Freddie Hubbard(tp),Hubert Laws(fl),Hank Crawford,Grover Washington(as),Stanley Turrentine
Joe Farrell(ts),Milt Jackson(vbs),Deodato,Johnny "Hammond" Smith,Bob James(keyb),George
Benson(g),Ron Carter(b),Jack DeJohnette(dr),Airto Moreira(perc),Esther Phillips(vcl).
                                        Live."Hollywood Bowl",LA.July 30,1972

Grits Bowl	CTI 7076
Inner City Blues/What's Going On	-
California Dreaming	
First Light	-
Blues Force	CTI 7077
Rock Steady	-
Theme From:	-
Love Story	
Pavane	
Fire And Rain	
People Make The World Go Round	-
Funkfathers	CTI 7078
Cherry	-
Bowl Full O'Blues(no tp)(ep(?))	-
Cherry Red(no tp)(ep)	-
God Bless The Child(no tp)(ep)	-

All titles on CTI 7076 also on CTI(Eu)63026.
All titles on CTI 7077 also on CTI(Eu)63027.
All titles on CTI 7078 also on CTI(Eu)63028.

CUBAN JAM SESSION

Alejandro "El Negro" Vivar(tp),Juan Pablo Miranda(fl),Edilberto Serich(?)(as),Emilio Pe-
nalver,José "Chombo" Silva(ts),Osvaldo "Mosquifin" Urrutia(bars),Julio Gutierrez,Pedro
"Parrachin" Justiz(p,co-leaders),Salvador Vivar(b),Walfredo de los Reyes,Jr.(dr),Jesus
Ezquijarrosa,Oscar Valdes,Marcelius Valdes(perc).
                                        Havana,Cuba. 1950's

Introduction	Panart CLP8000
Theme On Perfidia	-
Theme On Mambo	-
Cimarron	-
Theme On Cha Cha Cha	-
Opus For Dancing	-
Theme For Conga	-

Same.
                                        Havana,Cuba. 1950's

Jam Session (Descarga Caliente)	Panart (unknown issueno.)
Rhumba Theme	-
Listen To The Rhythm	
Of The Cha Cha Cha	-
Bata Rhythm	-

All titles also on Panart(Venezuelan)102-28042.
Note:Three LPs were issued in US as CUBAN JAM SESSION; the above titles were poss. issued
    on Panart CLP3055 or CLP3090 - details for these LPs are not available.

RONNIE CUBER

See also XANADU ALL STARS.

Ronnie Cuber(bars),Barry Harris(p),Sam Jones(b),Albert Heath(dr).
                                    NYC.August 20,1976
Star Eyes	Xanadu 135	
Rifftide	- ,5001,(Eu)197150	
Tin Tin Deo	-	
Samba d'Orfeo	-	
Misty	-	
Sudwest Funk	-	
Prince Albert	-	

All titles also on Xanadu(Eu)197.114,(J)ULX86.

Tom Harrell(tp,flh),Ronnie Cuber(bars),Mickey Tucker(p),Dennis Irwin(b),Eddie Gladden(dr).
                                    NYC.January 31,1978
Klepto	Xanadu 156	
Open Air	-	
Sunburst	-	
Taurus Lullaby	-	
Commit To Memory	-	
Cumana	-	

All titles also on Xanadu(F)JX6622,VG405.506622,ULX111.

RON CUCCIA

RON CUCCIA AND THE JAZZ POETRY GROUP:
Ron Cuccia,Leigh Harris(vcl) acc. by Charles Neville(sax,vcl),Johnny Magnie(p,vcl),Ramsey
McLean(b,cello),Ricky Sebastian(dr,perc).
                        Live.Contemporary Arts Center,NYC.July 13/14,1979
Jazztown/Fastfood	Takoma TAK7072	
Streets/My Darlin' New Orleans	-	
Who Pushed The Button/		
Children Of Creation	-	
Summer Ain't No Secret Anymore	-	
Spring Rendezvous/		
Splendid Company	-	
The Scuffle	-	
Love Song	-	

HENRY CUESTA

Henry Cuesta(cl),Brian Browne(p),Pearson "Skip" Beckwith(b),Alex Lazaroff(dr).
                        Toronto.May 3,1966
Michelle	Canadian Talent Library(Ca)M1077/S5077	
Lazy Bones	-	
Yellow Dog Blues	-	
Autumn Leaves	-	
Washington Square	-	
You Forgot Your Gloves	-	
Spain	-	

Henry Cuesta(cl),Peter Appleyard(vbs),Jimmy Coxson(p),Hank Monis(g),Murray Lauder(b),
Mickey Shannon(dr),strings.   Toronto.April 23,1968
      We're At Home   Canadian Talent Library(Ca)S5101
      Fate   -

Both titles also on RCA-Victor(Ca)CTLS1101,Camden(Ca)CAS2407.

Hagood Hardy(vbs) replaces Appleyard;omit Coxson.
                                  Toronto.April 25,1968
      Just A Closer Walk With Thee   Canadian Talent Library(Ca)S5101
      At A Georgia Camp Meeting   -

Both titles also on RCA-Victor(Ca)CTLS1101,Camden(Ca)CAS2407.

Henry Cuesta(cl,bars),Peter Appleyard(vbs),Jimmy Coxson(p,hcs,org),Hank Monis,Kenny Gill,
Bobby Edwards(g),Bob Price(b),Don Vickery(dr).
                                  Toronto.May 1971
      The Promised Land   Canadian Talent Library(Ca)477-5147
      Help Me Make It Through The Night   -
      Royal Garden Blues   - ,477-806
      Skyline Stomp   -   -

Henry Cuesta(cl),rest unknown.   LA.c. 1975/76
      Unknown titles   Ranwood R8166

DEXTER CULBERTSON

U.S. NAVY BAND:
Dexter Culbertson(tp,ldr),John Coltrane(as),Norman Poulshock(p),Willie Stader(b),Joe Time
(dr),Benny Thomas(vcl).   Hawaii.July 13,1946
      Embraceable You(bt)
      Ornithology
      Sweet Miss
      It's Only A Paper Moon(bt)
      Sweet Lorraine(bt)
      Koko
      Now's The Time(bt)
      Hot House

Note:The above titles are on 4 unnumbered discs (only 4-5 copies of each). An excerpt of
    "Koko" (22 sec.) was incl. in a Coltrane video (Video Arts(J)VAVJ165).

CUL CULLEN (Australian)

(vcl) acc. by Bob Barnard(tp,flh),Lloyd Adamson(tp),Norm Wyatt(tb),Johnny McCarthy(reeds
Terry Wilkinson(p),Norm Day(g),Darcy Wright(b),Louis Burdett(dr).
                                  Sydney.September 26,1974
      How Long Blues   Earth(Au)ELF003
      Nobody Knows You   -
      Black Eye Blues   -
      Rich Folks Hoax   -
      Lonely At The Top   -
      Drinking Again   -
      More Alcohol   -
      Sometimes   -
      Rhubarb Song   -
      Wanderings   -
      Forget It   -

FRANK "FLOORSHOW" CULLEY

Unknown tp,tb,Frank Culley(ts),sax,p,g,b,dr. Unknown location. 1948

HS4010	The Pig Is Diggin'(1)	Lennox 513,Plymouth 12-122
HS4012	Ready For Action(2)	Lennox 513,Remington L1037,Plymouth 12-113,12-122,
		Palace M737.LPM672
HS4220	Potato Salad	Lennox 525,Plymouth 12-115
HS4221	Jackson Is Jivin'	-

-1.As "Ready For Action" on Plymouth 12-122.
-2.As "Harlem Hop" and "House Rocking" on Plymouth issues; Remington L1037 issued as by
  EDDIE LOCKJAW DAVIS.

Frank Culley(ts),prob. Randy Weston(p),unknown g,b,prob. Connie Kay(dr).
                                  NYC.January 17,1949

175	The Snap	Atlantic 880
176	Floor Show	-
177	Cole Slaw	Atlantic 874,SD8161
178	Central Avenue Breakdown	- ,81293-1,81293-2(CD)

All titles also on Official OFF6057.

Similar.   NYC.August 3,1949

255	Peas And Rice	Atlantic unissued
256	Fast Blues	
257	Miss Meal Cramp	
258	Let Her Roll	
259	Slow Blues	
285	Fast Blues	
286	Little Caesar	

Incl. Frank Culley(ts),Harry Van Walls(p). NYC.September 19,1949

294	Waxie Maxie Boogie	
	(Boogie Woogie No.1)	Atlantic 902,Official OFF6057
295	Boogie Woogie No. 2	unissued
296	After Hours Session	Atlantic 888,Official OFF6057
297	Rhumboogie Jive	- -
298	Train	unissued
298A	Coffee Grind	-
298B	Peas And Rice No.2	-
299	Hop 'N' Twist (Fishtail)	Atlantic 902,LP/SD8013,81666-1,Official OFF6057

Frank Culley(ts),Harry Van Walls(p),unknown g,b,dr,Arlene Talley(vcl).
                                  NYC.August 12,1950

501	My Silent Love	Atlantic 918,Official OFF6057
502	Mona Lisa	- -
503	Original Jump No.1	unissued
504	Original Jump No.2	-
505	Gone After Hours (After	
	Hours Session No.2,pt.1)	Atlantic 922,LP/SD8013,81666-1,(J)P6191,Official
		OFF6057
506	Little Miss Blues(at)	Atlantic 922,Official OFF6057
507	After Hours Session No.2,pt.2	unissued

Wallace Wilson(tp),Walter Morris(tb),Frank Culley(ts),Randy Weston(p),Count Edmondson(b),
Connie Kay(dr).   NYC.February 27,1951

472	I've Got You Under My Skin	Atlantic 935,Official OFF6057
473	Culley Flower	- ,LP8013,81666-1,Official OFF6057
474	Leap Frog	unissued
475	Saints	-

ARLENE TALLEY - FRANK CULLEY:
Add Arlene Talley(vcl).   Same date
576   I Cried For You   Atlantic unissued
577   Just One Moment Blues

Frank Culley(ts),unknown(bars),poss. Harry Van Walls(p),unknown g,b,dr.
                                              NYC. 1955
          Nine O'Clock Express   Baton BC1201,Krazy Kat(E)KK784
          Lindy Rock   -   -
          Go,Floorshow   -   -
          Bubbles   -   -
          Speed Limit   -   -

Note:"After Hours Express,I/II" issued on Baton 226 may be an edited version of "Nine
     O'Clock Express".

No details.   Unknown location.c. 1959
9488   I Ain't Sorry   Chess unissued
9489   Troubles
9490   Cool Breeze
9491   Come And Get It

JIM CULLUM

(JIM CULLUM'S) HAPPY JAZZ BAND (OF SAN ANTONIO,TEXAS):
Jim Culllum,Jr.(cnt),Gene McKinney(tb),Jim Cullum,Sr.(cl),Cliff Brewton(p),Ben Valfrey
(bj),Wilson Davis(tu,sousaphone),Harvey Kindervater(dr).
                                         San Antonio,Texas. 1963
          Cake Walking Babies From Home   Happy Jazz HJ63
          Ole Miss   -
          Riverboat Shuffle   -
          Original Jelly Roll Blues   -
          Just A Closer Walk With Thee   -
          Copenhagen   -
          Sweet Substitute   -
          Ostrich Walk   -
          Blues For B-Flat Clarinet   -
          Original Dixieland One Step   -

All titles also on Audiophile AP115.

Note:When the Audiophile label - excluding the items recorded by Jim Cullum - was sold to
     George H. Buck's Jazzology label in the mid-1970s, some of the issuenumbers were re-
     used - e.g. AP115 (new series) is a Ian Whitcomb LP.

Cliff Gillette(p) replaces Brewton.   San Antonio,Texas.c. 1964
          Peculiar Rag   Audiophile AP86
          Tishomingo Blues   -
          Royal Garden Blues   -
          Clarinet Marmalade   -
          Milenberg Joys   -
          The Chant   -
          Sister Kate   -
          Bogalusa Strut   -
          The Pearls   -
          Panama   -

Same.   San Antonio,Texas.c. 1965
        Fidgety Feet   Audiophile AP87
        Winin' Boy Blues   -
        Tia Juana   -
        John Jennings Blues
          (Terrible Blues)   -
        New Orleans Stomp   -
        Papa Dip   -
        Melancholy   -
        San   -
        Mabel's Dream   -
        Down In Jungle Town   -

Curly Williams(bj) replaces Valfrey.   San Antonio,Texas.c. 1966
        Willie The Weeper   Audiophile AP93
        Sunset Cafe Stomp   -
        Someday Sweetheart   -
        Angry   -
        Susie   -
        Pelican Panic   -
        Singin' The Blues   -
        I Ain't Gonna Give
          Nobody None Of This Jelly Roll -
        All Night Blues   -
        Lizard On A Rail   -

THE HAPPY JAZZ BAND WITH BOBBY HACKETT:
Add Bobby Hackett(cnt).   San Antonio,Texas.c. 1967
        Goose Pimples   Audiophile AP96
        Memphis Blues   -
        Louisiana   -
        Sorry   -
        Buddy Bolden's Blues   -
        Wang Wang Blues   -
        Mood Indigo   -
        Chloe   -
        You've Got To See
          Mama Every Night   -
        A Bientot   -
        Westmoreland Weave   -

'IM CULLUM'S HAPPY JAZZ BAND:
mit Hackett.   Live.World's Fair.Unknown location. 1968
        I'm Comin' Virginia   Happy Jazz HJ200
        Blues My Naughty
          Sweetie Gives To Me   -
        Smiles   -
        Margie   -
        Oh!Baby   -
        Alexander's Ragtime Band   -
        Yellow Dog Blues   -
        Rose Of Washington Square   -
        Falling Tears   -
        High Society   -
        Winin' Boy Blues   -

im Culllum,Jr.(cnt),Gene McKinney(tb),Jim Cullum,Sr.(cl),Cliff Gillette(p),Curly Williams
bj),Bill Chapman(tu),Wilson Davis(sousaphone),Harvey Kindervater(dr).
                                         San Antonio,Texas.c. 1969
session cont. next page).

(session cont. from previous page):

Zacatecas	Happy Jazz HJ201
Savoy Blues	-
Sweet Georgia Brown	-
Cornet Chop Suey	-
Just Make Me A	
Pallet On The Floor	-
Wolverine Blues	-
Limehouse Blues	-
Skylark	-
Eccentric Rag	-
New Orleans	-
Come Back Sweet Papa	-
Shreveport Stomp	-

George Pryor(b) replaces Chapman;McKinney plays (tb,b);Williams plays (bj,g).
San Antonio,Texas.c. 1970

Way Down Yonder In New Orleans	Happy Jazz HJ202
I Guess I'll Have	
To Change My Plan	-
She's Cryin' For Me	-
Blue Orchids	-
Mo Honey's Lovin' Arms	-
Jitterbug Waltz	-
I'll Be A Friend With Pleasure	-
King Porter Stomp	-
Melancholy Baby	-
Vilia	-
Canal Street Blues	-
Song Of The Wanderer	-

JIM CULLUM,Sr:
Jim Cullum Jr. -1(cnt),Jim Cullum Sr.(cl),Spud Goodall,Curly Williams(g),Gene McKinney(b).
San Antonio,Texas.c. 1970

Oh!What It Seemed To Be	Audiophile AP107
Once In A While	-
I Remember You	-
Sugar Foot Strut(1)	-
It's Easy To Remember	-
Every Day (I Fall In Love)	-
Exactly Like You	-
Love Lies	-
Roses Of Picardy	-
Drinking Again	-
Moonlight On The Ganges(1)	-
September In The Rain	-
Moon Song(1)	-

JIM CULLUM'S HAPPY JAZZ BAND:
Jim Culllum,Jr.(cnt),Gene McKinney(tb),Jim Cullum,Sr.(cl),Cliff Gillette(p),Spud Goodall,
Curly Williams(bj,g),Warren Lewis(b),Wilson Davis(sousaphone),Harvey Kindervater(dr).
San Antonio,Texas.c. 1971

Royal Garden Blues	Audiophile AP114
Russian Roulette(1)	-
Just A Little While To Stay Here	-
Ol' Man River	-
Black And Blue	-
Everybody Loves My Baby	-
Struttin' With Some Barbecue	-
Dark Eyes	-

(session cont. next page).

JIM CULLUM

(session cont. from previous page):
Mississippi Mud	Audiophile AP114
My Gal Sal	-
Shine	-
Bye Bye Blackbird	-
The Japanese Sandman	-
That Da-Da Strain	-

-1.Add El Curro(g).

mit Spudd Godall. San Antonio,Texas. 1972
Bourbon Street Parade(1)	Audiophile AP116
Aggravatin' Papa(1)	-
Riverboat Shuffle	-
China Boy	-
At The Jazz Band Ball	-
Willow Weep For Me	-
Rose of The Rio Grande	-
Sugar	-
I'm Gonna Stomp Mr. Henry Lee	-

1.Add Mark Hess(p,cnt,vtb).

im Cullum,Jr.(cnt),Gene McKinney(tb),Mark Hess(p,vtb),Jim Cullum,Sr.(cl),Cliff Gillette
p),Curly Williams(g),Warren Lewis,George Pryor(b),Harvey Kindervater,Kevin Hess(dr).
San Antonio,Texas.April 1973
Swing That Music	Audiophile AP117
Stardust	-
Dixieland Shuffle	-
My Inspiration	-
Old Spinnin' Wheel	-
Waltzing Matilda	-
Old Folks	-
Washboard Blues	-
Am I Blue	-
Mine	-
Li'l Liza Jane	-

rob. same. Live."The Landing",San Antonio,Texas.April 1973
Canal Street Blues	Audiophile AP118/19
Skylark	-
Milenberg Joys	-
Dream	-
Old Man River	-
China Boy	-
Stardust	-
Corrine,Corrina	-
Papa Dip	-
St. Louis Blues	-
Muskrat Ramble	-
Unknown titles	-

E HAPPY JAZZ BAND - THE WORLD GREATEST JAZZ BAND:
m Cullum,Jr.(cnt),Yank Lawson(tp),Gene McKinney(tb),Jim Cullum,Sr.(cl),Bud Freeman(ts),
lph Sutton(p),Bob Haggart(b),Harvey Kindervater(dr).
Live."The Landing",San Antonio,Texas.April 8,1973
Royal Garden Blues	Audiophile AP119

M CULLUM'S HAPPY JAZZ (BAND):
m Cullum,Jr.(cnt),Mark Hess(vtb),Gene McKinney(tb),Bobby Gordon(cl),Cliff Gillette(p),
m Newell(bj),Buddy Apfel(b),Harvey Kindervater(dr).
ession cont. next page).

(session cont. from previous page):

	Live.Meriden,Connecticut.February 8,1974
The Eel	Connecticut Traditional Jazz Club SLP10
Westmoreland Weave	-

Prob. same.   San Antonio,Texas.c. 1974

The Eel	Audiophile AP120
PLayin' Hooky	-
Westmoreland Weave	-
Savoy Blues	-
All My Love	-
Kansas City Stomps	-
Wherever There's Love	-
High Society	-
Winin' Boy Blues	-

Prob. same.   San Antonio,Texas.c. 1975

Black Bottom Stomp	Audiophile AP121
Squeeze Me	-
Some Sunny Day	-
Lover Come Back To Me	-
Pee Wee's Tune	-
Panama	-
Apex Blues	-
Lullaby Of The Leaves	-
Don't Leave Me,Daddy	-
Emperor Norton's Hunch	-

Similar.   Live.New Jersey. 1970's

Pee Wee's Song	Jersey Jazz JJ1001

Jim Cullum,Jr.(cnt),Randy Reinhart(tb,flh),Allan Vache(cl),Cliff Gillette(p),Bobby Black (bj),Buddy Apfel(tu),Mike Masessa(dr).   San Antonio,Texas.September 19/20,1976

Wrought Iron Rag	American Jazz AJ125
Hagar's Blues	-
Mabel's Dream	-
Kakapu Rag	-
Lazy Bones	-
Rhythm King	-
Morning Glory	-
The Albatross	-
Dixieland Shuffle	-
Sage Hen Strut	-

Same.   Live.Meriden,Connecticut.February 18,1977

Aunt Hagar's Blues	Connecticut Traditional Jazz Club SLP13

Jim Cullum,Jr.(cnt),Randy Reinhart(tb,cnt),Herb Gardner(tb),Allan Vache(cl),Cliff Gillett (p),Bobby Black(bj,g),Bill Chapman(tu),Mike Masessa(dr).

	San Antonio,Texas.c. 1977
Milenburg Joys	American Jazz AJ126
The Mooche	-
Thou Swell	-
Gatemouth	-
Lonesome Me	-
I Would Do Anything For You	-
When There's Time	-
Enterprise Rag	-

Jim Cullum,Jr.(cnt),Michael Pittsley(tb),Allan Vache(cl),John Sheridan(p),Howard Elkins
(bj,g),Jack Wyatt(b),Kevin Hess(dr).   Live.Breda,The Netherlands.May 25,1979
    Wrought Iron Rag   Jazz Crooner(Du)JC242526579
    Tia Juana   -

Same.   Live.Prob. San Antonio,Texas. 1979
    Big Boy   American Jazz AJ127
    Take Your Tomorrow   -
    I've Got A Crush On You   -
    Canal Street Blues   -
    Irish Black Bottom   -
    Bienville Blues   -
    Ole Miss   -
    Swing That Music   -

FRANK CUNIMONDO

Frank Cunimondo(p,el-p),Ron Fudoli,Spider Rondenelli(b/dr).
                                              Pittsburgh. 1970's
    Milestones   Mondo M101
    Lush Life   -
    Gentle One   -
    Of Wine And You   -
    Gentle Is My Lover   -
    Watch What Happens   -

Frank Cunimondo(p,el-p),Mike Taylor(b),Roger Humphries(dr).
                                              Pittsburgh. 1970's
    Echoes   Mondo M102
    Seven Steps To Heaven   -
    Bonnie B.   -
    Remembering Your Love   -
    You've Made Me So Very Happy   -
    We've Only Just Begun   -
    Wichita Lineman   -
    Love Story   -
    Beyond The Clouds   Mondo M103
    Pretty,Pretty   -
    Love So Fine   -
    A House Is Not a Home   -
    Animal Crackers   -
    What Are You Doing
       The Rest Of Your Life   -
    Feelin' Good   -
    Until It's Time For You To Go   -
    Soon It's Gonna Rain   -
    We've Only Just Begun   -
    Two For The Road   Mondo M104
    The Lamp Is Low   -
    Girl Talk   -
    Here's That Rainy Day   -
    Alfie   -
    Dindi   -

Frank Cunimondo(p,el-p),Ray Russell(b),Lenny Rogers(dr).
                                              Pittsburgh. 1970's
(session cont. next page).

(session cont. from previous page):
```
        Sagitarius                    Mondo M105
        Slalom                        -
        Chameleon                     -
        Samba Nove                    -
        Aqua De Beber                 Mondo/Sound Idea 90175
        Misty                         -
        Close To You                  -
        Touch Me In the Morning       -
        Eleanor Rigby                 -
        Blue Bossa                    -
        Hullo Bolinas                 -
```

ENRICO CUOMO (Italian)

Aldo Rossi(cl),Giorgio Gaslini(p),Franco Pisano(g),Battista Pezzaglia(b),Enrico Cuomo(dr).
Milan,Italy.April 4,1948
```
        Opus One                      Fonit(I)12692
        Tutti Amici                   -
75871   Frenesia                      Fonit(I)12693
        Swing In China                -
```

MIKE CUOZZO

MIKE CUOZZO WITH THE COSTA - BURKE GROUP:
Mike Cuozzo(ts),Eddie Costa(vbs),Ronnie Ball(p),Vinnie Burke(b),Kenny Clarke(dr).
NYC.November 22,1955
```
69093   There Will Never Be Another You  Savoy MG12051
69094   What Is This Thing Called Love   -
69095   Nancy                            -
69096   An Evening At Papa Joe's         -
69097   Undecided                        -
69098   Walk Up                          -
```

All titles also on Savoy(J)KIJJ2013.

MIKE CUOZZO WITH THE COSTA - BURKE TRIO:
Mike Cuozzo(ts),Eddie Costa(p),Vinnie Burke(b),Nick Stabulas(dr).
NYC. 1956
```
        Fools Rush In                 Jubilee JLP1027
        Lover Man                     -
        Ten A.M.                      -
        That Old Feeling              -
        I Cover The Waterfront        -
        Easy To Love                  -
        Blue Jeans                    -
        Bounce For Mike               -
```

All titles also on Jubilee(J)YW7568,Roulette(J)TOCJ5414 (CD),Josie JJM/JJS3509 (issued under Costa's name).

GILBERTO CUPPINI (Italian)

See also SERGIO FANNI,SESTETTO BEBOP DI MILANO.

SESTETTO JAZZ GILBERTO CUPPINI:
Renato Grimaldi(tp),Glauco Masetti(as),Carlo Donida(p),Piero Visano(g),Beppe Termini(b),
Gilberto Cuppini(dr).   Milan,Italy.June 6,1947
OBA6257 Boogie Drums Woogie   HMV(I)HN2193
OBE6259 Opus One-Half   -
        Occhie Neri   HMV(I)HN2192
        Take The "A" train   -

SESTETTO BE-BOP GILBERTO CUPPINI:
Nino Impallomeni(as "N. Harry")(tp),Marcello Boschi(as),Eraldo Volonté(ts),Giorgio Gaslini
(p,arr),Antonio De Serio(b),Gilberto Cuppini(dr).
                                              Milan,Italy.June 10,1948
OBA6548 Night In Tunisia   HMV(I)HN2328
OBA6549 Salt Peanuts   -
OBA6553 Bop-Bop   HMV(I)HN2355
OBA6554 Drums Be-Bop   -

SESTETTO JAZZ CUPPINI:
Claude Dunson(tp),Athos Ceroni(tb),Gino Stefani(cl),Giorgio Gaslini(p),Antonio De Serio
(b),Gilberto Cuppini(dr).   Milan,Italy.November 24,1948
OBA6724 Memphis Blues   HMV(I)HN2425,3065,RCA-Victor EPA492
OBA6729 Basin Street Blues   -   -   -

GIL CUPPINI E IL SUO COMPLESSO:
Giulio Libano(tp),Leonard Principe(cl),Alessandro Rocchi(ts),Pino Spotti(p),Franco Pisano
(g),Antonio De Serio(b),Gilberto Cuppini(dr,arr).
                                              Milan,Italy.February 22,1949
OBA6833 Swing Club   HMV(I)HN2464
OBA6834 Nelly Bop   -

Giulio Libano(tp),Glauco Masetti(as),Pino Spotti(p,arr),Franco Pisano(g),Antonio De Serio
(b),Gilberto Cuppini(dr,arr).   Milan,Italy.March 25,1949
OBA6852 Esophagus   HMV(I)HN2474
OBA6853 Egyptology   -

GIL CUPPINI AND HIS ALL STARS:
Hazy Osterwald(tp),Ernst Höllerhagen(cl),Flavio Ambrosetti(as),Francis Coppieters(p),Toots
Thielemans(g),Sunny Lang(b),Gilberto Cuppini(dr).
                                              Milan,Italy.October 11,1949
BA7093 Perdido,I   HMV(I)HN2594,HN3066,RCA-Victor EPA492
BA7094 Perdido,II   -   -   -

GILBERTO CUPPINI E LA SUA ORCHESTRA MAMBO:
Raoul Ceroni(tb),Glauco Masetti(as),Sandro Bagalini(ts),Pino Calvi(p,arr),Gilberto Cuppini
(dr,arr),Tino Soto,Marino Barreto(bg).   Milan,Italy.November 10,1950
BA7509 Manteca   HMV(I)HN2067
BA7510 Mama Yo Quero Una   -

GIL CUPPINI E IL SUO COMPLESSO:
Raoul Ceroni(tb),Sergio Valenti(cl),Vittorio Paltrinieri(p),Elvio Favilla(org,vbs),Franco
Pisano(g),Battista Pezzaglia(b),Gilberto Cuppini(dr,arr).
                                              Milan,Italy.May 20,1953
BA8357 On The Sunny Side Of The Street HMV(I)HN3145,Columbia(I)33QPX8017

Mario Midana(tb),Giancarlo Barigozzi(as),Eraldo Volonté(ts),Sandro Bagalini(bars),Silvio
Romensoli(vbs),Gianfranco Intra(p),Antonio De Serio(b),Gilberto Cuppini(dr,arr).
                                              Milan,Italy.September 8,1954
BA8770 You Go To My Head   HMV(I)HN3404
BA8771 Auld Lang Syne   HMV(I)HN3381
BA8772 Things To Come   -
BA8773 Little George   HMV(I)HN3404

Glauco Masetti(as),Alberto Baldan(vbs),Tony De Vita(p,arr),Beppe Termini(b),Gilberto Cup-
pini(dr,arr),José Montery(cg).   Milan,Italy.May 1958
       Over The Rainbow   Fox(I)EPF119
       Buttercup   -
       Congo Square   -

GIL CUPPINI QUINTET:
Oscar Valdambrini(tp),Gianni Basso(ts),Renato Sellani(p),Giorgio Azzolini(b),Gilberto Cup-
pini(dr,arr).   Milan,Italy.November 28,1958
       L'Uomo Dal Braccio D'Oro   Astraphon(I)Y1755,Meazzi(I)BW4000
       There's A Small Hotel   -   -
       Hula Hoop Song   Astraphon(I)Y1756,LPA10004
       Il Nord   - ,Meazzi(I)BW4000

GIL CUPPINI AND HIS FRIENDS:
Enrico Intra(p) replaces Sellani.   Milan.December 18,1958
       Il Nord   Astraphon(I)LPA10001

GIL CUPPINI E IL SUO COMPLESSO:
Loreto Ficorilli,Balso Panfili,Giuliano Bernicchi,Oscar Valdambrini(tp),Gianni Basso(ts),
Renato Sellani(p),Bruno De Filippi(g),Beppe Termini(b),Gilberto Cuppini(dr).
                                     Milan,Italy.January 11,1959
       Per Tutta La Vita   Astraphon(I)Y1789
       La Luna E Un'Altra Luna   -

GIL CUPPINI QUINTET:
Oscar Valdambrini(tp),Gianni Basso(ts),Renato Sellani(p),Giorgio Azzolini(b),Gilberto Cup-
pini(dr,arr).   Milan,Italy.March 15,1959
       Bernie's Tune(no p)   Astraphon(I)Y1784,Meazzi(I)BW4000
       Il Vecchio   -   -

Add Lars Gullin(bars).   Same date
       Topsy   Astraphon(I)Y1785,HLP4000,Meazzi(I)BW4000
       I'll Remember April   - ,Meazzi(I)BW4000

GIL CUPPINI QUINTET:
Sergio Fanni(tp),Eraldo Volonté(ts),Ettore Righello(p),Giorgio Buratti(b),Gilberto Cuppin
(dr).   Milan,Italy.March 1960
       Moanin'   Meazzi(I)BW4000
       Duo   -
       Circeo   -
       Walkin'   -
       Lover man   -
       The Drums(1)   -

-1.Cuppini(dr),Liliana Feldman(recitation).

All titles on BW4000 also on Broadway(I)BW4000,Hollywood(I)HLP4000.

Same.   Milan,Italy.April 19,1960
       Duo   Cetra(I)EPD38
       Circero   -
       Non Ti Scordar Di Me   -
       P.N. Blues   -

Same.   Poss. same session
       Lover Man   RCA(I)LPM10083

Dusko Goykovich(tp),Barney Wilen(ts,ss),George Gruntz(p),Karl-Theodor Geier(b),Gilberto
Cuppini(dr).   Milan,Italy.September 1/2,1961
(session cont. next page).

(session cont. from previous page):

Hatch Tag-Blues(no tp)	Meazzi(I)MLP04012
Vinnie's Components(no tp)	-
Blue Daniel(no tp,ts)	-
I Love You(no p)	-
What's New(no p,dr)	-
What Is This Thing	
Called Love(no tp,ts)	-
John's Ballade(no tp)	-
Blue Waltz(no p)	-
Confirmation	Meazzi(I)ME03028
Solar	-

All titles on MLP04012 also on Broadway(I)BW04012.

GIL CUPPINI BIG BAND:
Dusko Goykovich(tp,flh),Fermo Lini,Alberto Corvini,Emilio Soana,Oscar Valdambrini(tp),Dino
Piana,Mario Pezzota,Nicola Castriotta,Cesare Gagliardi(tb),Glauco Masetti,Sergio Valenti,
Gianni Basso,Eraldo Volonté(ts),Sergio Rigon(bars,fl),Ettore Righello(p),Giorgio Azzolini
(b),Gilberto Cuppini(dr).   Live."Universal Club",Marina di Carrara,Italy. 1968

Opening "The Stretch"	Meazzi(I)MLPS04048
Flip Top	-
Sof' Stroke	-
A Crystal Dream	-
Tronicorum	-
Well Said!	-
Making Love	-
Sweet Lips	-
When The Angels Listen To Mario	-
Hot D.O.G.	-
Ending Lady Of The Lavender Mist	-

Note:"Sweet Lips" issued on Grandi del Jazz(I)GdJ99 may be the above version.

Rudy Migliardi,Beppe Bergamasco(tb),Cesare Bergonzi,Enzo Nardini(sax) replace Piana,Pez-
zota,Volonté,Rigon;add Carlo Sola(bg);omit Goykovich.
                                 Live.Teatro Linico,Milan,Italy.October 27,1969

A New Day - A Jazz	
Suite For Big Band	Red Record(I)VPA154

Fermo Lini,Emilio Soana,Oscar Valdambrini,Sergio Fanni(tp,flh),Nicola Castriotta,Palmiro
Mautino,Beppe Bergamasco(tb),Glauco Masetti(as,ts),Sergio Rigon(ts,fl),Nando Nebuloni(ts),
Athos Poletti(bars),Ettore Righello(p,arr),Carlo Milano(el-b),Gilberto Cuppini(dr,arr).
                                 Milan,Italy.May 1971

Blows	Jump(I)J0118
Blues For Duke	
Free Bossa	
My Mood	
Miss Up	

Fermo Lini,Emilio Soana,Sergio Fanni,Luciano Biasuitti(tp),Nicola Castriotta,Beppe Berga-
masco(tb),Eraldo Volonté(ss),Sergio Rigon,Giancarlo Barigozzi(ts),Athos Poletti(bars),Al-
berto Pizzigoni(g),Carlo Milano(el-b),Gilberto Cuppini(dr,arr).
                                 Milan,Italy.May 1971

Caprice	Jump(I)J0118

Emilio Soana,Franco Corvini,Bruno Moretti,Sergio Fanni(tp),Rudy Migliardi,Nicola Castriotta,Palmiro Mautino,Beppe Bergamasco(tb),Glauco Masetti,Nando Nebuloni,Leandro Prete,Eraldo
Volonté,Sergio Rigon(sax),Carlo Milano(b),Gilberto Cuppini(dr).
                                 Live.Cinisello Balsamo,Milan,Italy.March 13,1974

Flakes	Red Record(I)VPA 154

Emilio Soana,Franco Corvini,Bruno Moretti,Sergio Fanni(tp),Rudy Migliardi,Nicola Castriot-
ta,Claudio Barbieri,Beppe Bergamasco(tb),Glauco Masetti,Gianni Basso,Leandro Prete,Sergio
Rigon,Stelio Licudi(sax),Mario Bosi(vbs),Ettore Righello(p),Piero Gosio(synth),Alberto
Pizzigoni(g),Carlo Milano(b),Gilberto Cuppini(dr).

		Live."Tarantello",Locarno,Switzerland.September 23,1977
01' Man River	Red Record(I)VPA154	
Caceres		-
Laura		-
3th(!) Dimension		-

CURLEW

George Cartwright(as,ts,ss,fl),Nicky Skopelitis(g),Tom Cora(cello),Bill Laswell(el-b),Bill
Bacon(dr,perc).

	NYC(?).February 6/29,March 1/2,1980
Panther Burn	Landslide LD1004
The Bear	-
Bitter Thumbs	-
The Victim	-
The Hard Wood	-
Sports	-
Bruno	-
But Get It	-
Rudders	-
Binoculars	-
The Ole Miss Exercise Song	-

ALVIN CURRAN

See also ANDREA CENTAZZO.

Alvin Curran(synth,flh,hca,vcl,electronics),Margherita Benetti(vcl,etc.).

	Rome. 1973
Songs And Views From The Magnetic Garden	Ananda(I)1

Alvin Curran(p,recorder).

	Rome.April 1975
Light Flowers,Dark Flowers	Ananda(I)4

Alvin Curran(p,vcl,synth,etc.)

	Minneapolis.February 1980
The Works	Fore 80(I)Two

ED CURRAN

ED CURRAN QUARTET:
Marc Levin(cnt,flh,mellophone),Ed Curran(as,cl),Kiyoshi Tokunaga(b),Robert Pozar(dr).

	NYC.March 17,1967
Cire	Savoy MG12191
Why	-
Mid Tempo	-
Looking Back	-
Duos	-
Lady A	-
Nicole	-
Drac	-

HAWLEY ADAMS CURRENS

Hawley Adams Currens(vln),J.P. Richards(perc,vbs).
                                        San Francisco.June 1979
        Particles   TIWA 555
        Winding   -
        Kinetic Dance   -
        Jig   -
        Integration   -
        Resolution(1)   -

-1.Add Robert Haven(fl).

IRMA CURRY

(vcl) acc. by DON ELLIOTT'S ORCHESTRA:
Details unknown,Al Cohn(arr).   NYC.c. 1961
        Forget About The Boy   Columbia CL1754
        Love Is A Necessary Evil   -
        A Stranger In The City   -
        Too Much,Too Soon   -
        When Sunny Gets Blue   -
        Goin' Back To Joe's   -
        Forgetful   -
        Can't Help It   -
        No Spring This Year   -
        Ain't Nobody Home   -
        No One Came To My Party   -
        Leavin' Town   -
        Love Is A Necessary Evil,II   -

(vcl) acc. by orchestra,Benny Carter(arr,cond).
                                        LA.c. 1964/65
        Undecided   Exodus 6003,EXS3

Note:The above title is prob. from a VeeJay LP; information on the LP is not available.

(vcl) acc. by orchestra,Benny Carter,Ernie Freeman(arr).
                                        LA.c. 1964/65
        We Were In Love   VeeJay 669
        A Heart Must Learn To Cry   -

PAUL CURRY

PAUL CURRY AND THE FRIENDS OF "FATS":
Paul Webster(tp),Paul Curry(p,vcl),Al Casey(g),Al Hall(b),Herbie Lovelle(dr).
                                        NYC(?). 1959
        Organ Grinder's Swing   Golden Crest CR(SP)3070
        I Can't Give You
            Anything But Love   -
        Stars Fell On Alabama   -
        Truckin'   -
        If It's True   -
        15 Minutes Intermission   -
        Never Had It So Good   -
        Pardon Me,Pretty Baby   -
(session cont. next page).

(session cont. from previous page):
```
        There'll Come A Time          Golden Crest CR(SP)3070
        How Come You Do Me Like You Do           -
        Does The Chewing
           Gum Lose Its Flavor                   -
        I Heard                                  -
```

TED CURSON

See also BILL BARRON,NICK BRIGNOLA,GUSTAV BROM,ANDRZEJ TRZASKOWSKI.
Note:On some of the recordings Curson plays piccolo-tp or pocket-trumpet.

TED CURSON QUINTET:
Ted Curson(tp),Eric Dolphy(fl),Kenny Drew(p),Jimmy Garrison(b),Dannie Richmond(dr).
```
                                      NYC.April 11,1961
        Bali Hai                      Old Town OTLP2003
        The Things We Did Last Summer          -
```

Bill Barron(ts),Roy Haynes(dr) replace Dolphy,Richmond.
```
                                      Same date
        Ahma (See Ya)                Old Town OTLP2003
        Flatted Fifth                          -
```

Pete LaRoca(dr) replace Haynes.
```
                                      Same date
        Caravan                      Old Town OTLP2003
        Nosruc (Waltz)                         -
        Dem's Blues                            -
        Antibes                                -
        Mr. Teddy                              -
```

All titles on OTLP2003 also on Old Town(J)YQ7501,YS7131,YW7577,20EL5037,EDJC00078,32ED5053
(CD),Jazz View COD016 (CD).

TED CURSON QUINTET:
Ted Curson(tp),Al Doctor(as),Maury Kaye(p),Charles Biddle(b),Charles Duncan(dr).
```
                                      Live."La Tête de l'Art",Montreal.September 15,1962
        Cracklin' Bread              Trans World(Ca)TWJ7000
        Ted's Tempo                            -
        Playhouse March                        -
        Straight Ice                           -
        Quicksand                              -
```

All titles also on Can-Am CA1700.

Ted Curson(tp),Gildo Mahones(p),George Tucker(b),Roy Haynes(dr),Montego Joe(cg).
```
                                      NYC.December 10,1962
3677    Fire Down Below              Prestige 45-241,PRLP/ST7263
3678    The Very Young(no cg)                  -              -
3679    Baby Has Gone Bye Bye        Prestige PRLP/ST7263
3680    Show Me                                    - ,Moodsville MVLP38,Status
                                     ST8325
3681    Falling In Love With Love    Prestige PRLP/ST7263
3682    Only Forever(no cg)                    -
```

All titles on PRLP7263 also on Original Jazz Classics OJC1744,OJCCD1744-2 (CD).
Note:Prestige session books shows master numbers as 3647-52 - this may be an error.

TED CURSON QUARTET:
Ted Curson(tp),Bill Barron(ts,cl),Herb Bushler(b),Dick Berk(dr).
                                        Paris.August 1,1964
        Kassim   Fontana(Eu)688.310ZL
        East Sixth Street   -
        7/4 Funny Time   -
        Tears For Dolphy   -
        Quicksand   -
        Reava's Waltz   -   ,Polydor(J)25MJ3533(?)
        Searchin' For The Blues Arista/Freedom AL1030
        Desolation   -
        Light Blue   -

All titles on 688.310ZL also on Fontana(Eu)888.310ZY,(J)SFON7099,Arista/Freedom AL1021,(J)
PA9711,K18P9389,32JDF173 (CD).

Add Georges Arvanitas(p).   NYC.March 25,1965
1790   Ted's Tempo   Atlantic LP(SD)1441
1791   Straight Ice   -
1792   Nublu   -
1793   Kaleidoscope(no p)   unissued

same.   NYC.March 29,1965
1798   Elefant Walk   Atlantic LP(SD)1441
1799   Star Eyes(no ts/cl)   -
1800   Reava's Waltz(no p)   -

All titles on LP/SD1441 also on Atlantic(J)PA4514.

TED CURSON - JUNIOR TRIO:
Ted Curson(tp),Jan Hammer(p),Miroslav Vitous(b),Alan Vitous(dr).
                                        Prague.October 19,1965
        Caravan   Supraphon(Cz)DV10195,SV9013,SUA1/55733
        Marjo   -   -   -

TED CURSON QUARTET:
Ted Curson(tp),Booker Ervin(ts),Jimmy Woode(b),Edgar Bateman(dr).
                                        Baarn,Holland.May 13,1966
        Roy's Boys   Fontana(Eu)683.910ZL
        You Don't Know What Love Is   -
        Cinq Quatre   -
        Musis Sacrum   -
        Latino   -

All titles also on Fontana(Eu)883.910ZY,(E)FJL910,(J)SFON7099,195J27,PHCE1008 (CD).

TED CURSON WITH THE ZAGREB RADIO ORCHESTRA:
Ted Curson(tp),Zagreb Radio Orchestra,Zita Carno(arr),Miljenhko Trohaska(cond).
                                        Live.Ljubljana,Yugoslavia. 1966
        Quicksand   Arista/Freedom AL1030,(J)PA7187
        Straight Ice   -   -
        Flip Flop   -   -
        Tears For Dolphy   unissued

TED CURSON QUARTET:
Ted Curson(tp),rest unknown.   Cologne,Germany.September 17,1967
        The Leopard   Columbia(G)SMC74334

Ted Curson(tp),Nick Brignola(ss),Pentti Hietanen(p),Pekka Sarmanto(b),Esko Rosnell(dr).
                                        Helsinki.July 1968
         Vallinkorvan Laulu   RCA(Fi)unissued
         Ol' Kaunis Kesäilta   -
         Kun Kerran Kannella Fregatin -
         Liljankukka   -
         The Flame   -
         Unknown titles

Note:Nick Brignola is not present on all titles.

TED CURSON QUINTET:
Ted Curson(tp),Pentti Hietanen(p,b),Dero Koivistoinen(ts,as,ss),Pekka Sarmanto(b),Reino
Laine(dr).   Helsinki.September 3,1970
         Ode To Booker Ervin   Columbia(Fi)5E.062-34201
         LSD Takes Holiday   - ,Polydor(J)25MJ3533(?)
         Airi's Tune   -
         Montreux   -
         Festival Blue   -
         Typical Ted   -
         The Leopard   -

TED CURSON WITH GEORGES ARVANITAS TRIO:
Ted Curson(tp,picc-tp),Georges Arvanitas(p),Jacky Samson(b),Charles Saudrais(dr).
                                        Paris.June 18,1971
         Pop Wine   Futura(F)GER26
         LSD Takes Holiday   -
         Song Of The Lonely One   -
         Quartier Latin   -
         Flip Flop   -

All titles also on Futura(J)ECPL12,Spotlite(E)SPLP18,Musica(F)2021.

Ted Curson(tp),Christer Eklund -1(ts,ss),Björn J-son Lindh -2(fl),Lee Schipper(vbs),Art
Lande(p),Jan (Janne) Schaffer(g),Stefan Brolund(el-b),Ola Brunkert(dr).
                                        Stockholm.August 31,1973
         For Jackie(1)   Four Leaf (Clover)(Sd)FLC5019,Polydor(J)25MJ3533
         Piccolo Blues   -   -
         Harvest Machine(1)(no tp)   -
         Phunky Physicist(1,2)   - ,Polydor(J)25MJ3533
         Transmogification(2)(no tp,p)   -
         Still Life(no g)   - ,Polydor(J)25MJ3533

Note:The above LP issued as "Jazz Meeting 1".

TED CURSON QUINTET:
Ted Curson(tp,flh),Chris Woods(as,fl),Georges Arvanitas(g),Jacky Samson(b),Charles Sau-
drais(dr).   Paris.October 26,1973
         Flatted Fifth   Marge(F)01
         Marjo   -
         Airi Tune   -
         Searchin' The Blues   -
         Cattin' Curson (Typical Ted) -

All titles also on Trident TRS503.

Ted Curson(tp),Robin Kenyatta(as,ss),Nick Brignola(bars,ts,saxello),Kenny Barron(p,el-p)
Herb Bushler(b,el-b),Albert Heath(dr),Lawrence Killian,Chicky Johnson,Butch Curson(perc)
                                        NYC.May 13,1974
(session cont. next page).

```
(session cont. from previous page):
28926  Greasy As A Porkchop         Atlantic(J)P7532
28927  Spiderlegs(1)                     -
28928  Sugar 'N' Spice                   -
28929  Typical Ted                       -

-1.Butch Curson(dr) replaces Heath.

Ted Curson(tp,flh),Robin Kenyatta(as),Kenny Barron(p),Richard Davis(b),Albert Heath(dr).
                                   NYC.May 16,1974
28930  Quicksand                    Atlantic(J)P7532
28931  Tears For Dolphy                  -

Ted Curson(tp,flh),Jim McNeely(p),Cecil McBee(b),Steve McCall(dr).
                                   NYC.July 1,1976
       All The Things You Are      Why Not(J)PA7153,(J)32ED5015(CD)
       Blue Piccolo                      -                  -
       Playhouse March                   -                  -
       Song Of The Lonely                -                  -
       Dwackdi Mun Fudalick
        (Open The Door)                  -                  -
       Ted Tempo                    (J)32ED5015(CD)
       'Round Midnight                   -
       Gary G                            -

All titles on PA5153 also on India Navigation IN1054,(J)20EL5015.

TED CURSON AND COMPANY:
Ted Curson(tp,flh),Chris Woods(as,fl),Nick Brignola(bars,saxello),Andy LaVerne(p),David
Friesen(b),Steve McCall(dr),Sam Jacobs(cg).  Live.Philadelphia.October 16,1976
       Reava's Waltz                Inner City IC1017
       Ted's Tempo                       -

Jim McNeely(p),Bob Merigliano(dr) replace LaVerne,McCall.
                                   NYC.October 17,1976
       Song Of The Lonely          Inner City IC1017
       Airi's Tune                       -
       Searchin' For The Blues           -
       Marjo                             -

All titles on IC1017 also on Inner City(J)RJ7131.

TED CURSON - DIZZY REECE:
Ted Curson(tp,flh),Dizzy Reece(tp),Claude Williamson(p),Sam Jones(b),Roy Haynes(dr).
                                   NYC.June 9,1978
       Stella By Starlight(1)       Interplay IP7716
       All The Things You Are(2)         -
       Bass Conclave                     -
       Moose The Mooche(1,2)             -
       Marjo                             -
       Walkin'                           -

1.Omit Curson.
2.Omit Reese.

ed Curson(tp,flh,perc),Ray Drummond(b),Roy Haynes(dr).
                                   NYC.January 3,1979
       Snake Johnson                Interplay IP7722
       Pent Up House                     -
       Quicksand                         -
session cont. next page).
```

(session cont. from previous page):
```
            Straight Ice                Interplay IP7722
            'Round Midnight                   -
```

All titles also on Trio(J)PAP9166.

Ted Curson(tp,flh,perc),Bill Saxton -1(ts),Mike Morgenstern -1(bars),Jim McNeely(p),Roy
Kawasaki(g),Mike Richmond(b,el-b),Adam Nussbaum(dr),Montego Joe(perc).
```
                                        NYC.January 14,1980
            I Heard Mingus              Interplay IP7729
            Please,Please,Please
               Don't Put The Pigfoot
               In The Kreplach Soup(1)        -
            Lost Her                          -
            Lin's Garden                      -
```

All titles also on Trio(J)PAP9217.

Ted Curson(tp,flh),Bill Barron(ts),Charlie Williams(as),Nick Brignola(bars,ss),Jim McNeely
(p),David Friesen(b),Steve McCall(dr),Lawrence Killian(perc).
```
                                        NYC.c.  1980
            Snake Johnson               Chiaroscuro CR2028
            Searching For The Blues          -
            Blue Piccolo                     -
            Dwackdo Mun Fudalik              -
            Marjo                            -
            LSD Takes A Holiday              -
```

CURTIS BAY COAST GUARD TRAINING STATION DANCE BAND

Tom Arthur,Tony Faso,Irving Goodman,Johnny Laone(tp),Tom Ellwein,Bob Kirscher(tb),Bill
Schallen(tb,cond),Kai Winding(tb,arr),Jerry Sanfino,Bob Walters(as),Ted Hyland,Leroy New
(ts),Pete Brendel(bars),Paul Smith(p),Wade Grove(g),Johnny Frigo(b),Charlie Perry(dr),Ken
Hopkins,Danny Hurd(arr).
```
                                        NYC.March  1944
            My Heart Isn't In It        V-Disc 186
            Annie Laurie                     -
            Mary Lou                         -
            Shine                            -
            Available Jones             V-Disc 263,Navy 43,I.A.J.R.C.  IAJRC51
```

KING CURTIS (OUSLEY)

See also OLIVER NELSON.

KING CURTIS/MELVIN DANIELS:
King Curtis,poss. Vonzell Tucker(ts),unknown(bars),Melvin Daniels(p,vcl),Webster Armstrong
(g),Dobbs(b),Vernon Lewis(dr).
```
                                        Fort Worth,Texas.  1953
1948   I'll Be There(1)                 RPM 383,Crown CL5294
1949   Boogie In The Moonlight               -
       If You Don't Want My Loving      Crown CL5294
       Lean Chicks(1)                        -
       Hey Hey Little Girl                   -
```

-1.Poss. a retitling of "Boogie In The Moonlight".

Omit Tucker,unkown bars.   Fort Worth,Texas. 1953
6120   Tenor In The Sky   Gem 208
6121   No More Crying On My Pillow(md)   -

Note:The above masters were sold to Savoy.
     Monark 702 issued as by "KING" CURTIS is in fact an Eddie Curtis item.

Jonah Jones(tp),Elmer Crumbley(tb),King Curtis(ts),Haywood Henry(bars),George Rhodes(p),
Jerome Barr(g),Al Lucas(b),Bobby Donaldson(dr).
                               NYC.March 1,1956
G5WB2162 Open Up   RCA Camden CAS2242
G5WB2163 Movin' On   Groove 0160,   -
G5WB2164 Rockabye Baby   -   -
G5WB2165 I'm With You   -

King Curtis(ts),Haywood Henry(bars),Ernie Hayes(p),Mickey Baker(g),Lloyd Trotman(b),Panama
Francis(dr).   NYC.November 26,1956
R1509 Rush Hour   Delmark DD452(CD)
R1510 King's Rock   Apollo 507,LP490
R1511 Dynamite At Midnight   -   - ,Delmark DD452(CD)
R1512 Happy Times   unissued

King Curtis(ts),unknown org,p,g,b,dr.   NYC. 1956
M7176 Guitar Rag   DeLuxe 6142,King 5647,LP884
M7177 The Stranger   -
M7178 Wicky Wacky I(1)   DeLuxe 6157,King 5647,LP882
M7179 Wicky Wacky II   -

-1.As "King Curtis Stomp" and "Surfin' In Blue" on King issues.

KING CURTIS AND COUNT HASTINGS WITH LEROY KIRKLAND AND HIS HI-FLYERS:
Jimmie Cleveland,Freddie Zito(tb),King Curtis,Lowell "Count" Hastings(ts),Haywood Henry
(bars),Ernie Hayes(p),Al Casamenti,Danny Perri,Everett Barksdale(g),Lloyd Trotman(b),
Panama Francis(dr),Leroy Kirkland(arr,cond). NYC.November 18,1957
H2PB7633 Night Before Battle   RCA EP4196,(F)430.279
H2PB7634 Royal Tenors   -
H2PB7635 The Count And The King   - ,(F)430.279
H2PB7636 Battle Royal   -

Note:RCA(F)430.279 issued as COUNT HASTINGS AND KING CURTIS.

King Curtis(ts) unknown p,b,dr.   Unknown location.c. 1960
      Perdito(!)(1)   Mount Vernon LP119
      Mr. Hip (Take Me)(1)   Mount Vernon LP109,LP119
      Relief Trio,pt.1(2)   Mount Vernon LP119
      Relief Trio,pt.2(2)   -
      Big Town Blues(1)   -
      The Blues (Soul Blues)(1) Mount Vernon LP109,LP119
      Walkin'(1)   Mount Vernon LP119
      The Track(2)   -
      Get Out(1)   -
      I'm So Very Weary(1)   -

1.Unknown(g) overdubbed - except on LP109 issues.
2.Unknown tamb,bg overdubbed.

KING CURTIS AND HIS BAND:
Nat Adderley(as "Little Brother")(cnt),King Curtis(ts),Wynton Kelly(p),Paul Chambers(b),
Oliver Jackson(dr).   NYC.April 21,1960
(session cont. next page).

(session cont. from previous page):
```
2181   Have You Heard                      New Jazz NJLP8237
2182   Da-Du-Dah                                 -
2183   Little Brother Soul                       -
2184   Willow Weep For Me(no tp)                 -
2185   Shout Up                            unissued
2186   In A Funky Groove                   New Jazz NJLP8237
```

All titles - except "Shout Up" - also Prestige PR7789,P24033,Original Jazz Classics
OJC198,Esquire 32-161.

Nat Adderley(cnt),King Curtis(ts),Wynton Kelly(p),Sam Jones(b),Belton Evans(dr).
                                       NYC.September 18,1960
```
2471   Do You Have Soul Now?               Prestige PRLP/ST7222
2472   Jeep's Blues                              -
2473   Soul Meeting                              - ,New Jazz 45-510
2474   What Is This Ting Called Love             -
2475   Lazy Soul                                 -
2476   All The Way                               - ,New Jazz 45-510
```

All titles also on Prestige PR7833,P24033.

King Curtis(as,ts,g,vcl),Paul Griffin(p),Al Casey,Mac Pierce (Hugh McCracken)(g),Jimmy
Lewis(b),Belton Evans(dr),The Cookies(vcl). NYC.April 25,1961
```
2989   Trouble In Mind                     Tru-Sound 45-401,TRU15001
2990   Bad Bad Whiskey                           -
2991   Don't Deceive Me(tc)                      -
2992   But That's All Right                Tru-Sound 45-401,      -
2993   I Have To Worry(tc)                 Tru-Sound 45-406,      -
2994   Nobody Wants You
          When You're Down And Out               -
2995   Woke Up This Morning                      -
2996   Ain't Nobody's Business                   -
2997   Deep Fry                                  -
2998   Jivin' Time                         Tru-Sound 45-406,      - ,Prestige PR7709,
                                           Bellaphon(G)BJS4055
```

All titles also on Red Lightning RL0042,Original Blues Classics OBC512.

King Curtis(ts),Paul Griffin(p),Al Casey(g),Jimmy Lewis(b),Belton Evans(dr),Ray Barretto
(cg).   NYC.July 11,1961
```
3135   Slow Motion                         Tru-Sound TRU15008
3136   Firefly                                   - ,Prestige PR7709,Bellaphon(G)
                                           BJS4055
3137   Something Frantic                   Tru-Sound TRU15008,Prestige PR7775
3138   Keep Movin'                               -                    -
```

Omit Barretto.   Live."Smalls Paradise",NYC.Mid-1961
```
       Jay Walk                            JSP(E)JSP1091
       Trouble In Mind                           -
       African Waltz                             -
       What'd I Say                              -
       I Have To Worry                           -
       The Twist                                 -
       Canadian Sunset                           -
       Hiw High The Moon                         -
       KC Special (Smooth Sailing)               -
```

King Curtis(as,ts),Jack McDuff(org),Billy Butler,Eric Gale(g),Bob Bushnell(b),Ray Lucas
(dr),Willie Rodriguez(cg,bg).   NYC.September 19,1961
(session cont. next page).

(session cont. from previous page):

3216	Night Train	Tru-Sound TRU15006,Prestige PR7775
3217	You Came A Long Way From St. Louis	- ,Prestige PR7709,Bellaphon(G) BJS4055
3218	Honky Tonk	Tru-Sound TRU15006,Prestige PR7709,Bellaphon(G) BJS4055
3219	Fever	Tru-Sound TRU15006,Prestige PR7775
3220	Tuxedo Junction	- -
3221	Lean Baby	- -
3222	The Hucklebuck	Tru-Sound 45-412,TRU15006, -

same   NYC.September 22,1961

3223	Soft	Tru-Sound TRU15006
3224	Tippin' In	-
3225	So Rare	Tru-Sound 45-412,TRU15006
3226	Harlem Nocturne	Tru-Sound TRU15006,Prestige PR7709,Bellaphon(G) BJS4055

King Curtis(as,ts),Sam Taylor -1(ts),Ernie Hayes(org),Paul Griffin(p),Billy Buttler(g),
Jimmy Lewis(b),Ray Lucas(dr).   NYC.January 5,1962

3339	Low Down(1)	Tru-Sound 45-422,TRU15008,Prestige PR7775
3340	The Hully Gully Twist	- ,Prestige PR7709, Bellaphon(G)BJS4055
3341	The Party Time Twist(1)	Tru-Sound TRU15008,Prestige PR7709,Bellaphon(G) BJS4055
3342	Free For All(1)	Tru-Sound 45-415,TRU15008,Prestige PR7775
3343	Easy Like(1)	-
3344	I'll Wait For You	Tru-Sound 45-422, -
3345	Hot Saxes(1)	- ,Prestige PR7709, Bellaphon(G)BJS4055

Britt Woodman(tb),King Curtis(ts),Paul Griffin(p),Billy Butler,Carl Lynch(g),Jimmy Lewis
(b),Ray Lucas(dr).   NYC.February 15,1962

3386	Alexander's Ragtime Band(1)	Tru-Sound TRU15009
3387	A Shanty In Old Shany Town	-
3388	Basin Street Blues	-
3389	When The Saints Go Marching In	Tru-Sound 45-415,TRU15009,Prestige PR7709,Bella- phon(G)BJS4055
3390	St Louis Blues	Tru-Sound TRU15009
3391	Royal Garden Blues	- ,Prestige PR7775
3392	Up A Lazy River	-
3393	Sweet Georgia Brown	- ,Prestige PR7709;Bellaphon(G) BJS4055
3394	Muskrat Ramble	Tru-Sound TRU15009
3395	St. James Infirmary	- ,Prestige PR7775

.Add unknown(bg).

KING CURTIS - CHAMPION JACK DUPREE:

King Curtis(ts),Champion Jack Dupree(p,vcl),Cornell Dupree(g),Jerry Jemmott(el-b),Oliver
Jackson(dr).   Live.Montreux Jazz Festival,Switzerland.June 17,1971

3593	Get With It	Atlantic SD1637,(G)ATL20052
3594	Poor Boy Blues	-
3595	I'm Having Fun	-
3596	Junker's Blues	-
3597	Sneaky Pete	-
3598	Everything's Gonna Be Allright	-

, titles also on Atlantic(G)ATL40434,(E)K40434.
Note:Additional recordings by this artist are not included.

PETER CUSACK (British)

Simon Mayo(cl),Peter Cusack(g).   London. 1975
    Hundreds And Thousands   Bead(E)1
    Rosin And Squeah   -
    String Of Beads   -
    Geese   -
    Lickspittle   -

Note:The above recording also includes(!) the dancing of Shelley Lee.

(g-solo).   Live.Tienhoven,The Netherlands.April 1976
    Recorded Near Tienhoven   Bead(E)5

Peter Cusack(g,whistling).   Live(?).Utrecht,The Netherlands.June 1976
    Whistling With Guitar
      Accompaniment   Rift 001,Red 008(?)

(g-solo).   Live.Unknown location,The Netherlands.June 197
    About Nice Dutch
      Improvisatory Music   Bead(E)5

(g-solo).   Live.Unknown location,The Netherlands.March 197
    Some Guitar Playing,pt.1,2 Bead(E)5
    Maarsseveenseplassen   -

(g-solo).   Live.Unknown location,The Netherlands.May 197
    A Dutch Landscape   Bead(E)5

(g-solo).   Live.Unknown location,The Netherlands.June 197
    Some More Guitar Playing   Bead(E)5

Evan Parker(ss,ts),Guus Janssen(p),Peter Cusack(g),Maarten van Regteren Altena(b),Terry
Day(dr,perc).   Live.Utrecht,The Netherlands.January 29,197
    Utrecht   Bead(E)15

Same   Live.Amsterdam.January 31,1978
    De Kroeg   Bead(E)15

Omit Parker.   Live.Rotterdam.March 4,1978
    Rotterdam   Bead(E)15

Guus Janssen(p),Peter Cusack(g),Maarten van Regteren Altena(b,cello),Paul Lovens(perc).
                        Leuven,The Netherlands.March 8,1978
    Leuven,I   Bead(E)14
    Leuven,II(no p)   -
    Leuven,III   -

Note:Bead(E)14/15 issued as "Groups In Front Of People" - the music is collective improv
    sation.

ALTERATIONS:
David Toop(fl,g,perc,etc.),Steve Beresford(p,g,tp,euphonium,vln,etc.),Peter Cusack(g),
Terry Day(perc,cello,as,etc.).   Live.The Premises Art Centre,Norwich,England.May 13,19
    Norwich 1-4   Bead(E)9

Same.   Live.London Musicians Collective.London.June 22,19
    London 1-3   Bead(E)9

Paul Termos(cl),Guus Janssen(p),Peter Cusack(g),Paul Lytton(perc).
Live.Delft,The Netherlands.June 30,1978

       Delft I(no p,g)   Bead(E)15
       Delft II   -

Guus Janssen(p),Peter Cusack(g),Maarten van Regteren Altena(b,cello),Paul Lovens(perc).
Live.Amsterdam.November 22,1978

       Bimhuis   Bead(E)14

Add Günter Christmann(tb).   Live.Alkmaar,The Netherlands.February 7,1979
       Alkmaar I   Bead(E)14
       Alkmaar II   -
       Alkmaar III   -

Note:Bead(E)14/15 issued as "Groups In Front Of People" - the music is collective improvi-
    sation.

ALTERATIONS:
David Toop(fl,g,el-b,etc.),Steve Beresford(p,g,el-b,tp,voice,etc.),Peter Cusack(g),Terry
Day(perc,cello,as,hca,etc.).   Live."Bimhuis",Amsterdam.January 30,1980
       He Feels Like A Doris Day   !Quartz(E)006
       Trail Of Traps   -

Same.   Live.Palais des Beaux Arts,Brussels.February 2,1980
       The Life And
          Opinion Of Masseur Ichi   !Quartz(E)006

Same.   Live.London Musicians Collective.London.March 9,1980
       Not So Deaf,Dumb And Mute   !Quartz(E)006
       Fear Of Mayonnaise   -
       Stand By Your Sheep   -
       Party Political   -

CHRIS CUTLER (British)

See FRED FRITH,HENRY COW.

CUTTY CUTSHALL

See ART FORD'S JAZZ PARTY,JAZZ IN THE TROC.

LEO CUYPERS (Dutch)

See also WILLEM BREUKER.

(p-solo).   Baarn,The Netherlands.June 6,1972
       Monk's Raus   BASF 14.25182
       Het Cowboylied Van Ome Piet   -
       One Million Dollar Song   -
       Cynisch Sjabloon Theater   -
       Zes Ongelikte Beertjes   -

Same.   Baarn,The Netherlands.October 19,1972
       Tristano Song   BASF 14.25182
(session cont. next page).

(session cont. from previous page):
      Lovely Rita   BASF 14.25182
      Weet Ik Nog Niet Hans   -
      De Kruidenier Deelt Spliterwten   -

Willem van Manen(tb),Piet Noordijk(as),Willem Breuker(as,ts,ss),Hans Dulfer(ts),Leo Cuypers(p),Arjen Gorter(b),Rob Verdurmen(dr).
                                Live."Shaffy Theater",Amsterdam.September 24,1974
      Johnny Rep Suite: BV Haast(Du)001
        Floris And Rosa
        Kirk
        Rank Jump
        Rep Mars
        Swing Along With Babe

Leo Cuypers(p),Rob Verdurmen(dr).   Live."Shaffy Theater",Amsterdam.September 25,1974
      Freule Pinard(p-solo)   BV Haast(Du)001
      Love You Tenderly(p-solo)   -
      Cowboylied Van Ome Piet   -

Willem van Manen,Bernard Hunnekink(tb),Jan Wolff(frh),Willem Breuker(as),Ronald Snijders(fl),Koen van Slogteren(oboe),Maurice Horsthuis(vla),Leo Cuypers(p),Martin van Duynhoven(dr).   Same date
      Russell   BV Haast(Du)001

Willem van Manen(tb),Willem Breuker(cl),Leo Cuypers(p),Rob Verdurmen(dr).
                                  Live."Shaffy Theater",Amsterdam.September 27,1974
      Ham & Ego Stango   BV Haast(Du)001

Note:Additional recordings with Cuypers from these September 1974 concerts - see BREUKER.

Willem van Manen(tb),Willem Breuker(bcl,ss,as,ts),Bob Driessen(ss,as,bars),Leo Cuypers(p),Harry Miller,Arjen Gorter(b),Martin van Duynhoven(dr).
                                  Hilversum,The Netherlands.September 19,1977
      Zeeland Suite: BV Haast(Du)012
        Impromptu
        Something Else
        Joplin
        Two Bass Shit(!)
        Bach II And Bach I
        No Plooi At All Blues
        Bob's Lick
        Memories
        Calypsooi

Willem Breuker(cl,bcl,ss,recorder,perc),Leo Cuypers(p,synth),Arjen Gorter(b,p),Martin van Duynhoven(dr).   Amsterdam.September 21,1977
      Jan Rap At 8:30 A.M.   BV Haast(Du)017
      The House   -
      Jan Rap At Noon   -
      Triste   -
      Early In The Morning (drums)   -
      Early In The Morning (1)   -
      Tristissime   -

Omit Breuker.   Amsterdam.October 13,1977
      Hijgen Voor Een Ander   BV Haast(Du)017
      Jaap Van De Merwe Song   -
      G.L.T.   -
      Jarrett   -

All titles on BV Haast(Du)017 also on Pläne(G)32000017.

Willem van Manen(tb),Keshavan Maslak(as),Maarten van Norden(ts),Leo Cuypers(p),Harry Miller(b),Martin van Duynhoven(dr),Linda van Dyck(vcl).
Amsterdam.February 10,1979

Nachtrit(lvd)	Theater Unie EP(unnumbered)
Drivin' Through The Night	-

(p-solo). Live."De Brakke Grond".Amsterdam.May 19,1979

Mattox Medley	BV Haast(Du)028
Saint Michel	-
Prinsengracht	-
De Riem	-
Romance	-
Skinned Ahead/Jarrett	-

All titles also on Pläne(G)32000028.

CYCLOP (German)

Wolfgang Engstfeld(ss,ts),Ulrich Engstfeld(g,perc),Günther Müller(b),Peter Weiss(dr).
Düsseldorf,Germany.September 1972

On The Road	Unknown label/unnumbered
Coloured	-
Some Kind Of Peace	-
River Roots	-
Nervous One	-
Abgesang	-

CYKLAMIUM (Danish)

Willy Jagert(tp,btp,ophicleide,melodica,perc),Morten Sivertsen(tp,perc),Christian Kyhl (sopranino-sax,as,bars,fl,hand-dr,perc),Uffe Markussen(as,ts,perc),Ole Thilo(p,org,prepared-p,perc),Peter Friis Nielsen(b),Jørgen Thorup(dr,perc),Kjeld Kemp(vcl,perc).
Copenhagen.February 26/27,1973

Mikalas Sang	Sweet Dragon(D)ML5
Ewe People Funeral March	-
Ude I Den Grønne Skov	-
Boble 1	-
Der Var Engang En Baron	-
Negeren Bob (Wottle/Clark Kents March)	-
Boble 2	-
Vejen Er Rød (Beat Til Bolle)	-
Boble 3	-
Konkubinat	-
Zip-Zap	-
Epeleptika	-
Kamæleonernes Kampsang	-

ANDREW CYRILLE

Andrew Cyrille(dr,perc,voice), Paris,August 11,1969

What About	Byg(F)529.316
From Whence I Came	-
Rhythmical Space	-
Rims And Things	-

(session cont. next page).

(session cont. from previous page):
        Pioneering   Byg(F)529.316

All titles also on Byg(J)BYG17,Affinity(E)AFF75.

ANDREW CYRILLE - MILFORD GRAVES:
Andrew Cyrille,Milford Graves(dr.perc).   Live.Columbia University,NYC. 1974
        Message To The Ancestors   Institue of Percussive Studies ST001
        Blessing From The Rain Forest   -
        Nagarath   -
        Rejuvenation   -
        The Soul Is The Music   -
        The Substance Of The Vision   -
        Call And Response   -

Ted Daniel(tp),David S. Ware(ts),Donald Smith(p),Romulus Franceschini(synth),Stafford
James(b),Alphonse Cimber(Haitian-dr),Andrew Cyrille(dr,perc),Jeanne Lee(vcl),Elouise
Loftin(poet).   NYC.February 26/May 14,1975
        Haitian Heritage (Part 1)   Institue of Percussive Studies ST002
        Haitian Heritage (Part 2)   -
        Fate   -
        Gossip   -
        Non-Expectation Celebration   -

All titles also on Trio/Nadja(J)PA7136.

ANDREW CYRILLE AND MAONO:
Ted Daniel(tp,flh,synth,fl),David S. Ware -1(ts,fl),Lisle Atkinson -1(b),Andrew Cyrille
(dr,perc,sansa,vcl).   Live.Studio Riverbea,NYC.May 23,1976
        Okurimono (Gift From Japan)(1) Institue of Percussive Studies ST003,Trio(J)PA715
        Interlude(1)   Trio(J)PA7157
        Sidi Ahmed-Siddy   Institue of Percussive Studies ST003
        Short Short(1)   Douglas NBLP7047,Casablanca 7047,Polydor(Eu)
                                        815.112

Omit Ware,Atkinson.   Live.Columbia University,NYC.June 12,1976
        Junction: Institue of Percussive Studies ST003,Trio(J)PA715
            Do You Know Where "1" Is
            Do You Know Where "2" Is
            Connaturally
        Ginakus "M"(1)   -   -

-1.Omit Daniel.

Andrew Cyrille(dr,perc,voice).   Pistoia,Italy.July 1978
        Excerpt From Spencyrspell   Ictus(I)0009
        5000 B.C.   -
        The Loop   -
        Some Sun   -
        The News   -
        Classical Retention   -

ANDREW CYRILLE AND MAONO:
Ted Daniel(tp,flh,wood-fl,perc),David S. Ware(ts,fl),Nick Di Geronimo(b),Andrew Cyrille
(dr,perc).   Milan,Italy.September 1978
        Metamusicians' Stomp   Black Saint(I)BSR0025
        My Ship   -
        5-4-3-2   -
        Spiegelgasse 14:   -
            Reflections & Restaurants
            The Park
            Flight

ANDREW CYRILLE - JEANNE LEE - JIMMY LYONS:
Jimmy Lyons(as),Andrew Cyrille(dr,perc),Jeanne Lee(vcl).
                                        Milan,Italy.June 1979
        Nuba 1   Black Saint(I)BSR0030
        Cornbread Picnic (Maize)   -
        The One Before Zero   -
        J.J. And A.   -
        In These Last Days   -
        Sorry   -
        Nuba 2   -

ANDREW CYRILLE QUARTET (MAONO):
Ted Daniel(tp,flh),David S. Ware(ts),Nick Di Geronimo(b),Andrew Cyrille(dr).
                                        Milan,Italy.October 21/22,1980
        A Girl Named Rainbow   Soul Note(I)SN1012
        High Priest   -
        Fortified Nucleolus   -
        Baby Man   -
        Special People   -

CZECHOSLOVAK DIXIELAND JAZZ BAND (Czech)

Karel Danda(cnt),S. Franc(tb),Miroslav Rücker(cl),J. Slitr(p),M. Frauenberg(g),O. Pokorny
(b),Frantisek Hruza(dr).   Prague.Autumn 1948
        At The Jazz Band Ball   Supraphon(Cz)DV10178

WOLFGANG CZELUSTA

see HERBERT JOOS.

GER DAALHUYSEN (Dutch)

WEST COAST DANCE ORCHESTRA:
Gert Grijsen -1(tp),Rudy Bosch -1(tb),Cees Verschoor(cl,ts),Eddie de Jong -2(vbs),Wim San-
ders(g,bj),Ger Daalhuysen(b),Kees Kranenburg(dr).
                                        Hilversum,The Netherlands.February 15,1962
        When The Saints
          Go Marching In(1)   Unknown label F106806,Maestoso(Du)CBS 5004
        Charleston(1)   -
        Schwarze Augen (Black Eyes)(2)   Unknown label F106808,Maestoso(Du)CBS 5004
        Twist(2)   -

Note:Additional recordings by this artist are not included.

ANDRZEJ DABROWSKI (Polish)

(vcl) acc. by KWINTET PAWEL PERLINSKIEGO:
Andrzej Olejniczak(sax),Pawel Perlinski(p),Marek Blizinski(g),Zbigniew Wegehaupt(b),Czes-
law Bartkowski(dr).   Live."Akwarium",Warsaw.October 1-10,1980
        Thou Swell   Poljazz(P)PSJ95
        The Good Life   -
(session cont. next page).

(session cont. from previous page):
      I Was Telling Her About You   Poljazz(P)PSJ95
      Bye Bye Blackbird   -
      Walkin'   -
      Like Someone In Love   -
      When I Fall In Love   -
      Autumn Leaves   -

PAULINHO DA COSTA (Brazilian)

Steven Huffstetter,Gene Coe(tp,flh),Frank Rosolino,Mike Julian(tb),Larry Williams(sax,fl),
Gregory Phillinganes(p,el-p),Lee Ritenour(g),Octavio Bailly(b,vcl),Claudio Slon(dr,perc,
synth,vcl),Paulinho Da Costa(perc,vcl).   LA.August 6/9/11/12/16,1976
      Simbora   Pablo 2310.785
      Terra   -
      Toledo Bagel   -
      Berimbau Variations   -
      Belisco   -
      Ritmo Number One   -

All titles also on Pablo 2335.747,Original Jazz Classics OJC630,OJCCD630-2.

Chuck Findley(tp,flh,arr),Steven Madaio,Gary Grant(tp,flh),Bill Reichenbach(tb,arr),Eric
Culver,Dick Hyde,Lew McCreary,Tom Malone(tb),Gary Herbig(fl,oboe,sax),Gregory Phillinganes
(keyb),John Barnes(keyb,arr),Michael Boddicker(synth),Marlo Henderson,Al McKay,Larry Carl-
ton(g),Nathan Watts(b),James Gason(dr),Paulinho Da Costa(perc),Philip Bailey,Bill Champlin
Carl Carwell(vcl,arr),Deborah Thompson,Jeanette Hawes,Clarence Ford,Venette Cloud,Carmen
Twillie(vcl),Erich Bulling,Bruce Miller(arr).
                                        LA.c. 1977/78
      Deja Vu   Pablo 2312.102
      Take It On Up   -
      Love Till The End Of The Time   -
      Seeing Is Believing   -
      Dreamflow   -
      Carnival Of Colors   -
      Let's Get Together   -
      Happy People   -
      Put Your Mind On Vacation   -

RITA DA COSTA

(vcl) acc. by THE CEDAR WALTON TRIO:
Cedar Walton(p),Herman Wright(b),"Scoby" Clarence Stroman(dr).
                                       NYC(?). 1976
      Let Me Love You   Finite 1976-3
      If You Walked Into My Life Again   -
      Quiet Nights   -
      On A Clear Day   -
      Easy To Love   -
      Boy(!) From Ipanema   -
      Travelin' Light   -
      I Didn't Know What Time It Was   -
      The Right To Love   -

Note:The jazz content of the above recording may be limited.

TONY DAGRADI

Gary Valente(tb),Tony Dagradi(ts,ss),Kenny Werner(p),Ed Schuller(b),D. Sharpe(dr).
Woodstock,NYC.March 1980

Urban Disturbance	Gramavision GR8001	
Oasis		-
Juanita		-
Radiation		-
Esther		-

Note:The LP lists Kenny Warner(p).

James "Snake" Harvey(p) replaces Werner.   Same date

Ghana Folk Song	Gramavision GR8001	
Green Jacket(1)		-

"JOMAR DAGRON"

JOMAR DAGRON QUARTET:
Ron Washington(ts),Marvin Halliday(bars),Dag Walton(org),Jo Jo Williams(dr).
Denver.Early 1960's

A Genie N' Bag-Dag	Golden Crest CR3018	
Froggy		-
Nothin'		-
One And Three More		-
Five Moods Five Points		-
Relaxation		-
Vince's Tune		-
Gene's Idea		-
Minor Mo		-
Cherry		-

Note:The name "Jomar Dagron" is constructed from the musicians' first names.

PAT DAHL

(vcl) acc. by unknown orchestra incl. Harry Edison(tp),Buddy Collette(reeds),Don Abney(p),
John Gray(g),Shelly Manne(dr),Benny Carter -1,Billy May -2,Lyn Murray -3,Marty Paich -4,
Shorty Rogers -5,Pete Rugolo -6(arr,cond).   LA.c. 1966

It's All Right With Me(1)	Audio Fidelity AFLP2157/AFSD6157	
Lonely Woman(1)		-
Stout-Hearted Men(2)		-
What Now,My Love(2)		-
I Who Have Nothing(3)		-
Ten Cents A Dance(3)		-
On The Good Ship Lollipop(4)		-
Show Me(4)		-
Oh Johnny(5)		-
Someone To Watch Over Me(5)		-
I'm In Love With The Honorable Mister So & So(6)		-
There's No Fool Like An Old Fool(6)		-

NILS-BERTIL DAHLANDER (Bert Dale) (Swedish)

NILS-BERTIL DAHLANDER QUARTET:
Sune Svensson(vbs),Rune Gustafsson(g),Bengt Carlsson(b),Nils-Bertil Dahlander(dr).
Gothenburg,Sweden.Autumn 1952

2210	Strike Up The Band	Poseidon(Sd)unknown issuenumber
2211	Move	Poseidon(Sd)22
2212	Moon Over Miami	Poseidon(Sd)unknown issuenumber
2213	Bei Mir Bist Du Schoen	Poseidon(Sd)22

Stig Larsson(vbs) replaces Svensson.　　　　　Gothenburg,Sweden.Autumn 1952

2224	Love Walked In	Decca(Sd)F44205
2225	Little White Lies	-
2226	All The Things You Are,I	Decca(Sd)F44224
2227	All The Things You Are,II	-

Sune Svensson(vbs),Scott Lunde(p),Ivar Börsum(b),Nils-Bertil Dahlander(dr).
Oslo.March 26,1953

K803	Undediced	Harmoni(N)AAS,Modern Music(Sd)M21
K804	Take The "A" Train	- -

Note:The above issuenumber may be AA5.

Stig Larsson(vbs),Rune Gustafsson(g),Bengt Carlsson(b),Nils-Bertil Dahlander(dr).
Stockholm.June 10,1953

494	Carioca	Metronome(Sd)J267,MEP21
495	Somebody Loves Me	- -

Same　　　　　　　　　　　　　　Stockholm.February 8,1954

Summertime	Metromone(Sd)MEP59
Someone To Watch Over Me	-
Frenesi	-
Lullaby Of The Leaves	Metronome MEP60, Esquire EP9
What Is This Thing Called Love	- -
Laura	- -

Knud Jørgensen(p),Bengt Carlsson(b),Nils-Bertil Dahlander(dr).
Stockholm.April 4,1956

Blue Lou	Philips(Sd)421.503PE,Epic LN3309
Walkin' Cheese	- -
Stompin'At The Savoy	-
Please Don't Talk About Me When I'm Gone	- ,BO8200L,(E)BB27102

Victor Feldman(vbs,p),Howard Roberts(g),Curtis Counce(b),Nils-Bertil Dahlander(dr).
LA.September 16,1957

21450-5	How Do You Do	Verve MGV8253
21451-15	Johnson's Wax	-
21452-7	When Lights Are Low	-

Same.　　　　　　　　　　　　　LA.September 17,1957

21459-3	Hip Soup	Verve MGV8253,HMV(E)7EG8693
21460-9	But Not For Me	-
21461-9	Emma	- ,HMV(E)7EG8693
21462-9	Room 608	-
21463-4	Medley: Everything Happens To Me Moonlight In Vermont Flamingo	-

Note:Master 21459 issued on HMV(E)7EG8693 as "Hip Sound".

Erik Nordström -1,Gunnar Nilson -2(ts),Staffan Nilsson -3(p),Hakån Berghe -4(org),Stig-
Olof Magnusson(acc) -5,Bengt Åke Anderson(b),Nils-Bertil Dahlander(dr).
                                    Gothenburg,Sweden.October 5,1976
    Good Old Swinging(1,2,3)   Everyday(Sd)31309
    Keep On Marching(1,2,3)   -
    How Do You Do(1,2,4,5)   -
    Answer Me(3,5)   -
    With The Help Of The Lord(3,5)   -
    Winter Waltz(4)   -

Vincent Lindgren -1(oboe),Bob Dahlqvist -2(ts),Staffan Nilsson -3,Gunnar André -4(p),Bengt
Åke Anderson(b),Nils-Bertil Dahlander(dr).   Same date
    After A Busy Day(1,3)   Everyday(Sd)31309
    Around Eight At Night(2)   -
    A Very Special Day(2,4)   -
    Little Bit(2,4)   -

ALBERT DAILEY

Albert Dailey(p),Richard Davis(b),Mel Lewis(dr).
                                    NYC.October 13,1966
    The Shadow Of Your Smile   United Artists unissued
    Untitled original
    There Is No Greater Love
    Insensitive
    Untitled original (waltz)
    Funkque Phondue
    New Orleans

Albert Dailey(p),Richard Davis(b),David Lee(dr).
                                    NYC. 1972
    A.D.   Columbia KC31278
    Dailey Double   -
    A Lady's Mistake   -
    Encounter   -
    September Of My Years(p-solo)   -

Brooks Tillotson(frh),Art Kaplan(fl),George Marge,Phil Bodner(oboe),Ray Shanfeld(bassoon),
Albert Dailey(p),Jack Wilkins(g),Charles McCracken(cello),Lisle Atkinson(b),Roy Haynes
(dr).   NYC. 1972
    Theme From "Clockwork Orange"   Columbia KC31278
    Bittersweet Waltz(p,g,b,dr only)   -

Percy Heath(b),Mickey Roker(dr) replace Atkinson,Haynes;omit Wilkins.
                                    NYC. 1972
    The Day After The Dawn   Columbia KC31278

Albert Dailey(p,el-p,synth,b,dr)(overdub). NYC. 1972
    Free Me   Columbia KC31278

Carter Jefferson(as,ts),Albert Dailey(p),Cecil McBee(b),Charlie Persip(dr),Cheary Alex-
ander(vcl).   NYC.November 1/2,1977
    Black Raspberry   Catalyst(J)KUX98
    I Love You   -
    Mimosa   -
    Gee Monatti   -
    Autumn   -

Adam Nussbaum(dr) replaces Persip.   Same date
    Cues We Have To Pay   Catalyst(J)KUX98
    Mr. Pogo   -

All titles on KUX98 also on VeeJay(J)20YB7017,30YD7017(CD).

ALBERT DAILEY TRIO:
Albert Dailey(p),Buster Williams(b),Billy Hart(dr).
                                      NYC.July 13,1978
    Music That Makes Me Dance   SteepleChase(D)SCS1107
    Yesterdays   -
    That Old Feeling   -
    Lover Man   -
    Body And Soul   -
    Michelle   -
    Night And Day   unissued

All titles on SCS1107 also on SteepleChase(J)RJ7487.

PETE DAILEY (DAILY)

See also BILL WILLIAMS.

PETE DAILEY AND HIS CHICAGOANS:
Pete Dailey(cnt),Bud Wilson(tb),Rosy McHargue(cl),Joe Rushton(bassax),Don Owens(p),Dick
Fisher(bj),Country Washburne(tu),Sleepy Kaplan(dr).
                                        LA.November 10,1945
SRC128 Skeleton Jangle   Sunset 7566,Decca 27038
SRC129 Sugarfoot Stomp   Sunset 7559,Decca 27037,Parlophone(E)R3141,MCA-
                                          Coral(G)6.22569
SRC130 Red Light Rag   Sunset 7559,Decca 27037,Parlophone(E)R3141
SRC131 Roundhouse Rag   Sunset 7566,Decca 27038

All titles also on Eclectic E71,Decca DL5261,Brunswick(E)LA8515,MCA-Coral(G)COPS7442,
6.22048.

Red Cooper(dr) replaces Kaplan;omit Fisher,Washburne.
                                        LA.October 18,1946
J45-1 Bluin' The Blues   Jump JL-2,J12-5
J45   Bluin' The Blues   Jump 14,Tempo(E)A28
J46-1 Lazy Daddy   Jump JL-2,J12-5
J46-2 Lazy Daddy   Jump 24
J47-2 Shake It And Break It   Jump JL-2,J12-5
J47-3 Shake It And Break It   Jump 24
J48-1 Livery Stable Blues   Jump JL-2,J12-5
J48-2 Livery Stable Blues   Jump 12,Tempo(E)A5
J49-1 You're Driving Me Crazy   Jump JL-2,J12-5
J50-1 Four Or Five Times   -   -
J51-2 Wolverine Blues   Jump 12,J12-5,Tempo(E)A5,Ampersand(Au)R102
J52-1 5.30 A.M. Blues   Jump 14,J12-5,Tempo(E)A28
J52-2 Jazz Me Blues   Jump JL-2,J12-5

Pete Dailey(cnt),Warren Smith(tb),Rosy McHargue(cl),Skippy Anderson(p),Len Esterdahl(g),
Jimmy Stutz(b),George Defebaugh(dr).   LA.November 24,1947
2588   When The War
       Breaks Out In Mexico   Capitol 15315,(E)CL13153
2589   I Want To Linger   Capitol 15095,1233,1624,EAP1-183,H/T183,W2139,(E
                                        LC6525,(Au)CLP028

(session cont. next page).

PETE DAILEY (DAILY)

(session cont. from previous page):
2590   Circus Slide   Capitol 15315
2591   What's Your Story   Capitol 15095,EAP1-183,H/T183,(E)LC6525,(Au)CLP028

Same.   LA.November/December 1947
2682   Panama   Capitol 15035,1588,EAP1-321,H321,(E)LC6562

PETE DAILEY`S RYTHM KINGS:
Omit Esterdahl,Stutz.   LA.December 24,1947
CPM1026 Sobbin'Blues   Jazz Man 29,Good Time Jazz 61
CPM1027 Jazz Man Strut   -   -
CPM1028 Yelping Hound Blues   Jazz Man 30,Good Time Jazz 68
CPM1029 Clarinet Marmalade   -   -

All titles also on Good Time Jazz EP1009,L12005,Vogue(E)EPG1178,LDG12023.

PETE DAILEY AND HIS CHICAGOANS:
Same.   Live."Sardi's",LA.November 26,1948
     Tin Roof Blues   Jump J12-5
     Clarinet Marmalade   -

Same.   Live."Sardi's",LA.November 1948
     St. Louis Blues   Eclectic E71
     That's A Plenty   -
     Ballin' The Jack   -
     After You've Gone   -
     I Want To Linger   -

PETE DAILEY'S CHICAGOANS:
Pete Dailey(cnt),Warren Smith(tb),Rosy McHargue(cl),Don Owens(p),Nappy Lamare(g),Jimmy
Stutz(b),Country Washburne(tu),George Defebaugh(dr).
                           LA.March 22,1949
4106   South   Capitol 57-60008,1233,1624,T794,(E)CL13170,(Eu)
                           1J.060-80154
4107   She Looks Like Helen Brown Capitol 57-60008,(E)CL13153
4108   Sailing Down The Chesapeake Bay Capitol 57-728
4109   Red Rose Romp   Capitol 1055,T385
(849) Green Light Rag(1)   Capitol 57-728

-1.Prob. from this session.

Stan Story(cl),Bernie Billings(tu) replace McHargue,Stutz.
                           LA.September 12,1949
4735   Down Home Rag   Capitol 57-760,H/T385,(E)LC6603,(G)C80062

Same   LA.September 29,1949
4962   O Katharina(1)   Capitol 57-760,T385,(G)C80062
4963   Doo Wacka Doo   Capitol 942,(E)CL13380
4964   Ook McGlook   -

-1.Add unknown vcl-group.

PETE DAILEY AND HIS CHICAGOANS:
Pete Dailey(cnt),Warren Smith(tb),Stan Story(cl),Don Owens(p),Nappy Lamare(g,bj),Phil Ste-
phens(tu,b),George Defebaugh(dr).   La.October 19,1949
5099   At A Georgia Camp Meeting Capitol 15434,EAP2-183,(E)CL13404
5100 When The Saints Go Marchin' In   -   -   -
5101 Dixieland Shuffle   Capitol 15433,   -
5102 Sensation Rag   Capitol 15432,EAP1-183

All titles also on Capitol H/T183,(E)LC6525,(Au)CLP028.

Same.   LA.October 20,1949
5103 Minnie The Mermaid   Capitol 1055
5104 Original Dixieland One-Step   Capitol 15432,EAP1-183,H/T183,(E)LC6525,(G)C80135,
                                               (Au)CLP028
5105 Daily Rag   Capitol 805,(G)C80120,Folkways RBF39
5106 Careless Love   Capitol 15433,EAP2-183,H/T183,(E)LC6525,(G)C80120,
                                               (Au)CLP028
5107 Big Bass Horn Blues   Capitol 805,EAP3-183,T183,(G)C80135

Pete Dailey(cnt),Burt Johnson(tb),Pud Brown(cl,ts),Skippy Anderson(p),Len Esterdahl(g,bj),
Budd Hatch(b,tu),Hugh Allison(dr).   LA.August 22,1950
6534 Daily Double   Capitol 1238,H/T385,(E)LC6603
6535 Basin Street Boogie   -   -   - - ,(Au)CEP003
6536 Put On Your Grey Bonnet   Capitol EAP3-183,T183
6537 Roamin'In The Gloamin'   Capitol 1486

Same or similar.   LA. 1950
      Over The Waves   Camay CA3035
      Daily Double
      Goat Blues
      O Tannenbaum
        (Maryland,My Maryland)
      Please Don't Talk
        About Me When I'm Gone

Note:The above titles are from Snader Telescriptions.

Pete Dailey(cnt),Burt Johnson(tb),Joe Darensbourg(cl),Pud Brown(ts),Skippy Anderson(p),
Jack Coss(g,bj),Bud Hatch(b,tu),Hugh Allison(dr).
                                          LA.December 20,1950
6927 Walkin' The Dog   Capitol 1486,H/T385,(E)LC6603
6928 Johnson Rag   Capitol 1370,T385
6929 Chicken Rag   Capitol 1820,EAP3-183,T183
6930 Louis-i-an-ia   Capitol 1370

Same   LA.May 14,1951
7554 Gramophone Rag   Capitol 2302
7555 Take Me Out To The Ball Game   Capitol 1588,T385
7556 Harmony Rag   - ,H/T385,(E)LC6603,(Au)CEP003
7557 Peggy O'Neil   Capitol 1820   -   -   -

Pete Dailey(cnt),Rolly Furnas(tb),William Sousa Martinez(cl),Skippy Anderson(p),Len
Esterdahl(bj,g),Phil Stephens(b,tu),Hugh Allison(dr).
                                          LA.March 3,1952
9821 The Wearin' Of The Green   Capitol EAP3-183,T183
9822 Asleep In The Deep   Capitol 2302,T385
9823 North   Capitol 2041,H/T385,(E)LC6603,(Au)CEP003,(J)Z229
9824 China Boy   -   -   - ,(J)Z229

Note:Some of the 1949-52 Capitol recordings issued as PETE DAILEY AND HIS DIXIELAND BAND.

Pete Dailey(cnt),Warren Smith(tb),Jerry Fuller(cl),Skippy Anderson(p),Len Esterdahl(bj),
Bernie Miller(tu,b),Hugh Allison(dr).   LA.November 1954
DB117 (There's A
        Quaker In) Quaker Town   Jazz Man EJ451
DB118 Just A Closer Walk With Thee   -
DB119 New Tin Roof Blues   -
DB120 Swanee River   -

All four titles also on Jazz Man LJ333,Tempo(E)EXA60,Storyville(D)SEP320.

LESLI DALABA

Leslie Dalaba(tp),Polly Bradfield -1(vln),Wayne Horvitz -2(b).
                                Unknown location.June/August 1978,January/March 1979
    Suite For Hopalong Cassidy: Parachute(E)10
      A Stop In Town
      Back On The Trail
    Two Up(2)   -
    Two Down(1)   -

Note:The jazz content of the above recording may be limited.

BARRY DALE (Canadian)

Réal Mathieu(tp),Bill Dadson(tb),Barry Dale(cl,vcl),Rod Tremblay(p),Gilles Forget(b),
Claude Resther(dr).   Montreal.c. 1963
    Misery(no cl)(bd)   Fonorama(Ca)FM302
    What's The Use Of Making Love   -
    Midnight In Moscow   -
    Loulou's Birthday   -
    Aupres De Ma Blonde   -
    Bal Petit Bal(bd)   -
    76 Trombones   -
    My Lord (Milord)   -
    That Big,Tall Thing   -

All titles also on Fonorama(Ca)MF604.
Note:The jazz content of the above recording may be limited.

BERT DALE (Swedish)

See NILS-BERTIL DAHLANDER.

FRED DALE

FRED DALE ORCHESTRA:
Fred Dale(tp,vbs),Vernon Cressler,Alan Kieger,Doug Mettome(tp),Buddy Baker,Dave Barker,
Urbie Green(tb),Leonard Graves(as,ts),Jerry Coker,Al Cohn(ts),Ray Pappi(bars),Al Planck
(p),Dick Wagner(b),Richard Dickenson(dr).   NYC.April 28,1954
46217 I Only Have Eyes For You   Coral 61261
46218 Laura   Coral 61194
46219 Mean To Me   -
46220 Ginger   Coral 61261

JOE DALEY

Joe Daley(ts),Russell Thorne(b),Hal Russell(dr).
                                       NYC.June 3,1963
PA1-5137 Helicon No.2   RCA-Victor unissued
PA1-5138 Ballad   RCA-Victor LPM/LSP2763
PA1-5141 Knell   -
PA1-5142 Dexterity   -
PA1-5144 Helicon No.1   unissued
PA1-5145 The Clown From Naptown   -

```
Same                                    Live.Newport Jazz Festival,R.I.July 5,1963
PPA5-5407 Ode To Blackie                RCA-Victor LPM/LSP2763
PPA5-5408 One Note                          -
PPA5-5409 Ramblin'                          -
```

All titles from LPM2763 also on RCA(E)RD/SF7606.

DALLAS JAZZ CLUB BAND

Don Potter(cnt),Lynn Barton(tb),Rupert Murphy(ts),Jim Cullum,Sr.(?)(bars),Shub Fuertes(cl)
Vincent Parrino(p),John Gilliland(tu),Bob McClendon(dr).
```
                                        Dallas.  1944
        At The Jazz Band Ball          Dallas Jazz Club(no number)
        Royal Garden Blues                 -
```


DALLAS JAZZ ORCHESTRA

Galen Jeter(tp,cond),Byron Parks,Fred Ralston,Dennie Kemp,Tom Wirtel(tp),Nick Keelan,Lloyd
Hebert,Toppy Hill,Bob Hurst(tb),Thom Mason(as,ss,cond),Bruce Thompson(sax),Fred Greenwell,
Don Daniels(ts),Bill Gutekunst(bars),Gloria Morgan(p,vcl),Jack Petersen(g),Billy Michaels
(b),Dale Cook(dr),A.D. Washington(cg).   Live."Maxine Kent's Club",Dallas.February 9,1975
        Four-Five-Six
        For The Last Time(gm)
        M'Lady
        Falling In Love With Love(gm)
        A Patchwork Blue
        Loving
        Hey,Man

Note:The above LP was issued - unnumbered (with 54X05A/B in the wax) - by the Dallas Jazz
     Orchestra (as "the first DJO album").

Mac Doughterty(g),Dave Hunt(dr),Bobby Sickles(perc) replace Peterson,Cook,Washington;Jeter
also (vcl).   Live."Maxine Kent's Club",Dallas.c. 1976
        Well You Needn't
        Monaghan
        I Had To Give Up On You(gm)
        Joshua
        Spain
        You Don't Know What Love Is
        Tuesday,The Fifteenth(gj)

Note:The above LP was issued - unnumbered (with 65X112A/B in the wax) - by the Dallas Jazz
     Jazz Orchestra (as "the second DJO album").

Galen Jeter(tp,cond),John Auletta,Byron Parks,Bob Eidenier,Chuck Willis(tp),Ed Wright,Kim
Corbet,Chuck Mandernach,Bob Hurst(tb),Bruce Thompson,Peter Profilet(as),Peter Vollmers,
(ts,ss),Billy Tillman(ts,fl),Alan Beutier(bars),Leon Ziligson(p),Mac Dougherty(g),Glenn
Moon(b),Joel Fulgham(dr),Rusty Wells(perc). Dallas.c. 1980
        Super Chicken
        Chiffon Dresses
        Typical New,And Tyler Too
        All In A Dream(2)
        Camel Rise(1)
        Vadar's Vaccination
        The More I See You
(session cont. next page).
```
```

(session cont. from previous page):
         Friends Last
            Longer Than Lovers(1)
         Lady From Oregon(1)
         Nothing Grows In The Shade
         Triple Sec(1)
         Icing(2)

1.Paul Baker(bars) replaces Beutier (or is added).
2.Bob Wilkinson(perc) replaces Wells (or is added).

Note:The above LP was issued - unnumbered (with JSS107 Side One/Two/Three/Four in the wax)
      - by the Dallas Jazz Orchestra (as "the third DJO album").

THELLA DALLAS (STROZIER)

ee MAC STRITTMATTER.

AVE DALLWITZ (Australian)

ee also GRAEME BELL,THE SOUTHERN JAZZ GROUP.

AVE DALLWITZ' SOUTHERN JAZZ GROUP:
eith Hounslow(tp),Mal Wilkinson(tb),Tas Brown(cl),Dave Dallwitz(p),Ron Carson(bj),Gubby
llen(tu),Brian Wright(dr).   Adelaide,Australia.June 7,1951
C39/FSZ699-1 Blues For Rex   Swaggie(Au)S1010

ame   Adelaide,Australia.June 17,1951
C43/FSZ703-1 Emu Strut   Swaggie(Au)S1010
C44/FSZ704-1 Shabby Gal Rag   -
C44/FSZ704-2 Royal Terminus Rag   -

ame   Adelaide,Australia.June 19,1951
C47A/FSZ705-2 Crocodille Creep   Swaggie(Au)S1010

ame   Adelaide,Australia.June 25,1951
C46A/FSZ707-1 That Imbo Thing   Swaggie(Au)S1010
C46A/FSZ707-2 Captivation   -

me   Adelaide,Australia.June 28,1951
C53A/FSZ696-2 Turquoise Twilight   Swaggie(Au)S1010

te:The June 1951 titles were recorded for radio transcriptions.

E DALLWITZ - MONSBOURGH JAZZMEN:
b Barnard(tp),Tas Brown(cl),Ade Monsbourgh(cl,as,ts,vcl),Neville Stribling(cl,as,bars),
c Connor(p),Peter Cleaver(g,bj),Ron Williamson(tu),Len Barnard(dr),Dave Dallwitz(arr).
                                               Adelaide,Australia,March 18/19,1972
         Nullabor(1)   Swaggie(Au)S1303
         Don't Monkey With Me(am)   -
         Tell The Boys You Saw Me   -
         Sprightly Nightly   -
         Stomp Miss Hannah   -
         Crocodile Creep   -
         Whim Creek Wobble   -
         Clarinet Sugar(2,3)   -
ession cont. next page).

(session cont. from previous page):

Murray Cod(1)	Swaggie(Au)S1303
Brandy Cruster(3)	-
Clever Feller	-
Takin' No Risks	Swaggie(Au)S1321
Purple Myrtle	-
Hessian Rag	
Heart Throb(1)	Swaggie(Au)S1343

-1.Joe McConechy(b) replaces Williamson.
-2.Omit Bob Barnard.
-3.Omit Stribling.

DAVE DALLWITZ AND HIS JAZZMEN:
Bill Munro(tp),Tas Brown,Bob Cruickshanks,Bruce Gray(reeds),Graham Coyle(p),Norm Koch(bj)
Bob Wright(tu),Len Barnard(dr).   Adelaide,Australia.August 19,1972

Stompology	Swaggie(Au)S1321
Coorong	-
Jack O'Lantern(p,dr only)	- ,Bill Haesler Coll. H001
Burning Off	-
Willochra Haze	-
Eucla Nymph	-
Rameses II	-
Butterfly(p,dr only)	- ,Bill Haesler Coll. H001
Piping Hot	-

DAVE DALLWITZ AND HIS JAZZ BAND:
Graham Eames(tp),Deryck Bentley(tb),Tas Brown(cl),Bob Cruickshanks(cl,as,bars),Dave Dall-
witz(p),Tony West(bj),John Bradsen(tu),Ken Farmer(dr),Penny Eames(vcl).
                                          Adelaide,Australia.February 1973

It Don't Mean A Thing	Jazznote(Au)JNLP008
The Moooche	-
Shipshape	- ,World Record Club(Au)R03167
Marrakesh(pe)	-
Climax Rag	-
Swanston Street Shuffle	-

DAVE DALLWITZ JAZZMEN:
Bob Barnard,Alan Nash(tp),John Costelloe(tb),Johnny McCarthy(cl,ss,ts),Graham Coyle(p),Ed
Gaston(b),Len Barnard(dr),Beverley Hay(vcl). Sydney.August 24,1973

Tullamarine	Swaggie(Au)S1342
Jolly Roger - A	
Portrait Of Roger Bell(bh)	-
Butterfly(1)	-
St. Kilda Sunset	-
Swanston Street Shuffle	-
Russell Street Rag	-
Lazy Ade - A Portrait	
Of Ade Monsbourgh(bh)	-
Nimrod - The Mighty Hunter(1)	-
Andamooka	Swaggie(Au)S1343
Peach Pie(bh)	-
Marrakesh(bh)	-(?)
Dreamtime(1)	-

-1.Add Johnny Sangster(vbs).

Bob Barnard,Bill Munro(tp),John Costelloe(tb),Johnny McCarthy(cl,ss),Ade Monsbourgh(as,t
John Sangster(vbs),Graham Coyle(p),Norm Koch(bj),Ron Williamson(tu),Len Barnard(dr),Roge
Bell(vcl).   Melbourne.March 9,1974
(session cont. next page).

(session cont. from previous page):
      Brancusi Bird(rb)   Swaggie(Au)S1343
      Don't Monkey With It(rb)   -
      Forgotten Woman's Blues(rb)   -
      Mootwingie(no vbs)   -
      Midnight Crawl(no vbs)(1)   -
      Gold Coast Mama   Swaggie(Au)S1410

-1.Omit Monsbourgh.

DAVE DALLWITZ AND HIS JAZZ BAND:
Bill Munro(tp,flh),Graham Eames(tp),Deryck Bentley(tb),Tas Brown(cl),Rod Porter(cl,as),
Dave Dallwitz(p),Johnny Malpas(bj),Bob Wright(tu),Reg Bassett(dr),Penny Eames(vcl).
                             Adelaide,Australia.September 7,1974
      Saltbush Rag   Swaggie(Au)S1354
      Peach Pie(pe)   -
      You Took The Words
         Right Out Of My Mouth(pe)   -
      The Sycamore   -
      Downtown man(pe)   -

Same.   Adelaide,Australia.September 8,1974
      Bunyip   Swaggie(Au)S1354
      Illawarra Flame   -
      Billabong(1,2,3)   -
      Clarinet Shimozzle(2,3)   -
      Three's A Crowd(1,2)   -
      The Entertainer   Swaggie(Au)S1410

-1.Omit Munro.
-2.Omit Eames.
-3.Omit Bentley.

Same.   Adelaide,Australia.August 16/17,1975
      Portrait Of Ern Malley   Swaggie(Au)S1360
      Portrait Of Sid Nolan   -
      Boult Upright(pe)   -
      Stagnant Fragment(pe)   -
      Obscene Unforgivable Rag   -
      Chiaroscuro(pe)   -
      Patterns Of Slatterns(pe)   -
      Portrait Of Max Harris   -
      I Shall Be Raised Up(pe)   -
      It Makes No Difference Now   Swaggie(Au)S1407

Keith Conlon(dr) replaces Bassett.   Adelaide,Australia.June 1977
      Gold Fever   Swaggie(Au)S1377
      Impending   -
      Blue(pe)   -
      Castlemaine Rag   -
      Lola's Assets(pe)   -
      Welcome Stranger   -
      Ghost Town   -
      Ev'ry Time   -
      Hill End Hush(pe)   -
      Gulgong Shuffle   Swaggie(Au)S1378
      Bendigo   -
      Dusk(pe)   -
      Who Can Explain(pe)   -
      Clunes Ruse(pe)   -
 session cont. next page).

(session cont. from previous page):
```
        Wedderburn Wag              Swaggie(Au)S1378
        Walhalla(pe)                       -
        Where You Find It(pe)              -
        Miners Rest(1)                     -
        Never Quite Catching The Tune  Swaggie(Au)S1407
```

-1.Omit Eames,Bentley.

Note:Some of the titles on S1378 were recorded October 1977.

DAVE DALLWITZ AND THE SCHAMPUS ALL STARS
Klaus Schmedtmann(tp),Erwin Kuckartz(tb),Giseller Spath(ss,as,ts,bars),Dave Dallwitz
(p,arr),Klaus Hochkeppel(bj,g),Manfred Weise(b),Ingold Schneider(dr).
```
                                   Dusseldorf,Germany.September 17,1978
        Fly-By-Night               Dawn Club DCS33002
        Facade                             -
        Sunday Morning Rag                 -
        Green Walley - Low Groovey         -
        Mundoo                             -
        Backslider                         -
        Was A Time                         -
        Casablanca                         -
```

THE DAVE DALLWITZ EUPHONIC SOUND RAGTIME ORCHESTRA:
Ross Smith(tp),Deryck Bentley(tb),Tas Brown(cl),Dave Dallwitz(p),Peter Hooper(bj),Brian
Green(tu),David Bentley(dr).   Adelaide,Australia.February 7/14/21,1979
```
        Panama Rag                 Swaggie(Au)S1393
        Elvish Tea Party                   -
        Bells Of Baghdad                   -
        Chimes                             -
        Baby Tank(1)                       -
        Hessian Rag(1)                     -
        Temptation Rag             Swaggie(Au)S1398
        Euphonic Sounds                    -
        Shipshape Rag                      -
```

-1.Keith Conlon(dr) replaces David Bentley.

Colin Doley(tp) replaces Smith.   Adelaide,Australia.February 7/14/21,1979
```
        Snake Rag                  Swaggie(Au)S1393
        Down Home Rag                      -
        Copenhagen                         -
        Giles Farnaby's Humour             -
        Russell Street Rag                 -
        Sunflower Slow Drag(1)             -
        Oriental                   Swaggie(Au)S1398
        Birdsville Rag                     -
        Chinese Blues                      -
```

-1.Johnny Malpas(bj) replaces Hooper.

Keith Conlon(dr) replaces David Bentley.   Live.Mildura,Australia.November 3/4,1979
```
        Chinese Blues              Nolon(Au)unnumbered cassette
        Baby Talk                          -
        Hessian Rag                        -
```

Ross Smith(tp) replaces Doley.   Live.Mildura,Australia.November 1/2/3,1980
```
        Baby Tank                  Nolon(Au)unnumbered cassette
```

LAILA DALSETH (Norwegian)

(vcl) acc. by Jim Berger(g),Erik Amundsen(b).
                                Oslo.November 14,1963
    Guess Who I Saw Today   Harmoni(N)H505
    Like Someone In Love   Harmoni(N)468

(vcl) acc.by Lars Martin Thomassen(flh),Ove Stokstad(ts,bars),Per Hubsy(p),Bjørn Alterhaug
(b),Svein Christiansen(dr).   Trondheim,Norway.February 10,1975
    Just Friends   EMI(Sd)7E.062-38217
    Old Folks   -
    I Can't Get Started   -
    It Could Happen To You   -
    Willow Weep For Me   -
    God Bless The Child   -
    More Than You Know   -
    Poor Butterfly   -
    I Remember Clifford   -
    Fooling Myself   -
    There Is No Greater Love   -

(vcl) acc. by ARNE DOMNERUS SEXTETTE:
Arne Domnerus(as),Claes Rosendahl(ts,fl),Bengt Hallberg(p),Rune Gustafsson(g),Georg Riedel
(b),Egil Johansen(dr).   Live."Konserthuset",Oslo.April 16,1978
    My Romance   Talent(N)TLS3045
    If You Were Mine   -
    I Got It Bad   -
    Have You Met Sir Jones   -
    But Beautiful(vcl,p only)   -

(vcl) acc. by Frode Thingnæs(tb,arr),Harald Halvorsen(tb),Erling Andersen -1(bars),Einar
Iversen(p),Nipe Nyrén(g),Bjørn Jacobsen(b),Svein-Erik Gaardvik(dr),strings.
                                Oslo.June 28/29,1978
    Like Someone In Love   Talent(N)TLS3045
    Every Time We Say Goodbye(1)   -
    Drinking Again(1)   -

(vcl) acc. by Finn Eriksen -1,Atle Hammer -1(tp),Tore Nilsen -1(tb),Erik Andresen -1(as),
Knut Riisnæs -2(ts),Roy Hellvin(p),Terje Venaas(b),Eyvind Olsen(dr),strings -2.
                                Same dates
    There Will Never
      Be Another You(1)   Talent(N)TLS3045
    Fine And Dandy(2)   -
    I'm Glad There Is You(vcl,p only)   -

DEREK DALTON (Australian)

Derek Dalton(cnt),Ernie Alderslade(tb),Ron Dalton(cl),Malcolm Bills(p),John Cavanagh(bj,g,
cl),Frank Mulders(b),Darion Powell(dr).   Adelaide,Australia. 1974
    Phoenix On Parade   Polydor(Au)2486.078
    What'll I Do(jc)   -
    Muskrat Ramble   -
    Royal Garden Blues   -
    Twelfth Street Rag   -
    New Orleans Function(band-vcl)   -
    Bourbon Street Parade(jc)   -
    After You've Gone(jc)   -
    Tin Roof Blues   -
session cont. next page).

(session cont. from previous page):
```
      South                          Polydor(Au)2486.078
      Alexander's Ragtime Band(jc)                -
      All The Girls Go Crazy                      -
      Just A Closer Walk With Thee                -
      That's A Plenty                             -
```


LES DALTONIENS (Belgian)

Jean Linsman(tp),Jacques Baily(ts,as),Jean-Marie Troisfontaines(p),José Bedeur(b),Dany
Carly(dr).   Namur,Belgium.c. March 1963
```
1F1   Entre Les Étoiles             Discofilia(B)106671DF
2F1   Fireman's Blues                         -
```


GÉO DALY (GEORGES DALIBON) (French)

See also JOHN ADDINGTON SOCIETY ORCHESTRA.

GÉO DALY ET SON QUARTETTE:
Géo Daly(vbs),Bernard Peiffer(p),Jean Bouchety(b),Roger Paraboschi(dr).
                                    Paris.November 24,1949
```
OSW635-1 Nine O'Clock Jump          Swing(F)329
OSW636-1 Crazy House                EMI/Jazztime(F)780.373-2(CD)
OSW637-1 Moonglow                   Swing(F)329
```

GÉO DALY ALL STARS:
Christian Bellest(tp),Maurice Meunier(cl),Michel De Villers(bars),Géo Daly(vbs),Raymond
Fol(p),Jean Bonal(g),Jean Bouchety(b),Roger Paraboschi(dr).
                                    Paris.March 1,1950
```
OSW655-1 Cobra                      Swing(F)343
OSW656-1 Cross Winds                        -
```

Note:See MAURICE MEUNIER for additional titles from this session.

GÉO DALY ET SON QUARTETTE:
Géo Daly(vbs),Raymond Fol(p),Jean Bouchety(b),Roger Paraboschi(dr).
                                    Paris.April 17,1950
```
OSW675-1 Odalisque                  Swing(F)348
OSW676   Anatol(1)                  unissued
OSW677-1 Sun Kiss(1,2)              Swing(F)348
OSW678   Avril(1,3)                 unissued
```

-1.Add Maurice Meunier(as)
-2.Roby Poitevin(p) replaces Fol.
-3.Add Roby Poitevin(vbs).

GEO DALY ET SON ENSEMBLE:
André "Cousin" Ross(ts),Géo Daly(vbs),André Persiany(p),Alix Bret(b),Bernard Planchenault
(dr).   Paris.November 15,1950
```
OSW710-1 Sonny Home                 Swing(F)367
OSW711-1 Farewell Glance                    -
OSW712   Willy Willy                unissued
OSW713   Winter Serenade                    -
OSW714   Portrait Of Doriane Gabin          -
OSW715   Clock Wise                         -
```

Christian Chevallier(p,org) replaces Persiany.
                                      Paris.Spring 1952
EK017 Groovy   Eko 3
EK018 Sentimental Daly   -
       Blue Moon   Eko 4
       Tenderly   -

GÉO DALY ET SON QUARTETTE DE "LA ROSE ROUGE":
Géo Daly(vbs),André Persiany(org),Alphonse Masselier(b),Bernard Planchenault(dr).
                                      Paris.September 10,1952
52V4284 Indian Love Call   Vogue(F)V3217,LD105
52V4285 Love For Sale   -
52V4286 Lady Be Good   Vogue(F)V3218,LD106
52V4287 I Can't Give You
           Anything But Love   -
52V4288 Old Man River   Vogue(F)V3221
52V4289 Body And Soul   -
52V4290 My Melancholy Baby   Vogue(F)V3222
52V4291 Stardust   -
52V4292 The Man I Love   Vogue(F)V3225
52V4293 Confessin'   -

Note:V3217,V3218 and V3225 were never issued.

Bill Tamper(tb),André Ross(ts),Michel De Villers(bars),Géo Daly(vbs),Christian Chevallier
(p),Alix Bret(b),Bernard Planchenault(dr).   Paris.April 5,1953
53V4491 Prez Wiggins   Vogue(F)LD184
53V4492 Wedding Day   -
53V4493 Day Dream   Vogue(F)V3327
53V4494 I Got It Bad And
           That Ain't Good   -
53V4495 Illya   Vogue(F)LD184
53V4496 Cat Trick   -

Omit Tamper,Ross,De Villers.   Paris.December 4,1953
         Golden Skies   Vogue(F)LD184
         A La New Dalhy   -
53V4746 Tabou   Vogue(F)V3405,LD184
53V4747 Katie   -   -

GÉO DALY - SON VIBRAPHONE ET SON ORCHESTRE:
Incl. Maurice Meunier(cl),Géo Daly(vbs).   Paris.December 20,1954
         Silver Moon   HMV(F)7EMF50
         Smile   -
         Farewell Glance   -
         Three Coins In The Fountain   -

same   Paris.February 8,1955
         Le Rififi   HMV(F)7EMF60
         September Song   -
         Magic Tango   -
         Garden Lane   -

same   Paris.March 5,1955
         Si Tu Es Jolie   Columbia(F)ESDF1042
         Mister Sandman   -
         The Man That Got Away   -
         Merci,Monsieur Schubert   -

GÉO DALY BIG BAND:
Fred Gérard,Bernard Hulin,Jean Liesse(tp),André Paquinet,Benny Vasseur,Charles Verstraete,
Gaby Vilain(tb),Francis Weisc(as,cl),Marcel Cauvin,André Ross,Pierre Guillotin(as,ts,bars)
Géo Daly(vbs),Raymond Le Sénéchal(p),René Duchossoir(g),Alix Bret(b),Bernard Planchenault
(dr).   Paris.June 27,1955
      The Night Of A Cat   Columbia(F)FP1059
      The Day Of A Dog   -

GÉO DALY TRIO:
Géo Daly(vbs),René Duchossoir(g),Alix Bret(b).
                                               Paris.June 29,1955
      The Nearness Of You   Columbia(F)FP1059
      I Remember You   -
      Sweetheart   -
      Mory's Tune   -

GÉO DALY QUARTET:
Géo Daly(vbs),Jean Bonal(g),unknown b,dr.   Paris.December 5,1956
      Encore   Columbia(F)ESDF1138
      Amoureux De L'Amour   -
      A Woman In Love   -
      Tu Me Vois   -

GÉO DALY ET SON QUINTETTE:
Géo Daly(vbs),prob. Jean-Pierre Sasson(g),rest unknown.
                                               Paris. 1957
      Summertime   President(F)KV13
      Mu Funny Valentine   -
      Basin Street Blues   -
      I Love You,Yes I Do   -
      Pete Kelly's Blues   -
      Moonlight In Vermont   -
      Canadian Sunset   -
      Sass Is Groovy   -
      A Woman In Love   -
      Slightly Old Fashioned   -

Note:Additional recordings by this artist are not included.

WARREN DALY (Australian)

WARREN DALY - ED WILSON ORCHESTRA
Don Raverty,Alan Nash,Bernie Wilson,Kel Brady(tp),Dieter Vogt(tp,flh,barh),John Costelloe
George Brodbeck,Merv Knott(tb),Ed Wilson(tb,btb),Doug Foskett,Don Reid,Col Loughnan,Ken
Dean,Tony Buchanan(reeds),Mark Bowden(vbs,tymp,perc),Col Nolan(p,el-p,org),Ned Sutherland
(g),Ford Ray(el-b),Warren Daly(dr).   Live."Cell Block Theatre",Sydney.September 23,197
      Kanga   Columbia(Au)SCX07979,Festival(Au)L70145
      Hip Walk   -
      Something Better Than This   -
      WD And HO Blues   -
      Queen Street   -
      Kaleidoscope   -
      All The Things You Are   -
      Kings Step Out   -

All titles also on Columbia(Au)TC-SCX07979.
Note:Additional recordings by this orchestra are not included.

MEREDITH D'AMBROSIO

Meredith D'Ambrosio(vcl,p).		Boston.July/October 1978
I Got Lost In His Arms	Spring,Inc. SPR1980A/B	
Baltimore Oriole	-	
Land Where The Good Songs Go	-	
In Love In Vain	-	
Alone Together(1)	-	
It Never Entered My Mind	-	
Once In A Blue Moon	-	
Blame It On My Youth(2)	-	
Rip Van Winkle(2)	-	
Everytime We Say Goodbye	-	
Never-Never Land(1)	-	
I Get Along Without You Very Well	-	
Up Jumped Spring	-	
Spring Is Here		
Funny Girl	-	

-1.(vcl) acc. by Ray Santisi(p),Chris Rathbun(b),unknown(dr).
-2.Add Norman Coles(g).

Note:The issuenumber is listed as SPR1980 on the spine of the LP and as SPR (only) on the
     label and in the liner notes (and as SPR A/B in the vax).

TADD DAMERON

See also BABS GONZALES,JAMSESSION (BIRDLAND),ANITA O'DAY.

KAY PENTON(vcl) acc. by TADD DAMERON AND HIS GROUP:
Doug Mettome(tp),Ernie Henry(as),Allen Eager(ts),Terry Gibbs(vbs),Tadd Dameron(p,arr),
Nelson Boyd(b),Kenny Clarke(dr).   NYC.Late August/early September 1947
          I Think I'll Go Away   V-Disc 794
          Don't Mention Love To Me   -

Note:The above titles are from a special V-Disc recording session.

TADD DAMERON SEXTET:
Fats Navarro(tp),Ernie Henry(as),Charlie Rouse(ts),Tadd Dameron(p,arr),Nelson Boyd(b),
Shadow Wilson(dr).   NYC.September 26,1947

BN304-0 The Chase	Blue Note BLP1531
BN304-2 The Chase	Blue Note 541,BLP5004,BLP1531,(J)W5501
BN305-0 The Squirrel	Blue Note BLP1531
BN305-1 The Squirrel	Blue Note 540,BLP5004,BLP1531,Vogue(E)1105,Jazz Selection(F)JS562,Jazz Parade(E)B7,Franklin Mint 85
BN306-0 Our Delight	Blue Note BLP1531
BN306-5 Our Delight	Blue Note 540,BLP5004,BLP1531,BST2-84433,(J)W5501, K18P-9124,Vogue(E)EPV1105,Jazz Selection(F) JS562,Jazz Parade(E)B7
BN307-0 Dameronia	Blue Note BLP1531
BN307-2 Dameronia	Blue Note 541,BLP5004,BLP1531,BLP1001,BLP2001, BST89902,BN-LA158,(Eu)1A.158-83385/8

All titles/takes also on Blue Note BST84554,BN-LA507,CDP7.81531-2 (CD),(J)GXK8060,
LNJ70071.
Note:Some of the above were issued under Navarro's name.

TADD DAMERON AND HIS BAND:
Fats Navarro(tp),Ernie Henry(as),Tadd Dameron(p,arr),Curley Russell(b),Kenny Clarke(dr),
Kay Penton(vcl).   NYC.October 28,1947
S3465-1 A Bebop Carroll   Savoy SJL2216,(F)2C.162-60486
S3465-6 A Bebop Carroll   Savoy 931,XP8026,MG9019,   -
S3466-1 The Tadd Walk   - ,MG9019,   -
S3467-3 Gone With The Wind(kp)   Savoy MG9023,   -
S3468-3 That Someone Must Be You(kp)   Savoy MG9024,   -

All titles - except master S3465 - also on Savoy MG12011,SJL2216,SJC416,Realm(E)RM192,CBS
(Eu)52192,Byg(F)529.102,Musidisc(F)JA5129.

TADD DAMERON QUINTET:
Allen Eager,Wardell Gray(ts),Tadd Dameron(p,arr),Curley Russell(b),Kenny Clarke(dr).
                                    Broadcast."Royal Roost",NYC.c. August/September 1948
        Now's The Time   Spotlite(E)108
        Lady Be Good (Rifftide)   -
        Just You,Just Me (Spotlight)   -

All titles also on Zim ZIM1002,Poljazz(P)ZSX699.

TADD DAMERON QUINTET:
Fats Navarro(tp),Allen Eager(ts),Tadd Dameron(p,arr),Curley Russell(b),Kenny Clarke(dr),
Kenny Hagood(vcl).   Broadcast."Royal Roost",NYC.August 29,1948
        Jumping With
          Symphony Sid (theme)   Beppo(E)BEP505
        Anthropology   Jazzland JPL50,Riverside RS3019,Sneaker TDFN829,
                                       Beppo(E)BEP505,Fun House(J)30YD7004(CD)
        Kitchenette Across The Hall(kh) Sneaker TDFN829,Beppo(E)BEP505,Fun House(J)
                                       30YD7004(CD)
        Lady Be Good (Rifftide)   Jazzland JPL50,Sneaker TDFN829,Beppo(E)BEP505
        The Squirrel   Sneaker TDFN829,Beppo(E)BEP505
        Good Bait   Jazzland JPL50,Sneaker TDFN829,Beppo(E)BEP505,
                                       Musidisc(F)CCV2521(?)

        Pennies From
          Heaven(no tp,ts)(kh)   Sneaker TDFN829,Fun House(J)30YD7004(CD)
        Jumping With
          Symphony Sid (theme)   Beppo(E)BEP505

All titles - except the themes - also on Ozone LP5,Musidisc(F)JA5176,Spotlite(E)109.
All titles - except "Pennies From Heaven" - also on Jazz View COD010 (CD).
All titles on JLP50 also on Jazzland(J)R5043,Riverside RS3019,(J)MW2007,Milestone M47041,
(F)68.118.

TADD DAMERON SEXTET:
Add Milt Jackson(vbs).   Broadcast."Royal Roost",NYC.September 4,1948
        Jumping With
          Symphony Sid (theme)
        The Tadd Walk   Sneaker TDFN829,Beppo(E)BEP505,Fun House(J)
                                       20YB7004,30YD7004(CD),Jazz View COD010(CD)
        Symphonette   Jazzland JLP68,Sneaker TDFN829,Beppo(E)BEP505,
                                       Milestone M47041,(F)68.118,Fun House(J)
                                       20YB7004,30YD7004(CD),Jazz View COD010(CD)
        The Squirrel   Sneaker TDFN829,Beppo(E)BEP505,Jazz View COD010
                                       (CD)

TADD DAMERON SEPTET:
Fats Navarro(tp),Allen Eager,Wardell Gray(ts),Tadd Dameron(p,arr),Curley Russell(b),Kenny
Clarke(dr),Kenny Hagood(vcl).   NYC.September 13,1948
(session cont. next page).

(session cont. from previous page):
BN332-0 Jahbero(1)   Blue Note BLP1532
BN332-1 Jahbero   Blue Note 559,BLP1532,(Eu)1A.158-83385/8,Gazell
                                            (Sd)2019,New World 271,Franklin Mint 90,Album
                                            No.23
BN333-0 Lady Bird   Blue Note 559,BLP5004,BLP1532,(Eu)1A.158-83385/8,
                                            (J)W5501,Gazell(Sd)2019,Smithsonian P6.11891,
                                            RD033-3(CD)
BN333-1 Lady Bird   Blue Note BLP1532
BN334-1 Symphonette   Blue Note 1564,BLP1532,(Eu)1A.158-83385/8
BN334   Symphonette   Blue Note BLP1532
BN335-1 I Think I'll Go Away(kh)   Blue Note(Eu)1A.158-83385/8,(J)BNJ61008

-1.Add Chano Pozo(bg).

All titles/takes - except master BN335 - also on Blue Note BST84554,BN-LA507,CDP7.81532-2
(CD),(J)GXK8061,LNJ70074.
Note:Some of the above were issued under Navarro's name.

TADD DAMERON SEPTET:
Fats Navarro(tp),Rudy Williams(as),Allen Eager(ts),Tadd Dameron(p,arr),Curley Russell(b),
Kenny Clarke(dr).   Broadcast."Royal Roost",NYC.October 2,1948
        Jumping With
          Symphony Sid (theme)
        Good Bait   Talcrip TDFN10230
        The Squirrel   Jazzland JLP50,(J)R5043,Talcrip TDFN10230,River-
                                            side RS3019,(J)MW2007,Milestone M47041,(F)
                                            68.118

All titles - except "Jumping With Symphony Sid" - also on Beppo(E)BEP505,Spotlite(E)110,
Fun House(J)20YB7004,30YD7004 (CD),Jazz View COD010 (CD).
Note:See Anita O'Day for additional titles from this broadcast.

same.   Broadcast."Royal Roost",NYC.October 9,1948
        Jumping With
          Symphony Sid (theme)
        The Tadd Walk   Ozone LP5,Beppo(E)BEP506,Talcrip TDFN10230,Frank-
                                            lin Mint 85,Musidisc(F)JA5176
        Dameronia   Beppo(E)BEP506,Fun House(J)20YB7004,30YD7004(CD)

All titles - except "Jumping With Symphony Sid" - also on Spotlite(E)110,Jazzland JLP50,
(J)R5043,Riverside RS3019,(J)MW2007,Milestone M47041,(F)68.118.
Note:A few bars of "The Squirrel" is heard at end of "Dameronia".
     See Anita O'Day for additional titles from this broadcast.

same   Broadcast."Royal Roost",NYC.October 16,1948
        Jumping With
          Symphony Sid (theme)
        Anthropology   Sneaker TDFN829,Bop(F)7,Fun House(J)20YB7004,
                                            30YD7004(CD)
        Our Delight   Jazzland JLP50,(J)R5043,Sneaker TDFN829,Ozone LP5,
                                            Riverside RS3019,(J)MW2007,Milestone M47041,
                                            (F)68.118,Fun House(J)20YB7004,30YD7004(CD),
                                            Musidisc(F)JA5176
        The Tadd Walk   Sneaker TDFN829

All titles - except "Jumping With Symphony Sid" - also on Spotlite(E)111,Beppo(E)BEP506.
Note:A few bars of "The Squirrel" is heard at end of "The Tadd Walk".

Same.   Broadcast."Royal Roost",NYC.October 23,1948
    Our Delight(1)   Talcrip TDFN10230
    Good Bait(2)   Jazzland JLP68,Talcrip TDFN10230,Manor M503
    Eb-Pob   -   -
    The Squirrel   Talcrip TDFN10230
    Jumping With
        Symphony Sid (theme)

-1.As "Dameronia" on TDFN10230.
-2.As "Better Bait" on TDFN10230.

All titles - except "Jumping With Symphony Sid" - also on Spotlite(E)111,Beppo(E)BEP506.
All titles on JLP68 also on Milestone M47041,(F)68.118.

TADD DAMERON QUINTET:
Kai Winding(tb),Allen Eager(ts),Tadd Dameron(p,arr),Curley Russell(b),Kenny Clarke(dr).
                               Broadcast."Royal Roost",NYC.October 30,1948
    The Chase   Talcrip TDFN10230,Fun House(J)20YB7004,30YD7004(CD
    Wahoo   Talcrip TDFN10230,Ult-Tadd TDFN XX1500,Cicala(F)
                                   BLJ8032,Fun House(J)20YB7004,30YD7004(CD)
    Lady Be Good (Rifftide)   Talcrip TDFN10230,Fun House(J)20YB7004,30YD7004
                                   (CD)
    The Squirrel   Ult-Tadd TDFN XX1500
    Jumping With
        Symphony Sid (theme)

Note:"The Squirrel" is not listed on Ult-Tadd label - but included on the LP.

Same.   Broadcast."Royal Roost",NYC.November 6,1948
    Jumping With
        Symphony Sid (theme)
    Anthropology   Jazzland JLP68
    Wahoo   - ,Ozone LP5,Ult-Tadd TDFN XX1500
    Tiny's Blues   -

All titles on JLP68 also on Milestone M47041,(F)68.118.

Same.   Broadcast."Royal Roost",NYC.November 13,1948
    Lady Bird   Ult-Tadd TDFN XX1500
    Good Bait   -
    Dizzy Atmosphere   -

TADD DAMERON AND HIS ORCHESTRA/BIG TEN:
Fats Navarro(tp),Kai Winding(tb),Sahib Shihab(as),Dexter Gordon(ts),Cecil Payne(bars),Tadd
Dameron(p,arr),Curley Russell(b),Kenny Clarke(dr),Diego Iborra(bg),Vidal Bolado(cg),Rae
Pearl(vcl).   NYC.January 18,1949
3391-3D-2 Sid's Delight   Capitol 57-60006,Giants Of Jazz(I)LPJT54,53029(CD
3392-3D-2 Casbah(rp)   -

Both titles also on Capitol M11059,(E)CL13132,(F)80020,(I)CR8812,(G)C80020,(Eu)EAP1-20388
T20243,5C.052-80852,One Up(E)OU2006,Affinity(E)AFF149,Blue Note CDP7.81531-2 (CD).
Note:Some of the above were issued under Navarro's name.

TADD DAMERON BIG TEN:
Incl. Miles Davis(tp),Kai Winding(tb),Tadd Dameron(p,arr),John Collins(g).
                               Broadcast."Royal Roost",NYC.February 12,194?
    Good Bait   Ult-Tadd TDFN XX1500
    Webb's Delight(1)   -
    Focus   -
    Wahoo   -

-1.Basically identical to "Sid's Delight" (January 18,1949).

Miles Davis(tp),Kai Winding(tb),Sahib Shihab(as),Benjamin Lundy(ts),Cecil Payne(bars),Tadd
Dameron(p,arr),John Collins(g),Curley Russell(b),Kenny Clarke(dr),Carlos Vidal(cg).
Broadcast."Royal Roost",NYC.February 19,1949

Focus	Jung Cat RBD948,Cicala(F)BLJ8032	
April In Paris	-	
Good Bait	- ,Cicala(F)BLJ8032,Musica Jazz(I)	
	2MJP1041	
Webb's Delight(1)	Jung Cat RBD948,Cicala(F)BLJ8032	

-1.Basically identical to "Sid's Delight" (January 18,1949).

All titles also on Beppo(E)BEP503.
Note:A few bars of "The Squirrel" is heard at end of "Webb's Delight".

Prob. same.
Broadcast."Royal Roost",NYC.February 26,1949

Miles	Jung Cat RBD948,Beppo(E)BEP503
Casbah	- - ,Cicala(F)BLJ8032

Prob. same.
Broadcast."Royal Roost",NYC.March 5,1949

Good Bait	Ult-Tadd TDFN XX1500
The Squirrel(1)	-

-1.Even though "Symphony Sid" announces "The Squirrel" as the band's theme, it is a full-
length performance.

Miles Davis(tp),J.J.Johnson(tb),Sahib Shihab(as),Benjamin Lundy(ts),Cecil Payne(bars),Tadd
Dameron(p,arr),John Collins(g),Curley Russell(b),Kenny Clarke(dr),Kay Penton(vcl).
NYC.April 21,1949

3760-4D-2	John's Delight	Capitol 57-60015,W2149,M11059,(E)CL14201,(Eu)
		EAP1-20388,K83925
3761	What's New(kp)	Capitol M11059
3762	Heaven's Doors	
	Are Open Wide(kp)	-
3763-2D-3	Focus	Capitol 57-60015,M11059,(E)CL14201,(Eu)EAP1-20388

All titles also on Capitol (Eu)5C0.52-80852,(J)CR8812,ECJ50073,One Up(E)OU2006,Affinity(E)
AFF149,Blue Note CDP7.81531-2 (CD).

MILES DAVIS - TADD DAMERON QUINTET:
Miles Davis(tp),James Moody(ts),Tadd Dameron(p,arr),Barney Spieler(b),Kenny Clarke(dr).
Live."Salle Pleyel",Paris.May 8,1949

Rifftide	Columbia JC34804
Good Bait	-
Don't Blame Me(no ts)	- ,CJ40972,CBS(Eu)461096
Lady Bird	

Note:Though the above group basically was a Tadd Dameron group, it was presented as MILES
DAVIS - TADD DAMERON QUINTET.

same.
Live."Salle Pleyel",Paris.May 1949

All The Things You Are	Columbia JC34804
The Squirrel	Phontastic(Sd)NOST7602
Allen's Alley	Columbia JC34804
Wahoo	-
Crazy Rhythm	
Embraceable You	Columbia JC34804
All The Things You Are	
Ornithology	Columbia JC34804,Franklin Mint 25

11 titles on JC34804 also on CBS(Eu)82100,(J)18AP2051,23AP2551,25AP91.
Note:The group played at "Salle Pleyel" May 8/9/12/14/15,1949.

TADD DAMERON:
Clifford Brown,Idrees Sulieman(tp),Herb Mullins(tb),Gigi Gryce(as),Benny Golson(ts),Oscar
Estelle(bars),Tadd Dameron(p,arr),Percy Heath(b),Philly Joe Jones(dr).
                                         NYC.June 11,1953
490   Philly Joe Jones   Prestige PREP1353,PRLP159,PRLP7055,Esquire(E)EP71,
                                            20-044,Barclay(F)84014
491-1 Choose Now   Prestige PRLP7055
491-2 Choose Now   Prestige PRLP159,PRLP7055,Esquire(E)20-044,Barclay
                                            (F)84014
492   Dial B For Beauty   Prestige PREP1353,PRLP159,Esquire(E)EP71,20-044,
                                            Barclay(F)84014
493   Theme Of No Repeat   Prestige PRLP159,PRLP7055,Barclay(F)84014

All titles also on Prestige PR7662,PR16008,P24049,(J)SMJX10097,Status ST8301(unissued),
Stateside(E)SL10122,Barclay(F)BLP84.014,Original Jazz Classics OJC017.

Kenny Dorham(tp),Henry Coker(tb),Sahib Shihab(as),Joe Alexander(ts),Cecil Payne(bars),Tadd
Dameron(p,arr),John Simmons(b),Shadow Wilson(dr).
                                         NYC.March 9,1956
859   Fontainebleu   Prestige LP7037,Metronome(Sd)MEP298,Franklin
                                            Mint 35
860   Delirium   Prestige LP7037
861   Clean Is The Scene
          (The Scene Is Clean)   - ,Metronome(Sd)MEP298
862   Flossie Lou   -
863   Bula-Beige(!)   -

All titles also on Prestige PR7842,PR16007,(J)SMJ6537,SMJ7260,LPJ40007,Status ST8300,
Esquire(E)32-034,Original Jazz Classics OJC055,OJCCD055-2 (CD).
All titles - except master 863 - also on Prestige P24049.

TADD DAMERON QUARTET:
John Coltrane(ts),Tadd Dameron(p,arr),John Simmons(b),Philly Joe Jones(dr).
                                         NYC.November 30,1956
1025   Mating Call   Prestige PRLP/ST7070,Metronome 9009,Fantasy
                                            FCD60-013(CD),Giants Of Jazz(I)CD53038(CD)
1026   Soultrane   Prestige PRLP/ST7070,Giants Of Jazz(I)CD53038(CD)
1027   Gnid   -
1028   Super Jet   -
1029   On A Misty Night   - ,PR7426,Metronome(Sd)MEP299
1030   Romas   - ,Metronome(Sd)MEP299,(?)9009

All titles also on Prestige PRLP/ST7247,PR7745,PR24084,PCD4405-2 (16xCD set),(J)SMJ6538,
SMJ7557,LPR8878,VICJ23620 (CD),VICJ40017-34 (18xCD set),Bellaphon(G)BJS40154,Original Jazz
Classics OJC212.
Note:Some of the above were issued under Coltrane's name.

Kenny Dorham(tp),Julius Watkins(frh),Leo Wright(as,fl),Jerome Richardson(as),Cecil Payne
(bars),Milt Jackson(vbs),Tommy Flanagan(p),George Duvivier(b),Connie Kay(dr),Tadd Dameron
(arr).   NYC.c. 1961
          8 unknown titles   unissued

Note:The above session may not have been recorded under Dameron's name.

(p-solo).   NYC.November 5,1961
106   Improvisation No.1   unissued
107   Improvisation No 2
108   Improvisation No 3
109   Improvisation No 4
110   Improvisation No 5
(session cont. next page).

(session cont. from previous page):
111   Improvisation No 6
112   Autumn In New York

Note:The above titles were privately recorded by Chris Albertson.

Donald Byrd(tp),Curtis Fuller(tb),Julius Watkins(frh),Sam Rivers(ts),Cecil Payne(bars),
Tadd Dameron(p,arr),Paul Chambers(b),Philly Joe Jones(dr).
                                        NYC.December 14,1961
        The Elder Speaks   Blue Note unissued
        Bevan Beeps   rejected
        Lament For Livery   -
        Aloof Spoof   -

TADD DAMERON ORCHESTRA:
Joe Wilder,Clark Terry,Ernie Royal(tp),Jimmy Cleveland,Britt Woodman(tb),Julius Watkins
(frh),Leo Wright,Jerry Dodgion(as,fl),Jerome Richardson(ts,fl),Johnny Griffin(ts),Tate
Houston(bars),Bill Evans(p),George Duvivier(b),Philly Joe Jones(dr),Tadd Dameron(arr).
                                        NYC.February 27,1962
        Our Delight   Riverside RLP(9)419
        Dial B For Beauty   -
        Bevan's Birthday   -

Charlie Shavers(tp),Ron Carter(b) replace Wilder,Duvivier
                                        NYC.March 9,1962
        On A Misty Night   Riverside 45-474,RLP(9)419
        Swift As The Wind   -   -
        Fontainebleau   Riverside RLP(9)419,RLP3511,(J)SR7046

Clark Terry(tp),Jimmy Cleveland(tb),Jerry Dodgion(as,fl),Jerome Richardson(ts,fl),Johnny
Griffin(ts),Tate Houston(bars),Bill Evans(p),Ron Carter(b),Philly Joe Jones(dr),Tadd Dame-
ron(arr),Barbara Winfield(vcl).   NYC.April 16,1962
        Just Plain Talkin'   Riverside RLP(9)419
        If You Could See Me Now(bw)   -
        You're A Joy(bw)   -
        Look,Stop And Listen   - ,Franklin Mint 74 (Album No.19)

All titles on RLP(S9)419 also on Riverside(J)SMJ6288,Original Jazz Classics OJC143.

AOLO DAMIANI (Italian)

See STRUTTURE DI SUPPORTO QUARTETTO.

ANK D'AMICO

ANK D'AMICO SEXTET:
Frank Newton(tp),Hank D'Amico(cl),Don Byas(ts),Dave Rivera(p),Sid Weiss(b),Cozy Cole(dr).
                                        NYC.October 10,1944
SC9   Hank's Pranks   National 9047
SC10   Juke Box Judy   -
SC11   Shy Little Witch From Greenwich National 9004
SC12   Gone At Dawn   National 9003,EmArcy MG36017,(E)EJL1276,(F)MLP7167

All titles also on Savoy SJL2224.

HANK D'AMICO QUARTET:
Hank D'Amico(cl),Johnny Guarnieri(p),Sid Weiss(b),Cozy Cole(dr).
                                        NYC.October 23,1944
NSC13 East Of The Sun   National 9005
NSC14 Between The Devil
         And The Deep Blue Sea   - ,EmArcy MG36049
NSC15 Over The Rainbow   National 9006
NSC16 Cole Heat,Warm Feet   -

HANK D'AMICO ORCHESTRA:
No details.   Unknown location. 1940's
         At Sundown   Golden Era LP15078
         How High The Moon   -

HANK D'AMICO SEXTET:
Henry Levine(tp),Vernon Brown(tb),Hank D'Amico(cl),Mario Janarro(p),Victor Jody(b),George
Wettling(dr),Mindy Carson(vcl).   NYC. 1946
         After You've Gone   Muzak 60930
         Oh Baby   -
         If I Love Again   -
         Original In B-Flat   -
         'Deed I Do   -
         Maybe You'll Be There(mc)   -
         Who Cares What People Say(mc)   -
         Why Did It Have
           To End So Soon(mc)   -
         My Adobe Hacienda(mc)   -
         It's As Simple As That(mc)   -
         Love And The Weather(mc)   Muzak 60960
         Every So Often(mc)   -
         Fun And Fancy Free(mc)   -
         Everybody And His Brother(mc)   -
         Lazy Countryside(mc)   -
         Jeepers Creepers   -
         Shine   -
         Rockin' Chair   -
         Headin' Down Hill(?)   -
         Lazy River   -
         Farewell Blues   Muzak 61285
         Crazy Rhythm   -
         China Boy   -
         D'Amigo Demonstrates   -
         They're Off   -

HANK D'AMICO SEXTET:
Jimmy Morreale(tp),Hank D'Amico(cl),Arthur Rollini(ts),Buddy Weed(p),Tommy Kay(g),Felix
Giobbe(b),George Wettling(dr).   NYC.c. October 1947
47S342-4 I Would Do Anything For You   MGM 10325,10638
47S343-2 If Dreams Come True   MGM 10641
47S344-1 You're The Cream In My Coffee   MGM 10639
47S345-1 Deep Purple   -

HANK D'AMICO AND HIS ORCHESTRA:
Bobby Hackett(cnt),John Fallstich,G. Esposito,Jimmy Morreale(tp),Vernon Brown,C. Small,
John Grassi(tb),Hank D'Amico(cl),Arthur Rollini(ts),Nick Caiazza,Bill Vitale,Irving Horo-
witz,Lester Merkin(sax),Buddy Weed(p),Tommy Kay(g),Felix Giobbe(b),George Wettling(dr).
                                        NYC.November 7,1947
47S387-3 Let's Fall In Love   MGM 10325
47S388-4 I Only Have Eyes For You   MGM 10638
47S389   Isle Of Capri   unissued
47S390-1 Poor Butterfly   MGM 10641

HANK D'AMICO WITH BUDDY WEED TRIO:
Hank D'Amico(cl),Buddy Weed(p),Tommy Kay(g),Felix Giobbe(b).
NYC.November 28,1947

47S370-3	Lover Come Back to Me	MGM 10640	
47S471-3	They're Off	-	

Note:The above titles were recorded under Weed's name.

HANK D'AMICO QUARTET:
Hank D'Amico(cl),Bill Triglia(p),Milt Hinton(b),Charlie Smith(dr).
NYC.October 5/8,1954

Hank's Holiday	Bethlehem BCP1006,BCP7	
Billy's Bubble	-	-
Tomorrow	-	-
Grasshopper	-	-
Hank's Dilemma	-	-
The Nearness Of You	-	-
Bernie's Tune	Bethlehem BCP7	
Gone	-	

11 titles also on Polydor(J)MP2171.
11 titles on BCP1006 also on London(E)LZ-N14008,(J)LLF1003,Bethlehem(SA)LZ-N14008.

1 Mattaliano(tp),Will Bradley(tb),Hank D'Amico(cl,as),Nick Caiazza(ts,bcl),Moe Wechsler
p),Arnold Fishkin(b),Don Lamond/Morey Feld(dr).
NYC.September 9,1957

Ma	Golden Crest CR3031
When My Sugar	
Walks Down The Street	-
Hands Across the Table	-
Organ Grinder's Swing	-
Haunting Me	-
Blue Lou	-
Blues In E	-
Sweet Lorraine	-
Between The Devil	
And The Deep Blue Sea	-
I Can't Believe That	
You're In Love With Me	-
Smoke Rings	-
Happy As The Day Is Long	-
Take Me In Your Arms	-
I Can't Give You	
Anything But Love	-
I've Got The World On A String	-
One Morning In May	-
Lonesome And Sorry	-
Girl Of My Dreams	-
If It's True	-
Let's Get Together	-
Pardon Me Pretty Baby	-
'Long About Midnight	-
Lyin' In The Hay	-
Who's Sorry Now	-

NJA DAMM ("MADAM ZENJA") (Dutch)

JJA AND HER JAZZ HORNS:
cl) acc. by Fred Horn(cnt,as),Wik Horn(p). Haarlem,The Netherlands.May 12,1974
ssion cont. next page).

(session cont. from previous page):
    Get Up Off Your Knees Papa   Cat(Du)LP7
    Pile Of Logs And Stones   -

(vcl) acc. by Fred Horn -1(cnt,as),Remco van der Gugten -1(cl),Peter Rijkhoff(p).
                  Nederhorst den Berg,The Netherlands.January 24,1976
    Nobody Rocks Me Like My Baby Do Cat(Du)LP15
    Trouble In Mind(1)   -

(vcl) acc. by Fred Horn(cnt),Remco van der Gugten(cl),Wik Horn(p),Jan de Jong(g),Wim van
Zoeren(tu).   Same date
    Titanic Man Blues(no g)   Cat(Du)LP15
    Pickin' On Your
      Baby(acc. p,g only)   -

(vcl) acc. by Wim van Zoeren(tp,tb,mell,vcl),Ton Damm -1(cl),Fred Horn(as,cnt,bars,mell),
Remco van der Gugten -2(ts),Paul Koenen -3(vbs),Wik Horn(p),Jan de Jong(g),John Erich(b),
Bernard Otten(dr).   Same date
    Sunbonnet Blue(1,2)   Cat(Du)LP15
    I Need A Little
      Sugar In My Bowl(2)   -
    I Must Have That Man   -
    You Go To My Head(3)   -
    I Can't Believe(2)   -
    He's Funny That Way(3,4)   -
    Sad Times Come,Sad Times Go(2,3)   -

-4.Omit van Zoeren,Fred Horn.

(vcl) acc. by Fred Horn(cnt,bars),Wik Horn(p).
                 Nederhorst den Berg,The Netherlands.January 27,197
    There'll Be Some Changes Made Cat(Du)LP15
    It's A Mighty Tight Woman   -
    Last Night I Was Dreaming   -

(vcl) acc. by Ton Damm(as),Etienne Francois(vln,tp),Jan de Jong,Dick Kleyn(g),Ronald
Jansen Heytmajer(bassax,arr).   Haarlem,The Netherlands.January 6,1979
    Daddy,Won't You
      Please Come Home   Cat(Du)LP33

(vcl) acc. Ernst Bruins(tp),Ton Damm(cl,as),Wik Horn(p).
                 Same date
    Was It A Dream   Cat(Du)LP33

(vcl) acc. by Peter Rijkhoff(p).   Same date
    Georgia Man   Cat(Du)LP33

(vcl) acc. by Fred Horn(cnt),Remco van der Gugten -1(cl),Wik Horn(p).
                 Same date
    Don't You Turn Your Back On Me Cat(Du)LP33
    Victim Of The Blues(1)   -

(vcl) acc. by WIK'S BIG BAND:
Ernst Bruins,Rinus Havelaar,Etienne Francois,Fred Horn(tp,cnt),Jacques Van Ham,Piet Glas
(tb),Ton Damm(cl,as),Kees van Lier(as),Remco van der Gugten(as,ts),Jan van der Woors(ts)
Han Weezenaar(bars),Pieter Klop(p),Jan de Jong(g),Roel Aardse(b),Ger Booiman(dr),Wik Horn
(arr,cond).   Nederhorst den Berg,The Netherlands.January 10,19
    Stop You're Breaking My Heart Cat(Du)LP33
    I'm Pulling Through   -

(vcl) acc. by THE ROARING SEVEN JAZZ BAND:
Ernst Bruins(cnt,mell),Rinus Havelaar(cnt,flh),Piet Glas(tb),Ton Damm(cl,as,ss),Jan van
der Woors(ts),Martin Santink(p),Ernst Jacobs(bj,g),Emile van Kreveld(tu).

	Same date	
Button Up Your Overcoat	Cat(Du)LP33	
Am I Blue	-	
Junk Man	-	
Mandy Make Up Your Mind	-	
Georgia On My Mind	-	
Sugar	-	

(vcl) acc. by Peter Ivan(tp),Ton Damm(cl),Bob Hofstede(g),Martin Zand Scholten(el-b),Bob
Dekker(dr).   Zaandam,The Netherlands.March 30,1979

Alphonse And Gaston(no vcl)	VR(Du)55086
Can't Help Lovin' That Man	-

FRANCO D'ANDREA (Italian)

See also MODERN ART TRIO.

(keyb-solo).   Rome. 1972

Fermento	Fly(I)AS60
Inside	-
Contemplazione	-
Estroversione	-
Outside	-
Around	-
Rinascita	-

(p-solo).   Milan,Italy.November/December 1977

Antelao	Carosello(I)CLE21034
Tension	-
Nuvolao	-
It Ain't Necessarily So	-
Naif	-

FRANCO D'ANDREA TRIO:
Franco D'Andrea(p),Dodo Goia(b),Bruno Biriaco(dr).
                    Live."Jazz Jamboree",Warsaw.October 1978

Fegiz	Atlantic(I)T50691
Myosotis	-
Looping	-

Same.   Torino,Italy.November 1978

Footprints	Atlantic(I)T50691
Blue 'n Green	-

(p-solo).   Milan,Italy.March 3,1980

Nadir	Red(I)VPA157
Sorapis	-
Via Libera	-
Ortwein,15	-

(p-solo).   Milan,Italy.June 5,1980

Ymnus	Red(I)VPA158
No Idea Of Time	-
Bluesprint	- ,Paragon(I)CRP04/05(?)
Hard Steps	-

DOROTHY DANDRIDGE

(vcl) acc. unknown orchestra.   Unknown location.c. 1941/42
      Swing For Yours Supper
      Jungle Jig(1)   Storyville(D)SLP6003
      Yes,Indeed(2)
      Easy Street
      A Zoot Suit   Storyville(D)SLP6003
      Congo Clambake
      Blackbird Fantasy(3)
      Cow-Cow Boogie

-1.Incl. Cee Pee Johnson(dr).
-2.Add Five Spirits Of Rhythm(vcl).
-3.Add Billy Mitchell(vcl).

Note:The above titles are from "Soundie" short film soundtracks.
    "Jungle Jig" as "Jig In The Jungle" on SLP6003.

(vcl) acc. by unknown orchestra.   Unknown location.January 20,1958
21942 Easy To Remember   Verve unissued
21943 What Is There To say
21944 That Old Feeling
21945 The Touch Of Your Lips
21946 When Your Lover Has Gone
21947 The Nearness Of You
21948 I'm Glad There Is You
21949 I've Grown
        Accustomed To Your Face
21950 Body And Soul
21951 How Long Has This Been Going On
21952 I've Got A Crush On You
21953 I Didn't Know What Time It Was

(vcl) acc. by unknown orchestra.   LA(?).February 2,1961
23459 Somebody   Verve 10231
23460 Stay With It   -
23461 Beautiful Evening   unissued
23462 Smooth Operator   -

DANDY INN FIVE

Bill Gallaty(tp),Raymond Burke(cl),Roy Armand(p),Chink Martin(b),Charlie Stowe(dr).
                        New Orleans. 1949
OL1103 Mardi Gras Blues   Creole 1

ALAN DANDY (British)

ALAN DANDY GROUP:
Ian Schoenfield(cl),Alan Dandy(p),John Clarke(g),Les Williams(b),Dick Richard(dr).
                Live.Leeds University,England.c. February 195⬤
      Careless Love   Oriole(E)MG10010

BARBARA DANE
(section cont. next page).

(vcl) acc. by Pete Stanton(tp),Bob Mielke(tb),Darnell Howard(cl),Don Ewell(p),Pops Foster
(b),Joe Watkins(dr).   San Francisco.July 3/4,1957

Trouble In Mind	Barbary Coast/San Francisco BBC4515,BC(S)33014	
See See Rider	-	-
Special Delivery Blues	Barbary Coast/San Francisco BC(S)33014	
Ain't Nobody Got The Blues Like Me	-	
Misery Blues	-	
Mighty Rumbling(!) Blues	-	
Good Mornin' Blues	-	
Oh Papa	-	
Prescription For The Blues	-	
Muddy Water	-	

(vcl) acc. by EARL HINES AND HIS ORCHESTRA:
Benny Carter(tp),Herbie Harper/John Halliburton(tb),Plas Johnson(ts),Earl Hines(p),Leroy
Vinnegar(b),Shelly Manne(dr).   LA.January 9/12,1959

Livin' With The Blues	Dot DLP3177,DLP25878
How Long,How Long Blues	-
If I Could Be With You	-
In The Evenin'	-
Bye Bye Blackbird	-
A Hundred Years From Today	-
Mecca Flat Blues	-
Why Don't You Do Right	-
Porgy	-
Since I Fell For You	-

All titles also on Dot DLP25177,Rediffusion(F)0100174.

(vcl) acc. by Kenny Whitson(cnt,p),Billy Strange(g),Wellman Braud(b),Jesse Sailes(dr).
                                               LA.March/April 1961

37548	Take It Slow And Easy	Capitol(S)T1758
37550	Draggin' My Heart Around	-
37551	Goodbye,Daddy Goodbye	-
37557	Mama Don't Allow No Twistin'	-
37560	The Hammer Song	-
37561	Wild Woman Don't Have The Blues	-
37569	Cakewalking Babies From Home	-
37570	Crazy Blues	-
37574	Hurry Up Sundown,Let Tomorrow Come	-

Earl Palmer(dr) replaces Sailes.
                                               LA.March/April 1961

37589	Good Old Wagon(1)	Capitol (S)T1758
37592	Less Than Wonderful	unissued
37596	Pennies From Heaven	-
37656	I'm On My Way(2)	Capitol (S)T1758
37670	This Little Light Of Mine(2)	-

-1.Add Ray Johnson(p).
-2.Add Rocco Wilson(cg),The Andrews Sisters(vcl).

Note:The Andrews Sisters on this recording is a gospel-group from San Francisco.
     Additional recordings with this artist are not included.

CHRIS DANE

See SIMON BREHM.

CAROL DANELL

(vcl) acc. by ORCHESTRA DI PIERO UMILIANI:
Incl. Marcello Boschi(as),Piero Umiliani(p,cond).

Rome.March 8,1957

I Only Have Eyes For You	RCA(I)A72V0109
Ma L'amore No	-
The Darktown Strutters' Ball	-
T'amo Dolce Notte	-

(vcl) acc. by PIERO UMILIANI E LA SUA ORCHESTRA:
Incl. Piero Umiliani(p,cond),Franco Pisano(g),Berto Pisano(b),Gilberto Cuppini(dr).

Rome.October 11,1957

The Lady Is A Tramp	RCA(I)A72V0187
You Go To My Head	-
All Of Me	-
Moonglow	-

DANGER (Dutch)

Kees Neeteson(ts),Mike Floothuis(org,vcl),Jaap Lindijer(synth).

The Hague,The Netherlands.January 17,1973

Danger	Cow(Du)RCS315

TED DANIEL

Ted Daniel(p,flh,frh,Moroccan-bugle),Otis Harris(as),Hakim Jami,Richard Pierce(b),Kenneth
Hughes,Warren Benbow(perc).   Live.Columbia University,NYC.October 15,1970

Congratulations	Ujamaa U1001
Pagan Spain	-
O.C.	-

TED DANIEL QUINTET:
Ted Daniel(flh),Richard Daniel(el-p),Khan Jamal(vbs),Tim Ingles(el-b),Jerome Cooper(dr).

NYC.January 26,1974

Tapestry	Sun(F)SR112
Sweet Dreams (For Your Eyes)	-
Mozambique	-

BILLY DANIELS

(vcl) acc. by STUFF SMITH TRIO:
Stuff Smith(vln),Jimmy Jones(p),John Levy(b).

NYC.September 26,1944

S5729	Always	Savoy 531

Note:See STUFF SMITH for additional titles (without Daniels) from this session.
   Acc. to a 1965 interview with Stuff Smith it is possible that another title ("Inter-
   mezzo") was recorded at this session - but not listed in the Savoy files.

(vcl) acc. by JERRY JEROME'S ORCHESTRA:
Incl. Jerry Jerome(ts),Teddy Wilson(p),Sid Weiss(b),Cozy Cole(dr).

NYC.c. 1947-49

(session cont. next page).

(session cont. from previous page):
3029	That Old Black Magic	Apollo 1101
3114	Love's A Lovely Thing	-
3115	Butterfly	Apollo 1077
3116	Diane	-
3310	My Yiddische Mama,I	Apollo 1172
3311	My Yiddische Mama,II	-
	Charmaine	Apollo 1188
	Trees	-

(vcl) acc. by RUSS CASE ORCHESTRA:
Jimmy Maxwell,Bernie Privin,Buck Clayton(tp),Jack Lacy,Bobby Byrne(tb),Eddie Barefield(as)
Andy Brown(ts),Benny Payne(p),Barry Galbraith(g),Milt Hinton(b),Specs Powell(dr).

NYC.March 11,1952

4953	My Thrill Is Loving You	Mercury 5822
4954	Must You Go	Mercury 5868
4955	That's How It Goes	Mercury 5822
4956	Don't Want That Woman	rejected(?)

(vcl) acc. by RUSS CASE ORCHESTRA:
Similar;omit Clayton.   NYC.c. March 1952
4964	Don't Want That Woman	Mercury 5868

(vcl) acc. by BENNY CARTER'S ORCHESTRA:
Harry Edison,Buddy Childers,Shorty Sherock(tp),Bill Shaffer,Milt Bernhart,Tommy Pederson,
George Roberts(tb),Willie Smith,Mark Berlow(as),Buddy Collette(fl,ts),Ben Webster(ts),
Chuck Gentry(bars),Benny Payne(p),Howard Roberts(g),Joe Comfort(b),Milt Holland(dr),Frank
Caroldon(perc),Benny Carter(arr,cond).   LA.June 12,1957
21014	Blue Skies	Verve 10065,MGV2072,HMV(E)7EG8485
21015	Blue Prelude	-
21016	It's D'lovely	- ,HMV(E)7EG8485
21017	You Turned The Tables On Me	- -
21018	Comes Love	- -
21019	Hallelujah	-

All titles also on HMV(E)DLP1174.

(vcl) acc. by BENNY CARTER'S ORCHESTRA:
Harry Edison(tp),Jack Stacy,Buddy Collette,Harry Klee,Chuck Gentry(reeds),Benny Payne(p),
Bob Bain(g),Red Callender(b),Milt Holland(dr),Benny Carter(arr,cond).
LA.June 19,1957
21026	Just In Time	Verve MGV2072,HMV(E)DLP1174
21027	You're My Everything	-
21028	Time After Time	-
21029	Just Like A Melody Out Of The Sky	- ,HMV(E)DLP1174
21030	You Go To My Head	Verve 10065,MGV2072, -
21031	How Am I To Know	- -

(vcl) acc. by unknown orchestra incl. Stuff Smith(vln),Benny Payne(p,vcl).
LA.September 1957
Summertime	Verve MGV2085
On The Street Where You Live	-
I Could Have Danced All Night	-
Long Before I Knew You	-
On The Sunny Side	
Of The Street(1)	-
Around The World(1)	-
Blue Turning Grey Over You(2)	-
Kiss Of Love	-
The Masculine Touch	-

session cont. next page).

(session cont. from previous page):
```
    Bye Bye Baby(1)                      Verve MGV2085
    I Need Your Love(1)                      -
    One Hundred Years From Today(1)          -
    My Gal Sal(1)                            -
    You Were Meant For Me                    -
    That Old Black Magic(1)                  -
```

-1.Payne also (vcl).
-2.Payne also (vcl);omit Daniels.

All titles also on HMV(E)CLP1200,Polydor(E)2482.425.

(vcl) acc. by Benny Payne(p),rest unknown. Live."Crescendo Club",LA. 1950's
```
    Them There Eyes                      Gene Norman Presents GNP16(S)
    Love Is A Many-Splendored Thing          -
    Sway                                     -
    Autumn Leaves                            -
    'Deed I Do                               -
    Medley:                                  -
        Easy To Love
        My Blue Heaven
        It's All Right With Me
    My Yiddishe Momme (Mama)                 -
    You Were Meant For Me                    -
    Lady Of The Evening                      -
    If I Should Lose You                     -
    How Deep Is The Ocean                    -
    I Can Dream                              -
    I Live For You                           -    ,GNP20(S)
    That Old Black Magic                     -
```

All titles also on Pye(E)PKL5569.
Note:Additional recordings by this artist are not included.

CLARENCE DANIELS

Melvin Moore,Mac Johnson,Ike Williams,Calvin Harvey,Joe Mitchell(tp),Clinton Arnold,John
Ewing,Lester Robertson(tb),Edwin Pleasants,Curtis Peagler,Wallace Brodis(as),Eddie Davis,
Carrington Vosor,Chester Harris,Lucius Weathers(ts),Alex Nelson(bars),Roland Johnson(p,
vbs),Clarence Daniels(b),John Brown,Clarence Johnston(dr),Sandy Miller(vcl).
```
                                         Unknown location/date
    Do The Deal                          Affiliated 45-101
    And Then I'll Say                        -
    I'll Drive My Blues Away                 -
    Pastel                                   -
    I'll Never Let You Go                    -
    Baby I'm  Gone                           -
    What Can A Poor Boy Do                   -
    Street Girl                              -
```


EDDIE DANIELS

See also EUROJAZZ ORCHESTRA.

Eddie Daniels(ts,cl),Roland Hanna(p),Richard Davis(b),Mel Lewis(dr).
```
                                         NYC.September 8,1966
```
(session cont. next page).

(session cont. from previous page):
```
        Felicidad                       Prestige PR7506
        How Deep Is The Ocean                  -
        The Spanish Flee                       -
        That Waltz                             -
```

Same   NYC.September 12,1966
```
        Falling In Love With Love       Prestige PR7506
        Love's Long Journey                    -
        Time Marches On(1)                     -
        The Rocker                             -
```

-1.Clarinet overdubbing on this title.

All titles on PR7506 also on Prestige(J)SMJ7458.

Terumasa Hino(tp),Eddie Daniels(ts,cl),Masabumi Kikuchi(p),Kunimitsu Inaba(b),Motohiko
Hino(dr).   Tokyo.August 4,1968
```
        The Strut                       Takt(J)XMS10005
        Thirsty Soul                           -
        This Is New                            -
        Whistle Moment                         -
        Giant Steps                            -
        Why Did I Choose You                   -
```

EDDIE DANIELS - BUCKY PIZZARELLI:
Eddie Daniels(fl,cl,bcl),Bucky Pizzarelli(g).
                                        New York.February 1973
```
        Samia                           Choice CRS1002
        Afterthought                           -
        Entr'acte                              -
        Emily                                  -
        Etude No 14 In
           F Minor,Opus 25 No.2                -
        Variations On An Autumn Theme          -
        As Long As I Live                      -
        Two For The Road                       -
        Blue Bossa                             -
        Wistful Moment                         -
        Shine                                  -
        A Flower For All Seasons               -
```

EDDIE DANIELS QUARTET:
Eddie Daniels(fl,cl,ts),Andy LaVerne(el-p,synth),Rick Laird(b),Billy Mintz(dr).
                                        NYC.July 11,1977
```
        Brief Encounter                 Muse MR5154
        A Child Is Born                        -
        The Path                               -
        Sway                                   -
        There Is No Greater Love               -
        Ligia                                  -
```

Eddie Daniels(cl,as),unknown orchestra,rhythm,string,vcl-group.
                                        Unknown location.c. 1979
```
        Good Morning,Bahia              Columbia NJC36290
        Hold Tight                             -
        Don't Let It Go                        -
        Lost In The Rain                       -
        Morning Thunder                        -
        Carnival Lady                          -
```
(session cont. next page).

(session cont. from previous page):
```
        Lindas                      Columbia NJC36290
        Forget The Woman                     -
        Midnight At The Caravelle            -
```

Eddie Daniels(cl,ts),Sante Palumbo(p,el-p),Julius Farmer(el-b),Grady Tate(dr).
```
                                    Milan,Italy.October 1979
        Giant Steps                 Dire(I)FO356
        Just Friends                        -
        Isn't She Lovely                    -
        Demoiselle                          -
```

Eddie Daniels(ts),Franco Cerri(g).   Same date
```
        They Say It's Wonderful     Dire(I)FO356
```


HALL DANIELS

HALL DANIELS SEPTET:
Hall Daniels(tp),Dick Nash(tb),Zoot Sims(ts),Bob Gordon(bars),Paul Atkerson(p),Tony Rizzi
(g),Rollie Bundock(b),Jack Sperling(dr).   LA.February 14,1953
```
J154-1 The Way You Look Tonight       Zim ZM1008
J154-2 The Way You Look Tonight       Jump JLP9,Zim ZM1008
J154-4 The Way You Look Tonight       Zim ZM1008
J155-1 Nash-ville(1)                        -
J155-4 Nash-ville(1)                        -
J155-7 Nash-ville(1)                  Jump JLP9,Zim ZM1008
J155-9 Nash-ville                     unissued
J156-1 You Don't Know What Love Is    Zim ZM1008
J156-2 You Don't Know What Love Is    Jump JLP9,Zim ZM1008
J157-2 Compatibility                  Zim ZM1008
J157-4 Compatibility                  unissued
J157-5 Compatibility                  Jump JLP9,Zim ZM1008
```

-1.As "Nashville" on ZM1008.

Note:Zim ZM1008 issued as ZOOT SIMS-DICK NASH OCTET.
     Incomplete unissued takes are not listed.

JOE DANIELS (British)

JOE DANIELS AND HIS HOT SHOTS:
Max Goldberg(tp),Harry Lewis(cl),Pat O'Neil(p),Joe Young(g),Pat Reilly(b),Joe Daniels(dr).
```
                                    London.March 25,1942
CE10915 Time On My Hands       Parlophone(E)F1915,(Au)A7444,Saville SVL167
CE10916 My Melancholy Baby     Parlophone(E)F1945
CE10917 Lady Be Good           Parlophone(E)F1909,(Au)A7444,Saville SVL167
CE10918 When You're Smiling          - ,(Au)A7440,          -
CE10919 Swing Fan              Parlophone(E)F1939,(Au)A7589
CE10920 Down Beat              Parlophone(E)F1915,        - ,Saville SVL167
CE10921 Corn On The Cob        Parlophone(E)F1945,(Au)A7605
CE10922 Honeysuckle Rose       Parlophone(E)F1939
```

Dave Wilkins(tp),Nat Temple(as,cl),Cecil Norman(p),Archie Slavin(g),Lou Nussbaum(b),Joe
Daniels(dr).   London.August 12,1942
```
CE10977 Rose Petals            Parlophone(E)F1961,Purple Pumpkin(A)4792
CE10985 Pig In A Poke          Parlophone(E)F1951,(Au)A7491
CE10986 Snug As A Bug          Parlophone(E)F1994,(Au)A7679,Saville SVL167
CE10987 Rubber Ball Rhythm     Parlophone(E)F1951,(Au)A7491
```

Leslie Hutchinson(tp),Nat Temple(cl),Pat Dodd(p),Archie Slavin(g),Tom Bromley(b),Joe Da-
niels(dr).   London.October 14,1942
CE11014 Canzonetta   Parlophone(E)F1994,(Au)A7599,Saville SVL167
CE11015 Jazz Me Blues   Parlophone(E)F1956,MPE151,(Au)7599
CE11016 Swing Is The Thing   Parlophone(E)F1961,(Au)A7679
CE11017 Jazz Jamboree   Parlophone(E)F1956,MPE151,(Au)A7605

Chick Smith(tp),Nat Temple(as(?),cl),Pat Dodd(p),unknown(g),Pat Reilly(b),Joe Daniels(dr).
                                    London.October 1,1943
CE11126 Bond Street Bally Hoo   Parlophone(E)F1999,(Au)A7649
CE11127 'Sippy Parade   Parlophone(E)F2058
CE11128 Tight As A Drum   -
CE11129 South Rampart Street Parade Parlophone(E)F1999

Chick Smith(tp),Nat Temple(as,cl),Pat Dodd(p),Frank Deniz or Joe Young(g),Dick Ball(b),Joe
Daniels(dr).   London.January 13,1944
CE11171 Shandy   Parlophone(E)F2038,(Au)A7634,Saville SVL167,Purple
                                      Pumpkin(A)4792
CE11172 Bugle Boy Blues   Parlophone(E)F2019,(Au)A7634
CE11173 Alike As Two Peas   Parlophone(E)F2038,Saville SVL167
CE11174 Cow Cow Boogie   Parlophone(E)F2009,Odeon 295195
CE11175 Nattering Around   Parlophone(E)F2029,(Au)A7649
CE11176 At The Military Ball   -
CE11177 Drum Kit   Parlophone(E)F2019
CE11178 My Blue Heaven   Parlophone(E)F2009

Harry Lewis(cl),Pat Todd(p),Joe Daniels(dr). London.July 20,1944
E11252 Down Be That Way   Parlophone(E)F2045,Saville SVL167
E11253 Bei Mir Bist Du Schoen   Parlophone(E)F2066
E11254 If I Had You   -
E11255 Blues In Boogie   Parlophone(E)F2045,(Au)A7628

Chick Smith(tp),Derek Hawkins(cl),Pat Dodd(p),Frank Deniz(g),Lou Nussbaum(b),Joe Daniels
(dr).   London.February 23,1945
E11342 Drummer Boy Drum,pt.1 (quickst) Parlophone(E)F2075
E11343 Drummer Boy Drum,pt.2 (blues)   -
E11344 King For A Day   Parlophone(E)F2084
E11345 Clarinet Marmalade   -

Alan Franks(tp),Nat Temple(cl),Pat O'Neil(p),Eric Kershaw(g),Joe Nussbaum(b),Joe Da-
niels(dr).   London.July 16,1945
E11412 Ciribiribin   Parlophone(E)F2098
E11413 Nice Going   Parlophone(E)F2091,(Au)A7628,Purple Pumpkin
                                      (A)4792
E11414 It's The Talk Of The Town   Parlophone(E)F2091,Saville SVL167
E11415 Sweet Lorraine   Parlophone(E)F2199,Odeon(Br)2981

Similar.   London. 1945/46
E11455 Back Bay Shuffle   Parlophone(E)F2116
E11456 Boogie Boots   -
E11673 Alexander's Ragtime Band   Parlophone(E)F2157
E11674 Shreverport(!) Shuffle   -

Similar.   London.August 2,1946
E11724 Barrel House Boogie   Parlophone(E)F2184,Odeon(Br)2981
E11725 Blue Skies   -

Kenny Baker,Chick Smith(tp),Jock Bain(tb),John Dankworth(cl),Pat Dodd(p),Archie
Slavin(g),Pat Reilly(b),Joe Daniels(dr).   London.November 1,1949
(session cont. next page).

(session cont. from previous page):
CE12739 Donnell Blues   Parlophone(E)F2392
CE12740 Gin Mill Blues   -
CE12741 Sugarfoot Stomp   Parlophone(E)F2397
CE12742 Drummin' Dan   -

Max Goldberg,Chick Smith(tp),Don Macaffer(tb),Ralph Bruce(cl),Pat Dodd(p),Joe Young(bj),
Pat Riley(b),Joe Daniels(dr).   London.May 9,1950
CE12917 The Old Piano Roll Blues   Parlophone(E)F2413,Odeon(G)O-28075
CE12918 Dixieland Rag   -   -
CE12919 Shine   Parlophone(E)F2426
CE12920 Chicago   -

No details.   London. 1950/51
        Memphis Blues   Parlophone(E)F2438
        University Rag
CE13100 Who's Sorry Now   Parlophone(E)F2452
CE13178 Boogie For Googie   -
        At A Georgia Camp Meeting   Parlophone(E)F2458
        Washington And Lee Swing   -

Max Goldberg,Jimmy Watson(tp),Don Lusher(tb),Billy Amstell(cl),Stan Butcher(p),Joe Young
(g),Jack Fallon(b),Joe Daniels(dr).   London.June 6,1951
CE13887 Joint's A Jiving   Parlophone(E)F2466
CE13888 The Saints Are Here
CE13389 Ma,He's Making Eyes At Me   Parlophone(E)F2473,Odeon(G)O-28330
CE13390 Slightly On The Mellow Side   -   -

JOE DANIELS'JAZZ GROUP:
Alan Wickham(tp),Geoff Sowden(tb),Paul Simpson(cl),Norman Long(p),Nevil Skrimshire(g),
George Pacy(?)(b),Joe Daniels(dr).   Live.Royal Festival Hall,London.July 14,1951
CE13499 Barnyard Blues   Parlophone(E)R3425,Dormouse(E)DM10
CE13500 Wolverine Blues   -   -

Similar.   London. 1951
        Corrine,Corrina   Parlophone(E)F3462
        Wang Wang Blues   -

Alan Wickham(tp),Geoff Sowden(tb),Dave Shepherd(cl),Norman Long(p),Nevil Skrimshire(g),
George Davis(b),Joe Daniels(dr).   London.October 26,1951
CE13624 Doctor Jazz   Parlophone(E)R3495,PMC1067,King International
                                       LP2027
        Five Point Blues(1)   Parlophone(E)R3495

-1.Prob. from this session.

Stan Butcher(p) replaces Long.   London.April 8,1952
CE13917 The Dixie Band Stomp   Parlophone(E)R3527,GEP8616
CE13918 Weary Blues
CE13919 That Da-Da Strain   Parlophone(E)R3565
CE13920 Runnin' Wild(no tp,tb)   Parlophone(E)R3574,Odeon(G)O-28510

Pat Dodd(p),Cliff Dickens(b) replace Butcher,Davis.
                                       London.May 21,1952
CE14049 Can Can Boogie   Parlophone(E)R3565
CE14050 The Boogie Woogie March   Parlophone(E)R3574,Odeon(G)O-28510

Alan Wickham(tp),Don Lusher(tb),Tony Coe(cl),Stan Foster(p),Nevil Skrimshire(g),George
Davis(b),Joe Daniels(dr).   London.November 6,1952
CE14310 Riverboat Shuffle   Parlophone(E)R3608
(session cont. next page).

(session cont. from previous page):
```
CE14311 I Got Rhythm                    Parlophone(E)R3608
CE14312 Sobbin' Blues                   Parlophone(E)R3661
CE14313 Honey Babe                                 - ,Purple Pumpkin(A)4792
```

Alan Wickham(tp),Harry Brown(tb),Bernie Stanton(cl),Norman Long(p),John Oxley(b),Joe Da-
niels(dr).   London.May 11,1953
```
CE14563 So Black And Blue(!)            Parlophone(E)R3718
CE14564 Royal Garden Blues                         - ,PMC1067,King International
                                        LP2027
```

No details.   London. 1953
```
        Happy Boogie                    Parlophone(E)R3695
        Mama Don't Allow It                         -
```

No details.   London.September 6,1953
```
CE14698 I Wish I Could Shimmy
        Like My Sister Kate             Parlophone(E)R3888,MSP6111,Music For Pleasure(E)
                                        DL1137,CDDL1137(CD)
CE14699 Nobody Knows You
        When You're Down And Out        Parlophone(E)R3771
CE14700 Jazz Me Blues                               - ,Music For Pleasure(E)CDDL1137
                                        (CD)
CE14701 Susie                           Parlophone(E)R3888,MSP6111,Music For Pleasure(E)
                                        DL1137,CDDL1137(CD)
```

No details.   London.November 25,1953
```
CE14811 The Creepers' Creep             Parlophone(E)R3801
CE14812 Spain                           Parlophone(E)R3854
CE14813 Bugle Call Rag                              -
CE14814 Jelly Roll                      Parlophone(E)R3801
```

No details.   London.May 25,1954
```
CE15005 Little Brown Jug                 Parlophone(E)R3921,MSP6129
CE15008 Crazy Rhythm                     Parlophone(E)R3952,MSP6143
```

Both titles also on Music For Pleasure(E)DL1137,CDDL1137 (CD).

Alan Wickham(tp),Orm Stewart(tb),Don Francis(cl),Ray Barcley(p),Billy Bell(g),John Oxley
(b),Joe Daniels(dr).   London.January 11,1955
```
CE15239 Marie                           Parlophone(E)R4023,GEP8545,Music For Pleasure(E)
                                        DL1137,CDDL1137(CD)
CE15240 Rosetta                         Parlophone(E)R4023,GEP8545
```

Alan Wickham(tp),Don Lusher(tb),Don Francis(cl),Freddy Courtney(ts),Ray Barcley(p),George
Davis(b),Joe Daniels(dr).   London.May 17,1955
```
CE15316 Saint Louis Blues               Parlophone(E)R4072,GEP8545,PMC1067,King Intern.
                                        LP2027
CE15318 Talking Drums                   Parlophone(E)R4072,GEP8545
```

JOE DANIELS JAZZ GROUP:
Cyril Ellis(tp) replaces Wickham;add Barry Fox(g).
                                        London.March 19,1956
```
CE15543 Chicago                         Parlophone(E)R4173,GEP8616,
CE15544 Avalon                          Parlophone(E)R4324,PMC1067,King International
                                        LP2027
CE15545 Charleston                      Parlophone(E)R4173
CE15546 New Orleans Parade              Parlophone(E)R4324,Music For Pleasure(E)DL1137,
                                        CDDL1137(CD)
```

Note:Additional recordings by this artist are not included; the jazz content of some of
the above recordings may be limited.

JUNIOR DANIELS

(vcl) acc. by AL HAIG AND HIS TRIO:
Al Haig(p),Jimmy Raney(g),Tommy Potter(b),Roy Haynes(dr).

		NYC.July 15,1949
D180	Did I Remember	Discovery unissued
D181	Autumn Nocturne	Discovery 507
D182	The Lamp Is Low	-
D183	Goodnight My Love	unissued

MIKE DANIELS (British)

MIKE DANIELS AND HIS DELTA JAZZMEN:
Mike Daniels(tp),Bernie Newland(tb),Dave Webb(cl),Reg Sims(p),Freddy Legon(bj,vcl),Owen Maddock(tu),Roy Hardy(dr).   London.December 1948
1   Lovin' Gal Lucille   Delta(E)1
2   Belmont Strut   -

Mickey Ashman(b),Red Townsend(dr) replace Maddock and Hardy.
                                London.December 1948
10   House Of David Blues   Delta(E)unissued
11   Don't You Think I Love You   -

Same;Daniels plays (tp,cnt).   London.April 10,1949
19   House Of David Blues   Delta(E)9
20   Don't You Think I Love You   -

Mike Daniels(cnt),Charlie Galbraith(tb),Dave Webb(cl,ss),Cy Laurie(cl),Alan Johnston(p),Freddy Legon(bj),Mickey Ashman(b),Red Townsend(dr).
                                London.February 5,1950
       Muskrat Ramble   Delta(E)unissued
       Willie The Weeper   -
PRS3 Gatemouth   Delta(E)D2
PRS4 Savoy Blues   -
PRS1 1919 Rag   Delta(E)D1
PRS2 Snag It   -

Note:The above titles are listed in the order of recording.

Mike Daniels(cnt),Peter Hodge(tb,euphonium),Charlie Conner(cl),Mike Jefferson(p),Freddy Legon(g),Ken Hogston(b),Trevor Glenroy(dr). Live.Hammersmith Palais,London.March 19,1951
150   South   Esquire(E)10-128
151   Mahogany Hall Stomp   -

Mike Daniels(tp),Gordon Blundy(tb),John Barnes(cl),Des Bacon(p),Eddie Smith(bj),Don Smith (b,sousaphone),Arthur Fryatt(dr).   London.November 20,1956
CE15725 Hiawatha   Parlophone(E)R4285,PMC1067,King Internat. LP2027
CE15727 Don't You Think I Love You   -

Note:Additional masters from this session have been destroyed.

MIKE DANIELS' DELTA JAZZMEN:
Geoff Over(bj) replaces Eddie Smith;add Doreen Beatty(vcl).
                                London.September 12,1957
       You're Just My Type(1)   Harlequin(E)HQ3007
       Milenberg Joys   -
       At A Georgia Camp Meeting -
       Riverboat Shuffle   -
(session cont. next page).

MIKE DANIELS

(session cont. from previous page):
```
        Weather Bird Rag            Harlequin(E)HQ3007
        Aunt Hagar's Blues                  -
        You Made Me Love You               -
        I'm Confessin' That I Love You(1)  -
        Baby Doll(db)                      -
        The Blues Are Brewing(db)          -
```

-1.Add Derek Cooper,Teddy Layton(cl).

Unknown(bj) replaces Over.   London.June 10,1958
```
        I'm Coming Virginia          unissued
        Sidewalk Blues                     -
        Muddy Water(db)                    -
        There'll Be Some Changes Made(db)   -
        That's My Weakness Now(db)   Harlequin(E)HQ3007
        I Got Rhythm(db)             unissued
        Thou Swell(db)                     -
        Don't Forget To Mess Around When
           You're Doing The Charleston Harlequin(E)HQ3007
        West End Blues               unissued
        Shake It And break It              -
        Czerny's Tune                      -
        Deep Duke                          -
```

Geoff Over(bj) replaces unknown(bj);Fryatt also (vcl).
                                       London.March 10/17,1960
```
        Steamboat Stomp              Columbia(E)33SX1256
        Wildcat Blues                      -
        Jelly Bean Blues(db)               -
        Thick Lip Stomp                    -
        Soleil Perdu(1)                    -  ,Philips(Eu)830.787-2(CD)
        King Porter Stomp                  -             -
        Cushion Foot Stomp(af)             -
        Careless Love                      -
        Struggle Buggy                     -
        Moan,You Moaners(db)               -
        The Pearls                         -
        Deep Duke                          -
```

1.Bacon plays (cl).

Note:The LP erroneously lists Geoff Walker(bj).

Mike Daniels(tp),Gordon Blundy(tb),Terry Thompson(cl,ts),Des Bacon(p,cl),Geoff Over(bj,tb)
Jon Smith(b,sousaphone),Phil Franklin(dr),Doreen Beatty(vcl).
                                       Hanwell,Middlesex,England.November 7,1962
```
208     High Life                    V.J.M.(E)unissued
215     Sorry                              -
216     Cannon Ball Blues                  -
217     You're Driving Me Crazy      V.J.M.(E)LC6
```

Same;Daniels plays (tp,as).   London.October 10,1963
```
        Stay Out Of The South(db)    V.J.M.(E)VEP29
        Thou Swell(db)               unissued
        Blues With A Feeling         V.J.M.(E)VEP29
        High Life                          -
        Stevedore Stomp                    -
        Sunday                       unissued
        Buddy's Habits                     -
```

MIKE DANIELS BIG BAND:
Mike Daniels(tp,bars),John Chilton,Jake Spalding(tp),Ben Cohen(cnt),Keith Nichols,Trevor Adams(tb),Chris Walker,Jack Hughes(as,cl),George Bere(ts,cl),Terry Thompson(ts,cl,vcl),Des Bacon(p),Geoff Over(bj),Don Smith(b,sousaphone),Phil Franklin(dr).

Hanwell,Middlesex,England.February 17,1965

Ring Dem Bells	V.J.M.(E)unissued
Sent For You Yesterday(tt)	-
Call Of The Delta	V.J.M.(E)LC3
My Sweet Tooth Says(tt)	-
I'd Love It	-
Peggy	-
High Life	unissued
Give Me Your Telephone Number	V.J.M.(E)LC3
What You Want Me To Do	-
Jungle Jamboree	-
Saratoga Shout	-
One O'clock Jump	-
I Wonder	-

DENNIS DANIELS-SMALL (British)

DENNIS DANIELS-SMALL TRIO:
Dennis Daniels-Small(p),John Ford(el-b),Lennie Ware(dr).

Hartley,Kent,England.March 26,1977

But Not For Me	MBC Studios(E)MBC300
Here's That Rainy Day	-
Jubilee-Boogie	-
Something Big	-
Satin Doll	-
Woven	-
Stars Fell On Alabama	-
That's All	-
Autumn Leaves	-

No details.   Unknown location/date
          Unknown titles   MBC Studios(E)MBC400

Note:MBC300 and MBC400 are cassette issues.

PALLE DANIELSSON (Swedish)

See also WOLFGANG ENGSTFELD.

Roland Keijser,Lennart Åberg(ts,ss,fl),Bobo Stenson(p,el-p),Palle Danielsson(b),Bengt Berger,Jon Christensen(dr).   Stockhom.April 6,1971

Ulla	SR(Sd)RELP1117
Kring David	-
6/4	-
3+2+3	-

THE DANISH JAZZ ARMY

See RED RODNEY.

THE DANISH JAZZBALLET SOCIETY ENSEMBLE

Allan Botschinsky -1(tp,flh,arr),Ray Pitts -2(ss,ts,arr),Per Carsten -3(as,fl,arr),Uffe
Karskov -4,Jesper Thilo -4(ts),Flemming Madsen -5(bars),Ole Kock Hansen(org,p,arr),Ole
Molin -6,Ole Berendorf -7(g),Niels-Henning Ørsted Pedersen(b,el-b,arr),Bjarne Rostvold
(perc,dr,arr,cond),Perry Knudsen -8(perc),Phil Wilson,Kenny Drew(arr).
                                        Copenhagen.May 1970

Jive Samba(3,4,8)	Fona(D)F501
Child Song(6)	-
Memphis Underground(1,2,7,8)	-
Groovy Samba(3,6,8)	-
Conversation(1,6,8)	-
Desert Drag(1,2,7,8)	-
Chili Con Carne(1,2,7,8)	-
Run Away(3,4)	-
Southside(1,2,6,8)	-
Mercy,Mercy(3,4,8)	-
The Jazz Dancer(8,9)	-

9.Knudsen,Rostvold(perc) only.

Perry Knudsen(tp),Allan Botschinsky(tp,arr),Palle Bolvig -1,Arne Lamberth -2,Leif Johansen
-3(tp),Per Esbersen -2,Ole Kurt Jensen -2,Torolf Mølgaard -4,Axel Windfeldt -5,Erling Kroner -5(tb),Jesper Thilo(ss,ts),Erling Christensen -6(as),Per Carsten -2(as,fl,arr),Uffe
Karskov -2(ts),Flemming Madsen -2(bars),Ole Kock Hansen(p),Ole Molin(g),Niels-Henning Ørsted Pedersen(b),Bjarne Rostvold(dr),Ray Pitts,Dage Jonsson(arr).
                                        Copenhagen.January 28/29,1971

Wish I Knew(1,2,4)	Fona(D)F502
Point Blank(1,2,4)	-
The Piledriver(1,2,4)	-
Dancing Time(1,2,3,4,5,6)	-
Corrida De Jangada(1,2,3,4,5,6)	-
Don't Know Why(1,2,3,4,5,6)	-
Son Of Folk Music(2,3,4)	-
Why Am I Treated So Bad(1)	-

THE DANISH RADIO JAZZ GROUP (RADIOJAZZGRUPPEN)

See also PALLE MIKKELBORG,SAHIB SHIHAB.

Palle Mikkelborg,Allan Botschinsky(tp,flh),Torolf Mølgaard(tb,euphonium),Poul Hindberg(cl,
),Bent Jædig(ts,fl,picc),Niels Husum(ss,ts,bcl),Bent Nielsen(bars,cl,fl),Louis Hjulmand
rbs),Bent Axen(p),Fritz von Bülow(g),Niels-Henning Ørsted Pedersen(b),Alex Riel(dr),Erik
seholm(cond).   Copenhagen.September 28,1965

Voyage Of The Starbird	Debut(D)DEB1145
Sound Like Arnoldi(1)	-
Fujiyama(1,2)	-
Gizzy(1,2)	-

.Add Steffen Andersen(b);omit von Bülow.
.Add Hugh Steinmetz.

me.   Copenhagen.October 9,1965

Hanne	Debut(D)DEB1145

THE DANISH RADIO BIG BAND (RADIOENS BIG BAND)
ection cont. next page).

THE DANISH RADIO BIG BAND (RADIOENS BIG BAND)

Palle Mikkelborg(tp,cond),Palle Bolvig,Arne Lamberth,Allan Botschinsky,Perry Knudsen,Vagn
Elsberg(tp,flh),Torolf Mølgaard,Per Espersen,Helmuth Hjort Hansen,Axel Windfeldt(tb),Ole
Kurt Jensen(btb),Bent Nielsen(as,cl,fl),Erling Christensen(as,cello),Jesper Thilo(ts,ss,
cl,fl),Uffe Karskov(ts,fl,cl),Flemming Madsen(bars,bcl,fl),Ole Kock Hansen(p,keyb),Ole Mo-
lin(g),Niels-Henning Ørsted Pedersen(b,el-b),Vagn Sørensen,William Schiöpffe,Bjarne Rost-
vold(dr,perc),Ray Pitts(cond).   Copenhagen.December 9/10,1969
        Brownsville Trolley Line: Sonet(D)SLP1520
            Agba Variations/Cornered
            Fat Girl
            A Cool,Dry Place
            The Tie,That Binks
        Tempus Incertum Remanet   -

Thad Jones(cnt,cond),Benny Rosenfeld,Palle Bolvig,Idrees Sulieman,Allan Botschinsky,Perry
Knudsen(tp,flh),Vincent Nilsson,Erling Kroner,Richard Boone,Ole Kurt Jensen(tb),Axel Wind-
feldt(btb,tu),Jesper Thilo(ss,as,cl,fl),Per Carsten(as,fl,ss),Bent Jædig(ts,fl),Uffe Kar-
skov(ts,as,fl,cl),Flemming Madsen(bars,bcl,cl),Ole Kock Hansen(p,el-p),Bo Sylvén(g),Niels
Henning Ørsted Pedersen(b,el-b),Bjarne Rostvold(dr),Ethan Weisgard(perc,cg).
                                Live."Montmartre",Copenhagen.March 21/22,197
        Tip Toe   Metronome(D)MLP15629,Storyville(D)STCD4172(CD)
        Kids Are Pretty People   -   -
        New York City   -
        Ebbe Skammelsøn   -
        Day Dream   -   ,Storyville(D)STCD4172(CD)
        Dancing Girls   -
        The Farewell   Metronome(D)MLP15644,Storyville(D)STCD4172(CD)
        Old Folks   -   -
        Frelimo   -   -
        I Got Rhythm   -   -
        61st And Rich'it   -   -
        A Good Time Was Had By All   -   -

All titles on MLP15629 also on Atl(G)ATL50548.

HAROLD DANKO

HAROLD DANKO QUARTET:
Greg Herbert(ts,as,ss),Harold Danko(p,el-p),Dave Shapiro(b),Jimmy Madison(dr).
                                NYC.April/May 1975
        When She Smiles   Inner City IC1029
        Antiquanova(1)   -
        Mirth Song   -
        Intensity   -
        You Made Me Love You   -
        Sweet Georgia Brown   -

-1.Add Lawrence Feldman(fl);Danko plays (picc).

Tom Harrell(tp,flh),Frank Tiberi(ts,bassoon),Harold Danko(p),Rufus Reid(b),Joe LaBarbera
(dr).   NYC.April 1979
        Extractations Of Frank Tiberi Dreamstreet DR104
        Tidal Breeze   -
        Stardust   -
        Softly As In A Morning Sunrise   -
        Coincidence   -
        In Your Own Sweet Way   -
        Cape Verdean Blues(1)   -
        Have You Met Miss Jones   -

-1.Omit Harrell,Tiberi.

HAROLD DANKO AND THE GELTMAN BAND:
Lawrence Feldman(ts,ss,cl,fl),Harold Danko(p),David Katzenberg(el-b,b),Billy Mintz(dr),
Lotti Golden(vcl).   NYC.February 1979
  Clearly You(lg)   Inner City IC1069
  Chasin' The Bad Guys   -
  Dance Of The Brooding Slave   -
  Blue Swedish Wildflower   -
  Spinning Waltz   -
  Soarin' Thru Space   -
  Silly Samba   -
  Flight Of The Desperados   -

JOHN (JOHNNY) DANKWORTH (British)

See also ALAN DEAN,DICKIE HAWDON,CLEO LAINE,MELODY MAKER ALL STARS,LAURIE MONK,KENNY
WHEELER.

JOHNNY DANKWORTH QUARTET:
John Dankworth(cl),Eddie Thompson(p),Bert Howard(b),Victor Feldman(dr).
           London.February 17,1948
m7-14 Mop-Mop   Esquire(E)10-004
m7-15 Lady Bird   -
m7-16 Quaternity   Esquire(E)10-065
m7-17 Moonlight In Vermont Esquire(E)10-092
m7-18 Gone With The Wind   Esquire(E)10-065

All titles also on Esquire(E)ESQ100-4 (4xCD set).

John Dankworth(as),Norman Stenfalt(p),Joe Muddell(b),Laurie Morgan(dr).
        Live."King George's Hall",London.April 9,1949
80 Bremavin   Esquire(E)10-037
81 Lover Man   -
84 Second Eleven   Esquire(E)12-007
85 Body And Soul   -
90 Night In Tunisia(1) Esquire(E)12-011

-1.Tommy Pollard(p) replaces Stenfalt.

All titles also on Esquire(E)ESQ315,ESQ315 (CD),ESQ100-4 (4xCD set).

JOHNNY DANKWORTH SEVEN:
Jimmy Deuchar(tp),Eddie Harvey(tb),John Dankworth(as,cl),Don Rendell(ts),Bill LeSage(p),
Joe Muddell(b),Tony Kinsey(dr). London.May 18,1950
CPVD7-1 Lightly Politely Jazz Parade/Vogue(E)B8
CPVD8-2 Strike Up The Band Jazz Parade/Vogue(E)B9
CPVD9 Marmaduke   Jazz Parade/Vogue(E)B8
CPVD10-2 Little Benny   Jazz Parade/Vogue(E)B9

Eric Dawson(b) replaces Muddell;add Marion Williams(vcl).
        London.July 29,1950
n-7-114 Sam's Song(mw)   Esquire(E)5-005
n-7-115 Theme From
   "The Haunted Ballroom"   - ,S317
n-7-116 Seven Not Out (Tea For Me) Esquire(E)10-093,S317,ESQ100-4(CD),Cupol(Sd)9017,
            Blue Note BLP5019
n-7-117 Cherokee   Esquire(E)10-093,ESQ100-4(CD),Blue Note BLP5019

Frank Holder (vcl) replaces Williams. London.October 14,1950
(session cont. next page).

(session cont. from previous page):
m-7-118-2 Perhaps   Esquire(E)10-103,ESQ301,ESQ100-4(CD)
m-7-119-3 Get Happy   - ,S317,ESQ100-4(CD),World(E)
                                           EG2601871
m-7-120-2 Lament And Wild Dance   Esquire(E)5-010,S317,Cupol 9017
m-7-121-5 Don't Blame Me(fh)   -

Omit Holder.   London.February 3,1951
128   Strictly Confidential   Esquire(E)rejected
129   Treble Chance   -

Add Alan Dean(vcl).   London.April 27,1951
p-7-170 Marching Through Georgia   Esquire(E)5-030,S317
p-7-171 Blue Moon(ad)   Esquire(E)5-023
p-7-172 So In Love   -
p-7-173 Stardust   Esquire(E)5-030,ESQ301

Omit Dean.   London.July 12,1951
  m-7-209 I Hear Music   Esquire(E)10-163,ESQ301,Cupol(Sd)9024
T-m-7-210 Leon Bismarck   Esquire(E)10-173,S317
  m-7-211 The Slider   Esquire(E)10-163,20-011,ESQ301,Cupol(Sd)9024
T-m-7-212 Webb City   Esquire(E)10-173,ESQ301

All titles also on Esquire ESQ100-4 (4xCD set).

Eddie Blair(tp),Eddie Harvey(tb),John Dankworth(as),Don Rendell(ts),Bill LeSage(p),Eric
Dawson(b),Eddie Taylor(dr),Cleo Laine(vcl). London.November 8,1951
SSS.7.227 Mr. And Mississippi(cl)   Esquire(E)5-052,S317
SSS.7.228 Lush Life(1)(cl)   - -
SSS.7.229 Strictly Confidential   Esquire(E)10-193, - ,ESQ100-4(CD)
SSS.7.230 Allen's Alley   - ,ESQ301,ESQ100-4(CD)

-1.Add Harry McKinsey(cl).

Same.   London.December 17,1951
SSS.7.248 Sin(cl)   Esquire(E)5-056
SSS.7.249 Wedding Of The Painted Doll   - ,S317
SSS.7.250 Stomping At The Savoy   Esquire(E)10-203, - ,ESQ100-4(CD)
SSS.7.251 Myob   - ,ESQ100-4(CD)

Add Frank Holder(vcl).   London.March 4,1952
RPL-276   I've Got You Under My Skin(fh)Esquire(E)5-060
RPL-277   The Very Thought Of You(cl)   - ,S317
RPL-278-4 Bopscotch   Esquire(E)10-223,ESQ301
RPL-279-3 Our Delight   - -

JOHNNY DANKWORTH WITH STRINGS:
John Dankworth(as),Steve Race(p,arr),unknown(harp),Eric Dawson(b),Eddie Taylor(dr),Kathrar
Field(vcl),strings.   London.May 6,1952
307   The Belle Of The Ball   Esquire(E)5-066,S317
308   Someone To Watch Over Me   - -
309   I Never Knew(kf)   Esquire(E)5-063
310   Down Memory Lane(kf)   -

JOHNNY DANKWORTH SEVEN:
Eddie Blair(tp),Eddie Harvey(tb),John Dankworth(as),Don Rendell(ts),Bill LeSage(p),Eric
Dawson(b),Eddie Taylor(dr),Cleo Laine(vcl). London.February 10,1953
CE14418 Two Ticks   Parlophone(E)R3694,Encore(E)ENC165,I.A.J.R.C. LP3
CE14419 Moon Flowers(1)   -   -
CE14420 Honeysuckle Rose(cl)   Parlophone(E)R3660,GEP8613,World(E)EG2601871
CE14421 Swingin'   - ,Encore(E)ENC165
(session cont. next page).

(session cont. from previous page):
-1.Add Frank Holder(bg).

Add Frank Holder(vcl).   London.May 6,1953
CE14596 Easy Living(cl)   Parlophone(E)R3719,GEP8613,World(E)EG2601871
CE14597 Oo-Be-Doop   Parlophone(E)R3850,Encore(E)ENC165,Music For Plea-
                                   sure(E)DL1200
CE14598 I Get A Kick Out Of You(fh) Parlophone(E)R3719

JOHNNY DANKWORTH AND HIS ORCHESTRA:
Derrick Abbott,Eddie Blair,Bill Metcalf,George Boocock(tp),Maurice Pratt,Keith Christie,
Eddie Harvey,Gib Wallace(tb),John Dankworth,Lew Smith,Maurice Owen(as),Rex Morris,Freddy
Courtenay(ts),Alex Leslie(bars),Bill LeSage(p,vbs),Eric Dawson(b),Allan Ganley(dr).
                                          London.November 12,1953
CE14772 S'Wonderful   Parlophone(E)R3788,Sepia(E)RSCD2014(CD)
CE14773 Younger Every Day   -

Both titles also on Angel LP60004,Encore(E)ENC165,I.A.J.R.C. LP39.

Same.   London.December 23,1953
CE14845 The Slider   Parlophone(E)R3820,Encore(E)ENC165
CE14846 Talk Of The Town   - ,GEP8697,Music For Pleasure(E)
                                   DL1200,World(E)EG2601871

Both titles also on I.A.J.R.C. LP39.

Geoff Cole(as) replaces Lew Smith.   London.January 21,1954
CE14859 My Buddy   Parlophone(E)R3836,Encore(E)ENC165,Sepia(E)
                                   RSCD2014(CD)
CE14860 Runnin'Wild   Parlophone(E)R3850,Encore(E)ENC165,Music For
                                   Pleasure(E)DL1200,World(E)EG2601871,Sepia
                                   (E)RSCD2014(CD)
CE14862 The Jerky Thing   Parlophone(E)R3836

All titles also on I.A.J.R.C. LP39.

JOHNNY DANKWORTH AND HIS ORCHESTRA WITH CLEO LAINE:
Bill Geldard(tb) replaces Wallace;add Cleo Laine(vcl).
                                          London.April 14,1954
CE14947 Ain't Misbehavin'(cl)   Parlophone(E)R3964,GEP8613,World(E)EG2601871
CE14948 I Got Rhythm   Parlophone(E)R3871,   -   -(?)
CE14949 I Know You're Mine(cl)   - ,World(E)EG2601871
CE14950 I Got It Bad   Parlophone(E)R3964,MSP6147,   -(?)

JOHNNY DANKWORTH AND HIS ORCHESTRA:
Derrick Abbott,Eddie Blair,Bill Metcalf,George Boocock(tp),Maurice Pratt,Keith Christie,
Eddie Harvey,Bill Geldard(tb),John Dankworth,Geoff Cole,Maurice Owen(as),Tommy Whittle,Rex
Morris(ts),Alex Leslie(bars),Derek Smith(p),Jack Seymour(b),Allan Ganley(dr).
                                          London.June 1,1954
CE15035 You Go To My Head   Parlophone(E)R3935,GEP8697,MSP6139,World(E)
                                   EG2601871(?),Angel(J)OM1010
CE15036 Four Of A Kind   Parlophone(E)R3886,MSP6113,Encore(E)ENC165,Angel
                                   (J)OM1013,I.A.J.R.C. LP39
CE15037 Perdido   Parlophone(E)R3886,MSP6113,Encore(E)ENC165,Angel
                                   (J)OM1013
CE15038 Bugle Call Rag   Parlophone(E)R3935,MSP6139,Encore(E)ENC165,Angel
                                   (J)OM1010,Sepia(E)RSCD2014(CD)

Add Tony Mansell(vcl).   London.August 9,1954
E15104 Hold My Hand(tm)   Parlophone(E)R3919,MSP6130
E15105 The High And Mighty(tm)   -   -

Frank Holder(vcl) replaces Mansell.   London.October 6,1954
CE15126 Mambo In The Moonlight(fh)   Parlophone(E)R3928
CE15127 Stop!Proceed With Caution(fh)   -

Same.   London.November 3,1954
CE15189 Cole Storage   Parlophone(E)R4033,Encore(E)ENC165,I.A.J.R.C. LP39
CE15190 Get Happy   - ,I.A.J.R.C. LP39

JOHNNY DANKWORTH AND THE JAZZ PARADE TRIO:
John Dankworth(as),Dave Lee(p),Bob Hill(b),Gene Latimore(dr).
    Unknown location/date
PEA3-1 All The Things You Are   Parlophone(E)S.P.D.58
PEA4-1 Good Bait   -

Note:It has not been possible to get exact details on the above recording (which may be a
    test pressing of an unissued record).

Derrick Abbott,Bill Metcalf,Dougie Roberts,Colin Wright,Stan Palmer(tp),Bill Geldard,Dan-
ny Elwood,Garry Brown,Laurie Monk,Tony Russell(tb),John Dankworth(as),Bill Harrington(ts),
Alex Leslie(bars),Dave Lee(p),Eric Dawson(b),Kenny Clare(dr).
    Broadcast.London.c. 1954
    Coquette   BBC(E)REC144

Derrick Abbott,Bill Metcalf,Dougie Roberts,Jimmy Venn(tp),Maurice Pratt,Keith Christie,
Bill Geldard,Danny Elwood(tb),John Dankworth,Maurice Owen,Dougie Robinson(as),Rex Morris
Don Pashley(ts),Alex Leslie(bars),Derek Smith(p),Bill Sutcliffe(b),Allan Ganley(dr).
    London.January 6,1955
13431 Singin' In The Rain   Capitol 3079,F3079,Capitol(E)CL14285,(G)C3079

Same.   London.January 7,1955
13440 Waterloo Walk   Capitol 3079,F3079,(G)C3079
13441 Non-Stop London   Capitol(E)CL14285

Derrick Abbott,Bill Metcalf,Charlie Evans,Tommy McQuater(tp),Bill Geldard,Danny Elwood,
Garry Brown,Laurie Monk(tb),John Dankworth,Rex Rutley(as),Pete Warner,John Xerri(ts),Alex
Leslie(bars),Dave Lee(p),Bill Sutcliffe(b),Kenny Clare(dr).
    London.November 2,1955
CE15435 Feather Merchant   Parlophone(E)R4107,GEP8570,I.A.J.R.C. LP39
CE15436 Indiana   - - ,Sepia(E)RSCD2014(CD)

Frank Donlan(tp),Ronnie Fenwick(as) replaces McQuater,Rutley.
    London.December 15,1955
CE15490 Crazy Rhythm   Parlophone(E)rejected
CE15491 Moby Dick   Parlophone(E)R4148,GEP8570,I.A.J.R.C. LP39

Same.   London.January 20,1956
CE15494 Memories Of You   Parlophone(E)R4148,GEP8570,Music For Pleasure(E)
    DL1200,I.A.J.R.C. LP39
    Itinerary For An Orchestra   Parlophone(E)PMD1042

Dougie Roberts(tp) replaces Donlan.   London.March 7,1956
    Jersey Bounce   Parlophone(E)PMD1042,Music For Pleasure(E)DL1200

Derrick Abbott,Bill Metcalf,Stan Palmer,Colin Wright,Dougie Roberts(tp),Bill Geldard,Dann
Elwood,Garry Brown,Laurie Monk,Harry Buckles(tb),John Dankworth(cl,as,tymp,narration),Pet
Warner(ts),Alex Leslie(bars),Dave Lee(p,arr),Bill Sutcliffe(b),Kenny Clare(dr).
    London.May 10,1956
CE15569 Experiments With Mice(jd)   Parlophone(E)R4185,GEP8697,MSP6255,Capitol 3499,
    F3499,Music For Pleasure(E)DL1200,World(E)
    EG2601871
CE15570 Applecake   Parlophone(E)R4185,GEP8653,MSP6255,Capitol 3499,
    F3499

Eric Dawson(b) replaces Sutcliffe. London.August 9,1956
CE15648 Blues In The Night Parlophone(E)R4213,Encore(E)ENC165
CE15649 Adios   - ,PMD1042,Music For Pleasure(E)
           DL1200,World(E)EG2601871,Sepia(E)RSCD2014(CD)
  Take The "A" Train Parlophone(E)PMD1042,Music For Pleasure(E)DL1200,
           World(E)EG2601871

Tony Russell(tb),Bill Harrington(ts) replace Buckles,Warner.
          London.December 19,1956
CE15739 All Clare   Parlophone(E)R4274,Encore(E)ENC165,World(E)
           EG2601871
CE15740 Melbourne Marathon Parlophone(E)R4274,GEP8653

Both titles also on I.A.J.R.C. LP39.

Same.   London.February 1,1957
CE15763 Duke's Joke   Parlophone(E)R4294,Encore(E)ENC165
CE15764 Coquette   - ,GEP8653,Intercord(G)158001

Both titles also on I.A.J.R.C. LP39.

Dickie Hawdon,Derrick Abbott,Bill Metcalf,Stan Palmer,Colin Wright(tp),Jack Botterill,Gar-
ry Brown,Danny Elwood,Laurie Monk,Tony Russell(tb),John Dankworth(as,arr),Tommy Whittle
(ts),Alex Leslie(bars,cl),Dave Lee(p),Eric Dawson(b),Kenny Clare(dr),Cleo Laine(vcl),Dave
Lindup(arr).   London.March 21,1957
  Somebody Loves Me(cl) Parlophone(E)PMC1043,Verve MGV20006,World(E)
           EG2601871
  Limehouse Blues   Parlophone(E)PMC1043,Verve MGV20006

Ted Barker(tb),Danny Moss(ts,cl) replace Botterill,Whittle.
          London.May 15,1957
CE15824 Big Jazz Story(1) Parlophone(E)R4321,GEP8697,Music For Pleasure(E)
           DL1200,World(E)EG2601871
CE15825 Firth Of Fourths Parlophone(E)R4321,GEP8653,I.A.J.R.C. LP39

-1.Dankworth also (cl,narration).

Bert Courtley(tp) replaces Metcalf. London.August 29,1957
  Export Blues   Parlophone(E)PMC1043
  Hullabaloo   - ,Music For Pleasure(E)DL1200

Both titles also on Verve MGV20006.

Same.   London.September 2,1957
  Stompin' At The Savoy Parlophone(E)PMC1043
  Just A Sittin' And A Rockin' - ,Music For Pleasure(E)DL1200

Both titles also on Verve MGV20006.

Bob Carson(tp),Jack Botterill(tb) replace Bourtley,Barker.
          London.March 10,1958
  The Breeze And I   Parlophone(E)PMC1076,Sepia(E)RSCD2014(CD)
  How High The Moon   -   -
  Stardust   -   -

Same.   London.March 13,1958
  Swingin' The Blues Parlophone(E)PMC1076
  I Can't Get Started   -
  How Deep Is The Ocean   -

Same.   London.March 20,1958
        Crazy Rhythm   Parlophone(E)PMC1076,Sepia(E)RSCD2014(CD)
        Moonglow   -   -
        Jive At Five   -   -

Same.   London.March 27,1958
        Show Me   Parlophone(E)GEP8671
        I Could Have Danced All Night   -

Same.   London.April 1,1958
        On The Street Where You Live Parlophone(E)GEP8671
        I've Grown
            Accustomed To Her Face   -
        Idaho   Parlophone(E)PMC1076

Add Johnny Scott(fl),Bill LeSage(vbs),Jim Powell(tu).
                                           London.June 20,1958
CE16100 The Colonel's Tune   Parlophone(E)R4456
CE16102 Jim And Andy   -
        Don't Get Around Much Anymore Parlophone(E)PMC1076

No details.   Unknown location.Poss. 1958/59
        Falstaff's Hat Dance
        Dawn At Dover(1)
        Daffy-Down-Day
        Ruins At Stonehenge
        Partly Cloudy
        Land's End
        Revolutionary Ballet
        Gad-About
        My Friend,Big Ben
        Oxford Blues
        Waltz In Four
        Echo
        Piccadilly Parade

-1.Add Rita Williams Chorus(vcl).

Dickie Hawdon,Derrick Abbott,Stan Palmer,Colin Wright,Bob Carson(tp),Garry Brown,Danny
Elwood,Laurie Monk,Tony Russell(tb),Ron Snyder(tb,tu),John Dankworth(as,cl),Danny Moss
(ts,bcl),Alex Leslie(bars,cl,fl),Dave Lee(p),Eric Dawson(b),Kenny Clare(dr),Dave Lindup
(arr).   London.May 12/13/19,1959
14565 Tribute To Chauncey   Roulette(S)R52040,CDP7.96566-2(CD)
14566 Slow Twain   -   -
14567 Sunflower
14568 Dauphine Blues   -   ,CDP7.96566-2(CD),(E)2934.021
14569 Honeydew Melon   -   -
14570 Joe And Lol's Blues   -   -
14571 Caribe   Roulette CDP7.96566-2(CD)
14572 Kool Kate   Roulette(S)R52040,CDP7.96566-2(CD)
14573 New Forest   -   -   ,(E)2934.021
14574 Specs Yellow   -   ,(E)2934.021
14575 Desperate Dan   -   ,CDP7.96566-2(CD),(E)2934.021
14576 Bluer Furs   unissued
14577 Internationale   Roulette(S)R52040

All titles on (S)R52040 also on Roulette(J)L5124,Columbia(E)33SX1280,Top Rank(E)30/020.
Note:Top Rank(E)30/020 was announced but never issued.

Kenny Wheeler(tp) replaces Wright.   Live.Newport Jazz Festival,R.I.July 3,1959

Firth Of Fourths	Top Rank(E)30/019
Caribe	-
Royal Ascot	-
Don't Get Around Much Anymore	-
Doggin' Around	-
Jones	-
Take The "A" Train	-

All titles also on Top Rank R/RS614,Top Rank International LRM314.

Colin Wright(tp) replaces Wheeler;add Art Ellefson(ts),George Tyndale(sax).
Unknown location(s).c. 1959

Limehouse Blues	Big Band International LPS2703
Little Horace	-
I Can't Get Started	-
Bypass	-
How High The Moon	-
Royal Garden Blues	-
Somebody Loves Me	-
Jersey Bounce	-
The Breeze And I	-
Battered Chops	-
Bluesology	-
I've Grown	
Accustomed To Your Face	-
Take The "A" Train	-
A Fifth Of Fourths	-
9:20 Special	-
Allen's Alley	-
DBA Special	-
Blue Post	-
Cobwebs	-
So What	-
Moanin'	-
Esso Blues	-
Blue In The Night	-
You Do Something To Me	-

Similar.   London.Late 1959

Duet For Sixteen	Top Rank(E)45JAR209
We Are The Lambeth Boys	-

JOHNNY DANKWORTH WITH THE LONDON PHILHARMONIC ORCHESTRA:
Dickie Hawdon,Derrick Abbott,Kenny Wheeler,Gus Galbraith(tp),Tony Russell,Eddie Harvey,Ian
McDougall(tb),Ron Snyder(tu),John Dankworth,Peter King(as),Danny Moss,Art Ellefson(ts),
George Tyndale(bars),Dudley Moore(p),Spike Heatley(b),Kenny Clare(dr),The London Philhar-
monic Orchestra,Dave Lindup,Matyas Seiber(arr),Hugo Rignold(cond).
London.May 25,1960

15500	Improvisations For Jazz	
	Band And Symphony Orchestra	Roulette(S)R52059
	Rendezvous:	-
15501	High Life	
15502	One Way Street	
15503	Variations Peruvianos	
15504	South Bank	
15505	Rendezvous (Rondo Cubano)	

All titles also on Boulevard(E) (S)4123.

JOHNNY DANKWORTH AND HIS ORCHESTRA:
Omit London Philharmonic Orchestra;add Jimmy Deuchar(tp),Dennis Wilson(frh),Gervase de
Peyer(cl),Ronnie Ross(bars),Michael Jeffries(harp),Ray Dempsey(g),Igor Stravinsky(comp).
                                         London.May 26,1960
15497-99 Ebony Concerto   Roulette(S)R52059

All titles on (S)R52059 also on Roulette(J)SL5124,Saga(E)XIP7006,Society(E)SOC963.

Dickie Hawdon,Kenny Wheeler,Gus Galbraith(tp),Tony Russell,Eddie Harvey,Ian McDougall(tb),
Ron Snyder(tu),John Dankworth(as,arr),Peter King(as),Danny Moss,Art Ellefson(ts),George
Tyndale(bars),Dudley Moore(p),Spike Heatley(b),Kenny Clare(dr),Dave Lindup,Galt McDermot
(arr).   London.July 1-5,1960
15694   Treasure Drive   Columbia(E)SEG8037,Cinema LP8002
15695   Sweet Suspence   unissued
15696   Riverside Stomp
15697   After The Party   Columbia(E)SEG8037,Cinema LP8002
15698   Freedom Walk   -   -
15699   African Waltz(1)   Roulette 4353,(S)R52075,(E)2934.021,(G)RL21137,
                                             Columbia(E)DB4590,SEG8137,Music For Pleasure
                                             (E)CDMFP6019(CD),Compacts For Pleasure(E)
                                             CDB7.94226-2(CD)
15700   BBA Special   unissued
15701   Moanin'   Roulette 4353,(S)R52075,(E)2934.021,(G)RL21137,
                                             Columbia(E)DB4590,SEG8137
15702   They Can't Take That Away From Me unissued
15703   One For Daddy-O   -

-1.Ronnie Stephenson(dr) replaces Clare;add Johnny Scott(fl,picc);omit Snyder.

Note:The above titles were recorded by Roulette.

Ray Premru(tb),Ronnie Ross(bars),Alan Branscombe(p) replace McDougal,Tyndale,Moore;omit
Scott.   London. 1961
17224   Chano   Roulette (S)R52096,(E)2934.021
17225   The Avenger's Theme   - ,CDP7.96566-2(CD)

Both titles also on Columbia(E)DB4695,SEG8137.
Note:Masternumbers were added by Roulette.

JOHNNY DANKWORTH SEXTET:
Tommy McQuater,Kenny Wheeler(tp),John Dankworth(as),Alan Branscombe(ts),Spike Heatley(b),
Ronnie Stephenson(dr).   London.July 1961
        Fall Guy   Fontana(E)TFL5179,STFL501,(Eu)680.971TL,Epic
                                             LA16032,BA17032

Note:The above title is from the "All Night Long" film soundtrack.

JOHNNY DANKWORTH AND HIS ORCHESTRA:
Ron Simmons,Leon Calvert,Kenny Wheeler,Gus Galbraith(tp),Tony Russell,Eddie Harvey(tb),
John Dankworth(as,arr),Roy East(as),Danny Moss,Art Ellefson(ts),Ronnie Ross(bars),Alan
Branscombe(p),Spike Heatley(b),Ronnie Stephenson(dr).
                                         London. 1961
17218   String Of Camels(1)   Roulette (S)R52096,(E)2934.021,Columbia(E)DB4751
17219   Winter Wail   Roulette (S)R52096,   - ,CDP7.96566-2(CD),
                                             Columbia(E)DB4751
17221   Esso Blues(2)   Roulette (S)R52096,CDP7.96566-2(CD),(E)2934.021,
                                             Columbia(E)DB4852
17223   Cannonball   Roulette (S)R52096,CDP7.96566-2(CD),Columbia(E)
                                             DB4852

-1.Add Frank Reidy(bcl,as),Bob Efford(bcl).
-2.Listed as "S.O. Blues" in the Roulette files.

Kenny Napper(b) replaces Heatley.   London. 1961
17220 Daily Date   Roulette(S)R52096
17226 When My Sugar
       Walks Down The Street   Roulette(S)R52096,CDP7.96566-2(CD)

Vic Ash(cl,ts) replaces Moss.   London. 1961
17222 Curtain Up   Roulette (S)R52096,CDP7.96566-2(CD),(E)2934.021
17227 Sack O'Woe   -   -   -

All titles on (S)R52096 also on Roulette RE121,Columbia(E)33SX1572.

Add Ray Premru(tb).   London. 1962
       Abandonado   Columbia(E)DB4942
       O Pato   -

Omit Premru.   London.c. 1962
       Hoe-Down   Fontana(E)TF396
       Sing Sing Sing   -
       Off The Cuff   Fontana(E)TF422
       Avenger's Theme   -

Jimmy Deuchar,Gus Galbraith,Leon Calvert,Kenny Wheeler,Dickie Hawdon(tp,flh),Tony Russell,
Eddie Harvey(tb),John Dankworth,Roy East(cl,as),Vic Ash(ts,cl),Art Ellefson(ts,bcl),Tony
Coe,Tubby Hayes,Peter King,Ronnie Scott,Bobby Wellins,Dick Morrissey(ts),Ronnie Ross(bars)
Alan Branscombe(p,vbs,xyl),Kenny Napper/Spike Heatley(b),Johnny Butts,Ronnie Stephenson
(dr),Roy Webster(perc)(coll. pers.).   London.July 29/31,August 7,October 4,1963
       Prologue   Fontana(E)TFL5203
       Weller Never Did   -

       Little Nell   -
       The Infant Phenomenon   -
       Demdest Little Fascinator -
       Dotheboys Hall   -
       Ghosts   -
       David And The Bloaters   -
       Please Sir,I Want Some More -
       The Artful Dodger   -
       Waiting For Something To Turn Up -
       Dodson And Fogg   -
       The Pickwick Club   -
       Sergeant Buzfuz   -
       Finale   -

11 titles also on Fontana(Am)MGF27525,SRF67525,Sepia(E)RSR2010.

Clark Terry,Greg Bowen,Gus Galbraith(tp),Leon Calvert(tp,flh),Kenny Wheeler(tp,tenor-h),
Bob Brookmeyer(vtb),Tony Russell,Johnny Marshall,Chris Smith(tb),Ron Snyder(tu),John Dank-
worth(cl,as),Al Newman(as),Vic Ash(ts,cl),Art Ellefson(ts,bcl),Paul Carroll(bars,as,cl),
Alan Branscombe(p,vbs),Kenny Napper(b),Johnny Butts(dr).
                             NYC.October 9,1964
       Theme:Way With The Stars   Fontana(E) (S)TFL5229
       Gemini(1)   -
       Leo(2)   -
       Scorpio(3)   -
       Sagittarius   -

1.Add Lucky Thompson(ts) (overdubbed later).
2.Add Danny Moss(ts),Chuck Israels(b) (overdubbed later).
3.Add Phil Woods(as),Zoot Sims(ts) (overdubbed later).

```
Same.                              London.October 28,November 2/10,1964
        Aquarius(1)                Fontana(E) (S)TFL5229
        Pisces                                          -
        Aries                                           -
        Taurus(2)                                       -
        Cancer                                          -
        Virgo                                           -
        Libra(3)                                        -
        Capricorn(4)                                    -
        Coda(4)                                         -
```

-1.Add Ronnie Scott(ts) (poss. overdubbed later).
-2.Add David Snell(harp) (poss. overdubbed later).
-3.Add Ronnie Ross(bars) (poss. overdubbed later).
-4.Add Osie Johnson(dr) (poss. overdubbed later).

All titles also on Fontana(Am)MGF27543,SRF67543,Sepia(E)RSR2011.

Unknown orchestra,Ray Ellington,Cleo Laine(vcl),John Dankworth(comp,arr,cond).

```
                                   London.  1965/66
        Modesty                    Fontana(E) (S)TFL5347
        Doo-Bah-Doo                                     -
        Willie Waltz                                    -
        Theme (vocal)                                   -
        Theme (instrumental)       Fontana(E)TF700,     -
        The Moods Of Modesty                            -
        Ice Is Nice (Breen)                             -
        Nights And Days                                 -
        More Moods Of Modesty                           -
        Even More Moods Of Modesty                      -
        End Title (We Should've)(re,cl)  Fontana(E)TF704,  -
```

All titles also on 20th Century Fox TCF/TFS4182.
Note:The above titles are from the "Modesty Blaise" film soundtrack.

Derek Watkins,Les Condon,Kenny Wheeler(tp,flh),Henry Lowther(cnt,vln),Michael Gibbs,Chris
Pyne(tb),Dick Hart(tu),John Dankworth(as,arr),Ray Swinfield,Tony Roberts,Tony Coe(reeds),
Laurie Holloway(p),Kenny Napper(b),John Spooner(dr),Tristan Fry(perc).

```
                                   London.May 1/2/3,1967
        Winter Scene               Fontana(E)STL5445
        Sailor                                          -
        Two-Piece Flower           Fontana(E)TF857,-
        Little Girl In Blue                             -
        Composition With Colour                         -
        Face In The Crowd                               -
        La Cloanesse               Fontana(E)TF857,-
        Garden Of Delight                               -
        Madonna                                         -
        Hogstead Of Hogarth(1)                          -
```

-1.Alan Branscombe(p) replaces Holloway.

All titles also on Fontana(Am)SRF67575.

```
Similar.                           London.  1968
        Ja-Da                      Fontana(E)LPS16261
        Off Duty                                        -
        Little Brown Jig(!)                             -
        Sophisticated Lady                              -
        African Waltz                                   -
(session cont. next page).
```

(session cont. from previous page):
```
      Bernie's Tune                    Fontana(E)LPS16261
      Skyliner                                -  ,(S)XL6
      Basin Street Blues                      -
      To Emma                                 -
      Don't Get Around Much Anymore           -
      Song Of India                           -
      Holloway House                          -
```

All titles also on Fontana(Eu)886.611,(Am)SRF67603.

Trevor Barber,Butch Hudson,Hank Shaw,Henry Lowther,Martin Drover,Kenny Wheeler,Eddie Blair
(tp),Malcolm Griffiths,Michael Gibbs,David Horler(tb),Toni Cooke(frh),Dick Hart(tu),John
Dankworth(as,cl,arr),Don Fay,Stan Sulzmann,Tony Roberts,Tony Coe(reeds),Bruce Graham(p),
Martin Kershaw(g),Tony Campo,Daryl Runswick(el-b),John Spooner(dr),Ray Cooper(perc),Dave
Lindup,Mike Vickers(arr).   London.c. March 1970
```
      Eleven Plus                      Philips(E)6308.122
      Academy One                             -
      The Italian Girl                        -
      Earthman                                -
      You Are Too Beautiful                   -
      Family Joy                              -
```

Henry Lowther,Kenny Wheeler(tp),Chris Pyne(tb),John Dankworth(as),Stan Sulzmann,Duncan La-
mont,Roger Cawkwell(reeds),Alan Branscombe(vbs),John Taylor(p),Joe Moretti(g),Daryl Runs-
wick(el-g),Harold Fisher(dr),Michael Gibbs,Ken Gibson(arr).
                                             London.c. June 1971
```
      Grow Your Own                    Philips(E)6308.122
      Schmaltz Waltz                          -
      Triple Portrait                         -
```

Martin Drover,Trevor Barber,Hank Shaw(tp),Henry Lowther(tp,vln),Ken Gibson(tb,arr),Malcolm
Griffiths(tb),John Dankworth(as,arr),Stan Sulzmann,Don Rendell,Mike Page(reeds),Tony Hymas
(p,el-p),John Girvan(g),Daryl Runswick(b,el-b,arr),Harold Fisher(dr).
                                             London.February 19/20/21,1973
```
      Fighting The Flab                Philips(E)6308.169
      Darlington                              -
      Tomorrow's World                        -
      WRVR                                    -
      Lifeline(1):                            -
          Orinoco
          Studio Five
          Kite Flight
          Defrantisity
          Brass Roots
```

-1.Duncan Lamont(reeds) replaces Sulzmann;add strings,voices.

Martin Drover,Hank Shaw,Alan Fowney,Kenny Baker(tp),Ken Gibson,David Horler,Malcolm Grif-
fiths(tb),Geoff Perkins(btb),John Dankworth(as,arr),Don Rendell,Alan Wakeman(ts,fl),Roger
Cawkwell(bars,fl),Tony Hymas(p,el-p),John Girvan,Alan Sparkes(g),Paul Hart(el-b,vln),Ron-
nie Verrell(dr),strings.   London.September 16/17/19/20,1974
```
      Theme: Modesty Blaise            RCA(E)SF8405
      Theme: Darling                          -
      Theme: Morgan                           -
      Theme: Return From The Ashes            -
      Theme: All Gone
          (From "The Servant")                -
      East St. Louis Boogaloo                 -
      Round Table Round                       -
```
(session cont. next page).

(session cont. from previous page):
    Herbie Walks Again   RCA(E)SF8405
    Long John   - ,(Am)APL2-1984
    Look Stranger
      (From "Look Stranger")   -
    Whirly Bird
      (From "Bird's Eye Wiew")   -

All titles also on RCA(Am)LPL1-5092,DRG MRS507.

JOHN DANKWORTH - PAUL HART OCTET:
John Dankworth(ss,as,cl),Paul Hart(p,el-p,el-vln),Daryl Runswick,Dave Markee(b,el-b),Kenny Clare(dr),string quartet.   London.c. 1978/79
    Bottom Of The Barrel   Repertoire(E)RSR1001
    Guess The Rest   -
    Starters   -
    Octavius   -
    Long John   -
    Dregs Of The Keys   -
    1812   -
    Moonlanding   -
    Reedwarblers Lament   -
    Truck On Down   -

JOHN DANKWORTH ORCHESTRA:
No details.   London(?).c. 1979
    Telford's Change   BBC(E)RESL63,REH365
    Serenade For Sylvia   -

FRANKIE DANN (FRANS DANEELS)

Charlie Knegtel,Vital De Backer,Jacques Deschauwer(tp),Jeff Demey,Louis Beckx(tb),Frankie Dann,Fernand Herreman(as),Louis Seghers,Paul Goos(ts),Gaston Henriet(p),Frank Engelen(g, arr),Henri Faes(b),Harry Delcart(dr).   Brussels.February 10,1947
17327 Estrellita   Olympia(B)5293
17328 The Sergeant Was Shy   -

JAMES DAPOGNY

(p-solo).   Library Of Congress,Washington,D.C.c. 1975/76
    The Pearls   Smithsonian Collection N003
    New Orleans Blues
      (New Orleans Joys)   -
    Big Fat Ham (Ham And Eggs) -
    Kansas City Stomp   -
    Jelly Roll Blues   -
    Frog-I-More Rag   -
    Stratford Hunch
      (Chicago Breakdown)   -
    Hyena Stomp   -
    Frances   -
    Jungle Blues   -
    The Crave   -
    Black Bottom Stomp
      (Queen Of Spades)   -

All titles also on Columbia Special Products P13160.

James Dapogny(p),unknown 10-piece orchestra. Unknown location/date

Too Bad	University Of Michigan School Of Music SM1006
Deep Henderson	-
Tin Roof Blues	-
Fireworks	-
Jungle Blues	-
Milenberg Joys	-
The Chant	-
Willie The Weeper	-
Someday Sweetheart	-
Chimes Blues	-
Kansas City Stomps	-
St. Louis Blues	-

BOB DARCH

(p-solo).   Unknown location/date

Maple Leaf Rag	United Artists UAL3120/UAS6120
Alexander's Ragtime Band	-
The Georgia Camp Meeting	-
Pear Blossoms	-
The Russian Rag	-
The Florida Rag	-
Swipsey Cakewalk	-
That Da-Da Strain	-
Carbolich Acid	-
Original Rags	-
Creole Belles	-
Dill Pickles Rag	-

BOB DARCH AND HIS RAGTIME BAND:
No details.   Unknown location/date

Unknown titles	Jan Productions JLP160

Note:JLP160 incl. Eubie Blake,Joe Jordan(p),Sally Heiss,Steve Spracklen(unknown instr.) on
    some titles.

ARDANELLE (BRECKENBRIDGE)

ARDANELLE TRIO:
Ardanelle Breckenbridge(p,vbs,vcl),Tal Farlow(g),Paul Edenfield(b).
                                             NYC.July 12,1945

Gold Braid	Audiophile AP32
Oh!What A Beautiful Morning	-
C-Jam Blues	-

Note:The above titles are from World Transcriptions.

Same.   NYC.July 24,1945

The Man I Love	Audiophile AP32
It Had To Be You	-
The Very Thought Of You	-
Light Up	-
There's A Small Hotel	-
My Heart Stood Still	-
Tabu	-

Note:The above titles are from World Transcriptions.

Same.	NYC.July 31,1945	
Sophisticated Lady	Audiophile AP32	
Where Or When	-	
Absinthe	-	
These Foolish Things	-	

Note:The above titles are from World Transcriptions.

Dardanelle Breckenbridge(p,vbs,vcl),Joe Sinacore(g),Bert Nazer(dr).
NYC.August 12,1946

Boogie In Bee	Victor 20-1959	
After You Get What You Want	- ,Stash ST109(?)	
September Song	Victor 20-1993	
When A Woman Loves A Man	-	
As Long As You Think Of Me	Victor 20-2254	
You Gotta Crawl Before You Walk	-	

Dardanelle Breckenbridge(p,vbs,vcl),Bucky Pizzarelli(g),George Duvivier(b),Grady Tate(dr).
NYC.May 3,1978

It Could Happen To You	Stash ST202
That Old Devil Called Love	-
For A Girl	-
Quiet Nights Of Quiet Stars	-
Just The Way You Are	-
You Stepped Out Of A Dream	-
Spring Can Really	
Hang You Up The Most	-
I Concentrate On You	-
Come In From The Rain	-

All titles also on DIW(J)DIW1164.

Phil Bodner(ts),Dardanelle Breckenbridge(p,vcl),Howard Collins(g),George Duvivier(b),Grady
Tate(dr). NYC.c. 1980/81

Where Or When	Stash ST217
Out Of This World	-
The Need To Be	-
Something Cool	-
The Colors Of My Life	-
It's All Right With Me	-
Memphis In June	-
Baby,Baby All The Time	-
It Never Entered My Mind	-
You'll Never Fall In Love Again	-

Dardanelle Breckenbridge(p,vbs,vcl),George Duvivier(b),John Basile(dr).
NYC. 1980/81

Taking A Chance On Love	Audiophile AP145
Look At Me	-
I Can't Face The Music	
(Without Singing The Blues)	-
The Wine Of May	-
When A Woman Loves A man	-
Make The Man Love Me	-
Old Guitaron	-
Over The Rainbow	-
Lover Come Back To Me	-

JOE DARENSBOURG
(section cont. next page).

JOE DARENSBOURG AND HIS FLAT OUT FIVE:
Details unknown.   Unknown location.c. 1951
      Hot Rod Cowboy   Colossal 1002
      Hot Rod Harry   -
      Saturday Night Drag Race,pt.1 Colossal 1003
      Saturday Night Drag Race,pt.2   -

JOE DARENSBOURG AND HIS DIXIE FLYERS:
Mike Delay(tp),Warren Smith(tb),Joe Darensbourg(cl,vcl),Harvey Brooks(p,celeste),William
Newman(bj,g),Al Morgan(b),George Vann(dr,vcl).
                                          Live."The Lark",LA. 1957
      Bourbon Street Parade   Red Stick RSLP5080
      Blues For Al   -
      Royal Garden Blues   -
      Savoy Blues   -
      Huggin' And Kissin'   -
      Four Or Five Times   -
      Sassy Gal   -
      Go Back Where You
         Stayed Last Night   -
      Milenberg Joys   -
      Just A Closer Walk With Thee   -

same.   LA. 1957/58
      Yellow Dog Blues   Lark 452,LP331,Vogue(E)V2409,(F)45-580
      Martinique   -   -   -   -
      Rockin' In Dixie   Lark 456, -
      Just A Little Time To Stay Here Lark LP331
      How Long Blues   -
      That Da-Da Strain   -
      When My Dream Boat Comes Home -
      Dixie Flyers March   -
      Careless Love   -
      Copenhagen   -
      Winin' Boy Blues   -
      Sweet Georgia Brown   -

11 titles on LP331 also on Dixieland Jubilee DJ514,Vogue(E)LAE12149,LDM30083,Quality
-1612.

same.   LA. 1958
      Stumblin'   Lark 453,Vogue(F)45-481,Dixieland Jubilee DJ515
      Lou-I-Si-An-I-A(jd)   -   -   -
      Four Or Five Times   Lark 454,Dixieland Jubilee DJ515
      Go Back Where You
         Stayed Last Night   -
      Snag It   Lark 455,Dixieland Jubilee DJ515
      Sassy Gal   -
      Huggin' And Kissin'   Lark 456
      Stardust   Lark ???,Dixieland Jubilee DJ515
      Petite Fleur   Dixieland Jubilee DJ515
      Over The Waves   -
      Sleepy Time Gal   -
      Lazy River   -
      Chimes Blues   -

Note:Newman poss. omitted on some titles.

Louis Diamond(dr) replaces Vann.   LA. 1960
      St. Louis Blues   Lark EP1451,Dixieland Jubilee DJ515
      Beale Street Blues   -   -
      Careless Love   -

Ernie Carson(cnt),Charlie Bornemann(tb),Joe Darensbourg(cl),Ralph Goodwin(p),Bill Rutan
(bj),Shorty Johnson(tu),Joe O'Neal(dr).   Unknown location.c. 1971/72
    Yellow Dog Blues   G.H.B. GHB90
    They're Diggin' Willie's Grave   -
    Cake Walkin' Babies   -
    Lou-Easy-An-I-A   -
    Blues My Naughty
       Sweetie Gives To Me   -
    Floating Down
       That Old Green River   -
    Just A Little While To Stay Here   -
    Winin' Boy Blues   -
    Meet Me Tonight In Dreamland   -

Pat Halcox(tp),Tom Hurst -1,Chris Barber -2(tb),Joe Darensbourg(cl,vcl),Richard Simmons(p)
Terry Knight(b),Dave Evans(dr).   Basingstoke,Hampshire,England.August 24,1974
    Blues(1)   unissued
    Someday You'll Be Sorry(1)
    Lou-Easy-An-I-A(1)(jd)
    Rose Room(2)
    Ballin' The Jack(2)(jd)
    All Of Me(2)
    Blues(1,2)
    Sweet Georgia Brown(no tp)
    Lady Be Good(no tp)

No details.   Live.Pismo Beach. 1980
    Sweet Georgia Brown   Clambake 6-218

DARKTOWN ALL STARS (Danish)

Per Reck(tp,vcl),Thorlai Ishøy(tb),Uwe Jankowski(ss),Knud Fryland(bj),Finn Schmidt(b),Leo
Jensen(dr).   Haderslev,Denmark.February 11,1968
    When My Baby Smiles At Me   CSA(D)CEP 101
    I'm Gonna Sit Right Down   -
    I'm In The Jailhouse Now   -
    Shine   -

DARKTOWN DIXIECATS (Italian)

Antonio Cavazzuti(tp),Nick Muti(tb),Giordano Fontana(cl),Nino Zamboni(p),Pietro Barenghi
(g),Ciccio Pentangelo(tu),Claudio Gambarelli(dr).
                     Milan,Italy.April 1952
    At The Jazz Band Ball   Durium(I)J9967
    At The Darktown Strutters' Ball   -
    Dixie My Dear   Durium(I)J9968
    High Society   -

DARKTOWN JAZZ BAND (Dutch)

Dick Douma(tp),Max Rodrigues Nunes(tb),Henk van Deijk(cl,ts),Daan van Golberdinge(p),Thom
van Eck(g),Jan Beset(bj,g),Jan van Dam(b),Gerry Schoen(dr).
                     Amsterdam,The Netherlands.July 14,1960
(session cont. next page).

DARKTOWN JAZZ BAND (Dutch)

(session cont. from previous page):
TN2B5244 Ich Bin Nur
        Ein Armer Wandergesell   Tivoli(Du)42096,43015
TN2B5245 Blume von Hawai(1)   -   -
TN2B5246 Bei Mir Bist Du Schön   Tivoli(Du)42097,   -
TN2B5247 Till We Meet Again(2)   -   -

-1.Omit van Eck.
-2.Omit Beset.

HENK VAN DEIJK AND HIS DARKTOWN JAZZ BAND:
Henk Oet(p),Jack Koomans(dr) replace Golberdinge,Schoen;omit Best(bj,g);add Milly Scott,
Franci Queen(vcl).   Amsterdam,The Netherlands.September 20,1961
TN2C5437 South Of The Border(ms)   Tivoli(Du)42172
TN2C5438 Johnny Will You Be Mine(ms)   -
TN2C5439 Hush-a-bye My Baby(fq)   Tivoli(Du)42173
TN2C5440 It's A Sin To Tell A Lie(ms)   -

DARKTOWN JAZZ BAND (German)

Wolfgang Trattner(tp),Dieter Riempp(tb),Karl-Heinz Höllering(cl),Werner Lener(p),Ludwig
Stimmler(b),Elmar Wippler(dr).   Live.Düsseldorf,Germany.October 4/5,1963
     Dark Eyes   Capitol(G)C83556

Klaus Bühler(b) replaces Stimmler.   Stuttgart,Germany.December 7,1963
     Royal Garden Blues   Lyodon 071263

Siegfried Seyffer(cl),Ludwig Stimmler(b) replace Höllering,Bühler.
                       Ludwigsburg,Germany.July 17,1974
     Dixieland Medley: Darktown Jazz(G)SP1/74
        Original Dixieland One-Step
        I've Found A New Baby
     The Entertainer   - ,Intercord(G)26606,145.000
     Moten Swing   -
     West End Blues   -
     Pretty Little Missie   -
     Mississippi Rag   - ,Intercord(G)26606,145.000
     Medley: -
        Georgia On My Mind
        Willow Weep For Me
        Basin Street Blues
     High Society   -
     Rosetta   -
     Royal Garden Blues   -

Add Fatty George(cl).   Ludwigsburg,Germany.April 20,1975
     My Bucket's Got A Hole In It Intercord(G)26606,145.000,155.032,155.057
     You Should Come With Me(1)   -   -

-1.Fatty George(cl),p,b,dr only.

Omit Fatty George.   Live.Stuttgart,Germany.April 24,1975
     Alabama Jubilee   Intercord(G)26566,130.002
     Tin Roof Blues   -   -

Oscar Klein(tp,g) replaces Trattner.   Ludwigsburg,Germany.May 31,1975
     I Want A Little Girl   Intercord(G)26606
     Struttin' With Some Barbecue   -
     Alexander's
        Ragtime Band(tp,p only)   -

Wolfgang Trattner(tp),Charly Antolini(dr) replace Klein,Wippler.
                                Ludwigsburg,Germany.July 12,1975
        Sweet Georgia Brown   Intercord(G)26606,155.057
        Cute   -

Jimmy McPartland(cnt,vcl),Wolfgang Trattner(tp),Dick Cary(alth),Dieter Riempp(tb),Sieg-
fried Seyffer(cl),Werner Lener(p),Ludwig Stimmler(b),Elmar Wippler(dr).
                                Stuttgart,Germany.November 22,1975
        At The Jazz Band Ball(1)   Intercord(G)26606,155.057
        Baby,Won't You
            Please Come Home(2)   -   -
        I Gotta Right To
            Sing The Blues(jmp)   -

-1.Omit Trattner.
-2.Cary(alth),p,b,dr only.

All titles on Intercord(G)26606 also on Intercord(G)145.000.

Klaus Osterloh(tp,flh,vcl),Joe Gallardo(tb),Charly Höllering(cl),Werner Lener(p),Ludwig
Stimmler(b),Elmar Wippler(dr).   Ludwigsburg,Germany.May 14,1980
        Sellerie   DJB(G)150.001
        Sweet Lorraine   -
        Ory's Creole Trombone   -
        Pretty Little Missy   -
        Medley: -
            Georgia On My Mind
            Stars Fell On Alabama
            Stomping At The Savoy

Same.   Ludwigsburg,Germany.May 15,1980
        South Rampart Street Parade   DJB(G)150.001
        Pennies From Heaven   -
        Chicago   -
        Little Rock Getaway   -

DARKTOWN STOMPERS (German)

Horst Himsel(tp),Bart Bönschen(tb),Teddy Karupkat(cl),Gert Hauk(p),Bonny Schüten(bj),Bis-
mark Simon(b),Heinz Piek(dr).   Live.Frankfurt,Germany.May 21,1954
        Apex Blues   Brunswick(G)LPBM87001

THE DARKTOWN STRUTTERS (New Zealand)

Vendi Matter(tp),Bruce Foster(tb),John Tucker(cl),Ken Avery(cl,ts,vcl),Tommy Duncan(p),
Jack Claridge(b),Bob Waugh(dr).   Wellington,New Zealand. 1953
        At Sundown   Tartar 26

Vendi Matter(tp),Bruce Foster(tb),Vince Gray(ss),Ken Avery(cl,ts,vcl),Julian Russell(p),
Bill Hoffmeister(g),Jim Wilson(b),Franz Jackson(dr).
                                Wellington,New Zealand.March 29,1976
        The Shadow Of Your Smile   Tartar 35

John Tucker(cl),Harry Edgington(p),Jim Wilson(b),Franz Jackson(dr).
                                Wellington,New Zealand. 1980
        We'll Be Together Again   Tartar 26

THE DARKTOWN STRUTTERS (New Zealand)

Vendi Matter(tp),Bruce Foster(tb),John Tucker(cl),Vince Gray(ss),Ken Avery(cl,ts,vcl),
Julian Russell(p),Jim Wilson(b),Franz Jackson(dr).

	Wellington,New Zealand. 1980
Georgia On My Mind	Tartar 26
What's New	-
The Nearness Of You	-

Add Jim Davidson(vbs).

	Wellington,New Zealand. 1980
Someone To Watch Over Me	Tartar 26
In A Sentimental Mood	-
Sweet Lorraine	-
Avalon	-
Satin Doll	-
Rosetta	-
Russian Lullaby	-
Mood Indigo	-
Keepin' Out Of Mischief Now	Tartar 35
On The Street Of Dreams	-
Woodchoppers Ball	-
Tuxedo Junction	-
Stardust	-

Same.

	Tauranga,New Zealand. 1980
It Don't Mean A Thing(ka)	Tartar 26

Note:Additional titles on Tartar 26 and 35 were recorded after 1980.

THE DARKTOWN STRUTTERS (Swiss)

Lukas Burkhart("Cheese Burke")(tp),Balz Fischer(tb),Peter Wyss(cl),Roby Suter(p),Marcel
Magnin(b),Willy Bosshardt(dr).

	Basel,Switzerland.February 6,1950
That's A Plenty	Chant du Monde(Sw)unissued
Morning Mood	
Somebody Stole My Gal	
Darktown Blues	

(BODY BUSER PRESENTS JAZZ AT THE JAVA):

Same.	Basel,Switzerland.February 13,1950
ASB249 Georgia Cake Walk	Chant du Monde(Sw)29137,Max Lussi(Sw)EP485
ASB250 Blues Meets Hermit	- -
ASB251 That's A Plenty	Chant du Monde(Sw)29138
ASB252 Morning Mood	- ,Musica Helvetica(Sw)12/27,
	EMI(Eu)13C.152-33894/95

Wallace Bishop(dr) replaces Bosshardt.

	Basel,Switzerland.April 29,1950
Morning Mood	Chant du Monde(Sw)12138
Mahogany Hall Stomp	unissued
Ballin' The Jack	-

Willy Bosshardt(dr) replaces Bishop.

	Live.Zurich,Switzerland.September 1952
Perdido Street Blues	Elite Special(Sw)9187

Guido Cova(b),Stuff Combe(dr) replace Magnin,Bosshardt.

	Basel,Switzerland. 1957
Papa Dip	HMV(Sw)ZFLP113
Of All The Wrongs You've Done Me	-
Sobbins Blues	-
Clarinet Marmelade	-

(session cont. next page).

(session cont. from previous page):
```
        Kansas City Man Blues         HMV(Sw)ZFLP113
        Somebody Stole My Gal              -
        Queer Dance(cl,p,dr only)         -
        Talkin' With Pee(cl,p,dr only)    -
```

DARKWA'S JAZZ BAND (Danish)

Ove Larsen(cnt),Johnny Rasmussen(tb),Freddy Larsen(cl),Knud Børgesen(bj),Fritz Winther(tu)
Helmuth Nielsen(dr).   Copenhagen.February 27,1960
```
K672   Dr. Jazz                    Metronome(D)B1408
K673   Bourbon Street Parade            -
```

DAVID DARLING

David Darling(cello,el-cello,bells,gong,tymp,vcl).
```
                                    Ludwigsburg,Germany.October  1979
        Slow Return                 ECM(G)1161
        Bells And Gongs                 -
        Far Away Lights                -
        Solo Cello                     -
        Minor Blue                     -
        Clouds                         -
        Solo Cello (2)                 -
        Solo Cello And Voice           -
        Journal October,Stuttgart      -
```

DENVER DARLING

(vcl) acc. by WILD BILL DAVISON AND HIS RANGE RIDERS:
Wild Bill Davison(cnt),unknown cl,p,g,b,dr. NYC.January 25,1946
```
W73308 Deep Delta Blues             Decca 46042
W73309 When I Gets To Where I'm Goin'  Decca 9000
W73310 Silver Dew On The
        Blue Grass Tonight         Decca 9001
W73311 I Wish I Had Never Met Sunshine   -
```

Note:Additional recordings by this artist are not included;the jazz content of the above
     titles may be limited.

HENRYK DARLOWSKI (Polish)

See BOBBY STERN.

BILL DARNELL

See also GEORGIE AULD.

(vcl) acc. by Babe Russin(ts),Tommy Todd(p),Al Hendrickson(g),Jud De Naut(b),Jackie Mills
(dr).   LA.March 8,1946
(session cont. next page).

(session cont. from previous page):
KWC10-5 Let's Fall In Love   Keynote K665
KWC11-3 Walkin' My Baby Back Home   -

Note:See Babe Russin for additional titles from this session.

(vcl) acc. by ALVY WEST'S SEXTET:
John Plonsky(tp),Alvy West(as),Romeo Penque(bars),Bob Caudana(acc),Dick Hyman(p),George
Shaw(b),Irv Kluger(dr).   NYC.July 18,1949
75078 So Much   Coral 60093
75079 Sleeping   Coral 60108
75080 Hoe Cake,Homini And Sassafras   Coral 60093
75081 Everybody Loves My Baby   Coral 60108

Note:Some sources list John Plonsky as a pseudonym for Dizzy Gillespie - this is not the
    case.
    Additional recordings by this artist are not included.

ALICE DARR

(vcl) acc. by Mundell Lowe(g),George Duvivier(b).
                          NYC.May 18,1962
     I Only Know How To Cry   Charlie Parker PLP/PS811
     Yes,He's Gone   -
     Love Does Funny Things   -
     Leave Me Alone   -
     Under This Smile   -
     There He Goes   -
     The Lost And The Lonely   -
     I Can't Find My Way Home   -
     It's A Lovely World   -
     Try, Try Again   -
     Season's Lost Love   -
     You're So Far Away From Me   -

Note:All Titles also on Summit(E)AJS21.

DARTMOUTH INDIAN CHIEFS

Al Shapiro(tp),Larry Elliott(tb),Dave Cook(cl),John Perge(p),Pete Bullis(bj),Barry Backus
(b),Cliff Olds(dr).   Boston(?).March 23,1957
     Begin The Beguine   Transition LP23
     South Rampart Street Parade   -
     The Joyous(?) Advent Of
       The Everything Machine   -
     Last Year Blues   -
     Ol' Man River   -
     Body And Soul   -
     It's All Right With Me   -
     Blues Of The Emperor Jones   -
     I Could Have Danced All Night -
     Barados(?)   -

GARY DARTNELL (Australian)
(section cont. next page).

GARY DARTNELL JAZZ MEN:
Gary Dartnell(cnt),Peter Neubauer(cl),Geoff Gilbert(bj),Terry Fowler(tu),Dick Gillespie
(dr).   Sydney,Australia.November 6,1966
    Algiers Strut   Studio 20 S20-27
    Ay,Ay,Ay   -

JOHN DARVILLE (Danish)

See EDDIE DAVIS.

RUDOLF DASEK (Czech)

See also TOTO BLANKE,JIRI STIVIN.

Rudolf Dasek(g),Vincenc Kummer(b),Lubos Nyvit -1(el-b),Ivan Smazik(dr).
                                       Prague.March 9-16,1970
    Angel Eyes   Supraphon(Cz)0.15.0843/1.15.0843
    It Might As Well Be Spring   -
    Pohadka Pro Beritku
       (Fairy Tale For Beritku)   -
    Fasank II   -
    Bewitched   -
    One,Two,Free   -
    Stella By Starlight   -
    Blue Note   -
    Foukej(1)   -

Jiri Stivin(fl,bcl),Rudolf Dasek(g).   Prague.October 6,1972
    Mezitum (In Between)   Supraphon(Cz)1.115.2533

(g-solo).   Live.Bratislava,Czechoslovakia.December 1976
    Ako Na Dlani   Opus(Cz)9111.0761/62

Tony Scott(cl),Rudolf Dasek(g).   Prague.October 14,1977
    Koda Na Radost   Supraphon(Cz)1.115.2533

Rudolf Dasek(g),Günter Sommer(dr).   Prague.December 9,1977
    Uz Jde   Supraphon(Cz)1.115.2533

Rudolf Dasek,Toto Blanke(g).   Prague.January 18,1978
    Jestli Chces   Supraphon(Cz)1.115.2533

Jiri Stivin(fl,bcl),Rudolf Dasek(g).   Prague.May 29,1978
    Caromlynek   Supraphon(Cz)1.115.2533

Laco Deczi(tp),Rudolf Dasek(g).   Prague.June 5,1978
    Navrat   Supraphon(Cz)1.115.2533

Karel Velebny(vbs),Rudolf Dasek(g).   Prague.June 9,1978
    Toulky   Supraphon(Cz)1.115.2533

Karel Ruzicka(p),Rudolf Dasek(g).   Prague.June 20,1978
    Corrida   Supraphon(Cz)1.115.2533

JULIAN DASH
(section cont. next page).

JULIAN DASH AND HIS ORCHESTRA:
Julian Dash(ts),Billy Kyle(p),Art Ryerson(g),Sid Weiss(b),Bunny Shawker(dr).
NYC.December 12,1950

7132	My Silent Love	Mello-Roll 5001
7133	Creamin'	- ,Coral 65094
7134	Going Along	Mello-Roll 5002 -
7135	Long Moan	-

All titles also on Doctor Jazz FW39519,EPM(F)FDC5008 (CD).

Julian Dash(ts),Haywood Henry(bars),Freddy Jefferson(p),Everett Barksdale(g),Lee Stanfield
(b),Sonny Payne(dr).
NYC.February 7,1951

2285	Coolin' With Dash	Sittin' In With 594
2287	Dashin'In	-
	Preachin'	Sittin' In With 600
	Somebody's Gone	Sittin' In With 645

Leroy Kirkland(g) replaces Barksdale.   NYC.March 17,1951

	Hot Rod	Sittin' In With 600
	For Squares Only	Sittin' In With 614,Riverboat(F)900.267
	Creamin' Boogie	- -
	Open Up Them Pearly Gates	Sittin' In With 645

Ted Donnelly(tb),Bobby Smith(as),Julian Dash(ts),Harwood Henry(bars),Raymond Tunia(p),
Everett Barksdale(g),Lee Stanfield(b),Sonny Payne(dr).
NYC.July 31,1951

2381	Holiday In Cuba,I	Sittin' In With 619
2382	Holiday In Cuba,II	-
	Dance Of The Mother Bird	Sittin' In With 630,Riverboat(F)900.267
	Devil's Lament	- -

Ted Donnelly(tb),Julian Dash,Bobby Greene(ts),Haywood Henry(bars),Freddy Jefferson(p),Lee
Stanfield(b),Sonny Payne(dr),Bob Kornegay ("Texas Bob"),Carmen Taylor(vcl),Sammy Lowe
(arr).
NYC.October 11,1951

4589	Can't You See(bk,ct)	Mercury unissued
4590	Can't Understand It(bk,ct)	Mercury 8255
4591	Blue Velvet	-
4592	Midnight Rock	unissued

Bobby Johnson(tp),Bob Range,Ted Donnelly(tb),Bobby Smith(as),Julian Dash(ts),Haywood Henry
(bars),Freddy Jefferson(p),Lee Stanfield(b),Sonny Payne(dr),Carmen Taylor(vcl).
NYC.November 15,1951

4615	It's All Over Again(ct)	Mercury 8262
4616	Cry(ct)	-

Note:The above titles issued as by Carmen Taylor.

Omit Donnelly,Taylor.   NYC.January 11,1952

When You Surrender	Mercury unissued
Why Come To Me,Sad Lover	
Unknown title	
Unknown title	

Henry Coker,Bob Range(tb),Julian Dash(ts),Haywood Henry,Charlie Fowlkes(bars),Freddy Jef-
ferson(p),Lee Stanfield(b),Sonny Payne(dr). NYC.January 7,1953

9440	Burnin'	Mercury unissued
9441	Fire Water	Mercury 70087
9442	Deacon Dash	-
9443	Alabama Mambo	unissued

Julian Dash(ts),Hank Marr(p),Warren E. Stephens(g),Lee Stanfield(b),Bill English(dr).
                                        Chicago.August 13,1954
54-175 Dash Is It   Vee-Jay unissued
54-176 So Let It Be   Vee-Jay 117,Top Rank(F)RLP-110
54-177 Zig Zag   -   -
54-178 Mambo   unissued

Julian Dash(ts),Raymond Tunia(p),Jimmy Oliver(g),Lee Stanfield(b),Bill English(dr).
                                        Chicago.June 22,1955
55-278 Zero   Vee-Jay 144,Top Rank(F)RLP110
55-279 Rhythm Punch   -   -
55-280 Ballad   unissued
55-281 Mambo No.2   -

Julian Dash(ts),Cliff Smalls(p),Jimmy Shirley(g),Milt Hinton(b),George Foster(dr).
                                        NYC.May 9,1970
        Tuxedo Junction   Master Jazz Recordings MJR8106
        Willow Weep For Me   -
        Take The "A" Train   -
        Honeysuckle Rose   unissued
        Julian's Dash (I Got Rhythm) Master Jazz Recordings MJR8106
        Two Shades Of Blue(ts,g only)   -
        Don't Blame Me(ts,b only)   -

Note:See CLIFF SMALLS for additional titles - without Dash - from this session.

THE DATSUN DIXIELANDERS (Australian)

Keith Hounslow(cnt),Mal Wilkinson(tb),Denis Ball(cl),Geoff Bland(p),John Bergin(bj),Robin
McCulloch(b,vcl),John Halliday(dr).   Melbourne.June 1977
        Darktown Strutters' Ball   Jazznote(Au)JNLP017

Keith Hounslow(cnt),Harry Price(tb),Gavan Gow(cl,as),Frank Gow(p),John Bergin(bj,g),Robin
McCulloch(b)/Alan Stott(tu),John Fordham/John Halliday(dr).
                                        Melbourne.June 1977
        I Saw Stars   Jazznote(Au)JNLP017
        Bourbon Street Parade(no p)   -
        Nobody's Sweetheart   -
        Li'l Darlin'   -
        Avalon(no p)   -

Keith Hounslow -1(cnt,flh),Mal Wilkinson -1(tb),Denis Ball(cl),Alan Lee(vbs,g),Tony Gould
(p),Robin McCulloch(b),John Fordham(dr).   Melbourne.June 1977
        Love Me Or Leave Me(no g)   Jazznote(Au)JNLP017
        Memories Of You(no g)   -
        Basin Street Blues(1)(no vbs)   -
        Blues For Rex(1)(cnt,p only)   -
        Fluff Stuff(1)(flh,p only)   -

CARLO ACTIS DATO (Italian)

See ART STUDIO.

JACK DAUGHERTY
(section cont. next page).

Incl. Jim Horn(fl),Milt Jackson(vbs),Jack Daugherty(p,arr),Ray Brown(b),Hal Blaine,Jim
Keltner(dr),strings.   LA. 1970's

Theme For Susan	A&M SP3038	
You Got It	-	
Getting Up	-	
Someone To Love	-	
Feel So Good	-	
The Day We Met	-	
Brothers And Sisters	-	
Number Nine	-	
The Strip	-	
La Costa Drive	-	

Chuck Findley,Bobby Findley,Ron Gorow(tp,flh),Dick Hyde,Dave Dahlsten(tb),Don Switzer
(btb),Ron Starr(as,ts,vln),Tom Scott(ts,lyricon),Gary Herbig(ts,fl),David Luell(bars),Jack
Daugherty(keyb),Lennie Coltun(g),Dan Dean(b),Michael Buono(dr),Bill Berg,Marc Ross(perc).
                                        LA.c. 1976

When's It Gonna Hit	Monterey MS100	
Carmello	-	
Solo Flight	-	
You And I	-	
Wild Turkey	-	
Cleared For Take-Off	-	
Rsing Star	-	
King Pong	-	
Lush Life	-	

Note:The jazz content of the above recordings may be limited.

WOLFGANG DAUNER (German)

ee also GERMAN ALL STARS,JAZZ STUDIO,MARTIN KOLBE,HANS KOLLER.

oki Freund(as,ss),Wolfgang Dauner(p),Eberhard Weber(b),Charly Antolini(dr).
                                        Villingen,Germany.April 2,1964

Take The "A" Train	Saba(G)SB15035	
Waltz Limp	-	
Waltz For A Young Girl		
Take The Coltrane	-	,MPS(G)10.20844

olfgang Dauner(p),Everhard Weber(b),Fred Braceful(dr).
                                        September 14,1964

Dream Talk	CBS(G)BPG62478	
Bird Food	-	
A Long Night	-	
Dämmerung	-	
Zehn Notitzen	-	
Soul Eyes	-	
Free Fall	-	,L+R(G)40.012
Yesterdays	-	

ll titles also on L+R(G)LR41.004.

erd Dudek(ts,cl),Jean Luc-Ponty(vln),Wolfgang Dauner(p),Eberhard Weber(cello),Jürgen Karg
),Fred Braceful(dr),Mani Neumeier(dr,tabla).
                                        Villingen,Germany.May 2,1967

session cont. next page).

(session cont. from previous page):
```
      Sketch Up And Downer        Saba/MPS(G)15095
      Disguise                          -
      Free Action Shot                  -
      My Spanish Disguise               -
      Collage                           -
```

All titles also on MPS(G)21.20624,(F)15017,(J)ULS1717,YS2401.

WOLFGANG DAUNER SEXTET:
Manfred Schoof(tp),Gerd Dudek(ts),Wolfgang Dauner(org,melodica),Eberhard Weber(cello),Jür-
gen Karg(b),Fred Braceful(dr),Kantorei am St. Martin in Kassel,Klaus Martin Ziegler(cond)
                                        Live.Berlin.November 10,1968
```
      Psalmus Spei For
         Choir And Jazz Group       MPS(G)15205,21.20681
```

WOLFGANG DAUNER QUARTET/TRIO:
Wolfgang Dauner(p,prep.-p,synth,org,melodica,tb,perc,vcl etc.),Eberhard Weber(cello,b,vcl
Jürgen Karg(b,säge,vcl),Fred Braceful(dr,perc,vcl).
                                        Villingen,Germany.April 3/29,1969
```
      Über Musik                   Calig(G)CAL30603
      Voices                            -
      Arco                              -
      Blues                             -
      Karg                              -
      Pamukkale                         -
      4'38"                             -
      Beat                              -
      Opus 5                            -
      Bemerkung                         -
      Gespräch                          -
      Tape Two                          -
      ABC                               -
      Braceful                          -
```

WOLFGANG DAUNER QUINTET:
Wolfgang Dauner(p,org,vcl),Pierre Cavalli(g),Siegfried Schwab(g,sitar),Eberhard Weber
(cello,b,vcl),Roland Wittich(dr,vcl).   Villingen,Germany.February 1970
```
      Oh,Baby I Don't
         Love You Anymore          MPS(G)21.20710
      Take Off Your Clothes
         To Feel The Setting Sun        -
      My Man's Gone Now                 -
      Come On In,On In                  -
      Dig My Girl                       -
      Greensleeves                      -
      Uwiii                             -
      A Day In The Life                 - ,05.10855,HGBS(G)11.000
      Sun Is Rising(1)             MPS(G)05.10855
```

-1.Poss. from the above session.

WOLFGANG DAUNER TRIO:
Wolfgang Dauner(p),Eberhard Weber(b),Roland Wittich(dr).
                                        Villingen,Germany.February 1970
```
      Leap Tick                    MPS(G)21.20729
      The Things We Did Last Summer     -
      Diäthylaminoäthyl                 -
      Es Läuft                          -
      Here Come De Honey Man            -
```
(session cont. next page).

(session cont. from previous page):
```
      Blue Light                  MPS(G)21.20729,25.20842
      Golden Green                -
```

All titles also on MPS(J)ULX65.

Wolfgang Dauner(p,ringmodulator,clavinet),Eberhard Weber(b,cello,g),Fred Braceful(d,perc,
voice).   Ludwigsburg.September 15/October 1,1970
```
      Mutations                   ECM(G)1006
      Output                      -
      Bruch                       -
      Nothing To Declare          -
      Abraxas                     -
      Brazing The High Sky Full   -
```

All titles also on ECM(J)P8113.

WOLFGANG DAUNER QUINTET:
Wolfgang Dauner(p,el-p),Siegfried Schwab(g),Eberhard Weber(cello,b),Roland Wittich,Fred
Braceful(dr,perc).   Unknown location.December 1970
```
      Thursday Morning Sunrise    Global(G)630.6901
      Lady Blue                   -
      Melodrama To A Raga         -
      Milkstreets                 -
```

ET CETERA:
Wolfgang Dauner(keyb,synth,vcl),Larry Coryell(g,vcl),Günter Lenz(b,vcl),Jon Hiseman,Fred
Braceful(d,perc,vcl),Richard Ketterer(sounds,voice).
                                 Villingen(?),Germany.March 1972
```
      The Really Great Escape     MPS(G)21.21432,10.21688,HGBS(G)11.000
      Sun                         -
      Yan(!)                      -
      Tuning Spread               -
      Yin                         -
```

11 titles also on HGBS(G)15.356.

ET CETERA:
Wolfgang Dauner(p,el-p,clavinet,synth),Jürgen Schmidt-Öhm(vln,fl),Matthias Thurow(b,sitar)
Zala Kovacev,Fred Braceful(dr).   Live.Sielmingen,Ludwigsburg,Germany.May 1973
```
      Twelve And Nine             MPS(G)29.21754
      Introduction                -
      Es Soll Ein Stück Von Willi Sein   -
      Plumcoke                    -
      G x 3 And Blues             -
      The Love That
          Cannot Speak It's Name  -
      Nemo's Dream                -
```

11 titles also on MPS(G)88020.

Hans Koller(ss,ts),Wolfgang Dauner(p,el-p,synth,etc.),Zbigniew Seifert(vln,as),Adelhard
Roidinger(b,el-b),Janusz Stefanski(dr).   Ludwigsburg,Germany.January 21-23,1974
```
      Kunstkopfindianer           MPS(G)21.22019
      Suomi                       -
      Nom                         -
      Ulla M & 22/8               -
      Adea                        -
```

Wolfgang Dauner(p,synth,voice).   Frankfurt am Main,Germany.March-September 1978
    Changes   Mood(G)23333
    Für Flo   -
    Changes 2   -
    Stuck Für Piano
        Und Synthesizer   -
    Landscape   -
    Tanz Trans   -

Wolfgang Dauner(p,synth,perc).   Unknown location.c. 1978
    Fahrt Ohne Wiederkehr   Mood(G)23400
    War Was Karl   -
    Intellektuelles Skalpell   -
    Karl On Tour   -
    Pfister   -
    Karl's Song   -
    Die Versteigerung   -
    Nix Nie Weg Karl   -
    Grandison   -

DAVENPORT FIVE (Argentine)

Roberto Cora(tp),Oscar Pandolfi(cl,as),Hector Gutiérrez(bars),Luis Pasquet(p),Alfredo Sil
vera Lima(bj).   Live.Buenos Aires.November 11,1960
    Lila   Opus(Arg)OL7004,OJC20006

DAVENPORT JAZZ BAND

Ed Krenz(cnt),Don Odette(tp,ldr),Wingy Manone(tp),Bill Rank(tb),rest unknown.
        Live.Bix Beiderbecke Memorial Jazz Festival,Davenport,Iowa.August 4/5/6,197
    When You're Smiling   Bix Lives vol.1
    St. Louis Blues   -

Don Odette(tp,ldr),Bill Allred(tb),Jim Valentine(cl),Bill Krenz(p),Gene Mayl(b).
        Live.Bix Beiderbecke Memorial Jazz Festival,Davenport,Iowa.July 26/27/28,197
    Song Of The Wanderer   Bix Lives vol.3
    How Come You Do Me Like You Do(1)   -

-1.Add Wingy Manone(tp),Bill Rank(tb).

Tom Saunders(cnt),Don Odette(tp,ldr),Al Winters(tb),Ronnie Deal(cl),Paul Klinger(ss),Eddi
Metz(p),Rod McDonald(g),Trevor Williams(b),Wes Ralston(dr).
        Live.Bix Beiderbecke Memorial Jazz Festival,Davenport,Iowa.July 27/28/29,197
    Undecided   Bix Lives vol.6
    Louisiana   -

Don Odette(tp,ldr),Rex Allen(tb),Ronnie Deal(cl),Norma Teagarden(p),Jack Sedlachek(b),
Monte Mountjoy(dr).
        Live.Bix Beiderbecke Memorial Jazz Festival,Davenport,Iowa.July 25/26/27,197
    China Boy   Bix Lives vol.9
    Sweet Georgia Brown   -
    Who's Sorry Now   -
    Lover   -

WALLACE DAVENPORT
(session cont. next page).

See also EARL HINES,MANASSAS JAZZ FESTIVAL,NICE ALL STARS,THE WOLVERINES JAZZ BAND.

WALLACE DAVENPORT AND HIS BAND:
Wallace Davenport(tp),Nat Perilliat(ts),Edward Frank(org),Richard Payne(b),Ed Blackwell
(dr),Blanche Thomas(vcl).   New Orleans. 1958
80W-4838 Tippy   Ponchartrain (un-numbered)
80W-4839 This Love Of Mine(bt)   -

Edgar Willis(b) replaces Payne;add David Newman(as).
                                      New Orleans. 1958
     4 unknown titles   Ponchartrain unissued

Wallace Davenport(tp),Herb Gardner(tb),Tom Gwaltney(cl),Art Hodes(p),Eddie Condon(g),Van
Perry(b),Freddie Moore(dr).   Live.Manassas Jazz Festival,Va.December 5,1971
     St. Louis Blues   Fat Cat's Jazz FCJ130

Wallace Davenport(tp,vcl),Walter "Slide" Harris(tb),Herb Hall(cl),John Eaton(p),Van Perry
(b),Freddie Moore(dr),Johnson "Fat Cat" McRee(vcl).
                                      Live.Manassas Jazz Festival,Va.December 6,1971
     Darkness On The Delta   Fat Cat's Jazz FCJ122
     Sugar Babe   -
     Melancholy   -
     Just A Closer Walk With Thee   -
     My Monday Date   -
     Sleepy Time Down South   -
     Someday You'll Be Sorry   -
     Chloe   -
     When The Saints Go Marching In   -
     Doctor Jazz(jmr)   Fat Cat's Jazz FCJ125

All titles on FCJ122 also on G.H.B. GHB146,Storyville(D)SLP512.
Note:See Manassas Jazz Festival for additional titles incl. Davenport.
     FCJ125 issued under McRee's name.

Wallace Davenport(tp,vcl),Louis Nelson(tb),Louis Cottrell(cl),Jeanette Kimball(p),Chester
Jardis(b),Josiah "Cie" Frazier(dr).   New Orleans.September 7,1972
     Way Down Yonder In New Orleans   My Jazz LP133
     Margie   -
     Saint James Infirmary   -
     If I Had My Life To Live Over(wd)   -
     Saint Louis Blues   -
     All Of Me   -
     Down By The Riverside   -
     Who's Sorry Now   My Jazz LP134
     Sheik Of Araby   -
     Is It True What
          They Say About Dixie   -
     Chinatown   -

Wallace Davenport(tp),Bill Allred(tb),Jack Maheu(cl),Claude Hopkins(p),Bill Goodall(b),
Freddie Moore(dr).   Live.Manassas Jazz Festival,Va.December 2,1972
     Bourbon Street Parade   Fat Cat's Jazz FCJ130
     St. Louis Blues   -
     Down By The Riverside   -

Wallace Davenport(tp),Walter "Slide" Harris(tb),Wally Garner(cl),Art Hodes(p),Van Perry
(b),Freddie Moore(dr).   Live.Manassas Jazz Festival,Va.December 2,1972
     Tin Roof Blues   Fat Cat's Jazz FCJ130
     Is It True
          What They Say About Dixie   -

Wallace Davenport(tp),Bill Allred(tb),Jack Maheu(cl),John Eaton(p),Steve Jordan(g),Van
Perry(b),Skip Tomlinson(dr).   Live.Manassas Jazz Festival,Va.December 3,1972
    Who's Sorry Now   Fat Cat's Jazz FCJ130

Note:See Manassas Jazz Festival for additional titles incl. Davenport.

Wallace Davenport(tp),Jim Robinson(tb),Albert Burbank(cl),Lars Edegran(p),James Prevost
(b),Louis Barbarin(dr).   New Orleans.June 5,1973
    Rosetta   My Jazz LP134
    Some Of These Days   -
    What A Friend We Have In Jesus   -

Wallace Davenport(tp,vcl),Scott Hill(tb),Louis Jordan(as),Dini Clark(p),Lloyd Lambert(b),
Albert "June" Gardiner(dr),Aline White(vcl). New Orleans.May 2/22,1974
    Sweet Georgia Brown   My Jazz LP135
    Sugar Babe(wd)   My Jazz EP135,LP135
    Indiana   My Jazz LP135
    Melancholy Blues   -
    Tuxedo Junction   My Jazz EP135,LP135
    Jersey Bounce   My Jazz LP135
    Ain't Misbehavin'   -
    I Shall Not Be Moved(aw,band-vcl)   -

Wallace Davenport,Don Albert(tp),Isaac Edward "Snookum" Russell Jr.(p),Lloyd Lambert(b),
Stanley Williams(dr).   New Orleans.October 7/18,1974
    Up A Lazy River   My Jazz LP138
    Roses Of Picardy   -
    Our Blues   -
    Look Down That Lonesome Road   -
    After You've Gone   -
    He'll Understand
        And Say Well Done   -
    Who's Sorry Now   -

Wallace Davenport(tp,vcl),Waldron "Frog" Joseph(tb),John Defferary(cl,ts),Bob Barton
(p,vcl),Placide Adams(b),Trevor Richards(dr).
                                Ludwigsburg,Germany.March 15/17,1975
    Secret Love   My Jazz LP142
    Bill Bailey   -
    (I'm Afraid) The
        Masquerade Is Over   -
    Bugle Boy March   -
    Dr. Jazz   -
    I Wish I Could Shimmy
        Like My Sister Kate   -
    High Society   -
    Old Rugged Cross   -

WALLACE DAVENPORT AND THE JAZZ GREATS:
Wallace Davenport(tp),Freddie Lonzo(tb),Clarence Ford(ss),Jeanette Kimball(p),Frank Fiel
(b),Ernest Elly(dr).   New Orleans.c. 1977
    Jazz Me Blues   Shalom 643
    I'm Confessin'   -
    Wabash Blues   -
    China Boy   -
    Dixieland One Step   -
    Sweethearts On Parade   -
    I Cried For You   -
    Fidgety Feet   Shalom 2214
    Prelude To A Kiss   -
(session cont. next page).

(session cont. from previous page):
```
        Tin Roof Blues                    Shalom 2214
        That's A Plenty                      -
        I Love You                          -
        I Never Knew (I Could Love
            Anybody Like I'm Loving You)     -
```

Wallace Davenport(tp),Andrzej Czechowski(tb),Rafael Zydron(cl),Jan Boba(p),Teofil Lisiecki
(b),Zdzislaw Gogulski(dr).   Live "Jazz Jamboree",Warsaw.October 1976
```
        Who's Sorry Now              Muza(P)SX1529
        I Can't Give You
            Anything But Love            -
        Blues                            -
```

WALLACE DAVENPORT WITH TED EASTON'S JAZZ BAND:
Wallace Davenport(tp),Bob Wulffers(tp,alth),Henk van Muyen(tb),Sidney Pfeffer(cl,ts),Wim
Reekhuizen -1(p),Pim Hogervorst(bj),Jacques Kingma(b),Ted Easton(dr).
                                        Leiden,The Netherlands.November 4/5,1976
```
        Back Home Again In Indiana      Riff(Du)658.003
        Don't Blame Me(1)                  -
        It's Alright With Me               -
        Harmony Blues                      -
        Lover Come Back To Me              -
        Rose Room                          -
        More Than You Know(1)              -
        When You're Smiling               -
        I'm Confessin' That I Love You     -
```

Wallace Davenport(tp),Lucien Barbarin(tb),Orange(?) Kellin(cl),Edward Franck(p),Lloyd
Lambert(b),June Gardner(dr).   Nice.July 17,1980
```
        Royal Garden Blues          Black & Blue(F)33.172
        Blame It On The Blues              -
        That's A Plenty                    -
        Who's Sorry Now                    -
        Basin Street Blues                 -
        Messin' Around                     -
        Original Dixieland One Step        -
        Sweet Georgia Brown                -
        All Of Me                          -
        Tin Roof Blues                     -
```

All titles also on Black&Blue(F)591.721.

KENNY DAVERN

See also MANASSAS JAZZ FESTIVAL,MUSIC MINUS ONE,SOPRANO SUMMIT,RALPH SUTTON,DICK WELL-
WOOD.

KEN DAVERN AND HIS SALTY DOGS:
Frank Laidlaw(cnt),Steve Knight(tb),Ken Davern(cl),Carl Lunsford(bj),Arnold Hyman(b),Bob
Thompson(dr).   NYC.c. 1958
```
        Tiger Rag                   Elektra EKL7099,Aves(G)156.511
        The Streets Of The City           -
        In The Gloryland                  - ,Aves(G)156.511
        Shake It And Break It             -
        Just A Closer Walk With Thee      - ,Aves(G)156.511
        Willie The Weeper                 -
```
(session cont. next page).

(session cont. from previous page):
      Precious Lord   Elektra EKL7099
      The Old Rugged Cross   -

All titles also on Elektra EKL201,Columbia(E)33SX1410.
Note:The Columbia(E)33SX1410 sleeve gives rec.date as 1961 - this is not possible since
    Elektra EKL7099 was released in August 1958.

KENNY DAVERN - FLIP PHILLIPS QUINTET:
Kenny Davern(ss,C-mels),Flip Phillips(ts,ss,bcl),Dave McKenna(p),George Duvivier(b),Bobby
Rosengarden(dr).   NYC.October 23,1977
      Elsa's Dream   Chiaroscuro CR199
      Sweet Lorraine   -
      Mood Indigo   -
      If Dreams Come True   -
      Just Squeeze Me   -
      Candy   -
      Cottontail   -

KENNY DAVERN QUARTET:
Kenny Davern(cl,ss),Steve Lacy(ss),Steve Swallow(el-b),Paul Motian(perc).
                               NYC.May 30,1978
      Swirls   Kharma PK7
      Trio 3   -
      The Sunflower   -
      Predicament In Three Parts   -
      Synonym   -
      Statement   -
      Loops   -
      Unexpected   -

Kenny Davern(cl),Riccardo Zegna(p),Luciano Milanese(b),Roberto Gargani(dr).
                  Live."Louisiana Jazz Club",Genova,Italy.May 10,197
      Sweet Georgia Brown   FDC(I)FDC3002

Kenny Davern(cl),Art Hodes(p),Don DeMichael(dr).
                  Live.St. John's University,Annapolis.Md.,July 1,197
      Fidgety Feet   Monmouth/Evergreen MES7091
      Chimes Blues   -
      Shim-Me-Sha-Wabble   -
      Liberty Inn Drag   -
      Some Of These Days   -
      Ballin' The Jack   -
      See See Rider   -
      It Don't Mean A Thing   -
      Tennessee Waltz   -
      My Blue Heaven   -

KENNY DAVERN AND THE TOMAS ÖRNBERG BAND:
Bent Persson(tp,arr),Kenny Davern(cl),Tomas Örnberg(as),Ulf Lindberg(p),Holger Gross(bj)
Bo Juhlin(tu).   Järfälla,Sweden.June 7,1980
      El Rado Scuffle   Kenneth(Sd)KS2050
      Apex Blues   -
      You Rascal You   -
      Tight Like That   -
      My Monday Date   -
      My Daddy Rocks Me   -
      Shine   -
      Oh Sister, Ain't That Hot   -
      Trouble In Mind   -
      A Porter's Love Song   -
      Blues My Naughty Sweetie Gives -

GARY DAVID

See OLIVER NELSON.

MERLE DAVID

Merle David(vln),John Case(el-p),Jerry Case(el-b),Ron Thayer(dr).
                                    Fort Worth,Texas.November 29,1980
     Jumping With Symphony Sid   Priority PRS409
     Caravan   -
     Don't Take Your Love From me   -
     Undecided   -
     How High The Moon   -
     There Will Never Be Another You   -
     Misty   -
     Elevation   -

RUSS DAVID

Russ David(p),unknown b,dr.   LA.August 20/21,1951
L6357 Echoes Of Harlem   Decca DL5369
L6358 Prelude To A Kiss   -
L6359 Rockin' In Rhythm   -
L6360 Caravan   -
L6361 Don't Get Around Much Anymore   -
L6362 Sophisticated Lady   -
L6363 It Don't Mean A Thing   -
L6364 I Got It Bad
     (And That Ain't Good)   -

All titles also on Brunswick(E)LA8568.
Note:The jazz content of the above recording may be limited.

JAMES "TRUMP" DAVIDSON (Canadian)

Trump Davidson(cnt,vcl),Murray Ginsberg(tb),Jack Wachter(tb),Harvey Silver(p),Sam Levine
(b),Reef McGarvey(dr).   Toronto. 1961
     Maple Leaf Rag   Chateau(Ca)CLP1009
     Ace In The Hole(td)   -
     Ballin' The Jack   -
     Fidgety Feet   -
     Wise Guys(td)   -
     Storyville Blues   -
     My Best Girl(td)   -
     Georgia Camp Meeting   -
     When My Sugar
       Walks Down The Street   -
     Nobody Knows You When
       You're Down And Out(td)   -
     South   -
     Hoghead Shout   -

Same.   Toronto. 1962
(session cont. next page).

(session cont. from previous page):
```
        Theme                           Canadian Broadcasting Corp. RM84
        At The Jazz Band Ball                             -
        Tin Roof Blues                                    -
        I Love You Canada(td)                             -
        When The Saints Go Marching In                    -
        Storyville Blues                                  -
        Midnight In Moscow                                -
        Creole Rag                                        -
        Theme                                             -
```

JIMMY TRUMP DAVIDSON AND HIS DIXIELAND BAND:
Add Teddy Davidson(sax).   Toronto.April 16,1963
```
        South                       Canadian Talent Library M1021/S5021
        Oh Didn't He Ramble                               -
        Medley No.1:                                      -
            Rose Of Washington Square
            Yes Sir, That's My Baby(1)
            Sweet Georgia Brown(1)
        12th Street Rag(1)                                -
        Memphis Blues(td)                                 -
        When My Sugar
            Walks Down The Street                         -
        Fidgety Feet                                      -
        Wang Wang Blues                                   -
        Medley No.2:                                      -
            My Honey's Lovin' Arms
            Five Foot Two(1)
            Runnin' Wild(1)
        Black And Blue                                    -
        When Ragtime Alex Plays
            The Humoresque(1)(td)                         -
        Copenhagen                                        -
```

-1.Alex Read(p) replaces Silver.

Same;omit Teddy Davidson.   Toronto,October 31,1963
```
        The Dixieland Band(td)      Canadian Broadcasting Corp. RM109
        At The Jazz Band Ball                             -
        Nobody Knows You When
        .  You're Down And Out(td)                        -
        Clarinet Marmalade                                -
        Storyville Blues                                  -
        Jazz Me Blues                                     -
        Someday(td)                                       -
        Ballin' The Jack                                  -
        Way Down Yonder In New Orleans                    -
```

Trump Davidson(cnt,vcl),Bob Livingston(tb),Cliff McKay(cl,as),Teddy Davidson(ts),Harvey
Silver(p),Al Harris(g),Joe Niosi(b,tu),Reef McGarvey(dr)
```
                                            Toronto.  1969
        I Found You Out(td)         Sounds Canada SC7702
        Black And Blue                                    -
        Nobody Knows(td)                                  -
        Southern Comfort                                  -
        Travellin'(td)                                    -
        Torch(td)                                         -
        A Hundred Years From Today(td)                    -
        That's A Plenty                                   -
        Monday Date(td)                                   -
        Dead Man's Blues                                  -
        Step To The Rear(td)                              -
```

TRUMP DAVIDSON BAND (ORIGINAL TORONTO DIXIELAND BAND):
Trump Davidson(cnt),Bob Livingston(tb),Cliff McKay(cl),Teddy Davidson(ts),Harvey Silver
(p),Kenny Gill(g),Bill Turner(b),Reef McGarvey(dr).

	Toronto.September 1971
Maxwell's Silver Hammer	Canadian Broadcasting Corp. LM156
Wolverine Blues	-

LOWELL DAVIDSON TRIO

LOWELL DAVIDSON TRIO:
Lowell Davidson(p),Gary Peacock(b),Milford Graves(dr).

	NYC.Prob. June 12,1965	
"L"	ESP 1012,1012(CD)	
Stately I	-	-
Dunce	-	-
Ad Hoc	-	-
Strong Tears	-	-

Note:The sleeve notes list rec.date July 27,1965.

ALAN DAVIE (British)

See also TONY OXLEY.

Alan Davie(p),Frank Perry(perc).

	London(?). 1971
Suite For Piano And Mini-drums	ADMW(E)2

Ray Warleigh(reeds),Eddie Harvey(tb,vbs),Alan Davie(p,cl,sopranino-
sax,as,glockenspiel,xyl),Chris Laurence(b),Alan Jackson(perc).

	London(?). 1971
Unknown titles	ADMW(E)3

DENNIS RUSSELL DAVIES

Dennis Russell Davies(p-solo).

	Ludwigsburg,Germany.June 1977
Ritual,pt.1	ECM(G)1112
Ritual,pt.2	-

HUGH DAVIES (British)

See MUSIC IMPROVISATION COMPANY.

Hugh Davies(var. selfmade instruments).

	Berlin.March 3,1979
Spring Song	FMP(G)SAJ36
Salad	-

Same.

	Utrecht,The Netherlands.March 30,1979
Music For Bowed Diaphragms	FMP(G)SAJ36
Shozyg Sequence No.1	-

CARMELO DAVILA (Chilean)

(section cont. next page).

Tito Rodriguez(cnt),Angel Valdes(tb),Carmelo Davila(cl),Rafael Translavinia(p),Cabrera(g),
Ravello(b),Luis Cordova(dr).   Santiago.February 2,1949
      At The Darktown Strutters' Ball Victor(Chilean)unknown no.
      Farewell Blues   -

SIDNEY DAVILA

SID DAVILA QUINTET:
Tony Dalmado(tp),Charlie Harris(tb),Sidney Davila(cl),Ray Rossi(p),Tony Greco(b),Russ
Johnson(dr).   New Orleans(?).May 17,1950
      Hindustan   Robin Hood unissued(?)
      Milenburg Joys
      Canal Street Blues
      Stump Jump Rag

ANTHONY DAVIS

(p-solo).   Milan,Italy.June 7,1978
      Locomotif N1   Red Record(I)VPA134
      Of Blues And Dreams   -
      On An Azure Plane   -
      Crepuscule - A Suite For Monk: -
         Evidence
         Epistrophy
         Crepuscule With Nellie
      Past Lives   -

Jay Hoggard(vbs),Anthony Davis(p),Mark Helias(b),Ed Blackwell(dr).
                                        NYC.July 1978
      Behind The Rock(p-solo)   India Navigation IN1036
      Song For The Old World   -
      African Ballad   -
      59   -
      An Anthem For The
        Generation That Died   -
      Andrew   -

Leroy Jenkins(vln),Anthony Davis(p),Abdul Wadud(cello),Pheeroan Ak Laff (Paul Maddox)(dr).
                                        Toronto.July 30/31,1978
      Of Blues And Dreams(p-solo)   Sackville(Ca)3020
      Lethe   -
      Graef   -
      Madame Xola   -
      Estraven   -

ANTHONY DAVIS - JAMES NEWTON:
James Newton(fl),Anthony Davis(p).   Live."B.I.M Huis",Amsterdam.November 27,1978
      Pax   Moers Music(G)01048
      Crystal Texts   -
      Wayang No.1   -
      Someone Inside Her   -

ANTHONY DAVIS - JAMES NEWTON:
George Lewis(tb),James Newton(fl),Anthony Davis(p),Rick Rozie(b),Pheeroan Ak Laff(dr).
                                        NYC.March 1979
(session cont. next page).

(session cont. from previous page):
```
      Forever Charles                India Navigation IN1041,Franklin Mint 76
      Hocket In The Pocket(no tb)                    -
      Past Lives(no tb)                              -
      Crystal Texts Set One,
          Pre A-Reflexion                            -
      Sudden Death                                   -
```

George Lewis(tb),J.D. Parran(cl,bcl,fl),Anthony Davis(p),Abdul Wadud(cello),Rick Rozie(b),
Pheeroan Ak Laff(dr).   NYC.Poss. c. 1980
```
      Variations In Dream-Time        India Navigation IN1056
      Enemy Of Light:                                -
          1.Drones And Clones
          2.Romantic Interlude
          3.Fugitive Of Time
```

(p-solo).   NYC. 1980
```
      Beyond Reason                   India Navigation IN1047
      Lady Of The Mirrors                            -
      Five Moods From An English Garden
          (For Vasily Kandinsky)                     -
      Under The Double Moon (Wayang IV)              -
      Man On A Turqoise Cloud
          (For Edward Kennedy Ellington)             -
```

All titles also on India Navigation IN1047 (CD).

ANTHONY DAVIS - JAY HOGGARD:
Jay Hoggard(vbs),Anthony Davis(p).   Villingen,Germany.September 1/2,1980
```
      A Walk Throught The Shadow      MPS(G)68267
      Ujamaa:                                        -
          Spirit Of The Ancestors
          Perserverance
          Uhuru Ni Kazi
      FMW (For My Wife)                              -
      The Clothed Woman                             -
      Under The Double
          Moon (Wayang No.4)                         -
      Toe Dance For A Baby                           -
```

All titles also on Pausa MPS(G)15562,LP7120.

ART DAVIS

Hilton Ruiz(p),Art Davis(b),Greg Bandy(dr). NYC.January 3,1980
```
      Lovin' You                      Interplay IP7728
      I Can't Give You
          Anything But Love                          -
      Art's Boogie                                   -
      The Spirit                                     -
      Add                                            -
```


EN DAVIS JAZZ ENSEMBLE

Greg Hodnett,Bob Oliphant,Backy Bates,Dave Cardwell,Mark Moffatt(tp),Bob Findley,Jon Stout
Joe Meyers,Donna Akers,John Garrison(tb),Susan Burkes(frh),Jenni Francis(fl),Sherre Jones,
Greg Laib,Jim Sisil,Dan Ball,Bill Blackwood(sax),Steve Garland(p(?)),Gary Frownfelter(b),
Rick Overman(dr),Paula Fulton(vbs),Donald J. Dudine(cond).

(session cont. from previous page):

	Unknown location.c. 1973
Dancing Man	Custom Fidelity CFS3194
Flapjacks And Maple Syrup	-
Rock Odyssey	-
Dark Orchid	-
Somewhere	-
Channel One Suite	-
God Save The Queen	-

(WILD) BILL DAVIS

See also EDDIE DAVIS,AL GREY,JOHNNY HODGES,ILLINOIS JACQUET,GLORIA LYNNE,CHARLIE SHAVERS,
BUDDY TATE.

(org-solo).   NYC. 1949
2715   Payday   Mercury unissued
2716   Old Troubles Got Me   -
2717   Yes,You Know I Love You   Mercury 8136
2718   Oobie Yoobie Boogie   -

BILL DAVIS AND HIS REAL GONE ORGAN:
Wild Bill Davis(org),Duke Ellington(p),John Collins(g),Jo Jones(dr).
                                         NYC.October 1950
M4023 Things Ain't What
           They Used To Be   Mercer 1955,Vogue(F)LD497
M4024 Make No Mistake(no p)   -

Both titles also on Mercer LP1002,Vogue(E)V9008,(F)LD012,DP19,Jazz Selection(F)JS664.
Note:Some issues as DUKE ELLINGTON - WILD BILL DAVIS.

BILL DAVIS TRIO:
Wild Bill Davis(org,vcl),Bill Jennings(g,vcl),Chris Columbus(dr).
                                         NYC.June 14,1951
CO46387 Eyesight To The Blind(wbd)   Okeh 6808,4-6808
CO46388 Chicken Gumbo(wbd,band-vcl) Okeh 6836,4-6836,Epic LN3118
CO46389 Hi Diddle Diddle(wbd)   -   -
CO46390 Catch 'Em Young,Treat 'Em Rough,
           Tell Them Nothing(wbg,bj) Okeh 6808,4-6808

Same   NYC.December 20,1951
CO47589 Piccadilly Circus   Okeh 6879,4-6879,Epic EG7010,LG1004
CO47590 Azure Te   Okeh 6867,4-6867,Epic EG37315,LG1004,LN3308
CO47591 Turn Back(1)(tfl)   Okeh 6860
CO47592 Tired Of Loving You(1)(tfl)   -

-1.Add The Four Lads(vcl) - issued as THE FOUR LADS WITH THE BILL DAVIS TRIO.

Note:Masters CO47589, CO47591 and CO47592 dated February 28,1951 in CBS files.
     Master CO47590 dated February 20,1951 in CBS files.

Same.   NYC.February 4,1952
CO47654 Each Time(1)(dh,tfl)   Okeh 6903,4-6903
CO47655 Rocks In My Bed(1)(dh,tfl)   Okeh 6880
CO47656 Rough Ridin'   Okeh 6867,4-6867
CO47657 Without A Song   Okeh 6879,4-6879,Epic EG7010,EG7094,LG1004,LN3118

-1.Add Dolores Hawkins,The Four Lads(vcl) - issued as DOLORES HAWKINS AND THE FOUR LADS
   WITH THE BILL DAVIS TRIO.

Prob. same.   Broadcast."Birdland",NYC.March 15,1952
    Piccadilly Circus
    Azure Te
    Why Do I Love You
    Without A Song
    It's All In The Game

Prob. same.   Broadcast."Birdland",NYC.March 22,1952
    Piccadilly Circus
    Azure Te
    Super Romp
    Things Ain't What They Used To Be

Prob. same.   Broadcast."Birdland",NYC.March 29,1952
    Why Do I Love You
    Azure Te
    It's All In The Game

Prob. same.   Broadcast."Birdland",NYC.April 5,1952
    Smooth Sailing
    I'll Walk Alone
    Stopgap
    Unforgettable
    Caravan

Wild Bill Davis(org,vcl),Bill Jennings(g,vcl),Chris Columbus(dr).
                                   NYC.April 18,1952
CO47842 Ooh-Ah-De-De-De(band-vcl)   Okeh 6913,4-6913,Epic EG7095,LN3118
CO47843 Alexandria,Va.   -   - ,Epic LG1004

Prob. same.   Broadcast."Birdland",NYC.July 19,1952
    Azure Te
    Chicken Gumbo
    Dark Eyes
    Passion Flower
    Blue Tango
    Flying Home

Wild Bill Davis(org,vcl),Bill Jennings(g,vcl),Chris Columbus(dr).
                                   NYC.January 8,1953
CO48676 April In Paris   Okeh 6946,4-6946,Epic 9137,EG7024,LG1004,LN3118
CO48677 Lullaby Of Birdland   -   -   -   -   -   -
CO48678 Lena The Hyena(band-vcl)   Epic EG7024,LG1004
CO48679 Bring The Money In(band-vcl)   Okeh 7021,4-7021,Epic EG7024,LG1004

All titles on Epic LG1004 also on Philips(E)BBR8079.

Wild Bill Davis(org),Floyd Smith(g),Chris Columbus(dr).
                                   NYC.March 11,1953
CO48916 Pompton Turnpike   Okeh 6983,4-6983,Epic LN3308
CO48917 Nina Never Knew   Okeh 6965,4-6965
CO48918 Rhapsody In Blue   -   - ,Epic EG7010,LN3308
CO48919 The Jitterbug Waltz   Okeh 6983,4-6983,   -   -

Same.   NYC.September 2,1953
CO49792 It's Crazy,Wild And Wonderful   Okeh unissued
CO49793 Indian Summer   Okeh 6983,4-6983,Epic EG7094,LN3118
CO49794 Come Rain Or Come Shine   Okeh 7033,4-7033,LN3308,(Eu)22.030
CO49795 Wailin' For Moondog   -   -
CO49796 Theme From "The
          Joe Louis Story"   Okeh 7013,4-7013
CO49797 These Foolish Things   unissued

```
Same.                                        LA.November 21,1953
RHC010652 Passion Flover               Epic LN3308
RHC010653 I Ain't Feeling So Good      Okeh 7021,4-7021,Epic EG7094,LN3118
RHC010654 Chelsea Bridge                     unissued
RHC010655 Nice Work If You Can Get It  Epic LN1121,LN3308
RHC010656 Laura                        Epic EG7073,EG7096,LN3308
RHC010657 Things Ain't
          What They Used To Be         Epic 7047,4-7047,EG7073,LN3118
```

Note:Master RHC010657 issued on Epic 7047,4-7047 in two parts (masterno. RHC033217/18).

```
THE WILD BILL DAVIS TRIO:
Same.                                        LA.May 16,1954
RHC010911 Don't Get Around Much Anymore Okeh 7054,4-7054,Epic LN3121
RHC010912 Don't Worry 'Bout Me         Epic EG7096,LN3118
RHC010913 Caravan                      Epic LN1121
RHC010914 East Of The Sun              Okeh 7054,4-7054,Epic LN1121,LN3308

Same.                                        NYC.October 22,1954
C053120 Make No Mistake                Epic LN3118
C053121 Linger Awhile                     - ,EG7095
C053122 Night Train                       -     -
C053123 Jumpin' At The Woodside           - ,EG7096

Same.                                        Live."Birdland",NYC.October 22,1954
C054121 April In Paris                 Okeh 9137,4-9137
C054122 Lullaby Of Birdland               -     -

Same.                                        NYC.March 21,1955
C053103 Serenade To Benny              Okeh unissued
C053104 Syncopated Clock               Okeh 7059,4-7059
C053105 Land Of Dreams                    -      - ,Epic LN1121,LN3308
C053106 Love For Sale                  Epic LN1121,LN3308

Same.                                        NYC.November 15,1955
C054161 Trees                          Epic LN3308,(Eu)22.030

Same.                                        NYC.November 17,1955
C054169 Danny Boy                      Epic LN3308,(Eu)22.030
C054170 My Bewildered Heart                  unissued
C054171 Dancing On The Ceiling            -
```

All titles on Epic LN3118 also on Epic(F)EPC64847,Fontana(Eu)682.202ML

```
Wild Bill Davis(org),Floyd Smith(g),Joe Morris(dr).
                                             NYC.July 1956
IR3    Invitation                       Imperial LP9010
IR4    I Remember April                          -
IR5    I Let A Song Go Out Of My Heart  Imperial 5399,LP9010
IR6    Take The A Train                 Imperial LP9010,LP9233
IR7    Cubano Chant                              -      -
IR8    My Funny Valentine                        -
IR9    Perdido (IM1208)                 Imperial 5420,LP9010
IR10   I Miss You So                    Imperial LP9010
IR11   Ain't Misbehavin'                         unissued
IR12   Inter-modulation (IM4254)        Imperial LP9015,LP9201,LP12201
IR13   Love Is Here To Stay                      -
IR14   Mr. Wonderful                             -
IR15   Autumn Leaves (IM4255)           Imperial 5399,LP9010,LP9201,LP12201
IR16   Jealousy                         Imperial LP9015
(session cont. next page).
```

(session cont. from previous page):
IR17	The High And Mighty	Imperial LP9015		
IR18	Tenderly	-		
IR19	Let's Fall In Love	-		
IR20	Give Me The Simple Life	unissued		
IR21	All The Things You Are	Imperial LP9015		
IR22	Supposin'	-		
IR23	At Dawn With Davis (IM4253)	- ,LP9201,LP12201		
IM1209	Crosstown(1)	Imperial 5420,LP9201,LP12201		
	Night Time(2)	Imperial LP9201,LP12201		

-1.Poss. rec. at this session.
-2.Poss. a re-titling of one of the above titles.

Note:"Perdido" issued on Imperial LP9201,LP12201 may be an alternate take/version.

Similar.   Unknown location.February/March 1957
M1264	Wild Blues (Hard Blues)	Imperial 5435,LP9201,LP12201
M1265	Summer Dreams	Imperial LP9201,LP12201
M1266	West Of Allah	Imperial 5435
M1267	No Sweat	Imperial LP9201,LP12201

Maurice Simon(ts),Wild Bill Davis(org),Milt Hinton(b),Jo Jones(dr).
                          NYC.September 7,October 6/20,1958
Get Me To The Church On Time	Everest LPBR5014,(F)EVY45-7001		
I Could Have Danced All Night	-	-	
The Rain In Spain	-		
Ascot Gavotte	-		
I've Grown Accustomed To Your Face	-		
You Did It	-		
Wouldn't It Be Loverly	-	,(F)EVY45-7001,Sunset SUS5191	
On The Street Where You Live	-	-	-
Just You Wait	-	,Sunset SUS5191	
With A Little Bit Of Luck	-		
I'm An Ordinary Man	-		
Show Me	-	,Sunset SUS5191	

11 titles also on Everest SDBR1014.

George Clarke(ts),Wild Bill Davis(org),Bill Jennings(g),Grady Tate(dr).
                          NYC.August 27,1959
Low Bottom	Everest 19358,LPBR5052	
I Want A Little Girl	-	
But Not For Me	Everest LPBR5052,(F)EVY45-7006	
The Nearness Of You	-	-
Love For Sale	-	-
'Round About Midnight(no ts)	-	-
Cabato(no ts)	-	
Tea For Two	-	
I've Got The World On A String	-	
Always	-	
Satin Doll	-	
Blues for Joe	-	

11 titles also on Everest SDBR1052,Jazz Anthology(F)JA5132.

WILD BILL DAVIS AND HIS ORCHESTRA:
Same.   NYC.March 29/April 4,1960
| Madison,I/II | Everest BREP126,LPBR5094 | |
| Smooth Sailing | - | - |
(session cont. next page).

(session cont. from previous page):

Organ Grinder's Swing	Everest LPBR5094,Sunset SUS5191	
In A Mellow Tone	-	-
Flying Home	-	-
Blue Skies	-	-
It's All Right With Me	-	-
Intermission Riff	-	-

All titles also on Everest SDBR1094,LPBR5116,SDBR1116.

Prob. same.   NYC.August 1960

Boogie Woogie	Everest 19372
Blues For Barbara	-
Deep Echo	Everest 19397
The World Of Susie Wong	-

George Clarke(ts),Wild Bill Davis(org),Bill Jennings(g),Grady Tate(dr).
                                     NYC.September 1960

Wenkie	Everest LPBR5125
Cherokee	-
What's New	-
St. Louis Blues	-

George Freeman(g) replaces Jennings. NYC.September 1960

Dis Heah	Everest LPBR5125
Theme From Mr. Lucky	-
Ebb Tide	-
Like Young	-
Jo-Do	-
Angel Eyes	-

All titles on LPBR5125 also on Everest SDBR1125.

Wild Bill Davis(org),Calvin Newborn(g),Grady Tate(dr).
                                     NYC.April 30,1962

112135 April In Paris	Coral 65558,CRL(7)57417
112136 Canadian Sunset	-
112137 On A Slow Boat To China	-
112138 Hawaiian War Chant	-

Add unknown(perc).   NYC.May 1,1962

112139 Lisboa Antigua	Coral CRL(7)57417
112140 Arrivederci Roma	-
112141 Brazil	-
112142 The Poor People Of Paris	-

Omit unknown(perc);add Les Spann(fl),Paul Gonsalves(ts),Janet Putnam(harp).
                                     Same date

112143 On A Little Street In Singapore	Coral CRL(7)57417
112144 Manhattan	Coral 65558,CRL(7)57417
112145 African Waltz(no harp)	-
112146 Midnight In Moscow(no harp)	-

All titles on CRL57417 also on Coral(E)LVA9208,(F)LPCS119.

Details unknown.   Unknown location.c. 1962

Moon River	Coral CRL(7)57427
Stella By Starlight	-
That Old Black Magic	-
Love Letters	-

(session cont. next page).

(session cont. from previous page):
```
        My Ideal                   Coral CRL(7)57427
        Mona Lisa                         -
        Lady's In Love                    -
        The Nearness Of You               -
        I Remember You                    -
        Penthouse Serenade                -
        Out Of Nowhere                    -
```

Clayton "Bob" Brown(ts,fl),Wild Bill Davis(org),Dickie Thompson(g),Jimmy Hopps(dr).
```
                                   NYC.September 22,1964
RPA1-5161 Free,Frantic And Funky   RCA-Victor LPM/LSP3314
RPA1-5162 C.C. Rider                     -
RPA1-5163 Theme From Warsaw Concerto     unissued
RPA1-5164 Azure-Te (Paris Blues)   RCA-Victor LPM/LSP3314,(F)FXL1.7317
```

```
Same.                              NYC.September 23,1964
RPA1-5165 Make Love To Me          RCA-Victor LPM/LSP3314
RPA1-5166 Hit The Road Jack        rejected
RPA1-5167 Well, Git It                   -
RPA1-5168 I Can't Stop
          Loving You(no ts/fl)     Victor LPM/LSP3314
```

```
Same.                              NYC,September 24,1964
RPA1-5169 Sent For You Yesterday   RCA-Victor rejected
RPA1-5170 Tippin' In               RCA-Victor LPM/LSP3314
RPA1-5171 Just Squeeze Me                -
RPA1-5172 Don't Cry,Baby(org,dr only)    -
```

Jerome Richardson,Seldon Powell(fl,ts),Wild Bill Davis(org),Dickie Thompson,Mundell Lowe
(g),George Duvivier(b),Osie Johnson(dr).   NYC.December 3,1964
```
RPA1-5193 C Jam Blues               RCA-Victor LPM/LSP3314,(F)FXL1.7317,PL42026
          Hit The Road Jack               -
          Sent For You Yesterday          -
          Well,Git It                     -
```

All titles on LPM/LSP3314 also on RCA(E)RD7716.

WILD BILL DAVIS - JOHNNY HODGES:
Johnny Hodges(as),Wild Bill Davis(org),Dickie Thompson,Mundell Lowe(g),Milt Hinton(b),Osie
Johnson(dr).   NYC.January 7,1965
```
SPA1-1801 On The Sunny
          Side Of The Street       RCA-Victor LPM/LSP3393
SPA1-1802 The Jeep Is Jumpin'            -
SPA1-1803 I'm Beginning To See The Light -
SPA1-1804 Lil' Darling                   -
SPA1-1805 Sophisticated Lady             -
```

```
George Duvivier(b) replaces Hinton.     Same date
PA1-1806 No One                    RCA-Victor LPM/LSP3393
PA1-1807 Con-Soul And Sax                -
PA1-1808 Drop Me Off In Harlem           -
PA1-1809 On Green Dolphin Street         -
PA1-1810 Johnny Come Lately              -
```

11 titles on LPM/LSP3393 also on Camden(G)CAS10176,RCA(F)741.047,PM42414.

WILD BILL DAVIS:
Wild Bill Davis(org),Dickie Thompson(g),Freddie Waits(dr).
                                   Live."Count Basie's",NYC.February 3,1966
(session cont. next page).

(session cont. from previous page):
```
        Opening                      RCA-Victor LPM/LSP3578
        Impulsion                         -
        Stolen Sweets                     -
        On A Clear Day                    -
        Quiet Nights                      -
        Bernie's Tune                     - ,(F)FXM2-7217
        Organic                           -
        The Shadow Of Your Smile          -
        Low Bottom No.2                   - ,(F)FXL3.7343
        This Is All I Ask                 -
        The Trolley Song                  -
        Closing Theme (April In Paris)    -
```

All titles also on RCA(F)430.719,FXL1.7103.

Lawrence Brown(tb),Johnny Hodges(as),Bob Brown(ts,fl),Wild Bill Davis(org),Dickie Thompson (g),Bobby Durham(dr).   Live."Grace's Little Belmont",Atlantic City.August 10,1966
```
TPA5-5417 In A Mellotone            RCA-Victor LPM/LSP3706
TPA5-5418 L.B. Blues                      -
TPA5-5419 Good Queen Bess                 -
TPA5-5420 Belle Of The Belmont           -
TPA5-5421 I'll Always Be
          In Love With You                -
TPA5-5422 Taffy                           -
```

Same.   Live."Grace's Little Belmont",Atlantic City.August 11,1966
```
TPA5-5423 Rockville                 RCA-Victor LPM/LSP3706
TPA5-5424 It Don't Mean A Thing           -
TPA5-5425 It's Only A Paper Moon          -
```

Omit Lawrence Brown,Hodges.   Same location/date
```
TPA5-5431 Up Top                    RCA-Victor LPM/LSP3799,(F)FXL1.7317
TPA5-5432 Let It Be                       -
TPA5-5433 Jive Samba                      -
TPA5-5434 Straight No Chaser              - ,(F)FXL1.7317
TPA5-5435 Unknown title             unissued
TPA5-5436 Manha De Carnaval         RCA-Victor LPM/LSP3799
TPA5-5437 Little Tracy                    -
TPA5-5438 Unknown title             unissued
TPA5-5439 Adoration                 RCA-Victor LPM/LSP3799
TPA5-5440 Cute                            -
TPA5-5441 Soft Winds                      - ,(F)FXL1.7317
TPA5-5442 Summertime                      -        -
UPA5-6313 April In Paris                  -        -
```

All titles on LPM/LSP3706 also on RCA(F)730.702,PM42414.

Wild Bill Davis(org),Ray Charles(p),unknown b,dr,woodwinds,strings,Gerald Wilson,Marty Paich(arr,cond).   LA(?). 1966/67
```
      I Didn't Know What Time It Was  Tangerine TRCS1509
      There Is No Greater Love             -
      Someone To Watch Over Me            -
      Sunday,Monday Or Always            -
      I Wish I Didn't Love You So        -
      Just Friends                        -
      If I Should Lose You                -
      How Deep Is The Ocean              -
      I'm Getting Sentimental Over You   -
      I'll Never Smile Again             -
```
(session cont. next page).

(session cont. from previous page):

Note:In an interview - with Joël Dufour (France) - Wild Bill Davis told that the above album was recorded using a band track that was recorded in 1962 (in LA). The band track was previously used by singer Little Jimmy Scott (for Tangerine TRCS1501). Two of the above titles - "Just Friends" and "I'll Never Smile Again" - were not on the Scott LP but are prob. unissued titles from the original recording. Acc. to Davis the band track incl. Ray Charles - which has been aurally confirmed.

Bob Brown(as,ts,fl),Wild Bill Davis(org),Dickie Thompson(g),Orville Mason,Jymie Merritt (b),Bernard Purdie(dr).   NYC.November 13,1967

JPA1-8544	Weasel's Kid	RCA-Victor LSP4139
JPA1-8545	Funny Thing	-
JPA1-8546	Deedle Lum Bum	-
JPA1-8547	Generator	-

Wild Bill Davis(org),Dickie Thompson(g),Chris Columbus(dr).
                                                NYC.November 14,1967

JPA1-8548	Dinah	RCA-Victor LSP4139,(F)FXL1.7317
JPA1-8549	Unknown title	unissued
JPA1-8550	Cherry Orchard	RCA-Victor LSP4139,(F)FXL1.7317

Bob Brown(as,ts,fl),Wild Bill Davis(org),Dickie Thompson(g),Jymie Merritt(b),Earl Curry (dr).   NYC.November 15,1967

JPA1-8551	London Derry Air	RCA-Victor LSP4139
JPA1-8552	Unknown title	unissued
JPA1-8553	Dreaming By The Fire	RCA-Victor LSP4139
JPA1-8554	Bo Bee Ba Biff	-
JPA1-8555	Puss In Boots	-
JPA1-8556	The Groaner	-

Wild Bill Davis(org),Floyd Smith(g),Chris Columbus(dr).
                                                Paris.May 9,1972

Intermodulation	Black&Blue(F)33.037
In The Evening	-
I Ain't Feeling So Good	-

same.   Paris.May 10,1972

Impulsions	Black&Blue(F)33.037
Ooh!Ah!Dee-Dee	-
Night Train	-
In A Mellotone	-
Organ Grinder's Swing	-

All titles on Black&Blue(F)33.037 also on Black&Blue(F)59.037-2 (CD),233.037 (CD).

Note:See BUDDY TATE for additional recordings from the May 9/10,1972 sessions.

WILD BILL DAVIS - EDDIE DAVIS:

Eddie Davis(ts),Wild Bill Davis(org),Billy Butler(g),Oliver Jackson(dr).
                            Live.Châteauneuf-du-Pape,France.January 17,1976

Impulsions	Black&Blue(F)33.303
Cubano Chant	-
Avalon	-
The Shadow Of Your Smile	-
True Blue	-
Lester Leaps In	-

same.   Paris.January 22,1976

On Green Dolphin Street(no ts)	Black&Blue(F)33.133
When Your Lover Has Gone	- ,233.101(CD),59.004-2(CD)
Whispering(no ts)	-

(session cont. next page).

(session cont. from previous page):
     All Right,OK,You Win(no ts)   Black&Blue(F)33.133
     Exactly Like You(no ts)   -
     After You've Gone   - ,233.101(CD)
     Candy(no ts)   Black&Blue(F)233.101(CD),59.004-2(CD)

Note:See EDDIE DAVIS for one additional title on Black&Blue(F)33.133.
    The same group also recorded under Eddie Davis' name (January 21,1976).

Stéphane Guerault(ts),Dany Doriz(vbs),Wild Bill Davis(org),Gérard "Dave" Pochonet(dr).
                         Live."La Huchette",Paris.May 1977
     Struttin' With Some Barbecue   Jazz Time(F)253.620(CD)
     Lullaby Of Birdland   -
     Indiana(1)   -
     Body And Soul(no ts)   -
     Wild Bill At The Huchette   -
     Gone With The Wind   -
     Li'l Darling(no ts)   -
     Jumpin' With Symphony Sid(1)   -

-1.Kenny Clarke(dr) replaces Pochonet.

Dany Doriz(vbs),Wild Bill Davis(org),Michel Denis(dr).
                         Limoges,France.March 17,1978
     In A Mellotone   Jazzmosphere(F)JZ79.01
     Take The "A" Train   -
     In The Evening   -
     Jitterbug Waltz   -
     Cute   -
     Stolen Sweets   -
     After You've Gone   -
     Misty   Jazzmosphere(F)JZ79.02
     Indiana   -
     Blixx   -
     Rockville   -
     Things Ain't What They Used To Be   -
     Limoges Hot Club Blues   -

BOB DAVIS

BOB DAVIS QUARTET:
Bob Grea(as,ts,bars),Bob Davis(p),Stu Anderson(b),Bill Blakkestad(dr).
                         Minneapolis. 1957
     The Goose   Zephyr ZEP7001,ZP12001G
     The Way You Look Tonight   -   -
     Willow Weep For Me   -   -
     China Boy   -   -
     Nancy   Zephyr ZP12001G
     It's All Right With Me   -
     The Song Is You   -
     River Road   -
     Night In Tunisia   -
     The Lady Is A Tramp   -

Dave Karr(fl,ts,bars),Bob Davis(p,b),Johnny Frigo(b,vln),Bill Blakkestad(dr).
                         Minneapolis. 1958
     Adams' Evening   Stepheny MF4003/LR8003
     Windy City   -
(session cont. next page).

(session cont. from previous page):

Darn That Dream	Stepheny MF4003/LR8003
Blues In Orbit	-
Dr. Pepper	-
Cherokee	-
Buzzy	-
Star Eyes	-
I'll Remember April	-
Sometimes I'm Happy	-
Up In Ray's Pad	-
Deedee's Dream	-

Note:The above issuenumbers may be MF4000 and LR8000.

CHARLES DAVIS

Andrew "Tex" Allen(tp,flh),Gerald Hayes(as,fl),Charles Davis(bars),Ronnie Mathews(p,el-p),
Louis Davis(g),David Williams(b),Louis Hayes(dr).
NYC.July 15,1974

The Gems Of Mims	Strata-East SES7425
Little Miss Jump	-
Linda	-
Ingia	-

CHARLES DAVIS SEXTET:

Tex Allen(tp),Clifford Adams,Jr.(tb),Charles Davis(bars,ss,ts),Kenny Barron(p),Walter
Booker Jr.(b),Billy Hart(dr). NYC.March 1/2,1979

Monking	West 54 WLW8006
Eastern Vibrations	-
Mexico Street	-
Dedicated To Tadd	-
Love Gods	-
Sir Charles	-

COLERIDGE DAVIS

COLERIDGE DAVIS AND HIS ORCHESTRA:
prob. incl. Silas Johnson(cl,as),Teddy Sutton(ts),Coleridge Davis(p),Al Dunn(dr),Marva
Louis(vcl). NYC. 1945

442 Harlem Caballero(ml)	Hub 5001
443 If I Didn't Have You	Hub 5000
444 Broadway Stomp	- ,3010
445 Follies Fantasy	Hub 3010
Atlantic City	Hub 5002

JACK DAVIS

JACK DAVIS AND HIS BAND:
Jack Davis(ts),rest unknown. Chicago. 1947

Tenor-mental Moods	Miracle 101
Sorry We Said Goodbye	-

Jack Davis,Eddie Chamblee,Tommy "Mad" Jones(ts),Sonny Thompson(p),Lefty Bates(g),Eddie
Calhoun(b),Buddy Smith(dr). Chicago. 1947
(session cont. next page).

(session cont. from previous page):
```
UB21046 Memphis Train              Miracle 109
UB21047 Benson Jump                   -
UB21048 Screamin' Boogie           Miracle 108,Esquire(E)10-339
UB21049 Sonny's Blues                 -                     -
```

DICK DAVIS AND HIS COMBO:
Details unknown.   Unknown location. 1948
```
        You Tell Me                Gotham 182
        Double Talk                   -
```


EDDIE DAVIS

Note:This artist is not Eddie "Lockjaw" Davis.

EDDIE DAVIS AND HIS MODERN ORCHESTRA:
Eddie Davis(ts),unknown bars,p,b,dr.   LA.c. 1946
```
MM892  Famous Amos II               Modern 20-628
MM893  Famous Amos I                   -
```


EDDIE "LOCKJAW" DAVIS

See also HARRY EDISON,RED GARLAND,LEONARDO PEDERSEN,SONNY STITT,TENORS OF JAZZ.

EDDIE DAVIS AND HIS QUINTET:
Eddie Davis(ts),Argonne Thornton (Sadik Hakim)(p),Bill de Arango(g),Gene Ramey(b),Denzil
Best(dr).   NYC.May 1946
```
h-1919 Surgery (SRC841)             Haven 801,Signature 28129
h-1920 Lockjaw (SRC842)             Haven 800,Signature 28124
h-1921 Afternoon In A Doghouse (SRC843)    -                -
h-1922 Athlete's Foot (SRC844)      Haven 801,Signature 28129
```

All titles also on Doctor Jazz FW39519,Raretone(I)5009,EPM(F)FDC5009 (CD).
Note:Signature masternumbers are given in parenthesis.

EDDIE DAVIS AND HIS BEBOPPERS:
Fats Navarro(tp),Eddie Davis(ts),Al Haig(p),Huey Long(g),Gene Ramey(b),Denzil Best(dr).
                                           NYC.December 18,1946
```
S3367  Calling Dr. Jazz             Savoy 907
S3368  Fracture                     Savoy 933
S3369A Hollerin' And Screamin'(1)   Savoy 904
S3370  Stealin' Trash               Savoy 907,MG9026
```

-1.Originally issued as "Hollerin And Screaming".

All titles also on Savoy MG12133,SJL2216,SV0123 (CD)(F)460SV451,Byg(F)529.103,Vogue(F)
VG655.650115,Realm(E)RM208,CBS52208.
Note:SJL2216 and SV0123 issued under Navarro's name.

```
Same.                               NYC.December 20,1946
S3371A Just A Mystery               Savoy 705
S3372A Red Pepper                      -
S3373  Spinal                       Savoy 933,Artista Stomp 1
S3374A Maternity(1)                 Savoy 904,XP8026
```

-1.As "Lard Pot" on Savoy XP8026.
(session cont. next page).

(session cont. from previous page):
All titles also on Savoy MG12119,SJL2216,SV0169 (CD),Vogue(F)VG655.650115.
Note:SJL2216 issued under Navarro's name.

EDDIE DAVIS QUINTET:
Eddie Davis(ts),Al Haig(p),John Collins(g),Gene Ramey(b),Denzil Best(dr).
NYC.April 12,1947

R1206	Lover	Apollo 767,LP477
R1207	Licks-A-Plenty	-
A1208	Foxy	Apollo 779,LP477,Raretone(I)5009
A1209	Sheila	- -

All titles also on EPM FDC5170 (CD),Xanadu LP208.

EDDIE DAVIS QUARTET:
Eddie Davis(ts),John Acea(p),Gene Ramey(b),Butch Ballard(dr).
NYC. 1947/48

L4053	Real Gone Guy	Lenox 502,Continental CLP16001,Plymouth P12-113
L4054	But Beautiful	Lenox 528, - - ,
		Remington EP75,LP1037,Pontiac PLP523
L4055	Leapin' On Lenox	Lenox 502,Plymouth P12-113,Continental L160001,
		Remington EP75,LP1037,Palace PST675,803,Ember
		(E)CJS826
L4055	Leapin' On Lenox(alt.take)(1)	Pontiac PLP523

-1.Issued as "Real Gone Guy,pt.2" on PLP523 and Raretone(I)5009.

All titles/takes also on Raretone(I)5009.

Prob. same.
NYC. 1947/48

L4156	Minton's Madhouse	Lenox 515,Plymouth P12-115,Continental CLP16001
L4157	Ravin' At The Haven	- ,Plymouth P12-113, - ,
		Remington EP75,L1037,Pontiac PLP523,Raretone
		(I)5009

Similar.
NYC. 1947/48

	Huckle Buck	Plymouth P12-115,Palace PST675,803,Continental
		CLP16001,Ember(E)CJS826
	Music Goes Down Around	Continental CLP16001,Remington EP75,L1037,Plymouth
		P12-113,Pontiac PLP523,Raretone(I)5009
	Lockjaw's Bounce	Plymouth P12-122,Continental CLP16001

Note:The above titles may be from the two previous sessions. It has not been verified
whether additional horns are added on "Lockjaw's Bounce" and "Huckle Buck".
An unidentified title - "Ready For Action" - on Pontiac PLP523 may be from the above
sessions (the instrumentation for "Ready For Action" is tp,tb,ts,p,b,dr).

Shad Collins(tp),Milt Larkins(tb),Rudy Williams(as),Eddie Davis(ts),Dave McRae(bars),prob.
John Acea(p),Gene Ramey(b),prob. Butch Ballard(dr).
NYC. 1948

C301	Happy Birthday	Sittin' In With 520,Solid Sender SOL512
C302	Black Pepper	- -
C2016	Jumpin' With Maxie-Waxie	Sittin' In With 525
C2017	Randy's Boogie	-

All titles also on Raretone(I)5009.
Note:The pianist may be Earl Knight; the drummer may be Shadow Wilson.

KING CARL (CARL DAVIS)(vcl) acc. by EDDIE DAVIS ORCHESTRA:
Eddie Davis(ts),Kenny Kersey(p),Gene Ramey(b),Lee Abrams(dr),T. Rhodes,W.I, Edwards,Bob
Aviles(unkn. instr.).   NYC.March 17,1949
S36-114 In the Dozens   Regent unissued
S36-115 Sure Like To Run   Regent 1011
S36-116 She's My Gal   -
S36-117 Notoriety Woman   unissued

EDDIE DAVIS with BILL DOGGETT TRIO:
Eddie Davis(ts),Bill Doggett(org),John Simmons(b),Jo Jones(dr).
                                           NYC.August 16,1949
K5767 Mountain Oysters(1)   King 4321,KS1133
K5768 Huckle Boogie   -

-1.Poss. add unknown tp,ts,bars,unknown male-vocal; Doggett may play piano.

No details.   Unknown location/date
        How High The Moon   Domino
        Intermission Riff
        Lock Goes Latin
        This Is Always

EDDIE DAVIS AND HIS ORCHESTRA:
Eddie Davis(ts),Wynton Kelly(p),Al Casey(g),Frank Skeete(b),Lee Abrams(dr),Carl Davis
(vcl).   NYC.February 7,1950
BL1206 I'm Gonna Eat You
       With A Spoon(cd)   Birdland 6003
BL1207 Little Rock(1)   Birdland 6004,Prestige 866,P24081
BL1208 If The Motif Is Right(cd)   Birdland 6003
BL1209 The Rock(2)   Birdland 6004,Prestige 866,P24081

-1.As "Sweet And Lovely" on Prestige issues.
-2.As "Squattin" on Prestige issues.

All titles also on Prestige PCD24116-2 (CD).

EDDIE DAVIS QUARTET:
Eddie Davis(ts),Bill Doggett(org),Oscar Pettiford(b),Shadow Wilson(dr).
                                           NYC. 1952
R1120-3 My Blue Heaven   Roost 553,LP422,Vogue(E)VJD548
R1121-2 Please Don't Talk
        About Me When I'm Gone   Roost 559,Vogue(F)V3257
R1122-1 Bewitched   Roost 553,LP422,LP1201,Vogue(E)VJD548
R1123-3 Blues In My Heart   Roost 559,LP422,Vogue(E)VJD548,(F)V3257

Eddie Davis(ts),Billy Taylor(org),Freddie Green(g),Oscar Pettiford(b),Shadow Wilson(dr).
                                           NYC. 1952
R1142 There's No You   Roost 568
R1143 Slow Squat   Roost 572
R1144 Hey,Lock   Roost 568,LP422,Vogue(E)VJD548
R1145 I'm An Old Cowhand   Roost 572

Unknown(tp),Eddie Davis(ts),unknown p,org,b,dr.
                                           Live."Apollo Theatre",NYC.December 1,1952
        The Way You Look Tonight   Session 124
        Bewitched(no tp)   -

Eddie Davis(ts),Eddie Bonnemere(org),John Simmons(b),Charlie Rice(dr).
                                           NYC. 1953
(session cont. next page).

(session cont. from previous page):
R1188 I Only Have Eyes For You   Roost 587
R1189 Chihuahua   -
R1212 Nightingale   Roost 599
R1213 This Can't Be Love   unissued
R1214 Secret Love   Roost 599

All titles - except "This Can't Be Love" - also on Roost LP422,Vogue(E)VJD548.

EDDIE DAVIS TRIO:
Eddie Davis(ts),Doc Bagby(org),Charlie Rice(dr).
                                       NYC. 1954
R1228 Too Marvelous For Words   Roost 600
R1229 Heartaches   -

EDDIE DAVIS - SONNY STITT:
Add Sonny Stitt(ts).   Live."Birdland",NYC.Spring 1954
       Marchin'   Roost LP1203,Vogue(E)VJD548
       S.O.S.   -   -
       Jaws   -   -
       I Can't Get Started   -   -
       Roller Coaster   Phoenix Jazz LP19
       All The Things You Are   -
       Whoops   -
       Don't Blame Me   -
     · Indiana   unissued
       Lullaby Of Birdland   -
       Hoagie   -
       Strawberries And Cream   -
       Bop,Mop,Flop   -

All issued titles also on Roulette CDP7.97507-2 (CD).

No details.   Unknown location/date
       Metalmouth   Vogue(E)VJD548
       Locked In   -
       Hey,Jim   -
       Beano   -

EDDIE "LOCKJAW" DAVIS TRIO:
Eddie Davis(ts),Doc Bagby(org),Charlie Rice(dr).
                                       Cincinnati.April 11,1955
K9602 There's A Small Hotel   King LP606,Swingtime ST1021
K9603 Bean-O   King 4801,EP372,LP506,Parlophone(E)GEP8678
K9604 This Is Always   -   -   -
K9605 Leaping On Lenox   King LP506
K9605 Tenderly   King 4928,LP506,President(F)PRC144

Same.   Cincinnati.April 19,1955
K9607 I'll Remember April   King LP506,Parlophone(E)GEP8678
K9608 Moonlight In Vermont   -   - ,President(F)PRC144
K9609 Yesterdays   King LP606,Swingtime ST1021
K9610 Little White Lies   King LP526,LP637
K9611 Out Of Nowhere   King LP599
K9612 You Go To My Head   King LP506,President(F)PRC144
K9613 What Is This Thing Called Love King LP526,LP637,Parlophone(E)GEP8685
K9614 Holler   King LP599
K9615 Tickle Toe   -
K9616 Punch   King 4813,LP599
K9617 Smooth Ride (Fireball)   King LP606,Swingtime ST1021

```
Same.                                  Cincinnati.April 20,1955
K9622  Johnny Come Lately              King LP506,Parlophone(E)GEP8678
K9623  Dizzy Atmosphere                King 4828,LP506
K9624  Just Friends                    King LP526,LP637
K9625  It's The Talk Of The Town       King 4813,EP372,LP506
```

Note:See DOC BAGBY for additional titles from this session.

```
Same.                                  Cincinnati.August 16,1955
K9680  The Way You Look Tonight        King 4904,LP506,Parlophone(E)GEP8587
K9681  Together                        King 4863,LP606,              - ,(Fi)DPY1073,
                                       Swingtime ST1021
K9682  A Foggy Day                     King 4863,LP506,Parlophone(E)GEP8587,(Fi)DPY1073
K9683  Don't Know Why,I Just Do        King LP599
K9684  It's A Pity To Say Goodbye      King 4832,LP599
K9685  Hey,Jim                         King LP599
K9686  Night And Day                   King LP606,Swingtime ST1021
K9687  Scatter                         King 4904,LP599,Parlophone(E)GEP8587
```

All titles on LP506 also on King KCD506 (CD),President(F)KVP115,Sing(E)LP506.

```
Same.                                  NYC.February 2/3,1956
K8724  Love For Sale                   King LP526,LP637
K8725  People Will Say We're In Love     -     - ,Bethlehem BCP6069
K8726  Whispering                        -     - ,Parlophone(E)GEP8685
K8727  Things Ain't
         What They Used To Be          King LP599
K8728  Our Love Is Here To Stay        King LP526,LP637
K8729  You Are Too Beautiful             -     - ,Bethlehem BCP6069,Parlophone(E)
                                       GEP8685
K8730  Man With A Horn                 King LP526,LP637,President(F)PRC144
K8731  All The Things You Are            -     - ,Bethlehem BCP6069,Parlophone(E)
                                       GEP8685
K8732  I Wanna' Be Loved               King LP526,LP637,Bethlehem BCP6069
K8733  You've Been Alone Too Long        -     -
K8734  Lady Bird                       King LP599,Bethlehem BCP6069
K8735  Satin Doll                        -               -
```

```
Eddie Davis(ts),Shirley Scott(org),Charlie Rice(dr).
                                       NYC.July 16,1956
K8789  The Happy Whistler              King 4966,LP606,Swingtime ST1021
K8790  Scotty Boo                      King 5164,LP566,LP837,Bethlehem BCP6069
K8791  I Need Ya'                      King LP566
K8792  Tia Juana                         - ,Bethlehem 3026,BCP6069
K8793  Blues In The Night                -
K8794  Teach Me Tonight                King 4966,LP566
```

```
Add Carl Pruitt(b),Ray Barretto(cg). NYC.January 22,1957
K8832  I Wished On The Moon            King LP566,Bethlehem 3026
K8833  Speak Low                       King 5026,LP566
K8834  Sheila                          King LP566
K8835  Ebb Tide                          - ,LP837,Bethlehem BCP6069
```

Note:King LP837 issued under Shirley Scott's name.

```
Same                                   NYC.February 5,1957
K8836  Say What                        King 5980,LP566
K8837  From This Moment On             King LP599
K8838  It Ain't Necessarily So         King 5026,LP566
K8839  Eddie's Function                King 5164,LP566,Bethlehem BCP6069
```

All titles on BCP6069 also on Bethlehem BCP6035(new series),Affinity(E)AFF153.

EDDIE "LOCKJAW" DAVIS TRIO - JOE NEWMAN:
Joe Newman(tp),Eddie Davis(ts),Shirley Scott(org),Count Basie(p),George Duvivier(b),Butch
Ballard(dr).   NYC.December 17,1957

12551	Telegraph	Roulette (S)R52007
12553	Lock Goes Latin	unissued
12554	A Misty One	Roulette (S)R52007
12556	Street Of Dreams(no tp,ts)	-

Same.   NYC.December 18,1957

12552	Farouk	Roulette (S)R52007
12557	Save Your Love For Me	-
12558	Lock-Up(no tp)	-

Same.   NYC.December 19,1957

12555	Swingin' Till	
	The Girls Come Home	Roulette (S)R52007
12559	Broadway	-
12560	Marie	- ,Blue Note CDP7.99095-2(CD)
12561	Don't Blame Me(no tp,p)	-
12562	Don't Take Your Love From Me	unissued(?)

All titles on (S)R52007 also on Columbia(E)33SX1117,Versailles(F)STDX8019,Jazz Legacy(F)
JL68,500118.
All titles on (S)R52007 - except "Street Of Dreams" - also on Vogue(F)VG651.600123 (CD).
All titles on (S)R52007 - except "Lock-Up" - also on Vogue(F)LDM30.123.

EDDIE "LOCKJAW" DAVIS AND HIS TRIO:
Eddie Davis(ts),Shirley Scott(org),George Duvivier(b),Arthur Edgehill(dr).
                                               NYC.January 20,1958

21670	Day By Day	Roost RLP2227,Sonet(Sd)SXP2833
21671	Do Nothing Till You Hear From Me	- ,Sonet(Sd)SXP2847
21672	I Remember You	-
21673	Autumn In New York	-
21674	Penthouse Serenade	-
21675	Don't Get Around Much Anymore	- ,Sonet(Sd)SXP2833
21676	Scotty	- ,Sonet(Sd)SXP2847
21677	On The Street Where You Live	- ,Sonet(Sd)SXP2833

All titles also on CID(F)42003.

Same.   NYC.January 21,1958

	Dee Dee's Dance	Roost RLP2227,Sonet(Sd)SXP2847
	Land Of Dreams	-
1722	Everything I Have Is Yours	- ,Sonet(Sd)SXP2847
1723	Don't Worry 'Bout Me	- ,Sonet(Sd)SXP2833

All titles also on CID(F)42003.
Note:Earlier given information on the existence of a different version of RLP2227 - con-
    taining re-issues of the 1952-54 Roost recordings - is incorrect; the Roost label
    copy files only list the 1958 recordings for RLP2227.

Same.   NYC.March 1958

2753	A Gal In Calico	Roulette(S)R52019,Sonet(Sd)SXP2019
2754	Now That I Need You	-	-
2755	This Time The Dream's On Me	-
2756	Fine And Dandy	-
2757	Canadian Sunset	-
2758	There Is No Greater Love	-
2759	Night And Day	-
2760	What Is There To Say	-

(session cont. next page).

(session cont. from previous page):
```
12761  Snowfall                    Roulette (S)R52019
12762  Just One More Chance                - ,Sonet(Sd)SXP2019
12763  Afternoon In A Doghouse             -
12764  Close Your Eyes                     - ,Sonet(Sd)SXP2019
```

Eddie Davis(ts),Shirley Scott(org),Bill Pemberton(b),Arthur Edgehill(dr).
```
                                   NYC.June 14,1958
K8968  All God's Chillun Got Rhythm King LP606,Swingtime ST1021
K8969  This Can't Be Love                 -              -
K8970  Mean To Me                         -              -
K8971  Out Of Nowhere              King LP599,LP665,Bethlehem BCP6069
K8972  All Of You                  King LP606,Bethlehem BCP6069,Swingtime ST1021
K8973  If I Were A Bell                   -                              -
```

All titles also on King LP665,AudioLab AL1601.
All titles on BCP6069 also on Bethlehem BCP6035(new series),Affinity(E)AFF153.

EDDIE "LOCKJAW" DAVIS QUINTET:
Jerome Richardson(fl,ts),Eddie Davis(ts),Shirley Scott(org),George Duvivier(b),Arthur
Edgehill(dr).   NYC.June 20,1958
```
1524   The Chef(no ts/fl)          Prestige 45-126,PRLP7141,Esquire(E)EP237,Metronome
                                      (Sd)MEP449
1525   Have Horn,Will Blow         Prestige PRLP7141,Esquire(E)EP217,Metronome(Sd)
                                      MEP449
1526   In The Kitchen              Prestige 45-129,45-196,PRLP7141
1527   But Beautiful               Prestige 45-144,PRLP7141,Esquire(E)EP217
1528   Three Deuces                Prestige 45-126,      - ,Esquire(E)EP237
```

All titles also on Prestige PR7660,P24039,Esquire(E)32-104,Original Jazz Classics OJC652,
OJCCD652-2 (CD).

EDDIE "LOCKJAW" DAVIS QUARTET:
Omit Richardson.   NYC.September 12,1958
```
1582   Tangerine                   Prestige 45-148,PRLP7154
1583   Pots 'N' Pans               Prestige PR7301
1584   Old Devil Moon              Prestige 45-137,PRLP7154
1585   I'll Never Be The Same      Prestige 45-148,      - ,Metronome(Sd)MEP489
1586   I Let A Song Go Out Of My Heart Prestige 45-138    -              -
1587   You Stepped Out Of A Dream         -              -
1588   It's A Blue World           Prestige PR7301
1589   Blue Lou                           -
1590   Avalon                      Prestige PR7791,Original Jazz Classics OJCCD652-2
                                      (CD)
1591   Too Close For Comfort       Prestige PRLP7154
1592   Willow Weep For Me          Prestige 45-155,PR7791,Original Jazz Classics
                                      OJCCD653-2(CD)
1593   But Not For Me              Prestige PRLP7154
1594   Strike Up The Band          Prestige PRLP7219,Original Jazz Classics
                                      OJCCD756-2(CD)
1595   Just A Lucky So And So      Prestige PRLP7219,PR7710,Original Jazz Classics
                                      OJCCD756-2(CD)
1596   Body And Soul               Prestige 45-137,PRLP7154
1597   Pennies From Heaven         Prestige PR7301,PR7313
```

All titles on PRLP7154 also on Original Jazz Classics OJC218.
All titles on PR7301 also on Original Jazz Classics OJC705-2 (CD),HMV(F)FELP10018.

Jerome Richardson(ts,fl),Eddie Davis(ts),Shirley Scott(org),George Duvivier(b),Arthur
Edgehill(dr).   NYC. December 5,1958
(session cont. next page).

(session cont. from previous page):

1676	The Broilers	Prestige PRLP7161,Metronome(Sd)MEP498
1677	The Goose Hangs High	Prestige PRLP7219
1678	Simmerin'	-
1679	Heat 'N Serve	-
1680	My Old Flame	-
1681	Stardust	Prestige 45-155,PRLP7161
1682	High Fry	Prestige PR7301,PR7710
1683	Skillet	Prestige PRLP7161,PR7710
1684	Smoke This	Prestige PR7301
1685	I Surrender Dear	Prestige 45-146,PRLP7161,Metronome(Sd)MEP498
1686	Jaws	Prestige PR7301
1687	The Rev	Prestige 45-146,PRLP7161,Bluesville BVLP1010

All titles on PRLP7161 also on Prestige PR7782,P24039,(F)331.002,Original Jazz Classics
OJCCD653-2 (CD).
All titles on PRLP7219 also on Original Jazz Classics OJCCD756-2 (CD).
All titles on PR7301 also on Original Jazz Classics OJC705-2 (CD),HMV(F)FELP10018.

EDDIE "LOCKJAW" DAVIS - BUDDY TATE - COLEMAN HAWKINS - ARNETT COBB:
Eddie Davis,Buddy Tate,Coleman Hawkins,Arnett Cobb(ts),Shirley Scott(org),George Duvivier
(b),Arthur Edgehill(dr).   NYC.April 29,1959

1764	Light And Lovely	Prestige PRLP7167
1765	Very Saxy	- ,PR7710
1766	Foot Pattin'	-
1767	Fourmost	-
1768	Lester Leaps In	-

All titles also on Prestige PR7790,Bel Air(F)331.005,Esquire(E)32-117,Original Jazz Classics OJCCD458-2 (CD).
Note:PRLP7167 (and equivalents) issued as "Very Saxy".

EDDIE "LOCKJAW" DAVIS QUINTET:
Steve Pulliam(tb),Eddie Davis(ts),Shirley Scott(org),George Duvivier(b),Arthur Edgehill
(dr).   NYC.May 1,1959

1769	Intermission Riff	Prestige PRLP7171
1770	Our Delight	- ,Metronome(Sd)MEP9025
1771	Bingo Domingo	- ,PR7710, -
1772	Bahia	-
1773	Can't Get Out Of This Mood	-
1774	Foxy	-

All titles also on Esquire(E)32-128,Original Jazz Classics OJC322.

Omit Pulliam;add Ray Barretto(bg),Luis Perez(cg).
                                                 NYC.December 20,1959

1959	Come Rain Or Come Shine	Prestige PRLP7178
1960	Last Train From Overbrook	Prestige 45-171,PRLP7178
1961	Dobbin' With Redd Foxx	- -
1962	That Old Black Magic	Prestige PRLP7178
1963	Sometimes I'm Happy	-
1964	Dancero	-
1965	Fast Spiral	-
1966	When Your Lover Has Gone	-
1967	Yes Indeed(org,b,dr only)	Prestige PRLP7173

Note:PRLP7173 issued under Shirley Scott's name.

Eddie Davis(ts),Shirley Scott(org),George Duvivier(b),Arthur Edgehill(dr).
                                                 NYC.January 31,1960
(session cont. next page).

(session cont. from previous page):
2011	It Could Happen To You	Moodsville MVLP4	
2012	What's New	-	
2013	The Very Thought Of You	-	
2014	Serenade In Blue	-	
2015	Man With Horn	-	
2016	The Man I Love	-	
2017	Smoke Gets In Your Eyes	- ,MVLP33	
2018	I Cover The Waterfront	-	
2019	The Christmas Song	Prestige 45-186,Original Jazz Classics OJC6011	
2020	Santa Claus Is Coming To Town	-	-

EDDIE "LOCKJAW" DAVIS - SHIRLEY SCOTT:
Eddie Davis(ts),Shirley Scott(org),Wendell Marshall(b),Arthur Edgehill(dr),Ray Barretto
(cg).   NYC.April 12,1960
2161	I Wished On The Moon	Moodsville MVLP30
2162	From This Moment On	Prestige PR7456
2163	Give Me A Kiss Goodnight	Moodsville MVLP30
2164	Moon Of Manakoora	-
2165	Just Friends	-
2166	Speak Low	-

EDDIE "LOCKJAW" DAVIS - JOHNNY GRIFFIN QUINTET:
Eddie Davis,Johnny Griffin(ts),Norman Simmons(p),Victor Sproles(b),Ben Riley(dr).
                                                 NYC.September 2,1960
2429	Pull My Coat	Prestige 45-183,PRLP7282
2430	What's Happening	Prestige PRLP7282
2431	Abundance	-
2432	63rd Street Theme	-
2433	Hey,Jim	-
2434	If I Had You	-

All titles also on HMV/VSM(F)FELP10005.

EDDIE "LOCKJAW" DAVIS BIG BAND:
Clark Terry,Richard Williams,Bobby Bryant(tp),Jimmy Cleveland,Melba Liston(tb),Eric Dolphy
(as),Oliver Nelson(as,arr),Eddie Davis(ts),Jerome Richardson,George Barrows(ts,fl),Bob
Ashton(bars),Richard Wyands(p),Wendell Marshall(b),Roy Haynes(dr),Ernie Wilkins(arr).
                                                 NYC.September 20,1960
2498	Walk Away	Prestige PRLP7206	
2499	Trane Whistle	-	
2500	Whole Nelson	-	
2501	Stolen Moments	-	
2502	Jaws	-	
2503	You Are Too Beautiful	- ,Atlantis(E)ATSD14	

All titles on PRLP7206 also on Prestige PR7834,Esquire(E)32-174,XTRA(E)XTRA5019,Original
Jazz Classics OJC429,OJCCD429-2 (CD).

EDDIE "LOCKJAW" DAVIS - JOHNNY GRIFFIN QUINTET:
Eddie Davis,Johnny Griffin(ts),Junior Mance(p),Larry Gales(b),Ben Riley(dr).
                                                 NYC.November 4/10,1960
Funky Fluke	Jazzland 45-703,JLP(9)31,Milestone M47035			
Tickle Toe	Jazzland 45-704,	-	-	
Save Your Love For Me	-	-	-	,Frankl.
	Mint 88			
Twins	Jazzland JLP(9)31,JLP(9)1001			
Imagination	-			
Soft Winds	-			
Hey,Lock	Jazzland JLP(9)42			

(session cont. next page).

(session cont. from previous page):
```
        The Last Train From Overbrook    Jazzland JLP(9)42
        Midnight At Minton's                    -
        Second Balcony Jump                     -
        I'll Remember April                     -
        Good Bait                               - ,Milestone M47035,Riverside(J)
                                         SR7046
```

All titles on JLP(9)42 also on Original Jazz Classics OJC264.

```
Same.                                    Live."Minton's Playhouse",NYC.January 6,1961
        Light And Lovely                 Prestige PRLP7191,PR7357
        Straight,No Chaser                      -
        Woody'n You                             -
        Bingo Domingo                           -
        I'll Remember April                     -
        Billie's Bounce                  Prestige PR7309
        Epistrophy                              -
        Well,You Needn't                        -
        I'll Remember April(alt.vers.)          -
        In Walked Bud                    Prestige PR7330
        Land Of Dreams                          -
        Bean-O                                  -
        Robbins' Nest                           -
        Our Delight                             -
        Theme                                   -
        Dee Dee's Dance                  Prestige PR7357
        Billie's Bounce                         -
        Epistrophy                              -
```

All titles on PRLP7191 also on Prestige PR7407,P24099,Bel Air(F)331.007,Esquire(E)32-144.
All titles on PR7309 also Stateside(E)SL10102.
All titles on PR7330 also on Prestige P24099,Transatlantic(E)PR9000.

```
Same.                                    NYC.February 7,1961
        In Walked Bud                    Jazzland 45-707,JLP(9)39
        'Round Midnight(1)                      -            -
        Ruby My Dear(2)                  Jazzland 45-708,           -
        Rhythm-A-Ning                           -
        Epistrophy                       Jazzland JLP(9)39,Riverside RM(S)3503,Milestone
                                           M47035
        Stickball (I Mean You)           Jazzland JLP(9)39,Milestone M47035
        Well,You Needn't                        -                  -
```

1.Omit Davis.
2.Omit Griffin.

All titles on JLP(9)39 also on Riverside(J)VIJ5053.

EDDIE "LOCKJAW" DAVIS WITH RAY BARRETTO'S LATIN PERCUSSION AND BRASS:
Clark Terry,Ernie Royal,Phil Sunkel(tp),Eddie Davis(ts),Lloyd Mayers(p),Larry Gales(b),Ben
Riley(dr),Ray Barretto(cg,bg),additional unknown musicians(Latin-perc),Gil Lopez(arr).
```
                                         NYC.May 4/12,1961
        Wild Rice(1)                     Riverside 45-471,RLP(9)373
        Alma Alegre (Happy Soul)                -            -
        Guanco Lament                    Riverside RLP(9)373
        Tin Tin Deo(1)                          -
        Jazz-A-Samba(1)                         -
        Star Eyes                               -
        Afro-Jaws                               -
```
 session cont. next page).

(session cont. from previous page):
-1.John Bello(tp) replaces Sunkel.

All titles also on Jazzland JLP(9)97,Original Jazz Classics OCJ403,OJCCD403-2 (CD).

EDDIE "LOCKJAW" DAVIS - JOHNNY GRIFFIN QUINTET:
Eddie Davis,Johnny Griffin(ts),Lloyd Mayers(p),Larry Gales(b),Ben Riley(dr).
                                    NYC.June 5,1961
        Blues Up And Down   Jazzland JLP(9)60,Milestone M47035
        Leapin' On Lenox   -
        Nice And Easy   -
        Layin' On Mellow   -
        Walkin'   - ,Milestone M47035

Same.   NYC.August 17,1961
        Oh,Gee   Jazzland 45-717,JLP(9)60
        Camp Meeting   -   - ,Milestone M47035

All titles on JLP(9)60 also on Riverside(Eu)673.015.

EDDIE "LOCKJAW" DAVIS - JOHNNY GRIFFIN QUINTET:
Eddie Davis,Johnny Griffin(ts),Horace Parlan(p),Buddy Catlett(b),Ben Riley(dr).
                                    NYC.February 5,1962
        Bahia   Jazzland JLP(9)76
        Blue Lou   - ,Milestone M47035
        How Am I To Know   -   -
        Ow   -
        I Wished On The Moon   -
        Tin Tin Deo   - ,Milestone M47035
        From This Moment On   - ,Riverside(J)SR7072

EDDIE "LOCKJAW" DAVIS QUINTET:
Eddie Davis(ts),Horace Parlan(p),Buddy Catlett(b),Art Taylor(dr),Willie Bobo(cg).
                                    NYC.May 1,1962
3506   Yes,Yes   Prestige PRLP7242
3507   Please Send Me Someone To Love Prestige 45-220,PRLP7242
3508   Our Love Is Here To Stay   Prestige PRLP7242
3509   Goin' To The Meetin'   Prestige 45-220,PRLP7242
3510   Oh,Babee   Prestige PRLP7242
3511   Night And Day   -
3512   Pass The Hat   -
3513   Little Cougar   -
3514   People Will Say We're In Love   - ,Moodsville MVLP35

All titles also on Prestige(J)VIJ5066,Esquire(E)32-194.

Eddie Davis(ts),Don Patterson(org),Paul Weeden(g),George Duvivier(b),Billy James(dr).
                                    NYC.November 15,1962
3653   Day By Day   Prestige PRLP7271
3654   Robbins' Nest   Prestige 45-257,PRLP7271
3655   Beano   unissued
3656   Street Lights   Prestige PRLP7261
3657   Sweet And Lovely   Prestige 45-236,PRLP7261
3658   I Only Have Eyes For You   -   -
3659   The Way You Look Tonight   Prestige PRLP7261
3660   It's A Pity To Say Goodnight   -
3661   Time On My Hands   -
3662   There'll Never Be Another You Prestige PRLP7271
3663   Beano   Prestige 45-279,PRLP7271
3664   What's New   -
3665   Too Marvelous for Words   -
3666   A Foggy Day   Prestige 45-257,   -

Eddie Davis(ts),Cedar Walton(p),Kenny Burrell(g),Bob Cranshaw(b),Billie Brooks(dr).
NYC.December 8,1964
What's New   Columbia G30217,CBS(Eu)66266

Eddie Davis(ts),Ross Tompkins(p),Les Spann(g),Russell George(b),Chuck Lampkin(dr),Ray
Barretto(cg).   NYC.June 20,1966
TPA1-5115 West Coast Blues   RCA-Victor LPM/LSP3652
TPA1-5116 On Green Dolphin Street   - ,Bluebird 6463,(E)ND86463
TPA1-5117 Oh!Gee!   -   -   -
TPA1-5118 Speak Low   -   -   -
TPA1-5119 Nina Never Know   -

Same.   NYC.June 21,1966
TPA1-5120 Save Your Love For Me   RCA-Victor LPM/LSP3652,Bluebird 6463,(E)ND86463
TPA1-5121 On A Clear Day   -
TPA1-5122 The Days Of Wine And Roses   -
TPA1-5123 The Good Life   - ,Bluebird 6463,(E)ND86463
TPA1-5124 Midnight Sun .   -

All titles on LPM/LSP3652 also on RCA(F)NL89584.

Ernie Royal,Joe Newman,Thad Jones,Snooky Young(tp),Urbie Green,Wayne Andre,Jimmy Cleveland
(tb),Tony Studd(btb),Bobby Plater(as,arr),Jerome Richardson(as),Eddie Davis,Billy Mitchell
Frank Wess(ts),Danny Bank(bars),Hank Jones(p),Gene Bertoncini(g),George Duvivier(b),Grady
Tate(dr).   NYC.November 1,1966
TPA1-7836 I Wished On The Moon   RCA-Victor LPM/LSP3741,Bluebird 6463,(E)ND86463
TPA1-7837 When Your Lover Has Gone   -   -   -
TPA1-7838 This Is Always   -
TPA1-7839 People Will
          Say We're In Love   -

Burt Collins(tp),J.J. Johnson(tb),Roland Hanna(p) replace Thad Jones,Andre,Hank Jones;omit
Wess.   NYC.November 2,1966
TPA1-7840 Born To Be Blue   RCA-Victor LPM/LSP3741
TPA1-7841 Bye Bye Blackbird   - ,Bluebird 6463,(E)ND86463
TPA1-7842 Call Me   -   -   -
TPA1-7843 I Remember You   -

Ernie Royal,Joe Newman,Thad Jones,Snooky Young(tp),Urbie Green,J.J. Johnson,Jimmy Cle-
veland(tb),Tony Studd(btb),Bobby Plater(as,arr),Jerome Richardson(as),Eddie Davis,Frank
Foster(ts),Danny Bank(bars),Hank Jones(p),Billy Butler(g),George Duvivier(b),Grady Tate
(dr).   NYC.December 14,1966
TPA1-7844 Day By Day   RCA-Victor LPM/LSP3741,Bluebird 6463,(E)ND86463
TPA1-7845 Out Of Nowhere   -   -   -
          Invitation(?)   RCA(F)NL70120(?)

All titles on LPM/LSP3741 also on RCA(F)NL70120.

Eddie Davis(ts),Jan Johansson(p),Roman Dylag(b),Albert Heath(dr).
Stockholm.May 8,1967
          I'll Remember April   Storyville(D)STCD4123(CD)
          A Gal In Calico   -
          I'll Never Be The Same   -
          Oh,Gee   -
          I Only Have Eyes For You   -
          Intermission   -

Note:The above titles were recorded - and broadcast - by the Swedish Radio.

EDDIE "LOCKJAW" DAVIS - PAUL GONSALVES:
Eddie Davis(ts),Paul Gonsalves(ts),Roland Hanna(p),Everett Barksdale(g),Ben Tucker(b),
Grady Tate(dr).   NYC.August 2,1967
UPA1-6388 The Man With The Horn   RCA-Victor LPM/LSP3882,Bluebird 6463,(E)ND86463
UPA1-6389 Just Friends   -
UPA1-6390 A Weaver Of Dreams   - ,Bluebird 6463,(E)ND86463
UPA1-6391 Love Is Here To Stay   -
UPA1-6392 If I Should Lose You   -

Same.   NYC.August 3,1967
UPA1-6393 When Sunny Gets Blue   RCA-Victor LPM/LSP3882
UPA1-6394 Don't Blame Me(1)   -
UPA1-6395 We'll Be Together Again(2)   - ,Bluebird 6463,(E)ND86463
UPA1-6396 I Should Care   -
UPA1-6397 Time After Time   -
UPA1-6398 If I Ruled The World   -

-1.Omit Davis.
-2.Omit Gonsalves.

All titles on LPM/LSP3882 also on RCA(F)PL43192.

EDDIE "LOCKJAW" DAVIS - JOHNNY GRIFFIN:
Eddie Davis,Johnny Griffin(ts),Francy Boland(p),Jimmy Woode(b),Kenny Clarke(dr).
                                       Cologne,Germany.April 24,1970
          Again 'N' Again   Saba(G)SB15283
          Tin Tin Deo   -
          If I Had You   -
          Jim Dawg   -
          When We Were One   -
          Gigi   -

All titles also on MPS(G)21.20742,(E)BAP5003,(F)5C.064-61174,(J)ULX15,Pausa PR7063.

Eddie Davis(ts),Milt Buckner(p),Jimmy Leary(b),Gus Johnson(dr).
                                       Vallauris,France.July 20,1974
          Leapin' On Lenox   Black & Blue(F)33.072,Denon DC8520(CD)
          On Green Dolphin Street   - ,Denon DC8529(CD)
          Body And Soul   - ,Denon CDC9009(CD)
          Quiet Nights   -
          Just Friends   -
          Mean To Me   - ,950.502
          I Can't Get Started   -
          The Shadow Of Your Smile   -

All titles - except "The Shadow Of Your Smile" - also on Denon CDC9028 (CD),Giganti del
Jazz(I)GJ70.

EDDIE "LOCKJAW" DAVIS ET MICHEL ATTENOUX ET SON ORCHESTRE:
Patrick Artero(tp),Claude Gousset(tb),Michel Attenoux(as),Eddie Davis(ts),Gabriel Garva-
noff(p),Jean-Pierre Mulot(b),Teddy Martin(dr).
                                       Live.Antibes.July 24,1975
          Splanky   Mahogany(F)558.104,Storyville(D)STCD5009(CD)
          Moonlight In Vermont   -   -
          Gee Baby Ain't I Good To You   -   -
          Flying Home   -   -
          What Am I Here For   -   -
          What's New   -   -
          Midnite Blues   -   -
          Lush Life   -   -
          Shiny Stockings   -   -

EDDIE "LOCKJAW" DAVIS WITH GEORGES ARVANITAS TRIO:
Eddie Davis(ts),Georges Arvanitas(p),Jacky Samson(b),Charles Saudrais(dr).
                                        Live.Massy,France.October 23,1975
        Cherokee   Spotlite(E)SPJ15
        Stomping At The Savoy   -
        Ghost Of A Chance   -
        Green Dolphin Street   -
        Avalon   -
        I Can't Get Started   -
        Tangerine   -
        Oh!Gee!   -

Eddie Davis(ts),Wild Bill Davis(org),Billy Butler(g),Oliver Jackson(dr).
                                        Paris.January 21,1976
        Don't Worry About Me   Black&Blue(F)33.101
        The Man I Love   -
        Light And Lovely   -
        Stompin' At The Savoy   -
        When Sunny Gets Blue   -
        Blue And Sentimental   -
        Jumpin' With Symphony Sid
        Pennies From Heaven   Black&Blue(F)33.133,233.101(CD),59.004-2(CD)

All titles on Black&Blue(F)33.101 also on Black&Blue(F)233.101 (CD),59.004-2 (CD).
Note:"Pennies From Heaven" originally issued under Wild Bill Davis' name.
     The same group also recorded under Wild Bill Davis' name (January 22, 1976).

Eddie Davis(ts),Thomas Clausen(p),Bo Stief(b),Alex Riel(dr).
                                        Copenhagen.March 8,1976
        Bye Bye Blackbird   SteepleChase(D)SCS1058
        Swingin' Till
            The Girls Come Home   -
        Love For Sale   -
        Wave   -
        Ghost Of A Chance   -
        Locks   -
        Out Of Nowhere   -
        Indiana   -

All titles also on SteepleChase STCD31058 (CD),(J)RJ7411,32JD10127 (CD),Inner City IC2058.

Eddie Davis(ts),Tommy Flanagan(p),Keeter Betts(b),Bobby Durham(dr).
                                        LA.May 3,1976
        Lover   Pablo 2310.778,Pablo 2310.858
        Wave   -   -
        On A Clear Day
            (You Can See Forever)   -   -
        The Chef   -   -
        Gigi   -
        Last Train From Overbrook   -
        The Good Life   -
        I'll Never Be The Same   - ,Pablo 2310.858
        Watch What Happens   -

All titles also on Pablo(J)MTF1060,Original Jazz Classics OJC629,OJCCD629-2 (CD).

EDDIE "LOCKJAW" DAVIS AND HARRY EDISON WITH JOHN DARVILLE'S QUARTET:
Harry Edison(tp),John Darville -1(tb),Eddie Davis(ts),Kenny Drew(p),Hugo Rasmussen(b),
Svend-Erik Nørregård(dr).   Copenhagen.July 6,1976
(session cont. next page).

(session cont. from previous page):
```
        Lullaby For Dancers          Storyville(D)SLP276
        Angel Eyes(no tp)                           -
        Lester Leaps In(1)                          -
        Spotlite                                    -
        September Song(no ts)                       -
        Blues Walk(1)                               -
        Opus Funk                    Storyville(D)SLP281
        There Is No
           Greater Love(tp,b only)                  -
        Robbins' Nest(1)                            -
        Candy                                       -
        You Are Too Beautiful(no tp)                -
        C Jam Blues(1)                              -
```

All titles on SLP276 also on Storyville(D)SLP4004.
All titles on SLP281 also on Storyville(D)SLP4025.
Note:SLP281 issued under Edison's name.

EDDIE "LOCKJAW" DAVIS - HARRY EDISON:
Harry Edison(tp),Eddie Davis(ts),Gerald Wiggins(p),Major Holley(b,vcl),Oliver Jackson
(dr).   Paris.February 14,1977
```
        Jim Dawg                     Black&Blue(F)33.121,233.106(CD)
        The Good Life                            -          -
        Meditation                               -          -
        Intermission Riff                        -          -
        Land Of Dreams                           -
        Light And Lovely                         -
        Just Friends                 Black&Blue(F)33.106,233.106(CD)
        Sunday                                   -          -
        Yesterdays                               -          -
        Gimme Some                               -          -
        Super                                    -
        There Is No Greater Love(no ts)          -   ,233.106(CD)
        My Old Flame(no ts)                      -
```

All titles on Black&Blue(F)33.121 also on Classic Jazz CJ116.
All titles on Black&Blue(F)33.106 also on Classic Jazz CJ132.
Note:Black&Blue(F)33.106 was issued under Edision's name.

EDDIE "LOCKJAW" DAVIS QUARTET:
Eddie Davis(ts),Oscar Peterson(p),Ray Brown(b),Jimmie Smith (dr).
                                 Live.Montreux Jazz Festival,Switzerland.July 15,1977
```
        This Can't Be Love           Pablo 2308.214
        I Wished On The Moon                     -
        The Breeze And I                         -
        Angel Eyes                               -   ,Pablo 2310.858
        Telegraph                                -             -
        Land Of Dreams                           -             -
        Blue Lou                                 -             -
```

All titles also on Pablo 2620.107 (8xLP album),(J)MTF1810,Original Jazz Classics OJC384,
OJCCD384-2 (CD).

EDDIE "LOCKJAW" DAVIS - HARRY EDISON:
Harry Edison(tp),Eddie Davis(ts),Alain Jean-Marie(p),Pierre Michelot(b),Sam Woodyard(dr).
                                 Paris.November 30,1978
```
        It Could Happen To You       All Life(F)AL008
        Pumpin' "It" Up                          -
        Polka Dots And Moonbeams(no ts)
```
(session cont. next page).

(session cont. from previous page):
```
        Secret Love(no tp)              All Life(F)AL008
        Jumpin' With Symphony Sid             -
        All Of Me                             -
        Yesterdays                            -
        Don't Blame Me(no tp)                 -
```

Harry Edison(tp),Eddie Davis(ts),Alain Jean-Marie(p),Marc Michel(b),Sam Woodyard(dr).
                                    Villetaneuse,Paris.December 1,1978
```
        Shiny Stockings                 Jazz Today(F)JT2601
        Moonlight In Vermont                  -
        Ow                                    - ,Vogue(F)VG651.600123(CD)
        'S Wonderful                          -                    -
        Exactly Like You                      -                    -
        Tenderly                              -
        You Stepped Out Of A Dream            -
```

All titles also on Vogue(F)VG405.502601.

Eddie Davis(ts),Albert Dailey(p),George Duvivier(b),Victor Lewis(dr).
                                    NYC.January 18,1979
```
        When Your Lover Has Gone        Muse MR5202
        Just One Of Those Things              -
        Medley:                               -
            Old Folks
            Out Of Nowhere
        Secret Love                           -
        Comin',Home Baby                      -
        You Stepped Out Of a Dream            -
        Jim Dog                               -
```

EDDY DAVIS

EDDY DAVIS DIXIE JAZZMEN:
Norman Murphy(tp),Jug Berger(cl,vcl),Eddy Davis(bj,vcl),Ed Wilkinson(tu),Wayne Jones(dr,
vcl).   Live."Old Town Gate",Chicago.June 29,1966
```
        ODJB One Step                   Blackbird 701,M12001/S12001
        It Don't Mean A Thing                 -
        Sister Kate(jb)                       -
        More                                  -
        My Kind Of Town                 Blackbird 701,    -
        Louisiana                             -
```

Jack The Bear Brown(tp) replaces Murphy;add Jerry Lofstrom -1(b).
                                    Same date
```
        Medley(1)(no tu):               Blackbird M12001/S12001
            Mame(ed)
            Hello Dolly(ed)
        Jazz Me Blues(wj)                     -
        Limehouse Blues                       -
        Kansas City Torch(ed)                 -
        Bill Bailey(ed)                       -
```

Eddy Davis,Buck Kelly(bj),unknown(b,g).   Unknown location.c. 1974/75
```
        Cascades Rag                    Pa Da P7401
        Bethena Waltz                         -
        Euphonic Sounds                       -
        Magnetic Rag                          -
```
(session cont. next page).

(session cont. from previous page):
```
        The Entertainer            Pa Da P7401
        Stoptime Rag                   -
        Gymnopedies no 1              -
        Golliwog's Cakewalk          -
        Russian Rag                  -
        Original Rags(1)             -
```

Incl. Jackie Coon(cnt),Bobby Gordon(as),George Probert(ss,ocarina),Eddy Davis(bj,vcl).
```
                            Unknown location.c.  1974
        My Canary Has
            Circles Under His Eyes   Pa Da P7402
        Lovin' Sam,The Sheik Of Alabam'    -
        Santa Claus Blues            -
        Irish Black Bottom           -
        Take Your Tomorrows          -
```

Eddy Davis(bj),Howard Smith(tu),Bob Raggio(perc).
```
                            Unknown location.c.  1974
        The Pearls                   Pa Da P7402
        Kansas City Stomps           -
        Original Jelly Roll Blues    -
        King Porter Stomp            -
        Mr Jelly Lord                -
        Black Bottom Stomp           -
```

EDDY DAVIS AND THE HOT JAZZ ORCHESTRA:
Jack Maheu(cl),Don Ewell(p),Eddy Davis(bj),Bill Goodall(b),George Reed(dr).
```
                            Buffalo,New York.January 15,1976
        Riverboat Shuffle            Jazzology J88
        Sweet Substitute             -
        Cherry                       -
        Memphis Blues                -
        At The Jazz Band Ball        -
        Rhythm King                  -
        Hesitation Blues             -
        Crazy 'Bout My Baby          -
        Buddy Bolden's Blues         -
        'Deed I Do                   -
```

EDDY DAVIS AND THE HOT JAZZ ORCHESTRA OF EUROPE:
Herbert Christ(tp),René Franc(ss,cl),Eddy Davis(bj),Jean-Pierre Lumont(b).
```
                            Frankfurt,Germany.  1976
        New Orleans Shuffle          New York Jazz J005
        Because It's You That
            Put The Music In My Heart          -
        Minority Blues                         -
        Rene's Bar-B-Que                       -
        Ragtime Dance                          -
        Rocking Chair                          -
        Blame It On The Blues                  -
        China Boy                              -
        My Man                                 -
        I Can't Believe That
            You're In Love With Me             -
```

EDDY DAVIS AND THE HOT JAZZ ORCHESTRA:
Max Kaminsky(tp),Bobby Gordon(cl),Dill Jones(p),Eddy Davis(bj),Vince Giordano(bassax,tu).
```
                            Unknown location.September 18,1978
```
(session cont. next page).

(session cont. from previous page):
```
        Oriental Strut                    Jazzology J67
        Lazy Bones                            -
        (I Would Do) Anything For You         -
        Don't Cry,Joe                         -
        Turn On The Heat                      -
        Them There Eyes                       -
        Mandy,Make Up Your Mind               -
        Oh,Daddy                              -
        Honeysuckle Rose                      -
```

Note:The jazz content of some of the above recordings may be limited.

JACKIE DAVIS

JACKIE DAVIS TRIO:
Jackie Davis(org),unknown b,dr.   Unknown location.c. 1951
```
        Do,Baby,Do                       Victor 20/47-5111
        Coffee Time                           -
```

No details.   LA. 1952
```
        Autumn In New York               Trend 65,LP1010
        They Can't Take That Away From Me    -      -
        Oh,You Crazy Moon                Trend LP1010
        Did I Remember                        -
        My Romance                            -
        I Dream Of You                        -
        Aggravatin' Situation                 -
        There's A Lull In My Life             -
        I Concentrate On You                  -
        I Let A Song Go Out Of My Heart       -
        The Christmas Song                    -
        Better Luck Next Time                 -
```

All titles also on Kapp KL1030.

No details.   LA.c. September 1955
```
14414  Would You Like To Take A Walk     Capitol T686,T951
14415  The Night Is Young                    -
14427  Beau Nights In Hotchkiss Corner       -
14428  The Talk Of The Town                  -
14456  I'll Close My Eyes                    -
14457  Sleepy Head                           -
14458  For Heaven's Sake                     -
14459  Between The Devil
          And The Deep Blue Sea              -
14463  I Hear A Rhapsody                     - ,T948
14464  It All Comes Back To You             - ,T954
14465  Time Was                             - ,T944
14466  Taking A Chance On Love               -
```

Jackie Davis(org),Irving Ashby(g),Shelly Manne(dr).
                                             LA.c. 1956/57
```
        Chasing Shadows                  Capitol T815
        Central Park                          -
        You Keep Coming Back Like A Song      -
        I've Got Pocketful Of Dreams          -
        Irresistable You                      -
        Lovely Lady Waltz                     -
```
(session cont. next page).

(session cont. from previous page):
    Constantly   Capitol T815
    Unknown titles   -

Jackie Davis(org),Irving Ashby(g),Milt Holland(dr).
                                    LA.October 1957

17750	I Wonder When My Baby's Coming Home	Capitol T974
17751	Across The Alley From The Alamo	-
17752	Jumpin' Jackie	-
17753	Darn That Dream	-
17758	Isn't It Romantic	-
17759	What's The Trouble	-
17760	I Got The Sun In The Morning	-
17761	Coffee Time	-
17764	Moonlight Becomes You	-
17766	I'd Love To Take Orders From You	-
17768	I've Hitched My Wagon To A Star	-
	So Beats My Heart For You	-

Eddie Costa(vbs),Jackie Davis(org),Kenny Burrell/Mundell Lowe(g),Bertell Knox(dr).
                                 NYC.April 1958

22086	All Of You	Capitol (S)T1046,(Eu)74098
22087	Say,Darling	-
22088	It's Second Time	- ,(Eu)74098
22089	Wish	-
22090	Push De Button	-
22091	Long Before I Knew You	-
22092	Surprise	-
22093	Just My Luck	- ,(E)SLCT6184
22094	I Feel Pretty	-
22095	Jubilation T. Cornpone	- ,(Eu)74098
22096	Standing On The Corner	-
22097	Till There Was You	- ,(Eu)74098

JACKIE DAVIS AND FOUR TROMBONES:
Bob Fitzpatrick,Joe Howard,Ed Kusby,Nick DiMaio,Dick Nash,George Roberts,Lester Robinson,
Frank Rosolino,Ken Shroyer(tb),Vincent DeRosa(frh),Jackie Davis(org),Irving Ashby(g),Joe
Comfort(b),Milt Holland(dr),Weede Morris(bg)(coll. pers.).
                               LA.c. September 1959

30504	There's Something In The Air	Capitol (S)T1180
30505	My,My	-
30527	Gonna' Get A Girl	Capitol 4158,(S)T11180
30528	Fascinating Rhythm	Capitol (S)T1180
30529	Charleston Alley	-
30587	Yours Is My Heart Alone	-
30588	This Can't Be Love	-
30589	When I'm With You	-
30590	Falling In Love With Love	-
30591	Frenesi	Capitol 4158, -

No details.   LA. 1959

32466	Calypso Blues	Capitol (S)T1419
32467	You Forgot Your Gloves	-
32468	You Took Advantage Of Me	-
32479	Softly As In A Morning Sunrise	-
32480	You Do Something To Me	-
32481	I've Got The World On A String	-
32482	Should I	-
32487	I Don't Want To Walk Around	-
32489	You And The Night And The Music	-

(session cont. next page).

(session cont. from previous page):
32490 The Major And The Minor   Capitol (S)T1419
32491 Thou Swell   -
32492 In The Shade Of The Old Apple Tree   -

JACKIE DAVIS TRIO:
No details.   LA. 1959
32554 A Woman In Love   Capitol (S)T1338,(Eu)74098
32555 Rain On The Roof   -
32556 Manana   -
32557 Perfidia   -
32595 The Glow-Worm Cha Cha   -
32596 Lady Play Your Mandolin   -
32597 Heat Wave   -
32598 Ain't She Sweet   -
32614 I Got Plenty O'Nuttin'   -
32615 In A Little Spanish Town   -
32616 Love Is Just Around The Corner   -
32617 Then I'll Be Happy   -

Jackie Davis(org),Irving Ashby(g),Joe Comfort(b),Weede Morris(dr).
                                    LA.c. October 1960
34609 Sunday Punch   Capitol (S)T1686
34610 Honeysuckle Rose   - ,(Eu)74098
34611 Time On My Hands   -   -
34635 Stop Look And Listen   -   -
34626 Stompin' At The Savoy   -
34643 Shadow Waltz   -
34656 What Can I Say
       After I Say I'm Sorry   -
34657 The Song Is You   -
34658 Sweet Sue,Just You   -
34659 Strange Music   -

Prob. the same.   LA.November/December 1960
34681 Without A Song   Capitol (S)T1517
34682 Sweet And Lovely   -
34683 Walkin' My Baby Back Home   -
34684 I'll Never Stop Loving You   -
34685 I Would Do Anything For You   -
34686 Just Friends   -
34687 Stop At My House   -
34807 You Don't Know What Love Is   -
34808 I Hadn't Anyone 'Till You   -
34809 Star Eyes   -

Jackie Davis(org),Barney Kessel(g),Joe Comfort(b),Earl Palmer(dr).
                                    LA.January 15,1963
E13002 In The Wee Small Hours   Warner Bros. W(S)1492
E13004 'Round Midnight   -
E13005 Easy Does It   -
E13006 Midnight Sun   -
E13007 Lonely Wine   -
E13009 One For My Baby   -
E13010 Five Minutes More   -
E13011 If I Could Be With You   -
E13012 Blues In The Night   -
E13013 Sleepy Time Gal   -
E13014 St. Louis Blues   -
E13015 Night Train   -

All titles also on Warner Bros.(E)WM/WS8128.

Jackie Davis(org),unknown choir(vcl),Sid Bass(cond).

		LA. 1963	
F13257	I'll Buy That Dream	Warner Bros. W(S)1515	
F13258	If You're My Dream	-	
F13259	You're My Dream	-	
F13260	Street Of Dreams	-	
F13261	I Ain't Lazy,I'm Just Dreamin'	-	

Same.

		NYC. 1963	
FX50758	When My Dreamboat Comes Home	Warner Bros. W(S)1515	
FX50759	If Dreams Come True	-	
FX50760	All I Do Is Dream Of You	-	
FX50761	Did You Ever See A Dream Walking	-	
FX50762	Wrap Your Troubles In Dreams(?)	-	
FX50763	Something I Dreamed Last Night	-	
	My Dream Is Yours	-	

Jackie Davis/org),Louis Debij(dr).

	Heemstede,The Netherlands. 1980
Chicago	EMI(Du)1A.054-26474
Evergreen (A Star Is Born)	-
Young And Foolish	-
Change Partners	-
Ain't She Sweet	-
I'm Happy	-
You Make Me Feel So Young	-
An Old Piano Plays The Blues	-
And Russia Is Her Name	-
All I Do Is Dream Of You	-

Note:The jazz content of some of the above recordings may be limited.

JIMMIE "LOVERMAN" DAVIS

(vcl) acc. by Michel De Villers(cl,as),Aaron Bridgers(p),Heinz Grah(b),Bernard Planche-
nault(dr).

	Paris.c. 1953
Lover Man	Concertum(F)TCV40
J'ai De La Veine	-
Blue Valley	-
C'est Beau	-
Why Is A Good Girl	
So Hard To Find	-
Un Dia Sin Ti	-
L'Amour Est Venu	-
Darling You're So Delicious	-
En P'tit Coup De Chapau	-
Sugar,Sugar Lady	-

LEM DAVIS

LEM DAVIS SEXTET:
Emmett Berry(tp),Vic Dickenson(tb),Lem Davis(as),Dodo Marmarosa(p),John Simmons(b),Henry
Green(dr),Ernie Sheppard(vcl).

		LA.October 20,1945	
SRC122-3	Nothin' From Nothin'(es)	Sunset 7558	
SRC122-5	Nothin' From Nothin'(es)	Polydor(E)2660.137	
SRC123-5	Blues In My Heart	-	
SRC124-4	It Was Meant To Be	-	
SRC125-6	My Blue Heaven	Sunset 7558,	-

(session cont. next page).

(session cont. from previous page):
All titles - except master SRC122-3 - also on Black Lion(E)BLP30113.

Neal Hefti(tp),Lem Davis(as),Hal Singer(ts),Sanford Gold(p),John Simmons(b),Denzil Best
(dr).   NYC.March 6,1946
S5894 Theme On The Beam   Savoy SJL2224
S5895 Solace   -
S5896 Chitlin Strut   -
S5897 Daily Double   -

Courtney Williams(tp),Vic Dickenson(tb),Lem Davis(as),Sanford Gold(p),Al Hall(b),Denzil
Best(dr).   NYC.May 10,1946
S59038 I Don't Believe   Savoy SJL2224
S59039 I Never Knew   -
S59040 Lovely You(no tp)   Savoy 607,SJL2224
S59041 G-U-M-P-E-Y(band-vcl)   -   -

Lem Davis(as),Teacho Wiltshire(p),Leonard Gaskin(b),Teddy Lee(dr).
                                           NYC.October 16,1951
215   The Glory Of Love   Prestige 911
216   Sin   -
217   This Is Always   Prestige 915
218   Knock Hop   -
219   Problem Child   Prestige 912
220   She's A Wine-O   -

No details.   NYC.December 20,1951
291   Pretty   Prestige 776
292   Hoppy's Hop   -

MARTHA DAVIS

Martha Davis(p,vcl).   NYC.August 1946
       Martha's Boogie   Urban 120
       Why Am I   -
MAS359 Be-Bop Bounce   Urban 121
MAS360 I'm Fer It   -

Add unknown orchestra.   Same date
       Lovin' Blues   Urban 126
       Can't Be Bothered   -
       The Same Old Boogie   Urban 127
       Time For The Postman's Ring   -

Martha Davis(p,vcl),Ralph Williams(g),Calvin Ponder(b),Lee Young(dr).
                                         Unknown location. 1948
JRC262 Bread And Gravy   Jewell ON2002
JRC263 Little White Lies   -
JRC264 When I Say Goodbye(md)   Jewell ON2003
JRC265 Sarah,Sarah(md)   -

Martha Davis(p,vcl),unknown acc.   LA.December 9,1947
4639 Cincinnati   Decca 24335

Same.   LA.December 16,1947
4666 Ooh,Wee   Decca 24383
4668 Honey,Honey,Honey   Decca 24335

Same.		LA.December 26,1947
L4736	Kitchen Blues	Decca 48174
L4737	Trouble Is A Man	Decca 24383
L4738	I Ain't Getting Any Younger	Decca 48174

No details.		LA.February 13,1951
L6071	Would I Love You,Love You	Coral 65048
L6072	Get Out Those Old Records	-

Martha Davis(p,vcl),John Collins(g),Calvin Ponder(b),Art Blakey(dr).
NYC.May 10,1951

80993	Experience	Coral unissued
80994	How Could Anything Be So Bad	
80995	You're The Doctor	Coral 60506
80996	Piano Player Boogie	-

No details.		LA.December 10,1951
L6570	No Deposit,No Return	Coral 60890
L6571	What Became Of You?	-

No details.		Unknown location/date
	Unknown titles	ABC-Paramount ABC160

Martha Davis(p,vcl),Calvin Ponder(b),rest unknown.
Unknown location.c. 1955

Your Feet's Too Big	ABC-Paramount ABC213
Jitterbug Waltz	-
Ain't Misbehavin'	-
It's A Sin To Tell A Lie	-
The Spider And The Fly	-
How Can You Face Me	-
Honeysuckle Rose	-
Lulu's Back In Town	-
Blue Turning Grey Over You	-
Hold Tight	-
Handful Of Keys	-
S'posin'	-

MAXWELL DAVIS

No details.		LA.c. 1946
	Lonesome Road Blues	4. Star 1027
	Honey Dripper	-
	Don't Worry 'Bout Me	Supreme 1544
	September In The Rain	-

JO-JO ADAMS(vcl) acc. by MAXWELL DAVIS AND HIS ORCHESTRA:
George Orendorff(tp),Jewell Grant(as),Maxwell Davis(ts),Francis Midell(bars),Garland Finney(p),Herman Mitchell(g),Ralph Hamilton(b),Lee Gibson(dr).
LA.June 11,1946

Disgusted	Aladdin 142
Thursday Evening Blues	-
Jo-Jo's Trouble	Aladdin 143
Upstairs	-
When I'm In My Tea	Aladdin 144
Hard Headed Woman Blues	-

MAXWELL DAVIS AND HIS ORCHESTRA:
Joe Evans(vcl) replaces Adams;Maxwell poss. also (vcl).
                                         LA. 1947
   Goody Goody Baby(je)   Black&White 785,840
   Root Of All My Evil(je)   - ,858
   Give It Up(je)   Black&White 786
   Private Stock(je)   -
   M.T. Boogie   Black&White 858

Note:Black&White 785 and 786 issued under Evans's name.

JUANITA BROWN / MAXWELL DAVIS AND HIS ALL STARS:
Unknown tp,as,Maxwell Davis(ts),unknoen bars,p,g,b,dr,Juanita Brown(vcl).
                                    LA.February 12,1949
RR630 Key To My Door(jb)   Aladdin 3022
RR633 Real Nervous(1)   Aladdin 3174
   Red Hot(2)(jb)   Aladdin 3022

-1."Real Nervous" replaced "Gomen Nashai" (February 18,1953) on later pressings of Aladdin
 3174.
-2.Prob. from this session.

MAXWELL DAVIS AND HIS BLENDERS:
No details;Jimmy Grissom(vcl).   LA. 1940's
   Get Out(jg)   Gotham 267
   Welcome Baby(jg)
   Hung Out   Swingtime 191
   The Adams' Bop Hop   -

MAXWELL DAVIS AND HIS ORCHESTRA:
Jake Porter(tp),Jack McVea(as),Maxwell Davis(ts),Maurice Simon(bars),Austin McCoy(p),Chuck
Norris(g),Red Callender(b),Lee Young(dr). LA.c. 1950
MM1444 Boogie Cocktails   Modern 20-791,Ace CHAD239
MM1445 Bristol Drive   Modern 20-805, -
MM1446 Resistor   -   -
MM1447 Belmont Special   Modern 20-791, -
MM3111 Tempo Rock(1)   RPM 482,Ace CHAD239
MM3112 Cool Diggin'   -   -
   Rockin' With Maxie   Ace CHAD239

-1.Add vocal chorus.

Note:See note after Dexter Gordon June 9,1952 session.

Maxwell Davis(ts),unknown p,g,b,dr,bg. LA.November 9,1951
RR1796 Charmaine   Aladdin 3114,EP509,AL709
RR1797 Hey,Good Lookin'   - - - ,AL804,Score LP4016
RR1798 I'm Waitin' Just For You Aladdin 3115,EP510, -
RR1799 I'll Always Be In Love With You - - -

CALVIN BOZE WITH MAXWELL DAVIS ALL STARS:
Calvin Boze(tp),Maxwell Davis(ts),unknown p,g,b,dr.
                                    LA.July 3,1952
RR1943 Blue Tango(1)   Aladdin 3142,EP509
RR1944 Popsicle   Aladdin 3143
RR1945 Blue Shuffle   -
RR1946 The Glory Of Love   Aladdin 3142,EP509

-1.Add unknown(ts).

All titles also on Aladdin AL709,AL804,Score LP4016.

CALVIN BOZE / MAXWELL DAVIS:
Calvin Boze -1(tp,vcl),Maxwell Davis(ts),unknown p,g,b,dr,bg.
                                        LA.August 15,1952
RR1968 Looped(1)(cb)   Aladdin 3147
RR1969 Blow Man Blow(1)(cb)   -
RR1970 Strange Fascination   Aladdin 3201,EP510,AL709,AL804,Score LP4016
RR1971 Kiss Me Again   Aladdin AL804,Score LP4016

Note:Masters RR1968-69 issued under Boze's Name; masters RR1970/71 issued under Davis'
     name.

MAXWELL DAVIS:
Maxwell Davis(ts),unknown p,b,dr,bg.   LA.February 18,1953
RR2080 Gomen Nashai   Aladdin 3174
RR2081 Hot Point (Forgive Me)   - ,AL804,Score LP4016

Note:"Real Nervous" (February 12,1949) replaced "Gomen Nashai" on later pressings of
     Aladdin 3174.

Maxwell Davis(ts),unknown p,b,dr.   LA.July 24,1953
RR2188 No Other Love   Aladdin 3201,EP510,AL709,AL804,Score LP4016

Note:The above title is an instrumental from a Clarence Garlow session.

Maxwell Davis(ts),unknown bars,p,b,dr. LA.September 8,1953
RR2223 Look Sharp,Be Sharp   Aladdin 3252,AL804,Score LP4016

Note:The above title is an instrumental from a Norman Dunlap session.

Maxwell Davis(ts),unknown p,g,b,dr.   LA.November 4,1953
RR2244 The Joe Lou's Story Theme(1) Aladdin 3216,AL804,Score LP4016
RR2245 Hey Boy   -   -   -
RR2246 C'est Si Bon   Aladdin AL804,Score LP4016

-1.Add unknown horns

No details.   LA.c. 1953
       Side Car   RPM 382
       The Way You Look Tonight   -

MAXWELL DAVIS AND HIS ROCK&ROLL ORCHSTRA:
No details.   LA.c. 1954
MM2262 Thunderbird   RPM 449,Ace CHAD239
MM2263 Bluesville   -   -

MAXWELL DAVIS QUARTET:
No details.   LA. 1950's
       When The Saints
          Go Marching In   Crown CLP5227,CST527
       Down By The Riverside   -   -
       Careless Love   -   -
       Ida   -   -
       Bill Bailey   -   -

Note:During 1958-1960 Maxwell Davis organized, arranged and - in many cases - conducted a
     series of recordings titled: "A Tribute/Salute to..." various major big band leaders.
     Original sidemen were included among LA studio personnel for each leader's "tribute"
     session.

(TRIBUTE TO STAN KENTON)
Conte Candoli,Pete Candoli,Conrad Gozzo,Oliver Mitchell,Al Porcino(tp),Milt Bernhart,Bob
Fitzpatrick,John Halliburton,Frank Rosolino(tb),Mahlon Clark,Bud Shank(as),Bob Cooper,Bill
Holman(ts),Chuck Gentry(bars),Milt Raskin(p),Laurindo Almeida(g),Don Bagley(b),Mel Lewis
(dr),Chico Guerrero(cg).   LA.November 17,1958

Artistry In Rhythm	Crown CLP5093,CLP5140,CST173,Bright Orange BO725
Elegy	-
Estrellita	-
Martha	-
Peanut Vendor	-

Add Vido Musso(ts).   LA.December 4,1958

Come Back To Sorrento	Crown CLP5093,CLP5126,CST159,Modern M7005,MS805,
	Riviera STR003,Bright Orange BO722
Dark Eyes	Crown CLP5093
Intermission Riff	- ,Bright Orange BO721

All titles on CLP5093 also on Crown CST128,Bright Orange BO705.

(TOAST(!) TO JIMMY & TOMMY DORSEY)
John Best,Ray Linn,Mickey Mangano,George Seaberg,Zeke Zarchy(tp),Dick Noel,Jimmy Priddy,
Tommy Pederson,Paul Tanner(tb),Les Robinson,Wilbur Schwartz(as),Dave Harris,Babe Russin
(ts), Freddy Stulce(bars),Milt Raskin/Paul Smith(p),Dick Fisher/Tony Rizzi(g),Phil Ste-
phens/Rollie Bundock(b),Nick Fatool/Jack Sperling(dr),Al Cava,Adele Francis,Jack Travis
Singers(vcl).   LA.December 1958

Boogie Woogie	Crown CLP5047,Bright Orange BO714,BO723	
Deep River	-	-
Green Eyes(ac,af)	-	- ,BO724
I'm Gettin' Sentimental Over You	- ,Bright Orange BO711,	- ,BO725,
	Modern M7005,MS805	
Maria Elena(ac)	Crown CLP5047,Bright Orange BO714,BO722	
Om The Sunny Side		
Of The Street(jts)	- ,Bright Orange BO711	
So Rare(jts)	- ,Bright Orange BO714	
Song Of India	-	-
Swanee River	-	-
Swing Low Sweet Chariot	-	
Tangerine(ac,af)	- ,Bright Orange BO714	
Marie	Very Sonics 103	

All titles - except "Marie" - also on Crown CST104,Modern M7000,MS8000.
All titles - except "Deep River" also on Very Sonics 103.

TRIBUTE TO ARTIE SHAW)
Ray Linn,Mickey Mangano,Zeke Zarchy(tp),George Arus,Joe Howard,Tommy Pederson(tb),John
Cave(frh),Bob Keene(cl),Les Robinson,Morris Bercov(as),Bus Bassey,Babe Russin(ts),Chuck
Gentry(bars),Milt Raskin/Paul Smith(p),Al Henrickson/Tony Rizzi(g),Phil Stephens(b),Nick
Fatool(dr),strings.   LA.December 1958

Blues	Crown CLP5102,Modern M7005,MS805
Frenesi	- ,CLP5126,CST159,Bright Orange BO723
La Paloma	-
Moonglow	- ,Bright Orange BO724
Nightmare	- - ,BO725
Stardust	- ,CLP5140,CST173,Bright Orange BO722
Temptation	-
Ziguener	-

All titles also on Crown CST134,Bright Orange BO708.
Note:Some sources give rec.date as February 2/3,1959.

(CHARLIE BARNET(!) PRESENTS A TRIBUTE/SALUTE TO HARRY JAMES)
John Audino,Nick Buono,Ray Linn,Oliver Mitchell,Bob Rolfe,Rob Turk,Shorty Sherock(tp),
Hoyt Bohannon,Bob Edmondson,Ray Sims(tb),Ernie Tack(btb),Herb Lorden,Willie Smith(as),
Sam Firmature(ts),Bob Poland(ts,bars),Ernie Small(bars),Jack Perciful(p),Dave Koonse(g),
Marvin Shore(b),Jackie Mills(dr),strings-1. LA.December 1958

Two O'Clock Jump	Crown CLP5114,Modern M7005,MS805,Bright Orange BO720,Baccarola(G)77835
You Made Me Love You(1)	Crown CLP5114,CLP5140,CST173,Modern M7005,MS805, Bright Orange BO722
Cherry(1)	Crown CLP5114,Bright Orange BO724
Just Lucky	-
Palladium Party	-
Trumpet Blues(1)	- ,Bright Orange BO720
Ultra	-
Bangtail	-
Here's One	-
Ciribiribin	- ,Bright Orange BO725,Riviera STR003
One In The House	Crown CLP5127
Sleepy Lagoon(1)	-
Easter Parade(1)	-
One On The House	-
Flatbush Flanagan	-
Music Makers	-
Back Beat Boogie	- ,Bright Orange BO723
The Mole(1)	-
Blues For Sale	-

All titles on CLP5114 also on Crown CST146,Bright Orange BO710,Eros(E)ERL/ERLS50014.
All titles on CLP5127 also on Crown CST160,Bright Orange BO715.

(TRIBUTE TO BENNY GOODMAN)
Don Fagerquist,Irving Goodman,Mickey Mangano,Zeke Zarchy(tp),Hoyt Bohannon,Tommy Pederson
Murray McEachern(tb),Mahlon Clark(cl),Les Robinson,Heinie Beau(as),Dave Harris,Babe Russi
(ts),Jess Stacy(p),Allan Reuss(g),Sid Weiss(b),Nick Fatool(dr).
                                        LA.December 1958

Bugle Call Rag	Crown CLP5090,CLP5140,CST173,Bright Orange BO704, BO721,Riviera STR003
East Side West Side	Crown CLP5090,CLP5527,CST527,Modern M7001,MS801
King Porter Stomp	- ,Bright Orange BO704,BO720
Sing Sing Sing	- ,CLP5126,CLP5527,CST159,Modern M7001 MS801,Bright Orange BO704,BO720
Jersey Bounce	Crown CLP5097,Modern M7001,MS801,Bright Orange BO718
Stomping At The Savoy	Bright Orange BO718

Frank Beach(tp),Jimmy Rowles(p),Al Hendrickson(g),Curtis Counce(b),Ralph Collier(dr) replace Fagerquist,Stacy,Reuss,Weiss and Fatool.
                                        LA.December 1958

Loch Lomond	Crown CLP5090,CLP5527,CST527,Modern M7001,MS801
Jumpin' At The Woodside	- ,Bright Orange BO718,Riviera STR003
Down South Camp Meeting	Crown CLP5097,Modern M7001,MS801,Bright Orange BO718,BO724
Carry Me Back	Crown CLP5097,Bright Orange BO718
My Wild Irish Rose	- -
One O'Clock Jump	- -

Frank Beach,Irving Goodman,Conrad Gozzo,Zeke Zarchy,Don Fagerquist -1(tp),Milt Bernhart,
Bob Pring,Tommy Pederson(tb),Mahlon Clark(cl),Les Robinson,Heinie Beau(as),Dave Harris,
Vido Musso(ts),Jimmy Rowles(p),Allan Reuss(g),Sid Weiss(b),Nick Fatool(dr).
                                        LA.December 1958
(session cont. next page).

(session cont. from previous page):

And The Angels Sing	Crown CLP5092,Modern M7001,MS801,Bright Orange BO704,BO724
Christopher Columbus	Crown CLP5092,Modern M7001,MS801,Bright Orange BO704,Baccarola(G)77835
Let's Dance	Crown CLP5092,Modern M7001,MS801,Bright Orange BO704,BO722,BO725
Careless Love	Crown CLP5092,CLP5527,CST527,Modern M7001,MS801
Down Hill Special	- - - - - -
Bring Back My Bonnie	- - -
Don't Be That Way(1)	- - - ,Modern M7001,MS801, Bright Orange BO704
When The Saints Go Marching In	Crown CLP5092,Modern M7001,MS801,Bright Orange BO704
Sugar Foot Stomp(1)	Crown CLP5097,Modern M7001,MS801,Bright Orange BO704,Baccarola(G)77835
Frankie And Johnny	Crown CLP5097,Bright Orange BO718
Goodbye	Bright Orange BO718,BO725

Mahlon Clark(cl),Red Norvo(vbs),Jimmy Rowles(p),Al Hendrickson(g),Curtis Counce(b),Ralph Collier(dr). LA.December 1958

School Days	Crown CLP5090,CLP5527,CST527
In The Shade Of The Old Apple Tree	- - -
I Love You Truly	Crown CLP5092
Lonesome Road	-
Cuddle Up A Little Closer	Crown CLP5097
Hand Me Down My Walking Cane	-

All titles on CLP5090 also on Crown CST121.
All titles on CLP5092 also on Crown CST123.
All titles on CLP5097 also on Crown CST129,Eros(E)ERL/ERLS50008.
Note:Baccarola(G)77835 as by RAY McKENZIE ORCHESTRA.

(TRIBUTE TO CHARLIE BARNET)
Bob Clark,Don Fagerquist,Maurice Harris,Ray Linn,Al Porcino,Zeke Zarchy(tp),Milt Bernhart, Murray McEachern,Dick Nash,Dick Noel,Tommy Pederson,Dick Taylor(tb),Skeets Herfurt(ss,ss), Bob Jung,Ted Lee(as),Fred Fallensby,Plas Johnson(ts),Bob Dawes(bars),Claude Williamson(p), Allan Reuss(g),Phil Stephens(b),Dick Shanahan/Jack Sperling(dr),Bunny Briggs(vcl).
LA.December 23/24,1958

Cherokee	Crown CLP5094,Bright Orange BO721
Pompton Turnpike	- ,Bright Orange BO722
Skyliner	- ,CLP5140,CST173,Moder M7005,MS805, Bright Orange BO723
Redskin Rhumba	Crown CLP5094,CLP5126,CST159,Bright Orange BO723, BO725,Riviera STR003
Charleston Alley	Crown CLP5094
East Side West Side(bb)	-
Lonely Street	-
Really	-
Claude Reigns	-
Charlie's Other Aunt	-

All titles also on Crown CLP5531,CST131,Modern M7002,MS802,Eros(E)ERL/ERLS50012,Bright Orange BO706,FM Veri Sonics VS102.
All titles - except "East Side,West Side" also on Golden Hour(E)GH868.

(SALUTE TO WOODY HERMAN)
Danny Stiles,Bernie Glow,Hal Posey,Al Forte,Willie Thomas,Al Stewart(tp),Frank Rehak,Billy Byers,Wayne Andre,Charley Henry(tb),John LaPorta(cl,as),Al Cohn,Joe Romano,Don Lanphere (ts),Marty Flax(bars),Eddie Costa(vbs),Bill Potts(p),Jack Six(b),Jimmy Campbell(dr).
(session cont. next page).

```
(session cont. from previous page):        Prob. NYC.  1958/59
      Northwest Passage            Crown CLP5103,Bright Orange BO721
      Wild Root                          -
      Blue Flame                         - ,Bright Orange BO722,BO725
      Four Brothers                      -
      Blowin' Up A Storm                 -
      Woodchopper's Ball                 -
      Apple Honey                        - ,Bright Orange BO721,BO723
      Goosey Gander                      -
      Bijou                              -
```

All titles also on Crown CLP5533,Eros(E)ERL/ERLS50009,Bright Orange BO707,Baccarola(G)
80111 (as by RAY McKENZIE ORCHESTRA).

(TRIBUTE TO WOODY HERMAN)
Same or similar.   Prob. NYC. 1958/59
```
      Montmartre Bus Ride          Crown CLP5180
      Aruba                              - ,Modern MM7004,MS804
      Darn That Dream                    -
      Crown Royal                        -
      I Can't Get Started                -
      The Grind                          -
      Off Shore                          -
      Single O                           -
      After Glow                         - ,Modern MM7004,MS804
      Hermosa Beach                      -
```

All titles also on Crown CST113,CST205,Bright Orange BO717,Eros(E)ERL/ERLS50027,Ember(E)
FA2033.

(SALUTE TO TOMMY DORSEY)
Conte Candoli,Ray Linn,Ray Triscari,Zeke Zarchy(tp),Jimmy Henderson,Tommy Pederson,Dick
Noel(tb),Skeets Herfurt(as,cl),Jewell Grant(as),Don Lodice,Babe Russin(ts),Dave Pell/Chuck
Gentry(bars),Milt Raskin(p),Allan Reuss(g),Max Bennett(b),Jackie Mills(dr),Rickie Page,
B.B. King(vcl).   LA.January 1959
```
      Dry Bones                    Crown CLP5176
      Not So Quiet,Please                -
      Opus No. One                       -
      We'll Git It                       -
      Yes,Indeed(bbk,rp)                 -
      Everytime I Feel The Spirit        - ,Modern M7000,MS800
      Hawaiian War Chant                 -         -      -
      I'll Never Smile Again             -         -      - - ,Br. Orange BO722
      Someone's Knocking At My Door      -         -      -
      Wade In The Water                  -         -      -
```

All titles also on Crown CST201,Bright Orange BO711.

(MUSIC BY LIONEL HAMPTON AND OTHERS)
John Anderson,Billy Brooks,Conrad Gozzo,Oliver Mitchell,Al Porcino(tp),Lester Robertson,
John Ewing,Dick Noel,Dave Wells(tb),Jewell Grant,Jackie Kelso(as),Plas Johnson,Bill Green,
Bumps Myers(ts),Bill Woodman(bars),Larry Bunker(vbs),Gerald Wiggins/Willard McDaniel(p),
Irving Ashby(g),Curtis Counce,Red Callender(b),William Eperson/Earl Palmer(dr).
                                           LA.January 29/February 22,1959
```
      Air Mail Special             Crown CLP5107,Bright Orange BO720
      Cool Train                         -
      Flying Home                        - ,Bright Orange BO720
      Hamp's Boogie Woogie               - ,Bright Orange BO721
      Midnight Sun                       - ,CLP5126,CST150
```

All titles also on Crown CST139,Eros(E)ERL/ERLS50011,RCA PJL1-8130,Bright Orange BO716,
Sonopresse(F)66017.

(COMPOSITIONS OF COUNT BASIE AND OTHERS)
John Anderson,Snooky Young,Joe Newman,Pete Candoli(tp),Henry Coker,Dick Nash,Tommy Peder-
son(tb),Marshall Royal,Jewell Grant(as),Frank Foster,Frank Wess(ts),Charlie Fowlkes(bars),
Milt Raskin(p),Herman Mitchell(g),Eddie Jones(b),Sonny Payne(dr),B.B. King(vcl).

		LA.March 24,1959
Basie Boogie	Crown CLP51111,CLP51126,CST159	
Everyday I Have The Blues(bbk)	-	
John's Idea	-	
Jumpin' At The Woodside	- ,Bright Orange BO721	
Lester Leaps In	- ,Bright Orange BO723	
One O'Clock Jump	- ,Bright Orange BO720	
Red Bank Boogie	- ,CLP5140,CST173,Bright Orange BO721	
April In Paris	Crown CST143	

All titles also on Crown CST143,Eros(E)ERL/ERLS50015.
All titles - except "April In Paris" also on Bright Orange BO702.

(COMPOSITIONS OF DUKE ELLINGTON)
Conte Candoli,Ray Linn,Al Porcino,Jake Porter(tp),Juan Tizol(vtb),Lloyd Elliott,Dick Noel,
Jimmy Henderson,Tommy Pederson(tb),Mahlon Clark,Jewell Grant(as,cl),Bumps Myers,Ben Web-
ster(ts),Bill Hood(bars),Jimmy Rowles(p),Al Hendrickson(g),Red Callender/Curtis Counce(b),
Mel Lewis/Jackie Mills(dr),B.B. King(vcl).   LA.January 13/14,1960

Cottontail	Crown CLP5153,Bright Orange BO721
Don't Get Around Much Anymore(bbk)	-
East Side West Side	-
Jack The Bear	- ,Bright Orange BO723
Jeeps Blues	-
Main Stem	- ,Bright Orange BO721
Mood Indigo	-
Solitude	- ,Modern M7005,MS806,Br. Orange BO724
Take The "A" Train	- ,Bright Orange BO725
Sophisticated Lady	Crown CST183,Bright Orange BO722

All titles also on Crown CST183,Bright Orange BO7009,Eros(E)ERL/ERLS50012.

MEL DAVIS

Mel Davis(tp),Joe Spargo(g),Milt Hinton(b),Osie Johnson(dr).

		NYC.April 5,1956
055740 Fools Rush In	Epic LN3268	
055741 Alone Together	-	
055742 You've Changed	-	
055743 I Should Care	-	

add Barry Galbraith(g).   NYC.April 16,1956

055768 Love Your Magic Spell Is Everywhere	Epic LN3268
055769 Taking A Chance On Love	-
055770 My Heart Belongs To Daddy	-
055771 Gone With The Wind	-

add Phil Bodner(fl).   NYC.April 30,1956

055886 The Wang Wang Blues	Epic LN3268
055887 Jeepers Creepers	-
055888 Roses Of Picardy	-
055889 You're An Old Smoothie	-

no details.   Unknown location/date
        Unknown titles   Time M52070/S2070

MEL DAVIS SEXTET:
No details.   NYC. 1963
    What Kind Of Fool Am I   Time M52117/S2117
    Put On A Happy Face   -
    My Favorite Things   -
    Beyond The Stage Of Loving You   -
    The Sweetest Sounds   -
    A Lot Of Living To Do   -
    Gonna Build A Mountain   -
    Loads Of Love   -
    A The World Turns   -
    Flugel Bugle Blues   -

Note:Additional recordings by this artist are not included.

- 631 -

Greene,Burton 4:386,392
Greene,Flip 4:405
Greenlee,Charles Majid 4:202
Greenow,Bill 4:377
Greenwell,Fred 4:500
Greer,Sonny 4:254
Gregg,Jack 4:247
Gregory,Edmund
   see Shihab,Sahib
Greig,Stan 4:227
Gremier,Bernard 4:137
Grenu,Charles 4:328
Grenu,Georges 4:138
Greve,Bert 4:236
Grevet,Jean 4:360
Grey,Al 4:36,127,316
Grey,Dave 4:236
Griffin,Chris 4:441,447
Griffin,Dick 4:143
Griffin,Johnny 4:424,515,590,592,594
Griffin,Paul 4:403,484,485
Griffith,Derek 4:63
Griffiths,Malcolm 4:48,182,545
Grijsen,Bert 4:491
Grillon,Jean-Claude 4:333
Grimaldi,Renato 4:473
Grimes,Johnny 4:224
Grimes,Tiny 4:1,38,67,68,71
Grinsven,Frans van 4:17
Grissom,Jimmy 4:605
Grolnick,Don 4:42,43,365
Gros,Pascal 4:328
Gross,Holger 4:566
Gross,Sidney 4:8,309
Grossman,Steve 4:350
Grove,Bob 4:167
Grove,Wade 4:482
Groves,Bruce 4:345
Groves,Lani 4:405
Grunnet,Morten 4:358
Gruntz,George 4:474
Grusin,Don 4:184
Gruyer,Jean 4:241
Gryce,Gigi 4:19,141,514
Gualda,Sylvio 4:328
Guaraldi,Vince 4:457
Guarnieri,Johnny 4:24,66,67,310,516,517
Guarnieri,Mario 4:333
Gubin,Sol 4:317,337
Guerault,Stéphane 4:580
Guérin,Beb 4:386
Guérin,Roger 4:4,307,328,419
Guerrero,Chico 4:607
Guesnon,George 4:16
Gugten,Remco van der 4:518
Guilbeau,Phil 4:400,401
Guillot,Pierre 4:241
Guillotin,Pierre 4:508
Guin,Francois 4:136,137
Guizien,Christian 4:136
Gullin,Lars 4:474
Gumbley,Steve 4:393
Gumbs,Onaje Allen 4:324-326
Gunneman,Henk 4:245
Gustafsson,Rune 4:494,505

Gutekunst,Bill 4:500
Gutiérrez,Hector 4:562
Gutierrez,Julio 4:462
Gwaltney,Tom 4:305,563
Haas,Eddie de 4:133,316
Haas,Steve 4:361
Haavisto,Jukka 4:243
Habberjam,Derek 4:20
Hackett,Bobby 4:250,252-262,267-270,277,
   278,280-283,285,286,288,289,298,303,467,
   516
Haden,Charlie 4:144-146,151-155,157-161,
   194-196,200,215,216
Hadjo,Georges 4:2,167
Hafer,Dick 4:187
Hafer,John 4:70
Haffey,Kid 4:56
Hagans,Tim 4:408
Hageman,Rob 4:374
Haggart,Bob 4:244,250,255-262,264,265,268,
   279,280,302,341,423-427,429,430,432,440,
   441,443,447-449,469
Hagmann,Christoph 4:22,23
Hagood,Kenny 4:510
Haig,Al 4:530,582,583
Haines,Bud 4:245
Haines,Connie 4:109,441
Hajek,Petr 4:243
Hakeem,Bilal Abdul
   see Brooks,Billie
Hakim,Sadik
   see Thornton,Argonne
Hako,Alain 4:166
Halcox,Pat 4:550
Hale,Teddy 4:279,280
Hales,Bobby 4:347
Haley,Bruce 4:23
Hall,Al 4:297,302,477,603
Hall,Alice 4:112
Hall,Andrew 4:381
Hall,Bob 4:323
Hall,Bobby 4:326
Hall,Carlyle 4:110,114
Hall,Edmond 4:250,252,253,255,258-265,271,
   273,277,290-299,304
Hall,Herb 4:300,563
Hall,Jim 4:157,169,170,172
Hall,Rene 4:72,336
Hallam,John 4:184
Hallberg,Bengt 4:505
Halliburton,John 4:119,340,521,607
Halliday,John 4:558
Halliday,Marvin 4:493
Halsall,Ivan 4:381
Halvorsen,Harald 4:505
Hamilton,Bill 4:329
Hamilton,Charlie 4:16
Hamilton,Chico 4:169
Hamilton,Ian 4:20
Hamilton,Jeff 4:1,25,186,187
Hamilton,Jimmy 4:8,309,359
Hamilton,Ralph 4:604
Hamilton,Scott 4:25,26,248,249
Hammack,Bob 4:345
Hammalian,Dan 4:165

Ralston,Wes **4**:562
Ramage,Bob **4**:345
Ramey,Gene **4**:8,10,11,140,141,372,582-584
Randén,Povel **4**:338
Randle,Mac **4**:20
Rando,Arthur **4**:423,426,427,429,430
Raney,Jimmy **4**:51,52,530
Range,Bob **4**:557
Rank,Bill **4**:562
Ransy,Andrien **4**:26
Raskin,Milt **4**:607,610,611
Rasmussen,Hugo **4**:57,595
Rasmussen,Johnny **4**:554
Raso,George J. **4**:23
Rassinfosse,Jean-Louis **4**:26
Rathbun,Chris **4**:509
Ratip,Ahmed **4**:370
Rauch,Doug **4**:42
Raux,Richard **4**:306
Ravello,... **4**:570
Ravensberg,Bill van **4**:167
Raverty,Don **4**:508
Ray,Ford **4**:508
Ray,Johnny **4**:290
Ray Charles Singers (The) **4**:121
Rayman,Morris **4**:278,329
Raynal,Yves **4**:241
Razadu,Kaeef **4**:407
Razik,Boguslaw **4**:247
Read,Alex **4**:568
Rebillot,Pat **4**:321
Reck,Per **4**:550
Redd,Gene **4**:69
Redd,Sharon **4**:326
Reddick,Jeff **4**:189
Reddie,Louis **4**:28
Redford,Mike **4**:457
Redman,Dewey **4**:153-155,157,158,161
Reece,Dizzy **4**:420,481
Reed,George **4**:598
Reese,Cliff **4**:64
Regteren Altena,Maarten van **4**:245,246,486,487
Rehak,Frank **4**:51,54,56,316,317,609
Reichenbach,Bill **4**:492
Reichert,Stieg **4**:165
Reid,Don **4**:453,454,508
Reid,Neal **4**:423
Reid,Rufus **4**:534
Reidy,Frank **4**:542
Reilles,Mac Kac **4**:418
Reilly,Pat **4**:526-528
Reinhardt,Django **4**:241
Reinhart,Randy **4**:470
Remeta,Kresimir **4**:14
Remler,Emily **4**:1
Rémy,Pierre **4**:241
Renard,Alex **4**:3,242
Renard,Simon
    see Simmons,Richard
Renaud,Henri **4**:413
Rendell,Don **4**:386,420,535,536,545
Renfeldt,Steve **4**:357
Renzi,Paul **4**:128
Resther,Claude **4**:499

Return To Forever **4**:351,352
Reuss,Allan **4**:346,460,608-610
Rey,Eduardo **4**:308
Rhames,Arthur **4**:365
Rhodes,George **4**:34-36,483
Rhodes,T. **4**:584
Riat,Gérard **4**:333
Ricard,Fip **4**:40
Ricard,Gilbert **4**:333
Ricci,Paul **4**:440,441
Rice,Charlie **4**:584-586
Rich,Buddy **4**:279-283,285,288,289
Richard,Dick **4**:520
Richard,Marc **4**:138
Richards,Carol **4**:445
Richards,Charles **4**:167
Richards,Emil **4**:174,459
Richards,J.P. **4**:477
Richards,Red **4**:3,140
Richards,Trevor **4**:376,564
Richardson,Barney **4**:147
Richardson,Barry **4**:60
Richardson,Jerome **4**:18,19,70,141,196,447,514,515,577,588,590,593
Richardson,Wally **4**:409
Richman,Al **4**:115,119
Richman,Boomie **4**:53,310,327,341,432
Richmond,Bill **4**:168,170,171,451
Richmond,Dannie **4**:478
Richmond,June **4**:96
Richmond,Mike **4**:482
Rickson,Roger E. **4**:357
Ricotti,Frank **4**:47
Riddle,Nelson **4**:120,122,123,126,438
Ridge,Pete **4**:232,233
Ridley,Larry **4**:57,192,193
Ridone,Aldo **4**:243
Riedel,Georg **4**:505
Riel,Alex **4**:533,595
Riempp,Dieter **4**:551,552
Righello,Ettore **4**:474-476
Rignold,Hugo **4**:541
Rigon,Sergio **4**:138,475,476
Riisnæs,Knut **4**:505
Rijkhoff,Peter **4**:518
Rikkers,Ferdi **4**:385
Riley,Ben **4**:194-196,218,590-592
Riley,Dean **4**:59
Riley,Jim **4**:381
Riley,Teddy **4**:380
Rimington,Sammy **4**:60,63,231-233
Riska,Gustav **4**:243
Ritchie,Ruth **4**:167
Ritenour,Lee **4**:191,326,416,492
Rivera,Dave **4**:515
Rivera,Mario **4**:142,335
Rivera,Ramon **4**:373
Rivers,Sam **4**:65,515
Rizzi,Tony **4**:526,607
Rizzo,Pat **4**:333
Roach,Max **4**:18,50,141
Roach,Rahim **4**:407
Roane,Eddie **4**:423
Robbins,David **4**:347
Robbins,Steve **4**:405

JAZZ RECORDS, 1942-80

- a discography *by Erik Raben*

Vol. 4 (Cla-Da): *Just published* (see front cover for details)

Vol. 6 (Ellington, 1942-74): Edited by Ole J. Nielsen, this is the most comprehensive discography on Duke ever It includes every known studio- & concert recording, radio- & TV-appearance. Totalling 613 pages with complete indexes.

Vol. 3 (Bro-Cl): Includes sections with Clifford Brown (11 pages), Dave Brubeck (31 pages), Kenny Burrell (17 pages), Donald Byrd (10 pages), Benny Carter (24 pages) ... totalling 632 pages.

Vol. 2 (Bar-Br): Sections includes Art Blakey (24 pages) Sidney Bechet (30 pages - still the most complete available), Count Basie, 1942-84 (105 pages), Charlie Barnet (27 pages) ... totalling 650 pages.

Vol. 1 (A-Ba): Includes sections with Chris Barber (35 pages), Julian "Cannonball" Adderley (20 pages), Louis Armstrong (94 pages) ... totalling 644 pages.

Jazz Records, 1942-80 *is printed in the handy A5-forma on 120 gr paper. Each volume is strongly bound hard cove with gold-embossed lettering and contains an index o musicians!* **$50.00/volume** (+postage

---

The discographical basis for JAZZ RECORDS, 1942-80

The JAZZ RECORDS, 1942-80 project started in 1972 and during the following years draft-manuscripts - based on J.G. Jepsen's JAZZ RECORDS - were circulated to 20-25 collectors from several countries all over the world. More than ten years of discographical research followed until the manuscript for vol. 1 was prepared. This manuscript - as well as all later manuscripts - have been re-checked by a smaller group of people and a lot of specialists have been used to work on sections covering artists with a recorded output, that is "difficult" - seen from a discographical point of view.

This procedure - which is rather "heavy" - not only adds a lot of details that were never published earlier, but also corrects several errors which are found in the works of Jepsen and other discographers. The "cost" is that JAZZ RECORDS, 1942-80 volumes can not be published as fast as other discographies which are not - to the same degree - based on discographical research.

CHET -
The music of Chesney Henry Baker
by *Thorbjørn Sjøgren*

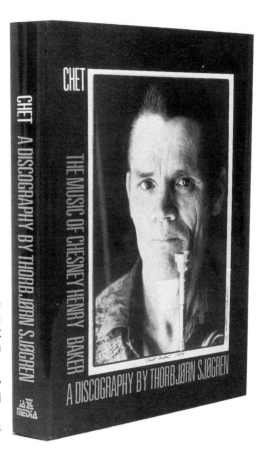

Though essentially a discography, the title of this book is chosen deliberately, for it contains far more than the usual discographical information:
An extended interview with Baker, reviews, a biography, and many previously unpublished photographs.

However, the main part is of course the discography that takes us through Baker's career from his first recordings in 1952 until his death in Amsterdam on May 13, 1988.

The evidence of 36 years as a highly original and gifted trumpeter and singer (plus occasionally piano player, and - in a few cases - drummer) is here:

■ Approximately 200 recording sessions. ■ 150 radio- and TV-broadcasts (from which much material has become available on LP, CD or video), and ■ 250 private tape recordings of concerts. ■ The 360-page book has indexes of musicians, song titles, and LP/CD titles.

336 pages. Size A5. Many previously unpublished photos. Hardcover with dustjacket. $31.00 (+ Postage).

JAZZMEDIA ApS, DORTHEAVEJ 39, DK-2400 COPENHAGEN NV, DENMARK
PHONE (+45) 3119 8259 - FAX (+045) 3119 0110

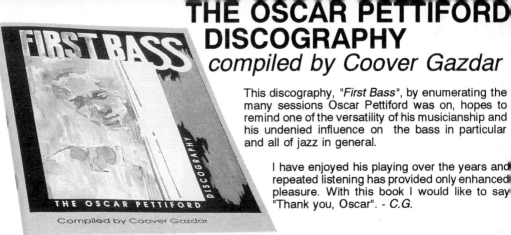

DUKE ELLINGTON
- Day by day and film by film
by Dr. Klaus Stratemann

This book is a first among the many publications devoted to Duke Ellington in that it recounts the entire range of his multiple professional activities in chronological order; almost, though not always, day by day!

Generously illustrated with reproductions of ads and rare original documents; and with over 300 photos, most of which have never been published before, the book also provides a visual record of Duke Ellington's distinguished career.

Special sections are devoted to his motion pictures, detailing his work on the screen, on the sound stages and as a film composer.

This is a book to browse through, or to turn to in search of information.

Access is provided with 60 pages of indexes on persons and music units; on compositions, venues, cities; and with a general index covering films, radio, TV, theatre and other subjects.

This is a book for the scholar and the jazz enthusiast; for the film lover and for anyone with an affinity for Americans show business.

And above all, it is a must for those with an interest in that genius of American music, Duke Ellington!

Excerpts from the reviews ...

■ "The detailing and analysing of every bit of film Duke ever made is so obviously exhaustive that one could not begin to criticise it... I remain breathless with admiration and amazement." - *Jazz Journal.*

■ "...where Stratemann scores is in the wealth of illustrative and archive material he has been able to reproduce, which brings to life the minutiae of the chronicle in an exceptionally vivid way". - *Jazz (UK).*

■ "...Besides many complete itineraries of foreign tours, there are reproductions of programs, recording contracts, ads, and rare photgraphs... All in all, it is the biggest single collection of factual information about Ellington yet accumulated... he has achieved something that would daunt anyone living in the U.S.". -*JazzTimes.*

792 pages. Size A4.
More than 300 photos!
Hardcover with dustjacket. $119.00 (+ postage).

The New Revised
STAN GETZ
DISCOGRAPHY
By Arne Astrup

BIDSTRUP DISCOGRAPHICAL PUBLISHING CO.

The Discography of

SONNY ROLLINS
COMPILED BY THORBJØRN SJØGREN

BIDSTRUP DISCOGRAPHICAL PUBLISHING COMPANY, DENMARK.

- The new revised STAN GETZ DISCOGRAPHY (3rd ed., 1991) by Arne Astrup. S/c, A4 format, 264 p. (many photos) incl. list of most important album titles plus indexes of musicians and tune titles. $33.7

- A discography of BREW MOORE by Arne Astrup. Publ. 1992. S/c, A4 format, 34 pages with photos and with indexes of tunes and musicians. $11.7

- The John Haley Sims - ZOOT SIMS discography by Arne Astrup Published 1980 *plus supplement*, publ. 1992. A4 formats, totalling 144 pages with photos plus indexes of musicians and tune titles. $23.5

- The GERRY MULLIGAN discography by Arne Astrup. A4 format. Published 1989. A4 format, 106 pages with indexes of tunes and musicians. $23.5

- The discography of SONNY ROLLINS compiled by Thorbjørn Sjøgren. Published 1993. S/c, A5 format, 130 pages (many photos) with indexes plus LP and CD-titles. $21.2

- LONG TALL DEXTER - the discography of Dexter Gordon compiled by Thorbjørn Sjøgren. Published 1986. S/c, A5 format, 206 pages with many photos plus album covers and indexes of tunes and musicians. $18.2

- The discography of DUKE JORDAN compiled by Thorbjørn Sjøgren. Published 1992. S/c, A5 format, 36 pages with many photos. With indexes of musicians and tune titles. $21.2